PRODUCTION AND OPERATIONS MANAGEMENT

A PROBLEM-SOLVING AND DECISION-MAKING APPROACH

FOURTH EDITION

PRODUCTION AND OPERATIONS MANAGEMENT

A PROBLEM-SOLVING AND DECISION-MAKING APPROACH

FOURTH EDITION

NORMAN GAITHER

College of Business Administration
Texas A&M University

THE DRYDEN PRESS
Chicago   Fort Worth   San Francisco   Philadelphia
Montreal   Toronto   London   Sydney   Tokyo

Acquisitions Editor: **Robert Gemin**
Developmental Editor: **Jan Richardson**
Project Editor: **Teresa Chartos**
Design Supervisor: **Rebecca Lemna**
Production Manager: **Barb Bahnsen**
Permissions Editor: **Cindy Lombardo**
Director of Editing, Design, and Production: **Jane Perkins**

Text and Cover Designer: **Vargas/Williams/Design**
Copy Editor: **Mary Englehart**
Indexer: **Leoni McVey**
Compositor: **Progressive Typographers, Inc.**
Text Type: **10/12 Times Roman**

Library of Congress Cataloging-in-Publication Data
Gaither, Norman.
    Production and operations management: a problem-solving and
    decision-making approach / Norman Gaither. — 4th ed.
        p.   cm.
    Includes bibliographies and index.
    ISBN 0-03-026342-5
    1. Production management.   I. Title.
TS155.G17   1990   89-1167
658.5 — dc19   CIP

Printed in the United States of America
901-039-987654321

Address orders:
The Dryden Press
Orlando, FL 32887

Address editorial correspondence:
The Dryden Press
908 N. Elm Street
Hinsdale, IL 60521

The Dryden Press
Holt, Rinehart and Winston
Saunders College Publishing

Cover Source: © The Photo File/Tom Tracy.

Dedicated to:

The professors who actually stand in classrooms and teach production and operations management.

While the faces of the students change from semester to semester, the challenge continues—to prepare students to cope and succeed in tomorrow's business world. Somewhat like our students, professors are trying to survive another semester, but something else is driving them. Knowing that our students can make a difference in the future of our manufacturing and service operations, we may often seem deadly serious, intense, and doggedly persistent. It is hoped that in some small way this text can make the teaching and learning of POM more effective.

THE DRYDEN PRESS SERIES IN MANAGEMENT

The American Assembly of Collegiate Schools of Business (AACSB) requires that all accredited schools include production and operations management (POM) in their curriculum. Schools of business in growing numbers have included POM courses in their academic programs at both the undergraduate and graduate levels. This book has been developed to meet the need for comprehensive text materials in these and other POM courses.

The fourth edition retains the distinctive features of the earlier editions:

1. **Production/operations function perspective.** The text places the student squarely in the production/operations function in a variety of organizations. The problems of operations managers in many diverse manufacturing, service, and government units are studied.

2. **Practical view of POM.** Most of the problems and examples in the text have been abstracted from actual situations that have been analyzed by the author or his associates. The view presented is one of realism about real-world problems.

3. **Nontheoretical approach.** The text presents the quantitative topics of POM side by side with managerial issues and concepts for a balanced view of POM problems. When quantitative approaches are appropriate, the text presents these approaches in a nontheoretical way. This objective is accomplished by emphasizing operational problems rather than the solution techniques and by using examples to demonstrate the techniques.

4. **Liberal use of examples with solutions.** Each chapter includes examples of POM problems with complete solutions. These examples are solved step by step so that students can follow every detail of the solutions.

5. **End-of-chapter problems and cases.** A strength of the text is its problem sets and cases. The problems and cases are numerous, are about practical POM situations, and can be worked directly from the information in the chapters. The problems exhibit a progression of difficulty as one proceeds through a set.

6. **Graduated-learning process.** Chapters are presented in a framework particularly suitable for learning by students. Concepts and solved examples are presented within chapters, level of difficulty increases as one proceeds through the chapters, and answers to odd-numbered problems are provided as an appendix. This process builds understanding and confidence to the point that students should be able to test their ability to solve problems without the assistance of supplied solutions and answers.

7. **Liberal use of graphics in text.** Many charts, graphs, tables, and other visual tools are used in the text to demonstrate the concepts presented. Students continue to report the usefulness of these aids in understanding the concepts of the chapters.

8. **Use of second color to add emphasis.** A second color is used to emphasize organization, to accentuate content, and to aid understanding. Similarly,

second color and shading are used in the graphics to facilitate comprehension.

9. **Emphasis of POM in services.** Service operations receive considerable discussion in this edition. Operations strategy, process planning, automation, quality, and other topics are cast in the setting of transportation, retailing and wholesaling, banking, and other service industries.

10. **Balanced view of behavioral concepts.** Readers will immediately notice that behavioral concepts are intertwined with other issues as early as Chapter 1. As the text unfolds, these concepts are integrated with other content to form a balanced view of operations management.

11. **Japanese management approaches.** Japanese manufacturing strategy, personnel relations and practices, robotry, JIT, quality control, and other concepts are integrated throughout the text. The view is one of comparison and understanding, rather than one of directly adapting Japanese methods to U.S. production systems.

12. **Comprehensive set of supporting materials.** The text continues to offer a wide range of supporting materials:

   - The *Instructor's Manual and Transparency Masters* presents a comprehensive set of materials to assist instructors in teaching the course. It includes suggested course schedules, chapter teaching notes, sample exams, answers to end-of-chapter review and discussion questions, and transparency masters of figures not included in the text as well as of key figures from the text.
   - The *Instructor's Solutions Manual* consists of complete solutions for all of the problems and cases in the text. These are presented in large ORATOR type so that they can be used as transparency masters.
   - The *Test Bank* includes true/false, multiple-choice, and short-answer questions and problems with detailed solutions. A computerized version for use with IBM PC microcomputers is also available.
   - The *POM Computer Library* includes computer programs that are geared to novice computer users. This package is intended to remove some of the computational drudgery from problem solving of the number-intensive topics in the text. The package is thoroughly consistent with the text in sequence of topics, notation, terminology, and approach. The programs frequently refer to tables, figures, examples, and formulas in the text. Being totally prompted by the programs, students can use them to solve problems or cases as they proceed through the text. An information packet and a disk for IBM PC microcomputers are free to adopters of the text.

Our goal in this fourth edition has been to make the text even better. Toward this end, we have made the following changes to the previous editions:

1. **Emphasis on operations strategy.** Chapter 2, Operations Strategy, introduces the student to strategic issues early in the text. This chapter also motivates the study of POM by examining the forces at work today in our global economy and sets up Part II of the text, Strategic Planning in Operations. Chapter 2 combined with the chapters in Part II form a thorough treatment of the strategic issues and decisions in POM today.

2. **Emphasis on production processes.** Chapter 4, Production Processes, consolidates much of the information about production processing early in the text. Students are shown several classic types of production schemes and the strategic capabilities of each type are explained.

3. **Video plant tours.** Three classic types of manufacturing schemes are illustrated by plant tours of IBM, R. R. Donnelley, and Wal-Mart. Chapter 4 includes a written tour and each is accompanied by a video tour that helps bring the plant to life. These three videos are provided free to adopters.

4. **Advanced production technology.** Chapter 1 introduces students to robotics, automation, computer-integrated manufacturing, CAD/CAM, flexible manufacturing systems, bar-coding systems, and other high-tech production equipment. Chapter 2, Operations Strategy, discusses the strategic implications of high-tech manufacturing. Chapter 5, Production Technology, discusses automated work cells, flexible manufacturing systems, automated assembly systems, automation in services, and other state-of-the-art automation concepts. These methods are described and illustrated from the perspective of the operations manager and how they affect the strategic performance of operations.

5. **Industry Snapshots.** Special accounts of industry applications are featured in most chapters. These Industry Snapshots are visually highlighted to indicate their importance to the topics being discussed. Where possible in these narratives, the real names of companies and people and their actual situations are used to demonstrate to students the relevance of what we teach in POM courses.

6. **Placement of quantitative supplements in appendixes.** Quantitative topics such as linear programming and queuing theory had appeared as chapter supplements in earlier editions. Many of the users of the third edition suggested that these supplementary materials would be more easily located from other chapters if they were placed at the end of the text. Accordingly, in this fourth edition they are placed at the end of the text as appendixes. The quantitative topics remain thoroughly integrated with the application areas within the chapters.

7. **Refinement of problems and cases.** In a continuing effort to keep the problem sets current and effective, new problems have been added to this edition and several of the old ones have been removed. Some of the problems and their solutions that were removed from earlier editions have been placed in the *Instructor's Manual* for professors' use.

8. **More special problems and cases to be solved by computer.** Where appropriate, the end-of-chapter problems and cases are specially designed to be solved with the use of the computer. These problems and cases, which are formulated to be consistent with the expanded capabilities of the *POM Computer Library*, are identified by a computer symbol preceding the problem number or case title.

9. **More photos and full-color layouts.** As in the third edition, the fourth edition uses full-color photos to illustrate robotics, advanced manufacturing methods, and other POM concepts. Additionally, in the fourth edition, the photos are better integrated with other topics in Chapter 5, Production Technology.

10. **Study Guide.** The *Study Guide* provides chapter outlines and review questions and problems, including answers and solutions, to help students master the text material and prepare for exams.
11. **Expansion of the *POM Computer Library.*** The fourth edition includes many improvements to the computer package available for the IBM PC. The package is more visually appealing while retaining its ease of use, and it continues to include automatic file maintenance. The library has been refined to reflect many improvements to individual programs and also contains some new programs. A major improvement is the ability of the programs to edit data and to store data between use sessions. This allows students to interrupt sessions without losing data and to shift to other computers to print their output. This computer package is free to adopters of the text.
12. **Test Bank.** An expanded *Test Bank* by Ray Boykin, Marcus Najem, Kathryn Ritchie, Carl Salmonsen, and Toni Schreder of California State University—Chico, William Corney, University of Nevada, and Norman Gaither, includes more than 1,000 questions and problems with detailed solutions. Nile Leach, Colorado State University, checked all questions and problems for accuracy and consistency with the text.
13. **Computerized test bank.** The *Computerized Test Bank* includes all of the questions and problems in the *Test Bank* and is provided free to adopters of the text. The package is available in disk form for the IBM PC. With this package instructors can design their own comprehensive quizzes and examinations covering the concepts and issues presented in the text.
14. **Videotapes.** Several videotapes of factory and service operations are provided free to adopters of the text. These tapes are in VHS format and are intended to reinforce the materials in several topic areas of the text. The *Instructor's Manual* suggests how these tapes may be integrated with the text and with the other ancillary materials provided.

As with the previous editions, students should have completed courses in college algebra and introductory statistics as prerequisites to courses using this text. Although the mathematical and statistical concepts in the text are not complex, students with a basic background in these topics tend to perform better.

As this fourth edition is completed, numerous persons deserve special recognition for their contributions to the project:

1. My faculty colleagues, graduate students, and students at Texas A&M University who have participated in Bana 364, the POM core course. These persons not only made many suggestions for the improvements that are incorporated into this edition, but they also shared their thoughts and philosophies of teaching. A special mention goes to Bob Davis, Benito Flores, Rob Bregman, Ted Anthony, Joe Munn, and Greg Frazier.
2. My family and friends who have continued to provide me with moral support and encouragement. Lynda, my wife, is an especially important contributor to my work through her support and understanding. She has allowed me to spend countless hours in my office working on manuscripts rather than on other activities that she would have considered more fun.

3. The great editorial team at The Dryden Press. They continue to demonstrate that they are unparalleled in their ability to convert a rough manuscript into a finished POM textbook. For their suggestions, cooperation, congeniality, diligence, professionalism, and talent, I am truly thankful.
4. The many friends and associates who have contributed to both formal and informal reviews of the text manuscript. A special mention goes to those reviewers who were actively involved in the fourth edition project:

- Steven F. Bolander, Colorado State University
- Ray Boykin, California State University—Chico
- Jonathan Burton, Drexel University
- Alec Calamidas, Baruch College
- William Corney, University of Nevada—Las Vegas
- C. W. Dane, Oregon State University
- Ellen Dumond, Miami University—Oxford, Ohio
- Barbara B. Flynn, Iowa State University
- Van Gray, Baylor University
- Raymond A. Jacobs, Clemson University
- Gopalan Kutty, Mansfield University
- Bangalore Lingaraj, Indiana University—Purdue University at Fort Wayne
- James Milleville, University of Colorado—Denver
- William H. Moates, Indiana State University
- Russell Morey, Western Illinois University
- Henry Person, University of Minnesota—Duluth
- Gary L. Ragatz, Michigan State University
- Roger D. Scow, Southwest Texas State University

To these and all of the other persons who have contributed to this work, I am grateful.

Norman Gaither

Texas A&M University

ABOUT THE AUTHOR

Norman Gaither is a professor in the Business Analysis and Research Department of Texas A&M University. He received his Ph.D. and M.B.A. from the University of Oklahoma and his B.S.I.E. from Oklahoma State University. He also taught at Northern Arizona University and the University of Oklahoma. Prior to teaching, Professor Gaither worked for eight years at Olin Corporation where he held the positions of chief industrial engineer, plant manager, and director of a multiplant operation and for three years at B.F. Goodrich Company as senior industrial engineer.

Professor Gaither's writings on a wide range of POM topics have appeared in *Management Science, Decision Sciences, International Journal of Production Research, Journal of Production and Inventory Management, Academy of Management Journal, Academy of Management Review, Simulation, Journal of Purchasing and Materials Management, Journal of Cost Analysis,* and *International Journal of Operations and Production Management.*

He serves on the editorial boards of the *Journal of Production and Inventory Management,* the journal of the American Production and Inventory Control Society, and the *International Journal of Production Research* and is an AACSB Federal Faculty Fellow. Professor Gaither has been actively involved in consulting for government agencies and major corporations, including Bell Telephone, Texas Instruments, Sector Research, and the U.S. Department of Commerce.

CONTENTS IN BRIEF

PART IV
PLANNING AND CONTROLLING OPERATIONS FOR PRODUCTIVITY, QUALITY, AND RELIABILITY   622

APPENDIXES

INDEX

CONTENTS

CHAPTER 6
FACILITY LAYOUT: MANUFACTURING AND SERVICES   224

CHAPTER 7
ALLOCATING RESOURCES TO STRATEGIC ALTERNATIVES   274

PART IV
*PLANNING AND CONTROLLING OPERATIONS FOR
PRODUCTIVITY, QUALITY, AND RELIABILITY   622*

CHAPTER 14
PRODUCTIVITY AND EMPLOYEES: BEHAVIOR, WORK METHODS, AND
WORK MEASUREMENT   624

APPENDIXES

PRODUCTION AND OPERATIONS MANAGEMENT
INTRODUCTION AND OVERVIEW

Today is an exciting time for the study of operations management. So many events of national and international significance have occurred recently that this field has become one of the most challenging in the world of business. Our national leaders are expressing concern that manufacturers from foreign countries are seriously threatening the future of such basic industries as automobiles, steel, electronics, and computers. The top managements of our leading corporations are urging their operations managers to get back to the basics of factory management so that this country's manufacturing costs, productivity, and product quality can compete with those of manufacturers from Asia, Europe, and other parts of the world. In addition, many of our industries are in a period of rapid technological change as robotics and computer-based technology innovations are applied to operations.

In such a heady environment, the study of operations management could not be more important to you or more relevant to your career opportunities. If you should choose to enter the operations management field when you finish college, what you will learn in this course should provide you with an important introduction to the field. If you enter another field, such as accounting, marketing, finance, computer/information science, personnel, or engineering, what you will study in this text can be important to you because your chosen field will most certainly interact with operations management and its problems, opportunities, and challenges.

Part I of this text provides the following:

1. An overview of the operations management field—its history, contemporary developments, and the strategic choices of today's production operations.

2. Different frameworks for studying operations management—production as a system, production as an organizational function, and decision making in POM are useful ways of viewing POM. From the decision-making perspective, each chapter in the text fits into this framework: strategic decisions (Part II), operating decisions (Part III), and control decisions (Part IV).

3. An examination of the strategic choices available to today's operations managers; an assessment of the present economic climate, approaches to developing strategies in today's business environment, and exploration of the strategies available to allow U.S. manufacturers to survive in tomorrow's world markets.

4. A survey of forecasting techniques and systems as a starting point for developing successful operations strategies, decisions, and plans.

CHAPTER 1

PRODUCTION AND OPERATIONS MANAGEMENT (POM)

AN INTRODUCTION

BUSINESS SCHOOLS EMPHASIZE POM AND TECHNOLOGY

Manufacturing, a subject that long ago fell from favor among students and professors at many business schools, is making a comeback. Academicians are recruiting professors and creating courses to treat production-related topics. MBA candidates who a year ago wouldn't have thought of getting their hands dirty on a factory floor are vying for top grades and recommendations that will land them jobs in manufacturing. Manufacturing companies are showing up on Ivy League and other college campuses to recruit not just marketing and finance majors, but also the best and brightest students majoring in what college course catalogs now call "production and operations management." It's all the result of the embarrassment and adversity U.S. manufacturers are suffering at the hands of foreign competitors.[1]

Another reason for the renewed interest in production and operations management at colleges and universities is the explosion of production technology and the need to deal with it in businesses. Lester C. Thurow, dean of MIT's Sloan School of Management, thinks that courses in production should teach students to understand manufacturing technology and its role in developing business strategy. "We have educated a generation of management people who in some very literal sense don't understand technology. A major technical change comes along and they won't bet on it before the numbers show it's right. Failure to recognize a revolution led to the downfall of the U.S. steel industry. We built our first continuous caster six years after the Japanese. A continuous caster is a billion dollar bet. Would you bet a billion dollars on something you don't understand?" Thurow is overhauling the curriculum at MIT to interweave the traditional management concepts with production technology.[2]

[1] "Schools Again Offer Courses on Production," *The Wall Street Journal,* Jan. 26, 1981.

[2] "New MIT Dean Seeking Better Technical Literacy," *Houston Chronicle,* June 15, 1987, sec. 2, 1.

As the previous newspaper articles suggest, production and operations management is reemerging as an important discipline in the struggle to make U.S. corporations competitive with manufacturers from Japan and other nations of the world. This book is about production and operations management. *Production and operations management (POM)* is the planning, organizing, staffing, directing, and controlling of all of the activities of production systems—those portions of organizations that convert inputs into products and services. In one sense, managers in POM, whom we shall simply call *operations managers,* do the same basic things that other managers do—plan, organize, staff, direct, and control. But the activities of production systems are often so different from the activities of finance, marketing, engineering, and other functions that the ways in which operations managers manage can be distinctly different. In general, production systems take raw materials, personnel, machines, buildings, and other resources and *produce* products and services.

The management of production systems today is different from what it was yesterday, and changes are already in the works that will modify the ways in which these operations managers go about their jobs next year. Because POM has evolved over the years to its present form by continually changing and adapting to the challenges of each new era, two factors are important to its understanding:

1. Operations managers today go about their jobs in ways that were developed by managers who preceded them decades, even centuries, ago. Many of today's POM practices were initiated by management pioneers who broke the trail as they encountered the new problems of their times.
2. Today's operations managers are facing new problems that are affecting the ways that they are managing. The ways of the past are being modified and new methods are being developed as managers attempt to cope with today's pressures and meet its challenges.

Figure 1.1 illustrates that POM today is an interesting blend of time-tested practices from the past that have been retained because they work, and of a continuing search for different ways to manage production systems in order to solve the new problems that arise daily. Consider the conditions that today's operations managers face—the reality of competing in worldwide markets, the rapid advance of production technology, foreign producers' cost and quality, the fluctuation of international financial conditions, the continued growth of the service sector, and if this were not enough, the scarcity of production resources. These challenges will be discussed in more detail in Chapter 2 of this text, Operations Strategy: Operations as a Competitive Weapon. In this chapter we shall explore both the past and the present so that we may develop a useful background for this introductory study of POM.

MILESTONE HISTORICAL DEVELOPMENTS IN POM

For an examination of their historical impact on POM, we have selected seven historical developments: the industrial revolution, the post–Civil War period, scientific management, the human relations movement, operations research, computers and advanced production technology, and the service revolution.

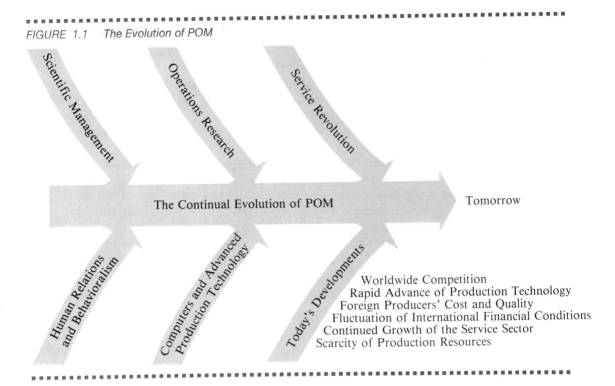

FIGURE 1.1   *The Evolution of POM*

The Continual Evolution of POM   Tomorrow

Scientific Management

Operations Research

Service Revolution

Human Relations and Behavioralism

Computers and Advanced Production Technology

Today's Developments

Worldwide Competition
Rapid Advance of Production Technology
Foreign Producers' Cost and Quality
Fluctuation of International Financial Conditions
Continued Growth of the Service Sector
Scarcity of Production Resources

THE INDUSTRIAL REVOLUTION

There have always been systems of production. The Egyptian pyramids, the Greek Parthenon, the Great Wall of China, and the aqueducts and roads of the Roman Empire attest to the ingenuity and industry of the peoples of ancient times. But the ways that these ancient peoples produced products were quite different from the production methods of today. Production systems prior to the 1700s are often referred to as the *cottage system,* because the production of products took place in homes or cottages where craftsmen directed apprentices in performing hand work on products.

In England in the 1700s, a development occurred that we refer to as the *industrial revolution.* This advancement involved two principal elements: the widespread substitution of *machine power* for human power and the establishment of the *factory system.* The steam engine, invented by James Watt in 1764, not only provided machine power for factories, but it also stimulated other inventors to devise methods of applying steam power to the production of products. The availability of machine power and machine tools made practical the gathering of workers in factories that housed the machines. The large number of workers congregated into factories created the need for organizing them in logical ways to produce products. The publication of Adam Smith's *The Wealth of Nations* in 1776 touted the economic benefits of the *division of labor,* also referred to as the *specialization of labor,* which broke the production of products into small, specialized tasks that were assigned to workers along production lines. Thus the factories of the late 1700s had developed not only production machinery, but also ways of planning and controlling the output of production workers.

The industrial revolution spread from England to other European countries and to the United States. Eli Whitney, the American inventor, in 1790 developed the concept of *interchangeable parts.* Whitney designed rifles to be manufactured for the U.S. government on an assembly line such that parts were produced to tolerances that allowed every part to fit right the first time. This method of production displaced the old method of either sorting through parts to find one that fit or modifying a part so that it would fit.

The first great industry in the United States was the textile industry. By the War of 1812, there were almost 200 textile mills in New England. The industrial revolution was advanced further with the development of the gasoline engine and electricity in the 1800s. Other industries emerged, and the need for products to support the Civil War stimulated the establishment of more factories.

By the middle 1800s, the old cottage system of producing products had been replaced by the factory system, but vast improvements to factories were yet to come.

POST–CIVIL WAR PERIOD

A new industrial era for the United States was ushered in with the coming of the twentieth century. The post–Civil War period set the stage for the great expansion of production capacity in the new century. The abolition of slave labor, the exodus of farm laborers to the cities, and the massive influx of immigrants in the 1865–1900 period provided a large work force for the rapidly developing urban industrial centers.

The end of the Civil War witnessed the beginning of modern forms of capital through the establishment of joint stock companies. This development led to the eventual separation of the capitalist from the employer, with managers becoming salaried employees of the financiers who owned the capital. During this post–Civil War period J. P. Morgan, Jay Gould, Cornelius Vanderbilt, and others built industrial empires. These entrepreneurs and the vast accumulation of capital in this period created a great U.S. production capacity that was to mushroom at the turn of the century.

The rapid exploration and settlement of the West created the need for numerous products and a means to deliver them to the product-hungry settlers. The post–Civil War period produced the large railroads, the second great U.S. industry. Rail lines were extended; new territories were developed; and with the coming of the twentieth century, an effective and economical transportation system, national in scope, was in operation.

By 1900 all these developments—increased capital and production capacity, the expanded urban work force, new Western markets, and an effective national transportation system—set the stage for the great production explosion of the early twentieth century.

TABLE 1.1   *Scientific Management: The Players and Their Parts*

Contributor	*Life Span*	*Contributions*
1. Frederick Winslow Taylor	1856–1915	Scientific management principles, exception principle, time study, methods analysis, standards, planning, control
2. Frank B. Gilbreth	1868–1924	Motion study, methods, therbligs, construction contracting, consulting
3. Lillian M. Gilbreth	1878–1973	Fatigue studies, human factor in work, employee selection and training
4. Henry L. Gantt	1861–1919	Gantt charts, incentive pay systems, humanistic approach to labor, training
5. Carl G. Barth	1860–1939	Mathematical analysis, slide rule, feeds and speeds studies, consulting to automobile industry
6. Harrington Emerson	1885–1931	Principles of efficiency, million-dollars-a-day savings in railroads, methods of control
7. Morris L. Cooke	1872–1960	Scientific management application to education and government

SCIENTIFIC MANAGEMENT

The economic and social environments of the new century formed the crucible in which scientific management was formulated. The one missing link was management—the ability to develop this great production machine to satisfy the massive markets of the day. A nucleus of men and women—business executives, consultants, educators, and researchers—developed the methods and philosophy called *scientific management.* Table 1.1 presents the main characters of the scientific management era.

Frederick Winslow Taylor is known as the father of scientific management. This title is well deserved when one considers his personal accomplishments in the face of great obstacles. Although Taylor did not originate most of the techniques that he used to analyze the shop management problems of his day (time study, motion study, and methods study), he brought their use into focus and popularized the notions of efficiency and productivity as had never been done before.

Taylor was born in 1856 in Pennsylvania, the son of a prosperous attorney. With a plan to follow in his father's professional footsteps, he attended preparatory school and applied such energy in his studies that he gradually impaired his eyesight. Although he passed the entrance exams to Harvard Law School with honors, his poor health prevented him from continuing in the legal profession. He turned instead to a four-year apprentice program for pattern makers and machinists. It was here in industry that Taylor found outlets for his interests—scientific investigation, experimentation, and improving and reforming things on the basis of fact. Taylor found industrial conditions that he could not tolerate—worker soldiering (loafing), poor management, and lack of harmony between workers and managers.

Although jobs were scarce in 1878, Taylor found work as a common laborer at the Midvale Steel Company in Philadelphia. In six years he rose from laborer to clerk, to machinist, to gang boss of machinists, to foreman, to master mechanic of maintenance, and finally to chief engineer of the works. While advancing through these positions, he attended Stevens Institute of Technology and received a degree in mechanical engineering. Taylor owed his rapid advancement at Midvale Steel in large part to his scientific investigations into improvements in efficient worker use that resulted in great labor cost savings.

Taylor's *shop system,* a systematic approach to improving labor efficiency, employed the following steps:

1. Skill, strength, and learning ability were determined for each worker so that individuals could be placed in jobs for which they were best suited.
2. Stopwatch studies were used to precisely set standard output per worker on each task. The expected output on each job was used for planning and scheduling work and for comparing different methods of performing tasks.
3. Instruction cards, routing sequences, and materials specifications were used to coordinate and organize the shop so that work methods and work flow could be standardized and labor output standards could be met.
4. Supervision was improved through careful selection and training. Taylor frequently indicated that management was negligent in performing its functions. He believed that management had to accept planning, organizing, controlling, and methods determination responsibilities, rather than leave these important functions to the workers.
5. Incentive pay systems were initiated to increase productivity and to relieve foremen of their traditional responsibility of driving the workers.

In 1893 Taylor left Midvale to form a private consulting practice in order to apply his system to a broader range of situations. Those analysts who followed Taylor were known as *efficiency experts, efficiency engineers,* and, finally, *industrial engineers.* In addition to the title of father of scientific management, Taylor is also known as the father of industrial engineering.

Taylor spent a total of twelve hours over a four-day period in the witness chair before a 1911 congressional investigating committee responding to labor, congressmen, and newsmen on charges that scientific management treated labor unfairly. It is interesting to note that while Taylor has been much maligned in his day and ours with charges of treating workers unfairly, there is no evidence that any company with which Taylor was associated ever experienced a strike over his methods. The great publicity from his testimony at these hearings and Louis Brandeis's call for the use of scientific management in the railroad industry to avoid railroad rate increases in 1910 gave scientific management the public attention it needed to gain widespread acceptance in a broad range of industrial settings in the United States and abroad.

The other scientific management pioneers listed in Table 1.1 rallied to spread the gospel of efficiency. Each of these individuals contributed valuable techniques

TABLE 1.2   *Scientific Management Legacy: Some Practices and Concepts Found in Today's Organization Functions*

Organization Function	Concepts and Practices from Scientific Management
Management	Exception principle Identifying management tasks that are distinctly different from worker tasks Placing responsibility for organizational performance on management Formal education of managers Staff experts Control systems as sensing mechanisms Decision making based on analysis Cost and budgeting systems
Industrial engineering	Time study Motion study Workplace layout and design Work sampling Standardization of tools and work methods Slide rules and mnemonic devices Assembly lines and mass production methods
Personnel management	Incentive pay systems Scientific selection of employees for jobs Employee training Cooperation between workers and management
Operations scheduling and control	Labor and material standards Graphic scheduling devices Planning departments Standardization of product designs

and approaches that eventually shaped scientific management into a powerful force to facilitate mass production. This force was so successfully applied during the U.S. buildup of output for World War I that after the war European countries imported scientific management methods to develop their factories.

Scientific management has dramatically affected today's management practices. Table 1.2 lists a few modern management concepts and practices that find their genesis in scientific management. Scientific management's struggle to find the *one best way* to operate factories leads logically to a questioning attitude on the part of managers in every phase of production systems. The questioning attitude and analytical investigations are perhaps scientific management's greatest legacy to modern management.

The high-water mark of scientific management occurred at the Ford Motor Company early in the twentieth century. Henry Ford (1863–1947) designed the "Model T" Ford automobile to be built on assembly lines that would soon become the basis for designing factories in the future. In Ford's assembly lines were embodied the chief elements of scientific management—standardized product designs, mass production, low manufacturing costs, mechanized assembly lines, specialization of labor, and interchangeable parts. Although Ford did not invent many of the production methods that he used, he did, perhaps more than any other industrial leader of his time, incorporate into his factories the best of that period's efficient production methods. In fact, he was responsible in large measure for popularizing assembly lines as *the* way to produce large volumes of low-cost products. Later this popularity spread to other industries in the United States and abroad.

Industry Snapshot 1.1 describes Ford's massive Rouge plant in the 1920s. The technology of assembly lines, refined to an art at the Rouge, expanded and grew throughout the buildup of production capacity in World War II. And Ford was concerned not only with mass production, he was also concerned for his workers. He paid his workers more than the going wage of the day so that they could afford to buy his cars, and he established "sociological departments" that were forerunners of today's personnel departments.

Scientific management's thrust was at the lower level of the organization's hierarchy—the shop floor, the foremen, the superintendents, and lower middle management. Taylor and his associates concentrated on the shop level because it was here that most management problems of the day were found. What was needed was production and *efficiency*, which means *doing things right* and implies focusing on the details of operations. Scientific management methods met that challenge. Later, Ford's Rouge plant and other firms would focus on the larger picture and attempt to develop organizational *effectiveness*, which means *doing the right things.*

THE HUMAN RELATIONS MOVEMENT

Factory workers of the industrial revolution were uneducated, unskilled, undisciplined, and starving peasants fresh off the farms. Although these workers had a basic dislike for factory work, factory jobs were all that stood between them and starvation. Factory managers developed rigid controls to force them to work hard. This legacy of a working environment structured around rigid controls carried over into the 1800s and early 1900s. Basic to this management method was the assumption that workers had to be placed in jobs designed to ensure that they would work hard and efficiently.

Between World War I and World War II, however, there began to emerge in the United States a philosophy among managers that workers were human beings and should be treated with dignity while on the job. The *human relations movement* began in Illinois with the work of Elton Mayo, F. J. Roethlisberger, T. N. Whitehead, and W. J. Dickson at the Hawthorne, Illinois, plant of the Western Electric Company in the 1927–1932 period. These *Hawthorne Studies* were initially begun by industrial engineers and were aimed at determining the optimal level of lighting to get the most production from workers. When these studies produced confusing results about the relationship between physical environment and worker productivity, the researchers realized that human factors must be affecting productivity. This was perhaps the first time that researchers and managers alike recognized that psychological and sociological factors affected not only human motivation and attitude but productivity as well.

INDUSTRY SNAPSHOT 1.1

Ford's Rouge Plant

At its maturity in the mid-twenties (1920s), the Rouge, located in Detroit, dwarfed all other industrial complexes. It was a mile and a half long and three-quarters of a mile wide. Its 1,100 acres contained 93 buildings, 23 of them major. There were 93 miles of railroad track on it and 27 miles of conveyor belts. Some 75,000 men worked there, 5,000 of them doing nothing but keeping it clean, using 86 tons of soap and wearing out 5,000 mops each month. The Rouge had its own steel mill and glass plant right on site.

Barges carrying iron ore would steam into the inland docks, and even as they were tying up, huge cranes would be swinging out to start unloading. The process was revolutionary. On Monday morning a barge bearing ore would arrive in a slip, and the ore would go to the blast furnace. By Tuesday it would be poured into a foundry mold and later that day would become an engine. John DeVenter, a business historian, wrote in awe: "Here is the conversion of raw material to cash in approximately 33 hours." Some 60 years later Toyota would be credited for its just-in-time theory of manufacturing, in which parts arrived from suppliers just in time to be part of the final assembly. But in any real sense, that process began at the Rouge. Toasting Philip Caldwell, the head of Ford who in 1982 was visiting Japan, Eiji Toyoda, of the Toyota company, said, "There is no secret to how we learned to do what we do, Mr. Caldwell. We learned it at the Rouge."

As the Rouge was switched from the Model T to the A in 1928, it became the most awesomely integrated plant in industrial history. The production of a complete car from raw material to finished item dropped from 21 days to only 4.[3]

---

[3] David Halberstam, *The Reckoning* (New York: Morrow), 87–88.

These early human relations studies and experiments soon gave way to a broad range of research into the behavior of workers in their job environments. The work and writings of Chester Barnard, Abraham Maslow, Frederick Herzberg, Douglas McGregor, Peter Drucker, and others disseminated to industrial managers a basic understanding of workers and their attitudes toward their work. From the work of these *behavioralists,* as they would soon be known, came a gradual change in the way managers thought about and treated workers. We are still learning how to utilize the great potential present in industrial workers today. That they have underutilized capabilities is not questioned, but how to tap this reservoir of energy, ingenuity, and skill remains the objective of many research experiments being carried out today.

OPERATIONS RESEARCH

With the advent of World War II, military, governmental, and industrial organizations in the United States and Europe grew to immense proportions. The European campaign of World War II used enormous quantities of men, supplies, planes, ships, material, and other resources that had to be deployed in efficient ways to accomplish a specific set of objectives in an extremely hectic environment. Perhaps never before had organizations faced such complex management decisions. These particular organizational situations created the need for a problem-solving approach aimed at solving management's problems with a top-of-the-organization perspective.

Because of this complexity, *operations research* teams were formed in all branches of the military services. These teams utilized many of the academic disciplines of the time. The concepts of a *total systems approach* and of *interdisciplinary teams* and the utilization of *complex mathematical techniques* evolved as a result of the chaotic conditions existing in the huge military organizations involved in World War II. Operations research (OR) met the needs of the time.

After World War II, military operations researchers and their approaches to complex organizational problems found their way back to universities, industry, governmental agencies, and consulting firms. These researchers introduced operations research into the curriculums of colleges and universities, developed consulting firms that specialized in operations research, and formed operations research societies. As time passed, operations research matured, and its characteristics (shown in Table 1.3) became those that we know today.

During the postwar era, operations research has been, and perhaps today still is, known chiefly for its quantitative techniques, such as linear programming, PERT/CPM, and forecasting models. One study of 1,398 manufacturing firms with 250 or more employees indicated that about half these firms used one or more of these techniques in their daily operations.[4] As firms become larger and use higher levels of technology, adoption of the techniques is more intense.

Operations research helps operations managers make decisions when problems are complex and when the cost of a wrong decision is high and long-lasting. Problems such as the following are commonly analyzed by using operations research techniques:

1. A company has 12 manufacturing plants that ship products to 48 warehouses nationwide. How many units of each product should be shipped from each plant to each warehouse? In other words, what is the optimal shipping plan to maximize profits?
2. A firm contemplates building a $157 million production facility. The project involves company resources, 2 prime contractors, and 75 subcontractors over a 4-year period. How can the company plan the completion of each activity of the project and the use of workers, materials, and contractors so that the cost and the duration of the project are minimized?

Operations research, like scientific management, seeks to replace intuitive decision making for large complex problems with an approach that identifies the optimal, or best, alternative through analysis. Operations managers, like managers of other functional areas in organizations, have adopted the approaches and techniques of operations research to improve their decision making.

---

[4] Norman Gaither, "The Adoption of Operations Research Techniques by Manufacturing Organizations," *Decision Sciences* 6(October 1975):808.

■■■

TABLE 1.3   *Characteristics of Operations Research (OR)*

1. OR approaches problem solving and decision making from the total system's perspective.
2. OR does not necessarily use interdisciplinary teams, but it is interdisciplinary; it draws on techniques from sciences such as biology, physics, chemistry, mathematics, and economics and applies the appropriate techniques from each field to the system being studied.
3. OR does not experiment with the system itself but constructs a model of the system upon which to conduct experiments.
4. Model building and mathematical manipulation provide the methodology that has perhaps been the key contribution of OR.
5. The primary focus is on decision making.
6. Computers are used extensively.

■■■

Although scientific management, human relations, and operations research have affected the ways that managers in POM manage today, perhaps no other development is as important to these managers as the growing presence of computers in their jobs.

COMPUTERS AND ADVANCED PRODUCTION TECHNOLOGY

Since the first computer was installed at the General Electric Appliance Park in Louisville, Kentucky, in 1954, the number of computers in businesses has increased enormously. Computers have become a growing force with which operations managers have had to contend, and as a consequence their day-to-day jobs have been tremendously changed. Table 1.4 traces the evolving use of computers in POM.

The early uses of computers were mainly for cost reduction purposes, replacing clerical jobs with machines. Payroll, billing, and other accounting applications are examples of this earlier cost reduction emphasis. In the 1960s, companies began to use software that provided operations managers with analyses of their operations. Forecasting, linear programming, and scheduling are examples of this analytical software. These applications made analyses of operations less costly and more timely. Also, analyses could be made that were previously impossible because of the number of calculations required.

In the 1970s, manufacturing planning and control software was developed, installed, and used by many companies. This use of computers forms the basis of *manufacturing information systems,* which are intended to provide operations managers with the information to manage operations more effectively. Information from such diverse areas as demand forecasts, purchasing, inventories, scheduling, and shop floor control are integrated into one information system. Such information systems are used to store massive quantities of data and to manipulate and retrieve these data as managers may require. These systems have improved the amount and quality of information available to operations managers. Material requirements planning (MRP) systems are an example of such information systems. We shall study more about MRP in Chapter 11.

TABLE 1.4   The Evolving Uses of Computers in POM

Years	Key Applications	Examples of Applications
1950s	Clerical duties	Payrolls, billings, inventory transactions, cost reports
1960s	Analysis of operations	Linear programming, scheduling, project planning and control
1970s	Manufacturing planning and control systems	Information systems for manufacturing that integrate forecasting, inventory planning, material requirements planning (MRP), scheduling, and shop floor control
1980s	Computer-integrated manufacturing (CIM)	Robotics, engineering design terminals, flexible manufacturing systems (FMS), automated storage and retrieval systems (ASRS), bar-coding systems, computer-aided design and computer-aided manufacturing (CAD/CAM)
1990s	Decision support systems (DSS), expert systems, and artificial intelligence (AI)	Computer systems that managers or analysts use to study operational problems and obtain solutions. These systems may provide computational support or imitate decision makers' thought processes.

In the 1980s, the term *factories of the future* became popular. In these factories, computers would be used extensively and would form the core of *high-tech* production methods. CAD/CAM, which means computer-aided design and computer-aided manufacturing, became the buzz word that was commonly used to describe this phase in the evolving use of computers in POM. Later, computer-integrated manufacturing (CIM) became the catch-all term for computer applications in manufacturing. Table 1.5 defines and describes some of the computer systems that are found in these factories of the future.

The U.S. companies Computervision, IBM, Intergraph, Calma-GE, and Applicon supply about three-quarters of the more than $3 billion annual market for these turnkey CAD/CAM systems. Many Japanese firms and other U.S. firms such as Westinghouse, General Electric, General Motors, and Ford have developed elaborate CAD/CAM systems, flexible manufacturing systems (FMS), and automatic storage and retrieval systems (ASRS) for their own use and are expected to be important suppliers of these systems to other companies in the future. Although the full impact of these systems is not expected to be immediate, these systems should allow U.S. manufacturing and service companies to become more cost and quality competitive with their foreign counterparts. We shall study more about the strategic importance of these systems in Chapters 2 and 5.

THE SERVICE REVOLUTION

One of the most startling developments of our time is the mushrooming of services in the U.S. economy. More than two-thirds of the U.S. work force is employed in

TABLE 1.5   *Some High-Tech Manufacturing Systems in Factories of the Future*

Term	Definition and Description
Computer-Aided Design (CAD)	Specialized software and hardware to allow engineers to design products directly on computer terminals. May be linked to larger computer system so designs can be communicated to others. Such companies as General Electric, Texas Instruments, Exxon, Eastman Kodak, Xerox, General Motors, Boeing, DuPont, and Caterpillar Tractor have these systems. Approximate cost is $300,000 to $500,000.
Computer-Aided Manufacturing (CAM)	Specialized computer systems that translate the CAD information into instructions for automated production machinery. This machinery performs the necessary production operations on the products with a minimum of direct worker involvement. CAM is not so well developed as CAD. The hardware that is required, such as the microprocessors that are the brains of the automated machinery, is available. But the software that is necessary to convert the designs into full manufacturing instructions is not yet widely available.
Flexible Manufacturing Systems (FMS)	Clusters of automated machines that are controlled by computers. These clusters produce a variety of products on the same machinery. Computers give the instructions, robots handle the parts and materials, and machine settings are automatically changed as required to produce the different products. Although there are few such systems so far, General Electric's electric-meter plant in New Hampshire produces 2,000 different meters on the same flexible equipment and is an example of this approach and perhaps a vision of what is coming in the future.
Automated Storage and Retrieval Systems (ASRS)	Computer-controlled warehouses that include automatic placement of parts into the warehouse, automatic removal of parts from the warehouse as needed in manufacturing or shipping, and automatic transportation of parts to and from the warehouse. An example of such elaborate systems is found at Westinghouse's College Station, Texas, plant.
Automatic Identification Systems (AIS)	Bar codes, radio frequencies, or optical characters that are designed to represent data are read by scanners that transmit data to computers. An example of these systems can be seen at many grocery checkout counters. The bar codes on items are passed across the scanner and price, item description, inventory number, and other data are read and stored in a computer for processing.

TABLE 1.6   Service Companies That Rank among the Top 15 U.S. Corporations

Measure of Size	Company	Rank
Market value	AT&T	4
	BellSouth	11
	Wal-Mart Stores	14
Profits	AT&T	6
	BellSouth	9
	Sears, Roebuck	10
	Nynex	14
Sales	AT&T	6
	Sears, Roebuck	7
	Citicorp	12
	K mart	14
Assets	Citicorp	1
	American Express	2
	Fannie Mae	3
	Chase Manhattan	4
	BankAmerica	5
	Chemical New York	7
	J. P. Morgan	8
	Sears, Roebuck	9
	Salomon	10
	Manufacturers Hanover	11
	Security Pacific	12
	Aetna	13
	Shearson Lehman	15

Source: *Business Week,* Apr. 15, 1988, 32–33.

services, roughly two-thirds of the GNP is produced by services, and investment per office worker now exceeds the investment per factory worker. Table 1.6 shows that some of our largest companies are service companies. These companies also cover a wide range of services. Consider the diversity of the private service industries and their companies listed in Table 1.7. Furthermore, these tables do not include the local, state, and federal government agencies that exist to provide public services to citizens.

The impact of this explosion of service organizations on operations management has been enormous. As we proceed through this text, we shall explore some of the difficulties and opportunities in managing these many private and public services for productivity, quality, and competitiveness.

Scientific management, human relations, operations research, and computer-based technology have all affected and *are continuing to affect* the ways that operations managers manage today. In our continued study of POM, let us consider some of the different ways of looking at the field.

TABLE 1.7   *Some Service Industries and Service Companies*

Service Industries	Representative Companies
Airlines	Delta Air Lines, Texas Air
Banks	Citicorp, J. P. Morgan
Discount, fashion retailing	Wal-Mart Stores, Sears, Roebuck
Food distribution	Super Value Stores, SYSCO
Food retailing	Food Lion, Kroger
Drug distribution	Henley Group, Walgreen
Health care	Hospital Corporation of America, Humana
Housing/real estate	Rouse, Kaufman & Broad
Eating places	McDonald's, Wendy's
Entertainment	Walt Disney, Warner Communications
Hotel and motel	Marriott, Hilton Hotels
Financial services	American Express, Loews
Insurance	American General, Aetna
Savings and loans	Great Western Financial, H. F. Ahmanson
Business services	Pitney-Bowes, Electronic Data Systems
Broadcasting	Capital Cities/ABC, CBS
Computer services	Microsoft, Lotus Development
Construction/engineering	Flour, Combustion Engineering
Industrial distribution	Genuine Parts, W. W. Grainger
Pollution control	Waste Management, Browning-Ferris Industries
Printing/advertising	R. R. Donnelley & Sons, Interpublic Group
Publishing	Dun & Bradstreet, Gannett
Railroads	Union Pacific, CSX
Telecommunications	MCI Communications, United Telecommunications
Telephone	AT&T, NYNEX
Transportation services	Ryder System, Federal Express
Trucking	Roadway Services, Consolidated Freightways
Utilities	Pacific Gas & Electric, Commonwealth Edison

Source: *Business Week,* Apr. 15, 1988, 233–292.

DIFFERENT WAYS OF VIEWING POM

Over the years, there have been many ways of approaching the study of POM. Among the traditional approaches, three viewpoints of POM have tended to dominate: production as a system, production as an organizational function, and decision making in POM.

PRODUCTION AS A SYSTEM

Russell Ackoff, a pioneer in systems theory, describes a system: "A *system* is a whole that cannot be taken apart without loss of its essential characteristics, and hence it must be studied as a whole. Now, instead of explaining a whole in terms of its parts,

TABLE 1.8   *Production Systems Concepts*

Concept	Definition
1. Production system	A system whose function is to convert a set of inputs into a set of desired outputs
2. Conversion subsystem	A subsystem of the larger production system where inputs are converted into outputs
3. Control subsystem	A subsystem of the larger production system where a portion of the outputs is monitored for feedback signals to provide corrective action if required

parts began to be explained in terms of the whole."[5] The concepts from the field of systems theory are helpful in understanding production as a system.

Table 1.8 gives the definitions of three important production systems concepts —a production system, a conversion subsystem, and a control subsystem. Production systems receive *inputs* in the form of materials, personnel, capital, utilities, and information. These inputs are changed in a *conversion subsystem* into the desired products and services, which are called *outputs.* A portion of the output is monitored in the *control subsystem* to determine if it is acceptable in terms of quantity, cost, and quality. If the output is acceptable, no changes are required in the system. If, however, the appropriate standards are not met, managerial corrective action is required. The control subsystem ensures a uniform level of system performance by providing feedback information so that corrective action can be taken by managers.

A Production System Model

Figure 1.2 illustrates a production system model. Inputs are classified into three general classes—environment, market, and primary resources. *Environmental inputs* generally are informational in character and tend to provide operations managers with knowledge about conditions outside of the production system. *Legal* or *political inputs* may establish constraints within which the system must operate.

Social and *economic inputs* allow operations managers to sense trends that may affect the production system in the future. *Technological inputs* may come from trade journals, government bulletins, trade association newsletters, suppliers, and other sources. This information provides managers with knowledge about important breakthroughs in technology that affect machinery, tools, or processes. Like environmental inputs, *market inputs* tend to be informational in character. Information concerning competition, product design, customer desires, and other aspects of the

---

[5] Russell L. Ackoff, "A Note on Systems Science," *Interfaces* 2(August 1972):40.

FIGURE 1.2   A Production System Model

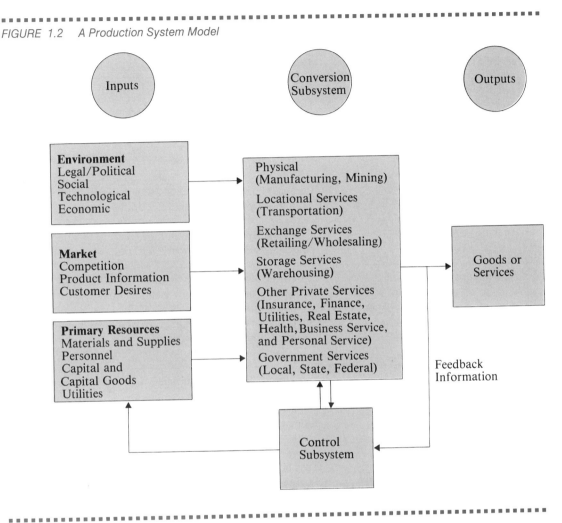

market is essential if the production system is to respond to the needs of the market. Inputs that directly support the production and delivery of goods and services are referred to as *primary resources*. These are materials and supplies, personnel, capital and capital goods, and utilities (water, gas, oil, coal, electricity).

Outputs of production systems can take one of two forms, tangible or intangible. An enormous array of *tangible goods* is produced each day — automobiles, hair dryers, toothpicks, calculators, rubber bands, clothes, tractors, vertical boring mills, typewriters, and agricultural products. Similarly, the services — the *intangible outputs* that pour from production systems seem inexhaustible: education, trash hauling, haircuts, tax accounting, hospitals, government agencies, banking, insurance, lodging, transportation, and so on. All of these goods and services are not the end but

TABLE 1.9   *Some Typical Production Systems*

Production System	**Primary Inputs**
1. Pet food factory	Grain, water, fish meal, personnel, tools, machines, paper bags, cans, buildings, utilities
2. Hamburger stand	Meat, bread, vegetables, spices, supplies, personnel, utilities, machines, cartons, napkins, buildings, hungry customers
3. Automobile factory	Purchased parts, raw materials, supplies, paints, tools, equipment, personnel, buildings, utilities
4. Trucking firm	Trucks, personnel, buildings, fuel, goods to be shipped, packaging supplies, truck parts, utilities
5. Department store	Buildings, displays, shopping carts, machines, stock goods, personnel, supplies, utilities, customers
6. Public accounting firm	Supplies, personnel, information, computers, buildings, office furniture, machines, utilities
7. Automobile body shop	Damaged autos, paints, supplies, machines, tools, buildings, personnel, utilities
8. College or university	Students, books, supplies, personnel, buildings, utilities
9. County sheriff's department	Supplies, personnel, equipment, automobiles, office furniture, buildings, utilities
10. National Marine Fisheries Service	Supplies, personnel, ships, computers, aircraft, utilities, office furniture, equipment

the beginning of production systems. It is because of outputs, the products and services, that production systems are established.

Interestingly, we often overlook indirect outputs of production systems. Taxes, waste and pollution, technological advances, wages and salaries, and community outreach activities are examples of indirect outputs. Although they do not receive the same attention as the goods and services outputs that generate the revenues which perpetuate the systems, the indirect outputs are a cause of both concern and pride. An awareness that such factors are indeed outputs of our production systems causes operations managers to perform their jobs more effectively.

Conversion Subsystem	Outputs
Converts raw materials into finished goods (physical)	Pet food products
Transforms raw materials into fast-food products and packages (physical)	Satisfied customers and fast-food products
Transforms raw materials into finished automobiles through fabrication and assembly operations (physical)	Automobiles
Packages and transports goods from sources to destinations (locational)	Delivered goods
Attracts customers, stores goods, sells products (exchange)	Marketed goods
Attracts customers, compiles data, supplies management information, computes taxes (private service)	Management information and tax services
Transforms damaged auto bodies into facsimiles of the originals (private service)	Repaired automobile bodies
Transmits information and develops skills and knowledge (private/public service)	Educated persons
Detects crimes, brings criminals to justice, keeps the peace (public service)	Acceptable crime rates and peaceful communities
Detects offenders of federal fishery laws, brings them to justice, preserves fishery resources (public service)	Optimal stock of fish resources

Production System Diversity

All organizations have at least one production system. A wide variety of these systems exist, several examples of which are shown in Table 1.9. The inputs, outputs, and conversion subsystems are not difficult to identify in production systems that produce physical goods. The components of service systems, however, tend to be more difficult to recognize. Why is it necessary or desirable to view these service systems as production systems?

Because the service sector represents such a large share of the nation's employment and GNP, efforts to improve the competitiveness of U.S. organizations must include services. Service organizations need better management as much or even more than our manufacturing organizations do. Being able to analyze service systems in the production system framework allows the application of tried and proven POM approaches and the development of new approaches to fit novel service system situations.

How a production system is manifested as part of an organization differs considerably from firm to firm. Let us examine some diverse organizational schemes for these production functions.

PRODUCTION AS AN ORGANIZATION FUNCTION

The core of a production system is its conversion subsystem, wherein workers, materials, and machines are used to convert inputs into products and services. This process of conversion is at the heart of production and operations management and is present in some form in all organizations. *Where* this conversion process is carried out and *what we call* the department or function where it is located vary greatly among organizations. Be assured, however, that every organization, regardless of its purpose, has a production function whose departments and personnel play a central role in achieving the objectives of the organization.

Table 1.10 compares the jobs and names of the production function departments of three different types of firms. This table shows the typical job titles given to the line and staff jobs within the production function, the name of the department where the production function is housed, and the jobs in other departments that are also a part of the larger production system but not directly assigned to the production function. Notice that services such as retailing and trucking tend to use the word *operations* rather than *production* for the name of the production function department, and also that the types of jobs that are considered line jobs tend to depend on the purpose of the organization.

Although the department names and job titles of production functions differ among diverse organizations, such production functions are nevertheless present and constitute important parts of all organizations. In this text we shall see many of the job titles and department names found in Table 1.10 as we study a variety of situations in real-world organizations.

It was stated at the beginning of this chapter that POM is reemerging as a central player in the struggle to make U.S. corporations competitive with companies from Japan and other foreign countries. There is a widely held consensus that in today's world of international competition and technological expansion, U.S. companies cannot compete with the Japanese organizations with marketing, finance, accounting, and engineering alone. Increasingly, attention is on POM because that is where the vast majority of a firm's workers and capital assets are. And, it is in POM that our ability to produce low-cost products and services of superior quality in a timely manner resides. We need new products, good marketing, and shrewd finance, but we must also have a strong operations function teaming with the other organization functions if we are to succeed in international competition.

Let us now turn to another way of viewing POM — decision making of operations managers.

TABLE 1.10 Production and Operations Functions and Jobs in Diverse Organizations

	Production Function Departments and Jobs			
Type of Firm	Some Line Jobs	Some Staff Jobs	Name of Production Function's Department	Some Production System Activities in Other Departments (Jobs—Department)
Manufacturing	V.P. manufacturing Plant manager Production manager Superintendent Foreman Team leader Crew chief	Manufacturing engineer Industrial engineer Quality control manager Quality control engineer Materials manager Inventory analyst Production scheduler	Manufacturing	Purchasing agent—purchasing Buyer—purchasing Personnel specialist—personnel Product designer—marketing or engineering Budget analyst—accounting Shipping specialist—shipping
Retailing	V.P. operations Store manager Operations manager Departmental supervisor Sales clerk Stocking clerk	Customer service manager Security manager Maintenance manager Supplies specialist Warehouse manager	Operations	Purchasing agent—merchandising Buyer—merchandising Merchandise control analyst—merchandising Budget analyst—accounting Inspector—merchandising
Trucking	Owner V.P. operations Branch manager Dock supervisor Truck operations manager Driver Dock worker	Rates specialist Maintenance director Truck scheduler Repair mechanic Dispatcher	Operations	Personnel manager—personnel Stores manager—administrative services Budget analyst—accounting Systems analyst—accounting Purchasing manager—administrative services

DECISION MAKING IN POM

Earlier in this chapter we defined POM in terms of what operations managers do. They plan, organize, staff, direct, and control all of the activities of production systems—those portions of organizations that convert inputs into products and services. This definition states in very general terms *what* POM is, but *how* operations managers manage may be just as important to understanding POM as what operations managers do. Perhaps no other approach helps us understand *how* operations managers manage than the examination of the decisions in POM, because, in large part, operations managers manage by making decisions about all of the activities of production systems.

Strategic, Operating, and Control Decisions

Classifying POM decisions is difficult, but in my experience as an operations manager, decisions tended to fall into three general categories:

- *Strategic decisions:* Decisions about products, processes, and facilities. These decisions are of strategic importance and have long-term significance for the organization.
- *Operating decisions:* Decisions about planning production to meet demand. These decisions are necessary if the on-going production of goods and services is to satisfy the demands of the market and provide profits for the company.
- *Control decisions:* Decisions about planning and controlling operations. These decisions concern the day-to-day activities of workers, quality of products and services, production and overhead costs, and maintenance of machines.

Strategic decisions concern operations strategies and the long-range game plan for the firm. These decisions are so important that typically people from production, personnel, engineering, marketing, and finance get together to study the business opportunities carefully and to arrive at a decision that puts the organization in the best position for achieving its long-term goals. Examples of this type of planning decision are:

1. Deciding whether to launch a new-product development project
2. Deciding on the design for a production process for a new product
3. Deciding how to allocate scarce raw materials, utilities, production capacity, and personnel among new and existing business opportunities
4. Deciding what new factories are needed and where to locate them

It seems that such decisions are always in the works. Those of us who are not tied directly to the supervision of workers in operations spend a good part of our time studying problems of this type. In the meantime, production is going on every day, and we must also be concerned with making decisions about the on-going activities of production.

Operating decisions must resolve all of the issues concerning planning production to meet customers' demands for products and services. The principal responsibility of operations is to take the orders for products and services from customers, which the marketing function has generated, and deliver products and services in such a way that we have *satisfied customers* at reasonable costs. In carrying out this responsibility, numerous decisions are made. Examples of this type of decision are:

1. Deciding how much finished goods inventory to carry for each product
2. Deciding what products and how much of each to include in next month's production schedule
3. Deciding whether to increase production capacity next month by having the foundry department work overtime or to subcontract part of the production to suppliers
4. Deciding the details of a plan for purchasing raw materials to support next month's production schedule

Such decisions are fundamental to the success of the production function and the entire organization.

Control decisions are concerned with a variety of day-to-day problems in operations. The facts of life for operations managers are that their workers do not always perform as expected, product quality tends to vary, and production machinery tends to break down and usually does so when it is least expected. Operations managers engage in planning, analyzing, and controlling activities so that poor worker performance, inferior product quality, and excessive machine breakdowns do not interfere with the profitable operation of the production system. Examples of this type of decision are:

1. Deciding what to do about a department's failure to meet the planned labor cost target
2. Developing labor cost standards for a revised product design that is about to go into production
3. Deciding what the new quality control acceptance criteria should be for a product that has had a change in design
4. Deciding how often to perform preventive maintenance on a key piece of production machinery

The day-to-day decisions about workers, product quality, and production machinery, when taken together, may be the most pervasive aspect of an operations manager's job.

Decision-Based Framework of This Book

This book is organized on the basis of the following general framework: *strategic decisions*—planning products, processes, and facilities; *operating decisions*—planning production to meet demand; and *control decisions*—planning and controlling operations. Table 1.11 outlines the remainder of the book in terms of this framework.

For a more in-depth discussion of decision making in POM, see Appendix F at the back of this book. This appendix provides a detailed examination of the characteristics of POM decisions, the levels of analysis of POM decisions, the nature of decision making in POM, and the techniques for analyzing decisions in POM.

TABLE 1.11   *Framework of This Book in Terms of POM Decisions*

Type of Decision	Chapter	Nature of Chapter Content
Part II Strategic Decisions: Planning products, pro- cesses, and facilities	4. Production Processes	Developing long-range production plans including process design
	5. Production Technology	Selecting and managing production technology
	6. Facility Layout	Planning the arrangement of facilities
	7. Allocating Resources to Strategic Alternatives	Planning for the optimal distribution of scarce resources among product lines or business units
	8. Long-Range Capacity Planning and Facility Location	Answering the *how much* and *where* questions about long-range production capacity
Part III Operating Decisions: Planning production to meet demand	9. Production-Planning Systems	Aggregate planning and master production scheduling
	10. Independent Demand Inventory Systems	Planning and controlling finished goods inventories
	11. Resource Requirements Planning Systems	Planning materials and capacity requirements
	12. Shop Floor Planning and Control	Short-range decisions about what to produce and when to produce at each work center
	13. Materials Management and Purchasing	Managing all facets of the materials system
Part IV Control Decisions: Planning and control- ling operations	14. Productivity and Employees	Planning for the effective and efficient use of human resources in operations
	15. Total Quality Control	Planning and controlling the quality of products and services
	16. Planning and Controlling Projects	Planning and controlling projects
	17. Maintenance Management and Reliability	Planning for maintaining the machines and facilities of production

SUMMARY

In this chapter we have discussed the reemergence of POM, defined POM, discussed historical developments in POM, and presented three ways of viewing POM.

The post–Civil War period, the scientific management era, the human relations movement, operations research, and computers and high-tech manufacturing represent five important historical developments for POM. As POM has adapted to these events of the past, so also is POM meeting contemporary challenges.

Viewing production as a production system is important because this scheme allows us to study a diversity of production situations having the same framework. These systems convert inputs such as materials, labor, capital, and utilities into outputs that are their products and services. A great variety of production systems exist in today's organizations. Understanding systems concepts (inputs, conversion subsystems, and outputs) should result in improved management of these systems.

Viewing production as an organization function helps us identify the conversion activity in a variety of organizations. All organizations, regardless of their purposes, have production functions — departments where the conversion process actually occurs. The location of these departments within organizations and the types of jobs in these departments vary greatly among organizations. Although such variance is nearly as great as the diversity of purposes among organizations, production functions and their personnel play central roles in achieving the objectives of their organizations.

Studying decision making in POM helps us understand how operations managers go about their jobs. Strategic decisions (planning products, processes, and facilities), operating decisions (planning production to meet demand), and control decisions (planning and controlling operations) have been described as a helpful way of viewing decision making in POM.

REVIEW AND DISCUSSION QUESTIONS

1. Define *POM*.
2. What role did the settlement of the American West play in the development of factories in the post–Civil War period?
3. Describe Frederick Winslow Taylor's shop management approach.
4. Why was scientific management in the early 1900s aimed at the shop floor level?
5. Who were the foremost pioneers in scientific management, and what were their contributions?
6. Write a brief biography of Frederick Winslow Taylor.
7. What are the characteristics of operations research?
8. To what extent are operations research techniques used in today's organizations?
9. Define these terms: *CIM, CAD, CAM, FMS, ASRS,* and *AIS.*

10. Explain what is meant by the term *service revolution*. Name five service industries. What approximate percentages of U.S. employment and GNP originate in the service sector?

11. Define *production system*. How does the concept of a production system help in the understanding of POM?

12. What are the inputs to production systems? How can they be classified?

13. Define *conversion subsystems*. How can they be classified?

14. Define *outputs* of production systems. Why does all production activity begin, rather than end, with outputs?

15. Define *control subsystems*. Do all organizations have them? Describe some of them. What do they control?

16. Describe the primary inputs, outputs, and conversion subsystems of the following organizations:
    a. a dry-cleaning business,
    b. a television factory,
    c. a medical clinic,
    d. a local fire department, and
    e. a public employment office.

17. Name two organizations that have no production functions. Defend your answer.

18. What are the probable job titles of the top operations managers at a retailing firm and a manufacturing firm? Compare and contrast the nature of their jobs.

19. Define *strategic decision*. Give an example of a strategic decision for:
    a. a retailer,
    b. a manufacturer, and
    c. a government agency.

20. Define *operating decision*. Give an example for:
    a. a computer center,
    b. a university, and
    c. a manufacturer.

21. Define *control decision*. Give an example for:
    a. a museum
    b. a ship, and
    c. a hot dog stand.

SELECTED BIBLIOGRAPHY

Ackoff, Russell L. "A Note on Systems Science." *Interfaces* 2(August 1972):40.

Andrew, C. G., et al. "The Critical Importance of Production and Operations Management." *Academy of Management Review* 7(January 1982):143–147.

Budnick, F. S., R. Mojena, and T. E. Vollman. *Principles of Operations Research.* Homewood, IL: Richard D. Irwin, 1977, 12–13.

Buffa, Elwood S. *Meeting the Competitive Challenge.* Homewood, IL: Dow Jones-Irwin, 1984, 93–94.

"Business Refocuses on the Factory Floor." *Business Week,* Feb. 21, 1981.

Bylinsky, Gene. "The Race to the Automatic Factory." *Fortune,* Feb. 21, 1983, 52–60.

Churchman, C. W. *Systems Approach.* New York: Dell, 1969.

Copely, F. B. *Frederick W. Taylor,* vol. 2. New York: Harper, 1923.

Economic Report of the President, February 1986.

Gaither, Norman. "The Adoption of Operations Research Techniques by Manufacturing Organizations." *Decision Sciences* 6(October 1975):797–813.

George, Claude S., Jr. *The History of Management Thought.* Englewood Cliffs, NJ: Prentice-Hall, 1968.

Gerwin, Donald. "Do's and Don'ts of Computerized Manufacturing." *Harvard Business Review* (March–April 1982): 107–116.

Ginzberg, E. "The Service Sector of the U.S. Economy." *Scientific American* 244(March 1981): 48–55.

Gold, B. "CAM Sets New Rules for Production." *Harvard Business Review* 60 (November–December 1982): 88–94.

Groover, Mikell P., and E. W. Zimmers, Jr. *CAD/CAM: Computer-Aided Design and Manufacturing.* Englewood Cliffs, NJ: Prentice-Hall, 1984.

Groover, M. P., and J. C. Wiginton. "CIM and the Flexible Automated Factory of the Future." *Industrial Engineering* (January 1986): 74–85.

Halberstam, David. *The Reckoning.* New York: Morrow, 1986.

"Hard Times Push B-Schools Into Basics." *Business Week,* Aug. 30, 1982, 23–34.

"IBM's Automated Factory—A Giant Step Forward." *Modern Materials Handling* (March 1985).

Kanet, J., and C. Mertens. "Expert Systems in Production Management: An Assessment." *Journal of Operations Management* 16, no. 4(August 1986): 393–404.

Mabert, V. A. "Service Operations Management." *Journal of Operations Management* 2, no. 4(August 1982): 203–209.

McClosky, Joseph F., and Florence N. Trefethen. *Operations Research for Management.* Baltimore: Johns Hopkins Press, 1954.

"New MIT Dean Seeking Better Technical Literacy." *Houston Chronicle,* June 15, 1987, sec. 2, 1.

Rosenthal, Stephen. "Progress Toward the Factory of the Future." *Journal of Operations Management* 4, no. 3(May 1984): 203–229.

"Schools Again Offer Courses on Production." *The Wall Street Journal,* Jan. 26, 1981.

Shostack, G. Lynn. "Designing Services That Deliver." *Harvard Business Review* 62(January–February 1984): 133–139.

Taylor, Frederick Winslow. *Shop Management.* New York: Harper, 1911.

———. *The Principles of Scientific Management.* New York: Harper, 1923.

Wren, Daniel A. *The Evolution of Management Thought.* New York: Ronald Press, 1972.

CHAPTER

2

OPERATIONS STRATEGY
OPERATIONS AS A COMPETITIVE WEAPON

HEALTH OF U.S. MANUFACTURING: A PESSIMISTIC VIEW FROM THE 1980s

In spite of stepped-up rhetoric about "competitiveness," U.S. manufacturers still lagged behind many of their foreign challengers in the late 1980s. Foreign manufacturers that once relied on low prices to sell their goods are moving upscale and testing traditional American strengths — high quality, extra features, skillful marketing, and rapid response to changing customer demands. Unless American manufacturers can reassert leadership in those areas, they will have to rely on a cheaper dollar and falling real wages to compete with the likes of Hong Kong and Taiwan. Edward Finein, Manager of Competitive Practices at Xerox Corporation, says that "most U.S. companies have not really faced up to the size of the challenge that they have in front of them, and have not really made the investment to go after it."[1]

---

[1] Peter Coy, Associated Press, "Manufacturing Dilemma: Low Wages, Foreign Competition Eroding Traditional U.S. Superiority in Productivity," *Houston Chronicle,* June 14, 1987, sec. 5, 2.

As the previous article suggests, throughout the 1980s many of our U.S. industries were in deep trouble. Their products were too costly and the quality of their products was too shoddy when compared to products from Japan and Western Europe. The majority of all products mass-produced in the United States were facing an uphill battle to maintain their share of world markets. Firms from Japan, Korea, Taiwan, China, Mexico, Hong Kong, Singapore, and Brazil were rapidly expanding their share of world markets. Meanwhile, U.S. producers in the steel, automobile, textile, shoe, copper, semiconductor, and electronics industries were losing world market share.

Annual U.S. trade deficits reached staggering proportions during the late 1980s, and the nation was frequently reminded of the severity of the problem by a steady stream of newspaper headlines such as these:

- Smokestack America Collapses, Ghost Plants Dot Landscape
- Steel Imports Capture Third of U.S. Market
- Minicars from Japan Flood U.S. Market
- Soviet-Made Farm Tractors Catching on in U.S.
- New Reality: U.S. Products Are Losing the Race
- NEC Gains on TI in Semiconductor Sales
- FTC Argues for Curbs on Auto Imports

The doom and gloom reflected in these headlines cast a pall over U.S. manufacturing in the last decade. From the depths of this manufacturing dilemma came calls for quick fixes and gimmicks. Some commentators said that just-in-time (JIT) manufacturing methods or better materials requirements planning (MRP) systems was the answer, and others said that we needed more robots in our factories. Some suggested that we needed more computers or that labor unions were responsible for much of manufacturing's problems. Still others said that if U.S. managers were closer to their workers and if they provided lifetime employment for their workers as did Japanese managers, we could somehow find our way out of this morass.

Considering our manufacturing problems of the 1970s and 1980s, we might well wonder about the prospects for U.S. manufacturers in the 1990s. Industry Snapshot 2.1 indicates that there are reasons for optimism about the future health of U.S. manufacturing. Although some U.S. industries are still in trouble, our manufacturing sector is predicted to generate a trade surplus in the 1990s, primarily because of a lower valuation of the dollar, increased research and development (R&D) spending, and productivity improvements.

While there are signs of optimism for U.S. manufacturing, we are not out of the woods yet. Nevertheless, we have moved beyond a profound pessimism about U.S. manufacturing and the simplistic answers and prescriptions of the last decade. What has emerged is a stark realization that if some of our U.S. manufacturing industries are to survive in the long run, quick fixes, gimmicks, slogans, and currency exchange rate swings are not the answers. We must make *fundamental* changes in the way we plan, structure, and manage our corporations, factories, and service operations.

The Japanese manufacturers may not be our only foreign competitors today, but it is perhaps true that for many of us they represent the greatest manufacturing success story that we have seen in our lifetime. As we explore ways to make U.S.

INDUSTRY SNAPSHOT 2.1

Health of U.S. Manufacturing: Optimistic Signals for the 1990s

Wharton Econometrics predicts trade in merchandise—including manufactured goods—will balance by 1996 and hit a surplus of $63 billion (in 1982 dollars) by the year 2000. Robert Malone, editor-in-chief of *Managing Automation* magazine, thinks the main reasons for this turnaround are a devalued dollar relative to other foreign currencies and smarter use of automation, but he warns that automation is also available to foreign competitors. If these sources are correct, the U.S. will run a trade surplus by the turn of the century, and the surplus will have to be generated by strong exports of manufactured goods, because agriculture and services make up a smaller part of international trade.[2]

Says the *Morgan Economic Quarterly,* published by the Morgan Guaranty Trust Company, American companies have become considerably leaner and more fit in the tough competitive environment of the 1980s. Labor productivity in manufacturing, often cited as evidence of the American decline, has risen in the past four years almost half again as rapidly as the long-term trend. Another complaint, that Americans aren't interested in plowing money into research and development (R&D), might have been true once. It isn't anymore. Outlays for R&D, the wellspring of new products are three times those of 20 years ago. The improvement in the economy was hidden for a while by the high valuation of the dollar in international trade. That the economy has been resurrected may be one of the reasons why the Japanese are putting their money into American plants, American real estate, and American stocks and bonds. They might see something that isn't entirely obvious to those nearer the scene.[3]

---

[2] Ibid.
[3] "Is U.S. Economy Stronger than Realized?" *Houston Chronicle,* Aug. 31, 1987, sec. 2, 3.

manufacturers more successful, it is worthwhile to consider the reasons for the success of the Japanese and other foreign manufacturers. The purpose of studying competitors' successes is not so much to mimic their methods, but rather to better understand why our corporations have been so vulnerable to their practices. Then we should be in a better position to develop business strategies that better fit tomorrow's competitive environment.

When puzzling over why the Japanese were so successful at producing and selling automobiles, television sets, and cameras, we have become accustomed to such pat answers as these:

1. Those people over there just work harder than our workers.
2. We bombed out all of their industry in World War II; therefore their machinery and production processes are technologically superior to ours.
3. Japanese labor rates are lower than ours.
4. Japanese managers use a more participative management style, which results in more committed workers.

5. Japanese quality is better than ours because they have more conscientious workers.
6. The Japanese have been producing small cars longer than we have.
7. The Japanese government, like the governments of Taiwan and Korea, subsidizes its industries; thus companies can produce at a loss.

Some of these simplistic answers may have had some impact in the past, but it is not at all clear how valid or how important they are today. In fact, when taken together, all of these answers do not fully explain why the Japanese have been so successful over the past two decades. Some U.S. experts today believe that their success has come primarily from the way that they approach the development of business strategy, the long-range game plan of how they achieve their corporate objectives.

THE JAPANESE APPROACH TO BUSINESS STRATEGY

Years ago, the leaders of Japan's industry determined that their country had certain strengths that could be used to compete in the larger world markets. Among these strengths, from their perspective, were an abundance of willing workers, low-cost labor, teamwork managerial styles, cultural uniformity, the emperor's mandate for economic survival, and an absence of destructive competition. To best use these strengths, these leaders believed that they should concentrate on *mass-produced consumer durable goods that either were in the mature stage of their product life cycles or soon would be.* Consumer durable goods are products that are directly used by consumers and are expected to last at least three years, like automobiles, television sets, and cameras. These products were selected because they:

1. Are produced in very high volumes.
2. Are price sensitive; thus low manufacturing costs allow low sales prices, which can increase market share and result in even higher volumes.
3. Have large established markets with standardized product designs; thus little money needs to be spent on product innovation and market development.

Japanese manufacturers studied, analyzed, and spent enormous sums of money to build systems of manufacturing that would allow them to compete in the growing world markets for mass-produced consumer durables. One of the key features of these systems was an infusion of automated equipment reflecting the latest production processing technology. An important obstacle that had to be overcome was the reputation of Japanese manufacturers for *shoddy product quality.* It was thought that once the obstacles were overcome and these systems of manufacturing were perfected, products could be found that would fit the systems and that the systems could be used as competitive weapons to capture larger shares of world markets. They were right. General Motors, General Electric, and Kodak all know that Toyota, Sony, and Canon are fierce competitors that have captured large shares of markets once dominated by the giants of U.S. industry.

Now, picture what it must have been like to sit in on a boardroom discussion at Nissan, Nikon, or Honda sometime in the last 20 years. Which function do you think would have dominated the development of business strategy—marketing, finance/accounting, or production? In the Japanese approach, marketing and finance/accounting reacted to production. It was the responsibility of marketing to go into world markets and find products that could be readily manufactured by their factories. Marketing had to be very selective, and many promising products were passed over because they were not compatible with the Japanese mass production manufacturing systems. Finance/accounting's responsibility was to acquire and provide the capital funds necessary to support the firm's long-range business strategy, which was dominated by the mass production manufacturing strategy.

This approach has allowed Japanese firms to plow great sums of money into automatic machinery and robots, long-range materials supply and shipping contracts, development of no-layoff personnel policies, and long-range production engineering projects aimed at reducing production costs. All of this effort and money was aimed at one central goal—build the most effective manufacturing system possible so that large market shares could be captured and so that continuous employment would result. This common goal was shared by workers, management, unions, and government.

How could the Japanese spend all of this money on developing their manufacturing systems when U.S. firms didn't seem to have sufficient funds to do so? Part of the answer lies in the savings rate of the Japanese people, which provided a great stock of capital for Japanese businesses. Part of the answer also lies in the type of products that the Japanese chose to produce. Mass-produced consumer durables that are in the mature stage of their product life cycles are essentially set in their design, and their markets are fully developed. Because little money needed to be spent for product innovation and market development, the Japanese firms had enormous amounts of funds to spend on manufacturing improvements.

Early in the 1980s Japanese manufacturers, who were so successful at using their production technology as a competitive weapon against their U.S. counterparts, added a new twist to their business strategy. They took what they had learned from their mass production of consumer durables in the 1970s and applied it to new arenas. Specifically, their ability to quickly develop and produce low-cost products of exceptional quality was applied to a wide range of products and industries. Construction, shipbuilding, publishing, robots and other automated manufacturing systems, mainframe and super computers, forklift trucks and other industrial durable goods, and high-quality and high-priced consumer durables are examples of this shift in business strategy. Additionally, they tended to take more market risks by entering markets before products reached the mature stage of their product cycles. Compact disc players, FAX systems, and videocassette recorders are examples of this development. It remains to be seen whether the Japanese manufacturers can be as successful in these new ventures, because of the changing conditions of international trade. Nevertheless, their attention to detail, their automated assembly lines, and the superior quality of their products are expected to be a continuing concern to U.S. industrial firms well into the 1990s.

With the approach of the Japanese manufacturers to business strategy as background, let us now consider the approach of U.S. manufacturers.

PRODUCTION'S TRADITIONAL ROLE IN U.S. BUSINESS STRATEGY

Business strategy in U.S. firms for the last 30 years has been dominated by two organization functions—marketing and finance/accounting. Marketing provided marketing information that became the principal basis for product designs. This marketing information included such things as what features customers want in products, what they are willing to pay for such features, the expected demand for products, and when products will be needed. Once the basic product designs were determined, they were turned over to production to determine how to produce them. Notice the *reactive* nature of production's role in this process. The finance/accounting function in these firms has provided the guidelines for the amount of capital funds that production could have to design, develop, and build the required processes and facilities to produce the products. All too often, the finance/accounting function's focus was on short-range monetary returns. True, production could recommend modifications to the basic product designs and propose exceptions to the capital-spending policies, but make no mistake about it, marketing and finance/accounting have swung the big sticks when business strategies have been planned in most U.S. corporate boardrooms.

RECOMMENDED CHANGES IN U.S. BUSINESS STRATEGY

Now the difficult question: How can U.S. manufacturers compete with foreign manufacturers in today's world markets? There are no easy answers and there are no quick fixes, but two fundamental things need to be done.

First, what is needed, perhaps more than anything else, is to put operations on an equal footing with marketing and finance/accounting in U.S. boardrooms where business strategy is set. In past eras when the United States was the preeminent producer in the world, manufacturing people held the central power in corporations. But we moved away from our emphasis on production as the glamorous professions of marketing and finance/accounting grew and developed in the 1960–1980 period when market and product innovation exploded. As Leighton F. Smith, of Arthur Andersen & Co., states: "Japanese manufacturers today are beating their U.S. counterparts over the head with a borrowed club—and we handed it to them a quarter-century ago when we freely exported our production technology."[4]

Second, U.S. manufacturers should not formulate business strategy to combat the successes of Japanese manufacturers in the 1970s and 1980s. The social, political, and economic climates of the world have already changed to the point that strategies designed to be appropriate two decades ago would surely fail. We must look to the present and the future world business conditions to formulate our business strategies. Therefore let us examine some of the important factors that are impacting business strategy formation.

---

[4] Leighton F. Smith, "Just-in-Case vs. Just-in-Time Production Systems," presented at the APICS Educational Liaison Workshop, St. Charles, IL, June 29–July 1, 1981, 12.

■■

TABLE 2.1   *Some of Today's Developments Affecting Business Strategy*

1. Reality of worldwide competition and the growing number of large international firms
2. Advanced production technology and a growing number of high-tech systems in both manufacturing and services
3. Foreign producers' cost and quality and their growing presence in world markets with increased market share
4. Continued fluctuation of international financial conditions, including currency exchange rates, interest rates, and financial markets
5. Continuing proliferation of service systems
6. Continuing prominence of government regulation of business
7. Growing scarcity of production resources as worldwide demand increases

■■

ASSESSMENT OF TODAY'S BUSINESS ENVIRONMENT

The starting point for developing business strategy—a long-range game plan for achieving corporate objectives—is to assess the nature of the business environment in which business strategy must be developed. As suggested earlier, Japanese manufacturers seem to be changing their business strategies to fit a changing economic, political, and sociological climate in the 1990s, and in order to compete, U.S. manufacturers must also change theirs. Developments in the world today are dramatically affecting the formation of business strategy. Table 2.1 lists some of these developments.

REALITY OF WORLDWIDE COMPETITION

Increasingly, firms are becoming more international in their scope of operations. We all know that Japan, Korea, Taiwan, Germany, and other foreign countries export many products into the U.S. markets. But many U.S. companies also export their products to foreign countries. Companies like Boeing, Caterpillar Tractor, International Minerals and Chemicals, McDonnell-Douglas, Northrop, Hewlett-Packard, A. E. Staley, Archer-Daniels-Midland, Digital Equipment, and Dresser Industries receive from 20 percent to 45 percent of their total sales revenues from exports to foreign countries.[5] Companies are not only shipping their finished products and services to foreign countries, they are also importing materials, parts, and products that are used in their production processes. International firms, therefore, are both exporters and importers as they buy and sell in world markets.

Production sharing, a term coined by Peter Drucker more than a decade ago, means that a product may be designed and financed by one country, raw materials

---

[5] *Arizona Republic,* Sept. 9, 1985, C5. (Data from *Fortune,* January 1985.)

INDUSTRY SNAPSHOT 2.2

World Cars Getting Worldlier

1. Ford's Festiva was designed in the United States, engineered by Mazda in Japan, and is being built by Kai in Korea for principally the American market.

2. The Mercury Capri was designed by Ghia and Italdesign in Italy and is assembled in Broadmeadows, Australia, principally of Japanese components, for the American market.

3. Ford's new Probe was designed in the United States, with input from Europe, engineered by Mazda and assembled by Mazda in the Japanese automaker's new Flat Rock, Michigan, plant.

4. The Mercury Tracer has a Ford design, but it is built on a Mazda 323 platform in Hermosillo, Mexico, where Ford already had been building engines. Some Tracer components are being shipped in from Taiwan.

5. The Chevrolet Nova is a joint venture of GM and Toyota. The car is assembled in Fremont, California, and GM is entering another joint venture with Suzuki at Ingersol, Ontario.

6. The Pontiac LeMans is a close cousin of the German-designed Opel Kadett, but LeMans is being built by Daewoo Motor Company in Korea.

7. Chrysler has imported Japanese-made Colts for years and has a venture with Mitsubishi going at Bloomington, Illinois.

8. Ford owns 25 percent of Mazda; Mazda owns 8 percent of Kai; Ford owns 10 percent of Kai; Ford and Volkswagen have a jointly managed holding company, Autolatina, involving some 15 plants in Latin America; Chrysler has an interest in Mitsubishi; and GM owns an interest in both Suzuki and Isuzu.[6]

[6] William Allan, Scripps Howard News Service, "World Car Is Here and Getting Even Worldlier," *Bryan-College Station Eagle,* Mar. 19, 1988, 4C.

---

may be produced in many countries and shipped to other countries for further processing, parts may be shipped to yet another country for assembly, and the product may be sold throughout world markets. The country that was the least-cost and highest-quality producer for a particular activity would perform that portion of the production of the product. We are seeing the idea of production sharing becoming a reality today. More and more companies are *international companies,* those that engage in production sharing and sell their products in world markets. Industry Snapshot 2.2 illustrates examples of production sharing in the auto industry.

Production sharing and the reality of international firms competing in world markets have made inefficient manufacturers even more vulnerable to more efficient foreign companies. The borders of a manufacturer's own country no longer provide the protection from foreign competition that they once did, and more and more marginally profitable manufacturers are folding under the pressures of this competition. Increasingly, business strategies of U.S. firms, particularly the successful ones,

TABLE 2.2   *Use of Industrial Robots by Country*

Country	Robots in Use (Thousands)
Japan	93.0
United States	20.0
West Germany	8.8
France	5.9
Italy	3.3
Sweden	3.1
Great Britain	3.0

Sources: Robot Institute of America, Japan Industrial Robot Association, 1985.

see importing and exporting of components and finished goods not as a risk imposed by foreign competitors; rather, they see importing and exporting as opportunities to compete on both production costs and product quality and as a means of capturing even larger market shares in today's expanded world business environment.

ADVANCED PRODUCTION TECHNOLOGY

The use of robots, automation, and other computer-based technology in production is one of the most far-reaching developments to affect manufacturing and services in this century. For small and large organizations alike, these systems of machines are revolutionizing many factories and service operations in the United States and other countries around the globe. Although the initial cost of these assets is tremendous, the benefits go far beyond a reduction in labor costs. Increased product quality, reduced scrap and material costs, and faster response time to customer needs are a few of the benefits claimed. Like most innovations, more may be claimed by this advanced technology than can actually be achieved for some of our factories and service operations, but the fact remains that these computer-based systems have raised the stakes for manufacturers and service companies in the 1990s.

The portability of this advanced production technology is a fact of life today. Japan produces approximately two-thirds of the world's robots and automated production machinery, and it sells about two-thirds of these products to other countries. Table 2.2 shows the distribution of industrial robots among the world's major trading partners. Automated production systems are available to all of the players in world markets for a price. This means that U.S. factories and service operations do not have a lock on the technological advantages that these systems offer. Our foreign competitors also have access to this technology.

According to Elwood S. Buffa, "U.S. manufacturers must take a long-term stance if they are to survive the competitive wars. They must invest heavily in advanced production technology as a part of their manufacturing strategies. The rewards will be lower, more competitive costs, as well as improved, more consistent quality."[7] For some U.S. manufacturers, these high-tech systems may form an important part of their business strategy because they may provide new life and continued survival in the high-stakes game of international manufacturing and world trade. For others, the cost of admission to the game may be prohibitive. We shall study more about these advanced production systems in Chapter 4, Production Processes, and Chapter 5, Production Technology.

FOREIGN PRODUCERS' COST AND QUALITY

Some foreign firms, particularly in Korea, Taiwan, China, Mexico, Hong Kong, and Singapore, use the latest production technology and have very low labor rates. Such high-tech advances and low labor rates, when combined with outstanding quality control, have resulted in high productivity, low production costs, and high product quality, thus making these foreign companies tough competitors for our U.S. manufacturers. There are indications that business strategies of U.S. firms have been formulated to attack these problems: U.S. firms are investing heavily in robotics and other advanced production technology, many are making progress in improving product quality, and the 1980s were characterized by unprecedented wage rate concessions by labor unions.

The successes of foreign competitors in markets once dominated by U.S. manufacturers have resulted in the loss of U.S. jobs. Jobs have been lost because some products formerly produced in the United States are now being produced in Japan, Taiwan, Korea, West Germany, Mexico, and other foreign countries. Also, high-tech production equipment installed by U.S. firms has eliminated many production jobs and created other jobs that require skills not possessed by the existing work force. Such developments have created the need for business strategies of U.S. firms to deal with *worker displacement, restructuring of jobs,* and *retraining of workers.*

FLUCTUATION OF INTERNATIONAL FINANCIAL CONDITIONS

The continued threat of inflation, rapidly fluctuating currency exchange rates, fluctuating interest rates, volatility of international stock markets, persisting huge national debts of many countries, and enormous trade imbalances between international trading partners have created a complex financial environment for U.S. businesses. The complexity of the international financial world is even more pronounced because of the rate at which these factors are changing.

Consider, for example, the effects of currency exchange rate changes in the 1970s and 1980s. The United States, Japan, and West Germany were the top three world exporters during this period. Table 2.3 illustrates the great variation in currency exchange rates among these three trading partners. Notice the particularly

---

[7] Elwood S. Buffa, *Meeting the Competitive Challenge* (Homewood, IL: Richard D. Irwin, 1984), 102.

■■■

TABLE 2.3   *The Dollar on a Roller Coaster: Dollar versus Yen and Mark*

Year	*Average Yen per Dollar*	*Average Marks per Dollar*
1974	302	2.4
1975	305	2.7
1976	295	2.3
1977	250	2.1
1978	200	1.9
1979	245	1.8
1980	215	2.0
1981	225	2.3
1982	230	2.4
1983	225	2.8
1984	260	3.2
1985	210	2.4
1986	160	1.9
1987	135	1.7

■■■

Source: Peter T. Kilborn, *The New York Times,* "Dollar Tumbles to New Depths," *Houston Chronicle,* Dec. 1, 1987, sec. 3, 1. Adapted from the International Monetary Fund.

volatile relationship between the value of the U.S. dollar and the value of the Japanese yen. The significance of this volatility is astounding. Consider, for example, *if we take into account only the effects of shifts in exchange rates,* a product produced and sold in the United States for $1 in 1984 would have sold for 260 yen if exported in that year to Japan. That very same product would have sold in Japan in 1987 for only 135 yen, a price reduction of 48 percent in only a 3-year period:

New Price = Old Price (New Exchange Rate/Old Exchange Rate)
= Old Price (135/260)
= Old Price (.519)

On the other hand, a product that was produced and sold in Japan for 260 yen in 1984 would have sold for $1 if exported to the United States in that year. That same product would have sold in the United States for $1.93 in 1987, a price increase of 93 percent in only a 3-year period:

New Price = Old Price (Old Exchange Rate/New Exchange Rate)
= Old Price (260/135)
= Old Price (1.93)

The relationship between the U.S. dollar and the West German mark was almost as volatile. Over the same 3-year period, *if only currency exchange rate changes were taken into account,* the prices of U.S. products sold in West Germany would have been reduced 47 percent, and the prices of West German products sold in the United States would have been increased 88 percent.

INDUSTRY SNAPSHOT 2.3

Korea, Japan Compete as Low-Price Supplier

Products made in South Korea are flooding the United States, and some experts say Korea is challenging Japan as the leading low-price supplier of everything from small cars to video recorders. Hyundai introduced its Excell subcompact car in 1986 and is the fourth best-selling import, having passed Mazda that same year. GM and Ford are planning to import Korean-made cars for sale in this country. In electronics, the Korean Lucky Gold Star Group opened an assembly plant in Alabama to produce up to a million microwave ovens a year. Gold Star and another South Korean company, Samsung, are already each producing a million television sets annually at American plants. And an Arizona company is marketing Hyundai's personal computers in this country, at a basic price of just $699. These developments remind us of the parallels between South Korean and Japanese trade activity, and South Korea is sometimes labeled "the new Japan" for its ability to increase market share in the United States by undercutting prices—even those of Japanese goods.[8]

---

[8] Nicholas D. Kristof, *The New York Times,* "Korea, Japan Compete as Low-Price Supplier," *Houston Chronicle,* Sept. 1, 1986, sec. 2, 6.

These swings in currency exchange rates had great long-term and short-term effects on both U.S. and foreign producers. In the short run, the expected price changes were by no means automatic. The prices of U.S. products abroad fell, but maybe not as much as we expected because U.S. manufacturers were anxious to recover profits lost during earlier periods when the value of the dollar was high. On the other hand, the prices of Japanese products in the United States did not increase as much as we would have ordinarily expected. Japanese manufacturers further reduced costs and accepted smaller profit margins to shore up their sales in an effort to maintain market share. As we shall discuss later in this section, several long-range effects are now apparent. U.S. manufacturers tended to move away from off-shore suppliers and Japanese manufacturers tended to build factories in the United States and Canada and also tended to move away from low-priced products and toward high-priced products.

With the prices of U.S. products falling precipitously in Japan, West Germany, and other foreign countries and the prices of Japanese and West German products rising dramatically in the United States during the middle and late-1980s, it is not surprising that the demand for U.S. manufactured goods abroad increased in the late 1980s. What may not be so obvious are other effects that these changes had on foreign manufacturers. In the late 1980s, partly because of the fall in the value of the dollar relative to the yen, Japanese manufacturers moved out of some of the low-priced consumer durables markets and moved toward the more expensive consumer durables markets in the United States. With the lower dollar, Japanese manufacturers no longer held great cost advantages in the U.S. markets over manufacturers from the United States and from Korea, Taiwan, and other foreign countries. Industry Snapshot 2.3 suggests that this situation created opportunities for Korean and other foreign manufacturers to fill the gap in the U.S. market for low-priced consumer durables that Japanese manufacturers had previously supplied.

Currency exchange rate shifts in the late 1980s, combined with the *growing fear of increased U.S. import quotas,* caused foreign producers to locate factories in the United States. Rather than producing products in Japan in yen and then selling them in dollars in the United States, Japanese manufacturers decided to produce products in the United States and thereby avoid the unfavorable conversion from yen to dollars. Industry Snapshot 2.4 shows the locations and capacities of foreign-owned automobile plants in the United States and Canada in the late 1980s and discusses the ramifications of this development for the automobile industry and other producers.

A significant impact of the low value of the dollar in the early 1980s was the overreliance of some U.S. firms on imports and the tendency to locate production facilities in foreign countries. The precipitous rise in the value of the dollar in the mid-1980s combined with concerns about the political instability and threat to nationalize private industry in foreign countries made many U.S. companies consider bringing the production of supplies back to the United States. Industry Snapshot 2.5 discusses this effect on manufacturers that imported large volumes of goods in the 1980s. After the dollar fell in value relative to the yen in the mid- to late-1980s, some imported goods were then more expensive to import than to produce domestically.

Wide swings in currency exchange rates such as those found in Table 2.3 could continue well into the 1990s. An important lesson should have been learned in the 1980s: U.S. manufacturers must develop business strategies with built-in flexibility and with an eye to the world financial markets. They must be ready to move quickly to shift strategies as world financial conditions change. Some strategic decisions are difficult to change quickly — for example, building a factory on foreign soil. Even in such a decision, however, opportunities are usually available to reduce risk. Smaller factories can be built that use mobile and flexible equipment, or parts and products can be bought outright from foreign suppliers. Also, careful planning and forecasting must be integral parts of strategic planning so that as many changes as possible can be anticipated and accounted for in long-range plans.

CONTINUED GROWTH OF THE SERVICE SECTOR

The emergence of a variety of private and public organizations to supply services to our growing population is one of the most compelling facts about the U.S. economy today. As mentioned in Chapter 1, more than two-thirds of the U.S. work force is employed in services, roughly two-thirds of the GNP is produced by services, and investment per office worker now exceeds the investment per factory worker. Services are indeed an important sector of the U.S. economy today.

As we focus on services, however, we should recognize the interrelationships between the manufacturing and service sectors. Many service companies exist only because the manufacturing sector buys their services; thus a strong and vigorous

INDUSTRY SNAPSHOT 2.4

Foreign-Owned Automobile Plants in the United States and Canada

Company	Location	Open	Capacity (Thousands)	Comments
Honda	Marysville, OH	1982	360	To make engines in U.S.
	Alliston, Ont.	1987	80	by 1991.
	E. Liberty, OH	1989*	150	
Toyota	Fremont, CA	1984	100	Fremont is joint venture
	Georgetown, KY	1988*	200	with GM. Georgetown to
	Cambridge, Ont.	1988*	50	grow to 500,000.
Nissan	Smyrna, TN	1983	265	More expansion planned.
Mazda	Flat Rock, MI	1987	240	Ford buys 40–60% of output.
Mitsubishi	Bloomington, IL	1988*	120	Joint venture with Chrysler.
Subaru-Isuzu	Lafayette, IN	1989*	240	Subaru cars, Isuzu trucks.
Hyundai	Bromont, Que.	1988*	100	Assembly only.

Source: "The Americanization of Honda," p. 96. Reprinted from April 25, 1988 issue of *Business Week* by special permission, copyright © 1988 by McGraw-Hill, Inc.

* Indicates the planned opening year for the factory.

Shifts in currency exchange rates and fears of U.S. import quotas have resulted in growing numbers of foreign producers moving to factories in the United States. After years of battling competition from imported Japanese vehicles, Detroit's automakers are girding for what may be their most dangerous competitive

manufacturing sector is necessary to support the service sector. Service companies in such industries as construction, industrial distribution, pollution control, printing and advertising, broadcasting, publishing, business services, financial services, insurance, lodging, health care, banking, telecommunications, utilities, railroads, and trucking could not survive if it were not for a healthy manufacturing sector.

Similarly, many manufacturing companies sell some of their products to service companies; thus a robust service sector helps support the manufacturing sector. Also, many technological innovations, such as computing and information processing, that have proven crucial to keeping services competitive were first developed in

threat yet—the manufacturing of Japanese automobiles on U.S. soil. Analysts say that U.S. production of Japanese vehicles, known as "transplants," will accelerate at rates that should alarm the domestic companies, and that the products likely will be well accepted by consumers. The Japanese either have built or are building dozens of car and light-truck assembly plants in the Midwest to serve the lucrative U.S. market.[9] Toyota has joined with GM at Fremont, California, to make Chevrolet Novas. Toyota has built a small-car plant near Georgetown, Kentucky. Chrysler and Mitsubishi have built a joint-venture plant to produce small cars in Bloomington, Illinois. GM and Suzuki have built a joint-venture plant in Canada. Isuzu and Fuji, which owns Subaru, have built an assembly plant in Lafayette, Indiana.[10] Honda has an automobile assembly plant in Marysville, Ohio, and Nissan has one in Smyrna, Tennessee.

The Japanese are making their presence known in other industries. Nippon Kokan took a 50 percent stake in National Steel Corporation. In many of the most basic manufacturing sectors—from ball bearings to industrial filters to machine tools—the Japanese are building factories in the United States, buying U.S. companies, and forming joint ventures. ATR Wire and Cable Company, a consortium of three Japanese companies, bought Firestone's Danville, Kentucky, tire factory. Bridgestone bought Firestone's tire plant in LaVergne, Tennessee. There is growing evidence that these transplants are producing products at production costs and quality levels comparable to their factories at home.[11]

---

[9] Rick Haglund, Newhouse News Service, "Japanese Autos Made in USA," *Houston Chronicle,* Aug. 30, 1987, sec. 5, 3.

[10] "Car Industry Sees Stiffer Competition," *The Daily Oklahoman,* Dec. 25, 1986, sec. B, 27.

[11] Aaron Bernstein, Dan Cook, Pete Engardio, and Gregory L. Miles, "Japan, U.S.A.," *Business Week,* July 14, 1986, 47–50.

---

manufacturing. This network of interrelationships between services and manufacturing calls into question the phrase *service economy,* because many services clearly could not exist without a strong manufacturing sector, and the reverse is undoubtedly true.

And yet, we must recognize the service sector as a large and growing presence in the U.S. economy. Its presence is all too often made known by the many examples of poor service quality. "Your shirt comes back from the laundry with a broken button. Within a week of paying an outrageous repair bill, that ominous rattle reappears in your car's engine. A customer service representative says he'll get back to you and

---

INDUSTRY SNAPSHOT 2.5

Drawbacks of Reliance on Imports as Dollar Falls

In the 1980s many U.S. manufacturers cut back their production and began importing components and even entire products from Japan and other foreign countries. As the value of the dollar fell dramatically relative to foreign currencies in this period, that strategy's drawbacks loomed large. The cost of these imported goods to U.S. manufacturers increased to the point of eliminating the previous cost advantage of importing. These added costs to companies like Ford, GE, and Cincinnati Milacron caused them to stop or reduce the importing of components or entire products. The production of components and products previously imported from Japan was either done in the United States or awarded to other foreign countries like Korea, Taiwan, Singapore, and Mexico, which had cheaper labor and more favorable currency exchange rates. Increasingly, manufacturers from importing nations are insisting on adjustment clauses to protect them from such currency exchange rate swings.[12]

---

[12] Barnaby J. Feder, *The New York Times,* "Swing in Currencies Points Up Drawbacks of Relying on Imports," *Houston Chronicle,* May 31, 1987, sec. 5, 2.

---

doesn't. An automatic teller swallows your card."[13] These reminders that all is not well in service operations motivates us to develop more effective ways of managing service operations.

Many operations managers are employed in services, and undoubtedly, even more will be employed in services in the future. These managers are adapting some of the planning, analyzing, and controlling approaches from manufacturing to service systems, and service systems have improved as a result. For example, the Methodist Hospital system in Houston has developed a very effective system of inventory control. The manager who developed this inventory system learned it first at Armco Steel Corporation. But many of the approaches developed in manufacturing are not easily applied directly in services, and new ones must be developed and tested.

What is needed in services, perhaps more than anything else, is a more effective way of developing operations strategies. This will be discussed later in this chapter.

GOVERNMENT REGULATION

The extent of government regulation of U.S. businesses reached staggering proportions in the 1970s. OSHA, EPA, affirmative action plans, and other federal agencies and their regulations were joined by a host of state and local agencies to form a long line of regulators and inspectors outside operations managers' doors. The trend

---

[13] G. Lynn Shostack, "Designing Services That Deliver," *Harvard Business Review* (January–February 1984): 133.

toward more and more complex and sometimes conflicting regulations that constrain operations managers in their day-to-day jobs may have been reversed in the 1980s, but it is too soon to tell at this point. Many observers believe that the frustration with overregulation may continue, given the tendency toward *government agency reincarnation.* The 60-day plant closing provision that was passed by the Congress in 1988 suggests that the trend toward federal government regulation of business is continuing.

With the trend toward international firms and production sharing, the need for standardizing government regulations seems obvious; otherwise, firms will tend to gravitate to the less-regulated countries. There may be some progress on this front, as evidenced by the more than 31 countries that signed a pact in 1988 regulating the release of industrial chlorofluorocarbons (CFCs), in an effort to curtail the effect of these compounds on the ozone layer in the upper atmosphere.[14]

Managers must adapt their strategic plans to the constraints imposed by government regulation and adopt contingency plans to allow their organizations to adjust to new regulations in the future.

SCARCITY OF PRODUCTION RESOURCES

The scarcity of production resources recently led one marketing executive to comment: "Manufacturing personnel used to call me and ask what they should produce. Now I call them and ask them what they *can* produce." Certain raw materials like titanium and nickel, personnel skills, coal, natural gas, water, oil products, and other resources are periodically unavailable or in short supply today and will probably become scarcer in the future. Given the finite supply of these scarce resources to firms and given an ever-increasing demand, an important issue in the formation of business strategy is how to allocate these resources among business opportunities. We shall study more about these allocation decisions in Chapter 7, Allocating Resources to Strategic Alternatives.

Such developments as those discussed here clearly demonstrate that the ways that operations managers manage must continue to evolve if U.S. businesses are to survive. Business strategies that reach far into the next century must take account of these developments and build long-range business plans that allow organizations to survive in an environment characterized by change. With these developments as a background, let us turn to the main topic of this chapter, the formulation of operations strategy.

OPERATIONS STRATEGY

As Figure 2.1 shows, operations strategies do not exist in a vacuum, independent of the rest of the organization; rather, they are derived directly from the corporate objectives and business strategies.

Corporate objectives are the long-range goals that are unique to each organization. These objectives are concerned with survival, growth, and profitability and are

---

[14] "An Ozone Hole Over Capital Hill," *Business Week,* Apr. 4, 1988, 35.

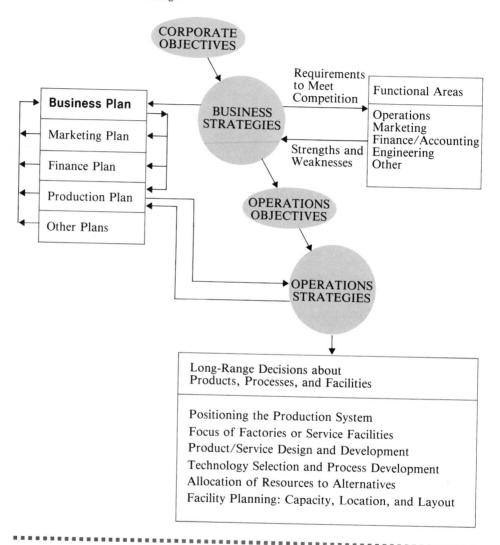

FIGURE 2.1 Developing Operations Strategies

developed at the highest levels of the organization. Corporate objectives express the central mission of the corporation that is established after due consideration of economic, political, technological, social, and market conditions. Business strategies form the long-range game plan of an organization that provides a road map of how to achieve the corporate objectives. These strategies are embodied in the company's business plan, which includes a plan for each functional area of the business, including a marketing plan and a production plan. Business strategies are developed while considering the requirements to meet competition in each major product line of the

TABLE 2.4   *Arsenal of Operations Function's Competitive Weapons*

Weapon	Definition	Some Ways of Creating the Weapon
Low production costs	Unit cost of each product/service, including labor, material, and overhead costs	Redesign of outputs New production technology Increase in output levels Reduction of scrap Reduction of inventories
Fast delivery of products/services	How fast customers may expect delivery of their products/services	Larger finished goods inventories Faster production rates Quicker shipping methods
On-time deliveries	Amount and timing of delivery of orders for products/services compared to promises	More realistic promises Better control of production of orders Better information systems

High-quality products/services	Customers' perceptions of degree of excellence exhibited by products/services	Improve product/services':
		  Appearance
		  Malfunction rating
		  Performance and function
		  Wear, endurance ability
		  After-sales service

Flexibility	Ability to change production to other products/services and other production volumes	Change in type of production process used Use of CAD/CAM Reduction of amount of work in process Increase in production capacity

business as well as the strengths and weaknesses of each of the company's functional areas. A central focus in forming business strategy is finding ways to capitalize on a firm's present strengths or strengths that can be developed to capture greater shares of segments of the market.

Operations objectives are the long-range goals for each major product line that the operations function must reach if the corporate strategies are to be successfully executed and corporate objectives are to be achieved. Table 2.4 lists the arsenal of weapons that operations functions can use to help the corporation win customers' orders in the marketplace. These weapons are also referred to as *distinctive competencies* and can be thought of as the things that customers want from products and services. It is a fact of life that all of these weapons may not be simultaneously used for a single product. For example, for a particular product, a company may not be able to provide great flexibility and at the same time provide very low cost production. With the use of computer-integrated manufacturing (CIM), however, some companies are claiming that all of these weapons can be utilized simultaneously for some products. Ordinarily, each company uses a different mix of these weapons to form the operations objectives for each major product line.

Operations strategies provide the road map for achieving the operations objectives and form the long-range game plan for production of the firm's products and services. Operations strategies include decisions about each major product line on such issues as what new production facilities are needed and when they are needed, what major production technologies and processes must be developed and when they are needed, and what production schemes will be followed to produce the sales forecasts. Operations objectives, and the strategies for achieving these objectives, are embodied in the *production plan*—the plan that will guide the operations function toward fulfilling its part of the business plan.

Let us now turn to a more detailed look at operations strategies.

ELEMENTS OF OPERATIONS STRATEGY

Operations strategy may be broken down into these major components: (1) positioning the production system, (2) focus of factories and service facilities, (3) product/service design and development, (4) technology selection and process development, (5) allocation of resources to strategic alternatives, and (6) facility planning: capacity, location, and layout.

Positioning the Production System

Positioning the production system in manufacturing means selecting the type of product design, type of production processing system, and type of finished goods inventory policy for each major product line in the business plan.

There are two basic types of product design, custom and standardized. *Custom products* are designed according to the needs of individual customers. The choice of this type of product results in many product models being produced in very small batches. The operations objectives for this type of product usually emphasize on-time delivery and flexibility. Low cost or price may matter but may not be of paramount importance. A specialized piece of medical equipment for a large hospital is an example of this type of product. The choice of *standardized products* results in only a few product models that are produced either continuously or in very large batches. The operations objectives for this type of product usually emphasize fast delivery of products and low production cost. A television set is an example of a standardized product. The determination of one of these two types of product designs has important implications for the design of the production processes.

There are two classic types of production processing systems, product-focused and process-focused. *Product-focused systems* group together all of the machines, tools, and workers needed to perform all of the tasks required to finish a product. These production systems are designed to produce a few standardized products in high volume at low cost. Assembly lines such as in auto manufacturing typify these systems. Because such systems are usually difficult and expensive to change to other product designs and production volumes, they are not very flexible. If the business plan calls for standardized products whose market strategy is based on low production cost and high volume, then product-focused systems are usually preferred. *Process-focused systems* are designed to produce many unique product designs in relatively low volumes. Production departments are ordinarily formed to perform only one kind of a task. For example, the painting of all products would be done in the painting department. Products must be transported from department to department to have the required tasks performed. Factories that produce industrial products to customer specifications are typically process-focused. Because such systems are relatively easy and inexpensive to change to other product designs and volumes, they offer the greatest flexibility. If the business plan calls for custom products whose market strategy is based on flexibility and on-time delivery, then process-focused systems are usually preferred.

There are two types of finished goods inventory policies: produce-to-stock and produce-to-order. In the *produce-to-stock policy,* products are produced ahead of time and placed in inventory. Then when orders for the products are received from customers, the products are shipped immediately from inventory. In the *produce-to-order policy,* operations managers wait until they have the customers' orders in hand before they produce the products. If fast delivery of products is important, then produce-to-stock is usually preferred because the products can be shipped directly from finished goods inventory.

Once the type of product, type of process, and finished goods inventory policy have been selected for a product line, much of the structure required of a factory has been established. To further explore factory structure, let us consider the scope of a factory's operations.

Focus of Factories and Service Facilities

An important element of operations strategy is a plan for each production facility to be specialized in some way. Specialization of a production facility allows it to excel at achieving a particular set of objectives. Wickham Skinner refers to this idea of the specialized factory as "the focused factory":

> *A factory that focuses on a narrow product mix for a particular market niche will outperform the conventional plant which attempts a broader mission. Because its equipment, supporting systems, and procedures can concentrate on a limited task for one set of customers, its costs and especially its overheads are likely to be lower than those of the conventional plant. But, more important, such a plant can become a competitive weapon because its entire apparatus is focused to accompany the particular manufacturing task demanded by the company's overall strategy and marketing objective.*[15]

---

[15] Wickham Skinner, "The Focused Factory," *Harvard Business Review* (May–June 1974): 113.

In the 1970s and 1980s we observed a trend toward corporate mergers that began in the 1960s. Corporations swallowed up other companies at an unprecedented pace. As Lee Iacocca states: "Nobody's building a better mousetrap anymore. They're trying to figure out how to do a leveraged buyout of the mousetrap company."[16] In many of these mergers, operations were eventually consolidated into large, diverse, and unfocused factories. Although the original aim of reducing the overhead cost per unit of output in such consolidations was sometimes achieved, too often the overall result has been factories that do not do anything particularly well. These large and unwieldy factories are at a competitive disadvantage compared to smaller and more specialized factories.

In contrast, Japanese firms have consistently stayed with smaller and more focused factories. An example of these smaller and more specialized factories is the emergence of minimills in the U.S. steel-making industry. These mills make a narrow range of steel products, are much smaller operations located near their markets, use significant amounts of scrap metal as base stock, and usually have incentive plans for their employees. These smaller mills have been very profitable and are capturing an increasing share of the U.S. market, even from Korean and Japanese companies.

Factories and service facilities can be specialized in several ways. The earlier statement by Skinner specified a plant that is designed to produce only a few product models. Factories may also specialize in particular types of processes. In fact, the opportunities for specialization of factories is almost unlimited, as they also are for service facilities. The key point is that it is generally desirable for factories and service facilities to be specialized in some way so that they will not be vulnerable to smaller and more specialized competitors that can provide customers with a better set of lower costs, faster product or service delivery, on-time delivery, high product and service quality, and flexibility.

Of course, we cannot conclude that smaller facilities are always better. Economies and diseconomies of scale have to be taken into consideration in choice of size of production facilities, as we shall discuss in Chapter 8, but the tendency for U.S. production facilities to be large and unwieldy is recognized. Now, let us examine the importance of designing and developing products and services as elements of operations strategy.

Product/Service Design and Development

Figure 2.2 illustrates the concept of a product life cycle. After a product is designed and developed, it enters the *introduction* stage of its life cycle. In this stage, sales begin, production methods are improved, marketing efforts evolve and develop, and profits are negative. Successful products move on to the *growth* stage. In this stage, sales grow dramatically, marketing efforts intensify and solidify, production concentrates on expanding capacity fast enough to keep up with demand, and profits begin to accumulate. Next comes the *maturity* stage. In this stage, production concentrates on high-volume production, efficiency, and low costs; marketing shifts to competitive

---

[16] Lee Iacocca with Sonny Kleinfield, *Talking Straight* (New York: Bantam Books, 1988): 96.

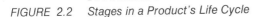

FIGURE 2.2   *Stages in a Product's Life Cycle*

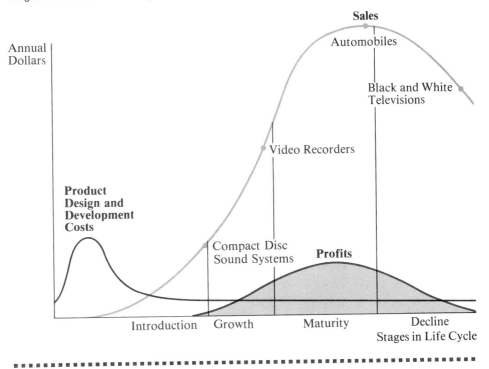

sales promotion and differentiation of the product and its promotion in order to increase or maintain market share; and profits are at their peak. Finally, the product enters the *decline* stage of its life cycle, which is characterized by declining profits and sales. Eventually the product is either dropped by the firm or replaced by improved products.

The activities in operations, marketing, and engineering functions related to product/service design and development are intense as new products and services are developed. As products and services move through the later phases of their life cycles, these efforts diminish somewhat in intensity and shift to concerns about redesigning products for maintaining market share and improving production.

There is a trend toward shortened product life cycles, particularly in industries such as electronics, computers, and consumer goods. Shortened product life cycles have had at least four important effects. First, the total amount of spending on product design and development is increased. Second, production systems tend to be whipsawed by continuously changing product models. This leads companies to prefer flexible production processing systems that can be readily converted to other products. Third, operations strategies emphasize the ability to bring new product designs on stream quickly. Computer-aided design (CAD), which was defined and described in Table 1.5, is allowing some companies to respond faster to designing and

FIGURE 2.3 The Design and Development of New Products

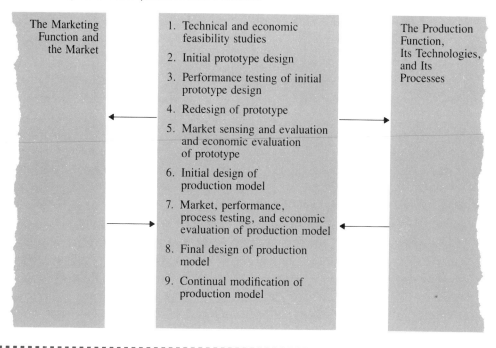

| The Marketing Function and the Market | 1. Technical and economic feasibility studies
2. Initial prototype design
3. Performance testing of initial prototype design
4. Redesign of prototype
5. Market sensing and evaluation and economic evaluation of prototype
6. Initial design of production model
7. Market, performance, process testing, and economic evaluation of production model
8. Final design of production model
9. Continual modification of production model | The Production Function, Its Technologies, and Its Processes |

redesigning these products. Fourth, computer-aided manufacturing (CAM) is allowing some companies to put these new product designs into production more rapidly.

In this study of product/service design and development, we shall focus on those issues that directly affect the management and design of production systems. In other words, we shall emphasize designing and developing products and services for producibility or ease of production.

Developing New Products/Services. Figure 2.3 shows some of the important steps in designing and developing new products. New-product ideas can come from almost any place—from customers, marketing, engineering, research and development (R&D), competitors' products, inventors outside the company, market surveys, letters from homemakers, and from personnel in operations. Because new-product ideas can come from almost anywhere, companies must develop a well-organized network for encouraging these ideas and quickly evaluating them.

Once a new-product idea has been recognized, initial *technical and economic feasibility studies* determine the advisability of establishing a project for developing the product. These studies seek to answer two questions: (1) Can the product be technologically produced? (2) Can the product be profitably produced and marketed?

If initial feasibility studies are favorable, engineers prepare an initial *prototype design.* This prototype design should exhibit the basic characteristics of the product's form, fit, and function that will be required of the final design. A prototype does not necessarily have the same weight, color, physical dimensions, materials, and other features of later designs, nor will it usually be made by the same production processes that will be used later.

Performance testing of prototype designs is aimed at determining the performance characteristics of the design. As tests show deficiencies, *redesign of the prototype* is undertaken until this design-test-redesign process produces a satisfactorily performing prototype.

When the prototype meets management expectations, the project is evaluated by its target market. This *market sensing and evaluation* can be accomplished by demonstrations to potential customers, market tests, market surveys, or other means. The objectives of these activities is to determine the desirability of the product in the marketplace and to learn what characteristics potential customers would like in the product.

If the response of the perceived market to the prototype is favorable, *economic evaluation of the prototype design* is performed to estimate production volume, costs, and profits for the product. If the estimated product profitability is acceptable to management, the project will enter the production design phase. While the prototype design was based solely on performance objectives, the production design must exhibit the product's ability to be effectively produced on production machinery. Also, it must have the weight, dimensions, color, appearance, corrosion resistance, and other characteristics desired in the final product.

The *initial production design* will evolve to a final production design through performance testing, production trials and testing, market testing, and economic studies. The *final production design* will exhibit low cost, competitive quality attributes, acceptable performance, and the ability to be produced efficiently in the desired quantities. Actually, final design is a misnomer, since no design is ever final. Product designs are dynamic because they must be modified to adapt to changing market conditions and changing production technology and to allow for manufacturing improvements.

This system of designing and developing physical products walks a tight line between marketing and the market on the one hand and the technologies and processes of the production function on the other. Although the market is the engine that drives the system, the capacity and capabilities of the production function, its technologies, and its processes must also be ever-present elements. How absurd it would be to propose a product that exhibits market acceptance if, because of its design, it could not be profitably produced.

The design and development of services tends to be aimed more at resolving questions of the degree of standardization of the service, the degree of customer contact, and methods of delivering the service rather than at product specifications and production process technologies. Additionally, because most services are intangible, market acceptability is usually determined from surveys rather than from testing and demonstration.

We must be concerned with how to cancel or modify projects for developing products and services. Otherwise, every design project will evolve into a produced product. When you consider that only about one out of ten new products is successful, new-product development projects must be scrutinized carefully to determine at the earliest possible moment if the product is likely to be unsuccessful in its present form. Each step in the procedure for designing products and services requires a decision: Should the project be continued? If the answer is no, the project should be either canceled or modified. It is best to cancel projects early so that human effort and development money can be directed toward more promising projects. Unfortunately, this is easier said than done, because managers, engineers, and marketers become emotionally caught up in their projects and are reluctant to dispose of them. This fact justifies the need for impartial management review boards for periodic reviews of the progress of new-product/service projects.

Designing Products/Services for Producibility.   Industry Snapshot 2.6 illustrates that product design has a tremendous impact on product quality, production cost, number of suppliers, and levels of inventories. Improvement of these performance measures through improved product designs may be a critical way that U.S. manufacturers can become more competitive with foreign manufacturers.

A study of designing and developing products and services for producibility or ease of production requires an understanding of four key concepts — specifications, standardization, simplification, and designing for quality.

A *specification* is a detailed description of a material, part, or product, including such measures as viscosity, surface finish, pH rating, particle size distribution, hardness, steel composition, strength requirements, and physical dimensions. These specifications provide production with precise information about the characteristics of each component of the product to be produced. Eli Whitney, although perhaps best known for his invention of the cotton gin, also invented and developed a *system of interchangeable parts.* This system required each part of a rifle, which Whitney was manufacturing under contract to the U.S. government in 1798, to be manufactured to specific physical dimensions that were expressed as *tolerances.* The rifles could be assembled by fitting a set of components together with the assurance that all components would fit and the assembled rifle would function as intended.

Tolerances are specified for each dimension of a physical product in a range from minimum to maximum. A shaft diameter, for example, could be specified as $4.000 \pm .001$ inches. This means that the minimum diameter is 3.999 inches and the maximum diameter is 4.001 inches. Tolerances and other forms of specifications are needed to allow both *ease of production* and *effective functioning* of the finished products.

Standardized and custom products were discussed earlier in this chapter. The motivation for more *standardization* of products and parts is higher production volume, lower production costs, higher product quality, greater ease of automation, and lower inventory investment. Although all of these advantages are certainly attractive, realistically we must recognize that many markets today are so competitive and segmented that some degree of variety in product models is usually necessary.

Even though a product is of the custom type, *modularity* of components allows standardized components. Modular designs permit a variety of final product models with only a few standardized components. A manufacturer of transmissions, for example, might use only three basic gear designs within its transmissions but arrange

---

INDUSTRY SNAPSHOT 2.6

Product Design Is Key to U.S. Manufacturing Competitiveness

Although underemphasized in the 1970s, U.S. manufacturers are rediscovering in the 1990s that product design is a key factor in international competitiveness. They are realizing again that product design is more than appearance. It is fundamental to the product being easy and economical to use, reliable, and economical to service. And perhaps more importantly, product designs should be simple to manufacture.

In American design today, simplicity of style and simplicity of assembly are being combined, with the purpose of slashing costs while producing higher-quality products. Much of Japan's superiority in the world competitiveness game has been acquired through its mastery of a process the Japanese know as "mechatronics." Its American equivalent is called *design-for-assembly,* or DFA. Although a few U.S. companies, such as Hewlett-Packard, IBM, and General Electric, have used the process for years, now many more are catching on. "The logic is very simple: Trim the number of parts that have to be assembled, and you reduce product costs," says W. Barton Huthwaite, president of Troy Engineering in Rochester, Michigan. "At the same time,

you pare inventories, cut the number of suppliers you have to deal with and shorten production time."

Because assembly usually accounts for about two-thirds of total manufacturing costs, designing for assembly really pays off. Reducing the number of screws, nuts, and bolts can trim 50 percent or more from the assembly costs of a product. This fact was proved by IBM with its Proprinter. IBM had been purchasing its dot-matrix printers from Seiko Epson Corporation in Japan, one of the lowest-cost producers in the world. But when IBM came out with the Proprinter, its manufacturing costs were well below Epson's former prices. This great reduction of cost came mainly from designing the printer so that it had 65 percent fewer parts and from cutting assembly time by about 90 percent, to only 3 minutes.

Similarly, GE reduced the number of parts in its refrigerator compressor from 51 to 29 by changing from a reciprocating to a rotary unit. Because the rotary unit is more efficient and smaller, it allows a lot more space for food storage. The redesign significantly lowered GE's production cost and cut the failure rate by one-third.[17]

---

[17] "Smart Design," *Business Week,* Apr. 11, 1988, 102–108.

---

the gears to provide numerous transmissions each having different performance characteristics. This approach offers the advantages of both specialization and the final product design variety that appeals to more customers.

Services can also be standardized to yield many economies. The largest single economy to be expected from service design standardization is usually reduced labor costs. The natural intrusion of the customer into the production system usually means lower levels of standardization for service organizations than for physical products. The degree of customer contact and the importance of customer–service interaction at the point of service delivery will have an unavoidable influence on the degree of service design standardization that is possible. High customer contact, such as in an expensive restaurant, is typically related to customized menus, whereas low customer contact, such as in a fast-food stand, is typically related to highly standardized menus.

Simplification of product/service design is the elimination of the complex features of a product or service so that the intended function is performed with reduced production cost while maintaining or even increasing customer satisfaction. Customer satisfaction may be increased through product/service design simplification by making a product or service easier to recognize, buy, install, maintain, or use.

Reduced operating costs can result from product/service design simplification when labor costs are reduced through easier assembly and through eliminated or simplified operations, and when material costs are reduced through substituted materials, when materials are in simpler configurations, and when less material is wasted as scrap.

Service designs can also be simplified. Services are usually simplified by transferring some of the work from the production system to the customers, eliminating or reducing the range of services offered, or increasing the response time of services to customers. It seems clear, however, that there can be a trade-off between customer satisfaction and the price or cost of simplified services. In other words, we may not particularly like the simplified services because more self-service is required, the range of services offered is reduced, or the time required to receive the services is increased. But we do like the reduced costs, reduced prices, or prices that do not increase as much as they would without the simplifications.

Examples of simplification of services are:

1. U.S. Postal Service — standardized envelope size, elimination of low-cost classes of mail, reduced number of deliveries, and elimination of weekend deliveries
2. Telephone companies — reduction of number of operators by initiating direct-dialing procedures
3. Universities — increase in class sizes, fewer course choices, and televised lectures for multiple locations
4. Service stations — reduction of number of service attendants by eliminating oil changes, lubrication, and maintenance services and by installing self-service gasoline pumps

Designing Products/Services for Quality.   The customer is the final judge of a product's quality, and this principle is stated in Table 2.4. Product quality is determined by the customer's perception of the degree of excellence exhibited by the product's or service's appearance, weight, size, color, operation, durability, and so on — the list is endless. But this definition provides little guidance for designing products, and more specifics are needed. Four specific aspects of quality are important considerations in product design — functionality, maintainability, reliability, and reproducibility.

Functionality refers to how well a product performs its intended function. For example, if the product is a hair dryer, it is designed to dry a person's hair quickly with ease and no undesirable side effects.

Maintainability refers to the ease of performing routine maintenance on the product, such as periodic lubrication, tightening belts, and replacing hoses. To remain in top operating condition, physical products must be maintained. The ease with which these maintenance activities can be performed is perceived to be an element of product quality by users of these products.

Reliability refers to the ability of a product to perform as desired under prescribed conditions without excessive frequency of failure from wear or other causes. Reliability is measured by the probability that a product or component of a product will not fail on any given trial. A reliability of .999, for example, indicates that a failure would ordinarily be expected once in 1,000 trials. A product composed of three independent components with reliabilities of .95, .90, and .99 would have a combined reliability of $.95 \times .90 \times .99 = .846$. This chain multiplication of component reliabilities further emphasizes the necessity of stringent design of components if the products are to have the desired level of reliability. Reliability is ordinarily improved through designs of higher precision, designs having fewer interacting components, designs having redundant or backup parts, and the more precise manufacturing of parts. Having fewer interacting components may actually reduce production costs in addition to improving reliability. On the other hand, redundant or backup parts, precision product designs, and precise manufacturing may be accompanied by increased production costs. Therefore care must be exercised in determining customer willingness to pay more for this increased reliability. These design approaches are further discussed in Chapter 17, Maintenance and Reliability.

Reproducibility refers to the ability of the production system to consistently produce products of the desired quality. Reproducibility must be considered when products are designed, because all other aspects of quality are directly affected unless the production system can effectively and efficiently produce the products at a consistent quality level. Selecting materials, setting tolerances, and specifying production procedures are examples of elements of product design that can directly affect reproducibility. When products are in the final stages of the design procedure, *pilot runs* of the product through the proposed production processes test the reproducibility of the design. Similarly, as materials, processes, and facilities change over time, a continuous monitoring of product quality gives feedback concerning design modifications needed to improve reproducibility.

An interesting issue concerns how a firm decides how to allocate its money and effort between developing and designing new products and redesigning existing products. It was here in the 1970s and 1980s that Japanese manufacturers differed dramatically from their U.S. counterparts. The Japanese firms tended to invest less in developing new products for unproven markets; rather, they invested more in modifying and improving the product designs of existing products for ease of production. This continuous drive to change product designs to allow them to be manufactured at lower cost and higher quality is at the heart of the Japanese firms' success in the past two decades. Now products from Korea, Hong Kong, Taiwan, and other countries have tended to crowd into the low-priced consumer durables markets. If they are to recapture market share in these markets, U.S. manufacturers must narrow their product lines through product and parts standardization, invest less in developing new products, and invest more in streamlining the designs of existing products to allow them to be produced with higher quality and lower costs.

Now that we have discussed the important issues of product/service design and development, let us turn to determining how to produce these products and services.

Technology Selection and Process Development

An essential part of operations strategy is the determination of how products will be produced. This involves deciding and planning every detail of production processes and facilities. The range of production technologies available to produce both products and services is great and is continuously increasing. Combining high-technology production equipment, such as robots, flexible manufacturing systems, and automated warehouses, with conventional equipment and devising effective overall production schemes are indeed challenges. This topic is of supreme importance today because of the international scope of operations and because the ability of U.S. firms to compete in world markets in the future will undoubtedly be affected. Chapter 5, Production Technology, contains the important concepts and issues related to this topic.

Allocation of Resources to Strategic Alternatives

Most companies today have limited resources available for the production function. Cash and capital funds, capacity, workers, engineering talent, machines, materials, and other resources are available in varying degrees to each firm. Because for most companies the vast majority of the firm's resources are used in production, shortages of these resources impact most severely on their production functions. These resources must be allocated in ways that maximize the achievement of the objectives of operations. Allocation decisions, which are constrained by the availability of resources, constitute a common type of decision to be made by operations managers today as they set operations strategies. These decisions are so important that an entire chapter, Chapter 7, Allocating Resources to Strategic Alternatives, is devoted to them.

Facility Planning: Capacity, Location, and Layout

How to provide the long-range production capacity to produce the products/services for a firm is a critical part of setting operations strategy. Enormous capital investment is required to make production capacity available. Land and production equipment may need to be purchased, specialized production technologies might have to be developed, and new factories may need to be located and built. The decisions involved have long-lasting effects and are subject to great risk. If poor decisions are made or if circumstances change after the company has committed to a choice of alternatives, companies will live with the results of these decisions for many years. These decisions are so important to operations managers that the whole of Chapter 8, Long-Range Capacity Planning and Facility Location, is devoted to them.

The internal arrangement of workers, production processes, and departments within facilities is a crucial part of positioning strategy that affects the ability to provide the desired volume, quality, and cost of products. Chapter 6, Facility Layout, is devoted to these issues and to their interrelationships with other elements of operations strategy.

TABLE 2.5   *Characteristics of Manufactured Products and Services*

Manufactured Products	*Services*
Tangible products	Intangible outputs
Products can be inventoried	Outputs cannot be inventoried
Little customer contact	Extensive customer contact
Long lead times	Short lead times
Capital-intensive	Labor-intensive
Product quality easily determined	Service quality determined with difficulty

Strategic Importance of Operating and Control Decisions

You should not assume from the foregoing discussion that the only issues in POM that are of strategic importance have been covered in this section. On the contrary, if we have learned anything from the Japanese manufacturers over the past two decades, it is that paying attention to the smallest details of production can be of strategic importance. Effectively planning the work force, maintaining good working relations with labor unions, managing personnel, looking after the details of the day-to-day production of products and services, making on-time deliveries, keeping on top of the management of product quality, and keeping the production machinery in top working condition can, when taken together, equal in importance any of the strategic decisions discussed in this section. Many of these issues are treated in Parts III and IV of this text.

OPERATIONS STRATEGY IN SERVICES

Most of what has been discussed about the elements of operations strategy in this section applies equally well to both manufacturing and services. But because of inherent differences between manufacturing and service organizations, the fundamental underpinnings of their operations strategies are also different. As a starting point for discussing operations strategies for service firms, therefore, we shall compare some of the fundamental characteristics of manufacturing and services.

Table 2.5 describes the characteristics of manufactured products and services, but this table really describes the polar extremes of a continuum because while some service organizations are strikingly different from manufacturers in some ways, they may be very much like manufacturers in other ways. Also, both manufacturing and service firms can provide both tangible products and intangible services. For example, a service organization like a restaurant provides food, a tangible good, for customers. A manufacturer like a computer manufacturer may provide customer services such as technical advice, credit, and field repairs.

Manufactured products are *tangible goods*—they have physical form, they can be seen and touched, and they ordinarily must be shipped to customers. Services, however, are *intangible*—they are usually without physical form. "Like light, they can't be physically stored or possessed and their consumption is often simultaneous with their production."[18]

Because manufactured products are tangible, customer demand can be anticipated and products may often be produced, transported, and held in inventory until customers need them. This allows manufacturers flexibility in deciding when to produce products. *Inventory can be used as a buffer between a stable production capacity and a highly variable customer demand.* This means that when production levels are held constant, in periods of low demand inventory levels of finished goods will climb, and in periods of peak demand inventory levels of finished goods will fall. This is not to say that all manufacturers inventory finished goods, because some manufacturers choose to wait until products are demanded, then produce the products and ship them directly to customers. Services cannot ordinarily be produced in advance of customer demand and must be delivered to customers when they want them. This means that services must somehow plan production levels to equal or exceed customer demand.

Customers ordinarily are not inputs into the manufacturing process. In fact, customers have little contact with the manufacturing system in most cases. In service organizations, however, customers are a primary input to the production of many services. In hospitals, restaurants, and banks, customers enter the production process, are routed to the necessary service operations, and exit from the service system. In high customer contact services, such as an expensive restaurant, operations personnel need training in people skills because the key element of quality control is the way that operations personnel conduct their transactions with customers.

Manufacturers ordinarily take several weeks from the time that a customer's order is received until the product is shipped. This requires that customers order products before they need them. Services, on the other hand, may need to be delivered immediately on the spot when customers want the service. In services with highly irregular demand patterns, such as doctors' offices, customers may need to make advance appointments to level out demand or "take a number" to set processing priorities.

We usually think of manufacturers as being located some distance from customers, highly automated, and capital-intensive, as with an automobile assembly plant. But the reverse could also be true, as with a small regional clothing manufacturer. Services are usually thought of as being located near customers and being labor-intensive, but the reverse could also be true, as with an electric utility company.

In manufacturing, determining the quality level of products is ordinarily based on objective evidence. A Gallup survey of recent purchasers of automobiles indicated that customers were interested in product performance, durability, ease of repair, customer service, and customer satisfaction. The first three of these elements of product quality can be measured, as objective evidence can be presented to determine the quality level of products. It is the last two factors, customer service and customer satisfaction, that are difficult to measure, and it is on factors such as these

---

[18] Shostack, "Designing Services That Deliver," *Harvard Business Review,* Jan./Feb. 1984, 133.

that service organizations must base much of the determination of the quality of their services. Pleasant surroundings, friendly operations personnel, speed of performing the service, craftsmanship of the repairman, skill of the physician, soundness of the financial advisor's advice, and other factors that are difficult to measure affect the perception of quality of services.

Given these differences between manufacturing and services, let us now discuss the kinds of competitive weapons available to services.

Competitive Weapons for Services

Table 2.4 listed these competitive weapons or distinctive competencies for firms: low production costs, fast delivery of products/services, on-time deliveries, high-quality products/services, and flexibility. As pointed out earlier, there are major differences between product quality and service quality. All of the weapons in Table 2.4 are available to service firms, however, and the similarities of their use in manufacturing and services are perhaps more striking than the differences. All organizations can seldom provide all of the weapons simultaneously to customers, and for each service must choose the set of weapons that will provide the greatest market advantage. The trade-off between cost and service quality is perhaps the most obvious. A small retailer that emphasizes close personal contact with customers may have high-quality services, but their cost may be higher than the cost of their high-volume discount competitors.

The fundamental nature of services requires a somewhat different approach to positioning strategies for service organizations.

Positioning Strategies for Services

We have shown that a positioning strategy in manufacturing includes the type of finished goods inventory policy (produce-to-stock or produce-to-order), type of product design (standard or custom), and type of production process (product-focused or process-focused). Such a positioning strategy would not be possible for services because of the differences listed in Table 2.5. These differences dictate that a positioning strategy for services include:

1. Type of service design, standard or custom
2. Type of production process, product-focused or process-focused
3. Amount of customer contact, high or low

The type of service design and the type of production process are very much like their manufacturing counterparts, but the amount of customer contact is distinctly different.

McDonald's has a very successful positioning strategy as evidenced by its long-term profitability. It has chosen to provide customers with standardized services, a product-focused production system, and a low amount of customer contact. An expensive restaurant, on the other hand, provides customers with more custom services, a more process-focused production system, and a high amount of customer contact.

Just as in manufacturing, the positioning strategy of the service firm determines the structure of the organization relative to the competition. This structure is crucial

FIGURE 2.4   *Evolution of Positioning Strategies for a Product*

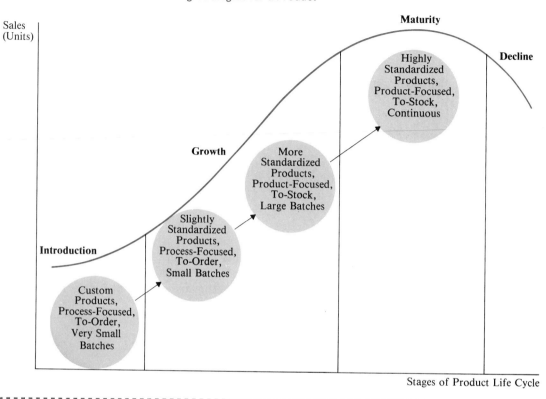

Stages of Product Life Cycle

to the success of service organizations. We shall discuss further the design of the production system for services in Chapter 4, Production Processes.

Now that we have examined the elements of operations strategy, let us consider how we go about integrating these elements into a comprehensive operations strategy.

GLOBAL OPERATIONS STRATEGIES

In this section we shall discuss the evolution of positioning strategies for products, consider the operations strategies preferred in North America, Europe, and Japan, and present suggestions for integrating the elements of operations strategy.

EVOLUTION OF POSITIONING STRATEGIES FOR PRODUCTS

Figure 2.4 illustrates that positioning strategies tend to evolve for some products as they move through their product life cycles. Such changes are particularly valid for

TABLE 2.6   *Ranking of Preferred Competitive Strategies: North America, Japan, and Europe*

Competitive Weapon	*North America*	*Japan*	*Europe*
Consistent quality	1	3	1
High product performance	2	6	2
On-time deliveries	3	4	3
Low price	4	1	5
Fast delivery	5	7	4
Rapid design changes	6	2	6
After-sales service	7	8	7
Rapid volume changes	8	5	8

Note: 1 is the highest ranking and 8 is the lowest.

Source: Arnaud DeMeyer, Jinchiro Nakane, Jeffrey G. Miller, and Kasra Ferdows, "Flexibility: The Next Competitive Battle," *Manufacturing Roundtable Research Report Series,* Boston University School of Management (Feb. 1987).

mass-produced products such as consumer durables. In the early stages of such a product's life cycle, it will typically be nearly custom-designed and will be produced in very small batches in a process-focused factory and on a produce-to-order basis. As the market demand for the product grows, the batch size of the product increases, and we see the positioning strategy shift to one of larger batches of a more standardized product design, produced in product-focused, assembly line factories on a produce-to-stock basis. Finally, when market demand for the product reaches its maturity, the highly standardized product is produced continuously in product-focused factories on a produce-to-stock basis.

The pattern of change illustrated in Figure 2.4 has important implications for operations strategy. Operations strategies must include plans for modifying production processing systems as products mature, and the capital and production technology required to support these changes must be provided.

COMPETITIVE STRATEGIES IN NORTH AMERICA, JAPAN, AND EUROPE

We have seen from Table 2.5 that the production function within a company has available the weapons of low production cost, fast delivery of products, on-time deliveries, high-quality products and services, and flexibility. Which combination of these weapons should be used to form a competitive strategy for the company in order to capture sales of a particular product in world markets? This is a complicated question, one whose answer depends on the company's perception of future world markets, which parts of the markets are its primary target, its own strengths and weaknesses compared to those of its competitors, and the relative importance of each weapon in increasing or maintaining market share and profitability.

Interestingly, the perspectives on these issues tend to differ in different parts of the world. Table 2.6 lists the competitive strategies preferred in North America,

Japan, and Europe in the mid-1980s. From this table we can see that companies from North America tended to emphasize product quality (consistency and high product performance) and service (on-time deliveries and fast service). Companies from Japan on the whole emphasized low production costs (low price), flexibility (rapid design changes), and product quality (consistency). Companies from Europe, somewhat like their U.S. counterparts, tended to emphasize product quality and service.

These rankings are not surprising, considering the performance of firms from these countries in the last two decades. The North American firms' emphasis on product quality reflects both their recognition of the ability of the Japanese firms to produce products of high quality and of the need for North American firms to improve the quality of their products. Also, the Japanese firms' high ranking of low price may reflect their true end objective, with high product quality representing a means to that end through reduced scrap. In other words, if products are produced right the first time, their quality is high and the scrap losses are low. As we shall discuss in Chapter 15, Total Quality Control, a key way to achieve low production costs is to emphasize high product quality so that the costs of scrap, rework, and product returns are low.

The high ranking of service (on-time deliveries and fast deliveries) by North American firms may reflect what they see as an exploitable strength relative to foreign competitors. The high ranking of low price by Japanese firms may reflect their concern about their vulnerability to market share loss to U.S. firms and from other Asian firms in the low-priced, mass-produced consumer durables markets. The high ranking of flexibility (rapid design changes and new-product introductions) by Japanese firms may reflect a key strength they have acquired as their manufacturing systems have matured. As they have moved toward the use of CAD/CAM systems, which are combined with flexible automation in their factories, the Japanese now have the ability to quickly launch new products into production. They may see this ability as a strength relative to their competitors, and they may intend to exploit this strength.

U.S. manufacturers must continue to look to the future. As they operate in an environment characterized by rapid change, they must set operations strategies that build on their strengths, reduce the impact of their weaknesses, and sense shifts in world business conditions.

Let us now consider how we go about pulling together all of the elements of operations strategies to form global operations strategies.

FORMING OPERATIONS STRATEGIES

The formation of positioning strategies is the starting point for determining operations strategy. This is because, as noted earlier, the determination of positioning strategy sets the fundamental structure of the production function. All of the other elements of operations strategy must follow from the decisions relating to the type of product, type of process, and type of finished goods inventory policy.

Table 2.7 presents two positioning strategies that are combinations of type of product, type of production process, and finished goods inventory policy that commonly occur together. These are often referred to as *pure positioning strategies*. Other

TABLE 2.7   *Pure Positioning Strategies*

Type of Product	*Type of Production Process*	*Type of Finished Goods Inventory Policy*
Standardized	Product-focused	Produce-to-stock
Custom	Process-focused	Produce-to-order

combinations of type of product, type of production process, and finished goods inventory policy are called *mixed positioning strategies.*

Table 2.8 presents a range of positioning strategies involving the type of product, type of production process, and finished goods inventory policy. An important principle is suggested in Tables 2.7 and 2.8: All of the elements of operations strategy (positioning strategies, focus of factories and service facilities, product design, production technology and processing plans, and facility planning) must be carefully matched. For example, the positioning strategy must be matched with the market strategy. In the 1970s and 1980s many Japanese manufacturers developed pure positioning strategies (highly standardized products, product-focused production, and produce-to-stock) for mass-produced consumer durables. This positioning strategy meshed perfectly with their market strategy, which was based on low price, fast product delivery, and high product quality. A key difference between U.S. firms and Japanese firms in the 1970s and 1980s was that some U.S. firms developed market strategies that required their operations functions to be all things to all people and did not take into account the structure of the operations functions and their positioning strategies. These U.S. market strategies may not have allowed the development of pure positioning strategies that could compete with their Japanese counterparts on either cost or product quality.

The decisions surrounding the structure of the production system are the domain of operations strategy. These decisions are fundamental to the future success and survival of our organizations that sell products and services in world markets. Part II of this book considers these strategic decisions.

SUMMARY

Many U.S. manufacturers suffered declining sales, market share, and profitability during the 1980s. One of the primary causes of this decline was ineffective operations strategy. Although there are mixed signals about the health of U.S. manufacturing as we enter the 1990s, one thing is sure. U.S. manufacturers must make fundamental changes in the way they plan, structure, and manage their corporations and factories. They must put the operations function on an equal footing with marketing and finance/accounting in the boardrooms where business strategy is set. Also, U.S. manufacturers should not formulate business strategy to combat the successes of Japanese manufacturers in the 1970s and 1980s; business conditions have already

TABLE 2.8   *Matching Positioning Strategies with Market Strategies*

Some Common Positioning Strategies	*Custom Products*		*Standardized Products*	
	Low Volume	*High Volume*	*Low Volume*	*High Volume*
Product-focused, to-stock				*Market Strategy:* Competition based largely on production cost, fast delivery of products, and possibly quality; *example:* TV sets
Product-focused, to-order			*Market Strategy:* Competition based largely on production cost, keeping delivery promises, and possibly quality; *example:* small-business computers	
Process-focused, to-stock		*Market Strategy:* Competition based largely on flexibility, quality, and fast delivery of products; *example:* medical instruments		
Process-focused, to-order	*Market Strategy:* Competition based largely on keeping delivery promises, quality, and flexibility; *example:* large supercomputers			

changed sufficiently to doom such an approach. They must look to future conditions as the basis for business strategy.

An assessment of today's world business environment is the starting point for developing more effective business strategy. International firms, high-tech manufacturing, foreign producers' productivity and product quality, fluctuation of international financial conditions, prominence of service systems, government regulation, and scarcity of production resources are the key factors affecting business strategy today.

Business strategies form the road map of how to achieve the corporate objectives of survival, growth, and profitability. Operations strategy is the plan for producing a firm's products and services. Operations strategy involves selecting the appropriate mix of competitive weapons for each major product line to be produced. These weapons include: low production costs, fast delivery of products/services, on-time deliveries, high-quality products/services, and flexibility. The elements of operations strategy are: positioning the production system, focus of factories and service facilities, product/service design and development, technology selection and process development, allocation of resources to strategic alternatives, and facility planning. Positioning means fitting together the type of product design (custom or standard), the type of production system (product-focused or process-focused), and the type of finished goods inventory policy (produce-to-stock or produce-to-order) so that the set of operations objectives is accomplished.

Because of shortened product life cycles, evolution of positioning strategies for products, rapidly fluctuating international financial conditions, and other factors, operations strategies in the future must include provisions for the fast development of new products and their introduction into production. Also, strategies must contain contingency plans in the face of uncertain future business conditions, and improved forecasting and planning methods are needed.

There were some differences in the early to mid-1980s in the competitive strategies of firms from North America, Japan, and Europe. North American and European firms emphasized product quality and service, and Japanese firms emphasized production costs, flexibility, and product quality. These disparities arose from the different perceptions of the firms' strengths and weaknesses, and their dissimilar views of which weapons would be important in winning future sales.

All of the elements of operations strategy must be perfectly matched for each product. Of particular importance is the need to match the positioning strategy with market strategy. More pure positioning strategies could then be developed.

REVIEW AND DISCUSSION QUESTIONS

1. Give some reasons why there is cause for optimism in predicting the health of U.S. manufacturers in the 1990s.
2. Describe the approach of Japanese manufacturers to the development of business strategy in the 1970s and 1980s.
3. Describe the traditional approach of U.S. manufacturers to the development of business strategy.
4. Give two basic things that U.S. manufacturers must do differently in the 1990s if they are to compete successfully with foreign producers.
5. Name seven developments that are affecting the formulation of business strategies today. Discuss their significance.
6. Arrange the developments listed in Table 2.1 in the order of their importance (in your opinion). Defend your choice.

7. Define, describe, and give an example of *production sharing.*

8. Discuss the pros and cons of U.S. manufacturers using high-tech manufacturing to combat foreign competition.

9. How have Japanese manufacturers changed their business strategy in recent years? What factors have prompted these changes?

10. Assume that a dollar could buy 125 yen in 1990 and 150 yen in 1992. If the only factor considered was the change in exchange rates, would the price of a Japanese product sold in the United States go up or down in this period? By what percentage would the price change?

11. What advice would you give managers today about developing business strategy, given that international financial conditions are changing rapidly? Justify your advice.

12. Give evidence of the prominence of service systems in the U.S. economy.

13. Name five resources in short supply to production functions today. What can managers do to combat these shortages?

14. Define these terms: *corporate objectives, business strategy, operations objectives, operations strategy.*

15. How is operations strategy related to business strategy?

16. Name and describe five competitive weapons of the operations function. How are these weapons created?

17. Name six elements of operations strategy.

18. Define and describe:
    a. positioning of the production system in manufacturing and in services,
    b. focus of factories and service facilities,
    c. product/service design and development,
    d. technology selection and development,
    e. allocation of resources to strategic alternatives,
    f. facility planning.

19. Define and describe the concept of a product life cycle. For each of the stages of a product life cycle, give an example of a product that is in that stage.

20. Name and describe the steps in developing new products. What are the key differences between a prototype and a production design?

21. Define these terms: *specifications, tolerances, system of interchangeable parts, modular design, maintainability, reliability, reproducibility, pilot run.*

22. What is product/service standardization? Give an example of product standardization. Give an example of service standardization.

23. What is product/service simplification? Why is simplification desirable? Give an example of product simplification. Give an example of service simplification.

24. Why is product/service design and development fundamental to efficient production systems?

25. Compare the development of products and services. How are they alike? How are they different?

26. How would you advise managers of U.S. manufacturing firms to apportion their spending between new-product development and redesign of existing products? Justify your advice.

27. Explain what is meant by "evolution of positioning strategies for products." What is the significance of this concept to operations strategy?

28. Compare and contrast the competitive strategies of manufacturing firms from North America, Japan, and Europe in the early to mid-1980s.

29. Define, describe, and give an example of these terms:
    a. pure positioning strategy,
    b. mixed positioning strategy.

30. Explain this statement: "All of the elements of positioning strategy must be perfectly matched to market strategy."

SELECTED BIBLIOGRAPHY

Buffa, Elwood. *Meeting the Competitive Challenge.* Homewood, IL: Richard D. Irwin, 1984.

Ferdows, K., and A. DeMayer. "The State of Large Manufacturers in Europe: Results of the 1984 European Manufacturing Futures Survey." *INSEAD,* 1984.

Sasser, W., R. Earl, Paul Olsen, and D. Daryle Wyckoff. *Management of Service Operations: Text, Cases, and Readings.* Boston: Allyn and Bacon, 1978.

Shostack, G. Lynn. "Designing Services That Deliver." *Harvard Business Review* 62(January–February 1984):133–139.

Skinner, Wickham. "The Focused Factory." *Harvard Business Review* 52(May–June 1974):113–121.

————. "Implementation of Operations Strategy." *Proceedings of the 4th Annual Operations Management Association Meeting* (Tempe, AZ, 1985):55–56.

————. *Manufacturing in the Corporate Strategy.* New York: Wiley, 1978.

————. *Manufacturing: The Formidable Competitive Weapon.* New York: Wiley, 1985.

————. "Manufacturing: The Missing Link in Corporate Strategy." *Harvard Business Review* 47(May–June 1969):136–145.

————. "Operations Technology: Blind Spot in Strategic Management." *Interfaces* 14, no. 1(January–February 1984):116–125.

————. "Reinventing the Factory: A Manufacturing Strategy Response to Industrial Malaise." In *Competitive Strategies Management,* Chapter 24. Englewood Cliffs, NJ: Prentice-Hall, 1984.

Stobaugh, Robert, and Piero Telesio. "Match Manufacturing Policies and Product Strategies." *Harvard Business Review* 61(March–April 1983):113–120.

————. "What Matters to Manufacturing." *Harvard Business Review* 66(January–February 1988):10–16.

Thomas, Dan R. E. "Strategy Is Different in Service Businesses." *Harvard Business Review* 57(July–August 1979):159–165.

Utterback, J., and W. J. Abernathy. "A Dynamic Model of Process and Product Innovation." *Omega* 3, no. 6(1976):639–656.

Wheelwright, Steven C. "Japan—Where Operations Really Are Strategic." *Harvard Business Review* 59(July–August 1981):67–74.

Wheelwright, Steven C., and Robert H. Hayes. "Competing Through Manufacturing." *Harvard Business Review* 63(January–February 1985):99–109.

CHAPTER

3

FORECASTING IN POM
THE STARTING POINT FOR ALL PLANNING

COMPAQ FORECASTS THE MICROCOMPUTER MARKET

Early in 1984 the Houston-based COMPAQ Computer Corporation faced a decision that would profoundly affect its future. Recognizing that IBM would soon introduce its version of the portable computer and threaten COMPAQ's dominance in this profitable market, the company had two options. It could elect to stick with its portable computers, or it could expand market offerings to include desktop microcomputers. The latter move would force the year-old company to confront IBM on its home ground. Moreover, COMPAQ would have to make a substantial investment in product development and working capital and expand its organization and manufacturing capacity.

COMPAQ's management faced several important unknowns, including the potential market's size, structure, and competitive intensity. If the expansion were successful, COMPAQ might enjoy economies of scale that could help ensure its survival in a dynamic and very competitive industry. If COMPAQ's market assumptions were incorrect, however, its future might be bleak.

COMPAQ's forecasts of the size, direction, and price trends of the microcomputer market were complicated by these factors: the entry of IBM's new portable computer, IBM's 23 percent price cut in June 1984 and its potential erosion of margins, the entry of lap portables introduced by Hewlett-Packard and Data General, the launch of IBM's new PC AT, and the introduction of desktop computers by Sperry, NCR, ITT, and AT&T.

COMPAQ entered the desktop segment of the market, and it succeeded both financially and competitively. During 1984 sales rose from $111 million to $329 million, and earnings increased from $4.7 million to $12.8 million. (Sales continued to rise in later years, to $625.2 million in 1986, $1.22 billion in 1987, and $2.1 billion in 1988.) COMPAQ's management attributes much of this success to its ability to correctly forecast future markets. Its approach to forecasting in the mid-1980s allowed COMPAQ to implement its plans for the development of new products, new technology, and marketing methods.[1]

---

[1] David M. Georgoff and Robert G. Murdick, "Manager's Guide to Forecasting," *Harvard Business Review* (January-February 1986): 110–111.

As the excerpt on the previous page suggests, it is imperative that companies today have effective approaches to forecasting and that forecasting be an integral part of managerial planning. When managers plan, they determine in the present what courses of action their organizations will take in the future. The first step in planning is therefore *forecasting* or estimating the future demand for products and services and the resources necessary to produce these outputs.

Estimates of the future demand for products and services are commonly called *sales forecasts*. Technically, *sales* means the value of shipments and *demand* means the value of what customers want shipped. For a variety of reasons, sales are almost never the same as demand. For example, orders cannot always be shipped when needed, customers occasionally cancel orders, and sales are sometimes lost. *Demand forecasts* would perhaps be a better term, but for consistency with industrial practice, we shall use the terms *sales forecasts* and *demand forecasts* interchangeably.

Sales forecasts drive all of the other forecasts in POM. Operations managers need long-range forecasts to make strategic decisions about products, processes, and facilities. They also need short-range forecasts to assist them in making decisions about production issues that span only the next few weeks. Table 3.1 summarizes some of the reasons why operations managers must develop forecasts.

Table 3.2 cites some examples of things that are commonly forecast in POM. In long-range forecasts in POM that span several years, sales forecasts may aggregate demand for entire product lines. For example, all garden products such as lawn mowers, garden tillers, and lawn edgers might be grouped into a single product line.

■ ■

TABLE 3.1   Some Reasons Why We Must Forecast in POM

1. **New Facility Planning.** It can take as long as five years to design and build a new factory or design and implement a new production process. Such strategic activities in POM require long-range forecasts of demand for existing and new products so that operations managers can have the necessary lead time to build factories and install processes to produce the products and services when needed.

2. **Production Planning.** Demands for products and services vary from month to month. Production rates must be scaled up or down to meet these demands. It can take several months to change the capacities of production processes. Operations managers need intermediate-range forecasts so that they can have the lead time necessary to provide the production capacity to produce these variable monthly demands.

3. **Work Force Scheduling.** Demands for products and services vary from week to week. The work force must be scaled up or down to meet these demands by using overtime, layoffs, or hiring. Operations managers need short-range forecasts so that they can have the lead time necessary to provide work force changes to produce the weekly demands.

4. **Financial Planning.** Sales forecasts are the driving force in the financial budget control process, the process that is used by so many operations managers to plan and control the financial performance of their production departments.

■ ■

TABLE 3.2   *Some Examples of Things That Must Be Forecast in POM*

Forecast Horizon	*Time Span*	*Examples of Things That Must Be Forecast*	*Some Typical Units of Forecasts*
Long-range	Years	New product lines	Dollars
		Old product lines	Dollars
		Factory capacities	Gallons, hours, pounds, units, or customers per time period
		Capital funds	Dollars
		Facility needs	Space, volume
Intermediate-range	Months	Product groups	Units
		Departmental capacities	Hours, strokes, pounds, gallons, units, or customers per time period
		Work force	Workers, hours
		Purchased materials	Units, pounds, gallons
		Inventories	Units, dollars
Short-range	Weeks	Specific products	Units
		Labor-skill classes	Workers, hours
		Machine capacities	Units, hours, gallons, strokes, pounds, or customers per time period
		Cash	Dollars
		Inventories	Units, dollars

Putting specific products into large classes reduces the number of forecasts that must be made and ordinarily improves the accuracy of the forecasts. By grouping product forecasts together in one class, errors of forecasting too high on some products and too low on other products would tend to offset each other. Long-range factory capacity needs are determined from the product-line demand forecasts. Capital funds requirements and facility needs are determined from the production capacity needs.

Intermediate-range forecasts span several months and group specific products into product families. For example, all lawn mowers could be lumped together as one product group, although there are many types of mowers within the group. Work force, production department capacities, purchased materials, and inventory forecasts would be determined from the product groups' demand forecasts. Short-range forecasts focus on specific products. For example, the demand for model #3559, a 3-horsepower push mower, would be forecast. The labor hours in each labor-skill class, the production rate needed for each major production machine, the cash needed in each week, and the inventory of each product in each time period are all determined from the product demand forecasts.

FIGURE 3.1 A Forecasting System in POM

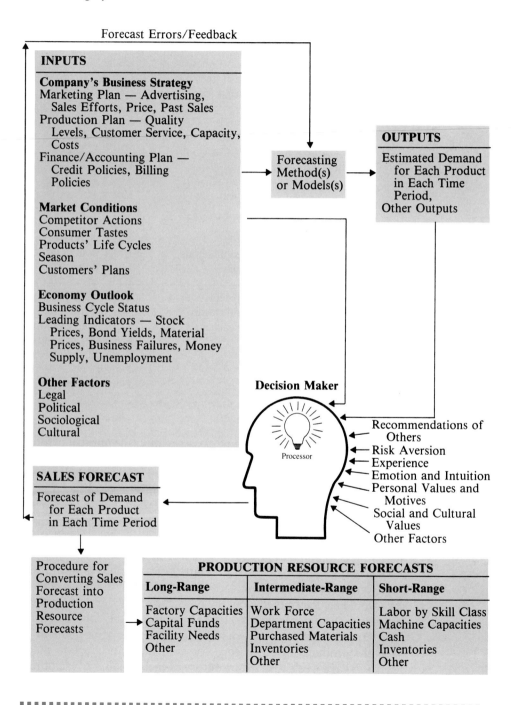

Forecasting is more than a technique, however, and most successful organizations have a comprehensive forecasting system in place. Figure 3.1 illustrates the idea of such a forecasting system. Some or all of the inputs are processed through one or more forecasting models to develop demand estimates. The decision maker uses these demand estimates as the starting point for developing a forecast. The original inputs, the demand estimates from the forecasting model(s), and several other inputs are used by the decision maker to finalize the sales forecast. These latter inputs can be as important as the demand estimates from the forecasting models: the recommendations of others, the aversion of the decision maker to risk, the experience of the decision maker in similar situations, the emotional mind-set of the decision maker at the time of the decision, the personal motives and values of the decision maker, and the social and cultural values that prevail. Figure 3.1 makes two key points: (1) the outputs of forecasting models are not the forecast, but rather a single input—admittedly an important one—to the sales forecast decision; and (2) the sales forecast is converted to the various production resource forecasts.

The forecasting methods or models used in a forecasting system may be either qualitative or quantitative in nature.

QUALITATIVE FORECASTING METHODS

Table 3.3 defines and describes several qualitative forecasting methods known to be used to develop sales forecasts today. As used here, a qualitative forecast is one that is not based exclusively on a mathematical model. These methods are usually based on judgments about the causal factors that underlie the sales of particular products or services and on opinions about the relative likelihood of those causal factors being present in the future. These methods may involve several levels of sophistication, from scientifically conducted opinion surveys to intuitive hunches about future events.

Executive committee consensus and the delphi method describe procedures for assimilating information within a committee for the purpose of generating a sales forecast and are useful for either existing or new products and services. On the other hand, the survey of sales force and survey of customers describe methods that are primarily used for existing products and services. Historical analogy and market surveys and tests describe procedures that are useful for new products and services. The forecasting method that is appropriate, therefore, depends on a product's life cycle stage.

Most sales forecasts in business today are based at least in part on qualitative forecasting methods. To learn more about these important and practical forecasting methods, refer to the Selected Bibliography at the end of this chapter.

QUANTITATIVE FORECASTING MODELS ✕

Quantitative forecasting models are mathematical models that are based on past data patterns. Such an approach assumes, of course, that past data are relevant to the

TABLE 3.3   *Qualitative Forecasting Methods*

1. **Executive Committee Consensus.** Knowledgeable executives from various departments within the organization form a committee charged with the responsibility of developing a sales forecast. The committee may use many inputs from all parts of the organization and may have staff analysts provide analyses as needed. Such forecasts tend to be compromise forecasts, not reflecting the extremes that could be present had they been prepared by individuals. This method is the most common forecasting method.

2. **Delphi Method.** This method is used to achieve consensus within a committee. In this method executives anonymously answer a series of questions on successive rounds. Each response is fed back to all participants on each round, and the process is then repeated. As many as six rounds may be required before consensus is reached on the forecast. This method can result in forecasts that most participants have ultimately agreed to in spite of their initial disagreement. For an interesting account of using the delphi method, see the Basu and Schroeder citation in the Selected Bibliography at the end of this chapter.

3. **Survey of Sales Force.** Estimates of future regional sales are obtained from individual members of the sales force. These estimates are combined to form an estimate of sales for all regions. Managers must then transform this estimate into a sales forecast to ensure realistic estimates. This is a popular forecasting method for companies that have a good communication system in place and that have sales persons who sell directly to customers.

4. **Survey of Customers.** Estimates of future sales are obtained directly from customers. Individual customers are surveyed to determine what quantities of the firm's products they intend to purchase in each future time period. A sales forecast is determined by combining individual customers' responses. This method may be preferred by companies that have relatively few customers.

5. **Historical Analogy.** This method ties the estimate of future sales of a product to knowledge of a similar product's sales. Knowledge of one product's sales during various stages of its product life cycle is applied to the estimate of sales for a similar product. This method may be particularly useful in forecasting sales of new products.

6. **Market Research.** In *market surveys,* mail questionnaires, telephone interviews, or field interviews form the basis for testing hypotheses about real markets. In *market tests,* products marketed in target regions or outlets are statistically extrapolated to total markets. These methods are ordinarily preferred for new products or for existing products to be introduced into new market segments.

future, which is not the case in all forecasting situations. Take, for example, the company that developed the first diet beer product. Few past data and little experience were available or relevant to projecting future sales. Instances where the past data are of no particular help in estimating the future are rare and should not cause us to abandon analysis by throwing out the baby with the bath water.

The times when some form of quantitative analysis can be utilized outnumber the times when it is inappropriate. Some relevant data can almost always be found.

TABLE 3.4   *Quantitative Forecasting Models*

1. **Regression.** A model that uses what is called the least-squares method to identify the relationship between a dependent variable and one or more independent variables that are present in a set of historical observations. In simple regression there is only one independent variable. In multiple regression there is more than one independent variable. If the historical data set is a time series, the independent variable is the time period and the dependent variable in sales forecasting is sales. A regression model does not have to be based on a time series; in such cases the knowledge of future values of the independent variable (which may also be referred to as the *causal variable*) is used to predict future values of the dependent variable. Regression is ordinarily used in long-range forecasting, but if care is used in selecting the number of periods included in the historical data and that data set is projected only a few periods into the future, regression may also be appropriately used in short-range forecasting.

2. **Moving Average.** A short-range time series type of forecasting model that forecasts sales for the next time period. In this model the arithmetic average of the actual sales for a specific number of most recent past time periods is the forecast for the next time period.

3. **Weighted Moving Averages.** This model is like the moving average model described above except that instead of an arithmetic average of past sales, a weighted average of past sales is the forecast for the next time period.

4. **Exponential Smoothing.** Also a short-range time series forecasting model that forecasts sales for the next time period. In this method the forecasted sales for the last period is modified by information about the forecast error of the last period. This modification of the last period's forecast is the forecast for the next time period.

The results of these models are usually modified by other relevant information before a final forecasting decision is made. As Figure 3.1 shows, analysis that projects past data into the future may not be used alone to determine a forecast. Still, analyses are important inputs to forecasting decisions.

Table 3.4 exhibits the quantitative forecasting models that we shall study in this chapter. Each of these models may be used with one or more quantitative or qualitative models. All of these models in Table 3.4 indicate that they can be used with *times series*. A time series is a set of observed values, usually sales, measured over successive periods of time.

FORECAST ACCURACY

Forecast accuracy refers to how close forecasts are to actual, but after-the-fact, data. Because forecasts are made *before* actual data become known, their accuracy cannot be determined at the moment they are made. Only after the passage of time will we know how accurate our forecasts have been. If they are very close to the actual data, we say that they have *high accuracy* and that the *forecast error* was very low. If, on the other hand, our forecasts miss the mark and depart from the actual data, we say that they have *low accuracy* and a very high forecast error. Forecast accuracy, unfortunately, cannot be determined until after the fact—after the future that we are forecasting becomes the past. Knowing whether a forecasting method has resulted in high-accuracy forecasts is fundamental to its continued use. We keep track of a forecasting method's accuracy by keeping a running tally of how far our forecasts have missed the actual data points over time. If the historical accuracy of a method's application has been low, we must consider whether to modify the method or select a new one. We usually monitor a forecasting method's accuracy with *mean absolute deviation* (MAD). We shall use MAD in evaluating the accuracy of forecasting methods later in this chapter. Forecast accuracy is not the only measure of a forecasting method's performance. We shall discuss impulse response, noise dampening, and tracking signal later in the chapter.

LONG-RANGE FORECASTS

Long-range forecasting means estimating future conditions over time spans that range from many months to many years. Estimates that span these long periods are necessary in POM to support most of the strategic decisions concerning planning products, processes, and facilities—the topics in Part II of this text. Such decisions are so important to the long-term success of production systems that intense organizational effort is applied to developing these forecasts.

Most of this effort involves estimating the future demand for products and services, or developing *sales forecasts.* From these sales forecasts comes most of the information that operations managers need to know about planning their production systems. Specifically, long-range forecasts provide operations managers with information to make important decisions such as the following:

1. Selecting a product design. The final design is dependent on the expected sales volume. Enormous production engineering design work is necessary, for example, for mass-produced products to ensure low-cost manufacture and ease of processing through automatic machines.
2. Selecting a production processing scheme for a new product. Because these forecasts determine the long-range production capacity that is necessary, the process designs are dependent on the forecasts.
3. Selecting a plan for the long-range supply of scarce materials. These forecasts allow operations managers to lock suppliers into long-range material supply contracts.
4. Selecting a long-range production capacity plan for all of an organization's product lines. How many manufacturing plants are needed and where should they be located?
5. Selecting a long-range plan for acquiring capital funds. Such a plan will be based on a long-range production capacity plan, which is in turn based on long-range forecasts.

These and other estimates of long-run requirements of production systems usually follow from long-range sales forecasts. To purchase and build new machines and buildings and to develop new sources of materials and capital funds takes time. And long-range forecasts give managers the time to develop these requirements.

FIGURE 3.2 *Data Patterns in Long-Range Forecasting*

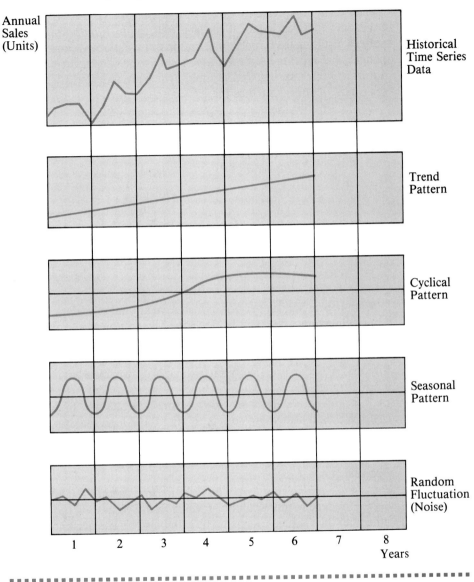

We shall now study some concepts and quantitative techniques of long-range forecasting.

Cycles, Trends, and Seasonality

Developing forecasts that can span several years usually involves historical data that exhibit complex patterns. It is often useful to be able to look beyond this complexity to identify fairly simple underlying data patterns. Figure 3.2 shows how historical sales data tend to be made up of several components. Among these components are trends, cycles, seasonality, and random fluctuation or noise. Long-range *trends* are illustrated by an upward- or downward-sloping line. A *cycle* is a data pattern that may cover several years before it repeats itself again. *Random fluctuation or noise* is a pattern resulting from random variation or unexplained causes. *Seasonality* is a data pattern that repeats itself after a period of time. The term suggests seasons such as autumn, winter, spring, and summer, which are repeated after a year has passed, but seasonality patterns such as these are also common:

Length of Time before Pattern Is Repeated	Length of Season	Number of Seasons in Pattern
Year	Quarter	4
Year	Month	12
Year	Week	52
Month	Week	4
Month	Day	29–31
Week	Day	7

In Figure 3.2, six periods of historical annual sales data are plotted on a graph. Long-range forecasts could be developed by graphically fitting a line through these past data and extending it forward into the future. The sales forecasts for Periods 7 and 8 could then be read off the graph. This graphical approach to long-range forecasts is used in practice, but its principal drawback is our inability to accurately fit a line through the past data.

Regression analysis provides a more accurate way to develop trend line forecasts. We shall also show how these trend line forecasts can be modified to reflect cycles and seasonality.

Regression Analysis

Regression analysis is a type of quantitative forecasting that establishes a relationship between a dependent variable, for which future values will be forecast, and a group of other variables, called independent variables. We use our knowledge about the relationship between the dependent and independent variables and about the future values of the independent variables to estimate the future values of the dependent variables. Thus we forecast values of the dependent variables. In *simple regression analysis* only two variables are involved in the analysis—one dependent variable (the one we want to forecast future values of) and one independent variable. If the underlying data form a time series, the independent variable is time periods.

Table 3.5 displays the variables, variable definitions, and formulas for simple linear regression analysis. The end product of simple linear regression analysis is the relationship between the dependent variable (y) and the independent variable (x). The formula for this relationship is called the *regression equation:* $Y = a + bX$. The

■ ■

TABLE 3.5   *Variable Definitions and Formulas for Simple Linear Regression Analysis*

x = Independent variable values	b = Slope of the regression line
y = Dependent variable values	Y = Forecast values in the regression
n = Number of periods of data	equation $Y = a + bX$
$\bar{x}$ = Mean value of the independent variable	X = Projected values of independent variable value associated with Y
$\bar{y}$ = Mean value of the dependent variable	r = Coefficient of correlation
a = Vertical axis intercept	r^2 = Coefficient of determination

$$a = \frac{\Sigma x^2 \Sigma y - \Sigma x \Sigma xy}{n\Sigma x^2 - (\Sigma x)^2}$$

$$b = \frac{n\Sigma xy - \Sigma x \Sigma y}{n\Sigma x^2 - (\Sigma x)^2}$$

or

$$a = \bar{y} - b\bar{x} \qquad Y = a + bX$$

$$b = \frac{\Sigma xy - n\bar{x}\bar{y}}{\Sigma x^2 - n(\bar{x})^2} \qquad r = \frac{n\Sigma xy - \Sigma x \Sigma y}{\sqrt{[n\Sigma x^2 - (\Sigma x)^2][n\Sigma y^2 - (\Sigma y)^2]}}$$

■ ■

Note: $\bar{x}$ and $\bar{y}$ must be carried out to *many* decimal places to achieve accuracy for a and b.

formulas listed in Table 3.5 show how to compute values of intercept (a) and slope (b). Once these constant values are known, a future value of X can be entered into the regression equation and a corresponding value of Y (the forecast) can be calculated.

Conceptually, this procedure is the same as that of Figure 3.2 except that in regression analysis we derive the mathematical formula for the trend line (Y = a + bX) and mathematically compute the future values of the dependent variable, whereas in Figure 3.2 we graphically extend the trend line and read off values of the dependent variable from the vertical axis.

To better understand the detailed procedures of simple linear regression analysis, study Example 3.1, which develops a forecast from time series data. Use your calculator to check each calculation in the example. The example shows how operations managers can plan facility capacities by developing long-range forecasts.

EXAMPLE 3.1   *Simple Linear Regression Analysis: A Time Series*

Specific Motors produces electronic motors for power-actuated valves for the construction industry. Specific's production plant has operated at near capacity for over a year now. Jim White, the plant manager, thinks that the growth in sales will continue, and he wants to develop a long-range forecast to be used to plan facility requirements for the next three years. Sales records for the past ten years have been accumulated:

Year	Annual Sales (Thousands of Units)	Year	Annual Sales (Thousands of Units)
1	1,000	6	2,000
2	1,300	7	2,200
3	1,800	8	2,600
4	2,000	9	2,900
5	2,000	10	3,200

Study the formulas and variable definitions in Table 3.5 carefully, and construct the following table to establish the values to use in the formulas:

Year	Annual Sales (Thousands of Units) (y)	Time Period (x)	x^2	xy	
1	1,000	1	1	1,000	
2	1,300	2	4	2,600	$\Sigma y = 21,000$
3	1,800	3	9	5,400	$\Sigma x = 55$
4	2,000	4	16	8,000	$\Sigma x^2 = 385$
5	2,000	5	25	10,000	$\Sigma xy = 133,300$
6	2,000	6	36	12,000	
7	2,200	7	49	15,400	$n = 10$
8	2,600	8	64	20,800	$\bar{x} = 55/10 = 5.5$
9	2,900	9	81	26,100	$\bar{y} = 21,100/10 = 2,100$
10	3,200	10	100	32,000	
Totals	21,000	55	385	133,300	

Solution

1. Let us now solve for the a and b values:

$$a = \frac{\Sigma x^2 \Sigma y - \Sigma x \Sigma xy}{n\Sigma x^2 - (\Sigma x)^2} = \frac{(385)(21,000) - (55)(133,300)}{10(385) - (55)^2}$$

$$= \frac{8,085,000 - 7,331,500}{3,850 - 3,025} = \frac{753,500}{825} = 913.333$$

$$b = \frac{n\Sigma xy - \Sigma x \Sigma y}{n\Sigma x^2 - (\Sigma x)^2} = \frac{(10)(133,300) - (55)(21,000)}{825}$$

$$= \frac{1,333,000 - 1,155,000}{825} = \frac{178,000}{825} = 215.758$$

or, alternatively, the other set of formulas for a and b may be used:

$$b = \frac{\Sigma xy - n\bar{x}\bar{y}}{\Sigma x^2 - n(\bar{x})^2} = \frac{133,300 - (10)(5.5)(2,100)}{385 - 10(5.5)^2} = \frac{133,300 - 115,500}{385 - 302.5} = \frac{17,800}{82.5} = 215.758$$

$$a = \bar{y} - b\bar{x} = 2,100 - (215.758)(5.5) = 2,100 - 1,186.667 = 913.333$$

2. Now that we know the values of a and b, the regression equation ($Y = a + bX$) from Table 3.5 can be used to forecast future years' sales:

$$Y = a + bX = 913.333 + 215.758X$$

3. If we wish to forecast sales in thousands of units for the next three years, we would substitute 11, 12, and 13, the next three values for x, into the regression equation for X:

$$Y_{11} = 913.333 + 215.758(11) = 3{,}286.7 \text{ thousand units}$$

$$Y_{12} = 913.333 + 215.758(12) = 3{,}502.4 \text{ thousand units}$$

$$Y_{13} = 913.333 + 215.758(13) = 3{,}718.2 \text{ thousand units}$$

4. Next, to simplify the calculations, modify the data for X so that $\Sigma X = 0$ and repeat the regression analysis to obtain forecasts for the next three years:

Year	Annual Sales (Thousands of Units) (y)	Time Period (x)	x^2	xy	
1	1,000	−9	81	−9,000	
2	1,300	−7	49	−9,100	$\Sigma y = 21{,}000$
3	1,800	−5	25	−9,000	$\Sigma x = 0$
4	2,000	−3	9	−6,000	$\Sigma x^2 = 330$
5	2,000	−1	1	−2,000	$\Sigma xy = 35{,}600$
6	2,000	+1	1	+2,000	
7	2,200	+3	9	+6,600	$n = 10$
8	2,600	+5	25	+13,000	$\bar{x} = 0$
9	2,900	+7	49	+20,300	$\bar{y} = 2{,}100$
10	3,200	+9	81	+28,800	
Totals	21,000	0	330	35,600	

$$a = \frac{\Sigma x^2 \Sigma y - \Sigma x \Sigma xy}{n\Sigma x^2 - (\Sigma x)^2} = \frac{\Sigma x^2 \Sigma y - 0(\Sigma xy)}{n\Sigma x^2 - (0)^2} = \frac{\Sigma x^2 \Sigma y}{n\Sigma x^2} = \frac{\Sigma y}{n} = \bar{y} = 2{,}100$$

$$b = \frac{n\Sigma xy - \Sigma x \Sigma y}{n\Sigma x^2 - (\Sigma x)^2} = \frac{n\Sigma xy - 0(\Sigma y)}{n\Sigma x^2 - (0)^2} = \frac{n\Sigma xy}{n\Sigma x^2} = \frac{\Sigma xy}{\Sigma x^2} = \frac{35{,}600}{330} = 107.879$$

$$Y = a + bX = 2{,}100 + 107.879X$$

$$Y_{11} = 2{,}100 + 107.879(11) = 3{,}286.7 \text{ thousand units}$$

$$Y_{12} = 2{,}100 + 107.879(13) = 3{,}502.4 \text{ thousand units}$$

$$Y_{13} = 2{,}100 + 107.879(15) = 3{,}718.2 \text{ thousand units}$$

As step 4 in Example 3.1 shows, there is a way to simplify the calculations in a regression analysis of a time series. In this example the independent variable X represents time and X initially has values that begin with 1, which represents the first year, and end with 10, which represents the tenth year. X could also have been given such values as 1986, 1987, 1988 . . . 1995. The only requirement that is placed on values of X, the independent variable in a time series, is that the values must be equally spaced from each other. With this requirement in mind, we could select values for X that make $\Sigma X = 0$; thus the calculation of a and b becomes much easier because ΣX would drop out of the regression equations. If there were an odd number of past periods of data, say 5, the values of X would be $-2, -1, 0, +1, +2$, values that are equally spaced one unit apart, and the value of X used in the regression equations for the next year would be $+3$. If there were an even number of past periods of data, say 10, as in Example 3.1, values of X would be spaced two units apart, and the value of X used in the regression equation for next year would be $+11$.

The independent variable in *simple linear regression analysis* does not have to be time periods. Example 3.2 demonstrates that the independent variable can be another variable believed to be a good predictor of the dependent variable. In this example a long-range forecast is developed to assist the manager in planning the number of engineers and facilities for the next year. This example also raises the question of the value of the predictive model developed through regression analysis. Coefficients of correlation and determination are measures of the expected precision of these forecasts.

EXAMPLE 3.2   Simple Linear Regression Analysis

Jack Williams, the general manager of Precision Engineering Corporation, thinks that his firm's engineering services supplied to highway construction firms are directly related to the amount of highway construction contracts let in his geographic area. He wonders if this is really so and if it is, can this information help him plan his operations better? Jack asked Bill Brandon, one of his engineers, to perform a simple linear regression analysis on historical data. Bill plans to do the following: **a.** Develop a regression equation for predicting the level of demand of Precision's services. **b.** Use the regression equation to predict the level of demand for the next four quarters. **c.** Determine how closely demand is related to the amount of construction contracts released.

Solution

a. Develop a regression equation:

1. Bill goes back through local, state, and federal records to gather the dollar amount of contracts released in the geographic area for two years by quarters.

2. He examines the demand for his firm's services over the same period.

3. The following data are prepared:

Year	Quarter	Sales of Precision Engineering Services (Thousands of Dollars)	Total Amount of Contracts Released (Thousands of Dollars)
1	Q_1	8	150
	Q_2	10	170
	Q_3	15	190
	Q_4	9	170
2	Q_1	12	180
	Q_2	13	190
	Q_3	12	200
	Q_4	16	220

4. Bill now develops the totals required to perform the regression analysis. The formulas and variable definitions are found in Table 3.5.

Time Period	Sales (y)	Contracts (x)	x^2	xy	y^2
1	8	150	22,500	1,200	64
2	10	170	28,900	1,700	100
3	15	190	36,100	2,850	225
4	9	170	28,900	1,530	81
5	12	180	32,400	2,160	144
6	13	190	36,100	2,470	169
7	12	200	40,000	2,400	144
8	16	220	48,400	3,520	256
Totals	95	1,470	273,300	17,830	1,183

$\Sigma y = 95$
$\Sigma x = 1,470$
$\Sigma x^2 = 273,300$
$\Sigma xy = 17,830$
$\Sigma y^2 = 1,183$
$n = 8$

5. Use these values in the formulas in Table 3.5 to compute a and b:

$$a = \frac{\Sigma x^2 \Sigma y - \Sigma x \Sigma xy}{n \Sigma x^2 - (\Sigma x)^2} = \frac{(273,300)(95) - (1,470)(17,830)}{8(273,300) - (1,470)^2}$$

$$= \frac{25,963,500 - 26,210,100}{2,186,400 - 2,160,900} = \frac{-246,600}{25,500} = -9.671$$

$$b = \frac{n \Sigma xy - \Sigma x \Sigma y}{n \Sigma x^2 - (\Sigma x)^2} = \frac{(8)(17,830) - (1,470)(95)}{25,500} = \frac{142,640 - 139,650}{25,500} = \frac{2,990}{25,500} = .1173$$

6. The regression equation is therefore $Y = -9.671 + .1173X$.

b. Forecast the level of demand for the next four quarters:

1. Bill calls representatives of the contracting agencies and prepares estimates of the next four quarters' contract releases in thousands of dollars. These were 260, 290, 300, and 270.

2. Next, Bill forecasts the demand for Precision's engineering services (in thousands of dollars) for the next four quarters by using the regression equation $Y = -9.671 + .1173X$:

$$Y_1 = -9.671 + .1173(260) \qquad Y_2 = -9.671 + .1173(290)$$
$$= -9.671 + 30.498 \qquad\qquad = -9.671 + 34.017$$
$$= 20.827 \qquad\qquad\qquad = 24.346$$

$$Y_3 = -9.671 + .1173(300) \qquad Y_4 = -9.671 + .1173(270)$$
$$= -9.671 + 35.190 \qquad\qquad = -9.671 + 31.671$$
$$= 25.519 \qquad\qquad\qquad = 22.000$$

The total forecast (in thousands of dollars) for the next year is the total of the four quarter forecasts:

$$20.827 + 24.346 + 25.519 + 22.000 = \$92.7$$

c. Evaluate how closely demand is related to the amount of the construction contracts released:

$$r = \frac{n\Sigma xy - \Sigma x\Sigma y}{\sqrt{[n\Sigma x^2 - (\Sigma x)^2][n\Sigma y^2 - (\Sigma y)^2]}} = \frac{2,990}{\sqrt{[25,550][8(1,183) - (95)^2]}}$$

$$= \frac{2,990}{\sqrt{[25,500][9,464 - 9,025]}} = \frac{2,990}{\sqrt{(25,500)(439)}} = \frac{2,990}{\sqrt{11,194,500}}$$

$$= \frac{2,990}{3,345.8} = .894$$

$$r^2 = .799$$

The amount of contracts released explains approximately 80 percent ($r^2 = .799$) of the observed variation in quarterly demand for Precision's services.

The *coefficient of correlation (r)* explains the relative importance of the association between y and x. The range of r is from -1 to $+1$. Minus 1 means a perfect negative relationship between the two variables; in other words, as y goes up, x goes down unit for unit and vice versa. Plus 1 means a perfect positive relationship between y and x: that is, as y goes up, x goes up unit for unit and vice versa. Zero means no relationship exists between y and x. Notice that the signs of b and r are always the same. Also, in Example 3.2, $b = +.1173$ and $r = +.894$. This means that there is a strong positive relationship between demand for engineering services and amount of contracts released. A smaller value of r, say .25, would have indicated a weak relationship between demand for engineering services and amount of contracts released. The larger the absolute value of r, the better the regression equation forecasts accurate values of Y.

Although the coefficient of correlation is helpful in establishing confidence in our predictive model, terms such as *strong, moderate,* and *weak* are not very specific measures of relationship. The coefficient of determination offers some improvement in specificity.

FIGURE 3.3   *Variation of Dependent Variable (y)*

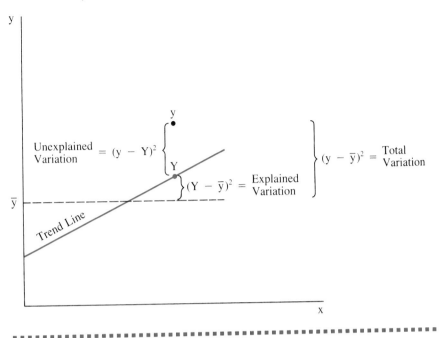

The *coefficient of determination (r^2)* is the square of the coefficent of correlation. The seemingly insignificant modification of r to r^2 allows us to shift from subjective measures of relationship between x and y to a more specific measure, *the percentage of variation in y that is explained by x.*

There are three types of variation in y: total, explained, and unexplained:

Total variation = Explained variation + Unexplained variation

$$\Sigma(y - \bar{y})^2 \quad = \quad \Sigma(Y - \bar{y})^2 \quad + \quad \Sigma(y - Y)^2$$

The total variation is the sum of the squared deviations of each value of y from its mean $\bar{y}$. The explained variation is the sum of the squared deviations of Y values that lie on the trend line from $\bar{y}$. The unexplained variation is due to chance, random, or as yet unidentified causes and accounts for all other sources of variation. It is computed by taking the sum of the squared deviations of y from its Y counterpart that lies on the trend line. Figure 3.3 illustrates these sources of variation.

The coefficient of determination is determined by the ratio of explained variation to total variation:

$$r^2 = \frac{\Sigma(Y - \bar{y})^2}{\Sigma(y - \bar{y})^2}$$

The coefficient of determination, therefore, illustrates how much of the total variation in the dependent variable y is explained by x or the trend line. If $r^2 = 80$ percent, as in Example 3.2, we can say that the amount of contracts released (x) explains 80 percent of the variation in sales of engineering services (y). Twenty percent of the variation in sales of engineering services is not explained by the amount of contracts released and thus is attributed to other variables or chance variation.

Both the coefficients of correlation and determination are helpful measures of the strength of the relationship between dependent and independent variables and thus of the value of regression equations as forecasting tools. The stronger the relationship, the more accurate the forecasts resulting from the regression equations are likely to be.

Simple linear regression analysis is limited in its ability to develop forecasts with high accuracy in the real worlds of government and business. Although there are instances where one independent variable explains enough of the dependent variable variation to provide management with forecasts having sufficient accuracy, more sophisticated models are usually required to increase forecasting accuracy. *Multiregression analysis* is used when two or more independent variables are incorporated into the analysis. An example of a multiregression equation is:

$$Y = 15.5 + 2.9X_1 + 12.8X_2 - 1.2X_3 + 8.5X_4$$

where:

Y = annual sales in thousands of units

X_1 = national freight car loadings in millions

X_2 = percent GNP growth $\times$ ten thousands

X_3 = unemployment rate in region $\times$ ten thousands

X_4 = population in county in thousands

Such an equation is used just as the simple regression equation ($Y = a + bX$): The values of the independent variables (X_1, X_2, X_3, and X_4) are substituted into the equation and the value of the dependent variable (Y) is directly calculated.

Another technique called *nonlinear multiregression analysis* is used when the relationship between the dependent variable and the independent variables is not linear. Other techniques such as *stepwise regression* and *partial* and *multiple correlation coefficients* are also part of the family of techniques called regression analysis, but these are beyond the scope of this text. The concepts presented here generally apply to these more sophisticated techniques. Additionally, Y, X, and r all have their counterparts in the more complex models.

Ranging Time Series Forecasts

Suppose that you have performed the forecasting analysis in Example 3.1 as part of your assignment from Jim White, Specific Motors, to recommend long-range forecasts for annual sales for three years into the future. You present your recommendations in thousands of units:

$$Y_{11} = 3,286.7 \qquad Y_{12} = 3,502.4 \qquad Y_{13} = 3,718.2$$

FIGURE 3.4   *Errors in Forecasting*

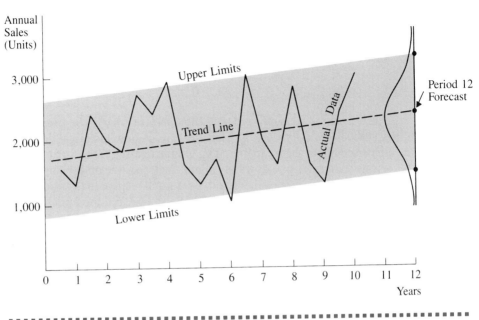

Mr. White considers the forecasts for a time and finally asks, "How sure are you of these figures?" Before you can respond, he asks, "How high and how low do you estimate the annual sales could be next year?"

When time series analysis generates forecasts for future periods, we must recognize that these are only estimates and that the actual annual sales to be subsequently realized may differ substantially from the forecasts. In fact, no one would be more surprised than the forecasters if they hit the forecasts on the nose. The presence of forecasting errors or chance variations is a fact of life for forecasters; it is a process permeated with uncertainty. How do forecasters deal with this uncertainty?

Figure 3.4 shows how we think about forecasting errors. Ten periods of data are used to develop a trend line. This analysis results in a forecast of 2,400 units for Time Period 12. The uncertainty surrounding this estimate is demonstrated by showing the forecast as a mean or central tendency of a frequency distribution of all of the possible values of annual sales during Time Period 12. By drawing upper and lower limits through the data parallel to the trend line such that actual annual sales only rarely exceed the limits, upper and lower limits can be estimated for the Time Period 12 forecast — 3,300 units and 1,500 units.

A graphic analysis of this type allows us to deal with the uncertainty of our forecasts in a very direct way. Questions about our confidence in our forecasts can be answered by stating how high (upper limit) or how low (lower limit) the annual sales are likely to be. If these limits are far apart, the historical data are highly scattered around the trend line and we have less confidence in our forecasts. If, on the other hand, the limits are close together, the historical data have been closely grouped about the trend line and we have more confidence in our forecasts.

Although this graphic approach is sometimes used to set upper and lower limits or ranges of forecasts, a more precise method is available. Example 3.3 uses this formula to estimate ranges:

$$s_{yx} = \sqrt{\frac{\Sigma y^2 - a\Sigma y - b\Sigma xy}{n - 2}}$$

The expression s_{yx} is referred to as the *standard error of the forecast* and the *standard deviation of the forecast*. s_{yx} is a measure of how historical data points have been dispersed about the trend line. If s_{yx} is large relative to the forecast, the historical data points have been spread widely about the trend line and the upper and lower limits are far apart. If, on the other hand, s_{yx} is small relative to the forecast, past data points have been tightly grouped about the trend line and the upper and lower limits are close together.

Forecast ranging allows analysts to face the reality of uncertainty that surrounds their forecasts by developing best-estimate forecasts and the ranges within which the actual data are likely to fall.

EXAMPLE 3.3   *Ranging Time Series Forecasts*

The annual sales data of Specific Motors from Example 3.1 resulted in these values: $\Sigma y = 21,000$, $\Sigma xy = 133,300$, $a = 913.333$, $b = 215.758$, and $n = 10$. The distribution of forecast values for a future time period has a standard deviation (s_{yx}), which is a relative measure of how the distribution is dispersed (spread out). The distributions of all future time periods are assumed to be normal distributions if n (number of observations) is large (usually ≥ 30) or Student's t distributions if n is small (usually < 30). Since we rarely have 30 or more observations in our data, and t and normal distributions tend to converge when n is large, it is assumed that we are dealing with t distributions.

Solution

1. From Example 3.1 we have computed all of these values: $\Sigma y = 21,000$; $\Sigma x = 55$; $\Sigma x^2 = 385$; $\Sigma xy = 133,300$; $n = 10$; $\bar{x} = 5.5$; and $\bar{y} = 2,100$. Let us now compute Σy^2:

Year	y (Thousands of Units)	y^2	Year	y (Thousands of Units)	y^2
1	1,000	1,000,000	6	2,000	4,000,000
2	1,300	1,690,000	7	2,200	4,840,000
3	1,800	3,240,000	8	2,600	6,760,000
4	2,000	4,000,000	9	2,900	8,410,000
5	2,000	4,000,000	10	3,200	10,240,000
			Totals	21,000	48,180,000

2. Now let us compute the value of s_{yx}:

$$s_{yx} = \sqrt{\frac{\Sigma y^2 - a\Sigma y - b\Sigma xy}{n - 2}}$$

$$= \sqrt{\frac{48,180,000 - 913.333(21,000) - 215.758(133,300)}{10 - 2}}$$

$$= \sqrt{\frac{48,180,000 - 19,179,993 - 28,760,541.4}{8}} = \sqrt{\frac{239,465.6}{8}} = \sqrt{29,933.2}$$

$$= 173.0 \text{ thousand units}$$

3. Now that we have the value of s_{yx}, let us compute the upper and lower limits of the forecast for Time Period 11:[2]

Upper limit $= Y_{11} + t\, s_{yx}$

Lower limit $= Y_{11} - t\, s_{yx}$

where t is the number of standard deviations out from the mean of the distribution to provide a given probability of exceeding these upper and lower limits through chance. Say, for example, that we wish to set the limits so that there is only a 10 percent probability of exceeding the limits by chance. Appendix B lists t values. Since the degrees of freedom (d.f.) $= n - 2$ and the level of significance is .10, the t value equals 1.860 and:

Upper limit $= 3,286.7 + 1.86(173) = 3,608.5$ thousand units

Lower limit $= 3,286.7 - 1.86(173) = 2,964.9$ thousand units

4. Now we can describe to Mr. White what we have: There is a 90 percent probability that our annual sales for next year will be between 3,608.5 and 2,964.9 thousand units. There is only a 10 percent probability that our sales will fall outside these limits. Our best estimate is 3,286.7 thousand units.

---

[2] A more precise expression of the upper and lower limits of the forecast Y is: Limits $= Y \pm t(s_f)$ where $s_f = s_{yx}\sqrt{1 + 1/n + [(X_0 - \overline{X})^2/\Sigma(X - \overline{X})^2]}$, and X_0 is the value of X for which a value of Y is being forecast.

Seasonality in Time Series Forecasts

We can incorporate seasonality into forecasts by using the regression analysis formulas. The method establishes seasonal patterns in the historical data and uses these patterns to modify the trend forecasts. *Seasonal patterns* are usually fluctuations that take place within one year and tend to be repeated annually. These seasons can be determined by weather, holidays, paydays, school events, and a multitude of other factors that can potentially affect demand for goods and services.

Example 3.4 demonstrates the procedures of seasonalized time series analysis. This example assumes that the last three years of data from Specific Motors in Example 3.1 are representative of what is expected in the near future. The example follows these steps:

1. Select a representative historical data set.
2. Develop seasonal indexes for each time period.
3. Use the seasonal indexes to deseasonalize the data; in other words, remove the seasonal patterns.
4. Perform a regression analysis on the deseasonalized data. This will result in a regression equation in the form $Y = a + bX$.
5. Use the regression equation to compute the forecasts for the future. These are based on deseasonalized data; in other words, the seasonal patterns have been removed.
6. Use the seasonal indexes to modify the forecasts, thereby reapplying the seasonal patterns to the forecasts.

When we develop forecasts, as in Example 3.4, by using seasonalized time series analysis and we wish to range these forecasts, the procedure is straightforward. The deseasonalized forecasts would be ranged and then these forecasts, along with their upper and lower limits, would be seasonalized by multiplying them by their seasonal indexes.

The seasonalized time series analysis technique may seem somewhat laborious because of the complex formulas and numerous arithmetic calculations required. Most forecasters in the real world of government and industry today, however, use computers to do their calculations.

EXAMPLE 3.4   Seasonalized Time Series Forecasts

Jim White, the plant manager of Specific Motors, is trying to plan cash, personnel, and materials and supplies requirements for each quarter of next year. The quarterly sales data for the past three years seem to fairly reflect the seasonal output pattern that should be expected in the future. If Mr. White could estimate quarterly sales for next year, the cash, personnel, and materials and supplies needs could be determined.

Solution

1. First, compute the seasonal indexes:

	Year	Q_1	Q_2	Q_3	Q_4	Annual Total
			Quarterly Sales (Thousands of Units)			
	8	520	730	820	530	2,600
	9	590	810	900	600	2,900
	10	650	900	1,000	650	3,200
Totals		1,760	2,440	2,720	1,780	8,700
Quarter average		586⅔	813⅓	906⅔	593⅓	725*
Seasonal index (S.I.)**		.809	1.122	1.251	.818	

* Overall quarter average = 8700/12 = 725.   ** S.I. = Quarter average/Overall quarter average.

2. Next, deseasonalize the data by dividing each quarterly value by its S.I.:

	Deseasonalized Adjusted Quarterly Data			
Years	Q_1	Q_2	Q_3	Q_4
8	642.8	650.6	655.5	647.9
9	729.3	721.9	719.4	733.5
10	803.5	802.1	799.4	794.6

3. Next, perform a regression analysis on the deseasonalized data (twelve quarters) and forecast for the next four quarters:

Time Period	*x*	*y*	y^2	x^2	*xy*
Year 8, Q_1	1	642.8	413,191.84	1	642.8
Year 8, Q_2	2	650.6	423,280.36	4	1,301.2
Year 8, Q_3	3	655.5	429,680.25	9	1,966.5
Year 8, Q_4	4	647.9	419,774.41	16	2,591.6
Year 9, Q_1	5	729.3	531,878.49	25	3,646.5
Year 9, Q_2	6	721.9	521,139.61	36	4,331.4
Year 9, Q_3	7	719.4	517,536.36	49	5,035.8
Year 9, Q_4	8	733.5	538,022.25	64	5,868.0
Year 10, Q_1	9	803.5	645,612.25	81	7,231.5
Year 10, Q_2	10	802.1	643,364.41	100	8,021.0
Year 10, Q_3	11	799.4	639,040.36	121	8,793.4
Year 10, Q_4	12	794.6	631,389.16	144	9,535.2
Totals	78	8,700.5	6,353,909.75	650	58,964.9

$\Sigma x = 78$
$\Sigma y = 8,700.5$
$\Sigma y^2 = 6,353,909.75$
$\Sigma x^2 = 650$
$\Sigma xy = 58,964.9$
$n = 12$

4. Now use these values to substitute into the formulas found in Table 3.5:

$$a = \frac{\Sigma x^2 \Sigma y - \Sigma x \Sigma xy}{n\Sigma x^2 - (\Sigma x)^2} = \frac{650(8,700.5) - 78(58,964.9)}{12(650) - (78)^2} = 615.421$$

$$b = \frac{n\Sigma xy - \Sigma x \Sigma y}{n\Sigma x^2 - (\Sigma x)^2} = \frac{12(58,964.9) - 78(8,700.5)}{12(650) - (78)^2} = 16.865$$

$$Y = a + bX = 615.421 + 16.865X$$

5. Now, substitute the values 13, 14, 15, and 16, the next four values for x, into the regression equation. These are the deseasonalized forecasts, in thousands of units, for the next four quarters.

$Y_{13} = 615.421 + 16.865(13) = 834.666$ $Y_{15} = 615.421 + 16.865(15) = 868.396$

$Y_{14} = 615.421 + 16.865(14) = 851.531$ $Y_{16} = 615.421 + 16.865(16) = 885.261$

6. Now use the seasonal indexes (S.I.) to seasonalize the forecasts:

Quarter	S.I.	Deseasonalized Forecasts	Seasonalized Forecasts [(S.I.) × Deseasonalized Forecasts] (Thousands of Units)
Q_1	.809	834.666	675.2
Q_2	1.122	851.531	955.4
Q_3	1.251	868.396	1,086.4
Q_4	.818	885.261	724.1

There are times in POM when managers develop plans to meet short-range goals such as high efficiency, cost and profit targets, and prompt customer deliveries. These plans require short-range forecasts.

SHORT-RANGE FORECASTS

Short-range forecasts are usually estimates of future conditions over time spans that range from a few days to a few months. Most short-range forecasts are sales forecasts. From these sales forecasts comes the information that operations managers need to have in order to make the decisions that we shall explore in Parts III and IV of this book: Proactively Planning Production to Meet Demand, and Planning and Controlling Operations for Productivity, Quality, and Reliability. Specifically, short-range forecasts provide operations managers with information to make such decisions as these:

1. How much inventory of a particular product should be carried next month, given the short-range forecast?
2. How much of each product should be scheduled for production next week, given the amount that is in the sales forecast and the amount in inventory?
3. How much of each raw material should be ordered for delivery next week, given the amount of products in the production schedule and the amount in inventory?
4. How many workers should be scheduled to work on a straight-time and overtime basis next week, given the production schedule and the number of workers available?
5. How many maintenance workers should be scheduled to work next weekend, given the production schedule and our breakdown experience?

The continued efficient operation of production systems requires accurate short-range forecasts. Two concepts are fundamental to these short-range forecasts — noise and impulse response.

Impulse Response versus Noise Dampening

Short-range forecasting involves taking historical data from a few periods of the past and projecting the estimated values for these data one or more periods into the future.

Forecasts that reflect every little happenstance fluctuation in the past data are said to include random variation, or *noise*. These forecasts can be erratic from period to period. If, on the other hand, forecasts are smooth with little period-to-period fluctuation, the forecasts are said to be *noise dampening.*

Forecasts that respond very fast to changes in the most recent historical data are described as having a *high impulse response.* On the other hand, when forecasts take several periods to reflect changes in historical data, these forecasts are said to have a *low impulse response.*

A forecasting system cannot be high both in noise-dampening ability and impulse response because we gain in impulse response only by giving up noise-dampening ability. In other words, a forecasting system that responds very fast to changes in the data, usually a desirable characteristic, necessarily picks up a great deal of noise associated with numerous chance variations in the data, which is usually undesirable. Conversely, a forecasting system that dampens noise does not respond fast to changes in the data. A trade-off between these two forecasting qualities is therefore always required.

We shall refer to impulse response and noise as we study some short-range forecasting techniques.

Mean Absolute Deviation (MAD)

In forecasting, MAD is often used to measure how closely forecasts are matching the actual data. MAD is computed with the formula below:

$$\text{MAD} = \frac{\text{Sum of absolute deviations for n periods}}{n}$$

$$= \frac{\sum_{i=1}^{n} |\text{Forecast demand} - \text{Actual demand}|_i}{n}$$

If MAD is large relative to the forecast, the forecast values of the dependent variable that have been computed do not closely match the actual values of the dependent variable. On the other hand, if MAD is small relative to the forecast, the forecast values of the dependent variable closely follow the actual values. MAD and the standard error of the forecast s_{yx}, described earlier, both measure the deviation of forecasts from the actual data points. When the forecast errors are normally distributed, the values of MAD and s_{yx} are related by the expression $s_{yx} = 1.25\text{MAD}$. These familiar values of s_{yx} have the following corresponding values of MAD:

s_{yx}	*MAD*
1	.8
2	1.6
3	2.4

Knowledge of this relationship allows forecasters to use MAD to develop ranges for forecasting methods similar to the procedures followed in using s_{yx} to range time series regression forecasts in Example 3.4. Also, as we shall discuss later in this chapter, MAD can be used to monitor and control the accuracy of specific forecasting models.

Moving Average Method

The *moving average method* averages the data from a few recent periods, and this average becomes the forecast for the next period. The key question is: How many periods of data do we include in the average? Example 3.5 addresses this question as it develops a system of short-range forecasts that are based on the moving average method.

EXAMPLE 3.5   Moving Average Short-Range Forecasting

Joseph Penny, the manager of the cash desk of a major corporation, wishes to develop a short-range forecasting system to estimate the demand for cash from the corporation's many divisions and departments. Mr. Penny thinks that the overall demand for cash has been generally steady, although it has fluctuated randomly from week to week. Orville Reach, a forecasting expert from corporate headquarters, also known as OR, has recommended that Mr. Penny use either a 3-, 5-, or 7-week moving average. The desk manager wonders which would be better. He decides to compare the accuracy of the 3-, 5-, and 7-week forecasts for the 10-week period that has just passed.

Solution

1. Compute the 3-, 5-, and 7-week moving average forecasts:

Week	Actual Cash Demand (Thousands of Dollars)	Forecasts		
		AP=3 Weeks	*AP=5 Weeks*	*AP=7 Weeks*
1	100			
2	125			
3	90			
4	110			
5	105			
6	130			
7	85			
8	102	106.7	104.0	106.4
9	110	105.7	106.4	106.7
10	90	99.0	106.4	104.6
11	105	100.7	103.4	104.6
12	95	101.7	98.4	103.9
13	115	96.7	100.4	102.4
14	120	105.0	103.0	100.3
15	80	110.0	105.0	105.3
16	95	105.0	103.0	102.1
17	100	98.3	101.0	100.0

Sample computations—forecasts for the tenth week:

$$F_3 = \frac{85 + 102 + 110}{3} = 99.0$$

$$F_5 = \frac{105 + 130 + 85 + 102 + 110}{5} = 106.4$$

$$F_7 = \frac{90 + 110 + 105 + 130 + 85 + 102 + 110}{7} = 104.6$$

Note: In order to forecast for the tenth week, remember that the only historical weekly actual cash demand data you have to work with is Weeks 1–9. Therefore you cannot include the actual data for the tenth week in computing the tenth-week forecasts.

2. Next, compute the mean absolute deviation (MAD) for the three forecasts:

| | | Forecasts | | | | | |
| | Actual Cash Demand (Thousands of Dollars) | AP = 3 Weeks | | AP = 5 Weeks | | AP = 7 Weeks | |
Week		Fore-cast	Absolute Deviation	Fore-cast	Absolute Deviation	Fore-cast	Absolute Deviation
8	102	106.7	4.7	104.0	2.0	106.4	4.4
9	110	105.7	4.3	106.4	3.6	106.7	3.3
10	90	99.0	9.0	106.4	16.4	104.6	14.6
11	105	100.7	4.3	103.4	1.6	104.6	.4
12	95	101.7	6.7	98.4	3.4	103.9	8.9
13	115	96.7	18.3	100.4	14.6	102.4	12.6
14	120	105.0	15.0	103.0	17.0	100.3	19.7
15	80	110.0	30.0	105.0	25.0	105.3	25.3
16	95	105.0	10.0	103.0	8.0	102.1	7.1
17	100	98.3	1.7	101.0	1.0	100.0	0
Total absolute deviation			104.0		92.6		96.3
Mean absolute deviation (MAD)			10.40		9.26		9.63

3. Mr. Penny should select an average period of 5 weeks because the MAD tends to be less than with 3 or 7 weeks. The accuracy of the 7-week average period forecast is very close to the 5-week one; therefore future checking is recommended.

4. OR now uses an AP of 5 weeks to forecast the cash demand for the next week, the eighteenth:

$$\text{Forecast} = \frac{115 + 120 + 80 + 95 + 100}{5} = 102, \text{ or } \$102{,}000$$

Figure 3.5 plots the three moving average forecasts against the actual data in Example 3.5. Note that the larger the averaging period (AP), the smoother the forecast. In other words, the AP = 7 forecast has a low impulse response and a high

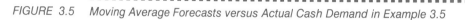

FIGURE 3.5   *Moving Average Forecasts versus Actual Cash Demand in Example 3.5*

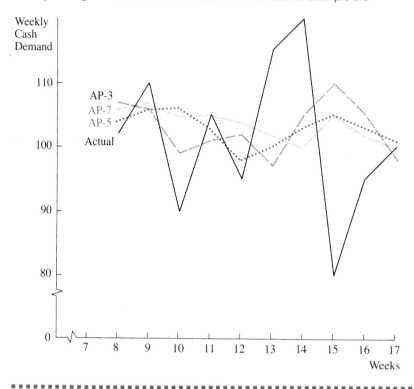

noise-dampening ability, whereas the AP = 3 forecast has a high impulse response and a low noise-dampening ability. The AP = 5 forecast ranks somewhere between the other two forecasts in these two characteristics.

So which AP do we select? This is a qualitative decision.

	Noise-Dampening Ability	*Impulse Response*	*Accuracy*
AP = 3	Low	High	Low
AP = 5	Mid	Mid	High
AP = 7	High	Low	Mid

The ultimate selection of an AP would depend on management's needs. What is more desirable, high impulse response or high noise-dampening ability? And how much accuracy can be given up to achieve either of these two characteristics? In the final analysis, the AP selected will depend on a complete knowledge of the intended management use of the forecasts and the nature of the forecasting situation.

TABLE 3.6   *Formulas and Variable Definitions for Exponential Smoothing Forecasts*

F_t = Next period's forecast A_{t-1} = Last period's actual data
F_{t-1} = Last period's forecast α = Smoothing constant

Next period's forecast = Last period's forecast +
α(Last period's actual − Last period's forecast)

$$F_t = F_{t-1} + \alpha(A_{t-1} - F_{t-1})$$

which can also be expressed as

$$F_t = \alpha A_{t-1} + (1 - \alpha)F_{t-1}$$

There are at least three drawbacks to the simple moving average method that we have presented: (1) all past periods in the AP are weighted equally, (2) no provision is made for seasonal patterns, and (3) several periods of historical data must be carried forward from period to period for calculating forecasts.

Weighted Moving Average.   The first disadvantage can be overcome by assigning weights, the sum of which would equal 1, to the past-period data. For example:

	Actual Data	*Weight*
Week 7	85	.20
Week 8	102	.30
Week 9	110	.50

Forecast for the tenth week = .5(110) + .3(102) + .2(85)
= 55 + 30.6 + 17
= 102.6

This simple modification to the moving average method allows forecasters to specify the relative importance of past periods of data. Recent periods are typically more heavily weighted than older data.

Exponential Smoothing Method

The variables, the variable definitions, and the formula for exponential smoothing forecasts are found in Table 3.6. *Exponential smoothing* takes the forecast for the last period and adds an adjustment to get the forecast for the next period. This adjustment is computed by multiplying the forecast error in the last period by a constant that is between zero and one. This constant alpha (α) is called the *smoothing constant*. Because only the forecast and forecast error from the last period are all the data required to prepare a forecast for the next period, exponential smoothing requires less data processing than the moving average method.

Example 3.6 demonstrates how we might set a value of α in a real forecasting situation.

EXAMPLE 3.6   Exponential Smoothing Short-Range Forecast

Joseph Penny, from Example 3.5, liked the recommendations from OR, the corporate head-quarters forecasting expert. As a goodwill gesture, OR was invited to the cash desk for consulta-tion. OR was flattered, not to mention relieved to be out of sight of corporate headquarters for a short period. OR reviewed the moving average forecasts in Example 3.5 and suggested to Mr. Penny that he try a similar experiment with ten periods of data using exponential smoothing. The only question was which alpha (α) is better: .1, .2, or .3?

Solution

1. First, study the formulas and variable definitions in Table 3.6. Compute the weekly forecasts for the eighth through the seventeenth weeks:

Week	Actual Cash Demand (Thousands of Dollars)	Forecasts $\alpha = .1$	$\alpha = .2$	$\alpha = .3$
7	85	85.0*	85.0*	85.0*
8	102	85.0	85.0	85.0
9	110	86.7	88.4	90.1
10	90	89.0	92.7	96.1
11	105	89.1	92.2	94.3
12	95	90.7	94.8	97.5
13	115	91.1	94.8	96.8
14	120	93.5	98.8	102.3
15	80	96.2	103.0	107.6
16	95	94.6	98.4	99.3
17	100	94.6	97.7	98.0

* All these seventh-week forecasts were selected arbitrarily. Beginning forecasts are necessary to use exponential smoothing. Traditionally, we set these forecasts equal to the actual data value of the period.

Here are sample calculations for the tenth-week forecasts:

$$F_{10} = F_9 + \alpha(A_9 - F_9)$$

$\alpha = .1$: $F_{10} = 86.7 + .1(110 - 86.7) = 89.0$

$\alpha = .2$: $F_{10} = 88.4 + .2(110 - 88.4) = 92.7$

$\alpha = .3$: $F_{10} = 90.1 + .3(110 - 90.1) = 96.1$

Note: When the tenth-week forecasts are made, the only historical data available are through the ninth week. Only the ninth-week actual data and the ninth-week forecasts are used to compute the tenth-week forecasts.

2. Next, compute the mean absolute deviation (MAD) for the three forecasts:

	Actual Cash Demand (Thousands of Dollars)	Forecasts					
		$\alpha = .1$		$\alpha = .2$		$\alpha = .3$	
Week		Fore-cast	Absolute Deviation	Fore-cast	Absolute Deviation	Fore-cast	Absolute Deviation
8	102	85.0	17.0	85.0	17.0	85.0	17.0
9	110	86.7	23.3	88.4	21.6	90.1	19.9
10	90	89.0	1.0	92.7	2.7	96.1	6.1
11	105	89.1	15.9	92.2	12.8	94.3	10.7
12	95	90.7	4.3	94.8	.2	97.5	2.5
13	115	91.1	23.9	94.8	20.2	96.8	18.2
14	120	93.5	26.5	98.8	21.2	102.3	17.7
15	80	96.2	16.2	103.0	23.0	107.6	27.6
16	95	94.6	.4	98.4	3.4	99.3	4.3
17	100	94.6	5.4	97.7	2.3	98.0	2.0
Total absolute deviation			133.9		124.4		126.0
Mean absolute deviation (MAD)			13.39		12.44		12.60

3. The smoothing constant $\alpha = .2$ gives slightly better accuracy when compared to $\alpha = .1$ and $\alpha = .3$.

4. Next, using $\alpha = .2$, compute the forecast (in thousands of dollars) for the eighteenth week:

$$F_{18} = F_{17} + .2(A_{17} - F_{17})$$
$$= 97.7 + .2(100 - 97.7) = 97.7 + .2(2.3) = 97.7 + .46 = 98.2 \text{ or } \$98,200$$

The selection of a value for alpha (α), the smoothing constant, is the only tricky part of the technique. Forecasters generally select values for α that work best for them in particular forecasting situations, as we see in Example 3.6. It is not always true that higher α levels result in more accurate forecasts. Each data set tends to have unique qualities, so that experimentation with different α levels is advised in order to maximize accuracy.

Figure 3.6 plots the exponential smoothing forecasts ($\alpha = .1, .2,$ and $.3$) against the actual weekly demand for cash from Example 3.6. When $\alpha = .1$, the forecast exhibits high noise-dampening ability but low impulse response. When $\alpha = .3$, the forecast exhibits higher impulse response but lower noise-dampening ability. This pattern is true over the entire $0 - 1.0$ range of α. The higher α is, the higher its impulse response and the lower its noise-dampening ability and vice versa.

FIGURE 3.6   *Exponential Smoothing Forecasts versus Actual Cash Demand in Example 3.6*

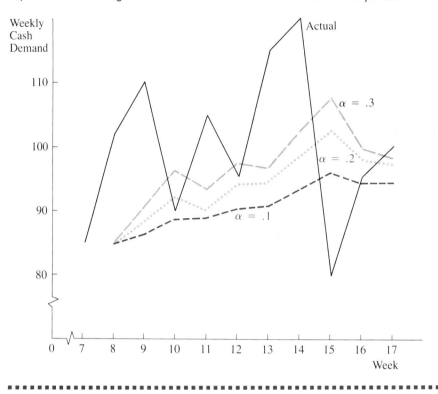

Let us summarize the results for selecting an α in Example 3.6:

	Noise- Dampening Ability	Impulse Response	Accuracy
$\alpha = .1$	High	Low	Low
$\alpha = .2$	Mid	Mid	High
$\alpha = .3$	Low	High	High

As in the case of moving averages (AP), the selection of a level of α would be based on a knowledge of management's needs and the nature of the particular forecasting situation.

Exponential smoothing weights data from recent periods heavier than data from more distant periods. Figure 3.7 illustrates the weights for some representative smoothing constants. The earlier term *exponentially weighted moving averages* for exponential smoothing describes this weighting of past data. Moving averages and

FIGURE 3.7   *Weighting of Past Data in Exponential Smoothing*

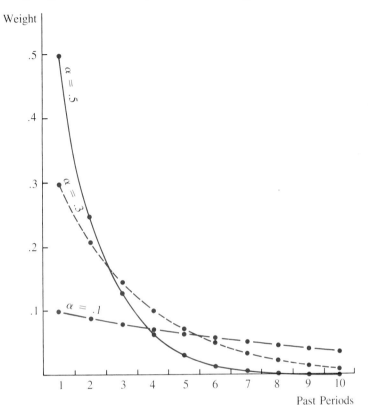

exponential smoothing are similar in this regard. Brown[3] relates the two methods by this expression:

$$\alpha = \frac{2}{AP + 1}$$

With this expression, we can see that if the averaging period (AP) in a moving average forecast is 3, then α would equal .5. This means that the *average* weighting of past data in an exponential smoothing forecast where $\alpha = .5$ would be the same as in a moving average forecast where AP = 3, or ⅓.

Exponential smoothing is really just one of a whole family of forecasting methods. We have presented only its simplest form here. At least two other enhancements can be offered:

[3] R. G. Brown, *Statistical Forecasting for Inventory Control* (New York: McGraw-Hill, 1959).

1. *Double smoothing.* This adaptation uses two smoothing constants. A new trend term is added to allow for nonhorizontal trend line data.
2. *Box-Jenkins.* Exponential smoothing is really just a special case of this approach. Its autocorrelation methods examine the actual historical data points and fit a mathematical function to these data. The mathematical function then becomes the forecasting model for future estimates. This method is available in many standard computer programming packages. The method is reported to be the most accurate of all the short-range forecasting methods, but about 60 data points are required, it requires some time to get forecast results, and it is moderately expensive to use.[4]

These and other developments in exponential smoothing forecasting make it a powerful force in short-range forecasting.[5]

Now that we have examined some forecasting methods and issues, we shall conclude the chapter by considering how to have a successful forecasting system and discussing the types of computer software available for forecasting.

HOW TO HAVE A SUCCESSFUL FORECASTING SYSTEM

Figure 3.1 illustrated a system of forecasting in POM. Some of the reasons that forecasting systems fail are found in Table 3.7. Relating to these reasons for failure, it is important for us to consider how to select the forecasting method and how to control the forecasting model.

HOW TO SELECT A FORECASTING METHOD

Several factors should be considered in the selection of a forecasting method: (1) cost, (2) accuracy, (3) data available, (4) time span, (5) nature of products and services, and (6) impulse response and noise dampening.[6]

Cost and Accuracy

There is ordinarily a trade-off between cost and accuracy. No method is totally accurate. Low-accuracy methods use little data, and the data are usually readily available and their cost is low. High-accuracy methods use more data, the data are ordinarily more difficult to obtain, and the models are more costly to design, implement, and operate. Such methods as simple statistical models, historical analogies,

---

[4] G. E. P. Box and G. M. Jenkins, *Time Series Analysis, Forecasting, and Control* (San Francisco: Holden-Day, 1970).

[5] For further discussion of this topic, see Everette S. Gardner, "Exponential Smoothing: The State of the Art," *Journal of Forecasting* 4(1985): 1–28.

[6] David M. Georgoff and Robert G. Murdick, "Manager's Guide To Forecasting," *Harvard Business Review* 64(January–February 1986):112–119.

TABLE 3.7 *Some Reasons That Forecasting Systems Fail*

1. Failure of the organization to involve a broad cross section of people in the forecasting system. Individual effort is important, but the need to involve everyone who has pertinent information and who will need to implement the forecast is also important.

2. Failure to recognize that the forecasting model is an element of the forecasting system and not the system. (See Figure 3.1.)

3. Failure to recognize that forecasts will always be wrong. There is no such thing as a perfect forecast. Estimates of future demand are bound to be subject to error, and the magnitude of error tends to be greater for forecasts that cover longer spans of time. When operations managers have unrealistic expectations of forecasts, the fact that the forecasts were not on the nose is often used as an excuse for poor performance in operations. Excuses will not result in improved forecasts and improved performance in operations.

4. Failure to forecast the right things. For example, it is all too common for organizations to forecast the demand for raw materials that go into finished products. The demand for raw materials need not be forecast because these demands can be computed from the forecasts for the finished products. Forecasting too many things can overload the forecasting system and cause it to be too expensive and time-consuming.

5. Failure to select an appropriate forecasting method.

6. Failure to track the performance of the forecasting models so that the forecast accuracy can be improved. The forecasting models can be modified as needed to control the performance of the forecasts.

and executive committee consensus tend to be of low or moderate cost, while complex statistical models, multiple regression and correlation, delphi, and market research tend to be high cost. Each organization must make the cost and accuracy trade-off that is appropriate to its own situation.

Industry Snapshots 3.1, 3.2, and 3.3 contrast three approaches to designing or selecting forecasting models. The first describes an expensive and complex forecasting system used by Texas A&M University to forecast the student enrollment at the university. The second describes an inexpensive and simple forecasting system used by the Olin Corporation to forecast the sales of railroad flares. The third describes a dynamic system for selecting forecasting models at American Hardware Supply. That all three organizations appear to be pleased with the accuracy and cost of their forecasting systems demonstrates that there is no single forecasting approach that is appropriate for all situations.

There is some evidence that in many POM situations simple and low-cost forecasting methods tend to provide forecasts that are about as accurate as more

INDUSTRY SNAPSHOT 3.1

Student Enrollment Forecasts Prove Accurate

Each fall, the Office of Planning and Institutional Analysis forecasts student enrollment for the coming year based on a system that has evolved over a 15-year period. Glenn Dowling, director of the office, points out that the forecasts are used in planning for the number of faculty, staff, and facilities required and that the forecasts must be very accurate.

The forecasting system uses a comprehensive set of data from several sources and processes the data on the university's computers. The system utilizes a rather large and sophisticated computer data base that includes these variables: the percentage of the market of Texas high school graduates that comes to the university, the retention rate of students in each classification at the university, the number of students currently enrolled in each classification at the university, and the number of anticipated graduates from the univer-

sity. There are several factors that must be forecasted accurately for the model to perform satisfactorily. First, the percentage of high school graduates that will come to the university: This percentage is forecasted using trend or regression analysis. Second, the percentage of students exiting each class at the university: These percentages are determined using the "cohort survival technique."

The forecasting system predicted the total enrollment this past fall with an error of only 31 students, an error of less than .1 percent. The system forecasted both the number of entering freshmen and the number of graduate students within 4 students each. Dowling says: "Our system really works." Although forecasts are ordinarily not as accurate as they were in 1987, a look at the preceding 14 years (Figure 3.8) shows that the average forecast error was less than 2 percent.[7]

[7] "Student Enrollment Projections Prove Accurate," *Fortnightly,* November 9, 1987, Texas A&M University, College Station, Texas. Reprinted with permission.

complex and high-cost forecasting methods. The choice between two forecasting methods can be based on mean absolute deviation (MAD), which is a common measure of the accuracy of a forecasting method. For instance, in Examples 3.5 and 3.6, MAD was used as the basis for choosing among several levels of AP in moving average models and for choosing among several levels of α in exponential smoothing models.

Data Available

The data that are available and relevant for forecasts are an important factor in choosing a forecasting method. For example, if the attitudes and intentions of customers are a relevant factor in forecasts and if the data can be economically obtained from customers about their attitudes and intentions, then a survey of customers may be an appropriate method for developing demand estimates. On the other hand, if we

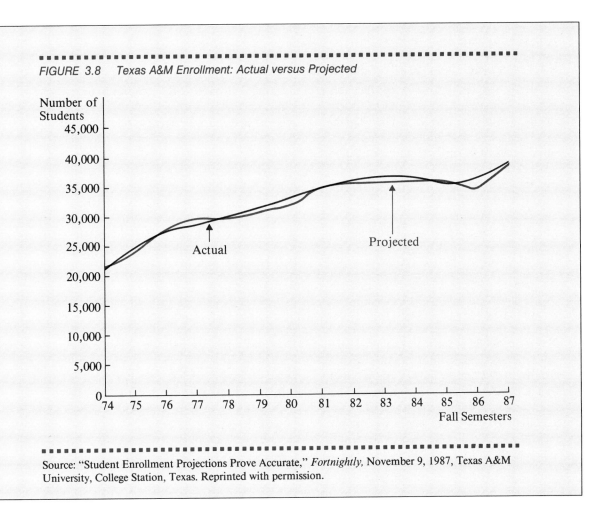

FIGURE 3.8   Texas A&M Enrollment: Actual versus Projected

Source: "Student Enrollment Projections Prove Accurate," *Fortnightly,* November 9, 1987, Texas A&M University, College Station, Texas. Reprinted with permission.

are attempting to forecast sales of a new product, then a survey of customers may not be a practical way for us to develop a forecast; historical analogy, market research, executive committee consensus, or some other method may have to be used.

Time Span
The choice of an appropriate forecasting method is affected by the nature of the production resource that is to be forecast. Short-range resource needs—for example, the number of workers in each skill class, cash, inventories, and machine schedules —can be estimated by the use of short-range time series techniques such as moving averages or exponential smoothing. Long-range production resource needs such as factory capacities and capital funds can be estimated by regression, executive committee consensus, market research, or other methods that are appropriate for long-range forecasts.

INDUSTRY SNAPSHOT 3.2

Forecasting Flare Sales at Olin Corporation

At the Morgan Hill Works of the Olin Corporation, located in Morgan Hill, California, plant manager Perry Spangler is planning the schedule for the production of railroad flares in the first quarter of next year. These products are sold to every major railroad in the United States and are used for signaling purposes. Mr. Spangler knows that sales forecasts need to be close to actual sales, but because the railroad flare is a produce-to-stock item, ample inventory is ordinarily on hand to ship to customers in case of minor inaccuracies in the forecasts.

For several quarters now, Mr. Spangler has been forecasting railroad flare sales using a simple graphing technique (Figure 3.9). On one side of the graph he plots the millions of national freight car loadings in each quarter, which is information that he finds in a U.S. Department of Commerce publication at his local library. On the other side of the graph he plots Olin's railroad flare sales in thousands of gross (a gross equals 144 flares). He has noticed a very close relationship between the previous quarter's national freight car loadings and the current quarter's sales of railroad flares: The national freight car loadings in millions in the previous quarter times .3 approximately equal the railroad flare sales in thousands of gross in the current quarter.

Accordingly, Mr. Spangler estimates the sales of railroad flares in the first quarter will be:

Sales = .3 × 55 million fourth-quarter loadings
    = 16.5, or 16,500 gross

He believes that this relationship is logical because railroad flare sales should be directly related to the number of railroad cars placed in service. He is pleased with the accuracy of the forecasts and the ease of preparing them.

Nature of Products and Services

Managers are advised to use different forecasting methods for different products. Such factors as whether a product is high volume and high cost, whether the product is a good or a service, and where the product is in its life cycle (introduction, growth, maturity, or decline) all affect the choice of a forecasting method.

Impulse Response and Noise Dampening

As pointed out earlier in our discussion of short-range forecasting, how responsive we want the forecasting model to be to changes in the actual demand data must be balanced against our desire to suppress undesirable chance variation or noise in the data. Each forecasting model differs in its impulse response and noise-dampening abilities, and the model selected must fit the forecasting situation. For example, let us say that we would like to keep the size of our work force reasonably stable. In this case we might want a forecasting model that has high noise-dampening ability: If the

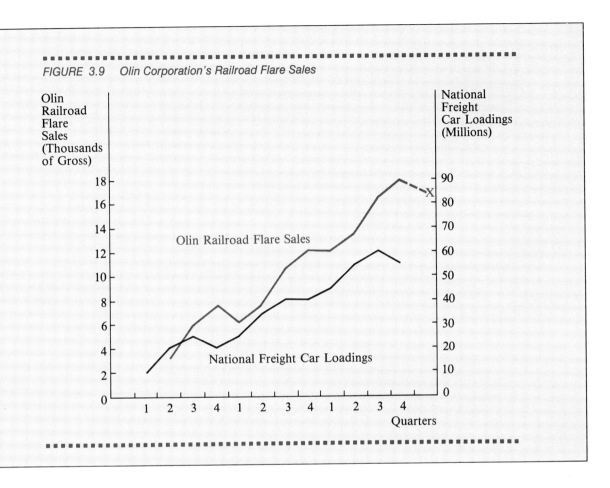

FIGURE 3.9   *Olin Corporation's Railroad Flare Sales*

forecast for the number of workers needed next week is too high, we could use the extra workers to build inventory, and if the forecast is too low, we could use overtime. On the other hand, a forecasting model that has a high impulse response and a low noise-dampening ability would result in forecasts that are too erratic for a planned stable work force.

Once managers have selected the forecasting models to use in their forecasting system, the performance of the models must be tracked.

HOW TO MONITOR AND CONTROL A FORECASTING MODEL

It is important that the performance of forecasting models be monitored and controlled. This means that we ordinarily set upper and lower limits on how much error the forecasting model can generate before we must change the parameters of the

---

INDUSTRY SNAPSHOT 3.3

Focus Forecasting at American Hardware Supply

Bernard Smith at American Hardware Supply developed a system for selecting forecasting methods. He called his approach *focus forecasting* and it was based on two principles: (1) More sophisticated and expensive forecasting methods do not always provide better forecasts, and (2) there is no single forecasting technique that should be used for all products and services.

The forecasting system at American Hardware Supply had to forecast purchase quantities for about 100,000 items purchased by the company's buyers. The buyers tended not to use the old exponential smoothing forecasting model to predict the purchase quantities because they did not understand or trust the model. Instead, they used very simple forecasting approaches, such as using an item's demand figure from the previous period for the order figure for the next period. Mr. Smith selected seven forecasting methods, including the simple ones that were used by the buyers, the old exponential smoothing model, and some new statistical forecasting methods. Each month every model was used to forecast the demand for each item. The model that provided the best forecast for an item was used to forecast the demand for that item for the next month.

Although buyers could override the forecasts from focus forecasting, the approach is said to be providing excellent forecasts for American Hardware Supply.[8]

---

[8] Bernard Smith, *Focus Forecasting: Computer Techniques for Inventory Control* (Boston: CBI Publishing, 1978).

---

model. One common way that we can track the performance of forecasting models is to use what is called a *tracking signal:*

$$\text{Tracking signal} = \frac{\text{Algebraic sum of errors over n periods}}{\text{Mean absolute deviation over n periods}}$$

$$= \frac{\sum\limits_{i=1}^{n}(\text{Forecast} - \text{Actual})_i}{\text{MAD}}$$

$$= \frac{\sum\limits_{i=1}^{n}(\text{Forecast} - \text{Actual})_i}{\left[\sum\limits_{i=1}^{n}|\text{Forecast} - \text{Actual}|_i\right]/n}$$

The tracking signal measures how much the forecast has been above or below the actual data for n periods in terms of MAD. For example, if the algebraic sum of errors for 12 periods has been a positive 1,000 units and the MAD in these same 12 periods is 250 units, then the tracking signal is +4. This indicates that the cumulative forecast error is 4 MADs, which can also be thought of as $5s_{yx}$ because of the relation-

TABLE 3.8   *Some Hypothetical Rules for Changing the Smoothing Constant (α) in Exponential Smoothing Models*

Limits for Absolute Value of Tracking Signal	*Do Not Change*	*Slight: Increase α by .1*	*Moderate: Increase α by .3*	*Panic: Increase α by .5*
0–2.4	✓			
2.5–2.9		✓		
3.0–3.9			✓	
Over 4.0				✓

ship $s_{yx} = 1.25$ MAD, above the actual demand data during these 12 periods. If the algebraic sum of errors for 12 periods has been a minus 1,250 units and the MAD in these same 12 periods is 250 units, then the tracking signal is -5. This indicates that the cumulative forecast error is 5 MADs, which can also be thought of as $6.25s_{yx}$, below the actual demand data during these 12 periods. If the forecasting model is performing well, the tracking signal should be nearly zero, which would indicate that there have been about as many forecasts above the actual demand data as there have been forecasts below the actual demand data. The ability of the tracking signal to indicate the direction of the forecasting error is very helpful.

Another valuable characteristic of the tracking signal is its magnitude. A firm can compare the magnitude of the tracking signal to predetermined limits to make the forecasting model adaptive to the changing nature of the actual demand data. For example, rules such as those found in Table 3.8 could be used to change the value of α in an exponential smoothing forecasting model. If a firm's policies set the limits for the tracking signal too low, then a forecasting model's parameters will need to be revised too often and the cost of the continual changing of the parameters can outweigh the value of improved forecasts. If, on the other hand, the limits for the tracking signal are set too high, then a forecasting model's parameters will be changed only infrequently and the accuracy of the forecasts will suffer.

COMPUTER SOFTWARE FOR FORECASTING

Forecasters in the real world of government and industry use computers to do their calculations. Numerous standard computer programs based on the forecasting models presented in this chapter are readily available to do these calculations.

This computer software is generally of two types. The first type includes only forecasting programs. Examples of this type of software are:

1. The *POM Computer Library* that accompanies this text. This library includes exponential smoothing, time series with ranging, seasonalized time series with ranging, simple linear regression with ranging, and multiple linear regression.

2. *Statistical Package for the Social Sciences (SPSS),* which is found in the Selected Bibliography at the end of this chapter (see the Nie, Bent, and Hull citation).
3. American Software Inc.'s *Product Group & Item Forecasting System* for mainframe computers and its *ForeThought*™ for personal computers.
4. General Electric's *Time Series Forecasting* program *FCST1*, a linear regression seasonalized forecasting model. Its *FCST2* program creates several forecasts with four different methods of exponential smoothing. The program then evaluates the performance of each forecast relative to past data and recommends a forecast.

A second type of computer software has forecasting programs embedded in a larger information system. Examples of this type of software are:

1. IBM's *Consumer Goods System (COGS),* a forecasting and inventory control information system.
2. IBM's *Inventory Management Program and Control Technique (IMPACT),* an information system for wholesalers and other users in distribution systems.
3. A host of other IBM software sets such as *INFOREM, COPICS, MAPICS, CAPOSSE,* and *PICS.*

Most quantitative forecasts made today make use of computer software such as that listed above.

SUMMARY

Forecasting in POM is estimating the future demand for products and services and the resources necessary to produce these outputs. Sales forecasts are used to determine the resources necessary for production. Operations managers participate in forecasting systems because accurate forecasts determine to a large degree the efficiency of the production system in the short range and the ultimate survival and profitability of the firm in the long range.

Operations managers may employ either qualitative forecasting methods or quantitative forecasting models. Long-range forecasting involves estimates over time spans that typically range from a few months to several years into the future. One of the most common long-range forecasting models is regression analysis. This model develops a trend line through past data that is closest to the historical data points and projects this long-range trend line into the future time periods. Short-range forecasting usually involves estimates of future conditions over time spans of a few months or less. Two commonly used models for short-range forecasting are moving averages and exponential smoothing. These models are appropriate for the day-to-day chance variation of short-range time series data.

It is not enough for operations managers to be familiar with some forecasting models to have a successful forecasting system. The common causes for failure of forecasting systems must be avoided. Most importantly, the appropriate forecasting method must be used, and the forecasting model must be effectively monitored and controlled.

REVIEW AND DISCUSSION QUESTIONS

1. What is forecasting?
2. Name three underlying reasons why operations managers must forecast.
3. Name three qualitative forecasting methods used in business today.
4. Describe a forecasting system in POM.
5. Describe briefly the steps in linear regression analysis.
6. What inputs are required in linear regression analysis? What are the outputs from this analysis?
7. What are the key advantages of moving averages and exponential smoothing? What are the disadvantages?
8. Regression analysis is based on identifying independent variables and gathering historical data for these variables. Name some independent variables to forecast these dependent variables:
   a. demand for hospital services,
   b. students entering colleges of business,
   c. local hamburger stand sales,
   d. county sheriff's department services.
9. Name the four components or data patterns of long-range demand in forecasting.
10. Explain what is meant by ranging a time series forecast.
11. Define the *coefficient of correlation* and the *coefficient of determination.*
12. What are the three types of variation of the dependent variable y in regression analysis? How are the three types of variation related? How are they calculated?
13. What is multiregression analysis? How is multiregression different from simple regression?
14. What is impulse response and noise dampening? How are they related?
15. What is mean absolute deviation (MAD)? How is it calculated?
16. What is the relationship between MAD and the standard error of the forecast? What do they measure? How may they be used?
17. Name three common reasons why forecasting systems fail.
18. What is the tracking signal? How is it calculated? How is it used?

PROBLEMS

Simple Regression

1. The Magneto Company manufactures magneto assemblies that generate direct electrical current when rotated. These assemblies are used by other companies in their products. The magneto is in the decline stage of its product life cycle. The historical data below reflect this decline and Magneto's management expects this trend to continue. Use these data to develop a time series regression forecast for next year's sales.

Year	Magneto's Sales (Millions of Dollars)	Year	Magneto's Sales (Millions of Dollars)
1	5.6	4	5.5
2	5.5	5	5.3
3	5.4	6	5.3

2. The We-Haul Trucking Company is authorized to haul local freight in the southern suburbs of Los Angeles. During the past five years the annual demand for We-Haul's services has grown steadily, requiring substantial outlays for trucking equipment. Laura Kennet, We-Haul's owner, has just managed to scrape together enough capital funds over the past five years to keep her head above water. These capital-raising projects have been spasmodic as the need for new equipment surfaced from time to time. Ms. Kennet realizes now that capital funds planning requires a long-range plan to provide steady and rational growth. Since she expects the past pattern of growth to continue, analyze the past five years of data using time series regression analysis to forecast the next two years' requirements for capital funds:

Year	Capital Funds (Thousands of Dollars)	Year	Capital Funds (Thousands of Dollars)
1	100	3	130
2	110	4	140
		5	160

3. The Halls of Ivy College, in a small town in upstate New York, is a private liberal arts college. Enrollments have grown steadily over the past six years since Marvin Cone assumed the presidency. The number of students has grown sufficiently to warrant expanded library facilities. Dr. Cone knows that the board of directors will not approve the library expansion unless it can be justified by forecasted increased enrollments in the future. Enrollments for the past six years have been:

Year	Student Enrollments (Thousands of Students)	Year	Student Enrollments (Thousands of Students)
1	2.5	4	3.2
2	2.8	5	3.3
3	2.9	6	3.4

Use time series regression to forecast enrollments for the next three years.

4. The top management of Computer Products Corporation (CPC) in San Jose is now going through the preliminary steps of its annual planning process to develop an

operating plan for next year. Jane Billingsley is one of the staff analysts charged with the responsibility of estimating the level of revenues for next year. Her approach is to develop individual product line forecasts and then combine the product line forecasts into an aggregate sales forecast for CPC. She is now in the process of examining the most recent six years of sales data for CPC's line of XT Personal Computers:

Year	Sales Revenues (Millions of Dollars)	Year	Sales Revenues (Millions of Dollars)
1	1.4	4	26.8
2	6.9	5	34.9
3	16.5	6	39.1

Assuming that the sales data above are representative of sales expected next year, use time series regression analysis to forecast next year's (Year 7's) sales revenues for the line of XT Personal Computers.

5. From Problem 4,
   a. determine the correlation coefficient for the data and interpret its meaning, and
   b. find the coefficient of determination for the data and interpret its meaning.

6. Jane Billingsley, the staff analyst in Problem 4, in attempting to develop a forecast of next year's sales revenues for the line of XT Personal Computers, wonders if time series regression analysis is perhaps not the best way to go about forecasting next year's sales. She is in the process of examining the following industry data:

Year	CPC's XT PC Sales Revenues (Millions of Dollars)	All Industry PC Sales Revenues (Billions of Dollars)
1	1.4	5.6
2	6.9	9.6
3	16.5	12.7
4	26.8	14.8
5	34.9	17.5
6	39.1	20.4

   a. Perform a regression analysis between the annual sales revenues of CPC's XT Personal Computers and all industry PC annual sales revenues. What is the forecast for next year's (Year 7's) sales revenues for CPC's XT Personal Computers if the Computer Machinery Association's estimate of next year's industry PC sales revenues is $22.9 billion?
   b. Which forecast — the time series forecast from Problems 4 and 5 or the forecast from this problem — seems to be "better"? Why is it better?

7. Hank Besnette, the manager of Railroad Products Company (RPC), is in the process of projecting the firm's sales for the next three years. As a unit in the holding company's budget system, RPC is required to develop three-year sales forecasts, operating costs, and profits. Two years ago Mr. Besnette discovered that RPC's long-range sales were tied very closely to national freight car loadings, and he wonders

if the railroad industry's projections of future freight car loadings can help him forecast his firm's sales. The following are seven years of historical data for RPC:

Year	RPC Annual Sales (Millions of Dollars)	National Freight Car Loadings (Millions)	Year	RPC Annual Sales (Millions of Dollars)	National Freight Car Loadings (Millions)
1	9.5	120	5	14.0	170
2	11.0	135	6	16.0	190
3	12.0	130	7	18.0	220
4	12.5	150			

a. Develop a simple linear regression analysis between RPC sales and national freight car loadings. Forecast RPC sales for the next three years if the railroad industry estimates freight car loadings of 250, 270, and 300 millions.
b. What percentage of variation in RPC sales is explained by freight car loadings?

8. Jewell Brown, of the First National Bank, is working on a long-range plan for the bank. Today, she needs to estimate the amount of revenue that will be generated next year from real estate loans. She knows that this revenue is directly related to the level of interest rates charged, but she is not sure of the precise nature of the relationship. She has developed these data for the last seven years:

Year	Interest Rate Charged (%)	Real Estate Loan Revenue (Millions of Dollars)
1	9.5	20.1
2	10.1	20.9
3	12.5	19.8
4	14.2	18.3
5	12.0	17.9
6	11.1	19.4
7	10.2	21.6

a. Use a simple regression analysis between First National's real estate loan revenue and interest rates charged to forecast next year's real estate loan revenue if the interest rate charged is expected to be about 12.0 percent.
b. What percentage of the variation in First National's real estate loan revenue is explained by the interest rate charged?
c. Evaluate the usefulness of simple regression analysis in this application.

Moving Averages

9. Computer Products Corporation's (CPC) plant in Austin, Texas, has been experiencing imbalances in its inventory of components used in the production of a line of computer printers. Both stock shortages and overstock conditions for the components seem to exist at one time or another, and the plant's production analysis staff

group is studying the pattern of demand for a particular component, CTR 5922 — a power supply assembly that is used in many of CPC's products and imported from a supplier in Japan. It is soon discovered that the heart of the problem is the forecasting method that the plant has been using to estimate weekly demand for the CTR 5922. The group believes that the most recent 12 weeks of demand for the CTR 5922 is representative of the future weekly demand:

Week	Demand (Units)	Week	Demand (Units)	Week	Demand (Units)	Week	Demand (Units)
1	159	4	161	7	203	10	168
2	217	5	173	8	195	11	198
3	186	6	157	9	188	12	159

Use the moving average method of short-range forecasting with an averaging period of 3 weeks to develop a forecast of the demand for the CTR 5922 component in Week 13.

10. Jane Montgomery is the manager in charge of maintenance for Rest-International, a large hotel in Las Vegas. She has observed that since the hotel is fairly new and is fully booked year-round, maintenance calls occur randomly, with almost no trend or seasonality. She is developing a system to forecast one month ahead the number of maintenance calls she will receive. She plans to use moving averages but wonders what AP to use in order to minimize the forecasting error. Two years of historical data are as follows:

Month	Maintenance Calls	Month	Maintenance Calls	Month	Maintenance Calls	Month	Maintenance Calls
1	95	7	89	13	97	19	82
2	85	8	84	14	95	20	102
3	92	9	97	15	93	21	100
4	100	10	101	16	105	22	101
5	80	11	82	17	102	23	95
6	91	12	92	18	89	24	90

a. Develop moving average forecasts for the past 10 months (Months 15–24) for AP = 2, 4, 6, and 8 months.
b. Which AP results in the lowest mean absolute forecasting error? MADValue
c. Use your recommended AP and forecast the number of maintenance calls for the next month (Month 25).

11. Jane Montgomery of the Rest-International thinks that the moving average forecast from Problem 10 looks pretty good but wonders if recent past data are more important in forecasting than older data. She thinks that the most recent month should be weighted at .5 and that the preceding months' weights should be sequentially reduced by a factor of .5 (i.e., .5, .25, .125, etc.) keep cut until to tal is one
a. Develop the weights for the weighted moving average forecast.
b. Use the weights developed in Part a to forecast the number of maintenance calls for Month 25 from the data in Problem 10.

12. The number of nurses required to staff the surgical wing at a large regional hospital varies from quarter to quarter. The last three years of data are shown below:

Year	Quarter	Number of Nurses	Year	Quarter	Number of Nurses
1	1	114	2	3	111
	2	110		4	112
	3	106	3	1	115
	4	114		2	113
2	1	116		3	110
	2	114		4	116

a. Use moving averages to forecast the number of nurses required in the first quarter of next year if AP = 2, 4, and 8.
b. Which of these forecasts exhibits the least forecast error over the last four periods of historical data?
c. Discuss the advantages and disadvantages of each of the forecasts.
d. It is possible that trend and seasonality may be present in these historical data. Considering this possibility along with your answers to Parts b and c above, which of the forecasts would you prefer? Defend your recommendation.

Exponential Smoothing

13. Bill O'Malley is a buyer in the purchasing department at Nilo Industries. His speciality is nonferrous metals. Bill is attempting to develop a system for forecasting monthly copper prices. He has accumulated 16 months of historical price data:

Month	Copper Price/Pound	Month	Copper Price/Pound	Month	Copper Price/Pound	Month	Copper Price/Pound
1	$.85	5	$.83	9	$.95	13	$.83
2	.82	6	.85	10	.90	14	.81
3	.90	7	.89	11	.90	15	.87
4	.79	8	.81	12	.85	16	.85

a. Use exponential smoothing to forecast monthly copper prices. Compute what the forecasts would have been for all the months of historical data for $\alpha = .1$, $\alpha = .3$, and $\alpha = .5$ if the forecast for all α's in the first month was $.90.
b. Which alpha (α) value results in the least mean absolute deviation over the 16-month period?
c. Use the alpha (α) from Part b to compute the forecasted copper price for Month 17.

14. Bill O'Malley wishes to compare two forecasting systems to forecast copper prices from the data in Problem 13: moving averages (AP = 3) and exponential smoothing ($\alpha = .5$).
a. Compute the two sets of monthly forecasts over the past ten months (7 through 16). The exponential smoothing forecast in Month 6 was $.832.

   b.   Which forecast system has the least forecasting error?

   c.   Plot on a graph the two forecasted system results against the actual copper prices for the past ten months. What conclusions can you reach about the graph?

   d.   Select the best system and forecast the copper prices for next month (Month 17).

15. In Problem 9, if a smoothing constant of .25 is used and the exponential smoothing forecast for Week 11 was 180.76 units, what is the exponential smoothing forecast for Week 13?

16. In Problems 9 and 15, which forecasting method is preferred (the AP = 3 moving average method or the $\alpha = .25$ exponential smoothing method)? The criterion for choosing between the methods is mean absolute deviation (MAD) over the most recent nine weeks. Assume that the exponential smoothing forecast for Week 3 is the same as the actual demand.

Multiregression

17. Elaine Sharp, a production engineer for Machine Products Inc. (MPI), a large general job shop servicing automotive customers in the greater Detroit area, has just completed a linear multiregression analysis:

$$Y = 25.00 + .025X_1 + 100X_2 + 10.500X_3$$

where:

Y = number of production engineering hours per order

X_1 = number of parts per order

X_2 = inverse of the number of past orders for the part

X_3 = number of gross pounds per part before machining

$R^2 = .795$

   a.   Estimate the number of production engineering hours required on the next order where $X_1 = 1,200$, $X_2 = \frac{1}{4}$, $X_3 = 2.5$.

   b.   What is the meaning of $R^2 = .795$?

18. Jane Billingsley, a staff analyst at Computer Products Corporation (CPC) in San Jose, has put a large quantity of industry, company, and U.S. economic data into her computer for a multiregression analysis. The purpose of this analysis is to develop a multiregression formula to forecast sales of CPC's line of XT Personal Computers for next year. The computer generates this regression formula:

$$Y = 4.95 + .545X_1 + 10.695X_2 + .068X_3$$

where:

Y = annual sales revenues of CPC's XT Personal Computers in millions of dollars

X_1 = annual industry sales revenues of personal computers in billions of dollars

X_2 = annual U.S. gross national product (GNP) in trillions of dollars

X_3 = annual U.S. discretionary spending levels in billions of dollars

Jane now has in her hands the U.S. Department of Commerce's predictions of next year's GNP and U.S. discretionary spending and the Computer Machinery Association's estimate of next year's industry sales revenues of personal computers:

Variable	Next Year's Predicted Value
(X_1) industry sales of PCs	$ 22,955,359,000
(X_2) U.S. GNP	1,350,895,000,000
(X_3) U.S. discretionary spending	270,003,000,000

a. Use the multiregression formula to develop a forecast of next year's sales revenues for CPC's line of XT Personal Computers.
b. Explain the assumptions implied in your forecast.

Forecast Ranging

19. From Problem 3:
    a. Develop time series forecasts of enrollments for the next three years.
    b. Compute the value of the standard error of the forecast.
    c. What upper and lower limits can be estimated for the third-year forecast if a significance level of .05 is used?

20. From Problem 4, what is the range of the forecast for next year if a 95 percent confidence interval is used?

21. From the data in Problem 6:
    a. If you have not already done so, compute the forecast of CPC's sales revenues for next year.
    b. What is the range of the forecast of CPC's sales revenues for next year if a significance level of .01 percent (confidence interval of 99 percent) is used?

22. From the data in Problem 8:
    a. If you have not already done so, compute the forecast of next year's real estate loan revenue.
    b. What is the range of the forecast of next year's real estate loan revenue if a significance level of .10 percent (confidence interval of 90 percent) is used?

Seasonalized Forecasts

23. Jane Billingsley, a staff analyst at the San Jose corporate headquarters of Computer Products Corporation (CPC), wants to develop next year's quarterly forecasts of sales revenues for CPC's line of XT Personal Computers. She believes that the most recent eight quarters of sales should be representative of next year's sales:

Year	Quarter	Sales (Millions of Dollars)	Year	Quarter	Sales (Millions of Dollars)
1	1	7.4	2	1	8.3
1	2	6.5	2	2	7.4
1	3	4.9	2	3	5.4
1	4	16.1	2	4	18.0

Use seasonalized time series regression analysis to develop a forecast of next year's quarterly sales revenues for CPC's line of XT Personal Computers.

24. CHEMCO, a firm that provides in-transit warehouse space to major chemical manufacturers, has a facility at Evansbrook, Illinois. This warehouse stores strontium nitrate for three firms that ship from the CHEMCO warehouse to local distributors. To double its capacity if it needs it, CHEMCO can lease another nearby warehouse that has recently become available, but the decision must be made now. CHEMCO will lease the warehouse for one year if at any time during the year the maximum quarterly inventory is expected to exceed the present warehouse capacity, which is 28.5 million pounds. The recent past inventory levels are:

Year	Quarter	Inventory (Millions of Pounds)	Year	Quarter	Inventory (Millions of Pounds)	Year	Quarter	Inventory (Millions of Pounds)
1	Q_1	10	2	Q_1	12	3	Q_1	14
	Q_2	8		Q_2	10		Q_2	14
	Q_3	12		Q_3	16		Q_3	18
	Q_4	14		Q_4	20		Q_4	22

a. Use seasonalized time series analysis to forecast inventory levels for Q_1, Q_2, Q_3, and Q_4 for next year.

b. Assume that when management refers to the maximum quarterly inventory levels, what it means is the upper limit of the quarterly forecasts with a probability of only .10 of exceeding the limit due to random variation. Find the upper limit or maximum quarterly inventory levels for next year.

c. Should CHEMCO lease the warehouse?

25. From the data in Problem 12:

a. If you have not already done so, use moving averages to forecast the number of nurses required in the first quarter of next year if AP = 4 and AP = 8.

b. Are these forecasts seasonalized or deseasonalized? Why?

c. Develop quarterly seasonal indexes and apply them to the deseasonalized moving average forecasts from Part *a*.

COMPUTER PROBLEMS/CASES

SWANK RETAILERS

Mary Demerick, chief operating officer of Swank Retailers in Phoenix, Arizona, is busy looking over the most recent sales information for the company. She has called a meeting of all salespersons in the region for one week from today, and she is attempting to estimate the sales levels that should be expected for their company over the next three months. She needs to have this information so that sales quotas can be set for the individual salespersons. Her staff has accumulated these historical sales data:

Year 1	Sales (Millions of Dollars)	Year 2	Sales (Millions of Dollars)	Year 3	Sales (Millions of Dollars)
Jan.	4.9	Jan.	5.1	Jan.	5.4
Feb.	6.1	Feb.	6.3	Feb.	7.5
Mar.	7.5	Mar.	7.9	Mar.	8.2
Apr.	7.4	Apr.	8.0	Apr.	8.7
May	5.2	May	5.5	May	6.1
Jun.	5.3	Jun.	5.9	Jun.	6.3
Jul.	5.6	Jul.	6.3	Jul.	6.9
Aug.	7.1	Aug.	7.7	Aug.	8.5
Sept.	8.0	Sept.	8.5	Sept.	9.0
Oct.	6.7	Oct.	7.1	Oct.	8.1
Nov.	8.2	Nov.	8.9	Nov.	10.2
Dec.	7.5	Dec.	8.7	Dec.	9.5

Ms. Demerick expects these sales patterns and trends to continue.

Assignment

1. Plot the sales data on a graph and examine the data.

2. From your graph in Part 1, if exponential smoothing were applied to these sales data for the purpose of developing short-range forecasts, would you recommend a low value of alpha, the smoothing constant, say .1, or a high value, say .5? Why?

3. Use the *POM Computer Library* that accompanies this text and determine for this data which value of alpha, the smoothing constant, results in the least value of mean absolute deviation (MAD) over the last 12 months of these data. Use this value of alpha to forecast next month's sales.

4. Use the *POM Computer Library* and seasonalized time series regression analysis to develop a forecast for the next three months' sales. How confident are you in these forecasts? Develop a statistical statement about next month's forecast (Year 4, January) that reflects your level of confidence if you use a 95 percent confidence interval.

5. Based on your findings in Parts 3 and 4 above, would you recommend that Swank use exponential smoothing or seasonalized time series regression analysis? What are the pros and cons of each method in this case?

SOUTH CITY HOSPITAL

The number of nurses needed in South City Hospital's surgical wing varies from quarter to quarter. This variation causes the hospital difficulty in hiring and scheduling nurses for the wing. It seems to Wanda Martin, the operations manager at the hospital, that there are always either too many nurses or not enough nurses scheduled to do the work in the surgical wing from quarter to quarter. Furthermore, nurses cannot be shifted to and from other departments due to the special surgical training required in the wing, and because of an understanding with the nurses union. If too many nurses are scheduled, the salary expense and fringe benefits are too high and personnel problems seem to increase. On the other hand, if too few are scheduled, overtime must be worked, increasing overhead costs and angering doctors.

The operations staff has been using a simple rule to schedule nurses: The average of the number of nurses needed in the last four quarters is the number scheduled to work next quarter. Ms. Martin wonders if there is a better way to forecast the number of nurses needed. She has had an operations analyst prepare historical data for the past three years for the number of nurses needed in the surgical wing:

Year	Quarter	Number of Nurses	Year	Quarter	Number of Nurses
1	1	114	2	3	111
	2	110		4	112
	3	106	3	1	115
	4	114		2	113
2	1	116		3	110
	2	114		4	116

Assignment

Using the *POM Computer Library,* develop forecasts for the number of nurses needed in the next quarter (Year 4, Quarter 1). Compute the value of the mean absolute deviation (MAD) over the last four quarters (Year 3) by using these methods:

1. Graph the data. What kinds of patterns do you observe? Before you analyze the data, decide which forecasting model(s) seem appropriate for these patterns.

2. Moving average with AP = 4. If you have already worked Problem 12, you can use your solution here.

3. Exponential smoothing, by finding the value of alpha, the smoothing constant, that results in the least value of MAD.

4. Time series regression analysis.

5. Seasonalized time series regression analysis.

6. Which forecasting method or methods would you recommend the hospital use to forecast the number of nurses needed in each quarter? What are the key factors on which you base this recommendation? Defend your recommendation.

FIRST NATIONAL BANK

In Problem 8, Jewell Brown of the First National Bank has just completed a simple regression analysis of the relationship between real estate loan revenue and the interest rate charged. She initially thought that the interest rates charged should be a good basis for forecasting the amount of revenue from real estate loans. Unfortunately, the amount of variation in loan revenue explained by interest rates charged was disappointingly low. Ms.

Brown set about to incorporate more variables into her analysis and developed the following historical data:

Year	Real Estate Loan Revenue (Millions of Dollars)	Interest Rate Charged (%)	Regional GNP (Billions of Dollars)	Regional per Capita Income (Thousands of Dollars)
0				7.9
1	20.1	9.5	12.1	8.1
2	20.9	10.1	13.2	7.8
3	19.8	12.5	13.4	7.6
4	18.3	14.2	12.8	7.5
5	17.9	12.0	12.4	7.9
6	19.4	11.1	12.9	8.0
7	21.6	10.2	13.6	8.1
8		12.0	13.8	8.2

Assignment
Use the *POM Computer Library* to help you answer these questions.

1. If you have worked Problem 8, you can use your solution here. If you have not, work that problem now. Perform a simple regression analysis on the data above by using the interest rate charged to forecast next year's (Year 8) real estate loan revenue. What is your forecast of next year's real estate loan revenue? What percentage of the variation in real estate loan revenue is explained by interest rate charged? Evaluate the usefulness of simple regression analysis in this application.

2. Perform a multiple regression analysis on the data above by using the interest rate charged and the regional GNP to forecast next year's (Year 8) real estate loan revenue. What is your forecast of next year's real estate loan revenue? What percentage of the variation in real estate loan revenue is explained by interest rate charged and regional GNP? Evaluate the usefulness of your forecast.

3. Perform a multiple regression analysis on the data above by using interest rate charged, regional GNP, and per capita income to forecast next year's (Year 8) real estate loan revenue. What is your forecast of next year's real estate loan revenue? What percentage of the variation in real estate loan revenue is explained by interest rate charged, regional GNP, and per capita income? Evaluate the usefulness of this forecast.

4. Regional per capita income may be a leading indicator of real estate loan revenue. Repeat your analysis from Part 3 above, except treat regional per capita income as a leading indicator of real estate loan revenue. This means that the regional per capita income in the immediately preceding period may tend to be more closely related to the real estate loan revenue in the current period than is the regional per capita income in the current period. Accordingly, each regional per capita income historical value is moved to the next year for the purposes of multiple regression analysis. Therefore the values of the three independent variables used to forecast real estate loan revenue would be 12.0, 13.8, and 8.1.

5. Which of the forecasts developed above do you recommend for First National? Defend your recommendation.

SELECTED BIBLIOGRAPHY

Bails, Dale G., and Larry C. Peppers. *Business Fluctuations: Forecasting Techniques and Applications.* Englewood Cliffs, NJ: Prentice-Hall, 1982.

Basu, Shankar, and Roger G. Schroeder. "Incorporating Judgments in Sales Forecasts: Application of the Delphi Method at American Hoist & Derrick." *Interfaces* 7, no. 3(May 1977):18–27.

Box, G. E. P., and G. M. Jenkins. *Time Series Analysis, Forecasting, and Control.* San Francisco: Holden-Day, 1970.

Brown, Robert G. *Smoothing, Forecasting and Prediction of Discrete Time Series.* Englewood Cliffs, NJ: Prentice-Hall, 1963.

Carpenter, James, Dennis Deloria, and David Morganstein. "Statistical Software for Microcomputers." *Byte* (April 1984):234–264.

Chambers, J. C., *et al.* "How to Choose the Right Forecasting Technique." *Harvard Business Review* 49, no. 4(July–August 1971):45–74.

"Forecasting Sales." *Studies in Business Policy,* no. 106. New York: National Industrial Conference Board, 1963.

Fox, Mary Lou. "Integrating Forecasting and Operations Planning in Promotion Driven Companies." *P & IM Review* (February 1988):42–45, 50–51.

Gardner, Everette S. "Exponential Smoothing: The State of the Art." *Journal of Forecasting* 4(March 1985):1–28.

———. "The Strange Case of the Lagging Forecasts." *Interfaces* (May–June 1984):47–50.

Georgoff, David M., and Robert G. Murdick. "Manager's Guide to Forecasting." *Harvard Business Review* 64(January–February 1986):110–123.

Gips, J., and B. Sullivan. "Sales Forecasting—Replacing Magic with Logic." *Production and Inventory Management Review* 2, no. 2(February 1982):25.

Kerlinger, Fred N., and Elazar J. Pedhazur. *Multiple Regression in Behavioral Research.* New York: Holt, Rinehart & Winston, 1973.

Makridakis, Spyros. "The Art and Science of Forecasting." *International Journal of Forecasting* 2(1986):15–39.

Makridakis, Spyros, and Steven C. Wheelwright, eds. *The Handbook of Forecasting: A Manager's Guide.* New York: Wiley, 1982.

Makridakis, Spyros, Steven C. Wheelwright, and Victor E. McGee. *Forecasting Methods and Applications.* 2nd ed. New York: Wiley, 1983.

Makridakis, Spyros, and R. L. Winkler. "Averages of Forecasts: Some Empirical Results." *Management Science* 29, no. 9(September 1983): 987–996.

Malinvaud, Edmond. *Statistical Methods of Econometrics.* New York: American Elsevier, 1970.

Nie, Norman, Dale H. Bent, and C. Hadlai Hull. *SPSS—Statistical Package for the Social Sciences.* New York: McGraw-Hill, 1982.

"Personal Computers Are Changing the Forecaster's Job." *Business Week,* October 1, 1984.

Plossl, G. W. "Getting the Most from Forecasts." *Production and Inventory Management* (First Quarter, 1973).

"Sales Forecasting." *Experiences in Marketing Management,* no. 25. New York: National Industrial Conference Board, 1971.

Smith, Bernard T. *Focus Forecasting: Computer Techniques for Inventory Control.* Boston: CBI Publishing, 1978.

II

STRATEGIC PLANNING IN OPERATIONS
PROCESSES, TECHNOLOGIES, AND FACILITIES

CHAPTER 4
Production Processes: Manufacturing and Service Operations

CHAPTER 5
Production Technology: Selection and Management

CHAPTER 6
Facility Layout: Manufacturing and Services

CHAPTER 7
Allocating Resources to Strategic Alternatives

CHAPTER 8
Long-Range Capacity Planning and Facility Location

Chapter 2 of this book presented the concept of operations strategy, which is embodied in the long-range plan for the operations function. This plan specifies positioning strategies, focus of the factories, product designs, process designs, production technology, allocation of scarce resources, and facility planning. Once these issues have been decided and set in place, the fundamental structure of the operations function is established. The basic principle that guides decisions about these strategic issues in operations is that operations functions exist in organizations to assist in achieving the broader organizational objectives. The fundamental structure of operations functions, therefore, must be designed to achieve the broader mission of the organization.

Decisions about the fundamental structure of operations functions are crucial to the long-range survival, growth, and profitability of organizations. This has never been more true than it is today. U.S. manufacturers in many industries are under immense pressure to improve the quality and cost of their products, while at the same time building and improving customer loyalty. The first step toward these ends is designing and structuring operations functions with these objectives in mind. Because the performance of operations functions must necessarily vary to fit the unique characteristics of market, industry, and firm, many structures are available to operations functions, making decisions about these structures more complex.

Many of the strategic decisions of operations are covered in Part II of this text. Chief among these are decisions about designing production processes, selecting production technology, allocating scarce resources to strategic alternatives, and long-range capacity and location of production facilities. In making these strategic decisions, issues such as the following must be resolved: Given our operations strategies, what basic types of production processes should be selected? How much vertical integration is appropriate for each of our major businesses? What level of production technology is appropriate for each major product line? What specific production technologies and processes are required to produce each major product line at the demanded volumes and the required costs, quality levels, flexibility, and customer service levels? How should the production process steps and departments be arranged within the production facilities? How should we allocate our capital, key people, and floor space to major product lines in order to maximize profits? How much production capacity is needed in each time period for each of our major product lines? What production facilities are necessary and where should they be located?

Chapter 4 considers the issues surrounding the determination of process designs of manufacturing and service operations. Chapter 5 discusses the selection and management of production technology. Chapter 6 is about facility layout — the arrangement of workers, departments, and production processes within facilities. Chapter 7 examines the trade-offs that are often necessary in the allocation of resources to strategic alternatives. Chapter 8 concerns long-range capacity planning and facility location.

CHAPTER

4

PRODUCTION PROCESSES
MANUFACTURING AND SERVICE OPERATIONS

OPERATIONS STRATEGY STRUCTURES OPERATIONS

Wickham Skinner, of Harvard University and a long-time proponent of improved operations strategies, recently summed up structuring operations as follows:

The manufacturing strategy (or operations strategy) process, which requires managers to dig into major, critical, and competitive issues, generally serves to revitalize manufacturing. I think of manufacturing strategy in three ways.

First, manufacturing strategy is simply a notion that you don't let the manufacturing function operate in isolation from the main corporate focus or strategic job the company has to do.

Secondly, manufacturing strategy says "manage the structure," not merely operations. Tailor the structure to the strategic task. Don't focus on operations management techniques such as MRP or total quality control or other fads without determining the proper structure of manufacturing. Manage the structure first to serve strategic, competitive needs.

Finally, the concept of manufacturing strategy is based on coherent, consistent, manufacturing structure. By structure I mean number of plants, size of plants, locations of plants, make-or-buy decisions, capacity, the basic choices in equipment and process technology, and main choices in design of the infrastructure, that is, production control, manufacturing organization, and work force management.

Those are the key, vital, long-term critical decisions that structure the operation. If they are wrong, heaven help you. You will work your head off and never get anywhere.[1]

---

[1] Wickham Skinner, "Implementation of Operations Strategy," *Proceedings of the 4th Annual Operations Management Association Meeting* (Tempe, AZ: November 1985), 55–56.

As the account on the previous page indicates, the development of effective operations strategies results in the structuring of operations. An important part of the structure of operations is the design of the production processes. In this chapter we shall study how to plan and design the processes that must *produce* the products and services of operations.

PROCESS PLANNING AND DESIGN

Process planning and design means the complete delineation and description of the specific steps in the production process and the linkages among the steps that will enable the production system to produce products/services of the desired quality, in the required quantity, at the time customers want them, and at the budgeted cost. Process planning is intense for new products/services, but replanning can also occur as capacity needs change, business or market conditions change, technologically superior machines become available, or as other changes occur. Although production processes and their technology do evolve, at any one point in time the essential character and structure of production processes is shaped by operations strategy.

OPERATIONS STRATEGY DRIVES THE CHOICE OF PROCESS DESIGN

The nature of production processes must necessarily follow directly from the operations strategies that were discussed in Chapter 2, Operations Strategy. Production processes must be planned and designed to provide the mix of competitive weapons embodied in the production plan, which reflects the operations strategy for the business. For example, let us say that our positioning strategy for a particular product line consists of producing small batches of custom-designed products and a produce-to-order inventory policy. In this case, production processes must be designed that allow us the flexibility of quickly shifting to other products and economically producing products in small batches. As we proceed through this chapter, therefore, we shall emphasize the abilities of each different type of process design to provide particular competitive advantages.

INTERRELATIONSHIP OF PRODUCT/SERVICE DESIGN AND PROCESS DESIGN

The design or redesign of products/services and the design or redesign of production processes are interrelated. Figure 4.1 illustrates that there is a continuous interaction between these activities. On the surface this means that production processes must be designed to accommodate the product/service design and that products must be designed for producibility. But more importantly, continuous interaction means that product/service designs are influenced and changed by what we learn as we design production processes. Also, production process designs are influenced and changed by what we learn as we design products/services. This point will be reinforced in Chapter 5, Production Technology, when we shall discuss the changes in product design that are required when products are assembled by automated equipment.

FIGURE 4.1   *Interaction between Product/Service Design and Process Design*

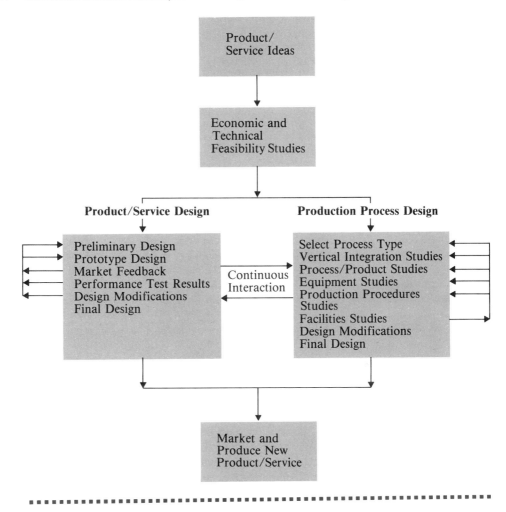

Process planning systems are established to guide an organization's efforts at designing and redesigning its production processes.

PROCESS PLANNING AND DESIGN SYSTEMS

Process planning and design brings together knowledge about operations strategies, product/service designs, technologies of the production system, and markets, and then develops a detailed plan for producing the products/services.

Figure 4.2 illustrates the inputs and outputs of process planning. The inputs to process planning come from information about products/services and their markets, from information about the production system and its technologies, and from operations strategies.

■■

FIGURE 4.2 *The Process Planning and Design System*

INPUTS	PROCESS PLANNING AND DESIGN	OUTPUTS
1. Product/Service Information Product/Service Demand Prices/Volumes Patterns Competitive Environment Consumer Wants/Needs Desired Product Characteristics **2. Production System Information** Resource Availability Production Economics Known Technologies Technology that Can Be Acquired Predominant Strengths Weaknesses **3. Operations Strategy** Positioning Strategies Competitive Weapons Needed Focus of Factories and Service Facilities Allocation of Resources	**1. Select Process Type** Coordinated with Strategies **2. Vertical Integration Studies** Vendor Capabilities Acquisition Decisions Make-or-Buy Decisions **3. Process/Product Studies** Major Technological Steps Minor Technological Steps Product Simplification Product Standardization Product Design for Producibility **4. Equipment Studies** Level of Automation Linkages of Machines Equipment Selection Tooling **5. Production Procedures Studies** Production Sequence Materials Specifications Personnel Requirements **6. Facilities Studies** Building Designs Layout of Facilities	**1. Technological Processes** Design of Specific Processes Linkages among Processes **2. Facilities** Building Design Layout of Facilities Selection of Equipment **3. Personnel Estimates** Skill Level Requirements Number of Employees Training/Retraining Requirements Supervision Requirements

■■

Process planning and design involves the selection of a process type, studies about the degree of vertical integration, process and product/service studies, equipment studies, production procedures studies, and facilities studies. The outputs of these studies is a complete determination of the individual technological process steps to be used and the linkages among the steps; the selection of equipment, design of buildings, and layout facilities; and number of personnel required, their skill levels, and supervision requirements.

Relation to Other POM Activities

Once process planning has been completed, the fundamental structure and character of the operations function is set. Figure 4.3 shows that process planning is the basis for the design of buildings, layout of facilities, and selection of production equipment. Additionally, process planning ultimately affects quality control, human resource requirements, job designs, and facility capacity. In short, this important activity determines in large measure the details of *how* products/services will be produced.

Process Planning Information Flows

Who does process planning? In complex manufacturing situations, this procedure may involve several departments, such as manufacturing engineering, plant engi-

FIGURE 4.3   *Process Planning: Its Relation to Other POM Activities*

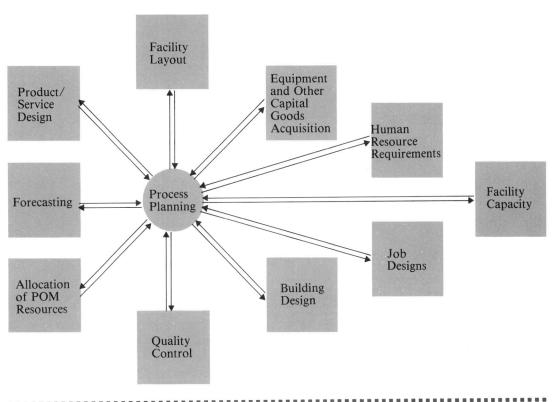

neering, tool engineering, purchasing, industrial engineering, design engineering, and, of course, production. Figure 4.4 shows how these functions work together to bring the product design into production through process planning. In less complex situations a single person may perform all of the activities of process planning.

Fundamental to process planning are the basic technological processes of organizations. For example, in the electronics industry, terms such as *flow soldering, component auto-insertion,* and *printed circuit (pc) acid baths* are part of the everyday language that everyone uses. A thorough understanding of the details of these processes in one's industry is an absolute must for effective process planning. They are the domain of process, product, manufacturing, tool, and industrial engineers. Organizations employ these engineers to use their specialized knowledge about these processes. Although staff personnel, employees from other departments, and managers are not expected to be experts in the processes of their firms, neither are they expected to be totally ignorant of them. Fortunately, most jobs afford opportunities to become informed about underlying technologies through daily on-the-job encounters. For most of us, this practical knowledge comes through years of experience.

■■

FIGURE 4.4   *Process-Planning Information Flows in Manufacturing*

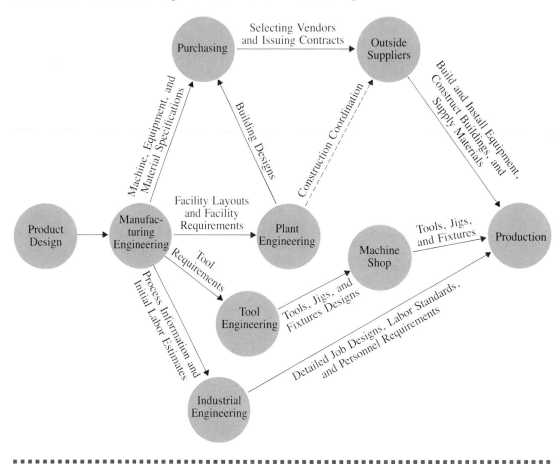

■■

MAJOR FACTORS AFFECTING
PROCESS DESIGN DECISIONS

Among the factors affecting process design decisions are the nature of product/service demand, degree of vertical integration, product/service and volume flexibility, degree of automation, level of product/service quality, and degree of customer contact.

NATURE OF PRODUCT/SERVICE DEMAND

Production systems exist to produce products/services of the kind that customers want, when they want them, and at a cost that allows the firm to be profitable. The place to start in designing production systems, therefore, is the demand for products and services. Of particular importance are the patterns of demand.

Patterns of Product/Service Demand

First, production processes must have adequate capacity to produce the volume of the products/services that customers want. In Chapter 3, Forecasting in POM, we discussed the ways that estimates of customer demand for products/services can be developed. These forecasts can then be used to estimate the amount of production capacity needed in each future time period. Seasonality, growth trends, and other patterns of demand, therefore, are important determinants of the production capacity necessary to satisfy demand.

Seasonality is an important consideration as we plan the type of production process appropriate for a product/service. For example, if a product's demand exhibits great variation from season to season, the production processes and inventory policies must be designed to allow the delivery of sufficient quantities of products or services during peak demand seasons, and yet still be able to produce products economically in slack demand seasons.

Similarly, the growth trends of product/service demand have important implications for designing production processes. For example, if a service is expected to show strong sales growth over a five-year period, provision must be made for designing production processes whose capacity can be expanded to keep pace with demand. Some types of processes can be more easily expanded than others, and the choice of the type of production process will be affected by the forecasted growth trends of product/service demand.

As with seasonality and growth patterns, random fluctuation and cyclical patterns will also impact on production process designs. In addition, the overall volume of the demand and the prices that can be charged for the products/services will affect the type and characteristics of the production processes.

Price – Volume Relationships

In the course of developing market plans for products/services, attempts are made to establish the relationship between prices and volume of demand. Figure 4.5 illustrates such a relationship with the well-known price–volume curve. As we can see from this graph for a hypothetical product/service, when price is set high, consumers tend to buy lower volumes of products/services. As prices are reduced, larger and larger volumes of products/services tend to be purchased until the curve becomes almost vertical.

There are several concepts implicit in price–volume curves that have important implications for designing production processes:

1. Every price along the price–volume curve assumes a combination of advertising, sales force, credit terms, customer services provided, a particular product/service design, inventory and shipping policies, quality requirements, and other elements of both the marketing and production plans.
2. At different price levels, different approaches to production must be taken so that the customer services provided, custom versus standard product/service

FIGURE 4.5   Price–Volume Relationship for a Product/Service

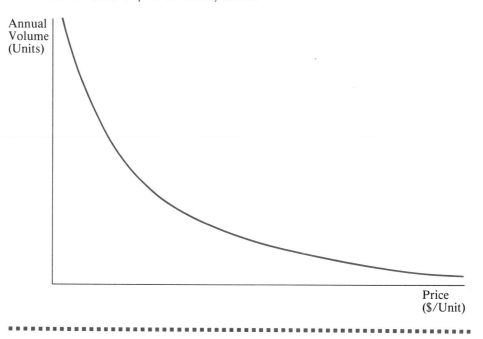

designs, inventory and shipping policies, product quality, and production cost requirements can be met.

As we shall discuss later in this chapter, different types of production processes provide a different mix of competitive advantages; therefore the choice of price and the choice of the design of production processes must be synchronized.

DEGREE OF VERTICAL INTEGRATION

One of the first issues to resolve when developing production processing designs is determining how much of a product/service a company will produce and how much will be bought from suppliers. *Vertical integration* is the amount of the production and distribution chain, from suppliers of components to the delivery of finished products/services to customers, that is brought under the ownership of a company. There are two types of vertical integration, forward and backward. *Forward integration* means expanding ownership of the production and distribution chain forward toward the market. *Backward integration* means expanding ownership of the production and distribution chain backward toward the sources of supply.

Generally speaking, there are three stages of production: component, subassembly, and final assembly. For most manufacturers of finished products—such as Ford, GM, and Chrysler that assemble automobiles—the major issue of vertical integration is whether they should enter into supply contracts with suppliers of

■■■

TABLE 4.1   Factors Affecting the Degree of Backward Integration

1. The cost of making or producing subassemblies or components in-house versus buying them from suppliers.
2. The amount of investment necessary to produce subassemblies or components in-house.
3. The availability of funds to support the necessary expansion or purchase of production capacity.
4. The effect on return on assets if production of subassemblies or components is undertaken.
5. The present technological capabilities of the company to produce subassemblies or components.
6. The need to develop technological capabilities to produce subassemblies or components to secure future competitive position.
7. The availability of excellent suppliers who are willing to enter into long-term supply relationships, particularly those who can provide high-quality subassemblies and components at low prices, who are well enough funded to ensure continuity of an adequate supply, and who are able to work with the company to continuously improve product and component designs and manufacturing processing.
8. The amount of market share held by the company.

■■■

subassemblies and components, or backward integrate to produce subassemblies and components themselves. On the other hand, for firms that are primarily subassembly suppliers — such as some divisions of Texas Instruments — the major issue of vertical integration is whether they should forward integrate and assemble and market their own finished products. In either case, the issue of whether to integrate vertically brings both opportunities and risks.

The amount of vertical integration that is right for a particular firm in one industry could be inappropriate for another firm in a different industry. For companies that would forward integrate toward the market, the predominant factor in such decisions is the ability of the company to market the products. For companies that would backward integrate toward subassemblies and components, Table 4.1 lists several factors that affect these decisions.

It should be clear from Table 4.1 that the decision whether to make products (backward integrate by bringing production of subassemblies and components in-house) or buy them from suppliers is not a simple decision. Among other things, all of the issues raised in Table 4.1 would have to be resolved. But the starting point in make-or-buy decisions is to resolve the first issue: What is the cost of making the subassemblies or components versus buying them from suppliers? Unless there are clear cost advantages to making subassemblies or components in-house, the other issues in Table 4.1 are not likely to be very important.

Make-or-buy analysis is explored in more detail in Chapter 13, Materials Management and Purchasing. Also, because make-or-buy decisions are likely to have long-lasting effects, the time value of money can be an important consideration. Appendix C, Financial Analysis in POM, explores the time value of money and related concepts in the context of several POM decisions. Example C.10, A Make-or-Buy Decision, is particularly appropriate to the topic of vertical integration.

On the opportunity side, profits may increase with vertical integration because of elimination of some purchasing and marketing functions, centralized overhead, pooling of R&D and design efforts, and economies of scale in production. However, return on assets may go up or down depending on the amount of investment necessary to integrate and the amount of increased profits. Generally, research has shown that return on assets is usually highest at the high and low extremes of vertical integration. Also, companies with small market shares should not vertically integrate.[2]

But there are also risks. For some firms, if they do not backward integrate, their suppliers may forward integrate and become formidable competitors. For others, if they do backward integrate, "[Managers] may suddenly discover that their decision to make rather than buy important parts has locked their companies into an outdated technology. They may find themselves shut off from the R&D efforts of suppliers by becoming their suppliers' competitor. Long-term contracts and long-term relationships with suppliers can achieve many of the same cost benefits as backward integration without calling into question a company's ability to innovate or respond to innovation."[3] Also, by attempting to vertically integrate, a firm may spread its management so thin that it does not do anything particularly well.

The choice of the degree of vertical integration sets the ballpark within which production processes must be designed. Within this scope, the degree of flexibility of the production system is an important factor in designing production processes.

PRODUCT/SERVICE AND VOLUME FLEXIBILITY

In Chapter 2, Operations Strategy, we discussed flexibility as one of the weapons that operations functions have for increasing or maintaining market share. Flexibility means being able to respond fast to customers' needs. Flexibility is of two forms, product/service flexibility and volume flexibility. *Product/service flexibility* means the ability of the production system to quickly change from producing one product/service to producing another. *Volume flexibility* means the ability to quickly increase or reduce the volume of products/services produced. Both of these forms of flexibility of production systems are determined in large part when the production processes are designed.

Product/service flexibility is required when business strategies call for many custom-designed products/services each with rather small volumes or when new products must be introduced quickly. In such cases production processes must ordinarily be planned and designed to include general-purpose equipment and versatile employees who can be easily changed from one product/service to another. The concept of a *flexible work force* involves training and cross-training workers in many

[2] Robert O. Buzzell, "Is Vertical Integration Profitable?" *Harvard Business Review* 61(January–February 1983):92–102.

[3] Robert H. Hayes and William J. Abernathy, "Managing Our Way to Economic Decline," *Harvard Business Review* 58(July–August 1980):67.

types of jobs. Although training costs obviously increase, the payoff is work that is perhaps more interesting for workers and a work force that can quickly shift from job to job and to other products/services with little loss in productivity.

As suggested earlier, in earlier times automation was not ordinarily used in production systems that required product flexibility because of the difficulty of changing the equipment to other products/services. However, as we shall discuss later, new forms of flexible automation allow great product/service flexibility.

Volume flexibility is needed when demand is subject to peaks and valleys and when it is impractical to inventory products in anticipation of customer demand. In these cases, production processes must be designed with production capacities that can be quickly and inexpensively expanded and contracted. Manufacturing operations are ordinarily *capital-intensive,* which simply means that the predominant resource used is capital rather than labor. Thus in the presence of variable product demand, capital equipment in production processes must be designed with production capacities that are near the peak levels of demand. This translates into either increased capital investment in buildings and equipment or the use of outside subcontractors and some provision for quickly expanding and contracting the work force. Over time, layoffs or the recall of workers from layoffs, use of temporary or part-time workers on short notice, and permanent overstaffing are options commonly used to achieve volume flexibility of employees.

The fundamental nature of services, as illustrated in Table 2.5, creates the need for volume flexibility. The fact that we cannot ordinarily store finished services in anticipation of demand means that we must produce and deliver services when demanded by customers or lose sales. Both the equipment capacities and the work force must be capable of producing and delivering enough services during peak demand periods. Many services are *labor-intensive,* which simply means that the predominant resource used is labor rather than capital. Many services use overstaffing to cover periods of small to medium demand peaks. As demand increases above these levels, part-time employees can be used routinely to cover the anticipated weekly variation in demand. Or if demand peaks occur unexpectedly, temporary or part-time employees can be used to produce and deliver services on short notice.

How much automation to use in production processes involves not only issues of flexibility, but also other issues crucial to remaining competitive in the 1990s.

DEGREE OF AUTOMATION

A key issue in designing production processes is determining how much automation to integrate into the production system. Because automated equipment is very expensive and managing the integration of automation into existing or new operations is difficult, automation projects are not undertaken lightly.

Historically, the discussion of how much automation to use in factories and services has centered on the cost savings from substituting machine effort for labor. Today, automation affects far more than the costs of production; in fact, for many companies automation is seen as basic to their ability to become or remain competitive. Industry Snapshot 4.1 discusses some of the effects of automation on the performance of production systems.

INDUSTRY SNAPSHOT 4.1

Justification of New Automation Requires Careful Study

Automation is reshaping the factory of tomorrow. "What we're finally beginning to admit is that if you don't treat automation as a strategic weapon, it becomes a strategic limitation," says David Clendennen, controller of Westinghouse Electric Company. You can't ignore it. There's no middle ground. But more often than not, the intangible benefits of advanced technology are ignored by corporate financial departments and by executive management. Convincing American management to invest in automation requires the backing of corporate financial divisions. "Old formulas for cost justification of automation focus on savings from direct labor costs,

rather than from improvements in the production processes," says William Rolland, director of the Automation Forum, a trade group based in Washington. But the price tag for direct labor is equivalent to only 5 percent to 10 percent of total manufacturing costs, citing a recent study by the National Electronic Manufacturers Association. "We've got to change our thinking," Rolland said, contending that new numbers indicating savings in scrap and rework, flexibility, shorter lead times and set-up times, and improved product quality, should be inserted in financial analyses.[4]

[4] John Barnett, "More Automation Seen as Business Necessity," *Houston Chronicle,* Dec. 22, 1986, sec. 2, 1. Copyright: Houston Chronicle. Excerpted with permission.

As indicated in Industry Snapshot 4.1, automation can reduce labor and related costs, but in many applications the huge investment required by automation projects cannot be justified on labor savings alone. Increasingly, it is the other benefits of automation that motivate companies to invest in automation. The need to quickly produce products/services of high quality and the ability to quickly change production to other products/services are the key factors that support many of today's automation projects. As with other factors affecting the design of production processes, the degree of automation appropriate for production of a product/service must be driven by the operations strategies of the firm. If those strategies call for high quality, product flexibility, and fast production of products/services, automation can be an important element of operations strategy. We shall consider more about automation and related technology later in this chapter.

LEVEL OF PRODUCT/SERVICE QUALITY

In today's competitive environment, product quality has become the chief weapon in the battle for world markets of mass-produced products. In earlier times, it was thought that the only way to produce products of high quality was to produce products in small quantities by expert craftsmen performing painstaking hand work. Mercedes and Rolls Royce are examples of automobiles that were produced with this approach. The implication from this scenario was that products that were mass-produced with little hand or touch labor were of inferior quality at worst and of questionable or unpredictable quality at best. In recent times, this scenario has proven to be a myth. Now, mass-produced products such as Japan's Toyota automobiles are considered to be of very high quality. And increasingly, many U.S. manufacturers of mass-produced goods are considered to be producing products whose quality is on a par with those of Japanese manufacturers.

The choice of design of production processes is certainly affected by the desired level of product quality. At every step of process design, product quality enters into most of the major decisions. For many firms the issue of how much product quality is required is directly related to the degree of automation integrated into the production processes. For, as we shall discuss later in this chapter, automated machines can produce products of incredible uniformity. And with proper management, maintenance, and attention, products of superior quality can be produced with automated production processes at low production costs.

DEGREE OF CUSTOMER CONTACT

For most services and for some manufacturers, customers are an active part of the processes of producing and delivering products and services. The extent to which customers become involved in the production systems has important implications for the design of production processes.

There is a wide range of degrees of interaction of customers with the production system. For example, at one extreme are barbershops, hair salons, and medical clinics. Here the customer becomes an active part of production, and the service is actually performed *on* the customer. In these cases the customer is the central focus of the design of production processes. Every element of the equipment, employee training, and buildings must be designed with the customer in mind. Also, courteous attention and comfortable surroundings must be provided to receive, hold, process, and release customers. In such systems, service quality, speed of performing the service, and reduced costs can be improved with automated equipment as long as the fundamental nature of the service is not materially affected.

At the other extreme of customer involvement, the design of production processes is affected little because of interaction with customers. Examples of this type of service are fast-food restaurants or back room operations at banks. In these operations, services are highly standardized, production volume of services is high, and cost, price, and speed of delivery tend to be predominant in operations strategies.

We have now discussed what process planning and design is, how it is achieved, and what factors affect it. Now let us study the major types of process designs we find in practice.

TYPES OF PROCESS DESIGNS ✳

At the earliest stages of process planning, we must decide on the basic type of production processing organization and which finished goods inventory policy to use

FIGURE 4.6   *Product-Focused Production*

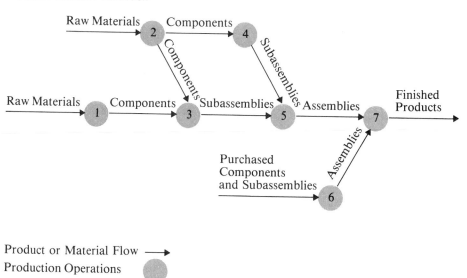

in producing each major product/service. The common types of production processing organizations are product-focused, process-focused, and group technology/cellular manufacturing. And, as we discussed in Chapter 2, Operations Strategy, produce-to-stock and produce-to-order are the finished goods inventory policies.

PRODUCT-FOCUSED

The term *product-focused* is used to describe a form of production processing organization in which production departments are organized according to the type of product/service being produced. In other words, all of the production operations required to produce a product/service are ordinarily grouped into one production department.

Product-focused production is also sometimes called *line flow production* or *continuous production*. Both of these terms describe the nature of the routes that products/services follow through production. In line flow production, products/services tend to follow along direct linear paths without backtracking or sidetracking. In continuous production, products/services tend to proceed through production without stopping. Figure 4.6 illustrates the rather direct linear and continuous paths that raw materials, components, subassemblies, assemblies, and finished products follow in the product-focused production of a hypothetical product.

Product-focused organization is applied to three general forms of production: discrete unit manufacturing, process manufacturing, and delivery of services. *Discrete unit manufacturing* means the manufacture of distinct or separate products such as automobiles or dishwashers. Such products may be produced in batches, requiring the system be changed over to other products between batches. Or a system may be dedicated to only one product, in which case the system is almost never changed over to other products. In discrete unit manufacturing, the term *product-focused* is also sometimes used synonymously with the term *assembly line,* as in the case of automobile assembly plants.

In *process manufacturing,* flows of materials are moved between production operations such as screening, grinding, cooking, mixing, separating, blending, cracking, fermenting, evaporating, reducing, and distilling. This form of production is common in the food, brewing, chemical, petroleum refining, petrochemicals, plastics, paper, and cement industries. As in discrete unit manufacturing, product-focused production in process manufacturing may also be referred to as either *line flow production* or *continuous production.* It is called *line flow* because materials tend to move through production in a direct, linear fashion without backtracking. It is called *continuous production* because materials tend to move through production in a linear fashion without much stopping, and because the term describes the nature of the materials, which are nondiscrete or without form, as in liquids or powders.

Services can also use the product-focused type of production, as, for example, in cafeterias and car-washing facilities. In these systems, services are administered to customers as customers continuously move through the systems while following rather direct, linear routes. Soviet doctors even perform radial keratotomy, a surgical procedure to correct nearsightedness, on patients in a product-focused production arrangement. "Lying on beds arranged like the petals of a flower, five patients undergo surgery simultaneously. Viewing the eye via computerized imaging systems, a surgeon makes tiny incisions on the eye to correct vision by changing the eyeball's shape. [Dr.] Fyodorov and his team perform 21,000 operations a year and plan to build other clinics. The surgical assembly line has brought fame and hefty revenues — including an estimated $1 million annually from foreigners."[5]

Compared to other types of production, product-focused systems in manufacturing usually require higher initial investment levels. This increased investment need stems from (1) the use of more expensive, fixed-position materials-handling equipment, such as overhead conveyors, and (2) the use of processing equipment that is specialized to a particular product/service, such as automatic welding machines especially designed and tooled for only one product. Additionally, the product/service flexibility of these systems tends to be rather low because they are ordinarily difficult to change over to other products/services. Offsetting these drawbacks are the advantages of low labor-skill requirements, reduced worker training, reduced supervision, and ease of planning and controlling production.

This arrangement of equipment and personnel was, until after World War I, uniquely American. Since World War II, product-focused production systems have been used in every industrialized country in the world. The main reason for the extensive use of this type of production is simple: It offers what most operations

---

[5] Peter Galuska, William D. Marbach, and Rose Brady, "What Will They Do When They Get the Right Stuff?" *Business Week,* Nov. 7, 1988, 83.

FIGURE 4.7   Process-Focused Production

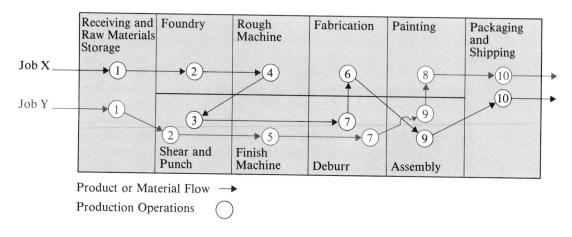

managers relish most—high-volume production, low unit costs, and ease of planning and controlling production.

PROCESS-FOCUSED

The term *process-focused* is used to describe a form of production in which production operations are grouped according to type of processes. In other words, all production operations that have similar technological processes are grouped together to form a production department. For example, all production operations throughout a factory that involve painting (the technological process) are grouped together in one location to form a painting department.

Process-focused systems are also sometimes known as intermittent production or job shops. They are referred to as *intermittent production* because production is performed on products intermittently, that is, on a start-and-stop basis. Process-focused systems are also commonly referred to as *job shops* because products/services move from department to department in batches (jobs) that are usually determined by customer orders. Figure 4.7 illustrates the routes of two hypothetical products through a job shop.

As we can see in Figure 4.7, in job shops, products/services do not follow continuous linear routes through production; on the contrary, highly irregular stop-and-go, zigzag type routes with sidetracking and backtracking are followed. In this figure, Job X and Job Y represent two distinctly different product designs. Because of their different designs, they require different production operations and must be routed through different production departments and in different sequences. Notice that in Figure 4.7 at times both Job X and Job Y must be processed through the same department, for example, the assembly department. Let us say that the assembly department does not have enough production capacity to work on both of these jobs simultaneously. This means that one of the jobs must wait its turn. This is the fundamental nature of job shops. Jobs spend the majority of their time waiting to be processed in production departments.

Process-focused production systems include hospitals, automobile repair shops, machine shops, and manufacturing plants. The key advantage of these systems is their product flexibility—the ability to produce small batches of a wide variety of products. Additionally, they usually require less initial investment since they typically use general-purpose equipment and mobile materials-handling equipment, which are usually less expensive. These systems do, however, require greater employee skill, more employee training, more supervision, more technically trained supervision, and more complex production planning and control.

Product-focused and process-focused systems represent two traditional approaches to organizing production. In practice, we also find blends and hybrids of these two approaches. For example, consider a factory that produces electric motors. In the upstream part of the factory that produces components and subassemblies, because of the great variety of component designs, a process-focused approach is used. But in the downstream part of the factory that produces finished goods, because of the relatively few finished product designs, a product-focused approach is used. Such blends of production types are not uncommon in practice and may tend to be more the rule than the exception. Other approaches to production have developed in recent times that are modifications of these traditional types. Group technology/cellular manufacturing is one such approach.

GROUP TECHNOLOGY/CELLULAR MANUFACTURING

Group technology/cellular manufacturing (GT/CM) is a form of production that has only recently been adopted in the United States. It is reported to have been used first in the Soviet Union in the late 1940s by Mitrofanov and Sokolovskii.[6] Since the end of World War II, it has been studied and applied in most of Eastern and Western Europe, and in India, Hong Kong, Japan, and the United States. Most of the applications of this form of production have been in metal-working applications.

Cellular manufacturing is a subset of the broader group technology concept. In *group technology,* a coding system is developed for the parts made in a factory. Each part receives a multidigit code that describes the physical characteristics of the part. For example, let us say that a part is cylindrical, 6 inches long, 1 inch in diameter, and made of aluminum. The part's code would indicate these physical characteristics. By the use of a coding system for parts, the following production activities are simplified:

1. It is easier to determine how to route parts through production because the production steps required to make a part are obvious from its code.
2. The number of part designs can be reduced because of part standardization. When new parts are designed, the codes of existing parts can be accessed in a computer data base to identify similar parts in the data base. New designs can be made like the existing ones.

[6] S. P. Mitrofanov, *Scientific Principles of Group Technology,* 1958, translated by E. Harris, National Lending Library for Science and Technology (England, 1966).

FIGURE 4.8   Cellular Manufacturing

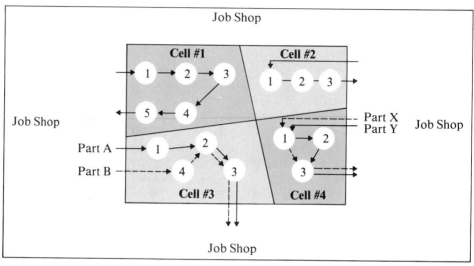

Product or Material Flow →
Production Operations ◯

3. Parts with similar characteristics can be grouped together into *part families.* Because parts with similar characteristics are made in similar ways, the parts in a parts family are typically made on the same machines with similar tooling.
4. Some parts families can be assigned to manufacturing cells for production, one part family to a cell. The organization of the shop floor into cells is referred to as *cellular manufacturing.*

In metal-working job shops, parts are made on equipment such as lathes, boring mills, drills, and grinders. Job shops make a great variety of part designs that are produced infrequently and in small batches. Through group technology, some part designs become more standardized, which tends to increase their batch sizes and requires that they be produced more often. Part families with parts that need to be produced more often in moderate batch sizes become candidates for cellular manufacturing.

Figure 4.8 illustrates a hypothetical cellular manufacturing system. The flow of parts within cells can take many forms. For example, in Cells #1 and #2, the parts in the part family flow through the same machines in a product-focused, line flow fashion. However, in Cells #3 and #4, parts take different routes through the cells because of the differences between the designs of the two parts. Two key features differentiate cellular manufacturing islands from the larger surrounding job shop:

There is a greater degree of similarity among parts within cells, and the flow of parts within cells tends to be more like the line flow of product-focused systems.

The advantages claimed for cellular manufacturing over job shops are many. Because the parts within a family in a cell require the same machines with similar tooling and require similar production operations:

1. Machine changeovers between batches of parts are simplified, thereby reducing costs of changeovers and increasing production capacity.
2. Variability of tasks is reduced, and training periods for workers are shortened.
3. There are more direct routes through production, allowing parts to be made faster and shipped quicker.
4. Parts spend less time waiting, in-process inventory levels are reduced.
5. Since parts are made under conditions of less part-design variability by workers who are more specifically trained for the parts, quality control is improved.
6. With shorter, more direct routes through production and with reduction of materials-handling costs, production planning and control are simpler.
7. As a result of reduced part variety and similarity of tooling and machines within cells, automation of cells is much simplified. The formation of cells may therefore be seen as an intermediate step in the automation of job shops.

As you would expect, GT/CM can also have some disadvantages. For example, duplicate pieces of equipment may be needed so that parts do not have to be transported between cells. Also, because not all parts from a job shop can be made in the GT/CM cells, producing the remaining parts in a job shop may not be as efficient once GT/CM cells have been established.

With the claims for GT/CM, we should be seeing more of this form of production in the future, but not all job shops will be converted to GT/CM. As we shall discuss later, only job shops that have a degree of parts standardization and moderate batch sizes are candidates for GT/CM.

PRODUCT DESIGN AND FINISHED GOODS INVENTORY POLICY

In Chapter 2, Operations Strategy, we discussed the concept of positioning strategy for manufacturers. Positioning requires that managers select a basic type of production design such as product-focused, process-focused, or GT/CM, as we have discussed in this section. Of equal importance in positioning decisions, however, are two interrelated decisions about each business:

1. Determining the type of product design — custom or standard.
2. Deciding the finished goods inventory policy — produce-to-stock or produce-to-order.

These two decisions are closely interrelated, because deciding between custom or standard designs necessarily affects the type of finished goods inventory policy that is either practical or possible.

FIGURE 4.9   Produce-to-Stock Systems

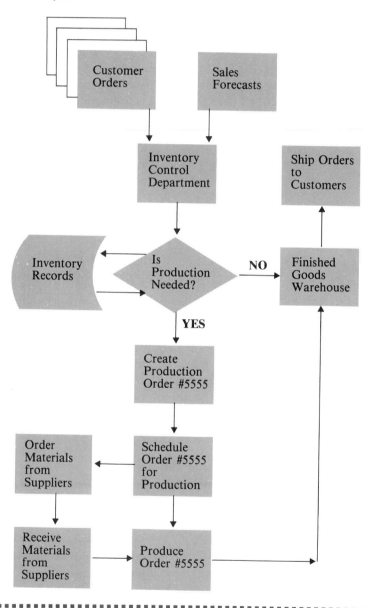

Standard product designs are usually linked with produce-to-stock finished goods inventory systems. Look at Figure 4.9 and see if you can tell why. This figure illustrates the procedures ordinarily followed in produce-to-stock finished goods inventory systems. Customer orders and sales forecasts give inventory control departments estimates of demand for particular products in future weeks and months. After consulting inventory records to determine the levels of inventory of finished goods, it can be determined if future production of particular products is required. If not, customers' orders for finished goods can be shipped directly from inventory in the finished goods warehouse. If inventory shortages appear likely, a production order is created. Raw materials, components, subassemblies, and assemblies are ordered from suppliers, and the order is scheduled for production. After the materials from suppliers are received and after the order has been produced, it is sent to the finished goods warehouse. Customers' orders are shipped from this warehouse.

If standard designs are chosen, shipping customers' orders from finished goods inventory is usually both possible and practical. Because the few standard product designs are well known, it is possible to produce products and place them in finished goods inventory before receiving customers' orders. Also, because there are only a few standard product designs, each with relatively high volume, it is practical to store these few product designs and ship customers' orders directly from finished goods inventory.

Custom product designs are usually linked with produce-to-order finished goods inventory systems. Look at Figure 4.10 and see if you can tell why. This figure illustrates the procedures ordinarily followed in produce-to-order finished goods inventory systems. Customer orders are received in production planning and control departments. After a customer order is created, it must be determined if a product design exists for this order. If products have been previously produced that meet the customer's specifications, products may not have to be designed. The same holds true for processing plans—the routes of products through the job shop. The design of products and the development of processing plans are referred to as *preproduction planning* in job shops. After scheduling the customer's order for production, notifying the customer of a promised delivery date, and ordering materials from suppliers, the order waits in an *order backlog* until it is produced and shipped to the customer.

As you can see from Figure 4.10, production of finished goods ordinarily does not begin until after a customer order is received, because the product design details may be supplied by the customer. Also, it is not uncommon to totally design a product for a customer *after* receiving the order, if the customer has submitted performance specifications (a detailed description of what the product must do). In such cases, therefore, it may not be possible to produce products before customers' orders are received. Also, because of the large number of product designs, the small demand for each design, and the infrequency of demand for each design, it may be impractical to store products in finished goods inventory while waiting for customers' orders.

Do not assume that companies follow only pure positioning strategies. Refer to Table 2.7 in Chapter 2 for a description of pure positioning strategies. We also find mixed positioning strategies in practice. As an example of a product-focused, produce-to-order production system, let us say that a firm has a few basic product designs that are highly standardized but have options or accessories that can be added to suit individual customers. Components can be produced ahead of time and inventoried in advance of customers' orders; then products may be assembled at the last minute according to customers' specifications. Most of the leading automobile man-

FIGURE 4.10 Produce-to-Order Systems

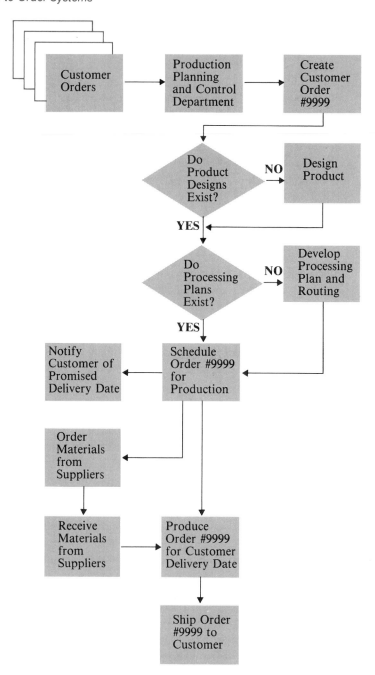

ufacturers have this form of process design and can build an automobile to a customer's order on an assembly line. The standardization of components, the standardization of the basic product design, and a very good information and communication system make this combination feasible.

On the other hand, a furniture manufacturer may use a process-focused, produce-to-stock production system. Because of the nature of the technology of wood preparation, sanding and surface preparation, painting, upholstering, and packaging, these operations are more compatible with a process-focused system. But because of the standardized product designs, a produce-to-stock finished goods inventory policy is used.

We have now discussed the different types of process designs and finished goods inventory policies. But how do we decide among the different types of process designs?

DECIDING AMONG PROCESSING ALTERNATIVES

In deciding on a particular type of production processing organization for a major product line, several factors must be considered. Among these are batch size and product variety, capital requirements, and economic analysis.

BATCH SIZE AND PRODUCT VARIETY

In choosing the type of process design, a major consideration would be the amount of product variety and the volume to be demanded of each product model. Figure 4.11 illustrates that the type of process design that is appropriate depends on the number of product designs and the size of the batches to be produced in a production system.

As a generalization, as we move from Point A to Point C in Figure 4.11, the production cost per unit and product flexibility increase. At Point A, there is a single product, and the demand for the product is very large. In this extreme case, a product-focused organization that is dedicated to only that product would be appropriate. Production costs per unit are very low, but this type of production organization is very inflexible because equipment specialized to the product and the specific training of the employees make it impractical to change to the production of other products. As the number of product designs increases and as the batch size of the products decreases, at some point, say Point B, a product-focused, batch system becomes appropriate. Although this system is relatively inflexible, employees are trained to shift to the production of other products, and equipment is designed to be changed to other products, but with some difficulty.

At the other extreme, Point C represents the production of many one-of-a-kind products. In this case, a job shop producing unique products in batches of a single item would be appropriate. This form of production is the ultimate in product flexibility. As the number of products decreases and as the batch size of the products increases from this extreme, at some point, say Point D, cellular manufacturing of some of the production of parts within a job shop becomes appropriate.

FIGURE 4.11 *Type of Process Design Depends on Product Diversity and Batch Size*

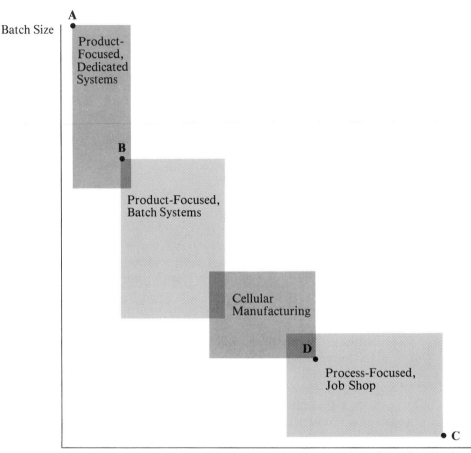

It would now be helpful if we referred to Figure 2.4 in Chapter 2, Operations Strategy. In this figure, the concept of a *process life cycle* was introduced. Simply put, production systems tend to evolve as products move through their product life cycles. Two principles are fundamental to the concept of process life cycles. First, product life cycles and process life cycles are interdependent; each affects the other. The production processes affect production costs, quality, and production volume, which in turn affects the volume of products that can be sold. Similarly, the volume of products that are sold affects the type of production processes that can be justified. Second, seldom do production processes move continuously along the ideal diagonal; rather, they evolve in fits and starts.

Thus as business strategies are developed for each major product line, the determination of the volume of demand that is expected for each product and the number of product models necessary to appeal to the market are important factors in choosing the type of process design. Other factors also have some impact on this decision.

CAPITAL REQUIREMENTS FOR PROCESS DESIGNS

The amount of capital required for the production system tends to differ for each type of production processing organization. In Figure 4.11, in general, the amount of capital required is greatest at Point A and diminishes as we move downward to the right toward Point C. The amount of capital available and the cost of capital to a firm could be important factors in choosing a type of process design, and business strategies would have to be adjusted accordingly.

For example, let us say that a firm has only a little capital available for a particular product, and a job shop may be the only type of process design that can be planned. Therefore the capabilities of a job shop production system must be integrated as part of the business strategy. Although product flexibility is a job shop's greatest strength, the production costs of this form of production organization tend to be higher than with other forms of production when production volumes are higher. Because fixed and variable costs tend to differ from one form of production organization to another, economic analysis is commonly used as a way of comparing alternative processing plans for the production of products.

ECONOMIC ANALYSIS

Among the factors to be considered when deciding among the types of production processing organizations, the production cost of each alternative is important. In this section, we shall discuss the cost functions of processing alternatives, the concept of operating leverage, break-even analysis, and financial analysis.

Cost Functions of Processing Alternatives

As mentioned earlier, each type of process design tends to require a different amount of capital. Capital costs are ordinarily fixed charges that occur every month and represent some measure of the cost of capital to the firm. Figure 4.12 graphically illustrates that different forms of process design for producing a hypothetical product have different cost functions. The greater the initial cost of equipment, buildings, and other fixed assets, the greater are the fixed costs. Also, different forms of production organizations have different variable costs — those costs that vary with the volume of products produced in each month.

As can be seen in Figure 4.12, the automated assembly line alternative has annual fixed costs of $2,250,000. Fixed costs are the annual costs when the volume of the product produced is zero. These costs are related to the very expensive robotics, computer controls, and fixed-position materials-handling equipment required for an automated assembly line. Also, it can be seen from Figure 4.12 that the variable costs

FIGURE 4.12   Cost Functions of Processing Alternatives

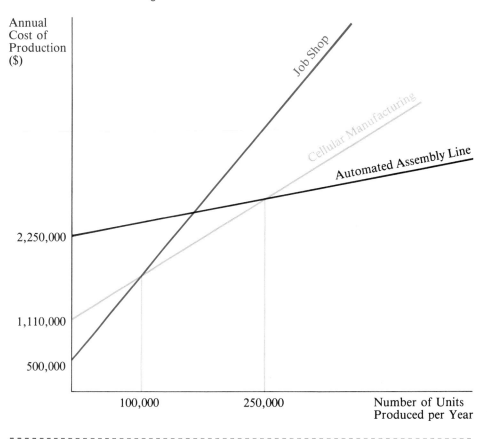

(labor, material, and variable overhead) for the automated assembly line are very low relative to the other forms of process design because the slope (rise over run) of its cost function is very flat. This means that annual costs do not climb very fast as annual volume of production grows. The cost function of a job shop usually exhibits very low fixed costs and very high variable costs. The fixed and variable costs of cellular manufacturing are usually intermediate to those of the other two process designs.

An important conclusion from Figure 4.12 is: If capital availability is not a factor and annual production costs are the predominant consideration, the process design that is preferred depends on the production volume of the product. In the example of Figure 4.12, if production volume is less than 100,000 units, a job shop would be preferred. If production volume of between 100,000 and 250,000 units is expected, cellular manufacturing would be preferred. And if production volume of greater than 250,000 units is expected, an automated assembly line would be preferred. We should remember, however, that the "no-go" alternative is always present: If none of the alternatives provides a satisfactory return, do not select any of the processing alternatives.

Operating leverage is another important concept related to economic analysis.

Concept of Operating Leverage

In an examination of the cost functions of processing alternatives, the concept of operating leverage has important implications. *Operating leverage* is a measure of the relationship between a firm's annual costs and its annual sales. If a high percentage of a firm's total costs are fixed, then the firm is said to have a high degree of operating leverage. A high degree of operating leverage, other things held constant, implies that a relatively small percentage change in sales will result in a large percentage change in operating income (the difference between annual sales and annual production costs).[7]

Figure 4.13 illustrates the concept of operating leverage. At production level BE_1, the annual production costs of cellular manufacturing equal annual sales revenues, the break-even point. The crosshatched areas to the right and left of BE_1 represent profits to the right and losses to the left. The concept of operating leverage relates to the angle between the cost function and the sales revenues lines. If operating leverage is small and the angle is therefore small, profits increase slowly to the right of the break-even point and losses increase slowly to the left of the break-even point. If operating leverage is large and the angle is therefore large, profits or losses increase rapidly to the right or left of the break-even point, respectively.

As you can also see in Figure 4.13, the operating leverage for automated assembly lines is represented by the shaded areas to the right and left, respectively, of volume BE_2, the break-even point. The operating leverage of the automated assembly line process design is greater than the operating leverage of the cellular manufacturing. The concept of operating leverage has the following important implications for the choice of process design:

1. Greater long-range profits can be realized from production processes with greater operating leverage once the production volume reaches a certain level (Point EP in Figure 4.13).
2. Greater long-range losses can result from production processes with greater operating leverage if the production volume is less than the break-even point (Point BE_2 in Figure 4.13).
3. The higher the operating leverage of a production process, the greater is the uncertainty of future profits.
4. The greater the uncertainty of sales forecasts, the greater is the risk of losses using production processes with high operating leverage.

---

[7] Eugene F. Brigham, *Fundamentals of Financial Management* (Hinsdale, IL: Dryden Press, 1986), 496.

FIGURE 4.13   Operating Leverage and Process Design Alternatives

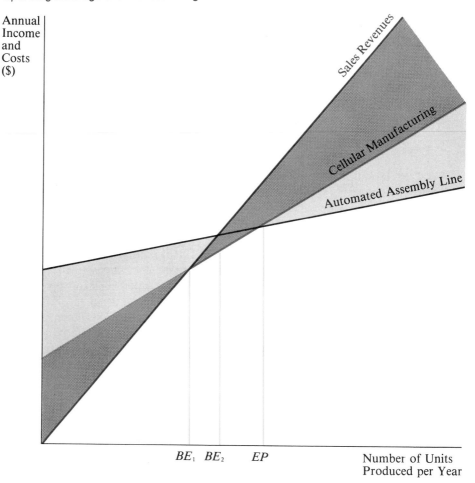

The practical significance of these implications is this: If there is a substantial amount of uncertainty concerning the forecast of number of products to be produced, process designs with lower levels of operating leverage tend to be preferred.

Break-Even Analysis

Break-even analysis is commonly used to choose between processing alternatives. Here we shall work our way through an example to refresh your memory of break-even concepts and to demonstrate how break-even analysis can be used to compare production processing alternatives.

Table 4.2 contains the variable definitions and formulas for straight-line break-even analysis. Example 4.1 compares the cost functions of three production processing alternatives.

■■■

TABLE 4.2   *Variable Definitions and Formulas for Break-Even Analysis*

p = Selling price per unit	Q = Number of units produced and sold per period
v = Variable cost per unit	P = Pretax profits per period
FC = Total fixed cost per period	TR = Total revenue per period
TVC = Total variable cost per period	TC = Total cost per period
	c = Contribution per unit
C = Contribution per period	

At break-even (P = 0)

1. $TR = pQ$
2. $c = p - v$
3. $C = Q(p - v) = TR - vQ = FC + P$
4. $TC = FC + TVC$
5. $TVC = vQ$
6. $P = TR - TC = pQ - (FC + vQ)$
7. $Q = (P + FC)/(p - v)$

8. $FC = pQ - vQ = Q(p - v)$
9. $Q = FC/(p - v)$
10. $TVC = TR - FC = pQ - FC$
11. $v = \dfrac{TR - FC}{Q} = \dfrac{pQ - FC}{Q} = p - \dfrac{FC}{Q}$
12. $TR = FC + TVC = FC + vQ$
13. $p = (FC + vQ)/Q = FC/Q + v$

■■■

EXAMPLE 4.1   *Break-Even Analysis: Selecting a Production Process*

Three production processes—A, B, and C—have the following cost structure:

Process	Fixed Cost per Year	Variable Cost per Unit
A	$100,000	$2.50
B	80,000	4.00
C	75,000	5.00

a. What is the most economical process for a volume of 10,000 units per year?

b. How many units per year must be sold with each process to have annual profits of $40,000 if the selling price is $6 per unit?

Solution

a. $TC = FC + v(Q)$

Process A $TC = \$100,000 + \$2.50(10,000) = \$125,000/\text{year}$

Process B $TC = \$80,000 + \$4(10,000) = \$120,000/\text{year}$

Process C $TC = \$75,000 + \$5(10,000) = \$125,000/\text{year}$

Process B has the lowest annual cost.

FIGURE 4.14   *Graphical Approach to Break-Even Analysis*

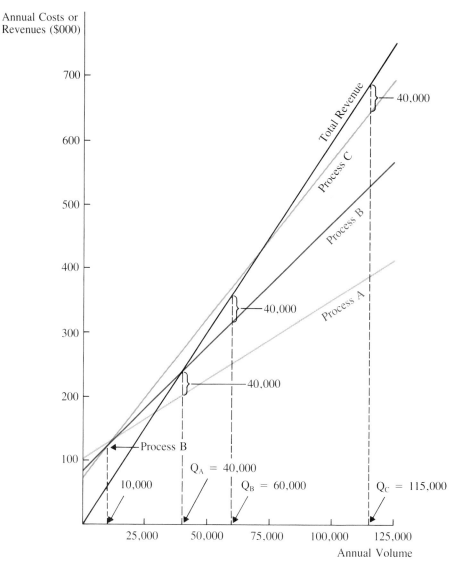

b. $Q = (P + FC)/(p - v)$

Process A $Q = (\$40{,}000 + \$100{,}000)/(\$6 - \$2.50) = \dfrac{\$140{,}000}{\$3.50} = 40{,}000$ units

Process B $Q = (\$40{,}000 + \$80{,}000)/(\$6 - \$4) = \dfrac{\$120{,}000}{\$2} = 60{,}000$ units

Process C $Q = (\$40{,}000 + \$75{,}000)/(\$6 - \$5) = \dfrac{\$115{,}000}{\$1} = 115{,}000$ units

Break-even analysis is widely used to analyze and compare decision alternatives. It does have some weaknesses, however, when compared to other methods. A primary weakness is the technique's inability to deal in a direct way with uncertainty. All of the costs, volumes, and other information used in the technique must be assumed to be known with certainty. Another disadvantage of the tool is that the costs are assumed to hold over the entire range of possible volumes. Additionally, break-even analysis does not take into account the time value of money.

Break-even analysis can be displayed either algebraically, as in Example 4.1, or graphically as in the familiar functions from Example 4.1. In either form, the results are easily explained. This is an important advantage, because managers would often rather live with a problem that they can't solve than implement a solution that they don't understand.

Financial Analysis

The amount of money to be invested in production processing alternatives is so great and the length of time these assets are expected to last makes the time value of money an important concept. In Appendix C, Financial Analysis in POM, the concepts of depreciation and the time value of money are applied to several POM problems. The payback period, net present value, internal rate of return, and profitability index are methods used to analyze POM problems involving long periods of time. Example C.9, A Choice of Equipment Decision, is particularly appropriate for this discussion because it uses an after-tax payback analysis to choose between production processing alternatives. But as noted in Industry Snapshot 4.1, long-term strategic consequences have to be considered along with the results of financial analysis.

In addition to economic analysis, two other techniques stand out in their frequency of use by process planners—assembly charts and process charts.

ASSEMBLY CHARTS

Assembly charts are typically used to provide an overall *macroview* of how materials and subassemblies are united to form finished products. These charts list all major materials, components, subassembly operations, inspections, and assembly operations. Figure 4.15 is an assembly chart that shows the major steps in assembling an electronic hand-held calculator. Follow through these steps and try to visualize the actual operations for producing this familiar product.

Assembly charts, sometimes called *gozinto charts* (from the words *goes into*), are ideal for getting a bird's-eye view of the process for producing most assembled products. They are also useful for planning production systems for services when those services involve processing tangible goods, as in fast-food restaurants, dry-cleaning shops, and quick tune-up shops for automobiles.

PROCESS CHARTS

Process charts provide more detail for process planners than do assembly charts. Figure 4.16 shows the individual steps required to process 1,500 pounds of prepared materials through a mixing operation. This chart is a detailed analysis of only one of

FIGURE 4.15 Assembly Chart for OK-20 Hand-Held Electronic Calculator

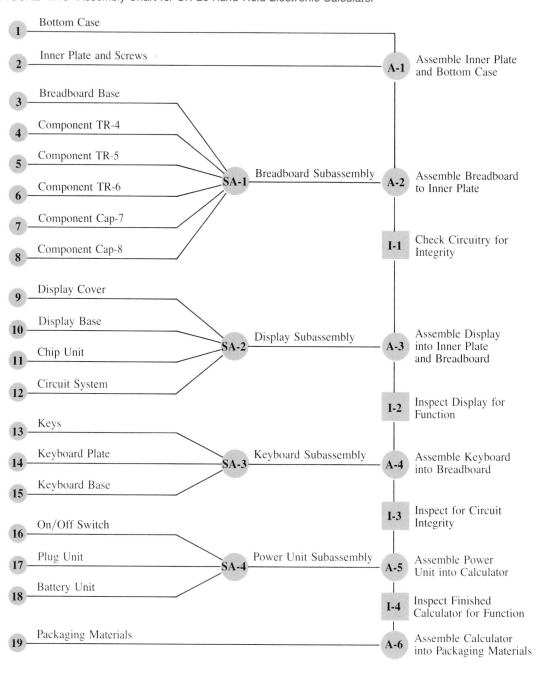

SA = Subassembly operation.   A = Assembly operation.   I = Inspection operation.

FIGURE 4.16 Process Chart for Mixing Aspirin

Operation __Mix aspirin materials__		Sheet __1__ of __1__ Sheets	Summary	
Product __Pronto aspirin (325)__		Charted By __B. Brown__	○ Operation	5
Depts. __Mixing__			⊃ Transport	5
Drawing No. __—__ Part No. __42200__		Date __3-16__	□ Inspect	1
Quantity __1,500 pounds of mixed materials__ __for Pronto 325 aspirin__		Approved By __M. Sharp__	D Delay	1
			△ Store	2
			Vertical Distance	—
Present __X__ Proposed __		Date __3-17__	Horizontal Distance	212
			Time (Hours)	1.041

No.	Dist. Moved (Feet)	Worker Time (Hours)	Symbols	Description
1	15	.200	○⊃□D△	Unload packages of material from truck to dock and place on pallet.
2	42	.033	○⊃□D△	Truck packages of material to storage area.
3			○⊃□D△	Store materials until needed.
4	25	.025	○⊃□D△	Move packages to charge chute.
5		.330	○⊃□D△	Unpackage materials and pour into charge chute.
6	20	.030	○⊃□D△	Transport charge to mixer.
7		.100	○⊃□D△	Charge mixer and begin mixing cycle.
8		.083	○⊃□D△	Wait until mixer completes cycle.
9		.017	○⊃□D△	Dump mixer charge into receiving vehicle.
10		.020	○⊃□D△	Inspect materials for proper mixing.
11	50	.033	○⊃□D△	Transport vehicle to weighing and packaging station.
12		.167	○⊃□D△	Operate machine to weigh and package 1,500 pounds of mixed materials.
13	60	.033	○⊃□D△	Transport materials to dock.
14			○⊃□D△	Store materials until truck arrives.

the operations required to produce aspirin tablets. This planning tool breaks the mixing operation down into fourteen elemental steps and segregates them into five classes — operation, transport, inspect, delay, and store. The frequency of occurrence of each class, distance traveled, and description and time for each step are recorded. When the heading of the chart is completed, the method of performing this mixing operation is thoroughly documented.

Process charts can be used to compare alternative methods of performing individual operations or groups of operations. Distance traveled and time to produce products/services can thus be reduced by examining alternative process charts for different production methods. This process-planning tool can be used for products/services that are produced in either continuous or intermittent production systems. Additionally, it is equally valuable for process planning when new products/services are being planned or when existing operations are being analyzed for improvement. Process charts will surface again in Chapter 14 when we study the analysis of human performance in production systems.

PROCESS DESIGN IN SERVICES

We have discussed much about the design of production processes for services in this chapter. We have specifically discussed these topics: estimating the nature of service demand, determining the degree of vertical integration, determining the amount of automation, setting the level of service quality, determining the degree of customer contact, and the various ways of deciding between processing alternatives.

Even with this discussion, there is the tendency of managers of service operations to leave the design of production processes for services at the verbal and subjective level. Industry Snapshot 4.2 discusses the need to bring a more quantifiable and objective approach to this activity. Such approaches as these are needed if the competitiveness of service organizations is to improve.

VIDEOTAPE-ACCOMPANIED PLANT TOURS

A PRODUCT-FOCUSED FACTORY: INTERNATIONAL BUSINESS MACHINES CORPORATION (IBM), LEXINGTON, KENTUCKY*

IBM Lexington develops and manufactures personal, systems printers, secretarial workstations, typewriters, keyboards, plastic parts, and related supplies. Established in 1956 as a typewriter-manufacturing operation, the facility has become one of the largest automated manufacturing plants in the world. The plant covers nearly 400 acres of land, has 4 million square feet under roof, and has approximately 5,400 employees.

The design of the facility is based on these principles:

1. Products must be designed for manufacturability on automated equipment to provide high product quality and low manufacturing costs.

---

* IBM publications, reprinted with permission from International Business Machines Corporation.

INDUSTRY SNAPSHOT 4.2

Developing a Blueprint for Services

G. Lynn Shostack, senior vice president in charge of the Private Clients Group at Bankers Trust Company, urges managers of services to move away from the traditional trial-and-error method of designing production processes for services. Shostack believes that:

1. Provisions must be made for customers in the production processes of services.
2. Designing production processes for services requires more judgment and a less mechanical approach when compared to products.
3. Managers must allow for special problems of market position, advertising, pricing, and distribution.

Toward these ends, Shostack urges managers to develop a more nonsubjective and quantifiable approach that is referred to as a *blueprint* for production processes of services. This approach is said to allow "a company to explore all the issues inherent in creating or managing a service." [8]

To explore the issues, the following steps should be taken:

1. *Identify processes.* Develop flowcharts or diagrams that connect the production steps in the overall production system. Include steps that the customer does not see, such as purchasing supplies.
2. *Isolate fail points.* Once the process is diagramed, determine the decision points where the production system

might fail. Build in corrective steps that avoid the consequences of possible errors.
3. *Establish time frame.* Estimate the amount of time that each step of the service should require. These time estimates become standards against which to measure performance of the system. If services are provided in more time than the standards, productivity and profitability will be lower than should be expected.
4. *Analyze profitability.* Continuously monitor the profitability of the service. This monitoring allows unprofitability to be avoided, productivity to be measured, uniformity to be maintained, and quality to be controlled.

"Such a blueprint approach to designing services is more precise than verbal definitions and less subject to misinterpretation. The alternative — leaving services to individual talent and managing the pieces rather than the whole — makes a company more vulnerable and creates a service that reacts slowly to market needs and opportunities." [9]

---

[8] G. Lynn Shostack, "Designing Services That Deliver," *Harvard Business Review* (January–February 1984), 135.

[9] Ibid., 139.

2. The production system must allow fast introduction of new products and have product and volume flexibility.

Computer-integrated manufacturing (CIM) is the production system employed at IBM Lexington. In CIM not only are product design (computer-aided design, or CAD) and manufacturing (computer-aided manufacturing, or CAM) automated or computer-augmented, but the introduction of products into manufacturing is also automated. Similarly, other functions such as accounting and marketing are also tied into the computer system. A network of computers guides the manufacturing processes all the way through the production of components, subassemblies, the just-in-time delivery of parts and subassemblies, and the use of automated storage and retrieval systems to final product assembly and packaging.

The manufacturing plant is organized into several plants within a plant or modules where each module produces components for assembly into finished products at the Lexington plant. Figure 4.17 illustrates the interrelationships among these automated modules; covers and injection molding, supplies, printed circuit boards, motors assembly and test, keyboard assembly and test, frame paperfeed transport, and final assembly and test. All planning and control at the plant focuses on these product-oriented departments or modules, and our discussion of the plant will also focus on these modules.

Covers and Injection Molding

IBM Lexington is the major technology center for plastics in IBM and is one of the major molding operations in the United States. The manufacturing processes in this module rely heavily on two- and three-dimensional computer modeling of parts to optimize plastics flow, cooling, and cycle times. Computer simulation provides "first time final" mold design. Approximately 80 injection mold presses range from 40 to 1,500 tons, and they mold parts that range from millimeter-size pivot plates to covers for typewriters and printers. These presses are controlled by a computerized shop floor monitoring system as raw materials are fed to presses from a central source and an automated materials-handling system moves molded parts to assembly and packaging. Plastic parts may be sent to other modules within the plant, shipped to other IBM plants, or shipped directly into the distribution system as a finished good.

Supplies

The principal products manufactured in the supplies module are ribbons, print wheels, print heads, correction tapes, electronic fonts, and typing elements. IBM Lexington manufactures three different families of high-quality, high-character-yield ribbons for typewriters and computer printers. The many technologies for ribbon cartridges include plastics and metalization, extruding and coating, mechanical and chemical processes, and automated final assembly. IBM print wheels use a variety of 150,000 characters to meet U.S. and overseas standards. Their manufacture includes molding processes, assembly, and laser identification. Electronic fonts featuring proportional spacing, letter expansion, bold-facing, and many typestyles for international use are also manufactured. Automatic function testing, image quality checking at $100 \times$ magnification, and environmental testing ensure the high quality of these

■■ ■■ ■■

FIGURE 4.17   Materials Flow at IBM

The Competitive Factory - From Pellets to Products

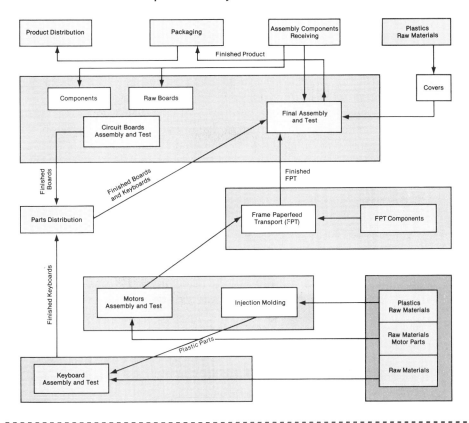

Source: Courtesy International Business Machines Corporation.

■■

products. The supplies module is located in another noncontiguous building and is not included in Figure 4.17.

Printed Circuit Boards

This department uses both surface-mount and pin-thru-hole technologies to assemble integrated printed circuit boards. First-pass quality is achieved by precise conformance to specifications and by computer control of machine operations, material transport, and process verification. Card assembly, soldering, shearing, and testing are computer controlled with built-in error checking. Over 50 automated insertion machines install into boards both standard components and nonstandard components such as transistors. The module manufactures a wide variety of boards and can be adapted to produce many more. As a board is passed along to the next operation, each operation recognizes the design of the board, retrieves the design specifications, performs its operation, tests its work, and communicates with other operations. Most boards manufactured are designed at the plant using CAD software. Rules of manufacture and circuit simulation are employed at the design stage to guarantee manufacturing ease, low cost, and conformance to specifications. The boards are used in IBM printers, computers, telecommunication products, and typewriters.

Motors Assembly and Test

The motor module manufacturers five types of motors that are used in IBM computers, printers, and typewriters. The motors feature standardized end caps, bearings, and stator laminates. Technologically advanced testing units automatically test the motors along 12 important mechanical and electrical parameters. The flexibility of this automated line can accommodate an even wider range of stepper motors. A streamlined method is used to design and manufacture motors that allows custom features to be entered into the design process.

Keyboard Assembly and Test

Keyboards are manufactured for IBM typewriters, terminals, and computers. Design of keyboards consider environmental extremes, human factors, electromagnetic compatibility, and product life. Automated manufacturing, statistical process control, and thorough testing of all parts and assemblies contribute to high product quality. Keyboards are assembled with several layouts, several different key nomenclatures, and with or without electronics and covers. An important feature of this module is the application of the principles of designing products for automation. Fewer parts, layered assembly, and vertical insertion of components has led to reduced assembly time, fewer bills of material, and lower production costs.

Frame Paperfeed Transport

The subassembly module uses state-of-the-art automation to manufacture the frame/paperfeed/transport (FPT) subassembly, which is the heart of IBM typewriters and printers. A variety of automated assembly machines and robots are used for manufacture, assembly, adjustment, and testing. A precision laser telemetric system scans and checks the platen at 30 points to ensure conformance to specifications. FPT subassemblies are delivered to the final assembly module.

Final Assembly and Test

The final-assembly department is a full-scale, flexible automation center. Approximately 20 different products are assembled here. Component parts and subassemblies from the other manufacturing modules reach final assembly via 7.5 miles of conveyor systems. Controlled by computers, each of the 18 autorobotic assembly stations, 12 automatic testing stations, and 74 autosupport stations on the assembly line recognizes the individual products and tailors its manufacturing operation to the specific product. Each robotic cell automatically tests its work before the product is sent to the next station. The final assembly module can assemble any IBM product within a $26 \times 22 \times 18$-inch envelope.

IBM Lexington's plant is said to be designed to provide the major keys to manufacturing competitiveness: exceptional quality and reliability in products, manufacturing flexibility, and low production costs.

A PROCESS-FOCUSED FACTORY: R. R. DONNELLEY & SONS, WILLARD, OHIO

R. R. Donnelley & Sons is the world's largest book manufacturer. Its factory is located in Willard, Ohio, in rural north central Ohio about equidistant from Columbus, Cleveland, and Toledo. The factory has been in operation for about 35 years and benefits from being adjacent to the main line of the Baltimore & Ohio Railroad and near an abundant local work force. R. R. Donnelley contracts with publishing companies to print hardcover books, softcover books, and software documentation products. There are many domestic and foreign competitors, and the business strategy of R. R. Donnelley is to provide custom production of book products with superior product quality, on-time deliveries, competitive prices, and manufacturing flexibility.

Superior quality is achieved by many means. First, top management has created an environment in which the attitude is "close is not good enough." A separate quality control department oversees the overall quality program at the factory. Strict material specifications are adhered to on all purchased materials. Teams of employees study and find solutions to quality-related production problems throughout the production process. Extremely high quality standards are applied to products at every step in the production process, and employees are conscientious in seeing that each product adheres to the standards. Employees seem sincerely dedicated to the company's quality control program.

The factory contains over 1 million square feet of floor space and has over 1,400 employees. Toward the goals of providing on-time deliveries and competitive prices, customers' orders for books are carefully planned, produced, shipped, and controlled as single batches or jobs. For example, if The Dryden Press placed an order for 5,000 of Gaither's *Production and Operations Management* book, the entire order would ordinarily be produced as a single batch flowing from department to department through the factory. This arrangement is often referred to as a *job shop* because customers' orders are treated as jobs that flow through the factory, and jobs become the focus of production planning and control.

Because enormous variety exists among the jobs that must be produced by the factory, great manufacturing flexibility is required. This means that in any particular production department, the employees, production machinery, and materials must be flexible enough to be quickly changed from one job to another. Employee flexibility is aided by cross-training among several jobs, training in the technical aspects of jobs, and rewards for employee initiative. Production machines must be designed so that they are general-purpose machines that can be quickly changed to other jobs to accommodate the great product variety. Because the myriad of materials necessary to produce the enormous variety of jobs must be ordered in large amounts from distant suppliers that require up to three months for delivery, large quantities of materials are warehoused until needed.

The production processes at the factory are illustrated in Figure 4.18. The major production steps are: (1) receiving, (2) plate making, (3) plate proofing, (4) printing, (5) drying, (6) slitting and collating, (7) binding, and (8) shipping.

FIGURE 4.18 *Flow of Printing Jobs at R. R. Donnelley & Sons*

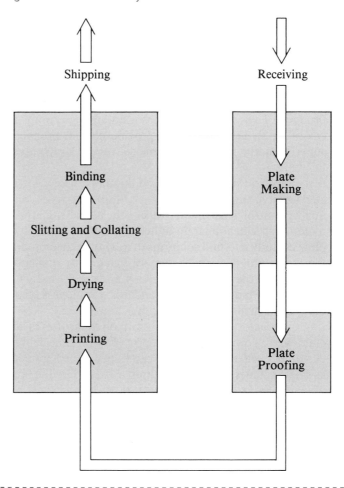

Receiving

Materials are received at the factory from suppliers that may be as near as the Ohio region or as far away as Seattle, Washington. These materials are paper stocks and inks, as well as maintenance, production, and office supplies. The material with the most weight and greatest storage needs, however, is paper, which comes in large heavy rolls. The factory uses 200 million pounds of paper each year, and it receives hundreds of different types of paper from over 25 different paper mills. Picture, if you can, the amount of warehouse space that would be needed to store such amounts of paper. Each material that is received must be checked by quality control personnel to determine if it meets the prescribed specifications and quality standards. Only after materials pass these inspections can they be placed in the warehouse to be made ready for use.

Plate Making

This operation makes the plates that are used in printing presses to print the books. These plates are produced by a photographic process in which a photographic image of an original page that is supplied by the publisher is transferred to a "plate." A plate is a sheet of metal with raised letters such that when ink is applied to the letters and pressed onto paper, the intended page of the book is transferred to the paper. The equipment used in this process is computer-controlled for better quality control. Very highly skilled labor is required in this production step, and in spite of computerization of the equipment, plate making remains labor-intensive.

Plate Proofing

This operation involves verifying that the images on the plates are exact duplications of the original pages supplied by the publisher. The original pages contain type text, line drawings, tables, photographs, mathematical equations, and all manner of material that you see in books today. Plate proofing of such material is painstakingly exacting, and microscopes are commonly used to inspect and compare the plates to the original pages. This operation is therefore also labor-intensive and requires employees who are dedicated to the highest standards of product quality.

Printing and Drying

Depending on its size, a job is routed to one of three different types of printing presses: a large press, a smaller automated press, or a sheetfed press. These presses incorporate the latest printing technology, with continuous computerized monitoring of paper stock, automated handling of rolls of paper stock, optical scanners, and computerized control of machine adjustments. Running sheets of paper through presses as wide as 10 feet at speeds of 1,500 feet per minute results in enormous production rates of printed pages. The printed paper stock is then run over a series of heated and cooled rollers until dry. The drying equipment requires a large amount of floor and overhead space. This production step, rather than labor-intensive, is very capital-intensive.

Slitting and Collating

Slitting involves cutting the sheets of printed paper stock into page-size sheets. Large shearing machines are used to slit stacks of sheets into successively smaller sheets. After slitting, pages are sorted into sequence and glued into small bundles of 16 sheets or 32 pages, which are called *signatures.* The signatures are exposed to an open flame to remove any excess scrap paper particles, and sets of signatures for each book are then gathered for binding.

Binding

Hard covers are assembled in a separate process. Back and front covers are printed on a single sheet, glued to a cardboard backing, and folded to fit. Soft covers are printed directly on the paper stock of the cover. In binding, casing-in equipment is used to wrap covers around preglued packages of signatures to form finished books.

Shipping

Finished books are placed either in boxes and then on pallets or directly on pallets. Pallets are wooden, paper, plastic, or fiberglass frames onto which products are stacked. Plastic shrink wrap is then wrapped around each pallet load to form a unitized load. Pallets of books are transported by forklift trucks from the shipping department to trucks or railroad cars for shipment to publishers' regional warehouses.

R. R. Donnelley's philosophy is to provide its customers with superior product quality, on-time deliveries, and competitive prices. The design, layout, and operation of its factory in Willard, Ohio, seem well suited to provide these distinctive competencies.

A REGIONAL DISTRIBUTION CENTER: WAL-MART STORES INC., NEW BRAUNFELS, TEXAS

Wal-Mart Stores Inc. is a regional retail discount chain operating in 24 states, with headquarters in Bentonville, Arkansas. The stores offer one-stop family shopping with a wide range of merchandise including electronics, toys, fabric and craft supplies, automotive supplies, lawn and patio equipment, sporting goods, jewelry, and shoes. Wal-Mart's stated merchandising philosophy is to offer name brand, quality merchandise at everyday low prices, not just during sales.

The first Wal-Mart store was opened in Rogers, Arkansas, in 1962 by Sam and Bud Walton. Its stock was first traded on the New York Stock Exchange in 1972. Today Wal-Mart has over 1,200 retail stores, 16 regional distribution centers, more than 200,000 employees (or *associates,* as Wal-Mart calls them), one of the largest private fleet of trucks in the United States, and annual sales of more than $20 billion.

Wal-Mart uses regional distribution centers to receive shipments of merchandise from suppliers, receive orders for merchandise from its stores, make up orders for the stores, and load and ship orders to the stores. The regional distribution center in New Braunfels, Texas, was built in 1988 and presently serves stores scattered throughout central and south Texas. After reaching its capacity, it will serve approximately 180 stores and employ about 800 associates.

It is difficult to imagine the size of this facility by reading about it in an account such as this, but consider these facts:

1. The facility has over 1 million square feet of floor space under roof. This is the rough equivalent of 23 football fields or more than 23 acres of floor space.
2. The facility has 96 dock doors for loading and unloading truck trailers.
3. The facility has 5.62 miles of conveyors for moving merchandise from incoming trucks, to and from storage, and to outgoing trucks.
4. The facility has 43.6 miles of rack width and 83,980 different address locations or rack slots within the warehouse where merchandise can be stored. The racks alone weigh 3.6 million pounds.
5. The site contains over 1,200 parking spaces for truck trailers, 110 parking spaces for trucks, and 700 parking spaces for associates.

■■■

FIGURE 4.19 Wal-Mart Regional Distribution Center

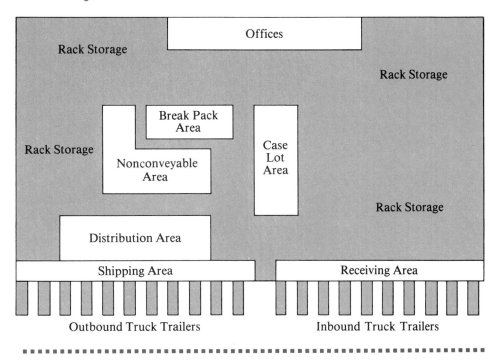

■■■

The facility is organized according to functions such as quality assurance, maintenance, traffic, distribution, loss prevention, data processing, and personnel. Quality assurance receives great emphasis at the center. Its main purpose is to make sure that the right quantity and type of merchandise has been received, that the merchandise has not been damaged in shipment, and that the right quantity and type of merchandise has been shipped to the stores. The traffic department is concerned primarily with scheduling and coordinating common-carrier trucks inbound from suppliers. The distribution department is concerned with scheduling and coordinating company-owned trucks outbound to the stores. The loss prevention department is responsible for security and safety.

Figure 4.19 illustrates the general layout of the center. The following operations of the facility will be discussed below: orders from the stores, inbound merchandise, order filling, conveyor/sort system, and outbound merchandise.

Orders from the Stores

Each Wal-Mart store has a direct computer connection with headquarters in Bentonville, Arkansas. At the end of every workday, associates at each store send in a list of merchandise orders over a computer terminal to Bentonville. The computer system at headquarters breaks down the list of orders and assigns the orders to regional distribution centers. Although most of the merchandise will be shipped from the nearest regional distribution center, certain specialty goods are stocked by only a few of the centers. A computer system at each of the regional distribution centers receives the orders by the next morning and prints the labels for the orders.

The labels play a crucial part in the operation of the center. Each package of merchandise that is to be shipped to a store must have a preprinted adhesive label attached. These labels are in bar-code form so that they can be read by optical scanning equipment and in printed form so that they can be easily read by associates. A label represents the authorization to ship the merchandise and contains all of the information relating to the order: store destination, name of merchandise, quantity of merchandise, name of supplier, and warehouse location or slot.

Inbound Merchandise

The purchasing department at the Bentonville, Arkansas, headquarters buys merchandise from suppliers on long-term contracts. The purchasing department keeps the traffic departments at the regional distribution centers informed about which supplier is to supply each type of merchandise. Almost all merchandise is made in the United States and literally comes from every region in the nation. As merchandise is shipped from regional distribution centers, inventory records are perpetually reviewed so that the traffic department will know when shipments of each type of merchandise are needed from suppliers. The traffic department then schedules shipments from suppliers to arrive before the regional distribution centers run out of each type of merchandise. Perhaps equally important, merchandise does not arrive at the distribution centers too early, thereby keeping inventory levels low and inventory investment controlled.

Order Filling

Order filling involves using the preprinted labels to locate within the warehouse each package of merchandise on a store order, attaching the label to the package, and transporting the package to the shipping area. Each label to be shipped each day is sent to one of four areas on the facility floor: case lot area, nonconveyable area, break pack area, or distribution area.

The case lot area contains merchandise that is shipped in whole-case multiples. In this area associates with rolls of labels walk between racks of merchandise and a continuously moving conveyor belt. The associates read the slot location number of the merchandise on the label, locate the slot, verify the accuracy of the quantity and type of merchandise information on the order label, pick up a case of merchandise and place it on the conveyor, and attach the self-adhesive label to the package. From there the packages are transported to the overhead conveyor/sort system.

The nonconveyable area contains merchandise that is too heavy, large, or bulky to fit on the conveyor/sort system. This merchandise — 50-pound sacks of dog food, for example — is usually received, handled, stored, and shipped in unitized loads. A unitized load is a batch of merchandise that is placed on a pallet (a 4-foot-square wooden frame) and shrink-wrapped in clear plastic. Filling orders of nonconveyable merchandise is achieved by attaching a label to the top of the unitized load and transporting the load to the shipping area with a forklift truck.

The break pack area contains merchandise that is to be shipped in less than whole-case quantities. Associates cut the tops off cases and place the cases in slot locations within racks that are adjacent to a continuously moving conveyor belt. Order-filling associates then use the labels to locate the slot, verify the information on the label, place the required quantity of merchandise on the conveyor, and attach the label to the merchandise. At the end of the conveyor, the merchandise is loaded into cases and checked by quality control. After this the packages of merchandise enter the conveyor/sort system.

The distribution area contains special merchandise that is currently receiving national promotion. For example, special merchandise to be stocked at stores for the Memorial Day holiday promotion would be found in this area. Store orders are filled from this area, and the merchandise either enters the conveyor/sort system or is moved to the shipping area with forklift trucks.

Conveyor/Sort System

The conveyor/sort system is used to transport packages from the storage areas of the warehouse, move them to the shipping area, and sort them to the appropriate loading bay. The conveyor/sort system is a network of conveyors, optical scanners, and package-diverting equipment. Packages are transported from the order-filling areas on the warehouse floor to an overhead conveyor system, which is approximately three stories high and just under the ceiling of the warehouse. Here the packages are turned so that their labels are facing upward, and they are then channeled through optical scanners. These scanners read all of the information from the bar codes on the labels, send the information to the inventory record system, and send to the package-diverting equipment information about which shipping bay should receive each package. The package-diverting equipment pushes packages off the main conveyor onto side conveyors that are bound for particular cargo bays in the shipping area.

Outbound Merchandise

Packages of merchandise exit the conveyor/sort system on apron conveyors that extend into outbound trucks. Associates scan each label with hand-held optical scanner wands to verify the information from the optical scanners of the conveyor/ sort system. Packages from the conveyor/sort system are placed by hand in the outbound trucks, and unitized loads of nonconveyable merchandise are placed in the outbound trucks with forklift trucks. The facility has the capacity of shipping to stores about 200 fully loaded trucks per day.

This regional facility, in combination with the computer information system at the stores and at the Bentonville headquarters, delivers orders to the stores no later than 48 hours after the orders have been placed. The breakdown of this 48-hour lead time is as follows:

1. Orders are transmitted from the stores to headquarters at the end of the working day.
2. Orders are assigned to regional distribution centers and labels are printed by the next morning.
3. Orders are filled, loaded into trucks, and shipped during the same day.

4. Orders are transported on company-owned trucks to the stores and arrive no later than the next day, depending on the distance between the store and the regional distribution center.

Because the stores do not have warehouses, the orders of merchandise go directly from the trucks to the shelves on the stores' display floors. This system of fast delivery of merchandise from regional distribution centers allows the stores to operate without warehouses. Also, stores can wait until merchandise on the shelves is almost gone before ordering, thereby permitting lower shelf inventories. This all translates into lower operating costs, higher productivity, and better customer service.

SUMMARY

Planning and designing production processes provides the foundation and the structure for the operations function to carry out the operations strategies. In deciding on the basic type of process design, several factors must be taken into account. Among these are: nature of product demand, degree of vertical integration, product and volume flexibility, degree of automation, level of product quality, and degree of customer contact.

There are three types of process designs: product-focused, process-focused, and cellular manufacturing. Product-focused (or line flow, continuous production) organizations are designed primarily for high-volume, standardized products. Process-focused (or intermittent production) organizations are designed primarily for low-volume, small-batch, custom products. There are hybrids of these types of designs, and new forms are emerging. For example, cellular manufacturing tends to evolve from job shop production settings by identifying families of parts with common characteristics that are produced in larger batches. A family of parts would be produced in a cell containing the machines necessary to produce the parts in that family.

The choice of processing alternative is usually based on batch size and product variety considerations, capital requirements, economic analysis, assembly charts, and process charts. Economic analysis entails the development of cost functions for the processing alternatives and then the comparison of those cost functions. Break-even analysis allows analysts to easily compare decision alternatives. The concept of operating leverage explains the relationship between the rate of profitability and production volume for each of the different processing alternatives. Financial analysis from Appendix C at the end of this book is often used in deciding between processing alternatives, because the time value of money plays a significant role in these important decisions.

REVIEW AND DISCUSSION QUESTIONS

1. Name three conditions that would cause process replanning to occur.
2. What is a *process life cycle?* Describe the typical stages as a process progresses through its life cycle.

3. Discuss the role of process design in operations strategy.

4. Describe the relationship between process design and product design.

5. What are the steps in process design? What inputs are required for process design? What are the outputs of process design?

6. Explain how these factors affect process design decisions:
   a. nature of product demand,
   b. degree of vertical integration,
   c. product/service and volume flexibility,
   d. degree of automation,
   e. level of product quality,
   f. degree of customer contact.

7. Explain why product-focused systems are sometimes called:
   a. line flow production,
   b. continuous production,
   c. assembly lines.

8. Explain the difference between:
   a. discrete unit manufacturing and process manufacturing,
   b. process-focused production and process manufacturing.

9. Explain why process-focused production is sometimes called:
   a. intermittent production,
   b. stop-and-go production,
   c. job shops.

10. What is the relationship between group technology and cellular manufacturing? What is a *family of parts?*

11. Under what conditions would a manager want to form manufacturing cells in a job shop?

12. As the number of product designs increases and as the batch sizes decrease, explain what happens to:
    a. production cost per unit,
    b. product flexibility.
    Give some reasons why this relationship exists.

13. Briefly explain how you would decide between two different process designs. What factors would you consider? What analysis tools would you use?

14. Give the important implications of the following statement: It is said that automated production systems have greater operating leverage. Define the term *operating leverage.* Explain why automated production systems tend to have higher levels of operating leverage.

15. Describe an assembly chart and a process chart. How are they different? Explain how they are used in process design.

16. What steps can be taken in designing production processes for services that would make this activity more quantifiable and more objective? Discuss the difficulties that could be encountered in following these steps.

PROBLEMS

Assembly Charts

1. Prepare an assembly chart for a flashlight with two batteries.
2. Prepare an assembly chart for a long-sleeved sports shirt with a collar and one pocket.
3. Prepare an assembly chart for a bicycle with these basic components: frame, front wheel, back wheel, brakes, power, and guidance.
4. A production analyst has prepared the following information for a new product that is to be put into production. Prepare an assembly chart for the product.

Component List for the ET90 Assembly

Component Description	*Component Code*	*Predecessor Component Code**	*Inspection Required after Component Is Installed?*
1. Motor shaft	1253	—	No
2. Internal field	1254	1253	No
3. Bearing assembly (2)	1255	1254	No
4. External field	1256	1255	No
5. Housing	1257	1256	Yes
6. Packaging	0065	1257	No

* The code of the component that must come immediately before.

5. A production analyst has prepared the following information for a new product that is to be put into production. Prepare an assembly chart for the product.

Component List for the A45 Horn

Component Description	*Component Code*	*Predecessor(s) Component Code(s)**	*Inspection Required after Component Is Installed?*
1. Left base housing	051	—	No
2. Wiring harness	064	051	No
3. Transducer	004	—	No
4. Diode	007	—	No
5. Power booster	015	004, 007	No
6. Ceramic receptacle	118	015, 064	No
7. Fastening clips (4)	001	118	No
8. Right base housing	052	001	Yes
9. Packaging	359	052	No

* The code or codes of the component or components that must come immediately before.

Process Charts

6. Prepare a process chart for replacing a flat automobile tire with a spare tire from the trunk.

7. Prepare a process chart for enrolling at your college or university.

8. Prepare a process chart for making a bed (use sheets and a pillowcase).

9. a. Prepare a process chart from the information below.
   b. Explain how such a process chart could be used.

Assembly Tasks for the ET90 Assembly

Task Description	Distance Moved	Worker Time
1. Get motor shaft and hold	13 in.	.04 min.
2. Slip internal field over shaft	5	.10
3. Install first bearing assembly	6	.12
4. Install second bearing assembly	6	.12
5. Rotate unit and install external field	12	.13
6. Place unit in housing and snap closed	8	.08
7. Position unit, connect to circuit test	10	.10
8. Wait for circuit test, stop if unit fails and sound alarm	—	.30
9. Place unit in package, close package, place in chute	23	.11

10. a. Prepare a process chart from the information below.
    b. Explain how such a process chart could be used.

Assembly Tasks for the A45 Horn

Task Description	Distance Moved	Robot Time
1. Get left base housing and hold	16 in.	.04 min.
2. Get wiring harness and snap into housing	12	.10
3. Get transducer, rotate 20 degrees	10	.06
4. Get diode, place in Position A	12	.09
5. Get power booster, prepare preassembly by installing transducer and diode	14	.15
6. Get ceramic receptacle, assemble with preassembly and wiring harness	11	.15
7. Insert 4 fastening clips in left base housing	9	.20
8. Get right base housing, fasten to left base housing	12	.12
9. Rotate unit 36 degrees, push into circuitry test machine, stop if unit fails and sound alarm	16	.30
10. Get packaging material, place unit in package, close package, place in chute	22	.18

Economic Analysis

⁴ 11. Oklahoma Instruments (OI) makes hand-held electronic calculators. A new model has been developed that requires a new design of display units. On the basis of the following estimates, OI is trying to decide if it should buy the units from a supplier, produce the units while using a manual assembly system, or produce the units while using an automated assembly system.

	Buy	Produce (Manual Assembly)	Produce (Automated Assembly)
Annual volume (display units)	100,000	100,000	100,000
Fixed cost per year	—	$300,000	$500,000
Variable cost per unit	$10	$8	$7

a. What should OI do—buy, produce with manual assembly, or produce with automated assembly?
b. At what volume would OI be indifferent between buying the units and producing them with manual assembly?
c. At what volume would OI be indifferent between manual and automated assembly?
d. What other considerations would be important in this decision?

✗ 12. The Beautiful Dreamer Mattress Company buys its spring foundation assemblies (SFAs) from the Springy Company. The present contract between the two companies requires the supply of SFAs on this basis:

Year	Volume (Units)	Price/Unit	Tooling Charges
1	100,000	$35.00	$10,000
2	200,000	37.50	20,000
3	250,000	39.50	30,000
4	350,000	42.00	35,000
5	400,000	45.00	50,000

Springy has informed Beautiful Dreamer that it has just filed for bankruptcy and that it cannot honor its previous supply agreements past the first year. Beautiful Dreamer's process engineers have designed two in-house alternative production process plans with these costs:

	Robotry Process			Conventional Process		
Year	First Cost	Tooling Charges	Cost/ Unit	First Cost	Tooling Charges	Cost/ Unit
2	$5,000,000	$20,000	$22.50	$2,000,000	$30,000	$27.50
3		30,000	25.00		40,000	32.00
4		35,000	27.50		45,000	36.00
5		50,000	30.00		60,000	42.00

Assuming that the volume of SFAs will be the same as projected in the Springy contract, use graphs and cost analysis to determine:

a. What should Beautiful Dreamer do now — install the robotry or the conventional process design? Why?

b. During what years would the robotry process begin to show a cost advantage over Springy and the conventional process design?

c. If Beautiful Dreamer follows your recommendation in Part *a*, how much money will be saved over that which would have been paid to Springy over the four-year period?

13. Southwestern University currently has 950 students in its MBA program. The present program is a lockstep approach that its students refer to as the "assembly line." In this system students "flow" through the program, each taking the same courses as every other student and in the same sequence. Martha Alief, the dean, estimates that the annual fixed cost of the MBA program is $900,000 and the variable cost per student per year is $1,000. Ms. Alief is considering a faculty proposal for modifying the MBA program to improve its academic standards. The suggested changes would allow students flexibility in selecting courses and the sequence in which the courses are taken. Under the new program, Ms. Alief estimates that the annual fixed cost would be only $500,000, but the variable cost per student per year would be $1,600.

If the school receives budget allocations of $2,000 per MBA student:

a. What is the present surplus or deficit of the MBA program?

b. What enrollment is required in the present program in order to balance the budget?

c. How many students would need to be in the proposed MBA program for Ms. Alief to be indifferent between the two programs if only budget factors are considered?

d. How many MBA students would be required in the proposed program in order for its total annual cost to be the same as in the present program?

14. Mary Johnson, a staff analyst at the corporate headquarters of Computer Products Corporation (CPC), is preparing for a presentation that her group will soon make to CPC's board of directors. The group is presenting an analysis and background report on a proposal that will mark a major change in the way that CPC bills its small-business customers for maintaining their CPC equipment. The proposal gives the customers the option of paying a flat monthly rate of $425 for a full-service CPC maintenance contract. Mary has determined from CPC's service records that without the flat rate, customers' monthly cost of service is normally distributed with a mean of $300 and a standard deviation of $50.

a. What is the probability that customers will pay more than the flat rate?

b. What is the expected monthly profit per customer for CPC from the proposal?

15. Grey's Manufacturing produces machined parts for the shipbuilding industry in Boston. Its factory is now a conventional process-focused job shop with departments built around the kinds of machining needed by the parts. After an engineering study, Grey's management is considering a proposal to take one family of parts from the job shop and place it in a new manufacturing cell. The demand for this family of parts

remains rather stable from year to year, and the orders for these parts are in moderate-sized batches. The cost of operating the job shop is expected to remain unchanged. The decision will hinge on whether the parts in the family can be manufactured more economically in a job shop or in a cellular manufacturing setting.

	Present Job Shop	Proposed Cellular Manufacturing
Annual production volume (parts in family)	80,000	80,000
Annual fixed costs	$25,000	$220,000
Variable cost per part	$10.40	$7.80

a. Should the manufacturing cell proposal be accepted?
b. What would the annual cost savings be if the proposal is accepted?
c. At what volume of parts would Grey's management be indifferent toward the proposal?
d. What other considerations would affect the decision to accept the proposal?

CASES

COMPUTER PRODUCTS CORPORATION

Abe Landers is a production planner at the Austin, Texas, plant of Computer Products Corporation (CPC). He has recently been studying for his American Production and Inventory Control Society (APICS) certification examination. One section of the examination requires that the candidates taking the test be familiar with assembly charts and process charts. Abe has developed two examples from the CPC plant to illustrate the use of these production-planning tools. He has gathered the following information about a microprocessor assembly that is used in one of CPC's floppy disk units:

Component List for the z44 Microprocessor Assembly

Component Description	Component Code	Predecessor Component Code	Inspection Required after Component Is Installed?
1. Printed circuit board	pc551	—	No
2. Transistor set	t6798	pc551	Yes
3. ROM chip set	i8088	t6798	Yes
4. RAM chip set	j88000	i8088	Yes
5. Packaging	p65	j88000	No

Assembly Tasks for the z44 Microprocessor Assembly

Task Description	Distance Moved	Worker Time
1. Get pc board and place in jig	14 in.	.05 min.
2. Insert transistor set in board	12	5.69
3. Seat, crimp, and trim	—	1.55
4. Inspect assembly	—	2.55
5. Insert ROM set	22	3.50
6. Seat, crimp, and trim	—	1.25
7. Inspect assembly	—	2.50
8. Insert RAM set	20	2.75
9. Seat, crimp, and trim	—	1.25
10. Inspect assembly	—	2.25
11. Place assembly into flow solder machine and retrieve	156	6.35
12. Inspect assembly	—	2.00
13. Place assembly in packaging for transport, and place in bin	35	.50

Assignment

1. Prepare an assembly chart for the z44 microprocessor assembly.

2. Prepare a process chart for the z44 microprocessor assembly.

3. To what uses could these charts be applied in process design?

PHELPS PETROLEUM REFINING

Phelps Petroleum Refining Corporation converts crude oil to refined petroleum products. The key process in its refinery is the cracking unit. This process heats the crude, drives off the refined products at different temperatures, and collects and cools the refined products. The present cracking unit is about 20 years old, is relatively inefficient, and costs much to maintain each year. Two competing proposals are being considered for its replacement.

The first proposal is for a low-cost *economy cracking unit.* This unit will produce refined products at 94 percent yield; in other words, 94 percent of the crude actually ends up in refined products and 6 percent is lost. The unit has semiautomatic controls and requires some degree of worker monitoring. The unit must be shut down, flushed out, and its controls calibrated before it can be changed to crudes with vastly different characteristics; thus the amount of refined products that can be produced each year is reduced. The type of construction used in the unit will require a moderate amount of annual maintenance.

The second proposal is for a high-cost *quality cracking unit* with 98 percent yield. The unit has fully automatic controls and requires only a small amount of worker monitoring. Because of its control system and type of holding vessels, the unit can easily be shifted to crudes with other characteristics. The construction used in manufacturing the unit minimizes the amount of annual maintenance.

These estimates have been developed for the two units:

	Economy Cracking Unit	Quality Cracking Unit
Annual volume (millions of gallons)		
First year	50	60
Second year	60	70
Later years	70	80
Annual fixed costs	$140,000	$1,650,000
Average variable cost per gallon	$.372	$.360

Assignment

1. If the sales price of the refined products averages $.425 per gallon at the cracking unit, which process would be preferred in each year?

2. At what annual volume of refined products would Phelps be indifferent between the two processes if the only consideration were economic analysis?

3. What other considerations would affect this decision?

SELECTED BIBLIOGRAPHY

Abernathy, William J. "Production Process Structure and Technological Change." *Decision Sciences* 7, no. 4(October 1976):607–619.

APICS Dictionary, 6th ed., prepared by Thomas F. Wallace and John R. Dougherty. Falls Church, VA: American Production and Inventory Control, 1987, 6.

Brigham, Eugene F. *Fundamentals of Financial Management.* Hinsdale, IL: Dryden Press, 1986, 496.

Buffa, Elwood. *Meeting the Competitive Challenge.* Homewood, IL: Richard D. Irwin, 1984.

Buzzell, Robert O. "Is Vertical Integration Profitable?" *Harvard Business Review* 61(January–February 1983):92–102.

Dasai, Dilip T. "How One Firm Put a Group Technology Parts Classification System into Operation." *Industrial Engineering* (November 1981):77–86.

Groover, Mikell P. *Automation, Production Systems, and Computer Integrated Manufacturing.* Englewood Cliffs, NJ: Prentice-Hall, 1987.

Hayes, Robert H., and William J. Abernathy. "Managing Our Way to Economic Decline." *Harvard Business Review* 58(July–August 1980):67–77.

Hayes, Robert H., and Steven C. Wheelwright. "Link Manufacturing Process and Product Life Cycles." *Harvard Business Review* 57(January–February 1979):133–140.

Hyer, N. L., and U. Wemmerlov. "Group Technology and Productivity." *Harvard Business Review* 62(July–August 1984):140–149.

Kantrow, Alan M. "The Strategy–Technology Connection." *Harvard Business Review* 58(July–August 1980):6–21.

Kumpe, Ted, and Piet T. Bolwijn. "Manufacturing: The New Case for Vertical Integration." *Harvard Business Review* 66(March–April 1988):75–81.

Levitt, T. "The Industrialization of Services." *Harvard Business Review* 54(1976):41–52.

Levitt, Theodore. "Production Line Approach to Service." *Harvard Business Review* 50(September–October 1972):41–52.

Mitrofanov, S. P. *Scientific Principles of Group Technology* (1958), translated by E. Harris. National Lending Library for Science and Technology, England, 1966.

Peters, Thomas J., and Robert H. Waterman, Jr. *In Search of Excellence.* New York: Harper & Row, 1982.

Sasser, W. Earl, R. Paul Olsen, and D. Daryle Wyckoff. *Management of Service Operations: Text, Cases, and Readings.* Boston: Allyn & Bacon, 1978.

Skinner, Wickham. *Manufacturing in the Corporate Strategy.* New York: Wiley, 1978.

5

PRODUCTION TECHNOLOGY
SELECTION AND MANAGEMENT

FLEXIBLE AUTOMATION WAVE OF THE FUTURE

In building No. 3 of General Electric Company's sprawling appliance works in Louisville, Kentucky, technology breeds dishwashers like rabbits. The automated assembly line is a blur of robots, machine tools, and a conveyor system that snakes its way through the building, toting high-tech plastic washer tubs that carry a 10-year warranty. GE is proud of this $40 million facility. It paid for itself in 3 years and has helped the firm gain 10 points in the market share for dishwashers, from 30 to 40 percent.

The irony is that technology experts do not consider this automated assembly line to be the wave of the future in American manufacturing. The reason: It's capable of making only dishwashers. The coming thing in manufacturing is the all-purpose factory, one that is linked together by computer and can produce several products on the same assembly line without costly or elaborate retooling. Flexible and efficient, it could make computers or toaster ovens of different sizes and shapes or of different parts. The ultimate flexible factory could be programmed to roll out many different types of products made on the same day to customer order, eliminating expensive inventory.

That day is not here yet, but scientists have made such dramatic strides in flexible manufacturing that some factories are capable of making a "family" of products or parts on the same line. It's an exciting concept, one that could prove the salvation of U.S. industry as the implementation becomes better developed.[1]

---

[1] William R. Neikirk, *Chicago Tribune*, "Factories Wrestling With Robots," *Bryan-College Station Eagle*, July 19, 1987, 1-F.

The previous article suggests that today is truly an exciting time to study operations management. We are increasingly optimistic about the economic future of the United States as we read such accounts of the use of leading-edge technology on the shop floors of our factories and in our service operations. Although it is on the shop floors that the ultimate battle for competitiveness must be waged, it is all too easy to neglect the shop floor production processes in today's heady environment of multi-billion dollar mergers, multimillion dollar advertising programs, international trade agreements, and huge shifts in currency exchange rates. Nevertheless, it is toward the shop floor that we look in this chapter as we explore the important issues of how to select and manage production technologies so that operations functions can serve as competitive weapons in achieving corporate objectives.

Automation has traditionally meant the replacement of human effort with machine effort. It has also meant a process of systematically replacing people with machines, a process that conjures up feelings of anxiety in workers and of hostility in labor unions. Even though workers are still concerned about their job security today, more and more we see cooperative efforts between management and labor unions to study the use of automation as a way of meeting an even greater immediate threat to job security — foreign competition. Also, as we shall discuss in this chapter, automation has come to mean far more than simply the replacement of human effort with machine effort.

PROLIFERATION OF AUTOMATION

That the field of industrial automation is mushrooming is evidenced by the number of automation projects recently undertaken by domestic and foreign manufacturers. Industry Snapshot 5.1 illustrates the extent of this development in the United States.

The United States is nevertheless far from the world leader in automation today. Japanese manufacturers of automated production systems are setting the pace and are probably destined to remain in the lead for many years to come. U.S. manufacturers were late in recognizing the full benefits to be realized through automation. At first, they seemed to think that the chief advantage of automation was labor cost savings. Thus U.S. firms tended to move production offshore to Japan, Taiwan, Korea, and other countries with lower labor rates, rather than investing in automation projects in their own factories. Chasing lower labor rates abroad resulted in transferring old technology abroad, getting locked into unfavorable currency exchange rates, and a failure to advance their own production technology. For a time, therefore, U.S. manufacturers grasped short-term labor savings but sacrificed the opportunity to obtain the many long-range performance advantages provided by automation. Today, automation projects are initiated not just for labor cost savings, but also for improved product quality, fast production and delivery of products, and, if flexible automation is used, increased product flexibility.

In this chapter we shall discuss types of automated machines, automated production systems, factories of the future, automation in services, and several other automation issues.

INDUSTRY SNAPSHOT 5.1

U.S. Manufacturers Turning to Automation

	1985	1986	1987	1988	1989	1990
U.S. robots (000)	18.7	26.4	37.0	52.2	72.8	101.0

In the next 5 years, it is projected that more than 80,000 new robots will be installed in U.S. factories, bringing the total in use to more than 100,000 by 1990.[2]

Auto manufacturers account for more than 50 percent of robotic systems working today, using the machines in painting, soldering, welding, and moving components from one location to another. The electronics industries use robots to assemble circuit boards and electronic components.[3] But automation is not limited to the big guys anymore. Increasingly, small manufacturers are installing automated machinery. Automation helps these small companies to respond to pressures from their large customers to improve product quality and to produce and deliver products faster.[4]

The spending on shop-floor automation is projected to be $32.3 billion by 1990.[5]

Where the Investments in Shop-Floor Automation Are Going (Millions of Dollars)

	1980	1985	1990*
Factory computers and software	$ 935	$2,861	$6,500
Materials-handling systems	2,000	4,500	9,000
Machine tools and controls	3,000	4,800	7,000
Programmable controllers	50	550	3,000
Robots and sensors	68	664	2,800
Automated test equipment	800	2,000	4,000
Total spending on CAM**	$6,853	$15,375	$32,300

* Estimates
** Computer-aided manufacturing
Source: Data from Dataquest Inc.

[2] Ibid.

[3] Kathie Price, "Robotics No Longer an 'Emerging' Field," *Arizona Republic*, Jan. 31, 1986, F-1,2.

[4] Russell Mitchell, "Automation Is Not Just for the Big Guys Anymore," *Business Week*, Jan. 27, 1986, 98.

[5] Richard Brandt and James B. Treece, "High Tech to the Rescue." Reprinted from June 16, 1986 issue of *Business Week* by special permission, Copyright © 1986 by McGraw-Hill, Inc.

■ ■

TABLE 5.1   *Types of Automated Machines*

Types of Machines	*Description*	*Examples*
1. Machine attachments	Machines that replace human effort with machine effort and typically perform from one to a few simple operations	Magazine feed attachments, quick centering and grasping devices for lathes, strip feeders for stamping machines, vibrating hoppers with scales that drop charges of chemicals into waiting containers
2. Numerically controlled (N/C) machines	Machines with control systems that read instructions and translate them into machine operations	Lathes, boring mills, tire-building machines, curing machines, weaving machines
3. Robots	General-purpose, reprogrammable, multifunction manipulators that possess some humanlike physiological characteristics	Machines that weld, paint, assemble, inspect for quality, grasp, transport, and store
4. Automated quality control inspection	Automated machines that perform part or all of the inspection process	Electronic circuit checks, computer-driven function checks, weighing robots, flexible inspection systems
5. Automatic identification systems (AIS)	Technologies used in automatic acquisition of product data for entry into a computer	Bar-coding systems, inventory counting, data entry for shop floor control, systems for adjusting settings of production machines
6. Automated process controls	Computer systems that receive data on the production process and send adjustments to process settings	Control systems for rolling mills in tire manufacturing, calenders in plastic film processing, cracking units in oil refineries

■ ■

TYPES OF AUTOMATED MACHINES

The enormous growth in the field of industrial automation has brought a myriad of automated machines with diverse features. These types of automated machines are particularly noteworthy: machine attachments, numerically controlled (N/C) ma-

One of the first demonstrations of a numerically controlled machine tool took place at MIT in the early 1950s. It was a Cincinnati vertical milling machine that had been modified at the servomechanism laboratory of MIT to operate from a punched-tape input. At the time, it was machining a wing-root fitting for a B47. The fitting was machined from a solid block of magnesium. The finished block was so complex that it weighed only 10 percent of the original block. The operator simply pushed a button to start the cycle. The machine then performed the rough-ing-cut cycle by operating in three planes simultaneously. When the cycle was completed, a bell rang to attract the attention of the operator. The operator then brushed some chips away and pressed the button for the finishing-cut cycle, which the machine quickly completed. The only operations the operator performed were to place the part in the machine, start it, brush away some chips, and remove the finished part. The operator, incidentally, was a law student from Harvard. This was the first machine tool he had ever operated.[6]

[6] H. B. Maynard, *Industrial Engineering Handbook* (New York: McGraw-Hill, 1963), 1/101.

chines, robots, automated quality control inspection, automatic identification systems (AIS), and automated process controls. Table 5.1 describes each of these types and gives examples of each type.

MACHINE ATTACHMENTS

Machine attachments are usually relatively inexpensive add-ons to machines that reduce the amount of human effort and time required to perform an operation. These appendages represent the oldest technology in automation and are commonly found in all production systems.

NUMERICALLY CONTROLLED (N/C) MACHINES

Numerically controlled (N/C) machines were the heroes among automatic machines in the 1950–1980 period as a broad range of applications were developed for this important technological achievement. These machines are preprogrammed through magnetic tape or microcomputers to perform a cycle of operations repeatedly. The machines have a control system that reads the instructions and then translates them into machine operations. Machine settings are achieved by the control system rather than by human beings. Industry Snapshot 5.2 describes an early experiment with N/C machines.

Figure 5.1 illustrates the evolution of N/C machines. N/C machines are important automated machines in their own right. When their programs are efficiently

FIGURE 5.1   *Evolution of Numerically Controlled Machines*

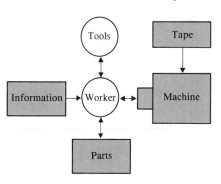 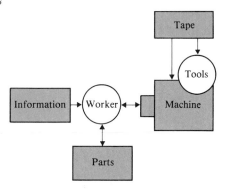

1. Numerically controlled machine tool developed at the Massachusetts Institute of Technology relieved the operator of the job of interpreting a blueprint in selecting machine settings. Machine motion is controlled by instructions on a punched tape. Operator must still select tools and load and unload the machine.

2. Automatic tool changing was the next step in raising the productivity of general-purpose machine tools. In this system the punched tape contains not only machine-guidance instructions but also information for selecting the right tool from a bank of from 20 to 100 tools. Tool-changing time can be as little as two seconds.

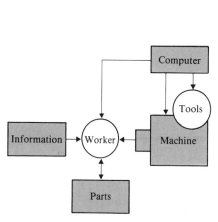 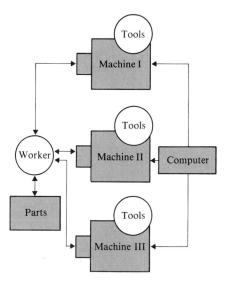

3. Computer numerical control transferred information storage from punched tape to the more capacious and flexible memory of a computer. This change not only made editing and altering programs easier but also made a computer available for a variety of other tasks, such as logging the time each tool is in use.

4. Direct numerical control places a battery of machines under the control of a single computer. Machines can be of different types and programmed to carry out different tasks. Such systems may or may not be provided with automatic tool-changing capabilities.

Source: Adapted with permission from "Computer-Managed Parts Manufacture," by Nathan H. Cook, *SCIENTIFIC AMERICAN,* February 1975, 21–29. Copyright © 1975 by *SCIENTIFIC AMERICAN, Inc.* All rights reserved.

produced and when their tools are effectively designed, they have great flexibility in being changed to other products and are therefore used extensively in process-focused job shops. Also, numerically controlled machines represent an important evolutionary stage in the advance toward the ultimate in automated machines — robots.

ROBOTS

Robotry is a fast-developing field in which humanlike machines perform production tasks. The Robotic Institute of America defines a robot as follows: *An industrial robot is a reprogrammable, multifunctional manipulator designed to move materials, parts, tools, or specialized devices through variable programmed motions for the performance of a variety of tasks.* The brain of these machines is a microcomputer that when programmed guides the machine through its predetermined operations. As the prices of robots fall with the increase in their numbers, these devices are sure to become as common in this country as they are now in Japan, Sweden, and other highly industrialized countries.

About 200 Japanese companies are now manufacturing industrial robots. Such U.S. firms as Cincinnati Milacron, Unimation Division of Condec Corporation, Prab Robots, Mobot Corporation, and Cross & Trecker are part of a group of robot manufacturers in the United States that numbered only about 75 in the early 1980s. But, according to the Robotic Institute of America, that number is expected to increase rapidly in the future. An interesting trend seems to have emerged; Japanese manufacturers use a far greater number of robots, but U.S. manufacturers are using more sophisticated and more costly robotic systems.

The variety of robots available today from suppliers is impressive. And the kinds of things that robots can do are truly amazing. Plates 1, 2, and 3 on the insert following page 198 illustrate three rather common robotic applications in manufacturing. Such robots can move their arms in vertical, radial, and horizontal axes and hold tools such as spot-welding guns, arc-welding tools, spray-painting guns, rotating spindles for metal-cutting machines, and assembly tools such as screwdrivers, heating torches, and water-jet cutting tools.

Robots have grippers at the end of their arms that are either vacuum, magnetized, or adhesive devices. Robots also have sensors that allow the grippers and arms to be positioned at precise locations as they perform their work. The common types of sensors are:

1. *Tactile sensors* are of two kinds: *touch* and *force.* Touch sensors indicate whether contact has been made. Force sensors indicate the magnitude of the force of the contact made with the object.
2. *Proximity sensors* indicate when an object is close to the sensor.
3. *Machine vision and optical sensors:* machine vision sensors are used for inspection, parts identification, guidance, and other uses; optical sensors are used to detect the presence or absence of objects.

Robots can operate in environments that are hostile to humans. Heat, noise, dust, skin irritants, darkness, and other conditions pose no threat to robots. Also, in many applications, robots can produce products of a quality higher than is possible with human beings because robots are more predictable and perform the same operations precisely and repeatedly without fatigue.

Increasingly, robots can be easily programmed to perform other tasks. Some of them can even be reprogrammed by simply attaching a stylus between the robot's arm and an experienced operator's arm. More typically, however, a program is stored on a diskette, magnetic card, or another magnetic storage medium. This arrangement allows the robot to be reprogrammed by simply inserting the diskette or card into a slot and returning the robot to the "run mode." This ability to be easily programmed and reprogrammed allows great flexibility in switching to other products and tasks. Robots are the basic building blocks for the automated production systems that we shall discuss later.

AUTOMATED QUALITY CONTROL INSPECTION

Automated quality control inspection systems are machines that have been integrated into the inspection of products for quality control purposes. These systems perform a wide range of tests and inspections and are found in many industries. They can be used to take physical dimensions of parts, compare the measurements to standards, and determine whether the parts meet quality specifications. Similarly, these machines can be used to check the performance of electronic circuits. For example, in the computer industry, computers are checked by software that tests every function that the computers must perform. Plate 4 of the insert illustrates the use of automatic quality control inspection systems in automobile manufacturing.

As we shall discuss further in Chapter 15, Total Quality Control, as quality control inspections are performed increasingly by automated machines, 100 percent inspection is becoming economically feasible for many products. This trend should lead to improved product quality and reduced quality control inspection costs.

AUTOMATIC IDENTIFICATION SYSTEMS (AIS)

Automatic identification systems (AIS) use bar codes, radio frequencies, magnetic stripes, optical character recognition, and machine vision to sense and input data into computers. Data are read from products, documents, parts, and containers without the need for workers to read or interpret the data. A good example of these systems is in checkout counters at grocery stores. The clerk passes the bar code on an item across the scanner. The system reads the identification number from the bar code on the item, accesses a computer data base and sends the price of the item to the cash register, describes the item to the customer through a speaker, and inputs the item identification number to the inventory system for the purpose of adjusting inventory counts.

AIS are becoming more commonplace in warehouses, shop floors of factories, retailing and wholesaling, and a variety of other applications. While the cost of the AIS hardware is not high, the cost of developing computer software and computer data bases is high, and such software is needed to make AIS effective.

AUTOMATED PROCESS CONTROLS

Automated process controls use sensors to obtain measures of the performance of industrial processes, they compare these measures to standards within stored computer software programs, and when the performance varies significantly from standards, they send signals that change the settings of the processes. Such systems have been in use for many years in the chemical-processing, petroleum-refining, and paper industries.

One example of automated process controls was recently observed in the paper industry. A large calender presses wood pulp between rolls to form a continuous sheet of paper. A large optical scanner is mounted above the paper sheet to monitor paper thickness and density. The readings from the optical scanner are fed into an expert system of a computer, which is a rule-based logical algorithm. This expert system decides whether the paper thickness and density are within tolerances. If they are not, the system decides what changes should be made and sends new machine settings to the calender machine, thus altering the paper thickness and density.

With the increasing use of computer-aided design and computer-aided manufacturing (CAD/CAM) systems, automated process controls have become important in other industries as well. Even in discrete-unit manufacturing, the settings of individual machines and groups of machines can now be sensed and changed as necessary to provide products of uniform dimensions and other characteristics.

As with other automated machinery, when automated process controls are installed, some flexibility is lost until software can be developed to accommodate different product characteristics. Also, although the initial cost of the hardware of these systems may not be very high, the cost of developing the supporting software and integrating the system with the remainder of the production system can be very costly. Nevertheless, the product quality necessary to support the business strategy may make such costs acceptable.

The automated machines described in this section are impressive, but the ultimate benefits from automation may not be achieved until the individual machines are integrated into automated production systems.

AUTOMATED PRODUCTION SYSTEMS

As the technology of automation has become more sophisticated, the focus has shifted away from individual machines and toward a broader concept. Today, whole systems of automated machines linked together for broader purposes are becoming more common. We shall discuss four general categories of these systems: automated flow lines, automated assembly systems, flexible manufacturing systems (FMS), and automated storage and retrieval systems (ASRS).

AUTOMATED FLOW LINES

An *automated flow line* includes several automated machines that are linked together by automated parts transfer and handling machines. The individual machines on the line use automated raw material feeders and automatically carry out their operations without the need for human attendance. As each machine completes its operations, partially completed parts are automatically transferred to the next machine on the line in a fixed sequence until the work of the line is finished. These systems are ordinarily used to produce an entire major component, for example, rear axle housings for trucks. They are common in the automobile industry. Plates 5 and 6 of the insert illustrate automated flow lines.

These systems are often referred to as *fixed automation* or *hard automation,* which means that the flow lines are designed to produce one type of component or product. Because of the very high initial investment required and the difficulty of changing over to other products, these systems are used when product demand is high, stable, and extending well into the future. If these conditions are met, the production cost per unit is very low. But because of shortened product life cycles and shifts in production technology, the popularity of fixed automation may be declining. Production systems are increasingly favoring production equipment that provides greater product flexibility. We shall discuss this trend later in this section when we discuss flexible manufacturing systems.

AUTOMATED ASSEMBLY SYSTEMS

An *automated assembly system* is a system of automated assembly machines that are linked together by automated materials-handling equipment. Materials are automatically fed to each machine, which is ordinarily some type of robot such as a robotic welder or a component insertion unit, which joins one or more materials, parts, or assemblies. Then the partially completed work is automatically transferred to the next assembly machine. This process is repeated until the whole assembly is completed. The purpose of these systems is to produce major assemblies or even completed products. Plate 7 illustrates such an automated assembly system, and Industry Snapshot 5.3 discusses the operation of one of Allen-Bradley's systems.

For an automated assembly system to be successful, major product design modifications are necessary. The product design and assembly methods appropriate for assembly by human hands cannot be directly applied to an automated assembly system because the capabilities of human beings cannot be duplicated by robots. For example, a worker can use a screw, lock washer, and nut to fasten two parts together, but in automated assembly new fastening procedures and modified product designs are necessary.

Principles such as the following are applied when redesigning products for automated assembly:

1. *Reduce the amount of assembly required.* For example, use one plastic molded part instead of two sheet metal parts that must be fastened together.
2. *Reduce the number of fasteners required.* For example, design parts that snap together or can be welded together rather than being fastened together by screws, nuts, and bolts.
3. *Design components to be automatically delivered and positioned.* This means designing parts so that they can be fed and oriented for delivery from parts

INDUSTRY SNAPSHOT 5.3

A Breakthrough in Automating the Assembly Line

It is 7:30 a.m. on the eighth floor of an 80-year-old Allen-Bradley Inc. building on Milwaukee's South Side. Two-and-a-half hours ago, an IBM mainframe computer at the company's headquarters relayed yesterday's orders to a master scheduling computer. Now, at the scheduling computer's command, what may be the world's most advanced assembly line comes to life with pneumatic sighs and birdlike whistles. Lights flash. Without human intervention, plastic casings the size of pocket transistor radios start marching through 26 complex automated assembly stations.

Bar code labels, computer-printed on the spot and pasted on each plastic cas-ing by a mechanical arm, tell each station which of the nearly 200 different parts to install in what combination. As the casings move along a conveyor belt, tiny mechanical fingers insert springs, another mechanical arm places covers over the casings, and automatic screwdrivers tighten the screws. At the end of the line a laser printer zaps detailed product information onto the side of each finished plastic box. The boxes are then packaged, sorted into customer orders, and shunted into chutes ready for shipment—all automatically.[7]

---

[7] Alicia Hills Moore, "A Breakthrough in Automating the Assembly Line," *FORTUNE,* May 26, 1986, 64.

hoppers, slotted chutes, vibratory bowls, and other continuous part-feeding mechanisms.

4. *Design products for layered assembly and vertical insertion of parts.* Products generally should be assembled from a base upward in layers to the top of the product. Parts should be designed so that they can be inserted vertically into the assembly.

5. *Design parts so that they are self-aligning.* Parts should have features like shoulders or protrusions that slide into matching features on adjacent parts that automatically position and align the parts as they are inserted into assemblies.

6. *Design products into major modules for production.* An automated assembly system would then be used to assemble each module. By breaking the assembly of the whole product into several assembly modules, downtime of the system is reduced.

7. *Increase the quality of components.* Components of high quality avoid jams in the feeding and assembly mechanisms.[8]

---

[8] Mikell P. Groover, *Automation, Production Systems, and Computer Integrated Manufacturing,* Englewood Cliffs, NJ: Prentice-Hall, 171.

FIGURE 5.2   A Flexible Manufacturing System

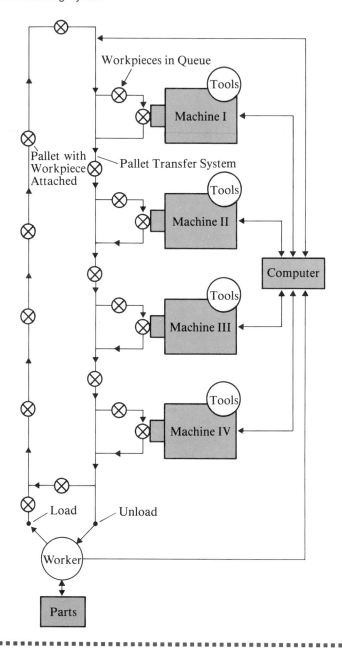

PLATE 1

LOADING/UNLOADING ROBOT

This GMF Robotics M1-A material-handling robot is performing a load/unload application on a diecasting machine. The robot unloads an automobile component, passes it through part intact sensors, a water spray booth, and then into a trim press where the flash is subsequently removed.

Source: Courtesy of GMFanuc Robotics Corporation.

PLATE 2

WELDING ROBOTS

These robotic welders work along an automobile assembly line. The chain
continuously moves bodies along the assembly line as each robot welds a distinct
pattern of fusion welds on a section of each body. Robotic welding is the
predominant method of attaching body parts in automobile manufacturing.

Source: Courtesy of Cincinnati Milacron Industrial Robot Division.

PLATE 3

PAINTING ROBOTS

Changes in the painting process contribute to product-quality improvement and an enhanced quality of work life in the production of today's automobiles. Here, robot painters go to work with a flourish in the main color booth. The body will pass nine pairs of robot painters teamed with other robot devices that open and close doors and paint inside surfaces.

Source: Courtesy General Motors Corporation.

PLATE 4

AUTOMATED QUALITY CONTROL INSPECTION

Computers are used extensively in quality control. Here, instruments are connected
to a computer for a complete check of all functions before the instrument panel
is sent by overhead conveyor to the point of installation.

Source: Courtesy General Motors Corporation.

PLATE 5

AUTOMATED FLOW LINE

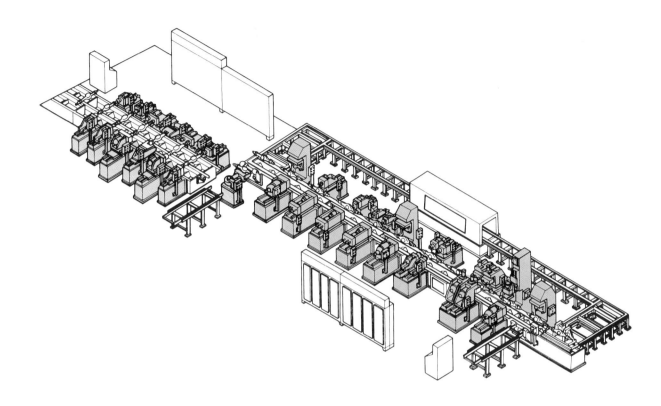

This drawing of a 20-station flow line system for machining truck rear axle housings consists of two sections: a 7-station free transfer section (green) and a 12-station palletized section (red). The station between the two sections (blue) reorients the workparts. Note the return loop for bringing pallets back to the starting point.

PLATE 6

AUTOMATED FLOW LINE

This automated flow line assembles electrical switches for toasters. Parts are moved among individual work stations that assemble, join, and test the switch assemblies.

Source: Courtesy Bodine Corporation.

PLATE 7

AUTOMATED ASSEMBLY SYSTEM

Shown here is a Bodine modular assembly system for automatically assembling videocassettes. The system operates in a semiclean room environment, and is integrated with automatic tape winders and parts conveyors.

Source: Courtesy Bodine Corporation.

PLATE 8

AUTOMATED STORAGE AND RETRIEVAL SYSTEMS

(a) Motorized robots combined with forklifts facilitate the Just-in-Time delivery of inventory as needed. The AGVS (automated guided vehicle system) directs the vehicles through the plant's expanse, following some 19,000 feet of wire buried in the floors. A computer sends signals through the wire to control automatic loading and unloading of parts. Sensors automatically stop the AGV if anything is in its path, then restart it when the way is clear.

Source: Courtesy of General Motors Corporation.

(b) This unit load stacker crane is one of six cranes that receives 2,500-pound pallet loads of grocery products from a conveyor belt system and automatically stores them on racks in the nine-stories high warehouse. The stacker cranes move vertically and horizontally, and can load and unload to either side. The facility has a capacity for 17,425 pallets that are stored and retrieved entirely under computer control. Each pallet is tracked by date of entry to assure that no item remains in storage longer than necessary, thus assuring the freshness of dated materials. Pallets received from the warehouse travel by conveyor belt to a truck-loading dock where they are broken down into truck loads matching delivery requirements.

Source: Courtesy SPS Technologies, Inc.

Automated assembly systems can provide manufacturers with low per-unit production costs, improved product quality, and faster production rates. Because some of the machines in these systems tend to be standard robots that are available from several suppliers today, the initial investment in equipment is not as high as we might imagine. Therefore these systems are not limited only to products of very high demand. Also, increasingly, these robots can be reprogrammed to other products and operations, thereby reducing the need for product demand to be stable and to extend well into the future.

FLEXIBLE MANUFACTURING SYSTEMS (FMS)

Flexible manufacturing systems (FMS) are groups of production machines, arranged in a sequence, connected by automated materials-handling and transferring machines, and integrated by a computer system. Figure 5.2 illustrates such a system.

In these systems, which are also sometimes called *flexible machining systems,* kits of materials and parts for a product are loaded on the materials-handling system. A code is then entered into the computer system identifying the product to be produced and the location of the product in the sequence. As partially completed products finish at one production machine, they are automatically passed to the next production machine. Each production machine receives its settings and instructions from the computer, automatically loads and unloads tools as required, and completes its work without the need for workers to attend its operations.

Although the initial cost of these systems is high, per-unit production costs are low, quality of products is high, and product flexibility is high. There are presently only a few FMS in use today, but they are growing in importance and many companies are now considering installing them. Industry Snapshot 5.4 discusses the use of FMS by several manufacturers.

AUTOMATED STORAGE AND RETRIEVAL SYSTEMS (ASRS)

Automated storage and retrieval systems (ASRS) are systems for receiving orders for materials from anywhere in operations, collecting the materials from locations within a warehouse, and delivering the materials to work stations in operations. There are three major elements of ASRS:

1. *Computers and communication systems.* These systems are used for placing orders for materials, locating the materials in storage, giving commands for delivery of the materials to locations in operations, and adjusting inventory records showing the amount and location of materials.
2. *Automated materials-handling and delivery systems.* These systems are automatically loaded with containers of materials from operations and deliver them to the warehouse. Similarly, they are automatically loaded with orders of materials at the warehouse and deliver the orders to work stations in operations. Powered and computer-controlled conveyors of several types are sometimes used, but *automated guided vehicle systems (AGVS)* are now being used in greater numbers for this purpose. AGVS are usually driverless trains,

---

INDUSTRY SNAPSHOT 5.4

FMS Switch to Other Products in Seconds

At the big Vought Aero Products plant in Grand Prairie, Texas, an automated wonder known as a flexible manufacturing system, or FMS, is drilling, grinding, and polishing parts for the aft fuselage of an air force bomber with startling efficiency. Except for the computer operator who sits in a glass-enclosed control booth and two workers who load and unload parts at the beginning and end of the process, the place practically runs itself. The system cost $10.1 million and makes 568 parts for the bomber in 40,000 square feet of floor space with 19 workers.

It now takes a General Electric locomotive plant in Erie, Pennsylvania, just 16 hours, rather than 16 days, to make locomotive motor frames. This system cost GE $16 million. Another GE plant, in Somersworth, New Hampshire, can be programmed to make up to 2,000 variations of 40 basic models of an electric meter. At the John Deere plant in Waterloo, Iowa, four types of transmissions for farm tractors are handled by the same FMS.

Japanese manufacturers are implementing FMS faster than U.S. firms. Yamazaki, Japan's largest machine tool builder, uses only 12 operators on the first and second shifts, compared with 215 who would be required in a conventional system. On the third shift, the plant runs by itself. Yamazaki's U.S. subsidiary, Mazak Corporation, opened a $25 million FMS plant in Florence, Kentucky.

The benefits from FMS are clear. Its ability to switch from making one kind of part to making another on virtually a moment's notice enables manufacturers to respond much faster to their markets and to custom-tailor their products to a degree never before possible. Moreover, companies increasingly see FMS as a key factor in accomplishing corporate objectives. A. J. Roch, Jr., director of industrial modernization at Vought, says, "We see flexible automation as a strategic weapon for enhancing our competitive position."[9]

---

[9] Carey W. English, "Factories That Turn Nuts Into Bolts," *U.S. News & World Report,* July 14, 1986, 44–45.

---

pallet trucks, and unit load carriers. AGVS usually follow either embedded guide wires or paint strips through operations until their destinations are reached.

3. *Storage and retrieval systems in warehouses.* Warehouses store materials in standard-size containers that contain fixed amounts of each material. For example, a container of a particular type of plastic molding would always contain 100 parts. These containers are arranged according to a location address scheme that allows the location of each material to be precisely determined by a computer. A *storage and retrieval (S/R) machine* receives commands from a computer, gets containers of materials from a *pickup point* in the warehouse, delivers materials to their assigned location in the

warehouse, and places them in their location. Similarly, S/R machines locate containers of materials in storage, remove containers from storage, and deliver containers to a *deposit point* in the warehouse.

Plates 8a & b of the insert illustrate the operation of both AGVS and S/R machines. The main purposes of installing ASRS are to:

1. *Increase storage capacity.* ASRS ordinarily increase the storage density in warehouses, that is, the total maximum number of individual loads that can be stored.
2. *Increase system throughput.* ASRS increases the number of loads per hour that the storage system can receive and place into storage and retrieve and deliver to work stations.
3. *Reduce labor costs.* By automating the systems of retrieving, storing, and delivering materials, labor and related costs are often reduced.
4. *Improve product quality.* Because of human error in identifying materials, the wrong parts are often delivered and assembled into products. These errors often occur because of similarity in the appearance of different materials. Automated systems that must identify parts based on bar codes or other identification methods are not as subject to these kinds of identification errors.

We have now discussed several automated production systems that are in common use today. What are production systems going to be like in the future?

FACTORIES OF THE FUTURE

To comprehend the nature of production that is likely to prevail in the coming decades, we must understand two rather complex computer-based systems: computer-aided design and computer-aided manufacturing (CAD/CAM) and computer-integrated manufacturing (CIM).

CAD/CAM

CAD and CAM were discussed in Chapter 1 and were cited as examples of state-of-the-art computer-based systems for planning product and process designs. These terms are defined as follows:

- *CAD:* The use of computers in interactive engineering drawing and storage of designs. Programs complete the layout, geometric transformations, projections, rotations, magnifications, and interval (cross-section) views of a part and its relationship with other parts.
- *CAM:* Use of computers to program, direct, and control production equipment in the fabrication of manufactured items.[10]

---

[10] *APICS Dictionary,* 6th Edition, prepared by Thomas F. Wallace and John R. Dougherty (Falls Church, VA: American Production and Inventory Control, 1987), 6.

CAD is concerned with the automation of certain phases of product design, and its use is growing as more and more powerful product design software is being developed. The increased availability of these engineering design work stations is revolutionizing the way products are designed. CAD systems are installed to increase the productivity of designers, improve the quality of the designs, improve product standardization and design documentation, and create a manufacturing data base.

CAM is concerned with automating the planning and control of production. It is coming along more slowly than CAD, but it is progressing. The ability to plan production, prepare product routings, generate N/C programs, fix the settings of production machinery, prepare production schedules, and control the operation of production processes with computers—all will undoubtedly continue to expand as computer software becomes more sophisticated. But it is the combination of these CAD and CAM systems into CAD/CAM that provides a vision of future production systems.

CAD/CAM implies a merger of CAD and CAM and an interaction between the two systems. The important result of this merger is the automation of the transition from product design to manufacturing. New products can be designed quickly as market demands change. And because these new product designs are stored in a common data base, through CAM the new products can be introduced into production much more quickly and with less expense. Thus CAD/CAM promises great product flexibility, low production costs, and improved product quality.

COMPUTER-INTEGRATED MANUFACTURING (CIM)

Computer-integrated manufacturing (CIM) is defined as "the application of a computer to bridge and connect various computerized systems and connect them into a coherent, integrated whole. For example, budgeting, CAD/CAM, process controls, group technology systems, MRP II, financial reporting systems, etc., would be linked and interfaced."[11] As we can tell from this definition, CIM has a broader application than CAD/CAM.

> *The CIM concept is that all of the firm's operations related to the production function [are] incorporated in an integrated computer system to assist, augment, and/or automate the operations. The computer system is pervasive throughout the firm, touching all activities that support manufacturing. In this integrated computer system, the output of one activity serves as the input to the next activity, through the chain of events that starts with the sales order and culminates with the shipment of the product.*[12]

In addition to the comprehensive computer systems described above, the term CIM has come to be associated with the use of the latest production technology. But

---

[11] Ibid.

[12] Groover, *Automation, Production Systems, and Computer Integrated Manufacturing,* 721–722.

as John J. Clancy, president of McDonnell-Douglas, points out, "CIM is not a piece of equipment, in fact, CIM is not technology, it is a way of using technology." [13] As production technology advances in the future, the intelligent use of this technology will surely dictate that CIM will become a fact of life for manufacturers.

With our understanding of CAD/CAM and CIM, let us consider the nature of future factories.

CHARACTERISTICS OF FACTORIES OF THE FUTURE

Although there are some factories today of the type known as *factories of the future,* an ever-increasing number of these organizations will be established in the future and will have these characteristics:

1. *High product quality.* The low quality and variability associated with manual operations will be avoided. Automation will allow consistent and high product quality. Market pressures for high product quality will ensure that this characteristic receives top priority.
2. *High flexibility.* New flexible technology will be used in the design of production processes. Many product models will be produced to appeal to markets that demand product variety. Small batches of many product models will be produced, and production processes will be economical to operate under these conditions.
3. *Fast delivery of customer orders.* With small batch sizes, operations that can be quickly changed to other products, and fast production rates, customer orders will be produced and shipped quickly.
4. *Changed production economics.* In the automated factory, costs that were formerly variable will become fixed, and costs that were formerly fixed will become variable. The majority of costs will be fixed costs. The only significant variable cost will be material and overhead. What labor costs there are, such as maintenance, will be considered fixed costs. The predominant cost will be overhead costs such as office and clerical, engineering, equipment, tooling, maintenance, utilities, and software.
5. *Computer-driven and computer-integrated systems.* CAD/CAM will be the basis for product design and process planning. CIM will integrate all phases of the business from a common data base.
6. *Organization structure changes.* In the automated factory, line personnel will become more like staff personnel, and staff personnel will become more like line personnel. Maintenance, product quality, engineering, management of technological change, software development and maintenance, and robotics and automation projects will become mainstream activities of the organization.

In factories of the future, job shops will evolve toward cellular manufacturing with increasing degrees of flexible automation. Product-focused production will

---

[13] Lee Green, "Gearing Up for CIM," *Information Week,* Apr. 13, 1987, 24–25.

evolve toward flexible manufacturing systems (FMS). At both of these ends of the present continuum, product flexibility, low unit costs, and high product quality will prevail.

Let us now consider the use of automation in the burgeoning service sector.

AUTOMATION IN SERVICES

Technological advance is perhaps one of the most profound developments of our time, and manufacturing is not the only sector to use it. When we consider the wide range of services supplied by companies in the following industries, the opportunities for applying automation are overwhelming: insurance, real estate, savings and loans and banks, trucking, airlines and air freight, construction, retailing and wholesaling, printing and publishing, advertising and broadcasting, business services, stock brokerages and financial services, health care, lodging and entertainment, communications, railroads, and utilities.

Consider, for example, what happened to the computer systems of the New York Stock Exchange on October 19, 1987, when the Dow Jones Industrial Average dropped 508 points and approximately 600 million shares of stock traded. Although the computer systems could not keep up with this enormous volume of transactions, it was surprising how well the system did perform. And now, larger and faster computer systems have been installed. The stock exchanges of the world could not possibly operate without the powerful computers and related automated equipment in use today.

Examples in other services are numerous. Table 5.2 gives some examples of automation in four service industries. Perhaps no other service industry is so dominated by the use of computers and automated equipment as is the banking and savings and loan industry. Automatic teller machines, electronic funds transfer systems, and computerized bank statements are only the tip of the iceberg. This entire industry is so dependent on computers and related equipment for its day-to-day operations that it literally could not operate without them.

As more and more advanced technology equipment and systems are integrated into service operations, an interesting trend toward more standardized services could be developing. Because automated equipment cannot possibly operate in an environment subject to the amount of variety and change that is present in some services, reducing and standardizing the variety of services offered allows the introduction of automated equipment. This standardization, however, brings trade-offs. On the one hand, from the customers' perspective, standardized services are not as appealing because the service is not specifically custom-designed for each customer. On the other hand, the cost of operations and the prices of services either are reduced or do not rise as rapidly, and they may be more convenient for customers. Consider, for instance, the emergence of the automated teller machines (ATMs) that are located in grocery stores, in shopping centers, and at drive-in branch bank facilities. Banking customers cannot obtain a wide range of banking services at ATMs, but their locations are convenient and their service is prompt.

TABLE 5.2   *Some Examples of Automation in Services*

Service Industries	Examples of Automation
Airlines	Air traffic control systems Autopilot systems Reservation systems Cargo containerization
Banks, savings and loans, and financial services	Automatic teller machines (ATMs) Electronic funds transfer Magnetic-ink character recognition codes (MICR) Optical scanners Computerized bank statements
Retailing/wholesaling	Point-of-sale terminals Bar code systems Optical scanners Automated warehouses
Health care	AGVS for waste disposal CAT scanners Magnetic resonance imaging (MRI) systems Automated patient monitoring

Generally speaking, where there is a large amount of customer contact in services, there tends to be less use of all types of equipment, including automated equipment. Figure 5.3 illustrates the relationship between the degree of customer contact and the amount of capital intensity. Capital intensity increases as we move from manual to mechanized to automated equipment. This figure suggests that automated equipment may not be appropriate for some service operations that have a high degree of customer contact. But as we discussed earlier, some service operations can be automated because of improved convenience and reduced costs. Also, services typically do not have a high amount of customer contact in all parts of their organization. For example, back room operations at banks, where customers seldom go, are prime candidates for automation.

One rather enduring complaint of today's society concerns the quality and costs of services. "Poor service" usually means that the personal delivery of the service is late, unfriendly, ineffective, or too costly. Through the use of automated equipment and standardized services, as in automatic teller machines, fast-food restaurants, and coin-operated and automatically vended services, the customers' perception of the "quality" of the service may improve and the efficiency of the delivery of the service is usually much improved.

The wide dissemination of automated systems in manufacturing and service industries has created many issues that require resolution.

FIGURE 5.3   *Degree of Customer Contact in Services and the Use of Automated Equipment*

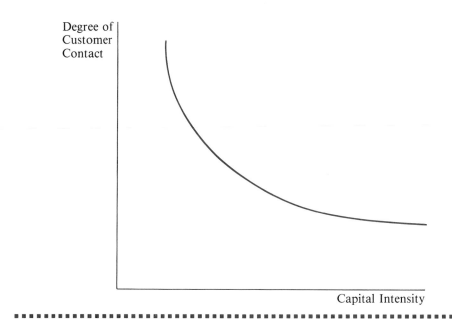

AUTOMATION ISSUES

Of the important automation issues that must be resolved, we shall discuss these: high-tech, mid-tech, or low-tech production?; building manufacturing flexibility; justifying automation projects; and managing technological change.

HIGH-TECH, MID-TECH, OR LOW-TECH PRODUCTION?

We can find examples of very successful companies that utilize the oldest known manual technology. We can also find examples of companies that are failing despite having the latest advanced technology. But we must not jump to the conclusion that the production technology used by a company is unrelated to its profitability or to other measures of success. Careful thought on this issue should lead us to these conclusions:

1. *Not all automation projects are successful.* Companies that launch major automation projects may poorly manage the implementation of the automated machinery. The result can be that they are worse off after automation than they were with their former production technology.
2. *Automation cannot make up for poor management.* Even if implementation of the automated production machinery goes well, the company may be so poorly managed that it fails anyway.

3. *Economic analysis cannot justify automation of some operations.* For example, if labor cost is very low and automated equipment is very costly, the extra cost of automating is not sufficiently offset by product quality and other improvements. This is the reason we find so many garment factories on both sides of the Mexican-U.S. border.
4. *It is not technically feasible to automate some operations.* In the garment industry, for example, the cloth that must be processed is so stretchable, flexible, and flimsy that certain production operations like cutting, assembling, and sewing are not yet automated. In these operations the chief obstacle to automation is imprecise positioning of the cloth relative to cutters, sewing heads, and other mechanical devices.

There are production operations that have not been automated, and there are undoubtedly operations that will never be automated. But for companies that are committed to long-term growth, survival, and profitability, the main reason for not automating cannot be because they have a closed mind on the subject. The truth is that all companies must keep their production processes updated as production technology advances. To do otherwise would put their companies' future in jeopardy, because they must assume that their competitors will seize the strategic advantages offered by switching to advanced technology. For many companies today, the question is not whether they will automate their operations. Rather, the questions are: Which operations will be automated? In what sequence will the operations be automated? When will the operations be automated?

BUILDING MANUFACTURING FLEXIBILITY

The term *flexible automation* means the opposite of the term *fixed manufacturing systems* or *hard automation,* as in automated flow lines or conventional assembly lines. In recent years, this use of the term has grown to refer to all types of equipment and production systems that provide the ability to respond to changing market needs. *Manufacturing flexibility* is the ability to improve or maintain market share because of the following:

1. Customer orders can be delivered soon after receipt of the orders. Sometimes this means modifying production schedules to respond to a customer's extraordinary request for a quick delivery.
2. Production can quickly be shifted from product to product because in a particular week customers may unexpectedly order relatively small batches of many product models.
3. Production capacity can be increased rapidly to respond to peaking market demands in a particular week.
4. New products can be developed and introduced into production quickly and inexpensively in response to shifting market needs.

As we have previously noted, manufacturing flexibility is of two general types, volume flexibility and product flexibility. Volume flexibility is usually provided by the use of overtime, extra finished goods inventory, and designing production processes with either *variable production rates* or *excess capacity.* As production systems have become more responsive to market demands, however, what used to be excess capacity is now considered to be only *enough capacity to respond to peak market demands.* But perhaps the more important form of manufacturing flexibility is product flexibility—the ability to quickly and inexpensively change the production system to other products.

As we discussed earlier in this chapter, process-focused production systems offer great product flexibility, although unit production costs can be high. Historically, the number of process-focused production systems has probably exceeded that of other forms of production. But many manufacturers today are looking for alternatives to job shops because these process-focused production systems will not allow them to compete with their foreign competitors on unit production costs. Owing to improved production technology, however, there are other ways to achieve product flexibility and still obtain low unit production costs.

Here are some machines or production systems that are understood to provide product flexibility:

1. N/C machines
2. Programmable and reprogrammable robots
3. Automated quality control inspection
4. Automatic identification systems (AIS)
5. Automated process controls
6. Automated assembly systems
7. Flexible manufacturing systems (FMS)
8. Automated storage and retrieval systems (ASRS)
9. Computer-aided design and computer-aided manufacturing (CAD/CAM)
10. Computer-integrated manufacturing (CIM)

These machines and production systems represent the core of what is referred to as *flexible automation.* Perhaps the most significant thing about them is their ability to produce products at low unit costs and simultaneously offer great product flexibility. Manufacturing flexibility has become the cornerstone of operations strategy in the 1990s, and production processes being designed today are increasingly being anchored to this cornerstone.

Flexible automation and other forms of automation require increased investment, however, and it is becoming increasingly apparent that the traditional approaches to justifying these huge investments are inadequate.

JUSTIFYING AUTOMATION PROJECTS

There is growing evidence that for several decades U.S. management policies and capital-budgeting approaches have led to only small improvements to existing products and production processes.

The turnover rate of our managers has been so high that long-term product improvement and production process changes have been avoided. It often takes five years or longer to drastically modify product designs and automate factories. There has not been much incentive for managers who plan to be with a company for only a few years to commit to these long-term projects.

The payback period, net present value, internal rate of return, and other conventional capital-budgeting approaches may, when taken alone, be inadequate tools upon which to base major product and process design and redesign decisions. These tools have tended to lead managers to expand present facilities with existing technology, rather than build new facilities with new production technology. Carrying this approach to its extreme, companies end up with huge, unwieldy, highly centralized production facilities based on outdated production technology.

Investment in product and process technology innovation must be taken out of the context of project-by-project investment decisions. Rather, investing in product and process technology must be seen as a long-term strategic choice for the company. These choices, like other major strategic business decisions, cannot be based solely on a simple payback formula. Although returns on investment will continue to be an important criterion for these investment decisions, the term *returns* will take on new and expanded meaning. Improved product quality, faster delivery of customer orders, increased product and volume flexibility, reduced production costs, increased market share, and other advantages will have to be factored into these future capital-budgeting decisions. Investment in product and process technology must be seen as a way of changing the factory into a competitive weapon that assists the corporation in achieving its strategic objectives.

MANAGING TECHNOLOGICAL CHANGE

Companies that have attempted ambitious automation projects have learned that implementing large automation projects is much more difficult and complex than they had anticipated. Automation projects almost always take longer and cost more than originally expected. Industry Snapshot 5.5 illustrates the difficulty of managing the change of production technology.

Given the difficulty of managing changes in production technology, what have we learned about how to manage the implementation of major automation projects? These suggestions are offered:

1. *Have a master plan for automation.* The plan should indicate what operations to automate, when and in what sequence to automate each area of the business, and how the organization and its products, marketing, and other business units will have to change because of automation.
2. *Recognize the risks in automating.* There are risks associated with every automation project. Among those that must be considered are: the risk of radical obsolescence, the danger that new technologies cannot be protected and will be easily transferred to competitors, and the possibility that a new production technology cannot be successfully developed.
3. *Establish a new production technology department.* This unit will disseminate information about new technology, become an advocate for new-technology adoption, lead the way in educating and training others about new technology, and provide the technical assistance necessary for the installation and implementation of advanced-technology equipment. An example of such an organization unit is the Department of Industrial Modernization at Vought Aero Products (see Industry Snapshot 5.4).

INDUSTRY SNAPSHOT 5.5

Technology Revolution or Evolution?

Many companies bought automated machines a few years ago as a quick fix. They tried for the instant cure without understanding how the new equipment would fit into their production systems. Sadly, they learned that buying a few robots in isolation without any idea of how they fit into the big picture of the business would result in failure.[14]

Also, companies learned that even if they have a grand plan, they can't just throw money at an automation project and expect it to be successful overnight. At best, they will waste a lot of money, and results from automation will be later than expected. At worst, an automated factory that is not wisely planned and precisely managed may perform worse than a well-managed conventional factory. General Motors, which led the world in robot purchases, found that its low-tech plants, such as its NUMMI joint venture with Toyota in California, were outper-

forming some of its state-of-the-art plants, such as Hamtramck and Buick City in Michigan.[15]

Part of GM's strategic plan in the late 1970s included the introduction of automated technology into all of its factories. GM faltered as it began to rely more heavily on robots and computers in its plants. Some automated equipment didn't work as well as expected. The company also bought Electronic Data Systems Corporation for $2.5 billion in 1984 to help develop a computer network. Unfortunately for GM, the road to automation has been bumpy, as witnessed by the Buick City complex in Flint, Michigan. Although management states that the $400 million refurbished plant cost only half as much as a new plant, carries only one-third the normal parts inventory, and is 30 percent more efficient than a conventional plant, it had one of the slowest startups of any automobile plant on record.[16]

---

[14] Neikirk, 1 F.

[15] "Firms Discover Trouble with Robots," *Houston Chronicle,* June 14, 1987.

[16] William J. Hampton and James R. Norman, "General Motors: What Went Wrong," *Business Week,* Mar. 16, 1987, 105–107.

---

4. *Allow plenty of time for the completion of automation projects.* Enough time must be allowed for learning how to install, tool, debug, program, and otherwise get an automated machine up to production speed. There is much to learn, and it always takes longer than expected. One automation expert recently suggested: "Estimate how long you expect it to take, then triple it." The key point: *What one learns about implementing one automation project is to be applied to the next one. There is a new technology associated with the implementation of automation projects, and it is best learned a little at a time.*

5. *Do not try to automate everything at once.* Glitches in automated equipment are inevitable. Try to phase in projects so that what is learned from one project can be applied to another project. By allowing plenty of time, the frequency

of missed schedule dates, organization frustration, and pressure to compress the schedule are somewhat reduced. By phasing in projects, an organization's resources can be more tightly focused on one or two projects at a time, thereby increasing the likelihood of success.

6. *People are the key to making automation projects successful.* If automation is being planned at the strategic level, the training and education of everyone in the organization about advanced production technology must be an ongoing activity. Frequent and intensive participation by all involved personnel must accompany automation projects. Union representatives must be brought into an active role in automation. Unions are particularly interested in advance notice of affected jobs, retraining and reassignment of displaced workers, and layoff policies associated with automation.

7. *If companies move too slowly in adopting new production technology, they may get left behind.* Being deliberate and careful as it moves from automation project to automation project does not give a company license to drag its feet. Doing so may mean that it will be beaten by the competition.

With the preceding discussion as a background, let us study some ways of deciding among automation alternatives.

DECIDING AMONG AUTOMATION ALTERNATIVES

As managers consider automation decisions, there are ordinarily several alternatives that must be considered. Here we present three approaches that are commonly used in industry today: economic analysis, rating scale approach, and relative-aggregate-scores approach.

ECONOMIC ANALYSIS

The approaches included in this kind of analysis were presented in some detail in Chapter 4, Production Processes. It is suggested that you reread the Economic Analysis section of that chapter. Of particular importance to this discussion are the topics of cost functions of processing alternatives, the concept of operating leverage, break-even analysis, and financial analysis.

Economic analysis will always be an important, if not a predominant, factor in choosing among automation alternatives. But other factors must also be considered. The incorporation of a variety of factors in these decisions requires the use of different approaches.

RATING SCALE APPROACH

Managers who make automation decisions know that the following important factors must be considered:

1. *Economic factors.* These factors provide managers with some idea of the *direct* impact of automation alternatives on profitability. Although the focus may be on cash flows, annual fixed costs, variable cost per unit, average production

cost per unit, or total annual production costs at the forecasted production levels, the intent is to determine the direct impact on profitability. Break-even analysis and financial analysis are frequently used for this purpose.

2. *Effect on market share.* How are automation alternatives likely to affect market share? Some alternatives require product redesign and product specialization, which can affect sales. Although some alternatives allow more product variety and greater customer appeal, the net effect of such changes upon market share is a difficult measure to obtain. Nevertheless, the effects are there and must be taken into account in such decisions.

3. *Effect on product quality.* How are automation alternatives likely to affect product quality? Measuring this effect is not easy. Scrap rates, market share changes, production costs, and other measures represent efforts to *indirectly* tie changes in product quality resulting from automation alternatives to profitability.

4. *Effect on manufacturing flexibility.* How are automation alternatives likely to affect product and volume flexibility? This factor is increasing in importance as product life cycles shorten and as competing organizations provide consumers with opportunities to order products with characteristics custom-designed for them. Measures of manufacturing flexibility are extremely difficult to develop. Cost of machine changeovers, overtime labor costs, and market share changes are measures that can be used to evaluate the effect of automation alternatives on manufacturing flexibility.

5. *Effect on labor relations.* How are automation alternatives likely to affect workers, their union, and the relationship between management and the work force? The number of workers that must be laid off, the amount of training and retraining required, and the availability of workers with the skills required to operate automated equipment are factors affecting the choice of automation alternatives.

6. *The amount of time required for implementation.* How much time will automation alternatives require to implement the automated machines and systems? Alternatives may have different time requirements for implementation because the alternatives have different levels of technology, organizational personnel may be unfamiliar with some types of technology, and alternatives require different kinds of changes in the rest of the production system.

7. *Effect of automation implementation on ongoing production.* If automation is to replace existing production operations, or if automation must share facilities with existing operations, how will automation alternatives affect existing production? It is a fact of life that production must go on in spite of automation projects. Products must be shipped, for customers will not wait just because of automation projects. Some automation alternatives affect existing operations less because they are to be installed in a different location, they do not require the use of existing production equipment, or they otherwise do not interact with existing production.

8. *Amount of capital required.* What is the amount of capital required for each automation alternative? If capital is in short supply, as it almost always is, this factor can be the predominant consideration in automation decisions.

■■

TABLE 5.3   *Rating Scale Approach to Comparing Automation Alternatives*

Automation Factors	Automated Flow Line	Flexible Manufacturing System
Economic factors		
Annual operating costs	$4,955,900	$5,258,100
Per-unit production costs	$59.40	$63.02
Other factors		
Market share	5	4
Product quality	4	4
Product flexibility	2	4
Volume flexibility	4	2
Labor relations	3	3
Implementation time	3	4
Existing operations	5	5
Capital requirements	3	4

■■

Note: A five-point rating scale is used: 5 = excellent, 4 = good, 3 = average, 2 = below average, and 1 = poor.

Given that factors such as these could all be important to deciding among automation alternatives, how can managers simultaneously consider all of these factors? Table 5.3 illustrates how the *rating scale approach* can be used as a manager attempts to decide between two automation alternatives.

We can see in Table 5.3 that if only economic factors were taken into account, the automated flow line would be preferred. But if other factors are considered, the choice is not so clear. The flexible manufacturing system rates better on product flexibility, implementation time, and capital requirements, and the automated flow line rates better on economic factors, market share, and volume flexibility. In such cases where no alternative is clearly superior on all factors, the appropriate choice will depend on which of the factors is of greater importance to the managers who must make the decision.

The rating scale approach requires decision makers to weigh the factors for each alternative, process this information through their unique mental calculus, and arrive at an overall rating of each automation alternative. Let us now consider another approach that directly develops this overall rating of each alternative.

RELATIVE-AGGREGATE-SCORES APPROACH

Table 5.4 illustrates the *relative-aggregate-scores approach* to the same decision depicted in Table 5.3. But in this approach, the overall aggregate scores for each automation alternative are developed as a part of the analysis.

We can see from Table 5.4 that the flexible manufacturing system appears to be a slightly better choice, .818 versus .770. This approach requires that managers state

■■■

TABLE 5.4   Relative-Aggregate-Scores Approach to Comparing Automation Alternatives

		Automated Flow Line			Flexible Manufacturing System		
Automation Factors	Factor Weights	Economic Data	Scores	Weighted Scores	Economic Data	Scores	Weighted Scores
Unit production costs	.30	$59.40	1.000*	.300	$63.02	.943*	.283
Market share	.10		1.000	.100		.800	.080
Product quality	.10		.800	.080		.800	.080
Product flexibility	.20		.400	.080		.800	.160
Volume flexibility	.05		.800	.040		.400	.020
Labor relations	.05		.600	.030		.600	.030
Implementation time	.10		.600	.060		.800	.080
Existing operations	.05		1.000	.050		1.000	.050
Capital requirements	.05		.600	.030		.700	.035
Total aggregate scores				.770			.818

■■■

* These scores are determined by dividing the lowest unit production costs by the actual unit production costs: $59.40/$59.40 = 1.000, and $59.40/$63.02 = .943; All other factor scores are estimated based on a maximum score of 1.000.

the factors that will be considered in the decision and the weights of each factor *before the decision is made.* Such considerations represent a decision structure imposed on decision makers that should be inherently superior to a purely subjective weighting of alternatives. It is assumed that each alternative included in the analysis has been required to meet certain qualifications. For example, if an alternative requires so much capital that it is impractical to consider it, that alternative should not be included in the analysis. In other words, all alternatives surviving to this point in the analysis are fundamentally sound and feasible, and in this approach we are attempting to determine which alternative is superior to the others.

The approaches to deciding among automation alternatives that we have discussed have all assumed we are attempting to achieve several objectives simultaneously. A series of mathematical programming techniques have been developed in recent years to analyze such problems. Goal programming and multiobjective programming have been applied to these problems, but these techniques are beyond the scope of this course.

SUMMARY

Planning and designing production processes enables the operations function to carry out the operations strategies. In deciding on the basic type of process design, the following factors must be taken into account: nature of product demand, degree of vertical integration, product and volume flexibility, degree of automation, level of product quality, and degree of customer contact.

There are three types of process designs: product-focused, process-focused, and cellular manufacturing. Product-focused, or line flow, continuous-production organizations are designed primarily for high-volume, standardized products. Process-focused, or intermittent-production, organizations are designed primarily for low-volume, small-batch, custom products. There are hybrids of these types of designs, and new forms are emerging. For example, cellular manufacturing tends to emerge from job shop production settings by identifying families of parts with common characteristics that are produced in larger batches. A family of parts would be produced in a cell containing the machines necessary to produce those parts. The choice of processing alternative is usually based on batch size, product variety, capital requirements, economic analysis, assembly charts, and process charts.

Numerically controlled machines, robots, automated quality control inspection, and automated process controls are types of automated machines. Automated flow lines, automated assembly systems, flexible manufacturing systems, and automated storage and retrieval systems are automated production systems. The future evolution of these systems into CAD/CAM and CIM systems is expected to result in factories that can produce small-batch, high-quality products that have great flexibility in responding to rapidly changing market needs. Several issues in automation must be resolved, among them manufacturing flexibility, justifying automation projects, and managing technological change.

REVIEW AND DISCUSSION QUESTIONS

1. Automation has traditionally meant the replacement of human effort with machine effort. Critique this traditional view of automation.

2. How much was planned to be spent on shop floor automation in the United States during 1990? Name the three shop floor automation applications that are expected to receive the greatest investment in the United States in the 1990s.

3. What benefits should be expected from automation projects? Discuss the overall impact on organizations from labor savings through automation.

4. Describe the conditions that would support the installation of a numerically controlled (N/C) machine.

5. Describe and give an example of each of these types of automated machines:
   a. automatic attachments,
   b. numerically controlled (N/C),
   c. robots,
   d. automated quality control inspection,
   e. automatic identification systems,
   f. automated process controls.

6. Describe and give an example of each of these types of automated production systems:
   a. automated flow lines,
   b. automated assembly systems,
   c. flexible manufacturing systems (FMS),
   d. automated storage and retrieval systems (ASRS).

7. What is meant by the term *hard automation?* Explain the difference between hard automation and *flexible automation.*

8. Explain why products must usually be redesigned if automated assembly systems are to be used in production.

9. Define and describe:
   a. CAD,
   b. CAM,
   c. CAD/CAM,
   d. CIM,
   e. characteristics of factories of the future.

10. Give three examples of the use of automation in services that you know about from your personal experience.

11. What is meant by the term *flexible automation?* What are four reasons that market share can be increased because of *manufacturing flexibility?* Name three machines or production systems that provide product flexibility.

12. If you could give managers who are considering automation projects advice on how to justify these projects, what would you tell them?

13. Give seven suggestions on how to better manage the implementation of major automation projects.

14. Name and describe two ways of analyzing automation alternatives.

15. What are the strengths and weaknesses of each of the two ways of analyzing automation alternatives presented in this chapter?

16. Identify the business conditions that would justify the use of a flexible manufacturing system.

PROBLEMS

Field Projects

1. Interview a manager of a manufacturing company that is considering installing automated equipment. Obtain the answers to these questions: What benefits are expected from this equipment? Who is responsible for supplying the engineering know-how for selecting and installing the equipment? How long is the implementation expected to take?

2. Interview a manager of a manufacturing company that has installed automated equipment. Obtain the answers to these questions: What benefits have been received from this equipment? How long did implementation take? Who supplied the engi-

neering know-how for selecting and installing the equipment? What would be changed if the project could be done over?

3. Interview a manager of a service company that plans to install automated equipment. Obtain the answers to these questions: What benefits are expected from this equipment? Who is responsible for supplying the engineering know-how for selecting and installing the equipment? How long is the implementation expected to take?

Economic Analysis

4. A manufacturing firm is considering two automation alternatives: semiautomatic and fully automatic. The fully automatic alternative is more capital-intensive, with annual fixed costs of $300,000 and variable costs of $95 per unit. The semiautomatic alternative has annual fixed costs of only $200,000 but variable costs of $116 per unit. If market share is not expected to be affected by this decision, what is the break-even production quantity beyond which the fully automatic alternative would be preferred? What other factors should be considered in this decision?

5. A savings and loan association must decide between two types of tellers: partially staffed and fully automatic. The automatic teller will result in an annual fixed cost of $120,000 and a variable cost of $1.49 per transaction. The partially staffed teller will result in an annual fixed cost of only $30,000, but its variable cost per transaction will be $2.60. The average revenue per transaction is $4.15. Because of differences in the speed of processing transactions and in the way that the tellers interact with customers, the annual number of transactions that can or will be processed by the fully automatic teller is expected to be only 80 percent of the number processed by the partially staffed teller. What number of annual transactions would cause the organization to be indifferent between the two alternatives? What other factors should be considered in this decision?

6. A manufacturing firm has made a particular component in-house for years while using a strictly manual production process. A supplier has an automated process for producing such components and has quoted a price of $42.50 per unit for any quantity. The company estimates that it could install a fully automated production process with annual fixed costs of $250,000 and a variable cost per unit of $38.40. If annual production volume is expected to be in the 100,000–200,000 range over the next five years, should the company install the automated production process? What other factors should be taken into account in this decision?

7. Gateway Manufacturing operates a job shop machining facility. Gateway manufactures parts for automobile manufacturers in the West Coast region of the United States. The company has decided that it must update its production technology if it is to compete with foreign suppliers of the parts. Three alternatives are presently being considered: cellular manufacturing (CM), numerically controlled (N/C) machines, and flexible manufacturing systems (FMS). The three alternatives have these costs:

	CM	*N/C*	*FMS*
Annual production (parts)	100,000	100,000	100,000
Annual fixed costs	$90,000	$190,000	$320,000
Variable cost per part	$29.40	$28.50	$27.30

a. On the basis of economic analysis, rank the alternatives from most desirable to least desirable.
b. Based on economic analysis, if 150,000 parts were produced in a year, rank the alternatives from most desirable to least desirable.
c. Based on your findings in Parts *a* and *b*, discuss the importance of accurate forecasting of production levels in decisions among automation alternatives. What practical ways can you suggest for including the uncertainty present in forecasts in analyses such as you have done in Parts *a* and *b*?
d. What other factors should be considered in this decision?

8. DAC Corporation must decide between two automation alternatives. The company has developed these cost estimates:

	N/C	*FMS*
Annual production (parts):		
Mean annual demand	50,000	50,000
Standard deviation of annual demand	8,000	8,000
Annual fixed costs	$290,000	$380,000
Variable costs per part	$19.40	$17.30

a. If the demand is assumed to be the mean demand, what is the production quantity at which the company would be indifferent between the two alternatives?
b. If the demand is assumed to be normally distributed, what is the probability that the FMS would be preferred?
c. What other factors should be considered in this decision?

Assembly and Process Charts

9. A production analyst has just completed a process chart for each of the two automation alternatives — robotic and semiautomatic — for an epoxy mixing and filling operation in manufacturing. Refer to the discussion of process charts in Chapter 4, Production Processes, and explain how the information on these two process charts might be used by a manager in deciding between the robotic and the semiautomatic mixer and filler.

10. A production analyst has just completed an assembly chart for each of the two automation alternatives for assembling a product in manufacturing — an automated assembly system and autoinsertion equipment. Refer to the discussion of assembly charts in Chapter 4, Production Processes, and explain how the information on these two assembly charts might be used by a manager in deciding between the two automated assembly alternatives.

Rating Scale Approach

11. Caldwell Manufacturing Company produces plastic molded products. A critical step in production is the injection-molding operation. To stay competitive with its com-

petitors, Caldwell needs to update its production technology in injection molding. Two automation alternatives (robots and N/C) seem feasible, but each has strengths and weaknesses. As an aid in deciding between these two alternatives, this information has been prepared:

Automation Factors	Robots	N/C
Economic factors:		
Annual operating costs	$3,600,000	$3,890,000
Other factors:		
Market share	5	4
Product quality	4	5
Product flexibility	3	4
Volume flexibility	4	4
Labor relations	3	3
Implementation time	3	4
Existing operations	5	4
Capital requirements	4	3

Note: A five-point rating scale is used: 5 = excellent, 4 = good, 3 = average, 2 = below average, and 1 = poor.

Which automation alternative would you recommend? Why?

12. The Eastmore Corporation is installing an automated storage and retrieval system (ASRS). The firm must decide between an automated conveyor system and an automated guided vehicle system (AGVS) for transporting materials to and from its warehouse. It has collected this information on the two alternatives:

Automation Factors	Automated Conveyors	AGVS
Economic factors:		
Annual operating costs	$540,000	$380,000
Average per-load transport costs	$19.40	$13.65
Other factors:		
Speed of delivery from warehouse	5	3
Ease of unloading in production	4	5
Product quality	4	4
Product flexibility	2	4
Volume flexibility	4	3
Implementation time	4	3
Existing operations	4	5
Capital requirements	3	4

Note: A five-point rating scale is used: 5 = excellent, 4 = good, 3 = average, 2 = below average, and 1 = poor.

Which automation alternative would you recommend? Why?

Relative-Aggregate-Scores Approach

13. The Cedar Creek Coal Company in Poteau, Oklahoma, is considering two different automated mining systems: a continuous mining system and a scowing system. Each of the two systems has its pros and cons. This information has been developed by one of Cedar Creek's mining engineers:

Automation Factors	Factor Weight	Continuous Mining System	Scowing System
Production cost per ton	.30	$9.60	$10.90
Coal ash content (%)	.10	.600	.800
Coal moisture content (%)	.10	.800	1.000
Coal size flexibility	.05	.400	.800
Volume flexibility	.05	.800	.700
Market share	.05	.700	.900
Labor relations	.15	.600	.600
Implementation time	.05	.500	.800
Existing operations	.05	1.000	.800
Capital requirements	.10	.600	.700

Use the relative-aggregate-scores approach to compare the two automation alternatives. Which alternative would you recommend? Why?

14. The Star Casting Company produces bronze castings that are sold to other manufacturing companies in its region. Star is considering two automation alternatives in its finishing department: flexible manufacturing system (FMS) and numerically control (N/C) machines. Each of the two systems has its pros and cons. The following information has been developed by one of Star's production analysts:

Automation Factors	Factor Weight	FMS	N/C
Production cost per casting	.40	$35.40	$38.20
Product quality	.10	.800	.850
Product flexibility	.10	.700	.950
Volume flexibility	.05	.900	.800
Market share	.10	.700	.900
Labor relations	.05	.600	.800
Implementation time	.05	.500	.800
Existing operations	.05	.500	.800
Capital requirements	.10	.600	.700

Use the relative-aggregate-scores approach to compare the two automation alternatives. Which alternative would you recommend? Why?

COMPUTER PROBLEMS/CASES

MORTON AEROSPACE

Morton Aerospace is producing components for the jet engines on commercial aircraft. One of its best-selling components is an aluminum alloy housing. Because of the many different jet engines that its customers use the housing on, about 18 different housings are presently produced. The company is considering two proposals for modifying the way it produces this part: an automated flow line and a flexible manufacturing system (FMS). The automated flow line would require standardizing the 18 models down to 5 models, but the FMS could produce all 18 models. Morton's management does not know how the reduction in the number of models would affect its customers' demand for the starting systems, but it suspects that at best some market turmoil would result. The following estimates were prepared on the two alternatives:

	Automated Flow Line	FMS
First-year volume (housings)	100,000	120,000
Second-year volume	80,000	120,000
Third-year volume	120,000	130,000
Annual volume after third year	120,000	140,000
Annual fixed costs	$500,000	$400,000
Average variable cost per housing	$29.30	$31.95

Assignment

1. If the sales price of the housings averages $42.50 per housing, which process would be preferred in each year?
2. At what annual volume of housings would Morton be indifferent between the two processes if the only consideration were economic analysis?
3. What other considerations would affect this decision?

FIRST NATIONAL BANK

The First National Bank (see the First National Bank case in the Computer Problems/Cases at the end of Chapter 3) is considering two automation alternatives related to real estate loans. The first alternative would allow customers to make payments on their loans through an automatic teller machine in a drive-in lane at the bank. The other alternative would allow customers to make transfer payments over the telephone. The following cost estimates for the alternatives have been developed:

	Drive-in	Telephone
Annual fixed costs	$275,000	$490,000
Variable costs per dollar of revenue	$.290	$.280

Assignment

1. Use the *POM Computer Library* that accompanies this text and work Part 4 from the First National Bank case at the end of Chapter 3. Regional per capita income (as a leading indicator), interest rate charged, and regional GNP are the independent variables in this regression problem. This should result in a forecast for real estate loan revenue for Year 8, along with its mean absolute deviation (MAD).

2. If we assume that the forecast of real estate revenue is normally distributed, the relationship between the MAD and the standard deviation can be estimated as was discussed in Chapter 3. What is the estimate of the standard deviation of the forecast of real estate revenue in Year 8?

3. Compute the amount of real estate revenue at which we would be indifferent between the two automation alternatives.

4. Given your answers in Parts 1 and 2 above, what is the probability that the telephone alternative would be preferred, based on your economic and statistical analysis?

5. What other factors should be considered in this decision?

SELECTED BIBLIOGRAPHY

Abernathy, William J. "Production Process Structure and Technological Change." *Decision Sciences* 7, no. 4(October 1976):607–619.

APICS Dictionary, 6th ed. Prepared by Thomas F. Wallace and John R. Dougherty, Falls Church, VA: American Production and Inventory Control, 1987.

Ayres, Robert U. "Future Trends in Factory Automation." *Manufacturing Review* 1, no. 2(June 1988):93–103.

Buffa, Elwood. *Meeting the Competitive Challenge.* Homewood, IL: Richard D. Irwin, 1984.

Bylinsky, Gene. "The Race to the Automatic Factory." *Fortune,* Feb. 21, 1983, 52–60.

Collier, David A. *Service Management: The Automation of Services.* Reston, VA: Reston Publishing, 1985.

"Flexible Manufacturing Systems." *Modern Materials Handling,* Sept. 7, 1982.

Gerwin, Donald. "Do's and Don't's of Computerized Manufacturing." *Harvard Business Review* 60(March–April 1982):107–116.

Gold, Bela. "CAM Sets New Rules for Production." *Harvard Business Review* 60(November–December 1982):88–94.

Groover, Mikell P. *Automation, Production Systems, and Computer Integrated Manufacturing.* Englewood Cliffs, NJ: Prentice-Hall, 1987.

Hayes, Robert H., and William J. Abernathy. "Managing Our Way to Economic Decline." *Harvard Business Review* 58(July–August 1980):67–77.

"IBM's Automated Factory—A Giant Step Forward." *Modern Materials Handling,* March 1985.

Jenkins, K. M., and A. R. Raedels. "The Robot Revolution: Strategic Considerations for Managers." *Production and Inventory Management* (Third Quarter 1982):107–116.

Kantrow, Alan M. "The Strategy–Technology Connection." *Harvard Business Review* 58(July–August 1980):6–21.

Levitt, T. "The Industrialization of Services." *Harvard Business Review* 54(1976):41–52.

Levitt, Theodore. "Production Line Approach to Service." *Harvard Business Review* 50(September–October 1972):41–52.

Peters, Thomas J., and Robert H. Waterman, Jr. *In Search of Excellence.* New York: Harper & Row, 1982.

Rosenthal, Stephen. "Progress Toward the Factory of the Future." *Journal of Operations Management* 4, no. 3(May 1984):203–229.

Sasser, W. Earl, R. Paul Olsen, and D. Daryle Wyckoff. *Management of Service Operations: Text, Cases, and Readings.* Boston: Allyn and Bacon, 1978.

Skinner, Wickham. "Operations Technology: Blind Spot in Strategic Management." *Interfaces* 14, no. 1(January–February 1984):116–125.

FACILITY LAYOUT

MANUFACTURING AND SERVICES

JAPANESE LAYOUTS: COMPACT AND FLEXIBLE

Japanese children grow up in a small, mountainous, island country that is densely populated. At an early age they learn to use to the fullest what little space they have. With space having a high value, it is not surprising that Japanese factories are about one-third as large as their U.S. counterparts. To save space, the Japanese try to eliminate inventory, design smaller pieces of equipment and place them closer together, squeeze down aisles, place work centers close together, and use areas and train workers for more than one task. These compact layouts have a dramatic strategic effect on the Japanese factory: materials travel shorter distances and products go through the factory faster so that customer orders can be produced faster; the cost of space, materials handling, and holding inventory is reduced; factories are more flexible to changes in customer orders, production schedules, and production rates; and workers are closer together, helping to improve communication and morale by developing tighter work groups.

The previous account reflects the interest of U.S. manufacturers in Japanese manufacturing methods in general and in Japanese approaches to facility layouts in particular. *Facility layout* means planning for the location of all machines, utilities, employee work stations, customer service areas, material storage areas, aisles, restrooms, lunchrooms, drinking fountains, internal walls, offices, and computer rooms, and for the flow patterns of materials and people around, into, and within buildings. Facility layout planning should be viewed as a natural extension of the discussion of process planning in Chapter 4. In process planning, we select or design processing machinery; in conjunction with product design, we determine the characteristics of the materials in the products, and we adopt new technology into operations. Through facility layouts, the physical arrangement of these processes within buildings, the space necessary for the operation of these processes and the space required for support functions are provided. As process planning and facility layout planning proceed, there is a continuous interchange of information between these two planning activities, because each affects the other.

Table 6.1 lists some of the objectives of facility layouts for manufacturing, warehouse, service, and office operations. The table is organized to show first the objectives for manufacturing operations, which also apply to warehouse, service, and office operations. Then the additional objectives for warehouse, service, and office operations are shown.

A thoughtful reading of the objectives for facility layouts in Table 6.1 should suggest that facility layout planning must be linked with operations strategy. Remember from Chapter 2, Operations Strategy, that the mix of competitive weapons that the operations function can provide are: low production costs, fast delivery of products, on-time deliveries, high-quality products and services, and product and volume flexibility. The objectives in Table 6.1 that drive our facility layouts must reflect an appropriate mix of these competitive weapons that are embodied in our operations strategy. Operations strategy drives facility layout planning, and facility layouts serve as a means of achieving our operations strategies.

Once they are in place, layouts are not often changed, for the cost of planning the changes, the very high cost of actually altering the arrangement of the facilities, and the necessity of curtailing operations may be prohibitive. Once the layouts for facilities are completed, operations managers' ability to direct the activities of production systems is locked in for a long time. Because of their strategic importance and their long-lasting effects, therefore, layout decisions are given close attention and thorough analysis by operations managers.

MANUFACTURING FACILITY LAYOUTS

Among the many objectives of facility layouts, the central focus of most manufacturing layouts is to minimize the cost of processing, transporting, and storing materials throughout the production system.

TABLE 6.1 *Some Objectives of Facility Layouts*

Objectives for Manufacturing Operation Layouts

Provide enough production capacity
Reduce materials-handling costs
Conform to site and building constraints
Allow space for production machines
Allow high labor, machine, and space utilization and productivity
Provide for volume and product flexibility
Provide space for restrooms, cafeterias, and other personal-care needs of employees
Provide for employee safety and health
Allow ease of supervision
Allow ease of maintenance
Control capital investment

Additional Objectives for Warehouse Operation Layouts

Promote efficient loading and unloading of shipping vehicles
Provide for effective stock picking, order filling, and unit loading
Allow ease of inventory counts
Promote accurate inventory record keeping

Additional Objectives for Service Operation Layouts

Provide for customer comfort and convenience
Provide appealing setting for customers
Allow attractive display of merchandise
Reduce travel of personnel or customers
Provide for privacy in work areas
Promote communication between work areas
Provide for stock rotation for shelf life

Additional Objectives for Office Operation Layouts

Reinforce organization structure
Reduce travel of personnel or customers
Provide for privacy in work areas
Promote communication between work areas

MATERIALS HANDLING

The materials used in manufacturing are many: raw materials, purchased components, materials-in-process, finished goods, packaging materials, maintenance and repair supplies, scrap and waste, and rejects or rework. These materials vary greatly in size, shape, chemical properties, and special features.

TABLE 6.2   *Materials-Handling Principles*

1. Materials should move through the facility in direct flow patterns, minimizing zigzagging or backtracking.
2. Related production processes should be arranged to provide for direct material flows.
3. Mechanical materials-handling devices should be designed and located and material storage locations should be selected so that human effort expended through bending, reaching, lifting, and walking is minimized.
4. Heavy or bulky materials should be moved the shortest distance through locating processes that use them near receiving and shipping areas.
5. The number of times each material is moved should be minimized.
6. Systems flexibility should allow for unexpected situations such as materials-handling equipment breakdowns, changes in production system technology, and future expansion of production capacities.
7. Mobile equipment should carry full loads at all times; empty and partial loads should be avoided.

Most of this variety in material characteristics is determined by product design decisions. The layout of facilities is directly affected by the nature of these materials. Large and bulky materials; heavy materials; fluids; solids; flexible and inflexible materials; and materials requiring special handling to protect them from conditions such as heat, cold, humidity, light, dust, flame, and vibration — all affect the layout of facilities for handling, storing, and processing these materials.

A *materials-handling system* is the entire network of transportation that receives materials, stores materials in inventories, moves them about between processing points within and between buildings, and finally deposits the finished products into vehicles that will deliver them to the ultimate customers.

Materials-handling systems are expensive to purchase and operate. Obvious expenses are those of initial costs, labor for operating the materials-handling devices, and maintenance and repair costs. Other expenses that are not so obvious result from damaged or lost materials, delays in material deliveries, and accidents. These and other expenses are so large that the successful operation of these facilities demands acute management attention to the design and selection of materials-handling systems.

The design and layout of buildings must be integrated with the design of the materials-handling system. For example, if overhead conveyors are to be used, the structure of the building must be strong enough to support the operation of these devices. Similarly, if heavy loads are to be transported on trucks, floors must have adequate support to withstand the constant stress of day-to-day pounding from these loads. Additionally, aisles must be wide enough to accommodate forklift trucks or other devices that will travel through the areas. Fixed-position devices such as conveyors must also be provided floor space.

Certain principles have evolved to guide facility layout to ensure the efficient handling of materials. Table 6.2 summarizes some of these fundamentals. Although

TABLE 6.3   *Materials-Handling Equipment*

1. **Automatic transfer devices**— Machines that automatically grasp materials, hold them firmly while operations are being performed, and move them to other locations.
2. **Containers and manual devices**
   Hand carts—Unpowered wagons, dollies, and trucks pushed about by workers.
   Pallets—Base structures on which materials are stacked and moved about by materials-handling vehicles.
   Tote boxes—Containers for holding loose parts or materials for storage and movements between operations.
   Wire bins—Containers for storing loose parts of materials in inventory.
3. **Conveyors**
   Belt—Motor-driven belt, usually made from rubberized fabric or metal fabric on a rigid frame.
   Chain—Motor-driven chain that drags materials along a metal slide base.
   Pneumatic—High volume of air flows through a tube, carrying materials along with the air flow.
   Roller—Boxes, large parts, or unitized loads roll atop a series of rollers mounted on a rigid frame. The rollers can be either powered or unpowered.
   Tube—Chain with circular scraper blades drags materials along inside a tube.
4. **Cranes**—Hoists mounted on overhead rails or ground level wheels or rails; they lift, swing, and transport large and heavy materials.
5. **Elevators**—A type of crane that, while in a fixed position, lifts materials —usually between floors of buildings.
6. **Pipelines**—Closed tubes that transport liquids by means of pumps or gravity.
7. **Turntables**—Devices that hold, index, and rotate materials or parts from operation to operation.
8. **Trucks**—Electric, diesel, gasoline, or liquefied petroleum gas powered vehicles equipped with beds, forks, arms, or other holding devices.
9. **Automated guided vehicle systems (AGVS)**—Driverless trains, pallet trucks, and unit load carriers. (See Chapter 5 of this book.)

these are not hard and fast rules, they do provide effective guidelines for the efficient movement of materials in most facility layouts.

The process design and the principles of efficient materials handling provide the framework for selecting specific materials-handling devices—the core of the materials-handling system. Table 6.3 describes some of these devices. Each of these devices has its own unique characteristics and advantages and disadvantages. Conveyors, for instance, are quite expensive to purchase, typically do not require operators, can be used to pace workers, follow fixed routes, and serve as temporary storage and holding devices. Trucks, on the other hand, are relatively inexpensive to purchase, follow no fixed routes, and provide the greatest materials-handling flexibility.

The four basic types of layouts for manufacturing facilities are process, product, cellular manufacturing (CM), and fixed position.

PROCESS LAYOUTS

Process layouts, functional layouts, or job shops as they are sometimes called, are designed to accommodate variety in product designs and processing steps. Figure 4.7 in Chapter 4 of this text depicts two jobs, X and Y, each with different product designs and different number, type, and sequence of processing steps. If a manufacturing facility produces a variety of nonstandard products in relatively small batches, as in a custom machine shop, the facility will probably use a process layout.

Process layouts typically use general-purpose machines that can be changed over rapidly to new operations for different product designs. These machines are usually arranged according to the type of process being performed. For example, all machining would be in one department, all assembly in another department, and all painting in another department. The materials-handling equipment generally consists of forklift trucks, cranes, and other mobile vehicles that allow for the variety of paths followed through the facility by the products produced. Because of their ability to be programmed to fit a variety of products and processing steps, automated guided vehicle systems (AGVS) are also being used in process layouts.

The workers in process layouts must change and adapt quickly to the multitude of operations to be performed on each unique batch of products being produced. These workers must be highly skilled and require intensive job instructions and technical supervision.

Process layouts require ongoing planning, scheduling, and controlling functions to ensure an optimum amount of work in each department and each work station. The products are in the production system for relatively long periods of time, and large in-process inventories usually are present. For more characteristics of process layouts, refer to Chapter 4 of this book.

PRODUCT LAYOUTS

Product layouts are designed to accommodate only a few product and process designs. Figure 4.6 in Chapter 4 of this text illustrates a product layout. Such layouts are designed to allow a direct material flow through the facility for products. Automobile-manufacturing plants are good examples of facilities that use an assembly line or a product layout.

Product layouts typically use specialized machines that are set up once to perform a specific operation for a long period of time on one product. To change over these machines to a new product design requires great expense and long down times. The machines are usually arranged into product departments. Within one product department several processes, such as forming, machining, and assembly, could be performed. Materials-handling equipment is most often permanently positioned, as conveyors, for example.

Workers in product layouts repeatedly perform a narrow range of activities on only a few product designs. The amount of skill, training, and supervision required is small. Although the planning and scheduling activities associated with these layouts are complex, they are not ongoing or continuously intense. Rather, planning and scheduling tend to be done intermittently as product changeovers, demand fluctuations, and special orders occur. For more characteristics of product layouts, refer to Chapter 4.

INDUSTRY SNAPSHOT 6.1

The Nature of Manufacturing Cells

From several studies of CM, we are beginning to gain an understanding of the nature of manufacturing cells. Here is a summary of the facts relating to these cells:

1. Most users of group technology and cellular manufacturing (GT/CM) produce parts in relatively small batches.
2. Most GT/CM uses are in metal-working production.
3. Cells are usually formed by taking production of parts from an existing job shop.
4. There is a full range of small and large firms using GT/CM. Users have from 300 to 17,000 total employees and from 90 to 3,000 total production machines.
5. Large percentages of users report that group technology (GT) is used in these activities: product design (55 percent), manufacturing engineering (75 percent), and cellular manufacturing (55 percent).
6. The number of cells in a CM layout is relatively small. The median is 5, the mean is 9, with a range of from 1 to 48.
7. The number of production machines per cell is relatively small. The mean is 6 with a range of from 3 to 24. Parts rarely are routed to all machines in a cell.
8. There are relatively few workers within cells. The range is from 2 to 15.
9. The percentage of parts produced in cells is a relatively small percentage of the total production. Production in cells averages only about 10 percent of the total. Cells usually appear as islands within larger job shops.
10. Typical CM arrangement is 5 cells, 6 machines per cell, 5 workers per cell. The majority of parts are produced outside the CM system in a job shop.[1]

[1] I. Ham and W. Reed, "First Group Technology Survey Reveals New Manufacturing Game Plan," *Machine and Tool Blue Book* 72, no. 5 (1977): 100–108; K. W. Tunnell Company, "Group Technology: A Review of the State-of-the-Art in the U.S.," An Intra-Company Report, 1978; T. J. Grayson, "An International Review of Group Technology," *SME Technical Paper MM71-186* (Dearborn, MI: Society of Manufacturing Engineers, 1971); N. Hyer, "The Potential of Group Technology for U.S. Manufacturing," *Journal of Operations Management* 4, no. 3 (May 1984).

CELLULAR MANUFACTURING (CM) LAYOUTS

In cellular manufacturing (CM), machines are grouped into cells, and the cells function somewhat like a product layout island within a larger job shop or process layout. Figure 4.8 in Chapter 4 illustrates a CM layout with four cells. Each cell in a CM layout is formed to produce a single *parts family*—a few parts all with common characteristics, which usually means that they require the same machines and have similar machine settings. Industry Snapshot 6.1 describes the nature of manufacturing cells in industry today.

Although the layout of a cell can take on many different forms, the flow of parts tends to be more streamlined when compared to a job shop. The reasons why a CM layout would be attempted are:

FIGURE 6.1   *Fixed-Position Layout*

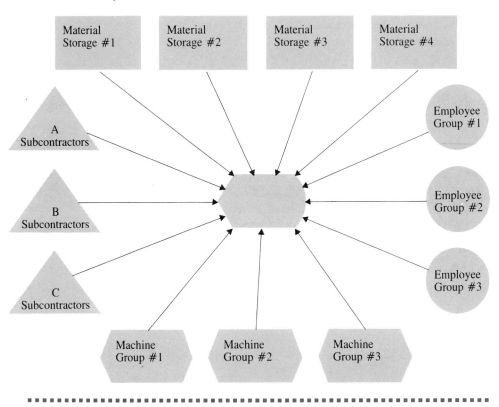

1. Machine changeovers are simplified.
2. Training periods for workers are shortened.
3. Materials-handling costs are reduced.
4. Parts can be made faster and shipped more quickly.
5. Less in-process inventory is required.
6. Production is easier to automate.

In developing a CM layout, the first step is the *cell formation decision,* the initial decision about which production machines and which parts to group into each cell. We shall discuss cell formation decisions later in this chapter. Next, the machines are arranged within each cell. For more about CM, refer to Chapter 4, Production Processes, in this book.

FIXED-POSITION LAYOUTS

Some manufacturing and construction firms use a layout for arranging work that locates the product in a fixed position and transports workers, materials, machines, and subcontractors to and from the product. Figure 6.1 demonstrates this type of

FIGURE 6.2   *Hybrid Layout for Producing Products X and Y*

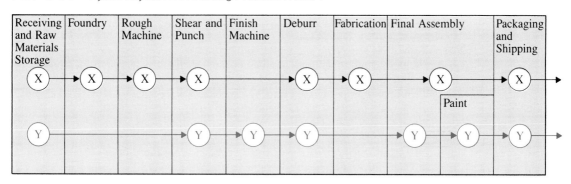

layout. Missile assembly, large aircraft assembly, ship construction, and bridge construction are examples of *fixed-position layouts.*

Although fixed-position layouts are not common, they are used when a product is very bulky, large, heavy, or fragile. The fixed-position nature of the layout minimizes the amount of product movement required. Fixed-position layouts are also used when special environmental conditions, such as "clean rooms," are required during assembly.

HYBRID LAYOUTS

Most manufacturing facilities use a combination of layout types. For example, one may basically adopt a process layout with one section of the facility using an assembly line. Figure 6.2 shows one such *hybrid layout* where the departments are arranged according to the types of processes but the products flow through on a product layout.

Although hybrids make the identification of layout types fuzzy, the importance of understanding the characteristics, advantages, and disadvantages of each type of layout should not be underestimated. As more complex production system layouts are designed, the ability to classify these into either product, process, CM, or fixed-position layouts enhances our ability to develop comprehensive and effective layout designs.

THE JAPANESE APPROACH AND TRENDS
IN MANUFACTURING LAYOUTS

The description of Japanese layouts that opened this chapter suggests that the Japanese are doing something different in their facility layouts. The business philosophy, objectives, and manufacturing methods of the Japanese are somewhat different from those of U.S. firms, and these differences are reflected in their facility layouts. Table 6.4 highlights some of these differences. In general, U.S. manufacturers' layouts have been designed for high worker and machine utilization, whereas Japanese layouts are

TABLE 6.4   *U.S. Layouts versus Japanese Layouts*

Characteristics of U.S. Layouts

Chief objective: High machine and worker utilization.

Means of achieving objective: Long production runs, fixed job assignments for workers in order to realize specialization-of-labor benefits, inventory to guard against machine breakdowns, constant production rates and with defects set aside for later rework, and large production machines that are kept fully utilized.

Appearance of layouts: Very large manufacturing-plant floor plans, extensive areas reserved for inventory, much space used for long conveyors and other materials-handling devices, large production machines requiring much floor space, L-shaped or linear production lines, and generally underutilized floor space.

Characteristics of Japanese Layouts

Chief objective: Manufacturing flexibility, the ability to modify production rates quickly and to change to different product models.

Means of achieving objective: Workers trained at many jobs, heavy investment in preventive maintenance, small machines easily changed over to different product models, workers encouraged to exercise initiative in solving production problems as they occur, workers and machines shifted as needed to solve production problems, production lines slowed down and machine breakdown or quality problems solved as they occur, little inventory carried, and work stations placed close together.

Appearance of layouts: Relatively small manufacturing-plant floor plans, compact and tightly packed layouts that sometimes appear to be overutilized, large percentage of floor space used for production, less floor space occupied by inventory or materials-handling devices, and U-shaped production lines.

---

designed for flexibility and the ability to quickly shift to different product models or to different production rates.[2]

Here are trends in layouts that can be observed in U.S. facilities:

1. Cellular manufacturing layouts within larger process layouts.
2. Automated materials-handling equipment, especially automated storage and retrieval systems, automated guided vehicle systems, automatic transfer devices, and turntables.
3. U-shaped production lines that allow workers to see the entire line and easily travel between work stations. This shape allows the rotation of workers among the work stations along the lines to relieve boredom and relieve work imbalances between work stations. Additionally, teamwork and improved

---

[2] For a more detailed discussion of the Japanese approach to facility layout, see Roger Schonberger, *Japanese Manufacturing Techniques: Nine Hidden Lessons in Simplicity* (New York: Free Press, 1982), 133.

morale tend to result because workers are grouped in smaller areas and communication and social contact are thereby encouraged.

4. More open work areas with fewer walls, partitions, or other obstacles to clear views of adjacent work stations.
5. Smaller and more compact factory layouts. With more automation such as robots, less space needs to be provided for workers. Machines can be placed closer to each other and materials and products travel shorter distances.
6. Less space provided for storage of inventories throughout the layout.

SERVICE FACILITY LAYOUTS

The fundamental difference between service facility and manufacturing facility layouts is that many service facilities exist to bring together customers and organizations' services. This chief difference results in service facility layouts that provide for easy entrance to these properties from freeways and busy thoroughfares. Similarly, large, well-organized, and amply lighted parking areas or garages are typically provided. Additionally, these facilities usually have wide, well-designed walkways to carry people to and from the parking areas.

Entryways and exits are typically well marked, easily located, and designed to accommodate large numbers of customers during peak visiting hours. Powered doors and escalators are often provided to ease the physical effort of opening doors and climbing stairs when armloads of merchandise must be transported.

A unique feature that often becomes the center for analyzing service facility layouts is lobbies or other such receiving or holding areas for customers, waiting lines, service counters, cash registers, and employee work stations. These direct customer receiving and service areas provide a basis for differentiating among types or classes of service facilities. Because of different degrees of customer contact, two extremes exist in layouts of service facilities: those that are almost totally designed around the customer receiving and servicing function and those that are designed around the technologies, processing of physical materials, and production efficiency.

Figure 6.3 shows a layout of a local branch savings and loan. The entire facility is primarily designed around customers — parking, easy entering and exiting, convenient waiting areas, waiting lines for standardized customer servicing, and individualized areas for customer savings account and loan customer servicing. The employee work areas for information processing and financial record keeping make up a secondary element of this type of service facility layout.

At the other extreme, some service facilities are designed much like manufacturing and warehousing facilities; the central focus is on the technologies or physical materials processing and production efficiency. Figure 6.4 depicts a layout of a small hospital. Although some area of the layout is devoted to receiving patients, settling accounts, and releasing patients, the dominant consideration in this layout is the application of medical technologies such as surgery, radiology, laboratory tests, patient rest and recovery, patient feeding, and the effective application of doctors' and nurses' healing skills.

FIGURE 6.3   A Savings and Loan Layout

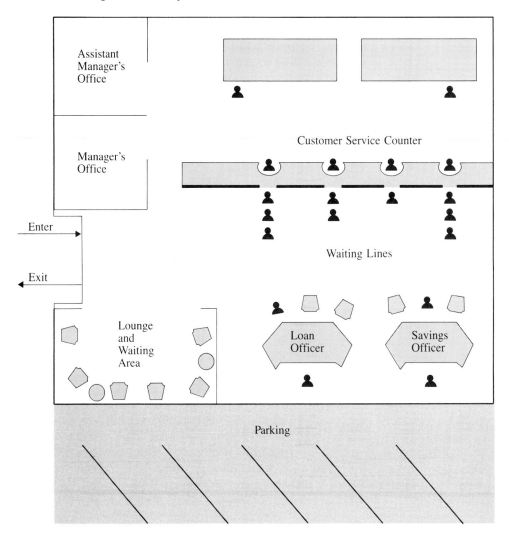

These two extremes in service facility layouts are near the endpoints of a continuum. Other service facilities blend the characteristics of these two layouts. Layouts of exclusive restaurants, for example, typically emphasize customer receiving and individualized servicing perhaps more than the processing and preparation of food products. On the other hand, fast-food restaurant layouts tend to emphasize the processing and preparation of food instead of customer receiving and individual servicing. The mix of customer or technology, physical materials processing, and production efficiency emphases varies according to the type of service offered and the operating strategies of each particular organization.

FIGURE 6.4   *A Hospital Layout*

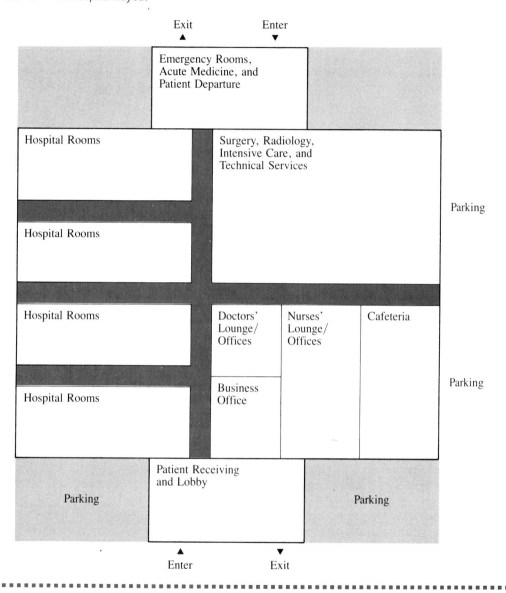

Another service facility that emphasizes both customer receiving and servicing and technologies and physical materials processing is the retail facility. Figure 6.5 shows a layout design for a retail grocery store. The entrance and exit, customer parking, the checkout channels, and the waiting areas near the front of the store have received the layout designers' intense attention. On the other hand, the layout design that displays the organization's products so that customers can easily locate them and

FIGURE 6.5 *A Grocery Store Layout*

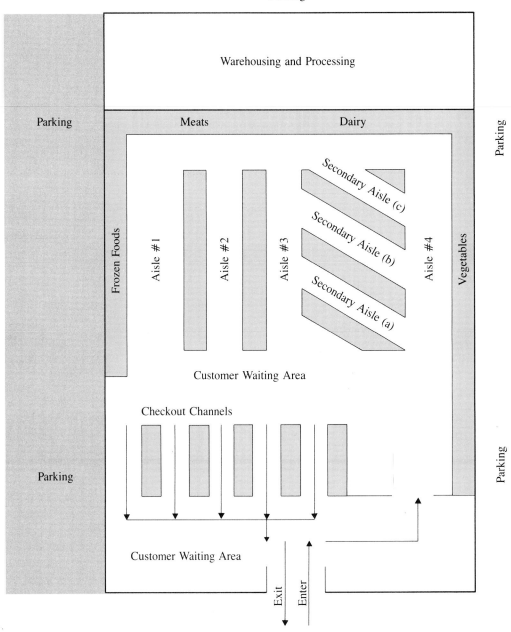

be encouraged to buy them is technology of retailing that also receives layout design emphasis. For example, use of angular aisles to focus customers' attention on items located off main aisles, diamond and circular walking patterns, placement of high-profit items on the floor's perimeter shelves, placement of sale items at the ends of aisles, and other store layout techniques are used to promote the sale of the organization's products.

Those service facility layouts that are primarily oriented toward the technologies, physical materials processing, and production efficiency can be viewed much like manufacturing layouts. Because service facilities almost always require great flexibility in accommodating a variety of processing paths through the facilities, the process layout dominates these layouts. Hospital layouts, for example, typically allow great variety in the processing steps for patients — surgery, radiology, blood chemistry testing, physical therapy, intensive care, and so on. The machinery and human work areas of hospitals are grouped and located according to their processing technologies in much the same way that a custom machine shop would lay out its machines and work stations. In both cases the layouts are designed to accommodate a variety of material (patient) flow patterns through the facilities while grouping employee skills and similar machinery logically according to the technical processes performed.

Let us now turn to some techniques that allow us to develop, analyze, and compare alternative layouts of facilities.

TECHNIQUES FOR DEVELOPING AND ANALYZING FACILITY LAYOUTS

Perhaps the most common facility layout technique is that of using two-dimensional *templates* or *machine cutouts* on a building floor plan. Analysts slide these cutouts of machines, desks, and other equipment — which are drawn to the same scale as the building floor plan — to various positions. They achieve, through trial and error, a detailed layout in which materials and personnel can flow from place to place with little excess travel. The floor plan/template method is particularly useful in developing a layout for an existing department or building or when the configuration of the building is already established through other layout analyses.

Other layout techniques differ among four types of layouts — process and warehouse layouts, product layouts, CM layouts, and customer service layouts.

PLANNING PROCESS AND WAREHOUSE LAYOUTS

The internal arrangement of buildings that use process layouts is usually first analyzed to determine the internal boundaries of operating departments and the external shape of the building. Operations sequence analysis, block diagram analysis, load-distance analysis, and systematic layout planning (SLP) are techniques used to develop these layouts.

ⅰ) *Operations Sequence Analysis*

An early approach to process layouts was the *operations sequence analysis.*[3] This technique develops a good scheme for the arrangement of departments by graphically analyzing the layout problem. Example 6.1 develops the arrangement of ten departments in a manufacturing facility. It shows how we might determine the location of operating departments relative to one another when the external shape and dimensions of the building are not limiting factors.

EXAMPLE 6.1   *Operations Sequence Analysis*

The Red Crystal Glass Products Company produces six products that are transported between ten operating departments within its present production plant. Red Crystal is planning to build a new production facility at a new location next year and wishes to design a plant layout for the new facility. Bill Dewey is given this important layout assignment. Critical to the new layout is the total number of products per month that travel between Red Crystal's operating departments:

		Department and Code					
Department Code	*Department Description*	*Grind 5*	*Paint 6*	*Drill 7*	*Rework 8*	*Glaze 9*	*Ship and Receive 10*
1	Blow and mold	1,000		5,000		3,000	3,000
2	Heat treat	2,000	2,000				3,000
3	Neck		2,000			2,000	
4	Package	1,000		4,000			5,000
5	Grind		2,000				
6	Paint					2,000	
7	Drill				1,000		
8	Rework						1,000
9	Glaze						
10	Ship and receive						

Bill must develop a schematic diagram of the product flows between the operating departments by operations sequence analysis.

Solution

First, develop an initial-solution schematic diagram with circles representing departments and lines representing product travel between departments. The number of products that travel per month between departments is written on the lines:

---

[3] E. S. Buffa, "Sequence Analysis for Functional Layouts," *Journal of Industrial Engineering* 6(March–April 1955):12–25.

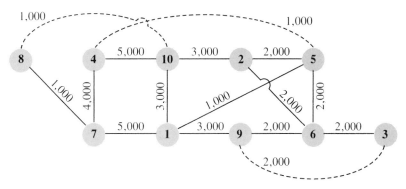

Next, restructure the initial schematic diagram to move departments closer to one another when the number of product movements between them is high, and move departments to form a near-rectangular shape. For example, from the previous diagram, Department 3 could be moved closer to Department 9, and Departments 8, 9, and 6 could be shifted to form a more rectangular shape:

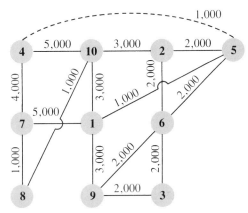

Further inspection of this schematic diagram reveals no other changes in department locations that will substantially improve the layout.

b) _Block Diagram Analysis_
  Example 6.2 takes the final schematic diagram from Example 6.1 and develops a *block diagram analysis,* which sets the general shape and dimensions of the building and the location of the interior departmental boundaries.

EXAMPLE 6.2   *Block Diagram Analysis*

Bill Dewey, at the Red Crystal Glass Products Company, wishes to develop a departmental layout from the schematic diagram of Example 6.1. Whereas the schematic diagram of the last example shows the general relationships among the operating departments, Bill must now determine the dimensions of the building and where the internal departmental boundaries will be. Critical to this building layout are the required areas for each department:

Department	Required Area (Square Feet)	Department	Required Area (Square Feet)
1. Blow and mold	200	6. Paint	200
2. Heat treat	200	7. Drill	400
3. Neck	400	8. Rework	200
4. Package	400	9. Glaze	200
5. Grind	900	10. Ship and receive	200

Bill wishes to use a block diagram analysis to develop a departmental layout for Red Crystal's new building.

Solution

First, use the schematic diagram from Example 6.1 and place each department circle at the center of a square with the same relative area shown in the above table:

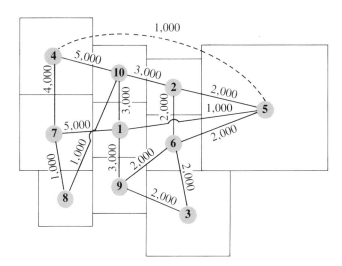

Notice that this layout retains the same general relationships among departments, but the external boundary of the facility is too irregular for functional building design.

Next, vary the shapes of the departments to fit the system into a rectangular building while retaining the required area of each department and the same relationships among departments:

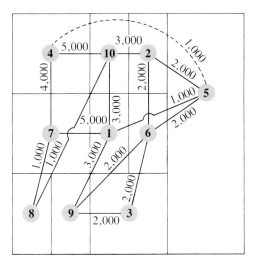

This block diagram is Bill's proposed departmental layout for the new building.

In the previous layout examples of this section, the objective is to develop a layout that minimizes the product or material travel among production processes. This objective is usually dominant in goods-producing systems, but when material travel is not so important, as in service systems, other layout techniques can be used.

Systematic Layout Planning (SLP)

In some production systems such as service systems, the amount of material that flows between departments may not be critical to developing a good facility layout. In these systems *systematic layout planning (SLP)* can be used.[4]

SLP first develops a chart to rate the relative importance of each department being close to every other department. The ratings range from the extremes of absolutely necessary to undesirable. The ratings are based on a variety of reasons—type of customer, ease of supervision, common personnel, common equipment, and so on. Next, an initial schematic diagram, similar to the one in operations sequence analysis presented in Example 6.1, is developed. But this diagram connects the operating departments with color-coded lines to indicate closeness rating. This initial schematic diagram is modified through trial and error until departments with high closeness ratings are adjacent to one another and department and building space limitations are satisfied.

SLP is quite similar to operations sequence and block diagram analyses in both procedures and end results. The only significant difference between these approaches is that SLP allows many reasons for assigning a closeness rating between depart-

[4] Richard Muther and John D. Wheeler, "Simplified Systematic Layout Planning," *Factory* 120(August 1962):68–77; (September 1962): 111–119; (October 1962): 101–113.

ments, whereas operations sequence and block diagram analyses allow a single reason—product or material travel per time period.

d) Load-Distance Analysis

Operations sequence analysis and block diagram analysis do not develop optimal— *the best*—layouts, only good layouts. It is not unusual for these analyses to develop two or more alternative block diagrams, each of which appears to be equally good. *Load-distance analysis* is useful in comparing alternative layouts to identify the one with the least product or material travel per time period. Example 6.3 compares two such layout alternatives.

EXAMPLE 6.3   Load-Distance Analysis

Two layout alternatives are shown below. The facility's products, their travel between departments, and the distances between departments for each layout alternative are also displayed. Which layout alternative minimizes the monthly product travel through the facility?

Layout A

8	4	10	2	5
3	7	1	9	6

Layout B

7	1	9	6	3
4	10	2	5	8

Department Movement Combinations	Distances between Departments (Feet)		Department Movement Combinations	Distances between Departments (Feet)	
	Layout A	Layout B		Layout A	Layout B
1 – 5	30	30	3 – 9	30	20
1 – 7	10	10	4 – 5	30	30
1 – 9	10	10	4 – 7	10	10
1 – 10	10	10	4 – 10	10	10
2 – 5	10	10	5 – 6	10	10
2 – 6	20	20	6 – 9	10	10
2 – 10	10	10	7 – 8	20	50
3 – 6	40	10	8 – 10	20	30

Products	Department Processing Sequence	Number of Products Processed per Month	Products	Department Processing Sequence	Number of Products Processed per Month
a	1 – 5–4–10	1,000	d	1–7–8–10	1,000
b	2 – 6–3– 9	2,000	e	2–5–6– 9	2,000
c	2 –10–1– 9	3,000	f	1–7–4–10	4,000

Solution

1. First, compute the total travel for each product through each layout alternative:

Product	Department Processing Sequence	Compute Distance per Product (Feet)	
		Layout A	Layout B
a	1– 5–4–10	30 + 30 + 10 = 70	30 + 30 + 10 = 70
b	2– 6–3– 9	20 + 40 + 30 = 90	20 + 10 + 20 = 50
c	2–10–1– 9	10 + 10 + 10 = 30	10 + 10 + 10 = 30
d	1– 7–8–10	10 + 20 + 20 = 50	10 + 50 + 30 = 90
e	2– 5–6– 9	10 + 10 + 10 = 30	10 + 10 + 10 = 30
f	1– 7–4–10	10 + 10 + 10 = 30	10 + 10 + 10 = 30

2. Next, compute the total distance traveled per month for each product through each layout alternative:

Product	Products per Month	Distance per Product (Feet)		Distance per Month (Feet)	
		Layout A	Layout B	Layout A	Layout B
a	1,000	70	70	70,000	70,000
b	2,000	90	50	180,000	100,000
c	3,000	30	30	90,000	90,000
d	1,000	50	90	50,000	90,000
e	2,000	30	30	60,000	60,000
f	4,000	30	30	120,000	120,000
			Total	570,000	530,000

3. Layout B results in the least total distance traveled per month through the facility by the products.

The four layout analysis techniques presented — operations sequence, block diagram, systematic layout planning, and load-distance analysis — can be used whether the analyst is or is not restricted in the building configuration. These analyses begin with the production processes and develop a layout that sets the building configuration. Such a procedure is generally preferred because the operation of the facility is likely to be far more efficient than if we first begin with the building configuration and then work backward to see how we can fit the production processes into the building.

I recently worked with a municipal government to develop an improved layout and more efficient operations methods in a newly built jail complex in a large Western city. The jail was designed by a leading architect and was quite an imposing structure. But when the sheriff's department moved into the new facility, the staff found that they needed twice as many law enforcement officers to operate the new facility. I explained to the city administrators that they had fallen into the trap of first setting the configuration of the building and then trying to fit the operations into the building. They will be paying about $400,000 per year in excess labor costs for that error.

This is not to say, however, that layout analysts never begin with the building configuration. Often they do. Existing buildings and departments must frequently be converted to other uses. Sites can be so small or unusual in shape that buildings of only a certain shape are possible. Existing departments must be expanded. All these are only a few examples of *relayouts*. In cases like these, it is unavoidable that we begin with the building configuration and back into the layout design.

Analyzing Layouts with Computers

In recent years many computer programs have been written to develop and analyze process layouts. In the last two decades, three well-known computer analyses have been developed—ALDEP, CORELAP, and CRAFT.[5]

ALDEP—automated layout design programs—and CORELAP—computerized relationship layout planning—are similar in that they use essentially the same procedures and logic as the systematic layout planning (SLP) that we discussed in the previous section. These programs maximize the total closeness rating for all the departments while complying with the required building characteristics. Very large and complex layout problems are feasible, and each analysis outputs a plotted floor-plan block layout.

CRAFT—computerized relative allocation of facilities—uses the same basic procedure and logic as operations sequence and block diagram analyses. CRAFT minimizes the total materials-handling cost per time period for the layout. The material movements per time period are converted to cost per time period for movements of each material between departments. Analysts input an initial block layout, and CRAFT modifies the initial layout until no cost improvements are possible. New initial layouts yield different CRAFT layouts, so some experimentation is advised. The program also can handle complex, quite large layout problems while adhering to complex building characteristics. The outputs of the program are a plotted floor-plan block layout and the cost of the layouts.

These and other computer programs can save time and effort in large and complex layout problems, but their outputs are only the beginning of a finished layout. Their layouts must be fine-tuned by hand and checked for logic, and machines and other elements of the layout must usually be hand-fitted with templates and cutouts.

X PLANNING PRODUCT LAYOUTS

The analysis of assembly lines characterizes much of the analysis of product layouts. The product design and the market demand for the products ultimately determine

---

[5] For further information about these analyses, see Jarrold M. Seehof and Wayne O. Evans, "Automated Layout Design Programs," *Journal of Industrial Engineering* 18(December 1967): 690–695; Robert S. Lee and James M. Moore, "CORELAP—Computerized Relationship Layout Planning," *Journal of Industrial Engineering* 18(March 1967): 195–200; and Elwood S. Buffa and Thomas E. Vollmann, "Allocating Facilities with CRAFT," *Harvard Business Review* 42(March–April 1964): 136–150.

TABLE 6.5   *Terminology of Assembly Line Analyses*

1. **Actual Number of Employees Required** — The number of employees that must be employed to staff a work station. This total number includes the equivalent number of employees working and the equivalent number of employees idle at a work station (see below).
2. **Cycle Time** — The time between units coming off the end of an assembly line.
3. **Equivalent Number of Employees Idle** — The amount of idle time at a work station that is expressed in number of employees. Four employee-hours among all of the employees assigned to a particular work station during an 8-hour shift would be the equivalent of one-half of an employee who is idle.
4. **Equivalent Number of Employees Working** — The amount of work for employees to do at a work station expressed in number of employees. Twenty-nine employee-hours of work at a particular work station during an 8-hour shift would be the equivalent of 29/8 or 3.625 employees working.

5. **Tasks** — Elements of an employee's work. *Grasp pencil, position pencil on paper to write,* and *write the number 4* is an example of a task.
6. **Task Time** — The amount of time required for a well-trained employee to perform a task. Task times are usually expressed in hundredths of a minute or minutes.
7. **Utilization of Employees** — The percentage of the time that employees at a work station or along an entire assembly line are working. This is usually calculated by dividing the equivalent number of employees working by the actual number of employees required.
8. **Work Station** — Physical location where tasks are performed by one or more workers. Tasks are combined into employee jobs at work stations. If more than one employee is assigned to a work station, all perform the same tasks.
9. **Order of Precedence** — The order or sequence in which tasks must be performed.

the technological process steps and the required capacity of assembly lines. The number of personnel and the amount of work per person working on the assembly lines must then be determined. These kinds of studies are known as line balancing.

Line Balancing

Line balancing is the phase of assembly line study that nearly equally divides the work to be done among the workers so that the total number of employees required on the assembly line is minimized. Table 6.5 summarizes some of the terms often used in line balancing. These terms will be used in the examples of this section.

The process that we follow to balance an assembly line is really conceptually quite simple. We determine what tasks are required to completely assemble one unit of the product, and then we divide up the tasks among the workers nearly equally so that all of the tasks get done. Because the work is nearly equally divided among the workers, there is little worker idle time. Table 6.6 explains this process in more detail.

Let us say that we need a product to come off the end of an assembly line every 5 minutes; then the cycle time is 5 minutes. This means there must be a product coming out of every work station along the assembly line in 5 minutes or less. If the amount of work to be done at a particular work station is great, then several workers may be needed to team up to finish the work in 5 minutes or less. On the other hand, if there is only a little work assigned to a work station, only one worker may be needed to complete the work in 5 minutes or less. Now, it is practically impossible to split the

■ ■

TABLE 6.6   The Line-Balancing Procedure

1. Determine what tasks must be performed to complete one unit of a finished product and the sequence in which the tasks must be performed; draw a precedence diagram.
2. Estimate task times (the amount of time it takes a worker to perform each task).
3. Determine the cycle time (the amount of time that would elapse between products coming off the end of the assembly line if the desired hourly production were being produced).
4. Assign each task to a worker and balance the assembly line. This process results in determining the scope of each worker's job or which tasks that he or she will perform. This combining of tasks into workers' jobs usually follows these steps:

a. Starting at the beginning of the precedence diagram, combine tasks into a work station in the order of the sequence of tasks so that the combined task times approach but do not exceed multiples of the cycle time.
b. When a sum of task times at a work station is found that is very close to but does not exceed a multiple of the cycle time, these tasks will be performed at the work station and will determine the scope of the worker's job or the tasks that he or she will perform.
c. When tasks are combined into a work station, the number of multiples of the cycle time is the number of workers required at that work station, all performing the same job.

■ ■

tasks up among work stations so that a unit is finished at every work station in exactly 5 minutes. For example, if the workers while working together at a work station could produce a finished unit in 4.90 minutes, there would be .10 minutes of idle time for each worker at that work station for each unit completed. In line balancing we want to assign tasks to these work stations so that there is little idle time. This means that each work station should be assigned tasks so that a finished unit is completed very close to but not exceeding the cycle time.

Line-Balancing Heuristics

Line balancing is not simple; in fact, there are usually many alternative ways that the work can be divided among the workers. Operations researchers have used linear programming, dynamic programming, and other optimal models to study line-balancing problems. But these solution methods are beyond the scope of this text and also beyond the abilities of most practicing operations managers. Because of the complexity of these problems, heuristic methods, those methods that depend on simple rules, are used to develop good solutions — not optimal, but good solutions. Among these methods are the *incremental utilization heuristic,* the *largest-number-of-following-tasks heuristic,* and the *longest-operation-time heuristic.*

The incremental utilization heuristic simply adds tasks in order of precedence one at a time to a work station until the worker utilization is 100 percent or is observed to fall, then we go to the next work station and repeat this same process for the remaining tasks. Figure 6.6 illustrates the steps in the incremental utilization heuristic, and Example 6.4 uses this heuristic to balance an assembly line that assembles hand-held calculators.[6]

---

[6] For a discussion of the largest-number-of-following-tasks and longest-operation-time heuristics, see R. B. Chase, "Survey of Paced Assembly Lines," *Industrial Engineering* 6, no. 2 (February 1974): 14–18.

FIGURE 6.6 *Steps in Incremental Utilization Heuristic*

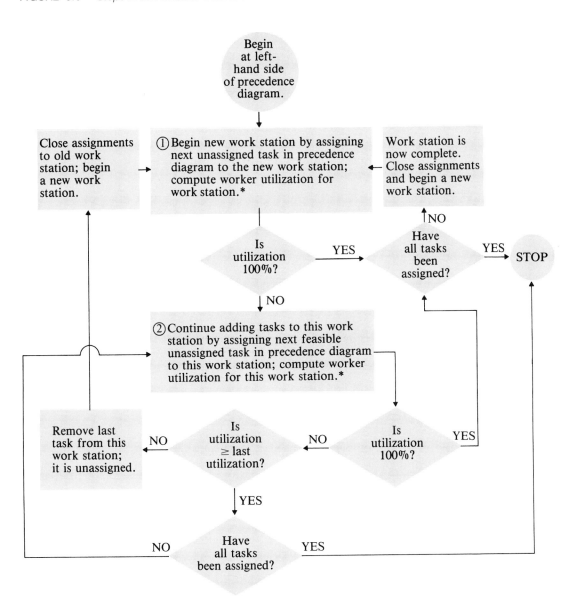

$$*\text{Worker utilization} = \frac{\text{Equivalent number of employees working}}{\text{Actual number of employees required}} \times 100$$

$$= \frac{\left(\begin{array}{c}\text{Sum of task times assigned}\\ \text{to work station}\end{array}\right) \div \text{Cycle time}}{\text{Numerator rounded to next whole number}} \times 100$$

EXAMPLE 6.4   *Line Balancing within Product Layouts*

Textech, a large electronics manufacturer, assembles Model AT75 hand-held calculators at its Midland, Texas, plant. The assembly tasks that must be performed on each calculator are shown below. The parts used in this assembly line are supplied by materials-handling personnel to parts bins used in each task. The assemblies are moved along by belt conveyors between work stations. If 540 calculators must be produced by this assembly line per hour: **(a)** Compute the cycle time per calculator in minutes. **(b)** Compute the theoretical minimum number of employees required. **(c)** How would you combine the tasks into workers' jobs to minimize operator idle time? Evaluate your proposal.

Task	Tasks That Must Immediately Precede	Time to Perform Task (Minutes)	Task	Tasks That Must Immediately Precede	Time to Perform Task (Minutes)
A. Place circuit frame on jig.		.18	I. Place and attach display to inner frame.	H	.30
B. Place Circuit #1 into frame.	A	.12	J. Place and attach keyboard to inner frame.	I	.18
C. Place Circuit #2 into frame.	A	.32	K. Place and attach top body of calculator to inner frame.	J	.36
D. Place Circuit #3 into frame.	A	.45	L. Place and attach power assembly to inner frame.	J	.42
E. Attach circuits to frame.	B,C,D	.51	M. Place and attach bottom body of calculator to inner frame.	K,L	.48
F. Solder circuit connections to central circuit control.	E	.55	N. Test circuit integrity.	M	.30
G. Place circuit assembly in calculator inner frame.	F	.38	O. Place calculator and printed matter in box.	N	.39
H. Attach circuit assembly to calculator inner frame.	G	.42	Total		5.36

Solution

a. Compute the cycle time per calculator:

$$\text{Cycle time} = \frac{\text{Productive time/hour*}}{\text{Demand/hour}} = \frac{54 \text{ minutes/hour}}{540 \text{ calculators/hour}} = .100 \text{ minute/calculator}$$

b. Compute the theoretical minimum number of employees:

$$\frac{\text{Theoretical minimum}}{\text{number of employees}} = \frac{\text{Time for all tasks} \times \text{Demand per hour}}{\text{Productive time per hour}}$$

$$= \frac{5.36 \text{ employee-minutes/calculator} \times 540 \text{ calculators/hour}}{54 \text{ minutes/hour}}$$

$$= 53.60 \text{ employees}$$

c. Balance the line:
   1. First, draw a precedence diagram for the assembly line. This diagram uses circles for tasks and arrows to show precedence relationships.

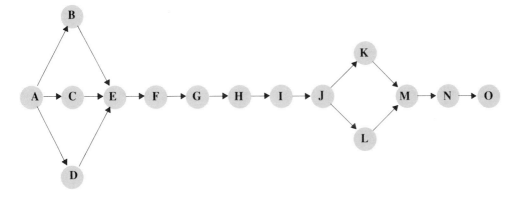

   2. Next, assign tasks to work stations. This is done by strictly following the sequence of tasks (D must follow A, G must follow F, and so on), and the *incremental utilization heuristic* is used to group the tasks into work stations. In this method tasks are combined in sequence until the utilization of the work station (equivalent number of employees working divided by the actual number of employees required times 100) is 100 percent or until the utilization of the work station is observed to fall, and then a new work station is started. Look at Work Station 1 and note that we first consider Task A alone [(1.8 ÷ 2.0) × 100 = 90%]; next we consider Task A and Task B together [(3.0 ÷ 3.0) × 100 = 100%]. Because this combination has a 100 percent utilization, Tasks A and B are combined into Work Station 1 and we now move to Work Station 2. In Work Station 2, as Tasks C, D, and E are combined one task at a time, the work station utilization increases from 80 percent to 96.3 percent and to 98.5 percent; but, when Task F is added to C, D, and E, utilization falls to 96.3 percent. Work Station 2 therefore includes Tasks C, D, and E, and we go on to Work Station 3.

---

* An average of 6 minutes per hour in this example is not productive because of lunch, personal time, machine breakdown, and start-up and shut-down time.

(1) Work Station	(2) Tasks	(3) Employee-Minutes/Calculator	(4) Equivalent Number of Employees Working [(3) ÷ Cycle Time]	(5) Actual Number of Employees Required	(6) Utiliza-tion of Employees [(4) ÷ (5)] × 100
1	A	.18	1.8	2	90.0%
1	A,B	.18 + .12 = .30	3.0	3	100.0
2	C	.32	3.2	4	80.0
2	C,D	.32 + .45 = .77	7.7	8	96.3
2	C,D,E	.32 + .45 + .51 = 1.28	12.8	13	98.5
2	C,D,E,F	.32 + .45 + .51 + .55 = 1.83	18.3	19	96.3
3	F	.55	5.5	6	91.7
3	F,G	.55 + .38 = .93	9.3	10	93.0
3	F,G,H	.55 + .38 + .42 = 1.35	13.5	14	96.4
3	F,G,H,I	.55 + .38 + .42 + .30 = 1.65	16.5	17	97.0
3	F,G,H,I,J	.55 + .38 + .42 + .30 + .18 = 1.83	18.3	19	96.3
4	J	.18	1.8	2	90.0
4	J,K	.18 + .36 = .54	5.4	6	90.0
4	J,K,L	.18 + .36 + .42 = .96	9.6	10	96.0
4	J,K,L,M	.18 + .36 + .42 + .48 = 1.44	14.4	15	96.0
4	J,K,L,M,N	.18 + .36 + .42 + .48 + .30 = 1.74	17.4	18	96.7
4	J,K,L,M,N,O	.18 + .36 + .42 + .48 + .30 + .39 = 2.13	21.3	22	96.8

Total   55

3. Summarize the assignment of tasks to work stations on the assembly line:

Tasks in work stations	A,B	C,D,E	F,G,H,I	J,K,L,M,N,O	
Work stations	→①	→②	→③	→④	
Actual number of employees required	3.0	13.0	17.0	22.0	55.0 Total
Equivalent number of employees working	3.0	12.8	16.5	21.3	53.6 Total
Equivalent number of employees idle	0	.2	.5	.7	1.4 Total

4. Next, compute the efficiency of your proposal:

$$\text{Efficiency} = \frac{\text{Equivalent number of employees working}}{\text{Total actual number of employees required}} = \frac{53.6}{55} = .975, \text{ or } 97.5 \text{ percent}$$

Mixed-Model Line Balancing

Thus far in our study of product layouts, we have assumed that each assembly line produces only one product model. If more than one model must be produced on the same production line, these questions arise:

1. How many of each product model should we produce when it is placed into production (what should be the length of the production run)?
2. In what sequence or order should the production runs of the models be placed into production?

If production runs are too large, models will be placed into production infrequently, in-process inventories of some models will be too high, and the inventory of the other models could be exhausted before they can be placed into production. If production runs are too small, the constant turmoil of so many model changeovers can drive up manufacturing costs.

Companies like Toyota divide the number of each product model included in the monthly production plan by the number of working days in the month. This gives the average number of each model to be produced each day. This number then is split up several times during the day and sequenced in with the other models. As a simple illustration, let us say that we need to produce 300 Ohno models and 200 Zuna models per day and the cycle time per Ohno is 45 seconds and the cycle time per Zuna is 65 seconds. If machine changeovers are negligible, here is a mixed-model balance scheme for this illustration:

Model sequence	20 Zunas	30 Ohnos
Production time (min.)	21.67	22.50
Time of the sequence (min.)	44.17	
Sequences per 8-hour shift	10	
Assembly line run time per shift (min.)	441.7	
Assembly line down time per shift (min.)	38.3	

In this scheme 20 Zuna models would be followed by 30 Ohno models, and this sequence would be repeated every 44.17 minutes, 10 times during an 8-hour shift. The assembly line would operate 441.7 minutes in 8 hours, leaving 38.3 minutes for maintenance, employee breaks, and other purposes. By providing 10 sequences of 20 Zuna models and 30 Ohno models in each 8-hour shift, employees are provided with variety in their work as they switch models. Additionally, because the production runs of each model are relatively small, excessive in-process inventories of each model do not occur.

Planning Cellular Manufacturing (CM) Layouts

As was discussed earlier in this chapter, the initial issue that must be resolved in CM layouts is the cell formation decision: Which machines are assigned to manufacturing cells and which parts will be produced in each cell? If the advantages claimed in Chapter 4, Production Processes, for cellular manufacturing are to actually materialize, this initial decision is crucial. Example 6.5 illustrates the essential elements of such decisions.

EXAMPLE 6.5   *Cell Formation Decisions in Cellular Manufacturing Layouts*

The Acme Machine Shop produces machined parts in a job shop. Acme has recently implemented a group technology (GT) program in its shop, and it is now ready to develop manufacturing cells on the shop floor. Production analysts have identified five parts that seem to meet the requirements of parts appropriate for CM: moderate batch sizes, stable demand, and common physical characteristics. The parts-machine matrix below identifies the five parts (1 through 5) and the machines (A through E) on which the parts are presently produced in the job shop. The Xs in the body of the matrix indicate the machines on which the parts must be produced. For example, Part 1 requires machine operations on Machines A and D.

<table>
<tr><td></td><td></td><td colspan="5" align="center">*Parts*</td></tr>
<tr><td></td><td></td><td>*1*</td><td>*2*</td><td>*3*</td><td>*4*</td><td>*5*</td></tr>
<tr><td></td><td>*A*</td><td>X</td><td></td><td>X</td><td></td><td>X</td></tr>
<tr><td></td><td>*B*</td><td></td><td>X</td><td></td><td>X</td><td>X</td></tr>
<tr><td>*Machines*</td><td>*C*</td><td></td><td>X</td><td></td><td>X</td><td>X</td></tr>
<tr><td></td><td>*D*</td><td>X</td><td></td><td>X</td><td></td><td></td></tr>
<tr><td></td><td>*E*</td><td></td><td>X</td><td></td><td>X</td><td>X</td></tr>
</table>

Acme wishes to assign the machines (and the parts that the machines make) to cells such that if a part is assigned to a cell, all of the machines required to make the part are also in the same cell. For example, if Part 1 were assigned to a cell, Machines A and D must also be assigned to that cell. Arrange the machines and the parts into cells.

Solution

1. **Rearrange the rows.** First, place the machines that produce the same parts in adjacent rows. Notice that Machines A and D are required by Parts 1 and 3; put these two machines in the first two rows. Also notice that Machines B, C, and E are required by Parts 2, 4, and 5; put these three machines in the next three rows.

Parts

		1	2	3	4	5
	A	X		X		X
	D	X		X		
Machines	B		X		X	X
	C		X		X	X
	E		X		X	X

2. **Rearrange the columns.** Next, rearrange the columns such that parts that require the same machines are put in adjacent columns. Notice that Parts 1 and 3 require Machines A and D; put these two parts in the first two columns. Also, notice that Parts 2, 4, and 5 require Machines B, C, and E; put these three parts in the next three columns.

Parts

		1	3	2	4	5*
	A	X	X			X
	D	X	X			
Machines	B			X	X	X
	C			X	X	X
	E			X	X	X

This part–machine matrix contains the solution to this cell formation problem. Parts 1 and 3 are to be produced in Cell 1 on Machines A and D. Parts 2 and 4 are to be produced in Cell 2 on Machines B, C, and E. Part 5* is called an *exceptional part* because it cannot be produced within a single cell: It requires Machine A, which is in Cell 1, and Machines B, C, and E, which are in Cell 2.

There are two fundamental requirements for parts to be made in cells:

1. The demand for the parts must be high enough and stable enough that moderate batch sizes of the parts can be produced periodically.
2. The parts being considered must be capable of being grouped into parts families. Within a part family, the parts must have similar physical characteristics and thus require similar production operations.

In Example 6.5, we assume that the five parts have undergone close scrutiny such that the nature of their demand complies with the first requirement above. Also, parts are assumed to have been chosen such that they require similar production operations. Requiring the same machines is perhaps the strongest indication that parts have similar production operations.

The solution in Example 6.5 would result in four of the parts and five of the machines being assigned to two cells. One of the parts, Part 5, is an exceptional part, which means that it cannot be entirely made within a single cell. The alternatives for producing this part are:

1. *Produce Part 5 by transporting batches of the part between the two cells.* The advantage of this alternative would be that the machine utilization (the percentage of time that the machines operate) of the cells would be higher. The disadvantages of this alternative are the additional materials-handling cost and the additional complexity in coordinating the scheduling of production between the cells.
2. *Subcontract the production of Part 5 to suppliers outside the company.* The advantage of this alternative is that it avoids the additional materials-handling cost and scheduling complexity caused by transporting batches of the part between the cells. The disadvantage is that this subcontracting may cost more than making the part in-house.
3. *Produce Part 5 back in the job shop, outside the CM cells.* The advantage of this alternative is that it avoids the additional materials-handling cost and scheduling complexity caused by transporting batches of the part between the cells and any additional cost of subcontracting. The main disadvantage of this alternative is that the machines on which Part 5 is made (A, B, C, and E) are already in use in the cells of the CM layout. If Part 5 is now to be sent back to the job shop for production, additional machines may have to be purchased.

The cell formation decision that is analyzed in Example 6.5 is not very complex, but many real problems in industry are solved in much the same way as in this example. For example, the Defense Systems Division of Texas Instruments in Dallas, Texas, has several cells in its machine shop that were formed in much the same way as in Example 6.5. In more complex problems, such issues as the following must be resolved:

1. If all of the parts cannot be cleanly divided between cells and we must choose from among several parts the ones that are to be exceptional parts, how will we decide? For example, let us say that we must choose one of two parts to be an exceptional part. How would we decide between the parts? In practice, the

part that has the least additional cost of subcontracting or the least additional cost of producing it in the job shop is chosen.

2. If inadequate production capacity is available to produce all of the parts in cells, which parts should be made outside the cells? Generally, the ones that require the least capacity and require the greatest additional cost to either subcontract or make in the job shop are chosen to remain in the cells.

Once we have made our cell formation decision, we know which machines and parts are assigned to which cells. But it remains to be decided how the machines will be arranged within the cells. Machine templates are often used to fit the machines within cells while considering such factors as the sequence of the machines that each part requires. It might be helpful to refer to Figure 4.8 in Chapter 4, Production Processes, of this text. In Cells #1 and #2 of that figure, all of the parts require the same sequence of machines. These are called *line flow cells:* The machines are arranged in an assembly line fashion, and a line-balancing approach to the within cell layout could be used. In Cells #3 and #4, the parts require a slightly different sequence of machines. Here, the machines are arranged so as to accommodate all parts, minimize part travel, allow smooth part flows while minimizing backtracking, avoid unnecessary congestion, and provide the necessary space for machines and workers.

We have now discussed several techniques for developing layouts for manufacturing operations. Let us now consider how we approach layouts for service operations.

PLANNING CUSTOMER SERVICE LAYOUTS

The customer waiting lines at grocery stores that we have become accustomed to in recent years are not a necessary part of buying groceries. We wait in these lines either because managers have not hired enough checkout employees or because they do not have enough checkout counters.

More personnel can be hired to staff checkout counters and an abundance of checkout counters can be constructed, but these actions result in increased costs. Fewer checkout counters cost less, but customers must then wait in lines. If we have to wait in line too long, we may not come back to a particular store, and this results in a cost to the store's management. Either too many or too few checkout counters can therefore become exorbitantly expensive. A balance must obviously be struck.

Managers are not, however, ordinarily restricted to using fixed-capacity service centers in POM. In fact, we observe that managers routinely vary the capacity of service centers by having standby personnel and machines that can be assigned to specific service centers either to prevent excessive waiting lines from forming or to quickly work off excessively long lines. In grocery stores, for example, workers who ordinarily stock shelves can be called to standby checkout counters to activate additional channels or to speed up operating channels that have excessively long lines.

Part-time workers who are on call, standby equipment, and other contingency measures to avoid excessive line lengths and excessive waiting times are commonly used in services. These service industries must avoid undesirable waiting line situations because their customers are the arrivals, and perhaps nothing irks customers more than to stand in line needlessly while waiting to be served.

The same management approaches to waiting lines may be used in both service industries and manufacturing. The factor of economics is present in both types of production systems: Balance the cost of more service center capacity against the savings resulting from shorter waiting lines. But in service industries the cost of long customer waiting lines may be so high that it cannot be tolerated. Thus alternative, flexible service capacities and other schemes are evolving. Appointment schedules, express checkout counters, standby workers and facilities, "take-a-number" procedures, and other approaches have developed to ease the effects of waiting lines on customer convenience.

Queuing theory, or waiting line theory, has evolved to assist managers in these kinds of questions: How many customer service channels should be staffed during each time period of the day? How much time will customers wait, on the average, if we staff a particular number of customer service channels during each time period of the day? How many customers will be in waiting lines on the average if we staff a particular number of customer service channels during each time period of the day? And how much maximum room will we need for waiting lines if we staff a particular number of customer service channels? These and other related questions can be important in customer service layouts, and they can be analyzed by queuing theory, which is treated in Appendix D at the end of this book.

SUMMARY

Facility layout means planning the arrangement of all of the elements of production in and around buildings. The objectives of layouts are to provide organizations with ways of achieving their operations strategies. Providing adequate production capacity, controlling materials-handling costs, allowing high labor productivity, promoting high volume and product flexibility, accommodating employee needs, and providing for employee safety and health are layout objectives common to manufacturing operations. Warehouse, service, and office operations have additional objectives beyond those of manufacturing.

Manufacturing facilities use product, CM, process, and fixed-position layouts. In product layouts, the overriding concern is for balancing the assembly line such that employee idle time is minimized. In CM layouts, the initial cell formation decision receives much attention. In process layouts, minimizing the total material travel and cost is the central focus. Operations sequence analysis, block diagram analysis, load-distance analysis, and systematic layout planning are used to analyze process layouts. CRAFT, CORELAP, and ALDEP are computer packages that have been used for over two decades to plan manufacturing layouts.

Customer-oriented layouts are commonly analyzed to determine the optimal number of customer service channels during each time period of the day. Alternatively, if the number of customer service channels is set, the average number of waiting customers, the average waiting time per customer, and the maximum waiting space can be calculated. The basis of these analyses is known as queuing theory or waiting line theory.

REVIEW AND DISCUSSION QUESTIONS

1. Define *facility layout.*
2. Name three objectives for these types of layouts:
   a. manufacturing operations,
   b. warehouse operations,
   c. service operations,
   d. office operations.
3. Which is the dominant objective for these types of layouts?
   a. manufacturing operations,
   b. warehouse operations,
   c. service operations,
   d. office operations.
4. Name four principles of materials handling.
5. Name and describe five types of materials-handling devices.
6. What are AGVS? Describe them and discuss their uses.
7. Name and describe four types of layouts for manufacturing operations.
8. What are the principal decisions that must be made in a CM layout? Define and describe the cell formation problem.
9. What are the objectives of cell formation decisions? Describe how we analyze cell formation problems. What is an exceptional part? What do we do with exceptional parts?
10. Compare and contrast the layout of a savings and loan with the layout of a hospital. How are they alike and how are they different?
11. Explain why we balance assembly lines. Describe the general procedure of line balancing.
12. Name three line-balancing heuristics. Explain the incremental utilization heuristic.
13. Describe the Japanese approach to manufacturing layouts. Compare and contrast the Japanese and U.S. approaches.
14. Name five trends in manufacturing layouts.

PROBLEMS

1. The Los Angeles plant of Computer Products Corporation (CPC) is planning to add a new wing to its existing production plant. The new wing will house the manufacture of electronic assemblies for CPC's own in-house use and for other firms in the electronics and computer industries. Practically all of the production from the new wing will be represented by five assemblies: P55 Power Unit, Z4 Converter, U69 Equalizer, K5 Audio, and T22 Stabilizer. The layout of the new wing will be based on the processes used to manufacture the assemblies. The following estimates have been developed for the number of trips of batches of assemblies between production departments for next year:

Department		Department Code						
Code	Department	1	2	3	4	5	6	7
1	Receiving		1,600	1,500	200			
2	Kitting			1,400	200			
3	Inspection				2,900			
4	Insertion					3,300		
5	Solder						3,000	300
6	Finish							3,000
7	Package and Ship							

Develop a schematic diagram of the general relationships among the production departments by using operations sequence analysis.

2. Use the schematic diagram developed in Problem 1 as a starting point and use block diagram analysis to develop a departmental layout for CPC's new building wing. The plant's engineering department has determined that the production departments in the new wing have these space requirements:

Department	Required Area (Square Feet)	Department	Required Area (Square Feet)
1. Receiving	1,200	5. Solder	2,400
2. Kitting	600	6. Finish	1,200
3. Inspection	600	7. Package and ship	1,200
4. Insertion	2,400		

3. The ABC Food Market has just purchased a building at a new location. This building has 80,000 square feet of floor space, measures 200 feet by 400 feet, and has ample parking. ABC's management has requested help from a local consultant to assist it in designing a facility layout for this store. The consultant is given this information:

Department	A	B	C	D	E	F	G	H
				Average Daily Customer Traffic between Departments				
A	—	2,000	1,000	0	500	1,500	200	300
B		—	500	1,000	500	500	0	500
C			—	500	1,500	200	0	300
D				—	0	500	500	500
E					—	0	500	0
F						—	500	1,000
G							—	500
H								—

Department	Required Area (Sq. Ft.)	Department	Required Area (Sq. Ft.)	Department	Required Area (Sq. Ft.)
A	5,000	D	8,000	G	16,000
B	5,000	E	4,000	H	12,000
C	10,000	F	20,000		

ABC's management has further indicated that the consultant could arrange the departments in any configuration within the building and that present entrances and exits could be modified to meet the needs of the layout. The firm wishes to minimize customer travel among departments.

a. Develop an initial schematic diagram for the arrangement of departments within the food store facility.

b. Use operations sequence analysis to develop a "best" schematic diagram for the departments.

c. Use block diagram analysis to develop a final departmental layout. (Note: The areas for departments listed earlier include provisions for aisles.)

4. A warehouse processes six products monthly: a, b, c, d, e, and f. Two alternative layouts for the warehouse are being considered, A and B:

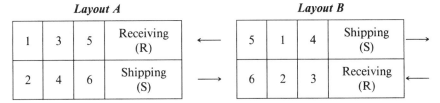

The products, their monthly production levels, their sequence of processing, and distances between processing departments are shown in the following table:

Product	Number of Products Processed/Month	Product Sequences	Sequence Distances (Feet) Layout A	Sequence Distances (Feet) Layout B
a	1,000	R–1–S	70	50
b	3,000	R–2–S	70	50
c	2,000	R–3–S	50	30
d	3,000	R–4–S	50	30
e	2,000	R–5–S	30	70
f	2,000	R–6–S	30	70

Which layout alternative minimizes the monthly warehouse travel? (Use load-distance analysis.)

5. A manufacturing plant is adding a new wing to its building to manufacture a new product line with five models: a, b, c, d, and e. Two layout alternatives are shown below. The new wing's product models, their movements through six departments, and the distances between departments are also shown.

Layout A

1	2	3
4	5	6

Layout B

4	1	3
2	5	6

Product Model	Product Model Processing Sequence	Number of Products Processed per Month	Product Model Movements	Distances between Departments (Feet)	
				Layout A	Layout B
a	1–2–3	2,000	1–2	15	25
b	4–5–6	2,000	1–5	30	10
c	1–5–6	3,000	2–3	15	35
d	2–5–6	1,000	2–4	20	10
e	2–4–3	3,000	2–5	15	15
			3–4	35	25
			4–5	15	25
			5–6	10	10

Which layout alternative minimizes the monthly product travel through the proposed new wing? (Use load-distance analysis.)

6. In Problem 5 the industrial engineers have just come up with some additional information — the materials-handling cost for each product. The cost of moving a single unit of each product between departments in the proposed wing differs because of the weight, bulkiness, and fragility of the products. These materials-handling costs increase as the distance moved increases:

Product Model	Materials-Handling Cost per Unit per Foot Moved	Product Model	Materials-Handling Cost per Unit per Foot Moved
a	$.005	d	$.010
b	.003	e	.007
c	.001		

Which layout, Layout A or Layout B, minimizes the monthly materials-handling cost for the proposed wing?

7. The Stratofit Manufacturing Company has just purchased an abandoned warehouse and plans to expand its manufacturing operations into this building. Two alternative layouts are being evaluated, Layouts 1 and 2, shown below. The company is a high-volume manufacturer of patented electromechanical devices used in several different industries. Because Stratofit's monthly volume is so high, the layout that is selected should minimize monthly product travel so that the cost and confusion of unnecessary materials handling is avoided. The two layouts shown are set on a 2,500-square-foot matrix background (in other words, the background squares are 50 × 50 feet), and products are assumed to travel in straight lines between centers of

Layout 1

	Package (8)			Paint (4)			
			Final Assembly (7)	Electronics (6)		Foundry (2)	
	Shipping and Receiving (1)						
		Fabrication (5)		Machine (3)		Office	

Layout 2

	Package (8)		Shipping and Receiving (1)		Final Assembly (7)		Paint (4)	
						Electronics (6)		
	Foundry (2)		Machine (3)		Fabrication (5)		Office	

departments. Stratofit manufactures eight products at this location. The product model codes, the sequence of processing products through manufacturing departments, and the estimated monthly production of each model are shown below:

Product Model Code	Processing Sequence	Monthly Production (Units)	Product Model Code	Processing Sequence	Monthly Production (Units)
5555	1–2–3–4–7–1	5,000	8960	1–5–7–8–1	2,000
5285	1–3–5–7–8–1	5,000	9110	1–7–4–6–1	6,000
9560	1–5–6–8–1	10,000	2955	1–2–3–8–1	3,000
9999	1–2–3–5–4–7–1	4,000	6666	1–6–4–7–1	5,000

a. Use load-distance analysis to determine which layout should be adopted by Stratofit.
b. Compare the two layouts; which one do you prefer? Why?

8. The Los Angeles plant of Computer Products Corporation (CPC) will soon add a new wing to its present manufacturing building to manufacture electronic assemblies. The plant's management is considering two alternative layouts:

Layout I

Layout II

The plant's electronic assemblies, the trips that batches of electronic assemblies make between departments, and the distances between departments are shown below:

	Distances between Departments (Feet)	
Trips between Departments	*Layout I*	*Layout II*
1–2	24	50
1–3	24	30
1–4	38	46
2–3	44	20
2–4	30	72
3–4	44	52
4–5	50	40
5–6	50	44
5–7	50	60
6–7	40	40

Sequence of Processing Assemblies through Departments

Electronic Assemblies	Department Processing Sequence	Batches of Assemblies to Be Produced per Year
P55 Power Unit	1–2–3–4–5–6–7	1,400
Z4 Converter	1–2–4–5–6–7	200
U69 Equalizer	1–3–4–5–6–7	1,200
K5 Audio	1–3–4–5–7	300
T22 Stabilizer	1–4–5–6–7	200

Use load-distance analysis to determine which layout minimizes the annual distance that batches of assemblies travel through the new wing.

9. A firm is planning to set up an assembly line to assemble 300 units per hour, and 50 minutes per hour are productive. The time to perform each task and the tasks that must precede each task are:

Task	Tasks That Immediately Precede	Time to Perform Task (Minutes)	Task	Tasks That Immediately Precede	Time to Perform Task (Minutes)
A	—	.69	F	B	1.10
B	A	.55	G	C,D,E	.75
C	B	.21	H	G,F	.43
D	B	.59	I	H	.29
E	B	.70			

   a. Draw a network diagram of precedence relationships.
   b. Compute the cycle time per unit in minutes.
   c. Compute the theoretical minimum number of assembly line employees required to produce 300 units per hour.

10. The Bulk Mail Specialty Company prepares, assembles, and mails advertising packages for customers on a contract basis. One such contract has just been signed, and Bulk's production planner, Jesse Brown, is developing a layout for the assembly line. These tasks, their predecessor tasks, and task times have been identified and estimated as shown below. Jesse knows that the contract specifies that 10,000 mailers must be processed in five working days, Bulk works only one 8-hour shift per day, and employees are allowed two 15-minute coffee breaks per shift.
   a. Draw a network diagram of the precedence relationships.
   b. Compute the cycle time in minutes.
   c. Compute the theoretical number of assembly line employees required for the contract.

Task	Tasks That Immediately Precede	Task Times (Minutes/Mailer)
A. Inspect materials for quality	—	.45
B. Prepare kits for assembly	A	.10
C. Get and fold industrial circular	B	.15
D. Assemble and glue envelopes	B	.22
E. Get and fold retail circular	B	.19
F. Put list of industrial outlets in circular	C	.31
G. Attach address to industrial envelope	D	.11
H. Attach address to retail envelope	D	.16
I. Put list of wholesale outlets in retail circulars	E	.20
J. Seal industrial circular into envelope	F,G	.41
K. Preassemble retail package into envelope	H,I	.10
L. Prepare plastic sleeve to fit over retail envelope	I	.05
M. Seal entire retail package into plastic sleeve	K,L	.19
N. Process addressed industrial and retail mailers through postage machine	J,M	.26
O. Combine mailers into bulk mail packages	N	.18

11. In Problem 10, combine the tasks into workers' jobs to minimize employee idle time by using the incremental utilization heuristic. Evaluate your solution.

12. Lectro Inc. assembles alternators for automobiles. Ten basic tasks must be performed along the assembly line. The time to perform each task and the tasks that must immediately precede each task are:

Task	Tasks That Immediately Precede	Time to Perform Task (Minutes)	Task	Tasks That Immediately Precede	Time to Perform Task (Minutes)
A	—	.10	G	D,F	.30
B	A	.15	H	G	.50
C	A	.20	I	H	.60
D	B,C	.30	J	I	.50
E	—	.40			Total 3.45
F	E	.40			

If 400 alternators per hour must be produced by the assembly line, 50 minutes per hour are productive, and a maximum of three tasks can be combined into each work station:

a. Draw a network diagram of the precedence relationships.

b. Compute the cycle time per alternator in minutes.

c. Compute the theoretical minimum number of assembly line employees required.

d. Combine the tasks into workers' jobs to minimize employee idle time by using the incremental utilization heuristic. Evaluate your proposal.

13. Serve Fast Inc., a fast-food restaurant in Los Angeles, will soon open its second store. Serve Fast's manager is now planning how to arrange the kitchen and food products assembly area in the new store. Of utmost importance in this layout is the arrangement of tasks into employee work stations so that a minimum amount of employee idle time is experienced. Toward this goal the manager wants to develop a line-balancing analysis. The time to perform each task in constructing Serve Fast's principal product, the Best Burger, and the tasks that must immediately precede each task are:

Task	Tasks That Immediately Precede	Time to Perform Task (Minutes)	Task	Tasks That Immediately Precede	Time to Perform Task (Minutes)
A	—	.19	H	—	3.05
B	—	.15	I	—	.50
C	—	.20	J	H,I,G	.60
D	—	.10	K	J	.30
E	A,B	.23	L	K	.25
F	C,D	.20			Total 6.05
G	E,F	.28			

Two hundred burgers per hour must be prepared by the crew and 50 minutes per hour are productive.

    a. Draw a network diagram of the precedence relationships.

    b. Compute the cycle time per burger in minutes.

    c. Compute the theoretical minimum number of assembly line employees required.

    d. How would you combine tasks into workers' jobs to minimize employee idle time? Use the incremental utilization heuristic. Evaluate your proposal.

COMPUTER PROBLEMS/CASES

ACUTE MEDICAL CLINIC LAYOUT

The Acute Medical Clinic needs to expand and has just purchased an existing one-story office building with 10,000 square feet of floor space. Acute is now developing plans for remodeling and equipping the building to fit its medical processes. A consultant has been hired to analyze the clinic's processes and recommend a layout for its building. The consultant has presented Acute with two alternative plans, Layout α and Layout β.

    Acute's staff must now decide between the two layouts. As a first step, they have agreed on closeness ratings for locating departments close to one another. On a scale from 1 (not important) to 10 (very important), the closeness ratings are as shown in the accompanying table. These closeness ratings reflect many factors that make it desirable to locate departments adjacent to one another. Among these factors are the number of patients expected to flow between departments per month, the need to transport patients quickly between departments, the need to conserve doctors' time, the acuteness of the type of cases that flow between departments, the amount of materials that flow between departments, and the usual sequence of processing patients through the building.

Layout α

	Surgery (7)	Emergency (8)
Doctors' Offices (4)	Laboratory (6)	Pharmacy (3)
		Admissions and Dismissals (2)
	Examination Rooms (5)	Waiting Room (1)

Layout β

Department \\ Department	Waiting Room (1)	Admissions and Dismissals (2)	Pharmacy (3)	Doctors' Offices (4)	Examination Rooms (5)	Laboratory (6)	Surgery (7)	Emergency Room (8)
1. Waiting room	—	8	8	1	5	4	1	6
2. Admissions and dismissals		—	8	3	5	4	1	7
3. Pharmacy			—	3	5	4	3	5
4. Doctors' offices				—	9	2	6	3
5. Examination rooms					—	5	6	7
6. Laboratory						—	9	8
7. Surgery							—	10

The two layouts are set on a matrix background where one square represents 100 square feet. Acute's staff wants to minimize the total distance between departments as weighted by the closeness ratings. In other words, the distance between two departments would be multiplied by the closeness rating for the pair to obtain a closeness-weighted distance. The distance between departments is assumed to be measured by straight lines that connect the approximate centers of the departments. The total closeness-weighted distance for the building would include the closeness-weighted distances for all possible combinations of pairs of departments:

$$\text{Number of combinations} = \sum_{i=1}^{n} (n - i), \text{ where n is the number of departments}$$

or 28 in this problem.

Assignment

1. Analyze the two layouts to determine which one minimizes the total closeness-weighted distance.
2. What changes in these layouts are suggested by your analysis?
3. Discuss how you would change the approach of this analysis in order to make it more realistic.

COMPUTER PRODUCTS CORPORATION (CPC)

Billie David, methods analyst at the Los Angeles plant of Computer Products Corporation (CPC), has been studying the assembly line at the plant that produces bar code scanners. She has been asked by her boss to recommend ways of decreasing worker idle time on the assembly line in order to reduce the labor cost of the scanners. Billie has developed this information:

Task	Tasks That Must Immediately Precede	Time to Perform Task (Minutes)
A. Kit the purchased assemblies	—	1.49
B. Inspect the kitted assemblies	A	3.58
C. Process controller board through auto-insertion equipment line	—	1.90
D. Process controller board through soldering equipment line	C	3.89
E. Trim and finish controller board	D	2.16
F. Assemble power unit into chassis	B	1.25
G. Assemble reader unit into chassis	F	.90
H. Assemble controller board into chassis	E,G	1.56
I. Assemble display unit into chassis	H	2.58
J. Inspect and test finished scanner	I	4.76
K. Package finished scanner	J	.69
	Total	24.76

Fifty bar code scanners must be produced by the assembly line per hour. An average of 55 minutes per hour are productive because of personal time, machine breakdown, and start-up and shut-down times. Because the union contract restricts the kinds of tasks that can be combined into work stations, Billie has grouped the tasks within these compatibility groups:

Compatibility Group	Tasks
Group I	A,B
Group II	C
Group III	D
Group IV	E
Group V	F,G,H,I,J,K

For example, Tasks F and G could be combined into one work station, but Tasks E and F could not. Tasks within compatibility groups may be combined while observing the precedence relationships; in other words, adjacent tasks along the network diagram may be combined.

Assignment

1. Draw a network diagram of the precedence relationships.
2. Compute the cycle time per bar code scanner.
3. Compute the theoretical minimum number of employees required.
4. Use the *POM Computer Library* that accompanies this text to solve this line-balancing problem. This package uses the incremental utilization heuristic and forms work stations.
5. How many employees are required on the assembly line? How many work stations are there? Describe *each* work station: How many employees are required, which tasks are performed, and what percentage of the time are employees idle?
6. What other factors should be considered in planning these work stations?
7. Discuss how you would implement your solution in a real manufacturing setting. What obstacles would you expect to encounter? How would you overcome these obstacles?

THE SUITCASE MANUFACTURING AND EXPORT COMPANY

The Suitcase Manufacturing and Export Company has just received an order for 1,500,000 leather briefcases from a large European distributor to be delivered over a period of 300 workdays. Because this product has never been produced before by the company, an assembly line must be planned to produce the order on a basis of one 8-hour shift per day. The company's employees are allowed to take two 15-minute coffee breaks per shift, they take 15 minutes per shift to clean up their immediate work area, and they lose an average of about 20 minutes per shift because of machinery breakdowns or material delivery delays. Suitcase's staff has identified these tasks and their predecessor tasks, and has estimated the time required for each task as shown in the table below. Four production departments will do the work on the cases: metals, woods, leather, and final assembly. The union contract does not allow workers to do work outside their own departments (for example, an individual employee could not do both leather and wood work), but they are allowed to do any work within their own production departments.

Task	Tasks That Immediately Precede	Task Times (Minutes/Case)
A. Process hide through cleaning bath	—	2.05
B. Cut wood components according to templates	—	.65
C. Process metal hinges through stamping operation	—	.45
D. Process metal closure components through stamping operation	—	.30
E. Process hide through tanning process	A	3.60
F. Trim wood components to dimension	B	.41
G. Tumble metal hinges to finish edges	C	.22
H. Tumble metal closure components to finish	D	.41
I. Cut hide into case blanks	E	2.15
J. Attach wood components into frame subassembly	F	1.02
K. Put metal hinges through plating process	G	.70
L. Put metal closure components through plating process	H	.80
M. Feather edges and sew corners of leather components	I	2.71
N. Rout out attaching grooves in wood frame subassembly	J	.79
O. Dye leather hide subassemblies	M	3.90
P. Bend metal handle and attach brackets	—	.61
Q. Assemble hinges, frame, closures, handle, and leather subassemblies	K,L,N,O,P	4.10
R. Assemble inner liner and shrink to case	Q	.71
S. Attach name plate	R	.30
T. Package for shipment	S	.21

Assignment

1. Draw a network diagram of the precedence relationships.
2. Compute the cycle time per briefcase in minutes.
3. Compute the theoretical minimum number of assembly line employees required.
4. Use the *POM Computer Library* to plan an assembly line for the briefcases. This package uses the incremental utilization heuristic for analyzing assembly lines.
5. How many employees are required on the assembly line? How many work stations are there? Describe *each* work station: How many employees are required, which tasks are performed, and what percentage of the time are employees idle?
6. What other factors should be considered in planning these work stations?
7. Discuss how you would implement your solution in a real manufacturing setting. What obstacles would you expect to encounter? How would you overcome these obstacles?

SELECTED BIBLIOGRAPHY

Buffa, E. S., G. C. Armour, and T. E. Vollmann. "Allocating Facilities with CRAFT." *Harvard Business Review* 42(March–April 1964):136–158.

Chase, R. B. "Survey of Paced Assembly Lines." *Industrial Engineering* 6, no. 2(February 1974):14–18.

Francis, R. L., and J. A. White. *Facility Layout and Location: An Analytical Approach.* Englewood Cliffs, NJ: Prentice-Hall, 1974.

Green, Timothy J., and Randall P. Sadowski. "A Review of Cellular Manufacturing Assumptions, Advantages, and Design Techniques." *Journal of Operations Management* 4, no. 2(February 1984):85–97.

Gunther, R. E., G. D. Johnson, and R. S. Peterson. "Currently Practiced Formulations of the Assembly Line Balance Problem." *Journal of Operations Management* 3, no. 3(August 1983):209–221.

Ham, I., K. Hitomi, and T. Yoshida. *Group Technology: Applications to Production Management.* Boston: Kluwer-Nijhoff Publishing, 1985, Chapter 9.

Hyer, Nancy Lea. "The Potential of Group Technology for U.S. Manufacturing." *Journal of Operations Management* 4, no. 3(May 1984):183–202.

Hyer, Nancy Lea, and U. Wemmerlov. "Group Technology and Productivity." *Harvard Business Review* 62(July–August 1984):140–149.

Jacobs, F. Robert, John W. Bradford, and Larry P. Ritzman. "Computerized Layout: An Integrated Approach to Special Planning and Communications." *Industrial Engineering* (July 1980):56–61.

Lee, Robert S., and James M. Moore. "CORELAP—Computerized Relationship Layout Planning." *Journal of Industrial Engineering* 18(March 1967):195–200.

Liggett, R. S., and W. J. Mitchell. "Interactive Graphic Floor Plan Layout Method." *Computer Aided Design* 13, no. 5(September 1981):289–298.

Muther, Richard, and John D. Wheeler. "Simplified Systematic Layout Planning." *Factory* 120(August, September, and October 1962):68–77, 101–113, 111–119.

Schuler, Randall S., Larry P. Ritzman, and Vicki L. Davis. "Merging Perspective and Behavioral Approaches for Office Layout." *Journal of Operations Management* 1, no. 3(February 1981):131–142.

Seehof, Jarrold M., and Wayne O. Evans. "Automated Layout Design Programs." *Journal of Industrial Engineering* 18(December 1967):690–695.

CHAPTER 7

ALLOCATING RESOURCES TO STRATEGIC ALTERNATIVES

ASSIGNING NEW-PRODUCT DEVELOPMENT PROJECTS

The director of new-product development at the corporate headquarters of Computer Products Corporation (CPC) in San Jose, California, is planning next year's projects. Five new products have been selected by top management to be developed next year. Each of the five projects will be assigned to a development team at the R&D center in San Jose. Five teams have been assembled from other projects that have been completed or nearly completed, from other divisions within CPC, and from outside CPC. Because the teams differ in the abilities of the team members and because each project requires a unique set of tasks, certain teams are better suited for assignment to certain projects. Although the director knows that every team could successfully complete any of the five projects, certain team–project matchups will be less efficient and cost more

money. There does not seem to be a simple assignment scheme. For example, it would be good to assign the new memory device project to Team #3, but it would also be good to assign Team #3 to either the graphics terminal or the portable PC project. The director knows that CPC's board of directors will be monitoring the progress of these projects because it is an important part of the long-range strategic plan of the corporation. Also, the board of directors has emphasized that each manager will be expected to use his resources efficiently in order to accomplish CPC's long-range strategic objectives. The director's problem is to assign each project to only one team and each team to only one project such that the total cost of developing the five new products is minimized.

Like the director of new-product development in the vignette on the previous page, all operations managers must use as little of their resources as necessary to accomplish as much of their operations strategies as possible. This is what managers mean by "getting the most bangs for their bucks." As operations managers develop operations strategies, they make decisions about positioning the production system, focusing the factories, designing products and developing production processes, determining production capacity and facility location, and facility layout. In these decisions they inevitably face up to the reality of limited resources.

When we refer to resources, we are talking about all of the things that are required for production. Included in this term are personnel, machines and equipment, cash and capital funds, materials and supplies, utilities, floor space, and other resources. These are the means of production, and each may be scarce to each operations manager's particular situation. These resources were not always as scarce as they are today. Shortly after World War II, production was taken for granted. New products were developed and introduced at a rapid pace into new and expanding markets. Operations managers were expected to produce the products and services that the customers demanded, at an acceptable quality level, on time, and at the budgeted cost. Operations managers measured up to these expectations largely because of the abundance of resources in the period. The highly developed wartime work force, materials stockpiles, and excess postwar production capacity all combined to make operations managers' jobs a little easier.

Conditions are different today. Certain supplies are scarce today. For example, strontium nitrate, a chemical used in the pyrotechnic (fireworks) industry, is produced by only one supplier in Britain. This material is rationed to the supplier's customers at a very high price. Titanium, nickel, and other materials used in steel making and other basic industries are similarly scarce. The dominant question for the users of these materials is: Can we get the quantities of materials we need when we need them? It used to be: Which supplier has the best price? Delivery times for machine tools such as lathes and boring mills are well over one year. As Industry Snapshot 7.1 illustrates, there is a growing shortage of people with certain skills, from managers to workers. The shortage of energy products (natural gas, electricity, gasoline, diesel fuel, and other fuels) is a long-term concern to all operations managers. Shortages of water in some states sometimes curtail production.

These and other resource scarcities are causing hectic shifts in operations strategies to meet objectives; additionally, many resource prices are skyrocketing. The limited quantity of resources available and their high prices act as a double-barreled incentive to use them to the greatest advantage in achieving operations objectives. Today, perhaps as never before, operations managers understand that operations strategies must be set and objectives must be achieved within constraints imposed on their organizations by the shortage of resources.

One of the ways that operations managers determine how best to allocate their scarce resources to various uses in operations strategy is with the use of linear programming (LP). There are five common types of LP problems encountered by operations managers: product mix, ingredient mix, transportation, production plan, and assignment. Table 7.1 describes each problem type by posing three questions

---

INDUSTRY SNAPSHOT 7.1

From Baby Boom to Baby Bust: The Coming Labor Shortage

People at Paine Webber believe that a lasting labor shortage is coming that will affect many U.S. corporations. The sectors most likely to be hit the hardest are labor-intensive manufacturing and services. A recent Paine Webber report entitled "Return of the Automat: Taking Advantage of the Coming Labor Shortage" stressed that U.S. businesses must learn to deal with the coming shrinkage in the U.S. work force. A labor shortage is approaching in spite of the facts that 55 percent of adult women are presently working and that the *baby boomers* have swelled the labor force. The key problem is that the baby boom has been followed by a *baby bust.* The number of workers aged 16 to 24 will have dropped about 21 percent (5.2 million workers) from 1980 to 1995, after having grown 42 percent (about 7.5 million workers) during the 1970s. What does Paine Webber say that businesses should do to deal with this labor shortage? Managers must do these four things:

1. Use labor more efficiently.
2. Upgrade recruiting and training standards.
3. Recruit from peripheral segments of the labor market such as disadvantaged inner-city workers.
4. Make operations less labor-intensive, particularly services.

Just as the automat reduced the amount of labor required to provide food to customers, so must mechanization and automation reduce the amount of labor required to provide services.

"Paine Webber states that direct labor on the factory floor now accounts for only 10 percent to 15 percent of total manufacturing cost. So most of the big labor savings must occur in offices, laboratories, and warehouses." [1]

---

[1] Robert Metz, "Making Money in Labor Shortage," United Feature Syndicate, *Houston Chronicle,* November 6, 1987, sec. 2, 1.

---

about each problem: What is the single management objective? What information do we need to know to achieve our objective? What factors restrain us from achieving our objective? Read the five types of LP problems in Table 7.1. Read the objective first, then the decision variables, and finally the constraints for each type of problem. Visualize how operations managers analyze these problems when they involve many constraints; large quantities of data; many products, services, warehouses, designs, time periods, and other decision elements; numerous decision alternatives; and other complications.

The complexity of these and other constrained POM decisions prompted the development of linear-programming (LP) methods. LP is a powerful tool in POM — powerful because of the variety of uses to which it is put by operations managers. Other operations research techniques such as PERT/CPM, computer simulation,

TABLE 7.1   Five Common Types of LP Problems in POM — Typical Features

Decision Type	Objective (What Is the Single Management Objective?)	Decision Variables (What Information Do We Need to Know to Achieve Our Objective?)	Constraints (What Factors Restrain Us from Achieving Our Objective?)
1. Product mix	To select the mix of products or services that results in maximum profits for the planning period.	How much to produce and market of each product or service for the planning period.	*Market*—maximum amount of each product or service demanded and minimum amount policy will allow. *Capacity*—maximum amount of resources available (personnel, materials, machines, utilities, cash, floor space).
2. Ingredient mix	To select the mix of major ingredients going into final products that results in minimum operating costs for the planning period.	How much of each major raw material or ingredient to use in the planning period.	*Market*—amount of final products demanded. *Technology*—relationship between ingredients and final products. *Capacity*—maximum amount of ingredients and production capacity available.
3. Transportation	To select the distribution plan from sources to destinations that results in minimum shipping costs for the planning period.	How much product to ship from each source to each destination for the planning period.	*Destination requirements*—minimum or exact amount of products required at each destination. *Source capacity*—exact or maximum amount of products available at each source.
4. Production plan	To select the amount of products or services to be produced on both straight-time and overtime labor during each month of the year to minimize costs of labor and carrying inventory.	How much to produce on straight-time labor and overtime labor during each month of the year.	*Market*—amount of products demanded in each month. *Capacity*—maximum amount of products that can be produced with straight-time and overtime labor and machinery in each month. *Inventory space*—maximum storage capacity in each month.
5. Assignment	To assign products to departments so that the total cost for all products is minimized during the planning period.	To which department each product is assigned.	Each product must be assigned to a department, and each department must be assigned a product.

TABLE 7.2   *Characteristics of LP Problems in POM*

1. A well-defined single objective must be stated.
2. There must be alternative courses of action.
3. The total achievement of the objective must be constrained by scarce resources or other restraints.
4. The objective and each of the constraints must be expressed as linear mathematical functions.

and queuing theory (all of which are covered in other sections of this book) cannot claim the great breadth of application that LP enjoys.

Much of this chapter is about LP: recognizing LP problems, formulating LP problems, solving LP problems, and interpreting LP solutions (what information do you have after you are finished?). The ability to think in terms of optimizing an objective within a set of constraints in real POM decision situations will definitely set you apart as a competent analyst. This *thinking* is at the heart of linear programming.

The first step is recognizing problems that are appropriate for LP solutions.

RECOGNIZING LP PROBLEMS

This section is perhaps the most important part of this chapter. Being able to recognize problems for which LP solutions are appropriate is fundamental — the very least that you should master and retain from this chapter.

What are the characteristics of problems suitable for LP solutions? Table 7.2 outlines briefly the four basic problem characteristics. When *all* of these requirements are met, LP can be a suitable tool of analysis.

Examples 7.1 and 7.2 are examples of problems appropriate for LP solutions in POM. Follow through these examples carefully and see if you can recognize the objective, the alternatives available, and the nature of the constraints (the first three characteristics of LP problems). Don't worry about the mathematical requirements just yet.

Once we have the feel of what an LP problem is and is not, the next step is to formulate the problem in the LP format.

EXAMPLE 7.1   *LP-1: Recognizing a Product Mix LP Problem*

As a part of its strategic planning process, Precision Manufacturing Company must determine the mix of its products to be manufactured next year. The company produces two principal product lines for the commercial construction industry, a line of powerful portable circular saws and a line of precision table saws. The two product lines share the same production capacity and are sold through the same sales channels. Although some product variety does exist within each product line, the average profit is $900 for each circular saw and $600 for each table saw. The production capacity is constrained in two ways, fabrication and assembly capacity. There is a maximum of 4,000 hours of fabrication capacity available per month, and each circular saw requires 2 hours and each table saw requires 1 hour. There is a maximum of 5,000 hours of assembly capacity available per month, and each circular saw requires 1 hour and each table saw requires 2 hours. The marketing department estimates that there is a maximum market demand next year of 3,500 saws per month for both product lines. How many circular saws and how many table saws should be produced monthly next year to maximize profits?

1. Is there a single managerial objective?
   Yes. The objective is to maximize profits for the year.

2. Are there alternative courses of managerial action?
   Yes. Management can decide to produce all circular saws or all table saws or any mix of the two product lines during the year.

3. Is the total achievement of the objective constrained by scarce resources or other restraints? If so, what is the nature of the constraints?
   Yes. Profits are constrained by the maximum amount of fabrication hours available per month, the maximum amount of assembly hours available per month, and the maximum amount of market demand per month.

EXAMPLE 7.2   LP-2: Recognizing an Ingredient Mix LP Problem

The Gulf Coast Foundry is developing a long-range strategic plan for buying scrap metal for its foundry operations. The foundry can buy scrap metal in unlimited quantities from two sources, Atlanta (A) and Birmingham (B), and it receives the scrap daily in railroad cars. The scrap is melted down, and lead and copper are extracted for use in the foundry processes. Each railroad car of scrap from Source A yields 1 ton of copper and 1 ton of lead and costs $10,000. Each railroad car of scrap from Source B yields 1 ton of copper and 2 tons of lead and costs $15,000. If the foundry needs at least 2½ tons of copper and at least 4 tons of lead per day for the foreseeable future, how many railroad cars of scrap should be purchased per day from Source A and Source B to minimize the long-range scrap metal cost?

1. Is there a single managerial objective?
   Yes. Management wishes to minimize the daily costs of buying scrap metal from which copper and lead can be extracted.

2. Are there alternative courses of managerial action?
   Yes. Management can buy all of its scrap from either Source A or Source B or any combination of amounts of scrap from both sources.

3. Is the total achievement of the objective constrained by scarce resources or other constraints? If so, what is the nature of the constraints?
   Yes. Daily costs are constrained upward by the minimum amount of copper and lead needed daily.

FORMULATING LP PROBLEMS

Although both recognition and formulation of LP problems tend to become intuitive after we gain experience, in the beginning a method to follow helps us to formulate them more effectively. Table 7.3 lists the steps to follow in formulating LP problems. These steps structure problems in a way that helps us better understand the problems we are dealing with. Additionally, the problems are then in a form necessary for LP solutions.

Example 7.3 follows the LP formulating steps and sets up Problem LP-1, which was discussed in Example 7.1. Read LP-1 again and follow through the example carefully to make sure that you understand the procedures for formulating LP problems.

TABLE 7.3 *Steps in Formulating LP Problems*

1. Define the objective.	6. Write =, ≤, or ≥ for each constraint.
2. Define the decision variables.	7. Write in all of the decision variables on the left-hand side of each constraint.
3. Write the mathematical function for the objective (objective function).	8. Write the coefficient for each decision variable in each constraint.
4. Write a one- or two-word description of each constraint.	
5. Write the right-hand side (RHS) of each constraint, including the units of measure.	

EXAMPLE 7.3   Formulating LP-1

You may find it helpful to study Figure 7.1 as you work through this example.

FIGURE 7.1   Formulation of Problem LP-1

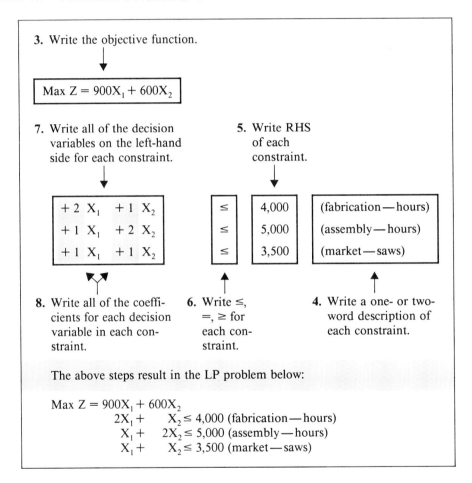

1. **Define the objective.** Precision Manufacturing Company seeks to maximize monthly profits. The problem is therefore a maximization problem.

2. **Define the decision variables.** What information does Precision need to know to maximize profits? The company needs to know how many circular saws and table saws to manufacture each month. Therefore let:

X_1 = number of circular saws to manufacture each month

X_2 = number of table saws to manufacture each month

X_1 and X_2 are the decision variables. When we know their values, the problem will be solved.

3. **Write the mathematical objective function.** Let Z equal the monthly profits; Z is a function of X_1 and X_2. In other words, the monthly profits depend on how many circular saws (X_1) and table saws (X_2) are manufactured each month. $Z = C_1X_1 + C_2X_2$, where C_1 and C_2 are the respective profits for each circular saw and table saw. C_1 = \$900 for each circular saw, C_2 = \$600 for each table saw, and $Z = 900X_1 + 600X_2$, where Z = total monthly profits, $900X_2$ = monthly profits for circular saws, and $600X_2$ = monthly profits for table saws. The objective function is therefore $Z = 900X_1 + 600X_2$ and suggests that we should select values of the decision variables X_1 and X_2 that result in the maximum value of Z. Were it not for production capacity and market constraints, Z monthly profits would be infinitely large.

4. **Write a one- or two-word description of each constraint.** There are three factors that constrain Precision from having infinite profits—fabrication hours available per month, assembly hours available per month, and market demand for saws per month. Therefore fabrication, assembly, and market are terms that describe each constraint.

5. **Write the right-hand side of each constraint.** The right-hand side (RHS) of each constraint is the maximum amount ($\leq$), exact amount ($=$), or minimum amount ($\geq$) of each constraint. Here the maximum amount of fabrication capacity is 4,000 hours per month, the maximum amount of assembly capacity is 5,000 hours per month, and the maximum market demand is 3,500 saws per month.

6. **Write $\leq$, $=$, $\geq$ for each constraint.** Since all of the constraints in this problem are maximum amounts, all of the constraints are the $\leq$ type. In other words, the amount of fabrication capacity that X_1 and X_2 use must be less than or equal to 4,000 hours per month, the amount of assembly capacity that X_1 and X_2 use must be less than or equal to 5,000 hours per month, and the amount of saws sold to the market must be less than or equal to 3,500 per month.

7. **Write in all of the decision variables on the left-hand side of each constraint.** In this problem there are only two decision variables—X_1 and X_2. If there were more X's, they would be written in with enough space between them to allow us to write in their coefficients in the next step. If a particular decision variable does not appear in a constraint, this is taken care of in the next step by assigning a zero coefficient to that decision variable in that constraint.

8. **Write the coefficients for each decision variable in each constraint.** Consider the first constraint, fabrication. What is the coefficient of X_1 in this constraint? It is the amount of fabrication hours per unit of X_1. In other words, it is the amount of fabrication hours used in manufacturing each circular saw, or 2 hours. Similarly, the coefficient of X_2 in this first constraint is the amount of fabrication hours used in manufacturing each table saw, or 1 hour. The coefficients of X_1 and X_2 in the assembly constraint are 1 and 2, and the coefficients of X_1 and X_2 in the market demand constraint are 1 and 1.

FIGURE 7.2   *Formulation of Problem LP-2*

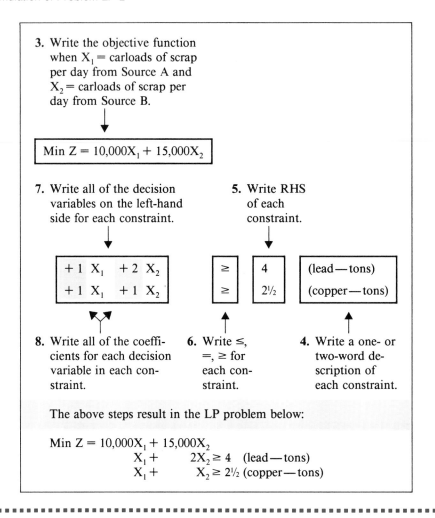

Figure 7.2 shows how the LP-formulating steps are applied to Problem LP-2. Read LP-2 again carefully and follow through Figure 7.2 step by step, as we did above in Example 7.3. Notice that LP-2 is a minimization problem and that the constraints are of the $\geq$ type.

Some observations are in order about LP problems in general. Let us use the LP-1 and LP-2 formulations to focus our comments:

1. The units of each term in a constraint must be the same as the RHS. For example, $2X_1$ in the first constraint of LP-1 must have the same units as 4,000:

$$\underset{\text{Units of } 2X_1}{\left(\frac{\text{Fabrication hours}}{\text{Circular saw}}\right)\left(\frac{\text{Circular saws}}{\text{Month}}\right)} = \underset{\text{Units of 4,000}}{\left(\frac{\text{Fabrication hours}}{\text{Month}}\right)}$$

2. The units of each term in the objective function must be the same as Z. For example, $15,000X_2$ in LP-2 must be the same as Z:

$$\underset{\text{Units of } 15,000X_1}{\left(\frac{\$}{\text{Carload}}\right)\left(\frac{\text{Carloads}}{\text{Day}}\right)} = \underset{\text{Units of Z}}{\left(\frac{\$}{\text{Day}}\right)}$$

3. The units *between* constraints do not *have* to be the same. For example, in LP-1, 4,000 fabrication hours and 3,500 saws per month are different units. The units *may* be the same between constraints, as LP-2 demonstrates, but they do not *have* to be.

4. An LP problem can have a mixture of constraint types. For example, minimization problems may have ≥, =, and ≤ constraints, and maximization problems may also have ≥, =, and ≤ constraints. However, maximization problems usually have more ≤ constraints, and minimization problems usually have more ≥ constraints.

Now that you have a grasp of how to recognize LP problems and how to formulate LP problems, you are ready to examine how LP problems are solved.

SOLVING LP PROBLEMS

Constrained operational decisions have been recognized and structured for analysis for several decades. In the 1930s W. W. Leontief developed his input–output economic analyses that were structured similarly to today's LP format. In the 1930s and 1940s F. L. Hitchcock and T. C. Koopsmans developed a method for structuring *and* solving transportation-type LP problems. In 1947 George Dantzig developed the simplex method of linear programming. Dantzig's simplex method was probably the beginning of the development of the present-day field of *mathematical programming.*

An early LP solution method was developed to solve facility location problems in POM. A physical model was built over a map of the geographic areas under examination. A string was threaded through a hole in the map over each proposed location, and a weight proportional to the location's total cost was tied to the end of the string. All of the strings were then connected on the top surface of the map by a sliding knot apparatus. When all of the weights were dropped simultaneously, the knot was pulled to a location point that minimized the total costs. While this "drop the string" method is archaic by today's standards, the time and effort plowed into these early methods emphasize the importance that managers place on the need for LP solution techniques.

The *graphical solution* approach conceptually demonstrates the process of LP solutions to those who have no experience with LP. Graphical solutions are therefore

■■

TABLE 7.4   *Steps in the Graphical Solution Method*

1. Formulate the objective and constraint functions.
2. Draw a graph with one variable on the horizontal axis and one on the vertical axis.
3. Plot each of the constraints as if they were lines or equalities.
4. Outline the feasible solution space.

5. Circle the potential solution points. These are the intersections of the constraints or axes on the inner (minimization) or outer (maximization) perimeter of the feasible solution space.
6. Substitute each of the potential solution point values of the two decision variables into the objective function and solve for Z.
7. Select the solution point that optimizes Z.

■■

intended as a teaching tool to assist you in understanding the process of LP solutions. The simplex, transportation, and assignment methods are the practical LP solution tools.

GRAPHICAL LP SOLUTIONS

Table 7.4 outlines the steps in the graphical method of solving LP problems. These steps are demonstrated in Example 7.4, a maximization problem, and Example 7.5, a minimization problem. Study these two examples and make sure you understand the basics of these solutions: plotting the constraint equations, outlining the feasible solution space, circling the solution points, and, finally, selecting the optimal solution.

EXAMPLE 7.4   *Graphical Solution of LP-1*

Problem LP-1 is used to demonstrate the steps of the graphical solution of a maximization problem. Read LP-1 again and Table 7.4 before beginning this example.

1. **Formulate the objective and constraint functions.** When LP-1 was formulated in Example 7.3, the decision variables were X_1 = number of circular saws to manufacture per month and X_2 = number of table saws to manufacture per month. The objective and constraint functions were:

Max $Z = 900X_1 + 600X_2$

$$2X_1 + X_2 \leq 4{,}000 \text{ (fabrication—hours)}$$

$$X_1 + 2X_2 \leq 5{,}000 \text{ (assembly—hours)}$$

$$X_1 + X_2 \leq 3{,}500 \text{ (market—saws)}$$

FIGURE 7.3   Graphical Solution of LP-1

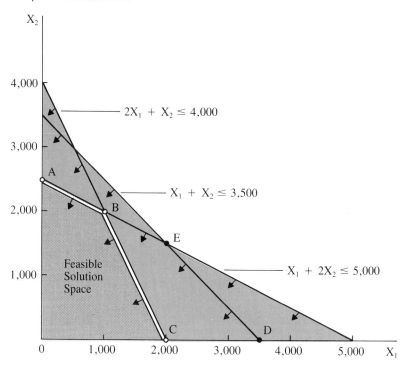

2. **Draw a graph.**

3. **Plot the constraint functions.**

4. **Outline the feasible solution space.**

5. **Circle the potential solution points on the perimeter of the feasible solution space. (See Figure 7.3.)**

   Note that the constraints are plotted by treating each constraint as an equality or a line. For each constraint line, let $X_1 = 0$ and solve for X_2, then let $X_2 = 0$ and solve for X_1; this gives two sets of X_1 and X_2 values or points. Connect each pair of points with a straight line. This process is repeated for each constraint.

   Note that all of the values of X_1 and X_2 must fall inside *all* constraints (toward the origin) because the constraints are $\leq$. Points D and E are not feasible because they both violate the first constraint. *While any point within the feasible solution space satisfies all of the constraints, only Points A, B, and C are candidates for the optimal solution because they are at the intersections of constraints or axes and lie on the outer perimeter of the feasible solution space.*

   Note also that Points A and C are formed by the intersection of a constraint and one of the axes. This is possible because the axes are implied constraints. In other words, X_1 cannot be negative; therefore the vertical axis $X_1 = 0$ is treated as a constraint. Similarly, $X_2 = 0$, the horizontal axis, is also treated as a constraint.

The values of X_1 and X_2 at Points A, B, and C are three potential solutions to Problem LP-1:

A: $X_1 = 0$ and $X_2 = 2,500$ **B**: $X_1 = 1,000$ and $X_2 = 2,000$ **C**: $X_1 = 2,000$ and $X_2 = 0$

How do we determine Point B accurately? If the coordinates cannot be read precisely, the two constraint equations can be solved simultaneously for X_1 and X_2:

The two equations that intersect at Point B:	Multiply the first equation by -2 and add the two equations together:	Substitute the value for X_1 back into either equation and solve for X_2:
$2X_1 + X_2 = 4,000$	$-4X_1 - 2X_2 = -8,000$	$2(1,000) + X_2 = 4,000$
$X_1 + 2X_2 = 5,000$	$\underline{X_1 + 2X_2 = \quad 5,000}$	$2,000 + X_2 = 4,000$
	$-3X_1 \qquad = -3,000$	$X_2 = 2,000$
	$X_1 = \quad 1,000$	

The intersection of the two constraints is therefore $X_1 = 1,000$ and $X_2 = 2,000$. Points A, B, and C are potential solutions to Problem LP-1. Which one is optimal?

6. **Substitute the solution point values of the decision variables into the objective function and solve for Z:**

Point A:	Point B:	Point C:
$X_1 = 0$ and $X_2 = 2,500$	$X_1 = 1,000$ and $X_2 = 2,000$	$X_1 = 2,000$ and $X_2 = 0$
$Z = 900X_1 + 600X_2$	$Z = 900X_1 + 600X_2$	$Z = 900X_1 + 600X_2$
$= 900(0) + 600(2,500)$	$= 900(1,000) + 600(2,000)$	$= 900(2,000) + 600(0)$
$= 1,500,000$	$= 2,100,000$	$= 1,800,000$

7. **Select the solution that optimizes Z.** To maximize Z, the optimal solution is Point B, where $X_1 = 1,000$ circular saws per month, $X_2 = 2,000$ table saws per month, and $Z = \$2,100,000$ profits per month.

EXAMPLE 7.5   Graphical Solution of LP-2

Problem LP-2 is used to demonstrate the steps in the graphical solution of a minimization LP problem. Read LP-2 again.

1. **Formulate the objective and constraint functions.** Recall that LP-2 was formulated in Figure 7.2 with these decision variables:

X_1 = carloads of scrap purchased from Source A per day

X_2 = carloads of scrap purchased from Source B per day

FIGURE 7.4   Graphical Solution of LP-2

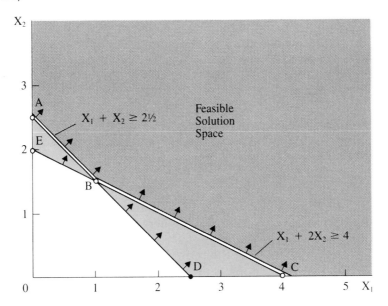

The objective and constraint functions were:

Min Z = 10,000X_1 + 15,000X_2

$$X_1 + \quad 2X_2 \geq 4 \text{ (lead—tons)}$$

$$X_1 + \quad X_2 \geq 2\frac{1}{2} \text{ (copper—tons)}$$

2. Draw a graph.

3. Plot the constraint functions.

4. Outline the feasible solution space.

5. Circle the potential solution points on the perimeter of the solution area. (See Figure 7.4.)
   Note that since both constraints are ≥, all possible values of X_1 and X_2 must lie outside both constraints, away from the origin. Point D is not possible because it violates the first constraint. Similarly, Point E violates the second constraint. *While any point within the feasible solution space satisfies all of the constraints, only Points A, B, and C are candidates for the optimal solution because they are at the intersections of constraints or axes and lie on the inner perimeter of the feasible solution space.*
   Points A, B, and C are three potential optimal solutions to Problem LP-2:

A: $X_1 = 0$ and $X_2 = 2.5$ **B:** $X_1 = 1$ and $X_2 = 1.5$ **C:** $X_1 = 4$ and $X_2 = 0$

6. **Substitute the solution point values of the two decision values into the objective function and solve for Z:**

Point A: Point B: Point C:

$X_1 = 0$ and $X_2 = 2.5$ $X_1 = 1$ and $X_2 = 1.5$ $X_1 = 4$ and $X_2 = 0$

$Z = 10,000X_1 + 15,000X_2$ $Z = 10,000X_1 + 15,000X_2$ $Z = 10,000X_1 + 15,000X_2$
$\ \ = 10,000(0) + 15,000(2.5)$ $\ \ = 10,000(1) + 15,000(1.5)$ $\ \ = 10,000(4) + 15,000(0)$
$\ \ = 37,500$ $\ \ = 32,500$ $\ \ = 40,000$

7. **Select the solution that optimizes Z.** To minimize Z, the optimal solution is Point B, where $X_1 = 1$ carload of scrap from Source A per day, $X_2 = 1.5$ carloads of scrap from Source B per day, and $Z = \$32,500$ total scrap cost per day.

Optimal solutions in the graphical solution method will always lie at intersections on the inner perimeter (min) or outer perimeter (max) of the feasible solution space. Figure 7.5 demonstrates why this is so. Beginning at the origin where $Z = 0$, we let Z, the profit function in LP-1, take on progressively larger values from 500,000 to 2,100,000. When these isoprofit functions, as they are sometimes called, are plotted, we can see that the *greatest* isoprofit function intersects the feasible solution space at Point B. The objective function Z will always intersect the perimeter of the feasible

FIGURE 7.5   *Isoprofit Lines in LP-1 Graphical Solution*

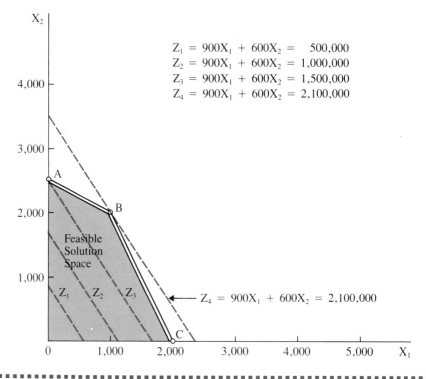

$$Z_1 = 900X_1 + 600X_2 = \ \ \ \ 500,000$$
$$Z_2 = 900X_1 + 600X_2 = 1,000,000$$
$$Z_3 = 900X_1 + 600X_2 = 1,500,000$$
$$Z_4 = 900X_1 + 600X_2 = 2,100,000$$

$$Z_4 = 900X_1 + 600X_2 = 2,100,000$$

INDUSTRY SNAPSHOT 7.2

Scientific American *Praises the Simplex Method of Linear Programming*

The simplex algorithm has enormous economic importance in government and industry. The algorithm determines the most profitable or least expensive course of action under a number of constraints. It is applied extensively in petroleum refining, papermaking, food distribution, agriculture, steelmaking and metalworking (see "The Allocation of Resources by Linear Programming," by Robert G. Bland; *Scientific American,* June, 1981).

Suppose a paper company makes 50 grades of paper, each grade requiring different quantities of wood pulp, chemical sizing, bleach and clay coating. If the company devoted production exclusively to its most profitable grade of paper (white bond, say), the supply of bleach might be exhausted long before the other resources were used up. Indeed, if at least some bleach is needed for all grades of paper, the allocation of all the bleach to the production of white bond would halt the manufacture of the other grades in spite of ample inventories of the remaining resources. The task of maximizing the paper company's return on its investment in the various resources is one of determining just how to allocate the resources most effectively to the entire range of products.[2]

---

[2] Source: From "Safety in Numbers," *SCIENTIFIC AMERICAN,* September 1982, 106. Copyright © 1982 by SCIENTIFIC AMERICAN, Inc. Reprinted with permission.

---

solution space at an intersection, and the optimal solution to the LP problem will be found at this intersection. Knowing this, we can find the optimal solution to an LP problem graphically by plotting isoprofit (max) or isocost (min) functions rather than algebraically substituting into the objective function the values of X_1 and X_2 at all of the intersections on the perimeter of the feasible solution space.

The graphical method is not a practical solution method because only two, or three at most, decision variables are allowed. Graphical solutions are a good place to begin solving LP problems, however, because the concepts learned are directly applied to the other practical solution methods that are described below.

OVERVIEW OF OTHER LP SOLUTION METHODS

Presented here are brief descriptions of three other LP solution methods: simplex, transportation, and assignment. A more detailed discussion of these methods is found in Appendix E at the end of this book.

Simplex Method

The *simplex method* is an analytical tool that is adaptable to numerous constrained decisions. It provides managers with precise solutions to complex problems that have many variables and constraints. Since its development in the 1940s, the simplex method has accumulated a large following among industrial and academic analysts. Industry Snapshot 7.2 illustrates the esteem in which the method is held in the scientific community.

INDUSTRY SNAPSHOT 7.3

The Startling Discovery at Bell Labs

Narendra K. Karmarkar is a scientist working at AT&T Bell Laboratories. He discovered a way to quickly solve huge linear programming (LP) problems that had been previously impossible to solve even on powerful supercomputers. AT&T is using his approach to estimate telephone customer needs over the next ten years in the countries rimming the Pacific Ocean. The number of pairs of switching points in the region is so large that a LP formulation of the problem has 42,000 variables. George B. Dantzig of Stanford University developed the simplex method over 40 years ago to solve LP problems, but the simplex method is not a practical approach to problems of the size being studied by Karmarkar. His method is estimated to require only about 1 percent of the computer time of the simplex method for such problems.

A linear programming problem can be viewed as a geodesic dome with a potential solution at each corner. To solve a LP problem, the many corners of the dome must be examined to determine which one is the best solution. In the simplex method, corners are examined in a sequence by moving to progressively better solutions until no better solutions can be found.

Karmarkar's method, using a radically different tactic, starts from a point within the structure and finds the solution by taking a shortcut that avoids the tedious surface route. From the interior vantage, it uses projective geometry to reconfigure the structure's shape. The method studies the new structure to determine in which direction the solution lies. After the problem-structure has been allowed to return to its original shape, the program jumps toward the solution, pausing at intervals to repeat the exercise and home in on the solution.

Karmarkar's approach to LP problems is reported to be so effective that AT&T is studying complex problems that have never before been studied. For example, an LP model of AT&T's domestic long-distance network is said to include 800,000 variables. Karmarkar's solution to this problem showed how AT&T could get another 9 percent to 10 percent of capacity out of the $15 billion system. Before Karmarkar's approach, such problems would have to be split into many small problems whose solutions would be patched together at the end. Karmarkar's technique solves the whole LP problem at one time in less than an hour.[3]

---

[3] William G. Wild, Jr., and Otis Port, "The Startling Discovery Bell Labs Kept In The Shadows," *Business Week*, Sept. 21, 1987, 69, 72, 76.

Although the simplex method is difficult to use, most real LP problems in POM are worked on computers anyway. Numerous standard computer programs are available to generate solutions to large LP problems quickly and accurately. Among these are IBM's MPSX, LINDO, and the LP program in the POM Computer Library that accompanies this text. A general familiarity with data processing will allow you to use these programs to input data and almost instantaneously receive solutions. Even though computer solutions are *the* method of solving real LP problems in POM, some experience with manual simplex solutions is desirable in order to understand better how to input data and interpret LP solutions when the computer is used.

There is a continuing effort to improve the simplex method. One area that is receiving particular attention is making the method more efficient to process on computers. As business and government problems become larger and more complex, the ability to process extremely large LP problems on our largest computers becomes more attractive. Industry Snapshot 7.3 discusses the work of Narendra K. Karmarkar in discovering a breakthrough in computer-processing efficiency in working large LP problems.

Transportation Method
One of the earliest LP solution methods was the *transportation method.* This method can solve only a special form of LP problem, those with *m* sources and *n* destinations and with these characteristics:

1. Number of variables is m × n.
2. Number of constraints is m + n.
3. Costs appear only in objective function.
4. Coefficients of decision variables in the constraints are either 0 or 1.

The simplex method can solve any LP problem that the transportation method can solve, but not vice versa.

A *transportation LP problem* is of a special form where the objective is usually to minimize the cost of shipping products from several sources to several destinations. The constraints are for source capacity and destination demand. Example 7.6 is an LP problem of this form. Note that the coefficients of the decision variables in the constraints are either 0 or 1. Additionally, the pattern of the appearance of the decision variables in the constraints in the example is characteristic of transportation problems.

EXAMPLE 7.6   *A Transportation LP Problem*

The Green Up Fertilizer Company ships fertilizer from two plants to three customers. The shipping cost per ton of fertilizer from each plant to each customer is:

Plant	Customer		
	A	*B*	*C*
1	$15	$30	$20
2	20	25	15

Plant 1 has a monthly capacity of 1,000 tons and Plant 2 has a monthly capacity of 2,000 tons. The monthly customer demand is: A = 500 tons, B = 1,500 tons, and C = 1,000 tons. Formulate an LP problem to determine how much fertilizer should be shipped from each plant to each customer per month to minimize monthly shipping costs.

1. **Define the objective.** Minimize monthly shipping costs.

2. **Define the decision variables.** Notice that there are m $\times$ n (2 $\times$ 3 = 6) decision variables.

   X_1 = tons of fertilizer to be shipped from 1 to A per month

   X_2 = tons of fertilizer to be shipped from 1 to B per month

   X_3 = tons of fertilizer to be shipped from 1 to C per month

   X_4 = tons of fertilizer to be shipped from 2 to A per month

   X_5 = tons of fertilizer to be shipped from 2 to B per month

   X_6 = tons of fertilizer to be shipped from 2 to C per month

3. **Write a mathematical function for the objective:**

   Min Z = $15X_1 + 30X_2 + 20X_3 + 20X_4 + 25X_5 + 15X_6$

4. **Write the constraints.** Notice that there are m + n (2 + 3 = 5) constraints.

$$X_1 + X_2 + X_3 \leq 1{,}000 \text{ (Plant 1 capacity in tons)}$$
$$X_4 + X_5 + X_6 \leq 2{,}000 \text{ (Plant 2 capacity in tons)}$$
$$X_1 + X_4 \geq 500 \text{ (Customer A demand in tons)}$$
$$X_2 + X_5 \geq 1{,}500 \text{ (Customer B demand in tons)}$$
$$X_3 + X_6 \geq 1{,}000 \text{ (Customer C demand in tons)}$$

The resultant LP problem is:

Min Z = $15X_1 + 30X_2 + 20X_3 + 20X_4 + 25X_5 + 15X_6$
$$X_1 + X_2 + X_3 \leq 1{,}000$$
$$X_4 + X_5 + X_6 \leq 2{,}000$$
$$X_1 + X_4 \geq 500$$
$$X_2 + X_5 \geq 1{,}500$$
$$X_3 + X_6 \geq 1{,}000$$

Assignment Method

Another LP problem of a special form occasionally occurs in POM: the *assignment problem.* The vignette at the beginning of this chapter is about an assignment problem. These problems usually seek to assign jobs or personnel to machines or departments. An assignment problem is just a special case of a transportation problem, having the characteristics of a transportation problem discussed earlier. Additionally, an assignment problem has these characteristics:

1. The right-hand sides of constraints are all 1.
2. The signs of constraints are = rather than ≤ or ≥.
3. The value of all decision variables is either 0 or 1.

For example, suppose that three persons must be assigned to three projects, each project must be assigned to only one person, and each person must be assigned to only one project. The costs are shown below. The objective is to determine an assignment scheme that minimizes costs.

Project	Persons		
	A	*B*	*C*
1	$20	$30	$10
2	40	30	40
3	30	20	30

REAL LP PROBLEMS

Real LP problems in POM typically have numerous variables, numerous constraints, and other complex characteristics. The real LP problem in POM presented and formulated in Example 7.7 will deepen your comprehension of LP in POM.

EXAMPLE 7.7   Oklahoma Crude Oil Company

An oil refinery in Oklahoma buys domestic crude oil from five sources: Oklahoma, Texas, Kansas, New Mexico, and Colorado. Six end products are produced: regular gasoline, premium gasoline, low-lead gasoline, diesel fuel, heating oil, and lubricating oil base. The accompanying table shows the crude oil distribution to each end product, the crude oil costs, and the market requirements for each end product.

Product	Crude Oil Source					Monthly Market Requirements (Thousands of Gallons)
	Oklahoma	*Texas*	*Kansas*	*New Mexico*	*Colorado*	
Regular gasoline	40%	30%	30%	20%	30%	5,000
Premium gasoline	20	30	40	30	20	3,000
Low-lead gasoline	20	10	—	30	10	3,000
Diesel fuel	10	10	10	—	20	2,000
Heating oil	—	10	10	20	10	1,000
Lubricating oil base	10	10	10	—	10	2,000
Totals	100%	100%	100%	100%	100%	16,000
Delivered cost/gallon	$.20	$.14	$.15	$.18	$.12	

    The sources of crude oil are captive within the company, and any quantity of each of the crudes can be purchased to satisfy the needs of this refinery up to these maximums:

Crude Source	Maximum Monthly Supply (Thousands of Gallons)	Crude Source	Maximum Monthly Supply (Thousands of Gallons)
Oklahoma crude	8,000	New Mexico crude	3,000
Texas crude	4,000	Colorado crude	6,000
Kansas crude	5,000		

How much crude oil should be purchased from each source to at least satisfy the market and to minimize crude oil costs?

1. **Define the decision variables:**

   X_1 = thousands of gallons of Oklahoma crude to be purchased per month

   X_2 = thousands of gallons of Texas crude to be purchased per month

   X_3 = thousands of gallons of Kansas crude to be purchased per month

   X_4 = thousands of gallons of New Mexico crude to be purchased per month

   X_5 = thousands of gallons of Colorado crude to be purchased per month

2. **Formulate the LP problem:**

   Min $Z = 200X_1 + 140X_2 + 150X_3 + 180X_4 + 120X_5$

$$.4X_1 + .3X_2 + .3X_3 + .2X_4 + .3X_5 \geq 5,000 \text{ (regular gasoline market requirement*)}$$

$$.2X_1 + .3X_2 + .4X_3 + .3X_4 + .2X_5 \geq 3,000 \text{ (premium gasoline market requirement*)}$$

$$.2X_1 + .1X_2 + .3X_4 + .1X_5 \geq 3,000 \text{ (low-lead gasoline market requirement*)}$$

$$.1X_1 + .1X_2 + .1X_3 + .2X_5 \geq 2,000 \text{ (diesel fuel market requirement*)}$$

$$.1X_2 + .1X_3 + .2X_4 + .1X_5 \geq 1,000 \text{ (heating oil market requirement*)}$$

$$.1X_1 + .1X_2 + .1X_3 + .1X_5 \geq 2,000 \text{ (lubricating oil base market requirement*)}$$

$$X_1 \leq 8,000 \text{ (Oklahoma crude supply*)}$$

$$X_2 \leq 4,000 \text{ (Texas crude supply*)}$$

$$X_3 \leq 5,000 \text{ (Kansas crude supply*)}$$

$$X_4 \leq 3,000 \text{ (New Mexico crude supply*)}$$

$$X_5 \leq 6,000 \text{ (Colorado crude supply*)}$$

_____

* In thousands of gallons.

The problem in Example 7.7 has five decision variables and eleven constraints. Many hours of laborious desk work would be required to manually solve such problems with the simplex method. Only about half an hour would be required to input the data for computer solutions. The speed and accuracy of computers just about rules out manual solutions today for real LP problems such as these.

INTERPRETING COMPUTER SOLUTIONS OF LP PROBLEMS

In this section we shall explain how to interpret the meaning of the printout of a solution of an LP problem from the *POM Computer Library* that accompanies this text. Figure 7.6 exhibits the solution to Problem LP-1 that was formulated and solved graphically earlier in this chapter. It may be helpful to review Examples 7.3 and 7.4 before you read this section.

In Figure 7.6, the first thing that you should notice is the formulation of the LP-1 problem — two decision variables and three ≤ constraints. In the next section of the printout, we find the solution that was accomplished in three interactions or simplex tables. The solution is deduced from the variables that appear in the variable mix column, which is also called the solution column or *basis:* $X_1 = 1,000$; $X_2 = 2,000$; $S_3 = 500$; $Z = \$2,100,000$; and all other variables not in the basis equal zero.

The meaning of the decision variables (the X's) and Z were discussed earlier in this chapter. The meaning of S_3, a *slack variable,* however, requires some explanation. The slack variable S_3 is associated with the third constraint, which is indicated by the subscript 3. The third constraint of LP-1 is $X_1 + X_2 \leq 3,500$, which limits the total number of circular saws (X_1) and table saws (X_2) that can be sold in each month to a maximum of 3,500. S_3 allows us to convert the third constraint from a ≤ to an =:

$$X_1 + X_2 \qquad \leq 3,500$$
$$X_1 + X_2 + S_3 = 3,500$$

As such, S_3 represents the amount of unused market per month that is not satisfied by the sales of X_1 and X_2 saws. Because $S_3 = 500$, we would have 500 saws of unused market per month if we produce and sell 1,000 circular saws and 2,000 table saws. Similarly, S_1 represents the amount of unused hours of fabrication capacity per month and S_2 represents the amount of unused hours of assembly capacity per month (the subscripts 1 and 2 refer to the first and second constraints). Because both S_1 and $S_2 = 0$ (because they did not appear in the basis or variable mix column), all available fabrication and assembly capacity hours would be used in each month.

Now let us turn to the Sensitivity Analysis section of Figure 7.6. For constraints, the shadow prices indicate the impact on Z if the RHS's of the constraints are changed. For example, in the first constraint, which is a ≤ constraint, if the RHS were changed by 1 unit, Z would change by \$400. Because Z is optimal when $S_1 = 0$, Z would become less optimal (profits would fall if the problem is a maximization or costs would rise if the problem is a minimization) if the RHS were reduced, and Z

FIGURE 7.6   *Computer Printout for Problem LP-1 from the* POM Computer Library

```
*****************************************************
*** LINEAR PROGRAMMING ***
*****************************************************


===================================================
*** ORIGINAL PROBLEM LP-1***
===================================================
MAX Z= 900 X 1 + 600 X 2

     2 X 1 + 1 X 2  <=  4000
     1 X 1 + 2 X 2  <=  5000
     1 X 1 + 1 X 2  <=  3500


===================================================
*** SOLUTION ***
===================================================
ITERATION NUMBER 3

VARIABLE MIX        SOLUTION
------------        ------------
X 1                  1000.00
X 2                  2000.00
S 3                   500.00
 Z                 2100000.00

---END OF SOLUTION---
===================================================
*** SENSITIVITY ANALYSIS ***
===================================================
CONSTRAINTS
---------------------------------------------------

                                    RANGE OF RHS
CONSTRAINT     TYPE OF      SHADOW   FOR WHICH SHADOW
 NUMBER      CONSTRAINT     PRICE    PRICE IS VALID
---------    ----------     ------   ----------------
    1            <=          400       2500 --  5500
    2            <=          100       2000 --  6500
    3            <=            0       3000 --  +INF
NOTE: THE SHADOW PRICE REPRESENTS THE AMOUNT Z WOULD
      CHANGE IF A CONSTRAINT'S RHS CHANGED ONE UNIT.


---------------------------------------------------
DECISION VARIABLES
---------------------------------------------------
NONBASIC    AMOUNT Z IS REDUCED (MAX) OR INCREASED
VARIABLE    (MIN) FOR ONE UNIT OF X IN THE SOLUTION
--------    ----------------------------------------
--------NONE----------
---------------------------------------------------
```

would become more optimal (profits would rise or costs would fall) if the RHS were increased. But this explanation is valid only if the RHS remains in the 2,500–5,500 range. If the RHS falls outside this range, the impact on Z cannot be deduced and a new solution to the problem would then be required.

The explanation of the shadow price for the second constraint is similarly deduced. The shadow price of the third constraint is zero, which means that Z will not change with upward (3,000–+ infinity) changes to the RHS of the third constraint. This follows because $S_3 = 500$, which means that we have unused market and increasing the market will not change Z.

For Decision Variables, the shadow prices indicate the change in Z if one unit of a nonbasic decision variable (an X variable that is not in the variable mix column or basis) is forced into the solution. Because both decision variables (X_1 and X_2) are in the basis above, there are no other decision variables to force into the solution. If there were, because Z is optimal, introducing any other X variable into the solution would cause Z to become less optimal (profits would fall or costs would increase).

LP-1 had only ≤ constraints. You may wonder how we would interpret a computer solution of a LP problem with ≥ constraints. Consider the first constraint of LP-2 from Example 7.2: $X_1 + 2X_2 \geq 4$, which represents the minimum daily number of tons of lead that must be provided. This constraint is converted to an equality by the introduction of S_1, where once again the subscript 1 refers to the first constraint:

$$X_1 + 2X_2 \quad \geq 4$$
$$X_1 + 2X_2 \quad = 4 + S_1$$
$$X_1 + 2X_2 - S_1 = 4$$

Notice that S_1 is added to the smaller side of the expression, which is the right side, to convert the expression to an equality. Also, note that S_1 is then subtracted from both sides to allow all of the variables to appear on the left-hand side. By looking at the middle expression above, we can see that S_1 represents the tons of lead that are provided above the minimum of 4 tons. If the minimum of 4 tons is provided, $S_1 = 0$. As S_1 is allowed to take on larger values, then a surplus of lead is provided above the 4-ton minimum. Thus when a constraint is of the ≥ type, a slack variable represents the amount of the constraint that is provided above the minimum.

If the RHS of a ≥ constraint is increased, the shadow price indicates the amount by which Z will change, or become less optimal (profits will fall and costs will increase). If the RHS is decreased, Z will become more optimal (profits will rise and costs will decrease). Thus we can see that if there is no slack, the optimality of Z *and the RHS move in opposite directions with ≥ type constraints.* And from our discussion of LP-1 above, if there is no slack, the optimality of Z *and the RHS move in the same directions with ≤ type constraints.*

In some computer solutions, artificial variables (A_1) may appear. They have no interpretive value.

SUMMARY

The resources of production systems—personnel, machines and equipment, cash and capital funds, materials and supplies, utilities, and others—are scarce. Both scarcity and rising resource prices cause shifts in POM strategies so that these resources can be used to the greatest advantage in achieving organizational objectives.

Today, perhaps more than ever before, operations managers understand that most decisions must be made and objectives achieved within constraints imposed on organizations. Customer demand for products and services, limited production resources, government regulations, quality requirements, and technological limitations are examples of typical decision constraints in POM. Within these and other constraints, managers seek to achieve such objectives as profit maximization and cost minimization.

The complexity of these constrained POM decisions prompted the development of a family of new analysis techniques. Among them, linear programming (LP) stands out in its frequency of use across various organizations. This chapter discusses several aspects of LP—recognizing LP problems, formulating LP problems, solving LP problems, and interpreting LP solutions.

LP problems have a singular well-defined objective, alternative courses of action, constraints, and linear objective and constraint mathematical functions. All of these characteristics must be present in decisions before LP is an appropriate tool of analysis. LP problems are solved with the graphical, simplex, transportation, and assignment methods. Among these solution methods, the simplex method stands out in frequency of use, breadth of application, and adaptability to computer programs. Computer solutions are *the* solution approach to real LP problems in POM.

This text and most others provide simple LP problems for solution solely to clarify the solution procedures. More complex real LP problems are typically solved on computers. Careful attention to problem recognition, formulation, and solution interpretation is perhaps more important than solution details.

REVIEW AND DISCUSSION QUESTIONS

1. What are production system resources?
2. What effects do scarce resources have on POM today?
3. Name five common types of constrained decisions in POM. Briefly describe each.
4. Define *objective function, constraint function, decision variable, objective function value, maximization LP problem, minimization LP problem.*
5. Name five characteristics of LP problems.
6. Name eight steps in formulating, or setting up, LP problems.
7. Name four solution methods to LP problems.
8. Describe the elements of a transportation LP problem.
9. Which LP solution method is used most often in POM? Why?
10. Why is the graphical method almost never used for real LP problems in POM?

PROBLEMS

LP-A. Agri-Gro, a large modern farming corporation in West Texas, plants milo and soybeans on a large tract of nonirrigated land. Soybeans require a special soil that is scarce, and only 100 acres are available for this crop. Milo can be planted on any of Agri-Gro's land but requires more fertilizer to condition the land. Agri-Gro is particularly worried about an adequate supply of fertilizer this year because the firm's supplier has been on strike for four months and only 200,000 pounds are available for this season's planting. Milo takes 2,000 pounds of fertilizer per acre and soybeans take 1,000 pounds of fertilizer per acre. How many acres should Agri-Gro plant in soybeans and milo, considering the shortages of fertilizer and land suitable for soybeans, if the profit per acre is $700 for soybeans and $500 for milo?

LP-B. Calchem is a supplier of specialty chemical products to petroleum and chemical industries in the San Francisco Bay area of northern California. Martha Sellmore, sales manager for Calchem, is trying to determine how the typical salesperson should divide time between petroleum and chemical industry customers. The following information seems pertinent to the sales manager:

	Petroleum Industry Customers	Chemical Industry Customers
1. Average profit per sales call	$500	$200
2. Salesperson's time required per sales call	8 hours	$\frac{8}{3}$ hours
3. Average entertainment cost per sales call	$40	$30

If less than 8 hours per day per salesperson is required for sales calls, other administrative duties can be performed to fill out the day. A maximum of $60 per salesperson per day for entertainment cost is allowed under company policy. How many daily sales calls to petroleum and chemical industry customers should each salesperson make, on the average, to maximize daily profits?

LP-C. Therm-co, a small private energy research firm in Tucson, Arizona, is planning the number of research personnel to assign to a new solar research project for the first and second quarters of next year. Because the firm has other research contracts, the number of personnel available for the new project during these two periods is severely limited. Maximums of 15 and 10 personnel are available during the first and second quarters, respectively. Additionally, a total personnel allowance of 20 personnel for the project means that a maximum of 20 personnel can be assigned to the project for the two periods (for example, if 15 personnel were assigned to the project during the first quarter, a maximum of 5 could be assigned during the second quarter). If the profit per person working on the project is estimated at $20,000 during the first quarter and $30,000 during the second quarter, how many personnel should be assigned to the project during each of the two periods?

LP-D. Moon City, a progressive municipal government in the western United States, is trying to decide among three community development projects—urban renewal, social health services expansion, and fire department services expansion. It is estimated that for each dollar spent next year in these three projects, the equivalent dollar amount in social returns is:

Project	Social Returns
Urban renewal	$.40
Health services	.30
Fire department	.35

Moon City can allocate no more than a total of $10 million to these projects. The nature of these projects sets these limitations on next year's spending:

Project	Minimum Cost Allocation	Maximum Cost Allocation
Urban renewal	No limit	$7 million
Health services	$3 million	No limit
Fire department	No limit	$8 million

Considering the project spending constraints, how much should Moon City spend on each of the three projects to maximize the social returns?

LP-E. Fat Quick, a huge cattle feedlot operation near Chicago, blends feeds mechanically to generate low-cost feeds for its cattle. Oats and corn are the principal ingredients of the cattle feed. The current costs for oats and corn are $.05 and $.03 per pound, respectively. Fat Quick requires a minimum of 4,000 calories, 10,000 units of minerals, and 5,000 units of vitamins per day for each head of cattle. Each pound of oats and corn supplies these quantities:

Feed	Calories per Pound	Mineral Units per Pound	Vitamin Units per Pound
Oats	100	200	200
Corn	100	400	100

How many pounds of oats and corn should be fed to each head of cattle per day to minimize feed costs?

LP-F. A manufacturer of electrical consumer products, with its headquarters in Burlington, Iowa, produces electric irons at Manufacturing Plants 1, 2, and 3. The irons are shipped to Warehouses A, B, C, and D. The shipping cost per iron, the monthly warehouse requirements, and the monthly plant production levels are:

	Destination				Monthly Plant Production
	A	B	C	D	Level (Units)
Plant 1	$.20	$.25	$.15	$.20	10,000
Plant 2	.15	.30	.20	.15	20,000
Plant 3	.15	.20	.20	.25	10,000
Monthly warehouse requirement (units)	12,000	8,000	15,000	5,000	

How many electric irons should be shipped per month from each plant to each warehouse to minimize monthly shipping costs?

LP-G. The Error Prone Publishing Company is a medium-size printing house in Gone Astray, Texas. It prints hardback and paperback books for publishing companies on a project basis. The printing industry backlog is now great and Error Prone can pick and choose from the available customers to develop the best mix of hardback and paperback books for its particular production environment. Because of its unique product-line design (one color, fixed book length, fixed book size, standard paper, etc.), Error Prone expects to earn $10 for each hardback and $6 for each paperback in contribution (fixed costs + pretax profits). The book cover department processes hardback books more slowly than paperback books. The cover department can complete eight paperback covers per minute but only four hardback covers per minute. The cover department cannot make both types of covers simultaneously, but it can easily switch from one type to the other. The printing line, on the other hand, can actually print hardbacks slightly faster than paperbacks because of the flimsy nature of the paperback paper stock. The printing department can produce six hardbacks per minute or it can produce four paperbacks per minute. The printing line can also easily be changed from one type of book to the other. Hardback books require a special framing operation that has a capacity of three and a half books per minute. For control purposes, Error Prone's management requires that any books that begin production in any eight-hour shift must be processed through the last operation in the plant before the end of that shift, so that no in-process inventory can accumulate between shifts. How many paperbacks and hardbacks should be produced per shift to maximize contribution?

LP-H. The Atlanta and El Paso plants of Computer Products Corporation (CPC) manufacture only two product lines: XT Personal Computers and BT Small-Business Computers. Beth Millman, Vice-President of Manufacturing at CPC's San Jose corporate headquarters, is working with her staff to decide the best product mix for these two product lines for the next year. She knows that the decision must be based on three important factors: (1) the profitability of each product line, (2) the amount of scarce production capacity that each product line requires, and (3) the amount of each product line that the market will demand. Harold Stark, one of the staff analysts researching the decision, summed it up when he said, "We want to produce the product mix that maximizes profits for the period within the production capacity and market constraints." Although some product variety does exist within each product line, the average contribution per product is $900 for each XT and $1,700 for each BT. The production capacity is constrained in two ways, labor and machine capacity. Because of labor agreements with the work force, a maximum of 40,000 labor hours is available next year to manufacture the two product lines. The manufacture of each XT product requires an average of 20 labor hours and each BT product requires an average of 40 labor hours. There is a maximum of 25,000 machine hours available next year in the auto-insertion process, the manufacturing operation that controls the maximum number of products that can be produced. Each XT product requires an average of 15 machine hours of auto-insertion machine time and each BT requires an average of 20 machine hours of auto-insertion machine time. The marketing department estimates that there is a maximum market demand next year of a total of 5,000 computers for both the XT and BT product lines.

LP-I. Warren Freeman, process engineer at the Boston plant of Computer Products Corporation (CPC), has been assigned the job of recommending the mix of ingredients that should go into the Wopac Resin. This resin is used in many of CPC's products and the purchasing department needs to know the quantity of each of the ingredients to include in an annual purchase contract from CPC's suppliers. Warren has this information on which to base his recommendation:

Ingredient	Cost/Pound	Mixing Instructions/Requirements
B22 Binder	$.30	No more than 4 pounds can be used for each pound of P55 Petroite
T90 Zinc Oxide	.20	Maximum of 60,000 pounds is available per year from sole source supplier
P55 Petroite	.40	At least 1 pound must be used for every 4 pounds of B22 binder

How much of each ingredient will provide at least 400,000 pounds of Wopac Resin next year with the minimum cost?

LP-J. Al Bergman, staff traffic analyst at the corporate headquarters of Computer Products Corporation (CPC), is developing a monthly shipping plan for the El Paso and Atlanta manufacturing plants to follow next year. These plants manufacture small-business computer systems that are shipped to five regional warehouses. Al has developed these estimated requirements and costs:

Plant	Monthly Capacity (Computers)	Warehouse	Monthly Requirements (Computers)
Atlanta	200	Chicago	75
El Paso	300	Dallas	100
		Denver	25
		New York	150
		San Jose	150

Plant	Warehouse	Shipping Cost ($/Computer)	Plant	Warehouse	Shipping Cost ($/Computer)
Atlanta	Chicago	$35	El Paso	Chicago	$50
	Dallas	40		Dallas	30
	Denver	60		Denver	35
	New York	45		New York	95
	San Jose	90		San Jose	40

a. What shipping plan will minimize monthly shipping costs?
b. What will be the monthly shipping costs of the optimal shipping plan from Part a?

Recognizing LP Problems

1. The Unfettered Lumber Mill in northern Alabama sells all of its products—oak, sycamore, and juniper hardwood slabs—to a local furniture manufacturer. The

customer will take any amount of each of the three hardwoods as long as the total equals 500,000 board feet a year. The customer will pay $150 for sycamore, $170 for oak, and $300 for juniper per 1,000 board feet. The mix of the three wood types is determined by the mix of woods found in the forest by the mill's contract woodcutters. The mill and log costs are $100 for 1,000 board feet of sycamore and oak, but $200 for the same amount of juniper. If the mill wishes to maximize annual profits, how much oak, sycamore, and juniper should it process each year?

   a. Review the requirements for a LP problem listed in Table 7.2 and determine if this problem meets each of these requirements.

   b. Is LP appropriate to use in this problem?

2. An expert diet planner for the U.S. Department of Health, Education, and Welfare (HEW) wishes to plan the ideal breakfast for first-grade schoolchildren. The diet would minimize the cost for a national breakfast program by providing a choice among three meals—A, B, and C. The dietetic quality of the three meals is:

Meal	Calories	Mineral Index	Costs/Meal
A	750	5.00	$1.25
B	1,200	7.00	$1.50
C	3,000	8.00	$3.00

What mix of A, B, and C meals provides the best balance of calories and minerals for minimum costs?

   a. Review the requirements for a LP problem listed in Table 7.2 and determine if each requirement is met.

   b. Is LP appropriate to use in this problem?

Formulating LP Problems

3. Formulate the objective function and constraint functions for Problem LP-A of this section. Define the decision variables.

4. Formulate the objective function and constraint functions for Problem LP-B of this section. Define the decision variables.

5. Formulate the objective function and constraint functions for Problem LP-C of this section. Define the decision variables.

6. Formulate the objective function and constraint functions for Problem LP-D of this section. Define the decision variables.

7. Formulate the objective function and constraint functions for Problem LP-E of this section. Define the decision variables.

8. Formulate the objective function and constraint functions for Problem LP-F of this section. Define the decision variables.

9. Formulate the objective function and constraint functions for Problem LP-G of this section. Define the decision variables.

10. Formulate the objective function and constraint functions for Problem LP-H of this section. Define the decision variables.

11. Formulate the objective function and constraint functions for Problem LP-I of this section. Define the decision variables.

12. Formulate the objective function and constraint functions for Problem LP-J of this section. Define the decision variables.

Solving LP Problems Graphically

13. Solve Problem LP-A graphically. What is the optimal solution? Explain what the solution means in terms of the original problem.

14. Solve Problem LP-B graphically. What is the optimal solution? Explain what the solution means in terms of the original problem.

15. Solve Problem LP-C graphically. What is the optimal solution? Explain what the solution means in terms of the original problem.

16. Solve Problem LP-E graphically. What is the optimal solution? Explain what the solution means in terms of the original problem.

17. Solve Problem LP-G graphically. What is the optimal solution? Explain what the solution means in terms of the original problem.

18. Solve Problem LP-H graphically. What is the optimal solution? Explain what the solution means in terms of the original problem.

COMPUTER PROBLEMS/CASES

SUNSHINE TOMATO SOUP SHIPPERS

The Sunshine Tomato Soup Shippers produces tomato soup at five West Coast canneries. The soup is shipped to four regional warehouses. The accompanying table shows the transportation cost per case from each cannery to each regional warehouse, the maximum and minimum monthly warehouse requirements, and the maximum monthly capacities of each of the canneries. The company wishes to ship *all* of its cannery capacity to the regional warehouses so that both the maximum and minimum monthly warehouse requirements are satisfied and the monthly total transportation cost is minimized.

	Destinations				*Maximum Monthly Cannery Capacities (Cases)*
Sources	*Seattle, Washington*	*Los Angeles, California*	*Denver, Colorado*	*Dallas, Texas*	
San Jose, California	$1.50	$ .70	$2.00	$2.50	50,000
Stockton, California	1.60	.80	1.80	2.50	80,000
Phoenix, Arizona	2.80	.60	1.20	1.50	60,000
Eugene, Oregon	.50	1.20	2.20	3.50	40,000
Bakersfield, California	1.80	.40	1.80	2.20	100,000
Maximum Monthly Warehouse Requirements (Cases)	90,000	100,000	80,000	100,000	
Minimum Monthly Warehouse Requirements (Cases)	60,000	80,000	50,000	70,000	

Assignment

1. Formulate the information in this case into a LP format. Define the decision variables, write the objective function, and write the constraint functions.

2. Using the LP computer program in the *POM Computer Library* that accompanies this book, solve the problem that you have formulated in No. 1.

3. Fully interpret the meaning of the solution that you obtained in No. 2. In other words, what should the management at Sunshine do? Fully explain the meaning of the slack variable values.

4. How would costs change if the capacity of the San Jose cannery increased to 60,000 cases? How would costs change if the capacity of the San Jose cannery decreased to 40,000 cases?

5. How would costs change if the minimum monthly requirements at the Dallas warehouse decreased to 69,000 cases? Increased to 71,000 cases?

6. Explain the caution that must be observed in answering Nos. 4 and 5.

COMPUTER PRODUCTS CORPORATION (CPC)

John Temple, director of new-product development at the corporate headquarters of Computer Products Corporation (CPC) in San Jose, California, is planning next year's projects. Five new products have been selected to be developed next year. Each of the new-product projects will be assigned to a development team at the R&D center in San Jose. Five such teams have just completed other development projects and are now ready to accept their new assignments. Because each team is made up of persons with unique abilities and experiences, and because each project requires persons with unique abilities and experiences, certain teams are better suited for assignment to certain projects. While John knows that every team could complete all of the projects, certain team–project matchups will be less efficient, take longer, and cost more money. John's staff has developed the estimated cost of each team completing each project:

| | New-Product Development Team | | | | |
| | 1
($000) | 2
($000) | 3
($000) | 4
($000) | 5
($000) |
Project					
A	$52	$120	$19	$39	$69
B	49	119	21	38	73
C	65	115	18	37	67
D	55	117	22	40	69
E	50	122	20	36	68

Which project should be assigned to each team to minimize the total cost of next year's new-product development budget?

Assignment

1. Formulate this case into a LP problem. Define the decision variables, write the objective function, and write the constraint functions.

2. Using the LP computer program in the *POM Computer Library* that accompanies this text, solve the problem that you formulated in No. 1.

3. Fully interpret the meaning of the solution that you obtained in No. 2. In other words, what should management at CPC do?

4. How would the solution change if further analysis resulted in increasing the development cost of Project C by Team 2 from $115,000 to $125,000? With the new information, to which teams would the projects be assigned?

5. Explain the caution that must be observed in answering No. 4.

DEMO ANCILLARY COMPANY (DAC)

Demo Ancillary Company (DAC) produces ancillary computer products such as printers, monitors, and specialty computer components. Charles Dallam, production scheduler at DAC's Austin, Texas, plant, is developing a production plan for the first two quarters of next year for producing XE2400 printers. The marketing department has estimated that 700 of the XE2400s will need to be shipped to customers in the first quarter and 1,000 in the second quarter. It takes 10 hours of labor to produce each of the printers, and only 8,000 hours of straight-time labor are available to produce the printers in each of the first and second quarters. Overtime labor can be used to produce the printers, but the plant has a policy that limits the amount of overtime to 10 percent of the straight-time labor available. Labor costs $10 per hour at straight-time and $15 per hour at overtime. If a printer is produced in the first quarter and shipped in the second quarter, the plant incurs a carrying cost of $100 per printer. How many printers should be produced on straight-time and overtime in each of the first and second quarters to minimize the total costs of straight-time labor, overtime labor, and carrying? The market requirements, the straight-time labor availability, and the overtime labor availability must be adhered to.

Assignment

1. Formulate the information in this case into a LP format. Define the decision variables, write the objective function, and write the constraint functions.

2. Using the LP computer program in the *POM Computer Library* that accompanies this book, solve the problem that you formulated in No. 1.

3. Fully interpret the meaning of the solution that you obtained in No. 2. In other words, what should the management at DAC do? Fully explain the meaning of the slack variable values.

4. If the labor union agreed to work up to 200 more hours of overtime during the first quarter, how would DAC's costs change? If the labor union wanted to work a maximum of 600 overtime hours in the second quarter, how much would it cost DAC?

5. How much would it cost DAC if 20 hours of overtime were worked in the first quarter producing printers to be shipped in the second quarter?

6. Explain the caution that must be observed in answering Nos. 4 and 5.

SELECTED BIBLIOGRAPHY

Balbirer, Sheldon D., and David Shaw. "An Application of Linear Programming to Bank Financial Planning." *Interfaces* 11, no. 5(October 1981):77–82.

Bierman, Harold, Jr., Charles P. Bonini, and Warren H. Hausman. *Quantitative Analysis for Business Decisions,* 6th ed. Homewood, IL: Irwin, 1981.

Brosch, Lee C., Richard J. Buck, William H. Sparrow, and James R. White. "Boxcars, Linear Programming, and the Sleeping Kitten." *Interfaces* 10, no. 6(December 1980):53–61.

Buffa, E. S., and J. S. Dyer. *Management Science/Operations Research: Model Formulation and Solution Methods,* 2nd ed. New York: Wiley, 1981.

Daellenbach, H. G., and E. J. Bell. *User's Guide to Linear Programming.* Englewood Cliffs, NJ: Prentice-Hall, 1970.

Hilal, Said S., and Warren Erikson. "Matching Supplies to Save Lives: Linear Programming the Production of Heart Valves." *Interfaces* 11, no. 6(December 1981):48–56.

Hollorann, Thomas, and Judson Byrn. "United Airlines Stationed Manpower Planning System." *Interfaces* 16, no. 1(January–February 1986):39–50.

Hooker, J. N. "Karmarkar's Linear Programming Algorithm." *Interfaces* 16, no. 4(1986):75–90.

Jackson, Bruce L., and John M. Brown. "Using LP for Crude Oil Sales at Elk Hills." *Interfaces* 10, no. 3(June 1980):65–70.

Karmarkar, N. "A New Polynomial-Time Algorithm For Linear Programming." *Combinatorica* 4, no. 4(1984):373–395.

Lee, Sang M. *Introduction to Management Science,* 2nd ed. Hinsdale, IL: Dryden Press, 1987.

Leff, H. Stephen, Maqbool Dada, and Stephen C. Graves. "An LP Planning Model for a Mental Health Community Support System." *Management Science* 32, no. 2(February 1986):139–155.

Oliff, Michael, and Earl Burch. "Multiproduct Production Scheduling at Owens-Corning Fiberglass." *Interfaces* 15, no. 5(September–October 1985):25–34.

Perry, C., and K. C. Crellin. "The Precise Management Meaning of a Shadow Price." *Interfaces* 12, no. 2(April 1982):61–63.

CHAPTER

8

LONG-RANGE CAPACITY PLANNING AND FACILITY LOCATION

COMPAQ PLANNING EXPANSION

Compaq Computer Corporation is a rapidly expanding computer products manufacturer. To meet the growing demand for its products, the firm's production capacity has been continuously growing. Compaq recently constructed 700,000 square feet of office space, 450,000 square feet of manufacturing space, and four new parking garages at its Houston headquarters.

As a part of its long-range capacity-planning program, Compaq has just announced another major production capacity expansion project. After flirting with offers from San Antonio, Dallas, and other cities, Compaq is locating this latest expansion of its manufacturing facilities in Houston. The long-range capacity expansion is expected to add 8,000 new employees to the company's payroll over the next seven years.

Local and state officials offered a generous package of inducements to convince the firm to expand its Houston facilities, including property tax abatements, road improvements, and a $253 million eight-lane freeway. The Houston Economic Development Council (HEDC), the Metropolitan Transit Authority, Mayor Kathy Whitmire, and other county and community representatives led the effort to keep the firm from locating the new facilities elsewhere. They met with Compaq officials for months to hammer out the package of inducements.[1]

[1] Bill Mintz and Ralph Bivins, "Compaq Planning Expansion," *Houston Chronicle,* June 30, 1988, sec. 1, 1, 8.

The previous vignette emphasizes the importance of facility-planning decisions in a company's strategy for competing in world markets. *Facility planning* includes determining how much long-range production capacity is needed, when additional capacity is needed, where the production facilities should be located, and the layout and characteristics of the facilities. Facility planning is based on the long-range strategic plan for the firm that delineates the product lines to be produced in each time period of the plan. For many firms long-range capacity and facility location plans are the most important strategic decisions that are made.

These decisions are crucial because, first, the capital investment in machinery, technology, land, and buildings for manufacturing and services is enormous. Once a firm has sunk several million dollars into a facility, it lives with the decision for a long time. These decisions therefore receive intense study and are made at the firm's highest level. Second, the long-range strategies are embodied in a firm's facility plans. Such issues as what product lines are to be produced, where they will be sold, and what technologies will be employed reflect the strategic plans of the firm, and these issues are also resolved at the firm's highest level. Third, the operating efficiency of operations is dependent on the capacity of the facilities. Maintenance costs, ease of scheduling, and economy of scale are among the factors affected by the capacity of facilities. Fourth, the capacity of facilities becomes a constraint on many other POM decisions. How much that can be economically produced in a specific time period is a limiting factor in short-range production planning.

In this chapter we shall develop a framework for planning long-range facility capacities, explore some of the important issues in capacity planning today, and study some of the methods used to analyze facility location decisions in POM.

LONG-RANGE CAPACITY PLANNING

Capacity-planning decisions usually involve these activities:

1. Estimating the capacities of the present facilities.
2. Predicting the long-range future capacity needs for all products and services.
3. Identifying and analyzing alternative sources of capacity to meet future capacity needs.
4. Selecting from among the alternative sources of capacity.

DEFINITION OF PRODUCTION CAPACITY

In general, capacity is the maximum production rate of an organization. Several factors underlying the concept of capacity make its use and understanding somewhat complex. First, day-to-day variations such as employee absences, equipment breakdowns, vacations, and material-delivery delays combine to make the output rate of facilities uncertain. Second, the production rates of different products and services are not the same. Thus 50,000 A's or 20,000 B's may be produced per month or some mix of A's and B's may be produced. The product mix must therefore be taken into account when capacity is estimated. Third, what level of capacity are we talking about? The maximum possible, the capacity based on a five-day-week work schedule, the practical capacity based on the use of existing facilities without the need to activate mothballed facilities, or some other level?

The Bureau of Economic Analysis defines *maximum practical capacity* as "that output attained within the normal operating schedule of shifts per day and days per week while bringing in high-cost inefficient facilities."[2] This definition is also used by the Federal Reserve Board and *The Wall Street Journal.* This commonly used definition does not rule out the use of inefficient standby equipment in estimating capacity.

MEASUREMENTS OF CAPACITY

For firms that produce only a single product or a few homogeneous products, the units used to measure *output rate capacity* are straightforward: Automobiles per month, tons of coal per day, and barrels of beer per quarter are examples of such measures. When a mix consisting of such products as lawn mowers, grass seed, and lawn furniture is produced from a facility, however, the diversity of the products presents a problem in measuring capacity. In such cases an *aggregate unit of capacity* must be established. This aggregate measure of capacity must allow the output rates of the various products to be converted to a common unit of output measure. For example, such measures as tons per hour and sales dollars per month are often used as aggregate measures of capacity among diverse products.

In capacity planning for services, output measures are particularly difficult. In these cases *input rate capacity* measures may be used. For example, airlines use available-seat-miles per month, hospitals use available beds per month, tax services use available accountant-days per month, and engineering service firms use labor-hours per month.

"U.S. factory use grew to 85 percent of capacity in December, the highest rate since 1975": What does this mean? *Percentage of capacity utilization* measures relate output measures to inputs available. For example, a tax service that had 10,000 labor-hours available during March used only 8,200 labor-hours to meet the demands of its customers. We divide the actual labor-hours used by the maximum labor-hours available during a normal schedule to arrive at the percentage of capacity utilization, or 82 percent in this example. Other commonly used percentage of capacity utilization calculations are: actual automobiles produced per quarter divided by the quarterly automobile production capacity, and occupied airline seats per month divided by the monthly airline seat capacity.

PREDICTING CAPACITY DEMAND

Predicting the sales levels of products and services five, ten, or twenty years into the future is very difficult. So much time is involved that fundamental changes in the economy, changes in consumer preferences, technological developments, demographic shifts, changes in government regulations, political and military events, and

---

[2] "Survey of Current Business," *U.S. Department of Commerce Journal,* 1982.

other developments can occur. Such shifts can dramatically affect the future demands for our products and services and the way that we produce them. As difficult as these forecasts are, we must nevertheless make them. Such long-range forecasts are necessary if we are to provide production capacity for our products and services, because it takes as long as five years to design, build, and activate a production facility today. If new technology is to be developed and incorporated into our production machines in a new building, it can take as long as an additional five years. These long lead times required to provide production capacity necessitate long-range forecasts of the demands for our products and services.

Some products or services for which we must develop long-range capacity plans are new, and others will have become obsolete and no longer need to be produced. The mix of products and services that will require production capacity five or ten years from now may therefore be quite different from the present mix. The product's life cycle (introduction — growth — maturity — decline) must be projected forward into the future for all products and services. This consideration must be built into the marketing plans and estimates on which the long-range forecasts and the capacity plans are to be based.

Technological developments must be anticipated because they can dramatically affect the way that we produce our products. Robotics, electronic computerized process controls, and bar coding technology are examples of such developments in our recent past. Because these and other technological advances are sure to affect the capacity of our facilities in the future, such developments must be an integral part of our long-range capacity predictions.

Another important consideration in estimating long-range capacity needs for a firm is the analysis of possible capacity additions by competitors. Capacity studies for a firm must also focus on the industry capacity if industry overcapacity situations are to be avoided. Video tapes, polyethylene film, semiconductors, automobiles, and personal computers are recent examples of how excess industry capacity can lead to depressed prices and/or unprofitability.

Fuji Photo Film, Hitachi Maxell, and TDK almost doubled their collective production capacity of videotapes in the early 1980s. While these capacity expansion decisions were being made, industry sales were expanding at a tremendous rate. The depressed consumer prices and company profits that resulted from the supply–demand imbalance (excess supply or capacity) within the industry persisted into the middle 1980s.[3] The excess production capacity in the personal computer industry is creating similar havoc for such firms as IBM, Texas Instruments, and Apple Computer. The excess capacity in the polyethylene film industry is expected to continue for several decades unless low profitability drives some of the capacity from the industry. Dow Chemical Company has cut back its capacity expansion projects in South Korea, Saudi Arabia, and Yugoslavia, which should help the capacity–demand imbalance in the industry.[4] Industry Snapshot 8.1 discusses the trends toward excess capacity in the global automobile industry in the late 1980s.

---

[3] "A Volatile Tape Market Has TDK on a Roller Coaster," *Business Week,* July 25, 1983.

[4] "Dow: Headed for Overcapacity, It Veers from Basic Chemicals," *Business Week,* Jan. 31, 1983.

INDUSTRY SNAPSHOT 8.1

Automakers Facing Challenge of the '90s: Overcapacity

Having modernized their factories and corporate structures, the Big Three face the more imposing task of making American cars that are better engineered and sell like Japanese cars. The dollar's slide against the Japanese yen and European currencies in the 1980s made some imports more expensive and temporarily helped level the playing field for General Motors, Ford, and Chrysler. So has a new United Auto Workers pattern contract that stresses job security over wage increases and gives the companies needed flexibility.

But by 1990 there could be 5.6 million more new cars and trucks than buyers worldwide, according to industry estimates. More than half the excess factory capacity will be in North America, and much of it in the United States. With an oversupply of production capacity, how will the Big Three automakers be able to compete?

Ford, losing $1 million a day at the beginning of the 1980s, made big adjustments, closing excess plants and running the rest on overtime while grabbing styling leadership from GM with a sleek, aerodynamic new lineup. Ford led U.S. automakers in earnings in 1986 and then set the world automotive industry record with $4.6 billion in 1987 profits. It also has a comfortable cash cushion available for acquisitions and new-product development.

Chrysler also has switched its focus from trimming costs to investing in new products. Chrysler has shed weight gained in its acquisition of ailing AMC. After squeezing more Jeeps out of a former AMC assembly plant in Toledo, Chrysler decided to close AMC's other U.S. assembly plant in Kenosha, Wisconsin. It also settled its UAW contracts five months early in 1988, eliminating the chance of a costly strike when its factories were pushing out 1989 models. Chairman Lee Iacocca is injecting extra money into R&D for new models and advanced engineering.

GM, which has spent $50 billion since the early 1980s to modernize or replace its factories, is also channeling resources into new-product development. The world's largest automaker is barely breaking even on its U.S. car and truck business despite cost-cutting, which may make additional plant closings necessary. GM lost market share in the 1980s to Ford and Chrysler as well as to foreign automakers. And the field of competitors only grows thicker. The sales of Mazda, which joined the ranks of Japanese automakers that operate U.S. plants when it opened a plant in Michigan, are booming. Toyota's huge Kentucky plant began making Camry sedans in 1988, and a Chrysler-Mitsubishi plant in Illinois began churning out sporty models in 1989.[5]

---

[5] Excerpted from "Automakers Facing Challenge of the '90s: Overcapacity," Associated Press, *Houston Chronicle*, sec. 2, p. 5, May 19, 1988. Excerpted with permission from Associated Press.

If significant excess capacity situations are to be avoided, firms must take extra care to predict future industry capacity needs, sense the capacity plans of the competition, and manage the capacity expansion/reduction process.

TABLE 8.1 | *Ways of Changing Long-Range Capacity*

Type of Capacity Change	Ways of Accommodating Long-Range Capacity Changes
Expansion	1. Subcontract with other companies to become suppliers of the expanding firm's components or entire products. 2. Acquire other companies, facilities, or resources. 3. Develop sites, build buildings, buy equipment. 4. Expand, update, or modify existing facilities. 5. Reactivate facilities on standby status.
Reduction	1. Sell off existing facilities, sell inventories, and lay off or transfer employees. 2. Mothball facilities and place on standby status, sell inventories, and lay off or transfer employees. 3. Develop and phase in new products as other products decline.

WAYS OF CHANGING CAPACITY

Once the long-range capacity needs are estimated through long-range forecasts, many avenues exist to provide for the capacity. Firms may either find themselves in a capacity shortage situation, where present capacity is insufficient to meet the forecast demand for their products and services, or have present capacity in excess of the expected future needs. Long-range capacity planning may therefore require either reduction or expansion of present capacity levels. Table 8.1 lists some of the ways that managers can accommodate the changing long-range capacity needs of organizations.

In cases where capacity reductions seem necessary, there may be a tendency to leave well enough alone. But operations managers should be just as concerned when their capacities are excessive as when they are insufficient. Excessive capacities result in unnecessarily high operating costs for several reasons. First, much of the facility investment is not being profitably used and could be sold, rented, or otherwise used to produce alternative sources of income. In times when interest rates are very high, businesses must make sure that every dollar of investment is being used to produce profits, either through producing products and services or through alternative investments. Second, operating expenses are excessive because of insurance costs, air-conditioning and heating costs, taxes, maintenance costs, security costs, and other costs that are directly related to the size and value of the facility. Third, as we shall discuss in the next section, facilities with production capacities greater than needed are often so unwieldy to operate that they are too inefficient to permit changeover to other product models. For these and other related reasons, labor, material, and overhead costs can be excessive when the production capacity of facilities is excessive. Operations managers therefore must adjust long-range capacities downward as required by declines in long-range demand for their products and services.

FIGURE 8.1   *Effects of Time-Phasing Products on Facility Capacity Utilization*

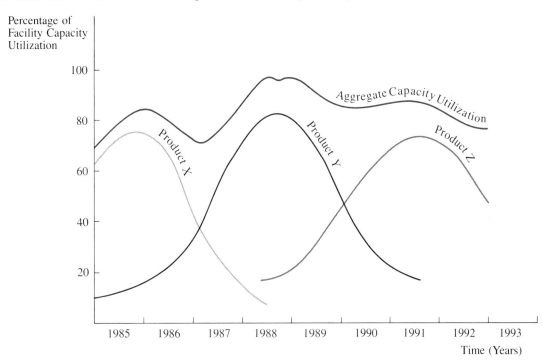

One avenue usually preferred by operations managers to maintain high levels of facility utilization in spite of declining long-range demand for their present products and services is the phasing-in of new products to replace older and declining ones. Figure 8.1 shows how a firm might design and develop new products as old ones decline over time. This time-phasing may be a key motivating force behind the development of new products and services in that the excess production capacity resulting from declining product demand that is not replaced by demand for new products becomes a millstone of high operating costs supported by a declining revenue base. Such a strategy, as demonstrated in Figure 8.1, does maintain a relatively stable long-range facility capacity utilization.

In the decades following the Great Depression of the 1930s in the United States, operations managers have tended to be more concerned with expanding capacity because of the extended growth patterns of our business sectors in this period. Although this tendency is now coming under increasing scrutiny because of the cost of funds and increasing shortages of resources of all types, capacity expansions remain a major concern to operations managers today. As can be seen in Table 8.1, the alternatives for providing additional capacity include outside contracting, acquisition, building new facilities from scratch, updating existing facilities, and reactivating old ones. G. Heileman Brewing Company used acquisition to provide capacity

FIGURE 8.2   *Economies and Diseconomies of Scale*

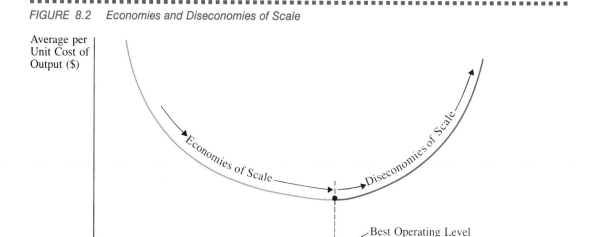

expansion in the early 1980s. Heileman, the fourth largest brewer in the United States, battled to acquire Pabst Brewing Company in order to expand its markets in the South and to gain additional production capacity at bargain prices. Although Heileman could have built new breweries in the South, it estimated that it could acquire the capacity for $17.50 per barrel by buying out Pabst, compared to paying $50 per barrel for building new breweries.[6]

If operations managers decide on building new facilities as the best alternative source of additional capacity, how to time-phase in the capacity remains an important issue.

ECONOMIES OF SCALE

For a given production facility, there is an annual volume of outputs that results in the least average unit cost. This level of output is called the facility's *best operating level.* Figure 8.2 illustrates this concept. Notice that as the annual volume of outputs increases outward from zero in a particular production facility, average unit costs fall. These declining costs result from fixed costs being spread over more and more units, longer production runs that result in a smaller proportion of labor being allocated to setups and machine changeovers, proportionally less material scrap, and other economies. Such savings, which are called *economies of scale,* continue to accrue as the volume of outputs increases to the best operating level for that particular facility.

Past this point, however, additional volume of outputs results in ever-increasing average unit costs. These increasing costs arise from increased congestion

---

[6] "Heileman Plans Big Expansion into South, Setting Stage for Bruising Beer-Sales Fight," *The Wall Street Journal,* Feb. 3, 1983.

FIGURE 8.3   *Increases in Incremental Facility Capacity*

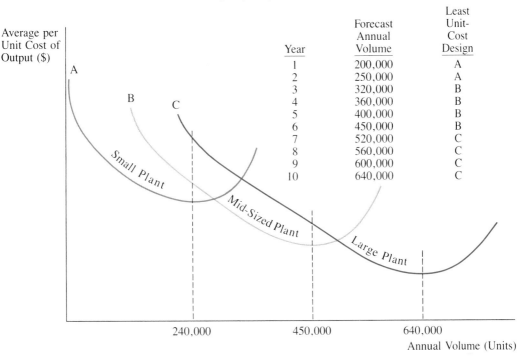

of materials and workers, which contributes to increasing inefficiency, difficulty in scheduling, damaged goods, reduced morale, increased use of overtime, and other diseconomies. The impact of such factors, which are called *diseconomies of scale,* increases at an accelerating rate past the best operating level for the facility.

Because each facility has its own unique best operating level and, all other things being equal, facilities with higher best operating levels require greater investments, operations managers must decide between two general approaches to expanding long-range capacity:

1. Invest heavily in one large facility that requires a large initial investment, but one that will have a higher best operating level and that ultimately will fulfill the capacity needs of the firm. In other words, build the ultimate facility now and grow into it.
2. Plan to invest in an initial facility design now and expand or modify that facility as needed to raise the best operating levels to meet the long-range demand for products and services. In other words, expand long-range capacity incrementally as needed to match future capacity demands.

Figure 8.3 compares these strategies. Notice that Designs A, B, and C exhibit best operating levels at 240,000, 450,000, and 640,000 annual volume, respectively. Let us suppose, for example, that our long-range capacity needs were estimated to be

640,000 annual volume 10 years from now. How do we best provide for this long-range capacity, incrementally or all at once?

As shown in Figure 8.3, the strategy of initially selecting Design A and subsequently modifying that design to Design B and then to Design C would seem to make sense because the average unit cost tends to be the lowest. Additionally, this incremental approach may be less risky because if our forecast capacity needs do not materialize, then the expansion program could be stopped in time to avoid unnecessary investment in unneeded expansion. On the other hand, one large construction project is likely to involve less investment and costs than several smaller projects because there would be no redundant construction work or interruptions of production. Because of inflation, construction costs may be less if we build all the needed capacity now. Furthermore, we avoid the risk of having to turn down future business if our long-range forecast turns out to be too low and our capacity is inadequate. But the chief concern about building the big facility now is that our funds will be tied up in excess capacity on which no return will be realized for several years. This results either in great additional interest expense or in income forgone owing to not having the funds committed to other types of investments that would generate revenue.

Choosing between expanding capacity all at once or incrementally is not a clear-cut choice for most firms. In cases of mature products with stable and predictable demand patterns, firms are more receptive to building the ultimate facility now. With new products, however, firms lean more toward an incremental expansion strategy because of the riskiness of forecasts and the unpredictable nature of their long-range demands. The eventual choice will differ from firm to firm because of the nature of their products, the availability of investment funds, their attitude toward risk, and other factors.

The Japanese Story

Japanese manufacturers have preferred relatively smaller facilities with less capacity. They, unlike their U.S. counterparts, have leaned away from vertical integration, where all operations required to produce a product are under one roof, and more toward *subcontractor networks.* In these arrangements the parent manufacturers develop long-range contractual relationships with several suppliers to provide a large proportion of the production of parts, components, and subassemblies. This system allows the parent manufacturers to operate with lower levels of capacity within their own facilities because much of their capacity needs have been "farmed out" to their supplier subcontractors. This pattern of subcontractor networks is evident in the size of Japanese manufacturing firms, as shown in the accompanying table.[7]

Number of Employees	Number of Firms	Percentage of Firms
1,000 or more	750	20%
30–999	60,000	30
Less than 30	180,000	50

---

[7] Leighton F. Smith, "Just-in-Time Production Systems," presented at the APICS Educational Liaison Workshop, St. Charles, IL, June 29–July 1, 1981, 9.

The principal advantage of subcontractor networks is that parent manufacturers can conveniently vary their capacity when business cycles or other factors would otherwise necessitate the hiring and layoff of employees. Since increases or decreases in capacity are ordinarily absorbed by subcontractors, the parent manufacturers can provide their lifetime-employed work forces with stable employment, an important objective of these Japanese firms.

A survey of the U.S. automotive industry conducted by Arthur Andersen & Co. and the University of Michigan reports that industry leaders plan to reduce vertical integration in the 1980s, implying a greater reliance on subcontracting in the future.[8]

ANALYZING CAPACITY-PLANNING DECISIONS

Facility-planning decisions can be analyzed using several different approaches. *Break-even analysis,* discussed in Chapter 4, is commonly used to compare the cost functions of two or more facility alternatives. If we can estimate the volume of outputs for any given year, we can determine from this type of analysis which facility alternative exhibits the least cost. *Present-value analysis* is also particularly useful in long-range capacity planning. Its usefulness stems from the long-term nature of the planning, which can span as many as 20 or more years. Over such long periods of time, discounting future sums back to present values puts all future actions and their costs or profits on an equal footing for purposes of comparison. Appendix C at the back of this book demonstrates the use of present-value analysis. *Computer simulation* and *waiting line analysis,* illustrated in Appendix D, can also be used to analyze capacity-planning decisions. *Linear programming,* which was discussed in Chapter 7, is also used in these decisions; this approach is used later in this chapter to analyze facility location decisions.

In addition to these techniques, decision trees are particularly helpful in analyzing facility-planning decisions.

DECISION TREE ANALYSIS

Decisions about facility planning are complex. They often are difficult to organize because they are *multiphase decisions,* those that involve several interdependent decisions that must be made in a sequence. Decision trees were developed for multiphase decisions as aids to analysts who must see clearly what decisions must be made, in what sequence the decisions must occur, and the interdependence of the decisions. This ability to structure the way we think about multiphase decisions simplifies the analysis.

Example 8.1 demonstrates the essentials of *decision tree analysis* in a decision that contains an alternative of providing production capacity for manufacturing. This form of analysis gives managers:

1. A way of structuring complex multiphase decisions by mapping decisions from the present to the future.
2. A direct way of dealing with uncertain events.
3. An objective way of determining the relative value of each decision alternative.

---

[8] Ibid., 6.

EXAMPLE 8.1   Decision Tree: To Manufacture or Not to Manufacture?

Biltmore Manufacturing has developed a promising new product. The firm's management faces three choices: It can sell the idea of the new product to a well-known company for $20,000, it can hire a consultant to study the market and then make a decision, or it can arrange financing for building a factory and then manufacture and market the product.

The study will cost Biltmore $10,000, and its management believes that there is about a 50-50 chance that a favorable market will be found. If the study is unfavorable, management figures that it can still sell the idea for $12,000. If the study is favorable, it figures that it can sell the idea for $40,000. But even if a favorable market is found, the chance of an ultimately successful product is about 2 out of 5. A successful product will return $500,000. Even with an unfavorable study, a successful product can be expected about once in every ten new-product introductions. If Biltmore's management decides to manufacture the product without a study, there is only a 1-in-4 chance of its being successful. A product failure costs $100,000. What should Biltmore do?

Solution

1. Draw a tree from left to right with squares (□) for decisions and circles (○) for chance events. These decisions and chance events are often called *nodes* or *forks.* Write the outcome values (profits or losses) in the right margin and write the probability of chance events in parentheses on the branches to the right of the circles.

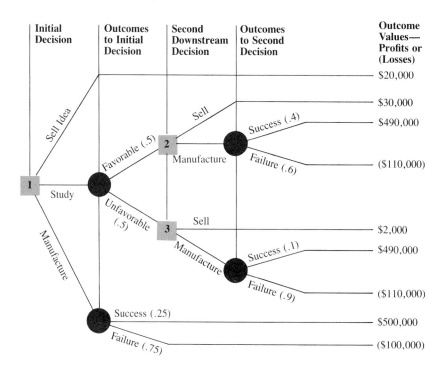

2. Working from right to left, compute the expected value (EV) at each circle for chance events to the second downstream decisions. Write the EVs to the right of each circle. For example, the EV of the chance events to manufacture—decision $\boxed{2}$—is computed: EV = .4($490,000) + .6(−$110,000) = $130,000. Continuing to work from right to left, decide which alternative of the second downstream decisions ($\boxed{2}$ and $\boxed{3}$) has the highest EV. Write the selected EV to the right of the decision boxes and prune ($\dashv$ $\vdash$) all other branches. Continue working from right to left as before and compute the EV for the initial decision. For example, the EV for the study alternative is computed: EV = .5($130,000) + .5($2,000) = $66,000.

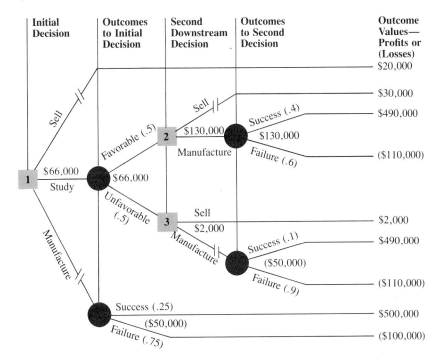

3. The EV for the initial decision is $66,000. The sequence of decisions is deduced by following the unpruned branches of the tree from left to right: study, if favorable, manufacture; if unfavorable, sell.

A note of caution should be observed in regard to the interpretation of expected value (EV) in decision tree analysis. One error that we might make is to interpret the EV for each decision literally and absolutely. The EV's are only *relative measures* of value and not *absolute measures.* Consider the profits (losses) in Example 8.1. These are possible outcomes to the study alternative: $30,000, $490,000, ($110,000), or $2,000. Only one of these values will ultimately be returned to the decision maker. The EV of $66,000 will never be returned to the firm. The EV is only a measure of value of this alternative relative to the other alternatives.

Expected value as a decision criterion varies in effectiveness depending on the decision situation. With a one-time decision, which is usually the case with facility-planning decisions in POM, expected value is at best only a relative measure of value. On the other hand, expected value as a decision criterion tends to be more meaningful when the decision is recurring. For example, when the number of standby machines is to be determined on the basis of weekly machine breakdown information, the average value of each alternative tends to approach its EV as the decision is applied over several trials.

But even if expected values or probabilities are not included in decision trees, the value of decision trees as a useful way of organizing the way we think about complex multiphase decisions must be recognized. This tool allows decision makers to see clearly what decisions must be made, in what sequence they must occur, and their interdependence. Expected value, if interpreted correctly, is a fringe benefit.

Regardless of the specific techniques employed to analyze long-range capacity-planning decisions, you may be assured that these decisions are among the most analyzed decisions that involve operations managers. The reasons for this involvement reside in the importance that these decisions hold for these managers, as we discussed early in the chapter.

When existing facility capacities are inadequate to meet the long-range capacity needs and new facilities are to be built, rented, or purchased, an important issue that must be resolved is where to locate the new facilities.

FACILITY LOCATION

Location decisions are particularly important — whether we are considering the location of warehouses, manufacturing plants, hospitals, fire stations, or retail outlets — because once the buildings are built, managers must live with their location decisions for a long time. The enormous first cost of most facilities and their subsequent low market value for resale purposes dictate that most organizations must continue to operate facilities for extended periods of time even though their locations are less than optimal.

Facility location decisions are not made lightly. On the contrary, they usually involve long and costly studies of alternative locations before the eventual site is selected. Those who have been through several of these location studies generally conclude that there is no clear-cut best location but rather that there are several good locations. If one site is clearly superior to all others in all respects, the location decision is an easy one. Typically, however, several site candidates, each with its strengths and weaknesses, emerge as good choices; and the location decision becomes a *trade-off decision:* You can gain one type of benefit only by giving up another. These trade-off decisions among sites can be agonizing and are usually resolved only after long and careful weighing of the pros and cons of each location.

No facility location decision in recent memory exceeds the notoriety given to General Motors Corporation's search for a location for a facility to produce its Saturn automobile. The Saturn was planned to be put into production in 1988 with the latest high-tech manufacturing methods to compete with the automobiles from Japan in both price and quality. GM planned to spend $3.5 billion to plan, build, and equip the facility, which would employ 6,000 workers when finished. Among the factors

GM considered in its location decision were: electric power costs, cost of workmen's compensation laws, cost of approximately 1,000 acres of land, local and state business climate, transportation facilities, utilities, proximity to suppliers, proximity to markets, and high-tech training opportunities for employees. GM fed all of this information and other facts about each potential location into their computers for help in determining the choice of locations. Twenty-four states were in the running, with several potential sites within each state. Eighty-four cities and 140 sites were known to be under consideration in the state of Texas alone.[9]

Location decisions can be better understood by examining the factors that commonly affect the final selection of facility locations.

FACTORS AFFECTING LOCATION DECISIONS

Selecting a facility location usually involves a sequence of decisions. This sequence can include a national decision, a regional decision, a community decision, and a site decision. Figure 8.4 shows this location decision sequence.

First, management must decide whether the facility will be located *internationally or domestically.* Only a few years ago, this choice would have received only minor consideration. Today, however, with the internationalization of business, managers are routinely considering *where in the world* their facilities should be located. Industry Snapshot 8.2 illustrates how facility location decisions transcend national boundaries. Including international location alternatives in these decisions provides economic opportunities, but the decisions also are more encompassing and complex.

Once the international-versus-domestic issue has been resolved, management must decide the general geographic region within the country where the facility is to be located. This *regional decision* may involve choosing among a few national regions, as in Figure 8.4, or among several regions within a much smaller geographic area. The scope of an organization's operations generally determines the size of the regions under consideration (county, state, or nation). Figure 8.5 illustrates the ranking of U.S. regions and states as desirable manufacturing locations, prepared by a Chicago-based international accounting and management consulting company.

Once the geographic region decision has been made, management must decide among several communities within the region. Figure 8.4 also lists some of the factors affecting the community decision. Most of the factors taken into consideration in the regional decision are also present in the community decision.

The *community decision* has some additional factors affecting the location choice. Community services and taxes, attitudes and incentives toward new facility locations, availability and costs of sites, environmental impact, banking services, and management preferences are important inputs in deciding among communities.

Finally, once a community has been selected, a site within that community must be chosen. Some additional factors emerge in *site selection:* size and cost of each site, proximity to transportation systems and related industries or services, availability of utilities and materials and supplies, and zoning restrictions.

---

[9] "Texas Cities Vie to Become Site for GM's Saturn," *Houston Chronicle,* Mar. 23, 1985, sec. 3, p. 1.

FIGURE 8.4 The Facility Location Decision

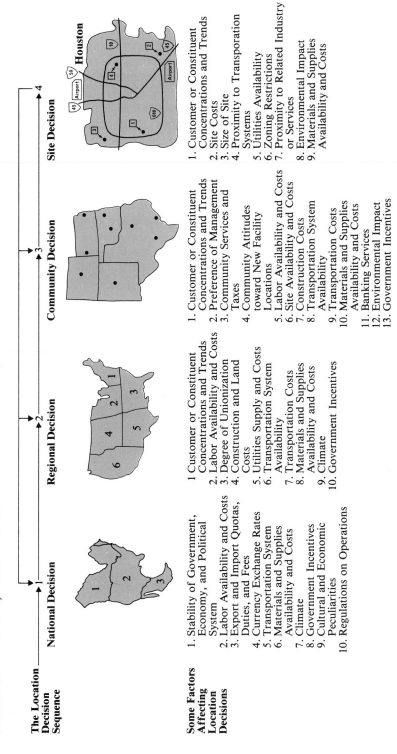

The Location Decision Sequence

National Decision → 1

Regional Decision → 2

Community Decision → 3

Site Decision → 4

Some Factors Affecting Location Decisions

National Decision

1. Stability of Government, Economy, and Political System
2. Labor Availability and Costs
3. Export and Import Quotas, Duties, and Fees
4. Currency Exchange Rates
5. Transportation System
6. Materials and Supplies Availability and Costs
7. Climate
8. Government Incentives
9. Cultural and Economic Peculiarities
10. Regulations on Operations

Regional Decision

1 Customer or Constituent Concentrations and Trends
2. Labor Availability and Costs
3. Degree of Unionization
4. Construction and Land Costs
5. Utilities Supply and Costs
6. Transportation System Availability
7. Transportation Costs
8. Materials and Supplies Availability and Costs
9. Climate
10. Government Incentives

Community Decision

1. Customer or Constituent Concentrations and Trends
2. Preference of Management
3. Community Services and Taxes
4. Community Attitudes toward New Facility Locations
5. Labor Availability and Costs
6. Site Availability and Costs
7. Construction Costs
8. Transportation System Availability
9. Transportation Costs
10. Materials and Supplies Availability and Costs
11. Banking Services
12. Environmental Impact
13. Government Incentives

Site Decision

1. Customer or Constituent Concentrations and Trends
2. Site Costs
3. Size of Site
4. Proximity to Transporation Systems
5. Utilities Availability
6. Zoning Restrictions
7. Proximity to Related Industry or Services
8. Environmental Impact
9. Materials and Supplies Availability and Costs

INDUSTRY SNAPSHOT 8.2

Mexico Is Attracting More Foreign Plants

Mexico is edging out Pacific Rim countries as the United States' favorite place for offshore assembly plants and is attracting an increasing number of Asian manufacturers. The devaluations of the peso in recent years have depressed Mexican wages in dollars, making them more competitive, while labor costs in the Far East have been on the rise. The information in the accompanying table indicates that Mexico is now among the lowest-wage countries in the world. Additionally, Mexico has abundant land mass for new-plant construction and a young population. More than 1 million new workers enter the Mexican labor force each year, and the largest segment of the population is between 10 and 19 years old, promising an even greater supply of labor for the 1990s.

The attitude of the Mexican government toward foreign factories in its country may be the most encouraging factor. With the blessings of the Mexican government, General Motors, Sylvania, General Electric, RCA, Honeywell, and other U.S. firms have established twin plants along the U.S.-Mexican border. Raw materials and components are shipped duty-free from the United States to U.S.-owned factories, called *maquiladora* plants, in Juarez, Tijuana, and Matamoros, where Mexican workers assemble finished or semifinished products. These products are then shipped back across the border to *twin plants* in San Diego, El Paso, and Brownsville for further work. The products are taxed by the U.S. Customs Service only on the basis of value added while the products were in Mexico. Such products as clothing, electronics, plastic bottles, dental braces, shoes, medical supplies, gift wraps, and automobile parts are produced in 1,220 twin plants that employ more than 325,000 workers on both sides of the border. The Mexican government has allowed maquiladora plants to be placed almost anywhere in the country, has enabled products made in the plants to be sold in the big domestic market of Mexico, and has permitted foreign companies to own 100 percent of the operations.[10]

U.S. firms are not the only ones interested. Japanese manufacturers are also

(continued)

---

[10] Daniel Benedict, "Mexico Attracting More Foreign Plants as Falling Peso Makes Wages Competitive," *Houston Chronicle,* Jan. 31, 1988, sec. 5, 1, 11. Copyright: Houston Chronicle. Excerpted with permission.

The process of selecting a specific location is complex. The decision sequence can be looping—backtracking to rethink community selection after sites have been examined, for example. Also, the analysis can compare Site X in Community A with Site Y in Community B. But regardless of the decision sequence and its complexity, these and other factors affect the eventual choice of nation, region, community, and site.

The type of facility and the nature of its products or services strongly affect the relative importance of each of these factors in location decisions.

INDUSTRY SNAPSHOT 8.2   (continued)

taking a good look at facility locations in Mexico. Four hundred Japanese firms are presently located in the border zone of California and Mexico's Baja California. Mitsura Misawa, the general manager of the Industrial Bank of Japan, assures us that the next 10 years will see a substantial Japanese investment in maquiladoras. Sixteen businessmen representing some of Japan's leading automotive, electronic, and industrial corporations toured McAllen–Reynosa, Laredo–Nuevo Laredo, San Antonio, Austin, and El Paso–Juarez in early 1988. Misawa indicated that with the fall of the dollar's value relative to the yen, shipping out of Japan is more expensive. Because Japanese labor costs have become very expensive, Japanese manufacturers would like to utilize the lower labor costs provided by Mexico.

Japan has invested $1.2 billion in Mexico as the two nations have nurtured closer economic ties. Locating factories on the border would put Japanese corporations closer to the huge consumer markets of the United States. Thus they would be saving not only on labor costs, but on transportation costs as well.[11]

	Average Wages per Hour	
	1982	*1987*
Mexico	$1.70	$ .60
Taiwan	1.10	1.30
Hong Kong	1.25	1.40
Singapore	1.50	1.90
South Korea	.85	1.05

Source: Sergio L. Ornela, director of a Chihuahua industrial park.

[11] "Japanese to Open More Mexico Plants," *Houston Chronicle,* March 13, 1987, sec. 1, p. 21. Reprinted with permission of United Press International, Copyright 1987.

TYPES OF FACILITIES AND THEIR DOMINANT LOCATIONAL FACTORS

Have you ever wondered why several steel mills are located right next door to one another in Pennsylvania, why several large mass-merchandising mail-order houses are located in Chicago, why most tire manufacturers are in Akron, why many automobile manufacturers are in Detroit, and why small convenience grocery stores are widely dispersed throughout communities? Are there compelling reasons why one type of facility with a particular product or service tends to be located close to its raw materials or centers of management, technical, and worker skills, while another facility with a different product or service is located close to its markets? These questions suggest that each type of facility under consideration has a few dominant factors that ultimately determine its location decision.

Table 8.2 rates the relative importance of some of the factors affecting location decisions for different types of facilities. Note, for example, that facilities for mining, quarrying, and heavy manufacturing tend to have Factors 3 to 6 and 8 to 10 rated as

FIGURE 8.5   Rankings of U.S. Regions and States as Desirable Manufacturing Locations

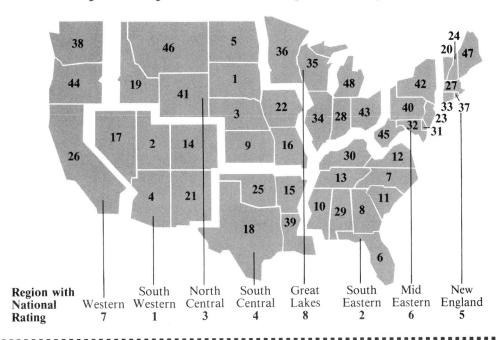

Source: "Seventh Annual Study of General Manufacturing Climates of the 48 Contiguous States of America," prepared by Grant Thornton, Chicago, 1986.

very important, while Factor 1 is rated as less important. These *capital-intensive* facilities usually are expensive to build, cover large geographic areas, and use great quantities of heavy and bulky raw materials. Additionally, their production processes discard large amounts of wastes, total finished outputs weigh much less than total raw material inputs, enormous quantities of utilities are absorbed, and products are shipped to only a few customers. These facilities consequently tend to be located near their raw material sources rather than near their markets so as to minimize the total transportation costs of inputs and outputs. Additionally, they tend to select sites where land and construction costs are relatively inexpensive and where waste disposal is not expected to harm the environment. The availability of an abundant supply of utilities and the proximity of railroad service are also necessary.

Light manufacturing facilities that make such items as electronic components, small mechanical parts, and assembled products do not typically locate near their raw material suppliers, because transportation costs of inputs are not typically dominant over transportation costs of outputs. In fact, these facilities do not necessarily locate near either raw material sources or markets. Rather, they strike a balance between transportation costs of inputs and outputs, and other locational factors therefore tend

TABLE 8.2   Relative Importance of Locational Factors in Types of Facilities

Factors Affecting Location Decisions	Types of Facilities						
	Mining, Quarrying, Heavy Manufacturing	Light Manufacturing	Ware-housing	Retailing	Customer Services for Profit	Local Government Services	Health and Emergency Services
1. Proximity to concentrations of customers or constituents	C	C	B	A	A	A	A
2. Labor availability and costs	B	A	B	B	A	B	B
3. Degree of unionization	A	A	B	B	B	C	B
4. Construction and land costs	A	B	B	B	B	B	B
5. Proximity to transportation facilities	A	B	A	B	C	C	C
6. Incoming transportation costs	A	B	A	B	C	C	C
7. Outgoing transportation costs	B	B	A	C	C	C	C
8. Utilities availability and costs	A	B	C	C	C	C	C
9. Proximity to raw materials and supplies	A	B	C	C	C	C	C
10. Zoning restrictions and environmental impact	A	B	C	C	B	C	C

Note: A = very important, B = important, C = less important.

to dominate the location decision. The availability and cost of labor and the degree of unionization can be dominant because labor tends to be a large part of total product cost for this type of *labor-intensive* facility. Light manufacturing facilities do not typically locate near their markets because they usually ship their products to only a few regional warehouses of wholesalers, who then distribute through their retailing network to the ultimate users of the products. Thus the shipment of outputs typically is in large quantities to a few locations and constitutes a relatively small part of total product costs. Industry Snapshot 8.2, "Mexico Is Attracting More Foreign Plants," is about light manufacturing companies. The availability and cost of labor is important in the location decisions of these facilities, whereas transportation cost is of lesser importance. The trend toward twin plants along the U.S. – Mexican border is likely to accelerate, given the high cost of labor within the United States. If the trend toward more factory automation accelerates as expected, labor cost could become less important in factory location decisions in the future. The trend could be toward more dispersed, decentralized production systems with many small plants that utilize flexible automation.

The location of warehouses is perhaps the most straightforward location decision among the various types of facilities. The dominant factors are those affecting incoming and outgoing transportation costs. Although it is desirable and indeed frequently necessary to be near enough to markets to both communicate effectively with recipients of outgoing products and react quickly to customer orders, transportation cost is the paramount locational factor for warehouses. These facilities are therefore often subjects of quantitative economic evaluations such as linear programming.

Retailing facilities are located near concentrations of target customers. All other locational factors are subordinate to this single factor. The studies of these facility locations typically involve the identification of target customer residential concentrations, traffic data on nearby streets, growth trends of communities and suburbs, discretionary spending levels of nearby neighborhoods, and other demographic information.

Facilities that provide customer services for profit, such as dry cleaners, laundromats, banks, welding shops, and hotels, are not unlike retailing facilities in their location decisions. These facilities are also located near concentrations of their target customers. These location studies therefore are also usually dominated by the identification of the target customers, their characteristics, and their present and future concentration locations. Because some service facilities such as dry cleaners, medical clinics, and photo processors can discard large quantities of waste paper, chemicals, and spent supplies, zoning restrictions and environmental impact can play more important roles than in retailing location decisions.

Local government service facilities also are usually located near concentrations of their constituents. Local government services are often grouped together so that constituents can economize in their time, effort, and transportation costs by making multiple calls with one trip. Additionally, these services are grouped in order to allow interagency interactions. For example, county jails tend to be located near county court buildings so as to minimize the transportation of prisoners between the jails and the courts.

Health and emergency services are traditionally located near concentrations of constituents because the key consideration in selecting locations is that such locations result in the lowest overall response times between the constituents and the services. The minimizing of property loss and loss of life is the overriding consideration in these locations. Fire stations are typically located near concentrations of residential constituents to minimize the time it takes for fire engines to arrive at fire scenes. Ambulance services are similarly located near these community neighborhood population centers to minimize the time required to transport patients to hospitals and health clinics. Hospitals are usually located near the centers of community population density concentrations.

The type of facility, the nature of its products and services, and the nature of its daily activities affect the importance that each locational factor plays in location decisions. Each location decision is unique because the nature of each facility and its daily operation is unique. The understanding of the factors that affect these decisions and of their relative importance in locating several classes of facilities provides a useful framework for analysis.

DATA, POLITICS, INCENTIVES, AND PREEMPTIVE TACTICS

The amount of data needed to compare facility location alternatives can be immense, and the sources of these data are numerous. One source is the *Business Site/Construction Planner* published by *Dun's Review.* Other valuable sources of location data are the chambers of commerce of the cities under consideration. Another surefire way for a firm to be inundated with facility location data is to prepare a press release to the news media announcing its intention of locating a new facility that will employ 500 people and have an annual payroll of $10 million.

Once governments, chambers of commerce, and communities get wind of a new facility being planned, the political aspects of facility location decisions become apparent. There seems to be no end to the extremes to which government and civic organizations will go to woo new facilities to their communities. Take, for example, the announcement by the U.S. government that it would build a super-collider facility for subatomic particle research at some U.S. location. The facility was expected to bring billions of dollars to the community and state lucky enough to be selected for its location. State legislatures began organizing teams for the purpose of promoting their locations in this high-stakes contest. The state of Texas, for one, allocated $500 million for the project so that its location would be more attractive. State, county, and community politicians regularly visited the appropriate federal agencies in Washington to make their case for locating the facility in their home states. After the long list was trimmed to seven finalists, the federal government went through an exhaustive site visitation program to evaluate the sites of the finalists. And all of this happened in 1988, a presidential election year. Industrial facility location decisions are no less free of political activity.

In 1985 and 1986 Chrysler-Mitsubishi was looking for a facility location for its Diamond-Star automobile assembly plant. The news media provided almost day-by-day and blow-by-blow accounts of where the research team was visiting, which communities had made presentations to the company, and which state politicians had visited the corporate offices. Community after community rolled out the red carpet for the visiting team, and the list of incentives offered to the company grew. The facility was finally located in Bloomington, Illinois. This account illustrates that economic incentives in the form of reduced income, property, and other taxes; free or discounted land, buildings, utilities, roads, parking lots; and other freebies are powerful factors in facility location decisions.

Once a firm announces that it intends to locate a facility somewhere, conversations begin at the various headquarters of the firm's competitors. Such an announcement is the first step in a *preemptive tactic,* and it usually has at least two effects. First, if competitors had been contemplating expanding their capacity, they may fear overcapacity within the industry and be scared off. Second, if a specific location choice is announced, competitors may be dissuaded from locating in the region of the announced location. Such a preemptive tactic is thus aimed at deterring competition.

Location decisions are very complex. So many variables are related in complicated ways and so much uncertainty is present that it is difficult to mentally juggle all of the information simultaneously. Because of this complexity, analysis techniques tend to analyze only part of the relevant information in sometimes rather simple ways; thus, in making the decision, the decision maker is left the task of intelligently integrating the results of the analysis with the remainder of the information. The analysis techniques that are presented in the following sections should be viewed with this perspective: They provide an orderly way of analyzing part of the relevant information present in a location decision. It is up to management to use the results of the analysis along with other information to make the final location decision.

ANALYZING RETAILING AND OTHER SERVICE LOCATIONS

Table 8.2 showed that the dominant factor in location decisions for some facilities is proximity to concentrations of customers. Facilities such as retailing, customer services for profit, and health and emergency services are types of facilities that attempt to locate near their customers/constituents.

Retailing and customer-service-for-profit organizations typically perform empirically based studies of alternative facility locations. Table 8.3 shows the basic steps in these studies. First, an organization's management must understand why customers buy its products and services. Next, market research must be performed to determine target customer characteristics. When large concentrations of target customers are identified, alternative locations near these concentrations can be considered. Enormous data-gathering activities can occur at this point in the study. Traffic patterns, local spending and income data, competition, and projected growth trends are estimated for each location. Revenues and operating costs are projected for each location. The projected profits based on empirical data become the basis for comparing the location alternatives under consideration.

Early retailing location studies were based on the *gravity model.* This model was structured on two principles: (1) customers are attracted to a location in direct proportion to the population in the immediate region of the location, and (2) customers are attracted to a location in inverse proportion to the square of the distance

■ ■

TABLE 8.3   *Steps in Analyzing Retailing and Customer-Service-for-Profit Facility Location Decisions*

1. **Consumer behavior research:** Why do customers buy our products and services?
2. **Market research:** Who are our customers and what are their characteristics?
3. **Data gathering for each location alternative:** Where are concentrations of target customers? What are their traffic and spending patterns? What are the growth trends and degree of present and projected competition?
4. **Revenue projections for each location alternative:** What are the relevant economic projections, discretionary spending projections, competition activity, and time-phased location revenue?
5. **Profit projections for each location alternative:** What are the projected revenues less time-phased operating costs?

■ ■

that customers must travel to a location. More recent retailing studies have been based on modern variations of these principles of the gravity model. Take, for example, the retailing model of Huff for evaluating the utility of shopping centers:[12]

$$E_{ij} = P_{ij}C_i$$

where

E_{ij} = expected number of customers at i likely to travel to shopping center j
C_i = number of customers at i
P_{ij} = probability of a customer at point of origin i traveling to shopping center j. P_{ij} is a function of the size of shopping center j, the travel time for a customer at point of origin i to travel to shopping center j, and the effect of travel time on various types of trips.

These and similar retailing models are aimed at estimating customer demand at retailing locations; thus the revenues at alternative retailing locations can be estimated.

Local government services typically do not systematically decide among locational alternatives for their facilities. To the contrary, geographic centers or conglomerations of these services tend to evolve over time. This is not necessarily bad, because once citizens learn that government services are concentrated in one location with centralized parking and other conveniences, they can maximize their utility in using the services. Satellite centers may develop when geographic constituent population centers shift outward as cities grow. The continuing threat of suburb incorporation may motivate central cities' services to move outward in order to service these outlying districts better.

---

[12] D. L. Huff, "A Programmed Solution for Approximating an Optimal Retail Location," *Land Economics* 42(August 1966): 293–303.

TABLE 8.4   *Some Common Types of Locational Problems*

Class of Locational Problem	Analysis Objective
1. Locating *a single plant facility* that will be serviced by one or more sources and that will in turn supply one or more destinations.	Minimize total annual costs (incoming and outgoing transportation costs and operating costs) or maximize annual profits while considering all these costs.
2. Locating *one or more source facilities* that will combine with existing source facilities to supply several existing destinations.	Minimize total annual costs (outgoing transportation costs and operating costs) or maximize profits while considering all these costs.
3. Locating *one or more destination facilities* that will combine with existing destination facilities to be serviced by one or more existing sources.	Minimize total annual costs (incoming transportation costs and operating costs) or maximize profits while considering all these costs.
4. Locating *one or more plant facilities* that will combine with existing plant facilities to be serviced by one or more existing sources and that will in turn supply one or more existing destinations.	Minimize total annual costs (incoming and outgoing transportation costs and operating costs) or maximize annual profits while considering all these costs.

Health and emergency services can analyze alternative locations much as industrial facilities do. The principal difference between these studies lies in their objectives. Health and emergency services usually attempt to minimize the overall time or distance traveled in responding to constituents' requests, whereas industrial facilities are usually located to minimize costs or maximize profits.

ANALYZING INDUSTRIAL FACILITY LOCATIONS

Industrial facility location decisions vary in their complexity. Table 8.4 classifies locational problems into four basic classes from the simplest to the most complex. In the first class, a single facility is assumed to receive materials from several existing sources and ship finished goods to several existing destinations. This class of problem is commonly analyzed with *conventional cost analysis.* Table 8.5 is a cost analysis for three alternative locations for a steel mill. The analysis develops the estimated total cost and per-unit cost for operating each location at production volumes expected one, five, and ten years into the future. The advantage of this type of cost analysis is its ease of communication and understanding. The approach assumes that annual revenues would be the same for each location; thus cost comparisons are as effective as profit comparisons. One disadvantage of this approach is that costs from one, five, and ten years in the future are being compared without considering the time value of money. Net present value (NPV) of costs or profits would avoid this shortcoming. It

TABLE 8.5   Cost Comparisons: Three Alternative Manufacturing Locations for a Steel Mill

Cost Element	St. Louis, Missouri			Cleveland, Ohio			Milwaukee, Wisconsin		
	Year 1	Year 5	Year 10	Year 1	Year 5	Year 10	Year 1	Year 5	Year 10
Transportation in	$18.5	$22.9	$28.4	$17.4	$21.5	$26.8	$16.4	$19.9	$24.6
Transportation out	6.1	7.6	10.2	6.0	7.6	10.0	6.1	7.6	10.1
Labor	14.7	19.4	26.2	18.6	22.7	30.5	21.5	25.4	33.9
Raw materials	30.3	39.4	57.1	29.5	39.1	56.3	28.9	38.6	55.2
Supplies	4.2	4.5	5.9	4.4	4.9	5.9	4.6	4.9	6.2
Utilities	6.0	9.2	18.5	8.4	12.6	29.2	10.1	16.3	32.1
Variable overhead	5.9	6.8	7.5	6.1	7.2	8.2	6.0	7.6	8.6
Fixed overhead	9.6	10.5	14.2	10.2	11.6	14.9	10.4	12.3	15.3
Total Operating Cost	95.3	120.3	168.0	100.6	127.2	181.8	104.0	132.6	186.0
Projected Volume	1.201	1.489	2.001	1.201	1.489	2.001	1.201	1.489	2.001
Per-Unit Production Costs ($/Ton)	$79.4	$80.8	$84.0	$83.8	$85.4	$90.4	$86.6	$89.1	$93.0

Note: Costs are in millions of dollars and volume is in millions of tons.

should also be recognized that relevant qualitative factors are not considered in this analysis.

When one or more facilities are to be located along with similar existing facilities, analyses become more complex. Some form of linear programming is usually employed to investigate simultaneously all the possible combinations of material shipments either from present and proposed sources to the required destinations or from sources to present and proposed destinations. These types of problems are described in Table 8.4 in Classes 2 and 3. Example 8.2 demonstrates that linear programming can be used to select a new warehouse location to team with two existing ones to supply four customer centers (an example of Class 2 in Table 8.4). The objective in this example is to minimize the total annual transportation and handling costs in operating the three warehouses. The procedure is to assume that one of the location alternatives teams with the existing warehouses to supply the four customer centers. This problem is formulated and solved as an LP problem. Next, another location alternative is assumed to team with the existing warehouses. This problem is also formulated and solved as an LP problem. After all the location alternatives have been considered in like manner, the results of the LP solutions are compared. While this approach identifies the least-cost warehouse location, relevant qualitative factors are not considered.

The location problems analyzed in Example 8.2 have also been analyzed with computer simulation. For example, Markland used computer simulation to study the complex flows of Ralston Purina Company products between plants, field warehouses, wholesalers, and retail grocers.[13] Computer simulation is discussed further in Appendix D at the end of this book.

EXAMPLE 8.2   Using LP to Analyze Industrial Facility Location Alternatives

Eco-Steel, a steel bar stock wholesaler specializing in imported assorted steel stock, must soon add another warehouse to its New York City area system in order to supply an increased demand from its customers. Eco now has two warehouses supplying four clusters of machine shop customers in the region. Two location alternatives, L_3 and L_4, are proposed, each with monthly capacities of 12,000 pounds. The actual monthly capacities for existing Warehouses 1 and 2, the minimum demand for each of the customer clusters, A, B, C, and D, and the transportation and handling costs per pound for supplying the demand are shown on the next page:

---

[13] R. E. Markland, "Analyzing Geographically Discrete Warehouse Networks by Computer Simulation," *Decision Sciences* (April 1973): 216–236.

Warehouse	Customer Clusters				Monthly Warehouse Capacity (Pounds)
	A	B	C	D	
Warehouse 1	$.10	$.10	$.15	$.20	12,000
Warehouse 2	.10	.10	.10	.20	12,000
Proposed Location L_3	.15	.15	.10	.10	12,000
Proposed Location L_4	.20	.10	.15	.15	12,000
Monthly Customer Demand (Pounds)	10,000	8,000	12,000	6,000	

a. If only one new warehouse will be built, which location (L_3 or L_4) will result in the lowest monthly transportation and handling costs?

b. What total monthly transportation and handling costs will result from all warehouses to all customers if your recommendation from Part *a* is followed?

c. How much steel should be shipped from the new warehouse to each customer cluster per month?

Solution

a. First, assume that proposed Warehouse L_3 will be combined with existing Warehouses 1 and 2, and formulate the linear programming problem:
  1. Define decision variables:

  X_1 = number of pounds of steel to be shipped from Warehouse 1 to Customer Cluster A per month

  X_2 = number of pounds of steel to be shipped from Warehouse 1 to Customer Cluster B per month

  X_3 = number of pounds of steel to be shipped from Warehouse 1 to Customer Cluster C per month
  $\vdots$

  X_{12} = number of pounds of steel to be shipped from Warehouse L_3 to Customer Cluster D per month

  2. Formulate the objective function:

  Min Z = $.10X_1 + .10X_2 + .15X_3 + .20X_4 + .10X_5 + .10X_6$
  $+ .10X_7 + .20X_8 + .15X_9 + .15X_{10} + .10X_{11} + .10X_{12}$

  3. Formulate the constraints:

  $X_1 + X_2 + X_3 + X_4 \le 12,000$ — Warehouse 1 capacity

  $X_5 + X_6 + X_7 + X_8 \le 12,000$ — Warehouse 2 capacity

  $X_9 + X_{10} + X_{11} + X_{12} \le 12,000$ — Warehouse L_3 capacity

  $X_1 + X_5 + X_9 \ge 10,000$ — Customer Cluster A requirements

$$X_2 + X_6 + X_{10} \geq 8,000 \text{—Customer Cluster B requirements}$$

$$X_3 + X_7 + X_{11} \geq 12,000 \text{—Customer Cluster C requirements}$$

$$X_4 + X_8 + X_{12} \geq 6,000 \text{—Customer Cluster D requirements}$$

4. This LP problem is solved by computer, with these results:

$X_1 = 10,000$	$X_4 = 0$	$X_7 = 6,000$	$X_{10} = 0$	$Z = \$3,600$
$X_2 = 2,000$	$X_5 = 0$	$X_8 = 0$	$X_{11} = 6,000$	
$X_3 = 0$	$X_6 = 6,000$	$X_9 = 0$	$X_{12} = 6,000$	

Next, assume that proposed Warehouse L_4 will be combined with existing Warehouses 1 and 2, and formulate the LP problem.

5. The objective function is:

$$\text{Min } Z = .10X_1 + .10X_2 + .15X_3 + .20X_4 + .10X_5 + .10X_6 \\ + .10X_7 + .20X_8 + .20X_9 + .10X_{10} + .15X_{11} + .15X_{12}$$

6. The constraints will not change from No. 3 above.
7. The solution to this new LP problem is:

$X_1 = 10,000$	$X_4 = 0$	$X_7 = 12,000$	$X_{10} = 6,000$	$Z = \$3,900$
$X_2 = 2,000$	$X_5 = 0$	$X_8 = 0$	$X_{11} = 0$	
$X_3 = 0$	$X_6 = 0$	$X_9 = 0$	$X_{12} = 6,000$	

Because the total monthly costs for L_3 are less than for L_4, Warehouse Location L_3 is preferred.

b. The total monthly transportation and handling costs for the three warehouses will be $3,600.

c. Eco should ship these quantities of steel per month from Warehouse L_3 to:

$A = 0$ $B = 0$ $C = 6,000$ pounds $D = 6,000$ pounds

Class 4 in Table 8.4 is often referred to as the *transshipment problem* and is of an order of magnitude more complex than the other types of location decisions considered thus far. There are several solution approaches to these and other complex location problems. Wagner and Geoffrion and Graves have developed advanced solution techniques for these problems.[14]

---

[14] Harvey Wagner, *Principles of Operations Research* (Englewood Cliffs, NJ: Prentice-Hall, 1975), 176–182; and A. M. Geoffrion and G. W. Graves, "Multicommodity Distribution System Design by Benders Decomposition," *Management Science* 20(January 1974): 822–844.

INTEGRATING QUANTITATIVE AND QUALITATIVE FACTORS INTO LOCATION DECISIONS

The techniques for analyzing and comparing alternative locations have thus far been based on locating concentrations of customers, as in the case of most service organizations, or on minimizing travel time, distance, or costs, as in the case of manufacturing plants, warehouses, and certain health and emergency services. These quantitative analyses provide invaluable quantitative inputs into location decisions, but many of these decisions may also involve factors that cannot be easily quantified.

Managers who make location decisions know that in some cases qualitative factors can be dominant when compared to quantitative ones. Some of these qualitative factors are housing, cost of living, availability of labor, climate, community activities, education and health services, recreation, churches, union activities, local transportation systems, proximity of similar industrial facilities, and community attitudes. These factors all work together with quantitative factors such as annual operations costs to determine the acceptability of a particular location.

Managers often wrestle with the task of trading off qualitative factors against quantitative ones. Methods for systematically displaying the relative advantages and disadvantages of each location alternative, both quantitative and qualitative, have evolved. Two general approaches are presented here. One approach is to develop quantitative and qualitative locational factor ratings independent of each other. This approach requires managers to subjectively weigh and relate the qualitative and quantitative factors for each location alternative in making their decisions.

Table 8.6 develops ratings for the locational factors for a steel mill. St. Louis, Missouri, obviously has a cost/ton advantage, whereas Cleveland, Ohio, has a local transportation system advantage and Milwaukee, Wisconsin, has a labor availability advantage. Managers must process these comparisons through their unique mental calculus and arrive at a relative rating for each of the location alternatives.

Another approach is demonstrated in Table 8.7. Here, quantitative factors are placed on the same scale as qualitative factors, and an aggregate weighted score is developed for each location alternative. Because production cost per ton is a continuous measure (ranges from zero to infinity in minute increments), the relative scores for this factor are computed by dividing the lowest cost ($79.40) by each of the location alternatives' costs per ton, thus reducing these continuous measures to relative measures (range from zero to one in minute increments). The qualitative factor scores are estimated on a zero-to-one scale. The relative weights (summing to one) are multiplied by these scores to yield weighted scores, and these are summed for each location alternative. This approach shows that Milwaukee, Wisconsin, barely squeezes out St. Louis, Missouri, as the preferred location (.870 versus .860). Approaches such as these can be helpful in comparing location alternatives, particularly when qualitative factors are important in the location decisions.

The concepts, locational factors, and analysis techniques for approaching facility location decisions presented in this chapter do not exhaust the subject. On the contrary, facility location can become a lifelong professional speciality through indepth research into this intriguing subject. What is presented here serves only as an introduction to a large topic.

TABLE 8.6   *Rating Scale Approach to Comparing Alternative Locations for Qualitative Factors for a Steel Mill*

Locational Factors	St. Louis, Missouri	Cleveland, Ohio	Milwaukee, Wisconsin
Economic Factors			
Annual operating costs	$95,300,000	$100,600,000	$104,000,000
Per-unit production costs	$79.40/ton	$83.80/ton	$86.60/ton
Qualitative Factors			
Housing availability	3	3	4
Cost of living	3	3	2
Labor availability	3	3	5
Community activities	3	2	4
Education and health services	3	3	4
Recreation	4	2	5
Union activities	3	1	3
Local transportation systems	3	5	3
Proximity to similar industry	3	4	4
Community attitudes	5	5	5

Note: A five-point rating scale is used: 5 = excellent, 4 = good, 3 = average, 2 = below average, 1 = poor.

SUMMARY

Long-range facility-planning decisions are made at the highest levels of organizations because of the enormous amount of capital funds required and the far-reaching impact that the decisions have on future operations. Once future capacity needs have been estimated, additional capacity can be obtained from subcontractors, acquisitions, building new facilities, expanding present facilities, and reactivating facilities that are on standby status. The alternative selected for additional capacity is usually selected after extensive analysis. Such techniques as break-even analysis, decision trees, present-value analysis, computer simulation, waiting line analysis, and linear programming are used to analyze and compare the alternatives. When new facilities are required, one fundamental issue in these decisions is where to locate the new facilities.

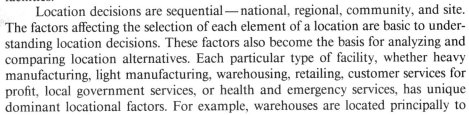
Location decisions are sequential — national, regional, community, and site. The factors affecting the selection of each element of a location are basic to understanding location decisions. These factors also become the basis for analyzing and comparing location alternatives. Each particular type of facility, whether heavy manufacturing, light manufacturing, warehousing, retailing, customer services for profit, local government services, or health and emergency services, has unique dominant locational factors. For example, warehouses are located principally to

TABLE 8.7 Relative-Aggregate-Scores Approach to Comparing Alternative Locations for a Steel Mill

Relevant Locational Factor	Weights of Factors	St. Louis, Missouri			Cleveland, Ohio			Milwaukee, Wisconsin		
		Economic Data	Scores	Weighted Scores	Economic Data	Scores	Weighted Scores	Economic Data	Scores	Weighted Scores
Production cost/ton	.60	$79.40	1.000*	.600	$83.80	.948*	.569	$86.60	.917*	.550
Cost of living	.05		.600**	.030		.650	.033		.500	.025
Labor availability	.20		.650	.130		.600	.120		.950	.190
Union activities	.10		.700	.070		.700	.070		.650	.065
Proximity to similar industry	.03		.600	.018		.650	.020		.850	.026
Local transportation	.02		.600	.012		.700	.014		.700	.014
Total Location Scores				.860			.826			.870

preferred (handwritten, by Milwaukee)

* These scores are determined by dividing the lowest cost/ton by the actual cost per ton:

$$\frac{79.40}{79.40} = 1.000 \qquad \frac{79.40}{83.80} = .9475 \qquad \frac{79.40}{86.60} = .9169$$

** Qualitative factor scores are estimated based on a maximum score of 1.000.

minimize transportation costs, whereas retailers are located to be close to concentrations of target customers.

Locations of single facilities usually are analyzed by comparing the per-unit operating costs for alternative locations. When a single facility is to be located to team with other like facilities and either to be supplied from suppliers or to supply customer centers, linear programming is typically used to identify the lowest-cost location alternative. Qualitative and quantitative factors can be combined in either rating-scale or aggregate-score comparisons.

REVIEW AND DISCUSSION QUESTIONS

1. Name four activities that are usually involved in any long-range capacity-planning decisions.

2. Define *production capacity.* How does the Bureau of Economic Analysis define *maximum practical capacity?*

3. How is the measurement of capacity of services likely to differ from the measurement of manufacturing capacity?

4. Define these terms: *output rate capacity, aggregate unit of capacity, input rate capacity,* and *percentage of capacity utilization.*

5. Name three ways that firms can reduce long-range capacity. Name five ways that firms can expand long-range capacity.

6. Define these terms: *best operating level, economies of scale, diseconomies of scale,* and *subcontractor networks.*

7. Name five techniques that are used to analyze long-range capacity decisions.

8. Name four sequential steps in location decisions.

9. What factors affect national location decisions?

10. What factors affect community location decisions?

11. What factors affect site location decisions?

12. List the dominant factors affecting the location of these facilities:
    a. mining, quarrying, and heavy manufacturing facilities,
    b. light manufacturing facilities,
    c. warehouses,
    d. retail and customer-service-for-profit facilities, and
    e. local government services and health and emergency services facilities.

13. Name five steps in analyzing retailing and customer-service-for-profit facility locations.

14. Describe four classes of location problems.

15. With what class of location problem can conventional cost comparisons and break-even analysis be appropriately used?

16. Name five qualitative factors commonly considered in facility location decisions.

17. Describe how managers may simultaneously consider both quantitative and qualitative factors in facility location analysis.

PROBLEMS

Long-Range Facility-Planning Decisions

1. The Nononsense Publishing Company intends to publish a textbook in production and operations management. Fixed costs are $125,000 per year, variable costs per unit are $32, and selling price per unit is $42.
   a. How many units must be sold per year to break even?
   b. How much annual revenue is required to break even?
   c. If annual sales are 20,000 units, what are the annual profits?
   d. What variable cost per unit would result in $100,000 annual profits if annual sales are 20,000 units?

2. Jane Pontac, facility engineer at the El Paso plant of Computer Products Corporation (CPC), is studying a capacity problem at the plant. The problem is insufficient production capacity in the electronic component insertion department. The problem is serious now and it is expected to become more serious in the long run if additional capacity is not added. Jane has developed these estimates for two alternatives for solving the capacity problem:

	Auto-Insertion Process	*Manual Insertion Process*
Annual fixed cost	$690,000	$269,000
Variable cost per product	$29.56	$31.69
Estimated annual production (in number of products):		
Year 1	152,000	152,000
Year 5	190,000	190,000
Year 10	225,000	225,000

   a. Which production process would be the least-cost alternative in Years 1, 5, and 10?
   b. How much would the variable cost per unit have to be in Year 5 for the auto-insertion process to justify the additional annual fixed cost for the auto-insertion process over the manual insertion process?

3. The Howsweetitis Manufacturing Company is considering expanding its production capacity to meet a growing demand for its product line of toilet bowl deodorizers. The alternatives are to build a new plant, expand the old plant, or do nothing. The marketing department estimates a 35 percent probability of a market upturn, a 40 percent probability of a stable market, and a 25 percent probability of a market downturn. Georgia Swain, the firm's capital appropriations analyst, estimates the following annual returns for these alternatives:

	Market Upturn	*Stable Market*	*Market Downturn*
Build new plant	$690,000	$(130,000)	$(150,000)
Expand old plant	490,000	(45,000)	(65,000)
Do nothing	50,000	0	(20,000)

    a. Use a decision tree analysis to analyze these decision alternatives.

    b. What should Howsweetitis do?

    c. What returns will accrue to the company if your recommendation is followed?

4. An engineer in the corporate R&D center at the corporate headquarters of Computer Products Corporation (CPC) in San Jose, California, has formalized a new product concept that applies fiber optics technology to robotic industrial controls. CPC must now decide whether to provide for long-range production capacity in its five-year plan or dispose of the project. If the idea is sold to another company now in its preliminary form, it is estimated that it would sell for these amounts, depending on the nature of the economic climate that exists:

Economic Climate	Likelihood	Amount of Sale
Positive	.4	$1,000,000
Neutral	.5	700,000
Negative	.1	500,000

It will cost approximately $500,000 to complete a new-product development project for the idea, and the R&D center estimates only a 50 percent likelihood of a successful project. If the project is unsuccessful, the idea could not then be sold and the entire cost of the project would be lost. If the project is successful, CPC may either produce and market the new product or sell the production and marketing rights for the new product. If the new product is produced and marketed, the amount of net present value of the returns (net present value means that the returns are expressed in terms of today's dollars), including the cost of the development project, is dependent on the size of the market that ultimately materializes:

Size of Market	Likelihood	Returns
Large	.3	$12,000,000
Marginal	.7	1,000,000

If CPC sells the newly developed product, the net present value of the returns (including the cost of the development project) is dependent on the economic climate at the time of the sale:

Economic Climate	Likelihood	Returns
Positive	.4	$6,000,000
Neutral	.5	4,000,000
Negative	.1	2,000,000

    a. Use a decision tree analysis and recommend a course of action for CPC for this new-product idea.

    b. If CPC follows your recommendation, what net present value of returns should CPC expect to receive?

5. The Sunshine Manufacturing Company has developed a unique new product and must now decide between two facility plans. The first alternative is to build a large

new facility immediately. The second alternative is to build a small plant initially and to consider expanding it to a larger facility three years later if the market has proven favorable. Marketing has provided the following probability estimates for a ten-year plan:

First Three-Year Demand	Next Seven-Year Demand	Probability
Unfavorable	Unfavorable	.2
Unfavorable	Favorable	.0
Favorable	Favorable	.7
Favorable	Unfavorable	.1

If the small plant is expanded, the probability of demands over the remaining seven years is ⅞ for favorable and ⅛ for unfavorable. These payoffs for each outcome have been provided by the accounting department:

Demand	Facility Plan	Payoffs ($000)
Fav-fav	1	$5,000
Fav-unfav	1	2,500
Unfav-unfav	1	1,000
Fav-fav	2 — expanded	4,000
Fav-unfav	2 — expanded	100
Fav-fav	2 — not expanded	1,500
Fav-unfav	2 — not expanded	500
Unfav-unfav	2 — not expanded	300

With these estimates, analyze Sunshine's facility decision and:

a. perform a complete decision tree analysis,
b. recommend a strategy to Sunshine, and
c. determine what payoffs will result from your recommendation.

6. Computer Products Corporation (CPC) owns a subsidiary company in Camden, New Jersey, that makes a variety of stamped steel products for CPC's in-house production operations and to supply other production plants in the Camden area. Increasingly, foreign producers are undercutting CPC's prices to CPC's customers for these stampings, and CPC is convinced that the technology of its production capacity at this plant must be upgraded to become competitive with the foreign firms. CPC's engineering department at the corporate headquarters has studied the alternatives available and has determined that the plant's processes should be converted to robotics, converted to a semi-automated system, or remain as they are and reviewed again in five years. If the production processes are upgraded, the net present value of the returns (net present value means that the returns are expressed in terms of today's dollars) to CPC is dependent on the market for the plant's products:

Process	Market Level	Likelihood	Returns
Robotics	High	.2	$8,000,000
	Med	.5	4,000,000
	Low	.3	1,000,000
Semi-automated	High	.2	$6,000,000
	Med	.5	4,000,000
	Low	.3	2,000,000

If CPC decides to do nothing now and review the situation five years from now, two alternatives will probably be present then — continue operating with the existing production processes or shut the plant down and liquidate its assets. If the plant continues to be operated in its existing condition after five years, the net present value of the returns is dependent on the market for the plant's products at that time:

Alternative	Market Level	Likelihood	Returns
Do nothing now, continue operating in existing condition	High	.2	$5,000,000
	Med	.6	4,000,000
	Low	.2	3,000,000

If CPC shuts the plant down and liquidates its assets after five years, the net present value of the returns is estimated to be $4,000,000.

a. Use a decision tree analysis and recommend a course of action for CPC.
b. What returns should CPC actually expect from following your recommendation?

7. The OK Trucking Company has a fleet of over-the-road trucks operating in southeastern Oklahoma. The fleet was purchased new ten years ago and is becoming obsolete and badly deteriorated. OK estimates that a new fleet would cost $650,000 and would save $200,000 per year in operating and maintenance expenses. If taxes are ignored, the old fleet has zero salvage value, and the new fleet has zero salvage value. What is the payback period on the new fleet?

8. Geotherm Research Corporation located in Jake Pass, Idaho, performs geothermal energy conversion research on federal and several state contracts. The firm is experiencing substantial growth and wishes to replace its old experimental facility with a new one. The new facility will cost $50,000 and will improve operating efficiency by $100,000 per year. If Geotherm has a tax rate of .45, the new facility is expected to have an economic life of 3 years, there is a 10 percent cutoff rate, and the old facility has a salvage value of zero, use net present value to recommend if the new facility should be acquired.

9. A local law firm, Amburep Associates, wishes to locate its offices nearer the county hospital where their investigative activities tend to be concentrated. A real estate broker has a professional building to Amburep's liking near the hospital and has agreed to either sell the building outright or provide a 50-year lease agreement. Here is the information affecting the analysis:

	Lease	*Buy*
Salvage value	—	0
Initial cost	—	$100,000
Economic life	50 years	50 years
Annual depreciation	—	$2,000
Annual lease payment	$20,000	—
Tax rate	.4	.4

If the after-tax payback period is less than six years, Amburep will buy the building; if it is greater than six years, it will lease the building. What should Amburep do?

Facility Location Decisions

10. Two locations are being examined for the construction of a new manufacturing plant. Two production processes, A and B, are also being studied. The annual operating costs for each process at the two locations are:

	Process A		*Process B*	
Location	*Fixed Costs*	*Variable Costs per Unit*	*Fixed Costs*	*Variable Costs per Unit*
New York	$1,500,000	$5.90	$3,400,000	$3.80
Philadelphia	1,250,000	6.40	3,000,000	4.10

In what range of outputs would each location and production process be preferred?

11. William Green, vice president of manufacturing for Computer Products Corporation (CPC), and his staff are studying three Midwestern alternative locations for a new production facility for producing bar code scanners. His staff analysts predict that the bar code scanners will be a growing market over the next ten years, and the analysis group shares marketing's enthusiasm for planning production facilities for producing this new product line. The analysts have developed these estimates for the three locations:

Location Alternative	*Annual Fixed Costs ($000,000)*	*Variable Cost per Bar Code Scanner*
Cleveland, Ohio	$3.9	$3,400
South Bend, Indiana	3.6	3,700
Grand Rapids, Michigan	3.1	4,000

The marketing department at CPC estimates sales for the bar code scanners will be 5,000 scanners in the first year, 20,000 in the third year, and 30,000 in the fifth year.
a. Use a break-even analysis to determine which location would be preferred in Years 1, 3, and 5.
b. In what range of production capacity would each of the locations be preferred?

12. The Big Shot Travel Trailer Manufacturing Company plans to establish another warehousing facility to strengthen its West Coast distribution system. Big Shot presently has three warehouses (San Diego, San Francisco, and Seattle). Two location alternatives are being considered for the new warehouse: Los Angeles and San Jose. The estimated shipping costs per trailer from the two manufacturing plants to each of the existing and proposed warehouses, the warehouses' annual trailer requirements, and the manufacturing plants' annual trailer capacities are shown below:

	Warehouse Locations					Annual Plant Capacity (Trailers)
Manufacturing Plant	San Diego (Existing)	San Francisco (Existing)	Seattle (Existing)	Los Angeles (Proposed)	San Jose (Proposed)	
Stockton	$170	$100	$190	$150	$120	50,000
Portland	200	160	130	180	170	50,000
Annual Warehouse Requirements (Trailers)	25,000	25,000	25,000	25,000	25,000	

If Big Shot wants to locate only one additional warehouse and wants to minimize the annual shipping costs from the two plants to the four warehouses:

a. Write the objective function and constraints for two LP problems that evaluate each of the proposed warehouse locations. Be sure to define your variables.
b. Use the LP computer program in the *POM Computer Library* that accompanies this book to solve the two LP problems.
c. What annual shipping costs result from selecting Los Angeles? San Jose?
d. Which of the two locations is preferable?
e. How many trailers will be shipped from each plant to each warehouse?

13. The Arizona County Sheriff's Department is proposing to locate an additional substation to service its constituents. The department presently has three substations (1, 2, and 3) that service three constituent centers (A, B, and C). Two alternative new substations are being considered: L_4 and L_5. The estimated response time in minutes from each of the existing and proposed substations to the three constituent centers, the minimum number of trips expected to each constituent center, and the maximum number of trips possible from each substation are shown below:

	Constituent Centers			Annual Substation Capacity (Trips)
Substation	A	B	C	
1	20 min.	5 min.	10 min.	10,000
2	20	10	5	10,000
3	5	20	20	20,000
L_4	8	12	12	10,000
L_5	12	10	8	10,000
Annual Minimum Constituent Center Requirements (Trips)	15,000	15,000	15,000	

If the Arizona County Sheriff's Department wants to locate only one additional substation and wants to minimize the total annual response time from the four substations to the three constituent centers:

a. Write the objective function and constraints for two LP problems that evaluate each of the proposed substation locations. Be sure to define your variables.

b. Use the LP computer program in the *POM Computer Library* that accompanies this book to solve the two LP problems.

c. What annual total response time results from selecting L_4? L_5?

d. Which of the two locations is preferred?

e. How many trips will be made from each substation to each constituent center per year?

14. Metroville, a fast-growing city in the Midwest, is trying to decide between two alternative locations (L_C and L_D) for one new emergency medical facility. Two such facilities (A and B) are now in existence, and it would be desirable to select a location for the new one that would minimize the distance traveled per year by people from the four major population centers in the city (1, 2, 3, and 4) to the three emergency medical facilities. The medical facilities' capacities (in patients per year), the minimum population expected to demand medical services in each population center per year, and the distance from each population center to each medical facility (in miles) are given below:

Population Center	Medical Facilities				Minimum Population from Each Population Center Expected to Demand Emergency Care per Year
	A	B	L_C	L_D	
1	1 mile	1 mile	2 miles	2 miles	10,000
2	1	1½	2½	2½	20,000
3	1	1	1	½	20,000
4	3	2½	2	2	10,000
Medical Facility Capacities (Patients per Year)	20,000	20,000	20,000	20,000	

a. Write the objective function and constraints for two LP problems that evaluate each of the proposed medical facilities. Be sure to define your decision variables.

b. Use the LP computer program in the *POM Computer Library* that accompanies this book to solve the two LP problems.

c. What total annual miles will be traveled one way if L_C is selected? L_D?

d. Which of the two locations is preferred?

e. How many people from each of the population centers will be serviced per year by each of the medical facilities?

15. Ramona Martin, staff analyst at the San Jose headquarters of Computer Products Corporation (CPC), is studying the alternative locations for a new facility for manufacturing small-business computers. Two alternatives seem to have emerged, Cleve-

land, Ohio, and Tulsa, Oklahoma. The economics tend to argue for Cleveland, but Ramona wonders if the qualitative factors might override in this particular decision. She has prepared this information on the location decision:

Rating Factors	*Locations*	
	Cleveland	*Tulsa*
Economic Factor		
Annual operating costs ($000,000)	23.1	24.4
Qualitative Factors		
Housing availability	3	4
Cost of living	3	4
Labor availability	4	4
Community activities	3	5
Educational and health services	4	4
Recreation	2	4
Union activities	2	5
Local transportation systems	4	4
Proximity to similar industry	5	3
Community attitudes	4	4
Zoning restrictions	3	4

Note: A five-point rating scale is used: 5 = excellent, 4 = good, 3 = average, 2 = below average, and 1 = poor.

Which location would you recommend? Why?

16. A large electronics R&D laboratory is investigating three alternative locations for a new facility. The rating scale and economic information for the locations are:

	Locations		
	Miami, Florida	*Cleveland, Ohio*	*San Francisco, California*
Economic Factor			
Annual operating costs (% of revenue)	76.5	69.5	81.0
Qualitative Factors			
Housing availability	5	2	3
Professional personnel availability and costs	5	3	5
Degree of unionization of hourly workers	5	2	3
Construction and labor costs	5	3	1
Urban transportation system	2	3	5
Proximity to customers	1	3	5
Zoning restrictions	3	5	1
Recreation	5	2	5
Cost of living	5	4	2

Note: A five-point rating scale is used: 5 = excellent, 4 = good, 3 = average, 2 = below average, 1 = poor.

Which location would you recommend? Why?

17. Ramona Martin, staff analyst at the San Jose headquarters of Computer Products Corporation (CPC), is studying the decision of where to locate the new plant to manufacture small-business computers. Cleveland and Tulsa have emerged as the top two contenders. Ramona has prepared rating factors and the scores of each of the two locations:

Locational Factor	Factor Weight	Location	
		Cleveland	Tulsa
Cost per computer	.50	$4,900	$5,190
Cost of living	.05	.60	.80
Labor availability	.15	.70	.70
Union activities	.15	.40	.80
Proximity to similar industry	.10	.70	.50
Local transportation systems	.05	.70	.70

Use the relative-aggregate-scores approach to compare the two alternative locations. Which location would you recommend? Why?

18. The Arkansas Cement Company plans to locate a new cement production facility at either Little Rock, Fort Smith, or Jonesboro. Six locational factors are important — cost per ton, labor availability, union activities, local transportation, proximity to similar industry, and proximity to raw materials. The weighting of these factors and the scores for each location are shown below:

Locational Factor	Factor Weight	Locations		
		Fort Smith Score	Little Rock Score	Jonesboro Score
Cost per ton	.55	$55.40	$62.30	$59.10
Labor availability	.15	.70	.90	.50
Union activities	.15	.80	.40	.90
Local transportation	.08	.70	.70	.60
Proximity to similar industry	.05	.80	.80	.40
Proximity to raw materials	.02	.70	.80	.50

Use the relative-aggregate-scores approach to compare the three alternative locations. Which location is preferred?

COMPUTER PROBLEMS/CASES

SPORTING CHARGE COMPANY

The Sporting Charge Company produces powder for shotgun shells in its only plant in St. Louis, Missouri. The plant was originally built in 1889 and with the great explosion of consumer demand for its product, growing environmental pressures from being located in a large city, and out-of-control production costs, Sporting Charge is considering three new location alternatives for its central offices and manufacturing plant: Clear River, Florida; Deerco, Nevada; and another location in the suburban St. Louis area. The production processes at Sporting Charge require about 300 production workers and 200 engineering and management personnel, large amounts of water and other utilities, large expanses of land, large volumes of materials to be shipped in and out of the plant, and fire- and explosion-tolerant areas.

The three locations under consideration have been analyzed by Sporting Charge's technical staff, and these operating costs have been developed for each location:

	Clear River	*Deerco*	*St. Louis*
Annual fixed costs	$5,000,000	$1,500,000	$3,500,000
Variable cost/pound	$.0200	$.0475	$.0290

These costs reflect all relocation costs, production costs, overhead costs, transportation costs, etc. Sporting Charge estimates these annual volumes for their powder over the next ten years:

Year	*Powder Sales (Millions of Pounds)*
1	70
5	140
10	200

The marketing staff for Sporting Charge does not think that sales volume or sales price will be affected by the location of the plant.

Assignment

1. What major factors should be considered in choosing one of the three location alternatives?

2. How would you weight the factors that you developed in No. 1 for Sporting Charge's plant? Which ones are more important and which ones should not be weighted heavily? Discuss and defend your answer.

3. Analyze the factors listed in No. 1 and recommend a course of action for Sporting Charge.

🖳 COMPUTER PRODUCTS CORPORATION (CPC)

Ramona Martin, staff analyst at the San Jose headquarters of Computer Products Corporation (CPC), is evaluating the economics of locating a new manufacturing plant at two alternative locations, Cleveland and Tulsa. CPC needs more production capacity for its line of small-business computers than its two present plants at Atlanta and El Paso can provide. Ramona knows that one of the most important factors in this decision is which location will result in the least annual shipping cost from the three manufacturing plants to the five regional warehouses. She has developed the following shipping cost and production capacity estimates:

Plant	Annual Capacity (Computers)	Warehouse	Annual Requirements (Computers)
Atlanta	2,400	Chicago	1,350
El Paso	3,600	Dallas	1,800
Cleveland or Tulsa	3,000	Denver	450
		New York	2,700
		San Jose	2,700

Plant	Warehouse	Shipping Cost ($/Computer)	Plant	Warehouse	Shipping Cost ($/Computer)
Atlanta	Chicago	$35	Cleveland	Chicago	$20
	Dallas	40		Dallas	45
	Denver	60		Denver	50
	New York	45		New York	40
	San Jose	90		San Jose	85
El Paso	Chicago	$50	Tulsa	Chicago	$40
	Dallas	30		Dallas	20
	Denver	35		Denver	40
	New York	95		New York	90
	San Jose	40		San Jose	60

Assignment

1. Formulate the two linear programming problems to determine the optimal shipping plan for each of the proposed location alternatives.
2. Solve the linear programming problems from No. 1 with the *POM Computer Library* that accompanies this text. What is the solution?
3. What does the solution mean in terms of the original problem?

BRIGHTCO MANUFACTURING

Brightco Manufacturing produces signal products for highway, railway, and marine use. The company has just closed out one of its line of products and now has some production capacity available. One of two product alternatives will be developed — a *marine signal kit* to be sold through marine products distributors or a *triangular reflective highway signal* to be sold to a mass merchandiser.

Brightco thinks that there is a 20 percent likelihood that the marine product cannot be successfully developed and that the idea would have to be scrapped. If the product development is only marginally successful, a likelihood of 30 percent, the product idea can be sold to a firm for about $50,000. The product development project is expected to cost $200,000, and if it is successful, a production process development project will be undertaken. Two processing alternatives, Process A and Process B, are being considered. Process A is a fully automated assembly line and Process B is a job shop arrangement. The differences between revenues and operating expenses for the processes at three levels of market acceptance for the product are expected to be:

	Level of Market Acceptance		
	High *(P = .3)*	*Medium* *(P = .4)*	*Low* *(P = .3)*
Process A	$1,500,000	$600,000	$(500,000)
Process B	1,000,000	700,000	400,000

The highway product has these likelihoods of development: successful, 70 percent; marginal, 20 percent; and unsuccessful, 10 percent. If the product cannot be developed, the idea will obviously have to be scrapped. If the development project is only marginally successful, the product can be produced on existing production equipment and marketed through existing marketing channels, or the product idea can perhaps be sold to a company for about $100,000, a likelihood of only about 60 percent. If the product line is produced and marketed, the differences between revenues and operating expenses at two levels of market acceptance are expected to be:

	Level of *Market Acceptance*	
	Medium *(P = .4)*	*Low* *(P = .6)*
Produce and market marginal product	$600,000	$200,000

If the product development project is successful, a mass merchandiser has agreed to a long-term purchase contract for all of Brightco's production of the highway product. Two processing alternatives are being considered for this production, with these expected differences between revenues and operating expenses at two yield levels:

	Level of Production Yield			
	High Yield		Low Yield	
	Value	Likelihood (P)	Value	Likelihood (P)
Process X	$ 800,000	.5	$600,000	.5
Process Y	1,100,000	.3	400,000	.7

The product development project for the triangular signal is expected to cost $300,000 and the process development project would cost about $150,000.

Assignment

1. Describe the nature of Brightco's problem. What issues must it decide? What is the general structure of its decision?

2. Which analysis techniques are most appropriate for analyzing this decision? Defend your answer.

3. Analyze Brightco's problem and recommend a course of action. What are the strengths and weaknesses of your analysis approach?

4. What risks are present if Brightco follows your recommendation in No. 3? How would your recommendation be modified if you knew that Brightco's management was a risk taker? A risk avoider?

SELECTED BIBLIOGRAPHY

Bulow, J. J. "Holding Idle Capacity to Deter Entry." *Economic Journal* 95(March 1985):178–182.

Coyle, John J., and Edward J. Bardi. *The Management of Logistics,* 2d ed., 294–298. St. Paul: West Publishing, 1980.

Craig, C. S., et al. "Models of the Retail Location Process." *Journal of Retailing* 60(April 1984):5–36.

"Dow: Headed for Overcapacity, It Veers from Basic Chemicals." *Business Week,* Jan. 31, 1983.

Ghosh, A., and C. S. Craig. "Formulating Retail Location Strategy in a Changing Environment." *Journal of Marketing* 47(Summer 1983):56–58.

"Heileman Plans Big Expansion into South, Setting Stage for Bruising Beer-Sales Fight." *The Wall Street Journal,* Feb. 3, 1983.

Leone, Robert A., and John R. Meyer. "Capacity Strategies for the 1980s." *Harvard Business Review* 58(November–December 1980):133–140.

Schmenner, Roger W. "Before You Build a *Big* Factory." *Harvard Business Review* 54(July–August 1976):100–104.

————. *Making Business Location Decisions.* Englewood-Cliffs, NJ: Prentice-Hall, 1982.

————. "Multiplant Manufacturing Strategies Among the Fortune 500." *Journal of Operations Management* 2, no. 2(February 1982):77–86.

"Small Is Beautiful Now in Manufacturing." *Business Week,* Oct. 22, 1984, 152–156.

Spohrev, George A., and Thomas R. Kmak. "Qualitative Analysis Used in Evaluating Alternative Plant Location Scenarios." *Journal of Industrial Engineering* (August 1984):52–56.

Sullivan, William G., and W. Wayne Claycombe. "The Use of Decision Trees in Planning Plant Expansion." *SAM: Advanced Management Journal* 40, no. 1 (Winter 1975).

"A Volatile Tape Market Has TDK on a Roller Coaster." *Business Week,* July 25, 1983.

Weston, F. C., Jr. "Quantitative Analysis of Plant Location." *Industrial Engineering* 4(April 1972):22–28.

OPERATING DECISIONS
PLANNING PRODUCTION TO MEET DEMAND

Part II of this text explored the ways that operations managers approach and analyze strategic decisions in operations. Designing products and processes, allocating scarce resources to business units, and long-range capacity and facility planning are so important that great attention and notoriety are focused on them. Important as these strategic decisions are, we must not allow them to overshadow other ongoing decisions in POM that can be of equal importance.

When I visit with operations managers, they say that the greatest source of pressure and tension in their jobs is the constant push to produce high-quality products and services to meet delivery promises to customers and at the same time keep the lid on costs. Products must be gotten out the back door on time and within cost budgets. Toward this end, operations managers engage in production-planning activities such as these:

1. Develop aggregate capacity plans that usually cover from 6 to 18 months. These intermediate-range plans should provide the production capacity necessary to meet the customers' demand for products.

2. Establish production-planning systems to guide the organization toward keeping delivery promises to customers, meeting inventory targets, and maintaining low production costs.

3. Provide sufficient inventory of finished products to meet the dual objectives of low operating costs and prompt delivery of products to customers.

4. Schedule the production of products and services necessary to meet delivery promises to customers and to load the production facilities such that production costs are low.

5. Plan for the purchase, storage, and shipment of materials so that the right materials are available in the right quantity at the right time to support the production schedules.

Because the cumulative effect of these intermediate- and short-range plans, issues, and decisions is immense, they are emphasized in Part III.

CHAPTER

9

PRODUCTION-PLANNING SYSTEMS

AGGREGATE PLANNING AND MASTER PRODUCTION SCHEDULING

AGGREGATE PLANNING AT NEW GENERATION COMPUTERS

An operations manager at New Generation Computers (NGC) is developing a six-month aggregate production plan for producing a line of computer printers. NGC's marketing department has estimated the demand for the printers for the six-month period. There are several printer models, and the amount of labor required to produce each printer depends on the characteristics of the model. Although overtime labor can be used, NGC has a policy that limits the amount of overtime labor in each month to 10 percent of the straight-time labor available. Overtime labor is more expensive than straight-time labor and NGC's union has resisted the use of overtime. NGC has a no layoff policy for its workers; thus the same number of straight-time labor-hours is available for producing the printers in each month. NGC incurs a carrying cost each time a printer is produced in one month and shipped in a later month. The objectives of the aggregate production plan are to fully utilize the work force, promptly ship customers' orders, and minimize the costs of overtime and of carrying inventory.

The previous account is an example of the classic *aggregate planning* problem. In such problems, operations managers must develop a plan for providing production capacity for the next 6 to 18 months given a forecast of demand for products. These plans specify the amount of straight-time and overtime labor, amount of subcontracting, and other sources of capacity to be used. Aggregate plans are directed toward the achievement of two principal goals:

1. Provide enough production capacity to satisfy market demand.
2. Keep production costs low.

Although other objectives may be important, both satisfied customers and low production costs are absolutely necessary to the survival and success of systems of production. This chapter is concerned with developing intermediate- and short-range production plans that achieve both of these goals.

PRODUCTION-PLANNING HIERARCHY

Production planning occurs at several organizational levels and covers several different time spans. Figure 9.1 illustrates how all of these long-range, intermediate-range, and short-range plans are connected. First, the vice president of operations, in collaboration with the firm's other top executives, develops long-range capacity and facility plans. These top-level plans usually focus on product lines, divisions, factories, markets, or other broad business units; they span several years; and they reflect the operations strategies of the business. These plans set in motion the activities required to develop facilities and equipment, production processes, and major subcontractors. These plans become constraints on how many products can be produced in the intermediate- and short-range plans.

At the next lower level in the organization, operations managers develop intermediate-term aggregate production plans. These plans focus on aggregations of products rather than on specific products. For example, Toro Corporation might aggregate all push mowers into one group for aggregate production-planning purposes. These aggregate plans usually span from six to eighteen months and specify the employment plans, machinery and utility plans, subcontractor and material supply plans, and facility modification plans. These aggregate plans impose constraints on the short-range production plans that follow. We shall study aggregate production planning later in this chapter.

Short-range schedules are usually developed at the factory level. These schedules specify the specific products to be produced in each week of a planning horizon, and usually span from a week to a few months. Because products can be inventoried or stored, the status of the inventory of each product must be known before it can be determined how many of each product to produce. The study of finished goods inventory decisions is included in Chapter 10.

Master production schedules are the short-range plans for producing finished goods, or end items, as they are sometimes called. Master production scheduling is the engine that drives all other short-range scheduling. As an introduction to short-

FIGURE 9.1   A Production-Planning System

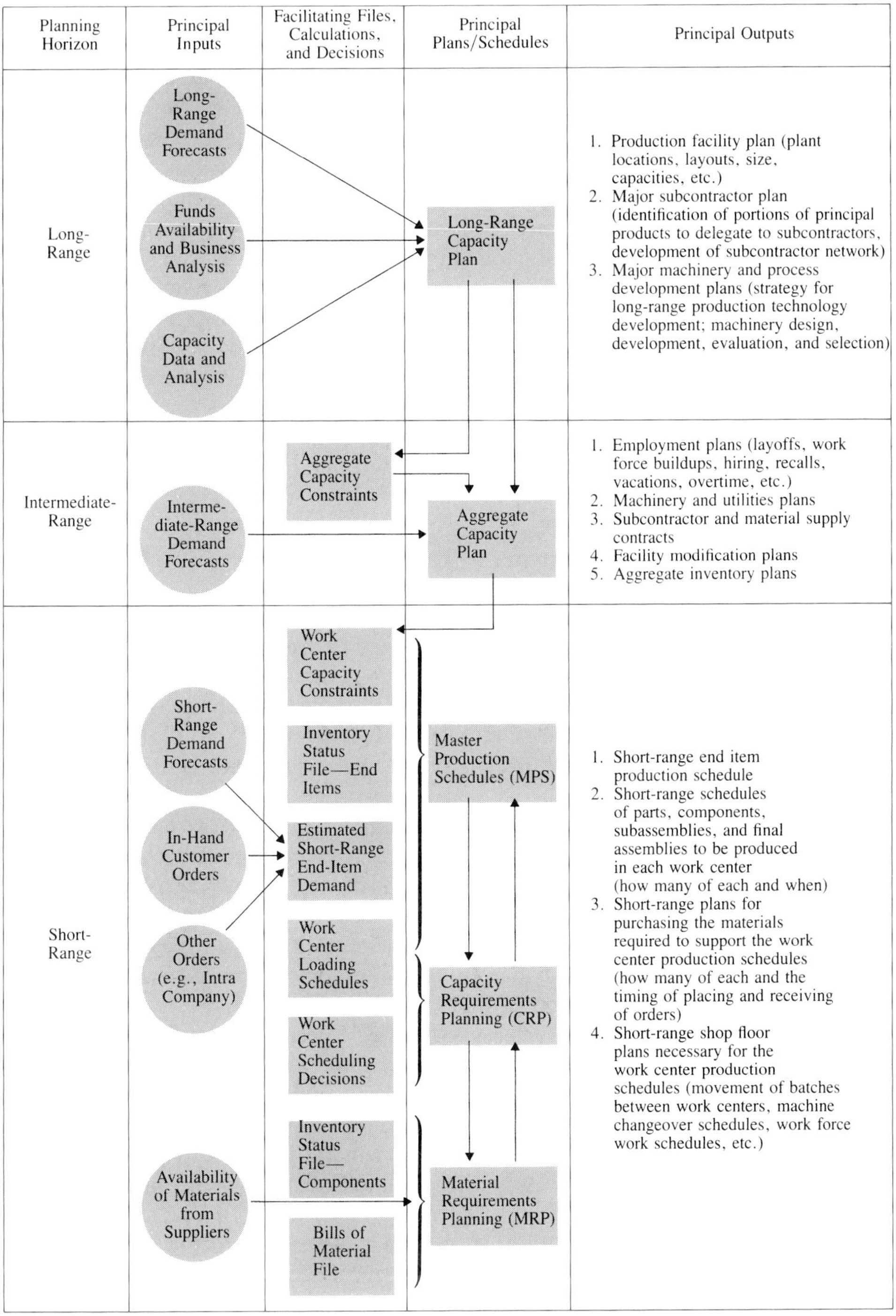

Planning Horizon	Principal Inputs	Facilitating Files, Calculations, and Decisions	Principal Plans/Schedules	Principal Outputs
Long-Range	Long-Range Demand Forecasts; Funds Availability and Business Analysis; Capacity Data and Analysis		Long-Range Capacity Plan	1. Production facility plan (plant locations, layouts, size, capacities, etc.) 2. Major subcontractor plan (identification of portions of principal products to delegate to subcontractors, development of subcontractor network) 3. Major machinery and process development plans (strategy for long-range production technology development; machinery design, development, evaluation, and selection)
Intermediate-Range	Intermediate-Range Demand Forecasts	Aggregate Capacity Constraints	Aggregate Capacity Plan	1. Employment plans (layoffs, work force buildups, hiring, recalls, vacations, overtime, etc.) 2. Machinery and utilities plans 3. Subcontractor and material supply contracts 4. Facility modification plans 5. Aggregate inventory plans
Short-Range	Short-Range Demand Forecasts; In-Hand Customer Orders; Other Orders (e.g., Intra Company); Availability of Materials from Suppliers	Work Center Capacity Constraints; Inventory Status File—End Items; Estimated Short-Range End-Item Demand; Work Center Loading Schedules; Work Center Scheduling Decisions; Inventory Status File—Components; Bills of Material File	Master Production Schedules (MPS); Capacity Requirements Planning (CRP); Material Requirements Planning (MRP)	1. Short-range end item production schedule 2. Short-range schedules of parts, components, subassemblies, and final assemblies to be produced in each work center (how many of each and when) 3. Short-range plans for purchasing the materials required to support the work center production schedules (how many of each and the timing of placing and receiving of orders) 4. Short-range shop floor plans necessary for the work center production schedules (movement of batches between work centers, machine changeover schedules, work force work schedules, etc.)

range scheduling, master production scheduling is presented in detail later in this chapter.

Material requirements planning and capacity requirements planning team with master production scheduling to form an integrated short-range production planning system. Material requirements planning develops a schedule for raw materials and parts to be produced in each work center of the factory or to be purchased from suppliers to support the master production schedule. Capacity requirements planning develops a loading plan for the factory and tests whether enough production capacity exists to produce the master production schedule. Both material requirements planning and capacity requirements planning are studied in Chapter 11.

Short-range production scheduling and shop floor planning involve the day-to-day, nitty gritty issues and decisions that operations managers must usually resolve on the factory floor. These topics, which result directly from material requirements planning and capacity requirements planning, are studied in Chapter 12. Purchasing, logistics, warehousing, expediting, and other materials management topics also result from material requirements planning, and these topics are treated in Chapter 13.

With this introduction to the hierarchy of production planning as a background, let us continue with a study of aggregate capacity planning.

AGGREGATE PLANNING

If we possessed perfect information about demand for the products of a production system for next year and if the demand were perfectly uniform from time period to time period, aggregate planning would be simple. We would hire just enough workers, buy just enough machines, and buy just enough materials to flow in to produce the exact amount of outputs in every time period to satisfy customer demand. Unfortunately, future demand is not known with certainty and is almost never uniform.

The forecasting techniques in Chapter 3 of this text are employed to estimate the quantity of products or services likely to be demanded in each time period of the planning horizon. *Aggregate planning* is the process of devising a plan for providing a production capacity scheme to support these intermediate-range sales forecasts. Then, as forecasted customer demand becomes known in the form of customers' orders, aggregate plans may have to be revised upward or downward to avoid either overloaded or underloaded facilities.

Aggregate planning is necessary in POM because: (1) it facilitates fully loaded facilities and minimizes overloading and underloading, thus keeping production costs low; (2) adequate production capacity is provided to meet expected aggregate demand; (3) orderly and systematic transition of production capacity to meet the peaks and valleys of expected customer demand is facilitated; and (4) in times of scarce production resources, getting the most output for the amount of resources available is enhanced. Aggregate planning is the key to managing change in POM because the changing patterns of customer demand and the plans for providing production resources that adapt to those changes are fundamental to aggregate planning.

■■ ■■ ■■

TABLE 9.1   Steps in Aggregate Planning

1. Begin with a sales forecast for each product that indicates the quantities to be sold in each time period (usually weeks, months, or quarters) over the planning horizon (usually 6 months to 18 months).
2. Total all of the individual product or service forecasts into one aggregate demand for a factory. If the products are not additive because of heterogeneous units, a homogeneous unit of measure must be selected that both allows the forecasts to be added and links aggregate outputs to production capacity.
3. Transform the aggregate demand for each time period into workers, materials, machines, and other elements of production capacity required to satisfy aggregate demand.
4. Develop alternative resource schemes for supplying the necessary production capacity to support the cumulative aggregate demand.
5. Select the capacity plan from among the alternatives considered that satisfies aggregate demand and best meets the objectives of the organization.

■■ ■■ ■■

Note: Step 5 assumes that the production system is compelled by management policy to produce the sales forecast. There are occasions when capacity cannot be sufficiently increased or when it would be more profitable to produce less than the sales forecast. It is assumed, for the purposes of this chapter, that these issues have already been resolved and that the sales forecast is the production goal.

In developing an intermediate-range aggregate capacity plan, management has several variables that may ordinarily be manipulated to vary the production capacity from month to month. Among these variables are: (1) the size of the work force; (2) the use of overtime; and (3) the use of inventories, back orders, subcontractors, and leaving demand unfilled to buffer the difference between production capacity and variations in demand from month to month.

Aggregate planning as a process generally follows the steps shown in Table 9.1. After a study of these steps, we shall demonstrate them through Industry Snapshot 9.1, Sherman-Brown Chemical Company, as we proceed through this section. After you have read Industry Snapshot 9.1, we will begin to explore how to go about developing an aggregate capacity plan.

AGGREGATE DEMAND

The aggregation of all of an organization's products or services into one aggregate demand that is expressed in homogeneous units may or may not be straightforward. Consider these aggregate demand situations: (1) systems that produce only one product—ammonium nitrate fertilizer, sand, coal, and crude oil; (2) systems that produce multiple outputs that are readily converted into common production capacity units—barrels, tons, press strokes, labor hours, dollars, and machine hours; (3) systems that produce diverse products with different production capacity units —electrical appliances, office supplies, and medical operations. This latter class of systems usually reduces its diverse outputs to common denominator production-

INDUSTRY SNAPSHOT 9.1

Aggregate Planning at Sherman-Brown Chemical Company

In 1989 the Sherman-Brown Chemical Company is about to finalize its aggregate capacity plan for 1990. The company produces three paint products—latex interior, latex enamel, and latex stain—on a produce-to-stock basis. The production plant is located in Cleveland, Ohio, where there is an abundance of workers who perform the duties of material preparation, mixing, and canning—the principal operations of the production line.

The latex carrier, pigments, cans, boxes, and other materials required to produce Sherman-Brown's products are also readily available from tried and proven suppliers in abundant quantities. The processing equipment in the production departments is operated on only one shift because Sherman-Brown's management bought out a competitor last year, and so an excess of machine capacity is available. Similarly, ample warehouse space for holding finished goods inventory is available.

The capacity situation at Sherman-Brown is this: Since the only limiting factor in capacity planning is the size of the work force, the only production capacity issue to be resolved is determining the number of workers to be employed during each time period to support the sales forecasts of the three paint products.

Two plans for providing production capacity are currently being considered by Sherman-Brown's plant manager: (1) level capacity and (2) matching capac-ity with aggregate demand. These alternatives must be evaluated in terms of which plan results in the lowest total annual cost while considering three elements of cost: (1) cost of hiring workers from time period to time period over the entire year, (2) cost of laying off workers over the same period, (3) cost of carrying the finished goods inventory for the entire year.

The pertinent data for this analysis are: Working days per quarter: 65; labor standard per gallon of paint: 2.311 worker-hours per gallon; working hours per shift: 8 hours per shift per worker; maximum machine and material capacity on one shift: 100,000 gallons per quarter.

The key analyses that must be performed by Sherman-Brown in developing an aggregate capacity plan are:

1. Develop an aggregate demand forecast from the three individual product forecasts.
2. Compare the two alternatives for providing production capacity in the number of workers hired, the number of workers laid off, and the average finished goods inventory levels for the entire year.
3. Develop an analysis of the two alternatives for providing production capacity in terms of their impact on worker employment levels and finished goods inventories.
4. Select the capacity plan alternative with the lowest annual cost.

planning units by developing conversion statistics such as labor-hours, machine-hours, dollars, standard processing units, and so on. For example, lawn mowers and Rototillers could be reduced to a common denominator of labor-hours by developing a historical relationship between the labor content of the two products: lawn mower = 21 labor-hours and Rototiller = 17 labor-hours. The aggregate plan for the

FIGURE 9.2   *Aggregating Individual Product Forecasts into Aggregate Demand: The Sherman-Brown Chemical Company*

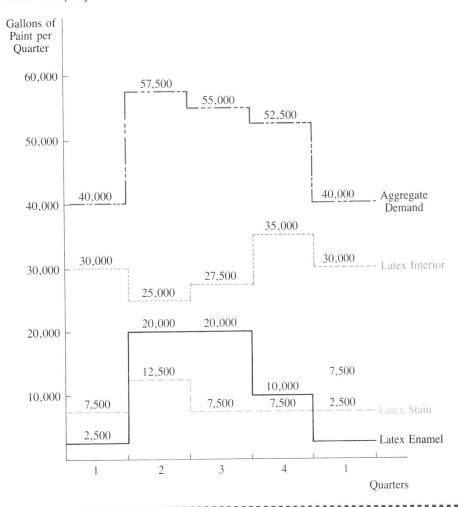

two products would be the total labor-hours for each time period required to produce the forecasted quantity of the two products. This example assumes that labor-hours is a good unit to measure production capacity. Machine hours, pounds per product, or other common-denominator units of measure might be better, but we could determine this only by being intimately familiar with a particular production system. The precision of aggregate plans that use artificially contrived common-denominator units of capacity is highly dependent on the accuracy of the conversion factors.

Figure 9.2 shows how the Sherman-Brown Chemical Company develops an aggregate demand with a one-year planning horizon. The three individual product quarterly forecasts are added together to form the aggregate demand for all products, expressed in gallons per quarter. It is important to note that the nature of the capacity of the processing steps in the production of paint must also be expressed in gallons of paint per quarter. For example, the material preparation, mixing, and canning operations at Sherman-Brown are known to have capacities expressed in gallons per quarter. The aggregate plan, which is also expressed in these same units, can therefore be readily compared to the capacities of the processing steps. These capacities can then be scaled up or down to approximately meet the aggregate demand.

DIMENSIONS OF PRODUCTION CAPACITY

As we have suggested, production capacity is dynamic — it can be changed from time period to time period, but at a cost. An essential part of aggregate planning is a comprehensive understanding of each production system's capacities. Of particular importance are the availability of production resources, the relationships between these resources and capacities, and the time and cost requirements to scale these capacities up or down.

The sources of labor are present employees, new hires, workers who have been previously released and are on recall lists, and overtime. The local labor market may or may not be a limiting factor in building up the work force. In some localities there are severe shortages of workers in some higher skilled-labor classes. When these shortages exist, expensive training programs must often be maintained to ensure an adequate supply of skilled workers.

Union contracts can limit management's flexibility in hiring new employees and laying off experienced workers. Personnel departments and industrial relations departments, the experts in these matters, play an important role in scaling the work force up or down in aggregate planning. The instability of the U.S. auto industry in the 1980s highlights the importance of this role and the economic impact of such planning on both the company and the workers.

Material supply can usually be varied up or down without great difficulty. However, when new sources of supply must be developed by the purchasing department to support increased capacity, these consequences can occur: (1) increased scrap rates while new suppliers are debugging their production processes, (2) spasmodic supply rates as suppliers struggle to increase their outputs, (3) increased material costs as new suppliers incur start-up costs. These and other outcomes are normally expected when capacities must be escalated.

Of all the factors that limit production capacity, machines are perhaps the most inflexible. Once a machine is operating 24 hours per day, 7 days per week, at its capacity, that is all the output you are going to get out of it. To get more output, you must either buy or rent another machine or you must subcontract out the machine operation to a subcontractor. Any one of these alternatives usually requires a long lead time.

How quickly can you scale the production capacity of an operation up or down, *and* what are the relative costs of accelerated changes and gradual changes to capacities? These questions suggest that if capacity is changed rapidly, more costs might be incurred than if capacities are allowed to shift gradually. In general, this is true. Production capacity can be increased almost instantaneously in most situations by using worker overtime. But overtime is usually prohibitively expensive if continued for long periods because of worker fatigue, reduced morale of workers, premium labor rates, and a tendency of managers to become increasingly dependent on this costly safety factor. On the other hand, an alternative to overtime may be the addition of another shift, say, for example, an evening shift. This alternative may take as long as a month or six weeks to execute if workers must be hired or trained, but it is usually less expensive than overtime if the additional capacity is planned for extended periods.

These time and cost characteristics of production capacity form the basis for developing alternatives for providing future aggregate production capacity.

SOME TRADITIONAL AGGREGATE PLANS

Production systems have developed traditional plans for responding to aggregate demand. Level capacity and matching capacity with aggregate demand are two plans that are commonly observed in POM practice.

Level Capacity

When managers develop aggregate production plans that have uniform capacities per day from time period to time period, these plans are called *level capacity plans*. Figure 9.3 shows how the seasonal quarterly aggregate demand of the Sherman-Brown Chemical Company is met by a level capacity plan. Begin at the first quarter and follow through the computation of finished goods inventory levels.

In the first quarter, aggregate demand is less than production. Thus finished goods inventory levels grow to a peak of 11,250 gallons at the end of the quarter. In the second and third quarters, inventories fall because production is less than aggregate demand. In the fourth quarter, inventory levels decline further until they are entirely depleted because demand still exceeds outputs. This is the underlying principle of level capacity in produce-to-stock firms: Operate production systems at uniform production levels and let finished goods inventories rise and fall as they will to buffer the differences between aggregate demand and production levels from time period to time period. Aggregate planning in produce-to-order firms will be discussed later.

The chief advantage of level capacity as an aggregate plan is that this approach usually promotes the least production costs. This is because: (1) the costs of hiring and laying off workers and using overtime are practically eliminated; (2) the cost of locating and developing new sources of material supplies is minimized; (3) only the most efficient production machinery is used; (4) labor and material costs per unit of output are low, as the rhythmic operation of the production system has eliminated the continual start-up and shutdown of operations; (5) supervision is simplified and scrap rates are low since workers are experienced in their jobs; (6) voluntary turnover and absenteeism may be lower. The Japanese use the concept of level capacity to the hilt through their "lifetime employment" personnel policies. It is believed that this idea results, at least in the Japanese system, in stable employment levels for personnel, reduced turnover and absenteeism, improved quality levels, and increased commitment of employees to company goals. Some U.S. companies are now adopting these employee guarantees, and this approach seems to favor level capacity as an aggregate planning strategy.

FIGURE 9.3   *Level Capacity: The Sherman-Brown Chemical Company — Produce to Stock*

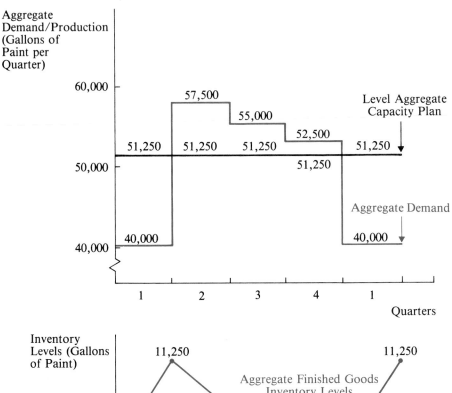

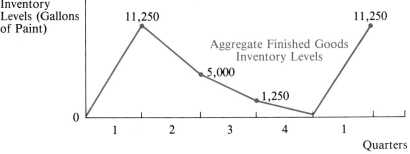

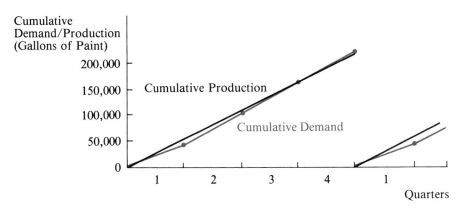

■■■

FIGURE 9.4   *Matching Capacity with Aggregate Demand: The Sherman-Brown Chemical Company*

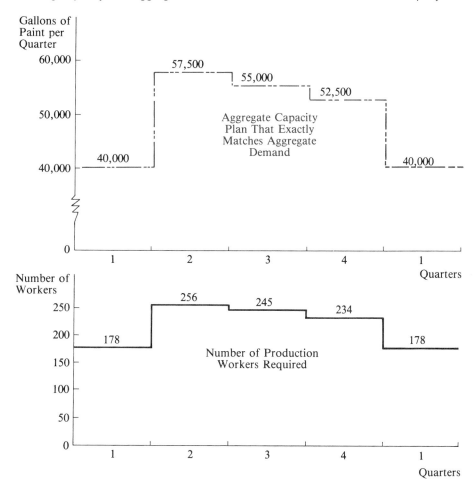

■■■

In short, operations managers like this approach because operating costs tend to be low, quality of outputs tends to be high and consistent, and production rates are usually dependable. Financial managers, however, typically do not prefer this alternative because this approach typically results in higher finished goods inventory levels, thus tying up cash and increasing the cost of carrying these inventories. Carrying costs are real, and the resolution of this finance versus POM conflict usually depends, finally, on the trade-off between additional carrying costs and the savings in labor and material costs that result from level capacity as an aggregate plan.

Matching Capacity with Aggregate Demand

Another traditional aggregate plan is to *match production capacity in each time period with the aggregate demand.* Figure 9.4 shows how the work force fluctuates to support this aggregate plan. Material flows and machinery capacity would similarly be allowed to change from quarter to quarter to just match the aggregate demand.

The labor standard at Sherman-Brown is 2.311 worker-hours per gallon of paint. The number of workers required in each quarter is therefore determined:

$$\text{Workers} = \frac{\text{Gallons of paint per quarter} \times \text{Labor standard per gallon}}{\text{Working days per quarter per worker} \times \text{Hours per day}}$$

$$\text{(1st quarter)} = (40{,}000 \times 2.311) \div (65 \times 8) = 178 \text{ workers}$$

$$\text{(2nd quarter)} = (57{,}500 \times 2.311) \div (65 \times 8) = 256 \text{ workers}$$

$$\text{(3rd quarter)} = (55{,}000 \times 2.311) \div (65 \times 8) = 245 \text{ workers}$$

$$\text{(4th quarter)} = (52{,}500 \times 2.311) \div (65 \times 8) = 234 \text{ workers}$$

The chief advantage of this plan is the lower levels of finished goods inventory that result. Carrying costs are therefore below those of the level capacity plan. However, labor and material costs tend to be higher because of the turmoil involved in frequently scaling the work force, material supplies, and production machine capacities up and down.

CRITERIA FOR SELECTING AGGREGATE PLANS

Example 9.1 develops and compares the number of workers hired per year, the number of workers laid off per year, and the average annual inventory level for each of the plans. The annual cost of hiring and laying off workers and the inventory carrying cost are computed and totaled for each plan. The level capacity plan is the lowest cost plan in this case. Although level capacity does seem to be favored among operations managers, it is not always the lowest-cost alternative. This can be demonstrated by increasing inventory carrying costs and decreasing hiring and layoff costs.

EXAMPLE 9.1   Analyzing Two Aggregate Plans at the Sherman-Brown Chemical Company

The Sherman-Brown Chemical Company is in the process of developing an aggregate capacity plan for next year. Two alternative plans are being considered, level capacity and matching capacity with aggregate demand. These plans were described in Industry Snapshot 9.1 and Figures 9.2 and 9.3 earlier in this chapter. For each of the plans, determine the cost of carrying inventory, hiring or recalling workers, and laying off workers.

Solution

First, compute for both plans the number of workers hired, the number of workers laid off, and the average inventory during the year:

(1)	(2)	(3)	(4)	(5)	(6)	(7)	(8)	(9)	(10)	(11)	(12)
Aggregate Plan	Quarter	Aggregate Demand (Gallons)	Planned Outputs (Gallons)	Workers Required $\left[\dfrac{(4) \times 2.311}{8 \times 65}\right]$	Workers Hired	Workers Laid Off	Inventory Additions or (Subtractions) $[(4)-(3)]$	Beginning Inventory (Gallons)	Ending Inventory (Gallons)	Average Inventory per Quarter (Gallons) $\left[\dfrac{(9)+(10)}{2}\right]$	Average Inventory per Year (Gallons) $\left[\dfrac{\Sigma(11)}{4}\right]$
Level capacity	1	40,000	51,250	228			11,250	0	11,250	5,625	4,375
	2	57,500	51,250	228			(6,250)	11,250	5,000	8,125	
	3	55,000	51,250	228			(3,750)	5,000	1,250	3,125	
	4	52,500	51,250	228			(1,250)	1,250	0	625	
Matching capacity with aggregate demand	1	40,000	40,000	178		56		0	0	0	0
	2	57,500	57,500	256	78			0	0	0	
	3	55,000	55,000	245		11		0	0	0	
	4	52,500	52,500	234		11		0	0	0	

Next, compute the annual costs for both plans:

(1)	(2)	(3)	(4)	(5)	(6)	(7)	(8)
Aggregate Plan	Total Annual Number of Workers Hired	Total Annual Number of Workers Laid Off	Average Annual Inventory (Gallons)	Annual Hiring Cost $[(2) \times \$250]$	Annual Layoff Cost $[(3) \times \$300]$	Annual Inventory Carrying Cost $[(4) \times \$5.00]$	Total Annual Incremental Operating Cost $[(5)+(6)+(7)]$
Level capacity	0	0	4,375	\$ 0	\$ 0	\$21,875	\$21,875
Matching capacity with aggregate demand	78	78	0	19,500	23,400	0	42,900

Hiring costs typically include personnel department costs incurred in the hiring process, training of new workers, and the cost of scrapped products while workers are learning their jobs. *Layoff costs* usually include personnel department costs, termination pay, unemployment benefits, and so on. Although Sherman-Brown considered only two alternative aggregate plans, several other alternatives exist in practice.

For instance, extra days per week, extra shifts per day, shifts longer than eight hours, overtime, and subcontracting could supply the required capacity in each quarter. Such alternatives may be differentiated according to overtime premium labor rates, evening and night shift premium labor rates, additional supervision and other supervision costs, subcontractor fees, and other factors. Example 9.2 compares two other alternative aggregate plans for Sherman-Brown. The two plans use either overtime or subcontracting to augment a constant straight-time work force. As the example illustrates, many factors, some of whose effects on costs and profits are difficult to quantify, can be used to evaluate aggregate plans.

EXAMPLE 9.2   *Overtime or Subcontracting in Aggregate Plans*

The Sherman-Brown Chemical Company has been considering keeping only enough workers employed on straight-time per quarter to produce 40,000 gallons. Either subcontracting or overtime would be used to supply the difference between the straight-time production capacity of 40,000 gallons per quarter and the highly variable quarterly demand. Sherman-Brown has a quote from a subcontractor for a price of $19.50 per gallon for each gallon supplied, and the subcontractor has guaranteed that it could supply up to 20,000 gallons a quarter. Sherman-Brown's labor union is more than willing to work as much overtime as necessary to avoid the use of the subcontractor. The extra cost of overtime over and above straight-time pay is $9.50 per hour of overtime worked. **(a)** Compute the overtime cost and the subcontracting cost per quarter for the two aggregate plans. **(b)** Which factors would be important in deciding between the two plans?

Solution

a. First, compute the amount of paint that would have to be supplied by either overtime or subcontracting and determine the cost of each of the alternative plans:

(1)	*(2)*	*(3)*	*(4)*	*(5)*
	Aggregate Demand	*Gallons to Be Supplied by Overtime or Subcontracting*	*Cost of Overtime*	*Cost of Subcontracting*
Quarter	*(Gallons)*	*[(2) − 40,000]*	*[(3) × 2.311 × 9.50]*	*[(3) × 19.50]*
1	40,000	0	$ 0	$ 0
2	57,500	17,500	384,204	341,250
3	55,000	15,000	329,318	292,500
4	52,500	12,500	274,431	243,750
		Total	$987,953	$877,500

b. Which factors would be important in deciding between the two plans?
  1. The costs developed in the table above are certainly an important factor.
  2. Maintaining positive management – union relations is also important. If the workers say that they want to work the amount of overtime that would be necessary, then allowing them to work overtime could prove to be a positive factor in future dealings. The benefits of this factor would have to be weighed against the additional cost of overtime over subcontracting.
  3. Fatigue, reduced morale, and increased costs could eventually result from working too much overtime on a continual basis. This factor would be an additional cost that would have to be added to Factor 2 above.
  4. Product quality might be better with the overtime plan because all production would be in-house and under the direct control of Sherman-Brown.
  5. The flexibility of increasing or decreasing production levels in any quarter appears to be about the same with both alternatives. However, if the subcontracting alternative is selected, overtime could be used to increase production. On the other hand, if the overtime alternative is selected, decreasing production levels could be easier by simply reducing overtime.

AGGREGATE PLANS FOR PRODUCE-TO-STOCK VERSUS PRODUCE-TO-ORDER FIRMS

In Figure 9.3 the Sherman-Brown Chemical Company level capacity aggregate plan assumed a produce-to-stock system. In produce-to-stock systems, finished goods inventory buffers the difference between the level production capacity and the variable quarterly demands. In produce-to-order firms, finished goods inventory cannot serve this purpose. Production cannot begin in produce-to-order firms until customers' orders are received because products may be custom-designed for customers. Level capacity aggregate plans can still be used in these produce-to-order firms, however, by letting a backlog of customers' orders buffer the difference between the level production capacity and the variable quarterly demand. A backlog of customer orders is simply a stack of customer orders that have been received but not yet shipped. Figure 9.5 illustrates how Sherman-Brown's backlog of customers' orders would fluctuate if it were a produce-to-order firm. During the first quarter, backlog would fall because demand is less than production capacity. In the remaining quarters of the year, backlog would rise because demand exceeds production capacity. This figure illustrates that backlog in produce-to-order firms can serve the same purpose as finished goods inventory in produce-to-stock firms — to buffer the difference between production capacity and demand, thus allowing a level capacity aggregate plan.

One difficulty that produce-to-order firms encounter as they develop aggregate plans is forecasting the demand levels of their products and then translating these demands into production capacities. This difficulty arises because of the lack of product standardization. For instance, let us say that a particular job shop has estimated that it should sell $10 million worth of its custom-designed products next

FIGURE 9.5   *Level Capacity: The Sherman-Brown Chemical Company — Produce to Order*

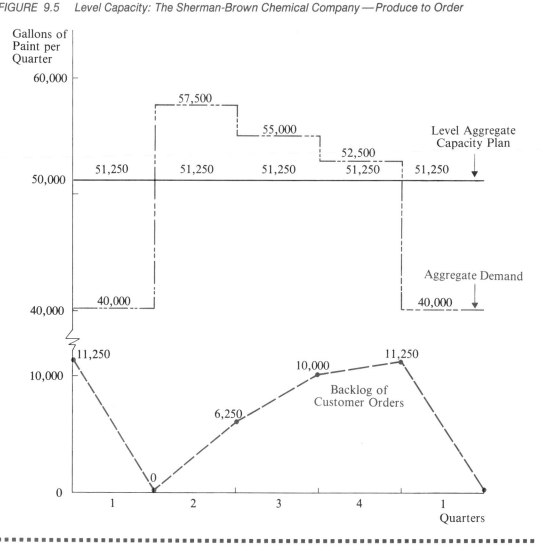

year. How is this aggregate demand translated into workers, pounds of steel stock, and machine-hours required in each month of the year? This translation is made particularly complex because it is often difficult to specify the detailed designs of the products before the customer orders are received. The problem is made a little easier if the industry tolerates using a backlog of customer orders, as illustrated in Figure 9.5. In these cases, because the designs of the products in the backlog are known before production planning is required, the firm can more readily estimate the required production capacity in each future time period.

AGGREGATE PLANS FOR SERVICES

Some service systems perform aggregate planning in almost the same way as we did in the Sherman-Brown case. In fact, in some of these systems that supply standardized services to customers, aggregate planning may be even simpler than in systems that produce products. Examples of these straightforward aggregate-planning situations in service systems are fast-food shops, trucking firms, and banks and savings and loans. Aggregate planning in these systems presents no additional problems beyond those faced by most manufacturing systems.

Some service systems that supply customized services to customers experience the same difficulty as job shops in specifying the nature and extent of services to be performed for each customer. Examples of these systems are hospitals, computer service centers, and automobile body repair shops. Another complicating factor with many of these customized service systems is that, unlike job shops, the customer may be an integral part of the production system, and scaling production capacity up or down may directly alter the perceived quality of the delivered services. Examples of these services are small private colleges and universities, exclusive dinner clubs, private country clubs, and private health clinics.

Also particularly worrisome to managers who must plan capacity levels for service systems is the absence of finished goods inventories as a buffer between system capacity and customer demand. This fact effectively takes away the aggregate plan of level capacity in many of these systems. This is particularly true in direct worker-to-customer services where no products are processed, stored, or transferred. Examples of these systems are income tax services, legal services, and emergency ambulance and fire-fighting services. However, some of these systems have developed certain techniques that encourage the use of level capacity aggregate plans. For example, the use of appointment schedules has tended to level the peaks and valleys of demand in medical clinics, thus facilitating level capacity plans. Similarly, after-hours windows at banks and savings and loans have facilitated level capacity plans. In spite of these innovations, however, many of these systems must develop capacity plans that nearly match the expected aggregate demand.

In service systems that deliver standardized services, we would perform aggregate capacity planning as in the Sherman-Brown case, with the exception that finished goods inventories are infeasible. In custom-designed services, we would suggest a two-step approach to aggregate planning. First, develop aggregate demand forecasts in some homogeneous units of measure such as labor-hours, machine capacity, and sales dollars. Second, try to discover common-denominator units of capacity that are helpful in transforming aggregate demand into production resource requirements. Such experimentation may be necessary to develop these conversion factors.

Next, particularly if the first suggestion is infeasible, develop alternative innovations for expanding the flexibility of production resource capacities. Examples of these innovations are standby workers who are on call for peak demand periods, machines and buildings that can be activated during peak demand periods, subcontractors who respond quickly, and retired supervisors who wish to work only part-time and can be recalled for short periods. These standby resources provide operations managers a near-level capacity aggregate plan with the extra capacity needed to respond to surges in demand.

MATHEMATICAL MODELS FOR AGGREGATE PLANNING

Several aggregate-planning methods have developed in recent years as the use of computers and the operations research discipline has grown. These methods seek to design capacity plans for production systems that achieve organizations' objectives within the availability of their production resources and aggregate demand constraints. A general description of four such methods is offered here to demonstrate their characteristics and general approaches: linear programming, linear decision rules (LDR), management coefficients, and computer search.

Linear Programming

Linear programming was discussed in Chapter 7 as a technique for applying scarce resources optimally to competing demands. In 1956 E. H. Bowman was one of the first analysts to apply linear programming to aggregate planning.[1] Linear programming models typically seek to minimize total operating costs over the planning horizon and include such costs as straight-time labor costs, overtime costs, subcontracting costs, worker-hiring costs, worker-layoff costs, and inventory-carrying costs. The constraints of the models usually include such factors as the maximum capacity available in each time period from straight-time workers, overtime workers, subcontractors, and new workers, and the minimum cumulative aggregate demand over the planning horizon.

Example 9.3 uses linear programming to develop an aggregate plan for a company. While this example is simpler than most real aggregate-planning problems, it does illustrate the structure of such problems and the linear programming approach to such problems.

EXAMPLE 9.3   *Using Linear Programming to Analyze an Aggregate-Planning Problem*

A production scheduler must develop an aggregate plan for his plant for the next two quarters of next year. The highly automated plant produces graphics terminals for the computer products market. The company estimates that 700 terminals will need to be shipped to customers in the first quarter and 3,200 in the second quarter. It is the policy of the company to ship customers' orders in the quarter in which they are ordered. It takes an average of 5 hours of labor to produce each terminal and only 9,000 hours of straight-time labor is available in each of the quarters. Overtime can be used, but the company has a policy of limiting the amount of overtime in each

[1] E. H. Bowman, "Production Planning by the Transportation Method of Linear Programming," *Journal of Operations Research Society* 4(February 1956):100–103.

quarter to 10 percent of the straight-time labor available. Labor costs $12 per hour at the straight-time rate and $18 per hour at the overtime rate. If a terminal is produced in one quarter and shipped in the next quarter, a carrying cost of $50 is incurred. How many terminals should be produced on straight-time and overtime in each of the first and second quarters to minimize straight-time labor, overtime labor, and carrying costs? The market requirements, straight-time labor availability, and overtime policy must be adhered to. **(a)** Formulate this aggregate-planning problem as a linear programming problem. Define the decision variables, formulate the objective function, and formulate the constraint functions. **(b)** Solve this problem using the computer-programming package in the *POM Computer Library* that accompanies this text. What is the solution to the problem? What is the aggregate plan?

Solution

a. Formulate this aggregate-planning problem as a linear programming problem. Define the decision variables:

X_1 = number of terminals to be produced on straight-time in the first quarter and shipped in the first quarter

X_2 = number of terminals to be produced on overtime in the first quarter and shipped in the first quarter

X_3 = number of terminals to be produced on straight-time in the first quarter and shipped in the second quarter

X_4 = number of terminals to be produced on overtime in the first quarter and shipped in the second quarter

X_5 = number of terminals to be produced on straight-time in the second quarter and shipped in the second quarter

X_6 = number of terminals to be produced on overtime in the second quarter and shipped in the second quarter

The coefficients of the objective function are computed as follows:

X_1: 5×12 = $ 60 X_4: $(5 \times 18) + 50 = \$140$

X_2: 5×18 = 90 X_5: 5×12 = 60

X_3: $(5 \times 12) + 50 =$ 110 X_6: 5×18 = 90

$\text{Min } Z = 60X_1 + 90X_2 + 110X_3 + 140X_4 + 60X_5 + 90X_6$

$$
\begin{aligned}
X_1 + X_2 &\geq 700 && Q_1 \text{ demand}\\
X_3 + X_4 + X_5 + X_6 &\geq 3{,}200 && Q_2 \text{ demand}\\
5X_1 + 5X_3 &\leq 9{,}000 && Q_1 \text{ st. labor}\\
5X_5 &\leq 9{,}000 && Q_2 \text{ st. labor}\\
5X_2 + 5X_4 &\leq 900 && Q_1 \text{ ot. labor}\\
5X_6 &\leq 900 && Q_2 \text{ ot. labor}
\end{aligned}
$$

The solution to this linear programming problem is:

X_1 = 580 terminals to be produced on straight-time in the first quarter and shipped during the first quarter

X_2 = 120 terminals to be produced on overtime in the first quarter and shipped during the first quarter

X_3 = 1,220 terminals to be produced on straight-time in the first quarter and shipped during the second quarter

X_4 = 0 terminals to be produced on overtime in the first quarter and shipped during the second quarter

X_5 = 1,800 terminals to be produced on straight-time in the second quarter and shipped during the second quarter

X_6 = 180 terminals to be produced on overtime in the second quarter and shipped in the second quarter

S_5 = 300 hours of unused overtime labor in the first quarter

Z = \$304,000 total cost of straight-time and overtime labor and carrying cost for the aggregate plan

S_1, S_2, S_3, S_4, and S_6 = 0

Linear Decision Rules (LDR)

Holt, Modigliani, Muth, and Simon of the Carnegie Institute of Technology developed the *linear decision rule* in the 1950s.[2] LDR develop a single quadratic mathematical cost function for a particular production system that includes these costs — regular payroll, hiring, layoff, overtime, inventory carrying, back order or shortage, and setup. This composite mathematical cost function covers each time period in the planning horizon and includes two principal decision variables — number of units of output to be produced and size of work force in each time period.

The quadratic composite mathematical cost function is differentiated by calculus methods to yield two linear mathematical functions; one is used to compute the number of units to produce during the next time period and the other is used to compute the work force size during the next time period. These two linear equations are typically used at the beginning of each period to plan the forthcoming production capacity and work force size; thus the number of workers to be hired or laid off, number of overtime hours required, expected fluctuations in inventories, and machine changeovers can all be deduced.

---

[2] Charles C. Holt, Franco Modigliani, John F. Muth, and Herbert A. Simon, *Planning Production, Inventories, and Work Force* (Englewood Cliffs, NJ: Prentice-Hall, 1960).

Management Coefficients

The *management coefficients* model is a capacity-planning technique that results in *heuristics*—useful guides to action. The basic assumption that underlies this approach is that managers develop capacity plans in practice by using complex criteria and gut feeling. This technique uses the historical data surrounding a manager's past capacity-planning decisions and develops a predictive regression equation to be used to formulate future capacity plans. This approach to capacity planning does not try to explain why managers make certain capacity-planning decisions, given that certain market and operations conditions are present. It attempts only to describe the decision processes of individual managers. Although there is some evidence that the technique performs rather well under some circumstances, numerous obstacles to its widespread use exist.[3] Chief among these weaknesses is the dependence of the technique on the individual expertise of analysts to effectively build a regression model that reflects a manager's decision-making behavior.

Computer Search

Computer search techniques sequentially examine thousands of combinations of production resources (overtime, layoffs, hiring, subcontracting, and so on) in each time period to meet the cumulative aggregate demand over a planning horizon. This method uses preprogrammed rules that control the way resources can be combined to select a low-cost capacity plan for each time period: What combination of production resources should be used in each time period?

These computer programs select a combination of sources of capacity in each time period that meets aggregate demand, computes the operating cost, follows search rules to select another combination of sources of capacity, costs out this new combination, and continues this process sequentially until no significant improvement in operating costs is observed. The last combination of sources of capacity in each time period is the *capacity plan.*

Mathematical models in aggregate planning do not dominate POM practice—not yet anyway. But you should know about these techniques because their approaches are fundamental and future models may become more important in capacity planning as you assume positions of responsibility in real-world production systems.

We have discussed the major concepts, issues, and techniques of aggregate planning—the development of intermediate-range capacity plans for production systems. These plans largely determine the volume of customer orders that *can* be economically produced during any specific time period. The upper limit of production capacity directly impinges on the day-to-day scheduling of products and services. Master production scheduling is the starting point for these day-to-day short-range schedules.

---

[3] E. H. Bowman, "Consistency and Optimality in Managerial Decision Making," *Management Science* 4(January 1963):100–103.

MASTER PRODUCTION SCHEDULING

The master production schedule (MPS) sets the quantity of each end item to be completed in each week of the short-range planning horizon. End items are finished products, or parts that are shipped as end items. End items may be shipped to customers, placed in inventory, or sent to others within the same firm. Operations managers regularly, usually weekly, meet to review market forecasts, customer orders, inventory levels, facility loading, and capacity information so that master production schedules can be developed. The MPS is a plan for future production of end items over a short-range planning horizon that usually spans from a few weeks to several months.

OBJECTIVES OF MASTER PRODUCTION SCHEDULING

As Figure 9.1 illustrated, short-range production capacity is constrained by the aggregate capacity plan. Master production scheduling takes this short-range production capacity that was determined by the aggregate plan and allocates it to orders for end items. The objectives of master production scheduling are twofold:

1. Schedule end items to be completed promptly and when promised to customers.
2. Avoid overloading or underloading the production facility so that production capacity is efficiently utilized and low production costs result.

RELATIONSHIPS WITH OTHER ELEMENTS OF PRODUCTION PLANNING

As Figure 9.1 further illustrated, the master production schedule drives the production schedules for all work centers in each week of the short-range planning horizon; thus the MPS is the beginning of all short-range production planning. From the MPS, material requirements planning (MRP) develops short-range schedules for producing parts that go into the end items in every work center of the production system. Also, MRP develops the short-range plans for purchasing the raw materials and components that are required to produce the products. In the words of Joseph Orlicky, "A MPS is to MRP what a program is to a computer." [4] In other words, the MPS is the driving force behind production planning in manufacturing.

TIME FENCES IN MASTER PRODUCTION SCHEDULES

Master production schedules can be viewed as being divided into four sections, each section separated by a point in time that is called a *time fence.* The first section includes the first few weeks of the schedule and is referred to as frozen, the next

---

[4] Joseph Orlicky, *Material Requirements Planning* (New York: McGraw-Hill, 1975), 231.

section of a few weeks is referred to as firm, the next section of a few weeks is referred to as full, and the last section of a few weeks is referred to as open.

Frozen means that this early part of the MPS cannot be changed except under extraordinary circumstances and only with authorization from the highest levels in the organization. Change in this section of the schedule is ordinarily prohibited because it would be costly to reverse the plans to purchase materials and produce the parts that go into the products. Moreover, when we change the MPS, we move one order in ahead of another one—why make one customer happy at the expense of making another one unhappy? *Firm* means that changes can occur in this section of the schedule, but only in exceptional kinds of situations. Changes are resisted in this section of the schedule for the same reasons as in the frozen section. *Full* means that all of the available production capacity has been allocated to orders. Changes in the full section of the schedule can be made and production costs will be only slightly affected, but the effect on customer satisfaction is uncertain. *Open* means that not all of the production capacity has been allocated, and it is in this section of the schedule that new orders are ordinarily slotted.

Here we observe another fundamental difference in the way that Japanese manufacturers schedule operations: The Japanese do not change production schedules in attempts to accommodate one customer at the expense of another. U.S. manufacturers have traditionally been more lax in allowing schedules to be changed, taking the attitude of "let's make a deal" when slotting customers' orders in schedules. Rising production costs and declining customer satisfaction have been the rewards of this prevalent tendency to change schedules.

PROCEDURES FOR DEVELOPING MASTER PRODUCTION SCHEDULES

Figure 9.6 describes the process for developing the MPS. Working from customer orders, forecasts, inventory status reports, and production capacity information, schedulers place the most urgent orders in the earliest available open slot of the MPS. Several important activities occur at this point. First, the schedulers must estimate the total demand for products from all sources, assign orders to production slots, make delivery promises to customers, and make the detailed calculations for the MPS. Example 9.4 illustrates how a scheduler might total the demands and perform the detailed calculations for a MPS. The activities of order entry and order promising are discussed in the demand management section below.

As orders are slotted in the MPS, the effects on the loading of the production work centers are checked. This preliminary checking of the MPS is sometimes called *rough-cut capacity planning.* The main goal in rough-cut capacity planning is to identify any week in the MPS where underloading or overloading of production capacity occurs and revise the MPS as required. *Underloading* means that not enough production of end items has been scheduled to fully load the facility. *Overloading* means that too much production of end items has been scheduled in the facility and that insufficient capacity exists to produce the MPS. Example 9.5 illustrates how rough-cut capacity planning can be carried out.

FIGURE 9.6   The Master Scheduling Process

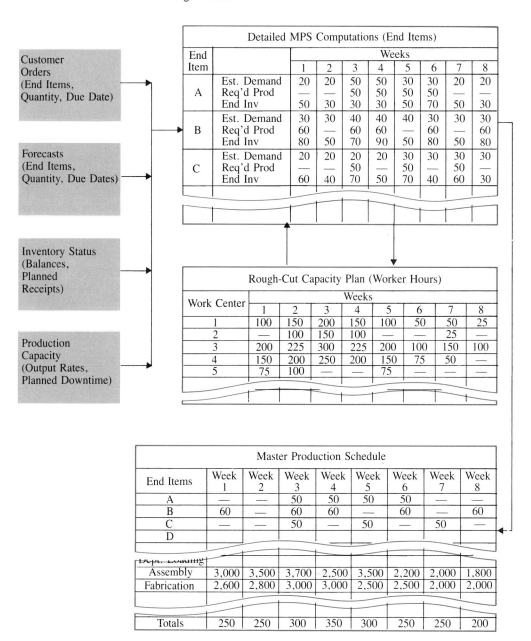

Inputs (left column):
- Customer Orders (End Items, Quantity, Due Date)
- Forecasts (End Items, Quantity, Due Dates)
- Inventory Status (Balances, Planned Receipts)
- Production Capacity (Output Rates, Planned Downtime)

Detailed MPS Computations (End Items)

End Item		1	2	3	4	5	6	7	8
A	Est. Demand	20	20	50	50	30	30	20	20
	Req'd Prod	—	—	50	50	50	50	—	—
	End Inv	50	30	30	30	50	70	50	30
B	Est. Demand	30	30	40	40	40	30	30	30
	Req'd Prod	60	—	60	60	—	60	—	60
	End Inv	80	50	70	90	50	80	50	80
C	Est. Demand	20	20	20	20	30	30	30	30
	Req'd Prod	—	—	50	—	50	—	50	—
	End Inv	60	40	70	50	70	40	60	30

(Weeks 1–8)

Rough-Cut Capacity Plan (Worker Hours)

Work Center	1	2	3	4	5	6	7	8
1	100	150	200	150	100	50	50	25
2	—	100	150	100	—	—	25	—
3	200	225	300	225	200	100	150	100
4	150	200	250	200	150	75	50	—
5	75	100	—	—	75	—	—	—

(Weeks 1–8)

Master Production Schedule

End Items	Week 1	Week 2	Week 3	Week 4	Week 5	Week 6	Week 7	Week 8
A	—	—	50	50	50	50	—	—
B	60	—	60	60	—	60	—	60
C	—	—	50	—	50	—	50	—
D								
Dept. Loading								
Assembly	3,000	3,500	3,700	2,500	3,500	2,200	2,000	1,800
Fabrication	2,600	2,800	3,000	3,000	2,500	2,500	2,000	2,000
Totals	250	250	300	350	300	250	250	200

EXAMPLE 9.4   Developing a Master Production Schedule

A firm produces two products, A and B, on a produce-to-stock basis. The demands for the products come from many sources. The demand estimates for the two products over the next six weeks are given below:

Demands for Product A from All Sources						
	Weekly Demand (Number of Product A's)					
Sources of Demand	*1*	*2*	*3*	*4*	*5*	*6*
Intracompany orders				20	10	10
Branch warehouse orders			20			
R&D orders			10	10		
Customer demand (forecasts and in-hand orders)	20	20	20	20	20	20
Total Demands for Product A	20	20	50	50	30	30

Demands for Product B from All Sources						
	Weekly Demand (Number of Product B's)					
Sources of Demand	*1*	*2*	*3*	*4*	*5*	*6*
Intracompany orders			10		10	
Branch warehouse orders				20		
R&D orders					10	10
Customer demand (forecasts and in-hand orders)	30	30	30	20	20	20
Total Demands for Product B	30	30	40	40	40	30

The safety stock is the minimum level of planned inventory. The safety stock for A is 30 and for B it is 40. The fixed lot size (the lot size is produced when production of the product occurs) for A is 50 and for B it is 60. The beginning inventory for A is 70 and for B it is 50. Prepare a MPS for these two products.

Solution

For each product, take the total demands, consider beginning inventory, determine in which weeks ending inventory would fall below the safety stock (SS) and thus require production, and schedule a lot of the product to be produced during those weeks.

Master Production Schedule (Number of Products A and B)							
End		*Weeks*					
Item		*1*	*2*	*3*	*4*	*5*	*6*
A	Total demands	20	20	50	50	30	30
	Beginning inventory	70	50	30	30	30	50
	Required production	—	—	50	50	50	50
	Ending inventory	50	30	30	30	50	70
B	Total demands	30	30	40	40	40	30
	Beginning inventory	50	80	50	70	90	50
	Required production	60	—	60	60	—	60
	Ending inventory	80	50	70	90	50	80

Note: Safety stocks are 30 for A and 40 for B, fixed lot sizes are 50 for A and 60 for B, and beginning inventory in Week 1 is 70 for A and 50 for B.

Let us take a closer look at the calculations for Product A in the MPS above. Follow through these computations and compare them to the MPS:

(1)	*(2)*	*(3)*	*(4)*	*(5)*	*(6)*
				Required Production [Fixed Lot Size If Column (4) Is Less Than Safety Stock; If Not, Then Zero]	*Ending Inventory*
Week	*Beginning Inventory*	*Total Demand*	*Balance [(2) − (3)]*		*[(2) + (5) − (3)]*
1	70	20	50	—	50
2	50	20	30	—	30
3	30	50	(20)	50	30
4	30	50	(20)	50	30
5	30	30	0	50	50
6	50	30	20	50	70

Note: For Product A, safety stock is 30, fixed lot size is 50, and beginning inventory in Week 1 is 70.

In Week 1 the balance exceeds the desired safety stock (50 > 30); therefore no production of A is needed. In Week 2 the balance is also enough to provide the desired safety stock (30 = 30) and no production of A is required. But in Weeks 3 and 4 the balances would actually be negative if production of A were not scheduled; therefore a fixed lot size of 50 Product A's is scheduled in both of these weeks. Weeks 5 and 6 are computed similarly.

The main idea in master production scheduling is to place orders as early in the MPS as possible to make customers happy, while at the same time taking care not to overload or underload the production capacities of the work centers. Two final checks of the MPS will be performed later. First, material requirements planning (MRP) checks to see if materials and parts can be purchased or produced to support the MPS. Next, capacity requirements planning (CRP) checks to see if production capacity can be made available to economically produce the MPS. MRP and CRP are discussed in Chapter 11, Resource Requirements Planning Systems.

Now that we have discussed the process of preparing a MPS and explained its detailed calculations, let us examine how to estimate the demands for products in the MPS.

EXAMPLE 9.5   Rough-Cut Capacity Planning

The firm in Example 9.4 now wishes to determine if the MPS that was developed underloads or overloads the final assembly line that produces both Product A and Product B. The final assembly line has a weekly capacity of 100 hours available. Each Product A requires .9 hour and each Product B requires 1.6 hours of final assembly capacity. **(a)** Compute the actual final assembly hours required to produce the MPS for both products; this is often referred to as the *load.* Compare the load to the final assembly capacity available in each week and for the total six weeks; this is often referred to as *rough-cut capacity planning.* **(b)** Does sufficient final assembly capacity exist to produce the MPS? **(c)** What changes to the MPS would you recommend?

Solution

a. Compute the load in each week and for the six weeks, and compare the load to the final assembly capacity:

End Item		**Weekly Final Assembly Hours**						
		1	*2*	*3*	*4*	*5*	*6*	*Total*
A	Production	—	—	(50)	(50)	(50)	(50)	
	Final assembly hours	—	—	45	45	45	45	
B	Production	(60)	—	(60)	(60)	—	(60)	
	Final assembly hours	96	—	96	96	—	96	
Load (Hours)		96	—	141	141	45	141	564
Capacity (Hours)		100	100	100	100	100	100	600

Note: The numbers in parentheses are the numbers of end items to be produced in each week. They come from the MPS in Example 9.4.

b. There is a total of 600 hours of final assembly capacity available over the 6-week schedule and the MPS requires only a total of 564 hours. However, the MPS overloads final assembly in Weeks 3, 4, and 6, and it underloads final assembly in Weeks 1, 2, and 5.

c. A better balance of weekly final assembly capacity is possible if some of the production lots are moved into earlier weeks of the schedule. Move lots of Product A from Weeks 4 and 6 into Weeks 3 and 5, and move the lot of Product B from Week 3 into Week 2:

End Item		Weekly Final Assembly Hours						
		1	2	3	4	5	6	Total
A	Production	—	—	(100)	—	(100)	—	
	Final assembly hours	—	—	90	—	90	—	
B	Production	(60)	(60)	—	(60)	—	(60)	
	Final assembly hours	96	96	—	96	—	96	
Load (Hours)		96	96	90	96	90	96	564
Capacity (Hours)		100	100	100	100	100	100	600

Note: The numbers in parentheses are the numbers of end items to be produced in each week.

This revised MPS would better load the final assembly line, but some additional inventory would be created by producing these lots earlier.

DEMAND MANAGEMENT

Estimating future demand is a crucial part of master production scheduling. The American Production and Inventory Control Society (APICS) describes this as *demand management,* which is defined as "the function of recognizing and managing all of the demands for products to insure that the master scheduler is aware of them. It encompasses the activities of forecasting, order entry, order promising, branch warehouse requirements, interplant orders, and service parts requirements."[5] Demand management includes establishing an effective forecasting system for the end items, monitoring the forecasts, and changing the system as required to improve forecasts.

Order entry and *order promising* are important functions within master production scheduling. Master schedulers must review the customer orders, check the requested delivery dates against the open production slots in the MPS, determine the priority of the orders, assign production slots in the MPS to the orders, and communicate the promised dates to the customers. Each promised date guides an order through the production processes and becomes an important goal of operations managers until the order is delivered to the customer. Interplant orders come from inside the company. Marketing orders products as samples to give to customers for promotion, R&D orders products to be used in tests, and branch warehouses order products. Service parts are ordinarily ordered by distributors to be used in warranty

[5] *APICS Dictionary,* 6th ed. (Falls Church, VA: American Production and Inventory Control, 1987), 8.

FIGURE 9.7   *Demand Estimates: A Blend of Orders and Forecasts*

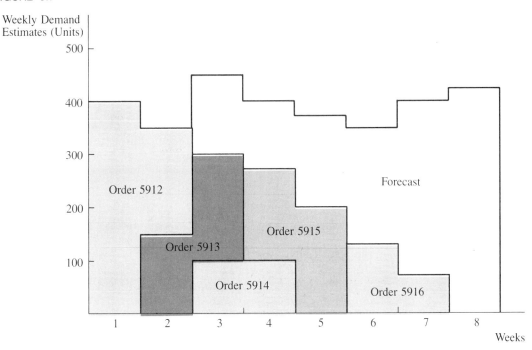

or repair work. For example, Briggs and Stratton ships many parts of its engines to repair centers that use the parts to repair customers' engines. The orders for these parts are treated in master production scheduling like other customer orders except that the parts are treated as end items and thus become part of the MPS.

WEEKLY UPDATING OF THE MPS

To truly understand the nature of demand management, we must understand the dynamic nature of the MPS. The MPS is usually updated weekly, meaning that after one week has passed, one week is taken off the front end of the MPS, one week is added on to the back end, and the demands for the whole MPS are estimated anew. Because the demands that are far out in the later periods of the MPS are likely to be changed as they undergo many updates while moving toward the early, frozen part of the schedule, the accuracy of the forecasts in the latter part of the MPS are not as critical as in the earlier part. Also, the early part of the MPS tends to be dominated by actual in-hand customer orders, whereas the latter part of the schedule tends to be dominated by forecasts. Thus the demand estimates of the early part of the MPS are by nature more accurate.

    Figure 9.7 illustrates this principle. In Weeks 1 and 2 the demand estimate is made up entirely of orders. In Week 8 the demand estimate is made up entirely of forecasts. In the middle of the schedule the demand estimate is a combination of actual orders and forecasts, but forecasts become more predominant as we move out into later periods. Through the weekly updating process, demand estimates in later periods of the MPS, which are based principally on forecasts, move forward in the MPS, and these demand estimates become more accurate for two reasons. First, much of the demand based on forecasts becomes based more on customer orders, and second, the forecasts become refined through the weekly updating process. Week after week as the MPS is updated, orders are flowing in and forecasts are being modified, and all of this is occurring before money must be committed to ordering materials, scheduling workers, and scheduling machine changeovers. By the time an order moves into the early, frozen portion of the MPS and money must be committed to the order, operations managers are able to place much confidence in the accuracy of the demand estimates.

MPS IN PRODUCE-TO-STOCK
AND PRODUCE-TO-ORDER FIRMS

Master production scheduling procedures differ according to whether a firm is a produce-to-stock or produce-to-order production system. The elements of the MPS that are affected most by the type of production system are *demand management, lot-sizing,* and *number of products to schedule.*

In produce-to-order systems, customer orders are the predominant focus in demand management. The master production scheduler usually works from a back-log of customer orders, and product demand forecasts may not be used. Customer orders in the backlog are assigned open production slots as we described earlier in the demand management section. The lot size, the number of products to produce on an order, is usually determined by the customer order. If a customer orders 500 of a particular product, ordinarily 500 of the products will be produced on the order. This approach to lot-sizing is called lot-for-lot (LFL). Because produce-to-order firms have many product designs, the number of products and orders that have to be placed in the MPS is great. The overall effort that must be expended in the MPS is therefore great.

In produce-to-stock firms, the orders for products come principally from ware-house orders within the company. These orders are based on forecasts of future demand for products from many customers. Forecasts therefore tend to play an important part in demand management in produce-to-stock firms. In the early part of the MPS, these warehouse orders that were based on forecasts may be backed up by actual customer orders. However, in produce-to-stock firms, customer orders only indirectly affect demand management by affecting warehouse orders. Thus ware-house orders are the important element in demand management in produce-to-stock firms.

The lot sizes of orders in produce-to-stock firms is a matter of economics. How many of a particular product should be produced, when we set up to produce the product, so that the average unit production cost is low? If we produce too few of the product, the fixed cost of getting ready to produce the order is spread over too few products and the average unit production cost is high. If we produce too many of the product, the inventory of the product will grow too large as we produce the order, the cost of carrying the inventory will be too high, and the average unit production cost will be too high also. A balance must be struck between these costs in determining economic lot sizes in produce-to-stock firms. We shall study further the concept of lot-sizing in Chapters 11 and 12. Because produce-to-stock firms produce only a few standard product designs, the effort expended on master production scheduling in these firms is usually less than in produce-to-order firms.

LENGTH OF PLANNING HORIZONS

The planning horizons in master scheduling may vary from just a few weeks in some firms to more than a year in others. How does a firm decide how long its planning horizon should be? Although several factors impinge on this decision, one factor tends to be dominant: The planning horizon should at least equal the longest cumulative end item lead time. *Cumulative end item lead time* means the amount of time to get the materials in from suppliers, produce all of the parts and assemblies, get the end item assembled and ready for shipment, and deliver it to customers. The end item with the greatest cumulative lead time therefore determines the least amount of time that a planning horizon should span. In practice, planning horizons are usually greater than this minimum.

The description of the MPS above often mentioned the activities of schedulers. In some applications of the MPS today, some of these activities are performed by computers.

COMPUTERIZED MPS

The MPS can be prepared by a computing system. In these cases end item demand information, inventory status information, capacity constraints, demand forecasts, lot sizes, and desired safety stock levels are used by the computer to perform the detailed MPS calculations, compare these figures to work center loads and capacity constraints, and finally generate an MPS. When many end items are produced in several production departments, the computer is not only economical, it is absolutely necessary to process all the data. Use of computers has actually allowed some to use what is called a *net change MPS.* These schedules show only changes to the last MPS.

The MPS is certainly the central focus in most computerized scheduling systems regardless of whether the programs are custom-designed for a production system or are a standard system from one of the computer hardware or software companies. IBM's *Communications Oriented Production Information and Control Systems (COPICS),* as illustrated in Figure 9.8, is an example of these computerized scheduling systems.[6] COPICS and similar systems are more than just computerized scheduling systems because they integrate forecasting, scheduling, inventory, and purchasing

---

[6] International Business Machines, *Communications Oriented Production Information and Control Systems (COPICS),* Vol. 1: *Management Overview,* Publication G320-1974 (White Plains, NY: IBM, 1972).

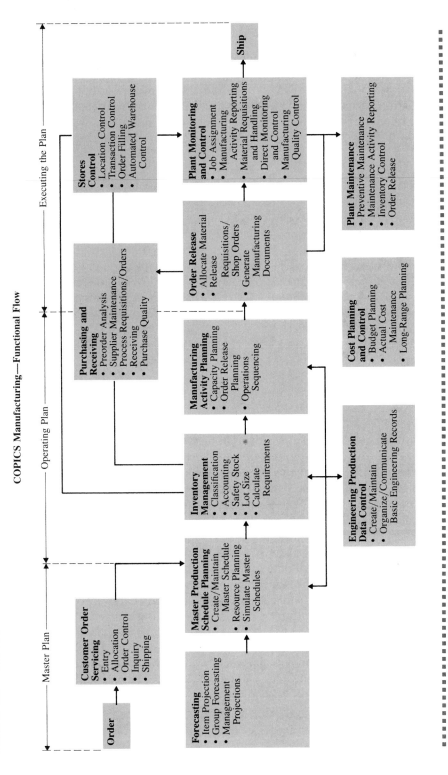

FIGURE 9.8   COPICS

decisions into one large information system for planning and controlling all facets of the production system.

Master production scheduling is an important activity in POM. When it is poorly done, these symptoms can occur: (1) overloaded facilities, (2) underloaded facilities, (3) excessive inventory levels on some end items and frequent stockouts on others, (4) unbelievable schedules that production personnel do not follow, (5) unreliable delivery promises to customers, and (6) excessive expediting. When MPS is properly done, positive customer relations are developed, inventory levels are low (because the right end items are produced in correct quantities), and production resources are fully utilized. Additionally, the MPS becomes the basis for detailed schedules for each production department and it anchors the material requirements planning system.

SUMMARY

Production planning is concerned with getting products and services out of production systems on time to meet customers' needs and doing so in ways that result in low production costs. Production planning spans several organizational levels and time periods. Long-range production planning occurs at the highest levels of organizations, spans up to several years, and constrains other intermediate and short-range plans. Intermediate-range production plans determine aggregate capacity while considering employment, machinery, and subcontractor plans. Short-range production plans are driven by master production schedules—schedules for the production of end items.

Aggregate planning begins with estimating aggregate demands for all products of a production system. These demand estimates, which usually cover from 6 to 18 months, require certain production capacities. The number of workers, how much straight-time and overtime labor to use, the amount of production to subcontract, and other issues must be decided and made a part of the plan. Two traditional aggregate plans are observed—level capacity and matching capacity with aggregate demand. The costs of these alternatives differ among production systems. The choice of an aggregate plan alternative is based on many criteria. Among these criteria are labor cost, inventory carrying cost, employment level stability, flexibility in changing capacity, worker–management relations, product quality, and other factors. Aggregate plans impose constraints on short-range production plans.

Master production scheduling (MPS) is the engine that drives all short-range plans. It is a schedule of all end items to be produced in the short-range plan. All work center production schedules that produce parts that go into end items are based on the MPS. Likewise, the MPS determines the quantity and timing of purchased materials delivery. Demand management with its order entry and order promising is aimed at prompt deliveries of customers' orders. Rough-cut capacity planning attempts to assign customers' orders to open production slots such that efficient facility loading results. Although differences in MPS exist because of differences between produce-to-stock and produce-to-order firms, the principles and many procedures of MPS are universal.

REVIEW AND DISCUSSION QUESTIONS

1. Production planning is aimed at two principal goals. What are these goals and how are they related?

2. What long-range plans result from long-range capacity planning? Who prepares these plans?

3. What is the main intermediate-range capacity plan? What types of resources are included in this plan? Who prepares these plans?

4. What are the main short-range production plans? How are they related? Who prepares these plans?

5. Explain the relationships among long-, intermediate-, and short-range production plans.

6. Define *aggregate planning*.

7. Describe how the following production resources can be increased to expand production capacity:
   a. work force,
   b. materials, and
   c. machines.

8. List the advantages and disadvantages of these traditional aggregate plans:
   a. level capacity, and
   b. matching capacity with aggregate demand.

9. Give three reasons why aggregate planning in produce-to-order firms is difficult. What can operations managers do to overcome these difficulties?

10. Give three reasons why aggregate planning in services is difficult. What can operations managers do to overcome these difficulties?

11. Explain how linear programming can be used in aggregate planning.

12. Explain how aggregate planning differs between produce-to-stock and produce-to-order firms.

13. What is a master production schedule? What inputs are needed? Describe the process of preparing a master schedule.

14. Explain the meaning of these master production scheduling terms:
   a. frozen,
   b. firm,
   c. full,
   d. open,
   e. lot sizes,
   f. rough-cut capacity planning,
   g. updating,
   h. demand management,
   i. order entry, and
   j. order promising.

15. Explain the process of weekly updating of the master production schedule.

16. Explain why operations managers have confidence in the demand estimates included in the early part of the master production schedule. Why does the updating of the MPS tend to build this confidence?

17. Explain the differences in MPS between produce-to-stock and produce-to-order firms.

18. What sets the length of planning horizons in master production scheduling?

PROBLEMS

Aggregate Planning

1. The Acme Engineering Company provides bridge design services to road construction companies. These projects are classified into three types of bridges — pedestrian, Class 1 vehicle traffic, and Class 2 vehicle traffic. Acme is planning its work force for next year and estimates that for every sales dollar .0156 engineering design hour will be required. The forecast of next year's sales of bridge design is:

Type of Bridge	Sales (Thousands of Dollars)			
	1st Quarter	2nd Quarter	3rd Quarter	4th Quarter
Pedestrian	$1,200 x .0156	$1,500	$1,200	$1,000
Class 1 vehicle	2,700 x .0156	2,500	3,000	2,500
Class 2 vehicle	5,500 x .0156	6,000	5,000	5,000

If there are 2,000 hours per year for each engineer, compute the number of engineers needed for each bridge type in each quarter and the total number of engineers needed in each quarter. Next, draw a composite graph that shows the number of engineers needed in each quarter for each bridge type and the aggregate demand (in engineers) for each quarter.

2. The Triple A Products Company produces three product lines: A_1, A_2, and A_3. Triple A is now doing its capacity planning for next year and wishes to develop an aggregate demand for its products. Billie Joe Kennedy, forecasting analyst, has developed a regression equation for each of the products' quarterly sales for next year:

Product	Quarterly Sales in Units
A_1	$Y = 550 + 333X$
A_2	$Y = 1,000 - 250X$
A_3	$Y = 250 + 267X$

Y is quarterly sales in units and X is the quarter (1, 2, 3, 4). The number of machine hours required in the calendering operation, which is the bottleneck operation in the entire facility (this operation has the least capacity among all the operations in the entire facility), for each of the products is:

Product	Machine Hours per Product
A_1	.50
A_2	1.00
A_3	.30

a. Compute the quarterly sales in units for each of the three products.
b. Compute the number of machine-hours in the calendering operation required to produce each of the products per quarter and all of the total aggregate demand (machine hours) per quarter.
c. Graph the information developed in Part *b*.

3. The Zapcom Computer Company manufactures small-business computers that are marketed nationally through a distributor network. Zapcom is now making its marketing and manufacturing plans for the next year, which are intermediate-range plans in their planning system. They have developed these sales forecasts and labor and machine standards for their products:

	Quarterly Sales (Units)				Labor Standard (Labor Hours/ Unit)	Machine Standard (Machine Hours/ Unit)
Product	1st Quarter	2nd Quarter	3rd Quarter	4th Quarter		
1. Z305 Business Computer	13,000	19,500	15,400	23,500	7.95	5.77
2. Z205 Business Computer	6,500	8,700	7,200	10,000	6.56	4.10
3. Z105 Business Calculator	12,500	23,500	16,500	25,000	3.22	2.55
4. Z1510 Floppy Diskette	8,700	12,200	10,500	15,750	4.90	3.15
5. Z1210 Floppy Diskette	4,500	6,000	4,900	7,000	3.11	2.10
6. Z620 CRT	11,500	14,700	12,800	16,500	2.60	1.50
7. Z520 CRT	10,500	14,000	11,500	17,500	2.20	1.21
8. ZROM Business Package	25,500	33,500	27,500	38,500	.56	.79

a. Compute the labor-hours required for each quarter.
b. Compute the machine-hours required for each quarter.
c. Graph the information developed in Parts *a* and *b*.

4. The Boston plant of Computer Products Corporation (CPC) manufactures a line of resins that is shipped to other CPC plants and other firms in the electronics and computer manufacturing industries. Lynda McDonald, production-planning manager at the plant, is in the process of planning the aggregate production capacity required at the plant to produce next year's sales forecast that was just issued from CPC's corporate headquarters in San Jose. The plant manufactures three lines of resin (Wopac, Ziptite, and Lockit), each line with several variations but each one

requiring the same amount of labor- and machine-hours to manufacture one pound. For example, the only difference between Wopac 3599 and Wopac 3674 is in the ingredients used for each. The same amount of production time is required by each.

	Sales Forecast (Thousands of Tons)			
Resin	*1st Quarter*	*2nd Quarter*	*3rd Quarter*	*4th Quarter*
Wopac	10.3	11.4	13.9	9.3
Ziptite	6.1	5.4	7.8	6.7
Lockit	3.0	1.4	4.2	5.7

Ample machine capacity exists to produce the forecast and each ton of resin requires 5 labor hours.
a. Compute the aggregate demand for resins in each quarter.
b. Compute the aggregate number of labor-hours in each quarter.
c. If each worker works 520 hours per quarter, how many workers will be required in each quarter?

5. In Problem 4, it costs $2,000 to hire a worker and $1,000 to lay off a worker, and inventory carrying cost is $150 per ton of resin (this means that if one ton of resin were held in inventory for a year, it would cost $150 for finance charges, insurance, warehousing expense, etc.). CPC's Boston plant works the same number of days in each quarter, 13 five-day weeks. Evaluate two aggregate plans for next year, level capacity and matching capacity with aggregate demand. Which plan would you recommend? Why?

6. The Rigid Strut Steel Company is trying to decide between two aggregate capacity plans, No. 1 and No. 2. The number of workers per quarter and the average annual finished goods inventory in thousands of pounds for the two plans are shown below. If hiring costs are $1,200 per worker hired, layoff costs are $600 per worker laid off, and inventory carrying cost is $.015 per pound per year, compute the annual hiring, layoff, carrying, and total incremental costs for each plan. Which plan would you prefer? Why?

Aggregate Plan	*Quarter*	*Workers Required*	*Average Annual Inventory (Thousands of Pounds)*
No. 1	1	150	1,500
	2	160	
	3	160	
	4	150	

Aggregate Plan	*Quarter*	*Workers Required*	*Average Annual Inventory (Thousands of Pounds)*
No. 2	1	155	2,950
	2	155	
	3	155	
	4	155	

7. In Problem 3, if the machine-hours were sufficient and employees worked 13 weeks in each quarter and 40 hours in each week, determine how many employees the Zapcom Computer Company would require in each quarter, using these aggregate plans:
   a. level capacity,
   b. matching capacity with aggregate demand.

8. The CM Underwear Company makes boys' stretch-fit briefs — one size fits all. CM is presently considering two capacity plans for next year — level capacity and matching capacity with aggregate demand. The quarterly aggregate demand is shown below for the two plans. The labor standard per brief is .25 hour, hiring cost is $200 per worker hired, layoff cost is $200 per worker laid off, carrying cost for finished goods is $.60 per brief per year, and working days per quarter is 65.

Quarter	Aggregate Demand (Thousands of Briefs)
1	150
2	200
3	400
4	200

   The beginning inventory in the 1st quarter and the ending inventory in the 4th quarter is 37,500 briefs for the level capacity plan. The beginning inventory in the 1st quarter is zero for the matching plan. Which plan exhibits the lowest total incremental operating costs?

9. The Austin, Texas, plant of Computer Products Corporation (CPC) produces printers and floppy disk units for personal and small-business computers. Gerald Knox, the plant's production-planning director, is looking over next year's sales forecasts for these products and will be developing an aggregate capacity plan for the plant:

Product Line	Sales Forecasts (in Printers and Disk Units)			
	1st Quarter	2nd Quarter	3rd Quarter	4th Quarter
Printer	1,000	1,200	1,400	1,200
Floppy disk unit	2,000	2,400	1,800	1,700

   Ample machine capacity exists to produce the forecast. Each printer takes an average of 20 labor-hours and each floppy disk unit takes an average of 15 labor-hours.
   a. Compute the aggregate number of labor-hours in each quarter.
   b. If each worker works 520 hours per quarter, how many workers will be required at the Austin plant in each quarter?

10. In Problem 9, it costs $1,000 to hire a worker, and $500 to lay off a worker, and inventory carrying cost is $200 per printer and $100 per floppy disk unit (this means that if one printer were held in inventory for a year, it would cost $200 for finance charges, insurance, warehousing expense, etc.). CPC's Austin plant works the same

number of days in each quarter, 13 five-day weeks. Evaluate two aggregate plans for next year, level capacity and matching capacity with aggregate demand. Beginning inventory is zero printers and 450 floppy disk units in the level capacity plan and zero for both products in the matching capacity with aggregate demand plan.

11. The Sherman-Brown Chemical Company in the chapter has just discovered more current and accurate information. The new data are:

Information Item	*New Data*
Aggregate demand	No change
Labor standard	2.650 worker-hours per gallon
Working days per quarter	No change
Beginning inventory	Zero in matching plan, 5,000 gallons in level plan
Working hours per shift	No change
Maximum capacity	No change
Carrying cost	$4 per gallon per year
Hiring cost	$200 per worker hired
Layoff cost	$250 per worker laid off

Using this new data, evaluate the level capacity and matching capacity with aggregate demand alternatives of Sherman-Brown.

12. In Problem 1, two aggregate plans are now being evaluated by the Acme Engineering Company: level capacity and matching capacity with aggregate demand. It costs Acme $.30 for every dollar of sales on any type of bridge design backlogged (delayed for completion at a later date) for one quarter. If it costs Acme $500 to hire and train an engineer and $300 to lay off an engineer, and the beginning backlog in the first quarter is zero, which plan exhibits the least cost?

13. In Problem 11, the production department wants to consider another aggregate capacity plan with the new information—use a stable work force of 250 workers and overtime and inventory (beginning inventory is 5,000 gallons) as needed to meet demand. Overtime costs $5 per hour over and above straight-time pay, and beginning inventory is 5,000 gallons. All other information in Problem 11 remains the same.
    a. What is the annual incremental cost of the proposed aggregate capacity plan?
    b. Which plan do you prefer?
    c. Why?

Master Production Scheduling

14. The Coverup Company is a produce-to-stock firm that produces products used by typists to correct typing mistakes. Coverup develops master production schedules with 10-week planning horizons for its many products. One such product, Snowpac Correcting Fluid, has a beginning inventory of 1,400 cases, a constant weekly demand of 500 cases, a fixed production lot size of 2,000 cases, and a minimum safety stock of 500 cases. Prepare the MPS detailed computations that result in the production schedule for Snowpac under the assumption that ample production capacity exists.

15. The Texprint Company makes a line of computer printers for personal computers on a produce-to-order basis for other computer manufacturers. Each printer requires an average of 24 labor-hours, and the manufacturing plant uses a backlog of orders to allow a level capacity aggregate plan. This plan provides a weekly capacity of 5,000 labor hours. Texprint has prepared this 6-week MPS:

	Master Production Schedule for the Texprint Plant				
	Weekly Production (Printers)				
Product	*1*	*2*	*3*	*4*	*5*
Printers	100	200	200	250	280

a. Compute the actual labor-hours required at the Texprint plant in each week and for the total 5 weeks to produce the MPS (this is often referred to as *load*). Compare the load to the labor-hours capacity in each week and for the total 5 weeks (this is often referred to as *rough-cut capacity planning*).
b. Does enough production capacity exist to produce the MPS?
c. What changes in the MPS would you recommend?

16. Scanco Corporation manufactures a line of bar code scanners on a produce-to-order basis for other computer companies. Scanco manufactures three models of the scanners on the same final assembly line at the plant. The final assembly has 12,000 hours of weekly capacity. The 6-week MPS and the final assembly standard for each model are:

	Master Production Schedule for the Scanco Final Assembly						
	Final Assembly Standard	*Weekly Production (Scanners)*					
Product	*(Hours per Scanner)*	*1*	*2*	*3*	*4*	*5*	*6*
Micro	30	100	50	200	300	100	200
Macro	20	200	200	300	200	200	300
Portable	25	50	100	50	100	50	100

a. Compute the actual final assembly hours required at the Scanco plant in each week and for the total 6 weeks to produce the MPS (this is often referred to as *load*). Compare the load to the labor-hours capacity in each week and for the total 6 weeks (this is often referred to as rough-cut capacity planning).
b. Does enough production capacity exist to produce the MPS?
c. What changes to the MPS would you recommend?

17. The Los Angeles plant of Computer Products Corporation (CPC) is in the process of updating its master production schedule (MPS) for its products. The plant produces bar code scanners for sale to consumers and other manufacturers on a produce-to-stock basis. Bill Freeland, production planner at the plant, is now in the process of developing a MPS for bar code scanners for the next 6 weeks. He has assembled these estimates of demand for the scanners:

Bar Code	Weeks					
Scanner Demand	1	2	3	4	5	6
Customers (forecasts and orders)	500	1,000	500	200	700	1,000
Branch warehouses	200	300	400	500	300	200
Market research		50			10	
Production research	10					

The safety stock level (inventory cannot fall below the safety stock level), minimum lot size (at least the minimum lot size must be produced when production of the product occurs), and beginning inventory level for the bar code scanners are:

Product	Minimum Lot Sizes	Safety Stock	Beginning Inventory
Bar code scanner	1,500	400	1,120

Prepare a 6-week MPS for the bar code scanner. Assume that there is ample production capacity at the plant.

18. The Pharmy Company produces and markets three pharmaceutical products: Cremo (antacid), Dullo (aspirin), and Bendo (backache) on a produce-to-stock basis. The demands (in gross) for these products over the 8-week planning horizon are:

Product Demand	Weeks							
	1	2	3	4	5	6	7	8
Customers (Forecasts and Orders)								
Cremo	2,000	1,000	500	2,000	2,000	1,000	500	500
Dullo	4,000	2,000	2,000	6,000	8,000	5,000	4,000	4,000
Bendo	1,000	500	500	1,000	1,000	500	500	500
Branch Warehouses								
Cremo	1,000		1,000			2,000		
Dullo	1,000		2,000			3,000		
Bendo		1,000					500	
Market Research								
Cremo	500			500			500	
Dullo		500			500			500
Bendo			500			500		

The safety stock levels (inventory levels cannot fall below the safety stock level), minimum lot sizes (at least the minimum lot size must be produced when production of the product occurs), and beginning inventory levels for the products are:

Product	Minimum Lot Sizes (Gross)	Safety Stock (Gross)	Beginning Inventory (Gross)
Cremo	5,000	3,000	4,000
Dullo	8,000	5,000	4,000
Bendo	2,000	1,000	2,000

Prepare the next 8-week MPS for Pharmy. Assume that ample production capacity exists.

COMPUTER PROBLEMS/CASES

AGGREGATE PLANNING AT THE TRIPLE A PRODUCTS COMPANY

In Problem 2, the Triple A Products Company, the marketing department has informed the production department that a competitor has just introduced a new product that will effectively destroy the market for the A_1 product. Triple A is now trying to determine, in light of this new information, if level capacity or matching capacity with aggregate demand would be the best aggregate capacity plan. It costs Triple A $25 for every A_2 or A_3 product either backlogged or placed in inventory at the end of a quarter. Triple A begins the year with zero backlog and inventory. Each calendering machine operates only 75 hours per quarter, on the average, because of frequent repairs necessitated by corrosion in its mixing chamber. It costs $5,000 to either start up a calendering machine or shut one down whenever capacity is changed from quarter to quarter. It is Triple A's policy to fully utilize calendering machines whenever they are in service; in other words, partial use of a machine is not economical. It is also Triple A's policy, when demand exceeds production capacity, to satisfy the demand for the A_2 products within a quarter before the demand for the A_3 products is satisfied. When production capacity exceeds demand, the A_3 products are produced with the excess capacity.

Assignment

1. Compute the quarterly aggregate calendering machine hours capacity required to meet sales demand for the A_2 and A_3 products.
2. Compute the number of calendering machines required per quarter to meet sales demand for the A_2 and A_3 products.
3. Compute the amount of production above or below the sales demand for the level capacity plan, and compute its annual cost.
4. Using the matching capacity with aggregate demand plan, compute the annual cost of starting up and shutting down calendering machines.
5. Which plan do you prefer? Justify your preference with as many factors as possible.

AGGREGATE PLANNING AT COMPUTER PRODUCTS CORPORATION (CPC)

Charles Dallam, production scheduler at the Austin plant of Computer Products Corporation (CPC), is developing an aggregate production plan for the first two quarters of next year for producing XE2400 printers at the Austin plant. The marketing department has estimated that 700 of the XE2400's will need to be shipped to customers in the first quarter and 1,000 in the second quarter. It takes 10 hours of labor to produce each of the printers and only 8,000 hours of straight-time labor are available in each of the first and second quarters. Overtime labor can be used to produce the printers, but the plant has a policy that limits the amount of overtime to 10 percent of the straight-time labor available. Labor costs $10 per hour at straight-time and $15 per hour at overtime. If a printer is produced in the first quarter and shipped in the second quarter, the plant incurs a carrying cost of $100 per printer. How many printers should be produced on straight-time and overtime labor in each of the first and second quarters to minimize straight-time and overtime labor cost and carrying costs. The market requirements, the straight-time labor availability, and the overtime labor availability must be adhered to.

Assignment

1. Formulate this aggregate-planning problem as a linear programming problem. Formulate the objective function and constraint functions. Define the decision variables.

2. Solve this linear programming problem using the computer program in the *POM Computer Library* that accompanies this text. What is the solution, and what does the solution mean in terms of the original aggregate-planning problem?

AGGREGATE PLANNING AT THE HIWAY TRUCKING COMPANY

The Hiway Trucking Company hauls commercial freight in Maricopa County, Arizona. Hiway estimates the aggregate quarterly demand for next year at 5,000, 7,500, 9,500, and 5,000 ton-miles. Trucking equipment owned by the company, rented trucks, and subcontracting can be used to supply capacity to meet Hiway's aggregate demand:

Source of Capacity	Capacity of Each Source (Ton-Miles per Quarter)	Cost of Capacity (Per Ton-Mile)
Company trucks:		
Straight-time	0–4,000	$.25
Overtime	0–2,000	.30
Work force changes	0–1,000	.35
Rented trucks (includes drivers and freight handlers)	0–3,000	.40
Subcontracting	0–5,000	.42

Assignment

1. Formulate this aggregate-planning problem in a linear programming formulation and define the decision variables. In other words, write each decision variable and explain what one unit of the variable means. (*Hint:* There are 20 decision variables—5 sources of capacity for each quarter and one of these for each quarter—and 20 constraints—5 maximum sources of capacity for each quarter and one for each quarter.) Write the objective function. Write the aggregate demand constraints. Write the straight-time operation of company truck constraints. Write the overtime operation of company truck constraints. Write the operation of company trucks with work-force-changes constraints. Write the truck rental constraints. Write the subcontracting constraints.

2. To solve this problem, use the computer program in the *POM Computer Library* that accompanies this text. What is the aggregate plan? Evaluate the plan.

SELECTED BIBLIOGRAPHY

APICS Bibliography. 11th ed. Falls Church, VA: American Production and Inventory Control Society, 1987.

APICS Dictionary. 6th ed. Falls Church, VA: American Production and Inventory Control Society, 1987.

Berry, William L., T. G. Schmitt, and T. E. Vollman. "Capacity Planning Techniques for Manufacturing Control Systems: Information Requirements and Operational Features." *Journal of Operations Management* 3, no. 1(November 1982):13–25.

Berry, William L., Thomas E. Vollman, and D. Clay Whybark. *Master Production Scheduling: Principles and Practice.* Falls Church, VA: American Production and Inventory Control Society, 1979.

Bowman, E. H. "Production Planning by the Transportation Method of Linear Programming." *Journal of Operations Research Society* 4(February 1956):100–103.

Buffa, E. S. "Aggregate Planning for Production." *Business Horizons* 10(Fall 1967):87–97.

Chung, C. H., and L. Krajewski. "Planning Horizons for Master Production Scheduling." *Journal of Operations Management* 4, no. 4(August 1984).

Eisemann, K., and W. M. Young. "Study of a Textile Mill with the Aid of Linear Programming." *Management Technology* 1(January 1960):52–63.

Gallagher, G. R. "How to Develop a Realistic Master Schedule." *Management Review* (April 1980): 19–25.

Holt, Charles C., Franco Modigliani, John F. Muth, and Herbert A. Simon. *Planning Production, Inventories, and Work Force.* Englewood Cliffs, NJ: Prentice-Hall, 1960.

Journal of Production and Inventory Management. Many articles on aggregate planning and master production scheduling are found in this journal.

Mangiameli, P., and L. Krajewski. "The Effects of Workforce Strategies on Manufacturing Operations." *Journal of Operations Management* 3, no. 4(August 1983):183–196.

McLeavey, D. W., and S. L. Narasimham. *Production Planning and Inventory Control.* Boston: Allyn & Bacon, 1985.

Proud, John F. "Controlling the Master Schedule." *Production and Inventory Management* 22, no. 2 (Second Quarter 1981):78–90.

Schwarz, Leroy B., and Robert E. Johnson. "An Appraisal of the Empirical Performance of the Linear Decision Rule for Aggregate Planning." *Management Science* 24(April 1978):844–849.

Vollman, T. E., W. L. Berry, and D. C. Whybark. *Manufacturing Planning and Control Systems.* Homewood, IL: Richard D. Irwin, 1984.

Wight, Oliver W. *Production and Inventory Management in the Computer Age.* Boston: Cahners Books, 1974.

CHAPTER 10

INDEPENDENT DEMAND INVENTORY SYSTEMS

SETTING INVENTORY POLICIES AT AIRCO DIVISION

The meeting was held at the Airco Division headquarters in St. Louis, and all of the division's plant and warehouse managers, its vice president of operations, and its vice president of marketing were present. The corporate vice president and general manager of the division, Mr. Milligan, called the meeting to order and opened the discussion. Needless to say, the meeting was a command performance. Everyone was to be present so that an agreement could be reached on inventory policies for the products of the division. Mr. Milligan stated that corporate headquarters was insisting that inventory investment in the division be reduced, but that at the same time some customers had indicated in recent months that their orders could not be delivered immedi- ately because Airco's warehouses were out of stock. The vice president of marketing stated that the division had plenty of products in the warehouses but they were the wrong ones. Also, he felt that the division was cutting corners on the amount of safety stock in the warehouses. The vice president of operations stated that the reason wrong products were in the warehouses was that marketing forecasts were always wrong. He asked the vice president of marketing what percentage of the time the warehouses should be out of products when customer orders are received. The vice president of marketing replied that enough inventory of products should always be on hand to fill customers' orders when they are received.

As the previous account suggests, inventory policies are important enough that operations, marketing, and financial managers work together to reach agreement on these policies at the highest levels in many corporations. That there are conflicting views concerning inventory policies underscores the balance that must be struck among conflicting goals—reduce manufacturing costs, reduce inventory investment, and increase customer satisfaction. This chapter concerns the integration of these seemingly irreconcilable views in setting inventory policies.

We shall examine in this chapter the nature of inventories and the inner workings of inventory systems, build an understanding of the various approaches to the fundamental issues in inventory planning, and develop several techniques for analyzing inventory problems.

NATURE OF INVENTORIES

Central to the understanding of the nature of inventories is a discussion of the reasons for holding inventories, the behavior of independent demand inventory systems, and inventory costs.

WHY HOLD INVENTORIES?

There is little argument that certain levels of inventory are necessary in any business. The important issue is how much inventory to hold. First, let us consider the reasons for *not holding* high levels of inventory. There are four fundamental reasons for keeping inventory levels low:

1. It costs to insure, finance, store, and manage inventories.
2. Inventories are an asset, and larger inventories reduce return on investment.
3. Inventory represents a form of waste. Materials that are ordered and held before they are needed waste production capacity, holding costs, storage space, and human effort.
4. Large in-process inventories clog up production systems. Production costs and the amount of time it takes to produce and deliver customer orders are increased.

On the other hand, inventory levels that are too low can result in increased production costs, higher raw material costs, lost sales, and dissatisfied customers. Let us consider the need for each type of inventory: finished goods, in-process, and raw materials. Table 10.1 summarizes the reasons for holding these inventories.

Finished Goods Inventories

The uncertainties of both supply of and demand for finished goods cause managers to hold a stock of finished goods to act as a buffer to be used when demand is greater than anticipated or when supply is less than expected. *Buffer stocks* are usually more economical than placing emergency special orders for meeting customer orders for out-of-stock items.

TABLE 10.1   *Why Are Inventories Necessary?*

Type of Inventory	Reasons for Holding Inventory
Finished goods	1. It can be infeasible or uneconomical to produce products when demanded by customers. 2. Customer orders may not be allowed to be backlogged in some situations. 3. Level production that may result in lower production costs is allowed. 4. Products can be displayed to customers.
In-process	1. Processing steps can be uncoupled, allowing flexibility in planning each step. 2. Production rates of processing steps are unequal. 3. Producing and transporting in larger batches may reduce materials-handling and production costs.
Raw materials	1. Raw material cannot be obtained from suppliers exactly when needed for production schedules. 2. Quantity discounts can result from larger purchase quantities. 3. Reduced incoming freight costs and materials-handling costs can result from larger shipments.

Tradition in some industries allows the *backlogging* of customer orders, which means holding orders for later shipment. Backlogging of orders occurs routinely in produce-to-order firms. This is not to say that produce-to-order firms carry no finished goods inventory; they certainly do. But inventory levels are usually much lower because the function of buffer stocks tends to be replaced by backlogging of orders. Backlogs, when acceptable to customers or when backlogging is relatively inexpensive, even in produce-to-stock firms, encourage generally lower finished goods inventory levels.

As we discussed in Chapter 9, finished goods inventories often occur because of conscious decisions to level production output even when demand patterns are seasonal. In periods when demand is less than production, finished goods inventory increases. In periods when demand is greater than production, inventory declines. Level production output allows manufacturers to stabilize employment levels and reduce production costs. These cost savings are somewhat offset by increased costs of holding the inventories.

In factories that produce many products—as in the printing, household appliance, and clothing industries—machines must be changed over to each product that is to be produced. The cost of these machine changeovers can be excessive if only a few products are produced between machine changeovers. Figure 10.1 illustrates an example of such an operation. The average cost per unit declines as the length of production runs increases. These conditions lead managers to produce for extended

■■■

FIGURE 10.1 Cost per Unit versus Length of Production Run

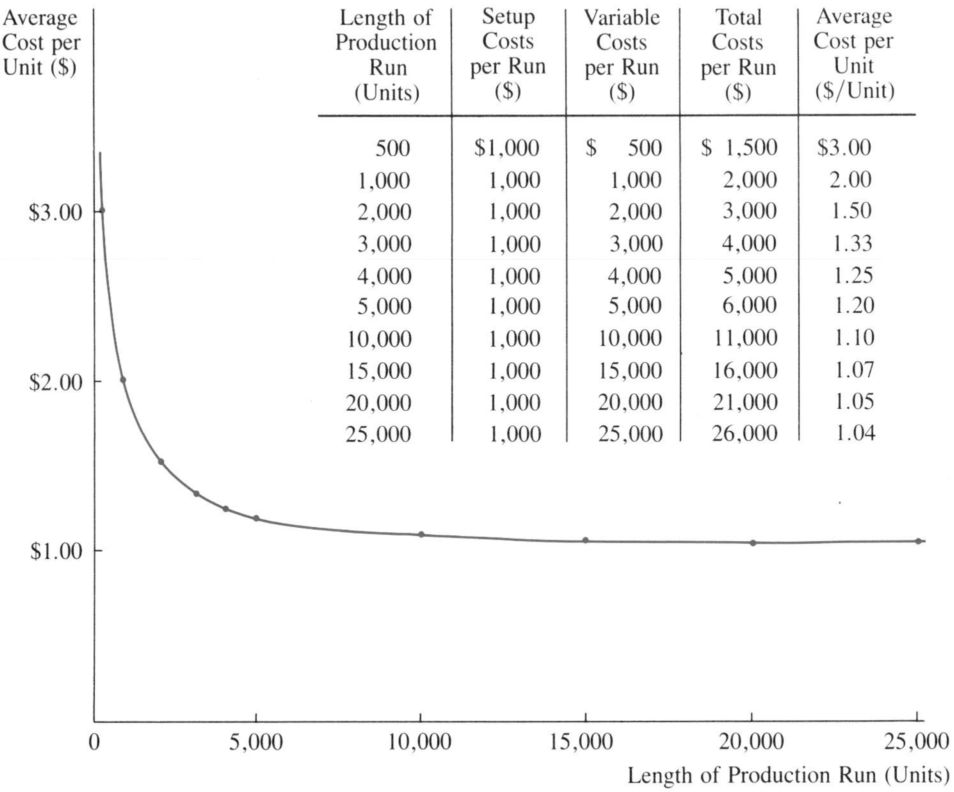

Length of Production Run (Units)	Setup Costs per Run ($)	Variable Costs per Run ($)	Total Costs per Run ($)	Average Cost per Unit ($/Unit)
500	$1,000	$ 500	$ 1,500	$3.00
1,000	1,000	1,000	2,000	2.00
2,000	1,000	2,000	3,000	1.50
3,000	1,000	3,000	4,000	1.33
4,000	1,000	4,000	5,000	1.25
5,000	1,000	5,000	6,000	1.20
10,000	1,000	10,000	11,000	1.10
15,000	1,000	15,000	16,000	1.07
20,000	1,000	20,000	21,000	1.05
25,000	1,000	25,000	26,000	1.04

Average Cost per Unit ($) plotted against *Length of Production Run (Units)*, with markers at $3.00, $2.00, $1.00 on the vertical axis and 0, 5,000, 10,000, 15,000, 20,000, 25,000 on the horizontal axis.

■■■

periods (long production runs) on one product; thus inventories of these products rise and fall as production switches from product to product.

In retailing and even in some manufacturing firms, finished goods inventories are kept in order to display products to customers. There is an old saying in retailing: "You can't sell from an empty wagon." Products must be displayed, and thus finished goods inventories are a fundamental fact of retailing.

In-Process Inventories

There is little in-process inventory in product-focused production systems. But in process-focused production, in-process inventories can be large because of the need to separate or uncouple successive processing steps. This uncoupling arrangement allows flexibility — the flexibility to continue operating even if one operation is idled because of mechanical breakdown, material shortage, or other delay, and flexibility in planning the activities of individual operations.

In process-focused production, in-process inventory inevitably builds up between successive processing steps because of the unequal production rates of the various operations. But the level of in-process inventory in these systems is also affected by two other factors: the number of batches of products that are started through the production system in each week, and the number of products in each batch. These two factors are issues that must be resolved as process-focused production is scheduled, and we shall discuss these issues in Chapter 12, Shop-Floor Planning and Control.

Raw Materials Inventories

The process of sensing the need for raw materials, ordering them from suppliers, monitoring their shipment, receiving and inspecting them, and moving them into production areas for use takes time and also involves some uncertainty. This uncertainty may justify carrying safety stock just in case materials arrive later than expected. Early arrivals of orders also cause raw materials inventories to climb.

Material requirements planning (MRP), as we shall see in Chapter 11, seeks to reduce raw materials inventories by more closely matching the inflow of materials with the expected usage rates of production. Even with the most successful MRP applications today, however, *perfect* meshing of raw materials inflows with outflows has proved impractical.

Materials are almost universally bought *in quantity.* These volume purchases have become standard operating procedures because of economics. Lower purchase prices, lower freight rates, and lower materials-handling costs motivate operations managers to buy materials in larger quantities. When these large batches of materials are received, a raw materials inventory is created because production does not use them instantaneously. Rather, they are used gradually, and the inventory levels decline until the next shipment is received.

We have shown that finished goods, in-process, and raw materials inventories are indispensable to the efficient and effective operation of production systems. Let us now turn to a discussion of how these inventory systems operate in practice.

BEHAVIOR OF INDEPENDENT DEMAND INVENTORY SYSTEMS

Two fundamental issues underlie all inventory planning:

1. How much to order of each material when orders are placed with either outside suppliers or production departments within organizations.
2. When to place the orders.

The determination of *order quantities,* sometimes also called *lot sizes,* and when to place these orders, called *order points,* determine in large measure the amount of materials in inventory at any point in time. The study of the *inventory cycle*— materials are ordered, received, used, and the process is repeated—uses a terminology all its own; refer to Table 10.2 for an understanding of the meanings of these terms.

●●

TABLE 10.2   Inventory Concepts and Terms

1. **Acquisition Cost (ac)**—The cost of purchasing or producing one unit of a material or product.
2. **Annual Acquisition Cost**—The total cost of either purchasing or producing a material for the entire year. Calculated by multiplying annual demand by acquisition cost per unit.
3. **Annual Carrying Cost**—The total cost of providing inventories for the entire year. Calculated for a material by multiplying average inventory level by carrying cost per unit per year.
4. **Annual Demand (D)**—The number of units of a material estimated to be demanded per year.
5. **Annual Ordering Cost**—The total cost of acquiring inventory replenishments for the entire year. Calculated for a material by multiplying the number of orders per year by the ordering cost per order.
6. **Backlogging**—The process of holding customer orders to be filled later when they cannot be shipped immediately because of stockouts.
7. **Carrying Cost (C)**—The cost of financing, warehousing, damaging or losing, and any other cost directly related to holding materials in inventory. Calculated by multiplying acquisition cost per unit by the estimated proportion of that cost attributed to carrying cost. Expressed in dollars per unit per year.
8. **Demand during Lead Time (DDLT)**—The number of units of a material demanded during the inventory replenishment process. The expected demand during lead time (EDDLT) is calculated by multiplying average demand per day by average lead time.
9. **Demand Rate (d)**—Also called the *usage rate*. The number of units demanded by customers or production departments per unit of time. Must be in the same units as the supply rate (p).
10. **Disbursement**—The act of physically removing a material from inventory. These transactions cause record-keeping adjustments that reduce inventory levels.
11. **Economic Order Quantity (EOQ)**—Also called *economic lot size* and *economic production quantity.* The quantity of materials

ordered at each point that minimizes the total annual stocking costs for a material in a fixed order quantity inventory system.
12. **Feasible EOQ**—In quantity discount problems, a computed EOQ is feasible if the EOQ can be purchased at the acquisition cost (ac) used to compute the EOQ. In other words, does the EOQ fit in the quantity range for the acquisition cost?
13. **Finished Goods Inventory**—The reservoir of products held for customer demand.
14. **Fixed Order Period System**—The system of inventory planning that takes physical counts of materials in inventory at equal fixed time intervals. Orders are placed at these equally spaced reviews for varying quantities of each material depending on inventory levels, upper inventory targets, and expected demand during lead time.
15. **Fixed Order Quantity System**—The system of inventory planning that places orders for a material when the inventory level falls to a preestablished critical level. These orders are for fixed quantities of each material.
16. **In-Process Inventory**—Also called *work in process.* Work in various stages of completion between the processing steps of the production system.
17. **Inventory Cycle**—The activities of sensing a need for ordering materials, placing an order, determining lead time for getting the material delivered, receiving the material, and using the material. This process is continuously repeated for a material and is thus cyclical.
18. **Inventory Level**—Amount of materials actually on hand in inventory that is ready for use.
19. **Inventory Planning**—All the management activities that result in stocking the right amount of each material. The principal concerns are order quantities, order points, and order periods.
20. **Lead Time (LT)**—The length of time required to replenish the inventory for a material from the time that a need for additional material is sensed until the new order for the material is in inventory and ready to use.
21. **Length of Production Run**—The number of units produced of a product at a processing step in the production system between

●●

━━

TABLE 10.2   (Continued)

machine changeovers.

22. **Level Production**—Stabilizing production output levels from time period to time period. Even though this plan tends to increase finished goods inventory levels during periods of low demand, this excess inventory tends to be dissipated during periods of high demand. Employment levels, materials flows, and machine schedules are levelized, resulting in reduced operating expenses.

23. **Material Requirements Planning (MRP)**— The management technique of developing a raw materials delivery schedule that approximately matches raw materials inflows with production's demand for materials.

24. **Optimal Order Period (T)**—Also called the *economic time interval* or *optimal time interval.* The time, in fractions of a year, between reviews of the status of a material that exactly balances annual ordering costs with annual carrying costs in a fixed order period inventory system.

25. **Order Point (OP)**—A point in time when an order is placed for a material in a fixed order period inventory system. In fixed order quantity systems, the order point refers to the preestablished inventory level that triggers a material order and is calculated by adding expected demand during lead time to safety stock.

26. **Order Quantity (Q)**—The quantity of a material ordered each time inventory is replenished. Q is constant in fixed order quantity systems and variable in fixed order period systems.

27. **Ordering Cost (S)**—The average cost of each inventory replenishment for a material. It includes such costs as those of processing purchasing requisitions, purchase orders, machine changeovers, postage, telephone calls, and receiving.

28. **Produce-to-Order**—Production systems are said to produce to order when production is not begun until customers' orders are in hand.

29. **Produce-to-Stock**—Production systems are said to produce to stock when production proceeds and standardized products are placed in finished goods inventory before customers' orders are received.

30. **Quantity Discount**—The reduction of purchase price if a raw material is ordered in greater quantities. *Price breaks* are those quantities where price per unit changes.

31. **Raw Materials Inventory**—The reservoir of raw materials held in warehouses until demanded by production or operations.

32. **Replenishment**—The process of adding materials to inventory. It includes sensing the need for an order of materials, placing the order, producing the order, and shipping and receiving the order.

33. **Safety Stock**—Also called *buffer stock.* Additional quantity of a material held in inventory to be used in time periods when demand is greater than expected or supply is less than expected.

34. **Setup Cost**—Also called *changeover cost.* The cost of changing a processing step in a production system over from one product to another.

35. **Stockout**—The reduction of the usable inventory level for a material to zero.

36. **Stockout Cost**—The cost of stockouts. It includes such costs as profits forgone through lost sales, cost of reclaiming disappointed customers, special expediting, special handling of backlogged orders, and additional production costs.

37. **Supply Rate (p)**—Also called *production rate.* The number of units per unit of time of a material supplied to inventory if delivered gradually. Must be in the same units as demand rate (d).

38. **Total Annual Material Cost (TMC)**—The total of annual acquisition cost and total annual stocking cost for a material.

39. **Total Annual Stocking Cost (TSC)**—The total cost of maintaining a material in inventory for one year. Includes annual carrying cost and annual ordering cost, but not annual acquisition cost.

40. **Two-Bin System**—A simple fixed order quantity system that uses two bins to physically hold a material in inventory. Material in the small bin is used only during lead time. Orders are triggered when the large bin is empty, and both are filled when inventory is replenished.

Inventories may contain materials that have either *dependent* or *independent demands.* In independent demand inventories, the demand for an item carried in inventory is independent of the demand for any other item carried in inventory. Examples of independent demand inventories are finished goods inventories and parts that are shipped as end items to customers for spare parts or repair. Demands for these items are based on actual customer orders or forecasts of what will be demanded. The remainder of this chapter is aimed at the order quantity and order point decisions of independent demand inventories. Dependent demand inventories contain items whose demand depends on the demands for other items also held in inventory. For example, the demand for a calculator case and shipping container, which are components, are both dependent on the demand for the calculator, a finished good. Typically, the demand for raw materials and components can be calculated if we know the demand for the finished goods that these materials go into. Order quantity and order point decisions for dependent demand inventories are therefore distinctly different from those of independent demand inventories; these decisions will be treated in Chapter 11, Resource Requirements Planning Systems.

Two simple models demonstrate the behavior of independent demand inventories: fixed order quantity system and fixed order period system.

Fixed order quantity systems place orders for the same quantity of a material in each inventory cycle. Order quantity (Q) is a constant. However, *when* the order is placed is allowed to vary. Figure 10.2 demonstrates how these systems operate.

Inventories fall until a critical inventory level (OP) triggers an order. The order point (OP) that triggers orders is determined by estimating expected usage during lead time plus safety stock. When the inventory is replenished (R_1, an order is received), the fixed order quantity (Q_1) is placed in inventory. Note that $Q_1 = Q_2 = Q_3$, but that the elapsed times between orders (T) are not usually equal.

The *two-bin system* of inventory control is a simple application of fixed order quantity systems. In the two-bin system each material has two bins that physically hold the material in the warehouse. As the material is used, material is withdrawn from a large bin until the large bin is empty. At the bottom of the large bin is a preprinted requisition for another order of the material. This replenishment requisition is sent out, and in the meantime, materials are used out of the small bin, which holds just enough material to last until the next inventory replenishment. The small bin contains the expected demand during lead time and safety stock. When the inventory is replenished, a requisition is placed in the bottom of the large bin, both bins are filled, and the cycle is repeated.

In fixed order quantity systems we usually assume perpetual inventory accounting. In *perpetual inventory accounting* additions and subtractions from inventory records are made at the time that materials are added to or removed from inventory. With this method we can determine the amount of a material in inventory at any point in time by looking at its *inventory record,* a display of all of the inventory transactions that have affected that material. Such displays today are usually a part of the company's computer system and appear on a computer terminal display when called. Visualize how a fixed order quantity system would use the inventory record: The computer could be programmed to identify materials whose inventory levels

FIGURE 10.2   *Fixed Order Quantity System*

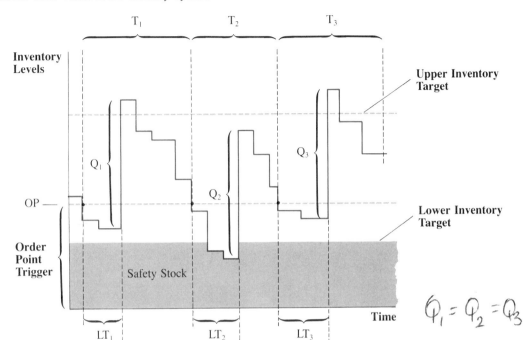

have fallen to their critical levels, the fixed order quantities could be printed on computer printouts, or orders could even be automatically prepared.

Fixed order period systems review inventory levels at fixed time intervals, and orders are placed for enough material to bring inventory levels back up to some predetermined level. Figure 10.3 demonstrates how these systems operate.

In Figure 10.3 orders are placed at equal time intervals so that $T_1 = T_2 = T_3$. The amount ordered in each cycle (Q_1, Q_2, and Q_3) is based on the inventory levels at the time of review, the upper inventory target including safety stock, and the expected demand during lead time. If at the time of review the inventory is relatively low, as at OP_1, larger order quantities (Q_1) are placed. If, on the other hand, inventories are high when reviewed, as at OP_2, smaller quantities (Q_2) are ordered.

In this inventory system, order quantities can be unequal but order intervals are equal ($T_1 = T_2 = T_3$). In most real situations lead times and demand patterns are usually relatively uncertain. Note that once the order interval has been set, inventory level need not be monitored until the next review (OP_1, OP_2, or OP_3). Between these reviews the uncertainties of both demand and lead time combine to make this system more subject to stockouts than the fixed order quantity system. This is because the

FIGURE 10.3 Fixed Order Period System

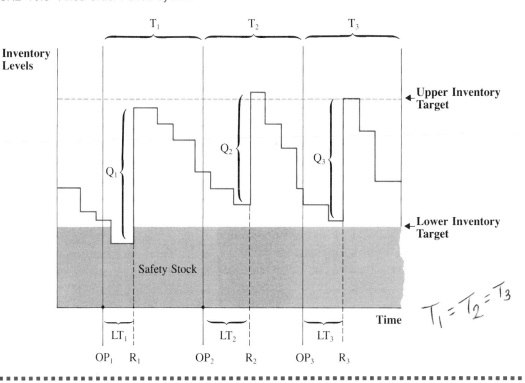

fixed order quantity system bases its order points on estimates of demand only during the lead time period, whereas the fixed order period system bases its order points on estimates of demand during the entire period between reviews. The fixed order period system therefore usually requires more safety stock to accommodate this increased risk of stockouts.

The fixed order period system lends itself to inventories where it is more desirable to physically count inventory on a regular periodic basis, as in some retail stores. In these situations, particularly with those goods that are in displays where perpetual inventory accounting may not be feasible, periodic counts of materials on hand may be the most practical system to use and the fixed order period system would be appropriate.

Both fixed order quantity and fixed order period systems have their strengths, and we observe both of these systems in practice. However, *hybrids* of these systems also exist. For example, some systems use inventory levels to trigger orders, as in fixed order quantity systems; but variable order quantities are based on inventory levels and other factors.

INVENTORY COSTS

How much should we order? The answer to this question is a function of the costs of ordering too much and the costs of ordering too little. The costs of ordering too much are those costs of carrying excessive quantities of materials in inventory for extended periods. These costs are *carrying costs,* and they include insurance, interest charges for financing the inventories, warehouse rental, utilities, taxes, lost and damaged materials, obsolescence, and any other out-of-pocket (cash actually expended) expense associated with holding materials in warehouses. Carrying costs are expressed either as a percentage of cost of a material—usually between 15 and 35 percent—or as the actual dollar amount to carry a material in inventory for a year.

On the other hand, when too few materials are ordered, excessive annual *ordering costs* and *stockout costs* are encountered. Ordering costs are all of the out-of-pocket costs associated with an inventory cycle—typing the purchase order, any expediting required, postage, any other purchasing and warehousing labor for placing each order, setup costs if produced in-house, record keeping, and receiving the order into the warehouse. Ordering costs are expressed as dollars per order.

Stockout costs are those costs directly attributed to running out of stock. A major part of these costs can be the lost profits of customer orders that cannot be filled. If the customers agree to backlogging of their orders—that is, holding the orders to be filled later—additional costs can result from extra paperwork, special handling of orders, and expediting. When raw materials arrive late and stockouts occur, production may have to shut down operations or take costly counteractions to avoid production delays. Additional sales costs can result when customers must be reclaimed after disappointments from unfilled orders.

Conceptually, managers order materials for raw materials and finished goods inventories so that the cost of ordering too few materials is balanced against the cost of ordering too many materials on each order. Figure 10.4 demonstrates that annual carrying costs climb as the order quantities rise. This results from the direct relationship between order quantity and average inventory level: As order quantities increase, so do average inventory levels. On the other hand, as order quantities increase, the number of orders per year declines and thus the annual ordering costs fall. Similarly, as order quantities increase, the number of times that inventory is replenished per year declines; therefore the number of stockouts that are likely to occur declines.

As Figure 10.4 shows, when the annual carrying cost curve is added to the annual ordering and stockout cost curve, an annual total stocking cost curve results. This total cost curve demonstrates an important concept in inventory planning: There exists for every material held in raw materials and finished goods inventories an optimal order quantity where total annual stocking costs are at a minimum. In this figure the optimal order quantity, traditionally called the *economic order quantity* (EOQ), appears to be approximately 524 units per order.

This concept is useful to operations managers, particularly if the fixed order quantity system is used.

FIGURE 10.4   *Balancing Carrying Costs against Ordering and Stockout Costs*

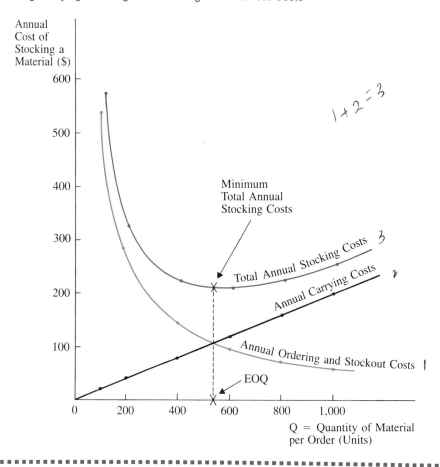

FIXED ORDER QUANTITY SYSTEMS

Two decisions are essential to fixed order quantity systems: order quantities and order points.

DETERMINING ORDER QUANTITIES

When operations managers must decide the quantity of a material to order in fixed order quantity systems, no single formula applies to all situations. Each situation requires analysis based on the characteristics of that particular inventory system. We shall develop here estimates of optimal order quantities for three inventory models: Model I—basic economic order quantity (EOQ), Model II—EOQ with gradual deliveries, and Model III—EOQ with quantity discounts.

TABLE 10.3   *Model I—Basic Economic Order Quantity (EOQ)*

Assumptions
1. Annual demand, carrying cost, and ordering cost for a material can be estimated.
2. Average inventory level for a material is order quantity divided by 2. This implicitly assumes that no safety stock is utilized, orders are received all at once, materials are used at a uniform rate, and materials are entirely used up when the next order arrives.
3. There are no stockout costs.
4. Quantity discounts do not exist.

Variable Definitions
  D = annual demand for a material (units per year)*
  Q = quantity of material ordered at each order point (units per order)
  C = cost of carrying one unit in inventory for one year (dollars per unit per year)*
  S = average cost of completing an order for a material (dollars per order)
TSC = total annual stocking costs for a material (dollars per year)

Cost Formulas

$$\text{Annual carrying cost} = \text{Average inventory level} \times \text{Carrying cost} = (Q/2)C$$

$$\text{Annual ordering cost} = \text{Orders per year} \times \text{Ordering cost} = (D/Q)S$$

$$\text{Total annual stocking cost (TSC)} = \text{Annual carrying cost} + \text{Annual ordering cost}$$

$$= (Q/2)C + (D/Q)S$$

Derivation of the Economic Order Quantity Formula
The optimal order quantity is found by setting the derivative of TSC with respect to Q equal to zero and solving for Q:

1. The formula for TSC is: $\qquad\qquad\qquad\qquad\qquad$ $TSC = (Q/2)C + (D/Q)S$
2. The derivative of TSC with respect to Q is: $\qquad$ $d(TSC)/d(Q) = C/2 + (-DS/Q^2)$
3. Set the derivative of TSC equal to zero and solve for Q:

$$C/2 + (-DS/Q^2) = 0$$
$$-DS/Q^2 = -C/2$$
$$Q^2 = 2DS/C$$

$$Q = \sqrt{2DS/C}$$

4. The EOQ is therefore: $\qquad$ *new* Q $\qquad$ $EOQ = \sqrt{2DS/C}$

* Note: In cases where a material has a seasonal demand, D could represent quarterly demand and C would represent per-unit carrying cost for one quarter. Thus the order policies would vary from quarter to quarter as the seasonal demand varies.

Model I—Basic Economic Order Quantity (EOQ)

Table 10.3 describes the assumptions, variable definitions, cost formulas, and derivation of the EOQ formula for Model I. The key question in applying this model is: Do the assumptions fit our inventory situation, or are the deviations from these assumptions only minor?

FIGURE 10.5 Average Inventory Level in Model I

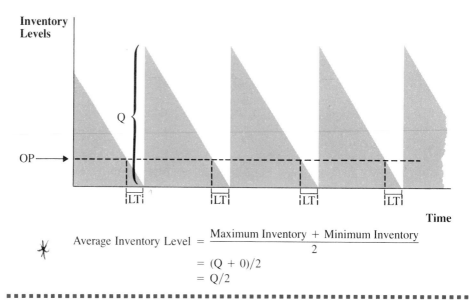

$$\text{Average Inventory Level} = \frac{\text{Maximum Inventory} + \text{Minimum Inventory}}{2}$$
$$= (Q + 0)/2$$
$$= Q/2$$

Three of these assumptions are critical: (1) Annual demand can be estimated. (2) Average inventory level equals order quantity divided by 2. (3) Quantity discounts do not exist. The number of units of a material expected to be demanded per year may be subject to great uncertainty, particularly if we have little experience on which to base our estimate. New products, products experiencing rapid growth or decline, and raw materials to support these highly variable products provide challenges to forecasters.

The demand for some materials and products is very stable, and the estimates of their demand tend to be very accurate. The resulting order quantities for these materials also tend to be very precise. What about the demand for those materials that we are not too sure about? The order quantity estimates will simply be less precise.

As demonstrated in Figure 10.5, an average inventory of $Q/2$ implies that there is no safety stock, orders are received all at once, materials are used at a uniform rate, and materials are entirely used up when the next order arrives. The presence of all these characteristics is rare in practice; but in spite of minor deviations, $Q/2$ may still be a reasonable estimate of average inventory levels for some materials. A quick check of the stock records of a material will either confirm or deny the validity of $Q/2$ as an estimate of average inventory levels. If another measure of average inventory levels is found to be a more precise estimate, this new value could be substituted for $Q/2$ in the cost formulas, thus resulting in a slightly different EOQ formula.

Example 10.1 applies the cost and EOQ formulas to one material purchased by a plumbing supply company. The simplicity of estimating an optimal order quantity, the present total annual stocking cost with present order quantity policy, and the new annual stocking cost by following the EOQ as a policy is demonstrated.

EXAMPLE 10.1   *Use of Model I in a Plumbing Supply Company*

The Call-Us Plumbing Supply Company stocks thousands of plumbing items sold to regional plumbers, contractors, and retailers. Mr. Swartz, the firm's general manager, wonders how much money could be saved annually if EOQ were used instead of the firm's present rules of thumb. He instructs Mary Ann Church, an inventory analyst, to conduct an analysis of one material only (Material #3925, a brass valve) to see if significant savings might result from using the EOQ. Mary Ann develops the following estimates from accounting information: $D =$ 10,000 valves per year, $Q = 400$ valves per order (present order quantity), $C = \$.40$ per valve per year, and $S = \$5.50$ per order.

Solution

1. Mary Ann calculates the present total annual stocking costs:

$$\text{TSC}_1 = (Q/2)C + (D/Q)S = \left(\frac{400}{2}\right).4 + \left(\frac{10,000}{400}\right)5.5 = 80 + 137.50 = \$217.50$$

2. The EOQ is calculated:

$$\text{EOQ} = \sqrt{\frac{2DS}{C}} = \sqrt{\frac{2(10,000)(5.5)}{.4}} = \sqrt{275,000} = 524.4 \text{ valves}$$

3. The total annual stocking costs if EOQ were employed are calculated:

$$\text{TSC}_2 = (Q/2)C + (D/Q)S = \left(\frac{524.4}{2}\right).4 + \left(\frac{10,000}{524.4}\right)5.5$$
$$= 104.88 + 104.88 = \$209.76$$

4. The estimated annual savings in stocking costs is calculated:

Savings $= \text{TSC}_1 - \text{TSC}_2 = 217.50 - 209.76 = \$7.74$

5. Mary Ann concludes that if the annual savings on this one material were applied to the thousands of items in inventory, the savings from EOQ would be significant.

Model II — EOQ with Gradual Deliveries
Model II, EOQ with gradual deliveries, offers only one slight modification to Model I: Orders are assumed to be delivered at a uniform rate rather than all at once. For example, an order for 1,000 units might be delivered 200 units per day over a 5-day period. Table 10.4 presents the assumptions, variable definitions, cost formulas, and derivation of the EOQ formula for Model II.

··

TABLE 10.4   Model II — EOQ with Gradual Deliveries

Assumptions
1. Annual demand, carrying cost, and ordering cost for a material can be estimated.
2. No safety stock is utilized, materials are supplied at a uniform rate (p) and used at a uniform rate (d), and materials are entirely used up when the next order begins to arrive.
3. There are no stockout costs.
4. Quantity discounts do not exist.
5. Supply rate (p) is greater than usage rate (d). $p > d$

Variable Definitions
All of the definitions in Model I apply also to Model II.* Additionally:

$$d = \text{rate at which units are used out of inventory (units per time period)}$$

$$p = \text{rate at which units are supplied to inventory (same units as d)}$$

Cost Formulas

Maximum inventory level = Inventory buildup rate × Period of delivery
$$= (p - d)(Q/p)$$

Minimum inventory level = 0

Average inventory level = ½(Maximum inventory level + Minimum inventory level)
$$= \tfrac{1}{2}[(p - d)(Q/p) + 0] = (Q/2)[(p - d)/p]$$

Annual carrying cost = Average inventory level × Carrying cost
$$= (Q/2)[(p - d)/p]C$$

Annual ordering cost = Orders per year × Ordering cost = (D/Q)S

Total annual stocking cost (TSC) = Annual carrying cost × Annual ordering cost
$$= (Q/2)[(p - d)/p]C + (D/Q)S$$

Derivation of the Economic Order Quantity Formula
Again, as in Model I, set the derivative of TSC with respect to Q equal to zero and solve for Q:

1. The formula for TSC is: $TSC = (Q/2)[(p - d)/p]C + (D/Q)S$
2. The derivative of TSC with respect to Q is: $d(TSC)/d(Q) = [(p - d)/2p]C - DS/Q^2$
3. Set the derivative of TSC equal to zero and solve for Q:

$$[(p - d)/2p]C - DS/Q^2 = 0$$
$$Q^2 = (2DS/C)[p/(p - d)]$$

$$Q = \sqrt{(2DS/C)[p/(p - d)]}$$

4. The EOQ is therefore: $EOQ = \sqrt{(2DS/C)[p/(p - d)]}$

■■

* Note: See the note to Table 10.3.

FIGURE 10.6   Average Inventory Level in Model II

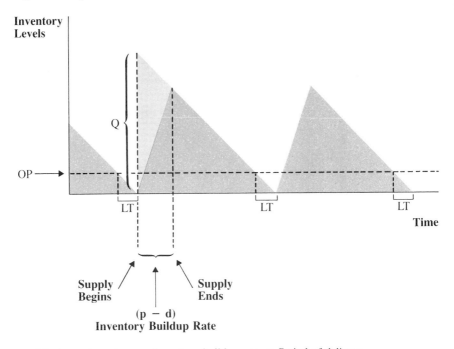

$$\text{Maximum inventory} = \text{Inventory buildup rate} \times \text{Period of delivery}$$
$$= (p - d)(Q/p)$$
$$\text{Minimum inventory} = 0$$
$$\text{Average inventory level} = \frac{\text{Maximum inventory} + \text{Minimum inventory}}{2}$$
$$= \tfrac{1}{2}[(p - d)(Q/p) + 0]$$
$$= Q/2[(p - d)/p]$$

Figure 10.6 shows that orders are received at a uniform rate (p) during the early part of the inventory cycle and used at a uniform rate (d) throughout the cycle. Inventory levels build at a rate of (p − d) during delivery and never reach the level Q as in Model I. Visualize a water tank with water flowing in at the top through a spigot at a rate of p and flowing out at the bottom through a spigot at a rate of d. The water level in the tank would rise at a rate of (p − d), if p is greater than d, while the top spigot is open. The maximum water level would be determined by multiplying the buildup rate (p − d, in gallons per hour) by the time period the top spigot is open

(Q/p, in hours). After the entire desired quantity of water (Q) is delivered, the top spigot is closed and the tank continues to empty at a rate of d. This analogy describes the dynamics of inventory levels when orders of materials are delivered gradually.

When materials are delivered gradually to either finished goods or raw materials inventories, two important developments result — larger order quantities and lower total annual stocking costs. Example 10.2 demonstrates these developments. Work through this example and compare the results to those of Example 10.1. Note that EOQ increases from 524.40 units to 642.26 units per order and TSC decreases

EXAMPLE 10.2   *Use of Model II in a Plumbing Supply Company*

Mr. Swartz of the Call-Us Plumbing Supply Company wonders what effect on annual stocking costs will result if he allows his supplier to deliver the #3925 valve orders gradually, as the supplier has proposed, rather than all at once. Mary Ann Church analyzes this request and develops these estimates: $D = 10,000$ valves per year, $C = \$.40$ per valve per year, $S = \$5.50$ per order, $d = 40$ valves per day (10,000 valves per year $\div$ 250 working days), and $p = 120$ valves per day.

Solution

1. Mary Ann calculates the EOQ:

$$EOQ = \sqrt{\frac{2DS}{C}\left(\frac{p}{p-d}\right)} = \sqrt{\frac{2(10,000)(5.5)}{.4}\left(\frac{120}{120-40}\right)} = 642.26 \text{ valves}$$

2. The new total annual stocking costs are calculated:

$$TSC_3 = (Q/2)\left(\frac{p-d}{p}\right)C + (D/Q)S = \frac{642.26}{2}\left(\frac{120-40}{120}\right).4 + \left(\frac{10,000}{642.26}\right)5.5$$

$$= 85.63 + 85.63 = \$171.26 \text{ per year}$$

3. The EOQ and total annual stocking costs from Example 10.1, when the #3925 valves were delivered all at once, were EOQ $= 524.4$ and $TSC_2 = \$209.76$.

4. The estimated savings to the plumbing supply company for allowing its supplier to deliver the #3925 valve gradually are calculated:

$$Savings = TSC_2 - TSC_3 = 209.76 - 171.26 = \$38.50 \text{ per year}$$

5. Mary Ann concludes that the supplier should be allowed to deliver the #3925 valves gradually.

from \$209.76 to \$171.26 per year as deliveries switch from orders received all at once in Example 10.1 to gradual deliveries of orders in Example 10.2.

Model II is particularly useful in situations where products must be ordered from a production department within the organization. Production usually occurs at a specific rate greater than demand ($p > d$) and finished products are typically transferred gradually from production to finished goods inventory as they are produced. Therefore this model is well suited for planning length of production runs or lot sizes for in-house production of products. Certain high-volume raw materials that are received in a specific shipping schedule arrangement often also fit the assumptions of Model II.

✗ Model III — EOQ with Quantity Discounts

Suppliers may offer their goods at lower unit prices if larger quantities are ordered. This practice is referred to as *quantity discounting* and occurs because larger order quantities are less expensive to produce and ship. A critical concern in most decisions of order quantities is ordering enough material on each order to qualify for the best price possible, but not buying so much that carrying costs consume the savings in purchase costs. Model III attempts to achieve this objective. The quantity purchased does not necessarily have to be the EOQ amount as formulated from Model I or Model II; rather, it is the quantity that minimizes the sum of annual carrying, ordering, and acquisition costs. Table 10.5 lists the assumptions, variable definitions, formulas, and procedures of this model.

Model III utilizes either Model I or Model II TSC and EOQ formulas. If deliveries of orders occur all at once, Model I formulas are used. If deliveries are gradual, Model II formulas are used. It is particularly important to recognize that the key quantities to consider are any feasible EOQ (is the EOQ in the quantity range for its price?) and the quantity at any price break with lower prices. Table 10.6 gives four different quantity-discount/order-quantity decision situations to demonstrate the procedures for identifying the quantities to be investigated by comparing the total annual material costs (TMC).

Example 10.3 applies Model III to our old friends at the plumbing supply company. In this example the manager must decide both the quantity and method of delivery — either gradual deliveries or orders received all at once — for one material. Follow through the steps of this example. It demonstrates both the procedures of Model III and the advantages of gradual deliveries.

Quantity discounts, when used with the EOQ formulas, begin to build more realism into these methods of analysis. Although some restrictive assumptions are still present in Model III, enough real inventory decisions approach the assumptions of this model to make it a valuable technique in POM. We have now estimated order quantities for materials in fixed order quantity inventory systems that operate under various assumptions. Let us now turn to the other fundamental issue in inventory planning — when to place the order.

•••

TABLE 10.5 *Model III—EOQ with Quantity Discounts*

Assumptions
1. Annual demand, carrying cost, and ordering cost for a material can be estimated.
2. Average inventory levels can be estimated at either:

   $Q/2$—if the assumptions of Model I prevail: no safety stock, orders are received all at once, materials are used at a uniform rate, and materials are entirely used up when the next order arrives.

   $Q/2[(p - d)/p]$—if the assumptions of Model II prevail: no safety stock, materials are supplied at a uniform rate (p) and used at a uniform rate (d), and materials are entirely used up when the next order arrives.

3. There are no stockout costs.
4. Quantity discounts do exist. As larger quantities are ordered, price breaks apply to all units ordered.

Variable Definitions
All the definitions in previous models apply to Model III.* Additionally:

TMC = total annual material costs (dollars per year)

ac = acquisition cost of either purchasing or producing one unit of a material (dollars per unit)

Formulas
The EOQ and TSC formulas from either Model I or Model II are applied to Model III, depending on which assumptions best fit the inventory situation.

Annual acquisition costs = Annual demand × Acquisition cost = (D)ac

Total annual material costs (TMC) = Total annual stocking costs
+ Annual acquisition cost = TSC + (D)ac

Model I—Orders Delivered All at One Time	*Model II—Gradual Deliveries*
EOQ = $\sqrt{2DS/C}$	EOQ = $\sqrt{(2DS/C)[p/(p - d)]}$
TMC = $(Q/2)C + (D/Q)S + (D)ac$	TMC = $(Q/2)[(p - d)/p]C + (D/Q)S + (D)ac$

Procedures
1. Compute the EOQ using each of the sales prices. Note that C is usually a function of sales price. For example, C may be defined as 20 percent of sales price. Therefore EOQ will change as C and ac change.
2. Determine which EOQ from Step 1 above is feasible. In other words, is the computed EOQ in the quantity range for its price?
3. The total annual material cost (TMC) is computed for the feasible EOQ and the quantity at any price break with lower sales prices.
4. The order quantity with the lowest total annual material cost (TMC) is the economic order quantity for the material.

•••

* Note: See the note to Table 10.3.

TABLE 10.6   Identifying Key Quantities to Investigate When Quantity Discounts Exist

Quantities	Prices	Feasible EOQ	Key Quantities to Investigate	Quantities	Prices	Feasible EOQ	Key Quantities to Investigate
0 – 399	$ 2.20			0 – 499	$ 6.95		
400 – 699	2.00	524.4	524.4*	500 – 999	6.50		
700 +	1.80		700*	1,000 – 1,999	6.25	1,700	1,700
				2,000 +	6.10		2,000
0 – 699	$43.50	590	590	0 – 599	$10.50		
700 – 1,499	36.95		700	600 – 749	7.50		
1,500 +	35.50		1,500	750 – 999	7.25		
				1,000 +	7.15	1,200	1,200

* See Example 10.3 and Figure 10.7.

EXAMPLE 10.3   EOQ with Quantity Discounts in a Plumbing Supply Company

The supplier of the #3925 valve has offered Mr. Swartz quantity discounts if he will purchase more than his present order quantities. The new volumes and prices are:

Range of Order Quantities	Acquisition Cost per Valve (ac)
0 – 399	$2.20
400 – 699	2.00
700 +	1.80

Mr. Swartz asks Mary Ann Church to investigate the new prices under two sets of assumptions: Orders are received all at once or deliveries are gradual.

Solution

Orders Received All at Once

1. Mary Ann has developed these estimates: $D = 10,000$ valves per year, $C = .2(ac)$ dollars per valve per year, and $S = \$5.50$ per order.

FIGURE 10.7 *Quantity Discount TMC Curves*

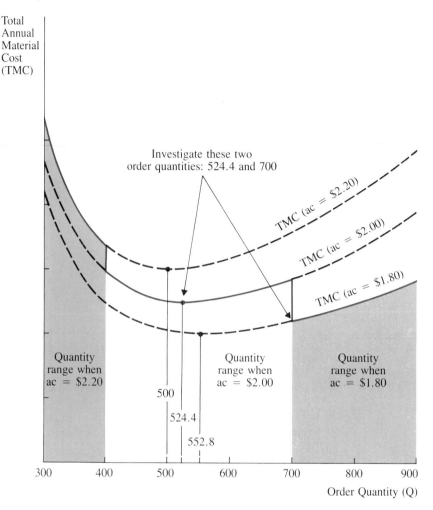

2. The EOQs are computed for each of the acquisition costs:

$$EOQ_{2.20} = \sqrt{\frac{2DS}{C}} = \sqrt{\frac{2(10,000)(5.5)}{.2(2.2)}} = 500$$

$$EOQ_{2.00} = \sqrt{\frac{2DS}{C}} = \sqrt{\frac{2(10,000)(5.5)}{.2(2.0)}} = 524.4$$

$$EOQ_{1.80} = \sqrt{\frac{2DS}{C}} = \sqrt{\frac{2(10,000)(5.5)}{.2(1.8)}} = 552.8$$

3. Mary Ann graphs the TMC for each acquisition cost (see Figure 10.7). For instance, $TMC_{2.2}$ can be graphed by substituting several values for Q in this TMC formula:

$$TMC = \left(\frac{Q}{2}\right)C + \left(\frac{D}{Q}\right)S + (D)ac$$

$$TMC_{2.2} = \left(\frac{Q}{2}\right)(2.2)(.2) + \left(\frac{10,000}{Q}\right)5.5 + (10,000)2.2$$

Mary Ann notes that only $EOQ_{2.00}$ is feasible because 524.4 valves per order can be purchased at \$2.00 per valve. The TMC at two quantities is therefore investigated: 524.4 and 700 units per order:

$$Q = 524.4: \quad TMC = \left(\frac{Q}{2}\right)C + \left(\frac{D}{Q}\right)S + (D)ac$$

$$= \left(\frac{524.4}{2}\right).4 + \left(\frac{10,000}{524.4}\right)5.5 + (10,000)2$$

$$= 104.88 + 104.88 + 20,000 = \$20,209.76 \text{ per year}$$

$$Q = 700: \quad TMC = \left(\frac{Q}{2}\right)C + \left(\frac{D}{Q}\right)S + (D)ac$$

$$= \left(\frac{700}{2}\right)(.2 \times 1.8) + \left(\frac{10,000}{700}\right)5.5 + (10,000)1.8$$

$$= 126.00 + 78.57 + 18,000 = \$18,204.57 \text{ per year}$$

4. Mary Ann concludes that if orders are delivered all at once, 700 valves should be ordered at each inventory replenishment.

Gradual Deliveries

1. Mary Ann has developed these estimates: $D = 10,000$ valves per year, $S = \$5.50$ per order, $C = .2$ (ac) dollars per valve per year, $p = 120$ valves per day, and $d = 40$ valves per day.

2. The EOQs are now computed:

$$EOQ_{2.20} = \sqrt{\frac{2DS}{C}\left(\frac{p}{p-d}\right)} = \sqrt{\frac{2(10,000)(5.5)}{.2(2.2)}\left(\frac{120}{120-40}\right)} = 612.4$$

$$EOQ_{2.00} = \sqrt{\frac{2DS}{C}\left(\frac{p}{p-d}\right)} = \sqrt{\frac{2(10,000)(5.5)}{.2(2.0)}\left(\frac{120}{120-40}\right)} = 642.3$$

$$EOQ_{1.80} = \sqrt{\frac{2DS}{C}\left(\frac{p}{p-d}\right)} = \sqrt{\frac{2(10,000)(5.5)}{.2(1.8)}\left(\frac{120}{120-40}\right)} = 677.0$$

3. Mary Ann notes that only $EOQ_{2.00}$ is feasible because 642.3 valves per order can be purchased at \$2.00 per valve. Two quantities are investigated, 642.3 and 700 units per order:

$$Q = 642.3: \quad TMC = \frac{Q}{2}\left(\frac{p-d}{p}\right)C + \left(\frac{D}{Q}\right)S + (D)ac$$

$$= \frac{642.3}{2}\left(\frac{120-40}{120}\right)(.2 \times 2.0) + \left(\frac{10,000}{642.3}\right)5.5 + (10,000)2.0$$

$$= 85.63 + 85.63 + 20,000 = \$20,171.26 \text{ per year}$$

$$Q = 700: \quad TMC = \frac{Q}{2}\left(\frac{p-d}{p}\right)C + \left(\frac{D}{Q}\right)S + (D)ac$$

$$= \frac{700}{2}\left(\frac{120-40}{120}\right)(.2 \times 1.8) + \left(\frac{10,000}{700}\right)5.5 + (10,000)1.8$$

$$= 84.00 + 78.57 + 18,000 = \$18,162.57 \text{ per year}$$

4. Mary Ann concludes that if gradual deliveries are used, 700 units per order should be purchased.

5. Given a choice, Mr. Swartz would prefer to have gradual deliveries of #3925 valves in quantities of 700 units per order because the TMC of gradual deliveries is less than that for orders delivered all at once.

DETERMINING ORDER POINTS

Table 10.7 contains many terms often used in setting order points. You may find it helpful to occasionally refer to the table as we progress through this section. When setting order points in a fixed order quantity inventory system, operations managers are confronted with an uncertain demand during lead time. *Demand during lead time (DDLT)* means the amount of a material that will be demanded while we are waiting for an order of a material to arrive and replenish inventory. The variation in demand during lead time comes from two sources. First, the lead time required to receive an order is subject to variation. For example, suppliers can encounter difficulty in processing orders, and trucking companies can have equipment failures or strikes that delay deliveries. Second, daily demand for the material is subject to variation. For example, customers' demands for finished products are known to be subject to great daily variation, and production departments' demands for raw materials can vary because of changes in production schedules. What makes this variation in demand during lead time particularly worrisome to operations managers is that this uncertainty hits them when they are most vulnerable — when they are waiting for an order of materials to arrive and inventory levels are low.

If orders arrive late or if demand for the materials is greater than expected while we are waiting for an order to come in, a stockout can occur. A *stockout* means that there is insufficient inventory to cover demands for a material during lead time. Operations managers carry safety stock so that if lead time or demand is greater than expected, stockouts will seldom occur. If we carry too much safety stock, the cost of carrying these materials becomes excessive; however, when too little safety stock is carried, the cost of stockouts becomes excessive. Operations managers want to balance these two costs as they set order points.

Figure 10.8 illustrates the relationships among the variables involved in setting order points and safety stock. The most important relationship for you to know is:

Order point = Expected demand during lead time + Safety stock

OP = EDDLT + SS

TABLE 10.7   *Terms Often Used in Analyses in Inventory Planning under Uncertainty*

1. **Continuous DDLT Distributions**—Probability distributions of all possible demand during lead time (DDLT) values where DDLT is a continuous random variable. In other words, DDLT can take on any value continuously between the extreme DDLT values of the distribution. Examples of these distributions are normal, Student t, and exponential.

2. **DDLT Distribution Parameters**—The measures that describe the DDLT distributions. For example:

   EDDLT—Expected demand during lead time is the mean of the DDLT distribution.

   σ_{DDLT}—Standard deviation of demand during lead time is the measure of how the DDLT values are dispersed about their mean.

3. **Demand per Day (d) Distribution Parameters**—The measures that describe the d distributions. For example:

   $\bar{d}$—Mean demand per day.

   σ_d—Standard deviation of demand per day is the measure of how the d values are dispersed about their mean.

4. **Discrete DDLT Distributions**—Probability distributions of all possible demand during lead time (DDLT) values, where DDLT is a discrete random variable. In other words, DDLT can take on only a few specific values between the extreme DDLT values of the distribution. Examples of these distributions are binomial, hypergeometric, Poisson, and a host of other empirically determined historical data distributions.

5. **Lead Time (LT) Distribution Parameters**—The measures that describe the LT distributions. For example:

   $\overline{LT}$—Mean lead time.

   σ_{LT}—Standard deviation of lead time, the measure of how the LT values are dispersed about their mean.

6. **Marginal Analysis**—A form of analysis of safety stock level and order point problems in inventory planning under uncertainty. This technique determines the cumulative probability that equates the expected long cost and expected short cost for DDLT. This probability is then used to identify the optimal DDLT in the cumulative DDLT probability distribution. The optimal safety stock level is deduced from the optimal DDLT or order point (SS = OP − EDDLT).

7. **Optimal Safety Stock Level**—The amount of safety stock, which is the order point (OP) minus the expected demand during lead time (EDDLT), that balances the expected long costs and expected short costs during lead time.

8. **Payoff Tables**—A form of analysis of safety stock level and order point problems in inventory planning under uncertainty. This technique computes the total of expected long and short costs per lead time for each order point strategy. The order point with the minimum total expected cost is the optimal order point. The optimal safety stock is then deduced (SS = OP − EDDLT).

9. **Risk of Stockouts**—The probability that *all* customers' or production departments' orders cannot be directly filled from inventory during lead time. Risk of stockouts is the complement of service level. For example, if there is a 10 percent risk of stockout, then the service level is 90 percent.

10. **Service Level**—The probability that a stockout will not occur during lead time. For example, a 90 percent service level means that there is a 10 percent probability that *all* orders cannot be filled from inventory during lead time.

FIGURE 10.8 *Relationships between DDLT, EDDLT, SS, OP, and Probability of Stockouts for Each Reorder Cycle*

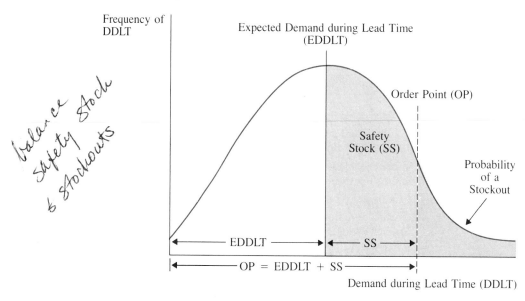

As you can see from the demand during lead time distribution in Figure 10.8, safety stock is added to the expected demand during lead time to determine the order point. If we assume that we can accurately estimate the value of the expected demand during lead time from historical records or other sources, then setting the safety stock also sets the order point. So when we set the safety stock level for a material, we also simultaneously set the order point. As we can see from Figure 10.8, increasing the safety stock for a material reduces the probability of a stockout during lead time. This reduces the cost of stockouts but has the disadvantage of increasing carrying costs.

In attempting to balance the costs of carrying too much or too little safety stock for each material, analysts have searched for optimal solutions to this problem. The main obstacle to determining optimal safety stock levels is estimating the costs of stockouts. We know that stockouts cost, but how much? How much profit is lost when we lose or disappoint customers because of stockouts? How much does it cost when production departments must change production schedules or shut down assembly lines when they experience stockouts of raw materials? Because of the difficulty in accurately determining the costs of stockouts, analysts have taken another approach to setting safety stocks — setting order points at service levels determined by management policy.

Setting Order Points at Service Levels
Service levels refers to the probability that a stockout will not occur during lead time. Managers might say, for example, "We want a 90 percent probability that *all* cus-

FIGURE 10.9 DDLT Distribution

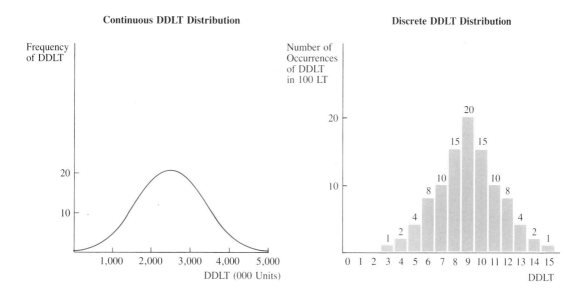

tomers' orders or production departments' orders can be immediately filled out of inventory." Such specifications of service levels are based on marketing policy in the case of finished goods inventory and on manufacturing policy in the case of raw materials inventory.

Discrete and Continuous DDLT Distributions. When DDLT ranges from 3 to 15 units as shown in the second part of Figure 10.9, a *discrete DDLT distribution* may more accurately describe the occurrence of DDLT since its values can only be integer values from 3 to 15 units. When the number of units in DDLT is very large, as shown in the first part of Figure 10.9, or when units are divisible, as in the case of barrels of crude oil, *continuous DDLT distributions* accurately describe the occurrence of DDLT. When enough historical data exist for the demand during lead time for a material, the setting of safety stock levels is straightforward. Example 10.4 sets the safety stock level for a material whose DDLT has been classified into discrete classes.

Example 10.5 demonstrates how we would set safety stock levels when DDLT is depicted by a continuous distribution. This example assumes that the historical DDLT for a raw material is actually from a normal distribution. Remember that we earlier defined order point as:

Order point = Expected demand during lead time + Safety stock

In this example we first use the historical data to compute the mean and standard deviation of the DDLT distribution (EDDLT and σ_{DDLT}). Next, we compute the

EXAMPLE 10.4   *Setting Safety Stock at Service Levels for a Discrete DDLT Distribution*

The Whipple Manufacturing Company produces office products that are sold through whole-saling distributors. One such product, a word-processing small-business computer, is produced to stock and held in finished goods inventory until ordered by Whipple's distributors. When finished goods inventory falls to the order point, an order for a production lot is placed with Whipple's manufacturing department. Whipple's management wants to determine how much safety stock should be carried on this item and has uncovered the following information: Average demand per day is 6.0 units, average production lead time is 10 days, and historical records show this frequency of actual demand during lead time:

Actual DDLT	Frequency
21–30	.05
31–40	.10
41–50	.15
51–60	.20
61–70	.20
71–80	.15
81–90	.10
91–100	.05

If Whipple's management wants to provide an 80 percent service level during lead time: **(a)** What is the order point? **(b)** What is the safety stock?

Solution

a. First, use the DDLT data to develop a cumulative probability distribution of the service level:

Actual DDLT	Frequency	Service Level (Probability of DDLT or Less)
11–20	0	0
21–30	.05	.05
31–40	.10	.15
41–50	.15	.30
51–60	.20	.50
61–70	.20	.70
71–80	.15	.85
81–90	.10	.95
91–100	.05	1.00

Next, graph this cumulative distribution:

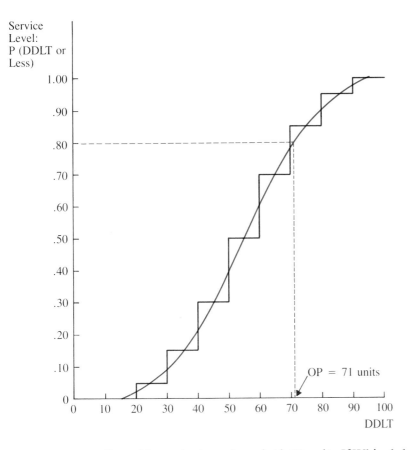

As we can see from this graph, the order point is 71 units. If Whipple begins a production lot of the computer when inventory falls to 71 units, stockouts will occur (DDLT > 71) about 20 percent of the time between the point in time when a production order for the units is begun and a production order is completed.

b. Determine the safety stock level:

$$OP = EDDLT + \text{Safety stock}$$

$$\text{Safety stock} = OP - EDDLT = OP - [(\text{Average demand per day}) \times (\text{Average lead time})]$$
$$= 71 - (6.0 \times 10) = 71 - 60 = 11 \text{ units}$$

value of DDLT that has a probability of 5 percent of being exceeded; this means that the probability of being less than or equal to this DDLT is 95 percent, the desired service level. This value of DDLT is our order point (OP). This approach to setting safety stock levels is valid only if service levels are precisely set and if accurate DDLT historical data are available.

EXAMPLE 10.5   *Setting Safety Stock at Service Levels for DDLT That Is Normally Distributed*

Billie Jean Bray, the materials manager for INJECTO Wholesale Plastics, is attempting to set the safety stock level for resin #942. This material is sold to INJECTO's customers, and its future use is believed to be accurately depicted by these historical DDLT data (in pounds): 632, 754, 429, 715, 949, 623, 555, 690, 740, and 850. Billie Jean believes that DDLT for resin #942 is really normally distributed and that these last ten DDLT occurrences are representative of the true DDLT normal distribution. **(a)** What is the EDDLT for resin #942? **(b)** What is the σ_{DDLT} for resin #942? **(c)** If the production manager specifies a 95 percent service level for resin #942 during lead time, what safety stock should be maintained?

Solution

a. EDDLT is the mean of the ten historical DDLT occurrences:

$$EDDLT = \frac{\Sigma DDLT}{n} = \frac{(632 + 754 + 429 + 715 + 949 + 623 + 555 + 690 + 740 + 850)}{10}$$

$$= 693.7 \text{ pounds}$$

b. Standard deviation of DDLT is:

$$\sigma_X = \sqrt{\frac{\sum_{i=1}^{n} (X_i - \overline{X})^2}{n}} \qquad \text{(This is the formula for standard deviation.)}$$

$$\sigma_{DDLT} = \sqrt{\frac{\sum_{i=1}^{n} (DDLT_i - EDDLT)^2}{n}} \qquad \begin{array}{l}\text{(This is the formula for standard deviation when applied} \\ \text{to DDLT.)}\end{array}$$

$$= \sqrt{\frac{1}{10} \begin{bmatrix} (632 - 693.7)^2 + (754 - 693.7)^2 + (429 - 693.7)^2 + \\ (715 - 693.7)^2 + (949 - 693.7)^2 + (623 - 693.7)^2 + \\ (555 - 693.7)^2 + (690 - 693.7)^2 + (740 - 693.7)^2 + \\ (850 - 693.7)^2 \end{bmatrix}}$$

$$= 139.27 \text{ pounds}$$

Therefore we have a normal distribution of DDLT with a mean of 693.7 pounds and a standard deviation of 139.27 pounds.

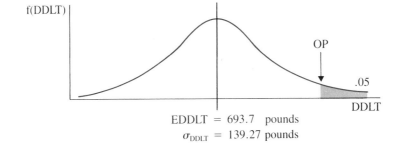

$$EDDLT = 693.7 \text{ pounds}$$
$$\sigma_{DDLT} = 139.27 \text{ pounds}$$

c. Compute safety stock (SS) to provide a 95 percent service level; in other words, what is the DDLT level that has a probability of only 5 percent of being exceeded? This is the order point:

$$OP = EDDLT + Z(\sigma_{DDLT})$$

Safety Stock

The Z value is read from Appendix A. Locate .95 (the area to the left of OP) in the body of the table and read off the Z value of 1.64. This is the number of standard deviations that OP is away from EDDLT:

$$OP = 693.7 + 1.64 (139.27) = 922.1 \text{ pounds}$$

The safety stock is then deduced:

$$SS = OP - EDDLT = 922.1 - 693.7 = 228.4 \text{ pounds}$$

Constant Lead Time and Normally Distributed Demand per Day. There are times when it is difficult to obtain DDLT data. In these instances it is often satisfactory to obtain demand-per-day data and assume a constant lead time. Because historical demand-per-day data are usually abundantly available and lead time is ordinarily subject to less variation than the daily demand, this approach can be useful.

Example 10.6 develops safety stock levels for a material while assuming constant lead time and a normally distributed demand per day. A normal DDLT distribution is developed by computing the expected demand during lead time (EDDLT) and standard deviation of demand during lead time (σ_{DDLT}):

$$EDDLT = LT(\bar{d}) \quad \text{and} \quad \sigma_{DDLT} = \sqrt{LT(\sigma_d)^2}$$

The resulting DDLT normal distribution is then analyzed to calculate the DDLT that provides the specified service level, and this DDLT is the order point (OP). The safety stock (SS) is then deduced: $SS = OP - EDDLT$.

All these approaches to explicitly dealing with uncertainty in inventory planning have relied on managers to specify service levels to comply with either manufacturing policy or marketing policy. Let us now examine some techniques for determining optimal order points and safety stock levels.

EXAMPLE 10.6   Setting Safety Stock Levels at Service Levels for Constant Lead Time and Normally Distributed Demand per Day

Mr. Bob Fero is an operations analyst for Sell-Rite Discount Stores of Washington, DC. He is currently studying the ordering and stocking policies at Sell-Rite's central warehouse for one of their best-moving items—the Zolo Blow Gun, a child's toy. An examination of historical supply and demand data for this item indicated an almost constant lead time (LT) of ten days, and abundant production capacity allowed very consistent production and delivery times. Bob also discovered that the demand per day (d) was nearly normally distributed with a mean (d) of 1,250 toys per day with a standard deviation (σ_d) of 375 toys per day. **(a)** Compute the order point for the toy if the service level is specified at 90 percent during lead time. **(b)** How much safety stock is provided in your answer in Part *a*?

Solution

a. Compute the order point:
1. First, compute the EDDLT and σ_{DDLT}:

   EDDLT = Lead time × Average demand per day = $LT(\bar{d})$ = 10(1,250)
           = 12,500 toys during lead time

   $\sigma_{DDLT} = \sqrt{LT(\sigma_d)^2} = \sqrt{10(375)^2} = 1,185.85$ toys during lead time

2. EDDLT and σ_{DDLT} totally describe the DDLT distribution:

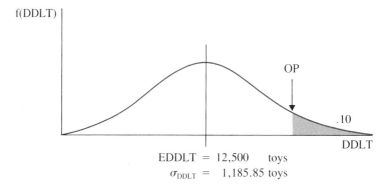

    EDDLT = 12,500   toys
    σ_{DDLT} =   1,185.85 toys

3. Next, we must determine Z, the number of standard deviations that OP is from EDDLT. Look up .900 in the body of the table in Appendix A and read off the corresponding Z value of 1.28.
4. Next, compute the order point:

   $$OP = EDDLT + \overbrace{Z(\sigma_{DDLT})}^{SS} = 12,500 + 1.28(1,185.85) = 12,500 + 1,517.89$$
       = 14,017.89 toys

   Orders for the toy would be placed when the inventory level falls to 14,018 toys.

b. Compute the safety stock (SS):

   SS = OP − EDDLT = 14,018 − 12,500 = 1,518 toys

Payoff Tables

Analysts may want to find an optimal balance between the costs of carrying too little and carrying too much safety stock for a product or material.

    Example 10.7 uses *payoff tables* to minimize the total of expected long costs and short costs for each discrete order point. This approach requires the following information:

1. Long cost—the cost of stocking one unit that is not demanded during lead time—is usually associated with carrying costs, the cost of special handling, and other expenses involved in carrying a unit from one period to another.

2. Short cost—the cost of not stocking a unit that is demanded during lead time—is ordinarily associated with stockouts—lost profits, special handling, expediting, and so on.

EXAMPLE 10.7   Developing Optimal Safety Stock Levels with Payoff Tables

A large hospital stocks supplies to support surgical operations. One such material, #711 surgical tape, is being studied. The following information has been developed: long costs = $20 per case not used during lead time, short costs = $60 per case short during lead time, and the following demand during lead time distribution:

DDLT (Cases of #711)	Occurrences	DDLT (Cases of #711)	Occurrences
3	1	6	2
4	4	7	1
5	3		

(a) What order point for #711 surgical tape is optimal? **(b)** What safety stock level is optimal?

Solution

a. Compute the optimal order point:
1. First, compute probabilities for each DDLT:

DDLT (Cases of #711)	Probability of DDLT	DDLT (Cases of #711)	Probability of DDLT
3	$1/11 = .091$	6	$2/11 = .182$
4	$4/11 = .364$	7	$1/11 = .091$
5	$3/11 = .273$		

2. Next, develop a long and short cost matrix:

DDLT (Cases)

		3	4	5	6	7	
	3	$ 0	$60	$120	$180	$240	← Short Costs
Order Point	4	20	0	60	120	180	
Alternatives (Cases)	5	40	20	0	60	120	
	6	60	40	20	0	60	
	7	80	60	40	20	0	

↑
Long Costs

For example, if an order point of 5 cases were adopted and 3 cases were actually demanded during lead time, a long cost of $40 ($20 × 2 cases long) would result. If, however, an order point of 5 cases were adopted and 7 cases were actually demanded during lead time, a short cost of $120 ($60 × 2 cases short) would result.

3. Next, compute the payoff table analysis to find the order point:

	SN_i					Total Expected Long and Short Costs $EC = \Sigma[P(SN_i)C_{ij}]$
	S_j	**DDLT (Cases)**				
		3	4	5	6	7	
	3	$ 0	$21.84	$32.76	$32.76	$21.84	$109.20
Order Point	4	1.82	0	16.38	21.84	16.38	56.42
Alternatives							
(Cases)	5	3.64	7.28	0	10.92	10.92	32.76
	6	5.46	14.56	5.46	0	5.46	30.94 ←
	7	7.28	21.84	10.92	3.64	0	43.68
	$P(SN_i)$	.091	.364	.273	.182	.091	

The probability for each DDLT is multiplied by the long and short costs in the matrix in Step 2 above and recorded in this matrix. For example, the column for DDLT = 3 is computed by multiplying .091 by 0, 20, 40, 60, 80 from the 3 DDLT column in Step 2 to yield 0, 1.82, 3.64, 5.46, and 7.28. Each of the columns is similarly filled. The expected costs for each order point alternative are added horizontally across the matrix. For example: $109.20 = $0 + $21.84 + $32.76 + $32.76 + $21.84.

4. The order point alternative with the lowest expected long and short costs is 6 cases.

b. Compute the optimal safety stock level:

Safety stock = Order point − Average demand during lead time

$$SS = OP - EDDLT = 6 - \frac{1(3) + 4(4) + 3(5) + 2(6) + 1(7)}{11} = 6 - 4.82$$

$$= 1.18 \text{ cases}$$

Because the order point computed by the approach in Example 10.7 is likely to be applied over and over from reorder cycle to reorder cycle, the minimization of total expected costs per reorder cycle is a useful criterion for selecting order points.

Payoff tables can also be used to analyze other stocking decisions in POM. We shall discuss other uses of payoff tables later in this chapter.

Marginal Analysis

In Example 10.8 the same surgical tape safety stock problem is solved, but this time by *marginal analysis*. This approach computes the probability (P) that makes the expected long cost equal to the expected short cost for any DDLT. This P is then compared to the cumulative probability distribution — probability of at least DDLT being demanded. The lowest DDLT whose cumulative probability is greater than or equal to P is the optimal order point alternative. The safety stock is then computed as in Example 10.7.

The data requirements for the marginal cost approach are exactly the same as with payoff tables—long cost per unit, short cost per unit, and discrete probability distribution of DDLT. Students seem to prefer the marginal cost approach over payoff tables because of its speed and ease of computation. The two methods give comparable results, but the payoff tables do offer an advantage: The total expected cost for each possible order point is clearly exhibited, thus allowing decision makers' insight into the sensitivity of total expected cost to changes in order points. For example, in the expected cost matrix in Example 10.7, managers can see that the total expected cost per lead time increases from $30.94 to $43.68 if the order point is increased from 6 to 7 cases. Such information may allow managers more flexibility in their decisions when considering warehouse capacities, marketing policies, customers' wishes, and other pressures not easily included in order point analyses.

EXAMPLE 10.8   *Developing Optimal Safety Stock Levels with Marginal Analysis*

The study of #711 surgical tape from Example 10.7 is now analyzed by using marginal analysis.

MLC = $20 per case—long cost per case, the marginal cost of not using a case of #711 surgical tape during lead time.

MSC = $60 per case—short cost per case, the marginal cost of being short a case of #711 surgical tape because of a stockout during lead time.

P — probability of needing the nth case of #711 surgical tape during lead time; DDLT is equal to or greater than n cases.

$(1 - P)$ — probability of not needing the nth case of #711 surgical tape during lead time; DDLT is less than n cases.

(a) Derive a formula for P that exactly balances expected long costs and expected short costs. **(b)** Compute the order point for #711 surgical tape. **(c)** Compute the safety stock for #711 surgical tape.

Solution

a. Derive the formula for P:

1. Set the expected short costs equal to the expected long costs and solve for P:

$$P(MSC) = (1 - P)(MLC)$$

$$P(MSC) = MLC - P(MLC)$$

$$P(MSC) + P(MLC) = MLC$$

$$P(MSC + MLC) = MLC$$

$$P = \frac{MLC}{MSC + MLC} = \frac{20}{60 + 20} = .250$$

2. When the probability of needing a unit is .250, the marginal cost of stocking that unit is exactly equal to the marginal cost of not stocking that unit.

b. Compute the order point for #711 surgical tape:

1. The optimal order point is determined by progressively increasing the order point, as long as the probability of needing the last unit added is equal to or greater than .250.
2. Develop the probability of at least each DDLT occurring:

DDLT (Cases of #711)	Probability of DDLT	Probability of at Least DDLT
3	.091	1.000
4	.364	.909
5	.273	.545
6	.182	.272
7	.091	.091

3. It seldom occurs that the probability of demanding at least any DDLT exactly equals the P computed in Part *a*. Ordinarily, the appropriate DDLT to select, therefore, is the lowest DDLT whose probability of being demanded is equal to or greater than P. An order point of 6 cases would be selected in this example because $P(DDLT \geq 6) = .272$, which is the lowest DDLT whose probability of being demanded is $\geq P$.
4. It can be shown that 6 units is the optimal order point by comparing the expected cost of stocking 6 units with the expected cost of stocking 7 units:

$OP = 6$:   Total expected cost = Expected long cost + Expected short cost
$$= .091(60) + .364(40) + .273(20) + .182(0) + .091(60)$$
$$= 5.46 + 14.56 + 5.46 + 0 + 5.46$$
$$= \$30.94 \text{ during lead time}$$

$OP = 7$:   Total expected cost = Expected long cost + Expected short cost
$$= .091(80) + .364(60) + .273(40) + .182(20) + .091(0)$$
$$= 7.28 + 21.84 + 10.92 + 3.64 + 0$$
$$= \$43.68 \text{ during lead time}$$

c. Compute the safety stock level:

Safety stock = Order point − Average demand during lead time

$$SS = OP - EDDLT = 6 - 4.82 \text{ (4.82 was computed in Example 10.7)}$$
$$= 1.18 \text{ cases}$$

While service levels, payoff tables, and marginal analysis are used to set order points, certain rules of thumb are also used.

Some Rules of Thumb in Setting Order Points
Perhaps the most common method involves setting safety stock levels at a *percentage of EDDLT*:

Order point = EDDLT + j(EDDLT), where j = a factor that varies from zero to 3.00

Materials are usually categorized according to classifications such as these:

Class	Description	j
1	Uncritical	.10
2	Uncertain–uncritical	.20
3	Critical	.30
4	Uncertain–critical	.50
5	Supercritical	1.00
6	Uncertain–supercritical	3.00

These classifications would be custom-designed for a firm's inventory system and uniformly applied to most materials in finished goods and raw material inventories. Another approach sets safety stock at *square root of EDDLT:*

$$\text{Order point} = \text{EDDLT} + \sqrt{\text{EDDLT}}$$

This method selects safety stock levels that are large relative to EDDLT when EDDLT is small and that are relatively small when EDDLT is large. This approach is usually applied when stockouts are not particularly undesirable or costly.

The percentage of EDDLT and square root of EDDLT methods for setting order points are demonstrated in Example 10.9.

EXAMPLE 10.9   *Using Rules of Thumb to Set Order Points*

Dapple Manufacturing Company produces bronze castings. A number of one type of casting, #699, is held in inventory until customers order it from Dapple. Mr. George Dapple, Dapple's materials manager, is dabbling with various approaches to setting order points for materials. The #699 casting is selected as the material for investigation. The following data were collected on #699: Average demand per day is 6 castings, and average lead time is 10 days, the time needed to produce a lot of castings. Mr. Dapple's study requires the following: **(a)** If safety stock is set at 20 percent of EDDLT, what is the order point? **(b)** If safety stock is set at square root of EDDLT, what is the order point?

Solution

a. Order Point = EDDLT + .2 (EDDLT)

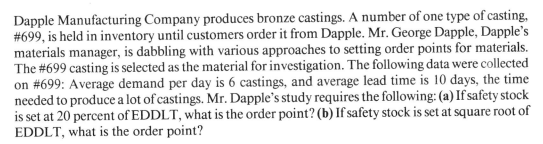

= Average demand per day × Average lead time + .2 (EDDLT)

= 6.0 (10) + .2 (6.0 × 10) = 60 + 12 = 72 castings

b. Order point = EDDLT + $\sqrt{\text{EDDLT}}$ = 60 + $\sqrt{60}$ = 60 + 7.75 = 67.75, or 68 castings

In Example 10.9 the two methods of computing order points develop safety stocks of 12 and 8 castings. Which one is correct? Both are mathematically correct, but the correctness of each of the order points can be tested only by experimentation —choose one and keep records on DDLT as time passes. This is the only true test of an order point: Does the safety stock give the level of protection against stockouts that is desired?

How does the use of safety stocks affect the order quantity (EOQ) in a fixed order quantity inventory system? Minimally if at all! However, total annual stocking costs would change because safety stocks cause these developments:

1. Increased annual carrying costs. This results from the fact that safety stocks are considered dead stock: On the average they are never used. The additional inventory therefore results in higher annual carrying costs.
2. Lower annual stockout costs. The basic EOQ models do not include stockout costs, and for good reason: They are difficult to estimate. But conceptually we know that the costs of stockouts are real, and these would be reduced by safety stocks.

We have considered the determination of order quantities and order points in fixed order quantity inventory systems for both raw material and finished goods inventories. Let us now consider techniques for computing optimal order periods in fixed order period inventory systems.

FIXED ORDER PERIOD SYSTEMS

The selection of an order period for materials in either raw material or finished goods inventories is the key decision in fixed order period inventory systems. If materials are reviewed too often, and therefore ordered too often, annual ordering costs are excessive. On the other hand, if the time between reviews of materials is too long, annual carrying costs are too high and the probability of stockouts is increased. Therefore we want to select an optimal time interval between reviewing materials so that annual carrying costs are balanced against annual ordering costs and total annual stocking costs are minimal.

Table 10.8 states the assumptions and variable definitions and develops the cost formulas and optimal order period formula for Model IV—fixed order periods. When we have estimated the optimal order period, only one other important consideration is necessary in these systems—the order quantity. The determination of order quantity is straightforward:

$$\text{Order quantity} = \text{Upper inventory target} - \text{Inventory level} + \text{EDDLT}$$

Order quantity is computed each time an order is to be placed for a material by subtracting the amount of a material in inventory or on order from the upper inventory target (including safety stock) and adding the expected demand during lead time. This basic computation can also be adapted to include materials that are

✓

TABLE 10.8   *Model IV — Economic Order Period*

Assumptions
1. Annual demand, carrying cost, and ordering cost for a material can be estimated.
2. Average inventory is average order size divided by 2. This implicitly assumes no safety stock, orders are received all at once, materials are used at a uniform rate, and materials are used up on the average when the next order is received.
3. There are no stockout costs.
4. Quantity discounts do not exist.

Variable Definitions
The variable definitions in Model I apply here.* Additionally:

$$T = \text{Time between orders in fraction of a year}$$

Cost Formulas

$$\text{Annual carrying costs} = \text{Average inventory} \times \text{Carrying cost} = (DT/2)C$$

$$\text{Annual ordering costs} = \text{Number of orders per year} \times \text{Cost per order}$$
$$= (D/DT)S = S/T$$

$$\text{Total annual stocking costs (TSC)} = \text{Annual carrying costs} + \text{Annual ordering costs}$$
$$= (DT/2)C + S/T$$

Derivation of the Optimal Order Period Formula
Set the derivative of TSC with respect to T equal to zero and solve for T:

1. The formula for TSC is: $\qquad\qquad$ $TSC = (DT/2)C + S/T$

2. The derivative of TSC with respect to T is: $\qquad$ $d(TSC)/d(T) = (D/2)C - (S/T^2)$

3. Set the derivative of TSC with respect to T equal to zero and solve for T: $\qquad$ $(D/2)C - (S/T^2) = 0$
$$T^2 = 2S/DC$$

4. The optimal T is therefore: $\qquad\qquad$ $T = \sqrt{2S/DC}$

* Note: See the note to Table 10.3.

promised but not shipped, large customer orders expected in the near future, and so on. These amounts would be added onto the order quantity.

$\qquad$ Example 10.10 applies the formulas for optimal order period and order quantity of this model to one material in a wholesaling company. Note that T, the optimal time interval for reviewing the status of a material and placing a material order, is expressed as a fraction of a year. This value must be adjusted to days, weeks, or months as desired. Note also that T is a computation that would be made only about once a year, whereas order quantity computations must be made for each order. In other words, T remains fixed for a long time and Q is allowed to vary from order to order.

EXAMPLE 10.10   Optimal Order Period in a Fixed Order Period Inventory System

The C, D, & F Retailing Company routinely reviews the inventory levels of its products on display monthly and places orders for these products, if needed, from their suppliers. Mr. Bill Bailey, the regional manager, wonders if monthly reviews are optimal when considering both carrying costs and order costs.

One product is selected to be the focus of investigation — Goo-Goo, a jarred baby food cereal. The following information was developed for Goo-Goo: D = 29,385 jars per year, C = 30 percent of acquisition cost, ac = $.29 per jar, and S = $10.90 per order. **(a)** How often should Goo-Goo be ordered? **(b)** At the first review after T has been computed in Part *a*, if inventory level = 985 jars, upper inventory target (including safety stock) = 3,220 jars, and expected demand during lead time = 805 jars, how many jars should be ordered?

Solution

a. C = .3 × .29

$$T = \sqrt{\frac{2S}{DC}} = \sqrt{\frac{2(10.9)}{(29,385)(.3 \times .29)}} = .0923 \text{ years} = 33.7 \text{ days}$$

b. Order quantity = Upper inventory target − Inventory level + EDDLT
= 3,220 − 985 + 805 = 3,040 jars

The following generalizations can be deduced from the formula for T:

1. More expensive materials are reviewed more frequently.
2. Materials with higher usage rates are reviewed more frequently.
3. Materials with higher ordering costs are ordered less frequently.

These seem to be rational criteria for determining order intervals for materials.

Now we shall turn from fixed order quantity and fixed order period inventory systems where we continuously reorder materials to a situation where we must determine order quantities for a material that is to be ordered for a single period.

✗ SINGLE-PERIOD INVENTORY MODELS

Some inventory problems involve determining an order quantity for an item to cover the demand for only a single period. This type of problem is common for short-lived materials such as fashion goods, perishable foods, and published matter such as magazines or newspapers. Such inventory problems have traditionally been called *newsboy problems.* The structure of these problems is particularly well suited for the use of payoff tables.

PAYOFF TABLES

Payoff tables are applied to a broad range of stocking problems when operations managers face an uncertain demand and it costs to stock too many or too few. For example, retailers must decide how many units of a particular product to stock for the next month, given the many possible levels of demand for the product. In such situations operations managers must evaluate the many alternatives available for meeting the uncertain states of nature.

How do operations managers choose among the alternatives? They usually use one of these rules or criteria: (1) Choose the alternative with the greatest expected profits. (2) Choose the alternative with the least total expected long and short costs. (3) Choose the alternative with the least total expected costs. Because operations managers ordinarily prefer to maximize expected profits, Rule 1 is usually preferred. Rule 2 is also often used by operations managers, and if profits are involved it gives results equivalent to Rule 1. When revenues are not involved, as in government agencies and not-for-profit organizations, or when revenues cannot be precisely attributed to specific products or units being stocked, Rule 3 is frequently used.

Because the choice of rule or criterion used for deciding among the alternatives can affect the alternative eventually selected, it is important to give careful thought to the most appropriate rule for the decision situation under analysis. Example 10.11 demonstrates how payoff tables are used by operations managers when different decision criteria are used.

One complication that students regularly encounter is the presence of *opportunity costs*. Such costs are incurred when, for example, not enough units are stocked at the beginning of the period and demand exceeds the number of stocked units sometime during the period. These costs are in the form of profits forgone. In this type of problem we are often confused about how to incorporate these opportunity costs into our payoff tables. Two equally acceptable approaches to these problems are demonstrated in Example 10.11:

1. Minimize the total expected long and short costs where short costs represent the profit per unit. Long costs are incorporated as usual.
2. Maximize the total expected profits. Notice in Example 10.11 that for stocking strategy 200, whenever demand is 200, 300, 400, and 450, the profits are $1,000. In this treatment, whenever demand exceeds supply, the number of units sold is the number of units stocked, and the profits are implicitly penalized by remaining the same regardless of increased demand. Therefore the implicit unit short cost is the entire per-unit profit. Long costs are incorporated as usual.

Payoff tables are an effective tool for analyzing single-period decisions under conditions of uncertainty. Their flexibility in evaluating a multitude of POM stocking decisions is perhaps their greatest strength. Cash, maintenance parts, workers, inventory items, production capacity, standby machines, and service capacity are all single-period stocking decisions that can be analyzed by payoff tables when demand levels or states of nature are uncertain.

EXAMPLE 10.11   Payoff Tables: A Retail Stocking Decision

Electronics Retailers Inc. is trying to decide how many #325 electronic calculators to stock for sale next month. The sales history of this item is as follows:

Number of Months	Units Demanded (SN)	Probability of Units Demanded P(SN)
1	100	.1
1	200	.1
4	300	.4
3	400	.3
1	450	.1
Total 10		1.0

The #325 calculator sells for $15 per unit and has a cost of goods sold of $10 per unit. If one of these calculators is stocked for sale but is not sold during the month, it costs $2 to carry it over into the next month's inventory, or long costs. **(a)** Use payoff tables to minimize the total expected long and short costs. What is the expected value of perfect information (EVPI)? Explain its meaning. **(b)** Use payoff tables to maximize the total expected profits. Compute the EVPI. **(c)** Which stocking strategy is best for the #325 calculator? Explain the equivalence of the solutions of Parts a and b above.

Solution

a. Use payoff tables to minimize the total expected long and short costs. What is the EVPI? Explain its meaning.

First, complete a payoff table that minimizes the total expected long and short costs where long costs are $2 per unit and short costs are $5 per unit, the lost profit on sales forgone.

	S_j \ SN_i	States of Nature					Total Expected Long and Short Costs $EC = \Sigma[P(SN_i) \times C_{ij}]$
		100	200	300	400	450	
Strategies	100	$ 0	$500	$1,000	$1,500	$1,750	$1,075
	200	200	0	500	1,000	1,250	645
	300	400	200	0	500	750	285
	400	600	400	200	0	250	205 ←
	450	700	500	300	100	0	270
	$P(SN_i)$	.1	.1	.4	.3	.1	

Note: C_{ij} is the costs of S_j and SN_i.

The procedures of payoff tables can be illustrated by explaining the three shaded elements of the table in detail, using S_j to mean *stocking strategies* and SN_i to mean *states of nature,* or uncertain levels of demand:

- **S of 200 and SN of 400:** The $1,000 found in this position means that if a stocking strategy of 200 units is selected and a demand of 400 units is experienced, this would put the firm 200 units short during the period. Since short costs are $5 per unit, the period short costs are $5 per unit times 200 units, which equals $1,000.

- **S of 300 and SN of 300:** The zero found in this position means that since the strategy exactly meets the state of nature, there are neither short nor long costs.

- **S of 400 and SN of 100:** The $600 found in this position means that if a stocking strategy of 400 units is selected and a demand of 100 units is experienced, this will yield an excess in inventory of 300 units at the end of the period. The period long cost is 300 units times $2 per unit, which equals $600.

All other elements of the payoff table are computed similarly. The expected cost column (EC) of the table is completed by summing along each strategy row (S_j) the products of the probability of the states of nature $P(SN_i)$ and their C_{ij}. For instance, the EC of $S_j = 400$ units is computed this way:

$$EC = .1(600) + .1(400) + .4(200) + .3(0) + .1(250) = 60 + 40 + 80 + 0 + 25 = 205$$

Now, what is the EVPI and what is its meaning? The EVPI is $205, the value of the minimum total expected long and short costs derived from the payoff table above. The EVPI means that if all of the uncertainty from the problem could be removed through perfect market research or some other means, an average of $205 per month could be saved by eliminating long and short costs altogether. In other words, as much as $205 per month could be spent for perfect market information to remove the uncertainty. The long and short costs for each level of demand under this perfect information condition are found on the diagonal of the payoff table. Because all of these values on the diagonal are zero, the total expected long and short costs are also zero. The difference between the total expected long and short costs under conditions of perfect information ($0) and under conditions of imperfect information or uncertainty ($205) is the EVPI.

b. Use payoff tables to maximize the total expected profits. Compute the EVPI.

First, complete a payoff table that maximizes the total expected profits (see the accompanying payoff table). The shaded elements of the table are explained below:

- **S of 200 and SN of 400:** The $1,000 found in this position means that if a strategy of 200 units is selected and a demand of 400 units is experienced, revenues would equal $15(200) or $3,000 and cost of goods sold would be $10(200) or $2,000 for a profit of $1,000 for the month.

- **S of 300 and SN of 300:** The $1,500 found in this position means that the strategy exactly meets the state of nature; revenues would be $15(300) or $4,500 and cost of goods sold would be $10(300) or $3,000 for a profit of $1,500 for the month.

	States of Nature					Total Expected Profits
S$_j$ \\ SN$_i$	100	200	300	400	450	EP $= \Sigma[P(SN_i) \times \pi_{ij}]$
100	$500	$ 500	$ 500	$ 500	$ 500	$ 500
200	300	1,000	1,000	1,000	1,000	930
300	100	800	1,500	1,500	1,500	1,290
400	(100)	600	1,300	2,000	2,000	1,370 ←
450	(200)	500	1,200	1,900	2,250	1,305
P(SN$_i$)	.1	.1	.4	.3	.1	

Strategies (label at left of rows)

Note: π_{ij} is the profits of S$_j$ and SN$_i$.

- **S of 400 and SN of 100:** The ($100) means that if a strategy of 400 units is selected and a demand of 100 units is experienced, revenues would be $15(100) or $1,500, cost of goods sold would be $10(100) or $1,000, and long costs would be $2(300) or $600. Profits would then be ($100) for the month.

All other elements of the payoff table are computed similarly. The expected profit column (EP) is completed by summing along each strategy row (S$_j$) the products of the probability of the states of nature P(SN$_i$) and their π_{ij}. For instance, the EP of S$_j$ = 400 units is computed this way:

$$EP = .1(-100) + .1(600) + .4(1,300) + .3(2,000) + .1(2,000)$$
$$= -10 + 60 + 520 + 600 + 200 = 1,370$$

Now compute the EVPI:

$$EVPI = [.1(500) + .1(1,000) + .4(1,500) + .3(2,000) + .1(2,250)] - 1,370 = \$205$$

The profits for each level of demand under conditions of perfect information are found on the diagonal of the payoff table. The total expected profits under conditions of perfect information minus the maximum total expected profits under conditions of imperfect information or uncertainty is the value of EVPI.

c. Which stocking strategy is best for the #325 calculator? Explain the equivalence of the solutions of Parts a and b above.

The best stocking strategy is 400 units of the #325 calculators. This alternative is preferred regardless of whether the total expected profits or the total expected long and short costs criterion is used. The equivalence of the two analyses is evident from a comparison of their payoff tables. For instance, it can be seen that the difference between the optimal strategy of 400 units and any other stocking strategy is the same in both analyses: for a strategy of 200 units, costs increase ($645 − $205 = $440) and profits decrease ($1,370 − 930 = $440) by the same amount. The criterion of minimizing the total expected costs (cost of goods sold, long costs, and short costs) would be inappropriate in this example because of the presence of revenues.

SOME REALITIES OF INVENTORY PLANNING

We have learned in this chapter how to analyze the *how much to order* and *when to order* questions for a material under a variety of operating conditions. Now we need to consider the magnitude of the problem and the difficulty that the typical operations manager has in making these decisions for all of the inventory items held in a company's warehouses. I recently visited a small manufacturing plant in Phoenix, Arizona, that produces pharmaceutical products. The plant employs about 200 workers and is a branch operation with headquarters in Illinois. The operations manager in charge of warehousing told me that the plant held over 45,000 different materials, each with a unique part number. To perform all of the analyses presented in this chapter for each of these materials would be an enormous undertaking for this operations manager. And yet he told me that some of these materials actually were analyzed more thoroughly than proposed in this chapter. Other operations managers are known to have as many as 500,000 unique inventory items that must be managed. In practice, operations managers must develop a system of classifying materials according to the amount of analysis that can be justified for each class of material.

ABC CLASSIFICATION OF MATERIALS

One scheme for classifying materials is the ABC method. In this scheme the 80–20 rule is applied to inventory items: In any aggregation of items, about 20 percent of the items will account for about 80 percent of a given characteristic. This rule, when used in inventory planning, states that only about 20 percent of the materials found in inventories account for about 80 percent of the total dollar value of the inventory. Now, strictly speaking, no one would argue these precise figures, but we do find with remarkable frequency that 15 to 25 percent of the materials in inventory account for 75 to 85 percent of the value of the inventory. Figure 10.10 shows that the ABC method of classifying materials is actually based on the 80–20 rule. These observations about the ABC classification explain the interpretation of Figure 10.10:

1. The A materials represent only 20 percent of the materials in inventory and 75 percent of the inventory value.
2. The B materials represent 30 percent of the materials in inventory and 20 percent of the inventory value.
3. The A and B materials represent 50 percent of the materials in inventory and 95 percent of the inventory value.
4. The C materials represent 50 percent of the materials in inventory and only 5 percent of the inventory value.

This classification suggests the question: What analysis is justified for each of these classes of materials? We would generalize by saying that the more inventory value a material represents, the more precision and more analysis can be justified. Class A materials would be analyzed extensively, Class B would be analyzed moderately, and Class C materials would be analyzed least.

FIGURE 10.10 ABC Classification of Materials

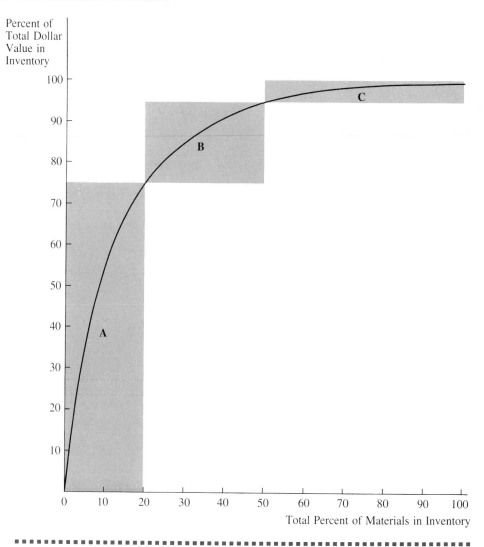

On the surface, linking levels of analysis to the value of inventories might seem like a good idea, but we must be careful. Here are some other factors that are also taken into account when determining order quantities and order points:

1. How critical is the item to production? Because an entire assembly line can be shut down when stockouts occur for such items, larger order quantities are justified.
2. What is the shelf life of the item? Because some components are subject to rapid obsolescence or deterioration, smaller order quantities are justified.

3. How much storage space is required by each unit of the item? Some components are so large and bulky that only a few of them are ordered at each order point.
4. Is the item subject to pilferage and theft? Because some materials are particularly subject to "inventory shrinkage," smaller order quantities are justified.
5. Does the item have particularly erratic lead times? Large order quantities of such items reduce the number of orders per year and mitigate the uncertainty of supply.
6. Is the item subject to wide fluctuation of demand? Larger order quantities and higher order points are justified for such items to allow for large peaks in demand.
7. Is the package, shipping container, or truckload size compatible with the EOQ? If the EOQ is not a multiple of the package or shipping container size, or if the EOQ is too small to obtain truckload shipping rates, then it will ordinarily be adjusted up or down.

EOQ AND UNCERTAINTY

Throughout this chapter uncertainties have lurked just below the surface. Annual demand, usage patterns, usage rates, carrying costs, lead times, ordering costs, and stockout costs—these are all uncertain in most inventory-planning situations.

Take annual demand, carrying costs, and ordering costs, for example. If we are in error when we estimate these values, what is the effect on our order quantity decision? Look at Figure 10.4 again. Note that estimation errors in demand (D), carrying cost (C), or ordering cost (S) would move us to the right or left of EOQ along the total annual stocking costs curve for a material. Moving in either direction increases our annual costs for stocking a material. In most circumstances this curve tends to be rather flat near the EOQ. For example, in Figure 10.4 if we order 400 or 600 units per order rather than 524 units, the EOQ, then the total annual stocking costs would be:

Q	TSC
400	$217.50
524	$209.60
600	$211.67

The total impact of errors in estimating Q for one material does not appear to be critical. If, however, tens of thousands of items are carried in inventory, this could expand the impact of estimation errors tremendously. Additionally, when quantity discounts are present, as in Figure 10.7, total annual costs can be much higher if we order the wrong quantity by just a slight amount if near a price break.

Of perhaps greater concern to inventory decisions in POM is the cost of stockouts. Much of the cost of stockouts may be profits forgone in lost sales, lost customer goodwill, interruption of production schedules, and other costs that are impossible to determine precisely. The inability to quantify precisely the costs of stockouts does not deter us from including them in our inventory planning in POM. We know that stockouts are costly and thus we attempt to avoid them. Safety stocks are routinely carried for most materials, but even these buffer stocks cannot eliminate stockouts entirely. The uncertainty of usage rates and usage patterns causes us to run out of stock periodically.

Another pragmatic POM tactic is to devise means to replenish inventories quickly through emergency procedures. These emergency procedures usually allow us to avoid stockouts and carry lower levels of safety stocks. One good example of the use of emergency replenishment procedures is in hospitals. Many hospitals in the Western states have National Guard helicopters available on extremely short notice to supply critical materials as needed from other hospitals or hospital supply warehouses. These procedures are necessary because many hospital materials, such as whole blood, for example, have such short shelf lives that only a very small quantity of these materials is ordered at a time. When unexpected demand for these materials forces inventory levels too low, emergency procedures can usually deliver the materials within a couple of hours. Although inventory planners in manufacturing may not have helicopters flying in emergency supplies of materials, other emergency procedures do exist to allow these systems to successfully meet the uncertainties of demand and to avoid stockouts or at least minimize their impact.

DYNAMICS OF INVENTORY PLANNING

Order quantities in fixed order quantity inventory systems may not be as fixed as we have led you to believe in this chapter. Although we suggested that hybrid systems exist that do not operate with fixed order quantities, we should probably add that so-called fixed order quantities may be rare in practice. Almost all inventory systems continually review their ordering practices and modify order quantities, order points, and time intervals as required to give the kind of inventory performance desired in their particular situation. When we view inventory planning as a dynamic system that is continually modified as needed, less emphasis must be placed on any one computation. This view makes us realize that we do not have to live with a computed order quantity from now on.

Actually, although many firms say that they use EOQ as the basis for setting order quantities, they are observed in practice to set *initial* order quantities based on tradition, rough estimates, or other means. This is not surprising or particularly disturbing because these decisions are continually modified as time passes; order quantities are increased or decreased to fit their demand and supply patterns and thus the inventory systems empirically develop order quantities and order points that work. Neither excessive stockouts nor excessive inventories result.

OTHER FACTORS AFFECTING INVENTORY PLANNING

The variables included in the models of this chapter for developing order points, order quantities, and time intervals are important, but in practice other variables also affect these decisions.

The quantity of a material that *can* be ordered may be determined by the capacity of an organization's warehouse. In the models of this chapter, warehouse capacity was implicitly assumed to be infinite or at least not a limiting factor. Another factor that may severely limit the size that an order for products *can* be is the capacity of the production department and the production schedules for other products. Once production schedules are set, they often cannot be changed quickly to work in an optimal order size for a material. We must often take the quantity of a material or product that we can get and not what we want because production capacity cannot be altered quickly, and the production department and its schedules are committed to producing quantities of other products.

Another factor that can give us more products or materials than we in POM would actually like to order is special buys on materials. When purchasing discovers a special buy, the savings from quantity discounts are often so spectacular that we just have to buy all we can get of that material. Many instances exist where we buy one or two years' supply of material on one order. Although this tends to play havoc with our warehousing and increases our annual carrying costs, ordering costs fall and the savings in purchase costs may be so great that we occasionally make these special buys.

These and other factors act on our order quantity and order point decisions in POM practice. These factors do not destroy the usefulness of the models presented in this chapter, but the results of these models are often modified as these other factors operate in the practical day-to-day operation of production systems.

AUTOMATION AND INVENTORY PLANNING

One of the first areas in business to receive the benefits of computerization was inventory planning. Computers' ability to store and retrieve huge quantities of information and to make lightning-quick and accurate calculations made them an almost sure success in inventory planning.

Today, inventory stock records are routinely maintained in the memories of computer systems. As changes in inventory levels occur, the computer files are modified to reflect the latest inventory transactions. Managers can query these files and instantaneously determine the status of each material's inventory level, what orders are outstanding, and other information critical to inventory management.

Computing order quantities, determining when orders should be placed, and automatic printing of purchase requisitions and purchase orders are routinely performed by computers in some organizations today. Now don't get the wrong idea — we can't totally turn over these inventory-planning decisions to computers. Someone must still describe in detail the basis for order quantities and order points. Computers just speed up the process and complete the calculations more quickly and accurately.

Complete computer software packages have been developed by the major computer producers and other software specialists that perform a wide range of inventory management functions. IBM's Inventory Management Program and Control Techniques (IMPACT), IBM's Communications Oriented Production Information and Control System (COPICS), and similar packages from Control Data Corporation, Xerox Computer Services, and other suppliers provide broad management information systems for operations managers.

■■ ■ ■ ■

TABLE 10.9 *Summary of Inventory-Planning Models*

Variable Definitions

  ac = acquisition cost — cost of producing or purchasing one unit of a material (dollars per unit)

  C = carrying cost — cost of carrying one unit in inventory for one year (dollars per unit per year)

  D = annual demand for a material (units per year)

  d = rate at which materials are used out of inventory (units per time period)

  $\bar{d}$ = mean of d, demand per time period (units per time period)

  DDLT = demand during lead time (units)

  EDDLT = expected demand during lead time (units)

  EOQ = economic order quantity — the optimal quantity of material to order (units per order)

  j = percentage of EDDLT as safety stock

  LT = lead time (number of time periods)

  OP = order point — the point at which materials should be ordered (units or point in time)

  p = rate at which materials are supplied to inventory (same units as d)

  Q = quantity of material ordered at each order point (units per order)

  σ_{DDLT} = standard deviation of DDLT

  σ_d = standard deviation of d

  S = average cost of completing an order for a material (dollars per order)

  SS = safety stock (units)

  T = order period — the time interval between orders for a material (fraction of a year)

  TMC = total annual material costs — the total annual costs of stocking and acquiring a material (dollars per year)

  TSC = total annual stocking costs — the total annual carrying and annual ordering costs for a material (dollars per year)

  Z = value from Appendix A, number of standard deviations that OP is from EDDLT

■■

SUMMARY

The inventory cycle is the central focus in independent demand inventory systems. In these systems, which include finished products and certain raw materials, materials are ordered, delivered, and used, and the cycle is repeated. The key issues are how much to order of each material and when to place the orders. The formulas and variable definitions of inventory planning that are developed in this chapter are given in Table 10.9.

Fixed order quantity inventory systems place orders for materials where the quantities are fixed from order to order. In these systems, material orders are trig-

---

Formulas

Fixed Order Quantity Inventory Systems

Model I — Basic EOQ (see Example 10.1)

$$EOQ = \sqrt{2DS/C} \qquad TSC = (Q/2)C + (D/Q)S$$

Model II — EOQ with Gradual Deliveries (see Example 10.2)

$$EOQ = \sqrt{(2DS/C)[p/(p-d)]}$$

$$TSC = (Q/2)[(p-d)/p]C + (D/Q)S$$

Order Points (see Examples 10.4, 10.5, 10.6, 10.7, 10.8, and 10.9)

$$OP = EDDLT + SS$$

$$OP = EDDLT + j(EDDLT) \qquad \text{Percentage of EDDLT}$$

$$OP = EDDLT + \sqrt{EDDLT} \qquad \text{Square root of EDDLT}$$

$$OP = EDDLT + Z(\sigma_{DDLT}) \qquad \text{Normal DDLT}$$

$$OP = LT(\bar{d}) + Z\sqrt{LT(\sigma_d)^2} \qquad \text{Constant LT and normal d}$$

Model III — EOQ with Quantity Discounts (see Example 10.3)
When assumptions of Model I apply:

$$EOQ = \sqrt{2DS/C} \qquad TMC = (Q/2)C + (D/Q)S + (D)ac$$

When assumptions of Model II apply:

$$EOQ = \sqrt{(2DS/C)[p/(p-d)]}$$

$$TMC = (Q/2)[(p-d)/p]C + (D/Q)S + (D)ac$$

In either case the procedures of Table 10.5 must be followed.

Fixed Order Period System

Model IV — Economic Order Period (see Example 10.10)

$$T = \sqrt{2S/DC} \qquad TSC = (DT/2)C + S/T$$

$$Q = \text{Upper inventory target} - \text{Inventory level} + EDDLT$$

---

gered when inventory levels fall to a particular level, the order point. In setting order points, the uncertainty of demand per day and lead times cause operations to carry safety stock. Both service level and optimal total expected cost per lead time are used in setting order points. Fixed order quantity systems assume that perpetual inventory accounting systems are in use.

In fixed order period systems, material orders are placed at equal time intervals for enough materials to last approximately until the next review. The key issue in these systems is how often to place an order for each material. At the time of the order a physical inventory count of the material will be taken and enough of the material will be ordered to bring the inventory level up to some predetermined upper target level. These systems tend to be used when perpetual inventory systems are impractical, as in the case of certain types of retailing operations.

When a material is ordered only once or when highly perishable materials are ordered at frequent intervals, single-period inventory models are used. Payoff tables and marginal analysis are used to analyze these inventory problems. The goal is to minimize the total of expected long costs (the expected costs of stocking too many) and expected short costs (the expected costs of stocking too few).

Although the total annual stocking costs of materials is an important criterion for making inventory-planning decisions, other factors can also be important. Among these are warehouse capacity, production schedules and capacity, and special buys on materials. Automation and computers play an increasing role in inventory planning.

REVIEW AND DISCUSSION QUESTIONS

1. Name three purposes of carrying these inventories:
   a. finished goods,
   b. in-process, and
   c. raw material.

2. Define these terms: *backlogging, produce-to-order, produce-to-stock, level production, order quantity, order point, inventory cycle, machine changeover, length of production run, uncoupling operations, lot size, order period, two-bin system.*

3. Compare and contrast fixed order quantity inventory systems with fixed order period inventory systems.

4. Define these terms: *carrying cost, ordering cost, stockout cost, annual carrying cost, annual ordering cost, total annual stocking cost.*

5. Name four assumptions of the basic EOQ—Model I.

6. Name five assumptions of the EOQ with gradual deliveries—Model II.

7. What units are these variables in?
   a. D,
   b. S,
   c. C,
   d. Q,
   e. EOQ,
   f. p,
   g. d.

8. Why is the maximum inventory level of a material greater when orders are received all at once than when orders are received gradually?

9. What are the purposes of safety stock? How will the use of safety stock affect the EOQ? How will the use of safety stock affect TSC?

10. Explain what is meant by this statement: "The uncertainties of inventory planning almost always affect operations managers when they are most vulnerable—when inventory levels are at their lowest points."

11. Give a brief explanation for each of the following:
    a. DDLT,
    b. EDDLT,
    c. σ_{DDLT},
    d. discrete DDLT distributions,
    e. continuous DDLT distributions,
    f. LT,
    g. σ_{LT}.

12. Define *service levels.*

13. Assuming the DDLT distribution is normal, write the formula for computing:
    a. EDDLT, and
    b. σ_{DDLT}.

14. What criteria are used to set optimal safety stock levels when payoff tables and marginal analysis are used?

15. Explain the relationship between these variables: order point, safety stock, and EDDLT.

16. What factors other than total annual stocking costs typically affect Q and T in practice?

PROBLEMS

1. Given: D = 300,000 units per year, C = 30 percent of acquisition cost per unit per year, S = $5.95 per order, and ac = $1.50 per unit. Required:
   a. EOQ, and
   b. TSC at EOQ.
   c. How much would TSC increase if the order quantity must be 3,000 units because of a standard shipping container size?

2. The Zartex Manufacturing Company produces ammonium nitrate fertilizer to sell to wholesalers. One raw material—calcium nitrite—is purchased from one supplier located near Zartex's plant; 5,750,000 tons of calcium nitrite are forecast to be required next year to support production. If calcium nitrite costs $22.50 per ton, carrying cost is 40 percent of acquisition cost, and ordering cost is $595 per order:
   a. In what quantities should Zartex buy calcium nitrite?
   b. What annual stocking cost will be incurred if calcium nitrite is ordered at the EOQ?
   c. How many orders per year must Zartex place for calcium nitrite?
   d. How much time will elapse between orders?

3. The Shady Lane Savings and Loan Company orders cash from its home office to meet daily counter transactions. If Shady Lane estimates that $5,000,000 will be needed next year, each order for cash costs $650 (which includes clerical and armored car delivery costs) and idle cash costs 10 percent:
   a. What quantities of cash should Shady Lane include on each order?
   b. What total annual stocking cost would result from Shady Lane's following your recommendation in Part *a*?
   c. How many days could Shady Lane operate with each order of cash if it stayed open 250 days a year and cash were ordered at the EOQ?

4. Swimco Inc., a swimming pool retail supply firm in Phoenix, stocks pelletized chlorine that is sold to local pool owners. Chlorine is ordered from a regional wholesaler in Los Angeles at a uniform price of $95.60 per 100 pounds. Thirty tons of chlorine are estimated to be needed next year. Swimco orders chlorine in the 0–5,000 pounds per order range. Carrying costs are 30 percent of acquisition cost per pound per year, and ordering cost is $55 per order. If chlorine is ordered in quantities greater than 5,000 pounds, then carrying cost falls to 20 percent of acquisition cost per pound per year because the supplier gives special late-payment privileges which reduce the interest charges that must ordinarily be paid to finance the chlorine inventory at a local bank, but ordering cost increases to $75 per order because of extra handling costs. How many pounds of chlorine should Swimco order at each order point?

5. Several executives of the Ramco Service Company, a maintenance-contracting firm that services hydraulic pumping equipment, are reviewing some rather disturbing news at their monthly financial review meeting. The vice president of finance states that the cost of financing the company's supplies inventories has increased 25 percent and the acquisition cost of its diaphragms has increased 5 percent. Increased labor rates and fringe benefits have caused ordering costs to rise 29 percent, and annual demand for diaphragms has declined 15 percent. Charlie McCullough, vice president of operations, sits quietly at the end of the conference table waiting for the inevitable question. Finally it comes from Ramco's president: "Charlie, how much, percentage-wise, will your order quantities change and how much will your total annual stocking cost change for diaphragms?" Can you answer for Charlie?

6. Given: $p = 500$ units per day, $d = 100$ units per day, $D = 10,000$ units per year, $S = \$20$ per order, and $C = \$.50$ per unit per year. Required:
   a. EOQ, and
   b. TSC at EOQ.

7. The Oklahoma Crude Oil Refinery buys crude oil from the Red Rock oil field located in eastern New Mexico, western Texas, and western Oklahoma. The refinery has been guaranteed through long-term supply contracts that its needs for crude will be supplied from this field at $18.90 per barrel as long as 5,000 barrels per day are accepted by the refinery during shipping periods. The refinery uses crude oil at a rate of 1,500 barrels per day and plans to purchase 450,000 barrels from the Red Rock field next year. If the carrying cost is 20 percent of acquisition cost per unit per year and the ordering cost is $2,500 per order:
   a. What is the EOQ for Red Rock crude?
   b. What is the TSC at EOQ?

   c. How many days of production are supported by each order of Red Rock crude?

   d. How much storage capacity is needed for the crude?

8. The Central Iowa Electric Company buys coal from the Cedar Creek Coal Company to generate electricity. Cedar Creek supplies coal at the rate of 3,500 tons per day at a price of $10.50 per ton. Central Iowa Electric uses the coal at a rate of 800 tons per day and works 365 days per year. The annual carrying cost and annual ordering cost functions for the coal are:

$$\text{Annual carrying cost} = (C/5) \text{ multiplied by average inventory}$$

$$\text{Annual ordering cost} = (S/1{,}000)(D/Q)$$

   a. Derive a formula for TSC.

   b. Derive a formula for the EOQ.

   c. What is the EOQ for coal if $C = \$2.50$ per ton per year and $S = \$5{,}000$ per order?

   d. What is the minimum TSC for coal?

9. Given: $D = 50{,}000$ units per year, $S = \$250$ per order, $C = .25$ (ac) dollars per unit per year, $p = 500$ units per day, $d = 200$ units per day, $ac_1 = \$5$ per unit for 0 to 5,999 units per order, $ac_2 = \$4.95$ per unit for 6,000 to 9,999 units per order, and $ac_3 = \$4.93$ per unit for 10,000+ units per order. Required:

   a. minimum TMC,

   b. EOQ,

   c. number of orders per year, and

   d. maximum inventory level.

10. The T. F. Goodwealth Auto Supply Stores Company has a regional tire warehouse in Atlanta, Georgia. One popular tire — H78-15, 4-ply polyester, is estimated to have a demand of 25,000 next year. It costs the warehouse $100 to place and receive an order and carrying cost is 30 percent of acquisition cost. The supplier quotes these prices on this tire:

Q	ac
0–499	$21.60
500–999	20.95
1000+	20.90

   a. What is the warehouse's EOQ?

   b. What is the minimum TMC?

   c. How much time will elapse between orders?

11. Electronic Computing Services Inc. (ECS) is a computer center selling computing services to banks in Miami, Florida. The center uses large quantities of computer printout paper #3225. ECS buys the paper from a regional warehouse of a large paper company. The warehouse has delivery trucks that make daily rounds to all the customers in its region. ECS receives 100 boxes of paper per day at a cost of $19.50 per box. ECS uses the paper at a rate of 50 boxes per day on a 5-day-per-week operation. It costs ECS $75 to place an order for the paper and carrying costs are 20 percent of acquisition cost. The supplier has recently put on extra delivery trucks and is offering

one half of 1 percent discount if its customers will take 200 or more boxes per delivery day. You may assume that ECS can receive less than 100 or 200 boxes on the last delivery day of an order.
   a.   What is ECS's present EOQ?
   b.   What is ECS's present TMC?
   c.   What would ECS's EOQ be if it accepted the supplier's discount offer?
   d.   What would ECS's new TMC be under the discount arrangement?
   e.   Should ECS accept the proposal?

12. Jay Houser is the director of maintenance at the United Silicon Chemicals plant in Baton Rouge. Jay is meeting with his materials manager, Dick Blake, to plan inventories for their neoprene 6-inch spring seal, a commonly used repair item at the plant. Under consideration is the order point for this item and the appropriate level of safety stock. Average demand per day is 5.4 seals and average lead time is 30 days. Dick suggests to Jay that United Silicon is accumulating so much data in its computer that now may be the time to institute a more sophisticated approach to setting order points. He shows Jay the following information on past demands during lead time for this seal:

Actual DDLT	*Occurrences*	*Actual DDLT*	*Occurrences*
80–99	3	160–179	9
100–119	4	180–199	12
120–139	7	200–219	5
140–159	8		

Dick suggests a service level of 90 percent, based on historical DDLT. Jay instructs Dick to recommend the safety stock level and order point for the seal under the 90 percent service level policy.
   a.   Compute the order point using the 90 percent service level.
   b.   What safety stock is provided with your answer to Part *a* above?

13. Given: EDDLT $= 55.5$ units, $\sigma_{DDLT} = 12.5$ units, DDLT is normally distributed, and service level is 95 percent. Required:
   a.   OP, and
   b.   SS.

14. The E–Z Mony Loan Company is a feeder operation servicing local Detroit industrial workers. It must periodically go to banks to trade loan paper for cash to use for short-term loans. E–Z wishes to know at what minimum level of cash inventory it should initiate order procedures for more cash from the banks. Mr. Slick, the president of E–Z, believes that the actual DDLT is really normally distributed and that the historical data for six previous periods are representative of what will be experienced in the future: 550, 520, 990, 780, 850, and 660, in thousands of dollars. If Mr. Slick specifies a service level of 85 percent:
   a.   What is the order point?
   b.   What is the safety stock level?

15. The maintenance department at the Blimp Tire Manufacturing Company stocks spare parts that are used to repair machines in production departments throughout the plant. One such part—#1520 bearing—has these demand-per-month historical data from ten previous periods: 21, 15, 22, 30, 18, 26, 23, 29, 25, and 19. If the lead time is so predictable that it can be considered a constant 1.25 months, d is normally distributed, and if a service level of 90 percent is specified:
    a. What is the order point?
    b. What is the safety stock level?

16. Given: Long cost per unit = $20, short cost per unit = $30, and historical DDLT data in units are:

DDLT (Units)	P(DDLT)
6	.1
7	.3
8	.5
9	.1

    Required:
    a. Use payoff tables to determine the order point.
    b. Use marginal analysis to determine the order point.
    c. Compute the safety stock.

17. The BIG University has a central work pool that supplies electrostatic copies for students at a price of $.10 per unit. The actual cost of making the copies is $.05. Ms. Stacey, the work pool manager, wants to determine what the optimal order point should be for the electrostatic paper if there are 20,000 sheets per case, the carrying cost from one reorder cycle to another is $.03 per sheet, and past DDLT has been:

DDLT (Cases)	P(DDLT)	DDLT (Cases)	P(DDLT)
10	.10	12	.25
11	.20	13	.35
		14	.10

    a. Compute the order point using payoff tables.
    b. Compute the order point using marginal analysis.
    c. Compute the safety stock.

18. Given: j = 20 percent and EDDLT = 500. Required:
    a. safety stock using percentage of EDDLT method,
    b. order point using percentage of EDDLT method,
    c. safety stock using square root of EDDLT method, and
    d. order point using square root of EDDLT method.

19. Jay Houser is the director of maintenance at the United Silicon Chemicals plant in Baton Rouge. Jay is meeting with his materials manager, Dick Blake, to plan inventories for their neoprene 6-inch spring seal, a commonly used repair item at the plant. Under consideration is the order point for this item and the appropriate level of safety stock. The plant operates under a policy of carrying 50 percent EDDLT as safety stock across all items in the same class as this seal. Average demand per day is 5.4 seals, and average lead time is 30 days.
   a. How much safety stock should be carried for this seal?
   b. At what inventory level should an order for the seal be processed?

20. Given: D = 30,000 units per year, S = $500 per order, and C = $5 per unit per year. Required:
   a. economic order period, and
   b. TSC at economic order period.

21. The General Services Administration (GSA) is a government agency that buys and distributes supplies to other agencies. GSA maintains a regional supply warehouse in Chicago. One of its items is Form GSA #35,665—a 15-part purchase order. GSA takes periodic inventory counts of its Chicago stock and places orders for materials needed. Inventory counts were taken today and the inventory level was 300,000 forms. The upper inventory target is 1,000,000, and EDDLT is 200,000. Annual demand in the region is approximately 5,500,000 forms, ordering cost is $1,000 per order, acquisition cost is $.05 per form, and carrying cost is 35 percent of acquisition cost.
   a. When should the physical inventory count be taken next?
   b. How many forms should be ordered today?

22. Computer Products Corporation (CPC) operates an electronic assembly plant in El Paso. CPC's production analysis group is investigating a recurring problem on the shop floor. The problem concerns frequent shortages of a material, Mira-bond 2301 —a gold alloy for plating various electrical components' exposed circuits. When the material is not available for use in production, it must be rushed in from outside suppliers at high cost in order to avoid costly shutdown of the production lines. According to the cost analysts in the production analysis group, this shortage cost averages about $50 per ounce short during any one week. Because of the high cost of the material, however, when too much of the material is stocked, a high carrying cost, which is a long cost, is borne by CPC. This long cost is estimated to be $20 per ounce stocked but not used in any one week and carried over into the next week. The weekly demand pattern for the material has been determined by studying recent production records at the plant:

Weekly Demand for Mira-bond 2301 (Ounces)	Probability of Weekly Demand
100	.2
150	.3
200	.3
300	.1
500	.1

a. How many ounces of the Mira-bond 2301 material should be stocked in each week with the objective of minimizing the total expected long and short costs for the material?

b. What is the EVPI?

23. Big Store sells A60 Strongcharge automobile batteries. Batteries are ordered weekly for delivery on Monday morning. The sales price for an A60 is $65 and its cost for Big Store is $45. If too many batteries are ordered and stock must be carried over the weekend, corporate headquarters charges Big Store $15 per battery for increased insurance, finance, and warehouse occupation costs. If Big Store is out of stock, it forgoes the profits from missed sales. How many A60 batteries should Big Store order each week if the weekly sales pattern is as shown below?

Number of Batteries Demanded	Probability
20	.2
30	.3
40	.4
45	.1

a. Work this problem by first minimizing the weekly total expected long and short costs (carrying and opportunity costs).

b. Next, work the problem by maximizing the total expected profits, and compute the EVPI.

c. Show the equivalence of your solutions in Parts a and b.

24. The Handtomouth Finance Company keeps cash on hand to meet short-term loans. If the firm keeps too much cash on hand, it forgoes some interest income that it could have earned in alternative investments; that is, idle cash has an opportunity, or long, cost. If Handtomouth keeps too little cash on hand, it must go to other lending institutions for cash, and this results in extra operating costs (short costs). The estimates of demand for the next period are:

Demand or SN (Thousands)	Frequency	P(SN)
$100	$1/10$	.1
200	$2/10$	.2
250	$3/10$	.3
300	$1/10$	.1
400	$3/10$	.3

The firm's estimates of long and short costs are:

$$SC = \$1,000 + .1X \qquad LC = \$500 + .05Y$$

where:

SC = total period short costs
LC = total period long costs
X = total number of units (thousands of dollars) short during the period
Y = total number of units (thousands of dollars) long during the period

How much cash should Handtomouth keep on hand for the next period to minimize total expected long and short costs?

COMPUTER PROBLEMS/CASES

THE PHOENIX WHOLESALE COMPANY

The Phoenix Wholesale Company sells dry goods to regional retailers. Jethro Bleu, the president of the company, has just addressed the company's management team and has stressed the absolute necessity of reducing the cost of their warehousing operations. Mary Montgomery, the director of warehousing operations, is already investigating ways to respond to Mr. Jethro's pronouncement.

Mary's staff is considering proposing that a minicomputer be installed to assist them in converting the present fixed order period inventory system that depends on periodic physical counts of inventory to a fixed order quantity system that assumes a perpetual inventory record system. The staff has developed these estimates for a single inventory item that is believed to be representative of the many items in their warehouses:

Acquisition cost: $9.55 per unit

Ordering cost: $21.50 per order

Carrying cost: (40 percent of acquisition cost) $ per unit per year

Estimated annual sales: 57,500 units per year

Annual cost of physical counts of inventory for the item: $1,200 per year

Annual cost of minicomputer perpetual inventory system (portion of total cost of the system allocated to this item based on cost of goods sold): $250 per year

Assignment

1. Compute the estimated annual cost of the present inventory system for this item.
2. Compute the estimated annual cost for the proposed perpetual inventory system for this item.
3. What annual savings for this single item are likely to result from installing the new inventory system?
4. What difficulties prevent us from extrapolating the savings for this single item to the entire inventory in the warehouses? How can the information developed in No. 3 be used effectively in deciding whether to adopt the new inventory system?
5. What difficulties are likely to be encountered in implementing the new inventory system?

🖳 *INVENTORY PLANNING AT COMPUTER PRODUCTS CORPORATION (CPC)*

Jane Boroughs, purchasing specialist in the purchasing department at the corporate head-quarters of Computer Products Corporation (CPC) in San Jose, is meeting with Bob Bliss, a production planner at CPC's Los Angeles plant. The purpose of the meeting is to develop ordering policies for some of the products that are warehoused and shipped from the Los Angeles plant. These products are electronic assemblies and components that are sold to the computer and electronics industries. The products are either bought and stocked or produced and held in a finished goods warehouse until ordered by CPC's customers. Jane and Bob must determine how often and how many of the products will be bought or produced and placed in inventory when each product is replenished. They have classified all of the products into three classes:

Class of Material	Example of Material	Description of Material Class
A	PS100 Power Supply Assembly	Materials that are of high cost, high volume, or otherwise of critical importance to customers. While these materials represent only about 20 percent of the *number* of materials, they represent about 80 percent of material *value.*
B	T55 Vertical Axis Chip	Materials that are of moderate cost, moderate volume, or otherwise moderately important to customers. These materials represent about 30 percent of the *number* of materials and about 20 percent of material *value.*
C	T90 Zinc Oxide	Materials that are of low cost, low volume, or otherwise of low importance to customers. They can usually be obtained on short notice or other materials can be substituted. They represent about 50 percent of the *number* of materials and only about 5 percent of material *value.*

Assignment

1. The PS100 Power Supply Assembly costs $14.95; CPC is forecasting that 90,000 of the assemblies will be sold annually; CPC estimates a 40 percent carrying cost for its inventory per year; it costs approximately $100 to process, receive, and inspect an order for these assemblies; and the Los Angeles plant uses a fixed order quantity inventory system for Class A materials. How many of the assemblies should be ordered when the material is replenished?

2. Jane Boroughs and Bob Bliss have just learned that CPC's supplier has offered to ship the PS100 Power Supply Assemblies at a rate of 500 per day during shipping periods via the supplier's own truck and that the Los Angeles plant works 300 days per year. If all other data in No. 1 above remain the same: **(a)** How many assemblies should be ordered when the material is replenished? **(b)** What annual savings will come to CPC if the new shipping policy is enacted?

3. The T55 Vertical Axis Chip costs $6.90; CPC is forecasting annual sales of 10,000 units; it costs approximately $50 to process, receive, and inspect an order for this material; and the Los Angeles plant uses a fixed order quantity inventory system for Class B materials. How many of the chips should be ordered when the material is replenished?

4. Jane Boroughs and Bob Bliss have just learned that CPC's supplier has offered to ship the T55 Vertical Axis Chip at a rate of 100 per day during shipping periods. The Los Angeles plant works 300 days per year. If all other data in No. 3 above remain the same: **(a)** How many chips should be ordered when the material is replenished? **(b)** What annual savings will come to CPC if the new shipping policy is enacted?

5. The supplier of the PS100 Power Supply Assembly has agreed to give CPC a quantity discount. The cost to CPC will be:

Quantity Ordered per Order	Cost per Assembly
0– 999	$14.95
1,000–4,999	14.85
5,000+	14.80

If all other data in No. 1 above remain the same: **(a)** How many assemblies should be ordered when the material is replenished? **(b)** What annual savings will come to CPC because of quantity discounts?

6. The supplier of the PS100 Power Supply Assembly has offered to combine its offer of gradual supply during shipping periods of No. 2 above and the quantity discount offer of No. 5. How many of the assemblies should be ordered when the material is replenished if all other data remain the same as in Nos. 2 and 5?

7. The supplier of the T55 Vertical Axis Chip has agreed to give CPC a quantity discount. The cost to CPC will be:

Quantity Ordered per Order	Cost per Chip
0– 999	$6.90
1,000–2,999	6.85
3,000+	6.82

If all other data in No. 3 above remain the same: **(a)** How many chips should be ordered when the material is replenished? **(b)** What annual savings will come to CPC because of quantity discounts?

8. The T90 Zinc Oxide costs $3.40 per pound; CPC is forecasting that 8,000 pounds will be sold annually; it costs approximately $25 to process, receive, and inspect an order for the material; and the Los Angeles plant uses a fixed order period inventory system for Class C materials. **(a)** How often should the material be ordered? **(b)** If Bob Bliss wants the upper inventory target for the material to be 1,000 pounds, the present inventory level is 540 pounds, and the EDDLT is 300 pounds, how many pounds of the material should be ordered when the material is replenished?

9. The expected demand during lead time (EDDLT) for the first two materials is:

Material	EDDLT
PS100 Power Supply Assembly	6,000
T55 Vertical Axis Chip	350

(a) Compute the order point for each of these materials by using a 20 percent of EDDLT method of computing safety stock. **(b)** Compute the order point for each of these materials by using the square root of EDDLT method of computing safety stock.

SAFETY STOCK LEVELS AT COMPUTER PRODUCTS CORPORATION (CPC)

The Austin plant of Computer Products Corporation (CPC) stocks C2900 printers in its finished goods warehouse. Abe Sanchez, materials planner at the plant, is studying the printer's demand during lead time (DDLT) so that he can set the order point for this important product. He has found these DDLT historical data, which he believes to be representative of future demand:

Actual DDLT	Frequency	Actual DDLT	Frequency
0–29	0	70– 79	.15
30–39	.05	80– 89	.10
40–49	.15	90– 99	.05
50–59	.25	100–109	.05
60–69	.20	110–120	0

Assignment

1. If Abe Sanchez wants to provide at least a 90 percent service level on these printers: **(a)** What is the order point? **(b)** What is the safety stock?

2. Abe Sanchez thinks that the DDLT for the C2900 printer is actually normally distributed with a mean of 65 and a standard deviation of 15. If he wants to provide at least a 90 percent service level on these printers: **(a)** What is the order point? **(b)** What is the safety stock?

3. Abe Sanchez thinks that the lead time on the C2900 printers is so stable that the lead time can be assumed to be a constant 10 days and that the demand per day is normally distributed with a mean of 6 and a standard deviation of 4. If Abe wants to provide at least a 90 percent service level on these printers: **(a)** What is the order point? **(b)** What is the safety stock?

4. Abe Sanchez has determined that in each reorder cycle it costs CPC approximately $100 whenever a C2900 printer is stocked as safety stock and not actually required to satisfy demand during lead time. Also, he estimates that it costs CPC about $300 whenever a printer is not available to satisfy demand during lead time. If you assume that the midpoints of the demand during lead time (DDLT) classes (35, 45, 55, etc.) are representative of the classes of DDLT: **(a)** Use a payoff table to determine the optimal order point for the C2900 printers. **(b)** Use marginal analysis to determine the optimal order point for the C2900 printers.

SELECTED BIBLIOGRAPHY

APICS Bibliography of Articles, Books, Films, and Audio-Cassettes on Production and Inventory Control and Related Subjects. 11th ed. Falls Church, VA: American Production and Inventory Control Society, 1987.

APICS Dictionary of Inventory Control Terms and Production Control Terms. 6th ed. Falls Church, VA: American Production and Inventory Control Society, 1987.

Buffa, Elwood S., and Jeffrey G. Miller. *Production-Inventory Systems: Planning and Control.* 3rd ed. Homewood, IL: Richard D. Irwin, 1979.

Fogarty, D. W., and T. R. Hoffman. *Production and Inventory Management.* Dallas: South-Western Publishing, 1983.

Harris, F. W. *Operations and Costs.* Chicago: A. W. Shaw, 1915.

Hoyt, J. "Order Points Tailored to Suit Your Business." *Production and Inventory Management* 14(Fourth Quarter 1973):42.

Mayer, R. R. "Selection of Rules-of-Thumb in Inventory Control." *Journal of Purchasing* 8(May 1972):19–24.

McLeavey, Dennis W., and Seetharama L. Narasimhan. *Production Planning and Inventory Control.* Boston: Allyn & Bacon, 1985.

Plossl, G. W., and O. W. Wight. *Production and Inventory Control.* Englewood Cliffs, NJ: Prentice-Hall, 1967.

Plossl, George W., and W. Evert Welch. *The Role of Top Management in the Control of Inventory.* Reston, VA: Reston Publishing, 1979.

Pursche, S. "Putting Service Level into Proper Perspective." *Production and Inventory Management* 16(Third Quarter 1975):69–75.

Silver, Edward A., and Rein Peterson. *Decision Systems for Inventory Management and Production Planning.* New York: Wiley, 1985.

Tersine, Richard J. *Principles of Inventory and Materials Management.* 2nd ed. New York: North-Holland, 1987.

Wight, Oliver W. *Production and Inventory Management in the Computer Age.* Boston: Cahnere Books, 1974.

RESOURCE REQUIREMENTS PLANNING SYSTEMS

MATERIAL REQUIREMENTS PLANNING (MRP) AND CAPACITY REQUIREMENTS PLANNING (CRP)

REDUCING INVENTORIES AT SC CORPORATION THROUGH MRP

At SC Corporation, the world's largest producer of evaporative coolers, sales had grown from $5 million to $20 million over the previous 15 years. This growth had resulted from the efficiency that evaporative coolers have over conventional refrigeration systems as the cost of electricity escalated. Mr. Gentry had owned SC for over 30 years, but he recently sold the company to a large, diversified electrical machinery manufacturer. The new owner sent in a team of young, aggressive operations managers to take over the factory, and their initial impression was not favorable. The factory was overloaded with inventory: $20 million in raw materials inventory to support $20 million in sales per year seemed out of line. Inventory occupied so much space in the factory that production capacity was being curtailed. With sales forecasted to be $30 million next year, it was clear that something had to be done to increase production capacity. The team of operations managers initiated material requirements planning (MRP) to reduce inventory levels. It was also hoped that by freeing up factory space through reduction of inventories, another assembly line could be installed without increasing the size of the physical plant. After two years, the results of the MRP project are spectacular. Annual sales are $40 million, total materials inventory is $9.8 million, profits have increased fivefold, and the factory now has enough capacity to support sales of about $50 million. All of this was accomplished with less investment. The machinery needed for the new assembly line required less investment than the reduction in inventory levels attributed to MRP.

As the previous success story indicates, material requirements planning (MRP) is being used increasingly as manufacturers strive to reduce inventory levels, increase production capacity, and increase profits. No course in POM is complete today without a thorough treatment of MRP. This chapter is about resource requirements planning systems, and MRP is an important part of these systems.

In Chapter 9 we described how employment plans, machinery and utility plans, subcontractor and material supply contracts, and facility modification plans are developed from aggregate capacity plans. These aggregate plans usually span periods of 6 to 18 months, and short-range master production schedules are developed within the capacity constraints formed by aggregate plans. These short-range master production schedules span periods of a few weeks to several months and delineate the finished products or end items to be manufactured. Master production schedules are the engine that drive the entire resource requirements planning system.

Resource requirements planning determines the quantity and timing of all of the production resources needed to produce the end items in the master production schedule. Production resources include raw materials, purchased parts, produced parts, personnel, cash, and production capacity. Resource requirements planning has a language that has evolved with its growing use in industry. The terms and their definitions that are a part of this language are found in Table 11.1. It may be helpful for you to refer to this table as these terms are used in this chapter.

Production functions do not do resource requirements planning alone. Figure 11.1 illustrates how the functional areas of a business work together to plan and control a firm's resource requirements. All of these functions supply information that makes the resource requirements planning system work, and then each of the functions receives information back so that it can do its job better.

■■

FIGURE 11.1 *Inputs and Outputs of a Resource Requirements Planning System*

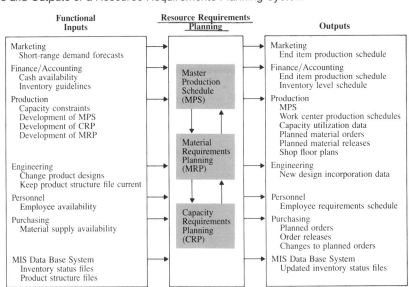

■■

TABLE 11.1   Terms Often Used in Resource Requirements Planning

Allocated Inventory — Materials that are in inventory or on order but have been assigned to specific production orders in the future. These materials are therefore not available for use on other orders.

Available Inventory — Materials that are in inventory or on order that are not safety stock or allocated to other uses.

Bills of Material File — A file containing the bills of material for all end items; a major element of the MRP system. A bill of material is a listing of all raw materials, parts, subassemblies, and assemblies that go into an end item. The amount of each component that is required to produce one end item is included. The way that the components go together, or product structure, is also included.

Bucket — The principal unit of time measurement in MRP systems. The term refers to a particular period of time in the planning horizon. For example, Time Bucket #6 means the sixth period, usually a week in duration, of the planning horizon.

Capacity Requirements Planning (CRP) — The process of reconciling the master production schedule to the labor and machine capacities of the production departments over the planning horizon.

Changes to Planned Orders — A primary output of MRP. These reports show how planned order schedules for a material should be changed. Orders may be delivered earlier, later, or canceled altogether, or quantities may be changed to adapt to a changed master production schedule.

Component — A term used to describe a subordinate relationship in a product structure. A component goes into a parent. For example, a part (component) goes into an assembly (parent).

Dependent Demand — Demand for a raw material, part, or other lower-level component that is dependent on the demand for the end item into which the component goes.

End Item — A product, service part, or any other output that has a demand from customers, distributors, or other departments and that is independent of the demands for other components or end items.

Frozen MPS — The early periods of the MPS that

can be assumed to not be subject to change. These frozen periods of the MPS allow operations managers to commit funds, order materials, and make other plans with the confidence that such plans will not need to be subsequently changed.

Gross Requirements — The quantity and timing of the total requirements for a particular material, not considering any availability of the material in inventory or scheduled receipts.

Independent Demand — Demand for a material that is independent of the demands for other materials. End items are usually assumed to have independent demands because they are not components of other parents; therefore their demands are determined by customers outside of the organization and not by the demand for other, higher-level parents.

Inventory Status File — A major input to the MRP computer program. Material on hand or on order, planned orders, planned order releases, materials allocated, lot sizes, safety stock levels, lead times, costs, and suppliers are among the information included in this file about each material in the material system.

Load Schedules — A method used in capacity requirements planning to compare the amount of production capacity required by the MPS to the capacity available. These schedules are usually prepared in a hierarchy from the beginning to the end of the manufacturing system, department by department.

Lot Size Decisions — Given a net requirements schedule, decisions on how to group these requirements into production lots or purchase lots. The decisions usually include both the size and timing of the lots.

Low-Level Coding — A convention that is followed in MRP. Because a component can appear at more than one level in product structures, each material is coded at the lowest level that it appears in any product structure. Because MRP computer programs process net requirements calculations for all products level by level from end items down to raw materials, low-level coding avoids redundant net requirements calculations.

(Continued)

• •

TABLE 11.1   Continued

Lumpy Demand — The demand for a material that exhibits an irregular period-to-period pattern.

Master Production Schedule (MPS) — A schedule of the number and timing of all end items to be produced in a manufacturing plant over a specific planning horizon. An important input to the MRP computer program.

Material Requirements Planning (MRP) — A POM computer information system that determines how much of each material, any inventory item with a unique part number, should be purchased or produced in each future time period to support the MPS.

MRP Computer Program — A computer program that is the central processor of MRP information. It receives inputs from the MPS, inventory status file, and bills of material file. The program yields these primary outputs: planned order schedule, planned order releases, and changes to planned orders. Additionally, the program supplies transaction data to the inventory status file and secondary reports to operations managers.

Net Change MRP — MRP systems that generate outputs emphasizing only the changes to the last MRP outputs. Planned order schedules in these systems, for example, would indicate only the changes to the previous report and not a completely new schedule.

Net Requirements — The amount and timing of the need for a material that must be satisfied from production or purchasing. It is calculated by subtracting material available from gross requirements.

Offsetting for Lead Time — A term used in both MRP and CRP to describe the need to account for the time required to produce a production lot in-house or to receive a lot purchased from a supplier. A requirement in one time period will necessitate the release of the order in some earlier time period. The number of periods between the requirement and the release is the offset and is equal to the lead time.

On-Hand Inventory — The amount of a material actually in inventory. It may include safety stock and materials allocated to other uses, but it may not include materials on order.

Parent — A term used to describe a superior relationship in a product structure. For example, a part (component) goes into an assembly (parent).

Planned Order Receipts — The quantity of each material to be received in each time period of the planning horizon.

Planned Order Releases — The quantity of each material to be ordered in each time period of the planning horizon. This schedule is determined by offsetting the planned order receipts schedule to allow for lead times.

Planning Horizon — The number of periods included in the MPS, CRP, MRP, departmental schedules, and all other production planning.

Product Structure Levels — Strata of the hierarchy of the product structure. Level 0, for example, would be the final assembled end items, Level 1 would be all components that go into the final assembly, and Level 2 would be all of the components that go into the Level 1 components.

Regenerative MRP — MRP systems that periodically generate one complete set of MRP outputs. In these systems, for example, a planned order schedule would be a complete report and not be comprised solely of changes to an earlier report.

Resource Requirements Planning — All of the planning that is directed at determining the amount and timing of production resources, usually including personnel, materials, cash, and production capacity, needed in the short-range planning horizon. MPS, CRP, and MRP are important elements in this planning.

Safety Stock — A given quantity of each material held in inventory that is dedicated to but one use — emergency shortages arising out of uncertain demand or lead times. When demand for the materials is greater than expected or when lead time is longer than expected during reorder periods, safety stock is intended to meet these extraordinary needs.

Scheduled Receipts — Materials that are on order from a supplier and scheduled to be received in a specific period of the planning horizon.

Service Parts — Materials that are demanded as end items when ordered by service centers to be used in repairing other end items. These materials usually also have dependent demands as they are assembled into other, higher-level components.

FIGURE 11.2 *Resource Requirements Planning Systems*

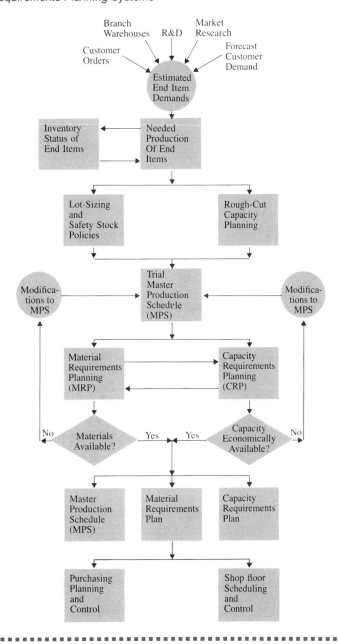

Figure 11.2 illustrates the major elements of resource requirements planning systems. Estimated end item demands, inventory status of end items, lot-sizing and safety stock policies of end items, and rough-cut capacity planning are integrated into a trial master production schedule (MPS). This trial MPS is tested by materials

requirements planning and capacity requirements planning (CRP). In other words, can enough materials be purchased and enough parts be produced in time to produce the end items in the MPS? If either purchased materials or production capacity is not economically available, the MPS must be changed. After MRP and CRP determine that a MPS is feasible, that MPS and its material requirements plan and capacity requirements plan become the nucleus of a short-range game plan for production. From the material requirements plan purchasing managers develop a plan for purchasing all of the purchased materials, and production managers develop a plan for scheduling and controlling the production of all of the parts on the shop floor to support the MPS.

In the remainder of this chapter, we shall study the two main elements of resource requirements planning systems — material requirements planning (MRP) and capacity requirements planning (CRP). In Chapter 12 we shall continue the study of resource planning with a discussion of scheduling and shop floor planning. In Chapter 13 we shall explore the field of materials management, which includes purchasing management.

MATERIAL REQUIREMENTS PLANNING (MRP)

MRP begins with the principle that many materials held in inventory have dependent demands, a concept introduced in Chapter 10. Materials in raw materials inventory and partially completed products held in in-process inventory are materials with dependent demand. The amount of a particular material with dependent demand that is needed in any week depends on the number of products to be produced that require the material. The demand for raw materials and partially completed products does not have to be forecast, therefore, because if it is known what finished products must be produced in a week, the amount of each material needed to produce these finished products can be calculated.

MRP is a computer-based system that takes the MPS as given; explodes the MPS into the required amount of raw materials, parts, subassemblies, and assemblies needed in each week of the planning horizon; reduces these material requirements to account for materials that are in inventory or on order; and develops a schedule of orders for purchased materials and produced parts over the planning horizon.

Why have so many production organizations today adopted MRP systems? The objectives of MRP help explain why its use has mushroomed.

OBJECTIVES OF MRP

Operations managers adopt MRP in order to:

1. Improve customer service.
2. Reduce inventory investment.
3. Improve plant operating efficiency.

Improving customer service means more than just having products on hand when customer orders are received. To have satisfied customers also means meeting

FIGURE 11.3 _Raw Materials Inventory Levels in MRP versus Fixed Order Quantity, Order Point_

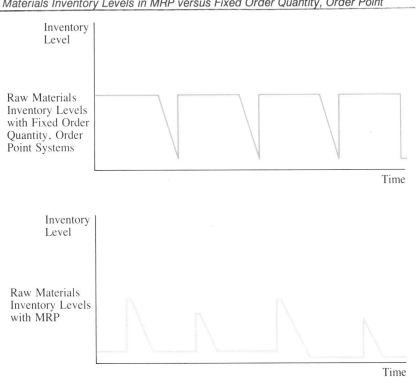

delivery promises and shortening delivery times. Not only does MRP provide the necessary management information to make delivery promises that can be kept, but also the promises are locked into the MRP control system that guides production. Therefore promised delivery dates become goals to be met by the organization, and the probability of meeting promised delivery dates is improved.

Figure 11.3 illustrates why MRP tends to reduce inventory levels. When fixed order quantity, order point systems are used to plan orders for a raw material, the order quantity plus safety stock remains in inventory until the raw material's end item appears in the master production schedule (MPS). Because these appearances may be several weeks apart, the pattern of inventory levels is long periods of full inventories interspersed with brief periods of low levels. In MRP, on the other hand, orders for raw materials are timed to arrive at approximately the time that the raw material's end item appears in the MPS. The pattern of inventory levels in MRP is long periods of low levels of inventory interspersed with brief periods of full inventories. The impact of MRP on raw material inventory levels is therefore dramatically reduced average inventory levels.

Because MRP better controls the quantity and timing of deliveries of raw materials, parts, subassemblies, and assemblies to production operations, the right

■ ■

TABLE 11.2   *Material Requirements Planning: How Can It Help?*

	Pre-MRP	*With MRP (Current)*	*With MRP (Future)*
1. Annual inventory turns*	3.2	4.3	5.3
2. Delivery promises met	61%	76%	88%
3. Orders that need to be split because of material shortages	32%	19%	9%
4. Number of expediters required	10	6	5
5. Lead time from order to delivery	71 days	59 days	44 days

■ ■

* Annual inventory turns = Annual sales dollars ÷ Dollar value of average inventory.
Source: Roger G. Schroeder et al., "A Study of MRP Benefits and Costs," *Journal of Operations Management* 2, no. 4(October 1981):1–9.

materials are delivered to production at the right time. Additionally, inflows can be slowed or accelerated in response to changes in production schedules. These controls of MRP result in reduced labor, material, and variable overhead costs because of:

1. Reduced numbers of stockouts and material delivery delays resulting in more output from production without corresponding increases in the number of employees and machines.
2. Reduction of the incidence of scrapped subassemblies, assemblies, and products resulting from the use of incorrect parts.
3. Increase in capacity of the production departments by increasing throughput rates as a result of decreased production idle time, increased efficiency of the physical movement of materials, and reduced confusion and planning delays.

All of these benefits result mainly from the *philosophy of MRP systems.* Simply put, MRP systems are based on the philosophy that each raw material, part, and assembly needed in production should arrive simultaneously at the right time to produce the end items in the MPS. This philosophy results in expediting materials that are going to be late and slowing down the delivery of materials that are going to be early. For example, if one material is going to be late and nothing can be done about it, the other materials that are needed to assemble the end item will not be needed until the one late material arrives. The MRP system changes the due dates of all of the materials so that materials arrive simultaneously to assemble the end item. MRP systems recognize that all of the elements of production are interrelated and that changing one element necessarily affects the other elements. A chief benefit of MRP systems is that production operations work on parts that are really needed on their stated due dates, so that production capacity is being used to directly support the MPS. This avoids expediting the production of parts through the factory so that they arrive at final assembly to find that the parts' end items are not being assembled this week.

Table 11.2 illustrates many of the improvements that have resulted from the installation of MRP systems in 679 firms. Inventory turns, delivery promises met,

■■

FIGURE 11.4   The MRP System

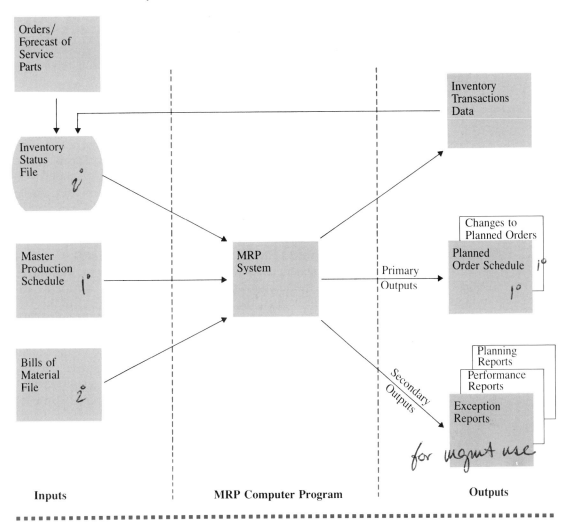

orders that need to be split because of material shortages, number of expediters required, and lead time from order to delivery have all improved. Furthermore, within these firms it is estimated that there is room for further improvement in the future. With such glowing reports of MRP successes, it is little wonder that companies in growing numbers are installing or gearing up to install these systems. Let us now examine the features of MRP systems.

ELEMENTS OF MRP

Figure 11.4 describes the operation of the MRP system. The *master production schedule* drives the entire MRP system. It is accepted as *given*. The *inventory status file* and *bills of material file* supply additional information about products included in the master production schedule. These inputs are fed into the MRP computer program, which generates the outputs. The inventory transactions resulting from the MRP actions are put back into the inventory status file so that current inventory records are maintained. The *planned order schedule* and *changes to planned orders* are the primary outputs of MRP. Exception, performance, and planning reports are also generated for management's use.

Master Production Schedule

A master production schedule (MPS) is devised to either replenish finished goods inventories or to fill customer orders. A MPS begins as a trial schedule to be tested for feasibility through MRP and CRP. As these schedules are proved feasible, they become the MPS that is put into action. The early weeks of the MPS are understood to be *frozen,* the middle weeks are described as *firm,* and the later weeks are said to be *full* or *open.* The early weeks are frozen so that production departments can depend on this portion of the plan to the extent that material can be ordered, personnel can be scheduled to work, and machine changeovers can be scheduled to support the MPS. If the early weeks of the MPS were allowed to be changed, material orders, personnel work schedules, and machine changeover schedules would also need to be changed. Such changes cause chaos in production departments and material control departments. After one period, usually a week, the MPS is updated by dropping off Week 1, since Week 1 would then be history, and adding a week onto the end of the schedule. This *rolling schedule* nature of the MPS must, however, observe the frozen character of the early weeks of the old MPS to allow for rational and systematic acquisition of material flows to support the schedule, *which is an absolute must in MRP.*

MRP cannot distinguish between feasible and infeasible master production schedules. That is to say, MRP assumes that the MPS can be produced within the production capacity constraints. MRP explodes the master schedule into material requirements. If these requirements cannot be met by the materials available from inventory or from materials on order, or if insufficient time is available for new orders, then the MPS will need to be modified to a new MPS. This process of MRP is performed parallel to the CRP process. Refer to Figure 11.2 to clarify this point.

The MPS drives the MRP system and is the primary basis for the MRP system's planning for the acquisition of the required materials and production. As the MPS is updated, the MRP results are also modified. Material orders are speeded up or slowed down or canceled. When the MPS is frozen, the plan for the inflow of materials emanating from MRP is also frozen.

Bills of Material File

A *bill of material* is a list of the materials and their quantities required to produce one unit of a product, or *end item.* Each product therefore has a bill of material. In POM, bills of material are the basis for planning the amount of each raw material for each time period given a production schedule of end items.

A *bills of material file,* or *product structure file* as it is sometimes called, is a complete list of all finished products, the quantity of each material in each product, and the structure (assemblies, subassemblies, parts, and raw materials and their relationship) of products. Another term for a bill of material is *indented parts list,* a list in which the parent is in the margin and its components are indented to show structure.

The bills of material file is an up-to-date computerized file that must be revised as products are redesigned. Accuracy of the bills of material files is a major hurdle that must be overcome in most MRP applications. With the confidence that the file is current, once the MPS is prepared, end items in the MPS can be *exploded* into the assemblies, subassemblies, parts, and raw materials required. These units may either be purchased from outside suppliers or produced in in-house production departments.

Inventory Status File

The *inventory status file* is a computerized file with a complete record of each material held in inventory. Each material, no matter at how many levels it is used in a product or in many products, has one and only one *material record.* A material record includes the *low-level code,* inventory on hand, materials on order, and customer orders for the item. These records are kept up to date by inventory transactions such as receipts, disbursements, scrapped materials, planned orders, and order releases.

Another part of the file includes planning factors that are used by the MRP system. These factors include such information as lot sizes, lead times, safety stock levels, and scrap rates.

Some parts, subassemblies, and assemblies are carried as end items supplied to customers as replacement parts. These materials may not be a part of the MPS because they are purchased directly from suppliers and placed directly in inventory for customer demand; in other words, they are not *produced* and so they are not included in the MPS. The orders or forecast orders for these materials, therefore, are fed directly into the inventory status file that directly becomes a part of the MRP system.

The inventory status file not only provides the MRP system with a complete status record for each material in inventory, but the planning factors are also used in the MRP computer program to project delivery dates of orders, quantities of each material to order, and when to place the orders.

MRP Computer Program

The MRP computer program operates this way:

1. First, with the MPS it begins to determine the number of end items needed in each time period. Time periods are sometimes called *buckets* in MRP terminology.
2. Next, the number of service parts not included in the MPS but deduced from customer orders are included as end items.
3. Next, the MPS and service parts are exploded into gross requirements for all materials by time period into the future by consulting the bills of material file.

4. Next, the gross materials requirements are modified by the amount of materials on hand and on order for each period by consulting the inventory status file. The net requirements of each material for each bucket are computed as follows:

$$\text{Net requirements} = \frac{\text{Gross}}{\text{requirements}} - \left[\frac{\text{Inventory}}{\text{on hand}} - \frac{\text{Safety}}{\text{stock}} - \frac{\text{Inventory allocated}}{\text{to other uses}} \right]$$

If the net requirements are greater than zero, orders for the material must be placed.

5. Finally, the orders are offset to earlier time periods to allow for lead times at each step in the production process and supplier lead times.

This procedure results in inventory transactions data (orders released, changes in orders, and so on), which are used to update the inventory status file, the primary output reports, and secondary output reports.

Outputs of MRP

The outputs of MRP systems dynamically provide the schedule of materials for the future—amount of each material required in each time period to support the MPS. Two primary outputs result:

1. Planned order schedule—a plan of the quantity of each material to be ordered in each time period. This schedule is used by purchasing to place orders with suppliers and by production to order parts, subassemblies, or assemblies from upstream production departments. The planned orders become a guide for future production at suppliers and for in-house production schedules.
2. Changes in planned orders—modification of previous planned orders. Quantities of orders can be changed, orders can be canceled, or the orders can be delayed or advanced to different time periods through the updating process.

The secondary MRP outputs provide this information:

1. Exception reports—reports that flag items requiring management attention in order to provide the right quantity of materials in each time period. Typical exceptions noted are reporting errors, out-of-bounds situations, late orders, and excessive scrap.
2. Performance reports—reports that indicate how well the system is operating. Examples of performance measures utilized are inventory turns, percentage of delivery promises kept, and stockout incidences.
3. Planning reports—reports to be used in future inventory-planning activities. Examples of such planning information are inventory forecasts, purchase commitment reports, traces to demand sources (pegging), and long-range material requirements planning.

These are the major elements of MRP—the inputs, the MRP computer program, and the outputs. Let us now work through an example to see how inventory planning can be affected by the use of MRP.

THE GREEN THUMB WATER SPRINKLER COMPANY

Industry Snapshot 11.1 demonstrates how MRP can be applied to one product of a manufacturing firm. Read the account and work your way through Figure 11.6, the MRP schedule. Make sure you understand how each piece of information is taken from the MPS (Table 11.3), the bill of material (Table 11.4), and the inventory status report (Table 11.5), to be used in the calculations of the MRP schedule.

   The planned order schedule (Table 11.7) is the primary output of MRP. The *planned order schedule* is a schedule of planned future order releases over the entire planning horizon. This report indicates to purchasing and production schedulers what materials to order, what quantities of materials to order, and when to place the orders for every material in the production system.

INDUSTRY SNAPSHOT 11.1

The Green Thumb Water Sprinkler Company

In the fall of 1989, Mr. James Verde, president of Green Thumb Water Sprinkler Company, has just called a meeting of his key personnel to discuss new approaches to inventory planning at Green Thumb. Mr. Verde starts the meeting:

Mr. Verde: I've called this meeting to explore new avenues for inventory planning in our organization. The incidences of stockouts in our raw materials inventory have led to lost business to the point that we just can't tolerate them any more. And the answer is not larger order quantities and higher safety stocks, because the interest charges for carrying our inventory are eating us alive. Somehow we've got to plan our acquisition of materials to mesh more closely with our customers' orders for finished products.

Bonnie Buck: I heartily agree, Mr. Verde. As production manager, may I say that when we in production place orders for materials from the warehouse, it seems it's out of stock as often as not. The warehouses are full—but of the wrong materials. Something has got to be done.

Bill Compton: Well, as materials manager, I'm obviously on the hot seat here. We've already concluded that our traditional system of fixed order quantities and order points is just not doing the job. Our individual customer orders are simply too large and spaced out to fit the assumptions of our present system. In anticipation of this problem, Joe Johnson, our inventory system analyst, has been attending a night class in material requirements planning (MRP) over at the university. Joe has selected the #377 lawn sprinkler to demonstrate the MRP technique. Joe, will you show us the results of your analysis?

Joe Johnson: Thank you, Mr. Compton. I've prepared an MRP schedule for the #377 based on our most recent master production schedule, #377 bill of material, and the inventory status of #377 and its components. The planned order schedule summarizes the recommended timing and size of orders of #377 components.

TABLE 11.3   Master Production Schedule: #377 Lawn Sprinkler

				Week Number				
	1	2	3	4	5	6	7	8
Gross requirements				1,000				2,000

TABLE 11.4   Bill of Material: #377 Lawn Sprinkler

Parent Code	Component Code	Level Code	Description	Components Required per Parent
	377	0	#377 Lawn Sprinkler	
377	M	1	Water motor assembly	1
	F	1	Frame assembly	1
	H	1	#699 hose recept. assembly	1
M	A	2	½″ dia. ⅟32″ alum. tube	10″
	B	2	½″ × ⅟16″ metal screws	3
	C	2	Water motor	1
F	A	2	½″ dia. ⅟32″ alum. tube	40″
	D	2	½″ × ½″ #115 plastic cap	3
	B	2	½″ × ⅟16″ metal screws	3

TABLE 11.5   Inventory Status Report: #377 Lawn Sprinkler

Item Code	On Hand	Safety Stock	Allocated	Lot Sizes*	Lead Times (Weeks)	Scheduled Receipts		Service Parts Orders	
						Qty.	Week	Qty.	Week
377	500	300		LFL	1				
M	200	0		LFL	1				
F	300	0		LFL	1				
H	1,500	200	1,000	1,000+	2				
A	30,000	5,000	15,000	50,000+	2	50,000	1		
B	5,000	0	2,500	10,000+	1				
C	1,000	500	800	1,000+	2	1,000	1	1,000	4
D	3,000	0	2,000	10,000+	2	10,000	1		

* Note: The plus (+) sign indicates that any quantity over the minimum may be ordered. For example, 1,000+ indicates that 1,000 or more may be ordered.

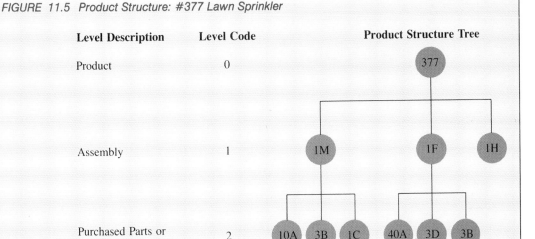

FIGURE 11.5 *Product Structure: #377 Lawn Sprinkler*

Level Description	Level Code	Product Structure Tree
Product	0	377
Assembly	1	1M 1F 1H
Purchased Parts or Raw Materials	2	10A 3B 1C 40A 3D 3B

After the group studies the results of the MRP analysis, Bonnie Buck has some clarifying questions:

Bonnie Buck: Joe, so I'll understand the mechanics of MRP, could you take just one component in the MRP schedule and explain your calculations?

Joe Johnson: Sure, Bonnie. Let's concentrate on Component C—the water motor. First, notice that our analysis of customer orders and forecasts of orders has resulted in Table 11.3, the master production schedule for the #377 lawn sprinkler. One thousand units are needed in Week 4 and 2,000 units are needed in Week 8. Next, from the bill of material for the #377 (Table 11.4), we can see that one unit of Component C goes into each unit of Component M (water motor assembly) and one unit of Component M goes into each #377. This relationship can perhaps be seen more clearly in Figure 11.5 — Product Structure: #377 Lawn Sprinkler. Next, looking at the MRP schedule for the #377 in Figure 11.6, note that the number of #377 units available going into Week 4 is 200 units (the difference between the on-hand inventory balance and the safety stock). Because we need 1,000 #377 units in Week 4 and 200 units are available from inventory, we have a net requirement of 800 units in Week 4. Because it takes one week to process a batch of #377 units through final assembly operations, the 800 units must be started through final assembly in Week 3, one week earlier.

If 800 #377 units must begin final assembly in Week 3, 800 Component M units are needed in Week 3 and this need shows up as a gross requirement for Component M in Week 3. When this same logic is applied to Component M, 600 units of Component M must be started into production in Week 2 and this creates a gross requirement of 600 units of Component C in Week 2. The gross requirement of 2,000 units of Component C in Week 6 similarly directly results from the #377 gross requirement in Week

FIGURE 11.6 MRP Schedule: #377 Lawn Sprinkler

Week Number

Item Code	Level Code	Lot Size	Lead Time Weeks	On Hand	Safety Stock	Allocated		1	2	3	4	5	6	7	8
377	0	LFL	1	500	300		Gross Requirements				1,000				2,000
							Scheduled Receipts								
							Available	200	200	200	200				
							Net Requirements				800				2,000
							Planned Order Receipts				800				2,000
							Planned Order Releases			800				2,000	
M	1	LFL	1	200			Gross Requirements			800				2,000	
							Scheduled Receipts								
							Available	200	200	200					
							Net Requirements			600				2,000	
							Planned Order Receipts			600				2,000	
							Planned Order Releases		600				2,000		
F	1	LFL	1	300			Gross Requirements			800				2,000	
							Scheduled Receipts								
							Available	300	300	300					
							Net Requirements			500				2,000	
							Planned Order Receipts			500				2,000	
							Planned Order Releases		500				2,000		
H	1	1,000+	2	1,500	200	1,000	Gross Requirements			800				2,000	
							Scheduled Receipts								
							Available	300	300	300	500	500	500	500	
							Net Requirements			500				1,500	
							Planned Order Receipts			1,000				1,500	
							Planned Order Releases	1,000				1,500			
A	2	50,000+	2	30,000	5,000	15,000	Gross Requirements		26,000				100,000		
							Scheduled Receipts	50,000							
							Available	60,000	60,000	34,000	34,000	34,000	34,000		
							Net Requirements						66,000		
							Planned Order Receipts						66,000		
							Planned Order Releases				66,000				
B	2	10,000+	1	5,000		2,500	Gross Requirements		3,300				12,000		
							Scheduled Receipts								
							Available	2,500	2,500	9,200	9,200	9,200	9,200	7,200	7,200
							Net Requirements		800				2,800		
							Planned Order Receipts		10,000				10,000		
							Planned Order Releases	10,000				10,000			
C	2	1,000+	2	1,000	500	800	Gross Requirements		600		1,000		2,000		
							Scheduled Receipts	1,000							
							Available	700	700	100	100	100	100		
							Net Requirements				900		1,900		
							Planned Order Receipts				1,000		1,900		
							Planned Order Releases		1,000		1,900				
D	2	10,000+	2	3,000		2,000	Gross Requirements		1,500				6,000		
							Scheduled Receipts	10,000							
							Available	11,000	11,000	9,500	9,500	9,500	9,500	3,500	3,500
							Net Requirements								
							Planned Order Receipts								
							Planned Order Releases								

8. The gross requirement of 1,000 units of Component C in Week 4 results from the need to ship service parts to customers. This information is found in Table 11.5 — Inventory Status Report: #377 Lawn Sprinkler. This explains how the gross requirement for Component C was determined. A further explanation of all the gross requirements in the MRP schedule of

TABLE 11.6   Gross Requirements Calculations for #377 Lawn Sprinkler

Component Code	Parent Code	Components Required per Parent	Components Required for Parents' Production		Service Parts Required		Total Gross Requirements	
			Quantity	Week	Quantity	Week	Quantity	Week
M	377	1	800	3			800	3
M	377	1	2,000	7			2,000	7
F	377	1	800	3			800	3
F	377	1	2,000	7			2,000	7
H	377	1	800	3			800	3
H	377	1	2,000	7			2,000	7
A	M	10″	6,000	2				
A	F	40″	20,000	2			26,000	2
A	M	10″	20,000	6				
A	F	40″	80,000	6			100,000	6
B	M	3	1,800	2				
B	F	3	1,500	2			3,300	2
B	M	3	6,000	6				
B	F	3	6,000	6			12,000	6
C	M	1	600	2			600	2
C	—	—			1,000	4	1,000	4
C	M	1	2,000	6			2,000	6
D	F	3	1,500	2			1,500	2
D	F	3	6,000	6			6,000	6

Figure 11.6 is contained in Table 11.6—Gross Requirements Calculations for #377 Lawn Sprinkler.

The gross requirement of 600 units of Component C in Week 2 is met by the scheduled receipt of 1,000 units in Week 1, although only 700 of these units are available for use in Week 2, as we were 300 units short entering Week 1 owing to an overallocation of the on-hand inventory beyond the safety stock. The gross requirement of 600 units in Week 2 combined with the 700 units available in Week 2 results in 100 units available to meet the gross requirement of 1,000 units in Week 4. This leaves a net requirement of 900 units in Week 4 and 1,000 units, the minimum lot size, are planned to be received in Week 4. After offsetting for the two weeks of lead time to receive the shipment of Component C, we should release the order for 1,000 units in Week 2.

The gross requirement of 2,000 units in Week 6 is similarly computed. Now do you see how we work our way through Figure 11.6, the MRP Schedule?

TABLE 11.7 Planned Order Schedule: #377 Lawn Sprinkler

Item Code	Week Number							
	1	2	3	4	5	6	7	8
377			800				2,000	
M		600				2,000		
F		500				2,000		
H	1,000				1,500			
A				66,000				
B	10,000				10,000			
C		1,000		1,900				
D								

Bonnie Buck: Yes. How do you know that the MPS and the planned order schedule are feasible? In other words, how do you know that we have the production capacity to produce the MPS, and how do you know that the materials will be available in time to allow us to produce the MPS?

Joe Johnson: That's a good question, Bonnie. We know that purchased materials will be available in sufficient quantities and in time to satisfy the planned order schedule (Table 11.7) because we have double-checked with our suppliers. This method of checking whether materials can be supplied in time to make the production of the MPS feasible will be a continuing requirement in MRP. If we discovered that a material could not be supplied in time or in sufficient quantities to conform to the planned order schedule, we would have only two alternatives: expedite the order and perhaps pay extra to have the order processed on an overtime basis at our suppliers, or change the MPS and go through the MRP process again. If the MPS is changed, the affected end item would have to be moved outward to later periods in the MPS.

The MPS has also been checked for production capacity feasibility. Load schedules were developed for each production department at the plant. All of the products in the MPS were included, and it was clear that sufficient production capacity exists in each department to allow us to produce the MPS. This brings up an interesting point: How do we develop detailed weekly production schedules from the MRP schedule that is shown in Figure 11.6? Only items 377, M, and F, which are higher-level items, require in-house production. All other items are purchased from our suppliers.

The production departments where the 377, M, and F items will be produced include the planned order releases for these items in their load schedules. For example, 600 and 2,000 units of Component M must enter production in the Mechanical Fabrication and Assembly Department in Weeks 2 and 6, respectively. The amount of labor per unit and the amount of machine-hours per unit are multiplied by these quantities, and the result is the amount of production capacity required in the department for Component M. When this same process is followed for all of our products, the loading can be compared to the labor and machine capacity of the department. The same loading analysis would also be applied to the Final Assembly Department and the Metal Fabrication and Assembly Department.

As you can see, capacity requirements planning (CRP), as this analysis is called, is a required part of the overall inventory-planning process. Additionally, the detailed production schedules of the production departments are picked off the MRP schedules. When all of the planned order releases are picked off all of the components of the MRP schedule that are to be produced in-house and classified according to their production departments, the result is departmental production schedules.

Do you see the connection between MRP and the departmental production schedules?

Bonnie Buck: Yes. Now would you summarize how MRP would be applied to all of our products in practice?

Joe Johnson: The procedure for our six major products would mechanically be the same as we demonstrated for #377. The big difference would be in computerizing the whole process. The figures that we've seen here today were all manually calculated. These could be the major tasks for us to get an MRP system operative: (1) Build an accurate computerized inventory status file for all our products. (2) Improve our forecasting methods so that we can combine forecasts with in-hand customer orders to form a reliable basis for an accurate master production schedule. (3) Build an up-to-date computerized bills of material file for all our products. (4) Buy the services of ABM Computer Services to assist us in installing the MRP computer program and debugging the MRP system after it's installed. I would estimate that we could have an MRP system operating for all our products in about six months.

Mr. Verde: Joe, what are the major advantages of MRP over our present inventory-planning system, which is tied to economic order quantities and order points?

Joe Johnson: (1) Better customer service, (2) lower inventory levels, and (3) higher operating efficiency in our production departments.

The group all agreed to give MRP a try by running the new system for one-half of Green Thumb's products while the present inventory-planning system was used simultaneously on the other products. It was thought that this approach should give a practical comparison of the results of MRP and the present inventory-planning system.

LOT-SIZING IN MRP

In both master production scheduling and MRP, whenever there is a net requirement for a material, a decision must be made concerning how much of the material to order. These decisions are commonly called *lot-sizing decisions.* In produce-to-order firms, the size of the customer's order is usually the lot size that will be produced because it cannot be assumed that there will be other orders for the custom-designed product in the future. On the other hand, in produce-to-stock firms, because only a few standard product designs are produced for inventory, the size of production lots is primarily a question of economics. Operations managers would ordinarily like to order and produce large lots of materials because:

1. The cost of changing over machines between production lots in the course of the year is less and production capacity is greater because of less downtime caused by machine changeovers.
2. The cost of placing purchase orders is less in the course of a year because only a few orders for large lots of materials are placed with suppliers.
3. By ordering large lots of materials from suppliers, price breaks and transportation cost breaks can be taken advantage of, resulting in lower purchasing costs of the materials.

On the other hand, operations managers would ordinarily like to produce small lots of materials because:

1. Smaller lots of materials result in lower average inventory levels and the annual cost of carrying inventories is less.
2. Lower inventory levels can reduce the risk of obsolescence when product designs are changed.
3. Smaller lots result in less in-process inventory and customers' orders can be produced faster.

Operations managers cannot have the benefits of both small and large lots. They must strike a balance between lots that are not too small and lots that are not too large. Much research has been conducted in developing methods of determining lot sizes. For example, in Chapter 10, the EOQ was used to compute lot sizes, but two restrictive assumptions of the EOQ make its use in MPS and MRP costly.

First, the basic EOQ assumes that the per-unit cost does not depend on the quantity of a material ordered, but we know that suppliers often offer quantity discounts for purchased materials. Likewise, for materials produced in-house, as illustrated in Figure 10.1 in Chapter 10, the size of the lot affects the unit cost of the material. Operations managers therefore either use the EOQ with quantity discounts or, perhaps more commonly, specify minimum lot sizes. For purchased materials these minimum lot sizes are typically at price breaks, and for materials produced in-house the minimum lot size is at a point like 5,000 units in Figure 10.1, where the unit cost goes up sharply when fewer than this number of units are produced. For instance, a minimum lot size of 5,000 units means that any quantity greater than or equal to 5,000 units may be ordered, but never less than 5,000 units. If there were a net requirement of 2,000 units of this material, a lot size of 5,000 units would be ordered. On the other hand, if there were a net requirement of 9,999 units, a lot size of 9,999 units would be ordered.

Second, the EOQ assumes that the demand for a material is uniform from week to week. In MRP and MPS the net requirements for materials have been described as lumpy demands. *Lumpy demand* means that demand varies greatly from week to week. In the presence of lumpy demands, other lot-sizing methods often exhibit lower costs than the EOQ. Additional lot-sizing methods are the *lot-for-lot method* and the *period order quantity (POQ) method.* Example 11.1 demonstrates the use of these methods when applied to a net requirements schedule. Other approaches have also been experimented with and may be used more extensively in the future. The methods of least total cost, least unit cost, and part-period balancing are discussed and described in Orlicky's book.[1] Heuristic methods by Gaither,[2] Groff,[3] and Silver and Meal[4] provide good cost performance and are very efficient to use. The Wagner and Whitin method yields optimal results, but it is based on dynamic programming and is difficult to understand, is very expensive to process on computers, and may not exhibit good cost performance when many changes to net requirements occur weekly.[5]

EXAMPLE 11.1   *Lot-Sizing Decisions for Materials with Lumpy Demands*

The net requirements for a material from an MRP schedule are:

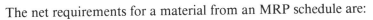

	Weeks							
	1	*2*	*3*	*4*	*5*	*6*	*7*	*8*
Net requirements	300	500	1,000	600	300	300	300	1,500

The annual demand for this end item is estimated to be 30,000 units over a 50-week-per-year schedule, or an average of 600 units per week. It costs $500 to change over the machines in the

---

[1] Joseph Orlicky, *Material Requirements Planning* (New York: McGraw-Hill, 1975), 120–138.

[2] Norman Gaither, "A Near-Optimal Lot-Sizing Model for Material Requirements Planning Systems," *Production and Inventory Management* 22(Fourth Quarter 1981):75–89.

[3] G. K. Groff, "A Lot-Sizing Rule for Time Phased Component Demand," *Production and Inventory Management* 20(First Quarter 1979):47–53.

[4] E. A. Silver and H. C. Meal, "A Heuristic for Selecting Lot Size Quantities for the Case of a Deterministic Time-Varying Demand Rate and Discrete Opportunities for Replenishment," *Production and Inventory Management* 14(Second Quarter 1973):64–75.

[5] H. M. Wagner and T. M. Whitin, "Dynamic Version of the Economic Lot Size Model," *Management Science* 5, no. 1(October 1958):89–96.

final assembly department to this end item when a production lot is begun. It costs $.50 per unit when one unit of this product must be carried in inventory from one week to another; therefore, when one unit of this product is in ending inventory, it must be carried over as beginning inventory in the next week and incurs the $.50 per-unit carrying cost. Determine which of these lot-sizing methods results in the least carrying and changeover (or ordering) costs for the eight-week schedule: **(a)** lot-for-lot (LFL), **(b)** economic order quantity (EOQ), or **(c)** period order quantity (POQ).

Solution

a. Develop the total carrying and ordering costs over the eight-week schedule for the lot-for-lot method.

	Weeks								*Costs*		
	1	*2*	*3*	*4*	*5*	*6*	*7*	*8*	*Carrying*	*Ordering*	*Total*
Net requirements	300	500	1,000	600	300	300	300	1,500			
Beginning inventory	0	0	0	0	0	0	0	0			
Production lots	300	500	1,000	600	300	300	300	1,500	$0	$4,000	$4,000
Ending inventory	0	0	0	0	0	0	0	0			

Ordering costs = Numbers of orders × $500 = 8 × $500 = $4,000

b. Develop the total carrying and ordering costs over the eight-week schedule for the EOQ lot-sizing method.

First, compute the EOQ:

$$EOQ = \sqrt{2DS/C} = \sqrt{2(30,000)(500)/(.50)(50)} = 1,095.4, \text{ or } 1,095 \text{ units}$$

	Weeks								*Costs*		
	1	*2*	*3*	*4*	*5*	*6*	*7*	*8*	*Carrying*	*Ordering*	*Total*
Net requirements	300	500	1,000	600	300	300	300	1,500			
Beginning inventory	0	795	295	390	885	585	285	1,080			
Production lots	1,095	—	1,095	1,095	—	—	1,095	1,095	$2,495	$2,500	$4,995
Ending inventory	795	295	390	885	585	285	1,080	675			

Carrying costs = Sum of ending inventories × $.50 = 4990 × $.50 = $2,495
Ordering costs = Number of orders × $500 = 5 × $500 = $2,500

c. Develop the total carrying and ordering costs over the eight-week schedule for the POQ lot-sizing method.

First, compute the POQ:

$$POQ = \frac{\text{Number of weeks per year}}{\text{Number of orders per year}} = \frac{50}{D/EOQ} = \frac{50}{30,000 \div 1095.4}$$

$$= 1.83, \text{ or 2 weeks per order}$$

	Weeks								Costs		
									Carry-ing	*Order-ing*	*Total*
	1	*2*	*3*	*4*	*5*	*6*	*7*	*8*			
Net require-ments	300	500	1,000	600	300	300	300	1,500			
Beginning inventory	0	500	0	600	0	300	0	1,500			
Production lots	800	—	1,600	—	600	—	1,800	—	$1,450	$2,000	$3,450
Ending inventory	500	0	600	0	300	0	1,500	0			

Carrying Costs = Sum of ending inventories × $.50 = 2,900 × $.50 = $1,450
Ordering Costs = Number of orders × $500 = 4 × $500 = $2,000

Among the lot-sizing methods considered, the POQ method exhibits the least carrying and ordering costs for the eight-week net requirements schedule.

The net requirements line in the MRP schedule for each component is analyzed to determine the timing and size of production lots or purchased lots by using one of the lot-sizing techniques mentioned earlier. The Planned Order Receipt line in the MRP schedule is the end result of these lot-sizing decisions.

Not all MRP systems are identical, and MRP is not equally applicable to all production systems. Several MRP issues are now being debated in POM. It is hoped that this debate will open new areas of application and clarify and refine MRP usage.

ISSUES IN MRP

Any comprehensive treatment of MRP should include a discussion of important issues yet to be resolved by consensus in POM practice. The following MRP issues are at present unresolved.

Lot-Sizing
One potential problem is said to exist when lot-sizing techniques are applied at every level in the product structure. Using lot-sizing in lower-level components (raw mate-

rials and parts) poses no serious problems, but with economic lot sizes for higher-level components (end items and assemblies), some MRP users believe that excessive inventory buildups in lower-level components can result. For example, three components are related as follows:

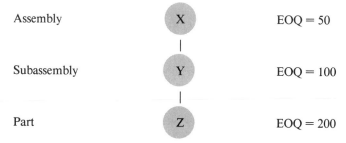

Assembly	X	EOQ = 50
Subassembly	Y	EOQ = 100
Part	Z	EOQ = 200

If a customer order of 25 units of Part X is received, if no inventory is on hand for Parts X, Y, and Z, and if orders equal to EOQ are ordered, then the inventory available for use immediately after shipping the customer order is:

$$\text{Inventory of Part X} = \;\;25 \text{ units}$$

$$\text{Inventory of Part Y} = \;\;75 \text{ units}$$

$$\text{Inventory of Part Z} = 175 \text{ units}$$

Some MRP users argue, however, that excessive inventory levels are not reached. The large economic lot size for Part Z in the example above is based on a higher average inventory for these lower-level components. The per-unit cost of lower-level components leads to higher lot sizes and consequently higher inventory levels. These MRP users contend that higher inventory levels of lower-level components should not be surprising or disturbing; the economic lot-sizing of all levels of components is therefore recommended.

The tendency in practice is to use lot-for-lot (LFL) at all levels for produce-to-order firms. Also, LFL is used in produce-to-stock firms for end items and assemblies, and minimum lot sizes are used for lower-level components such as raw materials and parts. The use of LFL in end items and assemblies avoids the inventory buildups in lower-level components described above. The use of minimum lot sizes for raw materials and parts suggests that for purchased components, some minimum amount of the material needs to be ordered to qualify for a price break or a transportation cost break. The minimum lot size for parts produced in-house suggests that at some minimum quantity the cost per unit of the item levels out.

Net Change versus Regenerative MRP Systems

Some organizations use what is called *net change MRP.* These systems update the master production schedule as changes in the MPS occur. The MRP system is then activated to generate one set of MRP outputs. These outputs, however, are only the net changes to past MRP runs and not an entire set of MRP outputs. The planned order schedule report, for example, would indicate only changes to previous planned order schedules, not a completely new schedule. Although this concept is indeed tempting in theory, because it promises to serve as one big exception report that would greatly reduce the amount of information generated on each run, its incidence of application has been disappointing.

Many organizations continue to use what is called *regenerative MRP*. In these systems a complete MRP run is processed periodically, usually every week. At these times a new MPS, an updated inventory status file, and an up-to-date bills of material file are fed into the MRP computer program, which generates a complete set of outputs. Although regenerative MRP systems are slightly more costly to prepare and process, they also apparently are easier to implement and manage. Only time will tell which of these approaches will gain favor.

Safety Stock

MRP users do not agree on whether safety stock should be used in MRP. Proponents for using safety stock in MRP argue that safety stock performs the same function in MRP systems as in other inventory-planning systems — avoiding excessive stockouts caused by uncertain lead times and daily demands. Those who oppose the use of safety stock in MRP argue that because MRP systems adapt to changing conditions that affect demand and lead times, safety stock will not actually be used under the vast majority of circumstances in MRP.

The use of safety stock can be justified only by the sources of uncertainty present during lead times. For higher-level items such as end items and components that are used as service parts, the uncertainty of demand compares with any other inventory item having independent demand. The uncertainty of lead times for these items seems more controllable if these items are produced in-house. On balance, the use of safety stock for end items in MRP systems can be justified on the same basis as in any other system — the presence of uncertain demand and uncertain lead times.

For lower-level items such as raw materials and parts, the uncertainty of demand is adequately controlled because the demand is a dependent demand. The MPS sets the weekly demand for these items. The only major uncertainties present during lead times are the uncertainty of lead time and the uncertainty of demand that occurs because of changes in the MPS. It appears that some safety stock can certainly be justified, even in raw materials, parts, and other lower-level items, although at significantly reduced levels.

MRP IN ASSEMBLE-TO-ORDER FIRMS

The *assemble-to-order firm* is a special type of produce-to-order firm. In these firms there can be millions of possible unique end items because customers have their choice of options and accessories. An automobile manufacturer is an example of an assemble-to-order firm. While only a few standard models are offered to customers, dealers can specify colors, engine types, transmission types, trim options, air-conditioning, power steering, power brakes, cruise control, and a host of other options. In these cases there are only a few hundred options and basic product models, but there are literally millions of possible unique finished products. A MRP system that attempted to develop a MPS for such unique end items would be swamped with the burden of trying to explode millions of bills of material for end items into the resources necessary to produce the MPS.

In assemble-to-order firms, therefore, the MPS and MRP are treated separately from the *final assembly schedule (FAS)*. The FAS is usually prepared only a week or two ahead, and it schedules the unique products ordered by customers. This is necessary because the customers must be shipped products that include the specific options that they have ordered. But the MPS, MRP, and all other elements of the resource requirements planning system require a much longer lead time and are not based on unique customer orders. Instead, the MPS explodes modular bills of material, which can be thought of as families of products. A *modular bill of material* for a particular product family will list the forecast percentage of customer orders that require each option along with the kit of parts that is common to all customer orders. These unassembled families of products with all of their options and kits of common parts are scheduled through the production operations such that the product families arrive at final assembly ready to be assembled into the specific products for customer orders. This greatly reduces the computational burden in the MRP system, although it creates the need to modify the way that final assembly schedules (FAS) and the bills of material are prepared.

FROM MRP I TO MRP II

Resource requirements planning systems are in a continuous state of evolution. The earlier systems were quite simple and unsophisticated, and the value of the information that was generated for operations was limited. In its most primitive form, MRP simply exploded the MPS into the required materials.

Then in the late 1970s Oliver Wight, George Plossl, and others began to talk about closing the loop in MRP systems. The term *closed-loop MRP* means:

> *A system built around material requirements planning and also including the additional planning functions of production planning (aggregate planning), master production scheduling, and capacity requirements planning. Further, once the planning phase is complete and the plans have been accepted as realistic and attainable, the execution functions come into play. These include the shop floor control functions of input – output measurement, detailed scheduling and dispatching, plus anticipated delay reports from both the shop and vendors, purchasing follow-up and control, etc. The term "closed loop" implies that not only are these elements included in the overall system but also that there is feedback from the execution functions so that the planning can be kept valid at all times.[6]*

Later the need for more sophisticated MRP systems led Wight, Plossl, and others to call for a move from MRP I to manufacturing resource planning (MRP II). The term *manufacturing resource planning* means:

---

[6] *APICS Dictionary,* 6th ed. (Falls Church, VA: American Production and Inventory Control Society, 1987), 5.

A method for the effective planning of all resources of a manufacturing company. Ideally, it addresses operational planning in units, financial planning in dollars, and has a simulation capability to answer "what if" questions. It is made up of a variety of functions, each linked together: business planning, production planning, master production scheduling, material requirements planning, capacity requirements planning, and the execution support systems for capacity and material. Output from these systems would be integrated with financial reports such as the business plan, purchase commitment report, shipping budget, inventory projections in dollars, etc. Manufacturing Resource Planning is a direct outgrowth and extension of closed-loop MRP.[7]

The evolution of resource requirements planning systems is continuing today. IBM has a software package called the *Communications Oriented Production Information and Control System (COPICS).*[8] This and similar packages from other companies are examples of MRP II systems.

HOW MRP ADAPTS TO CHANGE

You may have the impression that once an MRP system is in place it would be difficult to change the system. On the contrary, one of the cornerstones of MRP is that it must be a dynamic system and that it must adapt to change. By its very nature, MRP reflects the latest information in its planned order releases. In the updating procedures of the MPS, one week is added to the back end of the schedule and one week is taken off the front end, and all of the weekly demands are again estimated. This updating of the MPS is aimed at making the MRP system adaptive to changes in demands for the end items.

As the MPS is updated weekly, the MRP schedules are also updated weekly. Another reason for updating MRP schedules weekly is to allow any changes to the inputs to MRP to be reflected in the schedules. Since the inventory status file and its material records could have been changed since the last updating, the MRP schedules pick up these changes. For example, let us say that we have changed suppliers for a certain material and the purchasing lead time for the material has changed. The next updating of the MRP schedules will reflect this change. Similarly, if engineering were to change the bills of material file to effect product design changes, after the next updating the MRP schedules would reflect these changes.

One of the great improvements of MRP systems over the traditional order quantity, order point methods of planning material requirements is its dynamic nature. MRP effectively adapts to change and operations managers are provided with information based on present conditions rather than what conditions were several weeks or months ago.

---

[7] Ibid., 18.

[8] IBM, *Communications Oriented Production Information and Control System.* Publications G320-1974 through G320-1981.

■■■

TABLE 11.8   Desirable Characteristics of Production Systems Suitable for MRP

---

1. An effective computer system.
2. Accurate computerized bills of material and inventory status files for all end items and materials.
3. A production system that manufactures discrete products made up of raw materials, parts, subassemblies, and assemblies that are processed through several production steps.
4. Production processes requiring long processing times.

5. Relatively short and reliable lead times for materials purchased from suppliers.
6. The master schedule frozen for a period of time sufficient to procure materials without excessive expediting and confusion.
7. Top management support and commitment.

■■■

EVALUATION OF MRP

The advantages claimed for MRP over more conventional inventory-planning approaches such as fixed order quantities and order points have been demonstrated here and elsewhere in POM—improved customer service, reduced inventory levels, and improved operating efficiency of production departments. This sounds so good that we wonder why the whole world has not been "MRP'ed." There are good reasons that this isn't the case.

Table 11.8 lists the characteristics of production systems that support the successful implementation of MRP. The presence of an effective computer system is an absolute must. Two other characteristics that similarly seem almost automatic are accurate bills of material and inventory status files. The absence of these files and an ineffective computer system often pose the largest headaches for the implementation of MRP in practice. Correcting deficiencies such as these may take the bulk of implementation time.

MRP is conventionally applied only to manufacturing systems. These organizations process discrete products for which bills of material are possible, a requirement of MRP. This means that MRP is seldom applied to service systems, petroleum refineries, retailing systems, transportation firms, and other nonmanufacturing systems. Many of us in POM believe that MRP can be successfully applied to some of these nonmanufacturing systems. These applications would do what MRP is designed to do—improve customer service, reduce inventory levels, and improve operating efficiency. When service systems require sets of raw materials to deliver one unit of service (a pseudo bill of material), MRP potentially can be applied. Surgical operations in large hospitals, high-volume professional services, and other processes are likely to use MRP systems in the future.

MRP delivers the most benefits to process-focused systems that have long processing times and complex multistage production steps because inventory and production planning are more complex. Picture a hypothetical production system that converts raw materials into finished goods instantaneously, as is the case in some simple product-focused systems. Raw materials would be ordered in to exactly match finished goods requirements. In most process-focused systems, however, the in-house processing lead times can exceed the lead times required to obtain the raw materials from suppliers. MRP's ability to offset planned order receipts to planned order releases to account for long lead times and complex production processing steps greatly simplifies production and inventory planning.

In order for MRP to be effective, supplier lead times must be short and reliable. Also, the MPS must be *frozen* for a time before actual production to the MPS is begun, meaning that what is to be produced, the MPS, must be known with certainty and the timing and quantity of raw material receipts must be dependable. When lot sizes of raw materials are large and variability in demand is small, the conventional economic lot size and order point inventory-planning systems tend to work quite well because their assumptions of uniform demand apply. MRP therefore offers more improvement in inventory planning when lot sizes are small and demand variability is large.

MRP has not been and will not be applied to all production systems. In some POM applications, MRP is either unnecessary or economically unjustifiable. The frequency of MRP usage is, however, definitely on a dramatic upward trend. As we gain more experience with MRP, we realize that it is not a panacea. It doesn't solve all our inventory-planning problems. Basically, MRP is a POM computerized information system. When computer systems are ineffective, inventory status and bills of material files are inaccurate, master production schedules are undependable, and when the remainder of the organization is otherwise mismanaged, MRP—or any other technique—will not be of much help. It will generate greater volumes of inaccurate and unused information than previously thought possible. MRP is best applied when production systems are basically well managed and a more comprehensive production and inventory planning system is needed.

Implementation of an MRP system is not a painless process. Since MRP is an information system that is driven by information, merely buying software and maybe some hardware does not guarantee a successful MRP system. There are some significant start-up costs and some ongoing costs in implementing an MRP system. Many of these costs are associated with rectifying poor or inadequate information as well as instituting system discipline to ensure that correct information continues to flow into the MRP system. These are usually hidden costs that are often not formally recognized when the proposal for an MRP system is presented.

CAPACITY REQUIREMENTS PLANNING (CRP)

Capacity requirements planning (CRP) is that part of the resource requirements planning that tests the master production schedule (MPS) for capacity feasibility. In the process of this testing, a plan is developed for the assignment of orders to work centers, the use of overtime, standby equipment, and subcontracting. Figure 11.7 illustrates this process. CRP takes the *planned order releases* off the MRP schedules and assigns the orders to work centers by consulting the routing plans. *Routing plans* specify the sequence of production processes required for each order. Next, the lots of

FIGURE 11.7 The Capacity Requirements Planning Process

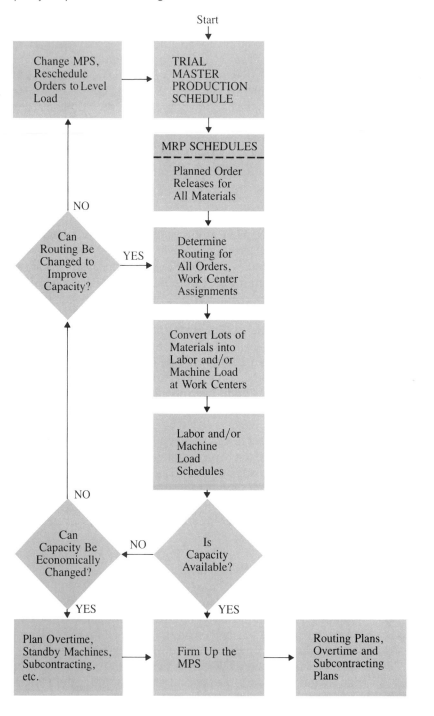

FIGURE 11.8   Loading Effects of MPS on Work Center Capacities

						Weeks				
	−2	−1	1	2	3	4	5	6	7	8
Final Assembly (Units)			800		1,600		600		1,800	
Labor-Hours			400		800		300		900	
Machine-Hours			240		480		180		540	
Assemble Frame (Units)		800		1,600		600		1,800		
Labor-Hours		320		640		240		720		
Machine-Hours		280		560		210		630		
Order Part #115 (Parts)	2,400		4,800		1,800		5,400			

materials are converted to capacity load data by using labor and machine standards, and then weekly *load schedules* are prepared for each work center that includes all orders. If enough capacity is available at all of the work centers in all weeks, then the MPS is firmed up. If not, then it must be determined if the capacity can be economically changed. If overtime, subcontracting, standby machines, or other means can be used to augment capacity, then the MPS can be firmed up. If capacity cannot be economically changed, then either the routing or assignment of orders to work centers must be changed to improve capacity, or the MPS must be changed by rescheduling orders to better level capacity, and the process is repeated.

The principal means of testing the feasibility of the MPS is through work center load schedules.

LOAD SCHEDULES

A *load schedule* is a device for comparing the actual labor-hours and machine-hours required to produce the MPS against the available labor-hours and machine-hours in each week. Load schedules are usually prepared in a hierarchy from work centers at the beginning of the manufacturing system through successive stages to the end of the manufacturing system.

Figure 11.8 demonstrates that when end items are included in the MPS, this inclusion causes activities to be undertaken at successively earlier stages in the production system. MRP schedules determine the planned order releases, and these releases are the basis for production in all work centers. Beginning at the top of the figure in Week 5 in the Final Assembly work center, we find that 600 units must be finished in Final Assembly in Week 5. One week earlier, in Week 4, 600 units must be

FIGURE 11.9 The Capacity Loading Hierarchy

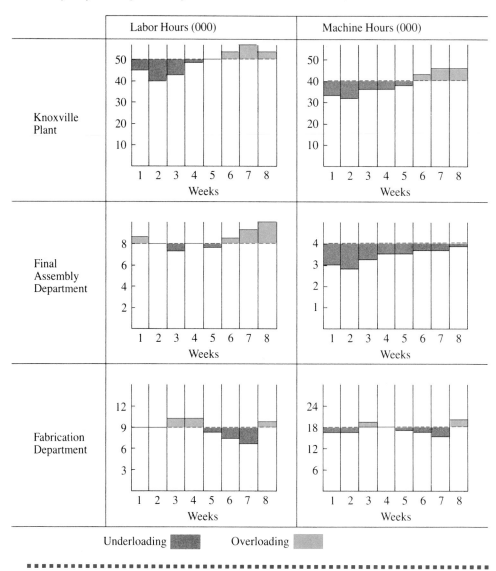

Underloading ▨   Overloading ▨

finished in the Assemble Frame work center. The one-week lead time is required to perform the operations in the Assemble Frame work center and transport the units to Final Assembly.

In Week 3, 1,800 #115 parts must be ordered from the supplier. Although ordering parts may not require any production capacity, the activity must begin in Week 3, thus demonstrating the need to offset the ordering activity by a lead time of one week from Assemble Frame. *Offsetting for lead times* between successive stages of the production system is fundamental to resource requirements planning.

Notice in Figure 11.8 that we can determine the actual number of labor- and machine-hours that the MPS will require weekly in each work center for this product. When all end items from the MPS are included, the total labor- and machine-hours required weekly in each work center can be compared to the number available. Such comparisons allow operations managers to determine the feasibility of the MPS in each work center weekly and also answer operating questions about overtime, standby machines, subcontracting, and other overloading and underloading issues.

Let us suppose that we have a trial MPS and we wish to test its feasibility through CRP. Load schedules such as the ones illustrated in Figure 11.9 may be used for this purpose. From such schedules we can determine the following:

1. The labor-hours loading is out of balance in the Fabrication Department. It appears that some fabrication work needs to be shifted from Weeks 3, 4, and 8 into Weeks 5, 6, and 7. A review of the machine loading in the Fabrication Department in these weeks indicates that such a shift would not cause machine overloading.
2. The change suggested in Fabrication above would not adversely affect Final Assembly because all units in Fabrication move to Final Assembly one week later and overtime could be used to alleviate the labor hours overloading in Weeks 6, 7, and 8 in Final Assembly. The machine-hour loading in all weeks in Final Assembly is not a limiting factor.
3. At the plant level, the later part of the schedule is overloaded on both machine- hours and labor-hours. Overtime could be used to relieve the labor-hours overloading, and subcontracting or the use of less efficient standby machines could reduce the machine-hour overloading. Another alternative is always present, however, and that is to modify the MPS to shift end items from the later part of the schedule to the earlier weeks.

If the MPS is modified, then the logic of the CRP would be applied again through a revised set of load schedules similar to Figure 11.9. In this process we develop a trial MPS and then modify it through CRP until not only is the MPS feasible, but also the work centers are economically loaded. This promotes internal operating efficiency and low unit costs throughout the entire manufacturing system.

One trend in CRP is to use one of the many standard computer programs available from computer software suppliers. An example of such a system is the *Capacity Planning and Operation Sequencing System — Extended (CAPOSS – E)* from IBM.[9]

We have now seen how the MPS attempts to achieve its dual objectives of satisfying customer demand on a timely basis and simultaneously promoting internal operating efficiency through CRP.

---

[9] IBM, *Capacity Planning and Operation Sequencing System — Extended,* Publications 5740 – M41 (OS/VS) and 5746 – M41 (DOS/VS), April 1977.

SUMMARY

Resource requirements planning is the planning for materials, machine capacity, personnel, cash, and other resources needed to produce the end items in a master production schedule.

Materials requirement planning is driven by the master production schedule. The inventory status file, bills of material, and the master production schedule are used by the MRP computer program to explode the end items into the gross requirements of raw materials, parts, and assemblies needed in each future time period. Gross requirements are converted to net requirements after considering the materials available and offsetting them to earlier time periods to allow for supply lead times. The primary outputs of MRP are the planned order schedule and changes to planned orders. Transactions affecting the inventory status file and exception, performance, and planning reports are also generated. MRP determines if materials can be made available to produce the master production schedule as it is, or if the production of end items needs to be moved into later periods.

Capacity requirements planning takes the planned order releases from the MRP schedules, assigns orders to work centers, and calculates the labor and machine load in each future time period at each work center. The load schedules indicate whether the master production schedule is feasible; whether overtime, subcontracting, or other means need to be used to change capacity; or whether the master production schedule should be changed.

Resource requirements planning systems have evolved from MRP I to closed-loop MRP to MRP II. The evolution of these systems from simple parts explosions to complete information systems that integrate all of the functions of the business through a common data base is continuing today. Although MRP-related issues remain to be resolved, there is little doubt that the MRP system is a powerful force in production and inventory planning and control now, and it is expected to remain so well into the future.

REVIEW AND DISCUSSION QUESTIONS

1. What is resource requirements planning?
2. Identify the major elements of resource requirements planning.
3. Describe the role of MPS, MRP, and CRP in resource requirements planning.
4. Describe the relationships between MPS, MRP, and CRP.
5. Describe the process of MRP.
6. Define these terms: *bills of material file, inventory status file, master production schedule, planned order schedule, changes to planned orders, MRP schedules, low-level coding, offsetting for lead time.*
7. What are the objectives of MRP? Explain how each of these objectives is achieved.
8. What is lumpy demand? Name three methods of lot-sizing that are used when demand is lumpy. How does a minimum lot size work?
9. Explain how net requirements for a material in a bucket are computed.

10. Explain the differences between regenerative and net change MRP systems. What are the advantages and disadvantages of each type of MRP system?

11. Explain these terms: *MRP I, closed-loop MRP, MRP II.*

12. Describe the process of CRP.

13. Name the characteristics of production systems that are suitable for MRP.

PROBLEMS

Material Requirements Planning (MRP)

1. If the beginning inventory for a product is 1,000 units, safety stock is 200 units, and estimated weekly demand is 500, 400, 300, 800, 1,000, and 500 units over a 6-week planning horizon, develop a net requirements schedule for the product.

2. The beginning inventory for floppy disk units at the Austin plant of Computer Products Corporation (CPC) is 500 units, and CPC ordinarily likes to carry a safety stock of 200 units. The estimated demand for the next 6 weeks is 355, 900, 810, 600, 600, and 600. Develop a net requirements schedule for the product.

3. Product A is made of two B assemblies and two C assemblies. Each C assembly is made of one D subassembly, 3 E parts, and one F raw material. Each D subassembly is made of 2 E parts and 3 G raw materials. Each B assembly is made of one F raw material and 3 H parts. Construct a product structure tree for Product A.

4. Complete this MRP schedule for a component:

Lot Size	Lead Time (Weeks)	On Hand	SS	Allo- cated		Week Number				
						1	2	3	4	5
					Gross requirements			10,000		7,500
					Scheduled receipts	5,000				
5,000+	2	5,000	2,500	2,000	Available					
					Net requirements					
					Planned order receipts					
					Planned order releases					

5. A product has this product tree:

Level Description	Level Code	Product Structure Tree
Product	0	A
Assembly	1	B C
Part	2	2D

Complete the MRP schedule on page 508.

Item Code	Level Code	Lot Size	Lead Time (Weeks)	On Hand	Safety Stock	Allocated		Weeks: 1	2	3	4	5	6
A	0	LFL	1	1,000	500		Gross requirements				1,000	2,000	1,000
							Scheduled receipts						
							Available						
							Net requirements						
							Planned order receipts						
							Planned order releases						
B	1	LFL	1	200	100	100	Gross requirements						
							Scheduled receipts						
							Available						
							Net requirements						
							Planned order receipts						
							Planned order releases						
C	1	LFL	1	500	100	100	Gross requirements						
							Scheduled receipts						
							Available						
							Net requirements						
							Planned order receipts						
							Planned order releases						
D	2	1,000+	1	1,000	500	200	Gross requirements						
							Scheduled receipts						
							Available						
							Net requirements						
							Planned order receipts						
							Planned order releases						

6. The P55 power unit is manufactured at the Los Angeles plant of Computer Products Corporation (CPC). The unit itself is made of one A9 assembly, one T99 part, and one D51 part. Each A9 assembly is made of one S6 subassembly and three C22 parts. Each S6 subassembly is made of one T39 part, two T41 parts, and two D31 parts. Construct a product structure tree for the P55 power unit.

7. Complete this MRP schedule for the S6 subassembly from Problem 6:

Lot size = 500 +	Safety stock = 100
Lead time = 1 week	Allocated = 200
On hand = 500	

	Weeks				
	1	*2*	*3*	*4*	*5*
Gross requirements		1,000	700	900	800
Scheduled receipts	1,000				
Available					
Net requirements					
Planned order receipts					
Planned order releases					

8. Each S6 subassembly from Problem 6 is made up of one T39 part, two T41 parts, and two D31 parts. Complete an MRP schedule for the S6 subassembly and all of its components:

	S6 Subassembly	T39 Part	T41 Part	D31 Part
Lot size	500 +	700 +	1,000 +	2,000 +
Lead time	1 week	1 week	1 week	2 weeks
On hand	500	200	600	600
Safety stock	100	—	—	400
Allocated	200	—	300	100

Component		Weeks				
		1	*2*	*3*	*4*	*5*
S6	Gross requirements		1,000	700	900	800
	Scheduled receipts	1,000				
T39	Scheduled receipts	700				
T41	Scheduled receipts	1,000				
D31	Scheduled receipts	2,000				

9. A product has this product tree:

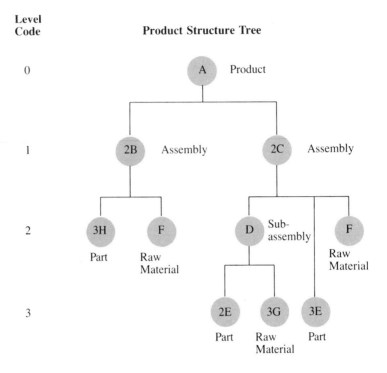

Level Code	Product Structure Tree

This inventory status report has just been issued for the product:

Item Code	On Hand	Safety Stock	Allo- cated	Lot Size	Lead Time (Weeks)	Scheduled Receipts		Service Parts Orders	
						Quantity	Week	Quantity	Week
A	500	500	500	LFL	1	1,000	1		
B	1,000	200	500	LFL	1	1,000	2	1,000	3
C	1,000	500	200	LFL	1				
D	1,500	500	500	500+	1				
E	500	500		5,000+	1				
F	2,000	500	500	5,000+	3				
G	3,000	1,000	500	6,000+	2	6,000	1		
H	2,500	500	1,000	4,000+	2	4,000	2	5,000	6

a. Prepare an MRP schedule for all of the components in the product to cover a 6-week planning horizon if the MPS for the product shows an estimated demand or gross requirements of 1,000 units in Week 5 and 1,500 units in Week 6.

b. Is the MPS feasible from a material supply perspective?

c. If not feasible, what actions could be taken to make the MPS feasible?

10. In the Green Thumb Water Sprinkler Company example in this chapter, the MPS is changed from 800 units in Week 4 and 2,000 units in Week 8 to 2,000 units in Weeks 4, 5, and 7. If all other data in the case remain unchanged:
    a. Prepare a MRP schedule.
    b. Is the MPS feasible from a material supply (purchased or produced components) perspective?
    c. What actions could be taken to allow Green Thumb to meet the material supply requirements of the MPS?

11. The Los Angeles plant of Computer Products Corporation (CPC) manufactures P55 power units for sale to other manufacturers in the electronics and computer industries. The P55 power unit is made of one A9 assembly, one T99 part, and one D51 part. Each A9 assembly is made of one S6 subassembly and three C22 parts. Each S6 subassembly is made of one T39 part, two T41 parts, and two D31 parts. The inventory status report exhibits this information for the P55 power unit:

Component	Lot Size	Lead Time	On Hand	Safety Stock	Allo-cated	Scheduled Receipts Amount	Week
P55	LFL	—	100	—	—	—	—
D51	1,500+	2 Weeks	1,300	200	200	1,500	1
A9	LFL	—	500	200	100	1,000	1
T99	2,000+	1 Week	1,000	300	300	1,000	1
S6	500+	1 Week	500	100	200	1,000	1
C22	3,000+	1 Week	2,000	500	500	3,000	1
T39	700+	1 Week	200	—	—	700	1
T41	1,000+	1 Week	600	—	300	1,000	1
D31	2,000+	2 Weeks	600	400	100	2,000	1

The MPS for the plant shows these quantities of the P55 power unit to be completed:

Product	Weeks				
	1	2	3	4	5
P55 power unit		2,300	700	900	800

a. Construct a product structure tree for the P55 power unit.
b. Complete a MRP schedule for the P55 power unit and all of its components.

12. If the weekly net requirements for a product are 0, 100, 300, 800, 1,000, and 500 units over a 6-week planning horizon, carrying cost per unit per week is $1 whenever a unit must be carried over into the next week, there are 52 work weeks per year, and ordering cost is $500 per order, develop a schedule of completed production lots and calculate the cost of your schedule by using these methods:
    a. lot-for-lot (LFL),
    b. economic order quantity (EOQ), and
    c. period order quantity (POQ).
    You may disregard the effects of initial inventory and safety stock on your calculations.

13. You are given this net requirements schedule:

	Weeks							
	1	*2*	*3*	*4*	*5*	*6*	*7*	*8*
Net requirements (units)	1,000	2,000	2,500	1,500	3,000	1,000	500	500

If it costs $5,000 to get the final assembly department ready to assemble batches of this product, it costs $26 to carry one unit in inventory for a year, and 52 weeks per year are worked by the final assembly department, develop a schedule of completed production lots for the product and calculate the cost of your schedule by using these methods:
a. lot-for-lot (LFL),
b. economic order quantity (EOQ), and
c. period order quantity (POQ).
You may disregard the effects of initial inventory and safety stock on your calculations.

14. James Moore, operations manager at the Austin plant of Computer Products Corporation (CPC), is looking over his staff's estimated net requirements for floppy disk units for the next six weeks:

	Week					
	1	*2*	*3*	*4*	*5*	*6*
Net requirements	55	900	810	600	600	600

If it costs $2,500 to set up the production line to produce this product and it costs $5 to carry one floppy disk unit in inventory for one week, develop a schedule of completed production lots for the product and compute the cost of your schedule by using these methods:
a. lot-for-lot (LFL),
b. economic order quantity (EOQ), and
c. period order quantity (POQ).
You may disregard the effects of initial inventory and safety stock on your calculations.

Capacity Requirements Planning (CRP)

15. The Ever-Pure Water Company sits atop a spring in Blackwater, Arkansas. The company bottles the water for shipment to customers through a distributor network. Ever-Pure's management has developed this master production schedule for the next six weeks:

	Weeks					
	1	*2*	*3*	*4*	*5*	*6*
Water (gallons)	100,000	150,000	200,000	150,000	150,000	100,000

If Ever-Pure's labor- and machine-hours available and its production standards are:

	Labor	Machine
Monthly capacity available (hours)	17,333	25,000
Production standard (hours/gallon)	.10	.15

a. Determine the percent utilization (standard hours $\times$ 100 $\div$ hours of capacity) of the labor and machine capacity in each week.

b. What suggestions would you make to Ever-Pure's management concerning its MPS?

16. The Silver Streak Iron Works produces three different models of wellhead valves for the petroleum industry. Each of the valves must be processed through three production departments: foundry, fabrication, and assembly. Approximately one week is required for a valve to be completely processed through each department. Silver Streak is now in the process of capacity requirements planning (CRP) and has just developed this MPS:

	Weeks							
Model	1	2	3	4	5	6	7	8
X-100	300	500	500	600	700	500	200	300
Y-101	500	300	400	200	300	500	300	400
Z-102	600	500	700	700	800	600	800	600

The weekly labor and machine capacities for the production departments are:

	Foundry		Fabrication		Assembly	
Models	Labor Standard (Hr./Unit)	Machine Standard (Hr./Unit)	Labor Standard (Hr./Unit)	Machine Standard (Hr./Unit)	Labor Standard (Hr./Unit)	Machine Standard (Hr./Unit)
X-100	2.0	3.0	1.5	2.0	1.5	1.0
Y-101	2.5	3.5	2.0	2.5	1.5	1.5
Z-102	3.0	3.5	1.5	2.5	2.0	1.5

a. Develop labor and machine load schedules for each department and the plant for the first six weeks of the MPS (remember to offset for lead times between departments).

b. Interpret the meaning of your load schedule: Is the MPS feasible? Are the production departments efficiently loaded? Can you make suggestions for changing the MPS to improve loading?

COMPUTER PROBLEMS/CASES

THE YOKO COMPANY: RESOURCE REQUIREMENTS PLANNING IN THE PROCESSING INDUSTRY

The Yoko Company is a pharmaceutical and food products manufacturer. Among its many products is an artificial egg product, called Yoko, which is produced in liquid bulk and sold to another company that markets it to persons who must have a low cholesterol diet. The company uses a seven-week planning horizon in its marketing and production plans and is now in the process of developing a master production schedule, material requirements planning, and capacity requirements planning. Its production-planning department has just gathered this information to be used in these plans:

1. Estimated weekly demands or gross requirements for the Yoko product are 200, 1,000, 500, 1,000, 2,000, 2,000, and 1,000.

2. The bill of material for the Yoko product is:

Parent Code	Component Code	Level Code	Description	Amount of Component per Unit of Parent
	Yoko	0	Artificial egg product	
Yoko	A	1	Amino protein	20 pounds
Yoko	B	1	Polychlorine sulfate CN#2	30 pounds
Yoko	C	1	Carrier base #3389	50 pounds
A	D	2	Yellow color stock EE#78	.25 pounds
A	E	2	Salicton thickener	.50 pounds
A	F	2	Thetscon carrier	.28 pounds

Note: The standard unit of measure for the Yoko product is a 20-gallon half-barrel.

3. The product structure for the Yoko product is:

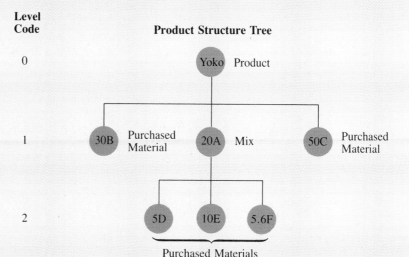

4. Capacity is limited in each week by 4,500 straight-time hours and 8,000 machine-hours, although overtime may be used. The company policy on overtime allows up to 10 percent of the total weekly labor-hours capacity to be supplied by overtime. The production-planning department has estimated the amount of labor- and machine-hours required by other products that must be manufactured to contractual schedules. The remaining hours may be used to manufacture the Yoko product.

Capacity Needed by Other Products	Weeks						
	1	*2*	*3*	*4*	*5*	*6*	*7*
Labor hours	3,635	4,050	3,800	3,400	3,100	3,700	4,500
Machine hours	6,645	7,050	6,900	6,000	6,100	6,700	7,900

Each 20-gallon half-barrel of the Yoko product requires .7 labor-hour and .9 machine-hour of capacity in the manufacturing plant. The production operation required to produce the Yoko product is a single mixing operation that is accomplished in two sequential steps: (1) Mix A is prepared by mixing D, E, and F materials, and (2) Mix A is combined with B and C materials. These mixing operations require only one week to complete. In other words, if 500 half-barrels of the Yoko product are required at the beginning of Week 3, all of the production of the product is begun in Week 2 and completed in Week 2.

5. The purchasing lead times for purchased materials are: B = 1 week, C = 1 week, D = 2 weeks, E = 2 weeks, and F = 2 weeks. D, E, and F can be shortened to 1 week with expediting and additional freight costs.

6. The inventory status report for the Yoko product is:

Item Code	On Hand	Safety Stock	Allocated	Lot Sizes	Scheduled Receipts	
					Quantity	Week
Yoko	500	250				
A	4,000#		1,500#	LFL		
B	3,000#		1,000#	LFL	30,000#	1
C	6,000#		2,000#	LFL	50,000#	1
D	5,000#	1,000#	2,000#	25,000#+	25,000#	1
E	4,000#	1,000#	1,000#	10,000#+	10,000#	1
F	3,500#	1,000#		5,000#+	5,000#	1

7. The Yoko Company operates 50 weeks per year and the annual demand for the Yoko product is 300,000 half-barrels. It costs $5,000 to flush the lines and set up to produce a production lot of the Yoko product, and it costs $10 whenever a half-barrel of the Yoko product must be carried in inventory into the next week.

Assignment

1. Prepare a set of master production schedule (MPS) calculations from estimated weekly demand (or gross requirements) to net requirements to production lots by using lot-for-lot (LFL), economic order quantity (EOQ), and period order quantity (POQ) as in Example 11.1. Select the lot-sizing method with the lowest total ordering and carrying costs. What are the total ordering and carrying costs of your production lot schedule?

2. Prepare a MRP schedule to test the MPS. The production lot schedule from the MPS in No. 1 above should be the same as the planned order receipts schedule for the Yoko product in the MRP schedule. Is the MPS feasible from the perspective of availability of

materials? What expediting, if any, is required to allow The Yoko Company to meet the material requirements of the MPS?

3. Prepare load schedules of The Yoko Company plant for both labor- and machine-hours. Does your capacity requirements planning indicate that the MPS is feasible from the perspective of production capacity? What overtime, if any, is required? Is the overtime plan within company policy?

4. Summarize your resource requirements plan for The Yoko Company and outline any extraordinary measures required to render the MPS feasible.

COMPUTER PRODUCTS CORPORATION (CPC)

The Austin plant of Computer Products Corporation (CPC) produces computer printers and floppy disk units for personal and small-business computers. Each of these products must be processed through two manufacturing departments: first through Component Fabrication and then through Assembly. Approximately one week is required to process one printer or one floppy disk unit through each of the two manufacturing departments. James Moore, operations manager at the Austin plant, is now reviewing the master production schedule (MPS) for the products:

	Weeks					
Product	*1*	*2*	*3*	*4*	*5*	*6*
Printer	700	700	800	900	1,000	800
Floppy disk unit	55	900	810	600	600	600

The weekly labor and machine capacities for the production departments are:

Department	*Labor-Hour Capacity (Labor-Hours per Week)*	*Machine-Hour Capacity (Machine-Hours per Week)*
Component fabrication	15,000	8,800
Assembly	11,000	2,000

The labor and machine standards for each of the products in the manufacturing departments are:

	Component Fabrication		*Assembly*	
Product	*Labor Standard (Hours/Unit)*	*Machine Standard (Hours/Unit)*	*Labor Standard (Hours/Unit)*	*Machine Standard (Hours/Unit)*
Printer	10.0	6.0	8.0	1.0
Floppy disk unit	8.0	5.0	6.0	1.0

The plant's personnel policy does not allow transfer of personnel between departments, and overtime hours may not exceed 10 percent of the straight-time hours.

Assignment

1. Develop labor and machine load schedules for each department for the first five weeks of the master production schedule (remember to offset for lead times between departments).

2. Interpret the meaning of your load schedule: Is the MPS feasible? Can you make suggestions for changing the MPS to improve loading?

3. Evaluate your proposal in No. 2.

SELECTED BIBLIOGRAPHY

APICS Bibliography. 11th ed. Falls Church, VA: American Production and Inventory Control Society, 1987.

APICS Dictionary. 6th ed. Falls Church, VA: American Production and Inventory Control Society, 1987.

APICS Special Report: Materials Requirement Planning by Computer. Falls Church, VA: American Production and Inventory Control Society, 1971.

Berry, W. L. "Lot Sizing Procedures for Requirements Planning Systems: A Framework for Analysis." *Production and Inventory Management* 13(Second Quarter 1972):19–34.

Bevis, George E. "A Management Viewpoint on the Implementation of a MRP System." *Production and Inventory Management* 17(First Quarter 1976):105–116.

Capacity Planning and Control. Falls Church, VA: American Production and Inventory Control Society, 1979.

Gaither, Norman. "A Near-Optimal Lot-Sizing Model for Material Requirements Planning Systems." *Production and Inventory Management* 22(Fourth Quarter 1981):75–89.

Groff, G. K. "A Lot-Sizing Rule for Time Phased Component Demand." *Production and Inventory Management* 20(First Quarter 1979):47–53.

International Business Machines Corporation. *Capacity Planning and Operation Sequencing System—Extended (CAPOSS-E).* Publications 5740-M41 (OS/VS) and 5746-M41 (DOS/VS), April 1977.

———. *Communications Oriented Production Information and Control Systems (COPICS).* Publications G320-1974 through G320-1981.

———. *The Production Information and Control System (PICS).* Publication GE 20-0280-2.

The Material Requirements Planning Application. IBM Systems/34 Manufacturing Accounting and Production Information Control Systems (MAPICS) Feature Education [ob]r[cb]SR30-0369-1, IBM(1979):4–29 through 4–50.

Miller, Jeffrey G., and Linda G. Sprague. "Behind the Growth in Material Requirements Planning." *Harvard Business Review* 53(September–October 1975):83–91.

Orlicky, Joseph. *Material Requirements Planning.* New York: McGraw-Hill, 1975.

Plossl, G. W., and Oliver W. Wight. *Material Requirements Planning by Computer.* Washington, DC: American Production and Inventory Control Society, 1971.

———. *Production and Inventory Control.* Englewood Cliffs, NJ: Prentice-Hall, 1967.

Schroeder, Roger G., et al. "A Study of MRP Benefits and Costs." *Journal of Operations Management* 2, no. 1(October 1981):1–9.

Silver, E. A., and H. C. Meal. "A Heuristic for Selecting Lot Size Quantities for the Case of a Deterministic Time-Varying Demand Rate and Discrete Opportunities for Replenishment." *Production and Inventory Management* 14(Second Quarter 1973):64–75.

Wagner, H. M., and T. M. Whitin. "Dynamic Version of the Economic Lot Size Model." *Management Science* 5, no. 1(October 1958):89–96.

12

SHOP FLOOR PLANNING AND CONTROL

JUST-IN-TIME (JIT), SCHEDULING METHODS, AND SERVICE OPERATIONS

SHOP-FLOOR DECISIONS AT SPECIFIC DATA CORPORATION

It was Monday morning at 8:05 a.m. of the day shift at Specific Data Corporation and Bill Johnson was looking over the orders waiting to be processed at his machine in the panel fabrication work center. He and his foreman studied the six waiting orders, trying to decide in what sequence Bill should process the orders. First, they looked at the planned order releases on the latest MRP schedule. One order had arrived early and was not scheduled to be released to (started through) the work center until next week; that order was placed at the back of the line. Another order was past due because it was scheduled to have been released to the work center last week; that order was put at the front of the line. According to the MRP schedule, only four orders were scheduled to be released to the work center this week. Now Bill and his foreman must decide in what sequence to process the four remaining orders. The foreman knew that such things as produc-

tion costs, capacity utilization, and delivery promises to customers could be affected by their decision. While the four orders could be processed on a first-come first-served basis, Bill preferred to work on the orders that could be completed the fastest so that more orders per shift could be completed. The foreman believed that the orders with the earliest promised delivery date and the most work remaining should be processed first. They turned to page 5 of the MRP report to find the critical ratio for each of the four orders. The foreman explained to Bill that this ratio is computed by dividing the time remaining to due date by the production time remaining; therefore those orders with low critical ratios should be processed first. Bill now had his instructions and the sequence in which to process the orders. The foreman wondered what effects his decision would have on production cost and capacity utilization.

Thus far we have studied aggregate planning, master production scheduling (MPS), and material requirements planning (MRP). These elements of production planning provide information about which products and components are to be produced in each week of the planning horizon. But the nitty gritty, day-to-day shop floor issues described in the previous account remain unresolved.

In this chapter we shall consider shop floor issues by discussing just-in-time (JIT) systems, scheduling methods, and scheduling service operations.

JUST-IN-TIME (JIT) SYSTEMS

Not all companies use the term *JIT*. For instance, IBM uses the term *continuous flow manufacture,* Hewlett-Packard calls it both *stockless production* and *repetitive manufacturing system,* GE calls it *management by sight,* and several Japanese firms use the term *the Toyota system.* Just as there is not a universal name for JIT, neither is there complete agreement about its meaning.

To some, JIT is simply a means of planning and controlling production on the shop floor. To others, it is a philosophy of production that permeates every facet of organizations. For our purposes, we discuss JIT in the section of this book that concerns shop floor planning and control, but we present JIT in its broadest terms. In this latter context, the JIT topic spills over into later chapters. In Chapter 13, Materials Management and Purchasing, we shall discuss JIT purchasing; in Chapter 15, Total Quality Control, we shall discuss the impact of JIT on product quality; and in Chapter 17, Maintenance Management and Reliability, we shall discuss the maintenance policies necessary for JIT.

JIT PHILOSOPHY

Behind JIT is the continuous drive to improve production processes and methods. Toward that end, JIT strives to reduce inventories because high inventory levels are thought to cover up production problems. For example, with high in-process inventories between operations, if a machine breaks down, if materials fail quality control tests, or if a stockout occurs, we can just shift to another machine or manufacture another product. The machine can be fixed when we get around to it, we can rework the defective parts when it is convenient and then determine why the parts failed the quality control tests, or we can find out later why we had a stockout. One main reason for in-process inventories is to allow us to continue manufacturing even if production problems occur; thus high machine and worker utilization is achieved. Proponents of JIT refer to the use of inventories for this purpose as *Just-in-Case systems.*

In JIT systems, when in-process inventories are drastically reduced, production stops until the production problem is solved. Only when the machine is fixed, the quality control problem is solved, or the reason behind the stockout is found and corrected — only then can production begin again. *JIT is really a system of enforced problem solving.* There are no safety factors in JIT. Every material is expected to meet quality standards, every part is expected to arrive exactly at the time promised and precisely at the place it is supposed to be, every worker is expected to work productively, and every machine is expected to function as intended without breakdowns. The willingness to tolerate interruptions to production so that management and worker attention can focus on production problems underscores JIT proponents' interest in solving those problems. Because such systems obviously cannot tolerate continuous interruptions of production, in JIT systems enormous effort is therefore put into permanently eliminating each problem as it arises so that production is not interrupted again for that problem.

It seems clear that JIT systems will not work unless certain conditions prevail.

PREREQUISITES FOR JIT

JIT does not come free—certain changes to the factory and the way it is managed must occur before the benefits are realized. Among these changes are changes in plant layout, supplier selection, materials-handling methods, scheduling methods, quality control, production equipment, and worker training. Of critical importance to the success of JIT are changes to the method of scheduling the factory.

At Toyota, for instance, where the notion of JIT may have started, there are both *stable and level production schedules.* The master production schedule (MPS) is frozen for the first month, and the entire MPS covers one year. The production schedule is exactly the same for each day of the month. This means that the same products are produced in the same quantities in the same sequence every day of the month. Toyota divides the total number of each automobile model to be manufactured during a month by the number of workdays in the month to get the number of that model to be produced daily. Even if only a few of a particular model were needed in a month, some would be assembled in each day of the month. This ensures that the same production schedule will be met daily. This approach to the MPS simplifies parts explosions, material planning, and worker job assignments. If JIT is to work, stable and level production schedules are a must.

Another important prerequisite for JIT systems is the need to have *smaller and more-focused factories.* Small, specialized factories are easier to manage, and JIT depends on the simplicity of these focused factories. Large, unfocused factories that employ thousands of workers in hundreds of manufacturing departments could be too complex to permit JIT systems to succeed.

A fundamental prerequisite for JIT is *the reduction of lot sizes.* This feature is universal to all JIT applications. Smaller lot sizes reduce inventory levels throughout the factory and are achieved primarily through reducing setup times. Setup time is the time it takes to adjust the machine settings so that a new part can be produced at a work center. This effort to reduce setup times throughout the factory must be made if the benefits of JIT are to be realized.

With stable and level production schedules, smaller and more-focused factories, and drastically reduced lot sizes as a starting point, let us now examine the elements of JIT systems.

ELEMENTS OF JIT

Although JIT is much broader in scope, Kanban is a key element of JIT systems.

FIGURE 12.1   *Kanban Cards*

Conveyance Kanban	
Part number: 33311-3501	Following work center: K123
	Stock location no.: A-12
Container capacity: 50	Stock location no.: A-07
No. of Kanban released: 7 of 12	Preceding work center: Y321

Production Kanban

Work center no.: Y321

Part number to be produced: 33311-3501

Container capacity: 50 units

Stock capacity at which to store: A-07

Materials required:

Material no. 33311-3504
Stock location: A-05

Part no. 33825-2474
Stock location: B-03

Source: R. W. Hall, *Driving the Productivity Machine: Production Planning and Control in Japan* (Falls Church, VA: American Production and Inventory Control Society, 1981), 35. Reprinted with permission, American Production and Inventory Control Society, Inc.

Kanban

At the core of JIT at Toyota is Kanban. *Kanban* means card, and perhaps the best thing about this noncomputerized method of planning and controlling production is its simplicity. There are two types of Kanban cards: a conveyance card (C-Kanban) and a production card (P-Kanban). Figure 12.1 shows examples of these types of cards. Basically these cards replace all other paper on the factory floor. It is important to note that with stable and level production schedules—a prerequisite for JIT— priority decisions (which orders are released each day, when orders are released, and the sequence of the orders) are routine; thus shop floor planning and control are reduced to movement of orders between work stations. In these simple scheduling situations, visual signals and Kanbans are the only devices needed.

Figure 12.2 illustrates how Kanban operates. When a worker on the shop floor at downstream Work Center #2 needs a container of parts for his operation, he does the following:

1.   He looks in the empty container at his work center and finds its C-Kanban; this card is his authorization to replace the empty container with a full one from storage.

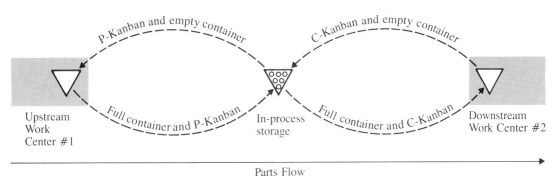

FIGURE 12.2 *Flow of Kanban Cards and Containers between Two Work Centers*

2. Next, he takes the empty container and its C-Kanban and finds a full container of the needed parts in storage.
3. Next, he removes the C-Kanban from the empty container and places it in the full container.
4. Next, he removes the P-Kanban from the full container and places it on a post at the upstream Work Center #1; this P-Kanban is the authorization to produce another container of the parts.
5. Then he takes the full container of parts with its C-Kanban to his downstream Work Center #2.

No parts can be produced or moved without a Kanban card. Kanban is based on the simple idea of replacement of containers of parts, one at a time. A container is not moved to a downstream production operation until it is needed, and a container of parts is not produced until it is needed. These containers are reserved for specific parts, are purposely kept small, and always contain the same standard number of parts for each part number. At Toyota the containers must not hold more than about 10 percent of a day's requirements. There is a minimum of two containers for each part number, one at the upstream producing work center and one at the downstream using work center. It is not unusual, however, for another container of safety stock to be held at the upstream producing work center in case a particular part number cannot be produced right away. Such delays can result because other P-Kanbans were there first and their parts need to be produced first. Workers produce exactly the quantity listed on the recycling Kanban cards, no more and no less. Producing one part more than the standard amount for the container would be considered as bad as producing one part less. Producing one part more than needed would be wasteful because labor, materials, and machine capacity would be spent on producing the extra part that is not needed now and could not be used until later.

Kanban in particular and JIT in general are referred to as a *pull* type of production-planning system because orders are triggered by the users of the parts at downstream production operations. On the other hand, MRP is called a *push* type system because the MRP schedule actually releases orders that push each other through the system.

Great variation exists among JIT systems. For example, at a Kawasaki motorcycle engine plant in Japan, workers communicate by means of painted golf balls that roll down pipes. At other plants, workers communicate with flashing lights. Regardless of the variation in JIT systems, workers must have cooperative attitudes for them to work. Similarly, programs to achieve excellence in preventive maintenance, product quality, and mutual trust with suppliers are musts.

These versions of pull systems greatly reduce in-process inventory of parts between work centers on the shop floor, but JIT is also aimed at reducing raw materials inventories.

JIT Purchasing

The same pull type approach in JIT is applied to purchasing shipments of parts from suppliers. In JIT purchasing, suppliers use the replacement principle of Kanban in that they also use small, standard-size containers and make several shipments daily to each customer. If Kanban is used by a supplier, Kanban cards authorize the movement of containers of parts between the supplier's shop and the customer. In such arrangements suppliers are ordinarily located near their customers. JIT therefore not only reduces in-process inventories by using Kanban, but raw materials inventories are also reduced by applying the same principles to suppliers.

The tendency to tie up suppliers in long-term supply contracts supports the concept of JIT purchasing. Japanese manufacturers refer to suppliers as *coproducers* and put together networks of subcontractors. These *subcontractor networks* involve a large number of suppliers who have signed long-term supply agreements. The networks hang together through good and bad times, and the lowest price is not the most important thing. Delivery times, dependability of supply, quality of products, and cooperation with the customer to reduce inventory levels are factors that are as important as price.

JIT purchasing makes a lot of sense when you think about it. The use of subcontractor networks, long-term supply contracts, and suppliers located near customers all work together to reduce the cost of ordering from suppliers. This reduction in ordering costs has the same effect on purchasing lot sizes as the reduction in setup costs has on production lot sizes — both are decreased.

Toward Reducing Inventories

If it costs a lot to set up a machine to produce a part, it makes sense to produce many units of the part each time it is produced. For perhaps too long, U.S. manufacturers have held to this conventional wisdom and have neglected to work on reducing setup times and reducing production lot sizes. Central to JIT is the reduction of production lot sizes so that inventory levels are reduced. But doesn't it seem that very small production lot sizes would result in too many machine setups, increased production costs, and lost capacity because of idle machines during setups? JIT systems spend large sums of money to reduce setup times to avoid these negative consequences of small lot sizes. Engineers study the setups, automatic devices are attached to the machines, workers are trained in more efficient work methods, and the result is very short setup times. In some cases computerized controls can make the new machine settings instantaneously, with the result that the setup time between different parts

FIGURE 12.3 *Effect of Reducing Changeover Times on Production Lot Size*

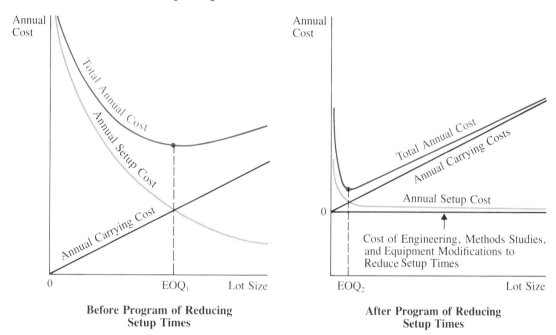

**Before Program of Reducing
Setup Times**

**After Program of Reducing
Setup Times**

approaches zero. Figure 12.3 shows that economic production lot sizes (EOQ) approach zero as the setup costs approach zero. JIT firms use the same EOQ formula to analyze lot sizes, but they turn it around. They treat a very small EOQ lot size as a given and then solve for the setup cost. In this way production lot sizes can be set very low and the resulting setup times can be used for targets as engineers develop programs for reducing setup times. Example 12.1 computes the setup time required to accommodate a small JIT production lot size. These types of computations would be the approach used in a factory-wide program to reduce changeover costs.

Not only do greatly decreased changeover costs in JIT result in reduced inventory levels, but also the factory begins to act very much like a repetitive manufacturing system.

EXAMPLE 12.1   *Computing Setup Time When a Small JIT Production Lot Size Is Given*

As a part of a factory-wide JIT program to reduce setup times so that production lot sizes can be smaller, a firm wants to determine how much the setup time of a manufacturing operation should be in order to accommodate an economic production lot size (EOQ) of 10 units of a part. A production analyst has developed these data for the operation:

D = 10,000 units annual demand

d =   250 units daily demand rate

p =   500 units daily production rate

EOQ = 10 units lot size for each production run

C = 5 dollars per unit per year carrying cost

S = cost per setup, which is unknown—to be determined from the EOQ formula with gradual deliveries

If the labor rate for the operation is $10 per hour, what setup time results in an economic production lot size of 10 units?

Solution:

$$EOQ = \sqrt{\frac{2DS}{C}\left(\frac{p}{p-d}\right)}$$

$$EOQ^2 = \frac{2DS}{C}\left(\frac{p}{p-d}\right)$$

$$S = \frac{C(EOQ^2)}{2D}\left(\frac{p-d}{p}\right) = \frac{\$5(10^2)}{2(10,000)}\left(\frac{500-250}{500}\right) = \$.0125$$

Setup time = S ÷ Labor rate = $.0125 per $10/hour
            = .00125 hour, or .075 minute or 4.5 seconds

Toward Repetitive Manufacturing

We traditionally think of two classic types of production systems—(1) product-focused/produce-to-stock/standardized product designs and (2) process-focused/produce-to-order/custom product designs. The first type is often referred to as *repetitive manufacturing.* These are systems in which products flow continuously along a direct route until they are finished and in which there are no in-process inventories and parts rarely stop moving. Most JIT applications have been in repetitive manufacturing.

Those companies that have worked hard to convert their factories to repetitive manufacturing find that JIT can be more readily adapted to their systems. Among the things that can be done to shape a factory to be more repetitive in its production are:

1. Reduce setup times and production lot sizes.
2. Change the layout of the factory to allow streamlined product flows through the plant.
3. Convert clusters of machines within process-focused layouts to cellular manufacturing (CM) centers or cells. In CM, groups of machines function as product-focused islands within the larger layout.

4. Install flexible manufacturing systems (FMS). These groups of machines can accommodate product variety without the necessity of worker-performed machine changeovers.
5. Standardize parts designs to reduce the number of parts and the number of changeovers.
6. Have workers trained for several jobs. These flexible workers can move from work center to work center as necessary to balance the work load in the factory.
7. Install effective preventive maintenance programs so that machine breakdowns do not interrupt product flows.
8. Install effective quality control programs so that defective products do not interrupt product flows.
9. Develop an effective subcontractor network so that materials flow into the factory smoothly to support the in-house production schedules, thereby allowing uninterrupted production.

Even if a firm cannot convert all of its operations to repetitive manufacturing, some parts of the system can be repetitive. For example, even if many custom-designed products are irregularly scheduled at final assembly, their component-part designs could be standardized, component-part production schedules could be made stable and level, and the component parts could be produced by repetitive manufacturing.

With such changes as these, even though a JIT system may not be of the repetitive manufacturing type, it has many of the same characteristics and enjoys many of the same benefits.

BENEFITS OF JIT

The proponents of JIT systems emphasize these benefits of installing such systems:

1. Inventory levels are drastically reduced.
2. The time it takes for products to get through the factory is greatly reduced, thus enabling factories to be more responsive to changing demands.
3. Product quality is improved and the cost of scrap is reduced. One reason that scrap cost is reduced is that with smaller production lots defective parts are discovered earlier.
4. With smaller production lots, less space is taken up with inventory and materials-handling equipment. Work stations are closer together, and workers can see each other, communicate more easily, work out problems more efficiently, learn each other's jobs, and switch jobs as needed. All of this promotes teamwork among workers and flexibility in work assignments.
5. Because the focus in manufacturing is on solving production problems, manufacturing operations are streamlined and problem-free.

Reduced production costs, increased worker productivity, and improved product quality are the bottom line of these benefits. Industry Snapshot 12.1 describes how these benefits accrue to JIT producers.

INDUSTRY SNAPSHOT 12.1

A Revolutionary Way to Streamline the Factory

The just-in-time (JIT) production system may be the most important productivity-enhancing management innovation since Frederick Winslow Taylor's time-and-motion studies at the turn of the century. It is a Japanese innovation, and key features were perfected by Toyota. But there is nothing uniquely Japanese about JIT production. It is usable anywhere.

JIT production means producing and buying in very small quantities just in time for use. It is a simple, hand-to-mouth mode of industrial operations that directly cuts inventories and also reduces the need for storage space, racks, conveyors, forklifts, computer terminals for inventory control, and material support personnel. More important, the absence of extra inventories creates an imperative to run an error-free operation because there is no cushion of excess parts to keep production going when problems crop up. Causes of errors are rooted out, never to occur again.

In some ways, JIT production is nothing new. High-volume continuous producers—for example, steel, chemical, and paper companies—employ it routinely. To do otherwise would bury them in inventory. Long-term predictability of materials needed makes it possible for continuous processors to arrange for materials to flow into and through their plants steadily without inventory buildups. The Anheuser-Busch brewery in St. Louis unloads a nearly continuous stream of trucks bringing in empty cans and uses them soon enough that, on the average, there is only a two-hour supply of unfilled cans on hand.

But cans of Budweiser don't come in many different models. In most of the rest of industry, plants produce an ever-changing variety of goods, and production scheduling is complicated and irregular. JIT streamlines and simplifies the stop-and-go production of most plant operations so that they resemble continuous processing. In so doing, it forces planners and analysts to get out of their offices and get out on the floor solving real problems.

The transformation begins with inventory removal. Fewer materials are bought, and parts and products are made in smaller quantities; so-called lot-size inventories thereby shrink. Buffer stocks or safety stocks—"just-in-case" inventory—are also deliberately cut.

The immediate result is work stoppages. Plenty of them. Production comes to a standstill because feeder processes break down or produce too many defectives—and now there is no buffer stock to keep things going. This is exactly what is supposed to happen. For now the analysts and engineers pour out of their offices and mingle with foremen and workers trying to get production going again. Now the causes—bad raw materials, machine breakdowns, poor training, tolerances that exceed process capabilities—get attention so that the problems may never recur.

When one round of problems is solved, inventories are cut again so that more problems crop up and get solved. Each round of problem exposure and solution increases productivity—and quality, too. In Japan extensive quality control measures blend nicely with just-in-time production because many of the problems uncovered by inventory removal are quality problems.

Some people who have studied the just-in-time system conclude that it is suitable for high-volume producers but not for smaller-volume "job shops." But many companies that call themselves job shops have some semblance of a product line; those companies can become more productive by producing in smaller lots as continuously as possible. If they don't, chances are that a Japanese competitor will emerge and capture enough market share to become a high-volume repetitive producer jeopardizing the position of the stop-and-go producers; this is what is happening to Harley-Davidson, International Harvester, and Hyster.

How can Western manufacturers become JIT producers? One way is "cold turkey": Remove inventories from the shop floor, dismantle distance-spanning conveyors, move machines close together, and permanently reallocate floor space that once held inventory. Spasms of work stoppages for lack of parts will soon get everyone involved in solving underlying problems.

Most companies will want to take a more incremental approach. One way is to cut the cost of machine setup, a major reason why companies make parts in large batches. Setup times can be cut by simplifying dies, machine controls, fixtures, and so forth. The term "quick die change" has been in the vocabulary of American production engineers for years. But American management only heard of it recently as stories have trickled in from Japan about "single setup," which means a single-digit number of minutes, and "one-touch setup," which means zero setup (only load and unload) time.

The Kawasaki plant in Lincoln, Neb., uses another experimental approach. Occasionally it will deliberately draw down buffer stocks to near zero. The kinds of problems exposed will be recorded and assigned as improvement projects. Stocks will be allowed to build back up, and the improvement projects will proceed. As underlying problems are solved, stocks will then be permanently cut and storage floor space reallocated.

Geography is the big obstacle to just-in-time deliveries of purchased parts. When your supplier is across the country, the economies of full truck and rail car shipments often dictate infrequent large-lot buying. The Japanese companies that have opened subsidiary plants in North America—Sony, Honda, Nissan, Sanyo, Kawasaki, etc.—deal with this hurdle by resolutely seeking nearby suppliers.

Establishing those arrangements may take years of effort. In the meantime, consolidated loads from clusters of remote suppliers may permit a load to be delivered every day. Common carriers may be rejected in favor of contract shippers or company trucks, so that the day and maybe the hour of delivery may be strictly scheduled. And manufacturers must not tolerate the standard practice among U.S. suppliers of delivering plus or minus 10 percent of the agreed-upon purchase quantity. With no excess inventory, nor space to store it, the just-in-time company must insist on deliveries in exact quantities.

It is clear that geography is a deterrent, though not an intractable one. Aside from that, there are few obstacles. More

continued

OTHER FEATURES OF JIT FACTORIES

Many observers and critics of JIT systems insist that all of the good things attributed to Japanese manufacturers result not only from JIT methods; rather, they result from a combination of JIT systems and other factors. Among these other factors are:

1. Japanese manufacturers use business strategies based on producing standardized products that can be mass-produced both at low cost and with outstanding product quality.
2. They use the latest production technology, including robotics, flexible manufacturing systems (FMS), group technology (GT), automatic storage and retrieval systems (ASRS), bar coding, computer-aided design/computer-aided manufacturing (CAD/CAM), and computer-integrated manufacturing (CIM).
3. They have focused factories that are specialized in particular technologies or products. These factories are smaller, more compact, and require less capital investment.
4. Their master production schedules are stable and level. Not only do they not vary in level of load from month to month, they also standardize and freeze the daily production schedules.
5. They enjoy the economies of reduced setup times. Less labor is used to make the setups and machines are not idle as long during the setups. This contributes to high machine capacity utilization.

6. Japanese workers, because they are trained on many jobs and are uninhibited by restrictive union rules, can move from one job to another as needed to balance the work load. This contributes to high worker utilization.
7. Because of the lifetime-employment policies of the company, less employee turnover results in a better-trained work force and in reduced hiring and training costs.
8. Their total quality emphasis integrates every worker in the quality control programs through *quality circles* and *quality-at-the-source* concepts. These concepts will be discussed later, in Chapter 15. Lower production costs result from reduced scrap.
9. Subcontractor networks have built trust relationships between customers and suppliers. These long-term arrangements have resulted in constancy of supply, improved quality of supplied materials, and, in the long run, reduced cost of materials.
10. Participative management styles, the attitude of managers toward workers, and benevolent company personnel policies have tended to develop cooperation between workers and management. Proponents of Japanese management styles claim that these factors, when combined with the unique culture of Japanese workers, have resulted in more committed workers.

Some argue that these factors alone, even without Kanban and JIT production-planning and inventory control methods, account for the success of Japanese manufacturers. Still others contend that the majority of these factors amount to nothing more than sound factory management, the way U.S. manufacturers did it in the "good old days" of the 1950s and 1960s. We shall probably never know which of these factors or combination of factors account for the success of the Japanese manufacturers, because they have all been blended and integrated with JIT by the manufacturers and it is impossible to separate them. In the end, maybe the Japanese are right: JIT and the other factors listed above comprise a total system and philosophy of manufacturing, and it is the whole rather than the parts that accounts for their success.

WILL JAPANESE MANUFACTURING METHODS WORK IN THE UNITED STATES?

Japanese manufacturing methods are already being used by several companies in the United States and *with U.S. workers.* Companies like Sharp, Sanyo, Hewlett-Packard, Kawasaki, Matsushita, Sony, Black & Decker, and IBM have successfully adopted the philosophy and practices of Japanese manufacturers in varying degrees. Industry Snapshot 12.2 describes the installation of a JIT system at the Buick City plant of General Motors Corporation in Flint, Michigan.

An interesting phenomenon associated with these successes occurs when a manufacturer succeeds with Japanese manufacturing methods after taking over a U.S. factory that has failed. Matsushita took over a Motorola television assembly plant in Franklin Park, Illinois. Within three years productivity increased 30 percent and defects were reduced from 150 down to 4 defects per 100 sets, and all of this with

INDUSTRY SNAPSHOT 12.2

Buick City Genuine JIT Delivery

Buick City contains about 1.8 million square feet of floor space, which is about half the size of other, comparable GM plants. Approximately 70 percent less floor space in Buick City is dedicated to materials storage than in the typical automobile plant. Major reductions are accomplished in labor, costs of materials, damage to parts, and repair operations. The most important benefit has been improvement in quality. The operators are responsible for doing their jobs correctly while the work is in their particular work station. There are no repair people at the end of the line.

Buick City contains 85 dock doors spread around the perimeter of the complex. The approach is to install docks as close as possible to the point where the parts will be used in the manufacturing process. Using *synchronized production* at Buick City, many parts, including metal stampings, are delivered to the line in the order that they are added to the automobile. Since suppliers are electronically linked to the scheduling computer, each part supplier knows the build sequence for the next ten days (the first five days are frozen). The facility uses rail as well as truck deliveries. At the docks robots are used to load and unload seats, transmissions, and engines into and from trucks. Bar coding is a basic premise on which much of JIT is built. All containers and most components are bar coded for automatic receiving and dispatch. Bar coding is coordinated with the suppliers so it is readable by both the factory and its suppliers. Buick City is using seven different standard containers, and it is headed toward 100 percent utilization of returnable containers.

Buick City believes that these benefits have come from the use of JIT: drastically reduced in-process inventories, improved product quality, improved labor relations, improved delivery and schedule performance, improved facility utilization, improved machine maintenance, improved shop floor problem solving, and reduced setup times.[2]

---

[2] Mehran Sepehri, "Case in Point: Buick City Genuine JIT Delivery," *P&IM Review* 8, no. 3(March 1988):34–36.

basically the same work force. Sanyo took over a Warwick television assembly plant in Forest City, Arkansas, that produced television sets for Sears Roebuck, and both productivity and product quality improved to the point that the plant was economically viable again.

Such success stories might lead us to believe that all of our U.S. factories should adopt the Japanese manufacturing methods immediately, but we would urge caution. There are some practices that may not soon be adopted in the United States because they simply do not fit our situations. For instance, lifetime-employment policies, company unions, and subcontractor networks may not be appropriate now because of cultural differences, well-entrenched U.S. unions, and the geographic distances between U.S. suppliers and their customers. Also, participative management styles and some facets of Japanese quality control programs that depend on cooperative worker attitudes may not be appropriate for some of our U.S. firms—at least not now. On the other hand, other practices do seem to be appropriate for U.S. industry. Among these are:

1. More selective business strategies with narrow product lines.
2. High-tech manufacturing methods and machinery.
3. Focused factories.
4. Stable and level production schedules.
5. Smaller lot sizes through reduced setup times.
6. Emphasis on solving shop floor production problems.
7. Workers trained in several jobs.
8. Quality control programs aimed at quality at the source.

Can U.S. manufacturers adopt some of these Japanese methods without adopting Kanban or JIT? In other words, can U.S. manufacturers continue to use MRP and also use some of the Japanese methods? It seems clear that the answer to this question is yes. In fact, many of these so-called Japanese methods never left the United States; they originated here. Japanese manufacturers have consistently maintained that the United States has been the great teacher and Japanese manufacturers have been the learners. Many of the Japanese methods are just sound factory management, and they are appropriate for U.S. manufacturers.

Whether U.S. manufacturers should adopt Kanban or other JIT systems of planning and controlling production is still an unanswered question. Unless and until small lot sizes are realized through factory-wide programs to reduce setup times, JIT just won't work. Also, unless product lines are narrowed through different business strategies, the nonrepetitive nature of production processes will argue against JIT. Although MRP handles great product variety extremely well, JIT simply will not work under these conditions.

U.S. manufacturers must be careful not to throw the baby out with the bath water. In their enthusiasm to gain the benefits that Japanese manufacturers enjoy, they should not give up the positive features of their production systems without assurances that the new methods will achieve better results. Presently, U.S. manufacturers accept high inventories as the price they must pay to achieve high worker and machine utilization. Although Japanese manufacturers have achieved high worker and machine utilization without high inventories, they are paying a different price—investing heavily in engineering studies and equipment modifications to achieve drastically reduced setup times, establishing training programs that train workers for several jobs, paying enormous sums for automated high-tech production machinery, and developing different business strategies with narrower product lines that allow stable and level production schedules. Unless U.S. manufacturers are willing to commit to this new price instead of the old price of high inventory levels, they cannot expect to reap the benefits of JIT.

Even in JIT factories, as in all other manufacturing, shop floor scheduling issues must be resolved. Because of the fundamental differences between process-focused and product-focused manufacturing, we shall separate the discussion of the scheduling issues related to these two forms of production.

SCHEDULING PROCESS-FOCUSED FACTORIES

Process-focused factories produce many nonstandard products in relatively small batches that flow along different paths through the factory and that require frequent machine changeovers. These factories are often called job shops. A *job shop* is defined as "a functional organization whose departments or work centers are organized around particular types of equipment or operations, such as drilling, forging, spinning, or assembly. Products flow through departments in batches corresponding to individual orders, which may be either stock orders (orders prepared for inventory) or customer orders."[3]

Figure 12.4 illustrates that scheduling and shop floor decisions in process-focused operations or job shops begin with the planned order releases report from the MRP system. An order is defined as the quantity of a unique part number. Because a part takes on a different part number as it passes through successive stages of production, an order for a unique part number can be tied to specific work centers within the factory. From the planned order releases report of the MRP system, it can be determined when orders for each part number must be released (production is authorized), and from the CRP system it can be determined to which work centers each order must go. Armed with this information, operations managers can make the day-to-day scheduling and shop floor decisions, which include deciding in what sequence orders should be processed at work centers, assignment of orders to machines within work centers, and shop floor control decisions.

Table 12.1 describes some of the characteristics of process-focused operations and their scheduling implications. One thing should be clear from reading this table —these characteristics make job shops complex to schedule. Since job shops may produce orders for customers who have been given promised delivery dates, customers can intrude into the production process. Also, production lots tend to be quite small and to require numerous machine changeovers. The network of work centers to which an order is assigned determines the production-processing plan for the order, and the number of possible networks for an order can be large. Workers and machines are so flexible that they are capable of being assigned and reassigned to many different orders. In such a flexible, variable, and changing environment, schedules must be specific and detailed in each work center to bring orderliness to a potentially hectic situation.

Perhaps if you have an idea about how orders are actually moved around a factory, it will be easier to see how work center schedules fit into the scheme of shop floor management. In job shops both of these types of *preproduction planning* may have to occur before production of an order can begin:

---

[3] *APICS Dictionary,* 6th ed. (Falls Church, VA: American Production and Inventory Control Society, 1987), 15.

FIGURE 12.4   *Scheduling and Shop Floor Decisions in Process-Focused Operations*

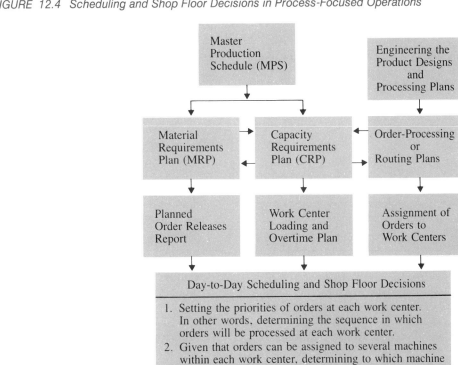

1.   Designing and redesigning of the product in a customer's order.
2.   Planning the network of work centers through which the order must pass before it is completed; this is an order's *routing plan.*

Production control departments then guide the movement of the order among the work centers on the routing plan. Material handlers are notified to move the order to the next work center by a *move ticket.* The order may be accompanied by engineering drawings, specifications, or job instructions so that workers at a work center have the necessary information about how to do their work on the order. A detailed schedule tells the production supervisor which order should be processed first at each work center and when the order should be finished. As the order is completed, the worker tells the production planning and control department, a move ticket is issued for the next work center on the order's routing plan, and the detailed schedules are updated.

TABLE 12.1   *Process-Focused Operations: Characteristics and Their Scheduling Implications*

Characteristics	*Scheduling Implications*
1. Similar operations are grouped with common supervision.	Numerous individual work center schedules must be developed and coordinated within production departments.
2. Products are diverse and sometimes custom-designed.	Much preproduction planning is necessary to establish routing, job instructions, processing plans, and product designs.
3. Processing steps are uncoupled and orders can follow a multitude of paths through production systems.	A complex production control system must be developed to plan, execute, and follow up the movement of orders through the production system.
4. In-process inventories build up between processing steps. Workers possess a variety of skills. Machines can adapt to a variety of products and operations.	Great flexibility is present in shifting workers and machines from order to order.
5. Work loads are typically unbalanced between processing steps.	An extra burden is put on schedules to fully load facility and minimize idle time and underloading.
6. When mechanical breakdowns, material delivery delays, and other interruptions occur, downstream operations typically are not immediately affected.	Fewer allowances for idle time from these factors need to be included in schedules.
7. Numerous orders can build up at each processing step.	A system of priorities must be established that determines which order should be scheduled first at each work center.
8. Products are typically of the produce-to-order type.	Long lead times are necessary for manufacture and material deliveries. Raw material input schedules (MRP) and output schedules (MPS) are used.

It is apparent, then, that work center schedules are an important part of shop floor management.

    With this description of the environment of scheduling in job shops as a background, we shall now discuss shop floor planning and control.

SHOP FLOOR PLANNING AND CONTROL

Shop floor control includes these activities:

1. Assigning a *priority* to each order, a measure of the relative importance of each order. This aids in setting the sequence of processing orders at work centers.
2. Issuing *dispatching lists* to each work center. These lists tell production supervisors which orders are to be produced at a work center, their priorities, and when each order should be completed.
3. Keeping the work-in-process (WIP) inventory updated. This includes knowing the location of each order and quantity of parts in each order in the system. It requires tracking the movement of orders between work centers when move tickets are used, knowing the number of good parts that survive each processing step, the amount of scrap, the amount of rework required, and the number of units short on each order. All of this information must be periodically reported to all interested parties.
4. Providing input – output control on all work centers. This means comparing the amount of work that was planned to be coming to a work center with the amount of work actually coming to the work center. Also, the amount of work actually coming out of a work center is compared with the amount of work planned to be coming out of a work center. From this information, production supervisors can monitor the capacity and work load relationship for each work center.
5. Measuring the efficiency, utilization, and productivity of workers and machines at each work center and reporting this information to production supervisors.

Production-planning and control departments perform these activities and report the results to operations managers so that corrective actions can be taken when orders are going to be late or when capacity or work load problems occur at work centers.

Input – Output Control

Input – output control is a key activity that provides operations managers with detailed information about how jobs are flowing between work centers. Problems such as insufficient capacity at work stations, production problems at work stations, and problems at upstream work stations can be identified through input – output control.

Example 12.2 illustrates an analysis of an input – output control report. From these reports operations managers can determine if the amount of work flowing to a work center is the planned amount and if the capacity of the work center is according to plan. If too much work is flowing to a work center compared to its capacity, then excessive WIP inventory will occur preceding the work center. When jobs pile up at work centers, not only does the work center become cluttered and crowded, but also downstream work centers become starved for jobs. If, on the other hand, too little work is flowing to a work center compared to its capacity, the work center will be underutilized and idle machines and workers could result.

The coordination of work center schedules aids in the orderly flow of jobs between work centers, and Gantt charts are useful for this purpose.

EXAMPLE 12.2   *Analyzing Input – Output Reports*

Input – Output Report at the End of Week 5 for Work Center 500						
		Weeks				
	−1	1	2	3	4	5
Planned input—labor-hours		300	300	300	300	300
Actual input—labor-hours		250	220	260	180	150
Cumulative deviation		−50	−130	−170	−290	−440
Planned output—labor-hours		300	300	300	300	300
Actual output—labor-hours		300	270	260	180	150
Cumulative deviation		0	−30	−70	−190	−340
Planned ending WIP—labor-hours		50	50	50	50	50
Actual ending WIP—labor-hours	100	50	0	0	0	0

Shown above is an input – output report for Work Center 500 as of the end of the fifth week. All of the values in the report are labor-hours. The jobs coming into the work center (input) have been converted to labor-hours, and the jobs coming from the work center (output) have also been converted to labor-hours with the use of labor standards. This conversion lets us compare different jobs, using a common measure that directly relates to capacity.

Notice that the planned input to the work center (jobs coming to the work center) is 300 labor-hours in each of the past five weeks, which is the same as the planned output (jobs coming from the work center). The actual output from the work center is far less than planned, which ordinarily might indicate that production problems have caused the capacity of the work center to be insufficient. A closer look at the input part of the report, however, tells a different story. Not enough jobs are coming from the upstream work centers to keep the work center fully utilized. The WIP at the work center was 100 labor-hours at the end of Week − 1 or at the beginning of Week 1, but this was depleted by the end of the second week to make up for the insufficient input to the work center.

The cause of the production problems at the upstream work centers must be found and corrected so that an increased flow of jobs can come into Work Center 500 to balance with the capacity of the work center.

Gantt Charts

Gantt charts can be used to display graphically the work loads in each work center in a department. Figure 12.5 is an example of a Gantt chart used to compare the weekly schedule for five work centers in a model shop (shops used to produce small quantities of experimental products for intracompany market research, engineering research, and process research). The jobs scheduled to be processed during the week are

FIGURE 12.5 Gantt Chart for Coordinating Work Centers' Schedules

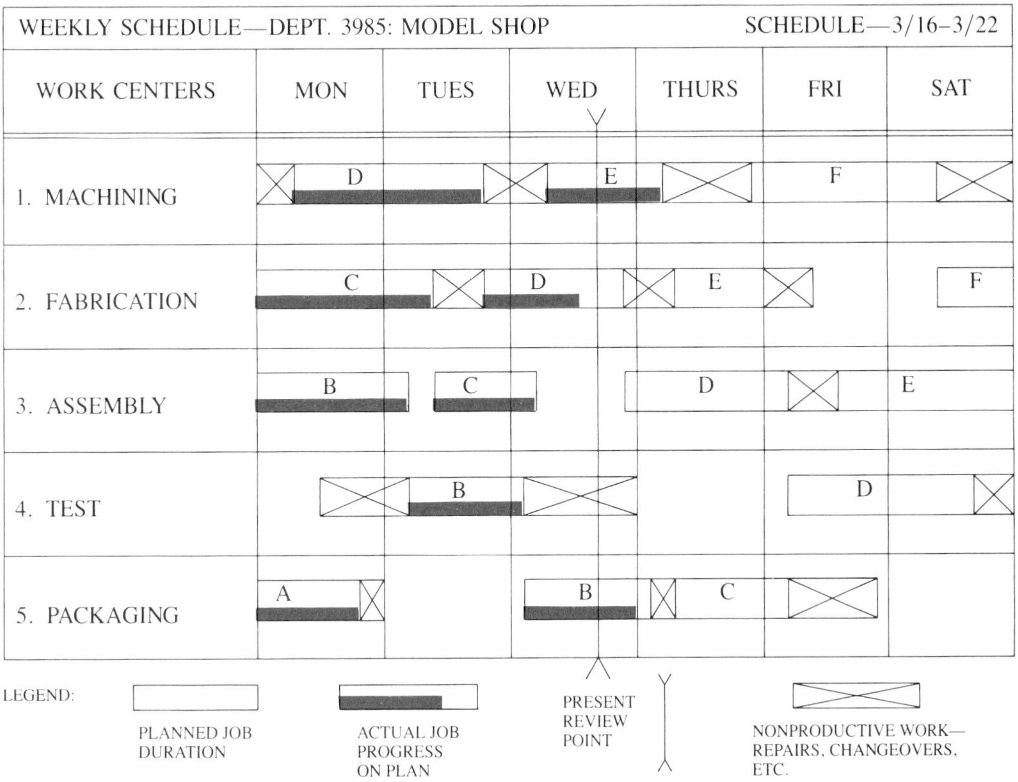

displayed with their beginning and ending times and allowed processing times represented by an open bar. As work progresses on a job, a solid bar shows how the work center is performing to the schedule. The time of the review is indicated by a vertical arrow.

Machine changes, routine maintenance projects, and other planned nonproduction work activities are indicated by an X. Blank spaces indicate planned idle time at the work center; work crews are not required during these periods and may be shifted to other work centers, or other jobs may be scheduled into these time slots later. Supervisors and production planners can see with a glance at the Gantt chart the progress of the work centers toward their schedules. For instance, Figure 12.5 shows that the time of the review is midafternoon on Wednesday. At this time the machining work center is ahead of schedule by about half a day on Job E, the packaging work center is ahead of schedule by about two hours on Job B, the test and assembly work centers are on schedule, and the fabrication work center is about two hours behind schedule on Job D. As a supervisor, how would information such as this guide your activities? These actions are suggested from Figure 12.5:

1. Check to see if Job F can be moved into the machining work center four hours early; also accelerate the changeover from Job E to Job F.
2. Investigate means of speeding up the performance of Job D in the fabrication work center. The use of packaging, testing, assembly, or machining workers may be feasible. If acceleration is infeasible, the schedules at fabrication and other downstream work centers must be slipped, that is, delayed.
3. Provide the workers at the packaging work center with two hours of other work.

Can you see now how Gantt charts provide operations managers with a practical way to coordinate the schedules of work centers? These graphic aids are found in most goods- and service-producing facilities, and although they are not often referred to as Gantt charts, they are extremely useful for coordinating a diversity of schedules of work teams, work centers, and major activities of projects.

Today, detailed schedules are increasingly the outputs of computerized scheduling systems. Computer programs do output all the same information commonly found on Gantt schedules, and some of these programs actually output the Gantt charts. Other organizations routinely take the information off computer outputs and construct Gantt charts for departmental use. This reinforces the contention that the graphic nature of these charts makes the scheduling information easy to grasp and apply.

Input–output control and Gantt charts provide operations managers with systematic ways of coordinating the flow of jobs between work centers. Let us now consider ways of setting priorities for jobs within individual work centers.

ORDER-SEQUENCING PROBLEMS

In order-sequencing problems we want to determine the sequence in which we will process a group of waiting orders at a work center. Order sequencing is also called *setting priorities for orders*. The term *priority* suggests the relative importance that one order has over another: Orders with higher priority are processed first.

We shall analyze these problems by discussing the various sequencing rules, the criteria for evaluating the sequencing rules, a comparison of sequencing rules, the control of changeover costs, and the minimization of total processing costs.

Sequencing Rules

Many rules can be followed in setting the priorities among orders or jobs waiting at work centers. Among the most common are:

1. **First-come first-served (FCFS)** — The next job to be processed is the one that arrived first among the waiting jobs.
2. **Shortest processing time** — The next job to be processed is the one with the shortest processing time among the waiting jobs.
3. **Earliest due date** — The next job to be processed is the one with the earliest due date (the date promised to the customer) among the waiting jobs.
4. **Critical ratio** — The next job to be processed is the one with the least critical ratio (time to due date divided by total remaining processing time) among the waiting jobs.

5. **Least changeover cost** — Since some jobs logically follow each other because of the similarity of their machine settings, the entire sequence of waiting jobs is determined by analyzing the total cost of making all of the machine changeovers between jobs.

Other rules such as most valued customer, most profitable job, and shortest waiting line at the next operation are also infrequently applied.

Criteria for Evaluating Sequencing Rules

In deciding which sequencing rule performs best in a particular job shop, the criteria that will be used to evaluate and compare the rules must be determined. While many criteria could conceivably be used, these criteria are common:

1. **Average flow time** — The average amount of time each job spends in the shop.
2. **Average number of jobs in the system** — The average number of jobs in the shop each day.
3. **Average job lateness** — The average amount of time that each job's actual completion date exceeds its promised due date.
4. **Changeover cost** — The total cost of making all of the machine changeovers in a group of jobs.

A Comparison of Sequencing Rules

Let us demonstrate the use of sequencing rules and evaluation criteria in a one-work-center production system. Example 12.3 describes a computer center that presently uses a first-come first-served sequencing rule in processing customers' computer programs. The example compares shortest processing time and the critical ratio sequencing rules with the present first-come first-served policy.

EXAMPLE 12.3   Evaluating Sequencing Rules

The Jiffy Computer Company processes computer programs for regional banks and savings and loans in Jacksonville, Florida. Numerous customer complaints have been received by Jiffy concerning excessive processing times for their jobs. Additionally, the computer center supervisors have complained that too many jobs seem to be in the center at any one time, thus confusing operations.

Jane Bergland, a systems analyst at the center, had taken some scheduling courses at the local university. She volunteered to study the problem. She suggested that a 24-hour period be studied at the center while using three sequencing rules — first-come first-served (the present policy), shortest processing time, and critical ratio. These rules would be evaluated according to three criteria — average flow time, average number of jobs in the system, and average job lateness. Jane recommended that whichever rule seemed to perform best to these three criteria during the 24-hour study period should be adopted as the sequencing policy to be used over a longer operating period.

TABLE 12.2   Data and Computations of Three Sequencing Rules at the Jiffy Computer Company

(1) Computer Jobs	(2) Estimated Processing Time (Hours)	(3) Time to Promised Completion (Hours)	First-Come First-Served			Shortest Processing Time			Critical Ratio			
			(4) Job Sequence	(5) Flow Time (Hours)	(6) Lateness (Hours) [(5) − (3)]	(7) Job Sequence	(8) Flow Time (Hours)	(9) Lateness (Hours) [(8) − (3)]	(10) Critical Ratio [(3) ÷ (2)]	(11) Job Sequence	(12) Flow Time (Hours)	(13) Lateness (Hours) [(12) − (3)]
A	2	4	1	2	—	1	2	—	2.00	2	6	2
B	5	18	2	7	—	5	18	—	3.60	5	20	2
C	3	8	3	10	2	2	5	—	2.67	3	9	1
D	4	4	4	14	10	3	9	5	1.00	1	4	—
E	6	20	5	20	—	6	24	4	3.33	4	15	—
F	4	24	6	24	—	4	13	—	6.00	6	24	—

TABLE 12.3   Comparison of the Performance of Three Sequencing Rules at the Jiffy Computer Company

Evaluation Criteria	First-Come First-Served	Shortest Processing Time	Critical Ratio
Average Flow Time	$= \dfrac{2 + 7 + 10 + 14 + 20 + 24}{6}$ $= 12.83$ hours **Rank = 2**	$= \dfrac{2 + 5 + 9 + 13 + 18 + 24}{6}$ $= 11.83$ hours **Rank = 1**	$= \dfrac{4 + 6 + 9 + 15 + 20 + 24}{6}$ $= 13.00$ hours **Rank = 3**
Average Number of Jobs in System	$= \dfrac{2(6) + 5(5) + 3(4) + 4(3) + 6(2) + 4(1)}{\underset{\substack{\text{TOTAL} \\ \text{FLOW TIME}}}{24}}$ $= 3.21$ jobs **Rank = 2**	$= \dfrac{2(6) + 3(5) + 4(4) + 4(3) + 5(2) + 6(1)}{24}$ $= 2.96$ jobs **Rank = 1**	$= \dfrac{4(6) + 2(5) + 3(4) + 6(3) + 5(2) + 4(1)}{24}$ $= 3.25$ jobs **Rank = 3**
Average Job Lateness	$= \dfrac{0 + 0 + 2 + 10 + 0 + 0}{6}$ $= 2.00$ hours **Rank = 3**	$= \dfrac{0 + 0 + 0 + 5 + 4 + 0}{6}$ $= 1.50$ hours **Rank = 2**	$= \dfrac{2 + 2 + 1 + 0 + 0 + 0}{6}$ $= .83$ hour **Rank = 1**

Jiffy's management authorized Jane to conduct the study. She selected a 24-hour period and prepared Tables 12.2 and 12.3.

Table 12.2 shows the estimated processing time remaining and the time to promised delivery for each of six computer jobs. The job sequence (order in which the jobs are to be processed), flow time (total time each job is in the system), and lateness (flow time minus time to promised delivery) are developed for each job under the three sequencing rules.

Table 12.3 compares the three sequencing rules according to three evaluation criteria—average flow time, average number of jobs in the system, and average job lateness. Average flow time is the average time that jobs are in the system and is computed by summing the flow times for all of the jobs and dividing by the number of jobs. The average number of jobs in the system is computed by taking a weighted average. For example, in the first-come first-served sequencing rule, 6 jobs are in the system for 2 hours, 5 jobs are in the system for 5 hours, and so on until only 1 job is in the system for 4 hours. Therefore the average number of jobs in the system is computed thus:

$$\frac{[2(6) + 5(5) + 3(4) + 4(3) + 6(2) + 4(1)]}{24} = 3.21 \text{ jobs}$$

The average job lateness is computed by summing the hours of lateness for each job and dividing by the number of jobs.

Jane reviewed the results of the study: Shortest processing time received 1, 1, and 2 ranks; critical ratio received 3, 3, and 1 ranks; and first-come first-served received 2, 2, and 3 ranks. She believed that shortest processing time should be recommended as the sequencing rule to be followed at Jiffy.

In the Jiffy Computer Company example, no single sequencing rule ranks first on all the evaluation criteria. This is also what we find in real-world applications. *No single sequencing rule excels on all evaluation criteria.* We know from experience that:

1. First-come first-served does not perform particularly well on most commonly used evaluation criteria. It does, however, in some cases give customers a sense of fair play, and equity can be an important consideration in service systems.
2. Shortest processing time does perform well on most evaluation criteria. It tends to perform best on average flow time and average number of jobs in the system. Although it does perform well in most circumstances on average job lateness, it may not do as well as critical ratio. The chief disadvantage of shortest processing time as a sequencing rule is that long-duration jobs may be continuously pushed back in the schedule in favor of short-duration jobs. Thus long-duration jobs may have excessive completion times from customers' viewpoints. Whenever this rule is used in practice, the long-duration jobs must be periodically moved ahead and processed.
3. Critical ratio usually performs well only on the average job lateness criterion. However, critical ratio is intrinsically appealing: We want to first work on jobs that are most likely to be required before they can be finished. Additionally, critical ratio is a useful aid in identifying jobs that are likely not to meet due dates in the schedule (their critical ratios would be less than 1).

Scheduling departments usually perform test runs on simulation models of their shops to measure the performance of different sequencing rules, as in our Jiffy Computer Company example. Once they have selected the rule that tends to perform best for them on the most important criteria, it is made a part of their information system. For instance, as the story at the beginning of this chapter indicates, the critical ratio or some other basis for setting priorities is provided for every order as a part of the MRP system.

Controlling Changeover Costs

There are numerous situations in which the sequence of processing jobs at a work center is dictated by the economies of machine changeovers. For example, two jobs may use exactly the same major machine settings, jigs and fixtures (holding devices), and raw materials, except for minor adjustments. Under ordinary circumstances, jobs that require similar machine setups and consequently require only minor adjustments to achieve a changeover from one job to another should follow each other at work centers.

Example 12.4 demonstrates a simple rule for determining job sequences in situations where the dominant factor in selecting a job sequence is minimizing the total cost of changeovers among the waiting jobs. The procedure selects the first and second job in the sequence by finding the lowest changeover cost among all the possible changeovers. From the second job on, the next job is always determined by selecting the lowest changeover cost from among the remaining jobs. This rule may not be optimal, but it usually performs well in practice.

Other more mathematically sophisticated procedures will achieve optimal results. *Integer linear programming* can be used to minimize total changeover costs within a set of constraints that require all jobs to be assigned to the sequence once and only once.

Computer search procedures follow simple procedural rules as the computer searches for good job sequences. Although these methods may not be optimal, they do give good results in practice. They are useful in very large problems because of their quick, efficient, and near-optimal results.

One of the chief disadvantages of all these methods is that they are designed to select job sequences at work centers with only one goal in mind: minimize the total changeover cost. Although this is a worthwhile goal, what about the other evaluation criteria that we discussed previously — average flow time, average number of jobs in the system, and average job lateness? These criteria are fundamental in POM because in-process inventory levels, shop loading, throughput rates, shop congestion, and customer service are directly affected. How do we simultaneously consider these criteria while we seek to minimize total changeover costs?

EXAMPLE 12.4   Changeover Costs and Job Sequence

The Quick Printing Company does custom printing jobs for local firms, political candidates, and schools. Quick Printing is in the middle of an election year boom, and numerous political poster jobs are waiting to be processed at the offset press. Tom Smith, who does Quick Printing's job planning, is currently developing a weekly printing schedule for the offset press. He has developed these changeover costs for the six waiting jobs. All jobs carry equal priority, so that the deciding factor in selecting a job sequence is the total changeover cost for the six jobs.

Jobs That Precede

		A	B	C	D	E	F
Jobs That Follow	A	—	$12	$15	$10	$35	$20
	B	$25	—	20	20	25	20
	C	27	15	—	12	20	15
	D	16	30	10	—	25	30
	E	35	20	25	30	—	30
	F	20	25	15	25	30	—

Tom uses this rule to develop a low-cost job sequence: *First, select the lowest changeover cost among all the changeovers. The next job to be selected will have the lowest changeover cost among the remaining jobs that follow the previously selected job.* Since there is a tie for the starting jobs (D–A and C–D), Tom develops two sequences:

1. A follows D ($10 is the minimum changeover cost, D is first and A is next).
   F follows A (read down A column: Job F has lowest changeover cost among the remaining jobs).
   C follows F (read down F column; Job C has lowest changeover cost among the remaining jobs).
   B follows C (read down C column; Job B has lowest changeover cost among the remaining jobs).
   E follows B (read down B column; Job E has lowest changeover cost among the remaining jobs).
   The job sequence is DAFCBE; its total changeover cost is $10 + 20 + 15 + 20 + 20 = \$85$.

2. Because there was a tie for the starting jobs above, the second job sequence is now developed: D follows C, A follows D, F follows A, B follows F, and E follows B.
   The job sequence is CDAFBE; its total changeover cost is $10 + 10 + 20 + 20 + 20 = \$80$.

Of the two sequences, CDAFBE is preferred because its total changeover cost is lower.

Now, Tom knows that this is not necessarily the lowest possible total changeover cost for the six jobs. In other words, the method does not guarantee an optimal solution. But the simple rule is easy to understand and it gives satisfactory results.

In practice, schedulers ordinarily first consider job sequences that result in low total changeover costs and then modify the sequence to a new compromise sequence as required to approximately conform to sequencing rules (critical ratio, shortest processing time, and so on) or special customer priority rules. **Because sequencing** decisions are increasingly an integral part of computerized scheduling systems in many organizations, the computation procedures must be programmed into the computer. These programs are written to select job sequences that perform well across many criteria — total changeover costs, average flow time, average number of jobs in the system, average job lateness, and special customer priorities. Of course, schedulers can override these sequences.

Minimizing Total Processing Time

We may want to set the sequence of a group of jobs such that the total time for processing all of the jobs is minimized. This objective results in low production costs and high worker and machine utilization. The ways that we analyze these decisions differ in the number of work centers or machines that must process the jobs.

Sequencing n Jobs through Two Work Centers.   When several jobs must be sequenced through two work centers, the job sequence at each work center may be determined by the procedures presented above. Two job sequences would ordinarily result, one for the first work center and one for the second. The two job sequences would not be expected to be the same since the two sequencing decisions would ordinarily be treated as independent of one another. We often want to select a job sequence that must hold for both work centers. This situation can be effectively analyzed by using *Johnson's rule.*[4]

Example 12.5 demonstrates the use of Johnson's rule in a two-work-center production system — the Jiffy Computer Company. Customers' jobs must be processed through data encoding (Work Center 1) and data processing (Work Center 2) *in the same job sequence, the only requirement of Johnson's rule.* The job sequence that results has the minimum total processing time through both work centers for all the jobs.

EXAMPLE 12.5   Sequencing Jobs through Two Work Centers with Johnson's Rule

There are two work centers at the Jiffy Computer Company, data encoding and data processing. Jiffy's management wishes to adopt a procedure that would routinely set the sequence in which jobs would be processed through both work centers. Jane Bergland has been experimenting with Johnson's rule; she believes that Jiffy's situation can be effectively analyzed with this technique. Jiffy's management wants both work centers to change over to new jobs at the same time. In other words, if Work Center 1 completes its work on a job, it must wait until Work Center 2 has completed the job that it has been working on so that both work centers can

---

[4] S. M. Johnson, "Optimal Two Stage and Three Stage Production Schedules with Setup Times Included," *Naval Research Logistics Quarterly* 1(March 1954):61–68.

begin new jobs simultaneously. The reason for this requirement is that supervisors can give job instructions to both work centers at the same time about how to process jobs.

Jane visits the computer center, noting that six jobs are waiting.

a. These data are developed for the six jobs:

Computer Job to Be Processed	Estimated Processing Times (Hours)	
	Work Center 1, Data Encoding	Work Center 2, Data Processing
A	1.50	.50
B	4.00	1.00
C	.75	2.25
D	1.00	3.00
E	2.00	4.00
F	1.80	2.20

b. Johnson's rule is:

1. Select the shortest processing time in either work center.
2. If the shortest time is at the first work center, do the job first in the schedule. If it is at the second work center, do the job last in the schedule.
3. Eliminate the job assigned in Step 2.
4. Repeat Steps 1, 2, and 3, filling in the schedule from the front and back until all jobs have been assigned a position in the schedule.

Jane then begins to follow the steps of the rule:

1. Select the shortest processing time—.50 for Job A at Work Center 2, A goes last.

2. Select the next remaining shortest processing time—.75 for Job C at Work Center 1, C goes first.

3. Select the next remaining shortest processing time—there is a tie between 1.00 for Job B at Work Center 2 and Job D at Work Center 1, B goes last and D goes first.

4. Select the next remaining shortest processing time—1.80 for Job F at Work Center 1, F goes first.

5. Only one job remains—E.

$$C \quad D \quad F \quad E \quad B \quad A$$

c. This CDFEBA job sequence is further studied by developing the cumulative time to process all six jobs through both work centers. Jane knows that Jiffy's management wants the jobs to begin at the same time in both work centers:

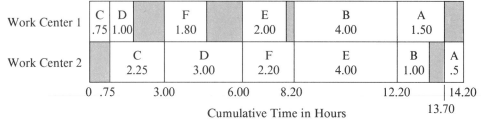

d. Jane can see that the CDFEBA job sequence allows both work centers to process all of the jobs in 14.20 hours. She plans to use this example to demonstrate to Jiffy's management the application of Johnson's rule.

Note in Example 12.5 that if a tie for the shortest processing time occurs in different work centers, no difficulty is encountered in determining the job sequence. If a tie should occur within the same work center, however, two job sequences would need to be evaluated by comparing their cumulative processing times as in Part *c* of the example. The job sequence with the lowest cumulative processing time would be the recommended job sequence. Note also in the example that if we wished to relax the requirement that all jobs must begin at the same time, *a constraint that is not required to use Johnson's rule,* the cumulative time for processing all jobs through both work centers would be reduced from 14.20 hours to 13.70 hours. Only the idle time (.50 hour) between Jobs B and A in Work Center 2 would be eliminated. Can you confirm the correctness of this 13.70 hours value by preparing a cumulative processing time figure as in Example 12.5? Johnson's rule can therefore be used with or without the requirement that all jobs must begin simultaneously in the two work centers.

Sequencing n *Jobs through* m *Work Centers.*   Job shops ordinarily must sequence many jobs through many work centers, a problem for which there are no easy analytical solutions. And yet operations managers and schedulers make these types of sequencing decisions daily; how do they go about making these complex decisions? Ordinarily, a sequencing rule such as shortest processing time, critical ratio, or earliest due date is uniformly applied periodically at each work center in the entire facility. This set of job sequences at each work center is then modified to take advantage of economies in changeovers. If some jobs are particularly late, changeover economies may have to be forgone in order to meet customer due-date commitments.

Surprisingly, this nonoptimal approach is effective in practice: Facilities are nearly fully loaded, high levels of customer service are maintained, low levels of in-process inventories result, and congestion in the shop is reduced to reasonable levels. Put simply, although this approach to setting job sequences is nonoptimal, it works in practice.

Research is continuing to explore mathematical methods for the optimal solution to these complex sequencing problems. Queuing theory, computer simulation, and computer search have all been used by operations research analysts to study sequencing problems.

ASSIGNMENT PROBLEMS

When many jobs are arriving in job shops that can be assigned to various work centers or machines within work centers, determining which jobs should be assigned to which work centers or machines is an important part of scheduling. These problems are commonly referred to as *assignment problems.*

In Appendix E, Linear Programming Solution Methods, the assignment method of linear programming is discussed and demonstrated in Example E.7. In that example, five jobs at the Mercury Electric Motor Company are assigned to five rewinding work centers. When n jobs must be assigned to only one downstream operation, as in the rewinding step at Mercury Electric, then the assignment method is an appropriate technique for analyzing such a problem. The assignment method is, however, seldom practical to use when job assignments must be made beyond the single-level case. Let us assume, for example, that each of the five jobs in the Mercury Electric example must be processed through four downstream work stations instead of the single rewinding operation. This assignment problem, involving four different sequential assignment decisions, is complex to analyze mathematically because the jobs tend to emerge from each operation at random times. Computer simulation, covered in Appendix D, is a technique that is appropriate for these analyses, but its application to multilevel job assignment problems is well beyond the scope of this text.

This concludes our discussion of shop floor planning and control topics in job shops. Let us now turn to the study of shop floor planning in product-focused factories.

SCHEDULING PRODUCT-FOCUSED FACTORIES

Table 12.4 lists some characteristics of product-focused factories and their scheduling implications. In product-focused factories there are only a few standardized product designs, the products are usually produced for finished goods inventory, and production rates of individual products are usually greater than their demand rates. These and the other characteristics in Table 12.4 determine the way that these factories are scheduled.

TABLE 12.4   *Product-Focused Factories: Characteristics and Their Scheduling Implications*

Characteristics	Scheduling Implications
1. Products are standard designs. The parts and raw materials, required processing steps, and sequence of operations are known.	Little preproduction planning concerning routing of products, job instructions, processing plans, and product designs is necessary.
2. Products are usually produced for inventory rather than to customer order.	Schedules can be based on near-economic production runs for products without pressure for deliveries to customers.
3. Processing steps are coupled together in product layouts.	The production process is scheduled much like a pipeline, concentrating on raw material input schedules and output schedules (MPS).
4. Workers and machines are specialized in only a few skills and operations.	Workers and machines cannot be readily shifted from operation to operation or from product to product.
5. Production rates are greater than demand rates for products.	The predominant scheduling concerns are timing of production line changeovers and length of production runs.
6. Because operations are coupled together, material supply delays, mechanical breakdowns, product scrap, and other factors that cause one operation to become idle also cause downstream operations to shut down.	Production schedules must have safety factors built in to allow for periodic idle time, must have preventive maintenance programs, and must have effective quality control programs.
7. The pipeline nature of the production line results in materials, once they have entered the line, flowing continuously from operation to operation until emitted at the end.	Production control does not ordinarily need to keep complex records of in-process material movements, authorize in-process material movements, or otherwise plan for the timing of in-process material movements along the line. The key planning and materials movement authorization activities concern the supply of materials to the line and discharge of finished units from the line.

The most common scheduling decisions for these factories are:

1. If products are produced in batches and multiple products are produced on the same assembly lines, how long should each product be produced before the line is changed over to another model? In other words, how long should the production run be for each product model and when should machine changeovers be scheduled?
2. If products are produced to a specific delivery schedule, at any point in time how many cumulative units of output should have passed each upstream process step if future deliveries are to be on schedule?

We shall now develop some techniques to assist managers in resolving these scheduling-related problems — batch scheduling, and scheduling and controlling production for delivery schedules.

BATCH SCHEDULING

In Chapter 10 we discussed the concept of an economic order quantity (EOQ) when deliveries were gradual (p) and usage was at a constant rate (d). The EOQ then was based on striking a balance between annual carrying costs and annual ordering costs. The perspective developed was in the finished goods warehouse looking backward into the production departments. How many units of Product X should we order to replenish our finished goods inventory?

This same EOQ formula can be useful in estimating the length of production runs by developing a slightly different view. Picture yourself in the production department looking toward the finished goods warehouse. How many units of Product X should we include in each production run to minimize annual carrying cost (still the same annual inventory carrying cost) and annual ordering cost (including ordering costs and machine changeover costs in production)? The length of production run problem is formulated in exactly the same way as the EOQ inventory replenishment problem from Chapter 10; the only difference is the perspective: $EOQ = \sqrt{(2DS/C)[p/(p-d)]}$. This EOQ formula is used in practice as a guide for determining the length of production runs for a single inventory item. As a comprehensive scheduling technique in batch scheduling, however, it is not entirely satisfactory because it fails to account for these facts:

1. Only so much production capacity is available in each time period.
2. Inventory items share common production capacity.
3. Length of production run decisions must be made simultaneously for all inventory items to be produced in each time period.
4. Length of production run decisions should be based on our most current information about demand rates and production rates and not on annual ballpark demand estimates as in EOQ.

These deficiencies of the EOQ in planning length of production runs have led to the development of the *run-out method* for planning production schedules in capacity-constrained production operations when batches of product models are produced on common assembly lines. This method attempts to use the total production capacity available in each time period to produce just enough of each product model so that if we stopped producing, the finished goods inventory for each product would be depleted, or would run out, at the same point in time.

Example 12.6 uses the run-out method to develop a production schedule for five products of a pet food company. Notice in this example that the run-out method does not attempt to set efficient lot sizes for individual products, a characteristic for which its approach is often criticized. In this example all 1,600 hours of extruder time per week are allocated among the five products so that if the weekly forecast demand materializes, the company would run out of each of the five products at exactly the same time.

EXAMPLE 12.6   Run-out Method of Production Scheduling

The Friendly Pet Food Company is planning its production for next week. All pet food products at Friendly must be processed through 20 mixer-extruders at its Hillsdale, Indiana, plant. Friendly has a total of 1,600 extruder hours per week of production capacity based on its 6-month aggregate capacity plan. Friendly's scheduling department is reviewing the inventory levels, machine hours required per 1,000 pounds, and forecast usage for its five principal products. Develop a production schedule for the extruders by using the run-out method.

Solution

1. First, convert inventory on hand and the forecasts into extruder hours:

(1) Product	(2) Inventory on Hand or in Production (000 Pounds)	(3) Extruder Time Required (Hours per 000 Pounds)	(4) Forecast Demand for Next Week (000 Pounds)	(5) Inventory on Hand (in Extruder Hours) [(2) × (3)]	(6) Forecast Demand for Next Week (in Extruder Hours) [(4) × (3)]
A	160.0	1.0	100.0	160.00	100.00
B	210.0	2.0	200.0	420.00	400.00
C	200.5	2.5	200.0	501.25	500.00
D	150.6	1.5	160.0	225.90	240.00
E	170.2	1.5	100.0	255.30	150.00
			Totals	1,562.45	1,390.00

2. Next, compute the aggregate run-out time (in weeks). This value represents the amount of time that the last unit of an item would remain in inventory *beyond the week being planned,*

assuming that future weekly demands are the same as the forecast demand for next week. This value is computed by dividing the inventory balance at the end of the week being planned (which is the numerator of the fraction that follows) by the demand per week:

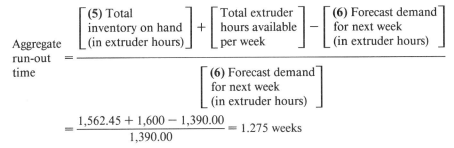

$$= \frac{1{,}562.45 + 1{,}600 - 1{,}390.00}{1{,}390.00} = 1.275 \text{ weeks}$$

3. Next, develop a weekly production schedule that uses the 1,600 hours of extruder time:

Product	*(7)* *Desired Ending Inventory at End of Next Week (000 Pounds)* *[(4) × 1.275]*	*(8)* *Desired Ending Inventory and Forecast (000 Pounds)* *[(7) + (4)]*	*(9)* *Required Production (000 Pounds)* *[(8) − (2)]*	*(10)* *Extruder Hours Allocated to Products* *[(9) × (3)]*
A	127.5	227.5	67.5	67.50
B	255.0	455.0	245.0	490.00
C	255.0	455.0	254.5	636.25
D	204.0	364.0	213.4	320.10
E	127.5	227.5	57.3	85.95
			Total	1,599.80

The run-out method is a useful technique for planning production schedules because it allocates production capacity to products in proportion to their demand and their inventory levels. However, if used as single-period short-run planning techniques, they may not allow rational materials requirement plans if material lead times are long relative to the planning horizon of the production schedule. In the Friendly Pet Food Company example, planning weekly production schedules would not allow sufficient lead time under ordinary circumstances for acquiring the necessary raw materials to support the production schedules. This problem has led most organizations to use more than single-period schedules. For example, the Friendly Pet Food Company could have developed weekly production schedules for five or six weeks in advance. Raw materials could then have been ordered and received in time to support the production schedules.

DELIVERY SCHEDULES: LINE OF BALANCE METHOD

Production systems often commit to a delivery schedule for their products. These *delivery schedules* can be a part of a purchase order or contract from a customer. If it is important that actual product deliveries match with the planned delivery schedule, a system must be devised to schedule and control all the processing steps of the production system.

All too often an organization may be on schedule in terms of deliveries, but about to be delinquent on deliveries because the production pipeline will soon run out of products. It is too late to take corrective action when this happens, because deliveries will necessarily suffer until the pipeline can again be refilled with products. POM has successfully used *line of balance (LOB)* in a variety of goods- and service-producing production systems to schedule and control upstream processing steps.

Example 12.7 shows how a snowmobile company uses a delivery schedule, manufacturing processing-step lead times, and cumulative production records at each processing step to develop a LOB analysis. Figure 12.6 shows the LOB charts for the company in the example.

Once a delivery schedule is set, the cumulative delivery schedule does not change unless the delivery schedule is modified. Periodically (every quarter-month in Example 12.7), a new line of balance is drawn on the progress chart and vertical bars are extended to reflect additional units passing each processing step since the last review. Thus a snapshot evaluation of each production step is taken at regular intervals. These periodic evaluations provide an operations manager with information about the performance of each step in the schedule.

This information is usually available well in advance of any deficiencies that might affect delivery schedules. Therefore management corrective action is possible to ensure the integrity of delivery schedules.

LOB achieves its greatest benefits when products or services are produced to specific delivery schedules, production involves many processing steps, and production lead times are long.

Although many service systems can and do approach scheduling in much the same way as manufacturing systems by using the scheduling approaches described above, enough diversity exists in these systems to justify special treatment.

EXAMPLE 12.7   *Line of Balance (LOB) in the Bigfoot Snowmobile Company*

The Bigfoot Snowmobile Company produces snowmobiles in its Iceberg, Wisconsin, manufacturing plant. Bigfoot has just signed a contract for its total output to be sold to one of the giant retailing chains in the eastern United States. One of the stipulations of the contract was an ironclad delivery schedule:

Month	Units to Be Delivered	Month	Units to Be Delivered	Month	Units to Be Delivered
January	1,000	May	1,000	September	2,000
February	1,000	June	2,000	October	2,000
March	1,000	July	2,000	November	2,000
April	1,000	August	2,000	December	2,000

The production-processing steps, the relationships among the steps, and the lead times are shown on the flow chart below:

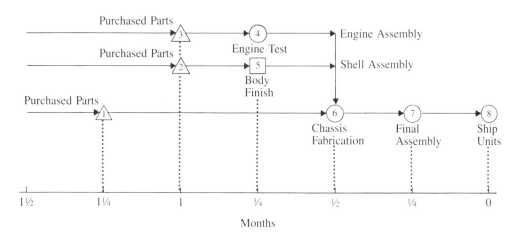

$\bigcirc$ = Company operation, $\square$ = Subcontracted operation, $\triangle$ = Purchased parts

After 8 months into the shipping schedule, these cumulative quantities of units have passed these processing steps in the production process:

Processing Step	Cumulative Production Quantity	Processing Step	Cumulative Production Quantity
⑧ Ship units	11,000	④ Engine test	12,000
⑦ Final assembly	11,000	③ Receive purchased parts	12,000
⑥ Chassis fabrication	11,500	② Receive purchased parts	14,000
⑤ Body finish	12,000	① Receive purchased parts	15,000

Develop a LOB chart and evaluate the status of production at each processing step.

Solution

1. First, construct a cumulative delivery schedule as shown in Figure 12.6.
2. Next, locate the review point on the cumulative delivery schedule in Figure 12.6. The review point is at 8 months. Proceed vertically upward until the cumulative delivery

FIGURE 12.6   Line of Balance Charts: Bigfoot Snowmobile Company

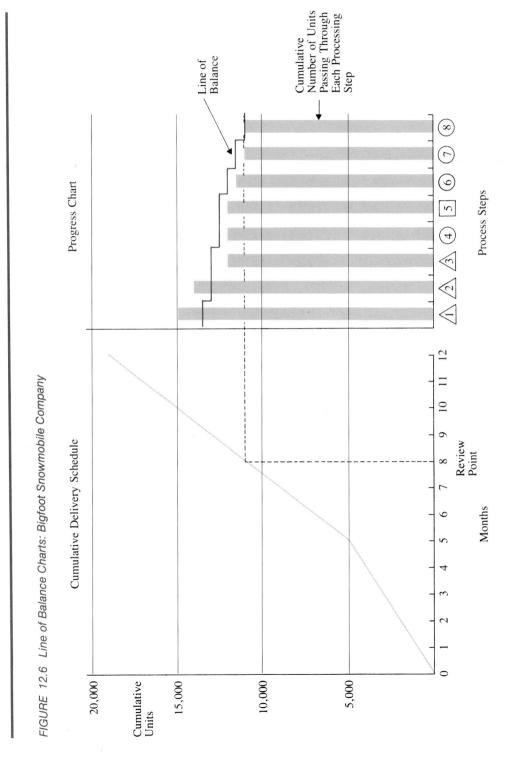

schedule curve is reached; proceed horizontally to the right until the last processing step ⑧ on the progress chart is reached. Draw a short horizontal line across the processing step ⑧ column at this level: This is the *line of balance* for processing step ⑧. To locate the line of balance for step ⑦, go *forward* (to the right) a quarter-month from the previous review point on the cumulative delivery schedule to $8\frac{1}{4}$ months and repeat the procedure. Why go forward in a schedule a quarter-month when step ⑦ is back upstream in the production process? Because the units that are at processing step ⑦ now should be shipped a quarter-month (the amount of lead time between steps ⑦ and ⑧) from now in the future, or at least $8\frac{1}{4}$ months in the schedule. The line of balance is similarly drawn for all processing steps.

3. Next, draw a vertical bar for each processing step on the progress chart to indicate the cumulative number of units that have passed each step.

4. Next, evaluate the progress chart: **(a)** Bigfoot is on its delivery schedule; the vertical bar for units shipped ⑧ exactly meets the line of balance. However, trouble looms ahead. **(b)** Processing steps △2 and △1 are on schedule or ahead of schedule; that is, their bars either meet or exceed the line of balance. **(c)** Processing steps ⑦, final assembly, and ⑥, chassis fabrication, are both 500 units behind schedule, probably because of engine assemblies and shell assemblies deficiencies. **(d)** Processing step ⑤, subcontracted body finish, is 500 units behind schedule. The fault lies with the subcontractor and not purchased parts. **(e)** Processing steps ④ and △3, engine assemblies, are 500 and 1,000 units behind schedule, respectively. Purchased parts is holding up engine test operation.

This evaluation suggests that management should immediately take corrective steps to accelerate purchase engines, engine test, and subcontracted body finish processing steps. Deliveries will be deficient by 500 units during the next review period (a quarter-month). Unless progress is made to accelerate △3 and ⑤, more serious delinquencies can be expected in the coming periods.

SCHEDULING SERVICES

Detailed schedules in services tend to be differentiated between custom and standard services.

Custom services are not unlike job shops in their characteristics. Consequently, their scheduling systems theoretically should be much like those found in job shops. However, in practice we find extremes in scheduling these systems. Small services, such as doctors' offices, small retailers, and local trucking companies, use almost no formal scheduling systems. Instead, such devices as appointment schedules, take-a-number systems, or first-come first-served rules are often used to assign priorities among customers. Part-time workers and standby equipment are also frequently employed during unexpectedly high demand periods.

At the other extreme, service systems such as hospitals have developed sophisticated scheduling systems that may surpass those found in job shop manufacturing. Because these systems are also produce-to-order systems and finished goods inventories cannot be maintained, capacities must be variable to meet wide variations in customer demand levels. Because customer demand is highly variable from week to week and because services must often be provided on short notice, these scheduling systems tend to work on a rather short planning horizon. It is not uncommon to observe schedules in these systems for only one week into the future.

Can you see the similarity in scheduling in hospitals and job shops? Several differences naturally exist—for example, setting priorities among patients at each work center in a hospital, though obviously based on different criteria than in a machine shop, would still follow the same general procedure. Job shops might use a first-come first-served criterion, whereas a hospital might use a most critical need criterion.

Much work has been devoted to developing scheduling systems in *standard services*. These production systems are much like product-focused manufacturing. Services are standard for most customers, and the processes employed are similar to production lines in that once they are begun they are carried through to completion without significant delays. They differ materially from product-focused manufacturing in only one respect: They produce to customer order rather than for finished goods inventory.

Examples of these systems are trucking companies, fast-food restaurants, the U.S. Postal Service, and airlines. The degree of sophistication achieved in scheduling some of these standard services has surpassed that in all other production systems. The airlines, for example, have on-line computer-based scheduling systems that are among the most effective today.

Service systems generally have these characteristics: They do not hold finished goods inventories; the demand for their outputs is highly variable from hour to hour, day to day, and week to week; and their operations are labor-intensive. Because the demand for services is so variable and because the services may be consumed as they are produced, great pressures rest on personnel scheduling because the principal means of performing the services is through personnel.

SCHEDULING PERSONNEL IN SERVICES

How do operations managers in services cope with these variable demand patterns as they schedule personnel? Four approaches are usually used:

1. Let waiting lines that use a first-come first-served priority buffer the difference between customer demand and the system capacity. This approach allows managers to schedule personnel such that the system's capacity is approximately uniform from period to period.
2. Use some means to level out the demand for services. Appointment schedules are commonly used in medical, legal, and other professional services for this purpose. Priority systems in medical clinics and hospitals allow certain types of patients, usually those cases that are emergencies or life-threatening, to be scheduled first, and the remaining patients are admitted by appointment. This approach also allows operations managers to schedule personnel so that the system capacity is approximately uniform.
3. Develop personnel schedules to allow system capacities that approximately match the pattern of customer demand. This approach attempts to vary the

FIGURE 12.7   Crew Schedules of California City Fire Department

JULY	S	M	T	W	T	F	S	S	M	T	W	T	F	S	S	M	T	W	T	F	S	S	M	T	W	T	F	S	S	M	T
	1	2	3	4	5	6	7	8	9	10	11	12	13	14	15	16	17	18	19	20	21	22	23	24	25	26	27	28	29	30	31
Crew A																															
Crew B																															
Crew C																															

Note: Shaded squares indicate a 24-hour shift.

system capacity by varying the number of personnel scheduled to work during each hour of the day. Because full-time personnel usually work 40 hours per week, some slack or personnel idle time is ordinarily introduced if full-time personnel are used exclusively.

4. For emergency services such as fire departments, schedule 24-hour full-crew coverage. During low-demand periods, have crews perform necessary but nonemergency tasks. During peak-demand periods, call in off-duty personnel and compensate them with overtime pay or compensatory time off.

As an example of this last approach, consider the California City Fire Department personnel schedules in Figure 12.7 and Table 12.5. This fire department has 5 stations that work a total of 21 fire-fighting personnel in providing round-the-clock fire protection. Each fire fighter is assigned to a crew. Figure 12.7 shows how the three crews, A, B, and C, are scheduled to work 24-hour shifts. This scheme is based on each crew working 96 hours per 12-day cycle, and then the cycle is repeated. Because severe emergencies require additional personnel, extra personnel can be called in on an overtime basis; personnel therefore actually average about 67 hours per cycle. Because some shifts will be low-demand periods, the fire fighters are scheduled to perform nonemergency tasks on a regular basis. Table 12.5 schedules some nonemergency tasks on every 24-hour shift.

From these scheduling approaches, we can see that operations managers may develop personnel schedules based on approximately uniform system capacities or highly variable system capacities. The uniform capacity approach must, however, be accompanied by other means of leveling out demand, such as appointment schedules, priority systems, and waiting lines.

Three general difficulties are encountered in scheduling personnel in services: demand variability, service time variability, and availability of personnel when they are needed. Consider, for example, how many attendants you would schedule to work during each hour of each day of the week in a health club. Figure 12.8 illustrates that the number of members at the club varies drastically throughout the day, the number of members at the club varies throughout the week, and the hourly pattern of the number of members at the club varies among the days of the week. If attendants are required to assist members in their exercises, provide guidance in their exercise programs, hand out supplies, and perform other duties, the number of attendants needed in each hour of the week is dependent on the number of members at the club.

TABLE 12.5   California City Fire Department Monthly Activity Schedule—July

Day	Cmdr.	Shift	Station 1		Station 2		Station 3		Station 4		Station 5	
			AM	PM	AM	PM	AM	PM	AM	PM	AM	PM
SUN 01	C2	B	SM	SM	SM	SM	SM	SM	SM	SM	SM	FB
MON 02	C5	A	FM	FM	FM	FM	FM	FM	FM	FM	FM	FM
TUE 03	C2	B	HM	HM	HM	HM	HM	HM	HM	HM	HM	HM
WED 04	C3	C	PC	PC	PC	PC	PC	PC	PC	PC	PC	PC
THU 05	C2	B	FP	FP	FP	FP	FP	FP	FP	FP	FP	FP
FRI 06	C3	C	DS	DS	CD	CD	DS	DS	FP	FP	FP	FP
SAT 07	C2	B	EM	EM	EM	EM	EM	EM	EM	EM	EM	FB
SUN 08	C3	C	SD	SM	SD	SM	SD	SM	SD	SM	FB	SM
MON 09	C5	A	FP	FP	FP	FP	FP	FP	FP	FP	FP	FP
TUE 10	C3	C	FP	FP	DS	DS	CD	CD	DS	DS	CD	CD
WED 11	C5	A	SM	SM	SM	SM	SM	SM	SM	SM	SM	SM
THU 12	C2	B	FP	FP	FP	FP	HM	HM	HM	HM	FP	FP
FRI 13	C5	A	SD	SD	HM	HM	SD	SD	CD	CD	SD	SD
SAT 14	C2	B	PC	PC	PC	PC	PC	PC	PC	PC	PC	PC
SUN 15	C5	A	CD	CD	SD	SD	CD	CD	SD	SD	FB	FB
MON 16	C2	B	PC	PC	PC	PC	PC	PC	PC	PC	PC	PC
TUE 17	C3	C	HM	HM	FP	FP	HM	HM	HM	HM	DS	DS
WED 18	C2	B	EM	EM	EM	EM	EM	EM	EM	EM	DS	DS
THU 19	C3	C	SD	SD	SD	SD	SD	SD	SD	SD	SD	SD
FRI 20	C5	A	HM	HM	CD	CD	EM	EM	EM	EM	CD	CD
SAT 21	C3	C	PC	PC	EM	EM	EM	EM	PC	PC	PC	PC
SUN 22	C5	A	SD	SM	SD	SM	SD	SM	SD	SM	FB	SM
MON 23	C3	C	FP	FP	FP	FP	FP	FP	FP	FP	FP	FP
TUE 24	C5	A	CD	CD	FB	FB	CD	CD	HM	HM	HM	HM
WED 25	C2	B	FP	FP	FP	FP	FP	CD	FP	CD	FP	FP
THU 26	C5	A	FP	FP	FP	FP	HM	HM	HM	HM	FP	FP
FRI 27	C2	B	DS	DS	SD	SD	HM	HM	DS	DS	SD	SD
SAT 28	C3	C	EM	EM	EM	EM	EM	EM	EM	EM	EM	EM
SUN 29	C2	B	SM	SM	SM	SM	SM	SM	SM	SM	SM	FB
MON 30	C3	C	CD	CD	CD	CD	CD	CD	CD	CD	CD	CD
TUE 31	C2	B	SD	SD	DS	DS	DS	DS	SD	SD	SD	SD

AD—Administrative duties
CD—Captain's discretion
DS—Drill site training
FB—Fire boat training and maintenance
FH—Fire hydrants
HT—Hose testing
PC—Platoon commander's discretion
PP—Prefire plans
RT—Reserve training
ST—Simulator training

AM—Apparatus maintenance—monthly
CR—Certification training/testing
EM—Equipment maintenance
FP—Fire prevention
HM—Hydrant maintenance/service
PH—Paint/color-code hydrants
PI—Prefire inspection
PT—Pumper test
SD—Station drill
SM—Station/grounds maintenance

FIGURE 12.8   *Customer Demand Patterns for a Health Club*

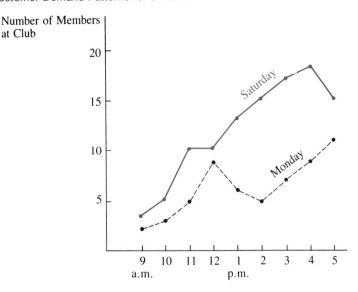

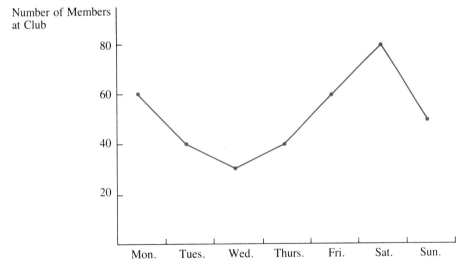

Because of the peaks and valleys in customer demand, operations managers are usually torn between two approaches to developing work schedules for employees in systems designed for variable capacity. The first approach is to use full-time employees exclusively. With this arrangement more than enough employees will be scheduled in some periods, which will result in employee idle time in these periods. In other periods not enough employees will be scheduled and overtime may be used or some means such as waiting lines will need to be used to level out demand. These periods when overstaffing and understaffing occur result from the inability of managers to develop work schedules that exactly match anticipated customer demand because of the desire of full-time employees for five consecutive days and eight consecutive hours per day work schedules.

The other approach to developing work schedules for service systems with variable capacity is to use some full-time employees and some part-time employees to staff the system. If the part-time employees can be called in to work on short notice, so much the better. This approach avoids much of the planned overstaffing and understaffing in work schedules and provides operations managers a safety valve, other than the use of overtime and waiting lines, to service unexpectedly high levels of customer demand during some periods.

APPOINTMENT SCHEDULES AND WORK SHIFT SCHEDULING

In some services even the use of appointment schedules and other efforts at leveling demand are not entirely feasible, or in some cases not desirable. Although it is true that leveling demand does simplify scheduling personnel to staff these services, the nature of the service may dictate how much that customer demand can or should be controlled through appointment schedules and other means. In Example 12.8 the health club that we discussed earlier is used to illustrate how appointment schedules can be used to make customer demand conform to patterns that are more conducive to personnel scheduling, even if the resulting demand pattern is not entirely uniform. In this example we reshape the customer demand into a more manageable pattern through appointment schedules; then we determine the number of attendants required in each day of the week, and schedule individual workers to work shifts.

EXAMPLE 12.8   Personnel Scheduling

Bob Bullit is studying the membership attendance records in Figure 12.8 with a view toward scheduling his attendants to work shifts at the Body Shop Health Club. The membership has recently voted to install a system of appointments at the club to avoid overcrowding during certain hours of the week and to avoid the extra cost of attendant overtime that has recently been used to excess at the club. Bob knows that the number of members at the club throughout the day tends to be low in the mornings and higher in the afternoons. In spite of this hour-to-hour pattern, Bob believes that the work load on the attendants is usually very uniform throughout the day because members who attend in the mornings tend to be on formal exercise programs and to require more assistance. Members who attend in the afternoons tend to

FIGURE 12.9 Requirements for Attendants at the Body Shop Health Club

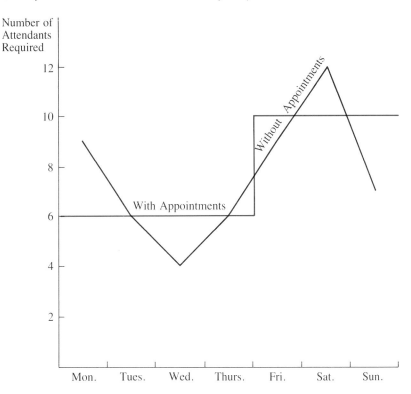

participate in recreation activities and to require less assistance. Therefore the hourly work load for attendants is approximately uniform.

Bob must now develop appointment and work shift schedules for the attendants.

Solution

1. First, Bob converts the attendance information in Figure 12.8 to the number of attendants required daily. This conversion is shown in Figure 12.9 in two ways: without appointments and with appointments.

2. Next, Bob develops the number of attendants required daily with the appointment system:

Mon.	Tues.	Wed.	Thurs.	Fri.	Sat.	Sun.	*Weekly Attendant Work Shifts*
6	6	6	6	10	10	10	54

From this information Bob knows that with each attendant working 5 shifts per week, he will need a theoretical minimum of 11 attendants. *Theoretical minimum* means that this

FIGURE 12.10 *Work Shift Heuristic Procedure for Work Shift Scheduling of Attendants at the Body Shop Health Club*

Attendant	Number of Attendant Work Shifts						
	Mon.	Tues.	Wed.	Thurs.	Fri.	Sat.	Sun.
1	6	6*	6	6	10	10	10
2	6	6	5	5*	9	9	9
3	5	5*	5	5	8	8	8
4	5	5	4	4*	7	7	7
5	4	4*	4	4	6	6	6
6	4	4	3	3*	5	5	5
7	3	3*	3	3	4	4	4
8	3	3	2	2*	3	3	3
9	2	2*	2	2	2	2	2
10	2	2	1	1*	1	1	1
11	1	1	1	1	0	0*	0**

* The pairs of days that are circled indicate the two consecutive days off for an attendant.

** This day will have one extra attendant. This is unavoidable slack because we have chosen to use all full-time employees and only 54 work shifts are required, but 55 work shifts result from employing 11 attendants for 5 days per week.

number may not actually be attained in practice because of the 5-consecutive-workdays, 2-consecutive-days-off, and 8-consecutive-hours-per-day constraint:

$$\text{Theoretical minimum number of attendants} = \frac{\text{Total number of attendant work shifts per week}}{\text{Number of work shifts per week per attendant}}$$

$$= 54/5 = 10.8, \text{ or } 11 \text{ attendants}$$

3. Next, Bob develops a work shift schedule for the attendants. Figure 12.10 shows the procedure used to develop the work shift schedule. This procedure uses the *work shift heuristic rule* to determine days off for each worker:

Work shift heuristic rule: Choose two consecutive days with the least total number of work shifts required. In the case of ties, arbitrarily select a pair and continue.

The number of attendant work shifts required each day when Attendant 1's schedule is planned is taken from Figure 12.8 and is the same as used in Step 2. One work shift is subtracted from Attendant 1's work shifts to yield the total attendant work shifts required when Attendant 2's schedule is planned. This process is repeated for each attendant's schedule.

4. Next, from Figure 12.10 Bob can now determine the shifts that each attendant will be scheduled to work during each week:

Attendant	Workdays	Days Off	Attendant	Workdays	Days Off
1	Wed.–Sun.	Mon.–Tues.	7	Wed.–Sun.	Mon.–Tues.
2	Fri.–Tues.	Wed.–Thurs.	8	Fri.–Tues.	Wed.–Thurs.
3	Wed.–Sun.	Mon.–Tues.	9	Wed.–Sun.	Mon.–Tues.
4	Fri.–Tues.	Wed.–Thurs.	10	Fri.–Tues.	Wed.–Thurs.
5	Wed.–Sun.	Mon.–Tues.	11	Sun.–Thurs.	Fri.–Sat.
6	Fri.–Tues.	Wed.–Thurs.			

Although the work shift heuristic procedure used does not guarantee optimal results, which means that the work shift schedule requires the least number of attendants possible, Bob knows that it does result in schedules with very little slack time. Additionally, Bob knows that other schedules may exist that are equally as good as the one developed by this heuristic procedure. He also knows that the work shift heuristic procedure may be used with or without appointment schedules.

Computer packages for scheduling are growing in both number and frequency of application in today's production systems.

COMPUTERIZED SCHEDULING SYSTEMS

Of course, you can buy or rent a computer and write your own computer programs that develop detailed schedules for each work center in your facility and macro schedules that provide coordination of all the jobs to be processed. Or you can do as many other organizations have done, buy the ready-made software packages that are already tried and proven in a variety of scheduling situations. IBM, Xerox, and many other computer manufacturers and software companies have their own versions.

In some cases the scheduling packages are an integral part of a larger manufacturing information system — cost analyses, inventory information, and scheduling. All the areas of POM are tied together in a neat package. There is no denying that these computer packages are appealing, but don't jump to the conclusion that they can be adapted to a particular production system quickly or easily just because the programs are already written and debugged. Many organizations have found, much to their disappointment, that it often takes months or even years to develop a system of information inputs that is necessary to feed the computerized system.

Other computer packages of less ambitious scope are principally designed to provide only scheduling information. Regardless of the scope of these packages, the scheduling portion of the programs ordinarily must:

1. Develop for each work center daily detailed schedules that indicate beginning and ending times for each order.
2. Develop departmental daily and weekly detailed schedules that are used to coordinate work centers.
3. Generate modified schedules as new customer or work center progress information surfaces.

Before these programs can be processed, priority rules for determining the sequence of jobs at work centers must be developed, the necessary set of rules for determining which jobs will be assigned to which work centers must be established, and a system of follow-up and feedback within the facility for modifying schedules must be developed. These are not easy tasks. When computerized systems are installed, managers cannot play fast and loose with their scheduling decisions. One of the most common complaints from schedulers is that managers always seem to be changing the rules to save them from the latest customer's telephone call. Schedulers seem to be whip-sawed between the changing orders from the top concerning which jobs are the hot ones in the current period. Computerized systems require that consistent rules must be developed and followed, rational approaches to routing and processing must be planned, and schedules must be followed if meaningful production-planning information is to be delivered.

These requirements are often forced on some managers by the necessity of installing a computerized scheduling system. In short, we must clean up our scheduling acts in POM when computers are used to develop detailed schedules. Substantial improvements in customer service and internal operating efficiency are possible in these production systems only if sequencing rules, routing plans, and other inputs are realistic and if schedules are followed.

Some recent computerized scheduling systems are gaining in popularity. Among these one stands out: Optimized Production Technology (OPT). OPT was developed by Dr. Eli Goldratt in Israel, and it is marketed in the United States by Creative Output Inc., of Milford, Connecticut. OPT is a complete production-planning and control information system that is particularly appropriate for complex job shop environments. Like MRP, OPT explodes the MPS into resource requirements. By developing loading schedules for all work centers, OPT, given a mix of products, finds the bottlenecks in the production processes. A bottleneck is any operation in a series of production operations that has the least capacity or lowest production rate. If a product must go through a series of operations, no matter how fast other operations in the series are, the capacity of the bottleneck determines the capacity of the series. It is at this point that OPT exhibits its advantage over other systems. Once the bottlenecks have been located, OPT uses a group of proprietary algorithms to schedule the workers, machines, and tools at bottleneck work centers. Companies in growing numbers seem impressed with the results that they have gained from using OPT.

To illustrate the effects of OPT, Dr. Goldratt has written *The Goal,* an intriguing and highly readable fictional work that dramatically illustrates the implementation of OPT in a factory. A factory manager, the main character of *The Goal,* searches for a way to save his factory, which is about to be deep-sixed by an uncaring and ignorant top management. By following the advice of Jonah, a consultant who continually asks easily understood questions that have very difficult answers, the factory survives.

The process followed by the factory manager in *The Goal* is at the heart of OPT. First, the factory manager measures the production rates of the major operations in the factory. He discovers one operation that is much slower than all of the others — a bottleneck. Next, he asks a team of his best people to come up with ways to increase the production rate of the bottleneck operation. Then after the production rate of the bottleneck operation is increased, the whole factory's production rate is observed to increase. The team then goes to the next slowest operation and repeats the process. The output of the factory increases as the production rate of each bottleneck operation is increased. This procedure results in the production rate of the factory being dramatically increased without additional costs and with a consequent rise in profits. For more information on OPT, see the group of articles by Robert Fox in the Selected Bibliography at the end of this chapter.

Q-Control was developed by William E. Sandman in his own company; he has since become a consultant applying his production-planning and control system to clients' operations. Like OPT, Q-Control is most appropriate in complex job shops and works on bottleneck operations. In this system overnight computer simulation studies are performed using the mix of end items from the MPS to be produced the next day. The objective of the simulation is to develop a schedule that maximizes the speed of work flow through the bottleneck operations. Q-Control also uses proprietary algorithms to schedule the bottlenecks. For more information on Q-Control, see Sandman's book in the Selected Bibliography at the end of this chapter.

SUMMARY

Just-in-Time production-planning and control methods in general and Kanban in particular seek to improve production methods by drastically reducing inventories and thereby exposing the problems that afflict production systems. This method of enforced problem solving is but one element of JIT systems. Many of these methods have been adopted by U.S. firms, but major shifts in operations have to occur before and be concurrent with their implementation.

The nature of scheduling decisions varies among the types of production systems. In process-focused factories, priorities must be set for each order at each work center, orders must be assigned to machines within work centers, and shop floor control must be applied to orders. Shop floor planning and control in process-focused factories includes setting priorities for orders, issuing dispatching lists to work centers, keeping work-in-process (WIP) updated, providing input–output control for work centers, and measuring and reporting performance of work centers.

In scheduling product-focused factories, the length of production runs, the timing of machine changeovers, and the planning and control of production for delivery schedules are important scheduling problems. Length of production runs can be determined by EOQ or the run-out method. Line-of-balance charts are helpful in planning and controlling production for delivery schedules.

Personnel schedules dominate scheduling in services. Some services have used techniques such as appointment schedules and priority systems to level out customer demand. Work shift scheduling—determining the scheme for consecutive workdays and consecutive days off for personnel, given a certain demand pattern—is commonly used.

Increasingly, scheduling information and scheduling decisions are a part of a computer information system. OPT and other computerized information systems impose structure on scheduling decisions. Operations managers may not be able to make as many ad hoc scheduling decisions as before.

REVIEW AND DISCUSSION QUESTIONS

1. Define *JIT systems.* Define *Kanban* and describe how a Kanban system works.

2. Describe the features of Japanese manufacturing methods. Discuss which of the features is most responsible for the success of Japanese manufacturers.

3. Discuss whether JIT is a method of production planning and control as in Kanban, or whether it is a philosophy and system of manufacturing.

4. Discuss whether Japanese manufacturing methods can be adopted by U.S. manufacturers. Why would U.S. manufacturers want to adopt Japanese manufacturing methods? What are the obstacles to the adoption of these methods in the United States?

5. Compare and contrast MRP with JIT. Under what conditions would each be preferred? What are the conditions necessary for JIT?

6. Explain the relationship between MRP and scheduling decisions. From where in the MRP system does the information for making shop floor scheduling decisions come?

7. Describe a process-focused factory. What are the implications of the characteristics of such a factory for scheduling decisions?

8. What are two key scheduling problems in job shops?

9. Explain how an operations manager would select and use a sequencing rule in practice.

10. What are the conditions that would make the use of Johnson's rule appropriate?

11. What scheduling decisions must operations managers resolve in product-focused factories?

12. Evaluate EOQ as a method of setting length of production runs. What are its strengths and weaknesses?

13. Explain how the run-out method improves upon the EOQ. What are its disadvantages?

14. Explain why the scheduling of services is difficult.

15. Describe some ways that operations managers cope with variable demand for services as they schedule personnel.

16. What is input–output analysis? What information does it provide operations managers? What is its main purpose?

PROBLEMS

1. An engineering team is working on a year-long plantwide project to reduce production lot sizes. The team is now studying the punch press work center that is producing part number Z225, a metal telephone base plate. It now takes 45 minutes to change the die tooling on the punch press and 1.25 minutes to produce each plate by passing

it through several dies. If the labor rate for the operation is $10.50 per hour, what must the lot size be to achieve an average labor cost per unit of $.50?

2. An engineering team has set a target lot size of 5 when part number Z225 is produced at the punch press work center. The production rate is 25 per hour, the usage rate is 5 per hour, the carrying cost is $1.50 per unit per year, the labor rate is $10.50 per hour, and the annual demand is 8,000 per year.
   a. What must the setup time be for the part at the work center?
   b. Is such a setup time possible? Discuss what could be done at the work center to achieve such a setup time.

3. Given this input–output report for Work Center 1301 at the end of Week 4:
   a. What production difficulties does the report indicate?
   b. What corrective actions do you recommend?

			Week		
	− 1	1	2	3	4
Planned input (labor-hours)		200	300	300	200
Actual input (labor-hours)		250	300	350	300
Cumulative deviation		50	50	100	200
Planned output (labor-hours)		200	300	300	200
Actual output (labor-hours)		200	300	300	200
Cumulative deviation		0	0	0	0
Planned ending WIP (labor-hours)		200	200	200	200
Actual ending WIP (labor-hours)	200	250	250	300	400

4. Given this input–output report for Work Center 65 at the end of Week 4:
   a. What production difficulties does the report indicate?
   b. What corrective actions do you recommend?

			Week		
	− 1	1	2	3	4
Planned input (labor-hours)		100	50	20	100
Actual input (labor-hours)		50	40	30	80
Cumulative deviation		− 50	− 60	− 50	− 70
Planned output (labor-hours)		120	70	50	100
Actual output (labor-hours)		110	50	20	70
Cumulative deviation		− 10	− 30	− 60	− 90
Planned ending WIP (labor-hours)		20	30	20	20
Actual ending WIP (labor-hours)	70	10	0	10	20

5. The Gospel Bible Company prints bibles for churches, book companies, and other organizations on a seven-day-per-week basis. A production schedule is now being prepared for September. The printing jobs, estimated processing times, estimated changeover times, and the 12:00 noon, September 15, progress are shown below:

Work Center	Job Processing Times (Days)					Changeover Times (Days)	Sept. 15 Progress [Days Ahead or (Behind)]
	A	*B*	*C*	*D*	*E*		
Photo	—	—	9	13	10	2	—
Typeset	—	10	8	10	8	1	(2½)
Printing	5	5	5	5	5	3	½
Binding	6	4	5	5	4	1	½
Packaging	3	3	3	3	3	—	—

The printing company is just coming off a one-month vacation in August; therefore work centers will be phased in as needed. The jobs will be sequenced in this order: ABCDE. Prepare a Gantt chart for the Gospel Bible Company that displays the September schedules for the work centers.

6. The Los Angeles plant of Computer Products Corporation (CPC) produces electronic assemblies for other manufacturers in the electronics and computer industries. The plant now has accepted customer orders for the next work week, Monday through Friday, eight hours per day. The customer orders, estimated processing times, estimated changeover times, and the Wednesday 5:00 p.m. progress are shown below:

Work Center	Order-Processing Time (Days)				Change-over (Hours)	Wednesday Progress [Hours Ahead or (Behind)]
	414	*398*	*555*	*449*		
Kitting	8	8	4	13	1	2
Inspection	8	8	2	4	1	(4)
Insertion	8	4	8	8	2	—
Soldering	8	8	12	12	2	—
Trimming	4	8	8	4	—	—
Packaging	4	4	4	2	—	—

The orders will be processed in this sequence: 414, 398, 555, and 449. Prepare a Gantt chart for one work week that shows how the work centers must be coordinated.

7. The Jailbound Tax Service processes industrial customers' tax jobs on a first-come first-served basis but wonders if shortest processing time would be better. The jobs that are now waiting to be processed are listed in the order in which they arrived, with their estimated processing times, time to promised completion, and the necessary computations:

			First-Come First-Served			Shortest Processing Time		
(1)	*(2)*	*(3)*	*(4)*	*(5)*	*(6)*	*(7)*	*(8)*	*(9)*
Cus-tomer Job	*Estimated Processing Times (Days)*	*Time to Promised Completion (Days)*	*Job Se-quence*	*Flow Time (Days)*	*Lateness (Days) [(5) − (3)]*	*Job Se-quence*	*Flow Time (Days)*	*Lateness (Days) [(8) − (3)]*
A	5	8	1	5	—	2	8	—
B	3	6	2	8	2	1	3	—
C	10	24	3	18	—	4	26	2
D	8	22	4	26	4	3	16	—

  a. Rate the two sequencing rules on three evaluation criteria—average flow time, average number of jobs in the system, and average job lateness.
  b. Which sequencing rule would you recommend? Why?

8. Bill Freeland, production planner at the Los Angeles plant of Computer Products Corporation (CPC), must decide the sequence in which to process four important customer orders for electronic assemblies. He has developed these estimates based on a first-come first-served sequencing rule:

Customer Order Number	Estimated Processing Times (Days)	Time to Promised Completion (Days)	First-Come First-Served Order Sequence	Flow Time (Days)	Lateness (Days)
44805	16	49	1	16	0
44980	32	30	2	48	18
44991	21	70	3	69	0
44999	19	85	4	88	3

Rate the first-come first-served, shortest processing time, and critical ratio sequencing rules on three evaluation criteria: average flow time, average number of jobs in the system, and average job lateness.

9. The Hardtimes Heat-Treating Service performs annealing, case hardening, water plunge, oil plunge, and other heat-treating services on its customers' metal parts. Each job usually requires a different setup, and these changeovers have different costs. Today Hardtimes must decide the job sequence for five jobs to minimize changeover costs. Below are the changeover costs between jobs:

Jobs That Precede

Jobs That Follow	A	B	C	D	E
A	—	$ 65	$80	$ 50	$62
B	$ 95	—	69	67	65
C	92	71	—	67	75
D	85	105	65	—	95
E	125	75	95	105	—

a. Use this rule to develop a job sequence: First, select the lowest changeover cost among all changeovers; this sets the first and second jobs. The next job to be selected will have the lowest changeover cost among the remaining jobs that follow the previously selected job.

b. What is the total changeover cost for all five jobs?

10. Bill Freeland is taking another look at the four customer orders in Problem 8. He has just discovered that the sequence in which the orders are processed affects the setup costs in the electronic assembly department. He has developed these setup cost estimates:

Orders That Follow	Orders That Precede			
	44805	44980	44991	44999
44805	—	$5,490	$2,600	$6,900
44980	$4,700	—	1,900	5,600
44991	3,450	4,960	—	3,900
44999	5,270	2,970	1,690	—

a. Use this rule to develop a job sequence: First, select the lowest setup cost among all setups; this sets the first and second orders. The next order to be selected will have the lowest setup cost among the remaining orders that follow the previously selected order.

b. What is the total setup cost for all four orders?

11. The Precise Manufacturing Company receives parts from suppliers to be used in its manufacturing departments. The quality control department must perform two operations when shipments are received: Operation 1—draw a random sample, package, and deliver to testing, and Operation 2—test the materials and issue a disposition report. The time estimates for processing six shipments through quality control are:

Shipment	Operation 1 (Hours)	Operation 2 (Hours)
A	.5	2.0
B	2.5	1.7
C	.2	2.4
D	1.7	.6
E	.5	.4
F	1.9	.9

a. Use Johnson's rule to set the sequence of processing the shipments through quality control. (Operations need not change over to new jobs at the same time.)

b. How much total time is required to process the six shipments through quality control?

12. Jane Rollins, production scheduler at the El Paso plant of Computer Products Corporation (CPC), must determine the sequence in which to process five customer orders for electronic assemblies. Each of the orders must be processed through two principal operations: component insertion and flow soldering. Jane has developed these processing-time estimates for the five orders:

Customer Order Number	Component Insertion (Days)	Flow Soldering (Days)
19501	4.9	3.9
19499	5.3	2.1
19387	2.7	2.9
19577	3.6	4.6
19409	3.1	3.5

If the operations need not change over to new jobs at the same time:

a. Use Johnson's rule to set the sequence of processing the orders through the two operations.
b. How many days will be required to process all of the orders through both operations?

13. The Los Angeles plant of Computer Products Corporation (CPC) produces several standard electronic assemblies on a produce-to-stock basis. The annual demand, setup or ordering costs, carrying costs, demand rates, and production rates for the assemblies are shown below:

Assembly	Annual Demand (000 Units)	Setup or Ordering Cost ($/Run)	Carrying Cost ($/Unit/Year)	Demand Rate (Units/Day)	Production Rate (Units/Day)
P55 Power Unit	5	$1,200	$6	20	200
Z4 Converter	10	600	4	40	300
U69 Equalizer	12	1,500	10	48	100
K5 Audio	6	400	2	24	50

a. Using the EOQ, compute the length of production run (number of units in the production run) for each assembly.
b. What percentage of the production run of P55s is being used during the run?
c. For the P55, how much time will pass between each setup?

14. The Mad Toy Company produces five models of toys. The annual demand, setup or ordering costs, carrying costs, demand rates, and production rates for the toys are presented below:

Toy Model	Annual Demand (Toys)	Setup or Ordering Cost ($/Run)	Carrying Cost ($/Toy/Year)	Demand Rate (Toys/Day)	Production Rate (Toys/Day)
A	10,000	$1,000	$2.50	40	250
B	5,000	2,000	6.25	20	200
C	15,000	2,000	1.25	60	300
D	20,000	3,000	3.50	80	300
E	10,000	2,000	3.00	40	200

a. Using the EOQ, compute the length of production run (the number of units in each production run) for each toy model.

b. Assuming that there are 300 working days per year and that the final assembly department processes only these toy models, what percentage of the year's capacity is required for Model A?

15. The Mad Toy Company produces five models of toys—A, B, C, D, and E. It is now June 15, and Mad is planning its final assembly department schedule for the fall quarter—July, August, and September. The inventory on hand, final assembly hours required per toy, and forecast demand are shown below:

(1) Toy Model	(2) Inventory on Hand or in Production (Toys)	(3) Final Assembly Hours Required (Hours/Toy)	(4) Forecast Demand for Fall Quarter (Toys)
A	5,000	.040	3,000
B	2,000	.050	2,000
C	5,000	.033	5,000
D	5,000	.033	6,000
E	5,000	.050	4,000

The winter quarter demand forecast is the same as the fall quarter. If there are 900 final assembly hours available in each quarter, use the run-out method to develop a final assembly production schedule for the fall quarter.

16. The Los Angeles plant of Computer Products Corporation (CPC) must develop a production schedule for March, the upcoming month, for producing electronic assemblies. The electronic assemblies are standard designs that are produced to stock for other manufacturers in the electronics and computer industries. The inventory of finished assemblies on hand, the hours required to flow-solder each of the assemblies (flow soldering is the bottleneck operation in the production of each of the assemblies, the operation with the least capacity), and the forecast demands for March and April are shown below:

Assembly	Inventory on Hand (Units)	Flow-Soldering Hours Required (Hours/Unit)	March Forecast Demand (Units)	April Forecast Demand (Units)
P55 Power Unit	100	.3	400	400
Z4 Converter	600	.2	900	900
U69 Equalizer	500	.6	1,500	1,500
K5 Audio	200	.1	500	500

If there are 1,000 flow-soldering hours available per month to produce these assemblies, use the run-out method to develop a schedule for March for the production of these assemblies.

17. The Rawhide Boot Company has a contractual delivery schedule for hiking boots with one of the oil-producing nations on the Persian Gulf. Rawhide must meet the delivery schedule or the country will buy the boot company and produce the boots

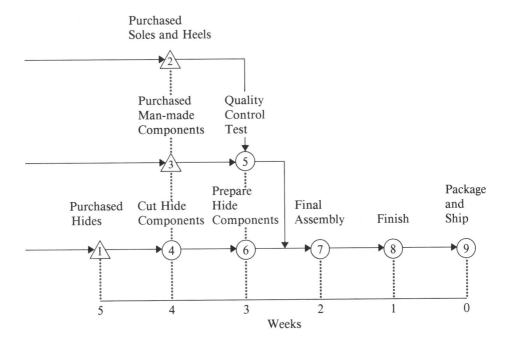

themselves. The delivery schedule calls for 5,000 pairs of boots to be delivered each week for 30 weeks. The production process for the boots has the lead times shown in the accompanying illustration. Ten weeks into the delivery schedule, production records indicate that these cumulative quantities have passed the processing steps:

Processing Step	Cumulative Quantities (Pairs of Boots)	Processing Step	Cumulative Quantities (Pairs of Boots)	Processing Step	Cumulative Quantities (Pairs of Boots)
1	87,000	4	77,000	7	57,000
2	63,000	5	63,000	8	57,000
3	72,000	6	67,000	9	52,000

a. Prepare a cumulative delivery schedule chart, a progress chart, and a line of balance.
b. Evaluate the prospects for future deliveries. Is the future bright for Rawhide, or are delivery problems looming on the horizon?

18. The Big State Plaza Savings and Loan operates a thriving business in Gardendale, California, offering savings, checking, bill-paying, and other money services. The cashier clerks work the cash drawer counters from 9 a.m. to 6 p.m. Monday through Saturday. Ms. Billie Davies is the manager of the cashier section and part of her responsibility involves developing work shift schedules for the cashier clerks. She has kept accurate records of customer demand and has estimated the number of cashier clerk work shifts required daily:

	Mon.	Tues.	Wed.	Thurs.	Fri.	Sat.	Total
Cashier clerk work shifts	8	6	4	5	8	10	41

All of the cashier clerks are full-time employees and according to company policy must be provided four consecutive days of work and two consecutive days off each week.
a. What is the theoretical minimum number of cashier clerks required?
b. Use the work shift heuristic procedure to develop weekly work shift schedules for the cashier clerks.
c. How many cashier clerk work shifts of slack per week are present in your proposed schedules? How could this slack be avoided? Are your schedules optimal?

19. Mary Perkins is the store manager for Seattle's largest Buy-Right Food Store. She is now developing weekly work shift schedules for the counter clerks. She has summarized the daily need for clerk work shifts:

	Mon.	Tues.	Wed.	Thurs.	Fri.	Sat.	Sun.	Total
Day shift	6	5	5	6	8	10	6	46
Evening shift	5	4	4	5	6	7	4	35

The shifts are scheduled independently, the clerks' union contract calls for schedules based on five consecutive days and eight consecutive hours per day, and only full-time clerks are employed.

a. What is the theoretical minimum number of clerks required on both the day and evening shifts?
b. Use the work shift heuristic procedure to develop work shift schedules for the clerks for both the day and evening shifts.
c. How many clerk work shifts of slack per week are present in your day and evening shift schedules? How could this slack be avoided? Is your solution optimal?

COMPUTER PROBLEMS/CASES

THE QUIK CLAIM SERVICES COMPANY

The Quik Claim Services Company provides claims adjustment services to insurance agents and insurance companies in the Atlanta, Georgia, region. The company's claims adjustors respond to insurance agents' requests for the resolution of damages to clients' properties in the region and collect fees from the insurance companies for this service. The service involves traveling to the client's property, observing the nature and extent of the damage, and affixing a reasonable amount that should be reimbursed by the insurance company. Quik Claim believes that the quick resolution of claims has been the cornerstone of its growth and success.

John Billingham is Quik Claim's operations manager in Atlanta. Recently numerous complaints have been received about the length of time required for a claims adjustor to complete the damage estimates. At a recent regional meeting, claims adjustors told John that they were working as hard and fast as humanly possible, but that on some days of the week the number of requests was so great that it could take a few days to get to some of these requests. All claims adjustors now work five days per week eight hours per day, Monday through Friday. John is considering a different scheduling arrangement for the adjustors that would result in their being available to answer requests six days per week, working four days per week and ten hours per day, and having two consecutive days off per week not including Sunday (Sunday is never worked). Such an arrangement would allow the number of adjustors available to answer requests to better match the daily pattern of the volume of requests.

John has researched the latest forecasts of requests for claims adjustments from Quik Claim's marketing staff, and these daily averages seem to be reasonable estimates for the next several weeks:

	Mon.	Tues.	Wed.	Thurs.	Fri.	Sat.	Total
Number of requests	42	36	24	32	38	46	218

Each request is expected to require an average of about four hours of an adjustor's time. John wants to plan work shifts for the adjustors to approximately match the requests for service, but he wonders how this will affect the utilization of adjustors, group morale, and the time required to resolve clients' claims.

Assignment

1. What is the theoretical minimum number of adjustors required?
2. Use the work shift heuristic procedure to develop work shift schedules for the adjustors.
3. How much slack per week is present in your work shift schedules?
4. What ways could be used to reduce the amount of slack in your work shift schedules?
5. What factors should be considered in changes in work shift schedules such as the one that John Billingham is considering? Which of these factors is most important? Can you suggest how John should go about making the schedule changes that he is considering?

COMPUTER PRODUCTS CORPORATION (CPC)

The Los Angeles plant of Computer Products Corporation (CPC) has contracted to supply a large consumer electronics distributor with CPC's P55 Power Unit on a strict shipping schedule. The agreed-to schedule is shown below:

Month	Units to Be Delivered	Month	Units to Be Delivered
January	1,000	April	1,500
February	1,000	May	2,000
March	1,500	June	2,000

The production-processing steps, the relationships among the steps, and the lead times are shown on the flow chart below:

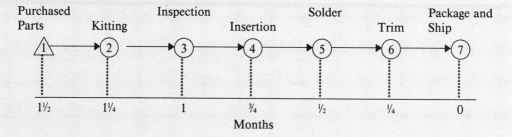

At the end of March these cumulative quantities of units have passed these production-processing steps:

Processing Step	Cumulative Units	Processing Step	Cumulative Units
1. Purchased parts	5,500	5. Soldering	3,600
2. Kitting	5,400	6. Trimming	3,400
3. Inspection	5,200	7. Package and ship	3,200
4. Insertion	5,000		

Assignment

1. Construct a cumulative shipping chart, a progress chart, and a line of balance as of the end of March.

2. What is the status of CPC's progress to the present?

3. What is the future status of CPC's progress likely to be? What corrective actions are likely to be required by the operations managers at CPC's Los Angeles plant if they are to live up to their shipping schedule?

4. Discuss the usefulness of LOB in planning and controlling CPC's shipments. How would an MRP system compare with LOB in this application? Defend your answer.

PONTIAC PLASTICS

Beverly Brady, production scheduler at Pontiac Plastics Corporation, must assign five factory orders for resins to five thermo-mixing machines. Because of the chemical properties of each of the resins and the unique capabilities of each of the thermo-mixing machines, the processing times of the resins differ among the machines. Beverly has developed these estimated times (in hours) for processing the resins in the thermo-mixing machines:

	Thermo-Mixing Machines				
Resin	1	2	3	4	5
Wopac	4.1	5.4	4.6	5.9	4.0
Ziptite	5.5	5.8	4.9	6.0	3.7
Lockit	2.6	2.8	2.7	3.2	2.4
Freezit	9.1	10.5	9.5	9.9	8.3
Sticktite	6.5	7.5	7.0	7.9	5.9

Which resins should be assigned to which thermo-mixing machines to minimize the total processing time for all the resins?

Assignment

1. Formulate the information in this case into a linear programming (LP) format. Define the decision variables, write the objective function, and write the constraint functions.

2. Using the LP computer program in the *POM Computer Library* that accompanies this book, solve the problem that you formulated in No. 1.

3. Fully interpret the meaning of the solution you obtained in No. 2. In other words, which resins should be assigned to which thermo-mixing machines to minimize the total machine processing time for processing all of the resins? How much total machine time will be required for the assignment?

4. Are there other assignments for which the total machine time will be nearly the same? What are those assignments and what are their costs?

5. Explain the caution that must be observed in answering No. 4.

SELECTED BIBLIOGRAPHY

Baker, K. R. "The Effects of Input Control in a Simple Scheduling Model." *Journal of Operations Management* 4, no. 2(February 1984):99–112.

Clark, Wallace. *The Gantt Chart: A Working Tool of Management.* New York: Ronald Press, 1922.

Day, James E., and Michael P. Hottenstein. "Review of Sequencing Research." *Naval Research Logistics Quarterly* 27(March 1970):11–39.

Fox, Robert E. "MRP, KANBAN, or OPT?" *Inventories & Production Magazine* 2, no. 4(July–August 1982).

———. "OPT—An Answer for America, Part II." *Inventories & Production Magazine* 2, no. 6(November–December 1982).

———. "OPT—An Answer for America, Part III." *Inventories & Production Magazine* 3, no. 1(January–February 1983).

———. "OPT—An Answer for America, Part IV." *Inventories & Production Magazine* 3, no. 2(March–April 1983).

———. "OPT vs. MRP: Thoughtware vs. Software." *Inventories & Production Magazine* 3, no. 6(November–December 1983).

Goddard, Walt. "Kanban versus MRP II—Which Is Best for You?" *Modern Materials Handling* (Nov. 5, 1982):40–48.

Goldratt, Eli Y., and Jeff Cox. *The Goal.* New York: North River Press, 1984.

Hall, Robert W. *Driving the Productivity Machine: Production Planning and Control in Japan.* Falls Church, VA: American Production and Inventory Control Society, 1981.

———. *Zero Inventory.* Homewood, IL: Dow Jones-Irwin, 1983.

Hershauer, James C., and Ronald J. Ebert. "Search and Simulation Selection of a Job-Shop Sequencing Rule." *Management Science* 21(March 1975):833–843.

Jacobs, R. "The OPT Scheduling System: A Review of a New Production Scheduling System." *Production and Inventory Management* 24(Third Quarter 1983):47–51.

Japan Economic Journal. Several articles of interest.

Johnson, S. M. "Optimal Two Stage and Three Stage Production Schedules with Setup Times Included." *Naval Research Logistics Quarterly* 1(March 1954):61–68.

Lee, Sang M., and Gary Schwendiman, eds. *Management by Japanese Systems.* New York: Praeger, 1983.

Monden, Yasuhir. *Toyota Production System, Practical Approach to Production Management.* Atlanta, GA: Industrial Engineering and Management Press, 1983.

————. "What Makes the Toyota Production System Really Tick?" *Industrial Engineering* 13, no. 1(January 1981):36–46.

Oral, M., and J. L. Malouin. "Evaluation of the Shortest Processing Time Scheduling Rule with Functional Process." *AIIE Transactions* 5(December 1973):357–365.

Sandman, William E. *How to Win Productivity in Manufacturing.* Dresher, PA: Yellow Book of Pennsylvania, 1980.

Schonberger, Richard J. *Japanese Productivity: Nine Hidden Lessons in Simplicity.* New York: Free Press, 1982.

————. "Some Observations on the Advantages and Implementation Issues of JIT Production Systems." *Journal of Operations Management* 2(November 1982):1–12.

Sunderland, F. O., and R. E. Fox. "Synchronized Manufacturing Challenge." *Production and Inventory Management Review* (March 1986):36–44.

Vollman, T. E. "OPT as an Enhancement to MRP II." *Production and Inventory Management* 27, no. 2(Second Quarter 1986):38–47.

Walleigh, Richard C. "Getting Things Done: What's Your Excuse for Not Using JIT?" *Harvard Business Review* 64, no. 2(March–April 1986):39–54.

Weiss, Andrew. "Simple Truths of Japanese Manufacturing." *Harvard Business Review* 62, no. 4(July–August 1984):119–125.

Wight, Oliver W. *Production and Inventory Management in the Computer Age.* Boston: Cahner's Books, 1974.

Zimmerman, H. J., and M. G. Sovereign. *Quantitative Models for Production Management.* Englewood Cliffs, NJ: Prentice-Hall, 1974.

13

MATERIALS MANAGEMENT AND PURCHASING

MOTOARC CENTRALIZES MATERIALS MANAGEMENT

Motoarc is an electronics, aerospace, electrical machinery, semiconductor, and computer products company. Its annual sales are $5.4 billion, it has manufacturing plants in 17 states and 12 foreign countries, and it employs 284,000 people worldwide. Although Motoarc's operations had expanded, its purchasing, warehousing, and shipping functions had lagged behind its other business units in effectiveness. Although a MRP system had been installed, problems with materials remained because no one seemed to be accountable when difficulties arose. For example, a recent order from a supplier arrived late at Motoarc's Indianapolis plant. Purchasing claimed that the warehouse did not place the order in time and that shipping gave the wrong shipping instructions to the supplier. The warehouse claimed that production control did not turn in the material requisition in time. Production control claimed that the requisition was turned in early enough, but that warehousing and purchasing sat on the order too long. Shipping claimed that the motor carrier lost the order for several days in Chicago, thus delaying delivery. Each function pointed an accusing finger at the other functions. Because of such difficulties, Motoarc has recently reorganized all of the materials management functions under a vice president of materials, who is responsible for all purchasing, logistics, warehousing, and expediting of materials in all divisions. Now the buck stops at the desk of the vice president of materials when any difficulties related to materials arise in any division of the company.

FIGURE 13.1   A Materials System in Manufacturing

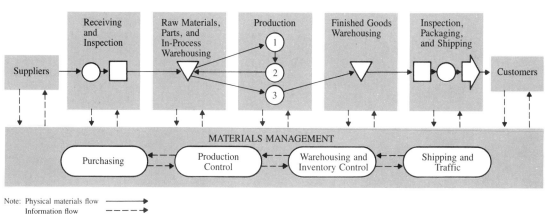

Note: Physical materials flow ———————▶
          Information flow   – – – – –▶

As the previous account illustrates, some companies today have reorganized their materials management functions under a top-level executive who is responsible for all activities related to materials. Such organizational changes focus management's attention on this function and underscore the importance of materials management.

Materials are any commodities used directly or indirectly in producing a product or service, such as raw materials, component parts, assemblies, and supplies. Managing materials in most companies is crucial to their success because the cost of buying, storing, moving, and shipping materials accounts for over half of a product's cost. Productivity basically means driving down the cost of doing business, and doing the job of materials management better is increasingly seen as the key to higher productivity in many U.S. firms today. Operations managers are working hard to develop better ways of managing materials so that costs can be controlled and so that their companies can survive in an increasingly competitive world.

A *materials system* is the network of material flows within a production system, including materials at suppliers, in transit from suppliers, in receiving, in raw materials warehouses, in in-process inventories, being processed in production departments, being moved between production operations, being inspected in quality control, in finished goods warehouses, and in transit to customers. In short, a materials system includes all of the materials present in the production system between the suppliers and the customers. Figure 13.1 illustrates a materials system of a manufacturing plant. Studying material flows—the acquisition, storage, movement, and processing of raw materials, components, assemblies, and supplies—is a good way to understand manufacturing. Also, services such as retailing, warehousing, and transportation companies can be viewed as systems of material flows. In these systems all organizational functions are critically affected by the planning and control of the materials system.

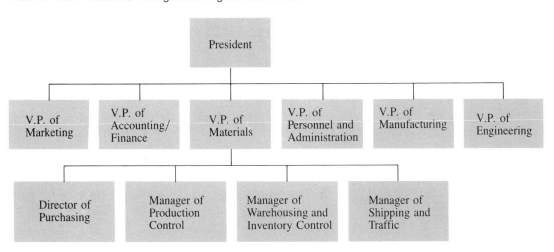

FIGURE 13.2 *Materials Management Organization Chart*

Materials management is all of the management functions related to the complete cycle of materials flows, from the purchase and internal control of materials to the planning and control of work in process to the warehousing, shipping, and distribution of the finished products.[1] Figure 13.2 illustrates how the materials management function fits into many organizations today. Some organizations have centralized their diverse materials management functions under one department headed by a *materials manager* or *vice president of materials.* This executive position coordinates all the activities of the materials system and bears total responsibility for the continuous supply of materials of low cost and specified quality when and where operating departments and customers require them. The responsibility of the materials manager is immense, a reality underscored by their typically high salaries, which rank with those of the highest industry positions.

It is important to recognize the relationship between the resource requirements planning system and materials management activities. Figure 13.3 illustrates the links between MPS, MRP, CRP, and certain materials management activities. For example, how do purchasing managers know when to place purchase orders for materials from suppliers? The planned order releases report provides this information. This report indicates the quantity and the date when every purchased material must be ordered if it is to be received in time to feed into the production operations without causing delays. Similarly, how does production control know when to issue move tickets to move orders from one operation to another in production? The routing plan indicates the path through the work centers that each order must follow,

---

[1] *APICS Dictionary,* 6th ed. (Falls Church, VA: American Production and Inventory Control Society, 1987), 18.

FIGURE 13.3 *Links between MPS, MRP, CRP, and Materials Management*

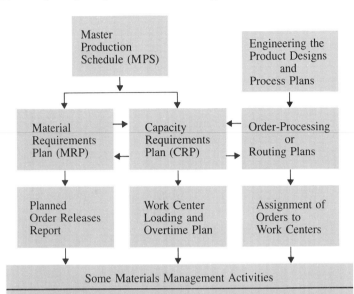

Master
Production
Schedule (MPS)

Engineering the
Product Designs
and
Process Plans

Material
Requirements
Plan (MRP)

Capacity
Requirements
Plan (CRP)

Order-Processing
or
Routing Plans

Planned
Order Releases
Report

Work Center
Loading and
Overtime Plan

Assignment of
Orders to
Work Centers

Some Materials Management Activities

1. Purchasing—Planned order releases report provides a schedule
   for ordering and receiving all materials from suppliers.
   Purchase orders are based on this quantity and timing information.
2. Production Control—Planned order releases report, routing
   plan, and scheduling decisions provide a timetable for the
   movement of orders between the production processes. Move
   tickets are issued to authorize physical movement of orders
   according to the routing plan.
3. Shipping and Traffic—Planned order releases report and
   scheduling decisions provide a timetable for shipment of
   customer orders. Purchase orders based on planned order
   releases report provide timetable for receipt of orders
   from suppliers.

and the planned order releases report indicates when and how many units of an order must be moved between work centers. Shipping and traffic know from the purchase orders when to plan shipments of materials from suppliers, and they know from the planned order releases report when to plan for shipments to customers. These and other important materials management activities occur naturally because of the information system provided by MPS, MRP, and CRP.

Materials management differs from organization to organization, but it usually includes these major activities—purchasing, logistics, warehousing, and expediting. These activities form the framework for studying the nature and scope of materials management.

PURCHASING

Purchasing departments buy the raw materials, purchased parts, machinery, supplies, and all other goods and services used in production systems — from paper clips to steel bar stock to computers. Stop and think about the immensity of this activity.

IMPORTANCE OF PURCHASING TODAY

Three factors are increasing the importance of purchasing today: the tremendous impact of material costs on profits, the increasing prominence of automated manufacturing, and increasing global competition.

On the average, about 60 percent of manufacturers' sales dollars are paid to suppliers for purchased materials. For example, automobile manufacturers spend about 60 percent of their revenues on material purchases, farm implement manufacturers spend about 65 percent, food processors spend about 70 percent, and oil refineries spend about 80 percent. And these percentages are going up.

As the automation of manufacturing continues, two developments enhance the importance of purchasing. First, it has been estimated that labor costs represent only about 10 to 15 percent of production costs in many mass production industries today. Some observers estimate that labor costs will decline to about 5 percent of production costs by the year 2000. It is thought, therefore, that in some industries labor costs will become almost trivial and material costs will become the central focus in the control of production costs. Second, automation requires rigid control of design, delivery schedules, and quality of purchased materials. In this setting, purchasing must establish and maintain vendor relations to ensure that materials of the right design and of perfect quality are delivered in the right quantities at the right times. Purchasing could be a key organization function affecting the success of automated manufacturing.

With the increase in global competition for world markets, all manufacturers are working hard to reduce production costs. The most lucrative area for this effort is in reducing materials costs. As the scope of business has expanded to global proportions, so the purchase of materials has moved to the world stage. Increasingly, materials are bought worldwide, transported to domestic and offshore manufacturing sites, and then shipped to markets throughout the world. This stretched-out supply chain has become necessary to offset increased competition for scarce materials. But the increased scope of supply has created an environment where materials are more subject to uncertain supply. This has also increased the importance of purchasing functions today.

Across the totality of our country's economy, the amount of annual expenditures for purchased materials is indeed staggering. Yet purchasing department employees represent less than 1 percent of the total employees of organizations. Can you think of a more influential group of employees whose performance is so critical to organizational success?

MISSION OF PURCHASING

The purchasing department is a key player in the achievement of a company's strategic objectives. It can affect fast delivery of products/services, on-time deliveries, production costs, and product/service quality, all of which are key elements in operations strategy. The mission of purchasing is to sense the competitive weapons necessary for each major product/service (low production costs, fast and on-time deliveries, high-quality products/services, and flexibility) and to develop purchasing plans for each major product/service that are consistent with operations strategies. One material, for example, may go into a product whose operations strategy calls for high volume, produce-to-stock production, and low production costs. For such a material, purchasing must emphasize developing suppliers that can produce the material at very low cost and in large quantities. On the other hand, another material may go into a product whose operations strategy calls for low volume, fast deliveries, high quality, and produce-to-order production. For this material, purchasing must emphasize fast response times by suppliers, very high quality, and dependable shipping schedules.

WHAT PURCHASING MANAGERS DO

Purchasing engages in these activities as it buys materials:

1. **Maintain a data base of available suppliers.** This data base includes information about the kinds of products that suppliers produce or are capable of producing, information about the quality of their products, and information about their costs or prices. An important aspect of maintaining this data base is the need to run periodic supplier surveys. These surveys include actual plant tours to assess the suppliers' ability to meet quantity, quality, and cost requirements.
2. **Select suppliers to supply each material.** This selection will ordinarily be based on several criteria. Price is important, of course, but quality, quantity, and promptness of deliveries may be of equal or greater importance.
3. **Negotiate supply contracts with suppliers.** This activity pins down the specific conditions that suppliers must adhere to as the materials are supplied. Such things as price, payment of freight charges, delivery schedule, quality standards, product specifications or performance standards, and payment terms are usually included in these contracts.
4. **Act as the interface between the company and its suppliers.** When production, engineering, accounting, production control, or quality control needs to communicate with a supplier, such communications must ordinarily go through purchasing. Similarly, all suppliers communicate with the company through purchasing.

Purchasing engages in these activities in most organizations, but the location of the purchasing department in organizations varies widely.

PURCHASING DEPARTMENTS IN ORGANIZATIONS

Purchasing departments can be located at any level of the organization hierarchy. The *manager of purchasing* or the *purchasing agent* may report to the president, vice president of materials, vice president of operations, plant manager, materials manager, or anyone in between. It is difficult to generalize about where purchasing will be assigned in the organization, except to say that its reporting level is generally directly related to the importance of its mission. In other words, if purchasing is critical to an organization's success — as with the large farm-implement manufacturer that spends 60 percent of its sales revenues on purchased materials — then we would expect to see the purchasing department report to a vice president of materials, vice president of operations, or even to the president. On the other hand, if purchasing has only a minor influence on organizational success, we would ordinarily expect the purchasing department to report relatively low in the organization, perhaps to the plant manager or manager of manufacturing.

Organizations tend to go through cycles of decentralization and centralization, and purchasing has been caught up in these cycles. The tendency toward centralization of purchasing today is probably encouraged by the advances both in communication between plants and divisions of companies and in the information-processing capabilities of computers. Among the advantages of centralization are:

1. Buying in larger quantities, which can mean better prices.
2. More clout with suppliers when materials are scarce, orders are delayed, or other supply difficulties are encountered. This clout translates into greater supply continuity.
3. Larger purchasing departments that can afford greater specialization of employees. For example, one buyer may specialize in buying only copper. This can lead to greater purchasing competence and lower material costs.
4. Combining small orders and thereby reducing duplication of orders, which can result in reduced clerical costs.
5. Reduction of transportation costs by combining orders and shipping larger quantities.
6. Better overall control and consistency of financial transactions.

On the other hand, operations managers often complain that centralized purchasing departments that do not report to them are slow, bureaucratic and cumbersome, and unresponsive to the needs of operations.

Large companies typically have centralized purchasing departments, particularly when the amount of annual purchases is large relative to revenues and when expert, technical purchasing knowledge is required. Additionally, even when other purchases are made at the plant level, the buying of large capital assets, such as expensive production machinery, is usually centralized because of the long-term nature of these assets and the amount of capital involved in their purchase.

Regardless of its organizational location, purchasing follows certain buying processes to acquire materials.

FIGURE 13.4   *Process of Acquiring Material Inputs*

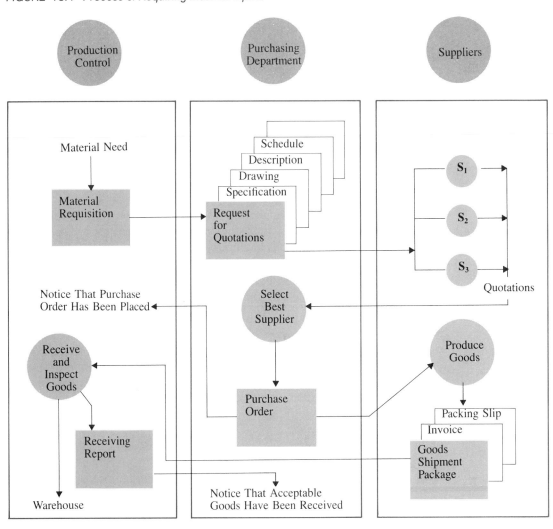

PURCHASING PROCESSES

Figures 13.4 and 13.5 illustrate the processes of acquiring materials and capital goods in production systems. These figures emphasize the interaction of the production department, purchasing department, finance department, and suppliers. Some variation of these procedures exists among organizations and among different types of goods.

FIGURE 13.5   *Process of Acquiring Capital Goods Inputs*

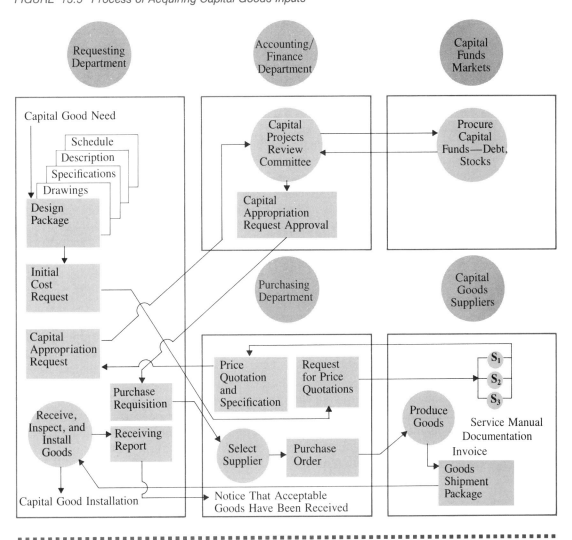

Basic Purchasing Instruments

The daily stock-in-trade of purchasing departments is material specifications, purchase requisitions, requests for quotation, and purchase orders. These instruments are fundamental to purchasing processes.

For every good to be purchased, the purchasing department must have a detailed description of that material. This detailed description is called a *material specification.* These instruments can include such descriptions as engineering drawings, chemical analyses, physical characteristics, and other details depending on the nature of the material. A material specification originates with the department requesting the material in its operations. Product engineers, process engineers, and other technical specialists of operations departments routinely supply purchasing departments with material specifications as products, parts of products, machinery, or other materials that will ultimately be purchased are designed. As these original designs are modified, revised material specifications are sent to the purchasing department so that the old specifications can be replaced with the new ones. *Value engineering* or *value analysis* is an activity that typically occurs jointly between purchasing and the technical specialists of production departments. This important activity is aimed at modifying the specifications of materials, parts, and products to reduce their costs while retaining their original function. Value engineering is a continuing activity within purchasing today because it provides companies with a way of holding the line on materials costs.

Material specifications are the fundamental means of communicating what materials production wants purchasing to buy and what purchasing authorizes suppliers to supply. Suppliers use the specifications to guide them in the production of the materials, and finally these same specifications become the basis for determining whether the requested materials were actually received. Material specifications are both the standards that purchasing buys to and the means of communication that guides the purchasing process.

Purchase requisitions originate with the departments that will use the materials. They authorize purchasing to buy the goods or services. The requisitions usually include: identification of what is to be purchased, amount to be purchased, requested delivery date or schedule, account to which the purchase cost is to be charged, where the purchased goods or services are to be delivered, and approval by the manager charged with authority to approve the purchase.

Requests for quotation are prepared by purchasing departments and sent to suppliers that are believed to be capable of meeting the cost, quality, and schedule requirements of the requesting departments. These instruments invite prospective suppliers to bid or quote on the goods or services. These forms usually include: material specification, quantity of purchase, delivery date or schedule desired, where goods or services are to be delivered, and date that supplier selection will be completed. Requests for quotation usually request the following from each prospective supplier: price per unit and total price, information on whether the supplier pays the freight charges, cash discounts and other terms of payment, delivery date or schedule, and any special conditions of the supplier.

Purchase orders are the most important purchasing instruments. They are the basis of the suppliers' authority to produce the goods or services, and they represent the buyers' obligation to pay for the items. A legal commitment by the buyer is present when a purchase order is issued in response to a quotation from a supplier. When a purchase order is issued in the absence of a request for a quotation, a legal commitment exists when a supplier acknowledges acceptance of the purchase order. These forms are usually designed to conform to the standards developed by the National Association of Purchasing Agents and the Division of Simplified Practice, National Bureau of Standards.

Purchase order forms usually include: purchase order number, quantity of the goods or services, material specifications, date and location for delivery, shipping and billing instructions, price per unit and total price, cash discount or other terms of payment, and any special terms of the purchase.

These instruments—specifications, requisitions, requests for quotation, and purchase orders—form the framework for the procedures of actually buying the goods or services.

Purchasing Procedures
Purchasing procedures differ depending on the nature of the good or service to be purchased. But these procedures tend to become more standardized as we classify the purchases into these homogeneous classes—high-volume continuously supplied materials, large unique purchases, small purchases, and regular purchases.

When materials are purchased in *high volume to be continuously supplied* throughout the year, purchasing departments typically issue requests for quotation to several prospective suppliers. When a supplier is selected, a *blanket purchase order* that covers the materials to be purchased for the entire year is issued. The authorization for purchasing departments to purchase these materials stems from the inclusion of these materials in their purchasing budgets. Purchasing budgets may be prepared months ahead and are based on approved production schedules.

When production departments need these materials, rather than issuing a purchase requisition to the purchasing department, a *release order* is sent directly to the supplier. The release order authorizes the supplier to ship a specific quantity of material in conformance to the original blanket purchase order. This procedure allows organizations to *tie up* suppliers for long-term supply arrangements, resulting in the likelihood of both quantity discounts and continuity of supply. Additionally, release orders can be processed quickly straight to the supplier, thereby reducing the possibility of needless delay in shipment. Suppliers usually like these release orders because the uncertainty of demand is reduced and better long-term production planning is possible.

Large computers, automated machinery, and consulting services are examples of *large unique purchases.* Although purchasing departments coordinate the overall procedures, as Figure 13.5 shows, their main function is to provide the interface between the technical specialists of the requesting department and the prospective suppliers. In these purchases price is often not the deciding factor in supplier selection. Instead, the ability to deliver quality goods and services on a timely basis and to meet unique technological requirements is critical to the eventual choice of supplier. In these situations purchasing departments bring the technical specialists who are requesting the purchase together with the prospective suppliers and coordinate the activities of these parties. Once the final supplier is selected, purchasing departments proceed to negotiate a contract with the supplier, and a purchase order is eventually issued.

Most purchasing departments do not wish to get involved with *small purchases* of such items as stationery supplies, blank checks, work gloves, and so on. These purchases are usually bought out of *petty cash accounts* by the originating departments directly from the supplier of their choice or from suppliers who hold *open purchase orders* that have been issued from the purchasing department. Under this latter arrangement the requesting department issues a *release order* to the supplier listing the items to be purchased, quantity requested, and date needed. The price and other conditions of sale are specified on the original open purchase order. Purchases from petty cash or releases of items on open purchase orders are usually limited to very small purchases, say $50 or less per order. Otherwise, they must be processed according to the procedures of regular purchases.

In *regular purchases* buyers in purchasing departments buy goods and services at the request of requesting departments. The procedure for these purchases is:

1.   The requesting department issues a purchase requisition to the purchasing department.
2.   The purchasing department issues requests for quotations to one or more suppliers.
3.   The suppliers submit quotations and a supplier is selected.
4.   A purchase order is issued by the purchasing department to the supplier.
5.   The supplier supplies the item to the requesting department.

Although the procedures for these various classes of purchases generally cover getting the goods and services to the requesting departments, the accounting department can pay for the items only after it has been notified by the requesting departments how much of the items received are of acceptable quality. The purchase order then becomes the basis for payment. One of the keys to the successful completion of these procedures is the competence of the buyers within purchasing departments.

BUYERS AND THEIR DUTIES

Buyers, as the name implies, do the buying in purchasing departments. They are typically specialized according to commodities. For example, one buyer may buy all ferrous metals, another may buy all nonferrous metals, and yet another may buy all machinery and tools. This specialization allows buyers to become experts at purchasing their particular commodities. To be effective, buyers must know both the manufacturing processes of their own companies and those of their supplier companies. This is typically possible only through specialization according to commodities.

Buyers must know their markets—the going prices of commodities and their availability. Additionally, they must be cost- and value-conscious, strong negotiators who constantly push for the lowest prices possible with their suppliers. Knowledge of the laws that govern their areas of responsibility in purchasing is also a must. Contract law, misrepresentation and fraud, infringement of patent rights, damage claims against suppliers, and shipping regulations are only a few of the areas where laws and regulations must be understood by buyers.

Buyers must interview salespersons who call on them daily. Because the buyers' time is precious, they must get the salespersons in and out as quickly as possible while maintaining a working relationship with the supplying organizations. They must be both courteous and expeditious in processing salespersons. This is a daily challenge. But from these interviews comes information concerning new products and new services that may be of great importance to future purchases. The buyers remain open to salespersons' suggestions and continually pass along important information about new developments to operations departments. This feedback is an important function of buyers.

Officially, buyers process purchase requisitions and requests for quotation, make supplier selections, place purchase orders, and follow up on purchase orders. Additionally, they negotiate prices and conditions of sale on open purchase orders, blanket purchase orders, adjustments to purchase orders, and all other purchasing contracts. Generally, all operations departments go through buyers to contact suppliers unless otherwise authorized by buyers to contact suppliers directly.

Buyers are the backbones of purchasing departments: They are in a unique position of very high visibility. As one vice president of operations recently stated: "The good news is that buyers can *make* you. The bad news is that buyers can *break* you. Competence among buyers can be the difference between being very profitable or folding."

MAKE-OR-BUY ANALYSIS

Not all requisitions for raw materials and parts that are received in purchasing departments are automatically ordered from suppliers. Production departments can often make parts in-house at lower cost, of higher quality, and with faster deliveries than would be possible in buying them from suppliers. On the other hand, because suppliers may specialize in certain types of production, some parts can be bought from these suppliers at lower cost, higher quality, and faster delivery times than would be possible if the company made them in-house. Buyers in purchasing departments, with assistance from engineers in production departments, routinely perform make-or-buy analyses for the raw materials and parts that go into existing products. In these instances they must ordinarily decide between the alternatives of vertically integrating and making a part in-house or buying the parts from outside suppliers. Example 13.1 illustrates a make-or-buy analysis in which an operations manager must decide between two different in-house production processes and buying the part from a supplier. This example serves only one purpose — to determine if the purchase cost of the part from a supplier is less than the production cost if the part were made in-house. In practice, such analyses must be accompanied by other considerations. For instance, which alternative offers the best combination of part cost, product quality, and on-time deliveries?

EXAMPLE 13.1   A Make-or-Buy Decision

Drasco, a medium-size manufacturer of oilfield pumps, is located in Houston, Texas. The firm has developed a new model of its high-pressure secondary-recovery purge pump with improved performance. Bonnie Nelson, manager of process engineering, is trying to decide whether

Drasco should make or buy the electronically controlled input valve for the new pump. Her engineers have developed the following estimates:

	Make (Process A)	Make (Process B)	Buy
Annual volume	10,000 units	10,000 units	10,000 units
Fixed cost/year	$100,000	$300,000	—
Variable cost/unit	$75	$70	$80

(a) Should Drasco make the valve using Process A, make the valve using Process B, or buy the valve? **(b)** At what annual volume should Drasco switch from buying to making the valve on Process A? **(c)** At what annual volume should Drasco switch from Process A to Process B?

Solution

a. Develop the annual cost of each alternative:

Total annual costs = Fixed costs + Volume (variable cost)

$$\text{Process A} = \$100{,}000 + 10{,}000\ (\$75) = \$850{,}000$$

$$\text{Process B} = \$300{,}000 + 10{,}000\ (\$70) = \$1{,}000{,}000$$

$$\text{Buy} = \$0 + 10{,}000\ (\$80) = \$800{,}000$$

If the annual volume is estimated to be stable at 10,000 units, Drasco should buy the valve.

b. At what annual volume should Drasco switch from buying to making the valve on Process A (Q = volume)?

Total annual cost using Process A = Total annual cost of buying

$$\$100{,}000 + Q(\$75) = Q(\$80)$$

$$\$5Q = \$100{,}000$$

$$Q = 20{,}000\ \text{units}$$

Drasco should switch when annual volume is greater than 20,000 units.

c. At what annual volume should Drasco switch from Process A to Process B (Q = annual volume, TC = total annual costs)?

$$TC_A = TC_B$$

$$\$100{,}000 + Q(\$75) = \$300{,}000 + Q(\$70)$$

$$\$5Q = \$200{,}000$$

$$Q = 40{,}000\ \text{units}$$

Drasco should switch when annual volume is greater than 40,000 units.

ETHICS IN BUYING

A nagging problem within purchasing departments is the question of ethics in buying. Salespersons deluge buyers with offers of free lunches, free liquor, free tickets to professional ball games, free evenings on the town, free weekends at resorts, and occasionally even free summer homes in the Sierras. These attempts at offering gifts to buyers raise the question of how much is too much. At what point do gifts to buyers become unethical? Buyers hold great power, sometimes even over the economic life or death of salespersons and their organizations. Furthermore, buyers are not always compensated equitably with their responsibilities. All the ingredients are present for temptation.

Some companies have laid down strict codes of conduct for buyers. Absolutely no gifts to buyers, no more than three bottles of liquor at Christmas, no gifts costing more than $25 per buyer per year from any one source, and no single gift exceeding $25 are examples of such rules of conduct. Policies covering gifts to company employees, whether they are buyers or not, certainly seem advisable. But perhaps more important is frequent communication within purchasing departments regarding what constitutes *ethical behavior.* The real worry here is that buyers may feel obligated to salespersons who have given them gifts and may not act in the best interests of their own organizations. This is a knotty problem that can start out small and grow to huge proportions. There is no solution other than diligence in keeping open the channels of communication and staying on top of problems to head off undesirable trends before the problems become irreversible. Generally, most companies strive to eliminate kickbacks, out-and-out bribes, and excessive gifts, which are carefully defined. Another good practice is the use of internal audits to ensure that a continuing organizational control of the purchasing function is provided.

Other unethical, illegal, or questionable buying activities include taking advantage of obvious clerical or computational errors in quotations, fixing prices, collusion among bidders, playing favorites among suppliers in awarding orders, failing to respect personal obligations, and upgrading product samples with the intention of supplying lower-grade products.

PURCHASING: THE EMERGING INTERNATIONAL FRONTIER

Increasingly, purchasing materials means intense involvement in international trade. For example, U.S. manufacturers in the electronics/computer industry buy materials from all over the world. This means that purchasing agents must engage in negotiations with companies in other countries. The laws of foreign countries, currency exchange rates, cultural differences, and a host of other factors affect these purchases. Additionally, purchasing agents and other personnel routinely travel to foreign countries in the process of selecting vendors and awarding supply contracts. Because these purchases are complex and because much is riding on the success of these activities, organizations must select, develop, and reward purchasing personnel accordingly.

Purchasing is experiencing an increasing emphasis in organizations today: "Purchasing is an emerging frontier. Purchasing will be receiving greater organizational recognition due to increasing concerns regarding worldwide depletion of natural resources, spot shortages, increasing energy costs, changes in the relative costs of purchased items from country to country, ethical issues, and the increasing awareness of the need to maintain competitive position by better purchasing and materials management."[2]

These and other developments make the field of purchasing a challenging one for professional managers to consider for future jobs. You may too. Look at the classified ads in your local urban newspapers; you may be surprised at the job opportunities in purchasing.

JUST-IN-TIME (JIT) PURCHASING

In Chapter 12 we discussed Just-in-Time (JIT) production systems. JIT purchasing is an important part of these systems. The essential elements of JIT purchasing are:

1. *Vendor development* and *vendor relations* undergo fundamental changes. The nature of the relationships between customers and suppliers shifts from being adversarial to being cooperative. The Japanese call these relationships *subcontractor networks* and refer to suppliers as *coproducers.* Sensitive information, assistance in reducing costs and improving quality, and even financing are often shared by customers and suppliers.
2. Purchasing departments develop long-term relationships with suppliers. The result is long-term supply contracts with a few suppliers rather than short-term supply contracts with many suppliers. Repeat business is awarded to the same suppliers, and competitive bidding is ordinarily limited to new parts.
3. Although price is important, delivery schedules, product quality, and mutual trust and cooperation become the primary basis for supplier selection.
4. Suppliers are encouraged to extend JIT methods to their own suppliers.
5. Suppliers are ordinarily located near the buying firm's factory or if they are some distance from the factory, they are usually clustered together. This causes lead times to be shorter and more reliable.
6. Shipments are delivered directly to the customer's production line. Because suppliers are encouraged to produce and supply parts at a steady rate that matches the use rate of the buying firm, company-owned hauling equipment tends to be preferred.
7. Parts are delivered in small standard-size containers with a minimum of paperwork and in exact quantities.
8. Delivered material is of near-perfect quality. Because suppliers have a long-term relationship with the buying firms and because parts are delivered in small lot sizes, the quality of purchased materials tends to be higher.

---

[2] Robert M. Monczka, "The Purchasing Frontier," *Perspectives* 5(Fall 1977): 2–4.

INDUSTRY SNAPSHOT 13.1

JIT Purchasing at Woodbridge Group

The Woodbridge Group in Wilmington, Delaware, manufactures car seats for a nearby automobile manufacturer. The factory has a three-and-a-half hour turnaround from the time an order is received to the time the part is installed in a car. It operates with zero finished goods inventory and a two- to three-day raw material supply. The plant receives a weekly electronic communication from the automaker that forecasts the customer's requirements for the next 12 weeks. Another communication is received every day at 5 a.m. telling Woodbridge how many vehicles the automaker will produce in the next 10 to 14 days. In addition, a continuous communication is broadcast every 54 seconds informing Woodbridge of the actual sequence and specifications of the seats needed in the next three hours.

When Woodbridge gets the weekly forecast, it runs it through MRP, issues a 12-week shipping forecast, and electronically sends this to its suppliers. This forecast tells the suppliers what Woodbridge is going to be producing for the next 12 weeks so that the suppliers can order their raw material. Thus the suppliers also carry as little inventory as possible.

The automaker's 54-second communication represents changes to its previous production plans. Woodbridge processes this information through MRP and sends it to its suppliers so that they know which materials in which sequence are needed by Woodbridge at any point in time.

Woodbridge groups the automaker's orders into truckloads. The system then issues bar-coded orders to the shop floor in reverse order of the customer's requirements so that the last seat built and loaded is the first seat needed on the assembly line. When Woodbridge ships a truckload to the automaker, the system electronically issues a shipping notice and an invoice to the customer, automatically relieves the inventory used in production, and updates production, accounts receivable, and shipping records.[3]

---

[3] "JIT Aids Woodbridge Group," *P&IM Review* (March 1988): 35.

Industry Snapshot 13.1 discusses how one firm is experiencing success with JIT purchasing. U.S. firms seem to be adopting many of the practices of JIT purchasing, but whether they can totally adopt these methods is in doubt. Industry Snapshot 13.2 discusses this issue.

Although the whole JIT purchasing package may not yet be accepted by U.S. manufacturers, their purchasing practices are being affected by JIT, and a U.S.–JIT hybrid seems to be developing that fits the unique U.S. purchasing environment. For example, the General Motors and Toyota joint venture operation in Fremont, California, places daily orders with Midwestern suppliers of materials. These suppliers ship their materials to a staging area at a railroad yard in the Midwest. There the materials are loaded onto trains, in the sequence that they will be used in production, for overnight delivery to the factory.

INDUSTRY SNAPSHOT 13.2

Obstacles to U.S. Adoption of JIT Purchasing

Robert E. Todd, president of the National Association of Purchasing Management, says: "Just-in-time delivery is best suited to an assembly line, where the truck pulls up 15 minutes before it's needed. It's been adopted by the automotive industry, most notably at General Motors' Buick City complex in Michigan, which clusters the auto plant with a steel distributor and other suppliers. It has been less applicable to oil, gas, and other industries that are more capital-intensive. It won't be as successful as the Japanese because they have smaller distances involved and because American buyers are more geared to more open competition and finding the lowest price. Still, buyers have reduced the number of suppliers and there's a recognition of the need to build closer ties. Buyers are also placing more demands on suppliers to put the shipment on the dock defect-free. Getting a supplier to deliver the right material at the right time may require sharing production plans or new-product strategies—information that might once have been kept closely guarded."[4]

---

[4] "Many U.S. Industries Correcting Buying Sins," *Houston Chronicle,* Apr. 11, 1985, sec. 3, 2.

Once the materials are bought, materials managers must then decide the least expensive and most effective method of shipping those materials to their organizations. Similarly, how to ship finished goods to customers is a critical question. These issues are central to the important materials management activity of logistics.

LOGISTICS

Logistics is the management of the movement of materials within the factory, the shipment of incoming materials from suppliers, and the shipment of outgoing products to customers.

MOVEMENT OF MATERIALS WITHIN FACTORIES

The movement of materials within the factory includes:

1. Removing materials from incoming vehicles and placing them on the receiving dock.
2. Moving materials from the receiving dock to inspection.
3. Moving materials from inspection to the warehouse and storing them until needed.
4. Retrieving materials from the warehouse and delivering them to production operations when needed.

5. Moving materials between production operations.
6. Moving finished products from final assembly and storing them in the finished goods warehouse.
7. Retrieving finished goods from the finished goods warehouse and delivering them to packaging and shipping.
8. Moving packaged finished goods to the shipping dock.
9. Loading finished goods into outgoing vehicles at the shipping dock.

The transportation of materials in services includes the type of movements described in Nos. 1–5 above, but usually not the type of movements described in Nos. 6–9. Materials are transported with all types of equipment from hand baskets to hand trucks to belt conveyors to forklift trucks to robotic carriers known as automated guided vehicle systems (AGVS).

The management of the movement of materials within the factory may involve decisions about how to route batches of materials between departments. In Chapter 7 we discussed how linear programming can assist operations managers in making such decisions when many materials originate at several work centers and must be delivered to several destination work centers. The objective of these decisions is to determine the network of material movements among departments that minimizes materials-handling costs and satisfies the production capacities of the work centers.

All of these movements of materials are coordinated by production control personnel and are critical to effective operations management.

SHIPMENTS TO AND FROM FACTORIES

Traffic departments in organizations routinely examine shipping schedules and select shipping methods, time tables, and ways of expediting deliveries. The shipping costs to today's organizations represent such a huge proportion of costs that manufacturing plants, warehouses, and other facilities are located with one overriding thought in mind: Minimize incoming and outgoing shipping costs. In spite of these efforts, shipping costs alone can account for 50 percent or more of the sales price of some manufactured items.

The enormity of these expenditures has increasingly motivated organizations to staff traffic departments with professional managers and operations analysts who continually search for better shipping techniques. Additionally, many companies have entered the transportation business (sometimes called *vertical backward and forward integration*), when economically feasible, in order to reduce their freight bills.

Industry Snapshot 13.3 demonstrates the savings that are possible through better logistics management. If this small manufacturer saved $175,000 annually in freight costs, think what large organizations could accomplish.

Traffic management is a specialized field requiring intensive technical training in the Department of Transportation (DOT) and the Interstate Commerce Commission (ICC) regulations and freight rates. This patchwork of *regs and rates* forms the complex constraints with which logistics experts must work in attacking shipping costs. They must know the ins and outs of this complicated and changing field.

INDUSTRY SNAPSHOT 13.3

Flash Inc. Manufacturing Plant: Reducing Freight Costs

A small plant in northern California, Flash Inc., got a new plant manager. Upon examining the operating budgets for the plant, the new manager discovered that over $325,000 per year was being spent on incoming and outgoing freight. He immediately initiated a study of shipping methods and found that all shipping method decisions were being made by two clerks, a shipping clerk in the finished goods warehouse and an office clerk in the ordering department. Almost no materials or finished goods were shipped in whole carload or truckload quantities. Shipments were allocated to several trucklines to keep them happy. Additionally, no effort was made to develop unitized loading of goods and other means of reducing freight costs.

Two months later a new materials manager had turned the situation around. Whole carloads and whole truckloads now accounted for 75 percent of incoming and outgoing shipments. Furthermore, the lowest-cost form of shipment was utilized when feasible—for example, rail rather than truck and water rather than rail. Additionally, palletizing and other means of unitizing loads qualified the company for the lowest possible freight rates.

The result was indeed overwhelming to the new plant manager, who had hired the new materials manager: Annual savings were $175,000 even after deducting the total expenses of the new materials manager's office.

Distribution Management

Distribution is the shipment of goods through the distribution system to customers. A *distribution system* is the network of shipping and receiving points starting with the factory and ending with the customers. Shipments of goods through distribution systems may or may not be under the direct control of a materials manager. In some companies the responsibility for managing the distribution system lies with the marketing function.

Distribution Requirements Planning (DRP)

Distribution requirements planning is the planning for the replenishment of regional warehouse inventories by using MRP-type logic to translate regional warehouse requirements into main-distribution-center requirements, which are then translated into gross requirements in the MPS at the factory. Example 13.2 illustrates the logic of distribution requirements planning.

Distribution resource planning extends distribution requirements planning so that the key resources of warehouse space, number of workers, cash, shipping vehicles, and the like are provided in the right quantities and when needed to satisfy customers' demands.

Using Linear Programming to Analyze Shipping Decisions

In Chapter 7 we discussed using linear programming to solve transportation problems. Example 7.6 illustrated how to *formulate* a linear programming problem to

EXAMPLE 13.2   Distribution Requirements Planning (DRP)

A company has two regional warehouses that are supplied products from a main distribution center at the factory. The DRP time-phased order point records below illustrate how the planned order releases to the factory from the center are determined for a particular product. The planned order releases to the factory become the gross requirements in the master production schedule (MPS) of the factory.

Regional Warehouse #1
Lead time for shipping products from the main distribution center at the factory to Warehouse #1 is 1 week, the standard shipping quantity is 50 units, and the safety stock is 10 units.

		Week				
	−1	1	2	3	4	5
Forecast demand (units)		30	40	30	40	40
Scheduled receipts		50				
Projected ending inventory	60	80	40	10	20	30
Planned receipt of shipments					50	50
Planned orders for shipments				50	50	

Regional Warehouse #2
Lead time for shipping products from the main distribution center at the factory to Warehouse #2 is 2 weeks, the standard shipping quantity is 60 units, and the safety stock is 15 units.

		Week				
	−1	1	2	3	4	5
Forecast demand (units)		70	80	50	60	50
Scheduled receipts		60				
Projected ending inventory	110	100	20	30	30	40
Planned receipt of shipments				60	60	60
Planned orders for shipments		60	60	60		

Main Distribution Center at the Factory
Lead time for final assembling of products and moving them into the main distribution center is 1 week, the standard production lot size is 200 units, and the safety stock is 40 units.

		Week				
	−1	1	2	3	4	5
Gross requirements (units)		60	60	110	50	
Scheduled receipts						
Projected ending inventory	110	50	190	80	230	230
Planned receipt of orders			200		200	
Planned order releases to factory		**200**		**200**		

INDUSTRY SNAPSHOT 13.4

Trucking Firms Use Computers

If ever there was an industry with a low-tech image, trucking is it: The popular picture of blacktop cowboys punching big rigs down the nation's highways doesn't include video display terminals. But many trucking companies are being driven to more and more computerization because of competitive pressures that have built since the industry was deregulated in 1980.

The use of computers in the financial end of the business is not new. What is new is applying computers to the daily management of trucking operations. With computers, dispatchers can determine the best routes for their trucks; dockworkers can figure out the most efficient way to unload a truck; and drivers can stay in closer contact with their home offices. Skyway Freight Systems of Santa Cruz, California, uses computers to track shipments constantly, and it gives its customers access to the company's computer system so that they can track their own shipments. But Skyway's specialty is *JIT shipping,* which allows companies to hold down shipping and inventory costs by ensuring that "a shipment arrives no later than it is needed in the production process and no sooner than it can be handled efficiently." Computers categorize supplies according to when they are needed for production, and they dictate different methods of transportation depending on how soon the supplies will be used. Among other things, Skyway's system can tap into the National Weather Bureau and the Federal Aviation Agency's weather service to determine if bad weather might delay commercial airline service or slow highway traffic.

Carrier Logistics has developed a set of computer software that finds the most effective route for a truck to take, even in city traffic. Another of Carrier's computer software packages helps a company determine at which loading-dock door to unload a truck so that materials from the truck can most efficiently be separated and transferred to nearby trucks.

While computers are not a panacea for a trucking company's problems, they can assist operations managers in achieving higher profitability and greater productivity.[5]

---

[5] Nancy Rivera Brooks, "Trucking Firms Utilize Computers," *Los Angeles Times,* appeared in *Houston Chronicle,* Aug. 3, 1986, sec. 5, 16.

---

determine the monthly plan for shipping a product from several plants to several customers. The objective of the example was to minimize monthly shipping costs subject to the monthly plant capacities and the monthly requirements of the customers. Examples E.4, E.5, and E.6 in Appendix E illustrate how such transportation problems can be *solved* by using the transportation method of linear programming. Perhaps it will help you to understand these shipping decisions better if you review these examples at this time.

Linear programming minimizes the total costs of shipping products from several manufacturing plants to several warehouses or customers. These complex shipping problems can be and are analyzed routinely by standard computer programs. Because of the great outlay for freight costs and the resulting savings possible through intensive analysis, the quantitative analysis of shipping problems will undoubtedly continue to grow.

COMPUTER APPLICATIONS IN LOGISTICS

New developments are continually affecting logistics. Piggyback rail shipments, truck trailers on ships, and other unique shipping methods are examples of hybrids that have resulted in great freight savings. Lighter-weight shipping containers, unitized loads, drop shipping, in-transit rates, consolidated shipments, deregulation of the trucking and air-freight industries, and fluctuating fuel costs are examples of developments that are affecting logistics today, and new ones are arising every day. With the prevalence of computers in today's organizations, up-to-the-minute information is available on the status of each shipment. Additionally, in complicated distribution problems, the computer can be used to plan better networks of shipping methods. Industry Snapshot 13.4 discusses the use of the computer in the trucking industry.

Integral to logistics are methods of warehousing materials and products once they are received from suppliers and before they are shipped to customers.

WAREHOUSING

Warehousing is the management of materials while they are in storage. It includes storing, dispersing, ordering, and accounting for all materials and finished goods from the beginning to the end of the production process. Warehousing facilities may range from small stockrooms to large, highly mechanized storage facilities for raw materials and finished goods.

WAREHOUSING OPERATIONS

Warehousing deals primarily with materials that directly support operations. The first problems that must be addressed are when to place an order for each material and how much to order. Orders are placed and shipments eventually appear in the receiving department, usually by either truck trailers or railroad cars.

Materials are routinely unloaded from delivery vehicles and held in temporary storage areas until quality control has tested them, confirmed their acceptability for use in operations, and released them. Materials-handling equipment such as forklift trucks, conveyors, straddle trucks, and pump-forced pipelines are used to place the materials into *raw materials inventory*. This inventory is stored on pallets (a small base frame on which bags and boxes of material are stacked), in high stacks, in storage tanks, or other means of holding raw materials. The raw materials inventory is the reservoir of materials that operations use as required to begin the production process.

In some firms, such as chemical-processing plants, bulk materials are used as needed by operations departments without asking warehousing. In other facilities, however, a *stock requisition* is prepared by production control and forwarded to warehousing, requesting that materials be delivered to specific locations within production departments. In production systems that use process layouts, where material moves intermittently through the facilities, *in-process inventories* are usually maintained. These partially completed products that are between processes are located at various designated locations throughout the production system.

Warehousing may or may not be responsible for accounting for these in-process inventories, managing their movement, receiving and disbursing them, and controlling what materials are put in and taken out. If the time that materials are in in-process inventory is short, production usually retains control. If the time delay is long, however, or if other prevailing reasons exist, such as safety, government regulation, and so on, warehousing takes charge and maintains storerooms at various points within the production system.

In systems that use product layouts, where material moves continuously through the facilities, in-process inventories are rare, and therefore production maintains control of the in-process materials until they become finished products. At that point, after the materials have been transformed into finished goods inventory, they are relinquished to the finished goods warehouse.

The record keeping within warehousing requires a *stock record* for each item that is carried in inventories. The individual item is called a *stock-keeping unit (SKU)*. Stock records are running accounts that show the on-hand balance, receipts, disbursements, and any other changes that actually affect the usable on-hand balance for each SKU. Additionally, stock records may show expected receipts, promises, or allocations of SKUs even though they are still in inventory. Computers have allowed managers to improve the accuracy of these records, post changes to records more frequently as they occur, and have on-hand balance information instantaneously. Inventory record keeping was one of the first areas within large companies to be widely computerized in the 1960s, and this trend is continuing on down even to small companies today.

METHODS OF INVENTORY ACCOUNTING

For hundreds of years inventory accounting was based on *periodic inventory accounting systems,* or periodic updating of manual stock records, and *physical inventory counts.* Stock records were updated by periodically (usually at the end of every workday) entering, by hand on cards filed in trays, the number of units added to and taken from inventory. If one wanted to know the number of units on hand of a particular material in inventory, one would go to the card tray, pull the material's stock record card, and see the inventory balance as of the last update. The accuracy of these systems depended on how often the stock records were updated and on how often the information on the stock records was verified or corrected through physical inventory counts. The more frequent the correction and the updating of the stock records, the more accurate was the information on the stock records. The annual or "end-of-the-year" physical inventory counts, in which all materials in the warehouses were physically counted, were traditional in many industries. Some companies today still use this type of inventory accounting because it is either more economical or the only feasible way to account for inventory.

Increasingly, however, firms are using *perpetual inventory-accounting systems* in which stock records are maintained in computers. In such systems stock records, rather than being periodically updated, are updated at the time materials are received into or dispensed from inventory. The time lag between the last updating of the stock records and the time the records are accessed to determine the inventory balance is practically eliminated. These records are also subject to error, however, and they too must be verified or corrected. It is customary today to use cycle counting to maintain stock record accuracy in perpetual inventory-accounting systems.

Cycle counting is an ongoing effort to count the number of units of each material in inventory, compare this number to the balance shown on stock records, and reconcile the difference. The twofold purpose of cycle counting is to correct the stock records and, more importantly, to identify shortcomings in all areas of the inventory system and initiate corrective actions. In cycle counting, *when* a material is counted is determined by a counting schedule for that material. A material may be counted when it reaches its reorder point, when a shipment of the material is received, or at a particular time interval.

High-value, fast-moving materials (such as Class A materials from Chapter 10, Figure 10.10) tend to be counted more frequently. But, how often we count an inventory item (monthly, quarterly, etc.) should depend on two factors: the history of the item's inaccuracies and the difficulties caused if an item's counts are inaccurate. An item that has a history of inaccurate counts and one that will cause big problems in production if counts are inaccurate should be counted more frequently. Fast-moving items that have inaccurate counts usually cause great difficulties in production because they appear in production schedules more often. And when they do appear, the count can cause major changes in the master production schedules, expediting, split orders, panic shipment procedures, extra transportation and production costs, and confusion on the shop floor.

In cycle counting, a specially trained crew of workers counts some materials every working day, and stock records are verified or corrected on an ongoing basis. The ultimate goal of cycle counting is to reduce the inaccuracy of stock records to a very small percentage. Since it is estimated that MRP systems require stock records that are accurate to within $\pm .5$ percent, cycle counting is an important part of MRP systems. Example 13.3 illustrates a common situation associated with cycle counting.

EXAMPLE 13.3   Number of Cycle-Counting Personnel Required

A company wants to improve the accuracy of the stock records used in its MRP system. A consultant has recommended that all Class A materials be counted an average of 24 times per year, all Class B materials be counted an average of 6 times per year, and all Class C materials be counted an average of 2 times per year. The consultant estimates that an experienced and well-trained cycle counter can count an average of 20 materials a day. The company works 260 days per year and it has determined that it has 1,000 A materials, 3,000 B materials, and 6,000 C materials. How many workers would be required to perform cycle counting?

Solution

Class of Materials	Number of Materials per Class	Number of Counts per Material per Year		Total Counts per Year
A	1,000	24		24,000
B	3,000	6		18,000
C	6,000	2		12,000
			Total	54,000

$$\text{Number of materials counted per day} = \frac{\text{Total counts per year}}{\text{Number of work days per year}}$$

$$= \frac{54,000}{260} = 207.7$$

$$\text{Number of counters required} = \frac{\text{Number of materials counted per day}}{\text{Number of materials per day per counter}}$$

$$= \frac{207.7}{20} = 10.4, \text{ or } 11 \text{ counters}$$

CONTEMPORARY DEVELOPMENTS IN WAREHOUSING

New developments are continuously modifying the management of warehousing systems. Advances in computing systems are allowing on-line instantaneous record-keeping transactions. The automatic registering of products and prices at grocery stores is an example of these developments. Inventories are automatically adjusted as groceries are bought. Managers can remotely query the computing system and obtain instantaneous inventory balances. Motorola, Honeywell, Westinghouse, and other companies already have similar on-line systems for keeping stock records for all SKUs. Ralston Purina and Westinghouse have almost totally removed the human element from the physical movement and storage of materials at some of their newer locations. These automated storage and retrieval systems (ASRS) remove materials from raw materials inventory, make up batches of complete material orders, and deliver them to the appropriate points within the production system, all without being touched by human hands. (See Table 1.5 in Chapter 1 for a description of these systems.) Other automated systems similarly assemble shipping orders and move them to shipping areas. These and other developments promise to make warehousing even more effective in the future in meeting the quantity and scheduling needs of customers and operations departments.

In spite of the advances made in computing systems, the establishment of materials manager positions, and centralization of materials management functions for greater control, foul-ups still occur. Materials are not where they should be when they are needed, a stockout occurs, or a stockout is anticipated. When these or similar situations arise, *and they do in all systems,* materials must be expedited.

EXPEDITING

Expediting is the focusing of one or more persons' attention on a particular order or batch of materials for the purpose of speeding up the order through all or part of the entire materials system. *De-expediting* means slowing down an order. Expediting or de-expediting is necessary usually because unforeseen events have caused an order for materials or products to be likely to be late or early. Examples of some of these events are:

1. A customer increased the quantity of products ordered. The expanded order quantity now exceeds finished goods inventory, and additional products must be quickly produced.
2. A supplier fails to ship an order for materials when promised. Emergency shipping procedures must be employed in order to get the parts in-house in time to avoid a stockout or disruption of the production processes.
3. Parts being processed in heat treat have encountered technical difficulties. The batch must be quickly transferred ahead of other materials if the annealing process is not to be delayed.

Expediting most often is necessary because of the uncertainties present in production systems; customer demand, material delivery times, and in-house processing times are but a few of these uncertainties. Materials management must be flexible enough to accommodate these uncertainties by reacting quickly when the unexpected happens. Expediting is periodically performed by all materials management employees, and this activity helps make materials systems flexible.

Some managers and their organizations routinely operate by crisis management. *Every* activity is expedited. This approach to management is an excuse for poor planning, poor procedures, and poor management in general. When expediting becomes the dominant activity in materials management, something is wrong. Everyone and every production system makes mistakes, and these mistakes can create the need for expediting when materials managers, buyers, warehousing managers, logistics personnel, or others in the materials system foul up. But expediting should be the exception to the rule, not the rule.

Expediting completes the materials cycle that proceeds from acquisition of materials to the delivery of finished goods into customers' hands. The means to change procedures, override policy, make telephone calls and collect past favors, devise quick solutions as they occur, and other tactics of expediting are some of the important ways that managers make materials systems work effectively and get the right quantity of the right material to the right place at the right time.

■■

TABLE 13.1   *Evaluating Materials Managers in Manufacturing*

Performance Criteria	*Percentage of Materials Managers Evaluated*
1. The level and value of in-house inventories	87%
2. The percentage of orders that are delivered to customers on time	80
3. The number and severity of stockouts in in-house inventories	71
4. The annual costs of materials purchased from suppliers	69
5. The annual costs of transportation for materials from suppliers and for products to customers	53
6. The annual costs of operating warehouses	29
7. The number of customer complaints about poor service	27
8. Other factors such as profitability and manufacturing costs	7–20

■■

Source: Jeffery G. Miller and Peter Gilmour, "Materials Managers: Who Needs Them?" *Harvard Business Review* 57, no. 4(July–August 1979), 151.

MEASURING THE PERFORMANCE OF MATERIALS MANAGERS

Given the importance of materials management today, how do organizations measure how well materials managers are doing their jobs? Table 13.1 shows how 137 materials managers are evaluated in manufacturing companies. From this table we can see that companies want to control the level of their inventories, meet customer delivery dates, control the number and severity of stockouts, and control the costs of purchased materials, transportation, and warehousing. These criteria for measuring the performance of materials management reflect the goals that organizations have for materials management.

SUMMARY

Materials management encompasses all of the management functions related to the complete cycle of material flows from suppliers to customers. It includes purchasing, logistics, warehousing, and expediting.

Purchasing departments buy the raw materials, parts, machinery, supplies, and services used by production systems. Purchasing must maintain a data base of available suppliers, select suppliers to supply all materials, negotiate supply contracts with suppliers, and act as the interface between the company and its suppliers. Buyers do the buying in purchasing departments. They frequently perform make-or-buy analyses to determine if a material should be made in-house or bought from a supplier.

Just-in-Time (JIT) purchasing is a set of purchasing methods that are increasingly being used by U.S. manufacturers. Fundamental changes to traditional purchasing methods are required in JIT. Suppliers are viewed as coproducers; long-term supply contracts with fewer suppliers; suppliers being chosen on the basis of delivery schedules, product quality, mutual trust and cooperation; and frequent shipments delivered directly to production lines—all are elements of JIT purchasing.

Logistics is the management of the movement of materials within the factory, the shipment of incoming materials from suppliers, and the shipment of outgoing products to customers. Production control departments guide the movement of materials within factories. Shipping and traffic departments guide the shipment of incoming materials and outgoing products. The management of the shipment of products through the distribution system is referred to as distribution management. Distribution requirements planning (DRP) is the planning for the replenishment of regional warehouse inventories by using MRP-type logic. Shipping decisions are perhaps the most analyzed of all of the materials management problems.

Warehousing is the management of materials while they are in storage. It includes storing, dispersing, ordering, and accounting for all materials. Stock records and the means of updating and correcting them are the heart of warehouse information systems. Firms may use either periodically updated manual stock records that are corrected by physical inventory counts or computerized stock records that are corrected by cycle counting.

Expediting is the act of speeding up or slowing down orders or the processing of batches of materials. It is necessary because of the uncertainties that exist in production systems—customer demand, material delivery times, and in-house processing times. Materials managers are evaluated on these criteria: levels of inventories, customer satisfaction, number and severity of stockouts, costs of purchased material, costs of shipping materials and products, and costs of operating warehouses.

REVIEW AND DISCUSSION QUESTIONS

1. Define these terms: *a material, materials system, materials management.*

2. What is the mission of purchasing? What factors are making purchasing more important today? Explain. In what activities does purchasing engage?

3. Explain the relationship between MRP and materials management. What is the link between purchasing and MRP? What is the link between production control and MRP? What is the link between shipping and traffic departments and MRP?

4. Define these terms: *material specification, purchase requisition, request for quotation, purchase order.*

5. What is vertical integration? Define *make-or-buy analysis.*

6. What is Just-in-Time (JIT) purchasing? What are the elements of JIT purchasing? What are the obstacles to its full adoption by U.S. firms? What are some ways of overcoming these obstacles?

7. What practices of purchasing departments are considered unethical? How can companies prevent or control unethical purchasing practices?

8. Define these terms: *logistics, distribution management, distribution requirements planning (DRP).*

9. List the activities included in logistics within a factory.

10. Define these terms: *warehousing, raw materials inventory, stock requisition, in-process inventory, stock record, stock-keeping unit (SKU).*

11. Describe two methods of inventory accounting. Define *cycle counting* and explain its purpose. What factors would necessitate counting a material more frequently?

12. Why do firms occasionally have to expedite orders for materials? Does expediting occur only when materials managers foul up?

13. List the most important criteria used in evaluating materials managers.

FIELD PROJECTS IN MATERIALS MANAGEMENT

1. Make an appointment with a materials manager or a manager directly affiliated with a materials system from one of these types of organizations:
   a. manufacturing—assembly line, such as garment making,
   b. manufacturing—continuous, such as chemical processing,
   c. health care,
   d. retailing,
   e. trucking, or
   f. warehousing.
   Interview this manager and describe in detail the three most important materials problems that plague his or her organization.

2. From any organization, interview one person from this list:
   a. purchasing agent,
   b. purchasing buyer,
   c. traffic or logistics manager,
   d. warehousing manager, or
   e. expediter.
   Describe as completely as possible this person's duties as he or she perceives them.

3. Interview a purchasing buyer from any organization. Determine the buyer's idea of what is and what is not ethical buying behavior in regard to gifts. Do you agree or disagree with his or her point of view? Why?

4. From any organization, interview one person from this list:
   a. purchasing agent,
   b. traffic or logistics manager,
   c. warehouse manager, or
   d. expediter.
   What new developments are expected to have an important effect on the performance of this employee's duties within the next five years? How will the person's duties be affected by these developments? To what extent has JIT purchasing practices been implemented in the employee's firm?

5. Investigate any manufacturing organization and gather information about its materials system. Prepare a flowchart similar to Figure 13.1, but with more details, that depicts the organization's materials system.

6. Investigate any firm to determine how the materials management function fits into its organization. Prepare an organization chart similar to Figure 13.2 for the firm.

PROBLEMS

7. A company produces a product that needs heat treating. A buyer in the purchasing department is trying to decide whether to buy the heat-treating service from a supplier or to recommend that the firm's production department gear up to do its own in-house heat treating. The buyer has developed the following estimates:

	Heat Treat In-House	Purchase Heat-Treating Service
Number of parts needing heat treating per year	5,000	5,000
Fixed cost per year	$25,000	$0
Variable cost per part	$13.40	$17.50

If product quality and delivery performance are about the same for the make-or-buy alternatives, should the company buy the heat-treating service?

8. Joseph Ortega is a materials buyer at the El Paso, Texas, plant of Computer Products Corporation (CPC). He is now reviewing the quotations from suppliers for a paper spacer used in shipping XT personal computers. Joseph plans either to place an order for 10,000 of the components from the supplier with the least-cost quotation or to make the components in CPC's El Paso plant. Relevant data for this make-or-buy decision are found below. Should CPC make or buy the component?

Source of the Component	Fixed Cost per Order	Variable Cost per Unit
Make	$2,000	$ .89
Buy	1,500	1.05

9. John Morton, director of materials management for Computer Products Corporation (CPC) in San Jose, is now reviewing next year's plans for the supply of a component that is now purchased from Osiega Ltd., a company in Japan. The component is the PS100 power supply assembly that is used in many of CPC's products. CPC pays the supplier more than $7 million per year for these units, and John wonders if money could be saved by developing another supplier for this component or if CPC should gear up to manufacture the power supply assemblies in-house within one of CPC's own production plants. John's purchasing-analysis staff has developed the following estimates:

Supply Source for PS100	Description of Cost	Annual Fixed Cost	Variable Cost per Unit
Osiega Ltd.	Annual tooling	$50,000	
	Inspection and rework		$ .16
	Shipping		.95
	Purchase price		11.88
Atlanta Spier	Annual tooling	95,000	
	Inspection and rework		$ 1.05
	Shipping		.15
	Purchase price		10.59
In-house	Annual tooling	70,000	
	Inspection and rework		$ .55
	Shipping		.25
	Production costs	5,000	11.50

The purchasing-analysis group has learned that CPC will need about 550,000 of the PS100 units next year.
a.   Which supply source provides the least cost for next year?
b.   How many PS100 units would have to be bought next year for each of the sources to be the least-cost source?

10. The purchasing department of the Silver Aircraft Company is developing plans for buying next year's requirements for stainless steel stock. Three alternatives are being considered—a blanket contract, a national contract, or individual orders. Five hundred thousand pounds of stock will be purchased next year. The firm estimates the costs and the associated probabilities for each of the three decision alternatives as follows:

	Probability	Cost per Pound
Blanket contract	.50	$.50
	.30	.60
	.20	.70
National contract	.75	.60
	.25	.50
Individual orders	1.00	.70

a.   Use a decision tree to analyze the decision alternatives.
b.   How should the firm purchase the steel stock?
c.   What will be the cost of the steel if the firm follows your recommendation?

11. White Aerospace Inc. is about to submit a proposal for a research contract to develop a new product for a government agency. The firm can bid three levels of price. White estimates the probability of winning the research contract and the value to the firm as follows:

Level of Price	Probability of Winning Research Contract	Research Contract Value
High	.25	$300,000
Mid	.50	250,000
Low	.75	200,000

The firm will lose $50,000 if it does not get the research contract. It is also trying to decide whether to bid on a production contract for the product that will be released later this year. The firm has ample capacity to respond on both the research and production contracts. The firm estimates that the value to itself for the production contract is $750,000 if the contract is won, but an unsuccessful bid would result in a $100,000 loss. James Trenton, the estimator, estimates the probability of winning the production contract as follows:

	Probability of Winning Production Contract
Research contract won	.6
Research contract lost	.3

a. Use a decision tree to analyze the decision alternatives.
b. What should White do?
c. What will be the value of this decision if White follows your recommendation?

12. A purchasing agent must award a supply contract to either Ajax or Modern, two local manufacturers. The part to be supplied must feed into the purchasing agent's company on a JIT basis. After a comprehensive evaluation process for both vendor candidates, the purchasing agent has prepared the information below:

Performance Factor	Factor Weight	Rating	
		Ajax	Modern
Price	.3	$156.10	$139.98
Product quality	.3	.8	.6
Delivery schedule	.2	.7	.8
Financial stability	.1	.6	.5
Production capacity	.1	.6	.8

Which vendor would you recommend? Why? (Hint: Look at Tables 5.3 and 8.7.) What other factors would be important in such a decision?

13. Windec Computers is a computer manufacturer that has implemented JIT systems throughout its organization. The company has decided to subcontract the production of a power supply unit rather than make it in-house. Two suppliers are finalists for the part, Suchow in Korea and Electex in El Paso. Tom Monrod, purchasing agent for Windec, must decide which supplier will be awarded the supply contract. The evaluation team has prepared the information below:

Performance Factor	Factor Weight	Rating	
		Suchow	*Electex*
Price	.20	$16.50	$15.98
Product quality	.30	.85	.70
JIT delivery	.20	.50	.65
Cooperation	.10	.70	.80
Engineering ability	.05	.80	.60
Financial stability	.05	.50	.80
Production capacity	.10	.60	.70

Which vendor would you recommend? Why? (*Hint:* Look at Tables 5.3 and 8.7.) What other factors would be important in such a decision?

14. Products are shipped from a company's main distribution center (adjacent to the factory) to two regional warehouses. The DRP records below indicate the forecast demand, scheduled receipts, and the last period's projected ending inventory (in units) for a single product. The planned order releases to the factory become the gross requirements in the master production schedule (MPS) of the factory.
    a. Complete the DRP records below.
    b. From these records, what gross requirements will show up in the master production schedule at the factory?

Regional Warehouse #1

Lead time for shipping products from the main distribution center at the factory to Warehouse #1 is 1 week, the standard shipping quantity is 100 units, and the safety stock is 50 units.

		Weeks					
	−1	1	2	3	4	5	
Forecast demand		80	100	80	60	100	
Scheduled receipts		100					
Projected ending inventory	200						
Planned receipt of shipments							
Planned orders for shipments							

Regional Warehouse #2

Lead time for shipping products from the main distribution center at the factory to Warehouse #2 is 2 weeks, the standard shipping quantity is 200 units, and the safety stock is 80 units.

		Weeks					
	−1	1	2	3	4	5	
Forecast demand		100	200	200	240	200	
Scheduled receipts		200					
Projected ending inventory	220						
Planned receipt of shipments							
Planned orders for shipments							

Main Distribution Center at the Factory

Lead time for final assembling of products and moving them into the main distribution center is 1 week, the standard production lot size is 500 units, and the safety stock is 200 units.

	Weeks					
	−1	1	2	3	4	5
Gross requirements (units)						
Scheduled receipts		500				
Projected ending inventory	250					
Planned receipt of orders						
Planned order releases to factory						

15. A product is shipped from a main distribution center to three regional warehouses and directly to customers. The DRP records below indicate the forecast demand, scheduled receipts, and the last period's projected ending inventory.
    a. Complete the DRP records below.
    b. What gross requirements will show up in the master production schedule at the factory from these records?

	Warehouse A					Warehouse B				
	Weeks					Weeks				
	−1	1	2	3	4	−1	1	2	3	4
Forecast demand		50	60	50	60		80	90	150	130
Scheduled receipts		80					150			
Projected ending inventory	60					200				
Planned receipt of shipments										
Planned orders for shipments										

	Warehouse C					Direct Customer Sales			
	Weeks					Weeks			
	−1	1	2	3	4	1	2	3	4
Forecast demand		30	60	40	50	100	150	100	160
Scheduled receipts		70							
Projected ending inventory	50								
Planned receipt of shipments									
Planned orders for shipments									

Main Distribution Center

	Weeks				
	−1	1	2	3	4
Gross requirements (units)					
Scheduled receipts		300			
Projected ending inventory	300				
Planned receipt of orders					
Planned order releases to factory					

The standard order quantities, lead times, and safety stocks for the warehouses are shown below:

	Order Quantity (Units)	Lead Time (Weeks)	Safety Stock (Units)
Warehouse A	80	1	60
Warehouse B	150	2	100
Warehouse C	70	1	50
Main distribution center	300	1	200

16. Toward improving the accuracy of its stock records, a company is implementing a cycle-counting system. Class A items would be counted monthly, Class B items would be counted quarterly, and Class C items would be counted annually. Seventy-five percent of the company's production items are Class C items, 20 percent are Class B items, and 5 percent are Class A items. If the firm has 40,000 different material and part numbers, how many items will need to be counted daily if there are 250 working days per year?

17. A company has a cycle-counting program, but it is not achieving the expected improvement in stock record accuracy. Joe Blane, warehousing and inventory control manager, believes it is because the materials are not being counted often enough. To improve stock record accuracy, Joe proposes to double the frequency of counting the A and B classes of materials. The present situation is:

Class of Material	Percentage of Items in Material Class	Frequency of Counting
A	10%	Monthly
B	30	Quarterly
C	60	Annually

The company has 30,000 materials of all types. If a worker who does cycle counting costs $20,000 per year, can count an average of 30 items per day, and works 250 days per year:

a. How many cycle counters does the present system require?
b. How much does the present crew of cycle counters cost per year?
c. How many cycle counters would the new system require?
d. How much more would the improved accuracy cost per year?

COMPUTER PROBLEMS/CASES

TRI-B CORPORATION

The Des Moines plant of Tri-B Corporation has three fabrication departments (A, B, and C). Each fabrication department produces a single unique product with equipment that is dedicated solely to its product. The three products are moved to four assembly departments (1, 2, 3, and 4), where they are assembled. Although any of the three products can be processed in any of the assembly departments, the materials-handling and assembly costs are different because of the varying distances between departments and because of the different equipment in each assembly department. Each fabrication and assembly department has a different monthly capacity, and it is desirable that each department operate at capacity. The monthly departmental capacities are:

Fabrication Department	Monthly Capacity (Units)	Assembly Department	Monthly Capacity (Units)
A	9,000	1	3,000
B	17,000	2	10,000
C	14,000	3	15,000
		4	12,000

The per-unit materials-handling and assembly processing costs are:

Fabrication Department	Assembly Department	Materials-Handling Cost ($/Unit)	Assembly Processing Cost ($/Unit)	Total Cost ($/Unit)
A	1	$.25	$.95	$1.20
	2	.15	.55	.70
	3	.10	.40	.50
	4	.15	.45	.60
B	1	.10	.60	.70
	2	.15	.35	.50
	3	.20	.30	.50
	4	.25	.35	.60
C	1	.10	.40	.50
	2	.15	.55	.70
	3	.30	.50	.80
	4	.40	.80	1.20

The production control department at Tri-B is now trying to develop a plan for allocating the fabricated products to the four assembly departments for next month. This allocation amounts to a shipping plan that specifies how many of each product should be moved from each fabrication department to each assembly department for the month. If the company can sell all it produces of the three products, how many of each product should be moved from each fabrication department to each assembly department to minimize total monthly costs?

Assignment

1. Formulate this shipping problem as a linear programming problem. Define the decision variables, write the objective function, and write the constraint functions.
2. To solve the LP problem, use the LP program in the *POM Computer Library* that accompanies this book. Take care to fully interpret the meaning of the solution. This means not only determining the value of the decision variables (X's), slack variables (S's), and the objective function (Z), but also fully interpreting the meaning of the solution to management.

SELECTED BIBLIOGRAPHY

Ammer, Dean S. *Materials Management and Purchasing.* 4th ed. Homewood, IL: Richard D. Irwin, 1980.

Ansarl, A., and Batoul Modarress. "Just-in-Time Purchasing: Problems and Solutions." *Journal of Purchasing and Materials Management* 22, no. 2(Summer 1986):11–15.

APICS Bibliography. 11th ed. Falls Church, VA: American Production and Inventory Control Society, 1987.

APICS Dictionary. 6th ed. Falls Church, VA: American Production and Inventory Control Society, 1987.

Burt, D. *Proactive Purchasing.* Englewood Cliffs, NJ: Prentice-Hall, 1984.

Colton, Raymond R., and Walter F. Rohrs. *Industrial Purchasing and Effective Materials Management.* Reston, VA: Reston Publishing, 1985.

Corey, E. Raymond. "Should Companies Centralize Procurement?" *Harvard Business Review* 56(November–December 1978):102–110.

Dobler, Donald W., Lamar Lee, Jr., and David N. Burt. *Purchasing and Materials Management: Text and Cases.* 4th ed. New York: McGraw-Hill, 1984.

Hahn, Chan K., Peter A. Pinto, and Daniel Bragg. "Just-in-Time Production and Purchasing." *Journal of Purchasing and Materials Management* 19(Fall 1983):2–10.

Jordan, Henry. *Cycle Counting: An APICS Training Aid.* Falls Church, VA: American Production and Inventory Control Society, 1980.

Leenders, M. R., H. E. Fearon, and W. B. England. *Purchasing and Materials Management.* 8th ed. Homewood, IL: Richard D. Irwin, 1985.

Miller, Jeffery G., and Peter Gilmour. "Materials Managers: Who Needs Them?" *Harvard Business Review* 57, no. 4(July–August 1979): 151.

Narasimhan, Ram. "An Analytical Approach to Supplier Selection." *Journal of Purchasing and Materials Management* 19(Winter 1983):27–32.

Schneider, Lewis M. "New Era in Transportation Strategy." *Harvard Business Review* 63, no. 2(March–April 1985):118–126.

Schonberger, Richard J., and James P. Gilbert. "Just-in-Time Purchasing: A Challenge for U.S. Industry." *California Management Review* (Fall 1983):54–68.

Shapiro, Roy D. "Get Leverage from Logistics." *Harvard Business Review* 62, no. 3(May–June 1984):119–126.

Vollman, Thomas E., William L. Berry, and D. Clay Whybark. *Manufacturing Planning and Control Systems.* Homewood, IL: Richard D. Irwin, 1984, Chap. 19.

PLANNING AND CONTROLLING OPERATIONS FOR PRODUCTIVITY, QUALITY, AND RELIABILITY

Part IV of this text concerns the day-to-day decisions that operations managers make. They have the responsibility of getting production out the back door on time, within cost targets and within quality standards. They work hard to control their costs and product quality, not only because it is the professional or right thing to do, but also because their jobs are on the line. The fundamental management principle in real-world organizations is: No alibis please, operations managers are accountable for everything that happens in their areas.

The objectives of operations managers (timely production, low costs, high productivity, and product quality) would be relatively simple to attain if it were not for the inherent uncertainties. Will key personnel perform as expected? Will major pieces of equipment break down during next month's production peak? Will the natural gas supply be interrupted next month? Such questions require production systems to be flexible and capable of adapting to these uncertainties so that quality products or services can be promptly and economically delivered to customers.

More than any other factor, people — the employees in production systems — directly affect costs, timely production, and quality. Because of employees' great impact, their jobs must be carefully planned and they must be skillfully managed. Employees have many of the answers to questions about how to improve productivity, and operations managers must draw out and implement these ideas. Maintaining the machines of production is another important aspect of controlling costs and quality. Knowing the concepts and techniques of preventive maintenance and related subjects helps to assure operations managers that machines will not interfere with their cost, timely production, and quality objectives.

The function of quality control is to ensure that the organization will produce products or services that meet its predetermined quality standards. The setting of these standards, inspecting outputs and comparing the actual product or service characteristics to these standards, and taking corrective actions as required are important parts of operations managers' daily jobs.

Although any one of these decisions about planning and controlling the day-to-day operations of the production system may not be critical in and of itself to the long-range success and survival of the organization, the overall effect of all of these decisions is immense. If our industries are to survive foreign competition in the long run, they must improve the ways that they are planning and controlling their day-to-day operations. What this means to us is that the topics in Part IV — Productivity and Employees, Total Quality Control, Planning and Controlling Projects, and Maintenance Management and Reliability — when taken together may indeed prove crucial to the success and survival of our production systems.

CHAPTER

14

PRODUCTIVITY AND EMPLOYEES

BEHAVIOR, WORK METHODS, AND WORK MEASUREMENT

IF YOU CAN'T BEAT 'EM, JOIN 'EM

In Fremont, California, members of the United Auto Workers union line up each day and exercise before spreading out along the assembly line to build automobiles at the United Motor Manufacturing Inc., a joint venture between Toyota and General Motors. At Buick City in Flint, Michigan, GM has adopted similar innovations, including using robots, giving workers more responsibility, and expecting workers to pass on to the next assembly line station only perfect work — even if it means stopping the line. Exercising before work is part of the Japanese team approach. Japanese workers are teamed, exercised, and disciplined like army platoons. If anyone had suggested a few years ago that U.S. workers would line up and exercise for 10 minutes before going to work, there would have been a major strike. But now, Fremont's workers are "team members" who not only exercise together but also eat together.

What does the union say about all of this? The union is all for it. Union assembly line workers have been visiting GM dealerships, talking with dealers, salesmen, and service people about what's wrong with the cars and what can be done to build them right in the first place. In the face of declining union employment in the auto industry and the threat of U.S. automakers moving small-car production out of this country altogether — to Mexico, Brazil, and the Orient — the United Automobile Workers (UAW) is beginning to see the light. The UAW is now cooperating with U.S. automakers in up-front planning to go after future business. For example, a key feature of GM's Saturn plant is new union work rules that are less restrictive of management's efforts to improve productivity.[1]

---

[1] "The All-New Industrial Revolution," *Bryan-College Station Eagle,* Jan. 20, 1985, sec. E, 1. (By William Allan, Scripps Howard News Service.) Reprinted with permission.

As the account on the previous page indicates, the attention of union members and managers in key industries is focused on improving the productivity of U.S. factories. The failure of U.S. productivity to keep up with the Japanese and the rest of the world's major industrialized nations is a growing national concern. Our national leaders have stated that the economic survival of our factories, our standard of living, and ultimately the survival of our economic, political, and governmental systems could be at stake.

We have big problems concerning our industrial employees today. On the one hand, we need our employees to work harder and to be more productive so that we can get our production costs in line with the foreign competition. On the other hand, our employees today, particularly the younger ones, seem uncommitted to their jobs, change jobs often, are frequently absent from work, and appear to be disinterested in hard work, high productivity, low production costs, and high product quality. Some say that workers *and* managers in U.S. factories are just too soft, that they have become too self-indulgent, lazy, and unwilling to make the sacrifices necessary to overcome the superiority of the Japanese manufacturers. These critics cite the average work week in the United States at just under 40 hours per week as compared with the standard 6-day, 48-hour work week in Japan as an example of how the Japanese employees and managers are willing to work harder and longer.

Others say that it is unfair to blame workers and production supervisors in the United States for all of our productivity problems. They say that there is more to the story. They contend that if we are to overcome the superiority of the Japanese manufacturers, we must get back to the basics of factory management, pay attention to the details of production, and *continuously* strive for low production costs and excellence in product quality. It is perhaps here that the Japanese factory managers outplay their U.S. counterparts — they have a relentless drive to continuously *improve* every facet of manufacturing. Improving labor productivity, automating operations, controlling inventories, improving quality, and reducing costs become no-holds-barred, push-it-to-the-hilt, total-commitment-every-day compulsion. And Japanese manufacturers operate with fewer executives, smaller offices with less walnut paneling, fewer company cars, smaller sales forces and advertising budgets, and less overhead in general. Although most would agree that the productivity problems in the United States involve more than just employees' and managers' attitudes, it is also clear that attitudes are an important productivity issue. The problem of the attitudes of our employees toward work and the problem of foreign competition are not new developments, but their simultaneous impingement upon operations management is causing us to look at the whole area of productivity today with a fresh and genuine interest.

In this chapter we shall first develop an understanding of what productivity is and how human behavior is related to productivity. Next, we shall study how operations managers design employees' jobs so that the jobs are efficient. Finally, we shall examine the methods of measuring employees' work with a view to setting labor standards. The overall purpose of this chapter is to explore the setting in which operations managers today must achieve productivity and to develop some of the techniques that can be used to improve productivity.

PRODUCTIVITY AND HUMAN BEHAVIOR

Productivity means the amount of products or services produced with the resources used. Productivity in a time period is usually measured with formulas such as:

$$\text{Productivity} = \frac{\text{Quantity of products or services produced}}{\text{Amount of resources used}}$$

Notice that there are two sides to the productivity equation—the amount of production and the amount of resources used. Productivity varies with the amount of production *relative* to the amount of resources used. Productivity can be increased in several ways:

1. Increase production using the same or a smaller amount of resources.
2. Reduce the amount of resources used while keeping the same production or increasing it.
3. Allow the amount of resources used to increase as long as production increases more.
4. Allow production to decrease as long as the amount of resources used decreases more.

Notice that the productivity formula above does not include provisions for the prices of the products or services or the costs of the resources. There are, however, important implications in this formula for prices and costs. We can observe from the formula that when the cost of a resource increases, if profits are to remain the same, some combination of increased production, decreased amount of resources used, or price increases of products or services must occur. For example, when wage rates increase, either more production must be realized for each labor-hour or product/service prices must increase if profits are not to fall. Because the costs of resources seem to be continuously rising and because product and service prices cannot be freely increased in competitive markets, managers work diligently to find ways to achieve higher production rates relative to the amount of resources used if profits are not to decline.

The substitution of capital equipment for labor has been going on for many decades. Then in the 1980s there was a dramatic shift to automation in manufacturing and services. For instance, one researcher reports: "By 1983, numerical controlled (NC) and computer numerical controlled (CNC) machines accounted for one-third of all *new* machine-tool purchases in the U.S., and over 103,000 NC and CNC machines were in service. Although this represented only about 5 percent of all machine tools in the U.S., it accounted for a much higher percent of output. It is likely that NC/CNC had achieved at least 25 percent penetration." [2] This shift to automation in many of our industries today is dramatically changing the mix of their costs. Industry Snapshot 14.1 discusses the impact of a rapidly changing cost picture for our manufacturers.

---

[2] Robert U. Ayres, "Future Trends in Factory Automation," *Manufacturing Review* 1, no. 2(June 1988):96.

INDUSTRY SNAPSHOT 14.1

Low Wages No Longer Give Competitive Edge

Blue-collar labor costs in U.S. manufacturing account for only 18 percent of total costs. They are down from 23 percent only a few years ago and they are dropping fast as productivity is rising at a good clip.

Toyota and Honda in their U.S. auto plants operate with less than 20 percent and expect to reduce this to 15 percent within a decade, as does Ford. "Mini-mills" steel operations operate at blue-collar costs of 10 percent or less, they now produce a fifth of all steel made in the United States, and they are likely to produce well over half within another 10 years. About half of the textile industry operates with 10 or 12 percent blue-collar costs, and this is competitive with firms from Malaysia and Indonesia.

In this restructuring of costs in which blue-collar wages cease to be a dominant factor — and almost cease to be a factor altogether — American and Japanese industry are neck and neck. The Japanese are ahead in reducing labor-cost content in traditional industries like automobiles and tires. What helps them is that they are largely unhampered by union restrictions. In the new, fast-growing industries like pharmaceuticals, specialty chemicals, biotechnology, communications, and computers — and some old industries such as paper turbines, the United States is ahead. Europe, by and large, has barely begun; but it is waking up.[3]

[3] Peter F. Drucker, "Low Wages No Longer Give Competitive Edge," *The Wall Street Journal,* Mar. 16, 1988, 30.

The hypothetical cost information below reflects this change in the composition of costs for many U.S. manufacturers:

	Percentage of Total Cost		
Element of Cost	*1930*	*1960*	*1990*
Direct labor cost	40%	20%	10%
Cost of materials	50	50	50
Overhead cost	10	30	40

Notice the tremendous reduction of direct labor cost and the great increase of overhead cost as percentages of total cost of manufacturing.

For some firms today, production workers, or *touch labor,* represent such a small part of the firms' total costs that product quality, inventories, engineering, materials, shipping, knowledge workers, and other overhead costs hold more promise for reducing costs and increasing productivity. Failing to recognize this fact can be a major pitfall in productivity improvement programs. "American manufacturers have boosted productivity for several years now, largely by closing old plants and laying off workers. But the U.S. still lags behind Japan and other countries in productivity growth. The problem: We focus on capital investment as a way to reduce labor—ignoring the huge benefits to be gained from improved quality, reduced inventories, and faster introduction of new products. We need a new math for productivity." [4]

MULTIFACTOR APPROACH TO MEASURING PRODUCTIVITY

Productivity of a resource is the amount of products or services produced in a time period divided by the amount of that resource required. The productivity of each resource can and should be measured. For example, measures such as the following could be used to determine productivity in a time period:

1. **Capital:** Number of products produced divided by the asset value.
2. **Materials:** Number of products produced divided by dollars spent on materials.
3. **Direct labor:** Number of products produced divided by direct labor-hours.
4. **Overhead:** Number of products produced divided by dollars spent on overhead.

Such measures are not perfect. For example, the measure for materials productivity includes price. This is generally undesirable, but there is no other practical way to combine the many different units of measurement for the diverse materials used in production. Although such measures of productivity have their shortcomings, they do provide a starting point for tracking productivity so that managers can be aware of productivity trends.

In decades past when labor cost was the predominant cost of production, productivity was measured only by the output per hour of direct labor. Today, however, there is a need to look beyond direct labor costs and develop a multifactor perspective. Industry Snapshot 14.2 discusses this development.

Our view of productivity today must be toward improving the productivity of all of the factors of production—labor, capital, materials, and overhead. Nationally, the Bureau of Labor Statistics, the primary source of productivity measures, publishes statistics on *worker productivity* that are computed by dividing the real dollar value of all goods and services produced in the United States in a given year by the direct labor-hours used in producing those goods and services. The Bureau of Labor Statistics also publishes the most common measure of worker productivity, the percentage of change from the previous year. If worker productivity goes up more than wage rates, inflationary pressures should subside, and everyone should be better off. If worker productivity goes down, the reverse is true. In recent years the worker

---

[4] Karen Pennar, "The Productivity Paradox," *Business Week,* June 6, 1988, 100–102.

INDUSTRY SNAPSHOT 14.2

Multifactor Approach to Measuring Productivity

The trouble with measuring productivity by *output per direct labor hour* alone is that the productivity of one factor can be increased by simply replacing it with another factor. For example, if a factory that formerly bought castings and machined them in-house decides to purchase the castings premachined, then the company can lay off skilled workers and sell its machine tools. What happens to productivity? Output will remain the same but the number of workers will fall, so labor productivity will increase. Capital productivity will also increase, because investment will be less and production levels will be unchanged. But materials productivity will decline because the value of purchased materials will increase while production levels will not change.[5]

---

[5] W. Bruce Chew, "No-Nonsense Guide to Measuring Productivity," *Harvard Business Review* 67(January–February 1988):110–117.

productivity of the United States has increased overall but at a slower rate of increase than that of its foreign competitors. The United Kingdom, Canada, France, Italy, West Germany, and Japan all have had higher average rates of worker productivity increases than the United States over the last two decades. Unless this trend can be reversed, industries in the United States can continue to expect severe competitive pressure from foreign competitors through lower prices made possible by their relatively lower labor costs. If our government agencies could obtain data on the productivity of materials, capital, and overhead, they probably would publish them. Individual companies can develop their own resource productivity measures, and they should.

Many U.S. companies today are pushing hard to improve their productivity. See Industry Snapshot 14.3 for a description of what four firms are doing.

We have emphasized ways of improving the productivity of capital and materials elsewhere in this text. In Chapter 5, Production Technology, we discussed better ways of selecting and managing production technology. Because these methods should result in greater production for each dollar invested in production facilities, capital productivity should increase as a consequence. In Chapter 10, Independent Demand Inventory Systems, and Chapter 11, Resource Requirements Planning Systems, we discussed how inventory levels could be reduced while increasing customer satisfaction, with a resultant increase in the productivity of materials and capital.

As we discussed earlier in this section, direct labor cost is becoming a relatively minor part of the total production cost for some of our manufacturers. The day may come when the productivity of direct labor will receive only a cursory discussion in

INDUSTRY SNAPSHOT 14.3

Productivity: How Four Firms Found It

New York Times—Confronted by tough economic times, many businesses are putting their operations under a microscope to identify ways to raise productivity. They are adding new machines, cutting workers and generally slimming down activities that grew fat during better times. Many have found it slow going. Here is a sampling of what four companies are doing—strategies of the sort that are being hailed for their effect on improving the nation's productivity.

In 1979, the Intel Corp., the Santa Clara, Calif., semiconductor manufacturer, discovered that 65 percent of its employees worked in administration and only 35 percent in manufacturing, the opposite of 10 years earlier. The company responded by putting together a group of productivity experts to tighten up its administrative side, analyzing jobs and simplifying them where possible. The specialists have been gradually working their way through the company's operations, trimming both paper work and bureaucracy.

One billing process, for example, that formerly took 199 steps and 44 hours a month to complete, has been reduced to 14 steps and 41 minutes. Ordering a $2.79 mechanical pencil used to require the same 12 forms as ordering a pound of gold. Today, it takes just one form. . . .

Intel says corporate productivity is up 33 percent, while its administrative payroll has shrunk by $17 million a year, to $225 million, mainly through attrition. . . .

For TRW Inc., a diversified manufacturer, the emphasis on productivity grew out of a desire to improve competitiveness. The Cleveland-based company has employed a variety of techniques.

At one 350-person plant, for example, it put its hourly employees on a merit system, achieving an 11 percent productivity improvement. In its electronics and defense sector, it found that moving computer software programmers out of a common bullpen and into cubicles resulted in a 40 percent gain. Shifting to computer-aided design has also improved the output of the company's engineers and designers.

TRW's total productivity improvement last year—about 1½ percent by the company's calculations—was below the national average of 3.1 percent. But the company expects to achieve a 2½ percent gain this year and larger increases in later years. "A 2½ percent improvement may not sound like much," said Edward Steigerwald, TRW's vice president for productivity, "but on a $6 billion sales base it's really a formidable task." Besides, he said, "We're really not talking about short-term changes."

At Boise Cascade Corp., a wood products manufacturer, the decision to try to raise productivity, said Robert Stolz, director of productivity, was prompted by the feeling that "if we didn't do something about the economy, we would all go down the tubes like Rome, and more recently, Britain."

The company, based in Boise, Idaho, has instituted productivity measures both at its plants and in its offices. A task force exists to inform senior executives of new techniques they can employ. Managers have been encouraged—and trained—to

continued

INDUSTRY SNAPSHOT 14.3   (continued)

be better communicators and less dicta-torial.

The old recipe for using newer ma-chinery and fewer people has also been tried. In recent years, for example, the company has added three new paper ma-chines that can each handle 2,000 tons of product a day, double the previous capac-ity, but with the same size work crew. Overall, the company's work force had been trimmed by about 7,000 . . . , from a total of nearly 36,000 four years before.

"There's no magic to this productiv-ity thing," said Stolz. "It's just a little dif-ferent way of looking at things, keeping careful measurements, and a lot of hard work." [6]

The Methodist Hospital System in Houston, Texas, is doing something about the problem of skyrocketing costs in the health care industry. Toward improving the productivity of its organization, the Management Systems Consulting Depart-ment was established. This department provides all other departments in the sys-tem with services such as these:

1. *Productivity consulting:* training, work measurement, work flow analysis, work simplification, employee sched-uling
2. *Microcomputer consulting:* forecasting models, statistical analysis, microcom-puter training, budget analysis
3. *Operational management consulting:* staffing analysis, facility layout, cost/benefit analysis, forms analysis, inven-tory analysis, flowcharting, equipment utilization

Michael Kuhn, manager of the de-partment, states that his people not only provide services to others, but they also serve as productivity activists in all areas of the system, thereby encouraging all to improve productivity. Mr. Kuhn reports that although there are great upward pres-sures on costs in the health care industry, his department has had remarkable suc-cess in its ability to control and reduce costs in the Methodist Hospital System.

[6] "The Elusive Boom in Productivity" by Karen W. Arenson, April 8, 1984. Copyright © 1984 by The New York Times Company. Reprinted by permission.

textbooks such as this, but that day is not yet here. For many U.S. manufacturers, such as job shops, direct labor cost remains a significant cost. Some manufacturing operations are not yet automated and never will be because of extreme product variability, the variable nature of some duties (such as materials handling), the nature of the materials being processed, and similar reasons. For these operations, either it is simply not cost effective to automate them or insufficient capital is available for automation. Moreover, most services remain direct-labor-intensive. For these rea-sons, the cost of labor and the need to improve the productivity of labor continues to

FIGURE 14.1 *Variables Affecting Labor Productivity*

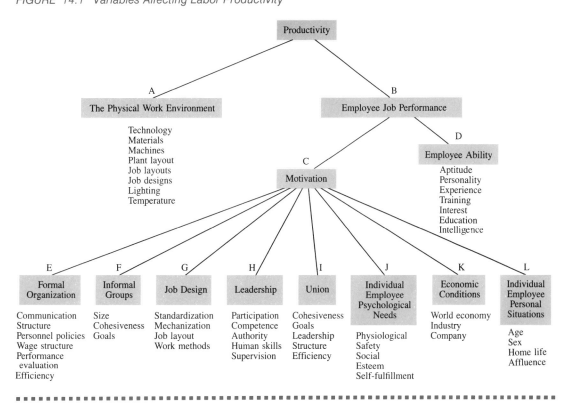

receive management attention. In the remainder of this chapter, therefore, we shall focus on labor productivity.

LABOR PRODUCTIVITY

Our discussion of labor productivity here will be broad enough to include direct labor, indirect labor, engineers and other knowledge employees, clerical employees, managers, and all other forms of labor in production organizations. This wide-angle view includes direct labor costs and a substantial portion of overhead costs in most organizations.

What causes employees to be more productive? Figure 14.1 shows the major factors that affect labor productivity. This illustration demonstrates an important truth: The causes of productivity are many. We have not yet developed a set of formulas that precisely predicts human behavior in general and productivity in particular. We have, however, begun to understand enough about employee behavior to remove some of the uncertainty about why employees are productive.

Two major factors affect labor productivity: employees' job performance and the machines, tools, and work methods that support and assist their work. Staff groups such as industrial, process, product, and systems engineering strive to develop better machines, tools, and work methods to enhance labor productivity. Increasing productivity through technological developments is at least as important as motivation and behavioral factors in improving employee job performance.

Employee job performance is a complex topic because all people are different. Abilities, personalities, interests, ambitions, energy levels, education, training, and experience vary widely. It is important for operations managers to consider these differences because blanket or universal approaches to improving job performance may not be effective for all employees. Personnel departments recognize these differences and attempt to select employees who have the desired abilities and to develop training programs to improve employees' skills.

Motivation is perhaps the most complex variable in the equation of productivity. Motivation is what prompts a person to act in a certain way. Maslow identified five levels of needs that prompt people to act: physiological, safety, social, esteem, and self-fulfillment.[7] These needs are arranged in a hierarchy from physiological at the lowest level to self-fulfillment at the highest level. Only unsatisfied needs are *motivators,* or cause people to act, and as each lower-level need becomes relatively satisfied, higher-level needs emerge as motivators. Today, employees' lower-level needs (physiological and safety) are mostly taken care of by the economic packages at work. The higher-level needs (social, esteem, and self-fulfillment) may hold more promise for managers in their attempts to motivate most employees.

How does an understanding of employees' needs help us to design a work environment that encourages productivity? If we can determine what class of needs is important to our employees, we can apply this framework: If productivity is seen by employees as a means of satisfying their needs, high productivity is likely to result. Once employees have their needs satisfied through rewards that have been conditional upon productivity, the process is likely to be repeated. Figure 14.2 illustrates this concept.

Labor unions and work groups can influence employees to be either productive or unproductive. If employees think that their work groups may treat them as outcasts because they have been productive, they may not cooperate with management in this productivity-reward-productivity cycle. Operations managers should recognize the influence that work groups have on labor productivity and develop cooperative work groups by carefully selecting employees for these groups and by influencing group norms through effective communication and supervision. *Japanese managers seem to be way ahead of us in their ability to get unions to support productivity improvement programs.* A major reason for Japanese productivity advances is that both the unions and managers share the same key objective — stable employment for their employees. See Industry Snapshot 14.4 for a description of how Toyota extends

---

[7] A. H. Maslow, "A Theory of Human Motivation," *Psychological Review* (July 1943):370–396.

FIGURE 14.2   *The Productivity Pathway to Satisfy Workers' Needs*

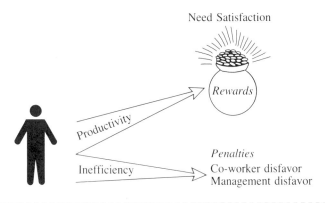

its concept of job security to "life security." Increasingly, U.S. companies like IBM are also applying the concept of "no layoffs." [8]

The concept of *lifetime employment* has not yet caught on in the United States as it has with large Japanese manufacturers, but there are some signs that managers in this country are beginning to come around. The new GM Saturn plant in Tennessee has adopted the lifetime employment concept — employees will not be fired because of economic conditions. Union–management–employee relations are sure to improve in this environment, and joint productivity programs are more likely.

If higher-level needs (social, esteem, and self-fulfillment) hold promise for motivating employees today, what rewards are likely to satisfy these needs and cause employees to want to be more productive? (1) Opportunities for social interaction, companionship, and friendship from co-employees and supervisors on the job. (2) Recognition, respect, and status given by supervisors and co-employees on the job. (3) A sense of accomplishment, growth, and achievement from the work and an expectation of personal development and advancement. These rewards are usually available for use by supervisors and thus can be offered as needed and deserved. Monetary rewards, on the other hand, can seldom be varied to adequately reward or penalize employees because wages are ordinarily set to apply universally to all employees and are beyond the day-to-day control of supervisors.

Why worry about satisfaction of employees' needs? What's in it for management and the organization? The obvious answer is an improvement in productivity, as we have discussed. Another equally important answer is that satisfied employees are less likely to be absent from work, less likely to leave their jobs for other ones, and more likely to produce high-quality goods and services. In today's working environ-

---

[8] "IBM: Model in People Utilization," Knight-Ridder News Service, *Bryan-College Station Eagle,* Nov. 9, 1988, 6B.

INDUSTRY SNAPSHOT 14.4

The Japanese Approach to Job Security and Lifetime Employment

Toyota City, Japan—Once known for its silkworm farms, Toyota City, Japan's automotive capital, is a model of how large Japanese industries wrap their workers in a cocoon of job and life security.

The paternal hand of Toyota Motor Co., Japan's largest automaker, reaches throughout this company town of 290,000, in facilities ranging from a free hospital to mountain resorts and cooking schools.

Cheap housing, a high school, a food cooperative, and a large sports center are also available to the families of the 52,000 workers who work at eight Toyota plants in this city in central Japan.

Like most Japanese companies with ample funds, Toyota is committed to keeping its "family" content as part of the lifetime employment system where workers dedicate their working careers to one company in exchange for job security. Toyota officials say job turnover on the assembly line is only about 3 percent or 4

percent a year, with almost all engineers and upper level office workers staying on until retirement.

Since Kiichiro Toyoda founded the plant here in 1938, one of the biggest benefits in becoming a Toyota man or woman is good housing, the most elusive of material dreams on these crowded islands.

For new and single workers, there is dormitory space for 19,000 people at $6.38 a month. Fifty percent of food costs is paid by the company, so workers can eat three meals for around $4.25 a day.

Young marrieds often live in one of about 4,500 company apartments. Comfortable by Japan's pinched standards, the four-room units rent from $30 to $42.50 a month.

With cheap living, a company savings plan paying almost twice normal interest rates, and average hourly wages of $9.75, it is easy for workers to save, Toyota officials say. By their early 30s, workers are ready to buy a home, and many choose

---

ment where absenteeism, turnover, and low quality of products and services are staggering problems, this reason alone seems sufficient to get operations managers interested in designing jobs in ways that provide for a broader range of employees' need satisfaction.

DESIGNING WORKERS' JOBS

Some behavioral scientists argue that assembly line jobs are boring and monotonous and that workers are not satisfying their needs for socialization, self-esteem, and self-fulfillment on these jobs. The high rates of absenteeism and turnover among our highly educated and affluent young workers seem to validate these contentions. This criticism of assembly line jobs is aimed at the high degree of labor specialization in

tracts developed by "Toyota Home," a company subsidiary which makes pre-fab units.

Prospective home owners can borrow $30,000 in low interest company loans, and another $12,766 if they buy a Toyota Home. A two-story house with a little land can be purchased for about $85,000.

Company spokesman Masamitsu Odaka also explained that residents of these "Toyota Heights" are always near a Toyota Cooperative, where food, clothing, and other necessities are available at reasonable cost. The Cooperative, founded in 1945 with company backing, has 100,000 members, including noncompany residents of the area.

There is free medical and dental care at the 403-bed, 23-doctor Toyota hospital, which costs the automaker about $15 million a year.

Hospital director Motoki Tanabe said about 10 Japanese companies have their own hospitals, "and ours is as good as any public hospital in the country." Pointing to a new, U.S.-made, million-dollar computer tomography machine for taking brain photos, Tanabe said, "you buy our cars, so we buy your medical equipment."

The outdoor showpiece is a 150-acre sports center including a 30,000-seat track and field stadium, completed six years ago at a cost of $14 million.

Workers and their families can unwind on 12 tennis courts, a 50-meter indoor swimming pool, two spacious baseball stadiums, an Olympic-quality gymnasium and athletic field, and individual playing grounds for soccer, rugby, archery, sumo and softball.[9]

---

[9] Jim Abrams, courtesy of the Associated Press.

these jobs. *Labor specialization* refers to the number of tasks that a worker performs. A highly specialized job is one in which the worker repetitively performs only a narrow range of activities, such as folding a sheet of paper and placing it in an envelope. On the other hand, a job that is not very specialized would be one in which the worker does a variety of tasks during the day. Table 14.1 lists some advantages and disadvantages of labor specialization.

Several proposals for modifying specialized jobs to provide for a broader range of needs satisfaction are:

1. **Job rotation** — Training workers to perform several jobs so that they can be moved about from job to job during the work shift.
2. **Job enlargement** — Adding additional similar tasks to workers' jobs; this is referred to as *horizontal job enlargement.*

■■■

TABLE 14.1   Some Advantages and Disadvantages of Labor Specialization

---

Advantages
1. Because of the repetitive work, production rates are high.
2. Because skill requirements of jobs are low:
    a. Wage rates are low.
    b. Workers can be trained quickly.
    c. Workers can be recruited easily.

Disadvantages
1. Worker dissatisfaction can cause total costs to be excessive because of high rates of turnover, absenteeism, tardiness, union grievances, job-related sicknesses, and sabotage.
2. Product quality can be low because:
    a. Workers are not motivated to produce high-quality products.
    b. Since workers make only a small part of a product, no single worker is accountable for the quality of the whole product.

■■■

3. **Job enrichment** — Adding more planning, inspecting, and other management functions to workers' jobs; this is referred to as *vertical job enlargement.*
4. **Sociotechnical system studies** — Attempts to design jobs that adjust production technology to the needs of workers. For more about these studies, see the Mumford and Weir listing in the Selected Bibliography at the end of this chapter.

These remedies have been experimentally applied with varying degrees of success and failure.

A burning issue remains: Can we simultaneously give workers the satisfaction they want from their work and still give the organization the productivity and efficiency it needs to survive economically? Is such a blend possible? How do we design jobs so that we integrate organizations' needs for high productivity and employees' needs for interesting work, self-direction, self-control, socialization, recognition, participation, and achievement? Are there practical guidelines that engineers and other technical specialists who design workers' jobs can follow to accomplish both of these necessary and worthwhile goals? Table 14.2 suggests several such guidelines for designing workers' job tasks, workers' immediate job settings, and the larger work environment.

Table 14.2 was developed with the assumption that individual worker jobs have first been designed to be technically efficient and productive. These suggestions for modifying worker tasks have been practically applied in real-world organizations to provide workers with opportunities for self-control, self-direction, and socialization. The remainder of this table offers other suggestions for modifying in positive ways both the immediate job setting and the larger work environment.

TABLE 14.2   Some Practical Guidelines for Designing Workers' Jobs and Work Environments That Accommodate Workers' Needs

Elements of Workers' Jobs	Suggested Design Guidelines	Workers' Needs Affected
Workers' job tasks (the work itself—arrangement of machines, workplace layouts, work methods, and sequence of work tasks)	1. Avoid machine pacing of workers. Workers should determine, when possible, rates of output. 2. When practical, combine inspection tasks into jobs so that workers inspect their own output. 3. Design work areas to allow open communication and visual contact with other workers in adjacent operations. 4. When economically feasible and generally desired by workers, combine machine changeovers, new job layouts, setups, and other elements of immediate job planning into workers' jobs. 5. Replace workers with automated equipment on boring, uncomfortable, or unsafe jobs.	Self-control Self-control Socialization Self-direction/control Dissatisfaction
Immediate job setting (the management policies and procedures that directly impinge on workers' jobs)	1. Rotate workers where practical between jobs that are repetitive, monotonous, boring, and short-cycled. 2. Assign new workers to undesirable jobs for fixed periods of time, then transfer them to more preferred jobs. 3. Recruit mentally or physically handicapped, hard-core unemployed, or otherwise disadvantaged persons for jobs with high absenteeism and high turnover. 4. To relieve monotony, provide workers with periodic rest periods away from repetitive jobs. 5. Set higher pay rates for undesirable jobs.	Variety and relief of boredom and monotony Equity Interesting work and basic needs Relief of boredom and social-ization Physiological, security, equity, and achievement
Larger work environment (organization-wide policies, climate, management philosophy, structure, facilities, and programs)	1. Select and train supervisors who openly communicate on most issues that affect workers. 2. Develop supervisors who are comfortable with a participative environment, both with their superiors and with workers. 3. Remove barriers between management and other employees, such as separate dining or washroom facilities. 4. Create an organizational climate and management philosophy that recognizes workers as important elements of the organization. This tends to give workers a sense of personal worth. 5. Develop formal and informal channels of communication between workers and all levels of management. These channels function best when used often, in all directions, and on a wide range of topics.	Recognition and socialization Participation, recognition, socialization, and achievement Equity and recognition Recognition and achievement Participation, self-control, and recognition

Labor unions are a strong force in affecting workers' attitudes toward work. Unions have been suspicious of managements' actions to make work more satisfying; thus workers and unions usually have not cooperated in implementing job design modification proposals. Also, over the years unions have negotiated labor agreements containing restrictive work rules. These rules control such things as pay, hours of work, overtime, seniority in filling vacancies, scope of jobs, incentive pay, layoff and recall procedures, and transfer between jobs. One common work rule inhibits a worker in one labor classification from doing work in another classification, as for example, when a production worker is not allowed to do any maintenance work. Such rules restrict management flexibility and reduce productivity.

In recent years, however, the loss of union jobs because of foreign competition has put great pressure on unions to change restrictive work rules in union contracts. These changes included eliminating unneeded jobs, more flexibility in moving workers around from job to job, modifications in seniority rules, and changing crew structure to be more appropriate for high-technology production equipment. Such changes are improving productivity in many industries.[10] Not only do work rule changes improve productivity by eliminating waste, but they also allow the formation of motivated work teams that were formerly impossible.

Although there do exist obstacles to designing workers' jobs that are both efficient and satisfying, experience shows that these obstacles can be overcome through education, cooperation, and persistence.

WORK METHODS ANALYSIS

Figure 14.1 illustrated that the technological development of the job, which means the machines, tools, materials, and work methods used in the job, directly affect labor productivity. As one supervisor put it: "Workers can work their tails off, but if the machines, tools, and materials they use are poorly designed and if their own work methods waste energy and time, they might as well be loafing. The effect is the same."

Pretend that you were just hired at a large automobile assembly plant to work on the assembly line. You would more than likely be trained by an experienced worker for a few days and then be assigned a job such as attaching right front doors onto automobile assemblies. Your first few days would probably be hectic, tiring, and confusing; but the muscle soreness would soon go away and things would begin to settle down into a more predictable routine. You would probably soon be amazed at the amount of work that gets done each hour—materials moved, labor expended, inspections made, instructions given, and all manner of activities.

---

[10] "Work-Rule Changes Quietly Spread as Firms Try to Raise Productivity," *The Wall Street Journal,* Jan. 25, 1983; and "A Work Revolution in U.S. Industry: More Flexible Rules on the Job Are Boosting Productivity," *Business Week,* May 16, 1983.

TABLE 14.3   The Questioning Attitude of Methods Analysis

1. *What* is done? *What* is the purpose of the operation? *Why* should it be done? *What* would happen if it were not done? Is every part of the operation necessary?
2. *Who* does the work? *Why* does this person do it? *Who* could do it better? Can changes be made to permit a person with less skill and training to do the work?
3. *Where* is the work done? *Why* is it done there? Could it be done somewhere else more economically?
4. *When* is the work done? *Why* should it be done then? Would it be better to do it at some other time?
5. *How* is the work done? *Why* is it done this way?

Source: Adapted by permission from Ralph M. Barnes, *Motion and Time Study,* 4th ed. (New York: Wiley, 1958), 31.

This systematic whir of assembly line work is the result of years of work methods studies that have been continuously refined by industrial engineers, supervisors, and employees themselves.

The employees themselves are perhaps the most important source for improving the way they do their work. These people do their jobs daily, and they are the experts when it comes to determining whether new work methods will work as planned. Besides offering some valuable suggestions, employees who are allowed to participate in improving their own jobs will be more likely to make the new methods work.

APPROACHING ANALYSIS OF OPERATIONS

Industrial engineers, methods engineers, supervisors, and other personnel in production systems usually attempt to improve work methods to increase productivity by increasing the production capacity of an operation or group of operations, reducing the cost of the operations, or both.

One key to successful methods analysis is the development of a questioning attitude about every facet of the job being studied. As the techniques of methods analysis that we shall cover later in the chapter are applied, every minute part of the work will be subjected to these questions: What? Who? Where? When? How? and Why? Table 14.3 presents questions that should be asked as work methods are analyzed. Adopting this questioning attitude leads analysts to accept nothing in an operation as sacred; everything about the job will be meticulously scrutinized.

When this questioning attitude is combined with tried and proven principles of motion economy, analysts can develop modifications in work methods that lead to increased output and reduced costs.

▪▪

TABLE 14.4   Principles of Motion Economy

Use of the Human Body	*Arrangement of the Workplace*	*Design of Tools and Equipment*
The two hands should begin, as well as complete, their motions at the same time.	There should be a definite and fixed place for all tools and materials.	The hands should be relieved of all work that can be done more advantageously by a jig, a fixture, or a foot-operated device.
The two hands should not be idle at the same time except during rest periods.	Tools, materials, and controls should be located close in and directly in front of the operator.	Two or more tools should be combined whenever possible.
Motions of the arms should be made in opposite and symmetrical directions, and should be made simultaneously.	Gravity feed bins and containers should be used to deliver material close to the point of use.	Tools and materials should be prepositioned whenever possible.
Hand motions should be confined to the lowest classification with which it is possible to perform the work satisfactorily.	Drop deliveries should be used wherever possible.	Where each finger performs some specific movement, such as in typewriting, the load should be distributed in accordance with the inherent capacities of the fingers.
Momentum should be employed to assist the worker wherever possible, and it should be reduced to a minimum if it must be overcome by muscular effort.	Materials and tools should be located to permit the best sequence of motions.	Handles, such as those used on cranks and large screwdrivers, should be designed to permit as much of the surface of the hand to come in contact with the handle as possible. This is particularly true when considerable force is exerted in using the handle. For light assembly work the screwdriver handle should be so shaped that it is smaller at the bottom than at the top.
Smooth continuous motions of the hands are preferable to zigzag motions or straight-line motions involving sudden and sharp changes in direction.	Provisions should be made for adequate conditions for seeing. Good illumination is the first requirement for satisfactory visual perception.	
Ballistic movements are faster, easier, and more accurate than restricted (fixation) or controlled movements.	The height of the workplace and the chair should preferably be arranged so that alternate sitting and standing at work are easily possible.	Levers, crossbars, and hand wheels should be located in such positions that the operator can manipulate them with the least change in body position and with the greatest mechanical advantage.
Rhythm is essential to the smooth and automatic performance of an operation, and the work should be arranged to permit easy and natural rhythm wherever possible.	A chair of the type and height to permit good posture should be provided for every worker.	

▪▪

Source: Reprinted by permission from Ralph M. Barnes, *Motion and Time Study,* 4th ed. (New York: Wiley, 1958), 214.

TABLE 14.5   *Procedures of Methods Analysis*

1. Make an initial investigation of the operation under consideration.
2. Decide what level of analysis is appropriate.
3. Talk with workers, supervisors, and others who are familiar with the operation. Get their suggestions for better ways to do the work.
4. Study the present method. Use process charts, time study, and other appropriate techniques of analysis. (These techniques will be discussed later in this section.) Thoroughly describe and evaluate the present method.
5. Apply the questioning attitude, the principles of motion economy, and the suggestions of others. Devise a new proposed method by using process charts and other appropriate techniques of analysis.
6. Use time study if necessary. Compare new and proposed methods. Obtain supervisors' approval to proceed.
7. Modify the proposed method as required after reviewing the details with workers and supervisors.
8. Train one or more workers to perform the proposed method on a trial basis. Evaluate the proposed method. Modify the method as required.
9. Train workers and install the proposed method.
10. Check periodically to ensure that the expected savings are being realized.

PRINCIPLES OF MOTION ECONOMY

Before we discuss the techniques of methods analysis, let us examine several principles of motion economy that have evolved. Although these fundamentals have their genesis in the work of Frank and Lillian Gilbreth, Frederick Taylor, and others of the scientific management period, they have since been profitably applied in almost every conceivable situation. Table 14.4 lists the principles of motion economy in the categories of use of the human body, arrangement of the workplace, and design of tools and equipment. Notice that the ideas in the principles not only provide for the efficient completion of work tasks (quick and timesaving) but also conserve the energy of workers, thus reducing fatigue. These concepts form a basis for a science of work (one of the elements in Taylor's principles of management) that can be applied through the techniques that follow.

TECHNIQUES OF METHODS ANALYSIS

How do we go about analyzing work methods? Table 14.5 lists ten steps that are generally followed by methods analysts.

The following points may seem minor, but they are actually critical: (1) Workers and supervisors should participate early in the study. (2) Sell the proposed method to workers and supervisors. (3) Be willing to modify the proposed method at every step to guarantee acceptance and/or practicality. (4) Adequately train workers. (5) Follow up. Methods analysts who ignore these points are probably doomed to failure. The best-proposed method may fall on its face unless workers and supervisors want it to work.

Some useful work methods analysis techniques are flow diagrams and process charts, operation charts, and multiactivity charts. These techniques will now be illustrated through examples that demonstrate the details of their use.

Flow Diagrams and Process Charts

Flow diagrams and *process charts* are perhaps the most versatile techniques available for analyzing work methods. When used together, these two tools allow analysts to investigate a variety of situations. Several operations being performed in sequence, flow of paper work, and a worker moving from place to place while doing work are examples of work that can be analyzed through the use of these techniques.

When we wish to eliminate or reduce delays, eliminate or combine tasks, reduce travel time or distance, or use other approaches that increase output or reduce costs, we first typically use flow diagrams and process charts. This larger view often enables analysts to look beyond the minute details of the work to identify major inefficiencies involved in unnecessary tasks, excessive travel, unnecessary delays, and other elements of jobs that contribute to reduced output and increased costs.

Example 14.1 illustrates how a large insurance company uses flow diagrams and process charts to improve work methods of clerks who repetitively prepare a certain type of form. Read the example and notice that first the present method is studied, then a new and improved method is developed, the two methods are compared, and the best one is selected.

EXAMPLE 14.1   *Methods Analysis at the American Insurance Company*

Work was piling up in the claims department of the American Insurance Company because so many authorization-to-investigate forms had to be processed. It was thought that the work load could be reduced if the method of processing the forms through the department could be streamlined.

Solution

1. Prepare a flow diagram and a process chart of the present method. (See Figure 14.3.)

2. Develop an improved method and prepare a flow diagram and a process chart of the proposed new method. (See Figure 14.4.)

3. Compare the two methods and select the best method. What are the main improvements in the new method? (See Table 14.6.)

FIGURE 14.3 *Flow Diagram and Process Chart: Present Method for Completing Authorization-to-Investigate Form*

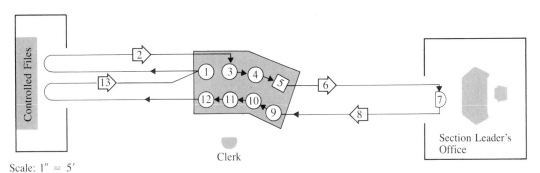

Scale: 1″ = 5′

			Summary	
Operation __Complete authorization__ | | | Operation | 7 |

Operation __Complete authorization to investigate form__
Product _____
Depts. __Property Loss__
Drawing No. __N.A.__   Part No. __N.A.__
Quantity __One form in triplicate__

Present __✔__   Proposed _____

Sheet __1__ of __1__ Sheets
Charted By __Joe Millard__
Date __9/14__
Approved By __Jim Street__
Date __9/15__

Summary
○ Operation — 7
⇨ Transport — 4
□ Inspect — 1
D Delay — 1
△ Store — —
Vertical Distance —
Horizontal Distance 180 ft.
Time (Min.) 16.000

No.	Dist. Moved (Ft.)	Worker Time (Min.)	Symbols	Description
1		.200		Remove Claim Dept.'s request from in-basket and identify client.
2	55	3.250		Walk to filing area, locate file, and return to desk.
3		.500		Locate pertinent information in client file.
4		4.750		Type information on authorization to investigate form (form no. 3355).
5		.500		Inspect form.
6	35	.200		Walk to section leader's desk.
7		.500		Wait for signature.
8	35	.200		Walk back to desk.
9		.200		Tear form apart into separate sheets.
10		1.750		Prepare regional investigator's copy for mailing, place in mail basket on desk.
11		1.500		Prepare Claims Dept.'s copy for routing, place in mail basket on desk.
12		.200		Place one copy in client's file.
13	55	2.250		Walk to filing area, refile, and return to desk.
14				

FIGURE 14.4 Flow Diagram and Process Chart: Proposed Method for Completing Authorization-to-Investigate Form

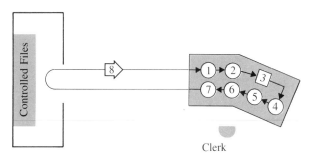

Clerk

Scale 1″ = 5′

Operation	Complete authorization	Sheet 1 of 1 Sheets	Summary		
Product	to investigate form	Charted By Joe Millard	Operation	6	
Depts. Property Loss		Date 9/20	Transport	1	
Drawing No. N.A. Part No. N.A.			Inspect	1	
Quantity One form in triplicate		Approved By Jim Street	Delay	—	
		Date 9/21	Store	—	
Present Proposed ✔			Vertical Distance	—	
			Horizontal Distance	55 ft.	
			Time (Min.)	12.250	

No.	Dist. Moved (Ft.)	Worker Time (Min.)	Symbols	Description
1		.200	○⇨□D△	Remove Claim Dept.'s request with client's claim form attached from in-basket.
2		4.750	○⇨□D△	Type information on authorization to investigate form.
3		.500	○⇨□D△	Inspect form.
4		.100	○⇨□D△	Attach routing slip to the completed form and place in mail basket on desk.
5		.200	○⇨□D△	Remove approved form from in-basket and tear apart into separate sheets.
6		1.750	○⇨□D△	Prepare regional investigator's copy for mailing, place in mail basket on desk.
7		1.500	○⇨□D△	Prepare Claim Dept.'s copy for routing, place in mail basket on desk.
8	55	3.250	○⇨□D△	Walk to filing area, locate client's file, place copy of form in file, and return to desk.
9			○⇨□D△	
10			○⇨□D△	
11			○⇨□D△	
12			○⇨□D△	
13			○⇨□D△	
14			○⇨□D△	

TABLE 14.6   Comparison of Present and Proposed Methods of Completing Authorization-to-Investigate Form — Property Loss Department

Comparison Factor	Present Method	Proposed Method	Estimated Savings
Feet traveled per form	180	55	125
Number of operations per form	7	6	1
Number of inspections per form	1	1	—
Number of delays per form	1	—	1
Minutes per form	16.000	12.250	3.750
Labor cost per form ($5 per hour)	$1.333	$1.021	$.312
Annual labor cost (300,000 forms per year)	$399,900	$306,300	$93,600

What are the principal improvements of the proposed method?

1. It eliminates retrieval of client's file by attaching claim department's claim form to request. All necessary client information is contained on this previously completed form.
2. It eliminates the necessity for clerk to obtain section leader's approval by utilizing existing interoffice mail service.

Operation Charts

The *operation chart,* sometimes called an *operator chart* or *right- and left-hand chart,* is a form of process chart that examines the coordinated movements of a worker's hands. This analysis tool is typically applied after the job has been studied through the use of flow diagrams and process charts. Next, the individual worker's job can be studied with operation charts (both present and proposed methods) to improve the efficiency of the worker's hand motions.

Figure 14.5 is an example of such an operation chart. In this chart the operator assembles U bolt cable clamps. This analysis clearly shows how the worker's two hands work together and separately to perform the operation, transportation, store, and delay elements of the assembly operation. The use of this technique gives analysts a microview of workers' work methods. Work methods can therefore be fine-tuned by removing even small inefficiencies.

Multiactivity Charts

There are several forms of *multiactivity charts,* but they all have one thing in common: They show how one or more workers work together and/or with machines. Figure 14.6, for example, is a *worker and machine chart.* This figure illustrates how a clerk in a grocery store works with a customer and with a coffee-grinding machine to produce ground coffee for the customer. We can see clearly from this chart how the

FIGURE 14.5 *Operation Chart and Workplace Layout: Assembly of U Bolt Cable Clamp — Present Method*

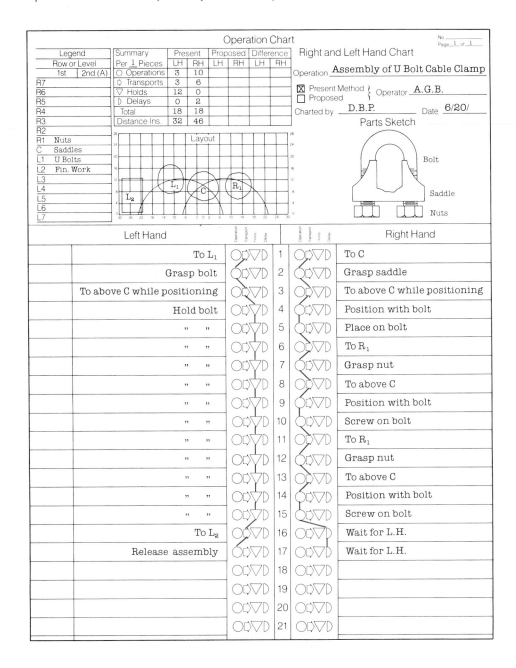

Source: H. B. Maynard, *Industrial Engineering Handbook* (New York: McGraw-Hill, 1963), 2–41. Reprinted by permission.

FIGURE 14.6 *Multiactivity Chart (Worker and Machine): Purchasing Coffee at*
Grocery Store — Present Method

Time in Sec.		Customer	Clerk	Coffee Grinder (Machine)
0	5	Ask grocer for 1 pound of coffee (brand and grind)	Listen to order	Idle
10	15	Wait	Get coffee and put in machine, set grind and start grinder	Idle
20 30 40	21	Wait	Idle while machine grinds	Grind coffee
50	12	Wait	Stop grinder, place coffee in package and close it	Idle
60 70	17	Receive coffee from grocer, pay grocer and receive change	Give coffee to customer, wait for customer to pay for coffee, receive money and make change	Idle

Summary

	Customer	Clerk	Coffee Grinder
Idle time	48 sec.	21 sec.	49 sec.
Working time	22	49	21
Total cycle time	70	70	70
Percent utilization	$\frac{22}{70} = 31\%$	$\frac{49}{70} = 70\%$	$\frac{21}{70} = 30\%$

Source: Reprinted by permission from Ralph Barnes, *Motion and Time Study,* 4th ed. (New York: Wiley, 1958), 80.

TABLE 14.7   *Fitting the Methods Analysis Techniques to the Operation under Consideration*

Characteristics of Operation Being Analyzed	Recommended Technique	Results Desired from Study
Several operations being performed in sequence	Flow diagram, process chart	Eliminate avoidable delays, reduce processing times by eliminating or combining tasks, reduce travel time and distance.
Flow of paper work	Flow diagram, process chart	Improve processing times, eliminate delays, reduce travel time and distance.
Worker moving from place to place while doing work	Flow diagram, process chart	Eliminate delays, reduce processing times, and reduce travel time and distance.
Worker performing work at fixed location	Operation chart, workplace layout	Reduce fatigue, reduce processing times by simplifying method and reducing idle time.
Worker operating one or more machines	Multiactivity chart, workplace layout	Balance worker and machine idle time, find optimal number of machines per worker.
Two or more workers working together as a team	Multiactivity chart, workplace layout	Reduce idle time, reduce processing times by eliminating or combining tasks and simplifying methods, reduce travel time and distance.

Source: Marvin E. Mundel, *Motion & Time Study,* © 1955, p. 46. Adapted by permission in *Handbook of Industrial Engineering and Management,* Ireson and Grant, Eds., © 1955, p. 288. Adapted by permission of Prentice-Hall, Inc., Englewood Cliffs, New Jersey.

clerk coordinates each step of the work with the customer and the machine and the resulting degrees of utilization of the clerk, machine, and customer. These charts are helpful in minimizing worker and machine delay and in determining the optimal number of machines per operator.

Once the general procedures of methods analysis are understood, we should consider the circumstances in which each of the methods analyses should be used. Table 14.7 describes several typical operations that are studied by methods analysis, appropriate analysis techniques, and the goals of these studies. Fitting the technique to the operation under consideration is fundamental to successful analysis.

WORK MEASUREMENT

Although methods analysis is an important element in achieving high labor productivity, another technique is also helpful in this worthwhile goal—work measurement.

What units of measurement shall we use to measure human work? Foot-pounds, calories per minute, and other units have been used historically in the physical sciences to measure work. But we must use a unit of work in operations that

TABLE 14.8   *Hierarchy of Labor Standards for Office Scissors #325*

Element Level		Operation Level		Product Level	
Element	**Element Standard (Minutes)**	**Operation**	**Operation Standard (Minutes)**	**Product**	**Product Standard (Minutes)**
a. Get	.100 ⎫				
b. Operate	.150 ⎪				
c. Turn	.050 ⎬	1. Forge	.650 ⎫		
d. Operate	.200 ⎪				
e. Trim	.150 ⎭		⎪		
		2. Grind	1.200 ⎬	#325	3.750
		3. Polish	.550 ⎪		
		4. Assemble	.700 ⎪		
		5. Package	.650 ⎭		

is both easily measured and easily understood. The unit of measure that has evolved is *worker-minutes per unit of output.* In other words, how many minutes does it ordinarily take a well-trained worker, on the average, to produce one component, subassembly, product, or service? *Work measurement* therefore refers to the process of estimating the amount of worker time required to generate one unit of output. The ultimate goal of work measurement is usually to develop labor standards that will be used for planning and controlling operations and thereby achieving high labor productivity.

LABOR STANDARDS

A *labor standard* is the number of worker-minutes required to complete an element, operation, or product under ordinary operating conditions. Standards are hierarchical. In other words, each product has a labor standard, each major operation within each product has a labor standard, and each elemental task within each operation has a labor standard. Table 14.8 shows some of the hierarchical levels of labor standards for manufacturing a pair of office scissors.

Ordinary Operating Conditions
The term *ordinary operating conditions* refers to a hypothetical *average* situation — workers' ability, workers' working speed, operation of machines, supply of materials, availability of information, and all other aspects of workers' jobs.

Dynamic Nature of Standards
Standards are dynamic. They must reflect the methods actually used in performing each element of work. When methods change, so must the labor standards change. If standards are not promptly modified as work methods change, their usefulness as planning and controlling aids is drastically diminished.

Planning and Controlling Aids

Standards are necessary as planning and scheduling tools. Estimating the number of workers required per week in each operation is computed thus:

$$\text{Workers needed} = \frac{\left(\begin{array}{c}\text{Number of products}\\\text{to be produced weekly}\end{array}\right) \times \left(\begin{array}{c}\text{Operation labor}\\\text{standard per product}\end{array}\right)}{\text{Minutes per worker per week}}$$

Additionally, standards are routinely used to monitor labor performance. In this regard, the performance of individual workers, production departments, and manufacturing plants is routinely measured and compared to standard. This labor performance is usually computed as a percentage of standard:

$$\text{August departmental labor performance} = \frac{\left(\begin{array}{c}\text{Number of products}\\\text{produced}\end{array}\right) \times \left(\begin{array}{c}\text{Labor standard}\\\text{per product}\end{array}\right)}{\text{Actual minutes of labor used}}$$

A 90 percent performance would, for example, indicate a subpar performance, and a 120 percent performance would indicate the efficient use of the department's personnel. Thus labor standards can provide operations managers with information about which individual workers, departments, and plants are performing above or below the labor standards.

Incentive Pay Systems

Standards are also used as the basis for paying workers. Although *incentive pay systems* have diminished in popularity in the United States in recent years, their use is still common, particularly in mature firms and industries where tradition dictates incentive pay. In Japanese firms such as Toyota, workers' pay checks are affected by "production allowances." These allowances are based on the production of the work team during a month. In the United States enormous variety exists in incentive pay systems, and as union–management contract negotiations evolve, so also do these systems change. However, some generalities may be summarized from this patchwork of pay systems:

1. First, the percentage performance for each worker is computed for the pay period:

$$\text{Performance} = \frac{\text{Units produced} \times \text{Labor standard per unit}}{\text{Number of minutes worked}}$$

2. Next, the worker's performance is applied to the worker's hourly base pay:

$$\text{Actual hourly pay} = \text{Hourly base pay} \times \text{Performance}$$

3. Next, the worker's pay for the period is computed:

$$\text{Worker pay} = \text{Number of hours worked} \times \text{Actual hourly pay}$$

The process for paying workers described above is commonly called *gain sharing* or *bonus plans. Halsey plans, Rowan plans,* and *Gantt task and bonus plans* are of this type.[11] The important difference among these plans is in Step 2 above: How do

---

[11] For a good discussion of these and other commonly used bonus plans, see Benjamin W. Niebel, *Motion and Time Study* (Homewood, IL: Richard D. Irwin, 1972), 605–617.

you adjust the hourly base pay? Some plans guarantee the base rate, whereas others have a sliding-scale bonus formula to determine actual hourly rates. *Piece rate plans* determine workers' pay by computing a standard payment for each unit of output at each operation:

$$\text{Operation piece rate} = \frac{\text{Hourly base pay} \times \text{Operation labor standard per unit}}{60 \text{ minutes}}$$

This piece rate (dollars/unit) is then multiplied by the units produced by a worker to compute the pay for the period.

Incentive pay systems for workers are carefully watched over by workers, unions, and management. Elaborate and precise work measurement systems have evolved to compute the labor standards used in these systems. Precision is demanded here because workers' pocketbooks are being affected.

Certain plans such as the Scanlon, Kaiser, and Eastman Kodak plans allow workers to participate in the development of cost-cutting programs.[12] Workers and work groups are subsequently rewarded on the basis of the incentive rates worked out in these management–worker committees. The savings are shared between workers and the companies. These group systems are believed to promote cooperation between workers and management in increasing productivity.

Accounting Cost Standards

Accountants routinely convert labor time standards to labor cost standards. These cost standards are particularly useful in cost estimates, labor cost variance reports, and pricing.

Cost estimates in POM occur routinely. How much will it cost to add an ear to our toy elephant? How much will it save if we eliminate Operation #104? These and other cost and savings questions must be answered, and labor cost standards help us to predict in advance of proposed actions what the cost outcomes will be. Labor variance reports are periodically prepared for each operating unit. For example, an August labor cost variance report may appear as follows:

	August Actual Labor Cost	*August Standard Labor Cost*	*August Labor Cost Variance*
Department 3251	$ 3,253	$ 3,100	$ (153)
Department 3252	4,922	5,522	600
Department 3253	10,153	8,965	(1,188)
Total section	$18,328	$17,587	$ (741)

These reports suggest potential labor performance problem areas. For example, the report above suggests that we should investigate why Departments 3251 and 3253 show unfavorable labor cost variances for August. Although rational explanations

---

[12] For good descriptions of these and other sharing plans, see A. J. Geare, "Productivity from Scanlon-Type Plans," *Academy of Management Review* 1(July 1976):99–108.

TABLE 14.9   Steps in Determining Labor Standards from Time Studies

1. Make sure that the correct method is being used to perform the operation being studied.
2. Determine how many cycles to time. A *cycle* is one complete set of the elemental tasks included in the operation. Generally, more cycles must be timed when cycle times are short, when cycle times are highly variable, and when the annual production of the product is high.
3. Break the operation down into basic tasks, which are also called *elements* (get part, hold against grinder, adjust machine, etc.).
4. Observe the operation and use a stopwatch to record the elapsed time for each element for the number of required cycles. The *observed element times* are recorded in minutes.
5. For each elemental task, estimate the speed that the worker is working. A *performance rating* of 1.00 indicates that the worker is working at normal speed, the speed at which a well-trained worker would work under ordinary operating conditions. A performance rating of 1.20 indicates 20 percent faster than normal, and a performance rating of .80 indicates 20 percent slower than normal.
6. Compute an *allowance fraction* for the operation. The allowance fraction is the fraction of the time that workers cannot work through no fault of their own. For example, if workers cannot work 15 percent of the time because of cleanup work, rest periods, company meetings, etc., the allowance fraction would be .15.
7. Determine the *mean observed time* for each element by dividing the sum of the observed element times for each element by the number of cycles timed.
8. Compute the *element normal time* for each element:

   Element normal time = Mean observed time × Performance rating

9. Compute the *total normal time* for the entire operation by summing the element normal times for all elements.
10. Compute the *labor standard* for the operation:

    Labor standard = Total normal time ÷ (1 − Allowance fraction)

may exist for these variances, these reports flag potential problem areas for management investigation.

Labor cost standards are also used to set prices of new products. Although pricing decisions are a function of many variables, such as competition, the lower limits of prices are usually set in practice by our estimates of production costs. Labor cost standards can thus be used to estimate the total labor cost for a product. When materials, overhead, shipping, and other costs are included, we have a good starting point for setting the lower limits of product and service prices.

TECHNIQUES OF WORK MEASUREMENT

If work measurement is primarily aimed at setting labor standards, how shall we go about setting these standards? Industry and government have traditionally used time study, work sampling, predetermined time methods, and subjective estimates.

Time Study

In *time study* analysts use stopwatches to time the operation being performed by workers. The results of these observed timings are then converted into labor standards that are expressed in minutes per unit of output for the operation. Table 14.9 lists the steps employed by analysts in determining labor standards based on time study. Example 14.2 demonstrates the steps in computing a labor standard from a time study.

EXAMPLE 14.2   Setting Labor Standards with Time Study

A new *Guide to Registration,* to be given to all entering students, is proposed for Metro University. The dean of student services wonders what the labor cost would be for 30,000 of the 12-page handouts.

The dean asked a business student to investigate the problem and report the results. The student thought that a good way to estimate the labor cost would be to:

1. Train a worker to collate the handouts.

2. Conduct a time study of the worker as a few of the handouts were collated.

3. Use the results of the time study to compute a labor standard for collating the handout.

4. Use the labor standard to estimate the labor cost of the entire project.

Solution

The student followed the steps of Table 14.9 and conducted a time study of the worker as the handouts were collated. The results of the time study are found in Figure 14.7. From the time study, the student knew that each handout would require .4482 minute of a worker's time. Also, the labor cost of workers in the work pool is $5 per hour, and about 15 percent of each worker's time is spent in cleaning up the work pool area, personal time, unavoidable delays, and other unproductive activities.

1. Compute the labor cost per handout:

$$\text{Labor cost per unit} = \text{Labor standard} \times \text{Labor cost per minute}$$
$$= .4482 \text{ minute} \times (\$5 \text{ per hour} \div 60 \text{ minutes per hour})$$
$$= \$.03735 \text{ per handout}$$

2. Compute the total labor cost for the project:

$$\text{Total-project labor cost} = \text{Number of handouts} \times \text{Labor cost per unit}$$
$$= 30,000 \times \$.03735 = \$1,120.50$$

FIGURE 14.7 The Study for Collating Handouts

Time Study

Operation	Collate Materials for University Handouts			
Dept.	University Work Pool	Start 12:10	Date 8/15	Operator Suzanne Ogden
Part		Stop 12:14	Shift 2	M. ___ F. ✓
Size	12-page 8½" x 11" handout	Diff. (Elapsed Time) 4 min.	Study 1	Analyst Mary Delaney
		Production 10 handouts	Sheet 1	
		Est. Time .400 min. per handout		

Remarks 12 stacks are arranged in two rows of 6 stacks each on a large table

Elements	1	2	3	4	5	6	7	8	9	10	11	12	13	14	15	Sum	Mean	Rating	Normal
1. Collate Row #1	.10	.09	.09	.08	.08	.09	.07	.10	.08	.09						.87	.087	1.00	.087
2. Tap handout on edge	.04	.03	.04	.05	.03	.04	.04	.04	.03	.05						.39	.039	.90	.035
3. Collate Row #2	.12	.09	.10	.09	.10	.10	.09	.08	.11	.10						.98	.098	1.00	.098
4. Tap handout on edge	.04	.02	.03	.05	.03	.04	.04	.03	.05	.04						.37	.037	.90	.033
5. Staple handout	.06	.06	.07	.05	.07	.06	.06	.06	.08	.05						.62	.062	1.10	.068
6. Aside	.02	.03	.04	.04	.03	.03	.03	.04	.04	.03						.33	.033	1.00	.033
7. Miscellaneous elements																			
a. Apply "stickum" to fingers					0.6											.06	.006	1.00	.006
b. Straighten stacks								.21								.21	.021	1.00	.021
															Total				.381

Labor standard = **Total normal time** ÷ **(1 – Allowance fraction)**

= **.381 ÷ (1 – .15) = .4482 minutes per handout**

Although time study offers precision in determining labor standards, in most situations it does require a competent staff of analysts. Additionally, the labor standard cannot be determined before the operation is actually performed. These deficiencies have led to the development of other work measurement techniques that are less expensive and/or may be used in advance of the performance of the operation.

Work Sampling

Work sampling is a work measurement technique that randomly samples the work of one or more employees at periodic intervals to determine the proportion of the total operation that is accounted for in one particular activity. These studies are frequently used to estimate the percentage of employees' time spent in unavoidable delays (commonly called ratio-delay studies), repairing finished products from an operation, supplying material to an operation, and so on. The results of these studies are commonly utilized to set allowances used in computing labor standards, in estimating costs of certain activities, and in investigating work methods.

Work sampling is also used to set labor standards. Example 14.3 uses a work-sampling study to set a labor standard for billing clerks to conduct credit checks on prospective customers. In this instance the purpose of the labor standard is to estimate the number of billing clerks that would be required if a new credit check department were established.

EXAMPLE 14.3   Setting Labor Standards with Work Sampling

The billing department at Gasco, the natural gas utility for the metropolitan Los Angeles, California, area, has clerks who perform these activities: (1) audit customers' bills, (2) make corrections to customers' bills, and (3) perform credit checks on prospective customers. Gasco has grown so rapidly in recent years that the credit-checking work load is mushrooming. The manager of the billing department forecasts that 150,000 credit checks will have to be made by the department next year and wonders how many clerks will be required to perform these credit checks. An analyst is assigned the job of estimating the number of clerks that would be required. This procedure is to be followed in the investigation:

1. Perform a work-sampling study to determine the proportion of time that a clerk does credit checks.

2. Compute a labor standard for each credit check based on the work-sampling study.

3. Compute the number of clerks required to perform credit checks next year.

Solution

1. Determine how many work-sampling observations are required:

TABLE 14.10 A Guide to Minimum Number of Work-Sampling Observations

Activity Percentage	Absolute Error		
[p or (1 − p)]	±1%	±2%	±3%
1 or 99	396	99	44
5 or 95	1,900	475	211
10 or 90	3,600	900	400
15 or 85	5,100	1,275	567
20 or 80	6,400	1,600	711
25 or 75	7,500	1,875	833
30 or 70	8,400	2,100	933
35 or 65	9,100	2,275	1,011
40 or 60	9,600	2,400	1,067
45 or 55	9,900	2,475	1,099
50	10,000	2,500	1,111

Note: This table is based on a 95 percent confidence interval. Absolute error means the actual range of observations of p, the percentage of the total job devoted to a particular activity. For example, if p = 25 percent and the ±2 percent column were used, we could say that we were 95 percent confident that p ranged between 23 percent and 27 percent. Smaller absolute errors require larger numbers of work-sampling observations.

Departmental personnel estimated that credit checks represented about 25 percent of clerks' jobs. The analyst referred to Table 14.10 and determined that a 95 percent confidence interval and ±3 percent absolute error would require 833 work-sampling observations. This means that the analyst would be 95 percent confident that between 22 and 28 percent of a clerk's job was credit checks.

2. Determine the time interval between work-sampling observations and the total time of the study:

The analyst planned to study a single clerk for 2½ hours with work-sampling snapshots every 10 seconds for a total of 900 observations (6/minute × 60 minutes/hour × 2.5 hours = 900). At each snapshot the analyst would record whether the clerk was doing credit checks.

3. Perform the work-sampling study and compute the labor standard for a credit check:

Type of Data	Data
Elapsed time of study (2.5 hours × 60 minutes/hour)	150 minutes
Total number of observations during study	900
Number of credit check observations during study	211
Proportion of clerk's work that was credit checks	.234
Number of credit checks completed during study	10
Performance rating of the clerk	1.10
Allowance fraction	.20

$$\begin{array}{l} \text{Time per} \\ \text{credit check} \end{array} = \left(\begin{array}{l}\text{Elapsed time}\\\text{of study}\end{array}\right) \times \left(\begin{array}{l}\text{Proportion of work}\\\text{that was credit checks}\end{array}\right) \div \left(\begin{array}{l}\text{Number of credit}\\\text{checks completed}\end{array}\right)$$

$$= 150 \times .234 \div 10 = 3.51 \text{ minutes}$$

Total normal time = Time per credit check × Performance rating
              = 3.51 × 1.10 = 3.861 minutes

Labor standard = (Total normal time) ÷ (1 − Allowance fraction)
            = 3.861 ÷ (1 − .20)
            = 4.82625 minutes per credit check

4. Compute the number of clerks required for credit checks next year:

$$\begin{pmatrix}\text{Number of}\\\text{clerks per year}\end{pmatrix} = \begin{pmatrix}\text{Number of checks}\\\text{forecast next year}\end{pmatrix} \times \begin{pmatrix}\text{Labor standard}\\\text{for credit checks}\end{pmatrix} \div \begin{pmatrix}\text{Minutes/year}\\\text{that clerks work}\end{pmatrix}$$

            = (150,000 × 4.82625) ÷ (50 weeks/year × 2,400 minutes/week)
            = 6.03, or slightly more than 6 clerks

Work sampling is less expensive than time study, but it usually offers less precision. Work sampling is usually preferred when many workers perform a single operation that is spread out over a large area. In these cases a single analyst could observe all workers at fixed time intervals, taking a snapshot every 10 seconds. This "sampling" of employees' activities allows analysts to break an operation into elements and record which element each employee is performing when the work-sampling snapshot is taken. The number of times that each element is performed in an 8-hour shift becomes the basis for the labor standard.

Predetermined Time Standards

When labor standards must be determined in advance of actually performing an operation, *predetermined time standards* can be used. These standards utilize data that have been historically developed for basic body movements, elements of operations, and entire operations. When cost estimates or pricing information is required for new operations or new products for which organizations have labor standard experience, these standards are commonly used.

Many predetermined time standard systems are used today—work factor, methods–time measurement (MTM), basic motion time study (BMT), and a host of systems custom-designed for individual companies. To demonstrate the use of these systems, we shall examine the development of MTM labor standards in Example 14.4. In this example a manager must estimate the labor cost for a newly imposed inspection and cleaning of electrical diodes. MTM is an excellent choice when ultra-light assembly work must be performed in a small geographic area and when quick, accurate, and low-cost labor standards are required.

EXAMPLE 14.4   Developing Labor Standards with MTM

Bill Rogers, production superintendent for Electec, which manufactures diodes for the electronics industry, has just requested an estimate of additional labor costs if the company's XG1500 diode were to be inspected and cleaned. This request resulted from a few recent

TABLE 14.11   *MTM Labor Standard Calculation for XG1500 Diode Inspection and Cleaning Operation*

Left Hand	MTM Code	TMU (1/100,000 Hour)	MTM Code	Right Hand
1. Reach to bin of electrical components.	R10C	12.9		
2. Grasp component to be tested.	G4B	9.1		
3. Move component to exposed inspection meter stop (10 inches).	M10A*	11.3		
4. Position component on test meter.	P2SS	19.7		
5. Observe electrical continuity light.	EF	7.3		
6. Transfer component to other hand.	G3	5.6	G3	Grasp component.
		9.2	M5C	7. Move component to abrasion wheel.
		19.7	P2SS	8. Position component on abrasion wheel.
		8.0	M5B	9. Move component to bin.
		2.0	RL1	10. Release component.

Total TMU = 104.8 units
= 104.8 ÷ 100,000 = .001048 hour
= .001048 × 60 = .0629 minute

* Look up this TMU in Table 14.12.

component failures in the field. Ruth Bell, an industrial engineer, is briefed on how the new inspection operation would be performed. She tells Bill that she will have an estimate for him in an hour and disappears to her office.

Ruth Bell knows that although Electec personnel had never performed the inspection and cleaning operation, a good labor estimate could be developed by using methods–time measurement (MTM). She got out her MTM manual, wrote down the right- and left-hand activities, estimated distances to be traveled, described the nature of the hand motions, and looked up the TMUs (time measurement units) for each activity. One TMU equals 1/100,000 of an hour. The results of this analysis are found in Table 14.11.

Because Ruth estimates that 80 minutes per shift will be unavoidably nonproductive, she calculates the following:

Allowance fraction = (Minutes of allowance) ÷ Minutes per shift
= 80 minutes ÷ 480 minutes = .1667

Labor standard = Normal time ÷ (1 − Allowance fraction)
= .0629 minute ÷ (1 − .1667) = .0755 minute per XG1500 diode

Standard cost = Labor standard × Labor cost per minute
= .0755 minute × $.129 per minute = $.0097 per XG1500 diode

TABLE 14.12   MTM—TMUs for Moving Objects with Hands and Arms (Move—M)

Distance Moved (Inches)	Time TMU				Wt. Allowance			Case and Description
	A	B	C	Hand in Motion B	Wt. (lb.) Up to	Dynamic Factor	Static Constant TMU	
¾ or less	2.0	2.0	2.0	1.7				
1	2.5	2.9	3.4	2.3	2.5	1.00	0	
2	3.6	4.6	5.2	2.9				A Move object to other hand or against stop.
3	4.9	5.7	6.7	3.6	7.5	1.06	2.2	
4	6.1	6.9	8.0	4.3				
5	7.3	8.0	9.2	5.0	12.5	1.11	3.9	
6	8.1	8.9	10.3	5.7				
7	8.9	9.7	11.1	6.5	17.5	1.17	5.6	
8	9.7	10.6	11.8	7.2				B Move object to approximate or indefinite location.
9	10.5	11.5	12.7	7.9	22.5	1.22	7.4	
10	11.3	12.2	13.5	8.6				
12	12.9	13.4	15.2	10.0	27.5	1.28	9.1	
14	14.4	14.6	16.9	11.4				
16	16.0	15.8	18.7	12.8	32.5	1.33	10.8	
18	17.6	17.0	20.4	14.2				
20	19.2	18.2	22.1	15.6	37.5	1.39	12.5	
22	20.8	19.4	23.8	17.0				
24	22.4	20.6	25.5	18.4	42.5	1.44	14.3	C Move object to exact location.
26	24.0	21.8	27.3	19.8				
28	25.5	23.1	29.0	21.2	47.5	1.50	16.0	
30	27.1	24.3	30.7	22.7				
Additional	0.8	0.6	0.85		TMU per inch over 30 inches			

Source: Copyrighted by the MTM Association for Standards and Research. No reprint permission without written consent from the MTM Association, 16-01 Broadway, Fair Lawn, NJ 07410.

Ruth returned to the meeting and told Bill the results of her MTM analysis: The estimated labor standard for the proposed inspection and cleaning operation was .0755 minute per diode, and the estimated labor cost was $.0097 per diode. She took along the MTM table for the basic *Move* motion (Table 14.12) to demonstrate how the standard was estimated. She explained the third left-hand activity, M10A. To find this, look up the distance moved of 10 inches, go across to Column A, and read the TMU — 11.3, which is in 100,000ths of an hour. This is converted to hours and minutes by dividing by 100,000 and multiplying the result by 60.

TABLE 14.13 *Appropriate Work Measurement Techniques for Some Jobs*

Job	Appropriate Work Measurement Technique
1. A job performed by a single worker in a fixed location. The job involves repetitive short cycles and is expected to continue relatively unchanged for long periods while producing large quantities of outputs. The resulting labor standards must be very accurate.	Time study
2. A job performed by a single worker in a fixed location. The job involves repetitive short cycles and will be changed periodically as customer orders for relatively small quantities of products change. The labor standards are used for accounting cost standards, pricing analyses, and production planning.	Predetermined time standards
3. A job performed by many workers over a compact area. The tasks may involve little repetition; but if repetitious, the cycles are usually very long. Workers must be observed by a single analyst. Although a moderate degree of accuracy in the labor standards is desired, time study would be too costly. Only large elements of work need to be observed; little detail is needed in setting the labor standards.	Work sampling
4. Any job or group of jobs in which very accurate labor standards are not required or in which the cost of time study, predetermined time standards, and work sampling is prohibitive.	Subjectively set labor standards

Subjectively Set Labor Standards

In some organizations labor standards are determined by rather gross estimates of the amount of work involved in each operation. In some cases *historical labor standards* are determined by using historical data from the actual performance of the operation. Although this procedure is low in cost, quick, and easy to understand, it has some rather fundamental flaws. First, this method implicitly assumes that past performance of the operation is *standard.* No formal methods studies are required as in time studies. Therefore work methods and labor standards are not explicitly related. Second, no attempt at performance rating is present. These and other weaknesses in historical labor standards generally lead operations managers to use these types of labor standards only when the use of the standards is not crucial and precision is therefore not critical.

Like historical labor standards, other rough estimates have evolved. *Crew size standards,* for example, are determined by estimating the total number of workers required to produce the necessary output per shift. This total number of worker minutes per shift is then divided by the required output per shift. *Supervisor estimates* are occasionally used. These standards are based on supervisors' intimate knowledge of the operations for which they are responsible. These and other roughly estimated standards are commonly used in industry today. Their uses are, however, usually limited to those situations where more expensive techniques cannot be justified. Although the precision of these methods leaves much to be desired, their cost and speed make their use common when rough estimates are better than no standards at all.

Time study, work sampling, predetermined time standards, and subjectively set labor standards may all be appropriate work measurement techniques, depending on the nature of the job being considered. Table 14.13 describes some jobs for which each of these techniques is appropriate. Regardless of the work measurement techniques employed to develop labor standards, their ultimate goals are the same:

1. To set benchmarks or standards against which to measure the actual performance of operations. The objective is to improve labor productivity.
2. To establish estimates of labor content in operations as planning aids for operations managers. Such estimates can be used to compare production methods, make cost estimates, determine product prices, and set incentive pay rates.

Labor standards are dynamic and must change as job conditions change. One type of change that affects all jobs is that workers learn, and as they learn, production times decrease.

LEARNING CURVES

In 1925 the commander of the Wright-Patterson Air Force Base in Dayton, Ohio, observed that workers exhibited definite learning patterns in manufacturing operations.[13] Since these first studies, we have learned that most aircraft-manufacturing tasks experience an 80 percent learning rate. In other words, the labor-hours required to assemble an aircraft is reduced by a factor of .8 as the production quantity is doubled. Figure 14.8 shows how the learning of workers causes the labor-hours per unit to fall as the number of units produced increases. If the first aircraft assembled requires 100 labor-hours, the second aircraft would require .8 × 100 = 80 labor-hours, the fourth would require .8 × 80 = 64 labor-hours, the eighth would require .8 × 64 = 51.2 labor-hours, and so on.

The concept of the learning curve rests well with operations managers because they know through experience that in the beginning of production runs workers are unfamiliar with their tasks and the amount of time required to produce the first few units is high. But as the workers learn their tasks, their output per day increases up to a point and then levels off to a rather constant output rate. Additionally, learning curve concepts are based on these underpinnings: (1) Where there is life, there can be learning. (2) The more complex the life, the greater the rate of learning. Worker-paced operations are more susceptible to learning or can give greater rates of progress

[13] Miguel A. Reguero, *An Economic Study of the Military Airframe Industry* (Wright-Patterson Air Force Base, Ohio: Department of the Air Force, October 1957), 213.

FIGURE 14.8 Aircraft Assembly 80 Percent Learning Curve

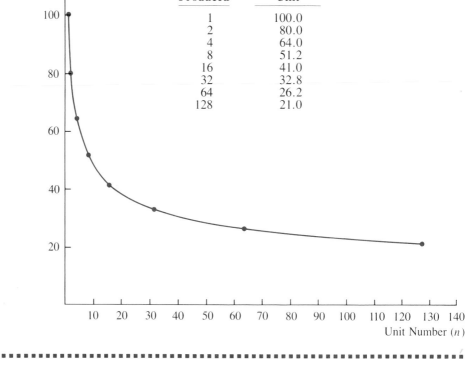

n^{th} Unit Produced	Labor-Hours for n^{th} Unit
1	100.0
2	80.0
4	64.0
8	51.2
16	41.0
32	32.8
64	26.2
128	21.0

than machine-paced operations. (3) The rate of learning can be sufficiently regular to be predictive. Operations can develop trends that are characteristic of themselves.[14] Workers are thus observed to improve eye and hand coordination, learn to perform tasks, and develop technical skills as they gain more experience in performing certain operations. It is helpful to be able to analyze these workers' learning situations and to be able to estimate: (1) the average number of labor-hours required per unit for N units in a production run, (2) the total number of labor-hours required to produce N units in a production run, and (3) the exact number of labor-hours required to produce the nth unit of a production run.

There are three approaches to learning-curve problems: arithmetic analysis, logarithmic analysis, and learning curve tables.

---

[14] Winfred B. Hirschmann, "Profit from the Learning Curve," *Harvard Business Review* 42(February 1964):118.

TABLE 14.14 Learning-Curve Values of b

Learning Rate	b
70%	−.515
75	−.415
80	−.322
85	−.234
90	−.152

ARITHMETIC ANALYSIS

Arithmetic analysis is the simplest approach to learning-curve problems because it is based on this fundamental concept: As the number of units produced doubles, the labor-hours per unit decline by a constant factor. This approach was introduced in Figure 14.8. For instance, if we know that the learning rate is 80 percent for a particular operation and that the first unit of production took 100 labor-hours, the labor-hours required to produce the eighth unit is:

nth Unit Produced	Labor-Hours for nth Unit
1	100.0
2	80.0
4	64.0
8	51.2

As long as we wish to find the labor-hours required to produce n units and n just happens to be a number that is one of the doubled values, then this approach works. But what if we want to find the labor-hours required to produce the seventh unit? Arithmetic analysis does not let us answer this question with precision, but logarithmic analysis does answer such questions.

LOGARITHMIC ANALYSIS

In logarithmic analysis this relationship allows us to compute T_n, which is the labor-hours required to produce the nth unit:

$$T_n = T_1(n^b)$$

where T_1 is the labor-hours to produce the first unit and b is the slope of the learning curve. The values of b are found in Table 14.14. For instance, if we know that the learning rate for a particular operation is 80 percent and that the first unit of production took 100 labor-hours, the labor-hours required to produce the eighth unit is:

$$T_n = T_1(n^b)$$

$$T_8 = 100(8^{-.322}) = 51.2 \text{ labor-hours}$$

TABLE 14.15 *Learning-Curve Coefficients*

Unit No.	75% Unit Time	75% Total Time	80% Unit Time	80% Total Time	85% Unit Time	85% Total Time	90% Unit Time	90% Total Time
1	1.000	1.000	1.000	1.000	1.000	1.000	1.000	1.000
2	.750	1.750	.800	1.800	.850	1.850	.900	1.900
3	.634	2.384	.702	2.502	.773	2.623	.846	2.746
4	.562	2.946	.640	3.142	.723	3.345	.810	3.556
5	.513	3.459	.596	3.738	.686	4.031	.783	4.339
6	.475	3.934	.562	4.229	.657	4.688	.762	5.101
7	.446	4.380	.534	4.834	.634	5.322	.744	5.845
8	.422	4.802	.512	5.346	.614	5.936	.729	6.574
9	.402	5.204	.493	5.839	.597	6.533	.716	7.290
10	.385	5.589	.477	6.315	.583	7.116	.705	7.994
11	.370	5.958	.462	6.777	.570	7.686	.695	8.689
12	.357	6.315	.449	7.227	.558	8.244	.685	9.374
13	.345	6.660	.438	7.665	.548	8.792	.677	10.05
14	.334	6.994	.428	8.092	.539	9.331	.670	10.72
15	.325	7.319	.418	8.511	.530	9.861	.663	11.38
16	.316	7.635	.410	8.920	.522	10.38	.656	12.04
17	.309	7.944	.402	9.322	.515	10.90	.650	12.69
18	.301	8.245	.394	9.716	.508	11.41	.644	13.33
19	.295	8.540	.387	10.10	.501	11.91	.639	13.97
20	.288	8.828	.381	10.49	.495	12.40	.634	14.61
21	.283	9.111	.375	10.86	.490	12.89	.630	15.24
22	.277	9.388	.370	11.23	.484	13.38	.625	15.86
23	.272	9.660	.364	11.59	.479	13.86	.621	16.48
24	.267	9.928	.359	11.95	.475	14.33	.617	17.10
25	.263	10.19	.355	12.31	.470	14.80	.613	17.71
30	.244	11.45	.335	14.02	.450	17.09	.596	20.73
35	.229	12.62	.318	15.64	.434	19.29	.583	23.67
40	.216	13.72	.305	17.19	.421	21.43	.571	26.54
45	.206	14.77	.294	18.68	.410	23.50	.561	29.37
50	.197	15.78	.284	20.12	.400	25.51	.552	32.14
60	.183	17.67	.268	22.89	.383	29.41	.537	37.57
70	.172	19.43	.255	25.47	.369	33.17	.524	42.87
80	.162	21.09	.244	27.96	.358	36.80	.514	48.05
90	.155	22.67	.235	30.35	.348	40.32	.505	53.14
100	.148	24.18	.227	32.65	.340	43.75	.497	58.14
120	.137	27.02	.214	37.05	.326	50.39	.483	67.93
140	.129	29.67	.204	41.22	.314	56.78	.472	77.46
160	.122	32.17	.195	45.20	.304	62.95	.462	86.80
180	.116	34.54	.188	49.03	.296	68.95	.454	95.96
200	.111	36.80	.182	52.72	.289	74.79	.447	105.0
250	.101	42.08	.169	61.47	.274	88.83	.432	126.9
300	.094	46.94	.159	69.66	.263	102.2	.420	148.2
350	.088	51.48	.152	77.43	.253	115.1	.411	169.0
400	.083	55.75	.145	84.85	.245	127.6	.402	189.3
450	.079	59.80	.140	91.97	.239	139.7	.395	209.2
500	.076	63.68	.135	98.85	.233	151.5	.389	228.8
600	.070	70.97	.128	112.0	.223	174.2	.378	267.1
700	.066	77.77	.121	124.4	.215	196.1	.369	304.5
800	.062	84.18	.116	136.3	.209	217.3	.362	341.0
900	.059	90.26	.112	147.7	.203	237.9	.356	376.9
1,000	.057	96.07	.108	158.7	.198	257.9	.350	412.2
1,200	.053	107.0	.102	179.7	.190	296.6	.340	481.2
1,400	.050	117.2	.097	199.6	.183	333.9	.333	548.4
1,600	.047	126.8	.093	218.6	.177	369.9	.326	614.2
1,800	.045	135.9	.090	236.8	.173	404.9	.320	678.8
2,000	.043	144.7	.087	254.4	.168	438.9	.315	742.3
2,500	.039	165.0	.081	296.1	.160	520.8	.304	897.0
3,000	.036	183.7	.076	335.2	.153	598.9	.296	1,047

The learning-curve table approach allows us to answer such questions as the one posed above. We can also answer other important questions.

LEARNING-CURVE TABLES

Table 14.15 gives us learning-curve coefficients that allow us to compute not only the labor-hours for the nth unit in a production run, but also the total labor-hours for the entire production run where the nth unit is the last unit in the production run. Example 14.5 illustrates the use of the coefficients in the table.

EXAMPLE 14.5   *Using Learning-Curve Tables*

A manufacturing plant must develop a cost estimate for a customer's order for eight large turbine shafts. It is estimated that the first shaft will take 100 hours of shop time and an 80 percent learning curve is expected. **(a)** How many labor-hours should the eighth shaft require? **(b)** How many labor-hours should the whole order for eight shafts require? **(c)** If the labor rate is $12.50 per hour and the pricing policy of the company is to double the labor cost of the order, what is the customer price for each shaft? **(d)** Trouble is encountered on the order and it is obvious that the original estimate was too low because it took 90 labor-hours for the third shaft. The company wants to approach the customer with a revised price for the order. What should the new customer price be for the whole order?

Solution

a. How many labor-hours should the eighth shaft require?

First, look up the unit time for Unit No. 8 in Table 14.15. This value is .512, and the labor-hours for the eighth shaft is:

$$\text{Labor-hours for eighth unit} = \left(\begin{array}{c}\text{Labor-hours}\\\text{for first}\\\text{unit}\end{array}\right) \times \left(\begin{array}{c}\text{Unit time}\\\text{for Unit}\\\text{No. 8}\end{array}\right)$$

$$= 100 \times .512 = 51.2 \text{ labor-hours}$$

b. How many labor-hours should the whole order for eight shafts require?

First, look up the total time for Unit No. 8 in Table 14.15. This value is 5.346, and the labor-hours for the whole order is:

$$\text{Labor-hours for whole order} = \left(\begin{array}{c}\text{Labor-hours}\\\text{for first}\\\text{unit}\end{array}\right) \times \left(\begin{array}{c}\text{Total time}\\\text{at Unit}\\\text{No. 8}\end{array}\right)$$

$$= 100 \times 5.346 = 534.6 \text{ labor-hours}$$

c. If the labor rate is $12.50 per hour and the pricing policy of the company is to double the labor cost of the order, what is the customer price for each shaft?

First, compute the labor cost for the order:

$$\text{Labor cost for order} = \left(\begin{array}{c}\text{Labor-hours}\\\text{for order}\end{array}\right) \times \left(\begin{array}{c}\text{Labor}\\\text{rate per}\\\text{hour}\end{array}\right)$$
$$= 534.6 \times \$12.50 = \$6,682.50$$

Next, double the labor cost to obtain the customer price for the whole order:

$$\text{Price for order} = 2 \times \text{Labor cost for order}$$
$$= 2 \times \$6,682.50 = \$13,365.00$$

Next, divide the customer price for the whole order by the number of units in the order to obtain a per-unit price:

$$\text{Price per shaft} = (\text{Price for order}) \div (\text{Units in order})$$
$$= \$13,365 \div 8 = \$1,670.63$$

d. What should the customer price be for the whole order if the third unit took 90 labor-hours?

First, compute a revised value for the first unit. The unit time for Unit. No. 3 in Table 14.15 is .702:

$$\text{Labor-hours for third unit} = \left(\begin{array}{c}\text{Labor-hours}\\\text{for first}\\\text{unit}\end{array}\right) \times \left(\begin{array}{c}\text{Unit time}\\\text{for Unit}\\\text{No. 3}\end{array}\right) = 90$$

$$= \left(\begin{array}{c}\text{Labor-hours}\\\text{for first}\\\text{unit}\end{array}\right) \times .702 = 90$$

Labor-hours for first unit = $90/.702 = 128.21$ labor-hours

Next, compute the labor-hours for the whole order by using the new 128.21 estimate for the labor-hours for the first unit:

$$\text{Labor-hours for whole order} = \left(\begin{array}{c}\text{Labor-hours}\\\text{for first}\\\text{unit}\end{array}\right) \times \left(\begin{array}{c}\text{Total time}\\\text{at No. 8}\\\text{Unit}\end{array}\right)$$
$$= 128.21 \times 5.346 = 685.41 \text{ labor-hours}$$

Next, compute the new customer price on the whole order by doubling the labor cost for the whole order:

$$\text{Customer price for order} = 2 \times 685.41 \text{ labor-hours} \times \$12.50 = \$17,135.27$$

SELECTING A LEARNING RATE

How does a firm select a learning rate for a particular operation? In many firms industrial engineers or other production analysts are trained to analyze an operation and fit a learning rate to that operation. They read trade journals that publish industry-wide data on specific types of operations and their learning rates. Also, they compare historical records with learning rates within their own companies and categorize their operations according to established learning rates. When new operations require learning rate estimates, the analysts can compare these operations to existing operations with known learning rates within their own companies, or they can fit the new operations to industry standards.

USES AND LIMITATIONS OF LEARNING CURVES

Experienced operations managers know that as production personnel gain experience with a new product/service or operation, the labor-hours per unit fall. Consequently, labor standards are expected to decline on many products and operations, and cost standards, budgets, production scheduling, staffing plans, and prices are necessarily affected.

In job shops and custom service operations, learning-curve theory is very important because:

1. Products and services tend to be custom designs that require workers to start near the beginning of small batches.
2. Batches tend to be small; thus labor-hours per unit improves dramatically from the first to the last unit.
3. Product/service designs tend to be complex; thus labor-hours per unit improves quickly.

The application of learning curves to mass production and standard service operations is less significant because entirely new products or services are rare, and long production runs and simplified tasks combine to cause labor-hours per unit to improve only slightly.

Industrial engineers and other staff specialists routinely use learning-curve theory to develop labor cost estimates for new products and services. For example, for companies that produce products for the U.S. military, NASA, and companies outside their own firms, learning curves are routinely used to estimate the amount of labor that will be required on each contract. This use allows the companies to prepare cost estimates and product prices for bidding purposes.

Applying learning curves in practice can be difficult because:

1. It may be impossible either to develop precise labor-hour estimates for the first unit or to determine the appropriate learning rate. Large unique projects exhibit both of these difficulties.
2. Different workers have different learning rates. In a pure sense, learning theory applies only to individual workers, but little difficulty is encountered in applying learning curves to groups of workers by developing an *average learning rate.* But we can get into trouble when we apply learning curves to further aggregations such as direct labor cost per unit, indirect labor cost per unit, material cost per unit, or even the labor-hours in a production department. Although these aggregations may be observed to improve as output increases, we must remember that individual workers learn and materials and machines do not. Application of learning curves to these aggregate measures must therefore be based on substantial evidence of improvement.

3. Few products are completely unique. Workers are usually well trained in the completion of tasks within their skill classifications. Past performance on related tasks therefore results in latent learning that is transferred to new products and services. As lot sizes are reduced through JIT programs, workers will produce about the same number of parts annually, but in many more and smaller lots. How much learning is carried over from lot to lot and what does the concept of a first unit mean in this setting?

These and other difficulties cause us to use great care in applying learning curves. The simplistic analyses of learning curves are tempting to apply universally in POM, but experience teaches us that judgment must be exercised in using the results of these studies. Have we used good labor-hour estimates for the first unit? Is an 80 percent learning rate appropriate? As the amount of touch labor in products decreases, how should learning curves be applied to knowledge workers? Is this really a new operation? In practice, these and other questions must be answered and the results of learning curve analysis appropriately adjusted before operations managers can act on these studies.

EMPLOYEES' HEALTH AND SAFETY

Hazards are inherent in most jobs. Employees can fall on slippery floors; fall from ladders; walk into protruding materials; get parts of their clothing or bodies caught in belts, gears, cutting tools, dies, and drill presses; be hit by flying pieces from grinding wheels and metal chips from lathes; and so on. Elevator shafts, stairs, balconies, heavy moving equipment, trucks, fires, explosions, high voltage electricity, molten metals, toxic chemicals, noxious fumes, dust and noise—all pose dangers to our employees. These and other hazards have always been around. They are not new. What perhaps is new is the growing body of government laws and regulations intended to provide employees with uniformly safe working conditions across all states, industries, and companies.

In modern times management has been concerned about the safety and health of employees. This concern was evident in the establishment of safety and loss prevention departments early in this century before laws rigidly forced employers to comply with government-imposed safety standards. The personnel management movement in the early 1900s and the human relations movement in the 1940s both contributed to this development. These movements emphasized the necessity to protect employees on the job and directly contributed to the growing number of formal safety programs in government and industry.

Two sets of laws have also critically affected employees' health and safety—the workmen's compensation laws and the Occupational Safety and Health Administration Act (OSHA). During the early 1900s the states gradually passed *workmen's compensation laws.* These laws provided for specific compensation amounts going to employees for various types of injuries incurred on the job. Employees no longer were required to bring suit through the courts and prove negligence by employers. Additionally, employers were protected by the maximum limitation on these settlements, and the number of court suits was reduced.

Although workmen's compensation laws went a long way toward compensating employees after they were injured on the job, three facts detracted from their effectiveness in ensuring safe working conditions:

1. Because the laws varied greatly among states and industries, this patchwork of regulations created great gaps in coverage and extreme variation in compensation for similar injuries.
2. Inflation and the enormous rise in the cost of health care have made compensation amounts of most of these laws inadequate.
3. The laws do not strike directly at the heart of the worker health and safety problem — creating a safe work environment for employees.

These and other deficiencies of the workmen's compensation laws and other contemporary developments led to the passage in 1971 of the *Occupational Safety and Health Administration Act (OSHA)*. OSHA established a federal agency whose primary functions were to set safety standards for all areas of the work environment for all industries and to enforce these standards through an inspection and reporting system. This law officially recognized, perhaps for the first time, the basic right of all employees to a safe working environment regardless of the state, industry, or firm in which they worked.

No company is beyond the reach of OSHA. Its inspectors routinely call on employers, conduct inspections, identify unsafe working conditions or violations of OSHA standards, require employer corrective actions, and the law can force compliance through the courts. OSHA is indeed a mighty force that management must deal with.

Cities, counties, and states also participate in regulating and/or inspecting the safety of working conditions of operations. In California, for example, a manufacturing plant can expect inspections concerning fire hazards on a regular basis from these sources: (1) in-plant inspectors, (2) division and corporate inspectors, (3) city fire marshal, (4) county fire marshal, (5) state fire marshal, (6) OSHA, (7) insurance carriers, and (8) union inspectors. These and other sources of regulation of operations form a network of worker safety protection that for all practical purposes provides a guarantee of managements' continual diligence in designing jobs that are safe for employees.

Experienced managers know, however, that even in this environment of over-inspection, employees can still be injured and their health damaged. Managers therefore establish *safety and loss prevention departments*. Not only do these departments interface with all of the sources of safety inspections, but also these specialists design safety devices and procedures aimed at protecting employees, raise employee awareness, and design advertising programs to minimize hazards resulting from human error. These and other activities are undertaken not just because it is the law, but because it is also the right and ethical thing to do. And besides — it is good business. When working conditions are safe, employee morale and labor productivity tend to be higher and the direct costs of accidents tend to be lower. Therefore management has a large stake in maintaining a safe working environment for employees.

SUMMARY

Today's production systems are made up of jobs designed primarily for efficiency, maximizing the output from each hour of employee effort. This tradition from the scientific management era is being modified, however, to account for employee and customer needs. Employees want more interesting work, and customers want low cost, timely deliveries, and high quality. The supreme challenge for POM today is to accommodate customer and employee needs while continuously trimming inefficiencies from operations and thereby surviving the onslaught of foreign and domestic competition.

Work methods analyses are studies of operations aimed at employee productivity and efficiency. These studies encompass the total working environment of employees—work methods, materials, machines, layout of workplaces, lighting, and so on. The employees themselves are perhaps the most important source for improving work methods. They know the intricacies of each operation, and they are an invaluable source of suggestions if they will participate. Once the appropriate level of analysis has been determined, the procedures to follow, a questioning attitude, and the principles of motion economy guide methods analysts in their work.

Work measurement involves the estimation of the actual amount of human work required to produce one unit of output from an operation. The universal unit of work measurement is the amount of time in minutes ordinarily required for a well-trained employee to produce one unit of output. These worker-minutes per unit become labor standards. Labor standards are dynamic and must change as work methods change. They are used for incentive pay systems, accounting cost standards, and other planning and controlling applications. Time study, work sampling, predetermined time standards, and subjectively set labor standards are commonly used techniques of work measurement.

Useful guidelines have evolved for designing jobs that are both efficient and satisfying to workers. This growing body of knowledge is a provocative area in POM. Although some work is being done on this important problem, much more remains to be done if we are to reduce employee turnover and absenteeism, increase quality of outputs, and improve morale.

REVIEW AND DISCUSSION QUESTIONS

1. Describe the general attitudes of younger employees in industry toward their work. What explanation can you give for these attitudes?
2. Define *productivity*. How should we measure productivity? Why should companies today be particularly concerned with productivity?
3. Given the makeup of production costs of U.S. manufacturers today, which resources should receive the focus of productivity improvement programs? Why?
4. Explain why a multifactor approach to measuring productivity is needed.
5. What two variables affect labor productivity? Explain how they affect productivity. Under what conditions should we expect employees whose needs are satisfied to be productive?

6. Describe Maslow's hierarchy of needs. What meaning does the hierarchy have for today's operations managers?
7. Make three suggestions for each of these:
   a. modifying employees' job tasks to improve employees' needs for self-control,
   b. modifying employees' immediate job settings to make jobs more satisfying, and
   c. modifying employees' larger work environments to make jobs more satisfying.
8. Define *job design.*
9. What two criteria must be used to evaluate proposals to remedy job design?
10. Name three key obstacles to achieving the integration of employees' needs with productivity in job design.
11. What are union work rules? Give examples of work rules and explain how they affect productivity.
12. Define and explain the questioning attitude of methods analysis.
13. Name five principles of motion economy relating to use of the human body.
14. Name five techniques of methods analysis.
15. Define *work measurement.* What is the universal unit of measure in work measurement? Name five causes of allowances.
16. Name three uses of work sampling.
17. Discuss the role of time study, work sampling, and other industrial engineering techniques in designing jobs.
18. As the number of aircraft doubles in production runs, what happens to the labor-hours per unit?
19. Why are learning curves perhaps more beneficial in job shops, custom services, and other intermittent production systems?
20. Give three reasons that problems can be encountered in using learning curves. Explain why care must be taken in applying learning curves to material costs, overhead costs, and departmental labor costs.

PROBLEMS

1. Bill Bonnet is Bratz Agricultural Chemicals' sales manager for the southern region. Twenty-two salespersons report to Bill and sell chemicals to jobbers throughout 12 southern states. During the past 5 years Bill has put together a team of salespersons that is second to none in its ability to cooperate. These salespersons appear to be happy with their jobs in all respects, including pay, supervision, attitude toward the company, and morale. Bill feels that he has done everything in his power to make each salesperson in his group happy with his particular job.

   In recent months Bratz's sales in the southern region have declined 10 percent when compared to comparable periods in the past. Bill has racked his brain to come up with some reason, such as decline in the overall economy or competitor activity, to explain the sales decline. After much investigation, however, Bill has concluded that there has been a drop-off in productivity among the salespersons because of lack of motivation.

    a. Use motivation theory to explain how employees who are happy with their jobs could be unproductive.

    b. What was Bill doing wrong?

    c. What should Bill do to correct this situation? Give the specific steps that he should follow in improving the productivity of the southern region sales staff.

2. Mercury Electric manufactures electric motors in Watertown, Connecticut. Mercury's industrial engineering department has been successful in designing assembly line jobs that are highly specialized and technically efficient. The assembly line at Mercury is so refined, in fact, that its labor cost per unit is lower than that of any of its competitors in spite of its workers receiving the highest average annual pay in the industry. When Mercury's workers were recently interviewed by a national television commentator, their comments were:

- We like working at Mercury; we wouldn't work anywhere else.
- The pay is good and besides we like the way management treats us.
- Our foremen are great guys; you know we work hard but you can depend on them giving you a square deal and they stick up for you.
- If you screw up, they don't crucify you; sure, they point out what we did wrong and tell us to avoid the problem in the future, but they don't make a federal case out of it.
- When we do a good job, they're down here in a hurry to let us know that they appreciate the good work.
- If we've got a problem, we can walk right in to the boss's office and level with him. That gets results around here. And if he's got a rush order that needs to be produced and shipped quick, he'll come right down on the line and talk to us about it. We appreciate the way we can talk openly around here. It's a two-way street, you know?
- Sure, the work on the assembly line can get monotonous, but taking everything into consideration, this is the best job I've ever had.
- Quality is good, absenteeism is low, and turnover is low around here. Why not? It's a good place to work.

    a. Are these workers satisfied with their jobs? Explain how these workers are satisfying their physiological, safety, social, esteem, and self-fulfillment needs.

    b. Why haven't the monotonous assembly line jobs at Mercury resulted in high absenteeism, high turnover, and low product quality?

    c. A new personnel manager at Mercury insists that he expects absenteeism and turnover to increase as new younger workers who have a lower tolerance for job boredom are gradually hired into the plant. What job design remedies should be tested at Mercury? Justify your proposals.

3. Mary Margret Tack manages a medium-sized garment factory in El Paso, Texas. Worker turnover and absenteeism have plagued her operation during the two years she has been plant manager. The cost of hiring new workers and having standby workers to fill in for absent workers is excessive. With the help of some personnel and engineering persons from the home office in Oklahoma City, the following estimates of cost savings and cost increases from alternative job design remedies were made:

Job Design Remedy	Average Per-Unit Cost Increase Due to Reduced Technical Efficiency	Average Per-Unit Cost Savings Due to Reduced Turnover and Absenteeism
Job rotation	$.059	$.085
Job enrichment	.092	.129
Time away from jobs	.065	.055
Supervisor training	.057	.090

   a. If only one of the proposals can be accepted, rank the remedies in order of desirability.

   b. Should Mary Margret reassign her industrial engineers to another plant because time studies will no longer be needed?

   c. Are the above remedies mutually exclusive, that is, in practice can only one of the remedies be applied at a time? What are some likely combinations?

4. Prepare a process chart for these operations:
   a. changing a flat tire on a bicycle, and
   b. patching a knee on a pair of work trousers.

5. Prepare an operation chart for making a double-dip ice cream cone. Can you make suggestions for improving your work method?

6. Prepare a flow diagram for processing a computer program at your school. How would you change this process to reduce travel distance and processing times?

7. Prepare a multiactivity or worker–machine chart for making three photocopies on a pay copy machine.

8. Using the principles of motion economy, design a method for these operations, documenting each method on an operation chart:
   a. buttering a piece of toast,
   b. replacing the ink element in a ballpoint pen, and
   c. filling a stapler with staples.

9. Go to your school's library. Study the procedure for checking out books at the main desk. Prepare a process chart for the present method and one for an improved proposed method. What are the estimated savings of the proposed method over the present method, in labor savings dollars and client time?

Time Study

10. Margaret Bower, production analyst at the Atlanta plant of Computer Products Corporation (CPC), has just completed a time study of a quality control test. The test is a circuit integrity and final performance check on personal and small-business computers. In this test the computer being tested is attached to a control computer that checks every possible performance attribute of the computer being tested and also checks the circuitry of the computer. Quality control operators perform the test

on all personal computers and small-business computers manufactured at the Atlanta plant. Therefore an accurate labor standard is needed to plan for and control the labor productivity at the operation. Margaret's time study found that the average time to complete the test was 41.5 minutes, the performance rating of the operators was 1.10, and the allowances were 80 minutes per 8-hour shift.

a. Compute a labor standard for the operation.
b. How many tests per 8-hour shift should an experienced operator be expected to perform under ordinary operating conditions?
c. If the labor rate for quality control operators is $11 per hour, what should the accounting department use as the standard labor cost per test?

11. A quality control technician performs a certain quality control (QC) test several times each day. A time study showed that the average time for the QC test is 12.55 minutes, the performance rating is 1.00, and allowances are 60 minutes per 8-hour shift:

a. Compute the labor standard for the operation.
b. If the technician performed only this test repeatedly, how many tests per 8-hour shift could be completed under ordinary operating conditions?
c. If the technician's labor rate is $9.75 per hour, what should the accounting department use as the standard labor cost per test?

12. A maintenance department of a large manufacturing plant routinely calibrates an electronic control unit for its production machines. A time study is performed on this operation, resulting in the data below (in minutes):

	Cycle								Performance
Element	1	2	3	4	5	6	7	8	Rating
1. Get and position unit	.10	.12	.15	.10	.09	.14	.12	.10	1.05
2. Perform calibration	1.50	1.90	1.60	1.80	1.70	1.90	2.00	2.00	1.20
3. Perform standard tests	4.90	3.85	5.19	4.50	5.50	4.72	4.60	5.21	.85
4. Update card and remove unit	.50	.60	.70	.60	.60	.50	.80	.60	1.00

Allowance per 8-Hour Shift
Clothes change	12 minutes
Unavoidable delay	20
Lunch	30
Shower and change	20
Total	82 minutes

a. Compute the mean observed time for each element in minutes.
b. Compute the normal time for each element and total normal time in minutes.
c. Compute the allowance fraction for the operation.
d. Compute the labor standard for the operation.

13. A bead-taping operation for 14-inch passenger tires is repeated continuously by 25 operators at the Quality Tire Company in Chevron, Michigan. This operation was time studied:

Element	Cycle										Performance Rating
	1	*2*	*3*	*4*	*5*	*6*	*7*	*8*	*9*	*10*	
1. Get bead, insert in clamp	.10	.08	.10	.12	.11	.09	.08	.10	.11	.10	.90
2. Operate to roll bead	.18	.20	.22	.25	.20	.22	.21	.19	.20	.20	.85
3. Get tape and insert	.15	.20	.17	.20	.17	.30	.19	.17	.19	.20	1.05
4. Operate to roll tape on bead	.40	.35	.30	.35	.38	.39	.41	.40	.38	.38	1.00
5. Straighten tape	—	.20	—	—	.22	—	—	.20	—	—	1.10
6. Remove finished bead	.10	.08	.06	.08	.09	.08	.08	.07	.08	.08	1.00

Allowance per 8-Hour Shift

Clothes change	10 minutes
Unavoidable delay	15
Rest periods	24
Area clean-up	10
Shower and change	20
Total	79 minutes

a. Compute the labor standard for this operation.
b. If the labor rate is $8.90 an hour, what is the accounting standard labor cost for taping beads for each 14-inch tire if each tire has two beads?
c. How many beads per operator should be expected for each 8-hour shift?

Work Sampling

14. Bobby White wants to study the 72 minutes allowed each operator for allowances during each 8-hour shift. He proposes to perform a work-sampling study of the operation with particular emphasis on the allowances. If a 95 percent confidence interval and a ± 3 percent absolute error are acceptable, how many work-sampling observations are required?

15. A time study is being performed on an operation to set a labor standard. Problems have been encountered, however, in developing an allowance fraction. The analyst knows that 60 minutes are normally devoted to coffee breaks and lunch, but an allowance for unavoidable delay must be estimated. A ratio-delay work-sampling study was conducted, with the following results:

Activity	Number of Observations
Unavoidable delay	52
Avoidable delay	39
Other	384

What allowance fraction should be used in setting the labor standard if allowances include unavoidable delay, lunch, and coffee breaks? Assume 480 minutes per shift.

16. Margaret Bower, production analyst at the Atlanta plant of Computer Products Corporation (CPC), has performed a work-sampling study of a manufacturing operation at the plant. In the operation the workers assemble keyboards for personal and small-business computers. The purpose of the study is to establish a labor standard for the operation. The results of the study are:

Activity	Percentage of Operators' Time
Assemble keyboards	90%
Allowances	10

If the workers who were performing the operation during the study each produced an average of 8.5 keyboards per 8-hour shift and received a performance rating of 1.05, what is the labor standard per keyboard?

17. A work-sampling study was conducted for a packaging operation in a mail-order shipping room over a 40-hour week. During the study the operator completed 390 finished packages and was rated at 1.15 performance while packaging. The results of the study were:

Activity	Number of Observations
Packaging	375
Unavoidable delay*	80
Rest periods*	45

* Included in allowances.

a. Determine the total normal time per package.
b. Determine the labor standard per package.

Incentive Pay Systems

18. A company has a wage incentive gain-sharing or bonus plan for its hourly employees. Joe Blare, an employee in the tube-splicing department, has just completed a one-week pay period. The information on his time card is:

Total hours worked = 39.5

Total production = 550

Labor standard per unit = 5.386 minutes

Hourly base pay = $8.75 per hour

If the company uses the following formula to compute actual hourly pay, what is Joe Blare's pay for the period?

Actual hourly pay = Hourly base pay × Performance

19. Bill Bray, an employee of Yelco Manufacturing's machining department, operates a boring mill. Yelco has installed a straight piece-rate incentive pay system for its employees. A two-week pay period has just ended and Bray is estimating his pay for the period from this information:

Total production $= 1,200$ units

Labor standard per unit $= 4.500$ minutes

Hourly base pay $= \$7.501$ per hour

a. Compute Bill Bray's piece rate for this product on the boring mill operation.
b. Compute his pay for the period.

20. John Blake, a production worker at the Atlanta plant of Computer Products Corporation (CPC), has finished a week of work at the plant in assembling keyboards for personal and small-business computers. The operation that he performs is included in a piece-rate compensation plan at the plant. He has just completed his production and time record to be turned in to his supervisor, and he wants to determine what his pay is for the week. His production and time record includes this information:

Production for week $= 45$ keyboards

Labor standard per keyboard $= 56.47$ minutes

Hourly base pay $= \$11$ per hour

a. Compute John Blake's piece rate per keyboard.
b. Compute his pay for the week.

Learning Curves

21. The Boston plant of Computer Products Corporation (CPC) has just received a customer's request for a price quotation for a year's supply of a custom-made resin. The order for 250 batches would be manufactured at regular intervals throughout the year. The plant's staff estimates that it would take 49 labor-hours to produce the first batch and that as their personnel became more experienced with the manufacture of the resin, the labor required per batch should conform to a 75 percent learning curve. CPC expects no follow-on orders for the resin. Estimate the average labor-hours per batch on which CPC should base its price quotation.

22. The Contrast Printing Company is now developing a price quotation on a special commemorative issue of *Life or Death Magazine.* The issue will have a special leather and gold leaf binding that involves all handwork for workers. It is estimated that the first unit will require 4 labor-hours, and a 90 percent learning rate is expected.
    a. Estimate the labor-hours for the sixteenth unit.
    b. Estimate the labor-hours for all 16 units.
    c. As the workers are producing the issue, the fifth unit actually requires 3.5 labor-hours. Was the estimate of 4 labor-hours for the first unit accurate? Estimate how many labor-hours the first unit actually required.

23. A valued customer has just called in a change in his order to Mercury Electric Motor Winding Service Company. The customer had first asked for a quote on repairing 20 electric motors. Now he wants only 12 or 13 motors repaired. To assist Mercury's management in responding to this customer:
    a. Estimate the labor-hours required for the original 20 units if the first unit is estimated to require 10 labor-hours and an 80 percent learning curve is expected.
    b. Estimate the labor-hours required for an order of 12 units.
    c. Estimate the labor-hours required for the thirteenth unit.

CASES

NILO SIGNAL COMPANY

Norbert Gailer is the new plant manager for the Nilo Signal Company of San Martin, California. The plant produces signal products for the highway, railway, and marine markets. Mr. Gailer is now confronted with a problem left over from his predecessor — low productivity within the bonnet operation. It is imperative to increase the output of this operation because it is the bottleneck operation for the entire assembly line of the plant. In fact, the bonnet operation's present production level is 20 percent below the capacity of all other operations on the assembly line. The excessive labor costs that result from underutilized personnel have caused the plant to operate in the red for several months and, furthermore, the plant's production level is inadequate to satisfy the demand of its customers.

Eight women per shift now staff the bonnet operation. In the distant past the operation was performed totally by hand and the workers' pay was based on the number of pieces produced by the group per shift. The workers now say that they never liked the incentive pay system. About a year ago some machines were installed in the bonnet operation as part of a plantwide program aimed at increasing plant capacity. It was estimated at the time that the production level of the bonnet operation would be increased by 30 percent. The number of women in the group was reduced according to plan, the machines were installed, the production levels did increase, but only by about 10 percent. About three months ago, when Mr. Gailer took over as plant manager, one of his first duties was to negotiate with the union representatives concerning the incentive pay system of the bonnet operation, the only such system in the plant. The system was done away with, and the bonnet operation workers were placed on hourly rates in line with similar work in other areas of the plant. The negotiations went well and all parties seemed satisfied with the outcome.

Mr. Gailer thought that the change in the pay system would trigger higher production levels in the bonnet operation, but the output remained below that of the other operations. Mr. Gailer met with the bonnet group and with individuals from the group to discuss the situation. Bernadine Murphy, the union steward for the plant and a member of the bonnet group, candidly indicated that the working relations between the former plant manager and the group had been strained. She seemed open and cooperative, not at all the troublemaker described by the previous plant manager. Mr. Gailer spoke plainly to the group. "The plant is in trouble profitwise. We can't produce enough products to satisfy our customers and they are beginning to turn to our competitors. As I see it, the output of the bonnet operation is presently at the center of our difficulties. Time studies indicate that we should be able to get another 20 percent of production per shift out of the operation with just a fair day's work for a fair day's pay. Can't we work together to get the production level of your operation up? If I can assist you in any way, my door is open. Just walk across and tell me your needs and we'll get going." The group did not deny that production levels of the operation could be substantially improved. No immediate response came from the group, but during the next two weeks several personal contacts were made between individuals and Mr. Gailer:

1. Mary Malviola walked into Mr. Gailer's office during an afternoon break and said that the bonnet room was so hot that the women were all wrung out by the end of the shift. She thought that two or three fans would solve the problem. Mr. Gailer believed that the room was warm, perhaps a little warmer than some of the other operations' locations.

2. Mioke Kisama walked up to Mr. Gailer in the parking lot before work one morning and showed him her hands. Her fingernails were torn and broken and her hands had several nicks, scratches, and scrapes. She said that the new machines were chewing up the workers' hands and that it was hard to make her own hands look pretty for her husband after they had been exposed to the machines all day long. She felt that some of the new-type gloves that she had seen at a local store would solve the problem and asked Mr. Gailer if he would supply the gloves to the group.

3. Mary Halalakala came into the main office during an afternoon break and asked Mr. Gailer if he would come over to the bonnet room. He accompanied her to a window on the west side of the room. She told him that the sun glared directly into the workers' eyes during the late afternoon and wondered if he would have a sunshade, blind, or awning installed.

4. Bernadine Murphy, the plant's union steward, entered Mr. Gailer's office during a morning break and asked him if he would support a plantwide Christmas party.

Assignment

1. Why is the production level depressed at the bonnet operation? Discuss the possible reasons for the development of the problem.

2. What should Mr. Gailer do about the requests from the bonnet group? Discuss the pros and cons of following your recommendations for responding to the requests. How are your recommendations directed toward the underlying problem?

3. What course of action should Mr. Gailer take to solve the problem of low productivity and to avoid its recurrence?

COMPUTER PRODUCTS CORPORATION (CPC)

Bobby White, production analyst at the Austin, Texas, plant of Computer Products Corporation (CPC), has just completed a time study of a quality control test of small-computer printers. Here are the results of his study (in minutes):

	Cycle						Performance
Element	1	2	3	4	5	6	Rating
1. Get and place	.15	.16	.12	.18	.12	.15	1.00
2. Connect probes	.30	.35	.20	.25	.36	.30	1.10
3. Computer test	2.50	2.50	2.50	2.50	2.50	2.50	1.00
4. Record results	.50	.55	.60	.50	.58	.55	1.00
5. Aside printer	.20	.25	.22	.28	.30	.25	.90

Bobby has determined that for an 8-hour shift the nonproductive time for the operation should be 10 minutes for unavoidable delay, 10 minutes for starting up the operation at the beginning of the shift, and 30 minutes for cleaning up and straightening up around the operation.

Assignment

1. Compute the labor standard for the operation.
2. How many tests should an experienced worker perform in an 8-hour shift under ordinary operating conditions?
3. If you were the operations manager in charge of this operation and the workers performing the test did fewer tests per shift than your answer to No. 2 above, what would you do?
4. How are the concepts of "normal speed" and "ordinary operating conditions" used in time studies? How do these concepts affect how you would use the labor standard developed in No. 1 above?
5. What is it about time studies that leaves workers and even some business students with a bad feeling? What could you as an operations manager do to help alleviate these feelings?

NORCOM ELECTRONICS

Betty Wright is the vice president of manufacturing at NorCom Electronics. The firm manufactures electronic components for the computer industry. Although the firm is profitable, the competitive pressure from foreign manufacturers has become intense. Betty believes that NorCom must improve its productivity in order to survive. Her staff analysts have prepared the following information (component sales in millions of components, labor in millions of hours, and dollar amounts in millions):

	1988	1989	1990
Component sales	49.1	50.9	57.3
Direct labor	93.3	99.3	120.3
Indirect labor	23.3	24.8	30.1
Materials cost	$373.2	$357.4	$389.8
Total capital investment	221.0	229.9	261.1
Inventory investment	43.1	41.6	39.5
Production equipment	156.3	159.6	174.3
Other investment	21.6	28.7	47.3
Total overhead spending	321.0	366.2	394.1
Sales revenue	441.9	470.8	550.1

Assignment

1. Where should NorCom focus its attention in improving its productivity? Why?
2. Develop a proposal of how to compute a measure of productivity for each of the factors of production for NorCom. What are the pros and cons of each measure?

3. Using your proposal from No. 2 above, compute the productivity for each factor of production in each of the three years.

4. Using your computations from No. 3 above, compute the percentage change from 1988 to 1989 and from 1989 to 1990 for each factor of production.

5. Based on your computations, what would you say are the major problems or opportunities related to productivity at NorCom?

SELECTED BIBLIOGRAPHY

Abernathy, W. J. "The Limits of the Learning Curve." *Harvard Business Review* 52(September–October 1974):109–119.

Adam, E. E., Jr., et al. *Productivity and Quality: Measurement as a Basis for Improvement.* Englewood Cliffs, NJ:Prentice-Hall, 1981.

Aft, Lawrence S. *Productivity Measurement and Improvement.* Reston, VA: Reston Publishing, 1983.

Andress, Frank J. "The Learning Curve as a Production Tool." *Harvard Business Review* 32(January–February 1954):87–95.

Barnes, Ralph M. *Motion and Time Study.* 8th ed. New York: Wiley, 1980.

Bell, Cecil H., Jr., Terence R. Mitchel, and Denis D. Umstot. "Goal Setting and Job Enrichment: An Integrated Approach to Job Design." *Academy of Management Review* 3(October 1978):867–879.

Charlisle, Brian. "Job Design Implications for Operations Managers." *International Journal of Operations and Production Management* 3, no. 3(1983):40–48.

Davis, Louis E., and Albert B. Cherns. *The Quality of Working Life.* Vols. 1 and 2. New York: Free Press, 1975.

Geare, A. J. "Productivity from Scanlon-type Plans." *Academy of Management Review* 1(July 1976):99–108.

Henrici, S. B. "How Not to Measure Productivity." *New York Times,* Mar. 7, 1982.

Hirschmann, Winfred B. "Profit from the Learning Curve." *Harvard Business Review* 42(February 1964):118.

Holdham, J. H. "Learning Curves—Their Applications in Industry." *Production and Inventory Management* 11(Fourth Quarter 1970):40–55.

Karger, Delmar W. *Advanced Work Measurement.* New York: Industrial Press, 1982.

Kirkman, Frank. "Who Cares about Job Design?" *International Journal of Operations and Production Management* 2, no. 1 (1981):3–13.

Konz, Stephan A. *Work Design: Industrial Ergonomics.* 2d ed. Columbus, Ohio: Grid, 1983.

Mali, Paul. *Improving Total Productivity; MBO Strategies for Business, Government, and Not-For-Profit Organizations.* New York: Wiley, 1978.

Mumford, Enid, and Mary Weir. *Computer Systems in Work Design—the ETHICS Method.* New York: Halstead, 1979.

Mundel, Marvin E. *Motion and Time Study: Improving Productivity.* 5th ed. Englewood Cliffs, NJ: Prentice-Hall, 1978.

Reguero, Miguel A. *An Economic Study of the Military Airframe Industry.* Wright-Patterson Air Force Base, Ohio: Department of the Air Force, 1957.

Sutermeister, Robert A. *People and Productivity.* 2d ed. New York: McGraw-Hill, 1969, ii.

U.S. Department of Labor, Occupational Health and Safety Administration. *All about OSHA.* OSHA publication No. 2056.

Yelle, Louis E. "The Learning Curve: Historical Review and Comprehensive Survey." *Decision Sciences* 10, no. 2(April 1979):302–328.

TOTAL QUALITY CONTROL

JAPANESE PRODUCTS SUPERIOR IN QUALITY

Elwood S. Buffa, in his book *Meeting the Competitive Challenge,* cites three examples of how Japanese manufacturers have achieved superior product quality.[1] "Matsushita bought the Motorola TV assembly plant in Franklin Park, Illinois, which had a poor record of both productivity and quality (more than 150 defects per 100 completed sets). Within three years, Matsushita was able to increase productivity by 30 percent and reduce defects to below 4 per 100 sets. This was an outstanding achievement but still not up to the .5 percent quality standards achieved in comparable Japanese plants.[2] Sanyo bought the ailing Warwick TV plant in Forest City, Arkansas — sales had declined to such an extent that 80 percent of the plant capacity had been closed. Sears owned 25 percent of the stock and had been buying most of Warwick's production under its own label, but quality was so poor that Sears turned to Japanese manufacturers for most of its needs. But within two months after Sanyo's takeover, quality had improved from a defect rate of about 30 percent to less than 5 percent, while productivity had improved substantially on the line.[3] David Garvin studied room air-conditioner manufacturers in the United States and Japan with conclusions that are no longer startling. The findings were: Failure rates of air conditioners made by the worst producers, all of which were American, were between 500 and 1,000 times greater than those made by the best producers, all of which were Japanese. The average American manufacturer had 70 times as many defects on the assembly line as the average Japanese manufacturer and made 17 times as many service calls during the first year following the sale. The defect percentages of air conditioners produced by the worst Japanese manufacturers were less than half of those produced by the best American manufacturers. Companies with the best quality records also had the highest labor productivity. The extra cost of making higher-quality Japanese goods was about half the cost of fixing defective products by American manufacturers."[4]

---

[1] Elwood S. Buffa, *Meeting the Competitive Challenge* (Homewood, IL: Dow Jones-Irwin, 1984) 123–124.

[2] S. C. Wheelwright, "Japan — Where Operations Really Are Strategic," *Harvard Business Review* (July – August 1981), 67 – 74.

[3] Y. Tsurumi, "Productivity: The Japanese Approach," *Pacific Basin Quarterly* (Summer 1981), 8.

[4] David A. Garvin, "Quality on the Line," *Harvard Business Review* (September – October 1983).

As the previous account clearly illustrates, U.S. manufacturers today have a big problem with the productivity of their workers and the quality of their products. Japanese manufacturers are beating us at what used to be our own game, low-cost mass production of manufactured products, and they have added a new dimension. Not only are they producing products at lower costs, but their product quality is superior to that of U.S. producers. At about the same time that the superiority of Japanese product quality has reached a peak, consumerism in the United States also is at an all-time high. U.S. consumers want products of high quality, and now the Japanese have given them a standard to use in defining high quality. In this environment consumers' demands for quality go well beyond manufactured goods to include all types of products and services.

All operations managers are concerned with the quality of both products and services today. The nature of each particular product or service determines the nature of this concern. Table 15.1 lists some common products and services and their principal quality control concerns. Managers usually want their products to meet certain physical, chemical, and performance specifications and tolerances, to be adequately packaged to protect their contents during shipment and handling, to be attractive in appearance, and to comply with government regulations and guidelines. Services must usually be delivered in courteous, prompt, and accurate ways, be within a total environment that is pleasing to customers, and be within government regulations.

Quality control begins long before products and services are delivered to customers. As Figure 15.1 shows, early in the production system raw materials, parts, and supplies must be of acceptable quality before they are allowed to be used. Materials must meet the appropriate specifications—strength, size, color, finish, appearance, chemical content, weight, and other characteristics. As the inputs of the production system proceed through production, the quality of these partially completed units is monitored to determine whether the system is operating as intended. This monitoring is aimed at alerting operations managers that corrective action is needed before poor-quality products and services are produced. Then finished products and services are examined to determine their acceptability. This span of quality control activities from the beginning to the end of production systems is an important part of POM, but quality control today must transcend even this broad view.

QUALITY DRIVES THE PRODUCTIVITY MACHINE

For many years operations managers held the traditional view that there was an inverse relationship between productivity and the quality of products and services. In other words, when the quality of products and services improved, productivity lessened and the cost of doing business grew. Increasingly, however, operations managers today believe that this traditional view is no longer valid. Japanese manufacturers are credited with popularizing the notion that *quality drives the productivity machine*. This means that if workers do it right the first time and produce products and services that are defect-free, waste is eliminated and costs are reduced. In this new way of thinking, when operations managers work to eliminate defects, the quality of products and services is improved and at the same time productivity also improves.

TABLE 15.1   *Some Products and Services and Their Principal Quality Control Concerns*

Product/Service Organization	Quality Control Concerns
1. Commercial chemical fertilizer manufacturer	Does the product contain the correct amount of each chemical? Does the packaging avoid the absorption of excess moisture under ordinary conditions of use? Is particle sizing correct?
2. Hospital	Is the patient treated courteously by all hospital personnel? Does each patient receive the correct treatments at the correct times? Is each treatment administered with precision? Does the entire hospital environment support patient recovery?
3. University	Does each student take the prescribed courses? Is each student achieving acceptable performance in courses? Is each faculty member contributing to the growth and development of students? Does the university environment support high scholarship?
4. Automobile manufacturer	Does the auto perform as intended? Is its appearance pleasing? Is each part of the auto within the manufacturing tolerances? Is the design safe to operate? Does the auto have the intended endurance? Is the auto's gas mileage, pollution control, and safety equipment within government guidelines?
5. Bank	Is each customer treated courteously? Are each customer's transactions completed with precision? Do customers' statements accurately reflect their transactions? Does the bank comply with government regulations? Is the physical environment pleasing to customers?
6. Construction lumber mill	Is the lumber properly graded? Is the lumber within moisture content tolerances? Are knotholes, splits, surface blemishes, and other defects excessive? Is lumber properly packaged for shipment? Does the lumber comply with strength specifications?

Raymond Wachniak, corporate director of quality assurance at Firestone Tire and Rubber Company, states that "for every dollar you spend on preventing defects, you save two dollars or more in reduced scrap, product failures, and other costs." Reduced scrap is not the only saved production cost. Fewer machines are shut down to investigate the causes of quality problems; thus interruptions to production and shop

FIGURE 15.1   Quality Control throughout Production Systems

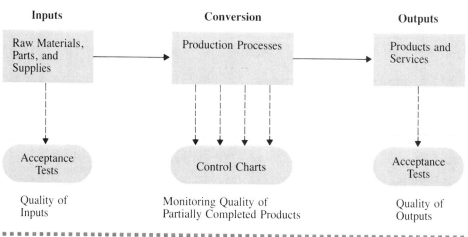

floor confusion are reduced as product quality improves. "It has been estimated that 20 to 25 percent of the overall cost of goods sold is spent on finding and correcting errors."[5] Quality control programs today, therefore, are viewed by many companies as productivity improvement programs.

In the following section we shall discuss the concept of total quality control, an organization-wide view of product quality. Next we shall examine the concepts of modern quality control. Then we shall discuss the statistical underpinnings of quality control as we develop control charts and acceptance plans. Finally, the use of computers in quality control and quality control in services will be explored.

TOTAL QUALITY CONTROL (TQC)

The quality problem in the United States is severe and pervasive enough that a Band-Aid approach will not solve the problem. We are well past the stage when slogans or quick-fix gimmicks are viable solutions. Some U.S. manufacturers have performed major surgery on their organizations from shop floors to boardrooms in an effort to put their organizations in positions to compete with superior Japanese products. Such efforts are often referred to as *total quality control (TQC)*. The Spectrum Control Inc. case at the end of this chapter is an example of such organization-wide efforts.

The underlying principle of TQC is to produce products of high quality in the first place, rather than depend on detecting defective products later through inspection. Here is how the entire organization gets behind this principle of TQC:

---

[5] Henry J. Johansson, "Factories, Services, and Speed," *New York Times,* Jan. 17, 1988.

1. **Top management policies.** Top management issues statements about how the quality of its products and services fits into the organization's business strategies. The level of quality of each of the organization's products and services is an important element and basic to the market strategy. Top management support is crucial to the total commitment of the organization to producing superior products and services. Fundamental to TQC is this philosophy: In order to achieve defect-free production, every piece of the business must be done right the first time and every piece of the business must continue to improve.

2. **Quality control training for everyone.** Toward implementing the TQC philosophy of top management, every employee—from the shop floor to the boardroom, both staff and line, as well as suppliers and major customers—should participate in a comprehensive training program. At the Ford Motor Company, for example, over 6,000 people attended 59 different courses in a two-year period and over 1,000 suppliers sent their employees to Ford for training programs on quality control methods. These programs were aimed not only at statistical quality control techniques, but also at the broader concepts of TQC.

3. **Product or service design.** Product design is important to product quality on several levels. First, the degree of product standardization can have important implications for product quality. Japanese manufacturers require standardized product designs and repetitive manufacturing for the application of their Just-in-Time (JIT) methods. Reduced lot sizes in these JIT systems account for much of the superior product quality of Japanese goods. Next, engineering designs determine how well a product functions, its level of reliability, and the customers' perceptions of its quality. Next, on the shop floor, ease of manufacturing and consistency of production are affected by the materials that go into products, by part tolerances, and by other product design characteristics.

4. **Quality materials from suppliers.** To ensure that materials from suppliers are of the highest quality, suppliers must be brought into a company's quality control program. The Ford Motor Company is a good example of how this should work. At Ford the initial selection of suppliers is based on how well suppliers can interface with Ford's quality control program. Suppliers send their personnel to Ford's training programs in quality control. Ford has about 300 suppliers on its Q-1 list, a list of suppliers with which Ford is willing to have long-term (usually three-year) supply contracts in order to achieve highest quality at competitive costs. Because Q-1 suppliers participate in the design of new Ford products, the designs reflect the suppliers' ability to produce high-quality materials.

5. **Control in production.** Production organizations must be totally committed to producing products and services of perfect quality. But more than this, there must be a commitment to strive relentlessly for improvement in product quality. It is this compulsion by the Japanese that has brought them to where they are now—the constant diligence applied to improving every detail of manufacturing. The idea of perfect quality should apply to every facet of the

production system, from every raw material at suppliers to every worker on assembly lines, to every warehouse worker. The responsibility for *producing* products of high quality does not rest with quality control personnel; on the contrary, the workers who produce the products are responsible. In this sense, therefore, quality control is not a staff function in the production organization; rather, it is a line function. Every worker is expected to pass on to the next operation products that are of perfect quality. If they do not, production is stopped and the worker who is producing inferior products corrects the problem. There are well-known inspection and control techniques of quality control that can assist in identifying these problems. But quality cannot be inspected into products; high-quality products must be *produced*.

6. **Distribution, installation, and use.** Packaging, shipping methods, and installation must be included in TQC because poor product performance is equated with poor product quality by consumers, even if the product was damaged in shipment or was improperly installed. This means that warehousing, marketing, and the distribution function also have to be committed to perfect quality.

Each of these elements is crucial to a successful TQC program. We shall be emphasizing the fifth element here—control in production—but let us not forget that top management policies, quality control training for everyone, product or service design, quality materials from suppliers, and distribution and installation methods are also important elements of product and service quality.

Although quality control programs provide the framework for achieving and improving the desired quality levels of products and services, several questions must ultimately be resolved in POM before these plans can be effective.

ROLE OF PRODUCT QUALITY IN BUSINESS STRATEGY

Setting the quality level of products and services is a strategic decision that involves most functional areas of organizations—marketing, accounting and finance, production, and engineering. When products and services are initially designed, a fundamental determination must be made about the outputs. How much quality will customers pay for? What quality level and price best position us in the market? What quality features allow us to best compete in the market?

Fundamentally, determining the appropriate level of quality is based on marketing considerations and estimated production costs. At one extreme, for example, nails are produced at very low quality levels, at very low production costs per unit, and in massive quantities. The resolution of the appropriate quality level of nails is therefore determined by the market: Customers prefer low-cost and low-quality nails to higher-cost nails that are masterpieces. At the other extreme, Rolls-Royce automobiles are built to the highest quality specifications because their customers want high quality and are willing to pay handsomely for it.

Determining the level of quality for a product or service is therefore a conscious business strategy that guides the entire quality control program. This strategy sets in large part the required organizational structure for quality control.

ORGANIZING FOR QUALITY CONTROL

Traditionally, quality control departments in organizations have been structured much like the production departments. This parallel relationship grew from the customary role of quality control, which was to monitor, measure, and report on the production department's quality performance. By designing quality control departments that paralleled the structure of the production departments, a balance of power was struck between the two functions. Quality control, on the one hand, pressed for production's conformance to quality standards; production, on the other hand, pushed for low costs, high production volume, and acceptable quality. This relationship placed quality control in a watchdog role over production.

Such a relationship has caused organizational difficulties. First, quality control personnel may not have the authority to shut down assembly lines when product quality is subpar; only production personnel can ordinarily do this. Also, assembly line workers felt that quality control personnel were always checking on them; thus production workers felt *controlled* rather than *in control,* which led to frustration and reduced morale. Next, this approach placed implicit responsibility for product quality on quality control. Quality control staff groups cannot accept responsibility for the performance of production workers. If production workers produce substandard products, how can quality control be responsible? These and other problems have caused operations managers to rethink this traditional approach to the structure, placement, and role of quality control departments in organizations.

Based on the concept of job enlargement and knowledge of the success of Japanese manufacturers, many production workers' jobs today are being redesigned to include primary quality control responsibility. This arrangement requires that each worker be responsible for passing parts of perfect quality to the next downstream operation, an approach that is often referred to as *quality at the source.* This arrangement does four things: First, it assigns responsibility for product quality to production workers and the production function, where it belongs. Second, it enlarges the jobs of production workers so that the workers inspect their own production, a task that was formerly performed by quality control personnel. Such an approach can lead to production workers who are more emotionally committed to high product quality. Third, it allows quality control personnel to do work, other than inspecting and testing, that will have direct impact on producing products of high quality. Some of these duties are monitoring production procedures to make sure that standard procedures are followed, working with production personnel to remove the causes of defects, training workers in quality control, and working with suppliers to improve their product quality. Fourth, it removes an obstacle to cooperation between quality control personnel and production workers so that they can better work together for higher product quality. We shall discuss the concept of quality at the source in more detail later in this chapter.

Quality control departments are often divided into subdepartments that are differentiated by scientific disciplines. One company, for example, has mechanical, chemical, electronic, and hydraulic quality control subdepartments. Employees are grouped together in these units so that the necessary supervision, training, and flexibility in personnel assignments are facilitated. Quality control personnel are usually highly trained physical scientists from such disciplines as mechanical, electrical, civil, and chemical engineering; physics; biology; mathematics; and chemistry.

These scientists engage in inspection, testing, and other duties. Inspections are performed at various points along the production system to determine the acceptability of incoming raw materials, to monitor the quality performance of production processes, and finally to determine the acceptability of the final products. Inspection involves the careful measurement of raw materials, in-process parts, or finished goods against prescribed quality standards. Go-no-go gauges, surface finish gauges, scales, circuit continuity meters, and other measurement devices are used in these inspections. Testing can be a highly specialized field within quality control. Chemical formulations are often verified in chemical tests, electronic instruments are tested for their resistance to vibration, concrete blocks are tested for their maximum compression pressure, and piston rings are tested for surface hardness. These and other quality control tests are usually performed in laboratories by scientists who are highly trained in their respective disciplines. Other routine tests may not require extensive scientific skills and may be performed by inspectors out in the production departments.

ROLE OF INSPECTION IN QUALITY CONTROL

Regardless of who does the inspection, production workers or quality control personnel, how many of an organization's outputs to inspect is to some degree a question of economics. Figure 15.2 demonstrates that as more and more outputs are inspected, the costs of inspection increase while the costs of undetected defects decline. At some point some particular level of inspection results in an optimal trade-off in which total quality control costs are minimized. Inspection costs include such costs as personnel training, supervision of inspectors, inspection labor, conducting tests, maintenance of testing and inspection facilities, scrap, and rework. The costs of undetected defects include such costs as customer complaints, loss of customer goodwill, product replacement costs, product liability suits, product recall programs, and returned products. Operations managers must balance these costs, conceptually at least, in deciding how many to inspect.

Practically speaking, for most products and services, we do not inspect all outputs. Not only would this be *uneconomical,* but it would also be impossible in cases where destructive testing is employed. For example, when concrete blocks are crushed to determine their maximum compression strength, the product is destroyed. Ammunition, fire extinguishers, and intercontinental missile systems are similarly destroyed when tested. Obviously, these products must be tested by using sampling plans, which we shall discuss later in this chapter.

When to inspect during production processes can usually be determined by following these general principles: (1) Inspect *after* operations that are likely to produce faulty items. (2) Inspect *before* costly operations. (3) Inspect *before* operations that cover up defects. (4) Inspect *before* assembly operations that cannot be undone. (5) On automatic machines, inspect first and last pieces of production runs but few in-between pieces. (6) Inspect finished products. The reasoning behind these principles is largely economic.

FIGURE 15.2   *Trading Off the Costs of Inspection against the Costs of Undetected Defects*

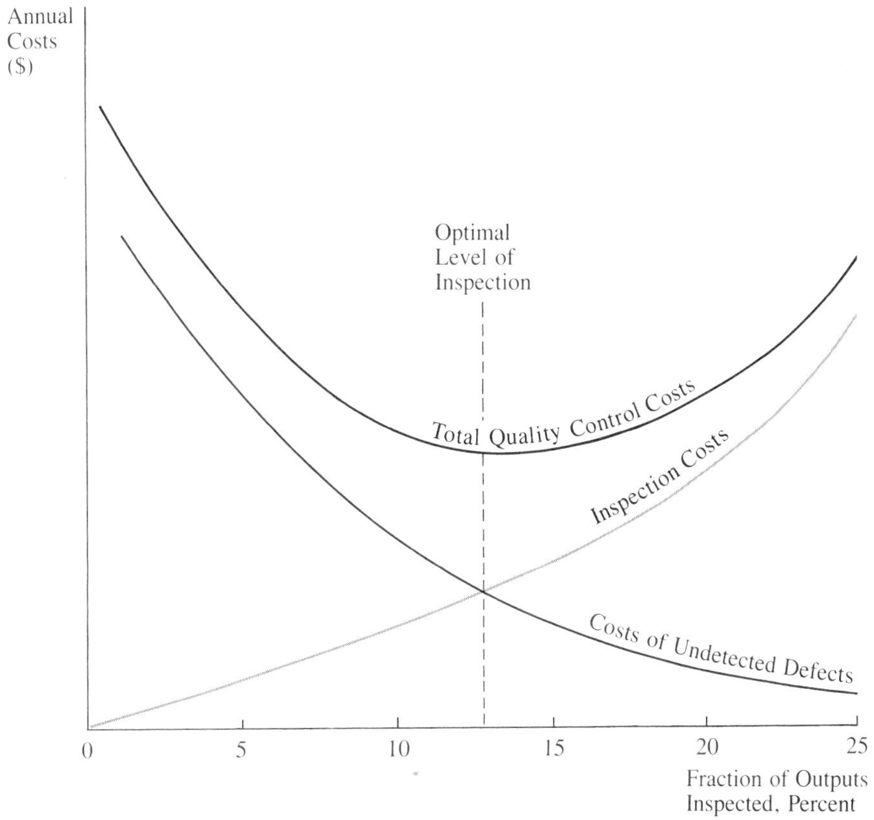

One story is told over and over about the human frailty of inspectors. A supervisor who wanted to check out the inspection skills of his inspectors purposely placed 100 defects in a lot of parts without telling his inspectors. The inspectors found only 68 of the defects on the first pass. Determined that the inspectors should be able to find the defects, he again put the lot with 32 defects through inspection. This time the inspectors found many of the defects, but not all. After this process was repeated for the third, fourth, and fifth times, 98 defects were found. The other two defects were never found. They went to a customer. Another version of this same story had the inspectors finding 110 defects.

Let us now discuss the approaches of today's operations managers to quality control.

MODERN QUALITY MANAGEMENT CONCEPTS

Shortly after World War II Japanese products competed with U.S. and other countries' products on the basis of very low prices and shoddy quality. For too long we continued to assume that the Japanese would be content to follow this marketing and manufacturing strategy. In the 1970s and 1980s it became apparent not only that the Japanese were now in a position to be competitive with U.S. manufacturers on price and quality, but also that the Japanese now actually enjoyed a substantial quality advantage in mass-produced products. Industry Snapshot 15.1 describes the extent of the Japanese quality advantage in the 1980s.

DEMING'S WAY

The turnaround in Japanese quality programs began in the 1950s but took a long time to develop to their successful status of today. Dr. W. Edwards Deming, a professor at New York University, traveled to Japan after World War II at the request of the Japanese government to assist its industries in improving productivity and quality. Dr. Deming, a statistician and consultant, was so successful in his mission that in 1951 the Japanese government established the Deming Prize for innovation in quality control to be awarded annually to a company that had distinguished itself in quality control programs. Industry Snapshot 15.2 discusses Deming's philosophy and approach to quality.

JUST-IN-TIME (JIT) SYSTEMS AND PRODUCT QUALITY

In Chapter 12, Shop Floor Planning and Control, JIT systems were described. Some of the features of JIT systems that contribute to high product quality are:

1. Because the same standardized products are produced every day, worker job assignments are well understood, workers are very familiar with their tasks, and product quality is therefore improved.
2. JIT has been called a system of enforced problem solving. Because in-process inventories have been drastically reduced by cutting lot sizes, any interruption causes production to stop until the problem has been solved. This tends to improve product quality in two ways. First, since only a few parts are in-process inventory, if a quality problem does occur, fewer defective parts are produced before they are discovered. Second, since production is stopped until the problem is corrected, everyone's attention is on solving the quality problem so that the problem will not be repeated.
3. JIT purchasing tends to develop suppliers that deliver parts of perfect quality, just as the in-house workers do. Many companies do not even inspect suppliers' deliveries of parts and materials; rather, the emphasis is on working with suppliers to produce perfect parts and materials.
4. The use of automated equipment and robots has played a major part in Japanese manufacturers' superior product quality. These machines consistently and predictably produce parts within quality standards. This fact

INDUSTRY SNAPSHOT 15.1

Foreign-Made Goods' Quality Surpasses U.S. Quality

New York (UPI)—At least half of all Americans are dissatisfied with American products and consider foreign products as good or better.

And to make domestic matters worse, the quality of American products has declined in the past five years while Japanese products have set new world standards for quality.

These are the conclusions of two surveys released recently, one by the American Society for Quality Control, based in Milwaukee, the other by *Fortune* magazine.

The Milwaukee society blamed industry's emphasis on profits, "uncaring workers," and the high costs of the present economy as the causes of the declining quality of American products.

The *Fortune* study put the blame on the same factors but added that Japanese cultural factors shape Japanese management attitudes.

"A Japanese executive expects to spend a lifetime with one company, so its long-term success is his success," the article said. On the other hand "an American takes a more self-centered view of his career."

The *Fortune* article also quoted Stephen Moss, an executive of Arthur D. Little, Inc., the Cambridge, Mass., research firm, as saying the contrasting American and Japanese management attitudes play a big role in the decline in quality.

"The U.S. manager sets an acceptable level of quality and then sticks to it. The Japanese are constantly upgrading their goals," Moss was quoted as saying.

The Society for Quality Control said its latest survey showed that the only American industry given high marks for quality by the public today is drugs and pharmaceuticals. Makers of frozen foods and television receivers get fair marks.

The automobile manufacturers got the lowest mark, with only 17.6 percent of respondents saying American cars are good and 36.5 percent saying they are definitely inferior. Makers of toys and games and household appliances got the next lowest marks.

On this score, *Fortune* noted that "a new American car is almost twice as likely to have a problem as a Japanese model. An American color TV needs repairs half again as often as a Japanese set and U.S.-made computer memory chips were judged in one test this year to be three times as likely to fail as Japanese chips." [6]

---

[6] *Houston Chronicle*, Aug. 9, 1981, sec. 3, p. 29. Reprinted with permission of *Houston Chronicle*.

flies in the face of our traditional view that real product quality resulted from handcrafted products. Mercedes advertisements, for example, have emphasized that its products were handcrafted. Such promotions and our recollections of the distant past have led to our perception that anything produced by those cold, mechanical machines can never have the same quality as products that have been handcrafted. Such perceptions are just not

INDUSTRY SNAPSHOT 15.2

Deming's Way

W. Edwards Deming is known as the father of quality control in Japan, but his recognition in his own country, the United States, was a long time coming. He taught the Japanese that higher quality meant lower cost, but the idea was so foreign to U.S. managers that they failed to listen until it was almost too late. Now they are listening in great numbers, and Deming's speaking and seminar schedule in the United States is unbelievably packed. He tells U.S. managers that they must:

1. Create consistency and continuity of purpose.
2. Refuse to allow commonly accepted levels of delay for mistakes, defective material, defective workmanship.
3. Eliminate the need for and dependence upon mass inspection.
4. Reduce the number of suppliers. Buy on statistical evidence, not price.
5. Search continually for problems in the system and seek ways to improve it.
6. Institute modern methods of training, using statistics.
7. Focus supervision on helping people to do a better job. Provide the tools and techniques for people to have pride of workmanship.
8. Eliminate fear. Encourage two-way communications.
9. Break down barriers between departments. Encourage problem solving through teamwork.
10. Eliminate the use of numerical goals, slogans, posters for the work force.
11. Use statistical methods for continuing improvement of quality and productivity and eliminate all standards prescribing numerical quotas.
12. Remove barriers to pride of workmanship.
13. Institute a vigorous program of education and training to keep people abreast of new developments in materials, methods, and technologies.
14. Clearly define management's permanent commitment to quality and productivity.[7]

Permeating these points is a philosophy based on the belief in the worker's desire to do a good job and the need to take power out of the boardroom and bring decision making to the factory floor. Factory workers are taught statistics so that they can keep control charts on their progress toward improved quality. Everyone in the organization, from board members to janitors, receives training in quality control concepts and statistics, and each and every one studies the organization and suggests ways to improve it. Workers, therefore, not only do work, but they also help improve the system.

---

[7] Myron Tribus, director of AKT Systems and Energy Company, founder and director of the American Quality and Productivity Institute, "Deming's Way," MECHANICAL ENGINEERING (January 1988): 26–30. Reprinted with permission from MECHANICAL ENGINEERING.

true today. In fact, Japanese manufacturers and, more recently, U.S. manufacturers have found that product quality actually improves when industrial robots have been installed. At the Ford Motor Company, robots installed at its truck assembly plant in Norfolk, Virginia, have improved product quality and have permitted a smaller work force. "Robotics is one of the most important technologies because the consistency of the robot ensures that the quality that is designed into the product will be built into it," said Robert S. Rennard, operations manager for Ford's body and assembly operations.[8] The use of robots as a competitive weapon in improving product quality may be an important factor for U.S. manufacturers in achieving parity with their Japanese counterparts.

5. Toward avoiding production interruptions, intensive preventive maintenance programs repair machines before they break down. This results in machines staying in adjustment and producing parts that are within quality standards.
6. Workers are responsible for producing parts of *perfect quality* or with *zero defects* before the parts are passed on to the next production operation.

The last concept of perfect quality is often referred to as *quality at the source.*

QUALITY AT THE SOURCE

The concept of quality at the source aims to put the production worker in the driver's seat in controlling product quality. Toward the goal of having each worker produce parts that are of perfect quality, quality at the source follows these principles:

1. Every worker's job becomes a quality control station. The worker is responsible for inspecting his own work, identifying any defects and reworking them into nondefectives, and correcting any causes of defects.
2. Statistical quality control techniques are used to monitor the quality of parts produced at each work station, and easy-to-understand charts and graphs are used to communicate progress to workers and managers.
3. Each worker is given the right to stop the production line to avoid producing defective parts.
4. Workers and managers are organized into *quality circles,* or *QC circles,* groups of people who analyze quality problems, work to solve the problems, and implement programs to improve product quality.

QUALITY CIRCLES

"Basically, a QC circle is a small group of employees, the average number is nine, who volunteer to meet regularly to undertake work-related projects designed to advance the company, improve working conditions, and spur mutual self-development, by using quality control concepts."[9] QC circles are encouraged by Japanese companies

---

[8] "Ford Says Robots Improve Quality of Truck Products," *Houston Chronicle,* Aug. 21, 1982, sec. 2, 3.
[9] "Japan: Quality Control & Innovation," *Business Week,* July 20, 1981, 32.

FIGURE 15.3   How QC Circles Work

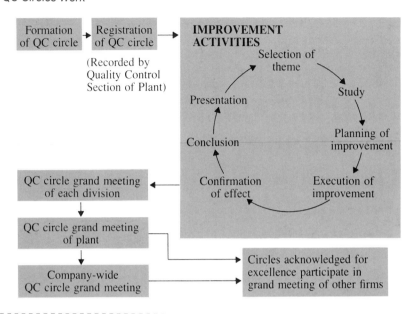

Source: "Japan: Quality Control & Innovation." Reprinted from the July 20, 1981 issue of *Business Week* by special permission, © 1981 by McGraw-Hill, Inc.

and receive substantial training in quality control concepts and techniques. These groups often meet away from the job and combine their meetings with social or athletic activities. They tend to select their own projects for investigation and can generally count on the support of management in implementing their recommendations. The types of projects are varied and may extend beyond quality to such areas as productivity, tool design, safety, or environmental protection.

Membership in QC circles is voluntary and there are no direct cash incentives. Members give the principal reasons for belonging to the groups as personal satisfaction from achievement and recognition given at regional and national quality control meetings. The success of these circles is no less than phenomenal and their use is expanding to the United States, Britain, Brazil, Indonesia, and other countries. Korea is estimated to have more than 40,000 circles operating.

Figure 15.3 shows how these circles operate. Ask yourself this question: If there is no cash benefit from participating in these groups, why is there an almost 50 percent participation rate in Japan?

Part of the difficulty in answering this and similar questions lies in the cultural differences between this country and Japan. In Japan many employees work in an environment where they are guaranteed lifetime employment. They are provided many health, recreational, social, and economic opportunities by the company (see Industry Snapshot 14.4 for one such company's program), and they generally view their relationship with the company with pride. In that environment the worker

---

INDUSTRY SNAPSHOT 15.3

Quality Circles Taking Shape in the United States

At 9:30 every Monday morning, nine workers who assemble electrical circuits for well logging equipment at Schlumberger put down their tools and plot strategy.

They are trying to rearrange and simplify instruction sheets designed by engineers to make them easier and quicker to use. The employees mull over the problems for weeks, possibly even months. Later, they may present their findings to management.

These workers form a "quality circle." From the same work area at Schlumberger, they voluntarily meet on a regular basis to identify, analyze, and solve problems. Their solutions may save money for the company, improve product quality, or simply boost morale.

Quality circles are most often found at manufacturers because concrete problems and product defects that develop on an assembly line or work station can be pinpointed and corrected.

The group of electrical assembly workers at Schlumberger, for example, found it difficult to find tools in good condition. There was no one responsible to see that the tools were kept in one place and that they were in good working order, said Eugenia Parker, a quality circle facilitator at the company.

So Schlumberger set up a special tool room and staffed it. . . .

Some manufacturers have expanded quality circles to include white collar and clerical employees. They also are spreading to service industries across the United States. At RepublicBank Houston, 19 groups meet once a week.

The groups at RepublicBank focus on procedures, forms, or filing systems. In one instance, a quality circle from accounts reconciliation was being buried each day by reports that sometimes exceeded 2,000 pieces of paper and took three hours to file. The department converted to microfiche, saving the bank more than $40,000 a year, Watson said.

Watson and others say that money savings are important, but aren't the only reason for quality circles. They help build morale and corporate culture — a kind of cohesion that is behind the success of many Japanese firms, as well as a number of U.S. companies in high technology.

"Bottom-line savings are fine, but if all (a quality circle) does is improve the quality of working life, we're going to win," Watson said.

A survey by the bank found job performance improved among more than 81 percent of workers who participated in quality circles.

"They develop a consciousness of quality," Watson said. Also, a problem

(continued)

---

strives for cooperation and accommodation with the company's representatives. In the United States all too often it appears that we see the worker–management relationship as an adversary relationship.

In spite of the cultural differences between Japan and the United States, QC circles are being organized in companies such as Motorola and Minnesota Mining and Manufacturing (3M). Industry Snapshot 15.3 illustrates the challenges of implementing such programs in the United States. If these experiments are to succeed, a

INDUSTRY SNAPSHOT 15.3   (continued)

solved by a worker, rather than by management decree, stays fixed, she said.

But having measurable results helps.

"There's a greater chance (of the program) surviving the ups and downs of the business cycle. Morale and culture are harder to track," Wexler said.

Executives who develop and guide quality circles say the groups usually start as gripe sessions. As they settle down, workers begin brainstorming to identify problems to be analyzed.

At the start, quality circles usually are headed by first-line supervisors. That can create problems because supervisors are used to giving orders, said Parker of Schlumberger. Some workers feel threatened.

"They have to change their tack and ask questions to bring issues out," Parker said. "They can't point fingers and ask, 'Why hasn't this been done?'" In time, workers replace supervisors as leaders of the group.

Executives involved in quality circles cite a number of pitfalls. Management must be willing to share information about operating costs and marketing strategies to enable workers to make meaningful judgments, according to Riggin.

"Steel workers didn't know steel was in big trouble," she said. "There's a lot of reluctance to give up information, because information is power."

Riggin said managers also are afraid information will leak out, but there's less of a risk if they're giving workers only a piece of the puzzle.

Workers often feel like they are being used as a tool to cut costs, Riggin said. They won't contribute ideas if they believe cost-cutting measures will do away with their jobs. In union shops, they have been viewed as work speedup programs or tools to weaken the influence of the union.

But quality circles can evolve to higher, more sophisticated forms. LaVine of Upjohn says he wants to shift emphasis from group dynamics to faster, more sophisticated analysis of problems.

Riggin cited experiments in timber and coal mining, where autonomous work teams are responsible for hiring and firing, budgeting and scheduling, evaluating peers, and approving pay raises.[10]

[10] Judith Crown, "Quality Circles Slowly Taking Shape Here," *Houston Chronicle,* Oct. 14, 1984, sec. 4, pp. 1, 9. Reprinted with permission of *Houston Chronicle.*

sincere trust and loyalty must exist between the worker and management. Such a relationship cannot be developed overnight, however; the groundwork for these programs had to have taken place years ago, and it is clear that the absence of positive labor–management relations will undoubtedly hinder efforts to establish QC circles in some companies. Nevertheless, companies in growing numbers are recognizing the importance of drawing their workers into the mainstream of their quality control programs. And this effort is sure to contribute to an overall elevation of quality control in the workers' consciousness, to result in unique and innovative solutions to quality problems, and to improve the likelihood of the workers cooperating in the implementation of programs to improve product quality.

Another important element of QC circles is training in the concepts and techniques of statistical quality control that was so strongly advocated to them by W. Edwards Deming in the late 1940s. Here too we shall need a brief review of certain statistical concepts that underlie quality control practices and thus are fundamental to the management of quality control programs.

STATISTICAL CONCEPTS IN QUALITY CONTROL

The ways that quality products and services are achieved today have evolved over the past 100 years. The statistical underpinnings of today's quality control practices stem principally from the work of Shewhart, Dodge, and Romig at the Bell Telephone Laboratories during the 1920s. The techniques of random samples, statistical control charts, and statistical acceptance of products based on samples were developed by these men during this period. Their statistical sampling tables, although slowly accepted at first, are now widely used by quality control specialists.

SAMPLING

Production departments routinely break the flow of products through their operations into discrete groups of units called *lots*. A lot of products will have been produced under the same conditions and will generally contain the appropriate number of units for economical control. For example, a lot of office scissors will include castings from a common lot, connecting rivets from a common lot, and paint from a common lot, and the scissors will be continuously produced under identical operating conditions. The maximum number of units in a lot of scissors may be limited to about 10,000 because of economics: As the number of units in a lot increases, the cost of physically keeping the lot together in production and storage becomes excessive. But as the number of units in a lot decreases, the sample represents too large a proportion of the lot and too large a percentage of the lot must be processed by inspectors and testing specialists; thus very small lots are resisted. A compromise between very large and very small lots is struck in practice.

Lots of materials, assemblies, and finished products are sampled to determine if the lots meet desired quality control standards. *Random samples* are removed from these lots by inspectors and measured against certain standards. A random sample is one in which each unit in the lot has an equal chance of being included in the sample; thus the sample is likely to be *representative* of the lot. Either attributes or variables can be measured and compared to standards.

Attributes are characteristics that are classified into one of two categories. In quality control, the two categories are usually *defective* and *nondefective.* For example, the lamp either lights up when connected to electrical current or it does not. *Variables* are characteristics that can be measured on a continuous scale. Inspectors who are inspecting for variables must measure the amount of a characteristic that is present and then determine if that amount is within the acceptable range before the

FIGURE 15.4 *Single-Sampling Plans*

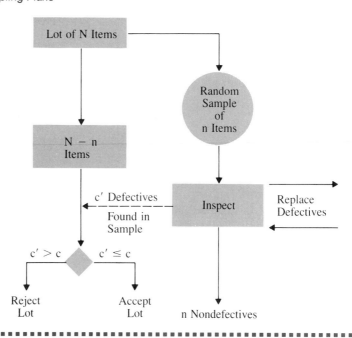

unit can be passed. For example, the diameter of a motor shaft can be measured by a dial micrometer. If the diameter is within the minimum and maximum allowable diameters, the shaft passes the inspection.

An *acceptance plan* is the overall scheme for either accepting or rejecting a lot based on information gained from samples. The acceptance plan identifies both the size and type of samples and the criteria to be used to either accept or reject the lot. Samples may be either single, double, or sequential. In *single-sampling plans,* an acceptance or rejection decision is made after drawing only one sample from the lot. If the number of defectives in the sample does not exceed the maximum number of defectives allowed in the acceptance plan, the lot is accepted. Figure 15.4 illustrates how such sampling plans operate.

In *double-sampling plans,* one small sample is drawn initially. If the number of defectives is less than or equal to some lower limit, the lot is accepted. If the number of defectives is greater than some upper limit, the lot is rejected. If the number of defectives is neither, a second larger sample is drawn. The lot is either accepted or rejected with the information from both of the samples. While the first sample in double-sampling plans is smaller than the sample in single-sampling plans, double-sampling plans overall tend to require a greater inspection load. The frequency of their use, therefore, is not high. Figure 15.5 illustrates how such sampling plans operate.

FIGURE 15.5 Double-Sampling Plans

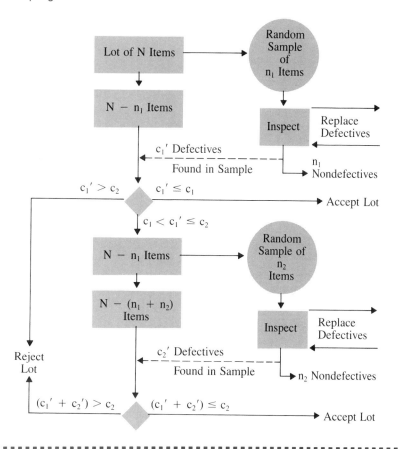

In *sequential-sampling plans,* units are randomly selected from the lot and tested one by one. After each one has been tested, a reject, accept, or continue-sampling decision is made. This process continues until the lot is accepted or rejected. Figure 15.6 illustrates how such plans operate. In this figure units are randomly drawn from the lot and tested. The first defective is the fifteenth unit, putting us in the *continue-sampling zone,* and so we continue to sample units from the lot. The second defective is the twenty-fifth unit, and we still must continue sampling. The third defective is the thirtieth unit, and we continue sampling. The fourth defective is the fortieth unit, and this puts us in the *reject lot zone;* therefore the lot is rejected. Conceivably, the whole lot could be tested unit by unit.

A concept that is important in applying sampling plans is the central limit theorem.

FIGURE 15.6 *Sequential Sampling Plans*

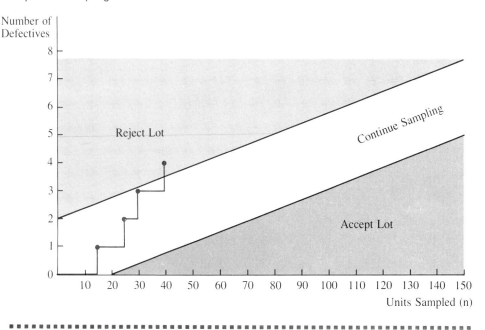

CENTRAL LIMIT THEOREM AND QUALITY CONTROL

The *central limit theorem* may well be the most important single statistical concept in POM. Stated simply, this theorem is: Sampling distributions can be assumed to be normally distributed even though the population distributions are not normal. The only exception to this theorem occurs when sample sizes are extremely small. Computer studies show that in some cases even when sample sizes are as small as five, however, their *sampling distributions* are very close to normal distributions.[11]

Figure 15.7 compares a population distribution with its sampling distribution of sample means. We are obviously referring to variables in this figure since the population distribution includes all the possible measures of the variable x. The sampling distribution includes all the possible measures of sample means ($\bar{x}$). We can make these generalizations about the sampling distribution:

1. The sampling distribution can be assumed to be normally distributed unless sample size (n) is extremely small.
2. The mean of the sampling distribution ($\bar{\bar{x}}$) is equal to the population mean (μ).
3. The standard error of the sampling distribution ($\sigma_{\bar{x}}$) is smaller than the population standard deviation (σ_x) by a factor of $1/\sqrt{n}$.

---

[11] Elwood S. Buffa, *Operations Management: Problems and Models,* 3rd ed. (New York: Wiley, 1972), 616–617.

FIGURE 15.7   *A Comparison of Population and Sampling Distributions*

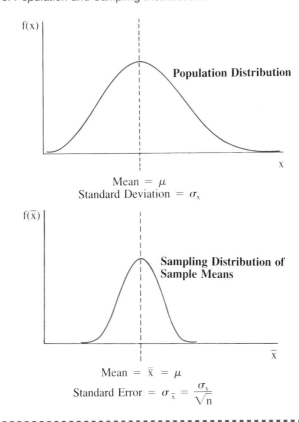

The power of the central limit theorem in quality control lies in its ability to allow quality control specialists to easily set limits for acceptance plans and control charts for both attributes and variables, which we shall discuss later in this chapter.

Two classes of quality control techniques are used almost daily in POM — control charts and acceptance plans.

CONTROL CHARTS

W. Edwards Deming in Industry Snapshot 15.2 stressed the need for *producing* products of high quality in the first place, rather than trying to find defective finished products after the fact. To produce products of high quality in the first place requires that we look farther back in the production processes, discover where quality problems lie, and correct those problems. Control charts help operations management do this. Control charts are used to monitor each major production operation continuously to determine if its outputs meet quality standards. If they do, no corrective

---

INDUSTRY SNAPSHOT 15.4

Statistical Process Control (SPC)

Traditional quality control typically came at the end of manufacturing. A product was made and then it was inspected. It either passed and was shipped, or it failed and went back for reprocessing, repairing, or scrapping. Statistical process control (SPC) attempts to fix the problem during and not at the end of manufacturing. Using SPC, those building the product make their measurements as the product flows through the manufacturing pipeline. By recording statistics, the quality of the product can be continuously monitored and corrections made at once, ensuring that what is produced meets all specifications. Although this procedure involves some mathematical work, over the years formulas, charts, and computer programs have been developed to make the mathematics easier.

Some companies have switched to SPC not only because they are convinced it is useful, but because of pressure from their customers. Ford Motor Company, for example, demands SPC reports from all its suppliers, who in turn demand such reports from their suppliers. Not only do many companies demand all suppliers practice SPC, they also want to look at the actual charting that is done.

Companies that have achieved success with SPC have been forced to change the attitudes of those at the sharp end of the problem—the production workers and their immediate superiors. These are the people who have to accept the responsibility for controlling product quality, and these are the people who have to be given the authority to do what is necessary to correct quality problems. SPC is among the list of measures that vanguard companies are adopting to boost manufacturing effectiveness today.[12]

---

[12] Jim Barlow, "No Quick Fix for Quality," business writer for the *Houston Chronicle,* sec. 2, Apr. 21, 1988. Copyright: *Houston Chronicle.* Excerpted with permission.

---

action is needed. But if they do not, the operation is quickly shut down until the problem can be corrected—by replacing worn tools, making machine adjustments, training and instructing workers, or dealing with other problems that may be causing subquality outputs. Industry Snapshot 15.4 discusses the growth in the use of control charts, which is also referred to as statistical process control (SPC).

Control charts are useful aids to managers and workers in monitoring the quality performance of the operations for which they are responsible. They can quickly glance at these charts and determine if the outputs of their operations are meeting quality standards and if unusual trends in quality should be investigated. Because of the flexibility of application of these tools, control charts are used in all types of businesses and government organizations today.

The way that control charts are constructed differs according to the quality characteristics that are to be controlled.

FIGURE 15.8 p *Chart for Controlling Percent Defectives in Samples*

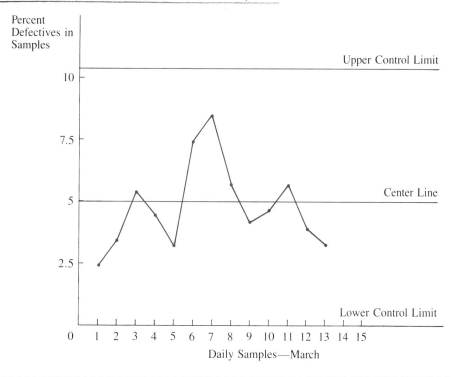

CONTROL CHARTS FOR ATTRIBUTES

Defective or nondefective, yes or no, open or closed, pass or fail, and go or no-go are examples of attributes. Perhaps the most common attribute measurement in quality control is defective or nondefective. A control chart for controlling the percentage of defectives in a sample, commonly called a *p* chart, is the principal chart for controlling attributes.

Constructing control charts involves three determinations: (1) center line, (2) upper control limit, and (3) lower control limit. After these three values are established, they become the benchmarks against which to compare future samples. Figure 15.8 is a *p* chart used to plot the percent defectives in daily samples for the month of March. The upper control limit is slightly over 10 percent, the center line is 5 percent, and the lower control limit is 0 percent. As the daily sample percent defectives are plotted on this control chart, we can see that all the points are within the upper and lower control limits and no undesirable trends are present. Therefore no management action to correct quality problems is necessary at this time.

Let us now try our hand at setting the center lines and control limits for control charts for controlling attributes. Example 15.1 requires a *p* chart for monitoring

TABLE 15.2   *Formulas and Variable Definitions for Computing 3σ Control Limits for Control Charts*

Type of Control Chart	*Center Line*	*3σ Lower Control Limit*	*3σ Upper Control Limit*
p	$\bar{p}$	$\bar{p} - 3\sqrt{\bar{p}(100-\bar{p})/n}$	$\bar{p} + 3\sqrt{\bar{p}(100-\bar{p})/n}$
$\bar{x}$	$\bar{\bar{x}}$	$\bar{\bar{x}} - A\bar{R}$	$\bar{\bar{x}} + A\bar{R}$
R	$\bar{R}$	$D_1\bar{R}$	$D_2\bar{R}$

p = percent defectives in a sample

$\bar{p}$ = average percent defectives across many samples

n = sample size — number of observations in sample

$\bar{x}$ = a sample mean

$\bar{\bar{x}}$ = mean of many sample means

R = a sample range

$\bar{R}$ = mean of many sample ranges

A, D_1, D_2 = factors from Table 15.3

keypunch errors. Table 15.2 displays the formulas and variable definitions for the necessary calculations for control charts. In this example the keypunch supervisor knows that experienced and well-trained operators should average 4 transactions that are in error in 100 keypunch transactions. This sets the center line at 4.0 percent for the *p* chart. Center lines are not always this easy to deduce. In cases when they are not, we usually draw samples from operators who are well trained and when processes are behaving normally. The mean percent defectives for several samples is then used as the center line.

The control limits in Table 15.2 are 3σ control limits. This means that the control limits are three standard deviations from the center line. Because of the central limit theorem, we know that sampling distributions (control charts are sampling distributions) are normally distributed. In normal distributions three standard deviations either side of the mean include 99.7 percent of the total observations. Therefore there is a 99.7 percent probability that sample data points will fall within the 3σ upper and lower control limits of control charts if the center line of the process being monitored has not changed. When data points are trending outside the control limits, the underlying process is changing and management investigation is in order. Control limits for attributes could similarly be set at 95 percent, 90 percent, or any other confidence interval by substituting the appropriate Z scores from the normal distribution for the 3 in the formulas for *p* charts in Table 15.2. For example, 95 percent Z score = 1.96, 90 percent Z score = 1.64, and so on.

Don't make this classic mistake in constructing control charts: Someone gives you 30 sample data points, asks you to compute the center line and upper and lower control limits, asks you to plot the 30 sample data points on the control chart constructed from your control limit computations, and then asks you this question: Is the process in control? You just can't answer that question with the information you have. It is assumed that the 30 sample data points that were used to compute upper and lower control limits were drawn from a process that *was* under control. Even though an occasional data point can be outside the 3σ control limits just through chance, you should not have enough points outside the limits to indicate an out-of-control process when those same points were used to set the control limits.

EXAMPLE 15.1   *Constructing Control Charts for Attributes*

Jane Morgan supervises 45 computer terminal operators in their work at a large commercial computer center. Because of increasing problems with input errors in recent months, Jane has decided to construct a control chart for each operator, draw samples of transactions for each operator, plot the sample error information on the control chart, and thereby monitor the quality performance of each operator. If the input errors of any operator appear to be trending upward, Jane intends to provide training and counseling to help correct the problem. If, however, an operator consistently produces low levels of errors, special recognition and even bonuses may be provided. Jane knows that a well-trained operator should average 4 transactions that are in error in the 100 transactions contained in each sample. Jane wishes initially to construct a *p* chart with three standard deviation control limits for one operator to be used for a month. She has kept ten daily samples for one operator:

Sample Number	Number of Transactions in Error	Sample Number	Number of Transactions in Error	Sample Number	Number of Transactions in Error
1	4	5	1	8	12
2	3	6	9	9	4
3	3	7	5	10	3
4	6				

Solution

1. Compute 3 σ control limits for *p*:
   First, from Table 15.2 observe the control limits for *p* charts:

$$\text{Upper control limits} = \bar{p} + 3\sqrt{\bar{p}(100 - \bar{p})/n} = 4 + 3\sqrt{4(96)/100} = 4 + 3(1.9596)$$
$$= 4 + 5.8788 = 9.88 \text{ percent}$$

$$\text{Lower control limits} = \bar{p} - 3\sqrt{\bar{p}(100 - \bar{p})/n} = 4 - 3\sqrt{4(96)/100} = 4 - 3(1.9596)$$
$$= 4 - 5.8788 = -1.88 \text{ percent, or 0 percent}$$

2. Construct a *p* chart and plot the ten data points that Jane has collected for the operator:

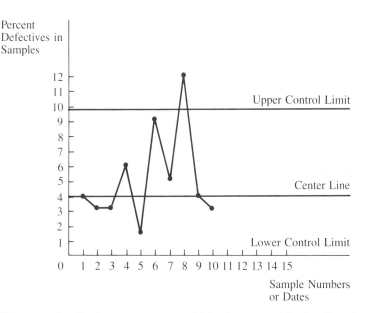

3. Although most of the samples for the operator are within the control limits, Jane intends to investigate the conditions surrounding Samples 6 and 8.

The lower control limit in Example 15.1 is negative. Therefore we set the limit at 0 percent defectives. Lower control limits do not have to be negative or zero. On the contrary, they are often positive values. As it happens, however, we are seldom interested in lower control limits when controlling defectives. Exceeding lower control limits would indicate that the process being monitored had changed and that products of better quality than expected were being produced. Managers do like to know when products of higher than expected quality are being produced. They may want to investigate the situation and determine the causes so that the condition can be continued and product quality thus improved.

CONTROL CHARTS FOR VARIABLES

Variables are characteristics that take on values in varying degrees. Variables are measured in such units as pounds, gallons, feet, inches, and minutes. Samples are drawn from populations of products being produced from production processes. These samples are usually described by sample means ($\bar{x}$) and sample ranges (R) for quality control purposes. Control charts are constructed for monitoring these variable values: $\bar{x}$ and R.

An $\bar{x}$ chart and an R chart are frequently used together to monitor the quality of products and services from a given production process. The $\bar{x}$ chart monitors the average value of the variable being measured. The R chart monitors the variation among the items within samples. This dual monitoring therefore controls both average values and variation of values from their mean. Take, for example, the weights of boxes of cornflakes from a production line. An $\bar{x}$ chart may indicate that the sample

■■■

TABLE 15.3 Control Chart Factors for Variables

Sample Size n	Control Limit Factors for Sample Means A	Control Limit Factors for Sample Ranges	
		D_1	D_2
2	1.880	0	3.267
3	1.023	0	2.575
4	.729	0	2.282
5	.577	0	2.116
10	.308	.223	1.777
15	.223	.348	1.652
20	.180	.414	·1.586
25	.153	.459	1.541
Over 25	$.75(1/\sqrt{n})$*	$.45 + .001(n)$*	$1.55 - .0015(n)$*

■■■

* These values are linear approximations for student use in constructing control charts.

Source: *Economics Control of Manufactured Products* (New York: Litton Educational Publishing, Van Nostrand Reinhold Co., 1931). Copyright 1931, Bell Telephone Laboratories. Reprinted by permission.

average box weights are on target, but without an R chart to monitor variation, box weights could range from zero to 10 pounds (assuming that a box would hold that much) within samples. This example demonstrates that we usually cannot conclude that a process is in control just by monitoring sample means, but that variation within samples must also be monitored.

Example 15.2 demonstrates the construction of $\bar{x}$ and R charts in monitoring fill weights of boxes of cornflakes. Table 15.3 lists the control chart factors A, D_1, and D_2 for variables.

Example 15.2 demonstrates an important truth in interpreting the information from control charts. Sometimes data trends are more important than the absolute values of the data. Trends can indicate the need for corrective action *before* products and services of substandard quality are actually produced. Thus managers and workers carefully monitor the trends of control charts to discover potential quality problems in operations before they actually occur.

In contrast with this substandard-quality prevention function of control charts, acceptance plans are devised to determine the acceptability of lots of products or materials *before* they are shipped to customers or used in production.

EXAMPLE 15.2   *Constructing Control Charts for Variables*

The High Fiber Cereal Company has recently had numerous customer complaints about the fill weight of one of its products — 16-ounce packages of Peppy Corn Flakes. These complaints combined with increased government interest in High Fiber's operations have caused Bill

Mallory, manager of High Fiber's quality control department, to direct Beverly Green to construct $\bar{x}$ and R control charts for the filling operation of 16-ounce Peppy Corn Flakes.

Beverly proceeds directly to the automatic filling operation. After first confirming that the process is operating properly, she begins to randomly select samples of 20 filled boxes hourly until 100 samples have been taken. The average of the 100 sample means is 16.1 ounces, and the average of the 100 sample ranges is 2.22 ounces.

Beverly now wishes to construct $\bar{x}$ and R charts and to begin plotting hourly sample means and ranges. These sample means and ranges were computed from samples later taken from the filling operation:

Sample Number	Sample Means (Ounces)	Sample Ranges (Ounces)	Sample Number	Sample Means (Ounces)	Sample Ranges (Ounces)
1	16.2	2.0	7	16.0	2.9
2	15.9	2.1	8	16.1	1.8
3	16.3	1.8	9	16.3	1.5
4	16.4	3.0	10	16.3	1.0
5	15.8	3.5	11	16.4	1.0
6	15.9	3.1	12	16.5	.9

Beverly must determine whether the process is in control.

Solution

1. Compute the upper and lower control limits for the $\bar{x}$ and R charts:

   First, from Table 15.2 observe the control limits for an $\bar{x}$ chart ($\bar{\bar{x}}$ is the center line and equals 16.1 ounces; A is found in Table 15.3, A = .180 when n = 20):

   Upper control limit = $\bar{\bar{x}} + A\bar{R}$ = 16.1 + .180(2.22) = 16.1 + .400 = 16.500 ounces

   Lower control limit = $\bar{\bar{x}} - A\bar{R}$ = 16.1 − .180(2.22) = 16.1 − .400 = 15.700 ounces

   Next, from Table 15.2 observe the control limits for an R chart (D_2 is found in Table 15.3, D_2 = 1.586 when n = 20; D_1 is found in Table 15.3, D_1 = .414 when n = 20):

   Upper control limit = $D_2\bar{R}$ = 1.586(2.22) = 3.521 ounces

   Lower control limit = $D_1\bar{R}$ = .414(2.22) = .919 ounces

2. Plot the sample means and ranges on the $\bar{x}$ and R control charts (see page 713).

3. Is the process in control when the 12 samples are drawn?

   Although none of the sample means exceeded the control limits, the trend of the last eight hours indicates a definite out-of-control situation. Unless this trend is reversed by management corrective action, excessive numbers of overfilled boxes will probably result. The R chart indicates that the sample ranges do not exceed the control limits. Curiously, however, the sample ranges of the last eight hours have narrowed. This trend could be associated with the out-of-control situation of the sample means and should be investigated.

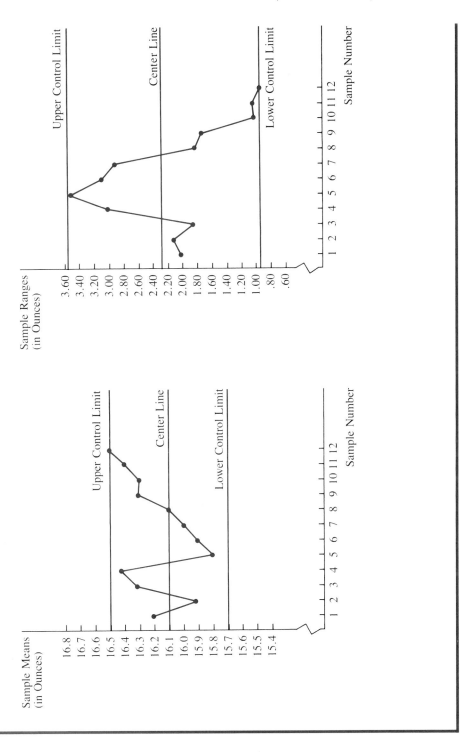

ACCEPTANCE PLANS

Acceptance plans are used to decide whether lots of raw materials, purchased parts, or finished products meet prescribed quality standards. Based on our acceptance plan, we must either accept or reject each lot. If a lot of raw materials is accepted, we place the materials in inventory for use. If a lot of raw materials is rejected, the materials are returned to the supplier, the price of the materials is adjusted downward to allow for increased inspection and reworking costs, or some other mutually acceptable disposition of the rejected lot is made.

When a lot of finished products is accepted, it is either placed in finished goods inventory or shipped directly to customers. Depending on the nature of the products, rejected lots may be thrown away or destroyed, ground up and reentered into the production system at an earlier step, 100 percent inspected to save nondefective products, or some other *scrapping-out* procedure.

The key information in an acceptance plan is the criteria for accepting or rejecting a lot based on information deduced from a sample. In the case of attributes, what is the maximum percent defectives that we can find in a sample and still accept the lot? For variables, what is the largest and smallest sample mean and sample range that we can find and still accept the lot? The answers to these questions provide inspectors with the information they need to decide whether to accept or reject lots of materials.

Two approaches to setting acceptance criteria for samples are ordinarily used — (1) MIL STD, Dodge Romig, or other tables for attributes, which we shall discuss later, or (2) statistics to compute acceptance criteria for both attributes and variables. We know that many quality control departments exclusively use what they call *QC tables* for these decisions. However, because statistics underlie the construction of these tables, and because the basic statistical computations best teach us the principles of the application of acceptance plans, we shall develop these statistical approaches here.

Two important concepts are needed as background to acceptance plans when the characteristics being measured are attributes — average outgoing quality curves and operating characteristic curves.

AVERAGE OUTGOING QUALITY (AOQ) CURVES

Acceptance plans in quality control provide managers with the assurance that the average quality level or percent defectives actually going to customers will not exceed a certain limit. Figure 15.9 demonstrates this concept.

As the actual percent defectives in a production process increases — that is, moves along the horizontal from left to right in Figure 15.9 — initially the effect is for lots to be passed even though the number of defectives has increased and the percent defectives going to customers increases. If this trend continues, however, the acceptance plan begins to reject lots. When lots are rejected, the lots are usually 100 percent inspected and the defective units are replaced with nondefective ones. The net effect of rejecting lots is therefore to improve the average quality of the outgoing lots because the rejected lots that are ultimately shipped contain *all* nondefective units. As the actual percent defectives increases, the average outgoing quality improves

FIGURE 15.9 *An Average Outgoing Quality (AOQ) Curve*

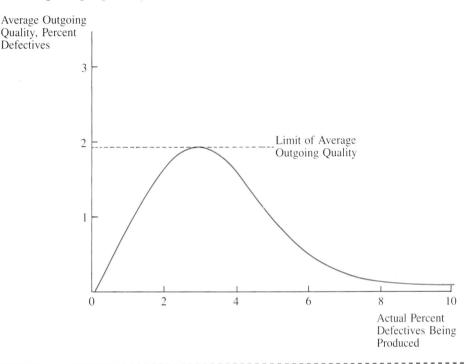

because more and more lots are rejected. The extreme condition exists when all lots are rejected and the percent defectives going to customers approaches zero.

Although each sampling plan exhibits a unique AOQ curve, this truth remains: Acceptance plans protect an organization through limiting the percentage of defective products that go to customers. This is an important consequence of acceptance plans and an important reason for implementing them.

OPERATING CHARACTERISTIC (OC) CURVES

Four things can happen in applying acceptance plans, and two of them are bad. First the good news: We can accept good lots and reject bad lots. Now for the bad news: We can accept bad lots and reject good lots. In the vast majority of cases, we do accept good lots and reject bad lots when we apply acceptance plans. But we know from experience that on rare occasions we also ship bad lots to customers even though our samples have met the acceptance criteria of our acceptance plans. Similarly, when we are reworking lots that have been rejected because the samples have not met the acceptance criteria, we occasionally find that these rejected lots were really good ones. These outcomes are unfortunate, but they are a fact of life in quality control programs.

When we stand before a lot of products, we just don't know with certainty the quality of all of the products. Even after drawing a random sample from the lot, we

FIGURE 15.10 An Operating Characteristic (OC) Curve

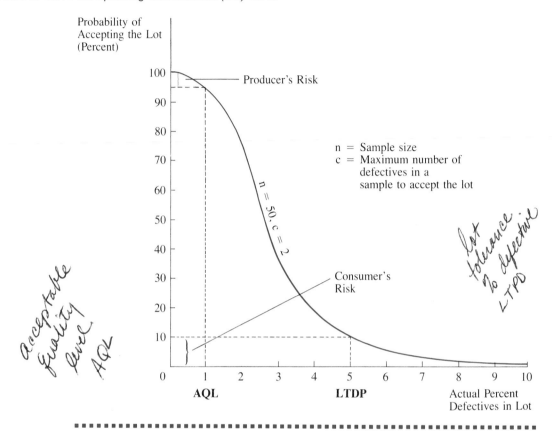

Note: A good lot in this acceptance plan is defined as a lot with 1 or less percent defectives, and a bad lot is defined as a lot with 5 or more percent defectives.

still don't know with certainty the quality of the products in the lot. All we do know is the quality of the products in the sample. From this information about the small proportion of the products in a lot, we must infer the quality of *all* the products in the lot. This is a risky inference, but it is the nature of acceptance plans.

The *operating characteristic curve (OC)* describes an important feature of acceptance plans: It shows how well an acceptance plan discriminates between good and bad lots. Figure 15.10 shows an OC curve, and we shall use this figure to illustrate the features of OC curves. From this figure let us say that we define a good lot as any lot having no more than 1 percent defectives; this is called the *acceptable quality level (AQL)*. If there is 1 percent actual defectives in a lot, the probability of accepting the lot is 95 percent. But the probability of rejecting the lot is 5 percent because we must either accept or reject the lot and the sum of the probabilities must equal 100 percent. The probability of rejecting the lot at the AQL is called a *producer's risk*. In any sampling plan there is always a risk that a good lot will be rejected, and this is the producer's risk. Let us say that we define a bad lot as any lot having 5 percent or more defectives; this is called the *lot tolerance percent defective (LTPD)*. The probability of accepting a lot with 5 percent defectives is only 10 percent; this is called the *consumer's risk*. In any sampling plan there is always a risk that a bad lot will be accepted and shipped to a customer, and this is the consumer's risk. But the probability of rejecting a lot with 5 percent defectives is 90 percent.

We want acceptance plans that pass good lots and fail bad lots. That is what we mean by an acceptance plan that discriminates between good and bad lots. We cannot, however, always have a sampling plan that achieves this objective to perfection. For instance, a good lot of 10,000 items with only 5 defectives could conceivably yield a random sample of 100 units that contains all of the 5 defectives. Thus the acceptance plan could reject the lot when the lot is actually good. Conversely, the lot could have 1,000 defectives and the random sample could have no defectives. In this case a bad lot could be passed by the acceptance plan. Since these examples demonstrate how all acceptance plans can fail to discriminate between good and bad lots because of sampling error (random chance), how can managers modify acceptance plans to minimize these occurrences?

Perhaps the most obvious way is to increase the sample size. Figure 15.11 compares three different sampling plans: $n = 100$, $c = 4$; $n = 50$, $c = 2$; and $n = 25$, $c = 1$, where n is the sample size and c is the maximum number of defectives in a sample from an acceptable lot. Note that even though each plan uses the same percent defectives as the maximum allowable for an acceptable lot (4/100, 2/50, 1/25 = .04, or 4 percent), the larger the sample size of the plan, the greater its discriminating power. Compare the $n = 25$ and $n = 100$ plans, for instance:

Sampling Plan	Actual Percent Defectives in Lot	Probability of Accepting the Lot (Percent)	Sampling Plan	Actual Percent Defectives in Lot	Probability of Accepting the Lot (Percent)
n = 100	1	97.5	n = 25	1	90.0
	5	3.0		5	17.5

When $n = 100$, the probability of accepting good lots (1 percent defectives) is 97.5 percent, and the probability of accepting bad lots (5 percent defectives) is only 3.0 percent. When $n = 25$, the corresponding probabilities are 90 percent and 17.5 percent. Acceptance plans with smaller sample sizes reject more good lots and accept more bad lots.

Why wouldn't we always have acceptance plans with large sample sizes? Because larger sample sizes cost more in inspection costs. Operations managers are therefore faced with this dilemma: We can avoid shipping bad lots and rejecting good lots but only at additional cost. Operations managers therefore must make trade-off decisions when designing acceptance plans. They must design acceptance plans with sample sizes that offer the balance between inspection costs and costs of undetected defects that best suits their situation. This trade-off was illustrated earlier in Figure 15.2.

FIGURE 15.11 OC Curves for Different Sample Sizes

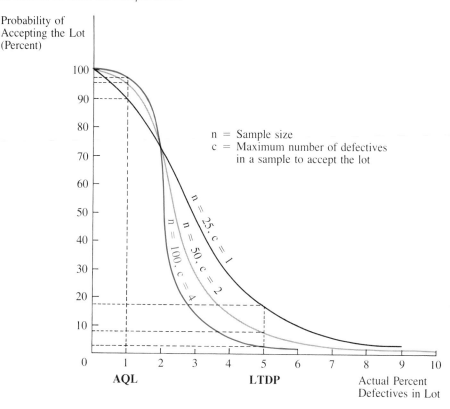

OC curves are not used to make day-to-day decisions about accepting or rejecting lots. OC curves simply depict graphically how a particular acceptance plan discriminates between good and bad lots. In practice all that operations managers must know to make accept-or-reject decisions about attributes in lots of materials is the sample size (n) and the maximum number of defectives in a sample to accept the lot (c) for each material. To determine these values, operations managers first use judgment in setting the values of these four parameters for each material:

1. Producer's risk. AQL
2. Consumer's risk. LTPD)
3. Acceptable quality level (AQL), or the percent defectives in a good lot.
4. Lot tolerance percent defective (LTPD), or the percent defectives in a bad lot.

With the values of these parameters known, the values of *n* and *c* can be found in Dodge and Romig, *Sampling Inspection Tables,* or in the U.S. Department of Defense tables. See the citations for these tables in the Selected Bibliography at the end of this chapter. OC curves and AOQ curves are useful in understanding the operation of acceptance plans, which we shall now discuss.

■ ■

TABLE 15.4   *Formulas and Variable Definitions for Computing Acceptance Criteria for Acceptance Plans*

Characteristic Being Measured	Sample Measure	Acceptance Criteria
Attribute	Percent defectives (p)	$\bar{p} \pm Z\sqrt{\bar{p}(100 - \bar{p})/n}$
Variable	Sample mean $(\bar{x})$	$\bar{\bar{x}} \pm Z\sigma_{\bar{x}}$

α = significance level or $(1 - \text{Confidence interval})$; always is given assuming a two-tailed test, and includes total area in both tails and corresponds to producer's risk

p = percent defectives in a sample

$\bar{p}$ = average percent defectives across many samples

n = sample size

$\bar{x}$ = a sample mean

$\bar{\bar{x}}$ = mean of many sample means

Z = Z scores. These values depend on the significance level (probability of sample measures exceeding acceptance criteria even though the lot is acceptable). $\alpha = .10$, $\alpha = .05$, $\alpha = .01$ are typically specified. The corresponding Z scores from the normal distribution are 1.64, 1.96, and 2.58.   *z = 3 at 99.7%*

$\sigma_{\bar{x}}$ = standard error of the mean of the sampling distribution. $\sigma_{\bar{x}} = \sigma_x/\sqrt{n}$ or $\bar{S}_x/\sqrt{n}$, where σ_x is the population standard deviation deduced from past production records and $\bar{S}_x$ is the mean of many sample standard deviations $[S_x = \sqrt{\Sigma(x - \bar{x})^2/(n - 1)}]$.

■ ■

ACCEPTANCE PLANS FOR ATTRIBUTES

Example 15.3 demonstrates the steps in setting acceptance criteria for the percent defectives observed in samples of ball bearings. Table 15.4 exhibits the formulas and variable definitions for attributes (percent defectives) and variables (sample means).

EXAMPLE 15.3   *Setting Acceptance Criteria for Attributes*

The Roll Perfect Bearing Company in Detroit produces ball and roller bearings of various sizes for automobile manufacturers. One such ball bearing, the ½″ 5525 Chrome Polished Bearing — No. 3580, has been the subject of numerous customer complaints in recent months because of surface defects. Marsha Pool, the director of Roll Perfect's quality control department, has decided that an acceptance plan based on random samples should be established for this product. Marsha carefully researches records of past periods when the surface polishing operation was known to be operating properly and finds that 2 percent of the No. 3580 ball bearings were defective. If a sample size of 200 bearings and a significance level of .05 is to be used: **(a)** Set the acceptance criteria for the percent defectives in a sample. **(b)** If a sample is drawn that has 7 defective ball bearings, should the lot be accepted?

Solution

a. Set the acceptance criteria for the percent defectives in a sample:

First, refer to Table 15.4 and observe that the acceptance criteria formula for the percent defectives is:

$$\bar{p} \pm Z \sqrt{\bar{p}(100 - \bar{p})/n}$$

where $\bar{p}$ is the average percent defectives across many samples and equals 2 percent in this example. Because $\alpha = .05$, $\alpha/2 = .025$ is assigned to either tail of the normal sampling distribution and this fixes Z at ± 1.96.

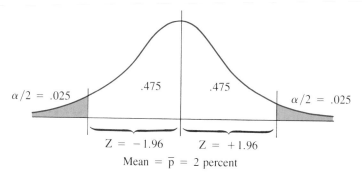

$$\alpha/2 = .025 \qquad .475 \qquad .475 \qquad \alpha/2 = .025$$

$$Z = -1.96 \qquad Z = +1.96$$

$$\text{Mean} = \bar{p} = 2 \text{ percent}$$

Therefore the acceptance criteria for *p* are:

$$\bar{p} \pm Z \sqrt{\bar{p}(100 - \bar{p})/n} = 2 \pm 1.96 \sqrt{2(98)/200} = 2 \pm 1.96(.9899) = 2 \pm 1.9403$$
$$= .0597 \text{ and } 3.9403, \text{ or } .06 \text{ and } 3.94 \text{ percent}$$

b. A sample of 200 ball bearings has 7 defectives. Should the sample be accepted?

Yes, because $7/200 = 3.5$ percent, which falls within the acceptance criteria of .06 and 3.94 percent defectives.

Notice that the formula for acceptance criteria for percent defectives in Table 15.4 includes *n*, which is the sample size. If sample sizes vary from sample to sample, the acceptance criteria must also vary with *n* and therefore must either be computed for each sample or be reduced to tabular form for quick referral.

Acceptance plans for variables are not as commonly found in books of tables as those for attributes. Statistical computations therefore tend to be fundamental for establishing these acceptance plans.

ACCEPTANCE PLANS FOR VARIABLES

Example 15.4 shows how to set the acceptance criteria for the mean compression strength of core samples taken from a section of a large interstate highway system. Setting acceptance criteria in this example requires that the mean of sample means ($\bar{\bar{x}}$), significance level (α), and the population standard deviation (σ_x) must all be known. This, realistically speaking, is seldom the case. Rather, quality control specialists must usually establish the $\bar{\bar{x}}$ and σ_x values through field research. The $\bar{\bar{x}}$ could be established, for example, by reviewing the historical records of many sample means ($\bar{x}$) and averaging these $\bar{x}$'s if the highway sections in these historical periods were good sections. Alternatively, the $\bar{\bar{x}}$ can be set as in this example by using a target, goal, or specification value. The σ_x must usually be deduced from historical information. A large group of cores from a number of acceptable sections could, for example, be tested and the standard deviation of these cores about their mean could be computed. This value could then be used as an estimate of σ_x.

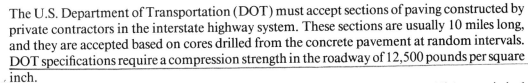

EXAMPLE 15.4   Setting Acceptance Criteria for Variables

The U.S. Department of Transportation (DOT) must accept sections of paving constructed by private contractors in the interstate highway system. These sections are usually 10 miles long, and they are accepted based on cores drilled from the concrete pavement at random intervals. DOT specifications require a compression strength in the roadway of 12,500 pounds per square inch.

Luis Gentry, head testing engineer for the third district, wishes to establish a statistical acceptance plan wherein sections of pavement would be accepted based on the mean compression strength of a sample of 50 cores removed from each section. Luis knows from experience that the standard deviation of compression strength for thousands of cores from hundreds of miles of pavement is 1,625 pounds per square inch. **(a)** Set the acceptance criteria of DOT's acceptance plan if $\alpha = .01$. **(b)** Fifty cores are pulled from a 10-mile section. The mean compression strength of the sample is 11,500 pounds per square inch. Should the section of pavement be accepted?

Solution

a. Set the acceptance criteria:

First, refer to Table 15.4 and observe that the acceptance criteria formula for sample means ($\bar{x}$) is:

$$\text{Acceptance criteria} = \bar{\bar{x}} + Z\sigma_{\bar{x}}$$

Because $\alpha = .01$, the Z score is 2.58.

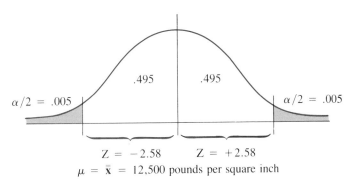

Because $\sigma_x = 1{,}625$ from the problem, $\sigma_{\bar{x}} = \sigma_x/\sqrt{n} = 1{,}625/\sqrt{50} = 229.81$ pounds per square inch. Therefore the acceptance criteria are:

Acceptance criteria $= \bar{\bar{x}} \pm Z\sigma_{\bar{x}} = 12{,}500 \pm 2.58(229.81) = 12{,}500 \pm 592.91$
$= 11{,}907.09$ and $13{,}092.91$ pounds per square inch

Luis Gentry is not concerned that a section of pavement might have a compression strength that is too high.

b. Should a section with a sample mean compression strength of 11,500 pounds per square inch be accepted?

No, because 11,500 falls outside the minimum sample mean acceptance criterion of 11,907.09 pounds per square inch.

The significance level (α) is commonly specified as a management policy. Its value is usually based upon this reasoning: (1) If we prefer to err on the side of accepting bad highway sections rather than rejecting good ones, we would select a small value of α, say about .01. (2) If, however, we prefer to err on the side of rejecting good highway sections rather than accepting bad ones, we would select a large value of α, say about .10. (3) If we wish to compromise between the two positions above, we would select an intermediate value of α, say about .05.

COMPUTERS IN QUALITY CONTROL

Total Quality Control programs require very large computer systems and data bases. Industries such as the automobile, pharmaceutical, food, and specialty chemicals industries are required under federal and state government regulations to be able to trace defects through the entire production and distribution systems. Even if an industry is not closely regulated by government agencies, however, such records are kept in order to limit a firm's exposure in the event of a product liability suit or the threat of such an action. Besides, it's just good business for a company to be able to track its products from production through consumer use, and this tracking is becoming feasible and economical with the use of computers. Highly publicized product recall programs in recent years highlight the importance of these computer systems. Such recall programs require that manufacturers (1) know the lot numbers of raw materials, assemblies, and parts that are responsible for the potential defects, (2) have an information storage system that can tie the lot numbers of the suspected raw materials, assemblies, and parts to the final product model numbers, and (3) have an information system that can track model numbers of final products to owners/consumers.

Computers also provide timely and economical information to managers about the quality of outputs coming from processes within production systems. Because control charts can be quickly prepared, the time lag is reduced between the time when materials, assemblies, parts, or products are inspected and the time when the results are posted on control charts. Similarly, computer programs are used in lot acceptance decisions. These programs set the criteria for acceptance, receive sample measure-

---

INDUSTRY SNAPSHOT 15.5

Computerized Quality Control Inspection

Employees at Garrett Pneumatic Systems in Phoenix, Arizona, who inspect products for quality now have the help of a computer system. An automatic video-inspection station is used to measure the close tolerance parameters of a fluidic laminate, a thin metal part that will be installed in a fluidic device. Fluidic devices use pressure and flow of fluids and gases to provide sophisticated sensing and control of such data as temperature or direction in flight instruments, missiles, or projectiles.

The video-inspection system is a computer-driven, electro-optical sensor with three-axis-measurement capabilities that allow the employee to see if a part has been machined properly. Combined with software developed by Garrett, the system allows a higher degree of accuracy and repeatability on a high-volume basis, eliminating chances for human error. The inspection equipment can be connected to a computer-aided design system to carry design data.[13]

---

[13] "Computer Aids Firm's Quality Checks," *The Arizona Republic,* Dec. 20, 1985, D-1. © The Arizona Republic, 1985. Reproduced by permission.

---

ments, and recommend an acceptance decision. Because the time lags are reduced in these decisions, products may be shipped to customers more quickly and materials may be moved more quickly into production. Also, because larger and more frequent samples can be taken economically, more precision can be attained in both control charts and lot acceptance tests.

There are even more dramatic uses of computers in quality control. Computers are used to test products as they come off the assembly line. Figure 5.5 in Chapter 5 illustrates a testing device that puts dashboard instrument panels through a series of functional checks. These tests are so fast that 100 percent inspection is now economical. Also, the tests are so thorough that every single function of the product can be quickly tested. Industry Snapshot 15.5 discusses a similar computer-assisted quality control inspection.

In addition to automatic inspections where computers are used to check the quality of products after they are made, computers are also being used to directly control the quality of products *while* they are being made. As discussed in Chapter 5, automated process controls measure the performance of production processes during production and automatically make corrections to the process settings to avoid producing defective products.

An indirect but related application of computers in quality control is the trend toward automated production that reduces the impact of human error on the production process. Robotics, numerically controlled machines, automatic identification systems, flexible manufacturing systems, automated assembly systems, automated storage and retrieval systems, and other automated and computer-assisted machines and systems are all believed to offer tremendous improvements in product quality.

The growth of computers in quality control has been spearheaded by a growing number of computer companies, manufacturing equipment manufacturers, and computer software firms. There is a growing list of quality control computer programs available today. For a list of quality control software, see the "Directory of Software for Quality Assurance and Quality Control" citation in the Selected Bibliography at the end of this chapter.

Computers and service industries are both becoming dominant forces in our economic system. Service systems must also be concerned with the quality of their outputs, but the nature of these systems prevents their straightforward adoption of quality control programs from manufacturing.

QUALITY CONTROL IN SERVICES

Services are usually intangible, and by their very nature it is difficult to determine their quality. Take, for example, the problem that airlines face when they try to determine the quality of the performance of flight attendants. The things about a flight attendant's performance that affect the customers' perceptions of quality are difficult to identify and measure, and in most cases standards for measuring the performance do not exist.

Another complicating factor is that the perceived quality of some services is affected by the surroundings. Quiet, soft music, pleasant decor, comfortable furniture, convenient parking, friendly servers, cleanliness of facilities, and other features can determine the perceived quality of services more than the quality of the actual service. Hospitals, banks, and restaurants, for example, all invest heavily in designing and maintaining facilities that develop particular feelings in their customers and leave them with specific impressions.

Services tend to be labor-intensive and workers tend to come in direct contact with customers. In many services, therefore, the performance of service employees determines in large part the quality of the services. And yet because services tend to be highly decentralized and geographically dispersed, direct supervision of employees can be difficult. Recognizing this difficulty, the cornerstone of quality control for many service organizations is an intensive continuing education and training program for their employees. McDonald's Hamburger University and Holiday Inn's University are examples of this development.[14]

Although some difficulty is encountered in developing quality control programs for services, such programs are in place in most service organizations and are receiving great attention today. Industry Snapshot 15.6 discusses the extent to which McDonald's is committed to training employees so that the quality of its products and services is maintained. But quality control in services extends far beyond employee training.

The difficulties we have discussed in establishing quality control programs for services are not insurmountable obstacles. Service organizations do develop sophis-

---

[14] W. Earl Sasser, R. Paul Olsen, and D. Daryl Wyckoff, *Management of Service Operations* (Boston: Allyn & Bacon, 1978), 17.

INDUSTRY SNAPSHOT 15.6

To Learn the Ins and Outs of QSCV, Enroll at Hamburger U.

Oak Brook, Ill. — The students could be goggle-eyed 19-year-olds or wizened Houston entrepreneurs, but they share unswerving loyalty to a bond thicker than blood.

"Around here," says Larry L. Coon, the hale, square-jawed dean of Hamburger University, "we say you get ketchup in your veins."

Coon ought to know. Like many a McDonald's executive, the director of America's quintessential management training academy started out as a humble part-time crew member at his local McDonald's.

When the ketchup started coursing, he gave up his career as a horticulturalist, started climbing the McDonald's corporate trellis, and now tends an ethic hardier than the hardiest perennial: QSCV.

Quality, Service, Cleanliness, Value — the four great mysteries in the theology of the hamburger were first revealed to Ray Kroc, and through him to enthusiastic acolytes at nearly 8,000 stores throughout the world, and through them to 17 million people daily who stop by for an Egg McMuffin or a Big Mac.

"We've got a great culture within McDonald's," says Coon, "and we spread that out among our customers. A guy with an eighth-grade education founded a business that's touched and impacted almost everyone in the world. It's an American success story."

His golden arches lapel pin glinting on his pin-stripe suit, his hands bedecked with a ring and a watch also bearing the soaring arches, Coon gestures around his corner office and says: "You can get more than hamburger at McDonald's. It's an experience."

Nowhere is the experience more lavishly presented or thoroughly studied than at Hamburger U.

The low-slung, new multimillion-dollar facility sits on 80 lush acres, cheek by jowl with a golf course and some polo fields, a stone's throw from McDonald's corporate headquarters here. It overlooks Lake Fred (named after Chairman of the Board Fred L. Turner) and commands a view of adjacent Lake Ed (named after Vice Chairman of the Board Edward H. Schmitt).

Clutching green plastic volumes embossed with the golden arches, students amble over Lake Fred on a gently curving bridge between Hamburger U. and their quarters in the Lodge, a posh Hyatt-run hotel.

Paintings from the McDonald's collection adorn every hotel and university wall, and are even more numerous than the framed maxims of founder Kroc — gems such as:

- "None Of Us Is As Good As All Of Us."
- "When You're Green You're Growing And When You're Ripe, You Start To Rot."
- "We Took The Hamburger Business More Seriously Than Anyone Else."

So do Hamburger U.'s students, from the lowliest assistant manager to the loftiest franchisee, all of whom must attend Hamburger U. and some of whom return for more sophisticated courses. . . .

"Most Hamburger U. students have worked their way up through the hierarchy for two or three years," says Coon.

In the two-week Advanced Operations Course, 2,000 students a year polish

(continued)

INDUSTRY SNAPSHOT 15.6 (continued)

their "human relations skills" with techniques derived from transactional analysis. They learn the fundamentals of time management and marketing, of scheduling shifts and calibrating soda dispensers.

Successful candidates . . . receive the Bachelor of Hamburgerology degree, a prerequisite to their continued rise in . . . McDonald's. . . .

The "degree," of course, carries no academic weight. But Hamburger U. has applied to Illinois education officials for permission to award authentic associate's degrees, the same degrees awarded by most two-year colleges.

Correspondence courses in personnel, finance, marketing, and management will be offered free to company employees through a Hamburger U. division called the McDonald's Management Institute.

Designed partly to induce McDonald's young labor force to remain at the company longer, the program also "will give our people a better perspective of McDonald's," says Coon.

"If there are, say, five marketing philosophies, we'll teach them all," he says, "but we'll always advocate the McDonald's philosophy." [15]

---

[15] "To Learn the Ins and Outs of QSCV, Enroll at Hamburger U." *Houston Chronicle,* Nov. 18, 1984, sec. 4, p. 20 (Scripps-Howard News Service). Reprinted with permission.

---

ticated quality control programs, and some of their features are very much like those found in manufacturing. Other aspects of their programs, however, are dramatically different. Table 15.5 gives five examples of quality control in a bank and a hospital. These examples suggest the presence of quality control programs that have broad and far-reaching impacts on the management of the firms. For most services the competitive weapon of choice is perceived service quality, because price, flexibility, and speed of delivery may not be much different from the competition; thus service quality becomes the primary focus of operations strategy.

Table 15.5 describes an important element of many quality programs in services, the use of *customer surveys.* This technique allows customers to fill out survey questionnaires or participate in interviews that are aimed at determining the customers' perceptions about several quality-related issues. Another way of gauging the quality of services is with the use of *mystery shoppers,* employees who pretend to be customers and monitor the quality of services. For example, at American Express about 250 quality control personnel monitor the quality of services worldwide. An important element of this program features the use of mystery shoppers. Also, as in other service organizations, American Express uses statistical control charts to monitor such things as the amount of time required to process a customer's application for an American Express Card. Similarly, statistical control charts are used to keep track of several measures of customer satisfaction using data gathered from customer surveys. The diversity of such measures emphasizes the flexibility of control charts in controlling the quality of services as well as cost and other dimensions of organization performance.

■■

TABLE 15.5   Examples of Quality Control in Services

Type of Organization	*Example*
Bank	Customers are randomly selected for a survey administered every three months to determine how satisfactory the bank's services are to customers. Areas of deficiency are identified, policies are reviewed, and corrective actions are taken to change operations and modify the nature of the services delivered.
	Control charts monitor the accuracy of customers' accounts. Customers' accounts are randomly audited each week to provide *p* charts (percentage of accounts that are in error) that are updated weekly to show trends. Operating procedures are reviewed and modified as necessary to bring deficiencies into an acceptable range.
Hospital	Patients are administered a survey as they check out. The purpose of the survey is to determine the perceptions of patients regarding quality of food, promptness of service, friendliness, competency of personnel, costs, comfort factors, and other quality-related issues. This information is used to revise policies and operations at the hospital as needed.
	Control charts are used extensively to monitor such things as billing accuracy, lab test accuracy, pharmacy prescription accuracy, and personnel absenteeism. Feedback is provided to the departments involved, and follow-up audits are conducted in areas that are trending out of control-chart limits.
	Suggestion boxes are provided at several locations in the hospital to provide patients, visitors, and personnel with on-the-spot opportunities to report on both satisfactory and unsatisfactory incidents and to make recommendations for improvements. This mechanism provides an overall check of service quality, but it requires diligence and interpretation to be effective.

■■

SUMMARY

Statistical concepts form the foundation of today's quality control discipline. Material lots; random samples, attributes, and variables; acceptance plans; single, double, and sequential sampling plans; and quality control tables are all based on the field of statistics. The central limit theorem allows quality control analysts to assume that sampling distributions are normally distributed. This is fundamental to control charts and acceptance plans.

Japanese firms have been very successful in encouraging their employees to participate in improving the quality of their mass-manufactured products. They have used JIT systems and the concepts of quality at the source and quality circles, which are volunteer groups of workers who develop projects for improving the quality of the products in their own areas. QC circles are now being used in this and other countries.

It is hoped that the benefits Japan has enjoyed from these groups can be experienced here and elsewhere.

Control charts are used to determine if the quality of products or services is in control during production processes or if worrisome trends are developing for which corrective action is needed. p charts are used to control percent defectives (an attribute) in a sample. $\bar{x}$ and R charts are used to control sample means and sample ranges (variables).

Average outgoing quality (AOQ) curves and operating characteristic (OC) curves help explain the workings of acceptance plans. Although these plans are not foolproof—they can on rare occasions reject good lots and accept bad ones—they do offer operations managers a good compromise between economy and quality control protection. These plans set the acceptance criteria for samples so that inspectors can either accept or reject lots of materials or products. Attributes (p) or variables ($\bar{x}$ and R) can be measured from samples, and appropriate acceptance criteria can be developed for these plans.

Computers are being used increasingly in quality control. The information storage and retrieval capabilities of computers are used to retain the massive volume of records for material and product lots. Control chart information is also processed on computers, thus providing information to managers and workers more quickly so that corrective action can be initiated while it is still possible to avoid production of poor quality products. Acceptance plan computations are also processed on computers. These uses of computers are providing quality control departments with lower costs and faster reaction time.

Quality control in services can be more difficult than in product systems because the outputs are often intangible and quality standards can be subjective. Additionally, the features of the service facilities may be more important in customer perception of quality than the quality of the actual service. Service firms are turning more and more to continuing education and training of their personnel as the key element of their quality control programs. Acceptance plans are commonly used in services to accept materials and supplies as inputs to these systems, but they are not used for the systems' outputs. Control charts are used to control a wide range of quality control measures in service systems.

REVIEW AND DISCUSSION QUESTIONS

1. Define *total quality control (TQC)*. Discuss how a firm would change if TQC were adopted.

2. What are four elements of most quality control programs? Discuss the meaning of this statement: "You can't inspect quality into products."

3. Name two sources of morale or cooperation problems that can occur as quality control and production personnel interact. How can these problems be avoided?

4. What two sources of cost do managers attempt to balance when deciding how many (what proportion of total) products to inspect?

5. Define these terms: *lot, random sample, attribute, variable, acceptance plan, single-sampling plan, double-sampling plan,* and *sequential sampling plan.*

6. Define the *central limit theorem.* What are its principal uses in quality control?

7. What is the meaning of *quality at the source*? On what principles is it based?

8. Who is W. Edwards Deming? What are his major contributions to quality control? Briefly describe the philosophy upon which his principles of quality control and productivity are built.

9. Explain how JIT affects product quality.

10. Define *quality circle.* Describe how it works. What benefits do companies enjoy from QC circles?

11. Define these values: p, x, and R. Are they variables or attributes?

12. Compare and contrast the purposes of control charts and acceptance plans. Discuss this statement: "The time is fast approaching when there will be no place for acceptance plans in manufacturing."

13. "Four things can happen in applying acceptance plans, and two of them are bad." Explain how these bad occurrences are possible.

14. Explain how you would decide what significance level to use in an acceptance plan.

15. What is the principal message that an average outgoing quality (AOQ) curve gives about an acceptance plan?

16. What is the most obvious way that acceptance plans can be modified to reduce the probability of accepting bad lots and rejecting good ones? Discuss the likely effects of increased automated manufacturing on the use of acceptance plans.

17. Name two factors that make quality control in service systems more difficult than in manufacturing.

18. What quality control strategy have service systems devised to deal with the fact that services tend to be labor-intensive and geographically dispersed?

PROBLEMS

Control Charts

1. Given: $\bar{p} = 2.5$ percent and n = 25. Required: Compute 3σ control limits for p.

2. Shirley Chides, quality control analyst at the Los Angeles plant of Computer Products Corporation (CPC), is studying a quality problem in manufacturing. A component purchased from an outside supplier has been causing CPC's bar code scanners to perform poorly. The component, a Y56 transistor, is tested and certified as meeting quality standards by the outside supplier. CPC does not presently test the component, but Shirley will propose that random samples of 100 components be subjected to a 500-watt fail test. She has determined that when the component is manufactured properly, only 2 percent of the components will fail the test. If Shirley prepares a control chart to monitor the progress of the outside supplier's quality performance on

the component, what 3σ upper and lower control limits should be used on the charts?

3. The southeastern distribution center for Jeans Inc. receives shipments of Western-style denim trousers from manufacturers, places its own labels on the jeans, packages them, and ships them to its retail outlets throughout the southeastern United States. In recent months the center has received numerous complaints about the quality of the labeling operation. Labels are said to be too loose and some have even fallen off the garments. Janie Hochevar, director of production at the center, has decided to record the number of defective labels in random daily samples on control charts. If Janie estimates that 1.5 percent of loose labels is about normal, on the average, the sample size is 200 pairs of jeans, and a p chart is to be used:
   a. Compute the center line for the p chart.
   b. Compute the 3σ control limits for the chart.
   c. Plot these recent data collected from daily samples and decide if the labeling operation is in control: Number of defectives per sample = 2, 3, 5, 2, 7, 8, 3, 0, 5, 7, 9, 2.

 4. At a recent staff meeting of the quality control department at the El Paso plant of Computer Products Corporation (CPC), it was decided to initiate a control chart program to monitor the quality performance of the plant's flow-soldering operation. All printed circuit boards that are soldered are processed through the operation. The boards are subjected to a circuit integrity test on a random basis, and those that fail the test are sent back for reworking and reprocessing. The control chart program that was adopted by the group included random samples of 20 boards taken twice per shift, control limits of 2σ, and a target of only 1 percent rework when the process is operating properly. Several weeks later Bill McClain, a quality control analyst, examined the records from the most recent five days from the flow-soldering operation. The percentage of boards that required rework from the ten random samples were: 2.1, 1.1, 0, 3.4, 1.9, .1, 1.2, 3.3, 5.4, and 2.6.
   a. Compute the center line and the upper and lower control limits for the chart.
   b. Plot the data from the ten samples and decide if the flow-soldering operation is in control.

 5. Bill O'Fallon, vice president for administrative services at Biltmore College, is concerned about the number of students who are dropping out of the college because of academic deficiencies each quarter. He believes that Biltmore should average about 285 academic drops per quarter out of a total stable student population of 9,500 students. Bill wishes to develop a control chart for the percentage of academic drops in quarterly random samples of 500 students. The last ten quarters' records show these numbers of drops in random samples: 18, 18, 13, 10, 12, 9, 11, 8, 14, 8.
   a. Compute the 95 percent control limits.
   b. Plot the ten quarters of sample data on a control chart.
   c. Has there been a change in the percentage of academic drops per quarter at Biltmore?

6. The average absenteeism rate for the clerical workers at the National Insurance Company (NIC) headquarters in Atlanta averages about 5 percent. Department heads voluntarily send data to the personnel department analytical records group to develop random samples of records for about 200 workers weekly out of a total

clerical work force of 5,000 workers. These sample sizes and number of absences are received:

Sample Number	Sample Size	Number Absent	Sample Number	Sample Size	Number Absent
1	200	10	7	200	12
2	150	10	8	180	10
3	170	12	9	220	10
4	220	12	10	200	11
5	180	13	11	160	10
6	120	8	12	100	6

   a. Construct a 3σ control chart for p and plot the sample data points. (*Hint:* The upper and lower control limits vary with sample size.)

   b. Has there been a change in the absenteeism rate at NIC?

7. Given: $\bar{\bar{x}} = 24$ inches, $\bar{R} = 5$ inches, and $n = 10$. Required:

   a. Compute 3σ control limits for $\bar{x}$.

   b. Plot these sample means on an $\bar{x}$ control chart: 24.1, 23.5, 24.7, 25.2, 25.8, 25.7, 26.1, 25.8, 26.7, 27.0.

   c. Decide if the process is in control.

8. Given: $\bar{R} = 5.0$ inches and $n = 10$. Required:

   a. Compute 3σ control limits for R.

   b. Plot these sample ranges on a 3σ control chart for R: 2.9, 4.6, 6.9, 5.4, 1.6, 2.7, 6.9, 6.5, 8.1, 3.6.

   c. Is the process in control?

9. The Bi-State Trucking Company, a local deliverer of freight in Durham, North Carolina, has been experiencing customer complaints about late deliveries. Bi-State's management strives for an average delivery of local freight in 24 hours. Weekly samples of 20 customers are taken and exhibit an average range of 3.5 hours. Bi-State's management thinks this is about right.

   a. Compute 3σ control limits for $\bar{x}$.

   b. Plot these sample means on a 3σ control chart for $\bar{x}$: 23.4, 24.5, 23.9, 25.6, 26.5, 23.8, 23.7, 24.1, 25.1, 24.9.

   c. Is management's target of an average 24-hour delivery being met?

10. The Atlanta plant of Computer Products Corporation (CPC) manufactures personal and small-business computers. These computers use the P22 power unit, the source of electrical power for the computers. Cooling of the P22 is accomplished by a small on-board fan. The fan is designed to cool the P22 under a variety of humidity and temperature environments as long as the P22 is not drawing too much wattage. Quality control personnel at the Atlanta plant remove random samples of 200 units of the P22 from the units going into production daily and measure the wattage drawn by the units. When the units are performing normally, the means of these samples average 22 watts and sample ranges average 3 watts. A 3σ control chart program is being used to monitor the quality performance of the P22 and these data from the ten most recent samples were collected:

Sample Number	Sample Mean (Watts)	Sample Range (Watts)	Sample Number	Sample Mean (Watts)	Sample Range (Watts)
1	21.5	2.1	6	21.6	2.5
2	22.2	1.1	7	22.1	3.5
3	22.7	.4	8	22.9	3.8
4	22.5	1.3	9	22.1	3.7
5	23.5	1.6	10	22.9	2.1

a. Compute the 3σ control limits and center line for an $\bar{x}$ chart.
b. Compute the 3σ control limits and center line for an R chart.
c. Plot the sample data on the $\bar{x}$ and R charts and decide if the quality performance of the P22 power unit is in control.

 11. The No-Cal Bottling Company bottles soft drinks for sale to government commissaries. The bottles come in only one flavor (chocolate-lemon) and only one size (32 ounces). Joan Stickler, the quality control officer for the commissaries, wants to keep track of the fill weights of No-Cal and begins to draw daily samples of 100 bottles from the daily receipts. The first ten sample means and ranges are:

Sample	$\bar{x}$	R	Sample	$\bar{x}$	R
1	31.5	2.1	6	31.5	.7
2	31.2	2.5	7	31.7	1.2
3	32.1	3.0	8	31.2	2.0
4	30.9	1.6	9	32.8	1.7
5	32.7	1.7	10	31.9	0

If sample ranges ordinarily average 2.5 ounces:
a. Compute 3σ control limits for sample means.
b. Compute 3σ control limits for sample ranges.
c. What would you conclude about the fill weights of No-Cal?

Acceptance Plans

12. Given: $\bar{p} = 10$ percent, $n = 200$, $\alpha = .10$, and c = number of defectives in a sample from a lot is 26 units. Required: Determine whether the sample percent defectives is large enough to reject the lot.

13. Betty Childress is the regional quality manager for McDougal's Hamburgers. She wishes to establish an acceptance plan for hamburger cartons, with particular emphasis on the cartons closing mechanisms. Several samples of normal carton shipments indicated that 5 percent of cartons from normal shipments had defective closing mechanisms. A sample of 500 cartons from a lot of 100,000 cartons had 6.5 percent defectives. If an α of .05 is used, should the lot be accepted?

 14. The Austin, Texas, plant of Computer Products Corporation (CPC) receives a component, the Z4 converter, from two outside suppliers. The component is used in the

computers and floppy disk units manufactured at the plant, and the quality of these products is affected by the quality of their components. The quality control department at the plant has determined that the assembly tests in manufacturing can catch all of the Z4 converter component defects if the quality of the batch of components is normal. This component ordinarily averages about 4 percent defective. If, however, the quality of the batch of components is too high, the quality of the printers and floppy disk units is affected. The quality control department must establish an acceptance plan for the Z4 component. If the sample size is to be 150 and you prefer to err on the side of rejecting good lots, what acceptance criteria would you recommend?

 15. The Rigid Beam Construction Company specializes in steel beam construction of high-rise buildings. Rivets are used by the thousands in this type of construction, and the tensile strength of the rivets is extremely important to the overall strength of these structures. Rigid draws random samples of rivets and subjects them to tensile force until they fail. If they fail after the force reaches 10,000 pounds, they pass. If they fail before the force reaches 10,000 pounds, they don't pass. Good lots of rivets average about 4 percent defectives. A lot of rivets from a new supplier has recently arrived. An inspector has just conducted a test of 100 rivets with 93 passing. If, given the choice, you would rather err on the side of rejecting good lots, should you accept the lot?

16. Given: $\mu = 28$ ounces, $\sigma_x = 4$ ounces, n = 196, $\bar{x} = 27.40$ ounces, and $\alpha = .10$. Required: Determine whether to accept or reject the lot.

 17. The Provo Steel Corporation buys coal from the Sun River Mining Company. Sun River ships low-volatility, low-sulfur coal from its mines at Howe, Oklahoma, via railroad cars. These cars are intended to hold precisely 60 tons because Provo Steel depends on this weight as the primary basis for its blending operations prior to charging its coke ovens. Provo's records show that when Sun River is attentive, their cars of coal average 60 tons, a contractual requirement of Provo, with a standard deviation of 1 ton, and then the cars of coal can go directly into the coke ovens; but when Sun River is not attentive, Provo must unload the cars, weigh out exactly 60-ton charges of coal, and then charge the coke ovens. Provo wishes to take daily sample car weights and determine whether unloading and weighing the entire daily shipment is necessary. Ten cars are randomly selected from a day's shipment, and the mean car weight is 61.5 tons. If Provo would rather err on the side of accepting out-of-weight cars, should they accept the day's shipment from Sun River directly into the coke ovens?

18. A professor keeps track of the grade point average (GPA) of his students from semester to semester. Overall he has found that his students average 2.5 out of 4.0 with a standard deviation of .25 among all his students, which is about the same as for the entire university. This semester, however, one of his classes of 75 students does not seem to be performing as well as they should on his standard exams. This class has a GPA of 2.43, and the professor wonders if this particular class might be academically below par. Use what you have learned in quality control analysis to help the professor resolve the issue.

COMPUTER PROBLEMS/CASES

GAS GENERATOR CORPORATION

Bill Blane has just received a big promotion to works manager and director of Gas Generator Corporation's largest plant, located in Carbondale, Illinois. The plant's products are gas generators that serve as power sources for the guidance systems for the most advanced U.S. missiles. After the euphoria of moving his family from California to the new location, meeting his new staff, and settling into his new office had passed, he got the bad news — one lot of the plant's products had just been rejected by its best customer. He noticed that the plant's staff members were not too concerned because, according to them, "it has happened before."

Mr. Blane called a meeting of all of the technical staff as soon as the test data from the customer had been received. He asked the following questions: (1) What was the nature of the test failure? (2) What caused the substandard products to be produced? (3) What should we have done differently in our production processes to have avoided the problem? (4) What is the impact of this failure on our operations? The staff summarized the nature of the failure this way. The products performed well under all conditions except the deep-freeze firing, and then the generators produced volumes of gas that were only slightly below standard. As for the other questions, the answers were the same: "We don't know!" Mr. Blane dispersed the group with instructions to develop the answers to his questions. He then called the home office to inform his boss, Mr. Don Billigan, that a potentially large problem loomed on the horizon and that he would keep him informed of the progress of the investigation.

The next morning the staff met again to discuss the problem. The news was much worse than Mr. Blane had thought. The entire finished goods inventory and in-process inventory back to the mixing stage of production were similarly substandard. Because it would take at least three months to introduce new materials at the mixing stage and process them through final assembly and delivery, the plant faced the prospect of three months of filling the pipeline without any revenue. The staff members were stumped, however, about the exact cause of the failure. Mr. Blane called Mr. Billigan and told him the bad news: "We won't have any finished products to ship for at least 90 days, we will have a net loss of about $500,000 before taxes during this period, we will be in default of our delivery contracts, and we don't know for sure what caused the problem or what needs to be done to correct it, but we are continuing the investigation."

Mr. Blane started with the mixing operation and worked forward through the production process to determine if their workers were following the *Manual of Standard Operating Procedures.* Two observers were assigned to every major operation in the process to verify that the procedures were being followed. It took only a week to determine that the workers were not following the procedures at the mixing operation. It took another week to verify that when the procedures were religiously followed, the in-process materials met the quality control performance specifications.

Assignment

1. What are the underlying causes of the quality control problem at the Gas Generator plant?

2. Discuss any deficiencies in the quality control program that are apparent from the case.

3. Why didn't the acceptance tests indicate the problem before the customer discovered it? Is such an occurrence possible? How would such a problem arise?

4. Discuss the appropriateness of the methods that Mr. Blane used to investigate the problem. How might he have acted to achieve better results?

5. Describe how a quality control program should operate so that such problems are avoided.

6. What changes should Mr. Blane make at the Gas Generator plant?

COMPUTER PRODUCTS CORPORATION (CPC)

The Boston plant of Computer Products Corporation (CPC) manufactures resins used in the electronics and computer industries. The Boston plant installed what it called *total quality control (TQC)* at the plant last year. The purpose of the new program was to involve everyone at the plant, from the plant manager to the shop floor workers in achieving excellent product quality. This program would feature *quality at the source* concepts and *quality circles.* A new resin has been developed by the R&D group at the CPC corporate headquarters in San Jose and will be put into production soon at the Boston plant. The quality control department at the plant is now developing a quality plan for the new product. Of particular importance is an acceptance plan for the finished resin before it is shipped to CPC's other plants or to customers. The key performance characteristic for the resin is its "pot life," the amount of time that it takes for the resin to be converted to its finished form after it is mixed with plasticizers. The "nominal pot life" of the resin is 35 seconds at 570 degrees Fahrenheit with a standard deviation of 5 seconds. The customary shipping unit of the resin is a 5-pound bag, and the quality plan calls for random samples of 160 bags drawn from finished production lots of 5,000 bags.

Assignment

1. What acceptance criteria for production lots would you recommend for the means of samples at a significance level of .01?

2. If a significance level of .01 is used, what does this say about management's attitude toward accepting bad lots as opposed to rejecting good lots? Does this attitude seem reasonable, considering the nature of the product?

3. Explain what total quality control (TQC) means. What are the major elements of TQC? What are the major benefits of TQC?

4. Explain the meaning of quality at the source. On what principles is it based? What are its major benefits?

5. Describe quality circles. What are their major benefits?

6. If TQC aims for perfect product quality, why should an acceptance plan be required for the new resin? Does not this violate a major principle of TQC—to produce products of high quality and not try to inspect quality into the products later? What is the appropriate role of acceptance sampling in a TQC environment?

TOTAL QUALITY CONTROL AT SPECTRUM CONTROL INC.

Spectrum, headquartered in Erie, Pa., was founded in 1968 by Thomas L. Venable, Glenn L. Warnshuis, and John R. Lane, three engineers who had met at Erie Technological Products Inc. In 16 years, the company grew from a $300,000 start-up housed in an old hardware store to a solid, $22-million public company. Today, Spectrum has four manufacturing plants and some 1,500 customers, including the likes of IBM Corp. and Hewlett-Packard Co. For the past three years, it has reported after-tax returns of about 10 percent of sales.

In the early days, quality wasn't an issue. Venable and Warnshuis designed and built Spectrum's sophisticated filters, while Lane marketed them. "There wasn't any point in making them wrong," Venable says with a chuckle. But, as the company began to prosper and grow, that kind of hands-on responsibility fell by the wayside.

Like most manufacturers—and like most businesses—Spectrum began to operate on the philosophy of acceptable-quality levels, or AQLs. The company regularly checked a sample of the product, then shipped the whole batch, so long as the number of bad units fell within accepted limits. If there were too many bad ones, the lot was rejected, or subjected to 100 percent inspection, an expensive process.

Then, slowly, Spectrum's marketplace began to change. A Japanese company, Murata Manufacturing Co., purchased Erie Technological Products (now Murata Erie North America Inc.), with which Spectrum competed, and raised the specter of Japanese-style quality. Several of Spectrum's customers began to make noises about quality as well. "About two or three years ago," says Venable, "Hewlett-Packard said that they were going to switch to the idea of 'zero defects'—no defects in any inbound materials." Soon IBM was joining the chorus—and implying, Venable remembers, that a business hoping to remain an IBM supplier better begin thinking seriously about quality.

Venable and other Spectrum managers began to assay likely strategies for attacking the newly discovered issue. They took a look at some Japanese quality techniques. . . . They bought 40 copies of *Quality Is Free* by management consultant Philip Crosby, a book that IBM had been pushing, and passed them out. They also bought and studied some videotapes featuring W. Edwards Deming, the dean emeritus of statistical control of quality.

Essentially, Crosby suggests that precise requirements be set for every business task, and that those standards be met each and every time. If problems occur, in either performance or product, permanent solutions must be found as soon as possible; temporary fixes won't do.

Crosby's evangelical approach paid off in at least one major way: It destroyed the shibboleth of AQLs. "I think the principal benefit," Venable says, "was that it convinced us that, given a structure, it was possible to work toward zero defects, toward error-free performance."

Venable's plan was to use Crosby's razzmatazz and routines to get things moving, then rely increasingly on Deming's techniques to control the process—modifying both, whenever it seemed necessary, with approaches of Spectrum's own design.

Some of the changes came easily, such as paying closer attention to customers' schedules. In the past, the company had often shipped its components too early, and the customers simply shipped them back. The cost of such errors, says Venable, was significant, particularly in the case of overseas deliveries—"$150 to $200 for transshipping, and $300 for paperwork." At the other end of the pipeline, Spectrum installed new order-entry checking systems, "so we've seen a tremendous improvement in our error rate there."

For the most part, though, the improvements came slowly. "Easy?" snorts one worker in the Electromagnetic Division. "It was like giving up smoking and drinking, plus going on a diet—all at the same time." Changing the habits and attitudes of Spectrum's workers was hard enough. But a thoroughgoing approach to quality involved the company's vendors and customers as well.

There was, for example, the matter of the bushings—small, threaded items used to connect glass-sealed filters to other devices. The bushings were manufactured by three screw-machine suppliers, inspected by Spectrum, sent to a plating vendor, and, once plated, inspected again. At that late date in the process, some 50 percent were rejected.

"After you'd gone through the QES classes," says Electromagnetic Division unit manager David Weunski, "you were supposed to go back to your unit and think of things that had been giving you problems over the years. . . . This one, of course, leaped out at me."

The solution, however, did not. Only after endless hours of brainstorming and conferences with suppliers did Weunski hit on a strategy. During the initial inspection, he realized, Spectrum employed gauges that indicated only when the bushings exceeded the correct dimensions of the finished product; not until later, after another layer of metal had been added in plating, did other problems show up. So Weunski ordered $7,000 worth of new gauges, one set to measure the raw bushing and another to measure the plated one, and donated duplicate sets of gauges to his vendors. "Before," he says, "we would probably have put the burden of buying the gauges on them. Now, the attitude is much more cooperative." And the early results, he adds, are dramatic. "When all of the gauges are in place, we could be talking about a *doubling* of productivity."

Then there was the matter of Department Number Nine at the Electromagnetic Division, which produces, among other things, shielded windows. These windows—artfully crafted panels of dark, curved glass that are fastened to the front of a computer screen—absorb the six or seven watts of radiated energy produced by some computer terminals, and thus prevent anyone from "reading" the screen's information at a distance. But they are inordinately difficult to manufacture. Composed of layers of glass, wire screening, and laminating materials, they tend to delaminate when exposed to temperature extremes. "At worst, rejects were running as high as 15 percent," says unit manager Cy Ley.

Although Number Nine already had been wrestling with the issue, Spectrum's quality initiative pushed it to take some radical steps, such as changing vendors. For instance, Homalite Inc., of Wilmington, Del., had once provided the parts for the plastic laminate, but had lost the contract to another supplier; then, when quality became a top concern, it got it back. "Basically," says Homalite general manager Rod J. Field, "we lost them on price, but won them back with quality. They sent a four- or five-man team down to review what we were doing here—and then we were back in business."

Department Number Nine supervisors have also become aggressively receptive to suggestions from line personnel. "No one is really an expert except the person who's out there building that window," Ley concedes. "One of their suggestions actually increased our productivity by something like 50 percent."

The net effect: a scant .08 percent reject rate on the newest line of windows. "Because of the dramatic improvement," observes Venable, "we were actually able to reduce our pricing on this product line."

Overall, there are few people, processes, or products that haven't in some way been affected by Spectrum's quality crusade. There is now a vendor-selection committee, for example, and the number of active vendors has been trimmed by 8 percent. The company is also more demanding of customers. When it felt that one client's specifications for a filter used in the B-1 bomber were unattainable, it said so, and lost the work, but promptly got it back when the competitor that got the job discovered (and proved) that the unit couldn't be built as designed. Not even the company's outside directors have escaped the reeducation process: Venable recently asked several of them to attend Crosby's Quality College.

Tom Venable, for his part, is happy with the results, despite the difficulties. "In our first quarter of Quality Response Process operation," says Venable, "we've seen a 75 percent reduction in sales returns and allowances; if you annualize that, you're looking at savings of something like $767,000." Even more telling is Spectrum's profit-sharing balance. Believing that employees should have a fiscal, as well as a psychological, incentive to get involved in the program, Venable earmarked about half of the savings realized for the company's profit-sharing plan. Last year, management had put $150,000 into the program, but, high on quality, had budgeted $525,000 this year. Now, observes Venable, "We have the feeling that it's going to be quite a bit higher—more like $1 million-plus." [16]

Assignment

1. What factors led Spectrum to undertake a total quality control (TQC) program?

2. Identify and describe the major elements of Spectrum's TQC program.

3. Did Spectrum abandon AQLs and other statistical quality control methods? Explain the role of statistical quality control methods in TQC.

4. What role did employee training and education play in Spectrum's TQC program? Assess the importance of employee training and education in TQC.

---

[16] Craig R. Waters, "Quality Begins at Home," *Inc.*, August 1985, 68–71. Reprinted with permission, *Inc.* magazine (August 1985). Copyright © (1985) by Inc. Publishing Company, 38 Commercial Wharf, Boston, MA 02110.

5. What factors must be present in an organization before a TQC program such as the one at Spectrum can succeed?
6. It has been said that the main philosophy of TQC is "Do it right the first time." Explain how this philosophy is present in Spectrum's TQC program.
7. What are the major benefits that Spectrum has derived from its TQC program?

SELECTED BIBLIOGRAPHY

Besterfield, D. H. *Quality Control.* 2nd ed. Englewood Cliffs, NJ: Prentice-Hall, 1986.

Buffa, Elwood S. *Meeting the Competitive Challenge.* Homewood, IL: Dow Jones-Irwin, 1984, 123–124.

Crosby, Philip B. *Quality Is Free.* New York: McGraw-Hill, 1979.

Deming, W. Edwards. *Out of Crisis.* Cambridge, MA: MIT, Center for Advanced Engineering Study, 1986.

"Directory of Software for Quality Assurance and Quality Control." *Quality Progress* (March 1984):33–53.

Dodge, H. F., and H. G. Romig. *Sampling Inspection Tables.* New York: Wiley, 1959.

Garvin, David A. "Quality on the Line." *Harvard Business Review* (September–October 1983):63–71.

Gitlow, H. S., and S. Gitlow. *The Deming Guide to Achieving Quality and Competitive Position.* Englewood Cliffs, NJ: Prentice-Hall, 1987.

Gitlow, H. S., and P. T. Hertz. "Product Defects and Productivity." *Harvard Business Review* 61, no. 5(September–October 1983).

Hostage, G. M. "Quality Control in a Service Business." *Harvard Business Review* 53(July–August 1975):98–106.

Ingle, Sud. *In Search of Perfection: How to Create/Maintain/Improve Quality.* Englewood Cliffs, NJ: Prentice-Hall, 1985.

Ishikawa, Kaoru. *What Is Total Quality Control?* Translated by David J. Lu. Englewood Cliffs, NJ: Prentice-Hall, 1985.

Sasser, W. Earl, R. Paul Olsen, and D. Daryl Wyckoff. *Management of Service Operations.* Boston: Allyn & Bacon, 1978.

Scanlon, Frank, and John T. Hogan. "Service Industry Quality Management—Part II." *Quality Progress* 60:6(June 1983), 30–35.

Swartz, Gerald E., and Vivian C. Comstock. "One Firm's Experience with Quality Circles." *Quality Progress* 12, no. 9(September 1979):14–16.

Tsurumi, Y. "Productivity: The Japanese Approach." *Pacific Basin Quarterly* (Summer 1981):8.

U.S. Department of Defense. *A Guide to Zero Defects: Quality and Reliability Assurance Handbook,* 4415.12. Washington, DC: Government Printing Office, 1965.

U.S. Department of Defense. *Military Standard (MIL-STD-414), Sampling Procedures and Tables for Inspection by Variables for Percent Defective.* Washington, DC: Government Printing Office, 1957.

U.S. Department of Defense. *Military Standard (MIL-STD-105), Sampling Procedures and Tables for Inspection for Attributes.* Washington, DC: Government Printing Office, 1963.

Wheelwright, S. C. "Japan—Where Operations Really Are Strategic." *Harvard Business Review* (July–August 1981):67–74.

Williamson, J. W. "Evaluating Quality of Patient Care." *Journal of the American Medical Association* 218(Oct. 25, 1971):564–569.

16

PLANNING AND CONTROLLING PROJECTS

MANAGING THE RATS PROJECT

Bill Williams, manager of the Power Systems plant in Marion, Illinois, received a telephone call from Ivor Kaney, vice president of marketing at divisional headquarters. Ivor inquired if Bill wanted to bid on a new product that could more than double the annual sales at the plant from $9.5 million to $20.6 million. The new product, called Rocket Aerial Target System (RATS), was an expendable, low-cost, rocket-propelled, aerial target that would be shot down on U.S. military gunnery ranges by heat-seeking missiles. The project would require putting together a technical proposal, submitting a budget proposal, building ten prototype rockets, and flying three rockets for the U.S. Army. And all of this had to be done in four and one-half months. After a meeting with the division's marketing staff and U.S. Army representatives, Bill decided to put to-gether a project team at his plant to respond to the proposal and development project. Bill appointed to the project team a project manager, a flight engineer, a system design specialist, a production engineer, a safety and security officer, and a cost engineer. These persons were among his best personnel and were permanently assigned to various departments at the plant. The project members would be assigned to the team for the duration of the project, which was expected to take no longer than five months. The project manager would report directly to the plant manager and would be responsible for the performance of the team in staying within budgets, meeting timetables, and successfully carrying out the objectives of the project team. The team had to quickly develop a plan for completing the activities of the project and then execute the plan.

FIGURE 16.1 *Project Organization*

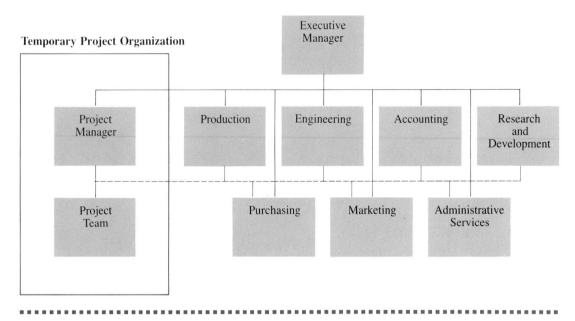

As the account on the previous page illustrates, operations managers must often organize project teams to plan and control projects. These teams must ordinarily work to tight time schedules, adhere to strict budgets, report high in the organization, and be temporarily removed from their regular jobs. While their project work is proceeding, the remainder of the organization must continue to produce the organization's products. Because of the difficulty of simultaneously managing such projects and producing the products and services, operations managers have developed new approaches to managing and controlling projects.

PROJECT MANAGEMENT

New organization forms have been developed to ensure both continuity of the production system in its day-to-day activities and the successful completion of projects. Foremost among these new organization forms is the *project organization*. Figure 16.1 shows that project teams are drawn from organizations' departments and temporarily assigned, full or part-time, to project teams.

A project manager is usually appointed to head the team, coordinate its activities, coordinate other departments' activities on the project, and report directly to the top of the organization. This executive management exposure gives the project high visibility within the organization, ensures the attention of the functional departments to the project, and encourages cooperation between the project team and other organizational units.

FIGURE 16.2   *Planning, Scheduling, and Controlling Projects*

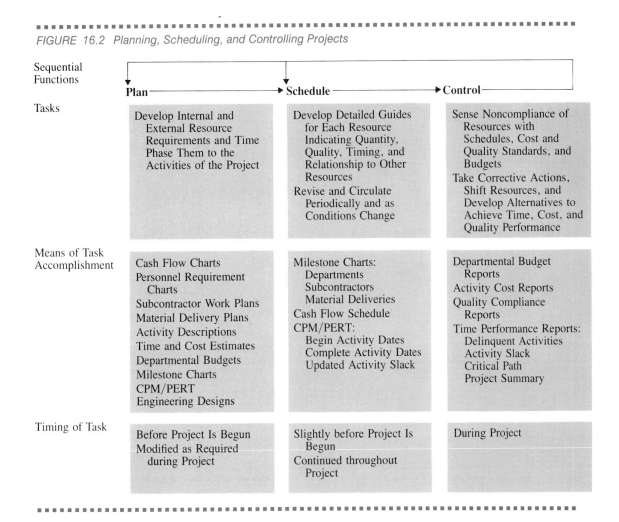

Sequential Functions	Plan ─────────────→	Schedule ─────────────→	Control ─────
Tasks	Develop Internal and External Resource Requirements and Time Phase Them to the Activities of the Project	Develop Detailed Guides for Each Resource Indicating Quantity, Quality, Timing, and Relationship to Other Resources Revise and Circulate Periodically and as Conditions Change	Sense Noncompliance of Resources with Schedules, Cost and Quality Standards, and Budgets Take Corrective Actions, Shift Resources, and Develop Alternatives to Achieve Time, Cost, and Quality Performance

Means of Task Accomplishment	Cash Flow Charts
	Personnel Requirement Charts
	Subcontractor Work Plans
	Material Delivery Plans
	Activity Descriptions
	Time and Cost Estimates
	Departmental Budgets
	Milestone Charts
	CPM/PERT
	Engineering Designs
		Milestone Charts:
		    Departments
		    Subcontractors
		    Material Deliveries
		Cash Flow Schedule
		CPM/PERT:
		    Begin Activity Dates
		    Complete Activity Dates
		    Updated Activity Slack
			Departmental Budget Reports
			Activity Cost Reports
			Quality Compliance Reports
			Time Performance Reports:
			    Delinquent Activities
			    Activity Slack
			    Critical Path
			    Project Summary

Timing of Task	Before Project Is Begun Modified as Required during Project	Slightly before Project Is Begun Continued throughout Project	During Project

The project organization is usually established well in advance of beginning the projects so that the project plan can be developed. Figure 16.2 shows the interrelationships among the planning, scheduling, and controlling functions of the project. Notice that the project plan is established before project activities begin and is modified as conditions change throughout the project. The plan is the blueprint and overall guide for achieving the successful completion of the project.

The scheduling and controlling functions of the project occur as the project proceeds. These ongoing functions ensure timely performance of the project's activities within cost and quality standards. The periodic generation of updated charts, reports, and schedules keeps all parties to the project informed about their particular work, when and how each activity must be done, corrective actions required, and particular problems to watch for.

The key ingredient in scheduling and controlling the project is the project team. Figure 16.3 shows that the project team is the hub around which the project rotates.

FIGURE 16.3 Scheduling and Controlling Projects with Project Teams

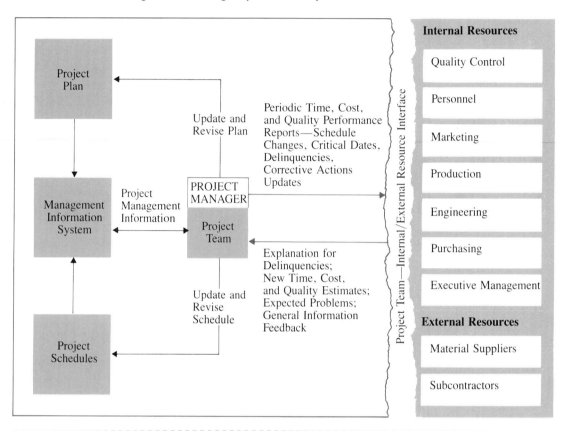

The project team supplies updated changes to the project plan and project schedules through the management information system. The project team sends periodic time, cost, and quality performance reports to the project's internal and external resources. The project team receives back from its resources information about progress on the project. This process continues throughout the project.

The concepts of the project team and its scheduling and control activities can be carried to the extreme in cases of massive projects such as the U.S. Department of Energy's super collider that is planned for the 1990s. The size of these massive projects justifies the formality of project organizations, because the stakes are high. On the other hand, smaller projects may utilize the concepts of the project team and its scheduling and controlling functions, but impose them more informally and flexibly on the existing organization. The degree of formality and dominance of the project team over project activities must be determined by management's confidence in the existing organization's ability to successfully accomplish the project.

One rather interesting development concerns the permanent institutionalization of the project organization form in organizations that predominantly depend on

TABLE 16.1 *Terms Used in Project Management*

1. **Activity**—An effort that is required to complete a part of the project.
2. **Activity duration**—In CPM, the best estimate of the time to complete an activity. In PERT, the expected time or average time to complete an activity.
3. **Critical activity**—An activity that has no room for schedule slippage; if it slips, the entire project completion will slip. An activity with zero slack.
4. **Critical path**—The chain of critical activities for the project. The longest path through the network.
5. **Dummy activity**—An activity that consumes no time but shows precedence between events.
6. **Earliest finish (EF)**—The earliest that an activity can finish, from the beginning of the project.
7. **Earliest start (ES)**—The earliest that an activity can start, from the beginning of the project.
8. **Event**—A beginning, completion point, or milestone accomplishment within the project. An activity begins and ends with an event.
9. **Latest finish (LF)**—The latest that an activity can finish, from the beginning of the project, without causing a delay in the completion of the project.
10. **Latest start (LS)**—The latest that an activity can start, from the beginning of the project, without causing a delay in the completion of the project.
11. **Most likely time (t_m)**—The time for completing an activity that is the consensus best estimate; used in PERT.
12. **Optimistic time (t_o)**—The time for completing an activity if all goes well; used in PERT.
13. **Pessimistic time (t_p)**—The time for completing an activity if bad luck is encountered; used in PERT.
14. **Predecessor activity**—An activity that must occur before another activity.
15. **Slack**—The amount of time that an activity or group of activities can slip without causing a delay in the completion of the project.
16. **Successor activity**—An activity that must occur after another activity.

products best managed as projects. Aerospace firms, construction firms, computer firms, and other types of firms have used the project organization form for so long that it has become a permanent part of their organizational structures. Project managers, project team members, and the project management information system continue to change and adapt to new project assignments.

New techniques have evolved to facilitate the timely completion of project activities within time, cost, and quality standards of the project plan. Some of the most often used scheduling and control techniques will be presented here.

PROJECT PLANNING AND CONTROL TECHNIQUES

Table 16.1 presents definitions of the terms we shall use in project planning and control. *These terms are the language of project management.* Additionally, we shall use them to explain the use of scheduling and control charts, CPM, PERT, and project cost control systems.

FIGURE 16.4 Horizontal Bar Chart — RATS Project Schedule Plan/Status Report Summary

Controlled Power Division/Acme Corporation

Project Schedule		
Project Manager __Cris Jacobs__	Schedule Approval Date __Apr. 10__	
Project __Rocket Aerial Target System (RATS)__	Status as of __July 15__	

Project Activities	April	May	June	July	August	September	October
a. Preliminary Propulsion Design							
b. Preliminary Flight System Design							
c. Static Tests A							
d. Propulsion Design Modifications							
e. Static Tests B							
f. Flight Tests A							
g. Flight System Design Modifications							
h. Flight Tests B							
i. Demonstrate to Customer							
j. Materials and Components Costs							
k. Labor and Overhead Costs							
l. Process Bid Package through Company							
m. Deliver Bid Package to Customer							

Status
Date

SCHEDULING AND CONTROL CHARTS

Scheduling and control charts are the tools most frequently used to manage projects. Each chart first plans and schedules some particular part of the project — what must be done and when it must be done. Second, as the project proceeds, each chart is updated to indicate the amount of accomplishment toward the plan. In this way project managers can compare actual project work accomplishment with planned project progress. This procedure allows rational changes in management's use of resources to complete the project within time, cost, and quality targets.

Perhaps the most frequently used chart is the horizontal bar chart. These charts are applications of Gantt charts, which were also applied in Chapter 12 of this text. One particularly useful horizontal bar chart is depicted in Figure 16.4. This chart is prepared in advance of the project to plan and schedule the activities of the project. Horizontal bars are drawn for each activity of the project along a time dimension. The letters at the beginning of each bar (left) indicate the activities that must be completed before that bar can begin.

After the bar chart is initially prepared, managers can be assured that all the activities of the project are planned for, the order in which the activities must be performed is taken into account, the time estimates for completing each activity are included, and, finally, the overall estimated time for completing the project is developed. The horizontal bar chart becomes the overall plan for the project.

As the project proceeds and activities are completed, actual progress is recorded by shading in the horizontal bars. How much of an activity bar to shade in is

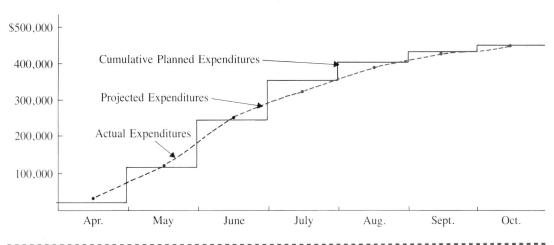

FIGURE 16.5   Expenditures Chart — RATS Project Expenditures Plan/Status Report: June 30

determined from estimates of the percentage of completion of work involved in each activity. If an activity is estimated to be one-third completed, for example, then one-third of the horizontal bar is shaded in.

Periodically, these charts are updated and distributed to all project participants. A vertical line is drawn on the chart corresponding to the date of the status report. Activity progress can be compared to the status date. In Figure 16.4, for example, Activity g, Flight System Design Modifications, can be observed to be on schedule because the horizontal bar is shaded up to the status date vertical line. Activity j, Materials and Components Costs, is approximately one week behind schedule, because its horizontal bar is shaded to a point about one week behind the status date. Similarly, Activity k, Labor and Overhead Costs, is approximately one week ahead of schedule.

These status reports allow managers to observe the progress of the project's activities, identify problem areas, and develop corrective action to bring the project back on target. These reports can be used alone or in conjunction with other techniques. When projects are not very complex, costly, or long-lasting, horizontal bar charts may be used alone to plan and control the timely completion of the project. On the other hand, on more complex and costly projects, the charts may be used as a summary of project status even though other, more detailed techniques are also used.

The key advantages of horizontal bar charts are their ease of understanding, ease of modification, and low cost. Their chief disadvantages are that on complex projects the number of activities may require either unwieldy charts or aggregation of activities, and the charts may not adequately indicate the degree of interrelationship among the project's activities.

Other charts are used to plan and control the acquisition and use of resources such as cash, personnel, and materials. Figure 16.5 shows one example of a chart used to plan and control expenditures accumulated through June and a projection of expenditures over the remainder of the project.

FIGURE 16.6 Personnel Chart — RATS Project Plan/Status Report: July 15

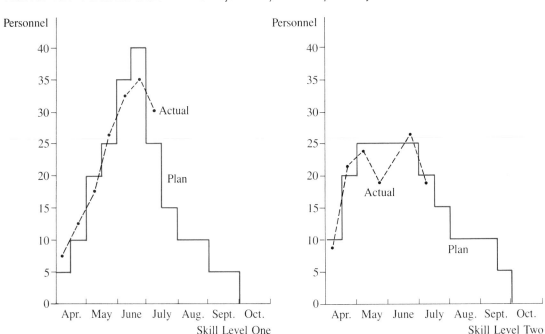

Managers typically seek answers to these questions from the charts:

1. Are we on our spending targets now?
2. Do we expect to be on our spending targets at the end of the project?
3. If we do not expect to be on our spending targets at the end of the project, should management corrective action begin in order to bring spending in on target?

The answer to the last question is complex. There are situations when management purposely allows project expenditures to overshoot spending targets in order to build new technical features into the project, improve project time performance, and other imperatives.

Figure 16.6 shows one chart used to plan and control two skill levels of employees on the RATS project. The project requires personnel peaks of 40 and 25 for Skills Levels One and Two, respectively. These charts are used by personnel departments and project teams to plan the acquisition of personnel and to develop corrective action as personnel needs change or as excess absenteeism, turnover, or other personnel-related developments occur.

The delivery of materials, components, and subcontracted parts presents special planning and control problems to project managers. First, the short duration and the unique nonrecurring nature of most projects rule out making components and

FIGURE 16.7 *Materials Chart—RATS Project Key Materials Acquisition Plan/Status Report*

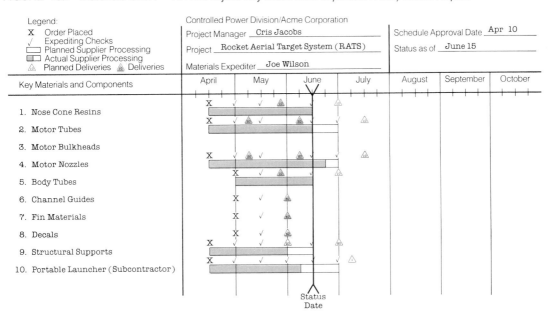

parts in-house; therefore most materials, components, and parts are purchased from suppliers outside the organization. Second, projects typically need the materials "yesterday," as the saying goes, because of severe time pressures. Third, materials of projects can be sufficiently different from the organization's other purchased materials so that regular suppliers may be passed over in favor of new, untried suppliers specializing in these new materials. These and other reasons often account for a most chaotic materials acquisition process for projects.

In spite of the uncertainty associated with finding new suppliers and severe time pressures, organizations have learned to successfully manage the acquisition of projects' materials, components, and subcontracted parts. Figure 16.7 shows one chart approach to planning and controlling the acquisition of materials for the RATS project. This materials chart, also called a milestone chart, shows the key materials to be acquired for the project, when orders are to be placed (x), when expediting checks are to be made (✓), when the supplier plans to process the order (an open horizontal bar), actual supplier processing progress (shaded portion of horizontal bar), and planned deliveries ($\triangle$10).

The charts presented here suggest that a wide range of these tools can be applied to an enormous number of project-planning and control situations. In fact, this flexibility probably is the key reason that charts are the most frequently used technique in project management. Flexibility, low cost, and ease of understanding—all contribute to the almost universal use of charts in project management.

FIGURE 16.8 A Manager's View of CPM

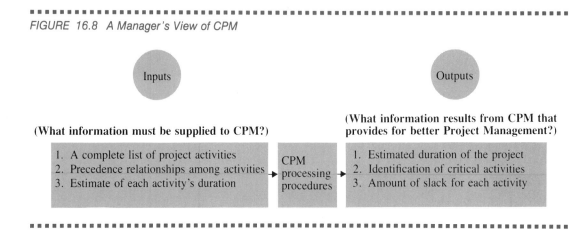

Some complex situations call for minute control of each elemental part of projects. CPM and PERT have evolved to fill this need for close microcontrol of the duration of projects.

CRITICAL PATH METHOD (CPM)

Developed in 1957 by J. E. Kelly of Remington Rand and M. R. Walker of Du Pont to help schedule maintenance projects in chemical plants, the critical path method (CPM) is today an important project-planning and control technique. Program evaluation and review technique (PERT) was developed at about the same time as CPM by the Navy Special Projects Office in cooperation with the management consulting firm Booz, Allen & Hamilton to plan and control the Polaris atomic-powered submarine and its intercontinental ballistic missile systems. PERT and CPM are alike in most respects, except for a few extra refinements incorporated into PERT and not found in CPM. Because of the great similarity of the two methods and because many users of CPM also refer to their method as PERT (the two terms tend to be used interchangeably), CPM will be presented first and everything covered in regard to CPM will also apply to PERT. The refinements in PERT will be covered in the next section.

CPM is designed for projects with many activities where on-time completion is imperative. Where the planning and control charts of the previous section offered overall macrocontrol, CPM is designed to provide intense microcontrol. In its original form, time performance was considered paramount; in other words, the legacy from government's use of CPM was the implicit assumption of unlimited funds. The federal government was racing to complete the Polaris program to avoid a possible Russian-imposed nuclear blackmail on the United States. Under this critical time pressure, it is no small wonder that unlimited funding was assumed.

CPM today is typically combined with other project cost control systems such as the charts of the previous section. The combination of macrocontrol from control

FIGURE 16.9   *The CPM Management Information System*

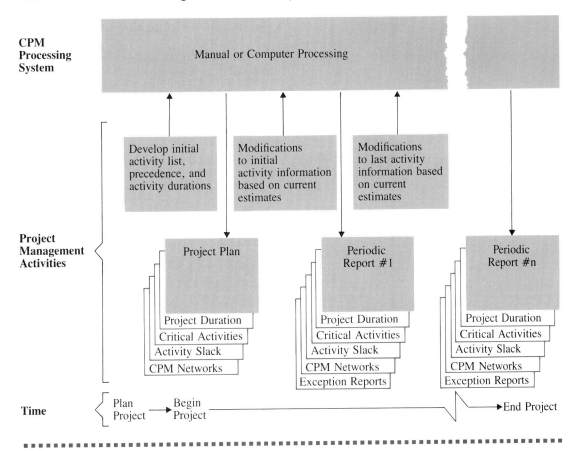

charts and microcontrol from CPM offers management both the big picture and minute detailed control.

Figure 16.8 shows a manager's view of CPM: What information must I supply CPM, and what project management information do I receive in return?

Some projects simply do not require the amount of detail provided by CPM. In these cases CPM typically would be passed over for scheduling and controlling techniques offering more macrocontrol.

CPM is not a scheduling and controlling system that is done once, set on the shelf, and never used again. Conversely, the system is dynamic. CPM continues to provide management with periodic reports as the project progresses. As Figure 16.9 shows, project managers update their original time estimates for completing each activity as time passes, and the computerized CPM system supplies management with current project management information: new estimates of project duration, a

---

TABLE 16.2   *Steps in CPM Analysis*

---

1. Draw a CPM network. This diagram gives a graphic view of the activities included in the project and the order of the activities.
2. Provide an overview of the project by analyzing the paths through the network. Determine the length of each path (the time required to complete each path), identify the critical path (the longest path through the network, the path that determines the time required to complete the project), and determine how much time to completion the project is expected to take.
3. Compute the earliest finish (EF) for each activity.
4. Compute the latest finish (LF) for each activity.
5. Compute the slack for each activity.
6. Compute the earliest start (ES) and latest start (LS) for each activity.

TABLE 16.3   *Activities and Events of the RAMOV Project*

Activity	Immediate Predecessor Activities	Activity Duration (Days)
a. Design RAMOV	—	20
b. Build prototype units	a	10
c. Perform tests of prototypes	b	8
d. Estimate material costs	a	11
e. Refine RAMOV design	c,d	7
f. Demonstrate RAMOV to customer	e	6
g. Estimate labor costs	d	12
h. Prepare technical proposal	e	13
i. Deliver proposal to customer	g,h	5

Event

---

1. The project is begun.
2. The RAMOV design is completed.
3. The prototype units have been built.
4. The prototype tests are completed.
5. The material cost estimates are completed.
6. The RAMOV design refinement is completed.
7. The technical proposal and the labor cost estimates are completed.
8. The RAMOV units have been demonstrated and the proposal has been delivered to the customer. The project is ended.

■■

FIGURE 16.10 CPM Network Conventions

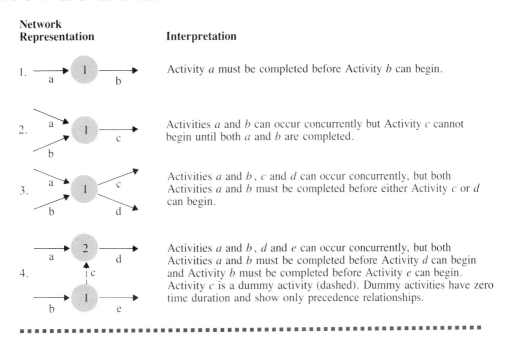

Network Representation	Interpretation
1.	Activity *a* must be completed before Activity *b* can begin.
2.	Activities *a* and *b* can occur concurrently but Activity *c* cannot begin until both *a* and *b* are completed.
3.	Activities *a* and *b*, *c* and *d* can occur concurrently, but both Activities *a* and *b* must be completed before either Activity *c* or *d* can begin.
4.	Activities *a* and *b*, *d* and *e* can occur concurrently, but both Activities *a* and *b* must be completed before Activity *d* can begin and Activity *b* must be completed before Activity *e* can begin. Activity *c* is a dummy activity (dashed). Dummy activities have zero time duration and show only precedence relationships.

■■

new list of critical activities, new activity estimates, and exception reports (e.g., new delinquent activities and compressed activities).

A series of examples will now be presented to demonstrate the inner workings of CPM. Table 16.2 lists the steps that are followed in a CPM analysis. Examples 16.1 through 16.5 will illustrate these steps.

In Example 16.1 the RAMOV project is described and a CPM network for the project is developed. Table 16.3 lists the activities and events for the project, the immediate predecessor activities, and the activity durations. An *activity* is a task or a certain amount of work required in the project, and an *event* just signals the beginning or ending of an activity. Activities require time to complete; events do not. Activities are represented by straight (not curved) arrows. Events are represented by circles. The first event of a project is always "the project is begun," and the last event of a project is always "the project is ended." The first activities (arrows) of a project are always drawn from the first event (circle), and the last activities of a project are always drawn to end in the last event. This convention avoids dangling arrows at the start and finish of CPM networks. The Immediate Predecessor Activities column in Table 16.3 indicates the order in which the activities must be performed. The activity durations are estimates of how much time will be required to complete each activity.

Study the conventions for drawing CPM networks in Figure 16.10 first, and then follow through Example 16.1. Notice that Convention 4 in Figure 16.10 uses a dummy activity. A *dummy activity* only indicates precedence relationships, or the order in which activities must be performed. Dummy activities do not require any time or effort. Once we have a CPM network, we have a graphic view of the activities that have to be completed in the project, the order in which the activities must be performed, and the interrelationships among the activities. To draw such networks, you are advised to first sketch a rough draft of the network on a sheet of paper. Then determine if the immediate predecessor activity information for the project fits your draft. If it does not, revise the draft and transfer it in its finished form to another sheet of paper.

EXAMPLE 16.1   *Drawing the CPM Network of the RAMOV Project*

A project team has been organized at Manufacturing Technology Inc. (MTI) to design and develop a slightly different version of one of the firm's industrial robots. The new robot is called the Random Access Mobile Orthonigal Vision (RAMOV) robot. RAMOV is mobile, has visual capabilities, is multiaxial, and is programmable on the shop floor. One of MTI's most important customers, a large automobile manufacturer, plans to replace a bank of machines with the new robots on its assembly lines in five factories. The customer wants to see a demonstration of the robot, a technical proposal, and a cost proposal in two months. The first thing that the project team did was list and describe the project's activities, determine the order of the activities, and estimate how much time each activity would take. This information about the activities and events of the project is presented in Table 16.3. Prepare a CPM diagram from the information in Table 16.3.

Solution

1. First, look at Figure 16.10. This figure contains the conventions that are followed in drawing CPM networks.

2. Next, start with the activity and event information in Table 16.3. *Activities* are tasks or work that must be done as the project progresses and are represented by straight arrows. *Events* are the beginning or ending of activities and are represented by circles. The project begins with Event 1, which is followed by Activity a. The order of the activities is found in the Immediate Predecessor Activities column of Table 16.3 and indicates which activity or activities must be completed just before each activity is begun. For instance, Activity b's immediate predecessor activity is Activity a. This means that Activity a must be completed before Activity b can begin.

3. Draw the CPM network and place each activity's letter under its arrow:

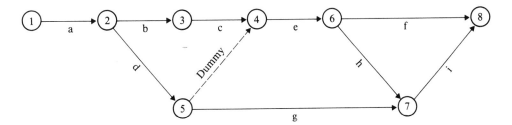

Note that both Activity c and Activity d are immediate predecessors to Activity e. To show that Activity d must be completed before beginning Activity e, a dummy activity is used. A *dummy activity* involves no work and no time; it simply shows the precedence relationship, or the order of the activities.

Example 16.2 provides an overview of the RAMOV project by performing an analysis of the project's paths. In this example the activity durations of each of the five paths are totaled to determine how much time each path is estimated to require. Notice that path a-b-c-e-h-i is estimated to require 63 days and that this is the longest path. All other paths are estimated to require less than 63 days. This longest path is therefore the critical path, and the project is estimated to require 63 days. If the critical path were to be delayed for any reason, the project would also be delayed by the same amount of time.

EXAMPLE 16.2   Providing an Overview of the RAMOV Project: Analyzing Its Paths

Now that the network diagram for the RAMOV project has been developed in Example 16.1, analyze the paths through the network. Determine which path is the critical path and how long the completion of the project is expected to take.

Solution

1. First, write the duration of each activity below its arrow. For instance, a = 20 is written below a's arrow:

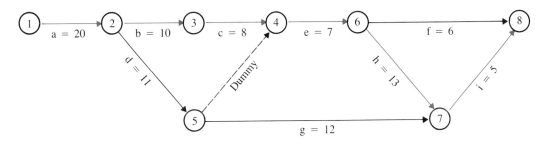

2. Next, identify the paths and compute the length of each path:

Paths	Length of Paths (Days)
a-b-c-e-f	$20 + 10 + 8 + 7 + 6 = 51$
a-b-c-e-h-i	$20 + 10 + 8 + 7 + 13 + 5 = 63*$
a-d-e-f	$20 + 11 + 7 + 6 = 44$
a-d-e-h-i	$20 + 11 + 7 + 13 + 5 = 56$
a-d-g-i	$20 + 11 + 12 + 5 = 48$

* Critical path.

The longest path is 63 days and it is the critical path. The critical path determines the length of the project; therefore the project is expected to take 63 days to complete.

Example 16.3 illustrates how the earliest finish (EF) values are computed for each activity in the RAMOV project. EF is the earliest elapsed time from the beginning of the project that we can finish an activity. By following along the CPM network *from left to right,* the EF values are written in the left-hand part of the box over each activity's arrow. Activities that begin a project always have EFs equal to their durations (D). For instance, the earliest that we can finish Activity a is 20 days, which is Activity a's duration; therefore $EF_a = D_a = 20$. For any other activity, its EF is the EF of its immediate predecessor activity plus its duration. For instance, $EF_b = EF_a + D_b$. If an activity has more than one immediate predecessor activity, its EF is computed by using the largest EF among the immediate predecessor activities. For instance, $EF_i = EF_h + D_i$ because $EF_h = 58$ is larger than $EF_g = 43$.

EXAMPLE 16.3   Computing Earliest Finish (EF) for the RAMOV Project's Activities

From the network in Example 16.1 compute the earliest finish (EF) for each activity. Write the EF for each activity in the left-hand part of the box over its arrow. Begin at Event 1 and move

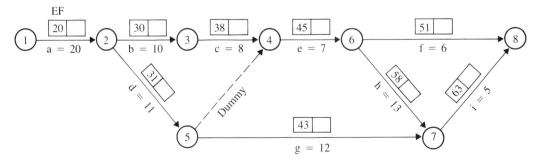

from left to right across the network and determine the EF value for each activity. EF represents the earliest elapsed time from the beginning of the project that we can finish an activity. For all activities that begin a project, their EFs are their durations. For instance, the EF of Activity a is 20, which is its duration, because it begins the project. For all other activities, an activity's EF is the EF of its immediate predecessor activity plus its duration (D). Let us compute the EF values:

$$EF_a = 20$$
$$EF_b = EF_a + D_b = 20 + 10 = 30$$
$$EF_c = EF_b + D_c = 30 + 8 = 38$$
$$EF_d = EF_a + D_d = 20 + 11 = 31$$
$$EF_e = EF_c + D_e = 38 + 7 = 45$$
$$EF_f = EF_e + D_f = 45 + 6 = 51$$
$$EF_g = EF_d + D_g = 31 + 12 = 43$$
$$EF_h = EF_e + D_h = 45 + 13 = 58$$
$$EF_i = EF_h + D_i = 58 + 5 = 63$$

Note that when an activity has two or more immediate predecessor activities, the *largest* EF among the immediate predecessor activities must be used in computing its EF. For instance, Activity i has two immediate predecessor activities—h and g. Because $EF_h = 58$ is larger than $EF_g = 43$, EF_h must be used to compute EF_i:

$$EF_i = EF_h + D_i = 58 + 5 = 63$$

Similarly, Activity e has two predecessors—c and d. Because $EF_c = 38$ is larger than $EF_d = 31$, EF_c must be used to compute EF_e:

$$EF_e = EF_c + D_e = 38 + 7 = 45$$

Example 16.4 illustrates how the latest finish (LF) and slack (S) values are computed for each activity in the RAMOV project. LF is the latest elapsed time from the beginning of the project that we can finish an activity without delaying project completion. By following along the CPM network *from right to left,* the LF values are written in the right-hand part of the box over each activity's arrow. Activities that end in the last event of a project always have LFs equal to the largest EF among the activities of the project. For instance, $LF_i = 63$ and $LF_f = 63$ because the greatest EF among all of the activities of the project is $EF_i = 63$. For any other activity, its LF is computed by subtracting the immediate successor activity's duration from the immediate successor activity's LF. If an activity has more than one immediate successor activity, its LF is the smallest LF − D among its immediate successor activities. For instance, $LF_e = LF_h - D_h$ because $LF_f - D_f = 57$ and $LF_h - D_h = 45$. The slack (S) value for an activity is computed by subtracting its EF from its LF and entering the value in the top part of the box over its arrow.

EXAMPLE 16.4   Computing Latest Finish (LF) and Slack (S) for the RAMOV Project's Activities

In Example 16.3, by means of a left-to-right pass through the network, the earliest finishes (EF) for all of the activities in the project have been completed. Now compute the latest finish (LF) and slack (S) for each activity.

Solution

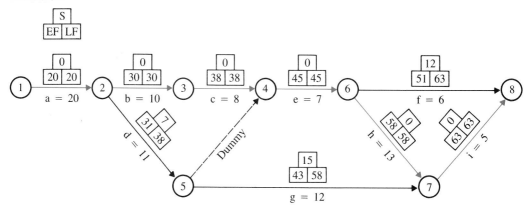

1. Compute the LF for each activity:

   Begin at Event 8 at the far right-hand side of the diagram and move *from right to left* through the network. Write the LF for each activity in the right-hand part of the box over its arrow. LF represents the latest elapsed time from the beginning of the project that we can finish an activity. The LF for all activities that end in the last event will always be the greatest EF of the project. The LF of Activities f and i is therefore 63 days, the same as EF_i, which is the greatest EF of all of the activities:

   $$LF_i = EF_i = 63$$

   $$LF_f = EF_i = 63$$

   The LF for any other activity is computed by subtracting the immediate successor activity's (the activity to its immediate right in the network) duration (D) from the immediate successor activity's latest finish (LF). The latest finish for the activities in the project are computed as follows:

   $$LF_h = LF_i - D_i = 63 - 5 = 58$$

   $$LF_g = LF_i - D_i = 63 - 5 = 58$$

   $$LF_e = LF_h - D_h = 58 - 13 = 45*$$

   $$LF_d = LF_e - D_e = 45 - 7 = 38*$$

   $$LF_c = LF_e - D_e = 45 - 7 = 38$$

   $$LF_b = LF_c - D_c = 38 - 8 = 30$$

   $$LF_a = LF_b - D_b = 30 - 10 = 20*$$

Note that when an activity has more than one immediate succeeding activity (activities to its immediate right in the network), its LF is computed by comparing the values of LF − D for all of the immediate succeeding activities. The *smallest* LF − D value is then used as its LF. For instance, Activities e, d, and a above have an asterisk (*) to indicate that these activities have more than one succeeding activity. Take Activity e, for instance: Both Activities f and h succeed Activity e. LF_e is computed thus:

$$LF_e = LF_f - D_f = 63 - 6 = 57 \quad \text{or} \quad LF_e = LF_h - D_h = 58 - 13 = 45$$

Therefore $LF_e = 45$.

2. Compute the slack (S) for each activity:

For each activity, $S = LF - EF$. For each activity, subtract its EF from its LF and write the value of S in the top part of the box over its arrow. The slack for all of the activities in the network is computed as follows:

$$S_i = LF_i - EF_i = 63 - 63 = 0*$$
$$S_h = LF_h - EF_h = 58 - 58 = 0*$$
$$S_g = LF_g - EF_g = 58 - 43 = 15$$
$$S_f = LF_f - EF_f = 63 - 51 = 12$$
$$S_e = LF_e - EF_e = 45 - 45 = 0*$$
$$S_d = LF_d - EF_d = 38 - 31 = 7$$
$$S_c = LF_c - EF_c = 38 - 38 = 0*$$
$$S_b = LF_b - EF_b = 30 - 30 = 0*$$
$$S_a = LF_a - EF_a = 20 - 20 = 0*$$

Notice that the asterisked activities above have zero slack. These activities are on the critical path a-b-c-e-h-i, which is denoted by the brown arrows through the network.

Example 16.5 completes the CPM analysis of the RAMOV project. In this example the EF, LF, and S values are transferred from the network in Example 16.4 to the table. Then the ES and LS values for each activity are computed from these formulas and entered into the table:

$$ES = EF - D$$
$$LS = LF - D$$

The table in Example 16.5 is typical of the outputs of CPM computer programs. The slack (S) values for each activity indicate how much an activity can be delayed without the completion time of the project being delayed. The activities with zero slack are the activities on the critical path. If any activities on the critical path are delayed, the project completion time will also be delayed by the same amount of time.

EXAMPLE 16.5   Computing Earliest Start (ES) and Latest Start (LS) for the RAMOV Project's Activities

From the network in Example 16.4, compute the earliest start (ES) and latest start (LS) for each activity.

Solution

Obtain the EF, LF, and S values for each activity in Example 16.4 and place them in the table below. Then compute the ES and LS values for each activity with these formulas:

$$ES = EF - D$$

$$LS = LF - D$$

Activity	Activity Duration (D)	Earliest Start (ES)	Earliest Finish (EF)	Latest Start (LS)	Latest Finish (LF)	Slack (S)
a	20	0	20	0	20	0
b	10	20	30	20	30	0
c	8	30	38	30	38	0
d	11	20	31	27	38	7
e	7	38	45	38	45	0
f	6	45	51	57	63	12
g	12	31	43	46	58	15
h	13	45	58	45	58	0
i	5	58	63	58	63	0

We have now demonstrated how CPM analysis develops information for management — project duration, critical activities, and activity slack. These computations are developed in the beginning of the project and modified when new estimates are provided as the project proceeds. Figure 16.9 illustrated how this updating of CPM takes place. These updates result in new periodic reports that are sent to project managers. CPM Exception Reports, Delinquent Activities Reports, and Compressed Activities Reports are examples of reports that provide project managers with current information about the details of the project, thus allowing close control of the activities.

Now that we have studied CPM, let us turn to PERT.

PROGRAM EVALUATION AND REVIEW TECHNIQUE (PERT)

PERT is almost identical to CPM in regard to its functions, network diagrams, internal calculations, and resulting project management reports. The minor exceptions surround the activity time estimates.[1]

In CPM an activity's duration is based on a single time estimate. In PERT three time estimates are made for each activity—pessimistic time (t_p), if bad luck were encountered; most likely time (t_m), the consensus best estimate; and optimistic time (t_o), if all goes well. From these three time estimates a mean (t_e) and variance (V_t) are computed for each activity:

$$t_e = (t_o + 4t_m + t_p)/6 \qquad \text{and} \qquad V_t = [(t_p - t_o)/6]^2$$

Why does PERT use multiple activity time estimates? Because this allows the development of an average duration and a variance for each path in the network, thus totally defining the paths' duration distributions. The mean duration of a path is equal to the sum of the activity mean durations, and the variance of the path is equal to the sum of the activity variances. When the duration distribution of a path is assumed to be normal and its mean and variance have been computed, we can make probabilistic statements about the path. For example: (1) There is only a 10 percent probability that the critical path will be greater than 35 weeks. (2) There is a 35 percent probability that the project can be completed in less than 50 weeks. The ability to make probabilistic statements about project path durations is the only difference between CPM and PERT. PERT uses t_e, the mean time based on three activity duration time estimates for activity durations, whereas CPM uses a single time estimate for activity durations; all other calculations of the two methods are identical.

Example 16.6 illustrates how PERT would be used to analyze the RAMOV project.

EXAMPLE 16.6   A PERT Analysis of the RAMOV Project

Refer to the description of the RAMOV project in Example 16.1. The project team has been asked by the customer to estimate the probability that the project could be completed within 65 days. Toward answering this question, the team developed three time estimates for each of the project's activities. Develop a PERT analysis of the project and answer the customer's question.

---

[1] Note to instructors: For simplicity of presentation, the activity-on-arrow (AOA) convention is used for both CPM and PERT.

Solution

1. First, compute the mean and variance for each activity:

Activity	Optimistic Time (t_o)	Most Likely Time (t_m)	Pessimistic Time (t_p)	Mean Duration $t_e = (t_o + 4t_m + t_p)/6$	Variance $V_t = [(t_p - t_o)/6]^2$
a	18	20	22	20.00	.44
b	8	10	14	10.33	1.00
c	5	8	9	7.67	.44
d	10	11	12	11.00	.11
e	7	7	7	7.00	0
f	4	6	7	5.83	.25
g	10	12	14	12.00	.44
h	12	13	15	13.17	.25
i	5	5	5	5.00	0

2. Next, draw the PERT network and compute the earliest finish (EF), latest finish (LF), and slack (S) for each activity. Determine the critical path.

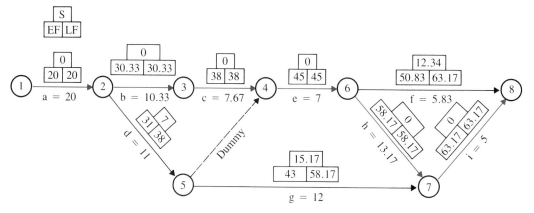

As we can see from the network above, the a-b-c-e-h-i path is the critical path and is expected to take 63.17 days.

3. Next, compute the standard deviation of the critical path:

Sum the variances of the activities along the critical path a-b-c-e-h-i:

$$V_{path} = V_a + V_b + V_c + V_e + V_h + V_i$$
$$= .44 + 1.0 + .44 + 0 + .25 + 0 = 2.13$$

$$\sigma_{path} = \sqrt{\text{Variance of Path a-b-c-e-h-i}}$$
$$= \sqrt{2.13} = 1.46 \text{ days}$$

4. Next, compute the probability of completing the project within 65 days:

Assuming that the distribution of the a-b-c-e-h-i path's completion time is normal with a mean of 63.17 days and a standard deviation of 1.46 days:

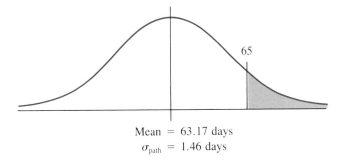

Mean = 63.17 days

σ_{path} = 1.46 days

Find how many standard deviations 65 days is from the mean:

$$Z = \frac{65 - 63.17}{\sigma_{path}} = \frac{65 - 63.17}{1.46} = 1.25$$

In Appendix A at the end of this book, locate $Z = 1.25$ in the left-hand margin of the table. The probability that the project will be completed in less than 65 days is .89435 (about 89.4 percent), but that is the good news. The bad news is that there is a .10565 (about 10.6 percent) probability that the project will take longer than 65 days.

PROJECT COST CONTROL SYSTEMS

CPM and PERT are designed to offer project managers planning, scheduling, and control aimed at only one project performance dimension—time performance. Most organizations today, whether goods producing or service producing, private industry or government, must also plan and control for another project performance dimension—cost or project expenditures.

Figure 16.5, the cash flow chart from the RATS project expenditures plan/ status report of June 30, is one approach to planning and controlling project expenditures. This chart has one distinct disadvantage, however: Time performance control and cost performance control are not integrated. If both these performance dimensions are important to project managers, wouldn't it be advisable to have a time and cost control system that showed time and cost performance simultaneously?

PERT/Cost was devised by the Department of Defense (DOD) and the National Aeronautics and Space Administration (NASA) in 1962 to tie together time and cost performance on government contracts. The term *PERT/Cost* is now commonly used not to identify the DOD and NASA system or any other specific cost system, but as a description of the general class of project time/cost planning and control systems. We will examine some of these by developing time/cost planning and control reports and charts for the RATS project that was described in the beginning of this chapter.

One common PERT/Cost report is depicted in Table 16.4: the RATS Time/ Cost Status Report. These computerized reports periodically show actual time and cost status compared to scheduled status for each activity of the project. For example,

■■■

TABLE 16.4   RATS Time/Cost Status Report

Activity			Time Status (Weeks)			Cost Status (Thousands of Dollars)		
Activity	Account Number	Scheduled Activity Duration	New Estimated Duration	Estimated vs. Latest Allowable Completion Date	Activity Slack	Scheduled Activity Cost	Actual Cost to Date	Estimated Cost (Over) or Under to Complete Activity
a	R-100	4	4	*		36.5	40.0	(3.5)
b	R-101	5	5	*		60.0	66.0	(6.0)
c	R-102	2	2	*		35.0	30.5	4.5
d	R-103	2	2	*		28.5	28.5	---
e	R-104	2	2	*		42.0	40.0	2.0
f	R-105	3	3	*		67.5	65.0	2.5
g	R-106	3	3	7/15 - 7/15	2	52.0	31.0	5.0
h	R-107	3	3	8/7 - 8/7	2	39.5	----	---
i	R-108	2	2	9/1 - 9/1	2	63.5	----	---
j	R-109	6	7	8/22 - 8/22	0	14.0	4.5	(4.0)
k	R-110	6	5	8/7 - 8/22	2	9.5	5.0	2.0
l	R-111	2	2	9/7 - 9/7	0	1.0	----	---
m	R-112	1	1	9/15 - 9/15	0	1.0	----	---
							Total	2.5

■■■

* Activity is complete.

Activity c can be evaluated as: (1) The activity is completed. (2) The actual duration of the activity was the same as the scheduled duration. (3) An amount $4,500 less than scheduled cost was actually expended on the activity. Similarly, Activity j can be evaluated as: (1) The activity is incomplete. (2) The activity duration has slipped from six weeks as scheduled to an estimated seven weeks. (3) The estimated completion date and the latest allowable completion date are the same — August 22. (4) There is zero slack for the activity. If the activity duration slips beyond the estimated seven weeks, the entire project will also slip by an equal amount of time. (5) Although the actual activity cost is well below the scheduled activity cost, the activity is estimated to be overspent by $4,000 at the completion of the activity. These evaluations of the project's activities give project managers information to better manage the project's activities. These and similar reports can be designed to offer much more refined exhibition of costs. The cost status of Table 16.4 could, for example, be broken into labor, materials, and overhead, or any other meaningful division of costs for each activity.

Charts and other visual devices are used to assess simultaneously the cost and time status of projects. Figure 16.11 is an example of a chart that summarizes a project's actual time and cost status compared to the project schedule. It shows that the RATS project on July 15 is about one week behind schedule and approximately

FIGURE 16.11 RATS Project Time/Cost Plan versus Actual Performance Chart

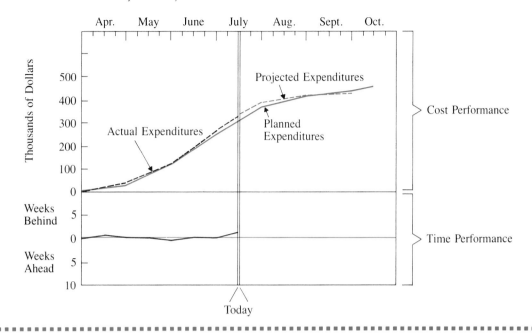

$30,000 overspent. Expenditures are projected to be about the same as scheduled at the end of the project.

Regardless of the format for time/cost status reports for projects, cost performance and time performance are both critically important elements of project management. The days when time performance dominated project management thinking are over for most organizations. Today cost performance is of at least equal importance in project management.

CPM/PERT IN PRACTICE

CPM/PERT is widely used across a great variety of organizations. Table 16.5 indicates that it tends to be used across a narrow range of applications. Project planning and control dominates all other applications, while production planning and control and maintenance planning and control round out 86 percent of the uses of PERT/CPM.

Target Slack versus Project Slack

Example 16.4, the RAMOV project, computes the slack for each activity—the amount of time that an activity can slip without causing a delay in the project completion. The slack is based on the duration of the critical path, which is 63 days. If the customer requirement were 65 days even if any critical activity slipped 2 days, the customer requirement would still be met. Each of the activities, then, in reality has 2

TABLE 16.5   *Uses of PERT/CPM*

PERT/CPM Use	*Frequency of PERT/CPM Use*
1. Project planning and control	46%
2. Production planning and control	22
3. Maintenance planning and control	18
4. All other	14

Source: Norman Gaither, "The Adoption of Operations Research Techniques by Manufacturing Organizations," *Decision Science* 6(October 1975):809.

additional days of slack if the standard is the customer requirement. Some organizations add this additional week of slack on to the project slack of each activity; thus activity slack is based upon a target project duration rather than critical path duration.

Activity Cost–Time Trade-offs

Project managers occasionally may have the option of *crashing* or *accelerating* activities, spending extra money to compress an activity's duration by using overtime, subcontracting, expediting materials, and so on. If projects are in danger of running over the allowable project duration, managers often consider crashing as a viable alternative.

Given that managers have several activities in the project that can be crashed or accelerated, how does one decide which activities not to crash, which activities to crash, if any, and in what order? The general rules are:

1. Do not crash noncritical activities. (This will not reduce the project's duration.)
2. Crash only critical activities — activities on the critical path, those activities with zero slack.
3. Crash activities with the lowest crashing cost per unit of time first until the desired project duration is achieved.
4. When parallel critical paths exist, each of the parallel paths must be compressed. Compressing only one of the paths will not reduce the project duration.

Example 16.7 illustrates the application of these principles in the RAMOV project.

EXAMPLE 16.7   *Cost–Time Trade-offs in the RAMOV Project*

MTI's customer in Examples 16.1 through 16.5 wants to shorten the completion time of the RAMOV project. The customer has indicated willingness to discuss paying for MTI's additional costs for shortening the length of the project. The RAMOV project team knows that overtime and other means can be used to accelerate some of the activities. Toward preparing for these discussions, the RAMOV project team has prepared these cost–time trade-offs:

Activity	Present Duration (Days)	Accelerated Duration (Days)	Present Cost	Accelerated Cost
a	20	15	$10,000	$15,000
b	10	5	12,000	16,500
c	8	5	6,000	10,500
d	11	10	4,000	5,500
e	7*	—	—	—
f	6*	—	—	—
g	12	9	9,000	11,000
h	13	10	12,000	16,000
i	5*	—	—	—

* These activities cannot be accelerated.

If the goal were to reduce the completion time of the project as much as possible, in what order would you accelerate the activities of the RAMOV project and what would be the cost of accelerating the activities?

Solution

1. First, develop a CPM network for the project without accelerating any of the activities. This CPM network was developed in Example 16.4:

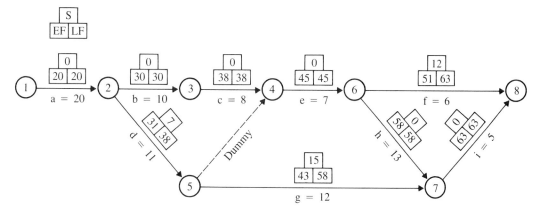

2. Next, compute the cost per day of accelerating each activity and arrange the activities in ascending order:

(1)	*(2)* Amount of Acceleration (Days)	*(3)* Cost of Acceleration	*(4)* Acceleration Cost per Day [$/Day = (3)/(2)]
Activity			
g	3	$2,000	$ 667
b	5	4,500	900
a	5	5,000	1,000
h	3	4,000	1,333
c	3	4,500	1,500
d	1	1,500	1,500

3. Next, develop the steps in accelerating the project.

   Let us examine three of the paths through the network:

Paths	*Length of Paths*	*Project Length*
a-b-c-e-h-i	20 + 10 + 8 + 7 + 13 + 5 = 63	63
a-d-e-h-i	20 + 11 + 7 + 13 + 5 = 56	
a-d-g-i	20 + 11 + 12 + 5 = 48	

Notice that these three paths contain all of the activities that can be accelerated. The activities that should be accelerated first are the ones that are on the critical path and have the lowest daily accelerating cost. Notice that while Activity g has the lowest daily accelerating cost, it is not on the critical path and would not shorten the project.

STEP 1: First, accelerate Activity b. Here is how the three paths change:

Paths	*Length of Paths*	*Project Length*
a-b-c-e-h-i	20 + ⑤ + 8 + 7 + 13 + 5 = 58	58
a-d-e-h-i	20 + 11 + 7 + 13 + 5 = 56	
a-d-g-i	20 + 11 + 12 + 5 = 48	

Notice that the critical path has been shortened by 5 days but the other paths remain the same.

STEP 2: Next, accelerate Activity a. Here is how the three paths change:

Paths	*Length of Paths*	*Project Length*
a-b-c-e-h-i	⑮ + 5 + 8 + 7 + 13 + 5 = 53	53
a-d-e-h-i	⑮ + 11 + 7 + 13 + 5 = 51	
a-d-g-i	⑮ + 11 + 12 + 5 = 43	

Notice that all of the paths have been shortened by 5 days.

STEP 3: Next, accelerate Activity h. Here is how the three paths change:

Paths	Length of Paths	Project Length
a-b-c-e-h-i	$15 + 5 + 8 + 7 + (10) + 5 = 50$	50
a-d-e-h-i	$15 + 11 + 7 + (10) + 5 = 48$	
a-d-g-i	$15 + 11 + 12 + 5 = 43$	

Notice that the two paths that include Activity h and the project length have been shortened by 3 days.

STEP 4: Next, accelerate Activity c. Here is how the three paths change:

Paths	Length of Paths	Project Length
a-b-c-e-h-i	$15 + 5 + (5) + 7 + 10 + 5 = 47$	
a-d-e-h-i	$15 + 11 + 7 + 10 + 5 = 48$	48
a-d-g-i	$15 + 11 + 12 + 5 = 43$	

Notice that although Activity c was shortened by 3 days, the project was only shortened by 2 days because path a-d-e-h-i is now the critical path.

STEP 5: Next, accelerate Activity d. Activity d is now on the critical path, and here is how the three paths change:

Paths	Length of Paths	Project Length
a-b-c-e-h-i	$15 + 5 + 5 + + 7 + 10 + 5 = 47$	
a-d-e-h-i	$15 + (10) + 7 + 10 + 5 = 47$	47
a-d-g-i	$15 + (10) + 12 + 5 = 42$	

There are now two paths tied for the critical path at 47 days, which is the length of the project. The only remaining activity that can be accelerated is Activity g, which can be shortened by 3 days. Notice, however, that it is not on the critical path and would not shorten the project beyond the present 47 days. Activity g therefore would not be accelerated.

The additional cost of accelerating the completion of the project is:

Activity	Additional Cost of Acceleration
b	$ 4,500
a	5,000
h	4,000
c	4,500
d	1,500
Total	$19,500

COMPUTER SOFTWARE
FOR PROJECT MANAGEMENT

Most project management applications today use computers extensively. Although our PERT/CPM calculations in this chapter have been performed manually, such applications are almost never calculated without computers.

The *POM Computer Library* that accompanies this book has both a CPM and a PERT computer program. The user inputs activity time estimates, and the programs output slack for each activity, duration and variance for critical paths, and other useful project management information. An issue of *P&IM Review* presented these ten software packages for project management:

1. *Harvard Project Manager,* Harvard Software Inc.
2. *Pertmaster,* Westminster Software Inc.
3. *PMS II/RMS II,* North America Mica Inc.
4. *Primavera,* Primavera Systems Inc.
5. *Project Scheduler 5000,* Scitor Corp.
6. *Pro-Ject 6,* Soft-Corp. Inc.
7. *Project Manager Workbench,* Applied Business Tech Corp.
8. *Project,* Microsoft Corp.
9. *MacProject & LisaProject,* Apple Computer Corp.
10. *VisiSchedule,* Paladin Software Corp.

Additionally, the citation "Buyer's Guide: Project Management Software," in the Selected Bibliography at the end of this chapter lists 67 software sets for project management, ranging from $100 to over $4,000.

Project management is an activity performed in many organizations today, and the computer software suppliers are offering a growing array of packages for these applications.

CRITICISMS OF CPM/PERT

As the use of CPM and PERT has grown, certain criticisms of these techniques have appeared. Among these criticisms are:

1. CPM/PERT assumes that the activities of the project are independent. In practice, we know that in some circumstances the duration of one activity is dependent on difficulties encountered in the performance of other, related activities. In these cases the duration of one activity is dependent on the duration of one or more other activities.
2. CPM/PERT assumes that there are precise breaking points where one activity ends and another begins. In practice, one activity may begin before a preceding activity is completed as long as some of the preparatory work has been performed.
3. CPM/PERT focuses too much on activities on the critical path. In practice, an activity that is not on the critical path early in the project may encounter

difficulty and delays. Such an activity may not receive the attention that it deserves until it appears on the critical path. By that time it may be too late to take corrective action to prevent delay of the project.

4. Activity time estimates can reflect behavioral issues that may diminish the usefulness of CPM/PERT. For instance, personnel who supply the activity time estimates, by being too optimistic or engaging in what is referred to as "blue sky" estimates, may develop activity times that are too short. On the other hand, they may be sandbagging, or developing activity times that are too long, thus giving themselves a cushion or fudge factor.

5. PERT has often been criticized because: (a) It may be unrealistic to expect three accurate time estimates from personnel. (b) It may be too much to expect personnel to understand its statistical underpinnings. (c) The assumptions of PERT concerning the probability distributions of activities and paths have been shown to cause errors in PERT's results. (d) The extra cost of PERT over CPM is not justified by the value of the additional information provided.

6. CPM/PERT is applied to too many projects, an overkill legacy from the government and the aerospace industry. In many of these applications the cost of CPM/PERT cannot be justified by the value of the information provided when compared to other project management techniques such as project charts.

In spite of these criticisms, CPM/PERT forms a family of techniques that are used widely in all organizations today. These techniques help operations managers to structure projects so that it is understood what activities must be done and when they must be done, to identify corrective actions that must be taken, to assign responsibilities for activities, to control costs, and to plan and control time performance. The bottom line is that they work and work well for operations managers in spite of their shortcomings, and that is the reason they are used so widely. The fact that so many low-cost CPM/PERT computer software packages are available today also supports their continued use.

SUMMARY

New organizational forms have evolved in recent years to accommodate simultaneously both projects and the production of goods and services. Foremost among these new forms is the project organization. Project teams are formed from personnel drawn from departments of organizations to manage and coordinate the activities of projects outside the conventional organization structures.

The planning and control of projects are sufficiently difficult to have fostered a variety of planning and control techniques. Additionally, a set of commonly used terms has developed into a language unique to project management. Some of these terms are: *activities, events, critical path, slack, predecessor activity, networks, CPM,* and *PERT.*

Scheduling and control charts are the most frequently used among these techniques. Simplicity, flexibility, and low cost are the key strengths of these devices.

These macrocontrol techniques offer project managers perhaps the quickest overall view of project performance at the lowest cost.

When more minutely detailed control is desired, CPM, PERT, and PERT/Cost can be used. PERT/CPM offers project managers an activity-by-activity planning and control system that is usually computerized. Periodic status reports give managers updated project duration, critical activities, activity slack, network diagrams, and exception reports from which to determine what must be done to ensure successful project completion.

REVIEW AND DISCUSSION QUESTIONS

1. Define *project management.*
2. Why is the management of projects a challenge for most managers in production systems? How do these managers meet this challenge?
3. What tasks must the project team perform before the project begins?
4. What tasks must the project team perform as the project progresses?
5. Why are the planning, scheduling, and controlling of materials, supplies, and subcontractors on projects more difficult than with these resources in production of the organization's usual goods and services?
6. Define these terms: *activity, event, critical activity, critical path, activity duration,* and *slack.*
7. Define these terms: *predecessor activity, dummy activity, earliest start, earliest finish, latest finish,* and *latest start.*
8. Define these terms: *most likely time (t_m), optimistic time (t_o),* and *pessimistic time (t_p).*
9. How does the activity duration differ between CPM and PERT?
10. Horizontal bar charts and other charting techniques offer operations managers macrocontrol of projects, whereas CPM and PERT offer microcontrol. Explain.
11. What are the inputs (information supplied) and outputs (information returned) of CPM?
12. Name three steps in CPM processing.
13. What are the four principles of crashing projects?

PROBLEMS

Scheduling and Control Charts

1. From Figure 16.12, describe fully the status of Stratophonic's new-product development project as of March 1.
2. From Figure 16.13, describe fully the spending status of Stratophonic's new-product development project as of March 1.

FIGURE 16.12 Project Schedule — New-Product Development Project: Stratophonic Sound Inc.

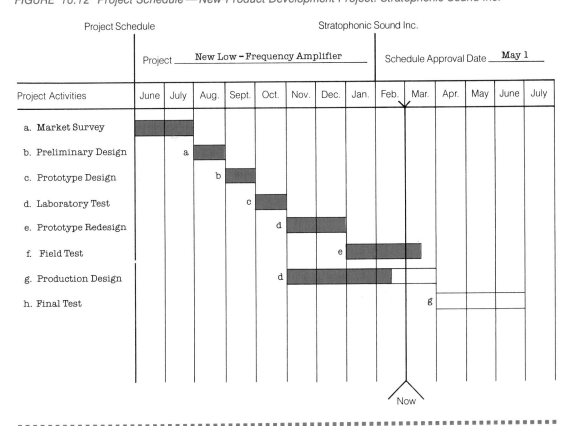

FIGURE 16.13 Expenditures Chart — New-Product Development Project: Stratophonic Sound Inc.

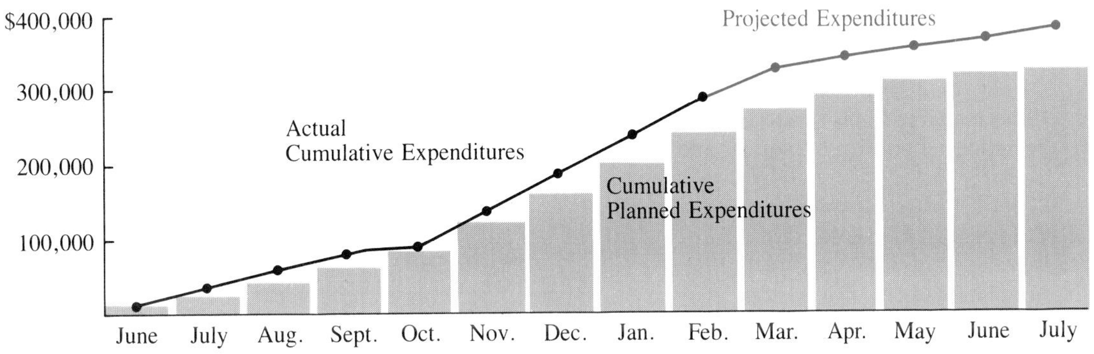

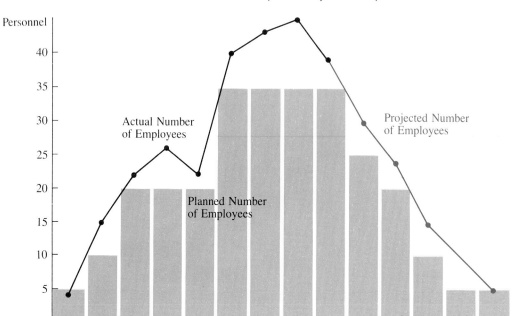

FIGURE 16.14   Personnel Chart — New-Product Development Project: Stratophonic Sound Inc.

3. From Figure 16.14, describe fully the status of project personnel on Stratophonic's new-product development project as of March 1.

4. From Figure 16.15, describe fully the status of key materials deliveries of Stratophonic's new-product development project as of March 1.

5. The Buildrite Construction Company is developing plans to build a new medical building in downtown Denver, Colorado. Buildrite has established these project activities, their precedence relationships, and their estimated activity durations:

Activity	Precedence Relationships (Immediate Predecessor Activities)	Estimated Activity Duration (Weeks)
a. Demolition of present structures	—	4
b. Excavation and filling of site	a	5
c. Forming and pouring of footings and foundation	b	5
d. Construction of structural steel skeleton	c	6
e. Construction of concrete structure	d	8
f. Construction of exterior skin	e	12
g. Installation of plumbing system	e	5
h. Installation of electrical system	e	3
i. Installation of heating/cooling system	e	4
j. Construction of interior partitions	g,h,i	3
k. Installation of lighting fixtures, and finish work	j	5

■■■

FIGURE 16.15 Materials Chart — New-Product Development Project: Stratophonic Sound Inc.

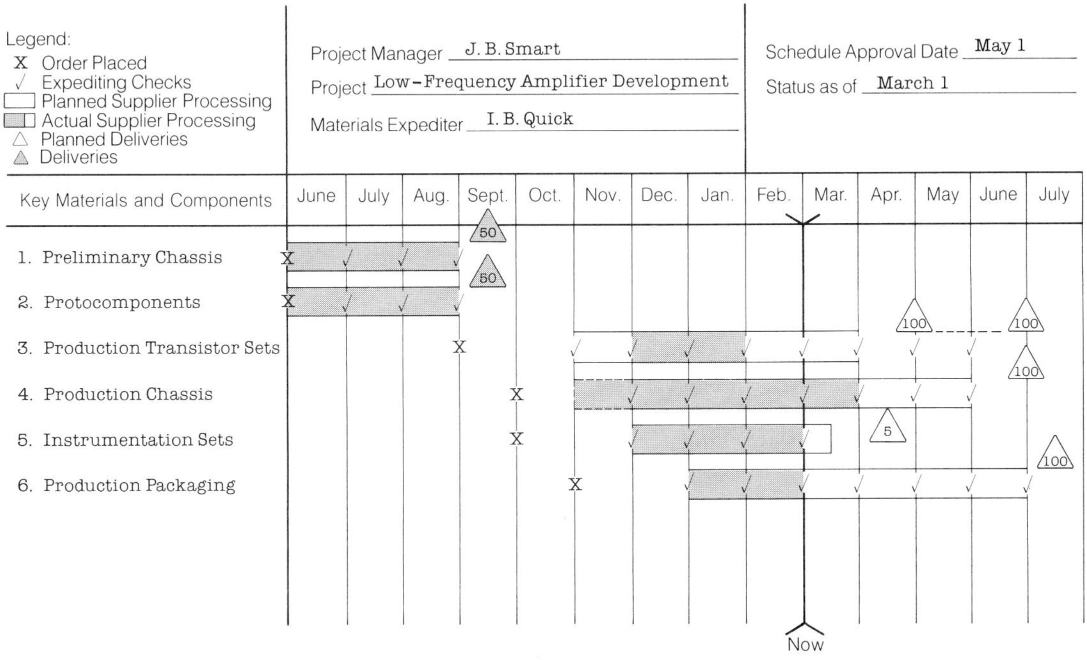

■■■

Prepare a horizontal bar chart to plan the schedule for this construction project if work is to begin January 1.

6. The Brownkraft Paper Mill in Ohno, Maine, has been experiencing increasingly excessive downtime and maintenance costs because of long-term machinery deterioration. Something has to be done. Brownkraft has decided to shift its production to a nearby mill on a subcontracted basis and shut down the Ohno mill in order to perform a massive repair and refurbishing program. These activities, their precedence relationships, and their estimated time durations have been established:

Activity	Precedence Relationships (Immediate Predecessor Activities)	Estimated Activity Duration (Days)
a. Development of machinery status reports	—	30
b. Engineering machinery renovations	a	60
c. Shutting down mill	b	7
d. Performance of mechanical renovations	c	90
e. Performance of electrical renovations	c	80
f. Performance of plumbing renovations	c	70
g. Test running refurbished facility	d,e,f	10
h. Debugging entire facility	g	7
i. Starting up mill	h	7

a. If the work is to begin June 1, prepare a horizontal bar chart to plan the schedule for this maintenance project.

b. How long will the Ohno mill be shut down?

CPM

7. A project has these activities, precedence relationships, and activity durations:

Activity	Immediate Predecessor Activities	Activity Duration (Weeks)	Activity	Immediate Predecessor Activities	Activity Duration (Weeks)
a	—	3	e	b	5
b	—	4	f	a	7
c	—	3	g	e,f	3
d	c	12			

a. Construct a CPM network for the project.

b. Provide an overview for the project by computing the duration of each path.

c. What is the critical path? What is the project's estimated duration?

8. A project has these activities, precedence relationships, and activity durations:

Activity	Immediate Predecessor Activities	Activity Duration (Days)	Activity	Immediate Predecessor Activities	Activity Duration (Days)
a	—	10	f	b	17
b	—	15	g	b	12
c	a	10	h	d,f	9
d	a	20	i	h,g	7
e	c	15			

a. Construct a CPM network for the project.

b. Provide an overview for the project by computing the duration of each path.

c. What is the critical path, and what is its duration?

 9. The Los Angeles plant of Computer Products Corporation (CPC) has just received the good news from its corporate headquarters in San Jose that it will manufacture a bar code scanner. This new product was developed and market-tested by the R&D center in San Jose, but the manufacturing processes required to produce the product have yet to be developed. The Los Angeles process-engineering group has been assigned the responsibility of this design project and has been given the target of 60 days to arrive at an overall process design. Although 60 days seemed very short to the process engineers at first, after some discussion it was concluded that they could probably pull it off because the product and its processes were so similar to the present processing technologies in use at their plant. These activities, their precedence relationships, and their durations were estimated by the engineers:

Activity	Activity Duration (Days)	Immediate Predecessor Activities
a. Initial study of the product design	12	—
b. Preliminary product redesign for production	10	a
c. Preliminary facility redesign for product	15	a
d. Preliminary process technologies study	9	a
e. Modification of facility for product redesign	6	b
f. Intermediate facility redesign	12	c,e
g. Intermediate product redesign	14	b
h. Specific process machinery design	21	b,d
i. Vendor involvement activity	15	b,d
j. Final facility, product, process design	10	f,g,h

a. Construct a CPM network for the design project.
b. Compute the EF, LF, and slack for each activity. Write the values on the CPM network.
c. Compute the ES and LS for all activities. Display the ES, EF, LS, LF, and slack values in a table.
d. What is the critical path? What is the project's estimated duration?

 10. A project has these activities, precedence relationships, and activity durations:

Activity	Immediate Predecessor Activities	Activity Duration (Weeks)	Activity	Immediate Predecessor Activities	Activity Duration (Weeks)
a	—	3	g	d	10
b	—	9	h	e,f	7
c	—	7	i	g,h	14
d	a	12	j	c	15
e	a,b	10	k	f,j	9
f	c	11			

a. Construct a CPM network for the project.
b. Compute the EF, LF, and slack for each activity. Write the values on the CPM network.
c. Compute the ES and LS for all activities. Display the ES, EF, LS, LF, and slack values in a table.
d. What is the critical path and its duration?

 11. The plant engineering group of the Los Angeles plant of Computer Products Corporation (CPC) has the responsibility of setting up the assembly line to manufacture the bar code scanner of Problem 9. The production processes have already been designed by the process-engineering group, and the machinery has been delivered to the plant from CPC's vendors. Sammy Brown, plant engineer, has been assigned the job of planning the installation of the machinery and laying out the assembly line. Because

the facility has been redesigned to contain the assembly line and because the machinery is already on-site, Sammy has been told that the assembly line must be ready for a dry run in three weeks. Sammy has identified these activities, determined their precedence relationships, and estimated their durations:

Activity	Activity Duration (Days)	Immediate Predecessor Activities
a. Organize machinery layout team	3	—
b. Organize facility modification team	5	—
c. Design personnel jobs	7	a
d. Set machinery in place	4	a
e. Connect utilities to machines	3	b
f. Modify overhead conveyor	9	b
g. Train personnel	5	c
h. Paint and clean up	6	f
i. Run pilot lot of products	3	d,e

   a.   Construct a CPM network for the project.
   b.   Compute the EF, LF, and slack for each activity. Write the values on the CPM network.
   c.   Compute the ES and LS for all activities. Display the ES, EF, LS, LF, and slack values in a table.
   d.   What is the critical path? What is the project's estimated duration?

PERT

12. An activity in a project has these time estimates: optimistic time $(t_o) = 15$ weeks, most likely time $(t_m) = 20$ weeks, and pessimistic time $(t_p) = 22$ weeks.
   a.   Compute the activity's expected time or duration (t_e).
   b.   Compute the activity's variance (V_t).
   c.   Compute the activity's standard deviation (σ_t).

13. An activity in a PERT network has these estimates: $t_o = 10$, $t_m = 12$, $t_p = 15$.
   a.   Compute the activity's expected time (t_e).
   b.   Compute the activity's variance (V_t).

14. Project Path a-c-e-f has these activity time estimates in days:

Activity	Optimistic Time (t_o)	Most Likely Time (t_m)	Pessimistic Time (t_p)
a	20	25	30
c	25	30	32
e	15	17	20
f	18	18	18

a. Compute the expected time or duration (t_e) for each activity.
b. Compute the variance (V_t) for each activity.
c. Compute the expected duration and variance for the path.

15. A path in a PERT network has these activity time estimates in days:

Activity	Optimistic Time (t_o)	Most Likely Time (t_m)	Pessimistic Time (t_p)
a	10	12	15
c	10	15	20
f	10	12	13
i	10	15	20

Compute the mean path duration and the path variance.

 16. A project has the following activities, precedence relationships, and time estimates in weeks:

Activity	Immediate Predecessor Activities	Optimistic Time (t_o)	Most Likely Time (t_m)	Pessimistic Time (t_p)
a	—	15	20	25
b	—	8	10	12
c	a	25	30	40
d	b	15	15	15
e	b	22	25	27
f	e	15	20	22
g	d	20	20	22

a. Compute the duration (expected time) and variances for each activity.
b. Construct a PERT network.
c. Compute the EF, LF, and slack for each activity. Write the values on the PERT network.
d. Compute the ES and LS for all activities. Display the ES, EF, LS, LF, and slack values in a table.
e. What is the critical path?
f. What is the probability that the project will take longer than 57 weeks to complete?

 17. Mary Yetter, staff analyst at the Los Angeles plant of Computer Products Corporation (CPC), is assigned to the team that is developing the process design for producing the bar code scanners of Problem 9. The corporate planning group in San Jose initially indicated that her group could take as long as 60 days to complete its design project. Now the corporate planning group has contacted her boss and has asked how confident the design group was about completing the project in 60 days. Her boss has now come to Mary and presented her with the same question. She has developed these estimated time durations in days for the project:

Activity	Predecessor Activities	Optimistic Time (t_o)	Most Likely Time (t_m)	Pessimistic Time (t_p)
a	—	10	12	15
b	a	9	10	11
c	a	10	15	20
d	a	9	9	18
e	b	5	6	8
f	c,e	10	12	13
g	b	12	14	16
h	b,d	18	21	24
i	b,d	10	15	20
j	f,g,h	8	10	14

a. Compute the duration (expected time) and variance for each activity.
b. Construct a PERT network for the project.
c. Compute the EF, LF, and slack for each activity. Write the values on the PERT network.
d. Compute the ES and LS for all activities. Display the ES, EF, LS, LF, and slack values in a table.
e. What is the critical path and its duration?
f. What is the probability that the project will take longer than 60 days? How would you answer Mary's boss's question?

18. Three paths of a PERT network have these mean durations and variances in weeks:

Path	Mean Duration (Σt_e)	Variance (ΣV_t)
1	45	2.75
2	44	5.50
3	46	1.20

Which path offers the greatest risk of overrunning a contract deadline of 48 weeks?

19. Two paths of a PERT network have these mean durations and variances in days:

Path	Mean Duration (Σt_e)	Variance (ΣV_t)
1	53.5	2.80
2	52.5	4.94

Which path offers the greater risk of taking longer than 55 days?

Time/Cost and Cost–Time Trade-offs

20. Larissa Gibson is the manager of new-product development at the Quality Underwear Company. She has just received the July 30 time/cost status report for Project XR-15-Nylon Brief:

Activity		Time Status (Weeks)			Cost Status (Thousands of Dollars)		
Activity	Account Number	Duration (D)	New D	Old/New Completion Date	Target Cost	Cost to Date	Estimated Cost (over) or under Target to Completion
a	X-100	10	10	*	—	10.5	8.5	2.0
b	X-110	12	12	*	—	12.0	13.5	(1.5)
c	X-120	5	6	8/15 – 8/22	0	10.0	9.0	(3.5)
d	X-130	16	18	12/15 – 1/7	0	22.0	5.5	(5.0)
e	X-140	12	10	10/1 – 9/15	4	6.5	0.0	1.0
f	X-150	5	5	11/1 – 11/1	3	5.0	0.0	1.0

* Activity is complete.

Describe fully the status of time and cost performance of the project's activities.

21. A project has the following activities, durations, costs, and precedence relationships:

Activity	Present Duration (Weeks)	Accelerated Duration (Weeks)	Immediate Predecessor Activities	Present Cost	Accelerated Cost
a	10	9	—	$11,000	$15,000
b	15	13	—	20,000	25,000
c	10	6	a	9,000	20,000
d	20	18	a	25,000	30,000
e	15	10	c	20,000	35,000
f	17	15	b	20,000	30,000
g	12	10	b	15,000	25,000
h	9	8	d,f	12,000	18,000
i	7	6	g,h	10,000	15,000

a. First, disregarding the acceleration information, perform a CPM analysis on the project. Draw a CPM network for the project. Compute the EF, LF, and S for each activity. Write the values on the CPM network. What is the critical path? How long is the project expected to take to complete?

b. Develop a cost–time trade-off analysis. Detail the steps that you would use to accelerate or crash the project to its minimum duration at the lowest cost. Determine each step's cost and the duration of the project.

COMPUTER PROBLEMS/CASES

MAXWELL CONSTRUCTION COMPANY

The Maxwell Construction Company is a large company that specializes in industrial and government construction projects. The company bids on only the largest projects at premium prices and tends to get its fair share because it has gained a reputation for doing work of outstanding quality within the time constraints of its contracts. Maxwell is now in the process of bidding on the construction of an addition to the Western State University football stadium, a project that will go for about $20 million. The only problem is that the project falls at a time when Maxwell has won several other large contracts and does not want to overextend itself and spread its resources too thin. If the project could be completed within 300 days of the beginning of the project, the company would feel confident in pursuing the contract. The cost estimator for Maxwell has developed the estimates of activity durations and their precedence relationships that are shown in the table below.

Assignment

1. Draw a CPM network diagram of the project.

2. Develop a horizontal bar chart that summarizes the plan for the project. Each activity should be "mapped out" on this chart. Discuss how this chart would be used as the project proceeds and how it would be used in the planning phases of the project.

3. Use a CPM computer program such as the one in the *POM Computer Library* that accompanies this text to develop a CPM analysis of the project. What is the estimated duration of the project? What activities are on the critical path? How much can Activity u slip without affecting the project completion date?

4. Discuss how the CPM analysis results compare with your chart in No. 2. What are the advantages and disadvantages of CPM as a planning and controlling technique when compared with the project chart or horizontal bar chart?

5. Should the Maxwell Construction Company bid on the project? Does the project require more time than Maxwell has available?

Activity	*Precedence Relationships (Immediate Predecessor Activities)*	*Activity Duration (Days)*
a. Demolish and salvage existing structures	—	10
b. Excavate and grade site	a	15
c. Pour concrete footings and foundation	b	17
d. Install in-ground plumbing	b	20
e. Install underground electrical service	b	8
f. Preassemble mid-level steel skeleton	b	14
g. Construct and pour concrete substructure	c,d,e	16
h. Pour lower-level concrete floors	g	12
i. Erect mid-level steel skeleton	f,h	9
j. Erect mid-level concrete columns and cross beams	i	21
k. Install aboveground phase 2 plumbing	j	18
l. Install aboveground phase 2 electrical service	j	14
m. Pour mid-level concrete floors	k,l	23
n. Preassemble top-level steel skeleton	i	14

Continues

Activity (continued)	Precedence Relationships (Immediate Predecessor Activities)	Activity Duration (Days)
o. Erect top-level steel skeleton	m,n	23
p. Erect top-level concrete columns and cross beams	o	36
q. Pour top-level floors	p	37
r. Construct press box complex	q	45
s. Erect field lights	p	14
t. Construct restrooms	m,n	48
u. Install seats	q	21
v. Paint and finish walls, floors, and ceilings	u	14
w. Clean up structure and grounds	v	7

ROCKET AERIAL TARGET SYSTEM (RATS)

An introduction to the RATS project is found at the beginning of this chapter.

Bill Williams immediately called a staff meeting of his key people to get their ideas on proceeding with the project. It was generally agreed that this was a piece of business the operation should pursue. The question was: How could the operation go after this new business and still successfully produce and deliver its other products? It was conceded that the new business was so important that if the key personnel were satisfied with what they heard from marketing tomorrow morning, an all-out effort should be expended to win the contract.

The meeting the next morning resolved most of the operation's questions. Ivor Kaney informed Williams that Corporate was so impressed with the prospects of RATS that the operation had Corporate's approval to spend up to a half-million dollars in securing the contract, a very high-trust, high-priority allotment. All the department heads agreed that some sacrifice would have to be made by them to succeed in this new effort. Each of them would be asked to give up one or two key employees to serve on the project team. Williams decided to commit the operation to an all-out effort on the project.

The next day the project team was announced:

Project manager—Cris Jacobs, a young recent MBA with an undergraduate degree in management. She was selected because she was perhaps the best administrator in the operation and she had great rapport with the other units of the company.

Flight engineer—Jim Sherry, head of quality assurance/propulsion.

System design specialist—Robert Brannon, expert design engineer, brilliant development specialist.

Production engineer—Jim Dawson, production manager of the propulsion generator department.

Safety and security officer — Irene Thompson, director of loss prevention.

Cost engineer — Wallace Potter, industrial engineer.

These individuals would be assigned to the project full-time for its duration. If the contract was won, all of them would carry their knowledge about RATS back to their home departments, thus aiding in the conversion from development to production.

The team developed the following list of project activities, time estimates, and precedence relationships as part of the project plan:

Activity	Precedence Relationships (Immediate Predecessor Activities)	Estimated Time to Complete Activity (Weeks)
Product Development		
a. Preliminary propulsion design	—	4
b. Preliminary flight system design	—	5
c. Static tests A	a	2
d. Propulsion design modifications	c	2
e. Static tests B	d	2
f. Flight tests A	b	3
g. Flight system design modifications	e,f	3
h. Flight tests B	g	3
i. Demonstration to customer	h	2
Bid Package		
j. Material and component costs	e,f	6
k. Labor and overhead costs	e,f	6
l. Processing of bid package through company	j,k	2
m. Delivery of bid package to customer	l	1

Assignment

1. Draw a CPM network for the project.

2. Use a CPM computer program such as the one in the *POM Computer Library* to develop a CPM analysis of the project. What is the estimated duration of the project? What activities are on the critical path?

3. How long would the project take to complete if Activity b were delayed two weeks? How long would the project take to complete if Activity f were delayed two weeks? How long would the project take to complete if both Activities b and f were delayed two weeks? Discuss the care that must be taken in interpreting the meaning of the activity slack values.

4. Explain how the project would be affected if some resources could be shifted to Activity j and that activity's duration were reduced by one week.

5. Discuss how the assumptions and criticisms of CPM should cause us to modify our interpretation of our analysis of the RATS project.

SELECTED BIBLIOGRAPHY

Baker, B. N., and D. L. Wileman. "A Summary of Major Research Findings Regarding the Human Element in Project Management." *IEEE Engineering Management Review* 9, no. 3(July 1981):56–62.

"Buyer's Guide: Project Management Software." *Industrial Engineering* 18, no. 1(January 1986):51–60.

Cleland, David I., and William R. King. *Project Management Handbook.* New York: Van Nostrand Reinhold, 1983.

Fawcette, J. E. "Choosing Project Management Software." *Personal Computing* 8, no. 10(October 1984):154–167.

Gaither, Norman. "The Adoption of Operations Research Techniques by Manufacturing Organizations." *Decision Science* 6(October 1975):794–814.

Harrison, F. L. *Advanced Project Management.* New York: Halsted, 1981.

Kelley, James E., Jr., and Morgan R. Walker. "Critical Path Planning and Scheduling." In *Proceedings of the Eastern Joint Computer Conference.* Boston: 1959, 160–173.

Kerzner, Harold. *Project Management for Executives.* New York: Van Nostrand Reinhold, 1984.

Kerzner, Harold, and H. Thamhain. *Project Management for Small and Medium-Sized Business.* New York: Van Nostrand Reinhold, 1984.

Levin, R. I., and C. A. Kirkpatrick. *Planning and Control with PERT/CPM.* New York: McGraw-Hill, 1966.

MacCrimmon, K. R., and C. A. Ryavec. "An Analytical Study of the PERT Assumptions." *Operations Research* 12(January–February 1964):16–37.

Meredith, J. R., and S. J. Mantel. *Project Management.* New York: Wiley, 1985.

Miller, Robert W. "How to Plan and Control within PERT." *Harvard Business Review* 40(March–April 1962):93–104.

Moder, J. J., C. K. Phillips, and E. W. Davis. *Project Management with CPM and PERT.* 3rd ed. New York: Reinhold, 1983.

Paulson, Boyd C. "Man–Computer Concepts for Project Management." *The Construction Institute,* Technical Report No. 148 (August 1971). Stanford, CA.: Stanford University.

PERT, Program Evaluation Research Task, Phase I Summary Report, 646–669. Washington, DC: Special Projects Office, Bureau of Ordnance, 7, Department of the Navy, July 1958.

Smith, Larry A., and Sushil Gupta. "Project Management Software in P&IM." *P&IM Review* (June 1985):66–68.

Smith, Larry A., and Joan Mills. "Project Management Network Programs." *Project Management Quarterly* (June 1982):18–29.

Smith-Daniels, Dwight E., and Nicholas J. Acquilano. "Constrained Resource Project Scheduling." *Journal of Operations Management* 4, no. 4(1984):369–387.

Wiest, Jerome D., and Ferdinand K. Levy. *A Management Guide to PERT/CPM.* Englewood Cliffs, NJ: Prentice-Hall, 1977.

CHAPTER

17

MAINTENANCE MANAGEMENT AND RELIABILITY

JAPANESE MANUFACTURERS ATTACK MAINTENANCE PROBLEMS

Japanese manufacturers detest interruptions to production. When a machine breaks down, a flashing red light goes off at the machine and production workers and repair specialists from maintenance departments work side by side to fix the machine fast so that production can resume. The breakdown also triggers another action: Co-workers meet after work for several days to study the problem and devise a program for eliminating the malfunction as a cause of future breakdowns. Also, as workers change over their own machines to other products, they repair the machines or assist repair specialists in repairs. Workers perform preventive maintenance on their own machines as a morning ritual. They methodically run down checklists for their machines much as pilots and flight crews check out aircraft before taking off. They listen intently as they operate the machines during the day, carefully listening for any hint of an impending malfunction. Machines are adjusted, serviced, and repaired before minor problems develop into larger problems that could interrupt production. This compulsion to avoid interruptions to production is shared by management and workers alike. The cornerstone of their maintenance programs is worker involvement.

The previous account illustrates the importance that Japanese manufacturers place on keeping production equipment adjusted, repaired, and in good operating condition. The reasons for this compulsion to have equipment in perfect operating condition are not only to avoid interruptions to production, but also to keep production costs low, keep product quality high, and avoid late shipments to customers. U.S. operations managers also recognize the importance of maintenance management today and are devising programs to improve the management of maintenance functions in their organizations.

Equipment malfunctions in manufacturing and service industries have a direct impact on:

1. **Production capacity.** Machines idled by breakdowns cannot produce; thus the capacity of the system is reduced.
2. **Production costs.** Workers idled by machine breakdowns cause labor costs per unit to climb. When machine malfunctions cause scrap products to be produced, unit labor and material costs increase. Also, maintenance department budgets include such costs as the costs of providing repair facilities, repair crews, preventive maintenance inspections, standby machines, and spare parts.
3. **Product and service quality.** Poorly maintained equipment produces low-quality products. Also, equipment in disrepair has frequent breakdowns and cannot provide adequate service to customers. The aging aircraft fleets of the U.S. airline and air freight industries have made the public aware of the dire need for better maintenance management.
4. **Employee or customer safety.** Worn-out equipment is likely to fail at any moment, and these failures can cause injuries to workers.
5. **Customer satisfaction.** When production equipment breaks down, products often cannot be produced according to the master production schedules. This means that customers will not receive products when promised.

Toward better maintenance management, maintenance departments are developed within organizations. A maintenance manager typically is a plant engineer who reports to either a plant manager or a manufacturing manager. The organizational level of the department depends on the importance of maintenance to the organization. Maintenance departments are usually split into two groups: buildings and grounds, and equipment maintenance. Buildings and grounds can include workers such as electricians, welders, pipefitters, steamfitters, painters, glaziers, carpenters, millwrights, janitors, and grounds keepers. It is the responsibility of the building and grounds group to maintain the appearance and functional utility of all buildings, lawns, planting areas, parking lots, fences, and all other facilities from the interior of the buildings to the perimeter of the grounds. The equipment maintenance group can include such workers as mechanics, machinists, welders, oilers, electricians, instrument calibrators, and electronic technicians. It is the responsibility of the equipment maintenance group to provide equipment repair crews, shops for repairing equipment, and the appropriate level of preventive maintenance for the equipment.

The degree of technology of the production processes, the amount of investment in plant and equipment, the age of the buildings and equipment, and other factors will affect how maintenance departments are organized, the required worker skills, and the overall mission of maintenance departments.

For most organizations, maintenance activities are directed at both repairs and preventive maintenance. The scope of these maintenance activities is outlined as follows:

1. **Repairs.** When buildings and equipment break down, malfunction, or are otherwise damaged so that normal operations are hindered, they are repaired, mended, overhauled, and put back into operating condition. Repair activities are reactive, that is, they are performed *after* a malfunction has occurred. A malfunction is indicated when a piece of equipment will not operate, operates at a less than normal speed, produces products below quality standards, or when workers think that the equipment is about to malfunction. Repair crews and repair shops work together with production workers to get the machine or building back into operation as fast as possible so that the interruption to production is minimized. Standby machines and spare parts are often used to speed this process.

2. **Preventive maintenance (PM).** Regularly scheduled inspections of buildings and all pieces of equipment are performed. At these times, machine adjustments, lubrication, cleaning, parts replacement, painting, and any needed repairs or overhauls are done. These activities are performed *before* the buildings or machines malfunction. The inspections and the needed repairs are usually performed during periods when the buildings and equipment are not needed for production. The inspection for a piece of equipment could be scheduled at a regular time interval, say, once a month, or after a certain number of operating hours, miles, or another measure of usage.

Operations managers make a trade-off between the amount of effort to expend on repairs and PM. As Figure 17.1 shows, some minimum amount of PM is necessary to provide the minimal amount of lubrication and adjustments to avoid a complete and imminent collapse of the production system. At this minimal level of PM, the cost of breakdowns, interruptions to production, and repairs is so high that total maintenance cost is beyond practical limits. Such a policy is simply a remedial policy: Fix the machines only when they break or will not operate any longer. As the PM effort is increased, breakdown and repair cost is reduced. The total maintenance cost is the sum of the PM and the breakdown and repair costs. At some point for each piece of equipment, additional spending for PM is uneconomical because PM costs climb faster than breakdown and repair costs fall. Operations managers seek to find the optimal level of PM where total maintenance costs are at a minimum both for each piece of equipment and for the entire production system.

The trade-off between PM and repairs is not simple because more than just production costs are involved in the decision. Production capacity, product quality, employee and customer safety, and customer satisfaction are also involved. The more money spent on PM, the higher we would expect production capacity, product

FIGURE 17.1   *Total Maintenance Costs as a Function of Repair Cost and Preventive Maintenance Cost*

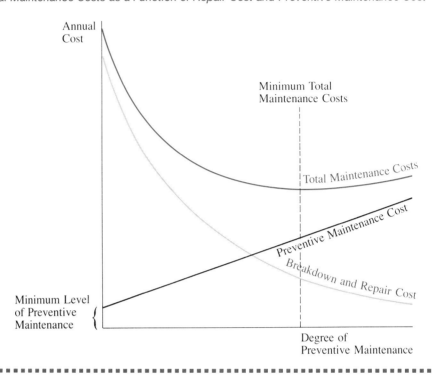

quality, employee safety, and customer satisfaction to be. Moreover, the amount of PM effort expended may be fundamental to a company's operating strategies and the positioning strategies selected. For example, in product-focused firms or in firms that are highly automated, the breakdown of one piece of equipment can idle an entire production system. It is important to note that even in firms with flexible automation such as FMS, a single machine breakdown can shut down all or a major part of the production system. Also, cellular manufacturing layouts experience similar problems. Such firms may emphasize preventive maintenance to avoid frequent breakdowns.

Process-focused firms, however, may have an abundance of in-process inventories, and work centers are buffered from interruptions of production at upstream work centers. Such firms may emphasize efficient and prompt repair programs to avoid the severity of breakdowns. The choice of the appropriate mix of emphasis on repairs and preventive maintenance is, therefore, a function of a number of factors, and this decision has strategic implications for the firm.

As an overview of maintenance management, Table 17.1 describes some maintenance policies often used by operations managers to reduce both the frequency and the severity of malfunctions in buildings and equipment.

TABLE 17.1   *Maintenance Policies That Reduce Frequency and Severity of Malfunctions*

Maintenance Policies	Reduces Frequency of Malfunctions	Reduces Severity of Malfunctions
1. Emphasize preventive maintenance.	✓	
2. Provide extra machines, reduce utilization to reduce wear rate.	✓	
3. Replace parts early to reduce number of breakdowns.	✓	
4. Train operators and involve them in machine care.	✓	
5. Train operators and involve them in machine repair.		✓
6. Overdesign machines for durability, precision, and redundancy so that likelihood of breakdowns is reduced.	✓	
7. Design machines for maintainability, emphasizing modular designs, quick-change parts, and accessibility, so that repairs can be made faster.		✓
8. Enhance maintenance department's capability: crew sizes, capacity of repair facilities, cross-training for personnel, flexibility, etc.	✓	✓
9. Increase supply of spare parts so that repairs can be made faster.		✓
10. Increase supply of standby or backup machines, devise alternative product routings, or arrange parallel production lines so that lost production is avoided in case of breakdowns.		✓
11. Increase in-process inventories.		✓

Enhancing preventive maintenance, providing extra machines so that all machines wear more slowly, replacing parts early, training operators in machine care, enhancing the maintenance department's capability, and overdesigning production machines are alternative policies to reduce the frequency of malfunctions. Speeding repairs by involving operators in repairs, simplifying repairs through innovative machine designs, enhancing the maintenance department's capability, increasing the supply of spare parts and standby machines, and increasing in-process inventories are alternative policies used by operations managers to reduce the severity of malfunctions.

In the remainder of this chapter we shall explore repair programs and PM programs in more detail. We shall also study about reliability, secondary maintenance department responsibilities, and trends in maintenance.

REPAIR PROGRAMS

Operations managers implement repair programs to achieve the following objectives:

1. To get equipment back into operation as quickly as possible in order to minimize interruptions to production. This objective can directly affect production capacity, production costs, product quality, and customer satisfaction.
2. To control the cost of repair crews, including straight-time and overtime labor costs.
3. To control the cost of the operation of repair shops.
4. To control the investment in replacement spare parts that are used when machines are repaired.
5. To control the investment in replacement spare machines, which are also called *standby* or *backup machines.* These replace malfunctioning machines until the needed repairs are completed.
6. To perform the appropriate amount of repairs at each malfunction. The decision about how far to go with a repair ranges from a Band-Aid and bubble gum fix to a complete overhaul. Some parts can be replaced early to extend the time until the next repair is required.

REPAIR CREWS, STANDBY MACHINES, AND REPAIR SHOPS

Production workers, repair specialists, spare parts and supplies, specialized tools and machines, repair shops, and standby machines are used to repair production equipment and buildings *after* malfunctions have occurred or when malfunctions are imminent. Repairs can be performed on an emergency basis to minimize interruptions to production, to correct unsafe working conditions, and to improve product quality. In these emergency situations, production workers and repair specialists may work overtime or they may be shifted from other, less critical projects. Maintenance supervisors and engineers are close at hand to collaborate with workers to make decisions as the repairs proceed. Malfunctioning machines may be quickly replaced by standby machines. The fundamental goal in repairs is to minimize the length of the interruption to production. Quick response times and fast repair jobs are therefore required.

Figure 17.2 illustrates how operations managers must trade off the cost of making repairs against the cost of interruptions to production. Large repair crews, the

FIGURE 17.2   *How Speedy Should Repairs Be?*

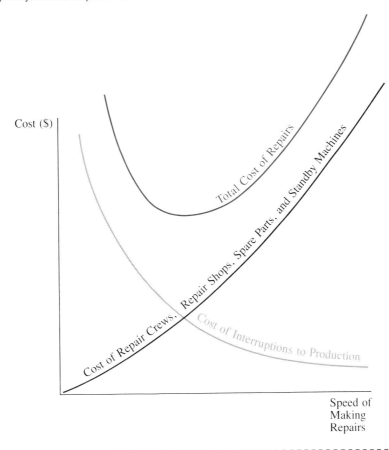

use of overtime to make repairs, maintaining large-capacity repair shops and large supplies of spare parts and standby machines all work together to speed up repairs and reduce the cost of interruptions to production. As Figure 17.2 shows, however, a point is reached where the cost of speedy repairs is not offset by savings in interruptions to production. The fundamental challenge in managing repair programs is to balance the cost of repair crews, repair shops, spare parts, and standby machines against the need for speedy repairs.

BREAKDOWNS TRIGGER REPAIRS AND CORRECTIVE ACTIONS

Ideally, an equipment malfunction should trigger two actions: first, a fast repair of the malfunction to get the equipment back into production as fast as possible, and second, and perhaps more importantly, the development of a program to eliminate the cause of the malfunction and the need for such repairs in the future. Such a program could include redesign and modification of the machine that malfunctioned, modification and redesign of the part or product being processed, training of the production workers to improve machine care, and more frequent adjustments, lubrication, and preventive maintenance inspections. It is here that Japanese manufacturers may be excelling over their U.S. counterparts. As the account at the beginning of this chapter depicts, such Japanese firms get everyone involved in programs of eliminating repairs that interrupt production, with the goal of keeping production equipment in perfect operating condition. All too often U.S. manufacturers depend too much on large repair staffs and not enough on eliminating the causes of machine malfunctions.

EARLY PARTS-REPLACEMENT POLICIES

When repairs to production machines are to be made, maintenance supervisors must decide how extensive the repairs should be. The extent of repairs can span this range:

1. Do just enough minor repairs to get the machine going again.
2. Repair the malfunction and replace some parts that are worn but have not yet malfunctioned.
3. Perform a major overhaul of the machine.
4. Replace the old machine with a newer one.

Operations managers should establish policies for how extensive repairs for each type of machine should be. For example, let us assume that a particular production machine has malfunctioned. Workers who are to perform repairs on the machine could follow one of these policies:

1. Replace or repair only parts that have malfunctioned.
2. Replace or repair parts that have malfunctioned and all Type A parts with more than 1,000 hours of service.
3. Replace or repair parts that have malfunctioned and all Type A parts with more than 1,000 hours of service and all Type B parts with more than 1,500 hours of service.

When operations managers have data on the frequency of malfunctions of parts, the cost of repairs or malfunctions, and the cost of early replacement of parts before malfunctioning, early replacement policies such as those above can be developed. Computer simulation is often used to analyze such problems.

LETTING WORKERS REPAIR THEIR OWN MACHINES

Traditionally, U.S. manufacturers have applied the principle of specialization to maintenance workers. Repair specialists are trained to do particular kinds of repairs. When the need for a certain type of repair occurs, the appropriate specialist is called upon to perform the repair. Increasingly, however, workers are being given the responsibility for repairing their own machines or assisting repair specialists in making repairs. Some of the advantages of enlarging workers' jobs to include repairs are:

1. Workers' jobs may be more satisfying because of the greater variety in work tasks and more challenging work assignments.
2. Because of their involvement in making repairs, workers are more sensitive to potential malfunctions, and major repairs may be avoided because workers sense the possibility of malfunctions before they actually occur.
3. Workers are more flexible when they have been trained at several jobs. They can be moved about to perform more tasks, and the production system is thus more flexible in responding to change.
4. Workers can often complete minor repairs before the arrival of the repair specialists.
5. Because of their involvement in making repairs, workers can often avoid even minor repairs by doing cleaning, lubrication, adjustments, and other servicing of their machines during their idle time.
6. Because of their involvement in making repairs, workers tend to operate their machines more carefully, thus avoiding the need for even minor repairs. For example, when excessive chip buildups are avoided, fewer cutting tools are broken.

Robert W. Hall makes a good case for workers' involvement in doing their own repairs:

> *It creates more pride in the machine, and it requires closer observation than if the operator merely watches it run. This also helps dispel the propensity for equipment abuse — the feeling that "I can operate it as I please, and someone else will figure out if something is wrong. The company has more than enough money for repairs anyway." (The author has watched operators deliberately jam machines just to take a break while someone else repaired them. That might not have happened had the operators felt that a machine breakdown was their responsibility and breakdowns caused them more work.)*[1]

The trend toward more direct worker involvement in maintenance activities in U.S. manufacturing firms may be a key factor in reducing production costs and in improving product quality and customer satisfaction.

Examples 17.1 and 17.2 are illustrations of how operations managers can analyze some important issues in repair programs. In Example 17.1 an operations manager uses queuing analysis to determine the size of repair crews that repair machines in a production department. This type of problem occurs when operations managers must estimate the amount of repair capacity to provide. Such problems ordinarily involve two types of repair capacity issues — size of repair crews and capacity of repair shops. Either of these issues can conveniently be analyzed by using queuing formulas. Care should be taken, however, to review the assumptions of the queuing formulas and make sure that they fit the problem being analyzed. Computer simulation is often used to analyze repair capacity problems when the assumptions of queuing formulas do not fit the maintenance problem.

---

[1] Robert W. Hall, *Zero Inventories* (Homewood, IL: Dow Jones-Irwin, 1983), 134–135.

EXAMPLE 17.1   *Determining the Size of Repair Crews*

Bill Willis is the maintenance supervisor at an automobile tire factory. Several years ago the plant installed over 200 tire-building machines of the same design, and Bill is the manager responsible for seeing that the machines are repaired when they break down. He supervises repair specialists who repair malfunctioning machines on the shop floor. Bill has been instructed by the plant manager that when the tire machines break down, they should be back in service in two hours on the average. Bill has collected data from historical records and has found that the machines break down at an average rate of 3.5 per hour and that each repair specialist can repair a machine in four hours on the average. Thus each repair specialist can repair .25 machine per hour on the average. How many repair specialists are required?

Solution

1. First, look at Table D.3 in Appendix D at the end of this book. If we assume that machine repairs are made according to the assumptions of Model 1, the formula for finding the value of the average repair rate (μ) is:

$$t_s = \frac{1}{\mu - \lambda}$$

2. Next, manipulate the formula so that the average repair rate (μ) is on the left-hand side of the expression:

$$t_s = \frac{1}{\mu - \lambda}, \quad (\mu - \lambda)t_s = 1, \quad \mu = \lambda + 1/t_s$$

3. Next, given that the average breakdown rate (λ) is 3.5 and the average time required for machines to be repaired (t_s) is 2, compute the required average repair rate (μ):

$$\mu = \lambda + 1/t_s = 3.5 + 1/2 = 4 \text{ machines per hour}$$

4. Next, since we now know the average repair rate (μ) and that each repair specialist requires four hours on the average to repair a machine, compute the number of repair specialists required:

$$\text{Number of specialists} = \mu \div \text{Machines per hour a specialist can repair}$$
$$= 4 \div .25 = 16 \text{ repair specialists}$$

EXAMPLE 17.2   *Determining the Number of Standby Machines*

Bill Willis from Example 17.1 is the manager responsible for the repair of 200 identical tire-building machines. When one of the machines breaks down, Bill's repair specialists replace the malfunctioning machine with a standby machine if one is available. When a standby machine is available, the length of time that the operation is out of production is greatly reduced. The plant manager has recently asked Bill to review the number of standby machines available and to recommend whether the number should be increased. Bill studies the historical records of breakdowns among the tire-building machines and finds this information:

Number of Machines Malfunctioning per Hour	Occurrences	Relative Frequency (Fraction and Proportion)
6	25	25/500 = .05
5	75	75/500 = .15
4	125	125/500 = .25
3	175	175/500 = .35
2	100	100/500 = .20
Total	500	1.00

Bill collaborates with the accounting and industrial engineering departments to develop cost estimates. When too few standby machines are provided, each breakdown for which a standby machine is not available costs the company $150 in lost production time and increased repair costs because of the emergency conditions. When too many standby machines are provided, each standby machine not in use costs the company $80 per hour in storage, special handling, and other costs. How many standby machines should be provided to minimize the total expected cost?

Solution

1. First, turn to Examples 10.7 and 10.11 in Chapter 10 and review how to solve payoff table problems.

2. Next, set up the payoff table and complete the calculations:

Number of Standby Machines Required per Hour

S_j \ SN_i	6	5	4	3	2	Total Expected Costs per Hour $EC = \Sigma[P(SN_i)C_{ij}]$
6	$ 0	$ 80	$160	$240	$320	$200.00
5	150	0	80	160	240	131.50
4	300	150	0	80	160	97.50 ←
3	450	300	150	0	80	121.00
2	600	450	300	150	0	225.00
$P(SN_i)$	.05	.15	.25	.35	.20	

(Number of Standby Machines Provided)

Note: C_{ij} is the costs of S_j and SN_i.

3. Next, recommend the number of standby machines to be provided.

The payoff table analysis indicates that four standby machines should be provided. Bill Willis recognizes, however, that costs are but one factor to be considered in his recommendation. He also has to consider the impact on production capacity (production capacity is reduced when machine repairs take longer owing to unavailability of standby machines) and on customer satisfaction (delivery promises to customers are broken when machine repairs take longer owing to unavailability of standby machines). Both of these factors argue for a larger number of standby machines. By looking at the payoff table, Bill can see that if he recommended five standby machines, hourly expected costs would increase by only $34. Bill believes that production capacity and customer satisfaction would be greatly improved if five standby machines are provided.

In Example 17.2 a payoff table is used to determine the number of standby machines to provide in order to minimize the cost of making repairs to machines that malfunction in a production department. This type of problem occurs when operations managers must provide:

1. A stock of spare parts for repairing machines *after* breakdowns.
2. A stock of spare parts for making unanticipated repairs during PM inspections.
3. A stock of standby machines for replacing machines *after* breakdowns.

In these problems operations managers do not know how many of each part will be needed in each time week. In the face of this uncertainty, they do not want to stock too many parts because it is expensive to store, insure, finance, maintain, and handle the stock. Similarly, they do not want to stock too few because of production downtime and other costs. When faced with such decisions, operations managers therefore attempt to provide the level of stock that balances the cost of stocking too few parts against the cost of stocking too many parts, given an uncertain demand for the stock.

These examples are common types of decisions that must be analyzed by operations managers as they strive to achieve the objectives of repair programs.

Let us now turn to a discussion of preventive maintenance issues.

PREVENTIVE MAINTENANCE (PM) PROGRAMS

In the case of machine breakdowns, operations managers have no choice — repairs must be made. On the other hand, the decision to have regularly scheduled inspections, machine adjustments, lubrication, and parts replacement as a part of a preventive maintenance (PM) program is discretionary. Operations managers do not *have* to have PM programs, but most do have them because they want to:

1. Reduce the frequency and severity of interruptions to production caused by machine malfunctions. This objective can directly affect production capacity, production costs, product quality, employee and customer safety, and customer satisfaction.
2. Extend the useful life of production machinery.

3. Reduce the total cost of maintenance by substituting PM costs for repair costs.
4. Provide a safe working environment for workers. Worn-out machines in poor operating condition create safety hazards for workers.
5. Improve product quality by keeping equipment in proper adjustment, well serviced, and in good operating condition.

PM AND OPERATIONS STRATEGIES

PM can be an important factor in achieving operations strategies. For example, a PM program can be essential to the success of a product-focused positioning strategy. In product-focused positioning strategies, standardized product designs are produced along assembly lines where there are little if any in-process inventories between adjacent operations. If a machine breaks down at one operation, all other down-stream operations will soon run out of parts to work on. An extensive PM program in such systems will reduce the frequency and severity of machine breakdowns.

AUTOMATION AND THE PROMINENCE OF PM

In automated factories PM programs are essential. Consider the concept of *worker-less factories.* In this concept systems of automated machines operate continuously without the need for production workers. In such an environment a large number of maintenance workers would be needed to keep the machines adjusted, lubricated, and in good operating condition. Although many of our factories will never become workerless, they will become more automated and we shall see a shift from large to smaller production work forces, but we shall also see a shift from small to larger PM work forces. Some of the production workers who will be displaced by automation will need to be retrained to become a part of the growing maintenance work force.

SCHEDULING PM ACTIVITIES

At some Ford, Toyota, General Motors, and other plants, production is scheduled on two 8-hour shifts per day along with one 4-hour minishift for PM activities. At other factories that produce on three shifts per day, the capacity of each machine used for production-planning purposes (master production scheduling and capacity requirements planning) is reduced to allow time for each machine to undergo its regular PM inspection, adjustment, lubrication, and parts replacement. Regardless of the arrangement devised to schedule PM activities, PM and production are increasingly viewed as being equally important, and therefore PM and production must be regularly scheduled on each machine.

PM DATA BASE REQUIREMENTS

For an effective PM program, detailed records must be maintained on each machine. An ongoing history of the dates and frequency of breakdowns, descriptions of malfunctions, and costs of repairs is fundamental to determining how often to schedule PM for each machine. Equipment specifications and checklists are needed for PM inspections and early parts replacement decisions. These records form the basis for improving PM programs, and the amount of data for a large factory can be great. Computers are often used to maintain a data base for maintenance departments to access as needed. Also, much of the data can be kept in a plastic pocket on each machine; then as repairs or preventive maintenance is performed, the cards in the pocket can be updated.

MODERN APPROACHES TO PM

Japanese manufacturers have pioneered the use of Just-in-Time (JIT) methods. A discussion of JIT was included in Chapter 12 of this book. In JIT, in-process inventories and production lot sizes are reduced to very low levels. The near absence of in-process inventories forces the attention of workers and managers to be focused on machine breakdowns. If a machine breaks down, all downstream machines will soon be out of parts and the whole production system will soon stop. Machine breakdowns simply cannot be tolerated in JIT systems; this is why manufacturers strive for *perfect machine maintenance.* We have discussed earlier how these manufacturers speed up repairs so that interruptions to production are minimized. Here we want to emphasize how they strive to *eliminate* machine breakdowns through PM.

A cornerstone of Japanese PM programs is worker involvement. Just as they developed the concept of quality at the source (placing the responsibility for product quality on the production worker), the Japanese have also similarly applied the concept of *PM at the source.* In this approach workers have the fundamental responsibility for preventing machine breakdowns by conducting preventive maintenance on their own machines. Workers have developed an aircraft mentality toward PM. You know how pilots and air crews go down checklists before an aircraft can take off? This meticulous attention to each small detail of the performance of the aircraft is to avoid the unthinkable — an air crash. Japanese workers also go down a PM checklist every morning, inspecting, lubricating, and adjusting their own machines with the same dread of the unthinkable — a machine breakdown. Industry Snapshot 17.1 illustrates the concept of PM at the source.

As workers operate their machines throughout the day, they listen intently as the machines operate, hoping to pick up any hints of machine irregularities so that they can correct the problem before a machine malfunction occurs. They fill out cards, which are kept in pockets attached to their machines, indicating PM, repair, and service data. If, during these PM inspections, parts replacement or other repairs are called for, the production workers assist repair specialists in this work. After a time these production workers are trained not only in several production jobs, but also in the maintenance of the machines of several jobs. Because workers know more than one job and can do more than one job, they are more valuable to the company and the company is more flexible in responding to change.

In Chapter 15 we discussed how Japanese manufacturers use quality circles to solve production problems. One of the production problems commonly attacked by these circles is the avoidance of machine breakdowns. PM activities are studied by co-workers to decide how often each machine should receive its PM inspection and to identify other PM activities that should be performed at these times. The use of worker study teams to solve maintenance problems is a key element of the PM

INDUSTRY SNAPSHOT 17.1

PM at the Source, or Total Preventive Maintenance (TPM)

A technique developed by Japanese manufacturers is being used more extensively by U.S. manufacturing today, say officials at H. B. Maynard Company, a management consulting firm. This technique is called *total preventive maintenance (TPM)* by Maynard. In this approach, machine operators in production are trained to perform preventive maintenance on the machines that they operate. In Japan, Seiichi Nakajima, vice chairman of the Japanese Institute of Plant Maintenance, claims that the approach has accounted for 50 percent increases in productivity, a 99 percent reduction of equipment failure rates, and a 90 percent reduction in product defects. Maynard thinks that the main difficulty in implementing similar programs in the United States is in altering the attitudes about the roles of machine operators in production and maintenance. Edward H. Hartmann, senior vice president at Maynard, says that "TPM abandons this division of labor and encourages equipment operators to accept responsibility for basic maintenance procedures like cleanup, lubrication, and basic preventive maintenance." Hartmann believes that such programs are even more important now that U.S. companies are turning to JIT and automated manufacturing.[2]

---

[2] Scripps Howard News Service, "U.S. Is Ripe for New Japanese Management Technique, Firm Says," *Bryan-College Station Eagle,* Sept. 27, 1987, E1.

---

programs of Japanese companies. U.S. manufacturers are coming around to letting workers participate more in maintenance activities, but they have not yet achieved the degree of worker involvement that the Japanese manufacturers enjoy.

A major obstacle to more worker involvement in PM at U.S. manufacturers is labor union work rules that restrict the kinds of tasks that each worker can do. For example, such rules may not allow production workers to change over their own machines or to perform maintenance on their machines. These rules evolved because of unions' interests in job protection, job security, and pay rate differences and have become traditional even in nonunion shops in the United States. Recent company–union negotiations have focused on eliminating many of these restrictive work rules. The General Motors assembly plant in Spring Hill, Tennessee, for instance, made sweeping changes to the traditional United Auto Workers (UAW) work rules.

Three examples illustrating the analysis of some common decisions in preventive maintenance are now presented. In Example 17.3 the problem of determining how many spare parts to stock for replacement parts during PM inspections is studied and discussed. This type of problem is perhaps unique to PM because the demand for replacement parts comes from two sources and the appropriate ways to estimate the two types of demands differ. Of particular interest in this example is the description of a system for scheduling orders for the planned replacement parts for PM inspections. This system utilizes logic that is similar to that used in material requirements planning (MRP).

EXAMPLE 17.3   Determining the Number of Spare Parts to Carry for PM

Bill Willis from Example 17.2 supervises the preventive maintenance program for 200 tire-building machines. The plant manager stopped by Bill's office the other day and asked how Bill's staff determined the number of spare parts to be used in PM inspections of tire-building machines. There seemed to be too much money tied up in spare parts used for PM, according to the plant manager, and he wondered if this inventory could be reduced somewhat without hindering the PM program overall. He was emphatic that he did not want the frequency of machine breakdowns to increase beyond present levels. Admitting that he did not fully understand how the appropriate number of spare parts for PM should be determined, he asked Bill to look into the matter, discuss it with his staff, and then report back to him. The plant manager wanted Bill to recommend a process for determining the appropriate number of spare parts for PM.

Solution

1. First, Bill called a meeting of his key people to discuss the problem. These basic points were established by the group:
   a. The need for each spare part originates from two types of demand. One type of demand is uncertain because the need for spare parts is not known until discovered during PM inspections. Another type of demand is certain and can be easily calculated because the spare parts scheduled to be replaced during PM inspections can be anticipated.
   b. The type of demand that is uncertain is created when, during a regularly scheduled PM inspection of a machine, it is determined that a particular part is wearing faster than expected or is otherwise not expected to last until the next scheduled inspection. An inventory of the part is stocked to meet this uncertain demand. Determining how much of this type of inventory of the part to hold is similar to determining how much inventory of a part to hold to make repairs during equipment breakdowns or computing the number of standby machines as in Example 17.1. In this approach the cost of stocking too few parts must be balanced against the cost of stocking too many parts while considering the uncertain demand for the part.
   c. The type of demand that is certain is created by regularly scheduled PM inspections of machines. For instance, if a particular part is to be replaced at every PM machine inspection, we know that one of the parts will be needed at every inspection, and orders for the part can be placed so that parts arrive when the PM inspections are scheduled. This type of demand can be satisfied by applying MRP-type logic.
   d. The number of each type of spare part in inventory at any point in time will be made up of two components. The first will be inventory stocked to meet uncertain demand during PM inspections. The second will be a transient inventory of parts flowing in as needed to be used in scheduled installations at regular PM inspections.

2. Next, Bill prepared an example of how the number of spare parts to hold for PM would be computed to meet the uncertain portion of demand.

a. First, Bill prepared this data for the example: Cost of stocking too many parts (the part is stocked, but not used during the week) is $20 per part to cover carrying, extra handling, and other costs. Cost of stocking too few parts (the part is needed but not stocked) is $50 per part to cover emergency supply of the part, extra production downtime, and other costs. The demand pattern for the part is:

Number of Parts Demanded per Week	*Occurrence*	*Relative Frequency (Fraction and Proportion)*
10	15	$15/100 = .15$
20	25	$25/100 = .25$
30	35	$35/100 = .35$
35	25	$25/100 = .25$
Totals	100	1.00

b. Next, Bill prepared a payoff table analysis of the data of the example:

Number of Spare Parts
Required per Week

S_j \ SN_i	10	20	30	35	Weekly Expected Costs $EC = \Sigma[P(SN_i)C_{ij}]$
10	$ 0	$500	$1,000	$1,250	$787.50
20	200	0	500	750	392.50
30	400	200	0	250	172.50 ←
35	500	300	100	0	185.00
$P(SN_i)$	.15	.25	.35	.25	

Number of Spare Parts Provided per Week (row label)

Note: C_{ij} is the costs of S_j and SN_i.

c. Next, Bill summarized the payoff analysis: The number of spare parts to be provided per week is 30 because this number provides the best balance between the cost of stocking too few and stocking too many. However, Bill pointed out that other factors such as production capacity and customer satisfaction would encourage a larger stock. In this example it can be seen that if 35 of the spare parts were carried, weekly expected costs would go up by only $12.50. Therefore Bill would recommend providing 35 of the parts per week.

3. Next, Bill explained how a system could be developed for ordering spare parts so that they would arrive for installation at regularly scheduled PM inspections.

a. First, all of the PM inspections to be made in each week of the planning horizon would be picked off the master production schedule and MRP records. Then these inspections would be classified according to the type of machines to be inspected in each week. This master PM schedule (MPMS) would be analogous to the master production schedule in MRP systems, and each type of PM machine inspection in the MPMS would be analogous to a product in the master production schedule.

    b. Next, a bill of spare parts would be prepared and kept up to date for each type of machine that receives a PM inspection. This bill is analogous to a bill of material in MRP systems. Although each spare part may not be replaced at each PM inspection, the planned frequency of replacement could be taken into account in the bill.

    c. Next, the bill of PM spare parts would be exploded by the MPMS into weekly PM demand for each type of spare part.

    d. Next, the parts explosion would be offset for lead time required to order and receive each type of spare part. The result would be a schedule for placing orders for each type of spare part for PM.

4. Finally, Bill prepared a summary of his recommendations. The demand for PM spare parts is made up of two components. The uncertain type can be estimated for each type of part based on the example prepared above. This analysis should take into account all of the factors affected by stocking too many or too few spare parts for unanticipated demand during PM inspections. Also, a system similar to an MRP system could be developed in which a weekly schedule would be prepared for placing orders for each type of spare part to be used in regularly scheduled PM inspections.

        In Example 17.4 the problem of determining how often to perform PM on a group of machines is analyzed. Such decisions are important because if PM inspections occur too frequently, the additional maintenance expense is not justified by the reduced frequency of breakdowns. On the other hand, if PM inspections occur too infrequently, too many breakdowns occur and production costs, production capacity, product quality, worker safety, and customer satisfaction suffer.

EXAMPLE 17.4   Determining the Frequency of Performing PM

It costs $2,000 to perform PM on a group of 5 machines. If one of the machines malfunctions between PM inspections, it costs $4,000. Records indicate this breakdown history on the machines:

Weeks between PM	Probability That a Machine Will Malfunction
1	.1
2	.2
3	.3
4	.4

If only costs are considered, how often should PM be performed to minimize the expected cost of malfunctions and the cost of PM?

Solution

1. First, compute the expected number of breakdowns for each PM policy. The formula for the expected number of breakdowns with the four PM policies is:

$$B_n = N \left(\sum_1^n p_n \right) + B_{(n-1)}p_1 + B_{(n-2)}p_2 + B_{(n-3)}p_3$$

where:

B_n = expected number of breakdowns for each of the PM policies

p_n = probability that a breakdown will occur between PM inspections when PM is performed every n period

N = number of machines in group

Therefore:

$$B_1 = N(p_1) = 5(.1) = .500$$

$$B_2 = N(p_1 + p_2) + B_1(p_1) = 5(.1 + .2) + .5(.1) = 1.550$$

$$B_3 = N(p_1 + p_2 + p_3) + B_2(p_1) + B_1(p_2)$$
$$= 5(.1 + .2 + .3) + 1.55(.1) + .5(.2) = 3.000 + .155 + .100$$
$$= 3.255$$

$$B_4 = N(p_1 + p_2 + p_3 + p_4) + B_3(p_1) + B_2(p_2) + B_1(p_3)$$
$$= 5(.1 + .2 + .3 + .4) + 3.255(.1) + 1.550(.2) + .5(.3)$$
$$= 5.000 + .326 + .310 + .150$$
$$= 5.786$$

2. Next, compute the expected breakdown cost, preventive maintenance cost, and total cost for each PM policy:

(1)	(2)	(3)	(4)	(5)	(6)
		Expected	*Weekly*		
		Number of	*Expected*		*Total*
PM	*Expected*	*Breakdowns*	*Cost of*	*Weekly*	*Weekly*
Every n	*Number of*	*per Week*	*Breakdowns*	*Cost of PM*	*Cost*
Weeks	*Breakdowns*	*[(2) ÷ (1)]*	*[(3) × $4,000]*	*[$2,000 ÷ (1)]*	*[(4) + (5)]*
1	.500	.500	$2,000	$2,000	$4,000
2	1.550	.775	3,100	1,000	4,100
3	3.255	1.085	4,340	667	5,007
4	5.786	1.447	5,788	500	6,288

3. The policy that minimizes weekly costs is to perform PM every week.

In Example 17.5 planning and controlling a large-scale PM project is studied. Large-scale projects occur commonly in maintenance departments. In fact, Table 16.5 in Chapter 16 indicated that one of the most common applications of CPM/PERT and other project management approaches is in maintenance. In many maintenance departments, banks of machines, whole production departments, and even entire factories are shut down periodically to perform PM. In such shutdowns the number and diversity of the PM tasks that must be performed is so great that some means is needed to plan and control the projects. As Example 17.5 illustrates, CPM is a useful way to plan and control large-scale maintenance projects.

Examples 17.3, 17.4, and 17.5 concern decisions about major issues in PM. Because PM is growing in importance today, an understanding of these examples is also important.

EXAMPLE 17.5   Planning and Controlling Large-Scale PM Projects

Jane Brown is a maintenance planner at Tex Inc.'s oil refinery in Baytown, Texas. She is developing a plan for the refinery's annual PM shutdown. She had identified these major PM activities, estimated their durations, and determined the precedence relationships among the activities:

Activity	Immediate Predecessor Activities	Activity Duration (Days)
a. Award subcontractor contracts	—	5
b. Call in Tex Inc. workers for PM	—	10
c. Drain storage tanks	—	8
d. Tear down cracking unit	b	7
e. Subcontractor cracking unit work	a	10
f. Painting subcontractor work	a	20
g. Clean and repair storage tanks	b,c	20
h. Reassemble cracking unit	d,e	12

Develop a CPM analysis of the PM project. Compute the critical path, the duration of the project, and the slack for each activity.

Solution

1. First, turn to Examples 16.1 through 16.4 in Chapter 16 and review the procedures for a CPM analysis.

2. Next, draw the CPM network diagram for the project. Compute the LS, LF, and S for each activity in the diagram.

3. Next, determine the critical path, the duration of the project, and the slack for each activity.

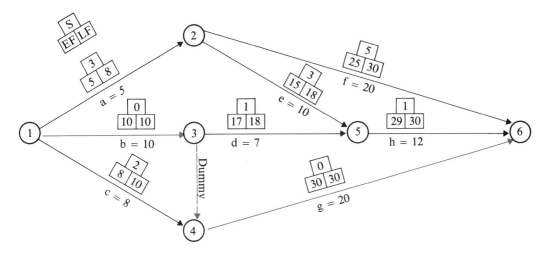

The critical path is path b-g. The PM project should require 30 days for completion. The slack for each activity is found in the top box over each activity arrow. All of the activities with zero slack are on the critical path.

Let us now discuss the concepts of reliability and their relationship to maintenance management.

RELIABILITY

Each part of a machine is designed for a given level of *component reliability,* which can be defined as the probability that a type of part will not fail in a given time period or number of trials under ordinary conditions of use. Component reliability is usually measured by: reliability (CR), failure rates (FR and FR_n), and mean time between failures (MTBF):

$$CR = (1 - FR)$$

where:

$$FR = \frac{\text{Number of failures}}{\text{Number tested}}$$

$$FR_n = \frac{\text{Number of failures}}{\text{Unit-hours of operation}}$$

$$MTBF = \frac{\text{Unit-hours of operation}}{\text{Number of failures}} \quad \text{or} \quad \frac{1}{FR_n}$$

For instance, for a particular type of automobile tire with an expected life of 30,000 miles, if only 1 percent of the tires fail within the 30,000-mile span, we would say that a tire has a reliability level of .99.

■■

FIGURE 17.3   *System Reliability as a Function of Component Part Reliability and Number of Component Parts*

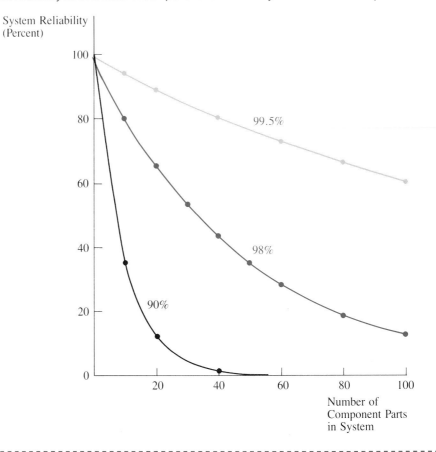

■■■

When component parts are combined into a larger system such as a machine, the combined reliability of all the components forms the basis for *system reliability (SR)*. When critical components — those that can directly cause the machine system to fail — interact during the operation of the machine system, the system reliability is determined by computing the product of the reliabilities of all the interacting critical components. For example, four automobile tires, each with a reliability of .99, would have a system reliability of:

$$SR = CR_1 \times CR_2 \times CR_3 \times CR_4$$
$$= .99 \ \times .99 \ \times .99 \ \times .99 = .961$$

The concept of system reliability is further demonstrated in Figure 17.3. If the critical components of a system have a reliability of 90 percent, the system reliability is almost zero if there are more than 50 critical component parts. Similarly, when component parts have a 99.5 percent reliability, system reliability falls to 60.6 percent when there are 100 critical component parts.

Considering the concept of system reliability, what are some of the ways that operations managers can increase the reliability of machines and reduce the frequency of machine breakdowns? There are three practical ways. First, overdesign of component parts to improve reliability may be a viable strategy in holding system reliability at acceptable levels. *Overdesign* means enhancing a design to avoid a particular type of failure. Let us say that if a part tends to corrode, overdesigning the part could mean machining the part out of stainless steel to reduce corrosion. Or if a part tends to wear over time, making the part out of forged steel that has been hardened could improve its wearing quality. Similarly, manufacturing parts to closer tolerances may improve fit of the parts during assembly and reduce the likelihood of improper meshing of parts during use.

When machines are relatively simple (have only a few critical interacting component parts) and when machines do not directly interact (as in job shops), overdesign may be a reasonable alternative for improving system reliability. But when machines are complex (have many critical component parts) and when many machines interact in complex machine systems (as in product-focused assembly lines or continuous production systems), overdesign of component parts may not significantly improve system reliability. Even if overdesign of critical component parts warrants consideration, the cost of designing, testing, and producing overdesigned parts may be exorbitant. Thus other alternatives must often be considered.

Second, *design simplification,* the reduction of the number of interacting parts in a machine, will ordinarily improve system reliability. Two examples of this approach from the field of product design are well known. In the IBM Proprinter (see the Plant Tours section in Chapter 4, Production Processes), the number of parts was halved to about 64. Similarly, in the mid-1980s the number of parts in the Ford Taurus and Mercury Sable autos was reduced by about one-third. One of the main reasons for such design simplification is to improve the reliability of the products.

Third, another practical approach to improving machine reliability is to provide *redundant components.* In this approach, a component with low reliability may have a backup built right into the system; thus if the first component fails, its backup is automatically substituted. The electronics industry commonly employs this approach. Example 17.6 illustrates the overdesign and redundancy approaches to improving machine reliability.

EXAMPLE 17.6   *Improving Machine Reliability with Overdesign and Redundancy*

Oklahoma Instruments (OI) uses several autoinsertion machines in its electronic assembly operations. In recent weeks, OI has experienced an excessive number of breakdowns of these machines. Most of these failures have been traced to an electrical circuit board in the main control panel of the machines. Two hundred of each of the four critical components in the circuit board were subjected to simulated accelerated operations tests. These tests have been proven to be the equivalent of 2,500 hours of normal operation, which is the advertised expected life of the components. The following data resulted from these tests:

Component	(1) Number of Failures	(2) FR [(1)/200]	(3) CR (1 − FR) [1 − (2)]	(4) FR_n [(1)/(200 × 2,500)]	(5) MTBF $1/FR_n$ [1/(3)]
155	2	.010	.990	.0000040	1,000,000
175	1	.005	.995	.0000005	2,000,000
205	22	.110	.890	.0000440	22,727
315	4	.020	.980	.0000080	125,000

The system reliability of the circuit board is computed as follows:

$$\begin{aligned} SR &= CR_{155} \times CR_{175} \times CR_{205} \times CR_{315} \\ &= .990 \times .995 \times .890 \times .980 \\ &= .8592 \end{aligned}$$

It was clear to the managers at OI that something had to be done to increase the system reliability of the circuit board by improving the reliability of Component 205. Two alternatives were suggested:

1. Redesign, develop, and test a new overdesigned configuration of Component 205 at an estimated cost of $50,000. It is believed that this project would result in a component reliability for Component 205 of about .960.

2. Modify the circuit board such that a backup Component 205 is automatically placed into service if the primary Component 205 fails. This use of redundancy in design is estimated to cost only $10,000, but OI wonders what the system reliability of the circuit board will be with this alternative.

Compute the system reliability of the alternatives and recommend a course of action for OI.

Solution

1. Compute the system reliability of the overdesign and redundancy alternatives:

$$\begin{aligned} SR_o &= CR_{155} \times CR_{175} \times CR_{205} \times CR_{315} \\ &= .990 \times .995 \times .960 \times .980 \\ &= .9267 \end{aligned}$$

$$\begin{aligned} SR_r &= CR_{155} \times CR_{175} \times CR_{205} \times CR_{315} \\ &= .990 \times .995 \times .9879 \times .980 \\ &= .9537 \end{aligned}$$

2. Compute the reliability of Component 205 in the redundancy alternative. What is the combined reliability of the two components working together?

$$\text{CR}_{205} = \begin{pmatrix} \text{Probability} \\ \text{of primary} \\ \text{component} \\ \text{working} \end{pmatrix} + \begin{pmatrix} \text{Probability} & \text{Probability} \\ \text{of backup} & \text{of needing} \\ \text{component} \times \text{backup} \\ \text{working} & \text{component} \end{pmatrix}$$

$$= \quad .890 \quad + \quad [.890 \quad \times (1 - .890)]$$
$$= \quad .9879$$

3. Because the system reliability is increased more with the redundancy alternative and at lower cost, the redundancy alternative is recommended.

Our knowledge of system reliability is also helpful in other areas of POM. Quality control is a particularly fruitful area for reliability applications. Today many U.S. manufacturers have set goals of producing products of near-perfect quality. In the achievement of such goals, the concepts of overdesign and redundancy are particularly relevant. Just as the reliability of production machines can be improved with the application of these concepts, so also can the reliability of products from manufacturers be improved. This is why products of the highest quality today exhibit the properties of overdesign, redundancy, parallel circuits, and backup capabilities of critical components.

SECONDARY MAINTENANCE DEPARTMENT RESPONSIBILITIES

All maintenance departments are responsible for the repair of buildings and equipment and for performing certain preventive maintenance inspections, repairs, lubrication, and adjustments. Additionally, certain secondary responsibilities have traditionally been assigned to these departments.

Housekeeping, janitorial, window washing, grounds-keeping, and painting services are usually performed by maintenance departments. These activities usually include all areas of the facility, from restrooms to offices to production departments to warehouses. In some plants, however, the area around each production worker's immediate workplace is cleaned by the worker. The appearance and cleanliness of all other areas are the responsibility of the maintenance department.

New construction, remodeling, maintaining safety equipment, loss prevention, security, public hazard control, waste disposal and transformation, and pollution control responsibilities have been assigned to some maintenance departments.

TRENDS IN MAINTENANCE

Production machinery today is far more complex than it was a decade or two ago. Computerized controls, robotics, new technology in metallurgy, more sophisticated electronic controls, new methods in lubrication technology, and other developments have resulted in many changes in the way complex machines are maintained.

INDUSTRY SNAPSHOT 17.2

If Your Lathe Is in a Lather, Maybe Charley Can Help

What does it mean when a machine starts making funny noises? Maybe you should ask Charley. That's the name for a new diagnostic system, developed by General Motors, that uses artificial intelligence to analyze vibration patterns. With Charley, any shop floor worker can troubleshoot machinery that has such rotating parts as bearings, pumps, motors, and gears. GM is testing the system in three plants and plans to add about a dozen more systems by 1990.

The computerized expert system is named for Charles Amble, a retired GM expert on machine tool diagnostics. His know-how makes a data base of some 1,000 "rules" of vibration analysis. A second data base contains details on the physical features—the number of teeth in gears, for example—for thousands of lathes, drills, and other pieces of industrial equipment.

Workers collect vibration data by touching a machine with a handheld device, then feeding the data into a personal computer for analysis by Charley. The system suggests preventive repairs and avoids "fixing" parts that aren't ailing.[3]

---

[3] "If Your Lathe Is in a Lather, Maybe Charley Can Help," p. 107. Reprinted from May 9, 1988 issue of *Business Week* by special permission, copyright © 1988 by McGraw-Hill, Inc.

Special training programs have sprung up to give maintenance workers the skills necessary to service and repair today's specialized equipment. An example of this training is found in the field of life support systems in hospitals. The engineers and technicians who design and perform maintenance programs for this sophisticated medical equipment must be involved in continuous training programs to stay abreast of new equipment developments. These training programs are conducted by individual hospitals, by cooperative health care groups, and by public and private educational institutions.

Subcontracting service companies have developed to supply specialized maintenance services. Computers, automobiles, office machines, and other products are increasingly serviced by outside subcontracting companies. Their specialized technical training and their fee structure, which is usually based on an as-needed basis, combine to offer competent service at reasonable cost.

Other technologies are developing that promise to reduce the cost of maintenance while improving the performance of production machines. An example is the network of computerized temperature-sensing probes connected to all key bearings in a machine system. When bearings begin to fail, they overheat and vibrate, causing these sensing systems to indicate that a failure is imminent. The massive damage to machines that can happen when bearings fail—snapped shafts, stripped gears, and so on—can thus be avoided. Industry Snapshot 17.2 illustrates this type of monitoring system, which promises to simplify the problem of when to perform preventive maintenance.

As computers have been almost universally absorbed into management information systems in all types of organizations, maintenance departments have also been affected by this development. Five general areas in maintenance commonly use computer assistance today: (1) scheduling maintenance projects; (2) maintenance cost reports by production department, cost category, and other classifications; (3) inventory status reports for maintenance parts and supplies; (4) parts failure data; and (5) operations analysis studies, which may include computer simulation, waiting lines (queuing theory), and other analytical programs. Information from these uses of computers can provide managers in maintenance with the necessary failure patterns, cost data, and other information fundamental to the key maintenance decisions discussed in this section.

Although computers, robotics, and high-tech machinery are important concerns in maintenance management today, people concerns may be at the heart of better maintenance. One important trend is the involvement of production workers in repairing their own machines and performing PM on their own machines. By enlarging production workers' jobs to include maintenance of their machines, not only is maintenance likely to improve, but many side benefits open up. Restrictive union work rules seem to be falling away at a record pace.

Maintenance today in POM means more than simply maintaining the machines of production. As POM has broadened its perspectives from minimizing short-range costs to other, long-range performance measures such as customer service, return on investment, product quality, and providing for workers' needs, so also has maintenance broadened its perspectives. Today maintenance means that the prompt supply of quality products and services is what is maintained, and not merely machines.

SUMMARY

It's a fact of life that buildings and equipment deteriorate; as they are used and grow older, age and wear eventually take their toll. Maintenance departments are established in both product and service industries to minimize the impact of this aging and wearing of machinery and buildings on production systems. Unless maintenance departments achieve this objective, capacity declines, production costs climb, product/service quality declines, and employee safety declines.

Maintenance involves two principal activities—repairs and preventive maintenance. Maintenance operations are frequently analyzed by staff specialists to determine repair crew sizes, repair project schedules, number of standby machines and spare parts, how often to perform preventive maintenance, and policies about when to replace parts before failure.

The nature of maintenance operations has supported extensive analytical studies. Probability theory, PERT/CPM, payoff tables, marginal analysis, queuing theory, and computer simulation techniques are frequently employed in these studies. The results of these and other analysis techniques become valuable inputs to management decisions about maintenance operations.

As production systems change, new trends are observed in maintenance—specialized training programs for maintenance workers, maintenance subcontracting, computerized sensing systems, and computerized maintenance information systems. These developments will provide managers with support to maintain the supply of products and services from production systems, the ultimate goal of maintenance operations.

REVIEW AND DISCUSSION QUESTIONS

1. Identify five factors or performance measures of production that are affected by maintenance management and equipment malfunctions.

2. Define *repairs*. Define *preventive maintenance*. Describe the relationship between repairs and preventive maintenance.

3. Name five ways that the frequency of equipment malfunctions can be reduced.

4. Name three ways that the severity of equipment malfunctions can be reduced.

5. Identify and explain five objectives of repair programs.

6. Explain the relationship between the costs of interruptions to production and the costs of making repairs.

7. What actions are triggered by a machine breakdown? Describe and discuss the actions and their role in maintenance management.

8. Explain the meaning and significance of early parts replacement policies in a repair program.

9. Identify and discuss the advantages of letting production workers repair their own machines.

10. What are the objectives of PM programs?

11. Explain and discuss how PM can be an important factor in achieving operations strategies.

12. Explain why the trend toward automation has increased the importance of PM.

13. Explain and discuss the modern approaches to PM.

14. Explain how an operations manager might determine how many spare parts to order for a PM program.

15. Define *component reliability*. Define *system reliability*. Describe the relationship between component reliability and system reliability. Explain the significance of reliability concepts to maintenance management.

16. Define and explain the meaning of *overdesign, simplification,* and *redundancy.* Discuss their roles in maintenance management.

17. What are some secondary responsibilities that are assigned to maintenance departments?

18. What are the trends in maintenance management?

PROBLEMS

1. A maintenance supervisor has just been told by his boss that machines that have malfunctioned should be out of production for no more than an average of one hour. Machines break down at a rate of five per hour on the average and the Model 1 queuing formulas apply. How many machines, on the average, must his repair crew be able to repair per hour?

2. Machines break down at a rate of 12 per hour on the average and each repair specialist can repair a machine in .75 hour on the average. Management states that each machine that has malfunctioned should be out of production for no more than 2 hours on the average. If Model 1 queuing formulas apply, how large should the repair crew be that repairs the machines?

3. A repair shop has three identical repair centers that repair machines independently. Machines arrive according to a Poisson distribution with a mean rate of 15 per hour. Each center repairs machines according to a Poisson distribution with a mean rate of 6 per hour. The space needed for waiting machines is considered to be adequate.
   a.   How long will machines be out of production on the average?
   b.   If each machine occupies 40 square feet of floor space, how much floor space should be occupied by waiting machines on the average?

4. A particular type of bronze bushing is stocked as spare parts to repair a number of different machines when they break down. If not enough of these bushings are on hand when needed, the production downtime, emergency supply procedures, and other short costs are $50 per bushing short. If too many of these bushings are stocked, it costs $30 per bushing per week for carrying, handling, and storage costs. The expected demand for these bushings for machine repairs is:

Demand per Week	Occurrence	Relative Frequency (Fraction and Proportion)
50	30	30/165 = .182
60	45	45/165 = .273
70	55	55/165 = .333
75	35	35/165 = .212
Totals	165	1.000

How many bushings should be stocked per week to minimize the total expected costs?

5. A repair shop uses #365 seals to repair machines. If the shop needs a seal and it is out of stock, it costs $25 to get one quickly from a local supplier. If a seal is stocked on Monday but not needed during a week, it costs $65 because the seals deteriorate so fast that they must be cleaned and treated if they are not used in five days. The demand history for the seals is:

Weekly Demand	Occurrence
30	5
40	10
50	25
55	25
60	15
Total	80

How many #365 seals should be stocked per week to minimize the total expected costs?

6. At the home office of Big Eight Accounting Inc., a type of desktop computer is stocked and used to replace computers that malfunction anywhere in the building. If one of the standby computers is not available when a malfunction occurs, it costs the company $300 in an employee's lost productivity. On the other hand, if one of the standby computers is not used, it costs $180 per week for extra handling, storage, carrying, and other costs. The demand pattern for these standby computers is:

Weekly Demand	Occurrence
10	15
20	25
25	35
35	30
Total	105

How many standby computers should be stocked by the accounting firm to minimize expected costs?

7. The Central Computing Services Company has ten regional computer centers in California. A preventive maintenance inspection and repair cycle costs a total of $7,000 on the average for all ten centers. If a breakdown occurs at any center, an average cost of $10,000 is incurred. The historical breakdown pattern for Central Computing is:

Weeks between PM	Average Number of Breakdowns between PM Cycles
1	.6
2	1.8
3	3.0
4	5.0
5	7.0

Recommend how often preventive maintenance should be performed.

8. It costs a total of $1,600 to perform preventive maintenance (PM) on five identical production machines. If one of the machines malfunctions between PM inspections, the cost averages $2,500. Here is the historical breakdown data for the machines:

Weeks between PM	Average Number of Breakdowns between PM Inspections
2	.5
3	1.2
4	2.5
5	6.6

What interval between PM inspections minimizes the total expected repair costs and PM costs?

9. It costs $400 for an engine overhaul, and the probabilities of an engine failure with varying intervals between oil changes are:

Thousands of Miles between Oil Changes	Probability of Engine Failure
20	.05
40	.10
60	.20
80	.30
100	.35

If you have ten automobiles in your fleet and a custom oil change with filters, long-wearing oil, and careful adjustments costs $50 per auto at each oil change, which interval between oil changes would you select? (*Hint:* Base your analysis on cost per 1,000 miles for the fleet.)

10. Preventive maintenance (PM) can be performed on six curing molds for a total cost of $3,000. If one of the molds malfunctions between PM inspections, it can be repaired for an average cost of $5,000. The probability of a machine malfunctioning between PM inspections is:

Weeks between PM	Probability of a Breakdown for Each Machine
1	.05
2	.15
3	.20
4	.25
5	.35

How often should PM be performed to minimize the total expected repair costs and PM costs?

11. If your car has four spark plugs, each with a probability of failure of .01 for a period of 10,000 operating hours:
    a. What is the reliability level of each spark plug?
    b. What is the reliability of the spark plug system of your car?

12. One hundred of a type of component in a machine is tested for 1,000 hours and 4 components fail.
    a. What is the reliability of the component?
    b. What is the mean time between failures for the component?
    c. How would you explain to a manager the meaning of your answers to Parts *a* and *b* above?

13. A machine has three critical component parts that interact. The three parts have component reliabilities of .96, .90, and .98.
    a. Compute the system reliability of the machine.
    b. If the machine could be redesigned to allow redundancy for the part that presently has a reliability of .90, what would be the new system reliability of the machine?

14. A plant for producing polyvinylchloride (PVC) will close soon for its annual PM shutdown. The PM activities, their durations, and their immediate predecessor activities are:

Activity	Immediate Predecessor Activities	Activity Duration (Days)
a. Instruct electrical repair team	—	3
b. Instruct mechanical repair team	—	5
c. Disassemble electronic controls	a	7
d. Modify computerized scale monitors	a	4
e. Disassemble and repair scales	b	3
f. Repair hopper vibrator mechanisms	b	9
g. Repair electronic controls	c	5
h. Reassemble automatic hoppers	f	6
i. Calibrate and adjust scales	d,e	3

    a. Construct a CPM network diagram for the PM shutdown.
    b. Compute the EF, LF, and slack for each activity.
    c. What is the critical path?
    d. What is the project's estimated duration?

15. A factory that produces precision polymer moldings is scheduled to have a plantwide PM shutdown soon. The PM activities, their durations, and their immediate predecessor activities are:

Activity	Immediate Predecessor Activities	Activity Duration (Days)
a. Train and instruct workers	—	12
b. Disassemble electronic controls	a	10
c. Disassemble curing molds	a	15
d. Modify mold tooling	a	9
e. Repair mold control panels	b	6
f. Repair defective molds	c,e	12
g. Repair electronic controls	b	14
h. Install mold tooling	b,d	21
i. Calibrate and adjust mold tooling	b,d	15
j. Reassemble curing molds	f,g,h	10

a. Construct a CPM network diagram for the PM shutdown.
b. Compute the EF, LF, and slack for each activity.
c. What is the critical path?
d. What is the project's estimated duration?

CASES

COMPUTER PRODUCTS CORPORATION (CPC)

The Boston plant of Computer Products Corporation (CPC) manufactures resins and molded plastic products. One production department has 20 injection-molding machines. Jerry Lee, the maintenance manager at the plant, is studying this group of machines with the goal of determining how often the department should shut down all of the machines and perform preventive maintenance (PM). The nature of the department and its processes causes PM to be performed on all the machines at one time at a cost of $5,000 for the entire group of machines. When a single machine breaks down, it costs about $500, on the average, to repair it. Jerry has gathered this data from production records about machine breakdowns between PM:

Months between PM	Probability of a Breakdown for Each Machine	Cumulative Probability of Breakdown
1	.10	.10
2	.15	.25
3	.20	.45
4	.25	.70
5	.30	1.00

Jerry notices that the probability that each machine will break down before the next PM inspection is 1.00 if there are five months between PM. This means that each machine is certain to break down before the next PM if there are five months between PM.

Assignment

1. Compute the expected number of breakdowns between PM with each of the PM policies.
2. Which PM policy minimizes the expected repair costs and PM costs?
3. What other factors should affect Jerry Lee's choice of a PM policy?
4. Explain the relationship between the choice of PM policy and its effect on: **(a)** production capacity, **(b)** product quality, **(c)** customer satisfaction, and **(d)** worker safety.
5. How much would an improvement in the factors listed in No. 4 have to be worth to justify changing the PM policy that minimized costs in No. 2?
6. Recommend the PM policy that should be adopted. Justify your recommendation.

CENTRAL MICHIGAN FABRICATORS INC.

The maintenance department of Central Michigan Fabricators Inc. presently provides 20 standby fabrication machines for the fabrication department. When a fabrication machine breaks down, it costs approximately $50 to remove the malfunctioning machine and replace it with a standby machine. When breakdowns occur and no standby machines are available, lost production costs (LPC) result:

$$LPC = 400 + 50X + X^2$$

where

$$X = \text{number of standby machines short per week}$$

The weekly LPC tend to justify a large number of standby machines. On the other hand, the weekly cost of providing standby machines forces management to control the number of standby machines provided. The cost per week of carrying standby machines (CC) when all are not needed is:

$$CC = Y^2 + 10Y - 40Z,$$

where

$$Y = \text{number of standby machines provided per week}$$

$$Z = \text{number of production machines that have failed during the week}$$

When CC is negative or when $Y = Z$, $CC = 0$. Maintenance records show the following pattern of breakdowns on these fabrication machines:

Breakdowns per Week	Number of Weeks
10	10
20	25
30	35
40	30

Assignment

1. How many standby machines should be provided to minimize the weekly total expected costs (installation costs, lost production costs, and carrying costs)?
2. The maintenance department believes that it could install and maintain a computerized sensing system that could determine with near-perfect accuracy the number of standby machines that would be needed in the next week. Assuming that the number of standby machines could be easily changed from week to week to exactly match the number of standby machines that the system indicated would be needed, how much could be spent per week on the sensing system?
3. What other factors should be considered in this analysis?

PRODUCT RELIABILITY AT VALVCO INC.

NASA is about to award a contract for a hydraulic valve to Valvco Inc. of Atlanta. But an obstacle has arisen in contract negotiations. NASA requires a reliability for this valve of at least .990. Valvco is studying its test data to determine if there is a practical way that its product can be made to meet NASA's requirements. The valve has four interacting component parts with the following test data:

Component Part	Number of Parts Tested	Number of Hours of Testing	Number of Failures
Z24	200	5,000	1
T19	190	3,000	0
A5	1,290	2,000	2
S113	323	1,000	3

Assignment

1. What is the present system reliability of the valve? Does the valve meet NASA's system reliability requirements?

2. NASA has suggested redundancy in design of the valve. Determine the reliability of the valve with each component as a candidate for redundancy. Can NASA's suggestion meet the system reliability requirements?

3. One of Valvco's engineers has suggested to NASA that it buy Valvco's valve as it is now and use two of the valves in parallel, one as the primary valve and one as a backup valve. Evaluate this proposal as a means of meeting NASA's system reliability requirements.

4. Which alternative would you recommend for meeting NASA's system reliability requirements? Why?

5. Discuss the concept of component redundancy as a practical means of increasing system reliability. What are the advantages and disadvantages of the approach?

SELECTED BIBLIOGRAPHY

Abbott, W. R. "Repair versus Replacement of Failed Components." *Journal of Industrial Engineering* 19(January 1968):21–23.

Cordero, S. T. *Maintenance Management.* Englewood Cliffs, NJ: Fairmont Press, 1987.

Gaither, Norman. "The Adoption of Operations Research Techniques by Manufacturing Organizations." *Decision Sciences* 6(October 1975):797–813.

General Electric Company. *Users' Guide to Preventive Maintenance Planning and Scheduling (FAME—Facilities Maintenance Engineering).* New York: General Electric Company, 1973.

Hardy, S. T., and L. S. Krajewski. "A Simulation of Interactive Maintenance Decisions." *Decision Sciences* 6(January 1975):92–105.

Hayes, R. H., and K. B. Clark. "Why Some Factories Are More Productive Than Others." *Harvard Business Review* 64, no. 5(Sept.–Oct. 1986):66–73.

Higgins, Lindley R. *Maintenance Engineering Handbook.* 3rd ed. New York: McGraw-Hill, 1977.

IBM. *General Information Manual: Preventive Maintenance and Cost Control.* Poughkeepsie, NY: IBM.

IBM. *Plant Maintenance Management System.* IBM Publication No. E20-0124-0. White Plains, NY: IBM, Data Processing Division.

Mann, Lawrence, Jr. *Maintenance Management,* Rev. ed. Lexington, MA: Lexington Books, 1983.

"Out of Order: Avoiding Plant Failures Grows More Difficult for Many Industries." *The Wall Street Journal,* Jan. 8, 1981, 1.

Tombari, H. "Designing a Maintenance Management System." *Production and Inventory Management* 23, no. 4(Fourth Quarter 1982):139–147.

Turban, Efraim. "The Complete Computerized Maintenance System." *Journal of Industrial Engineering* 1(March 1969):20–27.

Wilkinson, John J. "How to Manage Maintenance." *Harvard Business Review* 46(March–April 1968):191–205.

Wireman, Terry. *Preventive Maintenance.* Englewood Cliffs, NJ: Reston Publishing, 1984.

APPENDIXES

A NORMAL PROBABILITY DISTRIBUTION

The table Areas under the Normal Curve give the Z scores, or number of standard deviations from the mean, for each value of x and the area under the curve to the left of x. For example, in the figure below, if $Z = 1.96$, the .9750 value found in the body of the table is the total unshaded area to the left of x.

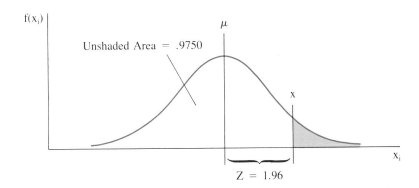

The Z scores in the table are signless; that is, the Z scores can be either negative $(-)$ or positive $(+)$. We determine the sign of Z in each problem. In the figure above, Z is positive because x falls to the right of the mean (μ). In the figure on the next page, x falls to the left of the mean (μ), and the area found in the body of the table lies to the right of x. In this figure, $Z = -2.28$ because x falls to the left of the mean.

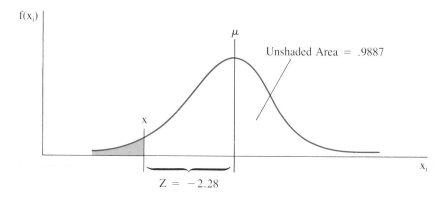

In these examples, Z scores of 1.96 and -2.28 were specified and the unshaded area to the left of x (positive Z scores) or to the right of x (negative Z scores) was read from the body of the table. The reverse process is often used: Either the shaded area or the unshaded area is specified and the Z score is read from the Z score column. For example, if the unshaded area $= .90$, the Z score is read from the table—$Z = 1.28$.

Areas under the Normal Curve

Z	.00	.01	.02	.03	.04	.05	.06	.07	.08	.09
.0	.50000	.50399	.50798	.51197	.51595	.51994	.52392	.52790	.53188	.53586
.1	.53983	.54380	.54776	.55172	.55567	.55962	.56356	.56749	.57142	.57535
.2	.57926	.58317	.58706	.59095	.59483	.59871	.60257	.60642	.61026	.61409
.3	.61791	.62172	.62552	.62930	.63307	.63683	.64058	.64431	.64803	.65173
.4	.65542	.65910	.66276	.66640	.67003	.67364	.67724	.68082	.68439	.68793
.5	.69146	.69497	.69847	.70194	.70540	.70884	.71226	.71566	.71904	.72240
.6	.72575	.72907	.73237	.73536	.73891	.74215	.74537	.74857	.75175	.75490
.7	.75804	.76115	.76424	.76730	.77035	.77337	.77637	.77935	.78230	.78524
.8	.78814	.79103	.79389	.79673	.79955	.80234	.80511	.80785	.81057	.81327
.9	.81594	.81859	.82121	.82381	.82639	.82894	.83147	.83398	.83646	.83891
1.0	.84134	.84375	.84614	.84849	.85083	.85314	.85543	.85769	.85993	.86214
1.1	.86433	.86650	.86864	.87076	.87286	.87493	.87698	.87900	.88100	.88298
1.2	.88493	.88686	.88877	.89065	.89251	.89435	.89617	.89796	.89973	.90147
1.3	.90320	.90490	.90658	.90824	.90988	.91149	.91309	.91466	.91621	.91774
1.4	.91924	.92073	.92220	.92364	.92507	.92647	.92785	.92922	.93056	.93189
1.5	.93319	.93448	.93574	.93699	.93822	.93943	.94062	.94179	.94295	.94408
1.6	.94520	.94630	.94738	.94845	.94950	.95053	.95154	.95254	.95352	.95449
1.7	.95543	.95637	.95728	.95818	.95907	.95994	.96080	.96164	.96246	.96327
1.8	.96407	.96485	.96562	.96638	.96712	.96784	.96856	.96926	.96995	.97062
1.9	.97128	.97193	.97257	.97320	.97381	.97441	.97500	.97558	.97615	.97670
2.0	.97725	.97784	.97831	.97882	.97932	.97982	.98030	.98077	.98124	.98169
2.1	.98214	.98257	.98300	.98341	.98382	.98422	.98461	.98500	.98537	.98574
2.2	.98610	.98645	.98679	.98713	.98745	.98778	.98809	.98840	.98870	.98899
2.3	.98928	.98956	.98983	.99010	.99036	.99061	.99086	.99111	.99134	.99158
2.4	.99180	.99202	.99224	.99245	.99266	.99286	.99305	.99324	.99343	.99361
2.5	.99379	.99396	.99413	.99430	.99446	.99461	.99477	.99492	.99506	.99520
2.6	.99534	.99547	.99560	.99573	.99585	.99598	.99609	.99621	.99632	.99643
2.7	.99653	.99664	.99674	.99683	.99693	.99702	.99711	.99720	.99728	.99736
2.8	.99744	.99752	.99760	.99767	.99774	.99781	.99788	.99795	.99801	.99807
2.9	.99813	.99819	.99825	.99831	.99836	.99841	.99846	.99851	.99856	.99861
3.0	.99865	.99869	.99874	.99878	.99882	.99886	.99899	.99893	.99896	.99900
3.1	.99903	.99906	.99910	.99913	.99916	.99918	.99921	.99924	.99926	.99929
3.2	.99931	.99934	.99936	.99938	.99940	.99942	.99944	.99946	.99948	.99950
3.3	.99952	.99953	.99955	.99957	.99958	.99960	.99961	.99962	.99964	.99965
3.4	.99966	.99968	.99969	.99970	.99971	.99972	.99973	.99974	.99975	.99976
3.5	.99977	.99978	.99978	.99979	.99980	.99981	.99981	.99982	.99983	.99983
3.6	.99984	.99985	.99985	.99986	.99986	.99987	.99987	.99988	.99988	.99989
3.7	.99989	.99990	.99990	.99990	.99991	.99991	.99992	.99992	.99992	.99992
3.8	.99993	.99993	.99993	.99994	.99994	.99994	.99994	.99995	.99995	.99995
3.9	.99995	.99995	.99996	.99996	.99996	.99996	.99996	.99996	.99997	.99997

B

STUDENT'S t PROBABILITY DISTRIBUTION

This t distribution is a two-tailed probability distribution. Follow these rules to use the table to set confidence limits:

1. Select the desired confidence interval. Subtract this confidence interval from 1. This will give the area in both tails outside the confidence interval. This area in the tails is shown in the figure below as the shaded area and is often referred to as the level of significance (α).

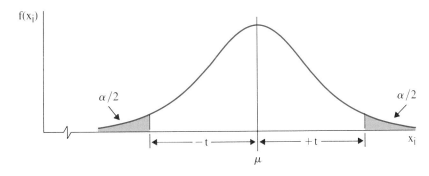

2. Find the column in the accompanying table with the appropriate level of significance heading.
3. Determine the degrees of freedom (d.f.). The d.f. usually equal $N - 1$ or $N - 2$, depending on the formula used, where N is the number of observations. Find the row in the table with the appropriate d.f.

4. The intersection of the level of significance column and the d.f. row is the t value. This t value means the number of standard deviations from the mean out to the shaded areas or the outer limits of the confidence interval.
5. The upper limit is computed by adding the product of the t value and the standard deviation to the mean. The lower limit is computed by subtracting this product from the mean.

EXAMPLE B.1

You have 25 observations with a mean of 32 and a standard deviation of 4.2. You wish to find the limits of a 90 percent confidence interval: $\alpha = .10$, N = 25, $\mu = 32$, and $\sigma_x = 4.2$. Upper limit = ? Lower limit = ?

1. Level of significance = .10.

2. d.f. = N − 2 = 25 − 2 = 23.

3. t = 1.714

4. Upper limit = $\mu + t(\sigma_x)$ = 32 + 1.714(4.2) = 39.20.

5. Lower limit = $\mu - t(\sigma_x)$ = 32 − 1.714(4.2) = 24.80.

Two situations usually occur in using the Student's t Distribution table:

a. You specify α and d.f. and you read t (the number of standard deviations to the right and left of the mean that spans the confidence interval or the unshaded area in the figure) from the body of the table.

b. You specify d.f. and t and read α from the top of the table.

Student's t Distribution

Level of Significance (α)

d.f.	.9	.8	.7	.6	.5	.4	.3	.2	.1	.05	.02	.01	.001
1	.158	.325	.510	.727	1.000	1.376	1.963	3.078	6.314	12.706	31.821	63.657	636.619
2	.142	.289	.445	.617	.816	1.061	1.386	1.886	2.910	4.303	6.965	9.925	31.598
3	.137	.277	.424	.584	.765	.978	1.250	1.638	2.353	3.182	4.541	5.841	12.941
4	.134	.271	.414	.569	.741	.941	1.190	1.533	2.132	2.776	3.747	4.604	8.610
5	.132	.267	.408	.559	.727	.920	1.156	1.476	2.015	2.571	3.365	4.032	6.859
6	.131	.265	.404	.553	.718	.906	1.134	1.440	1.943	2.447	3.143	3.707	5.959
7	.130	.263	.402	.549	.711	.896	1.119	1.415	1.895	2.365	2.998	3.499	5.405
8	.130	.262	.399	.546	.706	.889	1.108	1.397	1.860	2.306	2.896	3.355	5.041
9	.129	.261	.398	.543	.703	.883	1.100	1.383	1.833	2.262	2.821	3.250	4.781
10	.129	.260	.397	.542	.700	.879	1.093	1.372	1.812	2.228	2.764	3.169	4.587
11	.129	.260	.396	.540	.697	.876	1.088	1.363	1.796	2.201	2.718	3.106	4.437
12	.128	.259	.395	.539	.695	.873	1.083	1.356	1.782	2.179	2.681	3.055	4.318
13	.128	.259	.394	.538	.694	.870	1.079	1.350	1.771	2.160	2.650	3.012	4.221
14	.128	.258	.393	.537	.692	.868	1.076	1.345	1.761	2.145	2.624	2.977	4.140
15	.128	.258	.393	.536	.691	.866	1.074	1.341	1.753	2.131	2.602	2.947	4.073
16	.128	.258	.392	.535	.690	.865	1.071	1.337	1.746	2.120	2.583	2.921	4.015
17	.128	.257	.392	.534	.689	.863	1.069	1.333	1.740	2.110	2.567	2.898	3.965
18	.127	.257	.392	.534	.688	.862	1.067	1.330	1.734	2.101	2.552	2.878	3.922
19	.127	.257	.391	.533	.688	.861	1.066	1.328	1.729	2.093	2.539	2.861	3.883
20	.127	.257	.391	.533	.687	.860	1.064	1.325	1.725	2.086	2.528	2.845	3.850
21	.127	.257	.391	.532	.686	.859	1.063	1.323	1.721	2.080	2.518	2.831	3.819
22	.127	.256	.390	.532	.686	.858	1.061	1.321	1.717	2.074	2.508	2.819	3.792
23	.127	.256	.390	.532	.685	.858	1.060	1.319	1.714	2.069	2.500	2.807	3.767
24	.127	.256	.390	.531	.685	.857	1.059	1.318	1.711	2.064	2.492	2.797	3.745
25	.127	.256	.390	.531	.684	.856	1.058	1.316	1.708	2.060	2.485	2.787	3.725
26	.127	.256	.390	.531	.684	.856	1.058	1.315	1.706	2.056	2.479	2.779	3.707
27	.127	.256	.389	.531	.684	.855	1.057	1.314	1.703	2.052	2.473	2.771	3.690
28	.127	.256	.389	.530	.683	.855	1.056	1.313	1.701	2.048	2.467	2.763	3.674
29	.127	.256	.389	.530	.683	.854	1.055	1.311	1.699	2.045	2.462	2.756	3.659
30	.127	.256	.389	.530	.683	.854	1.055	1.310	1.697	2.042	2.457	2.750	3.646
40	.126	.255	.388	.529	.681	.851	1.050	1.303	1.684	2.021	2.423	2.704	3.551
60	.126	.254	.387	.527	.679	.848	1.046	1.296	1.671	2.000	2.390	2.660	3.460
120	.126	.254	.386	.526	.677	.845	1.041	1.289	1.658	1.980	2.358	2.617	3.373
∞	.126	.253	.385	.524	.674	.842	1.036	1.282	1.645	1.960	2.326	2.576	3.291

Source: Appendix B is taken from Table III of Fisher and Yates: *Statistical Tables for Biological, Agricultural and Medical Research,* published by Longman Group Ltd., London (previously published by Oliver and Boyd, Edinburgh), by permission of the authors and publishers.

C

FINANCIAL ANALYSIS IN POM

Operations managers are usually among the first to sense the need for *capital goods.*
These goods are all things bought by a business that have an expected life of more than
one year and are not bought and sold in the ordinary course of operations. These
goods include such items as production machinery, buildings, computers, trucks and
cars, and office equipment.

Operations managers often initiate proposals for buying capital goods because:

1. New products or services require new production equipment and buildings.
2. Existing production equipment and buildings are old and worn out and must be replaced.
3. Present production equipment has become obsolete and must be replaced with new and technologically superior designs.
4. Sales growth has resulted in the need for more production capacity that requires additional production machinery and buildings.

Sensing the need for capital goods is one thing; justifying that need to top-level executives who must approve such spending is quite another. Because of the scarcity of funds in most businesses and because of the volatility of interest rates and scarcity of funds in capital markets in the last decade, proposals for capital goods have undergone increased scrutiny by top management. If operations managers expect to win funds for capital goods, they must develop to a fine art the tools of financial analysis for justifying the acquisition of capital goods.

FINANCIAL ANALYSIS CONCEPTS

Table C.1 presents and defines some of the terms and concepts used in financial analysis in POM.

■ ■

TABLE C.1   Financial Analysis Concepts and Definitions

Capital good — An asset with a life of more than one year that is not bought and sold in the ordinary course of business.

Cutoff rate — The minimum rate of return on similar investments, set by management.

Depreciation — The annual noncash expense charged against profits to reduce taxes.

Economic life — The period over which an asset is expected to remain economically productive.

First cost — The total selling price of a capital good plus any delivery costs or costs of installation, tooling, and so on.

IRS depreciation category — The IRS classifies all capital goods put into service after 1986 into either 3, 5, 7, 10, 27.5, or 31.5 years of depreciation for tax purposes.

Operating expenses — The annual cost of operating the capital good, including labor, supplies, utilities, maintenance, and so on.

Opportunity costs — The highest return that will be forgone if the funds are invested in a particular capital good.

Salvage value — The market value of a capital good at the end of its economic life.

Taxes — Federal income taxes (usually means corporate income taxes).

■ ■

DEPRECIATION

Depreciation is perhaps the least understood concept in financial analysis. This is because of the noncash nature of depreciation expense. *Noncash* means that no cash has actually been spent for depreciation; the cash for the asset was paid at the time of the original purchase. Depreciation does not *directly* affect profits; rather, depreciation affects profits only indirectly through income tax savings. Example C.1 shows this impact. Note that in this example a $40,000 tax bill would have been paid by the business if there were no depreciation charged. With a $20,000 depreciation charge, however, the business paid only $32,000 in taxes, a savings of $8,000.

EXAMPLE C.1   *Effects of Depreciation on Cash Flows*

	Without Depreciation	*With Depreciation*
Profits before depreciation and taxes	$100,000	$100,000
Less depreciation	0	20,000
Taxable income	100,000	80,000
Taxes (t = .4)	40,000	32,000
Profits after taxes	60,000	68,000
Tax savings due to depreciation (t × depreciation)	—	8,000

Note: t is the tax rate, or 40 percent in this example.

The actual depreciation that can be claimed for an asset is strictly controlled by the Internal Revenue Service (IRS). Unfortunately, the IRS regulations have been changing rather rapidly in recent years. "Prior to 1954 the straight-line method was required for tax purposes, but in 1954 *accelerated* methods (double declining balance and sum-of-the-years'-digits) were permitted. Then, in 1981, the old accelerated methods were replaced by a simpler procedure known as the Accelerated Cost Recovery System (ACRS, which is pronounced 'acres'). And, the ACRS recovery allowances (depreciation rates) were changed again in 1986 as a part of the Tax Reform Act."[1] The most recent regulations pertaining to depreciation at the time of the writing of this edition is the 1986 Tax Reform Act. Although there will undoubtedly be other changes to depreciation methods allowable by the IRS in the future, these changes are not expected to affect the overall procedure of financial analysis in POM.

The 1986 Tax Reform Act stipulates that if a firm buys only up to $10,000 of assets in a year, the whole amount can be *expensed* or charged to depreciation in that

---

[1] Eugene F. Brigham, *Fundamentals of Financial Management,* 4th ed. (Hinsdale, IL: Dryden Press), 38.

year—a stipulation that applies only to very small businesses. Most firms purchase more than $10,000 of assets in a year, and for these firms the 1986 Tax Reform Act requires that assets be depreciated by the *double declining balance method,* the *straight-line method,* or a combination of these two methods. Table C.2 summarizes the classes of assets and the asset lives allowed for under the Accelerated Cost Recovery System (ACRS) in the 1986 Tax Reform Act. Table C.3 summarizes the percentage of the cost of assets that may be charged to depreciation in each year of an asset's life.

TABLE C.2   Classes and Asset Lives for Accelerated Cost Recovery System (ACRS) under the 1986 Tax Reform Act

Class	Type of Property
3-year	Computers and equipment used in research
5-year	Automobiles, tractor units, light-duty trucks, computers, and certain special manufacturing tools
7-year	Most industrial equipment, office furniture, and fixtures
10-year	Certain longer-lived types of equipment
27.5-year	Residential rental real property such as apartment buildings
31.5-year	All nonresidential real property, including commercial and industrial buildings

Source: Eugene F. Brigham, *Fundamentals of Financial Management,* 4th ed. (Hinsdale, IL: Dryden Press), 38.

TABLE C.3   Recovery Allowance Percentages under the Tax Reform Act of 1986

| Ownership Year | Class of Investment | | | |
	3-Year	5-Year	7-Year	10-Year
1	33%	20%	14%	10%
2	45	32	25	18
3	15*	19	17	14
4	7	12	13	12
5		11*	9*	9
6		6	9	7*
7			9	7
8			4	7
9				7
10				6
11				3

* Year in which the depreciation method was switched from double declining balance to straight line.
Source: Eugene F. Brigham, *Fundamentals of Financial Management,* 4th ed. (Hinsdale, IL: Dryden Press), 39.

The percentages in Table C.3 are computed while using double declining balance early in an asset's life, then switching to straight line in the year when the straight-line method allows a greater depreciation charge. Because the act assumes that an asset is purchased in mid-year, only a half-year of depreciation is charged in the first year and a half-year of depreciation is charged in the last year. This is referred to as the *half-year convention.* The double declining method allows twice the straight-line depreciation rate. For instance, consider the 5-year recovery class. Because the straight-line method would allow 20 percent of an asset's first cost in each year of a 5-year-asset's life, the double declining balance method allows an annual depreciation charge of 40 percent of the remaining undepreciated first cost of the asset. Here is how the percentages in Table C.3, which are rounded to whole numbers for simplicity, are calculated for the 5-year class of assets:

Year	Undepreciated First Cost	Double Declining Balance Multiplier	Annual Depreciation Percentage
1	100%	.4 (½ year)	20%
2	80	.4	32
3	48	.4	19
4	29	.4	12
5	~~17~~	~~.4~~	~~7~~
	17/1.5	Straight line	11
6	Remainder of unpreciated first cost		6

In Year 5 the double declining balance method would allow less depreciation ($17 \times .4 = 7\%$) than the straight-line method ($17/1.5 = 11\%$), so 11 percent is charged and we convert to straight line. The percentages in Table C.3 are applied to the full first cost of assets without considering the assets' salvage value.

The 1986 Tax Reform Act allows either 27.5 or 31.5 years for depreciating buildings. The half-year convention applies and only straight-line depreciation is allowed. As before, the full first cost of the assets is depreciated over the life of the assets without consideration of salvage value. If a depreciable asset is sold, regardless of the method of depreciation used, the sales price minus the then-existing undepreciated book value is added to operating income and taxed at the applicable rate.[2]

Example C.2 shows how the percentages in Table C.3 are used in computing the annual depreciation charges for an asset in the 5-year class.

TIME VALUE OF MONEY

The concept of the *time value of money* is based on two principles:

1. A sum of money in hand today will be worth more one year from now because of the earning power that money has in savings accounts and other

---

[2] Eugene F. Brigham, *Fundamentals of Financial Management,* 4th ed., (Hinsdale, IL: Dryden Press), 40–41.

EXAMPLE C.2   *Computing Annual Depreciation Charges*

The Star Coal Company purchased a light-duty truck for $20,000 on November 1. The truck is in the IRS 5-year class of assets. What are the annual depreciation charges allowed by the IRS for the truck?

Year	Depreciation Percentage	Annual Depreciation	Accumulated Depreciation
1	20%	$4,000	$ 4,000
2	32	6,400	10,400
3	19	3,800	14,200
4	12	2,400	16,600
5	11	2,200	18,800
6	6	1,200	20,000

forms of investments. The future value (f) of money is always more than the present value (p) by an amount that is equal to the *compounded interest* earned.

2. A sum of money in hand now is worth less than the sum one year from now because the sum of money one year from now implicitly includes compounded interest plus the value of the sum today. The future value must be stripped of its implicit interest earnings through discounting to compute the value of the sum today.

In compound interest calculations in business, an interest rate (i) may be selected for use in compounding or discounting that reflects any one of the following:

1. The *interest rate* that can be earned on such safe investments as savings accounts and government bonds. In this case *i* is an opportunity cost — the earnings passed up in other investments so that the money can be invested in the asset under consideration.
2. The *cutoff rate,* which is the lowest rate of return that management will accept on new investment opportunities for a business.
3. The *current* or *target rate of return* on the firm's assets.
4. The firm's *weighted cost of capital,* which is based on the inclusion of debt, stock issued by the firm, and retained earnings.

Regardless of the interpretation of the meaning of *i,* it is referred to as the *discount rate* in financial analysis.

Table C.4 presents some of the concepts and their definitions that are fundamental to a study of the time value of money. These concepts will be used in Examples C.3 and C.4 to demonstrate the calculation of present values and future values. Before studying the examples, however, turn to the end of this appendix and

TABLE C.4   *Compound Interest Concepts and Definitions*

Annuity—A series of payments of equal amounts for a specified number of time periods. **Compounding**—The arithmetic process of computing the final value of a payment or a stream of annuity payments when the interest is added. **Discounting**—The reverse of compounding: finding the present value of future cash flows.	**Future value**—The value at some specific time in the future of a present payment or a stream of annuity payments compounded at the discount rate. **Discount rate**—The interest rate applied in compound interest calculations in capital budgeting. It always refers to an annual interest rate basis. **Present value**—The value today of a stream of annuity payments or a future payment discounted at the discount rate.

EXAMPLE C.3   *Future-Value Calculations*

1. What is the future value of $1,000 invested today at 10 percent compounded annually for 5 years? Given: $p = \$1{,}000$, $i = 10\%$, and $n = 5$. Find: $f = ?$

Solution

$$f = p(f/p)_n^i = 1{,}000(f/p)_5^{10} = 1{,}000(1.611) = \$1{,}611$$

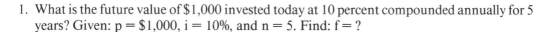

	1,000					$1,611
	↓					↑
End of Year	0	1	2	3	4	5

2. What is the future value 5 years from now of a stream of five $300 annuities paid in at the end of each year and compounded annually at 10 percent? Given: $a = \$300$, $i = 10\%$, and $n = 5$. Find: $f = ?$

Solution

$$f = a(f/a)_n^i = a(f/a)_5^{10} = 300(6.105) = \$1{,}831.50$$

		$300	$300	$300	$300	$300	
		↓	↓	↓	↓	↓	
End of Year	0	1	2	3	4	5	→ $1,831.50

become familiar with the compound interest tables. These tables are used in the examples of this section.

The factors in the compound interest tables are all multiplied by a known value such as p, f, or a to give the unknown value such as p, f, or a. For example, $(f/p)_5^{10}$ is the factor multiplied by the present value (p), which is known, to give the future value (f), which is unknown. In this scheme the known value is always found to the right of the

EXAMPLE C.4   *Present-Value Calculations*

1. How much would you have to pay in today to get back $1,000 five years from now if your payment is compounded annually at 10 percent? Given: $f = \$1{,}000$, $i = 10\%$, and $n = 5$. Find: $p = ?$

Solution

$$p = f(p/f)_n^i = f(p/f)_5^{10} = 1{,}000(.6209) = \$620.90$$

	$620.90					$1,000
	↓					↑
End of Year	0	1	2	3	4	5

2. What is the present value today of a sum worth $1,611 five years from now discounted annually at 10 percent? Note that this is the exact reverse of No. 1 in Example C.3. It demonstrates that discounting is the exact reverse process of compounding. Given: $f = \$1{,}611$, $i = 10\%$, and $n = 5$. Find: $p = ?$

Solution

$$p = f(p/f)_n^i = f(p/f)_5^{10} = 1{,}611(.6209) = \$1{,}000$$

Therefore the future value of $1,000 is $1,611, and the present value of $1,611 is $1,000.

3. What is the present value of a stream of five $300 annuities paid in at the end of each year for 5 years? The annuities are discounted annually at 10 percent. Given: $a = \$300$, $i = 10\%$, and $n = 5$. Find: $p = ?$

Solution

$$p = a(p/a)_n^i = a(p/a)_5^{10} = 300(3.791) = \$1{,}137.30$$

	$1,137.30					
	↑	300	300	300	300	300
		↓	↓	↓	↓	↓
End of Year	0	1	2	3	4	5

slash mark (/) and the unknown value is always found to the left. In the factor above, the discount rate is 10 percent and the total span of time over which the interest is compounded is 5 years. Now, take out your calculator, use a paper clip to mark the compound interest tables at the end of this appendix, and follow through the calculations in Examples C.3 and C.4.

In order to understand why the time value of money and depreciation are important concepts in financial analysis in POM, let us now study some of the ways that operations managers actually choose among capital goods.

METHODS OF FINANCIAL ANALYSIS

Among the methods of financial analysis used in business today, the following types will be studied and evaluated here: payback period, net present value (NPV), internal rate of return (IRR), and profitability index (PI). These methods may be used either to analyze and justify the purchase of individual capital goods or to analyze and compare several capital goods.

Payback Period

This method answers the question: How long does it take to get back our original investment through savings in operating expenses or other profit improvements for each capital good? The assumptions that underly this method are: (1) Investments that return the original investment faster are more profitable. (2) Investments with fast paybacks are less risky. (3) Investments with fast paybacks allow the firm to reinvest its capital in new revenue-generating projects and thus relieve capital funds shortages.

The payback period can be computed while using returns either before taxes or after taxes. An after-tax basis is more realistic and is preferred in most analyses. Example C.5 works through a comparison of investment alternatives using the payback period method. As Table C.5 summarizes, the payback period is quick and easy to compute, easily explained and understood, and considered a standard tool in financial analysis in business.

Ease of understanding is an important feature of the payback period method. A few years ago I hopped a plane to New York to meet with the board of directors of a major chemical manufacturer. I presented a proposal to build a new $20 million production facility in Florida. In summarizing, I explained that the investment promised a 12 percent internal rate of return (IRR, the discount rate that equates discounted cash inflows to cash outflows). I shall never forget the response of the chairman of the board, who was also a major stockholder in the corporation (he made or lost over $1 million when the corporation's stock price increased or decreased $1): He loudly asked, "What the hell does that mean?" While the financial vice president was desperately trying to explain the meaning of IRR, I was shuffling through my stack of transparencies for a payback period explanation. I finally found it and flashed it up on the screen. The tension was immediately eased, the chairman of the board and the rest of the board eventually approved the project, and I learned a valuable lesson in presenting the results of analytical studies. First, present the results in simple and understandable terms. Second, present the results in more detail and with more sophisticated techniques if required. This approach is also called the KISS principle (Keep It Simple, Stupid!), a principle that is commonly applied in business.

The payback period method is criticized by financial theorists because it doesn't consider any returns after the payback period and it doesn't consider the time value of money. Although one cannot deny the severity of these shortcomings, the method must have something going for it, considering its almost universal use in business.

Perhaps the greatest potential shortcoming of the payback period is that it tends to pass over investments that are big long-range winners in favor of investments with

EXAMPLE C.5   *Comparing Three Investments Using the Payback Period*

	End-of-Year Cash Flows		
Year	Investment A	Investment B	Investment C
0	($10,000)*	($20,000)*	($30,000)*
1	5,000	5,000	10,000
2	5,000	5,000	10,000
3	5,000	5,000	10,000
4	—	5,000	10,000
5	—	5,000	10,000
6	—	—	—
7	—	—	—
8	—	—	—
	$15,000	$25,000	$50,000

* Note: ( ) means an outflow, usually first cost if it occurs at the end of Year 0 or at the beginning of Year 1.

Solution

Payback period: 2 years   4 years   3 years

TABLE C.5   *Pros and Cons of Payback Period Method*

Advantages	Disadvantages
1. Quick and easy to compute; requires no compound interest or other complex calculations.	1. Does not consider returns after the payback period.
2. Easily explained and understood.	2. Does not compound or discount future earnings or costs; does not consider time value of money.
3. Universally used; considered a standard tool.	3. Builds a short-range investment bias.
4. Most effective for firms with cash shortages.	4. Inappropriate for capital assets with net cash outflows. For example, a new machine performing a new operation may have cash outflows throughout its entire life, and a payback period cannot be calculated.
5. Adapts to comparisons of investments of unequal first costs.	

modest short-range returns. Can businesses continually go for short-range payoffs or must they sometimes forgo short-range performance for long-range opportunities? The answer given by most businesses is that a balance must be struck in selecting investment alternatives between short-range and long-range performers. When used as the sole criterion for capital budgeting, the payback period may not allow this balance.

NET PRESENT VALUE (NPV)

This method of financial analysis discounts the value of the stream of after-tax cash flows back to the present. The capital good with the *least NPV* is preferred if we want the one with the least cost, and the one with the *greatest NPV* is preferred if we want the one with the greatest profits. The word *net* suggests that all cash flows are taken into account, both inflows and outflows.

NPV overcomes most of the disadvantages of the payback period method, as Table C.6 shows. It considers the time value of money and it considers all of the cash flows over the entire life of the asset. But it is more difficult to use, explain, and understand than the payback period. Moreover, when capital goods with unequal first costs are being compared, the method can give confusing results. In these cases the profitability index (PI) may be used. This method will be discussed in a later section. Because the 1986 Tax Reform Act lumps all similar capital goods into the same 3-, 5-, 7-, or 10-year categories, the lives of capital goods that would be compared by NPV will ordinarily be considered equal. In many cases, therefore, this act has eliminated a traditional objection to the use of NPV when capital goods have unequal lives.

Study Example C.6 and try to relate this example to the advantages and disadvantages of NPV from Table C.6.

TABLE C.6   *Pros and Cons of Net Present Value Method*

Advantages	Disadvantages
1. Considers time value of money; discounts future returns and costs back to the present.	1. Requires complex compound interest calculations.
2. Commonly used in business.	2. More difficult to explain and understand.
3. Considers all cash flows over the entire economic life of a capital good.	3. The selection of a discount rate is critical. Widely disparate rates can result in different investment decisions.
	4. Can be inappropriate for comparing investments with unequal first costs.

EXAMPLE C.6   Net Present Value (NPV) Method

Use NPV to select either Investment A or Investment B if the discount rate is 10 percent:

	End-of-Year After-Tax Cash Flows	
Year	Investment A	Investment B
0	($15,000)*	($15,000)*
1	7,000	10,000
2	6,000	5,000
3	6,000	5,000
4	6,000	5,000

* ( ) means a cash outflow.

Solution

	Investment A				
Year	End-of-Year After-Tax Cash Flows		Present-Value Factors $(p/f)_n^{10}$		Present Value
0	($15,000)	×	1.0000	=	($15,000)
1	7,000	×	.9091	=	6,364
2	6,000	×	.8264	=	4,958
3	6,000	×	.7513	=	4,508
4	6,000	×	.6830	=	4,098
				$NPV_A =$	$ 4,928

	Investment B				
Year	End-of-Year After-Tax Cash Flows		Present-Value Factors $(p/f)_n^{10}$		Present Value
0	($15,000)	×	1.0000	=	($15,000)
1	10,000	×	.9091	=	9,091
2	5,000	×	.8264	=	4,132
3	5,000	×	.7513	=	3,757
4	5,000	×	.6830	=	3,415
				$NPV_B =$	$ 5,395

Investment B is preferred. This results in spite of equal total cash inflows and equal first costs, because earlier cash inflows are discounted less severely than later ones.

INTERNAL RATE OF RETURN (IRR)

The internal rate of return method computes the discount rate that equates the present value of all annual net cash inflows with the first cost of the capital asset. Conceptually, IRR is similar to NPV except that in NPV the discount rate is specified and the excess of cash inflows over first cost is calculated, whereas in IRR the excess of cash inflows over first cost is set equal to zero and the discount rate is calculated. The computed IRR is then compared to either the specified cutoff rate (management's minimum rate of return for acceptable investments) or the rates of return on other investments. If the IRR for a specific investment is greater than the cutoff rate or greater than the IRR for comparable investments, the investment project is undertaken.

IRR is probably more difficult to compute, explain, and understand than NPV. Additionally, IRR applies only when present value of cash inflows is greater than first cost. This feature is a limitation in POM because when comparing two machines, for example, present value of cash outflows is almost always greater than first costs. Table C.7 indicates that IRR does overcome the major disadvantages of the payback period method and it is appropriate for comparing capital assets of differing first costs or economic lives.

TABLE C.7   *Pros and Cons of the Internal Rate of Return Method*

Advantages	*Disadvantages*
1. Considers time value of money; discounts future returns and costs back to the present.	1. Requires complex compound interest calculations.
2. Considers all cash flows over the entire economic life of a capital good.	2. Assumes that capital goods generate revenue (equates present values of cash inflows to first costs). This can be true for large groups of capital goods (profit centers), but it is usually not true for individual capital assets.
3. Is appropriate for comparing investments with unequal first costs and/or unequal lives.	3. Difficult to explain and understand.

Example C.7 uses IRR to work a problem of choosing between alternative investments. Notice that the example is simple to compute because there was one outflow of cash in Year 0 and equal annual inflows thereafter for both investments. This simple form allows us to equate the present value of a series of annuities to first cost. The computations would have been much more complex had the annual cash flows been positive, negative, and unequal.

The limited breadth of application, complexity of computations, and difficulty in explaining and understanding are impediments to business use of IRR.

EXAMPLE C.7   Internal Rate of Return (IRR) Method

Use IRR to select either Investment A or Investment B:

	End-of-Year After-Tax Cash Inflows	
Year	Investment A	Investment B
0	($50,000)	($30,000)
1	12,000	9,000
2	12,000	9,000
3	12,000	9,000
4	12,000	9,000
5	12,000	—

Solution

1. Note that Investment A has a $12,000 five-year annuity inflow stream. Find the value of the $(p/a)_n^i$ that equates the present value of the annuities to the first cost:

$$PV_A = a(p/a)_n^i = a(p/a)_5^i = \$12,000(p/a)_5^i$$

$$\text{First cost}_A = PV_A$$

$$\$50,000 = \$12,000(p/a)_5^i$$

$$(p/a)_5^i = \frac{\$50,000}{\$12,000} = 4.167$$

2. Interpolate to compute value of i_A:

$$7\%: \quad (p/a)_5^7 = 4.100$$

$$i_A: \quad (p/a)_5^i = 4.167 \left.\begin{array}{c} \end{array}\right\} .045 \left.\begin{array}{c} \end{array}\right\} .112$$

$$6\%: \quad (p/a)_5^6 = 4.212$$

$$i_A = 6\% + \frac{.045}{.112} = 6\% + .402\% = 6.40\%$$

3. Find the value of the $(p/a)_n^i$ for Investment B that equates the first cost to the present value of the annuities:

$$PV_B = a(p/a)_n^i = a(p/a)_4^i = \$9,000(p/a)_4^i$$

$$\text{First cost}_B = PV_B$$

$$\$30,000 = \$9,000(p/a)_4^i$$

$$(p/a)_4^i = \frac{\$30,000}{\$9,000} = 3.333$$

4. Interpolate to compute the value of i_B:

$$8\%: \quad (p/a)_4^8 = 3.312$$

$$\left.\begin{array}{l} i_B: \quad (p/a)_4^i = 3.333 \\[6pt] 7\%: \quad (p/a)_4^7 = 3.387 \end{array}\right\}.054 \Bigg\}.075$$

$$i_B = 7\% + \frac{.054}{.075} = 7\% + .72\% = 7.72\%$$

Investment B therefore has a higher IRR and should be selected.

PROFITABILITY INDEX (PI)

When capital goods that are being compared have unequal first costs and net cash inflows, NPV is an inappropriate financial analysis method. NPV could, for example, show that these two investments are equally attractive:

	Capital Good A	Capital Good B
First cost	$1,000,000	$200,000
NPV	100,000	100,000

We would obviously prefer Investment B because its return compared to its first cost is much greater than that of Investment A. The PI modifies the NPV to overcome this deficiency when there are unequal first costs and net cash inflows:

$$PI = \frac{\text{First cost} + \text{NPV}}{\text{First cost}}$$

$$PI_A = \frac{\text{First cost} + \text{NPV}_A}{\text{First cost}} = \frac{1,000,000 + 100,000}{1,000,000} = 1.10$$

$$PI_B = \frac{\text{First cost} + \text{NPV}_B}{\text{First cost}} = \frac{200,000 + 100,000}{200,000} = 1.50$$

Because Investment B has a greater PI, it is preferred.

When capital goods have unequal first costs and net cash outflows, NPV ordinarily is effective in comparing their cash flows and PI would not necessarily be preferred to NPV.

EVALUATION OF METHODS

All of the financial analysis methods presented in this section are used in business today, each with varying frequency. Because no single method applies universally in all situations, analysts must thoroughly understand the conditions under which each method is appropriate. Table C.8 summarizes the conditions appropriate for the use of each method when alternative investments are to be compared.

TABLE C.8 *A Comparison of Financial Analysis Methods: Which Methods Are Appropriate?*

Financial Analysis Method	*Equal Lives and Equal First Costs*	*Unequal First Costs*	*Cash Inflow ≥ Cash Outflow*	*Cash Outflow ≥ Cash Inflow*
1. Payback period	X	X	X	
2. NPV	X	X*	X*	X
3. IRR	X	X	X	
4. PI	X	X	X	

* Note: NPV is appropriate for comparing investments with unequal first costs only when the objective is to minimize the cash outflows over the economic lives. NPV is inappropriate when investments with unequal first costs have net cash inflows.

Now that we are equipped with an understanding of financial analysis concepts and methods, let us focus on some concrete examples of classic financial decisions in POM.

CLASSIC FINANCIAL ANALYSIS DECISIONS IN POM

Three financial analysis decisions stand out in frequency of occurrence in POM: equipment replacement, choice of equipment, and make-or-buy. These types of investment decisions are demonstrated in Examples C.8, C.9, and C.10. When studying these examples, you may find it helpful to refer to Table C.8 to determine which financial analysis methods are appropriate in each example.

EXAMPLE C.8 An Equipment Replacement Decision

Margaret Cooper is director of the product research department at Aerojet-Specific Corporation. She manages the department's personnel in their duties in determining the level of pressure at which the firm's products fail. One piece of equipment is critical in these tests — a 250-ton high-speed hydraulic press. The press has been fully depreciated and has a salvage value of $2,000. A new press is being considered that will reduce maintenance costs, reduce downtime, and increase the speed of the pressing operation. The new press falls into the 3-year

IRS depreciation category and is expected to have an economic life of 5 years. It has a first cost of $200,000, an annual operating cost savings of $60,000, and a salvage value of $30,000. The firm would use a discount rate of 10 percent and a tax rate of 40 percent. **(a)** Use net present value to determine if Ms. Cooper should recommend buying the new press. **(b)** Use the payback period method to determine if Ms. Cooper should recommend buying the new press if management uses 4 years as the maximum after-tax payback period for similar investments.

Solution

a. Net present value of new press:
   1. First, compute the tax savings from depreciation:

Year	IRS Depreciation Allowable	Annual Depreciation	Accumulated Depreciation	Tax Savings ($t \times$ Annual Depreciation)
1	33%	$66,000	$ 66,000	$26,400
2	45	90,000	156,000	36,000
3	15	30,000	186,000	12,000
4	7	14,000	200,000	5,600

   2. Now, compute the NPV:

	Pretax Amount	After-Tax Amount	Year of Occurrence	Present-Value Factor	Present Value
Cash Outflow:					
First cost	($200,000)	($200,000)	0	1.000	($200,000)
Cash Inflows:					
Cost savings	60,000	36,000	1–5	$(p/a)_5^{10} = 3.791$	136,476
Depreciation					
tax savings	66,000	26,400	1	$(p/f)_1^{10} = .9091$	24,000
	90,000	36,000	2	$(p/f)_2^{10} = .8264$	29,750
	30,000	12,000	3	$(p/f)_3^{10} = .7513$	9,016
	14,000	5,600	4	$(p/f)_4^{10} = .6830$	3,825
Salvage value					
(new)	30,000	18,000	5	$(p/f)_5^{10} = .6209$	11,176
Salvage value					
(old)	2,000	1,200	0	1.000	1,200
				NPV =	$ 15,443

Yes, the firm should buy the new press because a NPV of $15,443 means that the investment will return the 10 percent discount rate and still have a present value of cash inflows in excess of first cost.

b. Payback period:

Year	After-Tax Depreciation Tax Savings	After-Tax Operating Cost Savings	First Cost	After-Tax Salvage Value	Annual After-Tax Cash Flows	Accumulated After-Tax Cash Inflows
0	—	—	($200,000)	$1,200	($198,800)	
1	$26,400	$36,000	—	—	62,400	$ 62,400
2	36,000	36,000	—	—	72,000	134,400
3	12,000	36,000	—	—	48,000	182,400
4	5,600	36,000	—	—	41,600	224,000
5	—	36,000	—	$18,000	54,000	278,000

The payback period is 3.4 years [3 + ($198,800 − $182,400)/$41,600], which is within management's maximum payback period for similar investments. The firm should therefore purchase the new press.

EXAMPLE C.9   A Choice of Equipment Decision

Cal-Coop, a large agricultural corporation operating in the Imperial Valley of California, is now outfitting one of its divisions with tomato-harvesting equipment. Two designs are being considered: S, which is semiautomatic, and A, which is almost fully automatic. The two designs, both with equal capacities, exhibit the following costs:

	Design S	Design A
First cost	$400,000	$700,000
IRS life category	5-year	5-year
Estimated economic life	6 years	6 years
Labor cost per year	$85,000	$10,000
Annual maintenance and supplies	10,000	5,000
Salvage value	40,000	150,000

If Cal-Coop uses a standard 4½-year payback period for similar investments and its tax rate is 40 percent, use the payback period method to choose between the two equipment designs. The payback period can be used only if we assume that one of the two designs will be selected. Then we must determine if the additional investment required for Design A can be justified on the basis of annual labor cost savings and annual maintenance and supplies cost savings.

Solution

1. Compute depreciation for both designs:

Design	Year	IRS Depreciation Allowable	Annual Depreciation	Accumulated Depreciation	Tax Savings ($t \times$ Annual Depreciation)
	1	20%	$ 80,000	$ 80,000	$ 32,000
	2	32	128,000	208,000	51,200
S	3	19	76,000	284,000	30,400
	4	12	48,000	332,000	19,200
	5	11	44,000	376,000	17,600
	6	6	24,000	400,000	9,600
	1	20%	$140,000	$140,000	$ 56,000
	2	32	224,000	364,000	89,600
A	3	19	133,000	497,000	53,200
	4	12	84,000	581,000	33,600
	5	11	77,000	658,000	30,800
	6	6	42,000	700,000	16,800

2. Next, compute the tax savings from depreciation of the additional first cost for Design A over Design S:

Year	Tax Savings, Design A	Tax Savings, Design S	Difference in Tax Savings of A over S
1	$56,000	$32,000	$24,000
2	89,600	51,200	38,400
3	53,200	30,400	22,800
4	33,600	19,200	14,400
5	30,800	17,600	13,200
6	16,800	9,600	7,200

3. Next, compute the payback period for the additional investment for Design A. The annual after-tax cost savings of the automatic design over the semiautomatic design and the additional first cost are:

$$\text{Annual cost savings} = (1 - t)(\text{Annual operating cost savings})$$
$$= (1 - .4)(\text{Labor savings} + \text{Maintenance and supplies savings})$$
$$= (.6)(\$75,000 + \$5,000) = .6(\$80,000) = \$48,000$$

$$\text{Additional first cost} = (\text{First cost for A}) - (\text{First cost for S})$$
$$= \$700,000 - \$400,000 = \$300,000$$

$$\text{Additional salvage value} = (1 - t)[(\text{Salvage value for A}) - (\text{Salvage value for S})]$$
$$= .6(\$150,000 - \$40,000) = \$66,000$$

Year	After-Tax Depreciation Tax Savings	After-Tax Operating Cost Savings	First Cost	After-Tax Salvage Value	Annual After-Tax Cash Flows	Accumulated After-Tax Cash Inflows
0	—	—	($300,000)	—	($300,000)	—
1	$24,000	$48,000	—	—	72,000	$ 72,000
2	38,400	48,000	—	—	86,400	158,400
3	22,800	48,000	—	—	70,800	229,200
4	14,400	48,000	—	—	62,400	291,600
5	13,200	48,000	—	—	61,200	352,800
6	7,200	48,000	—	$66,000	121,200	474,000

The payback period is 4.1 years [4 + ($300,000 − $291,600)/$61,200]. The additional outlay for the automatic design is therefore within management's payback period guidelines of 4½ years and Design A should be purchased.

EXAMPLE C.10   A Make-or-Buy Decision

Niko Inc. manufactures hand-held electronic calculators. When the firm was small and growing, it purchased most of the components that go into calculators from outside suppliers. Now that Niko has grown to the point that funds for capital investment are available from profits, various investment opportunities are being investigated. One such opportunity involves establishing an automated production line for manufacturing electronic chips, a major component used in calculators and currently purchased from Florida Instruments. The present purchase price of chips is $4.25 per calculator. Niko estimates that the fully equipped department will cost $1.5 million; the equipment falls into the 5-year IRS depreciation category; a 6-year economic life is expected; the variable cost, including labor, materials, and overhead, will total $3 per calculator; the salvage value of the equipment will be $300,000; and 500,000 calculators per year can be sold. If a tax rate of 40 percent and a discount rate of 10 percent are used: **(a)** Use NPV to determine if Niko should make or buy the chips. **(b)** Use the payback period after taxes to determine whether Niko should make or buy the chips if management uses a 3-year maximum payback period for similar investments.

Solution

a. Compute the NPV:
   1. First, compute the tax savings from depreciation:

Year	IRS Depreciation Allowable	Annual Depreciation	Accumulated Depreciation	Tax Savings $(t \times Annual$ Depreciation)
1	20%	$300,000	$ 300,000	$120,000
2	32	480,000	780,000	192,000
3	19	285,000	1,065,000	114,000
4	12	180,000	1,245,000	72,000
5	11	165,000	1,410,000	66,000
6	6	90,000	1,500,000	36,000

   2. Compute the NPV:

	Pretax Amount	After-Tax Amount	Year of Occurrence	Present-Value Factor	Present Value
Cash outflow:					
First cost	($1,500,000)	($1,500,000)	0	1.000	($1,500,000)
Cash inflows:					
Cost savings ($1.25/ unit)	625,000	375,000	1–6	$(p/a)_6^{10} = 4.355$	1,633,125
Depreciation tax savings	300,000	120,000	1	$(p/f)_1^{10} = .9091$	109,092
	480,000	192,000	2	$(p/f)_2^{10} = .8264$	158,669
	285,000	114,000	3	$(p/f)_3^{10} = .7513$	85,648
	180,000	72,000	4	$(p/f)_4^{10} = .6830$	49,176
	165,000	66,000	5	$(p/f)_5^{10} = .6209$	40,979
	90,000	36,000	6	$(p/f)_6^{10} = .5645$	20,322
Salvage value	300,000	180,000	6	$(p/f)_6^{10} = .5645$	$ 101,610
				NPV =	$ 698,621

A NPV of $698,621 indicates that making the chips returns the 10 percent discount rate and $698,621 over the first cost. Thus Niko should make the chips.

b. Payback period:

Year	After-Tax Depreciation Tax Savings	After-Tax Operating Cost Savings	Additional First Cost	After-Tax Salvage Value	Annual After-Tax Cash Flow	Accumulated After-Tax Cash Inflows
0	—	—	($1,500,000)	—	($1,500,000)	—
1	$120,000	$375,000	—	—	495,000	$ 495,000
2	192,000	375,000	—	—	567,000	1,062,000
3	114,000	375,000	—	—	489,000	1,551,000

Year	After-Tax Depreciation Tax Savings	After-Tax Operating Cost Savings	Additional First Cost	After-Tax Salvage Value	Annual After-Tax Cash Flow	Accumulated After-Tax Cash Inflows
4	72,000	375,000	—	—	447,000	1,998,000
5	66,000	375,000	—	—	441,000	2,439,000
6	36,000	375,000	—	$180,000	591,000	3,030,000

The payback period is 2.9 years [2 + ($1,500,000 − $1,062,000)/$489,000]. The project is therefore within management's maximum payback period of 3 years for similar investments.

The NPV and payback period both confirm that the chips should be made rather than bought.

In these examples note that when changes in operating expenses are converted from pretax to after-tax amounts a $(1-t)$ factor is used. Let's use an example to demonstrate when $t = .4$:

	Situation A	Situation B
Pretax profits	$100,000	$100,000
Operating expenses	—	10,000
Taxable profits	$100,000	$ 90,000
Taxes	40,000	36,000
After-tax profits	$ 60,000	$ 54,000
After-tax impact of operating expenses		(6,000)

These two situations (A and B) are identical except that Situation A does not have the $10,000 in operating expenses. How do the after-tax profits differ? They differ by $6,000, which equals $(1-t) \times$ pretax operating expenses, or $(.6) \times \$10,000$. Anytime you encounter operating expenses or operating expense savings in financial analysis, these are converted to after-tax amounts by multiplying them by $(1-t)$. Depreciation, on the other hand, has been demonstrated to use t as the factor for converting pretax depreciation to after-tax savings.

The classic investment decisions demonstrated in these examples are realistic decisions that are made periodically in POM. These decisions are important for many reasons but particularly because they are long-lasting. How a company spends its investment dollars determines in large part its future course in terms of production capacity, diversification, expansion, and other elements of operations strategy. Wrong investment decisions in POM must be lived with for a long time by managers. Good investment decisions generate improved profits well into the future. The longevity of these decisions and a continuing condition of scarce and expensive capital funds cause companies today to scrutinize these decisions closely. The analysis methods presented in this appendix can serve you well in analyzing and justifying capital funds outlays in POM.

COMPOUND INTEREST TABLES

(5%)

	TO FIND F, GIVEN P: $(1 + i)^n$	TO FIND P, GIVEN F: $\dfrac{1}{(1+i)^n}$	TO FIND A, GIVEN F: $\dfrac{i}{(1+i)^n - 1}$	TO FIND A, GIVEN P: $\dfrac{i(1+i)^n}{(1+i)^n - 1}$	TO FIND F, GIVEN A: $\dfrac{(1+i)^n - 1}{i}$	TO FIND P, GIVEN A: $\dfrac{(1+i)^n - 1}{i(1+i)^n}$
n	$(f/p)_n^5$	$(p/f)_n^5$	$(a/f)_n^5$	$(a/p)_n^5$	$(f/a)_n^5$	$(p/a)_n^5$
1	1.050	0.9524	1.00000	1.05000	1.000	0.952
2	1.102	0.9070	0.48780	0.53780	2.050	1.859
3	1.158	0.8638	0.31721	0.36721	3.152	2.723
4	1.216	0.8227	0.23201	0.28201	4.310	3.546
5	1.276	0.7835	0.18097	0.23097	5.526	4.329
6	1.340	0.7462	0.14702	0.19702	6.802	5.076
7	1.407	0.7107	0.12282	0.17282	8.142	5.786
8	1.477	0.6768	0.10472	0.15472	9.549	6.463
9	1.551	0.6446	0.09069	0.14069	11.027	7.108
10	1.629	0.6139	0.07950	0.12950	12.578	7.722
11	1.710	0.5847	0.07039	0.12039	14.207	8.306
12	1.796	0.5568	0.06283	0.11283	15.917	8.863
13	1.886	0.5303	0.05646	0.10646	17.713	9.394
14	1.980	0.5051	0.05102	0.10102	19.599	9.899
15	2.079	0.4810	0.04634	0.09634	21.579	10.380
16	2.183	0.4581	0.04227	0.09227	23.657	10.838
17	2.292	0.4363	0.03870	0.08870	25.840	11.274
18	2.407	0.4155	0.03555	0.08555	28.132	11.690
19	2.527	0.3957	0.03275	0.08275	30.539	12.085
20	2.653	0.3769	0.03024	0.08024	33.066	12.462

(10%)

	TO FIND F, GIVEN P: $(1 + i)^n$	TO FIND P, GIVEN F: $\dfrac{1}{(1+i)^n}$	TO FIND A, GIVEN F: $\dfrac{i}{(1+i)^n - 1}$	TO FIND A, GIVEN P: $\dfrac{i(1+i)^n}{(1+i)^n - 1}$	TO FIND F, GIVEN A: $\dfrac{(1+i)^n - 1}{i}$	TO FIND P, GIVEN A: $\dfrac{(1+i)^n - 1}{i(1+i)^n}$
n	$(f/p)_n^{10}$	$(p/f)_n^{10}$	$(a/f)_n^{10}$	$(a/p)_n^{10}$	$(f/a)_n^{10}$	$(p/a)_n^{10}$
1	1.100	0.9091	1.00000	1.10000	1.000	0.909
2	1.210	0.8264	0.47619	0.57619	2.100	1.736
3	1.331	0.7513	0.30211	0.40211	3.310	2.487
4	1.464	0.6830	0.21547	0.31547	4.641	3.170
5	1.611	0.6209	0.16380	0.26380	6.105	3.791
6	1.772	0.5645	0.12961	0.22961	7.716	4.355
7	1.949	0.5132	0.10541	0.20541	9.487	4.868
8	2.144	0.4665	0.08744	0.18744	11.436	5.335
9	2.358	0.4241	0.07364	0.17364	13.579	5.759
10	2.594	0.3855	0.06275	0.16275	15.937	6.145
11	2.853	0.3505	0.05396	0.15396	18.531	6.495
12	3.138	0.3186	0.04676	0.14676	21.384	6.814
13	3.452	0.2897	0.04078	0.14078	24.523	7.103
14	3.797	0.2633	0.03575	0.13575	27.975	7.367
15	4.177	0.2394	0.03147	0.13147	31.772	7.606
16	4.595	0.2176	0.02782	0.12782	35.950	7.824
17	5.054	0.1978	0.02466	0.12466	40.545	8.022
18	5.560	0.1799	0.02193	0.12193	45.599	8.201
19	6.116	0.1635	0.01955	0.11955	51.159	8.365
20	6.727	0.1486	0.01746	0.11746	57.275	8.514

continued

■ ■

Compound Interest Tables (Continued)

(15%)

n	TO FIND F, GIVEN P: $(1+i)^n$ $(f/p)_n^{15}$	TO FIND P, GIVEN F: $\dfrac{1}{(1+i)^n}$ $(p/f)_n^{15}$	TO FIND A, GIVEN F: $\dfrac{i}{(1+i)^n-1}$ $(a/f)_n^{15}$	TO FIND A, GIVEN P: $\dfrac{i(1+i)^n}{(1+i)^n-1}$ $(a/p)_n^{15}$	TO FIND F, GIVEN A: $\dfrac{(1+i)^n-1}{i}$ $(f/a)_n^{15}$	TO FIND P, GIVEN A: $\dfrac{(1+i)^n-1}{i(1+i)^n}$ $(p/a)_n^{15}$
1	1.150	0.8696	1.00000	1.15000	1.000	0.870
2	1.322	0.7561	0.46512	0.61512	2.150	1.626
3	1.521	0.6575	0.28798	0.43798	3.472	2.283
4	1.749	0.5718	0.20027	0.35027	4.993	2.855
5	2.011	0.4972	0.14832	0.29832	6.742	3.352
6	2.313	0.4323	0.11424	0.26424	8.754	3.784
7	2.660	0.3759	0.09036	0.24036	11.067	4.160
8	3.059	0.3269	0.07285	0.22285	13.727	4.487
9	3.518	0.2843	0.05957	0.20957	16.786	4.772
10	4.046	0.2472	0.04925	0.19925	20.304	5.019
11	4.652	0.2149	0.04107	0.19107	24.349	5.234
12	5.350	0.1869	0.03448	0.18448	29.002	5.421
13	6.153	0.1625	0.02911	0.17911	34.352	5.583
14	7.076	0.1413	0.02469	0.17469	40.505	5.724
15	8.137	0.1229	0.02102	0.17102	47.580	5.847
16	9.358	0.1069	0.01795	0.16795	55.717	5.954
17	10.761	0.0929	0.01537	0.16537	65.075	6.047
18	12.375	0.0808	0.01319	0.16319	75.836	6.128
19	14.232	0.0703	0.01134	0.16134	88.212	6.198
20	16.367	0.0611	0.00976	0.15976	102.444	6.259

(20%)

n	TO FIND F, GIVEN P: $(1+i)^n$ $(f/p)_n^{20}$	TO FIND P, GIVEN F: $\dfrac{1}{(1+i)^n}$ $(p/f)_n^{20}$	TO FIND A, GIVEN F: $\dfrac{i}{(1+i)^n-1}$ $(a/f)_n^{20}$	TO FIND A, GIVEN P: $\dfrac{i(1+i)^n}{(1+i)^n-1}$ $(a/p)_n^{20}$	TO FIND F, GIVEN A: $\dfrac{(1+i)^n-1}{i}$ $(f/a)_n^{20}$	TO FIND P, GIVEN A: $\dfrac{(1+i)^n-1}{i(1+i)^n}$ $(p/a)_n^{20}$
1	1.200	0.8333	1.00000	1.20000	1.000	0.833
2	1.440	0.6944	0.45455	0.65455	2.200	1.528
3	1.728	0.5787	0.27473	0.47473	3.640	2.106
4	2.074	0.4823	0.18629	0.38629	5.368	2.589
5	2.488	0.4019	0.13438	0.33438	7.442	2.991
6	2.986	0.3349	0.10071	0.30071	9.930	3.326
7	3.583	0.2791	0.07742	0.27742	12.916	3.605
8	4.300	0.2326	0.06061	0.26061	16.499	3.837
9	5.160	0.1938	0.04808	0.24808	20.799	4.031
10	6.192	0.1615	0.03852	0.23852	25.959	4.192
11	7.430	0.1346	0.03110	0.23110	32.150	4.327
12	8.916	0.1122	0.02526	0.22526	39.581	4.439
13	10.699	0.0935	0.02062	0.22062	48.497	4.533
14	12.839	0.0779	0.01689	0.21689	59.196	4.611
15	15.407	0.0649	0.01388	0.21388	72.035	4.675
16	18.488	0.0541	0.01144	0.21144	87.442	4.730
17	22.186	0.0451	0.00944	0.20944	105.931	4.775
18	26.623	0.0376	0.00781	0.20781	128.117	4.812
19	31.948	0.0313	0.00646	0.20646	154.740	4.843
20	38.338	0.0261	0.00536	0.20536	186.688	4.870

REVIEW AND DISCUSSION QUESTIONS

1. Define *capital goods.* Give five examples of capital goods in POM.
2. Define the following terms: *depreciation, salvage value, first cost, taxes, operating expenses.*
3. Define the following terms: *compound interest rate, cutoff rate.*
4. Why is depreciation a noncash expense?
5. Does depreciation directly affect profits? Why or why not?
6. Define the following terms: *annuity, discount rate, future value, compounding, discounting, present value.*
7. Name the advantages and disadvantages of these financial analysis methods:
   a. payback period
   b. net present value (NPV)
   c. internal rate of return (IRR)
8. What disadvantages of the payback period method does NPV overcome?
9. What disadvantages of NPV does PI overcome?
10. Under what conditions should NPV not be used?
11. Under what conditions should PI not be used?

PROBLEMS

Depreciation

1. Design Corporation is an engineering service company servicing the greater Phoenix area construction contractors with structural testing. A new core failure machine has been purchased for $75,000. The new machine falls in the 7-year IRS depreciation category. The machine is expected to have a salvage value of $10,000 at the end of 8 years. If the firm is in the 30 percent tax bracket, what are the annual tax savings from depreciation of the machine?
2. The purchasing department of Expando Corporation, a company that produces highway bridge expandable joints, has just purchased a new minicomputer for instantaneously accessing inventory records. The computer costs $25,000, it is expected to have a salvage value of $5,000 at the end of its 5-year economic life, and it falls into the 3-year IRS depreciation category. What are the annual depreciation charges over its economic life?
3. The maintenance shop at the Bilt-Rite garment factory needs a new welding machine. A new machine costs $1,750 and falls into the 7-year IRS depreciation category. If the machine is expected to have a salvage value of $50 at the end of 8 years and the firm's tax rate is 45 percent, what are the annual tax savings from depreciation of the welding machine?
4. Speed-Flyte Corporation conducts air tunnel tests for aircraft and other airborne products. A new test facility is proposed that will cost $400,000 and will have a

salvage value of $70,000 at the end of 4 years. What are the annual depreciation charges if the facility falls into the 3-year IRS depreciation category?

Compound Interest

5. What is the future value of the following sums?
   a. Present value = $5,000 in 5 years at 10 percent compounded annually.
   b. Five annuities of $500 paid in at the end of each year at 5 percent compounded annually at the end of 5 years.
   c. Six annuities of $1,000 paid in at the end of each year at 20 percent compounded annually at the end of 6 years.

6. What is the present value of the following sums?
   a. Future value = $1,000 in 5 years at 10 percent compounded annually.
   b. Five annuities of $1,000 paid in at the end of each year at 5 percent compounded annually.
   c. Six annuities of $1,000 paid in at the beginning of each year at 20 percent compounded annually.

7. What single payment 10 years from now is equivalent to a $10,000 payment 2 years from now, if the discount rate is 15 percent compounded annually?

8. What five annuities beginning today are equivalent to two payments of $10,000, one made at the end of 2 years and the other one at the end of 4 years, if the discount rate is 10 percent compounded annually?

Financial Analysis Decisions

9. The OK Trucking Company has a fleet of over-the-road trucks operating in southeastern Oklahoma. The fleet was purchased new 10 years ago and is obsolete and badly deteriorated. OK estimates that a new fleet would cost $650,000 and would save $200,000 per year in operating and maintenance expenses. If taxes are ignored, the old fleet has zero salvage value, the fleet falls into the IRS 5-year depreciation category, and the new fleet is expected to have a zero salvage value at the end of 5 years, what is the payback period of the new fleet?

10. Bill Binton operates a small manufacturing company in Detroit. His firm manufactures side-view mirrors for one of the major auto manufacturers. He presently buys the bolts that are used to assemble the mirrors, but he wonders if he should make them since this business is expected to remain strong. He uses 10 million bolts per year at a price of $.01 each. He can buy, install, and debug a machine for $25,000. The machine will have an economic life of 6 years and a salvage value of $5,000, and will fall into the IRS 5-year depreciation category. Bill estimates that labor, material, and overhead would cost about $.009 per bolt. He will buy the machine only if it pays itself out in savings after taxes in 3½ years or less at a tax rate of 30 percent. Use payback period after taxes to recommend whether the bolts should be purchased or manufactured.

11. Geotherm Research Corporation, located in Jakes Pass, Idaho, performs geothermal energy conversion research on federal and state contracts. The firm is experiencing a substantial growth and wishes to replace its old experimental machines with new ones. The new machinery will cost $500,000 and will improve operating efficiency by $100,000 per year. If Geotherm has a tax rate of 45 percent, the machinery falls into the IRS 3-year depreciation category, a 10 percent cutoff rate is used, an economic life of 5 years is expected, and the old machinery and new machinery are expected to have a salvage value of zero, use NPV to recommend if the new machinery should be purchased.

12. The Cloud Kist Almond Wholesaling Company of Morgan Hill, California, warehouses enormous quantities of almonds and sells them to retailers. The company is building a new warehouse facility, and some disagreement has arisen concerning what type of forklift trucks to buy for the facility. Two designs appear to be the least costly to operate: electric and propane. The trucks have these characteristics:

	Electric	*Propane*
First cost	$14,500	$7,800
Economic life	8 years	8 years
IRS depreciation category	7 years	7 years
Salvage value	$1,000	$2,000
Annual fuel cost	300	2,500
Annual maintenance cost	1,500	200

If the discount rate is 15 percent, the tax rate is 40 percent, and NPV is used, recommend which forklift design Cloud Kist should purchase.

13. Debits Inc., a CPA firm, is about to buy a computer. Management is torn between two designs, each with unique costs and savings:

	Computer Y	*Computer Z*
First cost	$50,000	$75,000
Economic life	5 years	5 years
IRS depreciation category	3 years	3 years
Salvage value	$ 5,000	$10,000
Annual operating cost	12,000	14,000
Annual savings through increased efficiency	15,000	20,000

Use the after-tax payback period method to recommend which computer should be purchased if the company's tax rate is 35 percent and if the maximum payback period allowed is 5 years.

14. The electronic maintenance and calibration department at General Hospital in Glen Falls, New York, is trying to decide which of two designs for an electronic diagnostic unit to purchase. The designs, A and B, appear to have about the same performance features, but their unique designs result in different costs:

	Design A	*Design B*
First cost	$50,000	$25,000
Economic life	6 years	6 years
IRS depreciation category	5 years	5 years
Salvage value	0	0
Annual operating cost savings	$30,000	$14,000

If the tax rate is 45 percent and the discount rate is 20 percent, use PI to determine which design should be purchased.

SELECTED BIBLIOGRAPHY

Brigham, Eugene F., *Fundamentals of Financial Management,* 4th ed. (Hinsdale, IL: Dryden Press, 1986).

Kiess, Donald E., and Jerry J. Weygandt, *Intermediate Accounting,* 4th ed. (New York: Wiley, 1983).

Weston, J. Fred., and Thomas E. Copeland, *Managerial Finance,* 8th ed. (Hinsdale, IL: Dryden Press, 1986).

D WAITING LINES AND COMPUTER SIMULATION

WAITING LINES

Numerous situations occur in POM where waiting lines form while services are being performed. Here are just a few instances:

1. Computer programs are waiting to be processed at a computer center.
2. Workers are waiting to "clock in" at the company gate.
3. Customers are waiting to be served at a bank teller's window.
4. Parts are waiting to be processed at a manufacturing operation.
5. Machines are waiting to be repaired at a maintenance shop.
6. Customers are waiting to buy tickets at an airline ticket counter.
7. Trucks are waiting to unload their cargo at an unloading dock.

In these situations managers don't necessarily plan for waiting lines to form; rather, waiting lines are an inevitable characteristic of these operations.

What causes waiting lines to form? When people, parts, machines, computer programs, or trucks are arriving at service centers irregularly and the capacity of service centers cannot be expanded or contracted to exactly meet the needs of these arrivals, waiting lines will always result. Even if managers *could* expand service center capacities to exactly meet the demands of these irregular arrivals, the pattern of this irregularity is often so unpredictable that managers can't respond fast enough to expand service center capacities; therefore waiting lines form.

To further complicate the analysis of waiting lines, we don't usually know with certainty how long it will take to service each arrival. In banks, for example, some customers may take only about a minute to be served because they may only want to cash a small check or make a deposit. Other customers may require 15 to 20 minutes to service, particularly if they have a whole moneybag full of commercial transactions to complete.

Waiting lines typically have these characteristics:

1. Arrival patterns are irregular or random. Although we may know the average number of arrivals per time period to expect, we don't know for certain how many will arrive in any specific time period.
2. Service times vary among arrivals. Although we may know the average time required to service an arrival, we don't know in advance how long it will take to service each arrival.

Some managers plan service center capacities to meet the average condition plus a safety factor. For example, if a bank manager knows that about 50 customers per hour on the average must be serviced at teller windows, enough tellers, cash, supplies, open teller windows, and waiting areas would be provided to service an average of about 70 customers per hour. This safety factor approach is based upon the fact that, although 50 customers per hour arrive on the average, as few as 20 or as many as 90 customers can arrive in any one hour just through chance. Because arrival patterns are irregular or random, 20 minutes may go by without *any* customers and then 15 customers may flood through the doors.

Although the safety factor approach described above is observed in POM practice, more precise analysis techniques have evolved that provide managers with better information to plan waiting line service center capacities. The first recorded systematic study of waiting lines was performed by A. K. Erlang, a Danish mathematician working for the Copenhagen Telephone Company in 1917. Erlang's early work has been methodically expanded until today much is known about the behavior of waiting lines.

This body of knowledge about waiting lines is often referred to today as *queuing theory,* and waiting lines are called *queues.* Before we examine the concepts of queuing theory and its analysis techniques, study the terminology of queues in Table D.1. Figure D.1. shows four queuing system structures. A *single-channel, single-phase* system has only one waiting line, or channel, and the service is performed in only one step, or phase. Single-booth theater ticket sales, machines waiting to be repaired at a repair center, and parts waiting to be processèd at a manufacturing operation are examples of single-channel, single-phase queuing systems.

When more than one waiting line can form, as in checkout counters at supermarkets, *multichannel queuing systems* result. As the service performed becomes more complex, as in the case of two or more downstream manufacturing operations,

■■

TABLE D.1   *Terminology of Queues*

1. **Arrival**—One unit of the arrival rate distribution. Occurs when one person, machine, part, etc., arrives and demands service. Each of the units may continue to be called an arrival while in the service system.
2. **Arrival rate (λ)**—The rate at which things or persons arrive, in arrivals per unit of time (e.g., persons per hour). Arrival rate is usually normal or Poisson distributed.
3. **Channels**—The number of waiting lines in a service system. A single-channel system would have only one line and a multichannel system would have two or more lines.
4. **Queue**—A waiting line.
5. **Queue discipline**—The rules that determine the order in which arrivals are sequenced through service systems. Some common queue disciplines are first-come first-served, shortest processing time, critical ratio, and most valuable customers served first.
6. **Queue length**—The number of arrivals waiting to be serviced.

7. **Service phases**—The number of steps in servicing arrivals. A single-phase service system would have only one service step, whereas a multiphase system would have two or more service steps.
8. **Service (rate) (μ)**—The rate that arrivals are serviced, in arrivals per unit of time (e.g., per hour). Service rate is usually constant, normal, or Poisson distributed.
9. **Service time ($1/\mu$)**—The time it takes to service an arrival, expressed in minutes (or hours, days, etc.) per arrival. The measure does not include waiting time.
10. **Time in system**—The total time that arrivals spend in system, including both waiting time and service time.
11. **Utilization (P_n)**—The degree to which any part of a service system is occupied by an arrival. Usually expressed as the probability that *n* arrivals are in the system.
12. **Waiting time**—The amount of time an arrival spends in queue.

■■

FIGURE D.1 *Queuing System Structures*

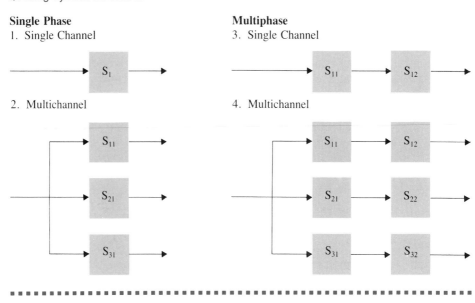

Single Phase
1. Single Channel

2. Multichannel

Multiphase
3. Single Channel

4. Multichannel

---

more than one step is needed in performing services. These are referred to as *multiphase queuing systems.*

Real-world waiting line situations in POM seldom fit the neat structures displayed in Figure D.1. Rather, real queuing systems tend to be combinations and hybrids of these structures. The fuzziness and complexity of real queuing systems have perhaps been the greatest obstacles to straightforward mathematical analysis of waiting lines in practice. As an introduction to queuing theory, we shall examine here some simple models that have been used to analyze waiting lines in POM. But first, what information do managers usually need to know about waiting lines?

1. Given that a service system has been designed to service a certain number of arrivals per hour on the average:
   a. What is the average number of units waiting?
   b. What is the average time each unit spends waiting?
   c. What is the average number of units waiting and being served — in other words, in the system?
   d. What is the average time each unit spends in the system?
   e. What percentage of time is the system empty?
   f. What is the probability that *n* units will be in the system?
2. Or, given that management sets policies that limit the average number of units waiting, average number of units in the system, average time each unit waits, average time each unit is in the system, or the percentage of time that the system is empty, what service center capacity is necessary to comply with these management policies?

■ ■

TABLE D.2   *Definitions of Variables for Queuing Models*

λ (lambda) = arrival rate — average number of arrivals per unit of time	N = number of channels in multichannel system
μ (mu) = service rate — average number of arrivals that can be serviced per unit of time	P_n = probability that there are exactly n arrivals in the system
n = number of arrivals in the system	Q = maximum number of arrivals that can be in the system (sum of arrivals being served and waiting)
$\bar{n}_1$ = average number of arrivals waiting	$\bar{t}_1$ = average time arrivals wait
$\bar{n}_s$ = average number of arrivals in the system	$\bar{t}_s$ = average time arrivals are in the system

■ ■

We shall present here four models that have been used to study particular queuing systems. Table D.2 above and Table D.3 on page D-7 show the characteristics of these queuing systems, the formulas for analyzing them, and the definitions of variables that are introduced.

MODEL 1: SINGLE CHANNEL, SINGLE PHASE

Waiting lines that are single channel, single phase can usually be analyzed by *Model 1*. When the arrival rate (λ) and service rate (μ) are known, then the average number of arrivals in the line ($\bar{n}_1$), average number of arrivals in the system ($\bar{n}_s$), average time each arrival waits ($\bar{t}_1$), average time each arrival is in the system ($\bar{t}_s$), and the probability of exactly n arrivals being in the system (P_n) can all be computed. Example D.1 demonstrates how the formulas of this model are applied.

EXAMPLE D.1   *Analyzing Waiting Lines at XYZ Manufacturing Company*

The XYZ Manufacturing Company produces artificial eardrum assemblies made of a specially developed material and processed through its own shop. The units are used in human eardrum transplant operations. The bottleneck operation (the operation with the lowest capacity) at XYZ is the ream, twist, and distort (RTD) operation. This information about the RTD operation is known:

$$\lambda = 50 \text{ units per hour arrive on the average}$$
$$\mu = 75 \text{ units per hour can be serviced on the average}$$

The arrival and service rates can be considered Poisson distributed, the system is single phase and single channel, and the maximum queue length is unlimited. **(a)** Compute the average queue length. (b) Compute the average number of units in the service system. (c) Compute the average time that units wait. (d) Compute the average time that units are in the system. (e) Compute the probability that one or more units are in the system.

Solution

a. Compute the average queue length (use the formula for Model 1):

$$\bar{n}_1 = \frac{\lambda^2}{\mu(\mu - \lambda)} = \frac{(50)^2}{75(75 - 50)} = \frac{2,500}{75(25)} = \frac{2,500}{1,875} = 1.33 \text{ units}$$

b. Compute the average number of units in the system:

$$\bar{n}_s = \frac{\lambda}{(\mu - \lambda)} = \frac{50}{75 - 50} = \frac{50}{25} = 2.00 \text{ units}$$

c. Compute the average time that units wait:

$$\bar{t}_1 = \frac{\lambda}{\mu(\mu - \lambda)} = \frac{50}{75(75 - 50)} = \frac{50}{75(25)} = \frac{50}{1,875} = .0267 \text{ hour} = 1.6 \text{ minutes}$$

d. Compute the average time that units are in the system:

$$\bar{t}_s = \frac{1}{(\mu - \lambda)} = \frac{1}{75 - 50} = \frac{1}{25} = .040 \text{ hour} = 2.4 \text{ minutes}$$

e. Compute the probability that one or more units are in the system.

First, compute the probability that the system is empty:

$$P_n = \left(1 - \frac{\lambda}{\mu}\right)\left(\frac{\lambda}{\mu}\right)^n, \text{ where } n = 0$$

$$P_0 = \left(1 - \frac{50}{75}\right)\left(\frac{50}{75}\right)^0 = \left(1 - \frac{50}{75}\right)(1) = 1 - \frac{50}{75} = 1 - .667 = .333$$

Next, because P_0 is the probability that the system is empty, $1 - P_0$ is the probability that one or more units are in the system:

$$1 - P_0 = 1 - .333 = .667$$

MODEL 2: SINGLE CHANNEL, SINGLE PHASE, AND CONSTANT SERVICE TIMES

When single channel, single phase waiting lines have *constant service times,* as in the case of an automobile car wash, an automatic coffee machine in an office building, or a machine-controlled manufacturing operation, *Model 2* is usually appropriate for studying these systems. The $\bar{n}_1$, $\bar{n}_s$, $\bar{t}_1$, and $\bar{t}_s$ measures are also computed from the formulas of this model. Note that these values are always less than in Model 1. Constant service times are therefore usually preferred over random service times. Example D.2 demonstrates the use of Model 2 formulas.

■ ■

TABLE D.3   Four Queuing Models and Their Formulas

Model Number	Number of Channels	Service Rate Distribution	Maximum Queue Length	Examples	Formulas
	Characteristics of Queuing System				
1	Single	Poisson	Unlimited	Single-booth theater ticket sales, maintenance repair center	$\bar{n}_1 = \dfrac{\lambda^2}{\mu(\mu - \lambda)}$ $\bar{t}_1 = \dfrac{\lambda}{\mu(\mu - \lambda)}$ $\bar{n}_s = \dfrac{\lambda}{\mu - \lambda}$ $\bar{t}_s = \dfrac{1}{\mu - \lambda}$ $P_n = [1 - (\lambda/\mu)](\lambda/\mu)^n$
2	Single	Constant	Unlimited	Machine-controlled manufacturing operation, automatic car wash	$\bar{n}_1 = \dfrac{\lambda^2}{2\mu(\mu - \lambda)}$ $\bar{t}_1 = \dfrac{\lambda}{2\mu(\mu - \lambda)}$ $\bar{n}_s = \bar{n}_1 + \dfrac{\lambda}{\mu}$ $\bar{t}_s = \bar{t}_1 + \dfrac{1}{\mu}$
3	Single	Poisson	Limited	Bank drive-in window, manufacturing operation with in-process inventories, parking lot of retail store, maintenance repair center	$\bar{n}_1 = \left(\dfrac{\lambda}{\mu}\right)^2 \left[\dfrac{1 - Q(\lambda/\mu)^{Q-1} + (Q-1)(\lambda/\mu)^Q}{[1 - (\lambda/\mu)][1 - (\lambda/\mu)^Q]}\right]$ $\bar{n}_s = \left(\dfrac{\lambda}{\mu}\right)\left[\dfrac{1 - (Q+1)(\lambda/\mu)^Q + Q(\lambda/\mu)^{Q+1}}{[1 - (\lambda/\mu)][1 - (\lambda/\mu)^{Q+1}]}\right]$ $P_n = \left[\dfrac{1 - (\lambda/\mu)}{1 - (\lambda/\mu)^{Q+1}}\right](\lambda/\mu)^n$
4	Multiple	Poisson	Unlimited	Toll road pay booth, bank teller window, maintenance repair shop	$P_0 = \dfrac{1}{\displaystyle\sum_{n=0}^{N-1}\left[\dfrac{(\lambda/\mu)^n}{n!}\right] + \dfrac{(\lambda/\mu)^N}{N!\left(1 - \dfrac{\lambda}{\mu(N)}\right)}}$ $\bar{n}_1 = P_0\left[\dfrac{\lambda\mu(\lambda/\mu)^N}{(N-1)!(N\mu - \lambda)^2}\right]$ $\bar{t}_1 = \left(\dfrac{\lambda}{\mu}\right)^N\left[\dfrac{P_0}{\mu N(N!)\left(1 - \dfrac{\lambda}{\mu N}\right)^2}\right]$ $\bar{n}_s = \bar{n}_1 + (\lambda/\mu)$ $\bar{t}_s = \bar{t}_1 + (1/\mu)$

■ ■

Note: All four models have single-phase services and Poisson arrival rate distributions.

■ ■

EXAMPLE D.2   Changing the RTD Operation to a Constant Service Rate

The XYZ Manufacturing Company of Example D.1 is considering installing an automatic machine at the RTD operation that could process a constant 75 units per hour. An average of 50 units per hour arrive at the operation, arrivals are Poisson distributed, the system is single channel and single phase, and queue length is unlimited.

If the present average time each unit is in the system is 2.4 minutes and each minute that each unit is in the system on the average represents $10,000 per year, how much will the proposed machine save annually over the present RTD operation?

Solution

Compute the annual savings for the proposed machine.

First, compute $\bar{t}_s$ with the formula for Model 2:

$$\bar{t}_s = \bar{t}_1 + \frac{1}{\mu} = \frac{\lambda}{2\mu(\mu - \lambda)} + \frac{1}{\mu} = \frac{50}{2(75)(75 - 50)} + \frac{1}{75} = \frac{50}{2(75)(25)} + .0133$$

$$= \frac{50}{3,750} + .0133 = .0133 + .0133 = .0266 \text{ hour} = 1.6 \text{ minutes}$$

Next, compute the average number of minutes saved per unit:

$$\bar{t}_{s_1} - \bar{t}_{s_2} = 2.4 - 1.6 = .8 \text{ minute}$$

Finally, compute the annual savings:

Annual savings = (Minutes saved)($ Annual cost/minute) = (.8)($10,000) = $8,000/year

MODEL 3: SINGLE CHANNEL, SINGLE PHASE, AND LIMITED WAITING LINE LENGTH

When single-channel, single-phase waiting lines are limited in the maximum length that they can have, *Model 3* can usually be used. Waiting line lengths may be limited by such factors as waiting room area, size of parking lots, and size of conveyors holding parts waiting to be processed at manufacturing operations.

MODEL 4: MULTICHANNEL, SINGLE PHASE

When more than one waiting line is used and services are single phase, *Model 4* can usually be used to provide managers with information about these systems. As in Model 3, however, the formulas of Model 4 are also more complex to use and apply. Computer programs such as those in the *POM Computer Library* that accompanies this book have greatly simplified the application of this model because complex calculations are relegated to the computer. Analysts supply the computer with arrival rates, service rates, and number of waiting lines. The computer then performs the necessary calculations to supply analysts with P_n, $\bar{n}_1$, $\bar{n}_s$, $\bar{t}_1$, and $\bar{t}_s$.

AN EVALUATION OF QUEUING THEORY IN POM

The chief benefit from understanding the models presented in Table D.3 is the insight into the behavior of waiting lines that is gained through the use of these relatively simple models. The specific use of these formulas in POM practice is limited, however, because we seldom observe waiting lines that precisely fit the assumptions of the models.

  The following assumptions particularly limit the wide use of the queuing theory formulas in POM:

1. Multiphase services may not be analyzed by the use of these formulas.
2. Arrival rates and service rates that are not from infinite Poisson distributions may not be analyzed by these formulas.
3. First-come first-served queue discipline is assumed. Other disciplines known to be commonly used in practice are shortest processing time, critical ratio, and most valued customers served first.
4. Line switching is not allowed in multichannel systems.

Another approach, though more involved and more time-consuming, has been developed that can be used to overcome the limitations noted above. *Computer simulation* has become the universal tool for analyzing most real waiting line problems that occur in POM. This tool of modern computer technology allows analysts in POM to analyze any queuing system and provide managers with information about the behavior of even the most complex queuing systems.

COMPUTER SIMULATION

Computer simulation may be emerging as one of the techniques most frequently employed by staff analysts in production and operations functions today. One study showed that among manufacturing firms that used operations research techniques, 52 percent used computer simulation.[1]

The flexibility of computer simulation in analyzing a variety of POM problems is perhaps its greatest virtue. These diverse problems, however, do share certain characteristics that make them targets for computer simulation analysis. Table D.4 lists six of these important characteristics. When these features are present, computer simulation can be an effective tool to support decision making in POM.

TABLE D.4   *Characteristics of POM Problems That Are Appropriate for Computer Simulation Analysis*

1. Experimentation with the real system is impossible, impractical, or uneconomical.
2. The system being analyzed is so complex that mathematical formulas cannot be developed.
3. The problem under consideration usually involves the passage of time. For example, policies are set and then executed as time passes. Although this characteristic is not absolutely mandatory, it is usually present.
4. The values of the variables of the problem are not known with certainty; rather, their values vary randomly through chance. We may know their average values and the degree of their variation, but their exact values at any point in time are not known in advance.
5. The severity of the problem justifies the expense of computer-based analysis.
6. The time available for analysis is long enough to permit computer-based analysis.

---

[1] Norman Gaither, "The Adoption of Operations Research Techniques by Manufacturing Organizations," *Decision Sciences* 6(October 1975):797–813.

To demonstrate the use of computer simulation here, we shall identify the key steps in performing a computer simulation, work through a case study of a manual simulation analysis, and finally evaluate the usefulness of the technique in POM.

PROCEDURES OF COMPUTER SIMULATION

Performing a computer simulation is not usually mathematically complex, but it can be very time-consuming. Table D.5 lists the procedures for developing a computer simulation analysis.

After the problem under consideration has been defined, the central activity of simulation is performed: building the mathematical model. Model building begins with determining which variables and parameters of the problem are important to its solution. Elements subject to variation when the real system operates are allowed to take on values that vary randomly in the model and are called *variables.* Elements that are constant in the operation of the real system (either because of management policies or for technological reasons) are assigned constant values and are called *parameters.* In most simulations the goal of the analysis is to produce a good set of parameter values (management policies) as the model simulates the operation of the real system.

Next, the *decision rules* of the model are specified. These rules answer questions such as: If this happens, then what? For example, if an arrival arrives at a multichannel queuing system, which line does it go to — the shortest one, the quickest-moving one, or the nearest one? These decision rules guide the operation of models and allow them to simulate how the real system operates.

Data gathering allows analysts to specify the frequency distributions of the variables and the constant values of the parameters. Next is a key part of the model, specifying the *time-incrementing procedures.* A simulation analysis is a series (usually a long series) of snapshots (usually a thousand or more) of the model operating as

---

TABLE D.5   *Procedures of Computer Simulation*

1. Thoroughly define the problem under consideration — its nature, scope, and importance.
2. Build a mathematical model of the problem. This usually involves these activities:
   a. Identify the variables and parameters.
   b. Specify the decision rules.
   c. Gather data so that variables and parameters can be assigned realistic values.
   d. Specify the probability distributions for each variable and the value of the parameters.
   e. Specify the time-incrementing procedures.
   f. Specify a procedure for summarizing the results of the simulation.
3. Write a computer program of the model and the summary procedures.
4. Process the program on the computer.
5. Evaluate the results of the computer simulation, modify parameter values, and rerun the program until a full range of parameter values has been evaluated.
6. Recommend a course of management action on the problem.

time passes between the snapshots. The time-incrementing procedure sets the time interval between these snapshots and the general rules for determining when a snapshot will be taken. At each snapshot each variable is randomly assigned a value, the decision rules are followed, and the results are recorded. The model is complete after a method of summarizing the results of all the snapshots is specified.

When the model has been written in a computer language such as BASIC or FORTRAN (or even some special computer simulation languages such as GPSS or SIMSCRIPT) and processed on a computer, the results are then evaluated. If other values of the parameters are to be analyzed, a new set of parameter values is established, the simulation is run again, and its results are again evaluated. When a full range of parameter values has been evaluated, the *best* set—those values that are recommended management policies to solve the problem—is selected.

These procedures will perhaps be more easily understood if we use them in a computer simulation case study.

A SIMULATION CASE STUDY

An outpatient clinic serves patients who arrive randomly. The number of patients arriving varies between 6 and 10 per hour while the clinic is open. The clinic's daily schedule is from 8 a.m. to 5 p.m. Any patients who are waiting for doctors inside are served before the clinic closes. It takes between 6 and 30 minutes for a doctor to serve each patient, depending on the nature of the patient's medical problem.

Two doctors presently serve on the staff of the clinic. But lately both patients and doctors have been complaining about the service. Patients complain about excessive waiting times before being served, and doctors complain about being overworked, not having any time between patients to rest or perform other duties such as charting, and not being able to leave work promptly at 5 p.m. The director of the clinic wonders how much patient waiting time and doctor idle time is being experienced now and how much things would improve if a third doctor were added to the staff.

A simulation will now be developed to analyze the director's staffing problem.

Define the Problem
What does the director of the clinic need to know in order to solve the problem? He or she needs to know how much patient waiting time and doctor idle time result when two and three doctors are on the clinic's staff. Then the director can decide which staffing arrangement is best.

Build a Model
A mathematical model of the clinic is developed by following the procedures of Step 2 in Table D.5.

Identify the Variables and Parameters.   The key variables of the model are the number of patients arriving each hour, the number of minutes required for a doctor to serve each patient, the time patients must wait before being served, and the time doctors are idle. The key parameter is the number of doctors on the clinic's staff.

Specify the Decision Rules. These rules will guide our simulation:

1. Patients are assumed to arrive uniformly through each hour. Patients do not wait and doctors are not idle because of irregular arrivals *within* each hour.
2. Doctors are assumed to serve patients on a first-come first-served basis. Any patients held over from previous periods are processed first before newly arriving patients are served.
3. Patient arrival patterns are assumed to be about the same for all hours of the day.
4. Patient waiting time or doctor idle time is computed hourly from this formula:

$$T_n = t_i - (60N - W_{n-1})$$

where

T_n = either patient waiting time or doctor idle time in Time Period n (if T_n is positive, it represents patient waiting time; if T_n is negative, it represents doctor idle time)

t_i = service times for the ith patient arriving in Time Period n

W_{n-1} = patient waiting time in last period or Time Period $n-1$

N = number of doctors on the staff

Gather Data and Specify Variables and Parameters. The simulation will compare two staffing arrangements: $N = 2$ and $N = 3$, the number of doctors on the staff. Records at the front desk of the clinic yield the historical information about patient arrivals and service times found in Figure D.2.

Specify Time-Incrementing Procedures. Each time increment will be one hour, and enough time intervals will be simulated to cover one operating day from 8:00 a.m. to 5:00 p.m.

Specify Summarizing Procedures. The patient waiting time and doctor idle time will be totaled across all time intervals of the simulation. Averages will then be computed for patient service time, patient waiting time, and doctor idle time.

Process the Simulation

Because this simulation example will be processed manually, no computer program needs to be written as would ordinarily be the case. What follows in this section would be the output of such a computer program. The essential elements in this simulation are determining how many patients arrive in each hour and how many minutes are required to service each patient.

Monte Carlo Arrivals. *Monte Carlo* is a technique for generating random values from discrete distributions, such as the discrete distribution of patients arriving per hour in Figure D.2. Monte Carlo uses uniform random numbers (*uniform* meaning that each number has an equal chance of being drawn) to randomly select the number of patients arriving during any hour. First, in Table D.6, we set up ranges of random numbers that correspond to the relative frequency of each class of the patient arrivals distribution.

FIGURE D.2   *Historical Data for Arrivals per Hour and Service Times*

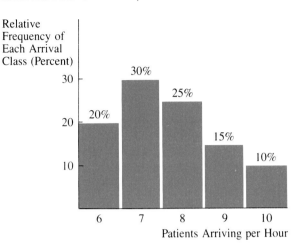

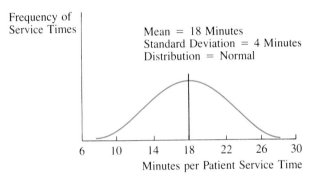

Under this scheme the range of random numbers allocated to each class exactly equals the relative frequency of that class. Thus 100 random numbers (zero to 99) are used to select one of the classes of patients arriving per hour from the distribution.

TABLE D.6   *Establishing Random Number Ranges for Each Class in Discrete Arrival Distribution for Monte Carlo*

Patients Arriving per Hour	Relative Frequency (Percent)	Random Number Range	Patients Arriving per Hour	Relative Frequency (Percent)	Random Number Range
6	20%	0–19	9	15%	75–89
7	30	20–49	10	10	90–99
8	25	50–74			

TABLE D.7   *Table of Uniformly Distributed Random Numbers*

6351	8348	2924	2414	8168	7280	0164	5466
1322	8739	0532	4546	2482	3980	1543	3442
6763	9603	6748	4061	3636	5266	8868	5817
5091	8188	3314	6192	7322	8207	3347	6218
7182	7128	8132	4638	4643	6119	4925	4476
2533	4910	6664	5793	4777	6530	6187	8349
4415	1347	8346	7957	2627	4151	1266	0237
0028	8040	7986	5559	1479	8844	9750	8901
5661	3854	2177	8376	0663	8592	5586	6187
6844	5383	0699	5749	8201	7467	0991	8737
3509	2418	2928	5803	8471	8598	5349	4714
0141	8418	9238	9667	4857	2140	9129	5517
0939	5977	7415	0690	7409	8244	2783	2502
9969	7295	4053	8663	5499	5024	0652	8698
6321	9644	0971	9037	5476	1527	9879	5530
4268	5837	6611	7137	3323	5702	4309	4533
8417	9699	2447	7390	2312	7368	3398	4075
3869	6536	4393	7533	5664	6182	6118	1073
1377	8599	9206	7842	4198	4608	9864	7713
7495	5559	5896	5344	8997	5889	4361	3166
9744	9971	2129	3036	9055	7011	0568	0312
6759	7744	5634	4107	3940	6674	4587	7455
3451	3612	0610	1156	1445	8261	6565	5042
1163	1599	9134	0409	0248	7807	4608	7382
2822	0493	7563	0939	7569	6966	3677	9366
3100	4307	7942	8883	1821	0982	9504	8185
3570	7757	4412	6664	0271	1656	7491	0047
2857	6721	4616	7207	1696	5314	6621	1898
1800	3717	6102	3159	4036	5780	8360	8142
3607	8366	7733	1108	7052	2340	0569	2354
9008	2860	6091	0800	9986	2712	6403	4006
6416	2438	6883	9360	4209	1018	8223	0181
7079	0844	1351	0508	0886	0747	6502	2293
5241	0807	7674	8782	3627	2728	3727	7805
3291	9499	7374	8751	6143	8100	3308	6951
1928	9013	6726	9241	4907	6275	3487	4448
5310	1826	3163	2545	6803	7911	6237	6225
1215	1270	6680	8651	1790	2881	1176	1130
6195	6999	6240	4452	0552	3239	4469	7658
5731	5461	1187	7973	7158	1193	2734	5666

■ ■

TABLE D.8   *Determining Number of Patient Arrivals for Each Hour of Simulation Using Monte Carlo*

Hour	Uniform Random Number (RN)	Patient Arrivals	Hour	Uniform Random Number (RN)	Patient Arrivals	Hour	Uniform Random Number (RN)	Patient Arrivals
1	00	6	4	40	7	7	55	8
2	28	7	5	79	9	8	59	8
3	80	9	6	86	9	9	14	6

■ ■

Note: Number of arrivals is determined by fitting RN into one of the random number ranges from Table D.6.

Table D.7 is a table of uniformly distributed random numbers. This means that any of the numbers from zero to 9 all occur with equal frequency. They are not arranged in any order, and thus they are random. To use the table to select random numbers from zero to 99, as we want to do here, just pick a starting point anywhere in the table. For our purposes, begin at Row 8 and read from left to right: 00, 28, 80, 40, 79, 86, 55, 59, and 14 are nine random numbers (RN) that will be used to establish the number of patient arrivals during the nine daily operating hours of our simulation.

Table D.8 uses these random numbers to set the number of patient arrivals for each hour of the simulation. The first RN = 00 falls in the 0–19 range of the random numbers in Table D.6; this sets six arrivals for the first hour. RN = 28 falls in the 20–49 range for seven arrivals; RN = 80 falls in the 75–89 range of numbers for nine arrivals, and so on. This procedure is used to set the number of arrivals in all nine hours of the simulation. Remember that you can read uniformly distributed random numbers from Table D.7 in any sequence from any starting point in the table: up, down, right, or left—but be consistent.

Normally Distributed Service Times.   Now we need to set the service times for our patients. But we cannot use Monte Carlo because our service times from Figure D.2 are normally distributed with a mean of 18 minutes and a standard deviation of 4 minutes. Table D.9 is a table of normally distributed random numbers that are Z *scores*—the number of standard deviations each service time is from the mean. This formula is used to compute the service time for each patient:

$$t_i = \mu + Z_i(\sigma) \qquad \text{or} \qquad t_i = 18 + Z_i(4)$$

Z is determined for each patient by selecting any starting point in Table D.9. For our purposes, let us begin at the upper left-hand corner and read from left to right: 1.21, −1.31, −1.12, 1.32, .86, and .31 are our Z scores for the six patients in the first hour of our simulation. Therefore we can now compute the service times for these patients:

$t_1 = 18 + 1.21(4) = 22.84$ minutes $t_4 = 18 + 1.32(4) = 23.28$ minutes

$t_2 = 18 − 1.31(4) = 12.76$ minutes $t_5 = 18 + .86(4) = 21.44$ minutes

$t_3 = 18 − 1.12(4) = 13.52$ minutes $t_6 = 18 + .31(4) = \underline{19.24 \text{ minutes}}$

Total   113.08 minutes

■ ■

TABLE D.9   *Normally Distributed Z Scores*

1.21	−1.31	−1.12	1.32	.86	.31	−.77	1.90
.40	−.11	−1.63	−.75	.92	−.81	−1.12	1.28
1.40	−.49	.56	.10	−1.05	.48	1.00	−.35
−.04	1.21	1.80	−.21	−1.58	.15	−2.75	.45
.47	−.28	2.02	3.00	1.14	−.54	1.72	.60
.11	.77	1.14	.46	1.01	.04	−1.05	−.11
.22	1.94	−.11	1.02	−.79	−.24	.52	1.66
−1.80	.97	−.76	.31	1.27	.81	−.17	−.28
.09	−.60	−.63	.56	.09	1.08	−.60	2.10
1.66	−2.26	.10	1.66	−.85	−.34	.02	.73

■ ■

Note: These numbers are not in any order and are normally distributed about a mean of zero.

By repeating this procedure, we can compute the service times for all patients and total these service times for each hour of the simulation: 113.1, 135.1, 160.6, 112.8, 197.1, 180.3, 154.7, 159.2, and 98.8.

Performing the Simulation.   Now we are ready to perform the simulation. Table D.10 lists the number of patients arriving and the total service time for each hour of the

■ ■

TABLE D.10   *Summary of Outpatient Clinic Simulation*

			Two-Doctor Staff		*Three-Doctor Staff*	
Hour	*Number of Patients Arriving*	*Total Service Time (Minutes)*	*Patient Waiting Time (Minutes)*	*Doctor Idle Time (Minutes)*	*Patient Waiting Time (Minutes)*	*Doctor Idle Time (Minutes)*
1	6	113.1	0	6.9	0	66.9
2	7	135.1	15.1	0	0	44.9
3	9	160.6	55.7	0	0	19.4
4	7	112.8	48.5	0	0	67.2
5	9	197.1	125.6	0	17.1	0
6	9	180.3	185.9	0	17.4	0
7	8	154.7	220.6	0	0	7.9
8	8	159.2	259.8	0	0	20.8
9	6	98.8	238.6	0	0	81.2
Totals	69	1,311.7	1,149.8	6.9	34.5	308.3
Average per patient		19.0	16.7	.1	.5	4.5

simulation. The patient waiting time and doctor idle time are computed for each hour for the two staffing arrangements. For example, in Hour 4:

Two doctors:

$$T_n = t_i - (60N - W_{n-1}) \qquad T_4 = 112.8 - (120 - 55.7) = 112.8 - 64.3 = 48.5$$

Because T_4 is positive, it represents patient waiting time.

Three doctors:

$$T_n = t_i - (60N - W_{n-1}) \qquad T_4 = 112.8 - (180 - 0) = -67.2$$

Because T_4 is negative, it represents doctor idle time.

After all the patient waiting times and doctor idle times have been similarly computed for all hours of the simulation, the totals and averages are computed. This summary information results:

	Two Doctors	*Three Doctors*
Average service time per patient	19.0 minutes	19.0 minutes
Average waiting time per patient	16.7 minutes	.5 minute
Average doctor idle time between patients	.1 minute	4.5 minutes

The director agrees with the patients — too much patient waiting time results with a two-doctor clinic staff. The doctors also presently are probably overworked. The three-doctor staffing arrangement alleviates both problems, but at a cost.

This example of a manual simulation demonstrates the essential steps in developing a computer simulation without overpowering you with complex calculations. You should realize, however, that this example is simple compared to most computer simulations on at least three points: (1) Most simulated systems are far more complex than a two- or three-doctor outpatient clinic. (2) Decision rules are seldom as simple as those of this example. (3) The number of random variables and their patterns of randomness are usually more extensive. Poisson, exponential, and other distributions frequently must be represented in addition to the discrete and normal distributions of this example. But in spite of the simplicity of our example, its procedures are similar in most respects to its real-world counterparts.

AN EVALUATION OF COMPUTER SIMULATION

Computer simulation deserves our attention on at least three counts:

1. It is perhaps one of the most flexible analytical tools in that it can be applied to a variety of POM problems.
2. It is frequently used in industry. Thus the likelihood of encountering it in your future jobs is relatively high.
3. It is not highly mathematical and complex; rather, it uses a relatively simple experimental approach to analyzing problems.

These reasons support the contention that the use of computer simulation in POM will grow in years to come.

Computer simulation does not always necessarily yield *best,* or optimal, answers, but good workable solutions can be developed by comparing alternative management policies. Although it is true that the technique requires well-trained staff specialists and an effective computer system, these elements are increasingly assumed in most organizations today.

REVIEW AND DISCUSSION QUESTIONS

1. Give five examples of waiting lines in production systems.
2. Why do waiting lines form?
3. List the assumptions of these queuing models:
   a. Model 1,
   b. Model 2,
   c. Model 3, and
   d. Model 4.
4. What techniques can be employed when queuing formulas are inappropriate?
5. What information about waiting lines do managers usually need to know?
6. How can managers vary service center capacities to avoid excessive waiting lines?
7. Name six characteristics of problems appropriate for computer simulation analysis.
8. Name six principal steps in computer simulation.
9. Name six activities in building a model for computer simulation.
10. Define *Monte Carlo.*
11. Define *uniformly distributed random numbers.*
12. Define *normally distributed random numbers.*

PROBLEMS

1. Given: Model 1, $\lambda = 5$ per hour, and $\mu = 10$ per hour. Required:
   a. $\bar{n}_1$,
   b. $\bar{n}_s$,
   c. $\bar{t}_1$,
   d. $\bar{t}_s$, and
   e. P_0.
2. Picture yourself as a teller at a single drive-in window at a local bank. If customers arrive one every 5 minutes on the average, and if you can serve customers in 3 minutes on the average:
   a. How long should customers expect to be at the bank facility on the average?
   b. How many cars would we expect to be in the drive-in facility on the average? (Assume one customer per car.)
   c. What is the probability that three or more cars will be in the drive-in facility?

3. The vice president of student services at Monroe University has ordered the operations manager to reduce the staff in the check-cashing booth at the student center. The average arrival rate of students to the single waiting line is expected to remain at 40 students per hour, but the average time required to cash a student's check is expected to increase from .5 minute to 1.4 minutes at the single cashing booth. Although the operations manager knows that the waiting line area is sufficient to accommodate the additional students, what changes will this staffing change cause in the average number of students in line, the average waiting time of students in line, and the proportion of the time that the staff will be at the window?

4. The Atlanta plant of Computer Products Corporation (CPC) ships personal and small-business computers by company trucks to regional warehouses in the eastern half of the United States. Trucks return from the warehouses to the plant for loading on the average of 4 per 8-hour day. The plant uses one loading crew in the shipping department that assembles customers' orders for personal and small-business computers and loads orders onto the outgoing trucks. The loading crew does warehouse work when no outgoing trucks are at the plant and loads the outgoing trucks on a first-come first-served basis. The loading crew can load 6 trucks per 8-hour day on the average. Each truck occupies about 200 square feet of parking space, each truck driver is paid $20 per hour including fringe benefits, and the loading crew is paid a total of $150 per hour including fringe benefits. CPC's union contract with its truck drivers does not allow drivers to assist in loading or unloading trucks.
   a. On the average, how much parking space should be necessary for trucks waiting to be loaded?
   b. How much does the union contract clause barring drivers from doing loading work cost CPC per year if the Atlanta plant works 250 days per year and if we assume that drivers' idle time could be put to a use that would be of equal value to their present pay?

5. You are a supervisor of a maintenance repair shop, and you have just attended a staff meeting. A policy was set at the meeting that established 4 hours as the average time that each production machine to be repaired should be out of production. If it takes 8 hours on the average for a repair worker to repair a machine, one machine per hour on the average is failing, and Model 1 applies (assume that 2 workers can repair a machine in 4 hours, 4 workers can repair a machine in 2 hours, etc.):
   a. How many repair workers are needed in the repair shop?
   b. If each machine requires 20 square feet of floor space, how much area should be provided on the average for the repair facility? (Assume that repaired machines leave immediately.)
   c. In your answer to Part *b*, what is the probability of overflowing the area?

6. Given: Model 2, $\lambda = 20$ per hour, and $\mu = $ a constant 30 per hour. Required:
   a. $\bar{n}_1$,
   b. $\bar{n}_s$,
   c. $\bar{t}_1$, and
   d. $\bar{t}_s$.

7. Billy White owns and operates White's Automatic Car Wash. The automatic washing mechanism takes exactly 12 minutes to wash each car. During weekdays the average

arrival rate of cars is 3 per hour and on weekends the rate is 4.5 per hour. Each car takes approximately 20 feet of driveway length.
   a. How much driveway length will be required on the average for cars waiting to be washed?
   b. For what length of time will each customer be at the car wash on the average?

8. The plant engineering staff at CPC's Atlanta plant in Problem 4 is studying a proposal to install an automatic truck-loading device. This system of loading trucks consists of a unit load being automatically loaded in each truck in exactly 10 minutes. It takes the loading crew an average of 30 minutes to prepare the unit load for the device, and the crew is required to be present when the device loads the truck. If the device costs $200,000 and the savings in loading crew time and driver idle time is to be used to justify the cash outlay, should CPC install the device?

9. The Security Bank would like to design an automatic night deposit box. The bank's board has set a policy of no more than two customers waiting to be served on the average. If ten customers per hour arrive on the average:
   a. In how many minutes should the automatic teller be designed to process each customer?
   b. How many minutes will each customer be at the bank on the average?
   [*Hint:* The formula for the quadratic equation is: $X = (-b \pm \sqrt{b^2 - 4ac})/2a$.]

10. Given: Model 3, $\lambda = 10$ per hour, $\mu = 20$ per hour, and Q = a maximum of 5 units in the system. Required: $\bar{n}_s$.

11. A popular student association, Business Students against Grade Inflation, is planning a car wash project to raise funds. A large shopping center has granted permission to use a portion of its parking lot with the understanding that no more than 100 feet of driveway length can be used. The students expect the 20-foot-long cars to arrive at the car wash one every 5 minutes on the average, and the car-washing team believes that it can wash a car in 4 minutes on the average.
   a. What proportion of the time will the students be able to rest?
   b. How many cars will be waiting in line at the car wash on the average?

12. In Problem 4, the warehouse manager at the Atlanta plant of CPC has established a policy that requires truck drivers to take their trucks to be serviced at the plant's maintenance center if one truck is waiting to be loaded, but each truck may be serviced a maximum of once per trip. Assume that the serviced trucks do not affect the arrival rate of 4 trucks per 8-hour day and that the truck-loading terminal operates much like a single-channel, limited queue-length waiting-line system. If each truck makes a trip every 10 days on the average, how often will the trucks be serviced?

13. Given: Model 4, $\lambda = 10$ units per hour, $\mu = 20$ units per hour, and N = 4 channels. Required:
   a. P_0, and
   b. $\bar{n}_1$.

14. In Problem 4, because of a large increase in sales, CPC has doubled the number of trucks that are hauling personal and small-business computers to regional warehouses. The trucks are now arriving at the rate of 8 trucks per 8-hour day on the average. Another loading crew has been added to the present one, and these two crews

work separate loading docks and each can load 6 trucks per 8-hour day on the average. With the extra trucks, should the drivers expect to spend more time at the plant now than previously?

15. Dixie Food Stores is opening a new store in Miami, Florida. Dixie has estimated that the new location will average 220 customers arriving per hour during peak shopping hours. During these peak periods all 6 checkout counters will be open and operating with a capacity of serving an average of 40 customers per hour per counter. All checkout counters are assumed to be identical.
    a. What proportion of the time would all of the checkout counters and waiting lines be empty of customers?
    b. How long would customers wait in line on the average?
    c. How many customers would be waiting in each line on the average?

16. Professor Bishop keeps office hours between 2 and 4 p.m. one day per week. The number of students who take advantage of the assistance available during these periods is given in this relative frequency distribution:

Number of Students (n)	Relative Frequency F(n) (Percent)	Number of Students (n)	Relative Frequency F(n) (Percent)	Number of Students (n)	Relative Frequency F(n) (Percent)
3	10%	5	20%	7	20%
4	10	6	30	8	10

The amount of time per student required to provide assistance is approximated by a normal distribution with a mean of 15 minutes and a standard deviation of 5 minutes. Use these uniform random numbers to establish the number of students arriving in ten office hours periods: 6, 5, 1, 0, 2, 9, 5, 4, 7, 3. Use the normally distributed Z scores in Table D.9 to establish service times per student. (Begin in the upper left-hand corner of the table and read horizontally across the first line, return to the left margin, go down to the next line, and repeat until completed.) Follow the procedures of the outpatient clinic case in this appendix to determine:
    a. The number of students arriving in each office hours period for ten periods.
    b. The total number of minutes required to assist students during each of the ten office hours periods.

17. The Red Snapper Fish Sales Company stocks fresh fish fillets daily for sale to its Boston customers. Its daily demand follows this pattern:

Cases of Fillets Demanded	Relative Frequency (Percent)	Cases of Fillets Demanded	Relative Frequency (Percent)
30	10%	60	40%
40	15	70	10
50	25		

Red Snapper can buy fillets only in multiples of 10-case quantities at a uniform cost of $25 per case. Red Snapper charges its customers $40 a case, and leftover fillets each day can be sold for cat food at $5 a case. Red Snapper's manager wishes to compare two rules for ordering fillets: (1) Order the quantity demanded today for tomorrow's sales. (Today's demand was 50 cases.) (2) Order a constant 60 cases per day. Use Monte Carlo to conduct a 20-day manual simulation to compare the average daily profit for the two decision rules. (These 20 uniformly distributed random numbers are read downward from the upper right-hand corner of Table D.7 — 66, 42, 17, 18, 76, 49, 37, 01, 87, 37, 14, 17, 02, 98, 30, 33, 75, 73, 13, and 66.)

18. The truck-loading dock described in Problem 4 has this arrival distribution:

(1) Trucks Arriving in an 8-hour day	(2) Minutes between Arriving Trucks [1/(1) × 480]	(3) Relative Frequency (Percent)
1	480	5%
2	240	15
3	160	20
4	120	30
5	96	20
6	80	10

The time that it takes the single loading crew to load the trucks is normally distributed with a mean of 80 minutes and a standard deviation of 20 minutes. Use these uniform random numbers to establish the number of trucks arriving in ten 8-hour days: 73, 52, 51, 45, 41, 51, 82, 08, 60, and 00. Use the normally distributed Z scores in Table D.9 to establish loading times for each truck. (Begin in the lower right-hand corner of the table and read horizontally to the left across the last line, return to the right margin, go up to the next line, read horizontally to the left across the line, and repeat until completed.) Follow the procedures of the outpatient clinic case in this appendix to determine:

a. The number of trucks arriving in each day for ten days.
b. The number of minutes required to load trucks in each day and the total for the ten days.
c. The number of minutes of driver idle time in each day and the total for the ten days.
d. The amount of loading crew idle time in each day and the total for the ten days.

SELECTED BIBLIOGRAPHY

Carlson, J. G., and M. J. Misshauk. *Introduction to Gaming: Management Decision Simulations.* New York: Wiley, 1972.

Christy, David P., and Hugh J. Watson. "The Application of Simulation: A Survey of Industry Practice." *Interfaces* 13, no. 5(October 1983):47–52.

Cooper, Robert B. *Introduction to Queuing Theory.* 2nd ed. New York: Elsevier-North Holland, 1980.

Cosmetatos, G. P. "The Value of Queuing Theory—A Case Study." *Interfaces* 9, no. 3(May 1979):47–51.

Gaither, Norman. "The Adoption of Operations Research Techniques by Manufacturing Organizations." *Decision Sciences* 6(October 1975):797–813.

Gross, Donald, and Carl M. Harris. *Fundamentals of Queuing Theory.* New York: Wiley, 1974.

House, William C. *Business Simulation for Decision Making.* New York: PBI Books, 1977.

Law, A. M., and W. D. Kelton. *Simulation Modeling and Analysis.* New York: McGraw-Hill, 1986.

McKeown, P. G. "An Application of Queuing Analysis to the New York State Child Abuse and Maltreatment Register Reporting System." *Interfaces* 9, no. 3(May 1979):20–25.

McMillan, C., and R. F. Gonzalez. *Systems Analysis: A Computer Approach to Decision Models.* 3rd ed. Homewood, IL: Richard D. Irwin, 1973.

Meier, R. C., W. T. Newell, and H. L. Pazer. *Simulation in Business and Economics.* Englewood Cliffs, NJ: Prentice-Hall, 1969.

Nanda, R. "Simulating Passenger Arrivals at Airports." *Industrial Engineering* 4, no. 3(March 1972):12–19.

Naylor, T. H., J. L. Balintfy, D. S. Burdick, and K. Chu. *Computer Simulation Techniques.* New York: Wiley, 1966.

Petersen, Clifford. "Simulation of an Inventory System." *Industrial Engineering* 5, no. 6(June 1973):35–44.

E

LINEAR PROGRAMMING SOLUTION METHODS

Although the graphical solution method that was presented in Chapter 7 is a useful learning device for those with limited knowledge of linear programming (LP), other methods are used daily in the worlds of business and government to solve real LP problems. Preeminent among these methods are *simplex, transportation,* and *assignment.*

SIMPLEX METHOD

Simplex does not mean *simple.* Nevertheless, the simplex method is used term after term by thousands of students just like you, and you can do it too. The main thing is to keep your eye on the big picture: Understand the overall procedures of the simplex method because it is easy to get bogged down in the nitty-gritty details and lose sight of the general process. Pay attention to the small details; this is necessary. But also constantly keep in mind the overall process.

The best way to learn the simplex method is to use it to work LP problems. "Experience is the best teacher" certainly applies here.

SIMPLEX MAXIMIZATION SOLUTIONS

Table E.1 presents the steps in the simplex method. Read them carefully and don't worry too much about being confused. Remember, get the big picture. Working through an example will demonstrate the meaning of each of these steps. Example E.1 uses the simplex method to solve Problem LP-1 from Chapter 7 while methodically following the steps of the simplex method. Work through every step in this example meticulously; this is absolutely necessary to an understanding of the method. Notice that the step numbers in this example correspond to the step numbers in Table E.1. You will not need a calculator, because calculators compute in decimals that require rounding or truncating. These sources of error are unacceptable in the simplex method, and therefore all calculations are carried out in fractions.

TABLE E.1   *Steps in the Simplex Solution Method*

1. Formulate the objective and constraint functions.	5. Check solution for optimality. If optimal, stop. If not, continue.
2. Add slack variables to convert each constraint to an equality (=).	6. Select a variable to enter to improve the solution.
3. Add artificial variables to constraints that were originally ≥ or = to produce a starting solution.	7. Select a variable to leave the solution.
	8. Perform row operations to complete the new solution.
4. Set up the first tableau, starting solution.	9. Return to Step 5 and continue until optimality is achieved.

EXAMPLE E.1   Simplex Solution of LP-1, a Maximization Problem

As part of its strategic planning process, the Precision Manufacturing Company must determine the mix of its products to be manufactured next year. The company produces two principal product lines for the commercial construction industry, a line of powerful portable circular saws and a line of precision table saws. The two product lines share the same production capacity and are sold through the same sales channels. Although some product variety does exist within each product line, the average profit is $900 for each circular saw and $600 for each table saw. The production capacity is constrained in two ways, fabrication and assembly capacity. There is a maximum of 4,000 hours of fabrication capacity available per month, and each circular saw requires 2 hours and each table saw requires 1 hour. There is a maximum of 5,000 hours of assembly capacity available per month, and each circular saw requires 1 hour and each table saw requires 2 hours. The marketing department estimates that there is a maximum market demand next year of a total of 3,500 saws per month for both product lines. How many circular saws and how many table saws should be produced monthly next year to maximize profits?

1. **Formulate the objective and constraint functions.**

   LP-1 was formulated in Chapter 7 as:

   $$\text{Max } Z = 900X_1 + 600X_2$$
   $$2X_1 + X_2 \leq 4{,}000 \text{ (fabrication — hours)}$$
   $$X_1 + 2X_2 \leq 5{,}000 \text{ (assembly — hours)}$$
   $$X_1 + X_2 \leq 3{,}500 \text{ (market — saws)}$$

   where

   X_1 = number of circular saws to be manufactured per month

   X_2 = number of table saws to be manufactured per month

2. **Add slack variables to convert each constraint to an equality (=):**
   a. $2X_1 + X_2 \leq 4{,}000$ (fabrication — hours)

   Note that the left-hand side of the expression is always less than or equal to the right-hand side (RHS). If the expression is to be an equality (=), something must be added to the left-hand side to increase its value up to the level of the RHS. We shall add a slack variable S_1 to take up the slack between the value of the left-hand side and the RHS. S_1 will take on the value of zero if the left-hand side exactly equals 4,000 and a value of 4,000 if X_1 and X_2 equal zero. When X_1 and X_2 take on values larger than zero, the value of S_1 will decrease accordingly so that the left-hand side of the expression exactly equals 4,000:

   $$2X_1 + X_2 + S_1 = 4{,}000$$

   Note that the subscript 1 in S_1 denotes that S_1 is the slack variable for the first constraint. When we proceed with and complete the simplex solution, and S_1 takes on some specific value at the end, we shall automatically know that S_1 belongs to the first constraint —

unused fabrication hours. Similarly, S_2 will belong to the second constraint — unused assembly hours.

b. The second constraint is converted to an equality by adding a slack variable S_2 to the left-hand side:

$$X_1 + 2X_2 + S_2 = 5,000 \text{ (assembly—hours)}$$

c. The third constraint is converted to an equality by adding a slack variable S_3 to the left-hand side:

$$X_1 + X_2 + S_3 = 3,500 \text{ (market—saws)}$$

We now have this LP problem:

$$\text{Max } Z = 900X_1 + 600X_2$$
$$2X_1 + \quad X_2 + S_1 \qquad\qquad = 4,000$$
$$X_1 + \quad 2X_2 \qquad + S_2 \qquad = 5,000$$
$$X_1 + \quad X_2 \qquad\qquad + S_3 = 3,500$$

3. **Add artificial variables to constraints that were originally $\geq$ or $=$ to produce a starting solution.** Since the constraints in this problem were all $\leq$, no artificial variables are required.

4. **Set up first tableau starting solution.**
   A tableau simply means a table. Each solution will be a tableau.
   a. First, let all variables appear in the objective function and constraint functions. This is achieved by assigning zero coefficients to all variables not appearing in these expressions:

$$\text{Max } Z = 900X_1 + 600X_2 + 0S_1 + 0S_2 + 0S_3$$
$$2X_1 + \quad X_2 + S_1 + 0S_2 + 0S_3 = 4,000$$
$$X_1 + \quad 2X_2 + 0S_1 + \quad S_2 + 0S_3 = 5,000$$
$$X_1 + \quad X_2 + 0S_1 + 0S_2 + \quad S_3 = 3,500$$

   b. Now put the problem above in the tableau format. The format is achieved by entering the set of coefficients for all the variables into the framework below:

First Tableau

C			900	600	0	0	0	
	SOL	**RHS**	X_1	X_2	S_1	S_2	S_3	ϕ
0	S_1	**4,000**	2	1	1	0	0	
0	S_2	**5,000**	1	2	0	1	0	
0	S_3	**3,500**	1	1	0	0	1	
	Z	**0**	0	0	0	0	0	
		(C − Z)	900	600	0	0	0	

   c. *Constraints.* The RHS value of each constraint is placed in the RHS column and the coefficients of the variables in the constraint are placed under the variables' columns.

d. *Objective function.* The coefficients of the variables in the objective function are placed in Row C above the appropriate variable columns.

e. *SOL column.* Note that the shaded matrix under the S_1, S_2, and S_3 is an identity matrix, a NW to SE diagonal of ones with all other elements zero. The variables over the columns of the identity matrix are always in the SOL column:

SOL	S_1	S_2	S_3
S_1	1	0	0
S_2	0	1	0
S_3	0	0	1

This condition will always hold: A variable found in the SOL column will have a one at the intersection of its row and column and all other elements in its column will be zero. This condition holds for all tableaus. When we are trying to determine what variables go into the SOL column later in this section, this rule can be helpful. Just look at all of the columns in the tableau and find the column that has a *one* in the first row with all other elements zero, and the variable of that column goes into the SOL column in the first row. All other SOL elements are determined in the same way.

f. *C column.* The zeros in the C column and opposite S_1, S_2, and S_3 are taken from Row C elements above S_1, S_2, and S_3. This will always hold — the values in the C column are the coefficients in the objective function that correspond to the variables found in the SOL column of the tableau.

g. *Row Z.* The elements in Row Z are all computed. Since the elements in the C column were zero, all the elements in Row Z were zero; however, the elements in the C column will not always be zero. Each element in Row Z is computed as follows:

$$Z_{RHS} = (0)(4,000) + (0)(5,000) + (0)(3,500) = 0$$
$$Z_{X_1} = \quad (0)(2) + \quad (0)(1) + \quad (0)(1) = 0$$
$$Z_{X_2} = \quad (0)(1) + \quad (0)(2) + \quad (0)(1) = 0$$
$$Z_{S_1} = \quad (0)(1) + \quad (0)(0) + \quad (0)(0) = 0$$
$$Z_{S_2} = \quad (0)(0) + \quad (0)(1) + \quad (0)(0) = 0$$
$$Z_{S_3} = \quad (0)(0) + \quad (0)(0) + \quad (0)(1) = 0$$

This step will become clearer in subsequent tableaus.

h. *Row (C − Z).* These values are computed by subtracting each element in Row Z from its counterpart in Row C:

$$(C - Z)_{X_1} = 900 - 0 = 900$$
$$(C - Z)_{X_2} = 600 - 0 = 600$$
$$(C - Z)_{S_1} = \quad 0 - 0 = \quad 0$$
$$(C - Z)_{S_2} = \quad 0 - 0 = \quad 0$$
$$(C - Z)_{S_3} = \quad 0 - 0 = \quad 0$$

i. *The starting solution.* This completes the explanation of the first tableau. The solution of the first tableau is:

$$X_1 = \quad 0 \text{ circular saws to be manufactured per month}$$

$$X_2 = \quad 0 \text{ table saws to be manufactured per month}$$

$$S_1 = 4{,}000 \text{ unused fabrication hours per month}$$

$$S_2 = 5{,}000 \text{ unused assembly hours per month}$$

$$S_3 = 3{,}500 \text{ unsatisfied market demand for saws per month}$$

$$Z = \quad \$0 \text{ profits per month}$$

Simplex tableau solutions always give the variables in the solution under the SOL column. Their associated values are found opposite them in the RHS column; therefore $S_1 = 4{,}000$, $S_2 = 5{,}000$, and $S_3 = 3{,}500$. All other variables not in the SOL column are equal to zero. The value of Z is found in the RHS column and Row Z.

5. **Check solution for optimality. If optimal, stop. If not, continue.**
Solutions are optimal when all of the values in Row $(C - Z)$ are either zero or negative. When any of the values in this row are nonzero positive numbers, the solution can be improved by continuing and the solution is not optimal. In our first tableau of LP-1, both X_1 and X_2 have Row $(C - Z)$ elements that are nonzero and positive. It is therefore not optimal, and we must continue to the next tableau.

6. **Select a variable to enter to improve the solution.**
Select the variable to enter that has the largest positive element in Row $(C - Z)$. X_1 will enter since its Row $(C - Z)$ element is the largest positive value in Row $(C - Z)$.

7. **Select a variable to leave the solution:**

First Tableau (Continued)

C			900	600	0	0	0	
	SOL	**RHS**	X_1	X_2	S_1	S_2	S_3	ϕ
0	S_1	4,000	②	1	1	0	0	$4{,}000/2 = 2{,}000 \leftarrow$ Leaving Variable
0	S_2	5,000	1	2	0	1	0	$5{,}000/1 = 5{,}000$ (Smallest Positive)
0	S_3	3,500	1	1	0	0	1	$3{,}500/1 = 3{,}500$
	Z	0	0	0	0	0	0	
	(C − Z)		900	600	0	0	0	

↑
Entering Variable
(Largest Positive)

The variable to leave this starting solution is determined by entering the column of the entering variable, X_1, dividing the number in each row into its RHS value, and recording this value in the ϕ column to the right. The leaving variable has the smallest positive ϕ value. If zero values or ties occur, do not worry. In the case of a tie, arbitrarily select one of the tying variables to leave, and in the case of a zero, let that variable leave. (Remember that a positive number divided by zero is a very large number at the limit.)

8. **Perform row operations to complete the solution.**
   This is perhaps the most confusing point in the simplex method. Table E.2 lists the steps in performing row operations. These steps will be followed to construct the second tableau.

TABLE E.2   *Steps in Performing Row Operations*

---

1. Identify the *pivot element* in the present tableau, which is found at the intersection of the column of the entering variable and the row of the leaving variable. Circle this element. Row operations convert the pivot column in this present tableau, element by element, to a new column in the new tableau. This new column always has these features: The element that is the pivot element in the present tableau will be a *one* in the new tableau, and all other elements in that column in the new tableau will be *zero.*
2. Convert the pivot element in the present tableau to a *one* in the new tableau by dividing the entire pivot row in the present tableau by the pivot element (element by element). This new row with a one in the pivot element is entered into the new tableau in the same row position as the pivot row of the present tableau.
3. Next, convert all other elements in the pivot column of the present tableau to *zero* in the new tableau. This is done by performing a separate operation on each remaining row of the present tableau. This operation involves the development of a special transitional row that is added to each remaining row in the present tableau. Each row in the present tableau for which we wish to convert its pivot column element to zero requires its own unique transitional row. This transitional row is developed by first determining the value of the element that we want to transform to zero. We then take the negative of the value of this element and multiply it by the row obtained in Step 2 above, element by element. When this transitional row is added to the row of the present tableau, a new row results that has a zero in the pivot column. This row is entered in the new tableau in the same row position as it occupied in the present tableau before it was transformed.

Second Tableau

C			900	600	0	0	0	
	SOL	**RHS**	X_1	X_2	S_1	S_2	S_3	ϕ
900	X_1	2,000	1	½	½	0	0	
0	S_2							
0	S_3							
	Z							
	(C − Z)							

a. Identify the pivot element. It is found at the intersection of the entering-variable column (X_1) and the leaving-variable row (S_1): the pivot element is ②.
b. Divide the pivot row, element by element, by the pivot element. Enter this new row in the next tableau: The first constraint row (4,000 2 1 1 0 0) is divided by 2 and the result is entered in the second tableau in the first-row position. The variable in the SOL column in

this row is the new entering-variable X_1, and its coefficient (900) in Row C is entered in Column C.

c. Reduce the other elements in the pivot column (X_2) to zero. Transform the second row in the first tableau (5,000 1 2 0 1 0) by multiplying the new row in the second tableau (2,000 1 ½ ½ 0 0) by −1 and adding this transitional row to the second row of the first tableau:

Multiply the row first entered in the second tableau by −1:

$$-1(2,000) \quad -1(1) \quad -1(½) \quad -1(½) \quad -1(0) \quad -1(0)$$

This gives values of

| −2,000 | −1 | −½ | −½ | 0 | 0 |

which are added to the row being transformed

| 5,000 | 1 | 2 | 0 | 1 | 0 |

to get values of

| 3,000 | 0 | 3/2 | −½ | 1 | 0 |

The third row in the first tableau (3,500 1 1 0 0 1) is now transformed by multiplying the row first entered in the new tableau (2,000 1 ½ ½ 0 0) by −1 and adding this transitional row to the third row of the first tableau:

Multiply the row first entered in the second tableau by −1:

$$-1(2,000) \quad -1(1) \quad -1(½) \quad -1(½) \quad -1(0) \quad -1(0)$$

This gives values of

| −2,000 | −1 | −½ | −½ | 0 | 0 |

which are added to the row being transformed

| 3,500 | 1 | 1 | 0 | 0 | 1 |

to get values of

| 1,500 | 0 | ½ | −½ | 0 | 1 |

d. These rows are entered into the second tableau in the second- and third-row positions. The variables in the SOL column for these rows do not change:

Second Tableau (Continued)

C			900	600	0	0	0	
	SOL	RHS	X_1	X_2	S_1	S_2	S_3	ϕ
900	X_1	2,000	1	½	½	0	0	
0	S_2	3,000	0	3/2	−½	1	0	
0	S_3	1,500	0	½	−½	0	1	
	Z	1,800,000	900	450	450	0	0	
	(C − Z)	0	150	−450	0	0	

e. Row Z is computed as follows:

$$Z_{RHS} = (900)(2,000) + 0(3,000) + 0(1,500) = 1,800,000$$
$$Z_{X_1} = (900)(1) \quad + \quad (0)(0) + \quad (0)(0) = \quad 900$$
$$Z_{X_2} = (900)(½) \quad + \quad (0)(¾) + \quad (0)(½) = \quad 450$$
$$Z_{S_1} = (900)(½) \quad + (0)(-½) + (0)(-½) = \quad 450$$
$$Z_{S_2} = (900)(0) \quad + \quad (0)(1) + \quad (0)(0) = \quad 0$$
$$Z_{S_3} = (900)(0) \quad + \quad (0)(0) + \quad (0)(1) = \quad 0$$

Row $(C - Z)$ is again computed by subtracting each element in Row Z from its counter-part in Row C.

f. The solution to the second tableau is:

$X_1 =$ 2,000 circular saws to be manufactured per month

$X_2 =$ 0 table saws to be manufactured per month

$S_1 =$ 0 unused fabrication hours per month

$S_2 =$ 3,000 unused assembly hours per month

$S_3 =$ 1,500 unsatisfied market demand for saws per month

$Z = \$1,800,000$ profits per month

The values of X_1, S_2, S_3, and Z are found in the body of the second tableau. X_2 and S_1 are not in the SOL column; therefore they both equal zero. Does this solution look familiar? It should, because it is identical to Point C in Example 7.4 of the graphical method.

9. **Return to Step 5 and continue until optimality is achieved:**
Steps 5, 6, and 7. Check solution for optimality. If optimal, stop. If not, continue. Select a variable to enter the solution. Select a variable to leave the solution:

Second Tableau (Continued)

C			900	600	0	0	0	
	SOL	RHS	X_1	X_2	S_1	S_2	S_3	ϕ
900	X_1	2,000	1	½	½	0	0	2,000/½ = 4,000
0	S_2	3,000	0	③	-½	1	0	3,000/¾ = 2,000 ← Leaving Variable
0	S_3	1,500	0	½	-½	0	1	1,500/½ = 3,000 (Smallest Positive)
	Z	1,800,000	900	450	450	0	0	
	(C − Z)	0	150	-450	0	0	

↑
Entering Variable
(Largest Positive)

The second tableau is not optimal since all Row $(C - Z)$ elements are not zero or negative. X_1 enters and, because the ϕ value for the second row is the smallest positive, S_2 leaves.

8. **Perform row operations to complete the solution.**
   a. The pivot element is $\frac{3}{2}$ because that element is at the intersection of the entering-variable column and the leaving-variable row.
   b. Divide the pivot row (second constraint row) of the second tableau through by the pivot element ($\frac{3}{2}$). Enter this new row into the third tableau in the same second-row position:

Third Tableau

C			900	600	0	0	0	
	SOL	RHS	X_1	X_2	S_1	S_2	S_3	ϕ
900	X_1							
600	X_2	2,000	0	1	$-\frac{1}{3}$	$\frac{2}{3}$	0	
0	S_3							
	Z							
	(C − Z)							

   c. Multiply this new row by a negative $\frac{1}{2}$ to transform the first constraint row in the second tableau:

$-\frac{1}{2}(2{,}000) \quad -\frac{1}{2}(0) \qquad -\frac{1}{2}(1) \quad -\frac{1}{2}(-\frac{1}{3}) \quad -\frac{1}{2}(\frac{2}{3}) \quad -\frac{1}{2}(0)$

This gives values of

$\qquad -1{,}000 \qquad 0 \qquad -\frac{1}{2} \qquad \frac{1}{6} \qquad -\frac{1}{3} \qquad 0$

which are added to

$\qquad 2{,}000 \qquad 1 \qquad \frac{1}{2} \qquad \frac{1}{2} \qquad 0 \qquad 0$

to give

$\qquad 1{,}000 \qquad 1 \qquad 0 \qquad \frac{2}{3} \qquad -\frac{1}{3} \qquad 0$

Multiply the first row entered in the third tableau by $-\frac{1}{2}$:

$-\frac{1}{2}(2{,}000) \quad -\frac{1}{2}(0) \qquad -\frac{1}{2}(1) \quad -\frac{1}{2}(-\frac{1}{3}) \quad -\frac{1}{2}(\frac{2}{3}) \quad -\frac{1}{2}(0)$

This gives values of

$\qquad -1{,}000 \qquad 0 \qquad -\frac{1}{2} \qquad \frac{1}{6} \qquad -\frac{1}{3} \qquad 0$

which are added to

$\qquad 1{,}500 \qquad 0 \qquad \frac{1}{2} \qquad -\frac{1}{2} \qquad 0 \qquad 1$

to give

$\qquad 500 \qquad 0 \qquad 0 \qquad -\frac{1}{3} \qquad -\frac{1}{3} \qquad 1$

   d. These rows are now entered into the first- and third-row positions of the third tableau:

Third Tableau (Continued)

C			900	600	0	0	0	
	SOL	**RHS**	X_1	X_2	S_1	S_2	S_3	ϕ
900	X_1	**1,000**	1	0	⅔	−⅓	0	
600	X_2	**2,000**	0	1	−⅓	⅔	0	
0	S_3	**500**	0	0	−⅓	−⅓	1	
	Z	**2,100,000**	900	600	400	100	0	
	(C − Z)		0	0	− 400	− 100	0	

e. Compute Rows Z and (C − Z) to complete the third tableau. Row Z is computed as follows:

$$Z_{RHS} = (900)(1,000) + (600)(2,000) + (0)(500) = 2,100,000$$

$$Z_{X_1} = (900)(1) \quad + (600)(0) \quad + (0)(1) \quad = \quad 900$$

$$Z_{X_2} = (900)(0) \quad + (600)(1) \quad + (0)(0) \quad = \quad 600$$

$$Z_{S_1} = (900)(⅔) \quad + (600)(−⅓) \ + (0)(−⅓) = \quad 400$$

$$Z_{S_2} = (900)(−⅓) \ + (600)(⅔) \quad + (0)(−⅓) = \quad 100$$

$$Z_{S_3} = (900)(0) \quad + (600)(0) \quad + (0)(1) \quad = \quad 0$$

Row (C − Z) is again computed by subtracting each element in Row Z from its counterpart in Row C.

f. The solution to the third tableau is:

$X_1 =$ 1,000 circular saws to be manufactured per month

$X_2 =$ 2,000 table saws to be manufactured per month

$S_1 =$ 0 unused fabrication hours per month

$S_2 =$ 0 unused assembly hours per month

$S_3 =$ 500 unsatisfied market demand for saws per month

Z = $2,100,000 profits per month

Does this solution look familiar? It should, because it is identical to Point B in Example 7.4 of the graphical method.

9. **Return to Step 5 and continue until optimality is achieved. Check solution for optimality. If optimal, stop. If not, continue.** The third tableau is optimal because all the elements in Row (C − Z) are either negative or zero.

The graphical solution of maximization Problem LP-1, Example 7.4, identified three solution points—A, B, and C. Each of these solutions was first identified as intersections of the constraints, and then each was substituted into the objective function to determine a value of Z. Finally, the optimal solution (maximum profit) was selected. The simplex method solution to LP-1 follows this same general process with one exception. The first tableau begins with $Z = 0$, and each subsequent tableau methodically exhibits higher values of Z. You can be assured that each tableau will exhibit progressively higher profits. This progression to better and better solutions is the only conceptual departure of the simplex method from the general process of the graphic method.

SIMPLEX MINIMIZATION SOLUTIONS

The graphical solution of minimization Problem LP-2, Example 7.5, identified three solution points—A, B, and C. The optimal solution to the problem was then determined by investigating Points A, B, and C. The simplex solution to this problem begins the first tableau with a very large value of Z. Subsequent tableaus exhibit progressively lower values for Z until optimality is achieved. This progression from high to low values of Z is characteristic of the simplex solution of minimization LP problems.

There are only two basic differences between maximization and minimization LP problem solutions with the simplex method:

a. Minimization LP problems are more likely to have $\geq$ and $=$ constraints, although the procedures for treating them apply to both minimization and maximization LP problems.
b. Minimization LP problems have different objective functions; Z is minimized.

In either minimization or maximization problems, $\geq$ and $=$ constraints are accommodated by adding artificial variables to these constraints. For example, in the case of $\geq$ constraints:

$$\textbf{1.}\ X_1 + 2X_2 \qquad\qquad \geq 500$$
$$\textbf{2.}\ X_1 + 2X_2 \qquad\qquad = 500 + S_1$$
$$\textbf{3.}\ X_1 + 2X_2 \qquad - S_1 = 500$$
$$\textbf{4.}\ X_1 + 2X_2 + A_1 - S_1 = 500$$

Note that in Step 2 above a slack variable (S_1) is added to the right-hand side, which must always be less than or equal to the left-hand side. The addition of S_1 to the smaller side of the expression allows us to convert the $\geq$ to $=$. In Step 3 the S_1 is moved to the left-hand side by subtracting S_1 from both sides. In Step 4 an artificial variable (A_1) is added to the left-hand side. Why do we do this? The only reason is to get a starting simplex solution. Remember when we said earlier that a requirement for each tableau was that the variable with a column which has a one in the first row and zeros for all other elements in its column is the variable that must go in the SOL column in the first row? What happens if no variable exists that has a column meeting this requirement? This is exactly the situation we have with $\geq$ or $=$ constraints. A $\geq$ constraint has a -1 coefficient for S_1, and this does not meet the requirement. Similarly, an $=$ constraint does not have a slack variable (as we shall soon see);

therefore we shall not be able to meet the requirement here either. When such conditions exist, we must add an artificial variable to $\geq$ or $=$ rows to meet the requirement and obtain a starting solution (complete the first tableau). The artificial variables appear in the SOL column of the first tableau and are then methodically driven from the solution in subsequent tableaus. The artificial variables have absolutely no meaning and we shall not be concerned with them again.

When $=$ constraints occur, an artificial variable must also be added. For example:

$$3X_1 + 2X_2 \quad\quad = 1{,}000$$
$$3X_1 + 2X_2 + A_2 = 1{,}000$$

Again, the purpose of A_2 is to achieve a starting simplex solution; A_2 will have no subsequent meaning.

The second basic difference is accommodated by converting objective functions from the *min* to the *max* form. For example:

$$\text{Min } Z = 5X_1 + 3X_2 \quad \text{becomes} \quad \text{Max } Z = -5X_1 - 3X_2$$

This is achieved by multiplying each term of the Min Z objective function by a -1. Minimization LP problems, after this conversion, are then solved as maximization problems. The exact same tableau procedures apply. After this conversion, slack variables and artificial variables are added to the objective function as required. Slack variables are assigned zero coefficients in the objective function as before. But what about the artificial variables? What coefficients should be assigned to the artificial variables? Would you believe a $-M$, where the M is a very large number? Now what the M actually represents is subject to speculation, but legend has it that Harvey Wagner first used the *big M method* in LP studies at the Mercury Motors Division of the Ford Motor Company more than 20 years ago. Regardless of its origin, each artificial variable is always assigned a $-M$ coefficient in the objective function in either max or min LP problems when the objective function conversion described above is used.[1] This $-M$ in Row C of the simplex tableau avoids an artificial variable entering back into the solution since $(C - Z)$ will always be zero or negative because the C value is $-M$ . . . , a negative very large number, say minus infinity. Since whatever is subtracted from minus infinity is either negative or zero, the artificial variable will never reenter the solution.

Example E.2 solves Problem LP-2 from Chapter 7, a minimization problem, using the simplex method.

---

[1] If this conversion of the objective function is not used, the objective function is left in its original form and the rule for the entering variable for minimization problems becomes: The entering variable is the one with the most negative number in Row $(C - Z)$. The artificial variables must then be assigned $+M$ coefficients in the objective function. All other procedures remain the same as in maximization problems. We prefer the conversion described above because the procedures are all exactly the same for both maximization and minimization problems, and we shall follow this convention throughout.

EXAMPLE E.2   Simplex Solution of LP-2, a Minimization Problem

The Gulf Coast Foundry is developing a long-range strategic plan for buying scrap metal for its foundry operations. The foundry can buy scrap metal in unlimited quantities from two sources, Atlanta (A) and Birmingham (B), and it receives the scrap daily in railroad cars. The scrap is melted down, and lead and copper are extracted for use in the foundry processes. Each railroad car of scrap from Source A yields 1 ton of copper and 1 ton of lead and costs $10,000. Each railroad car of scrap from Source B yields 1 ton of copper and 2 tons of lead and costs $15,000. If the foundry needs at least 2½ tons of copper and at least 4 tons of lead per day for the foreseeable future, how many railroad cars of scrap should be purchased per day from Source A and Source B to minimize the long-range scrap metal cost? LP-2 was formulated in Chapter 7 as:

$$\text{Min } Z = 10{,}000X_1 + 15{,}000X_2$$
$$X_1 + 2X_2 \geq 4 \text{ (lead—tons)}$$
$$X_1 + X_2 \geq 2\tfrac{1}{2} \text{ (copper—tons)}$$

where

$$X_1 = \text{carloads of scrap purchased from Source A per day}$$
$$X_2 = \text{carloads of scrap purchased from Source B per day}$$

1. **Add slack variables to constraints to convert from $\geq$ to $=$:**

$$\text{Min } Z = 10{,}000X_1 + 15{,}000X_2$$
$$X_1 + 2X_2 - S_1 \qquad = 4$$
$$X_1 + X_2 \qquad - S_2 = 2\tfrac{1}{2}$$

2. **Multiply objective function by -1 to convert to a maximization problem:**

$$\text{Max } Z = -10{,}000X_1 - 15{,}000X_2$$
$$X_1 + 2X_2 - S_1 \qquad = 4$$
$$X_1 + X_2 \qquad - S_2 = 2\tfrac{1}{2}$$

3. **Add artificial variables to constraints to obtain a starting solution, and include all variables in all functions:**

$$\text{Max } Z = -10{,}000X_1 - 15{,}000X_2 - MA_1 - MA_2 + OS_1 + OS_2$$
$$X_1 + 2X_2 + A_1 + OA_2 - S_1 + OS_2 = 4$$
$$X_1 + X_2 + OA_1 + A_2 + OS_1 - S_2 = 2\tfrac{1}{2}$$

4. **Place in first tableau and solve:**

First Tableau

C			$-10{,}000$	$-15{,}000$	$-M$	$-M$	0	0		
	SOL	**RHS**	X_1	X_2	A_1	A_2	S_1	S_2	ϕ	
$-M$	A_1	4	1	②	1	0	-1	0	$4/2 = 2$	← Leaving Variable (Smallest Positive)
$-M$	A_2	$2\frac12$	1	1	0	1	0	-1	$2\frac12/1 = 2\frac12$	
	Z	$-6\frac12 M$	$-2M$	$-3M$	$-M$	$-M$	M	M		
	(C − Z)		$2M$ $-10{,}000$	$3M$ $-15{,}000$	0	0	$-M$	$-M$		

↑
Entering Variable
(Largest Positive)

$$
\begin{array}{rrrrrrr}
-2 & -\tfrac12 & -1 & -\tfrac12 & 0 & \tfrac12 & 0 \\
2\tfrac12 & 1 & 1 & 0 & 1 & 0 & -1 \\
\hline
\tfrac12 & \tfrac12 & 0 & -\tfrac12 & 0 & \tfrac12 & -1
\end{array}
$$

Second Tableau

C			$-10{,}000$	$-15{,}000$	$-M$	$-M$	0	0		
	SOL	**RHS**	X_1	X_2	A_1	A_2	S_1	S_2	ϕ	
$-15{,}000$	X_2	2	$\tfrac12$	1	$\tfrac12$	0	$-\tfrac12$	0	$2/\tfrac12 = 4$	Leaving Variable (Smallest Positive)
$-M$	A_2	$\tfrac12$	(½)	0	$-\tfrac12$	1	$\tfrac12$	-1	$\tfrac12/\tfrac12 = 1$ ←	
	Z	$-\tfrac12 M$ $-30{,}000$	$-\tfrac12 M$ $-7{,}500$	$-15{,}000$	$\tfrac12 M$ $-7{,}500$	$-M$	$-\tfrac12 M$ $+15{,}000$	M		
	(C − Z)		$\tfrac12 M$ $-2{,}500$	0	$-\tfrac32 M$ $+7{,}500$	0	$\tfrac12 M$ $-15{,}000$	$-M$		

↑
Entering Variable
(Largest Positive)

$$
\begin{array}{rrrrrrr}
-\tfrac12 & -\tfrac12 & 0 & \tfrac12 & -1 & -\tfrac12 & 1 \\
2 & \tfrac12 & 1 & \tfrac12 & 0 & -\tfrac12 & 0 \\
\hline
1\tfrac12 & 0 & 1 & 1 & -1 & -1 & 1
\end{array}
$$

Third Tableau

C			$-10{,}000$	$-15{,}000$	$-M$	$-M$	0	0	
	SOL	**RHS**	X_1	X_2	A_1	A_2	S_1	S_2	ϕ
$-15{,}000$	X_2	$1\tfrac12$	0	1	1	-1	-1	1	
$-10{,}000$	X_1	1	1	0	-1	2	1	-2	
	Z	$-32{,}500$	$-10{,}000$	$-15{,}000$	$-5{,}000$	$-5{,}000$	$5{,}000$	$5{,}000$	
	(C − Z)	0	0	0	$-M$ $+5{,}000$	$-M$ $+5{,}000$	$-5{,}000$	$-5{,}000$	

The third tableau is optimal because all elements in Row (C − Z) are zero or negative.

5. **Interpret the solution:**

The solution is deduced from the SOL and RHS columns of the last tableau. All variables that do not appear in the SOL column are equal to zero:

$$X_1 = 1 \quad X_2 = 1\tfrac{1}{2} \quad S_1 = 0 \quad S_2 = 0 \quad Z = 32{,}500$$

The Gulf Coast Foundry should purchase 1 carload of scrap per day from Source A and $1\tfrac{1}{2}$ carloads of scrap per day from Source B. The total daily scrap cost will be $32,500 and no excess lead or copper above the minimum requirements will result. Note that the simplex method does not guarantee whole number (integer) answers. This is ordinarily not a serious difficulty. In this problem, for example, an average of $1\tfrac{1}{2}$ carloads of scrap from Source B could be accommodated by either 3 carloads one day and none the next or two carloads one day and one the next.

Pay particular attention to the conversion of $\geq$ constraints to the first tableau form by adding artificial variables and subtracting slack variables. Note also that the subscripts of the artificial and slack variables correspond to the order of the constraints. A_1 and S_1 belong to the first constraint, and A_2 and S_2 to the second.

The key complication in minimization problems is the more frequent inclusion of artificial variables. Negative M's, negative very large numbers, appear in the C row and column and consequently in Row Z and Row $(C - Z)$. If these M's are treated as any other very large number and are added, subtracted, and multiplied while the appropriate signs are observed, the minimization problems are as straightforward to solve as the maximization problems.

INTERPRETING SIMPLEX SOLUTIONS

Example E.1 used the simplex method to solve Problem LP-1. Let us now examine LP-1 and the last tableau from this example to determine what information is available to POM decision makers. LP-1 was formulated as:

$$\text{Max } Z = 900X_1 + 600X_2$$

$$
\begin{array}{llllll}
2X_1 + & X_2 + S_1 & & = 4{,}000 & \text{(fabrication — hours)} \\
X_1 + & 2X_2 & + S_2 & = 5{,}000 & \text{(assembly — hours)} \\
X_1 + & X_2 & + S_3 & = 3{,}500 & \text{(market — saws)}
\end{array}
$$

where

X_1 = number of circular saws to be manufactured per month

X_2 = number of table saws to be manufactured per month

S_1 = unused fabrication hours per month

S_2 = unused assembly hours per month

S_3 = unsatisfied market demand for saws per month

Z = profits per month

The last tableau in the simplex solution to LP-1 in Example E.1 was:

Third Tableau

C			900	600	0	0	0	
	SOL	**RHS**	X_1	X_2	S_1	S_2	S_3	ϕ
900	X_1	**1,000**	1	0	$\frac{2}{3}$	$\frac{1}{3}$	0	
600	X_2	**2,000**	0	1	$-\frac{1}{3}$	$\frac{2}{3}$	0	
0	S_3	**500**	0	0	$-\frac{1}{3}$	$-\frac{1}{3}$	1	
	Z	**2,100,000**	900	600	400	100	0	
	(C − Z)		0	0	-400	-100	0	

The solution to LP-1 is deduced as follows: X_1, X_2, S_3, and Z are in the SOL column and their values are shown in the RHS column. Because S_1 and S_2 are not found in the SOL column, their values are zero. This solution indicates that management should manufacture 1,000 circular saws and 2,000 table saws per month for a monthly profit of $2,100,000. All fabrication and assembly production capacity would be used and 500 additional saws could be sold to the market. To check this, let's examine the constraints of LP-1:

$$2X_1 + \quad X_2 + S_1 = 4,000 \text{ (fabrication — hours)}$$
$$2(1,000) + 2,000 + S_1 = 4,000$$
$$2,000 + 2,000 + S_1 = 4,000$$
$$S_1 = 4,000 - 2,000 - 2,000$$
$$S_1 = \quad 0$$

The fabrication of circular saws (X_1) and table saws (X_2) has used up all of the available fabrication hours per month; therefore $S_1 = 0$.

$$X_1 + \quad 2X_2 + S_2 = 5,000 \text{ (assembly — hours)}$$
$$1,000 + 2(2,000) + S_2 = 5,000$$
$$1,000 + \quad 4,000 + S_2 = 5,000$$
$$S_2 = 5,000 - 1,000 - 4,000$$
$$S_2 = \quad 0$$

The manufacture of circular saws and table saws has used up all of the available assembly capacity per month; therefore $S_2 = 0$.

$$X_1 + \quad X_2 + S_3 = 3,500 \text{ (market — saws)}$$
$$1,000 + 2,000 + S_3 = 3,500$$
$$S_3 = 3,500 - 1,000 - 2,000$$
$$S_3 = \quad 500$$

The sales of circular and table saws have fallen 500 saws short of completely satisfying the maximum monthly demand for saws; therefore $S_3 = 500$.

This explains the solution to LP-1. There is, however, some additional information in the last tableau that can be useful to operations managers. This information is called shadow prices and is found in Row $(C - Z)$:

	X_1	X_2	S_1	S_2	S_3
$(C - Z)$	0	0	-400	-100	0

The zeros in the X_1 and X_2 columns mean that these variables are in the solution column SOL in the last tableau. When nonzero shadow prices appear under X variables in Row $(C - Z)$, these values indicate the change in Z as a result of forcing one unit of an X variable into the solution. In maximization problems, the shadow prices under X variables indicate how much Z would be reduced by the introduction of one unit of the X variable into the solution. In minimization problems, the shadow prices under X variables indicate how much Z would be increased by the introduction of one unit of the X variable into the solution.

The value under an S variable in Row $(C - Z)$ represents the change in Z from a one-unit change in a constraint's RHS. S_1 refers to the first constraint because its subscript is 1 and represents fabrication hours. Since S_1 is not in the SOL column, $S_1 = 0$, which means that all of the monthly fabrication capacity is used. For example, assume that management wanted to know the following information:

1. How much would monthly profits (Z) increase if we could find one more hour of fabrication capacity per month (4,001 versus 4,000)?
2. How much would monthly profits (Z) decrease if we had one less hour of fabrication capacity per month (3,999 versus 4,000)?

The answer to both of these questions is found in Row $(C - Z)$ and the S_1 column: $400. The new monthly profits would be $2,100,400 and $2,099,600, respectively.

The element in Row $(C - Z)$ and the S_2 column indicates the change in Z if the RHS of the second constraint changes by one unit:

1. How much would monthly profits (Z) change if we could find one more hour of assembly capacity per month (5,001 versus 5,000)?
2. How much would monthly profits (Z) decrease if we had one less hour of assembly capacity per month (4,999 versus 5,000)?

The answer to both of these questions is $100; the new monthly profits would be $2,100,100 and $2,099,900, respectively.

How much would we be willing to pay to expand the market for our saw product lines through advertising or promotion? The answer to this question — nothing — can be found in Row $(C - Z)$ and the S_3 column. This answer is also obvious from the solution to Problem LP-1. If we could sell 500 more saws in the market than we are presently selling, we would not pay anything for more market demand.

An understanding of the shadow prices in Row $(C - Z)$ is valuable to management. This information allows managers to evaluate whether resources (production capacity and market demand in this example) should be shifted from other products or projects. If the cost of getting one unit of a resource is less than its shadow price, the resource should be acquired.

Interpreting simplex solutions of LP minimization problems is essentially the same as interpreting those of maximization problems. To demonstrate this similarity, let us examine Row $(C - Z)$ from the optimal tableau of Problem LP-2, a minimization problem:

	X_1	X_2	A_1	A_2	S_1	S_2
$(C - Z)$	0	0	$-M$ $+5{,}000$	$-M$ $+5{,}000$	$-5{,}000$	$-5{,}000$

The zeros under X_1 and X_2 mean that both X_1 and X_2 are in the solution. The values under A_1 and A_2 have no meaning. The 5,000 under S_1 means that if the lead requirement is raised or lowered one unit (1 ton per day), Z will change by \$5,000. If the RHS of the first constraint were increased from 4 to 5, Z would increase from \$32,500 to \$37,500. If the RHS were decreased from 4 to 3, Z would decrease from \$32,500 to \$27,500. The meaning of the 5,000 under S_2 is similarly the marginal impact of 1 ton of copper upon Z.

The minimization and maximization LP problems are interpreted exactly the same way. It is usually helpful to have the original problem formulated and in front of you when the last tableau is interpreted. The meanings of the variables in the solution and the shadow prices are then easier to understand.

Now, to further develop your ability to interpret simplex solutions, let us move on to a more realistic LP problem. Remember the Oklahoma Crude ingredient mix problem, Example 7.7, from Chapter 7? Example E.3 presents this problem and its simplex solution and fully interprets the meaning of the solution. Carefully reread the earlier problem before you begin this example.

EXAMPLE E.3   Interpreting Simplex Solutions: The Oklahoma Crude Oil Company Ingredient Mix Problem

The variable definitions of the Oklahoma Crude Oil Company problem are:

X_1 = thousands of gallons of Oklahoma crude to be purchased per month

X_2 = thousands of gallons of Texas crude to be purchased per month

X_3 = thousands of gallons of Kansas crude to be purchased per month

X_4 = thousands of gallons of New Mexico crude to be purchased per month

X_5 = thousands of gallons of Colorado crude to be purchased per month

S_1 = excess regular gasoline over minimum market requirement in thousands of gallons

S_2 = excess premium gasoline over minimum market requirement in thousands of gallons

S_3 = excess low-lead gasoline over minimum market requirement in thousands of gallons

S_4 = excess diesel fuel over minimum market requirement in thousands of gallons

S_5 = excess heating oil over minimum market requirement in thousands of gallons

S_6 = excess lubricating oil base over minimum market requirement in thousands of gallons

S_7 = unused Oklahoma crude supply in thousands of gallons

S_8 = unused Texas crude supply in thousands of gallons

S_9 = unused Kansas crude supply in thousands of gallons

S_{10} = unused New Mexico crude supply in thousands of gallons

S_{11} = unused Colorado crude supply in thousands of gallons

$A_1, A_2, A_3, A_4, A_5,$ and A_6 = no meaning

Min $Z = 200X_1 + 140X_2 + 150X_3 + 180X_4 + 120X_5$

$.4X_1 + .3X_2 + .3X_3 + .2X_4 + .3X_5 \geq 5,000$ (regular gasoline market requirement)*

TABLE E.3   Optimal Tableau from Ingredient Mix Problem: Oklahoma Crude Oil Company

C			−200	−140	−150	−180	−120	0	0	0	0
	SOL	RHS	X_1	X_2	X_3	X_4	X_5	S_1	S_2	S_3	S_4
−120	X_5	6,000	0	0	0	0	1	0	0	0	0
−180	X_4	1,333.33	0	0	0	1	0	0	0	−3.33	0
0	S_5	466.67	0	0	0	0	0	0	0	− .67	0
−150	X_3	2,000	0	0	1	0	0	0	0	0	0
0	S_2	2,200	0	0	0	0	0	0	1	−1	0
−140	X_2	4,000	0	1	0	0	0	0	0	0	0
−200	X_1	8,000	1	0	0	0	0	0	0	0	0
0	S_9	3,000	0	0	0	0	0	0	0	0	0
0	S_4	600	0	0	0	0	0	0	0	0	1
0	S_{10}	1,666.67	0	0	0	0	0	0	0	3.33	0
0	S_1	2,066.67	0	0	0	0	0	1	0	− .67	0
	Z	−3,420,000	−200	−140	−150	−180	−120	0	0	600	0
	(C − Z)		0	0	0	0	0	0	0	−600	0

* All requirements and supplies are in thousands of gallons.

$.2X_1 + .3X_2 + .4X_3 + .3X_4 + .2X_5 \geq 3{,}000$ (premium gasoline market requirement)

$.2X_1 + .1X_2 \qquad\quad + .3X_4 + .1X_5 \geq 3{,}000$ (low-lead gasoline market requirement)

$.1X_1 + .1X_2 + .1X_3 \qquad\quad + .2X_5 \geq 2{,}000$ (diesel fuel market requirement)

$\qquad .1X_2 + .1X_3 + .2X_4 + .1X_5 \geq 1{,}000$ (heating oil market requirement)

$.1X_1 + .1X_2 + .1X_3 \qquad\quad + .1X_5 \geq 2{,}000$ (lubricating oil base market requirement)

$X_1 \qquad\qquad\qquad\qquad\qquad \leq 8{,}000$ (Oklahoma crude supply)

$\qquad X_2 \qquad\qquad\qquad\qquad \leq 4{,}000$ (Texas crude supply)

$\qquad\qquad X_3 \qquad\qquad\qquad \leq 5{,}000$ (Kansas crude supply)

$\qquad\qquad\qquad X_4 \qquad\qquad \leq 3{,}000$ (New Mexico crude supply)

$\qquad\qquad\qquad\qquad X_5 \leq 6{,}000$ (Colorado crude supply)

TABLE E.3   (Continued)

0	0	-M	-M	-M	-M	-M	-M	0	0	0	0	0
S_5	S_6	A_1	A_2	A_3	A_4	A_5	A_6	S_7	S_8	S_9	S_{10}	S_{11}
0	0	0	0	0	0	0	0	0	0	0	0	1
0	0	0	0	3.33	0	0	0	-.67	-.33	0	0	-.33
1	-1	0	0	.67	0	-1	1	-.23	-.07	0	0	-.07
0	-10	0	0	0	0	0	10	-1	-1	0	0	-1
0	-4	0	-1	1	0	0	4	-.4	-.2	0	0	-.3
0	0	0	0	0	0	0	0	0	1	0	0	0
0	0	0	0	0	0	0	0	1	0	0	0	0
0	10	0	0	0	0	0	-10	1	1	1	0	1
0	-1	0	0	0	-1	0	1	0	0	0	0	.1
0	0	0	0	-3.33	0	0	0	.67	.33	0	1	.33
0	-3	-1	0	.67	0	0	3	-.03	-.07	0	0	0
0	1,500	0	0	-600	0	0	-1,500	70	70	0	0	90
0	-1,500	-M	-M	-M +600	-M	-M	-M +1,500	-70	-70	0	0	-90

A computer solution (last tableau) is presented in Table E.3.

a. What should management do? In other words, to management decision makers, what is the complete meaning of the values of the decision variables, slack variables, artificial variables, and Z in the optimal solution?

b. What is the meaning of each element in Row $(C - Z)$?

Solution

a. What should management do? What is the complete meaning of the values of the variables?

$X_1 = 8,000$ (buy 8 million gallons of crude oil per month from Oklahoma)

$X_2 = 4,000$ (buy 4 million gallons of crude oil per month from Texas)

$X_3 = 2,000$ (buy 2 million gallons of crude oil per month from Kansas)

$X_4 = 1,333\frac{1}{3}$ (buy 1⅓ million gallons of crude oil per month from New Mexico)

$X_5 = 6,000$ (buy 6 million gallons of crude oil per month from Colorado)

$S_1 = 2,066\frac{2}{3}$ (2,066,667 gallons of excess regular gasoline will be supplied monthly)

$S_2 = 2,200$ (2,200,000 gallons of excess premium gasoline will be supplied monthly)

$S_3 = \quad 0$ (no excess low-lead gasoline will be supplied monthly)

$S_4 = \quad 600$ (600,000 gallons of excess diesel fuel will be supplied monthly)

$S_5 = \quad 466\frac{2}{3}$ (466,667 gallons of excess heating oil will be supplied monthly)

$S_6 = \quad 0$ (no excess lubricating oil base will be supplied monthly)

$S_7 = \quad 0$ (all Oklahoma crude oil available will be purchased monthly)

$S_8 = \quad 0$ (all Texas crude oil available will be purchased monthly)

$S_9 = 3,000$ (3,000,000 gallons of Kansas crude oil will be available and not purchased monthly)

$S_{10} = 1,666\frac{2}{3}$ (1,666,667 gallons of New Mexico crude oil will be available and not purchased monthly)

$S_{11} = \quad 0$ (all Colorado crude oil available will be purchased monthly)

$A_1, A_2, A_3, A_4, A_5,$ and $A_6 =$ no meaning

$Z = 3,420,000$ ($3,420,000 crude oil cost per month will result)

b. Interpret Row $(C - Z)$:
   1. The values in the $A_1, A_2, A_3, A_4, A_5,$ and A_6 columns have no meaning.
   2. The zeros in the $X_1, X_2, X_3, X_4,$ and X_5 columns mean that all of these variables are in the solution.
   3. The zeros in the $S_1, S_2, S_4, S_5, S_9,$ and S_{10} columns mean that a 1,000-gallon change in the RHS of these constraints will not affect the monthly crude oil cost (Z), because each of these slack variables is in the solution. For example, $S_1 = 2,066\frac{2}{3}$ means that 2,066,667 gallons more than the 5,000,000 RHS of the regular gasoline minimum market requirement is supplied. Therefore raising or lowering the RHS a small amount will not affect Z.

Column	Row (C − Z)	Interpretation
S_3	−600	If the low-lead gasoline monthly market requirement were increased by 1,000 gallons, Z would increase $600.
S_6	−1,500	If the lubricating oil base monthly market requirement were increased by 1,000 gallons, Z would increase $1,500.
S_7	−70	If the amount of Oklahoma crude available each month were increased by 1,000 gallons, Z would decrease by $70.
S_8	−70	If the amount of Texas crude available each month were increased by 1,000 gallons, Z would decrease by $70.
S_{11}	−90	If the amount of Colorado crude available each month were increased by 1,000 gallons, Z would decrease by $90.

POST-OPTIMALITY ANALYSIS

Post-optimality analysis, or *sensitivity analysis* as it is often called, manipulates the elements of the last tableau of the simplex procedure to determine the sensitivity of the solution to changes in the original problem. Here are some of the questions that this analysis seeks to answer:

1. How will Z change if the RHS of any constraint changes? This question was addressed earlier in this section. The values in Row (C − Z) under the slack variables provide this information.
2. If a decision variable is not in the optimal solution (equals zero), how will Z change if one unit of the decision variable is forced into the solution ($X_i = 1$)? This question was also addressed earlier in this appendix. The values in Row (C − Z) under the decision variables provide this information.
3. Over what range can the RHS change and the shadow prices in Row (C − Z) remain valid?
4. How will Z change if one of the coefficients of a decision variable in the objective function changes by one unit?
5. How will Z change if one of the coefficients of a decision variable in a constraint changes by one unit?

These and other post-optimality questions are deduced from the optimal tableau, but the methods of analysis required to answer Questions 3, 4, and 5 are beyond the scope of this course. These questions assume that all other parts of the original problem remain unchanged and that only the singular change under consideration occurs. Although this is a popular topic with operations researchers, one rather obvious method for answering these and other post-optimality questions exists: Make the desired changes in the original problem, input the new problem to the computer, and interpret the new results.

UNUSUAL FEATURES OF SOME LP PROBLEMS

Two linear programming situations deserve special attention—degeneracy and alternate optimal solutions. *Degeneracy* is a condition in which there is a tie between two or more leaving variables in any maximization or minimization simplex tableau. For example, consider this problem:

$$\text{Max } Z = 5X_1 + 10X_2$$
$$X_1 + 3X_2 \leq 6$$
$$2X_1 + 2X_2 \leq 4$$

First Tableau

C			5	10	0	0	
	SOL	**RHS**	X_1	X_2	S_1	S_2	ϕ
0	S_1	6	1	3	1	0	$\frac{6}{3} = 2$
0	S_2	4	2	2	0	1	$\frac{4}{2} = 2$
	Z	0	0	0	0	0	
	(C − Z)		5	10	0	0	

$\uparrow$
Entering
Variable

In the first tableau a tie for the leaving variable exists. Therefore a condition of degeneracy is present. Why is this a problem? It usually poses absolutely no problem at all in arriving at an optimal solution. One of the variables is arbitrarily selected to leave, and the simplex method is continued. In rare instances, however, *looping* can occur. In other words, in the example above, if S_2 is selected to leave the first tableau, S_1 and X_2 are in the SOL column of the second tableau. S_1 could leave and S_2 could reenter the third tableau, and S_2 and X_2 would be in the SOL column. S_2 could leave and S_1 reenter the fourth tableau, and S_1 and X_2 would be in the fourth tableau. This switching could conceivably continue endlessly, thus prohibiting an optimal solution.

Looping situations almost never happen in nontrivial real LP problems in POM. When they do, a simple solution is to add or subtract an infinitesimally small amount to either the RHS or coefficient in the ϕ ratio to break the tie. For example, the original problem could be modified as follows:

$$\text{Max } Z = 5X_1 + 10X_2$$
$$X_1 + 3X_2 \leq 6.0001$$
$$2X_1 + 2X_2 \leq 4$$

This slight modification breaks the tie of leaving variables and removes the degeneracy condition.

Alternate optimal solutions exist when an element under a variable in Row $(C - Z)$ is zero and that variable is not in the solution. For example, consider this problem:

$$\text{Max } Z = X_1 + 7X_2$$

$$X_1 + 7X_2 \le 14$$

$$7X_1 + X_2 \le 14$$

Second Tableau

C			1	7	0	0	
	SOL	RHS	X_1	X_2	S_1	S_2	ϕ
7	X_2	2	$\frac{1}{7}$	1	$\frac{1}{7}$	0	$2/\frac{1}{7} = 14$ Leaving
0	S_2	12	$\textcircled{$\frac{48}{7}$}$	0	$-\frac{1}{7}$	1	$12/\frac{48}{7} = 1\frac{3}{4} \leftarrow$ Variable
	Z	14	1	7	1	0	
	$(C - Z)$	0	0	0	-1	0	

↑
Entering
Variable

Note that the zero under X_1 in Row $(C - Z)$ of this optimal tableau indicates that X_1 can enter the solution ($X_2 = 2, X_1 = 0, Z = 14$) with no change in Z. Let X_1 enter to check this out. X_1 enters and S_2 leaves:

$-\frac{1}{7}(1\frac{3}{4})$	$-\frac{1}{7}(1)$	$-\frac{1}{7}(0)$	$-\frac{1}{7}(-\frac{1}{48})$	$-\frac{1}{7}(\frac{7}{48})$
$-\frac{1}{4}$	$-\frac{1}{7}$	0	$\frac{1}{336}$	$-\frac{7}{336}$
2	$\frac{1}{7}$	1	$\frac{1}{7}$	0
$1\frac{3}{4}$	0	1	$\frac{49}{336}$	$-\frac{7}{336}$

A new alternate optimal solution emerges in the third tableau where $X_1 = 1\frac{3}{4}$, $X_2 = 1\frac{3}{4}$, and $Z = 14$. Z has not changed. Note that the zero in Row $(C - Z)$ under S_2 in the third tableau indicates also that an alternate optimal solution exists, the one in the second tableau.

Third Tableau

C			1	7	0	0	
	SOL	RHS	X_1	X_2	S_1	S_2	ϕ
7	X_2	$1\frac{3}{4}$	0	1	$\frac{49}{336}$	$-\frac{7}{336}$	
1	X_1	$1\frac{3}{4}$	1	0	$-\frac{1}{48}$	$\frac{7}{48}$	
	Z	14	1	7	1	0	
	$(C - Z)$	0	0	0	-1	0	

We should always examine Row (C − Z) to inspect for alternate optimal solutions. Why? Because these alternatives offer management the ultimate in flexibility—alternatives with the same profits or costs.

Now let us turn to a solution method designed to solve a special type of LP problem—the transportation problem.

TRANSPORTATION METHOD

In Chapter 7 we discussed selecting a set of shipments from sources to destinations that minimized period transportation costs. These problems can be analyzed by either the simplex method or the transportation method. We present the essential elements of the transportation method here.

CHARACTERISTICS OF TRANSPORTATION PROBLEMS

Transportation problems have these characteristics:

1. A finite and homogeneous set of discrete units must be shipped from several sources to several destinations in a particular time period.
2. Each source has a precise number of units that must be shipped in the time period.
3. Each destination has a precise number of units that must be received in the time period.
4. Each discrete unit to be shipped has a specific transportation cost from each source to each destination.
5. The objective is to minimize the total transportation costs for the time period.
6. The decision variables represent the number of units to be shipped from each source to each destination during the time period.

Such problems were first formulated in the 1940s, and the solution procedures that will be presented in this section were developed in the 1950s. Although the characteristics listed above accurately depict the problems as they were originally formulated and solved, later formulations and solutions allow a much broader range of problems. As we shall see later in this section, problems with ≥ and ≤ constraints, maximization objectives, demands greater than supply, and other characteristics are now routinely described as *transportation problems.* Solution procedures that constitute the *transportation method* also are used routinely to solve such expanded problems.

SOLUTION PROCEDURES OF THE TRANSPORTATION METHOD

The procedures of the transportation method are exhibited in Table E.4. To demonstrate these procedures, Example E.4 analyzes a problem of a manufacturing company that must select a new location for a factory to produce computer peripheral units.

TABLE E.4   *Procedures of the Transportation Method*

1. Formulate the problem in a transportation table. 2. Use the northwest corner rule or VAM to obtain a feasible starting solution.	3. Test the optimality of the solution by using the stepping-stone or MODI method. If the solution is optimal, stop. If not, continue to the next step. 4. Develop a new transportation table that is an improved solution. Go back to Step 3.

Notice in Steps 2 and 3 of Table E.4 that two alternative ways can be used to either test a solution for optimality or obtain a starting solution. Example E.4 uses only the northwest corner rule and the stepping-stone method so that you can get the overall picture of how the transportation method works. Later the same problem will be worked with the MODI and VAM methods so that you can appreciate the relationships among the methods.

EXAMPLE E.4   *The Northwest Corner Rule and the Stepping-Stone Method*

The Plain View Manufacturing Company presently has two factories at Amarillo and Waco, Texas, and three warehouses at Dallas, San Antonio, and Houston, Texas. In recent months Plain View has been unable to produce and ship enough of its computer peripheral units to satisfy the market demand at the warehouses. A new factory at Huntsville, Texas, is proposed to increase factory capacity. Bill Mayer, Plain View's president, wants to determine what Plain View's monthly shipping costs will be with the new factory located at Huntsville.

The monthly capacities of the old and new factories, the monthly warehouse requirements, and the transportation costs per unit from each factory to each warehouse are:

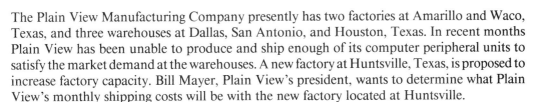

Factory	Monthly Capacity (Units)	Warehouse	Monthly Warehouse Requirements (Units)
Amarillo	400	San Antonio	300
Waco	1,000	Dallas	900
Huntsville	600	Houston	800
Total	2,000	Total	2,000

	Transportation Costs		
	Warehouses		
Factory	San Antonio	Dallas	Houston
Amarillo	$31	$21	$42
Waco	20	21	30
Huntsville	23	20	15

(a) Use the transportation method to determine the total monthly transportation costs if the new factory is located at Huntsville. **(b)** How many units per month should be shipped from each factory to each warehouse after the new factory is built? Follow the steps in Table E.4 for the transportation method. These steps are illustrated in Figure E.1.

Solution

1 and 2. **Formulate the problem in a transportation table and use the northwest corner rule to obtain a starting solution.** Note that the monthly factory capacities are placed on the right-hand side of the table opposite the appropriate factory row. Similarly, warehouse requirements are placed along the bottom of the table under the appropriate warehouse column. The per-unit shipping cost is shown in a box within each factory–warehouse cell. Note also that the total capacity for all factories equals the total warehouse requirements.

This starting solution shows how many units are shipped from each factory to each warehouse. When a cell is empty, zero units are to be shipped. The initial solution is obtained by beginning in the northwest cell (Amarillo–San Antonio) and allocating as many units as possible to this cell and proceeding likewise from left to right and downward. Only 300 units are possible in the Amarillo–San Antonio cell because this amount satisfies the San Antonio warehouse requirement. Moving to the right, we can allocate only 100 units to the Amarillo–Dallas cell because this completes the Amarillo factory capacity of 400 units. Next, we move downward and allocate 800 units to the Waco–Dallas cell, move right and allocate 200 units to the Waco–Houston cell, and so on until all 2,000 units have been allocated.

3. **Test the optimality of the solution by using the stepping-stone method.** This step requires systematically evaluating each of the empty cells in Transportation Table #1 to determine if monthly transportation costs can be reduced by moving any units into the empty cells. The stepping-stone evaluation method involves the procedures in Table E.5. As shown in Figure E.1, Transportation Table #1 is not optimal because we have a negative circuit cost for the Waco–San Antonio cell and we can reduce monthly transportation costs by moving some units into this empty cell.

4. **Develop a new transportation table that is an improved solution.** An improved solution is obtained by moving as many units as possible into the empty cell of the last transportation table with the most negative circuit cost. But how many units can be moved into the Waco–San Antonio cell, which had a negative circuit cost in Step 3? Let us again examine the stepping-stone circuit for this cell.

TABLE E.5   Stepping-Stone Method

Logic of the Stepping-Stones

In this procedure, we want to determine if the present transportation table is optimal, and if it is not, which variable should enter the solution. Each unfilled cell (a variable not in the solution) is investigated to determine if period costs would be reduced if units were moved from a filled cell (a variable in the solution) to an unfilled cell. The stepping-stone circuit is simply a logical way of determining the per-unit change in period costs if units are moved into an unfilled cell. This is analogous to examining the Row $(C - Z)$ in the simplex method to determine the entering variable.

Steps of the Stepping-Stone Method
1. Select an empty cell from the transportation table.
2. Draw a closed circuit between that empty cell and other stones (occupied cells) by using only straight vertical or horizontal lines. The circuit may skip over stones or other empty cells, but the corners of the circuit may occur only at stones (occupied cells) and the empty cell that is being evaluated.
3. Beginning at the empty cell being evaluated, move clockwise and alternatively assign positive (+) and negative (−) signs to the costs of the cells at the corners of the circuit from Step 2.
4. Total the per-unit costs of the cells at the corners of the circuit. The circuit total corresponds to the Row $(C - Z)$ values of the simplex method, and these values mean the amount of change in total shipping costs that can be realized by moving one unit to the empty cell under examination. Positive values mean costs will rise; negative values mean costs will fall.
5. Return to Step 1 and continue until all empty cells have been evaluated. The new cell to enter the solution is the cell whose circuit has the most negative circuit total cost.
6. If all the circuit totals are positive or zero, the solution is optimal. If negative circuit totals exist, develop an improved solution.

Determining the New Solution

Once we determine that period costs would be reduced if some units were moved into an unfilled cell, how many units should be moved? We should move as many as possible. The change in the solution is determined by examining the stepping-stone circuit with the most negative total circuit cost. In this circuit, among the filled cells with negative costs, locate the filled cell with the smallest number of units to be shipped. Subtract this number of units from all filled cells with negative costs and add this number to all filled cells with positive costs on that stepping-stone circuit. This is analogous to determining the value of the entering variable in the simplex method.

The maximum number of units that can be moved into the Waco–San Antonio empty cell is 300—the smallest number of units in a negative cell on the Waco–San Antonio stepping-stone circuit. To complete the improved solution, subtract the smallest number of units in negative cells, 300, from all negative cells and add this same number of units to the positive cells of the circuit. All other cells not on this circuit remain unchanged. This new solution is shown in Transportation Table #2 of Figure E.1.

This solution is an improved one—$43,200 in Transportation Table #1 versus $39,900 in Transportation Table #2—but is it optimal? Optimality can be determined once again by following the stepping-stone procedures. The stepping-stone circuit costs of the empty cells are shown in circles in Transportation Table #2 of Figure E.1. Because all stepping-stone circuit costs are either positive or zero, the solution in Transportation Table #2 is optimal.

Step 3—First, evaluate the Amarillo-Houston empty cell:
Circuit cost = +42 − 30 + 21 − 21 = +12. Place this cost in a circle.

To From	San Antonio	Dallas	Houston	Factory Totals
Amarillo	**300** 31	**100** 21 (−)	(+12) 42 (+)	400
Waco	20	**800** 21 (+)	**200** 30 (−)	1,000
Huntsville	23	20	**600** 15	600
Warehouse Totals	300	900	800	2,000 / 2,000

Next, evaluate the Waco–San Antonio empty cell:
Circuit cost = +20 − 31 + 21 − 21 = −11. Place this cost in a circle.

To From	San Antonio	Dallas	Houston	Factory Totals
Amarillo	**300** 31 (−)	**100** 21 (+)	42	400
Waco	(−11) 20 (+)	**800** 21 (−)	**200** 30	1,000
Huntsville	23	20	**600** 15	600
Warehouse Totals	300	900	800	2,000 / 2,000

Next, evaluate the Huntsville–San Antonio empty cell:
Circuit cost = +23 − 31 + 21 − 21 + 30 − 15 = +7. Place this cost in a circle.

To From	San Antonio	Dallas	Houston	Factory Totals
Amarillo	**300** 31 (−)	**100** 21 (+)	42	400
Waco	20	**800** 21 (−)	**200** 30 (+)	1,000
Huntsville	(+7) 23 (+)	20	**600** 15 (−)	600
Warehouse Totals	300	900	800	2,000 / 2,000

Next, evaluate the Huntsville–Dallas empty cell:
Circuit cost = +20 − 21 + 30 − 15 = +14. Place this cost in a circle.

To From	San Antonio	Dallas	Houston	Factory Totals
Amarillo	**300** 31	**100** 21	42	400
Waco	20	**800** 21 (−)	**200** 30 (+)	1,000
Huntsville	23	(+14) 20 (+)	**600** 15 (−)	600
Warehouse Totals	300	900	800	2,000 / 2,000

Steps 1 and 2—Starting Solution Using the Northwest Corner Rule

To From	San Antonio	Dallas	Houston	Factory Totals
Amarillo	**300** 31	**100** 21	42	400
Waco	20	**800** 21	**200** 30	1,000
Huntsville	23	20	**600** 15	600
Warehouse Totals	300	900	800	2,000 / 2,000

Step 4—Transportation Table #1

To From	San Antonio	Dallas	Houston	Factory Totals
Amarillo	**300** 31	**100** 21	(+12) 42	400
Waco	(−11) 20	**800** 21	**200** 30	1,000
Huntsville	(+7) 23	(+14) 20	**600** 15	600
Warehouse Totals	300	900	800	2,000 / 2,000

The monthly costs of Transportation Table #1 are:

Factory	Warehouse	Units to Be Shipped per Month	Monthly Transportation Cost ($)
Amarillo	San Antonio	300	$ 9,300
Amarillo	Dallas	100	2,100
Waco	Dallas	800	16,800
Waco	Houston	200	6,000
Huntsville	Houston	600	9,000
	Totals	2,000	$43,200

Step 5—Transportation Table #2

To From	San Antonio	Dallas	Houston	Factory Totals
Amarillo	(+11) 31	**400** 21	(+12) 42	400
Waco	**300** 20	**500** 21	**200** 30	1,000
Huntsville	(+18) 23	(+14) 20	**600** 15	600
Warehouse Totals	300	900	800	2,000 / 2,000

The monthly costs of Transportation Table #2 are:

Factory	Warehouse	Units to Be Shipped per Month	Monthly Transportation Cost ($)
Amarillo	Dallas	400	$ 8,400
Waco	San Antonio	300	6,000
Waco	Dallas	500	10,500
Waco	Houston	200	6,000
Huntsville	Houston	600	9,000
	Totals	2,000	$39,900

Now let us answer the questions of Plain View's location problem:

a. If the factory is located at Huntsville, Plain View's total monthly transportation costs will be $39,900.

b. Plain View should make these monthly shipments:

Factory	Warehouse	Number of Units
Amarillo	Dallas	400
Waco	San Antonio	300
Waco	Dallas	500
Waco	Houston	200
Huntsville	Houston	600
Total		2,000

Example E.4 uses the well-known *stepping-stone method* to determine optimality and to develop improved solutions. A newer and more frequently used method is the *MODI method* (modified distribution method). This procedure is similar to the stepping-stone method, but it is more efficient in computing the improvement costs (circuit costs in the stepping-stone method) for the empty cells.

Example E.5 uses the MODI method to test Transportation Table #1 in Figure E.1 for optimality. Before you begin this example, however, perhaps it would be helpful if you would do two things. First, review the procedures of the transportation method from Table E.4 to get the overall view of the procedure again. Notice that the only way that the MODI method affects the procedures of the transportation method is in testing each transportation table for optimality. Everything else in the procedure stays the same—formulating the transportation tables, using either the northwest corner rule or VAM to obtain a starting solution, and developing new transportation tables that are improved solutions. Next, review Step 3 in Figure E.1. This step uses the stepping-stone method to check for optimality.

In Example E.5 we first compute the R_i and K_j for the table. R_1 is always set equal to zero; this allows us to compute all other values of R_i and K_j *for filled cells.* After we know these values, we can directly calculate the circuit costs for the empty cells of the transportation table, but without the necessity of drawing the stepping-stone circuits for *all* of these cells as in the stepping-stone method. Next, if there are any negative circuit costs, we would draw the stepping-stone circuit for the empty cell that has the most negative circuit cost, just as we did in Figure E.1, and develop a new transportation table with an improved solution as before. Although the R_i and K_j must be recomputed for each transportation table, the MODI method is more efficient than the stepping-stone method and tends to be used more frequently in practice.

The northwest corner rule provides a starting solution to transportation problems, but one that is arbitrary. In most problems this results in too many transportation tables. This source of inefficiency may not seem too important to you now after having worked through Example E.4 in just two transportation tables, but in prob-

EXAMPLE E.5   *MODI Method of Testing Transportation Tables for Optimality*

Transportation Table #1

R_i \ K_j	To\From	$K_1 = 31$ San Antonio	$K_2 = 21$ Dallas	$K_3 = 30$ Houston	Factory Totals
$R_1 = 0$	Amarillo	300 $\quad$ 31	100 $\quad$ 21	(+12) $\quad$ 42	400
$R_2 = 0$	Waco	(−11) $\quad$ 20	800 $\quad$ 21	200 $\quad$ 30	1,000
$R_3 = -15$	Huntsville	(+7) $\quad$ 23	(+14) $\quad$ 20	600 $\quad$ 15	600
	Warehouse Totals	300	900	800	2,000 / 2,000

Calculating R_i and K_j for Filled Cells

$R_i + K_j = C_{ij}$, where C_{ij} represents the transportation cost of the ij cell

$R_1 = 0$
$R_1 + K_1 = C_{11}$
$0 + K_1 = 31, K_1 = 31$
$R_1 + K_2 = C_{12}$
$0 + K_2 = 21, K_2 = 21$
$R_2 + K_2 = C_{22}$
$R_2 + 21 = 21, R_2 = 0$
$R_2 + K_3 = C_{23}$
$0 + K_3 = 30, K_3 = 30$
$R_3 + K_3 = C_{33}$
$R_3 + 30 = 15, R_3 = -15$

Calculating Circuit Costs for Unfilled Cells

$$C_{ij} - R_i - K_j$$
Amarillo – Houston
$$= C_{13} - R_1 - K_3$$
$$= 42 - 0 - 30 = +12$$
Waco – San Antonio
$$= C_{21} - R_2 - K_1$$
$$= 20 - 0 - 31 = -11$$
Huntsville – San Antonio
$$= C_{31} - R_3 - K_1$$
$$= 23 - (-15) - 31 = +7$$
Huntsville – Dallas
$$= C_{32} - R_3 - K_2$$
$$= 20 - (-15) - 21 = +14$$

lems of more realistic proportions, say 25 sources and 40 destinations, *many* tables would be required if we used the northwest corner rule to obtain a starting solution. *Vogel's Approximation Method (VAM)* was developed to obtain a more efficient starting solution. In fact, in many problems the starting solution is optimal. Although the VAM method is more complicated than the northwest corner rule, in realistic problems that must be solved by hand, VAM is a much more practical way to obtain starting solutions.

EXAMPLE E.6 *Starting Solutions with Vogel's Approximation Method (VAM)*

To / From	San Antonio		Dallas		Houston		Factory Totals		D_1	D_2	D_3	D_4
Amarillo		31	**(4)** 400	21		42		400	10	10	10	
Waco	**(3)** 300	20	**(4)** 500	21	**(2)** 200	30		1,000	1	1	1	①
Huntsville		23		20	**(1)** 600	15		600	5			
Warehouse Totals	300		900		800		2,000	2,000				
D_1	3		1		⑮							
D_2	11		0		⑫							
D_3	⑪		0									
D_4												

D_i Column Calculations	D_i Row Calculations	Units Allocated at Iteration (i)
D_1 23 − 20 = 3, 21 − 20 = 1, 30 − 15 = ⑮	31 − 21 = 10, 21 − 20 = 1, 20 − 15 = 5	(1) 600/Huntsville – Houston
D_2 31 − 20 = 11, 21 − 21 = 0, 42 − 30 = ⑫	31 − 21 = 10, 21 − 20 = 1	(2) 200/Waco – Houston
D_3 31 − 20 = ⑪ , 21 − 21 = 0	31 − 21 = 10, 21 − 20 = 1 21 − 20 = ①	(3) 300/Waco – San Antonio
D_4 21 − 21 = 0		(4) 500/Waco – Dallas 400/Amarillo – Dallas

Example E.6 develops a starting solution to the transportation problem of our previous example. In working through the procedures of the VAM method, refer to Table E.6, which explains the steps of the method that are applied in Example E.6. In Step 1 from Table E.6 in the example, the D_1 row and column are first completed. These values represent the difference between the lowest unit cost and next lowest unit cost for each row and column. In Step 2 the Houston column has the largest

■ ■

TABLE E.6   *Steps of the VAM Method*

---

1. For each row and column of the transportation table, compute the difference between the lowest unit cost and the next lowest unit cost and record this difference. Place the row differences in a column to the right of the table under a heading of D_i and the column differences in a row across the bottom of the table with a heading of D_i, where i represents the number of times you have done this step.
2. Select either the row or column with the largest difference. If ties occur, arbitrarily select between tying elements.
3. Allocate as many units as possible to the cell with the lowest cost in the row or column selected in Step 2.

4. If the units in a row or column have been exhausted in Step 3, that row or column may be eliminated from further consideration in subsequent calculations by drawing a line through it.
5. When differences cannot be calculated in Step 1 because only one row or one column remains, this is not an unusual occurrence as we near the end of the process. Calculate the differences that are possible and continue.
6. Return to Step 1 and continue until the units in all of the rows and columns have been allocated.

■ ■

difference on the first iteration and it is selected. In Step 3 the Huntsville–Houston cell has the lowest unit cost within the Houston column, and we therefore allocate 600 units to that cell, the most possible. Because all of the Huntsville row has been allocated, you may draw a line all the way through this row to eliminate it from further consideration. This completes the first iteration.

Next, we begin the second iteration in the D_2 row and column. The Houston column has the largest difference and is selected, and 200 units are allocated to the Waco–Houston cell within the Houston column because this cell has the lowest remaining unit cost. This allocation exhausts the Houston column and a line may be drawn through the column. This completes the second iteration. The third and fourth iterations are similarly completed.

The starting solution obtained in this example is the same optimal solution obtained in Figure E.1 of Example E.4. This is not always the case and although the VAM method does yield an efficient starting solution when compared to the north-west corner method, it still must be considered only a starting solution and all of the steps of the transportation method listed in Table E.4 must be followed. In other words, in Example E.6, after the last iteration we would need to use either the stepping-stone or the MODI method to test the solution for optimality and proceed with the entire transportation method.

The reason that the VAM method yields better starting solutions than the northwest corner rule is that the northwest corner rule does not consider any cost information when the starting solution is determined — units are arbitrarily allocated on a northwest diagonal regardless of the costs. In the VAM method an opportunity cost principle is applied. At each iteration the difference between the lowest unit cost and the next lowest unit cost is the opportunity cost of not allocating units to a row or column. By selecting the largest difference, the largest opportunity cost is avoided. By taking into account the costs of alternative allocations, the VAM method yields very good starting solutions that are sometimes optimal, particularly in simple problems.

UNBALANCED PROBLEMS

Example E.4 involved a problem where the total number of units to be shipped from sources exactly equaled the number of units required at destinations. This is called a *balanced transportation problem.* It is not unusual to have an *unbalanced transportation problem,* where the number of units that can be shipped from sources exceeds the number required at destinations or vice versa. Figure E.2 is the optimal transportation table of such an unbalanced transportation problem.

FIGURE E.2   *An Unbalanced Transportation Problem*

To From	1	2	3	Dummy Destination	Source Totals
A	3.5	2.0 1,000	4.0	0	1,000
B	4.0	2.5 2,000	1.5 3,000	0	5,000
C	2.0 1,000	3.0 1,000	3.0	0 2,000	4,000
Destination Totals	1,000	4,000	3,000	2,000	10,000 10,000

A dummy destination column is entered into the table to account for the difference between destination requirements and source shipments. Note that the shipping cost from any source to the dummy destination is zero. The only function of the fictitious destination is to balance the problem. The interpretation of the 2,000 units in the Source C–dummy destination cell is that 2,000 units of the capacity at Source C will not be shipped. The dummy destination column therefore serves the same purpose as slack variables in the simplex method. All other solution procedures (the northwest corner rule, VAM, the stepping-stone method, or the MODI method) discussed earlier are followed to solve unbalanced transportation problems. The interpretation of the final solution is exactly the same in either balanced or unbalanced problems, with the exception of the dummy row or column interpretation.

DEGENERACY

Degeneracy is another complication that can be encountered in transportation problems. The number of occupied cells in a transportation table must be equal to the number of sources plus the number of destinations minus one. Thus in Example E.4 all transportation tables always had 5 occupied cells (3 sources + 3 destinations − 1 = 5). Degeneracy is present when less than this minimum number of occupied cells occurs. Degeneracy, if present, interferes with the drawing of stepping-stone circuits when the stepping-stone method is used, or it makes it impossible to compute the R_i and K_j if the MODI method is used to check for optimality of transportation tables. Therefore special procedures are necessary to solve these problems successfully.

If degeneracy occurs in the initial transportation table solution after employing either the VAM method or the northwest corner rule, a zero is assigned to one of the empty cells. The empty cell selected is usually one that creates an unbroken chain of occupied cells from NW to SE across the transportation table. The zero cell is treated as an occupied cell with zero units occupying the cell when stepping-stone circuits are drawn or R_i or K_j is calculated. This is analogous to having a variable in the solution, but with a zero value as in the simplex method. This manipulation allows us to complete our check for optimality without changing the nature of the transportation problem.

When degeneracy occurs in transportation tables beyond the initial solution, a slightly different procedure is used. Figure E.3 shows Transportation Tables #1 and

FIGURE E.3   *A Degenerate Transportation Table*

Transportation Table #1

To / From	Seattle	Denver	New Orleans	New York	Factory Totals
Miami	5,000 [1.2] (−)	5,000 [.7] (+)	[.5]	[.6]	10,000
Chicago	[.7]	5,000 [.5] (−)	10,000 [.5]	5,000 [.6] (+)	20,000
San Diego	[.5] (+)	[.7]	[.8]	15,000 [1.2] (−)	15,000
Warehouse Totals	5,000	10,000	10,000	20,000	45,000 / 45,000

Transportation Table #2

To / From	Seattle	Denver	New Orleans	New York	Factory Totals
Miami	0 [1.2]	10,000 [.7]	[.5]	[.6]	10,000
Chicago	[.7]	[.5]	10,000 [.5]	10,000 [.6]	20,000
San Diego	5,000 [.5]	[.7]	[.8]	10,000 [1.2]	15,000
Warehouse Totals	5,000	10,000	10,000	20,000	45,000 / 45,000

#2 of a transportation problem where degeneracy exists. Notice that the initial solution to this transportation problem has 6 occupied cells, exactly the required minimum (3 sources + 4 destinations − 1 = 6). The stepping-stone circuit of the San Diego – Seattle cell (superimposed on Transportation Table #1) has the most negative circuit cost of any empty cell in this table, and an improved solution must be developed from this circuit. Remember that we first identify the smallest number of units in the negative cells (5,000 units) and then subtract this number from all negative cells and add it to all positive cells on the circuit.

Ordinarily, this procedure makes one occupied cell go to zero units, but in this circuit both the Miami – Seattle and Chicago – Denver cells go to zero. That is what causes the solution in Transportation Table #2 to be degenerate, a condition comparable to a tie for leaving variables in the simplex method. We handle this degenerate situation in the transportation method by assigning a zero number of units to either one of the cells reduced to zero units. In Figure E.3 the zero is assigned to either the Miami – Seattle cell or the Chicago – Denver cell. The zero is then treated as an occupied cell, but with zero units, when applying either the stepping-stone or the MODI method of checking subsequent transportation tables for optimality. All other procedures of the transportation method are followed as before.

When more than two occupied cells are eliminated, more than one zero must be assigned to these cells to overcome the condition of degeneracy. Add enough zero cells so that the number of occupied cells equals the number of sources plus the number of destinations minus one. These problems are otherwise solved as before, with standard transportation method procedures.

ASSIGNMENT METHOD

The *assignment method* is another method for solving LP problems. Like the transportation method, the assignment method is easier to work than the simplex method, but it can be used only on LP problems with special characteristics. These characteristics are even more restrictive than those of LP problems using the transportation method:

1. *n* objects must be assigned to *n* destinations.
2. Each object must be assigned to some destination.
3. Each destination must be assigned an object.
4. The objective is to minimize the total cost of the assignment.

These problems can be solved by the transportation method where the units to be "shipped" is 1 for all rows and columns and the number of rows equals the number of columns. In this formulation the "sources" are the objects to be assigned. Although this formulation is straightforward, its solution with the transportation method can become difficult owing to extreme cases of degeneracy. Because of this complication, the assignment method offers computational advantages for solving assignment problems.

Example E.7 demonstrates the procedures of the assignment method. In this example the Mercury Electric Motor Company needs to assign five motor overhaul jobs to five motor rewinding centers. The assignment method is a simple and efficient method for solving such problems because it guarantees assignments that result in minimum processing cost, maximum profit, or minimum processing time for all of the jobs.

Example E.7 demonstrates the minimization algorithm that is appropriate for minimizing costs or processing times. If we wished to maximize profits, we would multiply all the profits in the first table by minus one (− 1) and then follow the same procedures as in the minimization case. Regardless of whether the problem is of the maximization or minimization type, the optimal job assignment — or job assignments, since multiple optimal solutions are possible — results from the use of the assignment method.

EXAMPLE E.7 *Using the Assignment Method to Assign n Jobs to n Work Centers*

Mercury Electric Motor Company overhauls very large electric motors used in industrial plants in its region. Bill Tobey has just received five electric motor overhaul jobs and is trying to decide to which rewinding work centers the jobs should be assigned. Because some of the work centers specialize in certain types of jobs, the cost for processing each job varies from work center to work center. Bill has estimated the processing costs for the five jobs at five rewinding work centers, and he uses the assignment method to make a minimum cost assignment of the jobs to work centers by following this procedure:

1. Place the cost information for assigning the jobs to work centers in an assignment table format. This is shown in Step 1 in Figure E.4.

2. Subtract the smallest cost in each row from all other costs in that row. The resulting table is shown in Step 2 in Figure E.4.

3. Subtract the smallest cost in each column from all other costs in that column. See Step 3 in Figure E.4.

4. Draw the least number of vertical or horizontal straight lines to cover the zero cells. See Step 4 in Figure E.4. Note that several different schemes may be possible, but the same number of minimum lines should result. If n lines (five in this example) were the minimum number of lines to cover the zero cells, the optimal solution would have been reached. If that were the case, the optimal job assignments would be found at the zero cells. Because less than n or only four lines were required, we must perform a modification to the table in Step 4 in Figure E.4.

5. Select the smallest cost not covered by lines in the table in Step 4 in Figure E.4 (the smallest cost is 50). Subtract this cost from all uncovered costs and add this cost to cells at the intersections of lines in Step 4. Then transfer these new costs and the costs that are unchanged in Step 4 to a new table in Step 5. Redraw the lines to cover the zero cells. Because five lines are required in Step 5, the solution is optimal. If fewer than five lines had been required, Step 5 would have to be repeated.

FIGURE E.4   Tables of the Assignment Method in Example E.7

Step 1

Work Centers

Jobs	1	2	3	4	5
A	$150	$300	$225	$350	$250
B	300	200	400	300	250
C	150	100	100	200	150
D	300	100	200	250	200
E	150	350	230	375	260

Step 2

Work Centers

Jobs	1	2	3	4	5
A	0	150	75	200	100
B	100	0	200	100	50
C	50	0	0	100	50
D	200	0	100	150	100
E	0	200	80	225	110

Step 3

Work Centers

Jobs	1	2	3	4	5
A	0	150	75	100	50
B	100	0	200	0	0
C	50	0	0	0	0
D	200	0	100	50	50
E	0	200	80	125	60

Step 4

Work Centers

Jobs	1	2	3	4	5
A	0	150	75	100	50
B	100	0	200	0	0
C	50	0	0	0	0
D	200	0	100	50	50
E	0	200	80	125	60

Step 5

Work Centers

Jobs	1	2	3	4	5
A	0	100	25	50	0
B	150	0	200	0	0
C	100	0	0	0	0
D	250	0	100	50	50
E	0	150	30	75	10

The zero cells in Step 5 of Figure E.4 indicate these assignments:

Possible Assignments			*Optimal Assignment*		
Job	*Work Centers*		*Job*	*Work Center*	*Processing Cost (from First Table)*
A	1 or 5		A	5	$250
B	2, 4, or 5		B	4	300
C	2, 3, 4, or 5		C	3	100
D	2		D	2	100
E	1		E	1	150
				Total cost	$900

REVIEW AND DISCUSSION QUESTIONS

1. Where in the optimal simplex tableau is the LP solution found?
2. Where are the shadow prices in the optimal simplex tableau?
3. What are shadow prices? What information do they provide managers?
4. Why must row operations be performed in the simplex method?
5. What purpose do artificial variables serve?
6. What are slack variables? What purpose do they serve?
7. What determines the subscripts for artificial and slack variables?
8. What are the characteristics of transportation problems?
9. What are the procedures of the transportation method?
10. What are the procedures of the northwest corner rule? Why is it used?
11. What methods may be used to test a transportation table for optimality?
12. What advantage does the MODI method have over the stepping-stone method? Explain.
13. What advantage does the VAM method have over the northwest corner rule? Explain.
14. What is an unbalanced transportation problem? What modifications are necessary in our ordinary transportation method when working unbalanced problems?
15. Why is degeneracy a difficulty in the transportation method? What specific difficulties are encountered in the northwest corner rule, stepping-stone method, and the MODI method?
16. What are the characteristics of assignment problems?
17. Describe the procedures of the assignment method.

PROBLEMS

Simplex Method

1. Perform row operations on this second tableau and complete the third tableau. Is the third tableau optimal? If not, which variables will enter and leave the third tableau?

Second Tableau

C			100	200	0	0	
	SOL	RHS	X_1	X_2	S_1	S_2	ϕ
200	X_2	500	1/4	1	1	0	
0	S_2	750	3/2	0	-1/2	1	
	Z	100,000	50	200	200	0	
	(C − Z)		50	0	−200	0	

2. Perform row operations on this second tableau. Complete the third tableau. Is the third tableau optimal? If not, which variables will enter and leave the third tableau?

Second Tableau

C			60	70	80	0	0	0	
	SOL	RHS	X_1	X_2	X_3	S_1	S_2	S_3	ϕ
0	S_1	50	1/8	1/2	0	1	0	0	
0	S_2	200	1	1/2	0	0	1	0	
80	X_3	60	1/4	1/4	1	0	0	1/2	
	Z	4,800	20	20	80	0	0	40	
	(C − Z)		40	50	0	0	0	−40	

Third Tableau

C			−20	−30	−M	−M	−M	0	0	0	
	SOL	RHS	X_1	X_2	A_1	A_2	A_3	S_1	S_2	S_3	ϕ
−20	X_1	100	1	1	0	1	0	0	1/4	0	
0	S_1	200	0	1	3	1/2	0	1	1/2	1/2	
−M	A_3	200	0	1	1	0	1	0	1	1/2	
	Z	−200M −2,000	−20	−M −20	−M	−20	−M	0	−M −5	−1/2 M	
	(C − Z)		0	M −10	0	−M −20	0	0	M +5	1/2 M	

3. Perform row operations on the third tableau on page E-42. Complete the fourth tableau. Is the fourth tableau optimal? If not, which variables will enter and leave the fourth tableau?

   (LP-A, B, C, D, E, F, G, H, I, and J problems are found at the end of Chapter 7.)

4. Solve LP-A using the simplex method. What is the optimal solution?

5. Solve LP-B using the simplex method. What is the optimal solution?

6. Solve LP-C using the simplex method. What is the optimal solution?

7. Solve LP-D using the simplex method. What is the optimal solution?

8. Solve LP-E using the simplex method. What is the optimal solution? (*Hint:* Convert the objective function to cents.)

9. Solve LP-G using the simplex method. What is the optimal solution?

10. Solve LP-H using the simplex method. What is the optimal solution?

11. Solve LP-I using the simplex method. What is the optimal solution? Fully interpret the meaning of the solution.

12. Below are the variable definitions and last (optimal) tableau for Problem LP-A:
    a. What should management do? In other words, to management decision makers, what is the complete meaning of the values of X_1, X_2, S_1, S_2, and Z in the optimal solution?
    b. What is the meaning of each of the elements in Row (C − Z)?

$$X_1 = \text{acres planted in soybeans this season}$$

$$X_2 = \text{acres planted in milo this season}$$

$$S_1 = \text{unused soybean acreage in acres}$$

$$S_2 = \text{unused fertilizer in pounds}$$

$$Z = \text{this season's profits on soybeans and milo in dollars}$$

Optimal Tableau

C			700	500	0	0	
	SOL	**RHS**	X_1	X_2	S_1	S_2	ϕ
700	X_1	**100**	1	0	1	0	
500	X_2	**50**	0	1	$-\frac{1}{2}$	$\frac{1}{2000}$	
	Z	**95,000**	700	500	450	$\frac{1}{4}$	
	(C − Z)	0	0	−450	$-\frac{1}{4}$		

13. Below are the variable definitions and last (optimal) tableau for Problem LP-B:
    a. What should management do? In other words, to management decision makers, what is the complete meaning of the values of X_1, X_2, S_1, S_2, and Z in the optimal solution?

b. What is the meaning of each of the elements in Row $(C - Z)$?

X_1 = daily sales calls per salesperson to petroleum industry customers

X_2 = daily sales calls per salesperson to chemical industry customers

S_1 = daily unused hours per salesperson on sales calls

S_2 = daily unused entertainment costs per salesperson

Z = average daily profits per salesperson in dollars

Optimal Tableau

C			500	200	0	0	
	SOL	RHS	X_1	X_2	S_1	S_2	ϕ
500	X_1	$6/10$	1	0	$18/80$	$-1/50$	
200	X_2	$1\,2/10$	0	1	$-3/10$	$3/50$	
	Z	540	500	200	$52\,1/2$	2	
	(C − Z)		0	0	$-52\,1/2$	-2	

14. Below are the variable definitions and last (optimal) tableau for Problem LP-C:
  a. What should management do? In other words, to management decision makers, what is the complete meaning of the values of X_1, X_2, S_1, S_2, S_3, and Z in the optimal solution?
  b. What is the meaning of each of the elements in Row $(C - Z)$?

X_1 = personnel assigned to the new project during the first quarter

X_2 = personnel assigned to the new project during the second quarter

S_1 = unused total personnel allowance

S_2 = unassigned first-quarter personnel

S_3 = unassigned second-quarter personnel

Z = total profits on the new project in dollars

Optimal Tableau

C			20,000	30,000	0	0	0	
	SOL	RHS	X_1	X_2	S_1	S_2	S_3	ϕ
20,000	X_1	10	1	0	1	0	−1	
0	S_2	5	0	0	−1	1	1	
30,000	X_2	10	0	1	0	0	1	
	Z	500,000	20,000	30,000	20,000	0	10,000	
	(C − Z)		0	0	−20,000	0	−10,000	

15. Below are the variable definitions and last (optimal) tableau for Problem LP-D:
    a. What should management do? In other words, to management decision makers, what is the complete meaning of the values of $X_1, X_2, X_3, S_1, A_2, S_2, S_3, S_4$, and Z in the optimal solution?
    b. What is the meaning of each element in Row $(C - Z)$?

> X_1 = next year's spending on urban renewal in millions of dollars
>
> X_2 = next year's spending on health services in millions of dollars
>
> X_3 = next year's spending on fire department in millions of dollars
>
> S_1 = unused urban renewal spending below the upper limit in millions of dollars
>
> A_2 = no meaning
>
> S_2 = excess health services spending above the lower limit in millions of dollars
>
> S_3 = unused fire department spending below the upper limit in millions of dollars
>
> S_4 = unused total spending in millions of dollars
>
> Z = total social returns for the three projects for next year in millions of dollars

Optimal Tableau

C			.4	.3	.35	0	−M	0	0	0	
	SOL	RHS	X_1	X_2	X_3	S_1	A_2	S_3	S_4	S_2	ϕ
.4	X_1	7	1	0	0	1	0	0	0	0	
.3	X_2	3	0	1	0	0	1	0	0	−1	
0	S_3	8	0	0	0	1	1	1	−1	−1	
.35	X_3	0	0	0	1	−1	−1	0	1	1	
	Z	3.7	.4	.3	.35	.05	−.05	0	.35	.05	
	$(C - Z)$		0	0	0	−.05	−M +.05	0	−.35	−.05	

16. Below are the variable definitions and last (optimal) tableau for Problem LP-E:
    a. What should management do? In other words, to management decision makers, what is the complete meaning of the values of $X_1, X_2, A_1, A_2, A_3, S_1, S_2, S_3$, and Z in the optimal solution?
    b. What is the meaning of each element in Row $(C - Z)$?

> X_1 = pounds of oats fed to each head of cattle daily
>
> X_2 = pounds of corn fed to each head of cattle daily
>
> A_1 = no meaning
>
> A_2 = no meaning
>
> A_3 = no meaning
>
> S_1 = excess calories per head of cattle daily in calories
>
> S_2 = excess minerals per head of cattle daily in units
>
> S_3 = excess vitamins per head of cattle daily in units
>
> Z = daily feeding cost per head of cattle in cents

Optimal Tableau

C			-5	-3	$-M$	$-M$	$-M$	0	0	0	
	SOL	RHS	X_1	X_2	A_1	A_2	A_3	S_1	S_2	S_3	ϕ
0	S_2	4,000	0	0	6	-1	-2	-6	1	2	
-3	X_2	30	0	1	$1/50$	0	$-1/100$	$-1/50$	0	$1/100$	
-5	X_1	10	1	0	$-1/100$	0	$1/100$	$1/100$	0	$-1/100$	
	Z	-140	-5	-3	$-1/100$	0	$-1/50$	$1/100$	0	$1/50$	
	(C − Z)		0	0	$-M$ $+1/100$	$-M$	$-M$ $+1/50$	$-1/100$	0	$-1/50$	

17. Below are the variable definitions for Problem LP-F. The last (optimal) tableau is found in Table E.7
   a. What should management do? In other words, to management decision makers, what is the complete meaning of the values of the decision variables, artificial variables, and Z in the optimal solution?
   b. What is the meaning of each element in Row (C − Z)?

$$A_1, A_2, A_3, A_4, A_5, A_6, \text{ and } A_7 = \text{no meaning}$$

The decision variables are the numbers of electric irons shipped from these sources to these destinations:

Decision Variable	Source	Destination	Decision Variable	Source	Destination
X_1	1	A	X_7	2	C
X_2	1	B	X_8	2	D
X_3	1	C	X_9	3	A
X_4	1	D	X_{10}	3	B
X_5	2	A	X_{11}	3	C
X_6	2	B	X_{12}	3	D

18. Below are the variable definitions and last (optimal) tableau for Problem LP-G:
   a. What should management do? In other words, to management decision makers, what is the complete meaning of the values of X_1, X_2, S_1, S_2, S_3, and Z in the optimal solution?
   b. What is the meaning of each of the elements in Row (C − Z)?

TABLE E.7 Optimal Tableau of LP-F

C			-.2	-.25	-.15	-.2	-.15	-.3	-.2	-.15	-.15	-.2	-.2	-.25	-M	-M	-M	-M	-M	-M	-M
	SOL	RHS	X_1	X_2	X_3	X_4	X_5	X_6	X_7	X_8	X_9	X_{10}	X_{11}	X_{12}	A_1	A_2	A_3	A_4	A_5	A_6	A_7
-.15	X_5	10,000	1	1	0	0	1	1	0	0	0	0	-1	-1	1	1	0	0	0	-1	-1
-.15	X_8	5,000	0	0	0	1	0	0	0	1	0	0	0	1	0	0	0	0	0	0	1
-.15	X_9	2,000	0	-1	0	0	0	-1	0	0	1	0	1	1	0	0	1	0	-1	0	0
-M	A_4	0	0	0	0	0	0	0	0	0	0	0	0	0	-1	-1	-1	1	1	1	1
-.20	X_{10}	8,000	0	1	0	0	0	1	0	0	0	1	0	0	0	0	0	0	1	0	0
-.20	X_7	5,000	-1	-1	0	-1	0	0	1	0	0	0	1	0	-1	0	0	0	0	1	0
-.15	X_3	10,000	1	1	1	1	0	0	0	0	0	0	0	0	1	-1	-1	1	1	0	0
	Z	-6,650	-.1	-.15	-.15	-.1	-.15	-.2	-.2	-.15	-.15	-.2	0	-.15	M	M	M	-M	-M	-M	-M
	(C - Z)		-.1	-.1	0	-.1	0	-.1	0	0	0	0	0	-.1	-2M	-2M	-2M	0	0	0	0

E-47

X_1 = number of hardback books to be produced per shift

X_2 = number of paperback books to be produced per shift

S_1 = unused minutes of cover capacity per shift

S_2 = unused minutes of printing line capacity per shift

S_3 = unused minutes of framing capacity per shift

Z = contribution dollars per shift

Optimal Tableau

C			10	6	0	0	0
	SOL	RHS	X_1	X_2	S_1	S_2	S_3
6	X_2	960	0	1	−4	6	0
0	S_3	68 4/7	0	0	−12/7	6/7	1
10	X_1	1,440	1	0	6	−3	0
	Z	20,160	10	6	36	6	0
	(C − Z)		0	0	−36	−6	0

Transportation Method

19. a. Use the northwest corner rule and the stepping-stone method to solve the transportation problem below.
    b. What is the optimal solution?
    c. Fully interpret the meaning of the solution.

From \ To	1	2	3	Source Totals
A	$.50	$ .90	$.50	100
B	.80	1.00	.40	500
C	.90	.70	.80	900
Destination Totals	300	800	400	1,500 / 1,500

20. The Apex Company produces electric transformers for electric distributors at two factories located in New York City and San Diego. Apex has four regional warehouses located in Seattle, Denver, Chicago, and Atlanta. The monthly warehouse requirements, monthly factor capacities, and per-unit transportation costs are:

Factory	Monthly Factory Capacity (Units)	Source	Destination	Transportation Cost per Unit
New York City	12,000	New York City	Seattle	$3.00
San Diego	14,000		Denver	2.00
			Chicago	1.00
	Monthly Warehouse Requirement (Units)		Atlanta	1.00
		San Diego	Seattle	1.00
			Denver	1.50
Warehouse			Chicago	2.00
			Atlanta	2.00
Seattle	9,000			
Denver	10,000			
Chicago	5,000			
Atlanta	2,000			

a. Use the northwest corner rule and the stepping-stone method to solve the transportation problem above.
b. What is the optimal solution?
c. Fully interpret the meaning of the solution.

21. a. Solve Problem LP-F using the northwest corner rule and the stepping-stone method. What is the optimal solution? Fully interpret the meaning of the solution.
    b. Solve Problem LP-F using the VAM and MODI methods. What is the optimal solution? Fully interpret the meaning of the solution.

22. a. Solve Problem LP-J using the northwest corner rule and the stepping-stone method.
    b. What is the optimal solution? Fully interpret the meaning of the solution.

23. a. Solve Problem LP-J using the VAM and MODI methods.
    b. What is the optimal solution? Fully interpret the meaning of the solution.

24. Three fabrication departments—A, B, and C—produce three slightly different products that are processed further in four assembly departments—1, 2, 3, and 4. Each fabrication and assembly department has a unique monthly capacity, and it is desirable that each department operate at capacity. Although any of the three products coming from the three fabrication departments can be processed in any of the four assembly departments, the assembly cost per unit differs among the products. Additionally, the materials-handling costs per unit differ among all the fabrication and assembly departments. The monthly fabrication department capacities, monthly assembly department capacities, and per-unit materials-handling and assembly processing costs are:

Fabrication Department	Monthly Capacity (Units)	Fabrication Department	Assembly Department	Materials-Handling Cost per Unit	Assembly Cost per Unit	Total Materials-Handling and Assembly Cost per Unit
A	9,000	A	1	$.25	$.95	$1.20
B	17,000		2	.15	.55	.70
C	14,000		3	.10	.40	.50
			4	.15	.45	.60
Assembly Department	Monthly Capacity (Units)	B	1	.10	.60	.70
			2	.15	.35	.50
			3	.20	.30	.50
1	3,000		4	.25	.35	.60
2	10,000					
3	15,000	C	1	.10	.40	.50
4	12,000		2	.15	.55	.70
			3	.30	.50	.80
			4	.40	.80	1.20

Develop a monthly production schedule for the three fabrication and four assembly departments. In other words, how many units should be processed in each fabrication department and moved to and processed in each assembly department so that monthly assembly and materials-handling costs are minimized?

a. Use the northwest corner rule and the stepping-stone method to solve the problem. What is the optimal solution? Fully interpret the meaning of the solution.

b. Use the VAM and MODI methods to solve the problem. What is the optimal solution? Fully interpret the meaning of the solution.

25. Three recycling plants—A, B, and C—receive and process scrap paper and ship paper stock to three regional warehouses—1, 2, and 3. The monthly recycling plant capacities, monthly regional warehouse requirements, and the shipping cost per 100 pounds are:

Recycling Plant	Monthly Capacity (100 Pounds)	Regional Warehouse	Monthly Requirement (100 Pounds)	Recycling Plant	Regional Warehouse	Shipping Cost per 100 Pounds
A	500	1	300	A	1	$3
B	1,200	2	900		2	2
C	800	3	800		3	4
				B	1	4
					2	3
					3	1
				C	1	2
					2	2
					3	3

How many pounds of paper stock should be shipped from each recycling plant to each regional warehouse per month to minimize monthly shipping costs?

a. Use the northwest corner rule and the stepping-stone method to solve this problem. What is the optimal solution? Fully interpret the meaning of the solution.

b. Use the VAM and MODI methods to solve this problem. What is the optimal solution? Fully interpret the meaning of the solution.

Assignment Method

26. Four jobs must be assigned to four work centers. Only one job can be assigned to each work center, and all jobs must be processed. The cost of processing each job through each work center is shown below:

Work Centers

		1	2	3	4
	A	$50	$45	$50	$65
Jobs	B	25	40	35	20
	C	65	60	55	65
	D	55	65	75	85

a. Use the assignment method to determine which jobs should be assigned to which work centers to minimize total processing costs.

b. What is the cost of your assignments in Part *a*?

27. Four employees must be assigned to four projects. Only one employee can be assigned to a project, and all projects must be performed. The cost of the employees performing the projects are:

Projects

		1	2	3	4
	Al	$300	$325	$500	$350
Employees	Ben	400	525	575	600
	Cal	350	400	600	500
	Dan	400	350	450	450

a. Use the assignment method to assign these employees to these projects.

b. What is the total cost of your assignment in Part *a*?

28. Five customers must be assigned to five stockbrokers in a brokerage house. The estimated profits for the brokerage house for all possible assignments are shown below:

Brokers

		1	2	3	4	5
Customers	A	$500	$525	$550	$600	$700
	B	625	575	700	550	800
	C	825	650	450	750	775
	D	590	650	525	690	750
	E	450	750	660	390	550

    a. Use the assignment method to assign the five customers to the five different brokers to maximize profits for the brokerage house.

    b. What are the profits from your assignment in Part *a*?

29. Use the assignment method to solve the Computer Products Corporation case at the end of Chapter 7. What is the optimal solution? Fully interpret the meaning of the solution.

COMPUTER SOLUTIONS

Several of the problems at the end of Chapter 7 and some of the problems in this appendix are appropriate for solution with a computer. The three computer problems/cases at the end of Chapter 7, Sunshine, CPC, and DAC, are especially intended for solution with the *POM Computer Library* that accompanies this book. In solving these problems, take care to define the decision variables, determine the solution of the problems using a computer, and fully interpret the meaning of the solution. This means not only determining the value of the decision variables (X's), slack variables (S's), and the objective function (Z), but also fully interpreting the meaning of the solution to management. In other words, what would you recommend that management do as a result of your analysis? This interpretation should also include an explanation of the meaning of the shadow prices. Also, you should be aware of unusual features in the solution; for example, you should determine if alternate optimal solutions are present.

SELECTED BIBLIOGRAPHY

Bierman, Harold, Jr., Charles P. Bonini, and Warren H. Hausman. *Quantitative Analysis for Business Decisions.* 6th ed. Homewood, IL: Irwin, 1981.

Buffa, E. S., and J. S. Dyer. *Management Science/Operations Research: Model Formulation and Solution Methods.* 2nd ed. New York: Wiley, 1981.

Daellenbach, H. G., and E. J. Bell. *User's Guide to Linear Programming.* Englewood Cliffs, NJ: Prentice-Hall, 1970.

Hillier, F. S., and G. J. Lieberman. *Introduction to Operations Research,* 4th ed. Oakland, CA: Holden-Day Inc., 1986.

Lee, Sang M. *Introduction to Management Science,* 2nd ed. Hinsdale, IL: Dryden Press, 1987.

Perry, C., and K. C. Crellin. "The Precise Management Meaning of a Shadow Price." *Interfaces* 12, no. 2(April 1982):61–63.

Taha, H. A. *Operations Research: An Introduction,* 4th ed. N.Y.: MacMillan Publishing Company, 1987.

DECISION MAKING IN POM

In this appendix we explore some of the concepts and techniques from the field of *decision theory.* This study of decision making is set in the context of production and operations management. Such an approach is intended to provide an understanding of decision making *and* insight into the nature of the decisions of operations managers.

THE DECISION-MAKING PROCESS

When we think of decision making, we typically envision a manager at some *moment of truth* deciding on or choosing a specific course of action. The mystique surrounding this highly charged moment can be so magnetic that it is sometimes hard to remember this is only the climax to decision making and not the total decision-making experience. While we cannot minimize the importance of this deciding phase of decision making, we must recognize that the process of arriving at this moment of choosing is of at least equal importance. Table F.1 lists the steps in the systematic process of decision making.

As the subtitle, *A Problem-Solving and Decision-Making Approach,* of this text suggests, in this book we attempt to place you squarely in the chairs of operations managers as they are forced to make decisions about a variety of operations problems. The decision-making process described in Table F.1 provides a useful framework for you to consider as you analyze the problems and recommend decision alternatives throughout the text.

TABLE F.1   *The Systematic Process of Decision Making*

1. Define and describe the problem and its magnitude.	4. Weigh and decide among the alternatives.
2. Generate alternative solution approaches.	5. Formulate a plan for implementation.
3. Analyze the alternatives.	6. Formulate a contingency plan.

NATURE OF DECISIONS IN POM

Here we shall attempt to give you an understanding of what it is like to make some of the decisions that operations managers have to make. To impart this understanding, we shall explore the characteristics of decisions in general, the level of analysis that is appropriate for different decisions, and the conditions that surround many operations management decisions.

CHARACTERISTICS OF DECISIONS

As we apply the systematic decision-making process to decisions, we find that the amount of analysis, amount of money spent on data gathering, degree of formality of implementation, and other specific details of the ways we make decisions differ, depending on the presence of the characteristics of the decisions found in Table F.2. For example, the amount of analysis applied to a nonrecurring decision having limited intensity and duration of impact would differ tremendously from a recurring decision having high intensity and long duration of impact. To understand the characteristics of a decision is, to a large degree, to know the specifics of how to perform each step of the decision process.

Uncertainty in decisions typically includes the lack of knowledge about what variables are important, about the relationships between the variables, and about the values of the variables. Uncertainty is typically dealt with by managers either subjectively or objectively. *Subjective methods* usually involve operating as if conditions of certainty were present by selecting the most important variables while ignoring the effect of all others, assuming the most likely relationships between the most important variables, and estimating as precisely as possible the values of the most important variables. When the analysis is completed while assuming conditions of certainty, the manager usually allows for uncertainty by dropping back and taking a somewhat more conservative stance than the analysis under assumptions of certainty may have indicated. *Objective methods* of dealing with uncertainty usually involve (1) spending money, time, and human effort to gather data in order to reduce the level of uncertainty; (2) developing analyses based on three or more levels of optimism — pessimistic, most likely, and optimistic; and (3) developing or estimating the probability of each outcome. The results of this latter analysis can be left in the form of outcome values (typically dollars), probabilities, or a combination of both into expected values.

Decision *complexity* refers to the number of variables, the network of relationships between the variables, and the relationships between decisions. A complex decision is described as one that involves a great number of variables, many of them in complicated relationships to one another, and one that stands in a series of decisions that must be made in sequence.

The *time frame* or the amount of time available to make a decision may determine how a decision can be made. Decisions with short time frames may not allow any more than a few minutes of consideration or analysis. Conversely, some decisions can take many weeks, months, or even years to complete.

TABLE F.2   *Some Characteristics of Decisions*

1. Degree of uncertainty	4. Expected returns relative to cost of analysis
2. Degree of complexity	5. Degree of recurrence
3. Decision time frame	6. Intensity of decision impact
	7. Duration of decision impact

A decision's *expected returns relative to cost of analysis* is important because the amount of money that should be spent on analysis is, to a large degree, a function of the returns expected from the decision. If few negative or positive consequences are expected from a decision, little analysis can be economically justified. Conversely, expected monumental consequences from decisions justify enormous outlays for data gathering and analysis.

Major decisions that happen only once are said to be *nonrecurring.* These decisions may receive intense organization attention throughout the decision process, but when the process is completed, the attention and activity end. Other decisions are *recurring* decisions. These decisions initially receive a high degree of organization attention and activity. Once the decision is reached, a pattern is set for all similar future decisions.

When decisions have prospects of either a high return if a good decision is made or a great loss if a poor decision is made, they are described as having an intense *impact.* The *duration* or time span over which the effects of decisions are expected to endure is an important consideration in the attention, effort, and formality that an organization devotes to them. A good or poor outcome concerning a certain decision may be over momentarily and never be experienced again. Another decision may, however, have potentially lasting effects extending 20 or more years into the future, and consequently that decision receives the highest level of decision effort.

Once we understand the characteristics of a particular decision, several levels of analysis exist for use in examining the alternatives of the decision.

LEVELS OF ANALYSIS

The full range of analytical possibilities consists of five classes or levels: intuition, quick-and-dirty, intensive computations, model building, and task force.

To call *intuition* a level of analysis is perhaps a misnomer. Making decisions on the basis of intuition applies no analysis at all to decisions. This approach uses hunches, gut feelings, or instinctive leanings to arrive at spur-of-the-moment decisions. When would you ever want to use this approach? Most managers would advise that you use it only when you cannot use any other basis or when the decision outcome is unimportant.

Practically speaking, there are almost always other possible bases for decisions. This is not to say that intuition is never used by managers, because it is present to varying degrees in all decisions. Additionally, when decisions must be made instantaneously, thus circumventing all other levels of analysis, intuition may be all that is left for the decision maker.

Crisis managers sometimes insist that all decisions must be made quickly. That is how they justify low levels of analysis, low degrees of participation in decision making by others, and poor decisions. They explain away these decisions with the excuse: "There wasn't enough time to . . . ."

The *quick-and-dirty* level of analysis typically assumes away most complexity and uncertainty. Simple calculations are performed on only the most critical variables under the assumption of the simplest of relationships. This level of analysis can usually be performed in a few minutes, or in a couple of hours at the most. This may be the method on which many of the day-to-day decisions in organizations are based.

When the relative importance of the decision is high, *intensive computations* are typically the lowest acceptable level of analysis. Many variables are quantified, manipulated, and compared in order to assess the decision alternatives. These analyses typically involve one or more persons gathering and examining volumes of data and assembling, calculating, and comparing various alternatives. Desk-top calculators or interactive computers are the dominant machines that are utilized.

The *model-building* method of analysis involves the construction of a model, usually a *mathematical model* that is a simplified abstraction from the real system under study.[1] Such a model forms the basis for most quantitative analysis of operations. For example, the familiar formula for period profits used in break-even analysis is a mathematical model:

$$\text{Period profits} = \text{Total revenue} - \text{Total costs}$$

$$P = Qp - (FC + Qv)$$

where P represents period profits, Q represents number of units sold in the period, p represents price per unit, FC represents period fixed costs, and v represents variable cost per unit. P would ordinarily be referred to as both a *dependent variable* and an *uncontrollable variable.* A dependent variable is one whose value depends on the value of other variables. An uncontrollable variable is one that cannot be directly manipulated by the model builder. Q would usually be called both an *independent variable* and a *controllable variable.* An independent variable is one on which the values of other variables depend. A controllable variable is one whose value can be set by the model builder. FC, p, and v ordinarily are referred to as *parameters.* A parameter is a measure of the conditions inherent in the problem and is usually treated as a *constant* reflecting these conditions. As the conditions change, the value of the parameter will be changed. The outcome of this profit model is said to be an *optimal solution* if the value of P is optimal, that is, the greatest value possible under the conditions defined by the parameters.

The underlying purpose of mathematical models is to allow us to estimate the effects of certain actions on the real system without the need to change the real system. For example, a mathematical scheduling model can be built that is a representation of a factory. Capacities, products, and machine speeds can be manipulated in the model to determine the approximate effect on the efficiency of the factory. Such analyses can be performed without the need to shut down production machinery, change the capacities and speeds of the machines, or introduce new products into production. Manipulating mathematical models is usually less expensive and quicker than manipulating the real system. The value of experimenting with a mathematical model depends on how closely the model represents the real system.

The profit model illustrated earlier is a very simple mathematical model. Other models in POM are much more complex. Linear programming, PERT/CPM, and

---

[1] Frank S. Budnick, Richard Mojena, and Thomas E. Vollman, *Principles of Operations Research* (Homewood, IL: Richard D. Irwin, 1977), 12–13.

queuing models are examples of more complex POM models; these models are studied in various places in this text. Linear programming is treated in Chapter 7 and PERT/CPM is studied in Chapter 16. Mathematical models such as these are usually programmed into a computer language so that they can be manipulated on a computer. By manipulation we mean *sensitivity analysis*—varying the values of the controllable variables and parameters of the model so that we can observe the effects on the dependent variables of the model. *Computer models* allow analysts to examine large numbers of variables simultaneously, to retrieve enormous blocks of data, and to perform these functions quickly. Still, model building takes more time and usually costs more than lower levels of analysis.

A *task force* is a group of high-level personnel who are assigned to collectively analyze a decision and arrive at a consensus on a course of action to be recommended to management. All of the various levels of analysis that have been mentioned above are likely to be used in this effort. This team usually has the mandate of the highest executive officers and carries the highest priority over most other activities of the organization. Large amounts of data are processed, many alternatives are analyzed, specialists are called into the effort as required, and the study typically spans several months or even years. Since the task force is the most intensive level of decision analysis, it is typically reserved for the most critical organizational decisions.

Knowledge of the characteristics of decisions and familiarity with the levels of decision analysis provide us with a good perspective to view decision making by operations managers.

MAKING DECISIONS IN POM

Strategic, operating, and control decisions were discussed in Chapter 1. The characteristics of decisions discussed earlier in this section are present in varying degrees in all these decisions. *Strategic decisions*—long-range decisions about products, processes, and facilities—are usually complex, one-time decisions that will have significant, long-lasting effects on the organization. Extensive analysis can be justified because enough time is available to do the analysis, the payoff is great relative to the cost of analysis, and the decisions are complex and must be made in an atmosphere of uncertainty. *Control decisions*—short-range decisions concerned with the planning and controlling of day-to-day operations—are, conversely, relatively simple decisions that must be made quickly. On the one hand, if the decisions are not recurring, little analysis can be justified because little time is available for analysis, the payoff for analysis is small, and the decisions involve little uncertainty. On the other hand, if the decisions are recurring, much analysis may be justified because the outcome of the decisions will be long-lasting and their cumulative effect can be great.

Table F.3 summarizes the frequency with which each level of analysis tends to be applied by operations managers to the three types of POM decisions. Strategic decisions concerned with products, processes, and facilities predominantly involve intensive computations, computer model building, and, occasionally, task forces. Control decisions concerned with planning and controlling daily operations principally involve intensive computations, and, to a lesser degree, quick-and-dirty and computer model building. If these control decisions are recurring, higher levels of analysis may be justified.

TABLE F.3   *Frequency of Use of Levels of Analysis for Three Types of POM Decisions*

Level of Analysis	Frequency of Use of Levels of Analysis		
	Strategic Decisions (Products, Processes, and Facilities)	*Operating Decisions (Planning Production to Meet Demand)*	*Control Decisions (Planning and Controlling Operations)*
1. Intuition	Very low	Very low	Very low
2. Quick-and-dirty	Low	Moderate	Moderate
3. Intensive computations	High	High	High
4. Computer model building	Moderate/high	Moderate*	Low*
5. Task force	Moderate	Low*	Very low*

* Except in decisions that are recurring; then the frequency of use would ordinarily be higher.

Figure F.1 illustrates that making decisions in POM is a complex activity. Many factors impinge on decision makers as they approach the moment of truth when a decision must be made. Analysis and logic, society and culture, emotions, experience and judgment, personal motives, intuition, uncertainty, and other inputs all affect the decision. Analysis plays an important part in almost all of the decisions in POM. Operations managers near the top of organizations make decisions about the long-range survival of their organizations with an open view of the external environment. They use judgment as the principal basis for these decisions. Judgment, as used here,

FIGURE F.1   *Decision Making in POM*

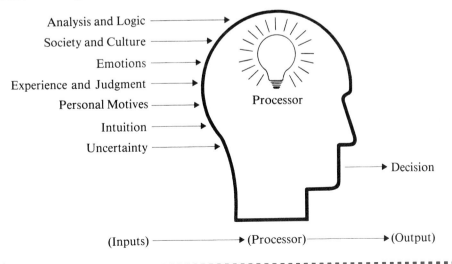

means using analysis performed by others, formulating the necessary linkages about what is known and unknown, and, finally, deciding on a course of action. Past experience, knowledge, common sense, and instinct are necessary ingredients of this decision making.

Operations managers who are further down in organizations may make some long-range decisions as top executives do, but many of their decisions are very different from those in the executive suite. These operations managers make some decisions that (1) are short-range, having effects that will not be long-lasting, (2) are about simple problems, having only a few variables that are related in relatively simple ways, and (3) deal with recurring problems. Because of the short time during which the decisions will affect the organization, the information available tends to be more predictable and certain, and a somewhat closed view of the external environment is taken. The limited number of variables and the recurring nature of the problems allow operations managers to better understand the relationships among the variables and to predict the probable outcomes from alternative courses of actions. Many such decisions of operations managers are based primarily on analysis.

Regardless of where we find operations managers in organizations, analysis plays an important part in their decision making. The techniques that they use to analyze their decisions are therefore an important part of this text.

DECISION-MAKING TECHNIQUES FOR POM

Many techniques associated with POM decisions are studied in this text. Among these, three stand out in their frequency of use: *break-even analysis, decision trees,* and *payoff tables.* These techniques could have been presented in this appendix because they are traditionally thought of as being related to *decision theory.* However, we have chosen to present them within the various topical chapters of this text so that their use could be more directly relevant to decision applications in POM. Break-even analysis appears in several places in the text, but it is prominent in chapter 4, Production Processes. See the discussion and explanation of break-even analysis in the section in which Example 4.1 appears. Decision trees are discussed and demonstrated in Chapter 8, Long-Range Capacity Planning and Facility Location. Read the treatment of decision trees in the section in which Example 8.1 appears. Payoff tables are treated in Chapter 10, Independent Demand Inventory Systems. Study the discussion of payoff tables in the section in which Examples 10.7 and 10.11 appear.

REVIEW AND DISCUSSION QUESTIONS

1. What is systematic decision making? What steps are included?
2. Name seven characteristics of decisions.
3. List the decision characteristics that would make it appropriate to analyze decision alternatives using these levels of analysis:
   a. intuition,

    b. quick-and-dirty,

    c. intensive computations,

    d. model building, and

    e. task force.

4. How do managers typically deal with uncertainty in decisions?

5. Define these terms: *mathematical model, dependent variable, independent variable, controllable variable, uncontrollable variable, parameter, constant, optimal solution, sensitivity analysis, computer model.*

6. Under what conditions would a manager analyze an operating decision as thoroughly as a strategic decision?

7. Discuss this statement: There is no room for intuition in systematic decision making.

PROBLEMS

Break-even Analysis

See Problems 4.11, 4.12, 4.13, 4.14, 4.15, Phelps Petroleum Refining case in Chapter 4, 5.4, 5.5, 5.6, 5.7, 5.8, Morton Aerospace case in Chapter 5, 8.1, 8.2, 8.10, 8.11, Sporting Charge Company case in Chapter 8, 13.7, 13.8, and 13.9.

Decision Trees

See Problems 8.3, 8.4, 8.5, 8.6, Brightco Manufacturing case in Chapter 8, 13.10, and 13.11.

Payoff Tables

See Problems 10.16, 10.17, 10.22, 10.23, 10.24, Safety Stock Levels at CPC case in Chapter 10, 17.4, 17.5, 17.6, and Central Michigan Fabricators case in Chapter 17.

SELECTED BIBLIOGRAPHY

Anderson, David R., Dennis J. Sweeney, and Thomas A. Williams. *An Introduction to Management Science: Quantitative Approaches to Decision Making.* 4th ed. St. Paul, MN: West Publishing, 1985.

Bierman, Harold, Charles P. Bonini, and Warren H. Hausman. *Quantitative Analysis for Business Decisions.* 6th ed. Homewood, IL: Richard D. Irwin, 1981.

Horowitz, I. *Decision Making and the Theory of the Firm.* Columbus, OH: Charles E. Merrill, 1969.

Jedamus, P., and R. Frame. *Business Decision Theory.* New York: McGraw-Hill, 1969.

Levin, Richard, Charles A. Kirkpatrick, and David S. Rubin. *Quantitative Approaches to Management.* 5th ed. New York: McGraw-Hill, 1982.

Pratt, J. W., H. Raiffa, and R. Schlaifer. *Introduction to Statistical Decision Theory.* New York: McGraw-Hill, 1965.

G ANSWERS TO ODD-NUMBERED PROBLEMS

CHAPTER 3

(1) a = 5.6333, b = −.0571429, Y_7 = $5.233 million. (3) a = 2.387, b = .180, Y_7 = 3.65 thousands, Y_8 = 3.83 thousands, Y_9 = 4.01 thousands. (5) a. r = .993; b. r^2 = .987. (7) a. a = .528, b = .0801, Y_8 = $20.55 million, Y_9 = $22.16 million, Y_{10} = $24.56 million; b. 96.6%. (9) 175 units. (11) b. F_{25} = 93.6 maintenance calls. (13) b. .5; c. F_{17} = $.851. (15) F_{13} = 178.55 units. (17) a. Y = 106.25 hours. (19) a. Y_7 = 3.647 thousands, Y_8 = 3.827 thousands, Y_9 = 4.007 thousands; b. s_{yx} = .0618; c. 3.84 thousands and 4.18 thousands. (21) a. Y_7 = $47.41 million; b. $33.8 and $61.02 million. (23) a = 8.357, b = .199; SI = .849, .751, .557, 1.843; Y_9 = $8.62 million, Y_{10} = $7.77 million, Y_{11} = $5.87 million, Y_{12} = $19.80 million. (25) a. $F_{ap=4}$ = 113.5 nurses, $F_{ap=8}$ = 113.375 nurses; c. SI = 1.021, .998, .968, 1.013; $F_{ap=4}$ = 115.9, $F_{ap=8}$ = 115.8.

CHAPTER 4

(11) a. buy; b. 150,000 units; c. 200,000 units. (13) a. $50,000 surplus; b. 900 students; c. 1,375 students; d. 844 students. (15) a. yes; b. $13,000 per year; c. 75,000 parts.

CHAPTER 5

(5) 155,172.41 transactions. (7) a. CM, N/C, and FMS; b. FMS, N/C, and CM. (13) CM: .760, SS: .804.

CHAPTER 6

(5) Layout A: 420,000 feet per month, Layout B: 380,000 feet per month, Layout B is preferred. **(7)** Layout 1: 34,245 thousand feet per month, Layout 2: 34,400 thousand feet per month. **(9)** b. .167 minute per unit; c. 31.86 employees. **(11)** (A), (B,C,D,E), (F,G), (H,I,J,K), (L,M,N,O); 15 personnel; 91.3%. **(13)** b. .250 minute per burger; c. 24.20 employees; d. (A), (B,C,D,E), (F,G), (H,I,J,K,L); 25 personnel; 96.8%.

CHAPTER 7

(1) a. no; b. no, there are no alternative courses of action. **(3)** Max $Z = 700X_1 + 500X_2$; $X_1 \leq 100$; $1{,}000X_1 + 2{,}000X_2 \leq 200{,}000$; $X_1 =$ acres to be planted in soybeans this season; $X_2 =$ acres to be planted in milo this season. **(5)** Max $Z = 20{,}000X_1 + 30{,}000X_2$; $X_1 + X_2 \leq 20$; $X_1 \leq 15$; $X_2 \leq 10$; $X_1 =$ number of research personnel to be assigned to new project during the 1st quarter; $X_2 =$ number of research personnel to be assigned to new project during the 2nd quarter. **(7)** Min $Z = \frac{5}{100}X_1 + \frac{3}{100}X_2$; $100X_1 + 100X_2 \geq 4{,}000$; $200X_1 + 400X_2 \geq 10{,}000$; $200X_1 + 100X_2 \geq 5{,}000$; $X_1 =$ pounds of oats fed to each head of cattle per day; $X_2 =$ pounds of corn fed to each head of cattle per day. **(9)** Max $Z = 10X_1 + 6X_2$; $\frac{1}{4}X_1 + \frac{1}{8}X_2 \leq 480$; $\frac{1}{6}X_1 + \frac{1}{4}X_2 \leq 480$; $\frac{2}{7}X_1 \leq 480$; $X_1 =$ number of hardback books to be produced per shift; $X_2 =$ number of paperback books to be produced per shift. **(11)** Min $Z = .3X_1 + .2X_2 + .4X_3$; $-X_1 + 4X_3 \geq 0$; $X_2 \leq 60{,}000$; $X_1 + X_2 + X_3 \geq 400{,}000$; $X_1 =$ number of pounds of B22 binder to purchase next year and include in the WOPAC resin; $X_2 =$ number of pounds of T90 zinc oxide to purchase next year and include in the WOPAC resin; $X_3 =$ number of pounds of P55 petroite to purchase next year and include in the WOPAC resin. **(13)** $X_1 = 100$, $X_2 = 50$, $Z = \$95{,}000$. **(15)** $X_1 = 10$, $X_2 = 10$, $Z = \$500{,}000$. **(17)** $X_1 = 1{,}440$, $X_2 = 960$, $Z = \$20{,}160$.

CHAPTER 8

(1) a. 12,500 textbooks; b. $525,000; c. $75,000; d. $30.75. **(3)** b. Build new plant; c. $690,000; ($130,000); or ($150,000). **(5)** b. Build large plant; c. $5,000,000; $2,500,000; or $1,000,000. **(7)** 3.25 years. **(9)** Payback = 7.81 years, lease the building. **(11)** a. Cleveland in Years 1, 3, and 5; b. Grand Rapids, $0 - 1{,}333.33$ scanners, and Cleveland, $1{,}333.33 +$ scanners. **(13)** L_4: $X_1, X_2, X_3 \cdots X_{12} =$ number of trips annually from Substation i (1, 2, 3, and L_4) to Constituent Center j (A, B, and C); Min $Z = 20X_1 + 5X_2 + 10X_3 + 20X_4 + 10X_5 + 5X_6 + 5X_7 + 20X_8 + 20X_9 + 8X_{10} + 12X_{11} + 12X_{12}$; $X_1 + X_2 + X_3 \leq 10{,}000$; $X_4 + X_5 + X_6 \leq 10{,}000$; $X_7 + X_8 + X_9 \leq 20{,}000$; $X_{10} + X_{11} + X_{12} \leq 10{,}000$; $X_1 + X_4 + X_7 + X_{10} \geq 15{,}000$; $X_2 + X_5 + X_8 + X_{11} \geq 15{,}000$; $X_3 + X_6 + X_9 + X_{12} \geq 15{,}000$; L_5: $X_1, X_2, X_3 \cdots X_{12} =$ number of trips annually from Substation i (1, 2, 3, and L_5) to Constituent Center j (A, B, and C); Min $Z = 20X_1 + 5X_2 + 10X_3 + 20X_4 + 10X_5 + 5X_6 + 5X_7 + 20X_8 + 20X_9 + 12X_{10} + 10X_{11} + 8X_{12}$; $X_1 + X_2 + X_3 \leq 10{,}000$; $X_4 + X_5 + X_6 \leq 10{,}000$; $X_7 + X_8 + X_9 \leq 20{,}000$; $X_{10} + X_{11} + X_{12} \leq 10{,}000$; $X_1 + X_4 + X_7 + X_{10} \geq 15{,}000$; $X_2 + X_5 + X_8 + X_{11} \geq 15{,}000$; $X_3 +$

$X_6 + X_9 + X_{12} \geq 15,000$; c. L_4: $Z = 295,000$ minutes per year, L_5: $Z = 265,000$ minutes per year; e. 10,000 from 1 to B, 10,000 from 2 to C, 15,000 from 3 to A, 5,000 from L_5 to B, and 5,000 from L_5 to C. **(15)** The strengths and weaknesses of the Tulsa location are the opposite of Cleveland. The selection will be based on weighing the strengths and weaknesses of each location. **(17)** $LS_c = .800$, $LS_t = .822$; Tulsa is preferred over Cleveland when both economic and qualitative factors are considered.

CHAPTER 9

(1) Total engineers by quarter: $Q_1 = 293.28$, $Q_2 = 312.00$, $Q_3 = 287.04$, $Q_4 = 265.20$. **(3)** a. $Q_1 = 310,145$, $Q_2 = 453,987$, $Q_3 = 363,461$, $Q_4 = 534,830$; b. $Q_1 = 220,490$, $Q_2 = 324,595$, $Q_3 = 258,658$, $Q_4 = 380,997.5$. **(5)** Total annual cost; level capacity = \$273,750; matching capacity with aggregate demand = \$225,000; matching plan is preferred. **(7)** a. 799.24 employees; b. $Q_1 = 596.43$, $Q_2 = 873.05$, $Q_3 = 698.96$, $Q_4 = 1,028.52$ employees. **(9)** a. $Q_1 = 50.0$, $Q_2 = 60.0$, $Q_3 = 55.0$, $Q_4 = 49.5$ thousand labor hours; b. $Q_1 = 96.2$, $Q_2 = 115.4$, $Q_3 = 105.7$, $Q_4 = 95.2$ employees. **(11)** Total annual cost: level = \$37,500; matching = \$40,500; the level capacity plan has the least cost. **(13)** a. \$72,160.50; b. level capacity plan is more economical and exhibits stable work force advantages. **(15)** a. 2,400, 4,800, 4,800, 6,000, 6,720; b. yes, but some production will need to be moved among the weeks. **(17)** 1,500 scanners in Weeks 2, 3, 5, and 6.

CHAPTER 10

(1) a. 2,816.6 units; b. \$1,267.48; c. \$2.52. **(3)** a. \$254,950.97; b. \$25,495.10; c. 12.75 working days per order. **(5)** a. EOQ will fall 8.6%; b. TSC will rise 20%. **(7)** a. 29,160.59 barrels; b. \$77,158.92; c. 19.44 days; d. 20,412.4 barrels. **(9)** a. \$251,447.50; b. 10,000 units; c. 5 orders per year; d. 6,000 units. **(11)** a. 1,000 boxes; b. \$255,450; c. 818.54 boxes; d. \$254,614.78; e. yes. **(13)** a. OP = 76 units; b. SS = 20.5 units. **(15)** a. OP = 35.01 bearings; b. SS = 6.51 bearings. **(17)** a. OP = 13 cases; c. SS = .85 case. **(19)** a. SS = 81 seals; b. OP = 243 seals. **(21)** a. 52.6 days; b. 900,000 forms. **(23)** a. Order = 40 batteries, weekly expected costs = \$115; b. order = 40 batteries, weekly expected profits = \$555.

CHAPTER 11

(1) 0, 100, 300, 800, 1,000, 500. **(5)** Planned order releases — A: 500, 2,000, 1,000 in Weeks 3, 4, and 5; B: 500, 2,000, 1,000 in Weeks 2, 3, and 4; C: 200, 2,000, 1,000 in Weeks 2, 3, and 4; D: 1,000, 3,700, 2,000 in Weeks 1, 2, and 3. **(7)** Planned order releases — 500, 900, 800 in Weeks 2, 3, and 4. **(9)** a. Planned order releases — A: 500, 1,500 in Weeks 4 and 5; B: 700, 3,000 in Weeks 3 and 4; C: 700, 3,000 in Weeks 3 and 4; D: 500, 2,700 in Weeks 2 and 3; E: 5,000, 5,000, 7,500 in Weeks 1, 2, and 3; F: 10,000 units in Week 1 (5,000 units of this order must be expedited); G: 6,000 in Week 1; H: 6,100, 5,000 in Weeks 2 and 4. b. No, not unless the order for 5,000 F items ordered for delivery in Week 1 can be expedited. c. The order for 5,000 F items ordered for delivery in Week 1 must be expedited from a 3-week LT to a 2-week LT.

(11) b. Planned order releases — P55: 2,200, 700, 900, 800 in Weeks 2, 3, 4, and 5; D51: 1,500, 1,500 in Weeks 1 and 3; A9: 1,000, 700, 900, 800 in Weeks 2, 3, 4, and 5; T99: 2,000 in Weeks 1 and 3; C22: 3,000 in Weeks 2, 3, and 4; S6: 500, 900, 800 in Weeks 2, 3, and 4; T39: 700 in Weeks 2 and 3; T41: 1,500, 1,600 in Weeks 2 and 3; D31: 2,000 in Weeks 1 and 2. **(13)** a. LFL: cost = $40,000; b. EOQ: lots of 5,477 in Weeks 1, 3, and 6, cost = $31,054.50; c. POQ: lots of 7,000 and 5,000 in Weeks 1 and 5, cost = $17,500. **(15)** a. Labor: 58, 87, 115, 87, 87, and 58%; machine: 60, 90, 120, 90, 90, and 60%.

CHAPTER 12

(1) 28 base plates. **(3)** a. Too much input to the work center; b. reduce upstream capacities or increase capacity of work center. **(7)** a. Shortest processing time ranks first on all three criteria; b. shortest processing time, but must deal with long jobs. **(9)** a. D-A-C-B-E; b. $286. **(11)** a. C-A-B-F-D-E; b. 8.2 hours. **(13)** a. $EOQ_1 = 1,490.7$, $EOQ_2 = 1,860.5$, $EOQ_3 = 2,631.2$, $EOQ_4 = 2,148.3$ units; b. 10%; c. 74.535 days. **(15)** Aggregate runout time = 1.273 quarters, final assembly hours for each toy — A: 72.76, B: 127.30, C: 210.05, D: 285.05, E: 204.60. **(17)** b. All steps are on schedule except 2, 5, and 7; delivery of purchased heels and soles seems to be the cause of the difficulty. **(19)** a. Day shift: 10 clerks, evening shift: 7 clerks; b. day shift: 10 clerks are required, evening shift: 8 clerks are required; c. day shift: 4 shifts of slack are required, evening shift: 5 shifts of slack are required.

CHAPTER 13

(7) Buy, $TC_{buy} = \$87,500$; $TC_{make} = \$92,000$. **(9)** a. Atlanta Spier, $TS_{as} = \$6,579,500$; b. Osiega Ltd: $0 - 36,231.9$ units, CPC: $36,231.9 - 39,215.7$, Atlanta Spier: $39,215.7+$. **(11)** b. Blanket contract has the least expected cost, $285,000; c. $250,000, $300,000, or $350,000. **(13)** Suchow relative aggregate score = .744, Electrix relative aggregate score = .760, Electrix is the preferred vendor. **(15)** b. 300 units in Weeks 1, 2, and 3. **(17)** a. 12 counters; b. $240,000; c. 22 counters; d. $200,000.

CHAPTER 14

(3) a. Remedies rank in this order: supervisor training, job rotation, job enrichment, and time away from jobs. **(11)** a. 14.343 minutes per test; b. 33.47 tests per shift; c. $2.331 per test. **(13)** a. 1.186 minutes per bead; b. $.352 per tire; c. 404.72 beads. **(15)** .2345. **(17)** a. 5.307 minutes per package; b. 7.076 minutes per package. **(19)** a. $.5626 per unit; b. $675.12. **(21)** 8.248 labor hours. **(23)** a. 104.9 labor hours; b. 72.27 labor hours; c. 4.38 labor hours.

CHAPTER 15

(1) 0 and 11.87%. **(3)** a. 1.5%; b. 0 and 4.08%. **(5)** a. 1.50 and 4.5%; c. number of academic drops is falling. **(7)** a. 22.46 and 25.54 inches; c. no, the mean in inches is changing rapidly and the process is out of control on the upward side. **(9)** a. 23.37 and

24.63 hours; c. no, too many sample means fall above the upper control limit. (**11**) a. 31.81 and 32.19 ounces; b. 1.375 and 3.500 ounces; c. within sample variation is within limits—sample means are experiencing extreme variation. (**13**) Yes, the sample's 6.5% defectives fall within the 3.09% and 6.91% acceptance criteria. (**15**) Yes, the sample's 7% defectives fall within the .79% and 7.21% acceptance criteria. (**17**) No, the sample mean of 61.5 tons falls outside the 59.18 and 60.82 tons acceptance criteria.

CHAPTER 16

(**1**) Activity F, field test is complete and is 2 weeks ahead of schedule; Activity G, production design, is 2 weeks behind schedule. (**3**) Project has been overstaffed since last July; project has 4 more personnel than planned and is projected to be overstaffed by 5 personnel through next July. (**7**) b. Lengths of paths: c-d = 15 weeks, b-e-g = 12 weeks, a-f-g = 13 weeks; c. path c-d, project is expected to take 15 weeks. (**9**) d. path a-b-h-j, project is expected to take 53 days. (**11**) d. path b-f-h, project is expected to take 20 days. (**13**) a. 12.17; b. .694; c. .83. (**15**) Path duration = 54 days, path variance = 6.500. (**17**) e. path a-d-h-j, project is expected to take 54 days; f. .00347 or .347%. (**19**) Path 1. (**21**) a. Without acceleration, the critical path is b-f-h-i and is expected to take 48 weeks; b. crash activities in this order: b, i, h, and d and f together, additional cost for crashing = $31,000.

CHAPTER 17

(**1**) 6 machines per hour. (**3**) a. 24.04 minutes; b. 140.4 square feet. (**5**) 50 seals. (**7**) Perform PM every 3 weeks; expected cost of this policy is $12,333 per week. (**9**) Perform PM every 40,000 miles; expected cost of this policy is $27.70 per 1,000 miles. (**11**) a. 99%; b. 96.1%. (**13**) a. .847; b. .931. (**15**) d. Path a-b-h-j and 53 days.

APPENDIX C

(**1**) $TS_1 = \$3,150$; $TS_2 = \$5,625$; $TS_3 = \$3,825$; $TS_4 = \$2,925$; $TS_5 = \$2,025$; $TS_6 = \$2,025$; $TS_7 = \$2,025$; $TS_8 = \$900$. (**3**) $TS_1 = \$110.25$; $TS_2 = \$196.88$; $TS_3 = \$133.88$; $TS_4 = \$102.38$; $TS_5 = \$70.88$; $TS_6 = \$70.88$; $TS_7 = \$70.88$; $TS_8 = \$31.50$. (**5**) a. $8,055; b. $2,763; c. $8,442. (**7**) $30,590. (**9**) 3.25 years. (**11**) NPV = ($104,208); no. (**13**) Additional first cost of Z exceeds a payback period of 5 years.

APPENDIX D

(**1**) a. .5 unit; b. 1 unit; c. 6 minutes; d. 12 minutes; e. .50. (**3**) Present: .167 student in line, .25 minute, and .333; proposed: 13.05 students in line, 19.6 minutes, and .933. (**5**) a. 10 workers; b. 80 square feet; c. .328. (**7**) Weekdays: a. 9 feet, b. 21 minutes; weekends: a. 81 feet, b. 66 minutes. (**9**) a. 4.97 minutes per customer; b. 16.97 minutes. (**11**) a. 27.1%; b. 1.25 cars. (**13**) a. .607; b. .000258 unit in line. (**15**) a. .001693; b. 2.34 minutes; c. 8.59 customers in all lines or 1.43 customers per line. **(17)** Order the quantity demanded today for tomorrow's sales; total profit for the 20 days is $10,500 and the average daily profit is $525.

APPENDIX E

(1) 3rd tableau is optimal; $X_2 = 375$, $X_1 = 500$, $Z = 125,000$. **(3)** 4th tableau is optimal; $X_1 = 50$, $S_1 = 100$, $S_2 = 200$, $Z = 1,000$. **(5)** e. $X_1 = .6$ sales call to petroleum customer per day on the average, $X_2 = 1.2$ sales calls to chemical customers per day on the average, $S_1 = 0$ unused salespersons' hours per day, $S_2 = 0$ unused entertainment costs per day, and $Z = \$540$ average daily profit. **(7)** e. $X_1 = \$7$ million urban renewal spending, $X_2 = \$3$ million health services spending, $X_3 = 0$ fire department spending, $Z = \$3.7$ million social returns, $S_1 = 0$ unused urban renewal spending, $S_2 = 0$ excess health services spending, $S_3 = \$8$ million unused fire department spending, and $S_4 = 0$ unused total spending. **(9)** e. $X_1 = 1,440$ hardback books to be produced per shift, $X_2 = 960$ paperback books to be produced per shift, $S_1 = 0$ minutes of unused cover capacity per shift, $S_2 = 0$ minutes of unused printing line capacity per shift, $S_3 = 68\frac{4}{7}$ or 68.571 minutes of unused framing capacity per shift, and $Z = \$20,160$ contribution per shift. **(11)** $X_1 = 272,000$ pounds of B22 binder, $X_2 = 60,000$ pounds of T90 zinc oxide, $X_3 = 68,000$ pounds of P55 petroite, $Z = \$120,800$, S_1, S_2, and $S_3 = 0$. **(13)** a. Each salesperson should make $\frac{6}{10}$ sales call on the average per day to petroleum industry customers and $1\frac{2}{10}$ or 1.2 sales calls on the average per day to chemical industry customers. The results will be $540 daily profits per salesperson, all 8 hours of each salesperson's day will be spent on sales calls, and all daily entertainment cost allowances for each salesperson will be spent. b. X_1 (0) and X_2 (0) mean that these two variables are in the optimal solution; S_1 ($-52\frac{1}{2}$ or -52.5) means that daily profit will change $52.50 for each one-hour change in the daily sales call hours per salesperson; S_2 (-2) means that daily profit will change $2 for each one-dollar change in the daily entertainment cost allowance per salesperson. **(15)** a. $7 million should be spent on urban renewal, $3 million should be spent on health services, and $0 should be spent on the fire department next year. The maximum amount would be spent on urban renewal and the minimum amount would be spent on health services. $8 million less than the maximum would be spent on the fire department. All available money would be spent. The total social returns for these projects would be $3.7 million. b. X_1 (0), X_2 (0), X_3 (0) mean that these three variables are in the optimal solution; S_1 ($-.05$) means that social returns would change $.05 for each one-dollar change in the maximum urban renewal spending; S_2 ($-.05$) means that the social returns would change $.05 for each one-dollar change in the minimum health services spending; S_3 (0) means that the social returns would not change if the maximum fire department spending were changed; S_4 ($-.35$) means that social returns would change $.35 for each one-dollar change in the maximum total spending for the three projects. **(17)** a. From Plant 1 ship 10,000 units to Warehouse C; from Plant 2 ship 10,000 units, 5,000 units, and 5,000 units to Warehouses A, C, and D; from Plant 3 ship 2,000 units and 8,000 units to Warehouses A and B. b. The values in the columns of the artificial variables have no meaning. The values in the X_3, X_5, X_7, X_8, X_9, X_{10} columns mean that these variables are in the optimal solution. The zero in the X_{11} column means that if one unit of X_{11} (one electric iron is shipped from Plant 3 to Warehouse C) were forced into the solution, total shipping cost Z would not be affected, which indicates an alternate optimal solution. X_1 (−.10), X_2 (−.10), X_4 (−.10), X_6 (−.10), X_{12} (−.10) all have the same meaning: If one unit of one of these variables were forced into the solution, Z would increase by $.10. **(19)** c. From Source A ship 100 units to Destination 1; from Source B ship 100 units and 400 units to Destinations 1 and 3; from Source C ship 100 units and 800 units to Destinations 1 and 2; total shipping cost will be $940. **(21)** There are two optimal solutions to this problem. *First solution:* From Source 1 ship 10,000 units to Destination C; from Source 2 ship 12,000 units, 3,000 units, and 5,000 units to Destinations A, C, and D; from Source 3 ship 8,000 units and 2,000 units to Destinations B and C; monthly transportation cost will be $6,650. *Second solution:* From Source 1 ship 10,000 units to Destination C; from Source 2 ship 10,000 units, 5,000 units, and 5,000 units to Destinations A, C, and D; from Source 3 ship 2,000 units and 8,000 units to Destinations A and B; monthly transportation cost will be $6,650. **(23)** c. Atlanta plant should ship 50 computers to Chicago and 150 to New York; El Paso plant should ship 25 computers to Chicago, 100 to Dallas, 25 to Denver, and 150 to San Jose; monthly shipping cost will be $19,625. **(25)** c. There are two alternate optimal solutions to this problem. *First solution:* From Plant A ship 50,000 pounds to Warehouse 2; from Plant B ship 80,000 pounds to Warehouse 3; from Plant 3 ship 30,000 pounds and 40,000 pounds to Warehouses 1 and 2; monthly shipping cost will be $3,200. *Second solution:* From Plant A ship 40,000 pounds to Warehouse 2; from Plant B ship 80,000 pounds to Warehouse 3; from Plant 3 ship 30,000 pounds and 50,000 pounds to Warehouses 1 and 2; monthly shipping cost will be $3,200. **(27)** Assign Al to Project 4, Ben to Project 1, Cal to Project 2, and Dan to Project 3; cost of the assignment will be $1,600. **(29)** There are two alternate optimal solutions to this problem. *First solution:* Assign Project 3 to Team 3, Project B to Team 1, Project C to Team 5, Project D to Team 2, and Project E to Team 4; cost of this assignment will be $288,000. *Second solution:* Assign Project A to Team 3, Project B to Team 1, Project C to Team 2, Project D to Team 5, and Project E to Team 4; cost of this assignment will be $288,000.

GLOSSARY

Acceptance plan Plan used to decide whether lots of raw materials, purchased parts, or finished products meet prescribed quality standards.

Acquisition cost Cost of purchasing or producing a unit of a material or product.

Aggregate planning Process of providing an intermediate-term production capacity scheme to support a sales forecast for a product.

Aggregate unit of capacity Measure that allows rates of various outputs to be converted to a common unit of output measure.

Assemble-to-order firm Firm that assembles, from a relatively few major assemblies or components, customer-ordered end items having many options.

Assembly chart Macroview chart listing all major materials, components, subassembly and assembly operations, and inspections for a product.

Assignment method Linear programming solution method used to assign jobs or personnel to machines or departments.

Assignment problem Scheduling problem related to deciding which jobs should be assigned to which work centers or machines.

Automated assembly system System of automated assembly machines linked together by automated materials-handling equipment; used to produce major assemblies or completed products.

Automated flow line Production line that includes several automated machines linked together by automated parts transfer and handling machines; designed to produce one type of component or product.

Automated process controls system System that uses sensors to obtain measures of the performance of industrial processes, compare them to predetermined standards, and then automatically signal changes in the settings of those processes.

Automated quality control inspection system System utilizing machines that have been integrated into the inspection of products for quality control purposes.

Automated storage and retrieval system (ASRS) System for receiving orders for materials, collecting the materials, and delivering them to work stations in operations.

Automatic identification system (AIS) System that uses bar codes, radio frequencies, magnetic strips, optical character recognition, and machine vision to sense and input data into computers.

Automation Replacement of human effort with automated machine effort.

Backlogging of orders Holding orders for late shipment.

Backward integration Expansion of the ownership of a company's production and distribution chain backward toward the source of supply.

Bill of material Listing of the quantities of all raw materials, parts, subassemblies, and assemblies that go into an end item.

Bills of material file Complete list of all finished products, quantity of each material in each product, and the structure of all products; may also be called an *indented parts list.*

Block diagram analysis Technique for planning facility layouts that sets the general shape and dimensions of a building and the location of the interior departmental boundaries.

Break-even analysis Process of determining the production volume needed to make revenues equal to costs.

Bucket Principal unit of time measurement in material requirements planning systems; usually one week.

Buffer stock Stock of finished products that can be used when demand is greater than anticipated or when supply is less than expected.

Business strategy Long-range plan of an organization and the methods to be used to achieve its corporate objectives.

CAD/CAM Computer-aided design and computer-aided manufacturing.

Capacity requirements planning (CRP) Process of reconciling the master production schedule to the labor and machine capacities of a production department.

Capital-intensive Depending on capital rather than labor as the predominant resource in an operation.

Carrying cost Total cost of holding a material in inventory; expressed in dollars per unit per year.

Cellular manufacturing (CM) Grouping of machines into cells that function like a product layout island within a larger job shop or process layout.

Central limit theorem Theorem that states that sampling distributions can be assumed to be normally distributed even though the population distributions are not normal.

Changes to planned orders Reports that show how planned order schedules should be changed to allow for earlier or later delivery, for cancellation, or for change in quantity.

Coefficient of correlation Measure of the expected precision of a forecast, explaining the relative importance of the association of two variables.

Coefficient of determination Measure of the expected precision of a forecast, explaining the percentage of variation in one variable that is explained by another variable.

Component A part that goes into an assembly.

Component reliability Probability that a type of part will not fail in a given time period or in a number of trials under ordinary conditions of use.

Computer search technique Capacity-planning method using preprogrammed rules that control the way resources are combined to select a low-cost capacity plan for a time period.

Computer-aided design (CAD) Computerized process for designing new products or modifying existing ones.

Computer-aided manufacturing (CAM) Use of computers to plan and program production equipment in the production of manufactured items.

Computer-integrated manufacturing (CIM) Total integration of all business functions associated with production through computer systems.

Continuous production Production in which products/services proceed through production without stopping.

Control chart Chart that continuously monitors a production operation to determine if its outputs meet quality standards.

Control decision Short-range, relatively simple decision about the planning and controlling of day-to-day operations.

Control subsystem Subsystem of a larger production system in which a portion of the outputs is monitored for feedback signals to provide corrective action if required.

Conversion subsystem Subsystem of a larger production system in which inputs are converted into outputs.

Corporate objectives Long-range goals, unique to each organization and developed at the highest organizational levels, that are concerned with survival, growth, and profitability.

Crash Accelerate an activity by adding resources; reduce the time required for a project.

Critical activity In project management, an activity that has no room for schedule slippage; an activity with zero slack.

Critical path In project management, a chain of critical activities for a project; the longest path through a network.

Critical path method (CPM) Network-based project management initially used in maintenance and defense projects; nearly identical to PERT.

Critical ratio Sequencing rule by which the next job to be processed is the one with the least critical ratio (time to due date divided by total remaining time) among the waiting jobs.

Custom product Product designed to meet the needs of an individual customer.

Cycle counting Verifying the accuracy of inventory records by periodically counting the number of units of each material in inventory.

Decision tree analysis Graphic aid in making multiphase decisions that shows the sequence and interdependence of decisions.

Delphi method Qualitative forecasting method used to achieve consensus within a committee.

Demand during lead time (DDLT) Number of units of a material demanded during the inventory replenishment process or lead time.

Demand management Recognizing and managing all demands for products and services to ensure that the master scheduler is aware of them.

Demand rate Number of units demanded by customers or production departments per unit of time; also called *usage rate.*

Dependent demand Demand for an item that depends on the demands for other inventory items.

Design simplification In product and machine reliability, the reduction of the number of interacting parts in a machine or product.

Disbursement Act of physically removing a material from inventory.

Discrete unit manufacturing Manufacturing distinct or separate products such as automobiles or dishwashers.

Diseconomies of scale Increase in unit cost caused by additional volume of outputs past the point of best operating level for a facility.

Distribution requirements planning (DRP) Planning for the replenishment of regional warehouse inventories.

Distribution resource planning Planning for the provision of the key resources of warehouse space — number of workers, cash, shipping vehicles, etc. — in the right quantities and when needed.

Distribution system Network of shipping and receiving points starting with the factory and ending with the customers.

Double-sampling plan Acceptance sampling plan in which a decision to accept or reject a lot can be made on the first sample drawn, but if it is not, a second sample is taken and a decision is made on the basis of the combined samples.

Earliest due date Sequencing rule in which the next job to be processed is the one with the earliest due date among the waiting jobs.

Earliest finish (EF) In project management, the earliest that an activity can finish.

Economic analysis Analysis based on the development of cost functions for the processing alternative and the comparison of these functions.

Economic order quantity (EOQ) Optimal order quantity that minimizes total annual stocking costs.

Economies of scale Reduction in unit cost as fixed costs are spread over increasingly more units.

End item Product, service, or other output that has a demand independent of the demands for other components or end items.

Expected demand during lead time (EDDLT) Average demand per day multiplied by average lead time.

Expediting Speeding up an order through all or part of the entire materials system.

Exponential smoothing model A short-range forecasting model that uses last period's actual and forecasted sales to forecast next period's sales.

Facility layout Plan for the location of all machines and utilities and for the physical arrangement within facilities of all manufacturing processes and their support functions.

Facility planning Determination of how much long-range production capacity is needed, when it is needed, where production facilities should be located, and the layout and characteristics of the facilities.

Factories of the future 1980s term for factories in which computers would be the basis for high-tech production methods.

Final assembly schedule (FAS) A schedule for assembling unique products ordered by customers.

Finished goods inventory Reservoir of end items or products held for customer demand.

First-come first-served (FCFS) Sequencing rule in which the next job to be processed is the one that arrived first among the waiting jobs.

Fixed order period system System of inventory planning that takes physical counts of materials in inventory at equal fixed time intervals.

Fixed order quantity system System of inventory planning that places fixed quantity orders for a material when the inventory level falls to a predetermined critical level.

Fixed-position layout Layout that locates the product in a fixed position and transports workers, materials, machines, and subcontractors to and from the product.

Flexibility Ability to change production to other products/services and to other production volumes.

Flexible automation Use of all types of automated equipment and production systems that provide the ability to respond to changing market needs.

Flexible manufacturing system (FMS) System in which groups of production machines are sequentially connected by automated materials-handling and transferring machines and integrated by a computer system.

Flexible work force Group of workers trained and cross-trained in several types of jobs.

Flow diagram Diagram of the flow of workers, equipment, or materials through a process.

Focused factory Factory that is specialized in some way; for example, one that concentrates on a narrow product mix for a particular market.

Forecasting Estimating the future demand for products/services and the resources necessary to produce them.

Forward integration Expansion of the ownership of a company's production and distribution chain forward toward the market.

Frozen master production schedule Early periods of the master production schedule that are not subject to change.

Gantt chart Chart that coordinates work center schedules by showing the progress of each job in relation to its scheduled finish date.

Group technology/cellular manufacturing (GT/CM) Form of production based on a coding system for parts that allows families of parts to be assigned to manufacturing cells for production.

Heuristic methods Methods based on simple rules.

Human relations movement Early twentieth-century development of a philosophy among managers that workers are human beings and should be treated with dignity in the workplace.

Hybrid layout Layout that uses a combination of layout types, as an assembly line combined with a process layout.

Impulse response In forecasting, the speed at which forecasts reflect changes in underlying data.

Incremental utilization heuristic Adding tasks to a work station one at a time in order of precedence until the worker utilization is either 100 percent or observed to fall, then repeating the process for the remaining tasks.

Independent demand Demand for an item that is independent of the demand for any other item carried in inventory.

Industrial revolution Widespread substitution of machine power for human power and the establishment of the factory system.

In-process inventory Inventory of partially completed products that are between processing steps.

Input Any raw material, personnel, capital, utilities, or information that is entered into a conversion system.

Input rate capacity Measure that allows rates of various inputs to be converted to a common unit of input measure.

Input–output control report Report detailing how jobs are flowing between work centers so that managers can determine if the capacity of the work center is as anticipated.

Intermittent production Production performed on products on a start-and-stop basis.

International company Company that engages in production sharing and sells its products in world markets.

Inventory cycle Activities of sensing a need for a material, placing an order, waiting for the material to be delivered, receiving the material, and using the material.

Inventory record Display of all of the inventory transactions that have affected a material.

Inventory status file Computerized file with a complete record of each material held in inventory.

Job design Description of a job's content and specification of the skills and training needed to perform that job.

Job shop Factory whose departments or work centers are organized around particular types of equipment or operations; products flow through departments in batches corresponding to stock orders or customer orders.

Just-in-time (JIT) system Production and inventory control system based on small lot sizes, stable and level production schedules, and focused factories; system of enforced problem solving.

Kanban Japanese work for *card;* used to describe a just-in-time system based on conveyance and production cards that determine the movement of production orders between work stations.

Labor intensive An operation in which labor is the predominant resource rather than machinery and equipment.

Labor standard Number of worker-minutes required to complete an element, operation, or product under ordinary operating conditions.

Lead time Length of time required to replenish the inventory for a material from the time that a need for additional material is sensed until the new order for the material is in inventory and ready to use.

Learning curve Curve illustrating the relationship between the number of units produced and the amount of labor required per unit.

Least changeover cost Sequencing rule by which the entire sequence of waiting jobs is determined by analyzing the total cost of making all of the machine changeovers between jobs.

Level capacity plan Aggregate production plan that has a uniform capacity per day from time period to time period.

Level production Stabilized production output levels from time period to time period.

Line balancing Phase of assembly line study that nearly equally divides the work to be done among the workers so that the total number of employees required on the assembly line is minimized.

Line flow production Production in which products/services follow direct linear paths without backtracking or sidetracking.

Linear decision rule Mathematical cost function for a particular production system that works with the number of units of output to be produced and the size of the work force in each time period.

Linear programming Technique for applying scarce resources optimally to competing demands.

Load schedule Comparison of the labor and machine hours needed to produce the master production schedule with the labor and machine hours actually available in each week.

Load-distance analysis Technique for planning facility layouts that compares alternative layouts to identify the one with the least product or material travel per time period.

Logistics Management of the movement of materials within a factory, shipment of incoming materials from suppliers, and shipment of outgoing products to customers.

Lot Discrete group of products that have been produced under the same conditions.

Lot-sizing Determining how many units of a product to produce to minimize unit cost.

Lumpy demand Demand for a material that has an irregular period-to-period pattern.

Machine attachments Add-ons to machines that reduce the amount of human effort and time required to perform an operation.

Maintainability Ease with which maintenance activities can be performed.

Make-or-buy analysis Analysis determining whether a material or part should be made in-house or bought from a supplier.

Management coefficients Capacity-planning technique that describes the decision processes of individual managers.

Marginal analysis Technique that computes the probability that expected long cost equals expected short cost for any DDLT.

Master production schedule (MPS) Schedule of the amount and timing of all end items to be produced over a specific planning horizon.

Material requirements planning (MRP) Computerized system that determines how much of a material should be purchased or produced in each future time period.

Material specification Detailed description of a good to be purchased; can include engineering drawings, chemical analysis, and a list of physical characteristics.

Materials management Management of all of the functions related to the complete cycle of materials flows, including the purchase and internal control of materials, the planning and control of work in process, and the warehousing, shipping, and distribution of end items.

Materials-handling system Entire network of transportation that receives, stores, moves, and delivers materials within a production facility.

Maximum practical capacity Output attained within the normal operating schedule of shifts per day and days per week while bringing in high-cost inefficient facilities.

Mean absolute deviation (MAD) Measure of forecast model accuracy; sum of absolute values of forecast errors over a number of periods divided by the number of periods.

Model building In decision making, a method of analysis that involves a model (usually mathematical) that is a simplified abstraction from the real system under study.

Modular design Design allowing a variety of final product models with only a few basic components.

Moving averages method Short-range forecasting method that averages the data from a few recent past periods to form the forecast for the next period.

Multiactivity chart Chart showing how one or more workers work together and/or with machines.

Multiregression analysis Form of regression analysis used when two or more independent variables are incorporated into an analysis.

Net change MRP system Materials requirement planning system in which changes to the master production schedule initiate an updating of only the affected inventory records.

Numerically controlled (N/C) machines Machines preprogrammed through magnetic tape or microcomputers to perform a cycle of operations repeatedly.

Objective function A mathematical function that describes an objective. Maximizing profits or minimizing costs are common.

Operating decision A short-range or intermediate-range decision about planning production to meet demand.

Operating leverage Measure of the relationship between a firm's annual costs and its annual sales.

Operations objective Long-range operations goal for a major product line.

Operations research (OR) World War II term for scientific investigations; sought to replace intuitive decision making with an analytical, systematic, and interdisciplinary approach.

Operations sequence analysis Graphic analysis technique for planning facility layouts that develops a scheme for the arrangement of departments.

Operations strategy Plan for achieving the operations objective for a major product line.

Operator chart Type of process chart that examines the coordinated movements of a worker's hands.

Opportunity cost Cost in the form of profits forgone.

Optimal order period Time, in fractions of a year, between reviews of the status of a material that exactly balances annual ordering costs with annual carrying costs in a fixed order period inventory system.

Order entry Acceptance of an order into the master production schedule; includes check of delivery date, assignment of production slot in the master production schedule, and communicating the promised date to the customer.

Order point (OP) Point when an order is placed for a material in a fixed order period inventory system; expected demand during lead time plus safety stock.

Order quantity Quantity of a material ordered each time inventory is replenished.

Output End product or service of a conversion system.

Overdesign Enhancement of a machine design to avoid a particular type of failure during production.

Parent Term that describes a superior relationship in a product structure; e.g., a part (component) goes into an assembly (parent).

Payoff table In decision making, a table showing the expected profits or expected costs for each alternative for meeting different levels of demand.

Percentage of capacity utilization Measure that relates output measure to inputs available.

Perpetual inventory-accounting system System in which stock records are continuously updated as materials are received into or dispensed from inventory.

Pilot run Initial run of a product through the proposed production process to test its reproducibility.

Planned order receipt Quantity of a material to be received in each time period of the planning horizon.

Planned order release Quantity of a material to be ordered in each time period of the planning horizon.

Planning horizon Number of periods included in the production-planning schedule.

Positioning strategy Manufacturing strategy that includes an inventory policy, type of product design, and type of production process.

Predecessor activity In project management, an activity that must occur before another activity.

Present-value analysis Process of determining the amount of money that must be invested now at a specified rate of interest to accumulate to a certain amount in the future.

Preventive maintenance (PM) Activities, such as machine adjustments, lubrication, cleaning, parts replacement, painting, and needed repairs and overhauls, that are performed before malfunction of facilities or machines occurs.

Process chart Chart documenting the elemental steps in one of the several operations in producing a product.

Process layout Layout for the production of a variety of nonstandard products in relatively small batches, as in a custom machine shop.

Process planning Determination of the specific technological process steps and their sequence that will enable the production system to produce the products/services of the desired quality and at the budgeted cost.

Process-focused factory Factory that produces many nonstandard products in relatively small batches flowing along different paths through the factory and requiring frequent machine changeovers; also called a *job shop.*

Produce-to-stock Produce products ahead of time and place in inventory until customers demand them.

Product layout Layout designed to accommodate only a few product designs as in product-focused production.

Product-focused production Factory or service operation in which there are only a few standardized product/service designs, the products/services are usually produced for finished goods inventory, and the production rates of individual products/services are usually greater than their demand rates.

Production and operations management (POM) The planning, organizing, staffing, directing, and controlling of all of the activities of production systems.

Production plan Plan that will guide the operations function in fulfilling its part of the business plan.

Production sharing Participation of several companies from various countries in the design, financing, production, assembly, shipment, and sale of a product.

Production system System whose function is to convert a set of inputs into a set of desired outputs.

Productivity Amount of products or services produced with the resources used.

Program evaluation and review technique (PERT) Project-planning method that uses multiple activity time estimates.

Project management Management of all of the functions relating to a specific set of activities that will result in a unique finished project.

Prototype design Initial product design exhibiting the basic characteristics of a product's form, fit, and function that will be required of the final design.

Purchase requisition Authorization to purchase a good or service.

Purchasing Process of buying the raw materials, purchased parts, machinery, supplies, and all other goods and services used in a production system.

Quality at the source Assignment of responsibility for product quality to production workers, who are expected to produce parts of perfect quality before those parts are passed on to the next production operation.

Quality circle Small group of employees who voluntarily and regularly meet to analyze and solve production and quality problems.

Quantity discount Decrease in unit price as larger quantities are ordered.

Queuing model In decision making, a complex model based on waiting lines.

Redundant component Backup component built into a machine or product.

Regenerative MRP system Material requirements planning system in which a complete MRP is processed periodically, resulting in a new master production schedule, an updated inventory status file, and an updated bills of material file that generates a complete set of outputs in the MRP computer program.

Regression analysis Long-range forecasting model that develops a trend line through past data and projects it into future time periods.

Reliability Ability of a product or machine to perform as desired under prescribed conditions without excessive frequency of failure from wear or other causes.

Repetitive manufacturing Product-focused, high-volume, and discrete-unit manufacturing.

Reproducibility Ability of a production system to consistently produce products of the desired quality and quantity.

Resource requirements planning Determination of the quantity and timing of all of the production resources needed to produce the end items in a master production schedule.

Robot A reprogrammable, multifunctional manipulator designed to move materials, parts, tools, or specialized devices through variable programmed motions for the performance of a variety of tasks.

Rough-cut capacity planning Preliminary checking of the master production schedule that identifies any week in the MPS where underloading or overloading of production capacity occurs and then revises the MPS as required.

Routing plan Network of work centers through which an order must pass before it is completed.

Run-out method Method for planning production and delivery schedules that allocates production capacity to products in proportion to their demand and their inventory levels.

Safety stock Quantity of a material held in inventory to be used in time periods when demand is greater than expected or when supply is less than expected.

Scientific management Application of scientific principles to the management of production systems.

Seasonality Seasonal patterns that are fluctuations, usually within one year and that tend to be repeated annually.

Sequential-sampling plan Acceptance sampling plan in which each time a unit is tested, an accept, reject, or continue-sampling decision is made.

Service level The probability that a stockout will not occur during lead time.

Service revolution Evolution of the service industry as the predominant sector of the U.S. economy.

Setup cost Cost of changing over a processing step in a processing system from one product to another.

Shop system Systematic approach to improving labor efficiency, introduced by Frederick Winslow Taylor in the late nineteenth century.

Shortest processing time Sequencing rule in which the next job to be processed is the one with the shortest processing time among the waiting jobs.

Simplex method Linear programming solution method that provides precise solutions to complex problems that have many variables and constraints.

Single-sampling plan Acceptance sampling plan in which an accept or reject decision is made after drawing only one sample from a lot.

Slack In project management, an amount of time that an activity or group of activities can slip without causing delay in the completion of the project.

Specification Detailed description of a material, part, or product that gives all of the physical measurements needed for its design.

Standardized product Product produced either continuously or in very large batches. Implies only a few product designs.

Stock-keeping unit (SKU) Any item that is carried in inventory.

Stockout Reduction of a material's usable inventory level to zero.

Strategic decision Long-range, one-time, complex decision about a product, process, or facility.

Subcontractor network Arrangement in which a manufacturer develops long-range contractual relationships with several suppliers of parts, components, and subassemblies.

Successor activity In project management, an activity that must occur after another activity.

System reliability (SR) Combined reliability of all of the interacting components of a machine.

Systematic layout planning (SLP) Technique for planning facility layouts that charts the relative importance of each department being close to every other department.

Task force Group of high-level personnel who are assigned to collectively analyze a decision and arrive at a consensus on a course of action.

Time series Set of observed values, usually sales, measured over successive periods of time.

Time study Method of establishing time standards by using stopwatches to time operations being performed by workers.

Tolerance Specification for each dimension of a physical product in a range from minimum to maximum.

Total quality control (TQC) A system of producing high-quality products and services initially rather than depending on detecting defective products later through inspection.

Tracking signal Measurement showing whether a forecast has had any built-in biases over a period of time.

Transportation method Linear programming solution method used to find the minimal cost of shipping products from several sources to several destinations.

Two-bin system   Simple, fixed-order quantity inventory control system that uses two bins to hold a material in inventory; orders are triggered when one bin becomes empty, and both bins are filled when inventory is replenished.

Value engineering   Modification of material specifications to reduce the costs of materials, parts, and products while retaining their original function.

Vertical integration   Amount of the production and distribution chain brought under the ownership of a company.

Work measurement   Process of estimating the amount of worker time required to generate one unit of output.

Work sampling   Work measurement technique that randomly samples the work of one or more persons at periodic intervals to determine the proportion of the total operation that is accounted for by one particular activity.

Worker productivity   Dollar value of all goods and services produced in a given year divided by the direct labor-hours used in producing those goods and services.

Workmen's compensation laws   Laws providing for specific compensation amounts to be given to employees for various types of injuries incurred on the job.

INDEX